The United States Government Manual 1995/1996

Office of the Federal Register
National Archives and Records Administration

Revised July 1, 1995

Richard L. Claypoole,
Director of the Federal Register.

John W. Carlin,
Archivist of the United States.

For sale by the U.S. Government Printing Office
Superintendent of Documents, Mail Stop: SSOP. Washington. DC 20402-9328
ISBN 0-16-048141-4

Preface

As the official handbook of the Federal Government, *The United States Government Manual* provides comprehensive information on the agencies of the legislative, judicial, and executive branches. The *Manual* also includes information on quasi-official agencies; international organizations in which the United States participates; and boards, commissions, and committees.

A typical agency description includes a list of principal officials, a summary statement of the agency's purpose and role in the Federal Government, a brief history of the agency, including its legislative or executive authority, a description of its programs and activities, and a "Sources of Information" section. This last section provides information on consumer activities, contracts and grants, employment, publications, and many other areas of public interest.

The 1995/96 *Manual* was prepared by the Legislative Unit, Office of the Federal Register. Gwendolyn J. Henderson was Managing Editor, assisted by Albert Kapikian, Kent Giles, and Alfred Jones.

COVER: This year's covers capture the sentiments and spirit of events surrounding World War II, commemorating the Allied victory at the end of the War and embodying the bravery and dedication of those who made it happen.

Special thanks is extended to the Office of Public Programs at the National Archives for supplying the original photos used in developing the covers.

THE FEDERAL REGISTER AND ITS SPECIAL EDITIONS

The *Manual* is published as a special edition of the *Federal Register* (see 1 CFR 9.1). Its focus is on programs and activities. Persons interested in detailed organizational structure, the regulatory documents of an agency, or Presidential documents should refer to the *Federal Register* or one of its other special editions, described below.

Issued each Federal working day, the *Federal Register* provides a uniform system for publishing Presidential documents, regulatory documents with general applicability and legal effect, proposed rules, notices, and documents required to be published by statute.

The *Code of Federal Regulations* is an annual codification of the general and permanent rules published in the *Federal Register*. The *Code* is divided into 50 titles that represent broad areas subject to Federal regulation. The *Code* is kept up to date by the individual issues of the *Federal Register*.

The *Weekly Compilation of Presidential Documents* serves as a timely, up-to-date reference source for the public policies and activities of the President. It contains the remarks, news conferences, messages, statements, and other Presidential material of a public nature issued by the White House during the week reported.

A companion publication to the *Weekly Compilation* is the *Public Papers of the Presidents,* which contains public Presidential documents and speeches in convenient book form. Volumes of the *Public Papers* have been published for every President since Herbert Hoover, with the exception of Franklin D. Roosevelt, whose papers were published privately.

OTHER OFFICE OF THE FEDERAL REGISTER PUBLICATIONS

The Office of the Federal Register publishes slip laws, which are pamphlet prints of each public and private law enacted by Congress. Slip laws are compiled annually as the *United States Statutes at Large*. The *Statutes* volumes contain all public and private laws and concurrent resolutions enacted during a session of Congress; recommendations for executive, legislative, and judicial salaries; reorganization plans; proposed and ratified amendments to the Constitution; and Presidential proclamations. Included with many of these documents are sidenotes, U.S. Code and statutes citations, and a summary of their legislative histories.

PUBLICATION AVAILABILITY

The publications of the Office of the Federal Register are available for sale by writing:

Superintendent of Documents
P.O. Box 371954
Pittsburgh, PA 15250–7954

and are also sold at Government Printing Office bookstores located in several major cities. Telephone inquiries should be directed to 202–512–1800.

Electronic Services

The Office of the Federal Register maintains a free electronic bulletin board service, FREND (Federal Register Electronic News Delivery), for public law numbers, Federal Register finding aids, and related information. To access by modem: phone, 202–275–0920.

In addition, the Federal Register's public inspection list and table of contents are also available on the National Archives' Fax-on-Demand system. Phone, 301–713–6905.

The texts of *The United States Government Manual* and the *Federal Register* are available in electronic format. For more information, contact Electronic Information Dissemination Services, U.S. Government Printing Office. Phone, 202–512–1530.

The Government Printing Office access user support internet e-mail address is <help@eids05.eids.gpo.gov>.

FURTHER INFORMATION

Information on *The United States Government Manual* and other publications of the Office of the Federal Register may be obtained by writing:

Office of the Federal Register
National Archives and Records Administration
Washington, DC 20408

Inquiries should be directed by phone to 202–523–5240 or faxed to 202–523–6866.

Contents

v

The Declaration of Independence

IN CONGRESS, JULY 4, 1776.

THE UNANIMOUS DECLARATION of the thirteen united STATES OF AMERICA,

WHEN in the Course of human events, it becomes necessary for one people to dissolve the political bands which have connected them with another, and to assume among the powers of the earth, the separate and equal station to which the Laws of Nature and of Nature's God entitle them, a decent respect to the opinions of mankind requires that they should declare the causes which impel them to the separation.—We hold these truths to be self-evident, that all men are created equal, that they are endowed by their Creator with certain unalienable Rights, that among these are Life, Liberty and the pursuit of Happiness.—That to secure these rights, Governments are instituted among Men, deriving their just powers from the consent of the governed,—That whenever any Form of Government becomes destructive of these ends, it is the Right of the People to alter or to abolish it, and to institute new Government, laying its foundation on such principles and organizing its powers in such form, as to them shall seem most likely to effect their Safety and Happiness. Prudence, indeed, will dictate that Governments long established should not be changed for light and transient causes; and accordingly all experience hath shown, that mankind are more disposed to suffer, while evils are sufferable, than to right themselves by abolishing the forms to which they are accustomed. But when a long train of abuses and usurpations, pursuing invariably the same Object evinces a design to reduce them under absolute Despotism, it is their right, it is their duty, to throw off such Government, and to provide new Guards for their future security.— Such has been the patient sufferance of these Colonies; and such is now the necessity which constrains them to alter their former Systems of Government. The history of the present King of Great Britain is a history of repeated injuries and usurpations, all having in direct object the establishment of an absolute Tyranny over these States. To prove this, let Facts be submitted to a candid world.—He has refused his Assent to Laws, the most wholesome and necessary for the public good.—He has forbidden his Governors to pass Laws of immediate and pressing importance, unless suspended in their operation till his Assent should be obtained; and when so suspended, he has utterly neglected to attend to them.—He has refused to pass other Laws for the accommodation of large districts of people, unless those people would relinquish the right of Representation in the Legislature, a right inestimable to them and formidable to tyrants only.—He has called together legislative bodies at places unusual, uncomfortable, and distant from the depository of their public Records, for the sole purpose of fatiguing them into compliance with his measures.—He has dissolved Representative Houses repeatedly, for opposing with manly firmness his invasions on the rights of the people.—He has refused for a long time, after such dissolutions, to cause others to be elected; whereby the Legislative powers, incapable of Annihilation, have returned to the People at large for their exercise; the State

1

remaining in the mean time exposed to all the dangers of invasion from without, and convulsions within.—He has endeavored to prevent the population of these States; for that purpose obstructing the Laws for Naturalization of Foreigners; refusing to pass others to encourage their migration hither, and raising the conditions of new Appropriations of Lands.—He has obstructed the Administration of Justice, by refusing his Assent to Laws for establishing Judiciary powers.—He has made Judges dependent on his Will alone, for the tenure of their offices, and the amount and payment of their salaries.—He has erected a multitude of New Offices, and sent hither swarms of Officers to harrass our people, and eat out their substance.—He has kept among us, in times of peace, Standing Armies, without the Consent of our legislatures.—He has affected to render the Military independent of and superior to the Civil power.—He has combined with others to subject us to a jurisdiction foreign to our constitution, and unacknowledged by our laws; giving his Assent to their Acts of pretended Legislation:—For quartering large bodies of armed troops among us:—For protecting them, by a mock Trial, from punishment for any Murders which they should commit on the Inhabitants of these States:—For cutting off our Trade with all parts of the world:—For imposing Taxes on us without our Consent:—For depriving us in many cases, of the benefits of Trial by Jury:—For transporting us beyond Seas to be tried for pretended offences:—For abolishing the free System of English Laws in a neighbouring Province, establishing therein an Arbitrary government, and enlarging its Boundaries so as to render it at once an example and fit instrument for introducing the same absolute rule into these Colonies:—For taking away our Charters, abolishing our most valuable Laws, and altering fundamentally the Forms of our Governments:—For suspending our own Legislatures, and declaring themselves invested with power to legislate for us in all cases whatsoever.—He has abdicated Government here, by declaring us out of his Protection and waging War against us.—He has plundered our seas, ravaged our Coasts, burnt our towns, and destroyed the lives of our people.—He is at this time transporting large Armies of foreign Mercenaries to compleat the works of death, desolation and tyranny, already begun with circumstances of Cruelty & perfidy scarcely paralleled in the most barbarous ages, and totally unworthy the Head of a civilized nation.—He has constrained our fellow Citizens taken Captive on the high Seas to bear Arms against their Country, to become the executioners of their friends and Brethren, or to fall themselves by their Hands.—He has excited domestic insurrections amongst us, and has endeavoured to bring on the inhabitants of our frontiers, the merciless Indian Savages, whose known rule of warfare, is an undistinguished destruction of all ages, sexes and conditions. In every stage of these Oppressions We have Petitioned for Redress in the most humble terms: Our repeated Petitions have been answered only by repeated injury. A Prince, whose character is thus marked by every act which may define a Tyrant, is unfit to be the ruler of a free people. Nor have We been wanting in attentions to our Brittish brethren. We have warned them from time to time of attempts by their legislature to extend an unwarrantable jurisdiction over us. We have reminded them of the circumstances of our emigration and settlement here. We have appealed to their native justice and magnanimity, and we have conjured them by the ties of our common kindred to disavow these usurpations, which, would inevitably interrupt our connections and correspondence. They too have been deaf to the voice of justice and of consanguinity. We must, therefore, acquiesce in the necessity, which denounces our Separation, and hold them, as we hold the rest of mankind, Enemies in War, in Peace Friends.—

    WE, THEREFORE, the Representatives of the UNITED STATES OF AMERICA, in General Congress, Assembled, appealing to the Supreme Judge of the world for the rectitude of our intentions, do, in the Name, and by Authority of the good People of these Colonies, solemnly publish and declare, That these United Colonies are, and of Right ought to be **FREE AND INDEPENDENT STATES;** that they are Absolved from all Allegiance to the British Crown, and that all political connection between them and the State of Great Britain, is and ought to be totally disolved; and that as Free and

Independent States, they have full Power to levy War, conclude Peace, contract Alliances, establish Commerce, and to do all other Acts and Things which Independent States may of right do.—And for the support of this Declaration, with a firm reliance on the protection of Divine Providence, we mutually pledge to each other our Lives, our Fortunes and our sacred Honor.

John Hancock	Benj. Harrison	Lewis Morris
Button Gwinnett	Thos. Nelson, Jr.	Richd. Stockton
Lyman Hall	Francis Lightfoot Lee	Jno. Witherspoon
Geo. Walton	Carter Braxton	Fras. Hopkinson
Wm. Hooper	Robt. Morris	John Hart
Joseph Hewes	Benjamin Rush	Abra. Clark
John Penn	Benj. Franklin	Josiah Bartlett
Edward Rutledge	John Morton	Wm. Whipple
Thos. Heyward, Jr.	Geo. Clymer	Saml. Adams
Thomas Lynch, Jr.	Jas. Smith	John Adams
Arthur Middleton	Geo. Taylor	Robt. Treat Paine
Samuel Chase	James Wilson	Elbridge Gerry
Wm. Paca	Geo. Ross	Step. Hopkins
Thos. Stone	Caesar Rodney	William Ellery
Charles Carroll of	Geo. Read	Roger Sherman
Carrollton	Tho. M: Kean	Sam. Huntington
George Wythe	Wm. Floyd	Wm. Williams
Richard Henry Lee	Phil. Livingston	Oliver Wolcott
Th. Jefferson	Frans. Lewis	Matthew Thornton

The Constitution of the United States

WE THE PEOPLE of the United States, in Order to form a more perfect Union, establish Justice, insure domestic Tranquility, provide for the common defence, promote the general Welfare, and secure the Blessings of Liberty to ourselves and our Posterity, do ordain and establish this Constitution for the United States of America.

Article I

Section 1. All legislative Powers herein granted shall be vested in a Congress of the United States, which shall consist of a Senate and House of Representatives.

Section 2. The House of Representatives shall be composed of Members chosen every second Year by the People of the several States, and the Electors in each State shall have the Qualifications requisite for Electors of the most numerous Branch of the State Legislature.

No Person shall be a Representative who shall not have attained to the Age of twenty five Years, and been seven Years a Citizen of the United States, and who shall not, when elected, be an Inhabitant of that State in which he shall be chosen.

Representatives and direct Taxes shall be apportioned among the several States which may be included within this Union, according to their respective Numbers, which shall be determined by adding to the whole Number of free Persons, including those bound to Service for a Term of Years, and excluding Indians not taxed, three fifths of all other Persons. The actual Enumeration shall be made within three Years after the first Meeting of the Congress of the United States, and within every subsequent Term of ten Years, in such Manner as they shall by Law direct. The Number of Representatives shall not exceed one for every thirty Thousand, but each State shall have at Least one Representative; and until such enumerations shall be made, the State of New Hampshire shall be entitled to chuse three, Massachusetts eight, Rhode-Island and Providence Plantations one, Connecticut five, New-York six, New Jersey four, Pennsylvania eight, Delaware one, Maryland six, Virginia ten, North Carolina five, South Carolina five, and Georgia three.

When vacancies happen in the Representation from any State, the Executive Authority thereof shall issue Writs of Election to fill such Vacancies.

The House of Representatives shall chuse their speaker and other Officers; and shall have the sole Power of Impeachment.

Section 3. The Senate of the United States shall be composed of two Senators from each State, chosen by the Legislature thereof, for six Years; and each Senator shall have one Vote.

Immediately after they shall be assembled in Consequence of the first Election, they shall be divided as equally as may be into three Classes. The Seats of the

Senators of the first Class shall be vacated at the Expiration of the second Year, of the second Class at the Expiration of the fourth Year, and of the third Class at the Expiration of the sixth Year, so that one third may be chosen every second Year; and if Vacancies happen by Resignation, or otherwise, during the Recess of the Legislature of any State, the Executive thereof may make temporary Appointments until the next Meeting of the Legislature, which shall then fill such Vacancies.

No Person shall be a Senator who shall not have attained to the Age of thirty Years, and been nine Years a Citizen of the United States, and who shall not, when elected, be an Inhabitant of that State for which he shall be chosen.

The Vice President of the United States shall be President of the Senate, but shall have no Vote, unless they be equally divided.

The Senate shall chuse their other Officers, and also a President pro tempore, in the Absence of the Vice President, or when he shall exercise the Office of President of the United States.

The Senate shall have the sole Power to try all Impeachments. When sitting for that Purpose, they shall be on Oath or Affirmation. When the President of the United States is tried, the Chief Justice shall preside: And no Person shall be convicted without the concurrence of two thirds of the Members present. Judgment in Cases of Impeachment shall not extend further than to removal from Office, and disqualification to hold and enjoy any Office of honor, Trust or Profit under the United States: but the Party convicted shall nevertheless be liable and subject to Indictment, Trial, Judgment and Punishment, according to law.

Section 4. The Times, Places and Manner of holding Elections for Senators and Representatives, shall be prescribed in each State by the Legislature thereof; but the Congress may at any time by Law make or alter such Regulations, except as to the Places of chusing Senators.

The Congress shall assemble at least once in every Year, and such Meeting shall be on the first Monday in December, unless they shall by Law appoint a different Day.

Section 5. Each House shall be the Judge of the Elections, Returns and Qualifications of its own Members, and a Majority of each shall constitute a Quorum to do business; but a smaller Number may adjourn from day to day, and may be authorized to compel the Attendance of absent Members, in such Manner, and under such Penalties as each House may provide.

Each House may determine the Rules of its Proceedings, punish its Members for disorderly Behaviour, and, with the Concurrence of two thirds, expel a Member.

Each House shall keep a Journal of its Proceedings, and from time to time publish the same, excepting such Parts as may in their Judgment require Secrecy; and the yeas and Nays of the Members of either House on any question shall, at the Desire of one fifth of those Present, be entered on the Journal.

Neither House, during the Session of Congress, shall, without the Consent of the other, adjourn for more than three days, nor to any other place than that in which the two Houses shall be sitting.

Section 6. The Senators and Representatives shall receive a Compensation for their Services, to be ascertained by Law, and paid out of the Treasury of the United States. They shall in all Cases, except Treason, Felony and Breach of the Peace, be privileged from Arrest during their Attendance at the Session of their respective Houses, and in going to and returning from the same; and for any Speech or Debate in either House, they shall not be questioned in any other Place.

No Senator or Representative shall, during the Time for which he was elected, be appointed to any civil Office under the Authority of the United States, which shall have been created, or the Emoluments whereof shall have been encreased during such time; and no Person holding any Office under the United States, shall be a Member of either House during his Continuance in Office.

Section 7. All Bills for raising Revenue shall originate in the House of Representatives; but the Senate may propose or concur with Amendments as on other Bills.

Every Bill which shall have passed the House of Representatives and the Senate, shall, before it become a Law, be presented to the President of the United States; If he approve he shall sign it, but if not he shall return it, with his Objections to that House in which it shall have originated, who shall enter the Objections at large on their Journal, and proceed to reconsider it. If after such Reconsideration two thirds of that House shall agree to pass the Bill, it shall be sent, together with the Objections, to the other House, by which it shall likewise be reconsidered, and if approved by two thirds of that House, it shall become a Law. But in all such Cases the Votes of both Houses shall be determined by yeas and Nays, and the Names of the Persons voting for and against the Bill shall be entered on the Journal of each House respectively. If any Bill shall not be returned by the President within ten Days (Sundays excepted) after it shall have been presented to him, the Same shall be a Law, in like Manner as if he had signed it, unless the Congress by their Adjournment prevent its Return, in which Case it shall not be a Law.

Every Order, Resolution, or Vote to which the Concurrence of the Senate and House of Representatives may be necessary (except on a question of Adjournment) shall be presented to the President of the United States; and before the Same shall take Effect, shall be approved by him, or being disapproved by him, shall be repassed by two thirds of the Senate and House of Representatives, according to the Rules and Limitations prescribed in the Case of a Bill.

Section 8. The Congress shall have Power To lay and collect Taxes, Duties, Imposts and Excises, to pay the Debts and provide for the common Defence and general Welfare of the United States; but all duties, Imposts and Excises shall be uniform throughout the United States;

To borrow Money on the Credit of the United States;

To regulate Commerce with foreign Nations, and among the several States, and with the Indian Tribes;

To establish an uniform Rule of Naturalization, and uniform Laws on the subject of Bankruptcies throughout the United States;

To coin Money, regulate the Value thereof, and of foreign Coin, and fix the Standard of Weights and Measures;

To provide for the Punishment of counterfeiting the Securities and current Coin of the United States;

To establish Post Offices and post Roads;

To promote the Progress of Science and useful Arts, by securing for limited Times to Authors and Inventors exclusive Right to their respective Writings and Discoveries;

To constitute Tribunals inferior to the supreme Court;

To define and punish Piracies and Felonies committed on the high Seas, and Offences against the Law of Nations;

To declare War, grant Letters of Marque and Reprisal, and make rules concerning Captures on Land and Water;

To raise and support Armies, but no Appropriation of Money to that Use shall be for a longer Term than two Years;

To provide and maintain a Navy;

To make rules for the Government and Regulation of the land and naval Forces;

To provide for calling forth the Militia to execute the Laws of the Union, suppress Insurrections and repel Invasions;

To provide for organizing, arming, and disciplining, the Militia, and for governing such Part of them as may be employed in the Service of the United States, reserving to the States respectively, the Appointment of the Officers, and the Authority of training the Militia according to the discipline prescribed by Congress;

To exercise exclusive Legislation in all Cases whatsoever, over such District (not exceeding ten Miles square), as may, by Cession of particular States, and the Acceptance of Congress, become the Seat of the Government of the United States, and to exercise like Authority over all Places purchased by the Consent of the Legislature of the State in which the Same shall be for the Erection of Forts, Magazines, Arsenals, dock-Yards, and other needful Buildings;—And

To make all Laws which shall be necessary and proper for carrying into Execution the foregoing Powers, and all other Powers vested by this Constitution in the Government of the United States, or in any Department or Officer thereof.

Section 9. The Migration or Importation of such Persons as any of the States now existing shall think proper to admit, shall not be prohibited by the Congress prior to the Year one thousand eight hundred and eight, but a Tax or duty may be imposed on such Importation, not exceeding ten dollars for each Person.

The Privilege of the Writ of Habeas Corpus shall not be suspended, unless when in Cases of Rebellion or Invasion the public Safety may require it.

No Bill of Attainder or ex post facto Law shall be passed.

No Capitation, or other direct, Tax shall be laid, unless in Proportion to the Census or Enumeration herein before directed to be taken.

No Tax or Duty shall be laid on Articles exported from any State.

No Preference shall be given by any Regulation of Commerce or Revenue to the Ports of one State over those of another: nor shall Vessels bound to, or from, one State, be obliged to enter, clear, or pay Duties in another.

No money shall be drawn from the Treasury, but in Consequence of Appropriations made by Law; and a regular Statement and Account of the Receipts and Expenditures of all public Money shall be published from time to time.

No Title of Nobility shall be granted by the United States: And no Person holding any Office of Profit or Trust under them, shall, without the Consent of the Congress, accept of any present, Emolument, Office, or Title, of any kind whatever, from any King, Prince, or foreign State.

Section 10. No State shall enter into any Treaty, Alliance, or Confederation; grant Letters of Marque and Reprisal; coin Money; emit Bills of Credit; make any Thing but gold and silver Coin a Tender in Payment of Debts; pass any Bill of Attainder, ex post facto Law, or Law impairing the Obligation of Contracts, or grant any Title of Nobility.

No State shall, without the Consent of the Congress, lay any Imposts or Duties on Imports or Exports, except what may be absolutely necessary for executing it's inspection Laws: and the net Produce of all Duties and Imposts, laid by any State on Imports or Exports, shall be for the Use of the Treasury of the United States; and all such Laws shall be subject to the Revision and Controul of the Congress.

No State shall, without the Consent of Congress, lay any Duty of Tonnage, keep Troops, or Ships of War in time of Peace, enter into any Agreement or Compact with another State, or with a foreign Power, or engage in War, unless actually invaded, or in such imminent Danger as will not admit of delay.

Article II

Section 1. The executive Power shall be vested in a President of the United States of America. He shall hold his Office during the Term of four Years, and, together with the Vice President, chosen for the same term, be elected, as follows

Each State shall appoint, in such Manner as the Legislature thereof may direct, a Number of Electors, equal to the whole Number of Senators and Representatives to which the State may be entitled in the Congress: but no Senator or Representative, or Person holding an Office of Trust or Profit under the United States, shall be appointed an Elector.

The Electors shall meet in their respective States, and vote by Ballot for two Persons, of whom one at least shall not be an Inhabitant of the same State with themselves. And they shall make a List of all the Persons voted for, and of the Number of Votes for each; which List they shall sign and certify, and transmit sealed to the Seat of the Government of the United States, directed to the President of the Senate. The President of the Senate shall, in the Presence of the Senate and House of Representatives, open all the Certificates, and the Votes shall then be counted. The Person having the greatest Number of Votes shall be the President, if such Number be a Majority of the whole Number of Electors appointed; and if there be more than one who have such Majority, and have an equal Number of Votes, then the House of Representatives shall immediately chuse by Ballot one of them for President: and if no Person have a Majority, then from the five highest on the List the said House shall in like Manner chuse the President. But in chusing the President, the Votes shall be taken by States, the Representation from each State having one Vote; A quorum for this Purpose shall consist of a Member or Members from two thirds of the States, and a Majority of all the States shall be necessary to a Choice. In every Case, after the Choice of the President, the Person having the greatest Number of Votes of the Electors shall be the Vice President. But if there should remain two or more who have equal Votes, the Senate shall chuse from them by Ballot the Vice President.

The Congress may determine the Time of chusing the Electors, and the Day on which they shall give their Votes; which Day shall be the same throughout the United States.

No Person except a natural born Citizen, or a Citizen of the United States, at the time of the Adoption of this Constitution, shall be eligible to the Office of President; neither shall any Person be eligible to that Office who shall not have attained to the Age of thirty five Years, and been fourteen Years a Resident within the United States.

In Case of the Removal of the President from Office, or of his Death, Resignation, or Inability to discharge the Powers and Duties of the said Office, the Same shall devolve on the Vice President, and the Congress may by Law provide for the Case of Removal, Death, Resignation or Inability, both of the President and Vice President, declaring what Officer shall then act as President, and such Officer shall act accordingly, until the Disability be removed, or a President shall be elected.

The President shall, at stated Times, receive for his Services, a Compensation, which shall neither be increased nor diminished during the Period for which he shall have been elected, and he shall not receive within that Period any other Emolument from the United States, or any of them.

Before he enter on the Execution of his Office, he shall take the following Oath or Affirmation:—"I do solemnly swear (or affirm) that I will faithfully execute the Office of President of the United States, and will to the best of my Ability, preserve, protect and defend the Constitution of the United States."

Section 2. The President shall be Commander in Chief of the Army and Navy of the United States, and of the Militia of the several States, when called into the actual

Service of the United States; he may require the Opinion, in writing, of the principal Officer in each of the executive Departments, upon any Subject relating to the Duties of their respective Offices, and he shall have Power to grant Reprieves and Pardons for Offences against the United States, except in Cases of Impeachment.

He shall have Power, by and with the Advice and Consent of the Senate, to make Treaties, provided two thirds of the Senators present concur; and he shall nominate, and by and with the Advice and Consent of the Senate, shall appoint Ambassadors, other public Ministers and Consuls, Judges of the supreme Court, and all other Officers of the United States, whose Appointments are not herein otherwise provided for, and which shall be established by Law: but the Congress may by Law vest the Appointment of such inferior Officers, as they think proper, in the President alone, in the Courts of Law, or in the Heads of Departments.

The President shall have Power to fill up all Vacancies that may happen during the Recess of the Senate, by granting Commissions which shall expire at the End of their next Session.

Section 3. He shall from time to time give to the Congress Information of the State of the Union, and recommend to their Consideration such Measures as he shall judge necessary and expedient; he may, on extraordinary Occasions, convene both Houses, or either of them, and in Case of Disagreement between them, with Respect to the Time of Adjournment, he may adjourn them to such Time as he shall think proper; he shall receive Ambassadors and other public Ministers; he shall take Care that the Laws be faithfully executed, and shall Commission all the Officers of the United States.

Section 4. The President, Vice President and all civil Officers of the United States, shall be removed from Office on Impeachment for, and Conviction of, Treason, Bribery, or other High Crimes and Misdemeanors.

Article III

Section 1. The judicial Power of the United States, shall be vested in one supreme Court, and in such inferior Courts as the Congress may from time to time ordain and establish. The Judges, both of the supreme and inferior Courts, shall hold their Offices during good Behaviour, and shall, at stated Times, receive for their Services, a Compensation, which shall not be diminished during their Continuance in Office.

Section 2. The judicial Power shall extend to all Cases, in Law and Equity, arising under this Constitution, the Laws of the United States, and Treaties made, or which shall be made, under their Authority;—to all Cases affecting Ambassadors, other public Ministers and Consuls;—to all Cases of admiralty and maritime Jurisdiction;—to Controversies to which the United States shall be a Party;—to Controversies between two or more States; between a State and Citizens of another State;—between Citizens of different States;—between Citizens of the same State claiming Lands under Grants of different States, and between a State, or the Citizens thereof, and foreign States, Citizens or Subjects.

In all Cases affecting Ambassadors, other public Ministers and Consuls, and those in which a State shall be Party, the supreme Court shall have original Jurisdiction. In all the other Cases before mentioned, the supreme Court shall have appellate Jurisdiction, both as to Law and Fact, with such Exceptions, and under such Regulations as the Congress shall make.

The Trial of all Crimes, except in Cases of Impeachment, shall be by Jury; and such Trial shall be held in the State where the said Crimes shall have been committed; but when not committed within any State, the Trial shall be at such Place or Places as the Congress may by Law have directed.

Section 3. Treason against the United States, shall consist only in levying War against them, or in adhering to their Enemies, giving them Aid and Comfort. No Person shall be convicted of Treason unless on the Testimony of two Witnesses to the same overt Act, or on Confession in open Court.

The Congress shall have Power to declare the Punishment of Treason, but no Attainder of Treason shall work Corruption of Blood, or Forfeiture except during the Life of the Person attainted.

Article IV

Section 1. Full Faith and Credit shall be given in each State to the public Acts, Records, and judicial Proceedings of every other State. And the Congress may by general Laws prescribe the Manner in which such Acts, Records and Proceedings shall be proved, and the Effect thereof.

Section 2. The Citizens of each State shall be entitled to all Privileges and Immunities of Citizens in the several States.

A Person charged in any State with Treason, Felony, or other Crime, who shall flee from Justice, and be found in another State, shall on Demand of the executive Authority of the State from which he fled, be delivered up, to be removed to the State having Jurisdiction of the Crime.

No person held to Service or Labour in one State, under the Laws thereof, escaping into another, shall, in Consequence of any Law or Regulation therein, be discharged from such Service or Labour, but shall be delivered up on Claim of the Party to whom such Service or Labour may be due.

Section 3. New States may be admitted by the Congress into this Union; but no new State shall be formed or erected within the Jurisdiction of any other State; nor any State be formed by the Junction of two or more States, or Parts of States, without the Consent of the Legislatures of the States concerned as well as of the Congress.

The Congress shall have Power to dispose of and make all needful Rules and Regulations respecting the Territory or other Property belonging to the United States; and nothing in this Constitution shall be so construed as to Prejudice any Claims of the United States, or of any particular State.

Section 4. The United States shall guarantee to every State in this Union a Republican Form of Government, and shall protect each of them against Invasion; and on Application of the Legislature, or of the Executive (when the Legislature cannot be convened) against domestic Violence.

Article V

The Congress, whenever two thirds of both Houses shall deem it necessary, shall propose Amendments to this Constitution, or, on the Application of the Legislatures of two thirds of the several States, shall call a Convention for proposing Amendments, which, in either Case, shall be valid to all Intents and Purposes, as Part of this Constitution, when ratified by the Legislatures of three fourths of the several States, or by Conventions in three fourths thereof, as the one or the other Mode of Ratification may be proposed by the Congress; Provided that no Amendment which may be made prior to the Year One thousand eight hundred and eight shall in any Manner affect the first and fourth Clauses in the Ninth Section of the first Article; and that no State,without its Consent, shall be deprived of its equal Suffrage in the Senate.

Article VI

All Debts contracted and Engagements entered into, before the Adoption of this Constitution, shall be as valid against the United States under this Constitution, as under the Confederation.

This Constitution, and the Laws of the United States which shall be made in Pursuance thereof; and all Treaties made, or which shall be made, under the Authority of the United States, shall be the supreme Law of the Land; and the Judges in every State shall be bound thereby, any Thing in the Constitution or Laws of any State to the Contrary notwithstanding.

The Senators and Representatives before mentioned, and the Members of the several State Legislatures, and all executive and judicial Officers, both of the United States and of the several States, shall be bound by Oath or Affirmation, to support this Constitution; but no religious Test shall ever be required as a Qualification to any Office or public Trust under the United States.

Article VII

The Ratification of the Conventions of nine States, shall be sufficient for the Establishment of this Constitution between the States so ratifying the Same.

> *done* in Convention by the Unanimous Consent of the States present the Seventeenth Day of September in the Year of our Lord one thousand seven hundred and Eighty seven and of the Independence of the United States of America the Twelfth *In witness whereof We have hereunto subscribed our Names,*
>
> G° Washington—Presid[t] and deputy from Virginia

New Hampshire	John Langdon
	Nicholas Gilman
Massachusetts	Nathaniel Gorham
	Rufus King
Connecticut	W[m] Sam! Johnson
	Roger Sherman
New York	Alexander Hamilton
New Jersey	Wil: Livingston
	David Brearley.
	W[m] Paterson.
	Jona: Dayton
Pennsylvania [1]	B Franklin
	Thomas Mifflin
	Rob[t] Morris
	Geo. Clymer
	Tho[s] FitzSimons
	Jared Ingersoll

[1] Spelled with one "n" on the original document.

	James Wilson
	Gouv Morris
Delaware	Geo: Read
	Gunning Bedford jun
	John Dickinson
	Richard Bassett
	Jaco: Broom
Maryland	James McHenry
	Dan of St Thos Jenifer
	Danl Carroll
Virginia	John Blair—
	James Madison Jr.
North Carolina	Wm Blount
	Richd Dobbs Spaight.
	Hu Williamson
South Carolina	J. Rutledge
	Charles Cotesworth Pinckney
	Charles Pinckney
	Pierce Butler.
Georgia	William Few
	Abr Baldwin

Amendments

(The first 10 Amendments were ratified December 15, 1791, and form what is known as the Bill of Rights)

Amendment 1

Congress shall make no law respecting an establishment of religion, or prohibiting the free exercise thereof; or abridging the freedom of speech, or of the press; or the right of the people peaceably to assemble, and to petition the Government for a redress of grievances.

Amendment 2

A well regulated Militia, being necessary to the security of a free State, the right of the people to keep and bear Arms, shall not be infringed.

Amendment 3

No Soldier shall, in time of peace be quartered in any house, without the consent of the Owner, nor in time of war, but in a manner to be prescribed by law.

Amendment 4

The right of the people to be secure in their persons, houses, papers, and effects, against unreasonable searches and seizures, shall not be violated, and no Warrants shall issue, but upon probable cause, supported by Oath or affirmation, and particularly describing the place to be searched, and the persons or things to be seized.

Amendment 5

No person shall be held to answer for a capital, or otherwise infamous crime, unless on a presentment or indictment of a Grand Jury, except in cases arising in the land or naval forces, or in the Militia, when in actual service in time of War or public danger; nor shall any person be subject for the same offence to be twice put in jeopardy of life or limb; nor shall be compelled in any criminal case to be a witness against himself, nor be deprived of life, liberty, or property, without due process of law; nor shall private property be taken for public use, without just compensation.

Amendment 6

In all criminal prosecutions, the accused shall enjoy the right to a speedy and public trial, by an impartial jury of the State and district wherein the crime shall have been committed, which district shall have been previously ascertained by law, and to be informed of the nature and cause of the accusation; to be confronted with the witnesses against him; to have compulsory process for obtaining witnesses in his favor, and to have the Assistance of Counsel for his defence.

Amendment 7

In Suits at common law, where the value in controversy shall exceed twenty dollars, the right of trial by jury shall be preserved, and no fact tried by a jury, shall be otherwise re-examined in any Court of the United States, than according to the rules of the common law.

Amendment 8

Excessive bail shall not be required, nor excessive fines imposed, nor cruel and unusual punishments inflicted.

Amendment 9

The enumeration in the Constitution, of certain rights, shall not be construed to deny or disparage others retained by the people.

Amendment 10

The powers not delegated to the United States by the Constitution, nor prohibited by it to the States, are reserved to the States respectively, or to the people.

Amendment 11

(Ratified February 7, 1795)

The Judicial power of the United States shall not be construed to extend to any suit in law or equity, commenced or prosecuted against one of the United States by Citizens of another State, or by Citizens or Subjects of any Foreign State.

Amendment 12

(Ratified July 27, 1804)

The Electors shall meet in their respective states, and vote by ballot for President and Vice-President, one of whom, at least, shall not be an inhabitant of the same state with themselves; they shall name in their ballots the person voted for as President, and in distinct ballots the person voted for as Vice-President, and they shall make distinct lists of all persons voted for as President, and of all persons voted for as Vice-President, and of the number of votes for each, which lists they shall sign and certify, and transmit sealed to the seat of the government of the United States, directed to the President of the Senate;—The President of the Senate shall, in the presence of the Senate and House of Representatives, open all the certificates and the votes shall then be counted;—The person having the greatest number of votes for President, shall be the President, if such number be a majority of the whole number of Electors appointed; and if no person have such majority, then from the persons having the highest numbers not exceeding three on the list of those voted for as President, the House of Representatives shall choose immediately, by ballot, the President. But in choosing the President, the votes shall be taken by states, the representation from each state having one vote; a quorum for this purpose shall consist of a member or members from two-thirds of the states, and a majority of all the states shall be necessary to a choice. And if the House of Representatives shall not choose a President whenever the right of choice shall devolve upon them, before the fourth day of March next following, then the Vice-President shall act as President, as in the case of the death or other constitutional disability of the President.—The person having the greatest number of votes as Vice-President, shall be the Vice-President, if such number be a majority of the whole number of Electors appointed, and if no person have a majority, then from the two highest numbers on the list, the Senate shall choose the Vice-President; a quorum for the purpose shall consist of two-thirds of the whole number of Senators, and a majority of the whole number shall be necessary to a choice. But no person constitutionally ineligible to the office of President shall be eligible to that of Vice-President of the United States.

Amendment 13

(Ratified December 6, 1865)

Section 1. Neither slavery nor involuntary servitude, except as a punishment for crime whereof the party shall have been duly convicted, shall exist within the United States, or any place subject to their jurisdiction.

Section 2. Congress shall have power to enforce this article by appropriate legislation.

Amendment 14

(Ratified July 9, 1868)

Section 1. All persons born or naturalized in the United States, and subject to the jurisdiction thereof, are citizens of the United States and of the State wherein they reside. No State shall make or enforce any law which shall abridge the privileges or immunities of citizens of the United States; nor shall any State deprive any person of life, liberty, or property, without due process of law; nor deny to any person within its jurisdiction the equal protection of the laws.

Section 2. Representatives shall be apportioned among the several States according to their respective numbers, counting the whole number of persons in each State, excluding Indians not taxed. But when the right to vote at any election for the choice of electors for President and Vice President of the United States, Representatives in Congress, the Executive and Judicial officers of a State, or the members of the Legislature thereof, is denied to any of the male inhabitants of such State, being twenty-one years of age, and citizens of the United States, or in any way abridged, except for participation in rebellion, or other crime, the basis of representation therein shall be reduced in the proportion which the number of such male citizens shall bear to the whole number of male citizens twenty-one years of age in such State.

Section 3. No person shall be a Senator or Representative in Congress, or elector of President and Vice President, or hold any office, civil or military, under the United States, or under any State, who, having previously taken an oath, as a member of Congress, or as an officer of the United States, or as a member of any State legislature, or as an executive or judicial officer of any State, to support the Constitution of the United States, shall have engaged in insurrection or rebellion against the same, or given aid or comfort to the enemies thereof. But Congress may by a vote of two-thirds of each House, remove such disability.

Section 4. The validity of the public debt of the United States, authorized by law, including debts incurred for payment of pensions and bounties for services in suppressing insurrection or rebellion, shall not be questioned. But neither the United States nor any State shall assume or pay any debt or obligation incurred in aid of insurrection or rebellion against the United States, or any claim for the loss or emancipation of any slave; but all such debts, obligations and claims shall be held illegal and void.

Section 5. The Congress shall have power to enforce, by appropriate legislation, the provisions of this article.

Amendment 15

(Ratified February 3, 1870)

Section 1. The right of citizens of the United States to vote shall not be denied or abridged by the United States or by any State on account of race, color, or previous condition of servitude.

Section 2. The Congress shall have power to enforce this article by appropriate legislation.

Amendment 16

(Ratified February 3, 1913)

The Congress shall have power to lay and collect taxes on incomes, from whatever source derived, without apportionment among the several States, and without regard to any census or enumeration.

Amendment 17

(Ratified April 8, 1913)

The Senate of the United States shall be composed of two Senators from each State, elected by the people thereof for six years; and each Senator shall have one vote. The electors in each State shall have the qualifications requisite for electors of the most numerous branch of the State legislatures.

When vacancies happen in the representation of any State in the Senate, the executive authority of such State shall issue writs of election to fill such vacancies: *Provided,* That the legislature of any State may empower the executive thereof to make temporary appointments until the people fill the vacancies by election as the legislature may direct.

This amendment shall not be so construed as to affect the election or term of any Senator chosen before it becomes valid as part of the Constitution.

Amendment 18

(Ratified January 16, 1919. Repealed December 5, 1933 by Amendment 21)

Section 1. After one year from the ratification of this article the manufacture, sale, or transportation of intoxicating liquors within, the importation thereof into, or the exportation thereof from the United States and all territory subject to the jurisdiction thereof for beverage purposes is hereby prohibited.

Section 2. The Congress and the several States shall have concurrent power to enforce this article by appropriate legislation.

Section 3. This article shall be inoperative unless it shall have been ratified as an amendment to the Constitution by the legislatures of the several States as provided in the Constitution, within seven years from the date of the submission hereof to the States by the Congress.

Amendment 19

(Ratified August 18, 1920)

The right of citizens of the United States to vote shall not be denied or abridged by the United States or by any State on account of sex.

Congress shall have power to enforce this article by appropriate legislation.

Amendment 20

(Ratified January 23, 1933)

Section 1. The terms of the President and Vice President shall end at noon on the 20th day of January, and the terms of Senators and Representatives at noon on the 3d day of January, of the years in which such terms would have ended if this article had not been ratified; and the terms of their successors shall then begin.

Section 2. The Congress shall assemble at least once in every year, and such meeting shall begin at noon on the 3d day of January, unless they shall by law appoint a different day.

Section 3. If, at the time fixed for the beginning of the term of the President, the President elect shall have died, the Vice President elect shall become President. If a President shall not have been chosen before the time fixed for the beginning of his term, or if the President elect shall have failed to qualify, then the Vice President elect shall act as President until a President shall have qualified; and the Congress may by law provide for the case wherein neither a President elect nor a Vice President elect shall have qualified, declaring who shall then act as President, or the manner in which one who is to act shall be selected, and such person shall act accordingly until a President or Vice President shall have qualified.

Section 4. The Congress may by law provide for the case of the death of any of the persons from whom the House of Representatives may choose a President whenever the right of choice shall have devolved upon them, and for the case of the death of any of the persons from whom the Senate may choose a Vice President whenever the right of choice shall have devolved upon them.

Section 5. Sections 1 and 2 shall take effect on the 15th day of October following the ratification of this article.

Section 6. This article shall be inoperative unless it shall have been ratified as an amendment to the Constitution by the legislatures of three-fourths of the several States within seven years from the date of its submission.

Amendment 21

(Ratified December 5, 1933)

Section 1. The eighteenth article of amendment to the Constitution of the United States is hereby repealed.

Section 2. The transportation or importation into any State, Territory, or possession of the United States for delivery or use therein of intoxicating liquors, in violation of the laws thereof, is hereby prohibited.

Section 3. This article shall be inoperative unless it shall have been ratified as an amendment to the Constitution by conventions in the several States, as provided in the Constitution, within seven years from the date of the submission hereof to the States by the Congress.

Amendment 22

(Ratified February 27, 1951)

Section 1. No person shall be elected to the office of the President more than twice, and no person who has held the office of President, or acted as President, for more than two years of a term to which some other person was elected President shall be elected to the office of the President more than once. But this Article shall not apply to any person holding the office of President when this Article was proposed by the Congress, and shall not prevent any person who may be holding the office of President, or acting as President, during the term within which this Article becomes operative from holding the office of President or acting as President during the remainder of such term.

Section 2. This article shall be inoperative unless it shall have been ratified as an amendment to the Constitution by the legislatures of three-fourths of the several States within seven years from the date of its submission to the States by the Congress.

Amendment 23

(Ratified March 29, 1961)

Section 1. The District constituting the seat of Government of the United States shall appoint in such manner as the Congress may direct:
A number of electors of President and Vice President equal to the whole number of Senators and Representatives in Congress to which the District would be entitled if it were a State, but in no event more than the least populous State; they shall be in addition to those appointed by the States, but they shall be considered, for the purposes of the election of President and Vice President, to be electors appointed by a State; and they shall meet in the District and perform such duties as provided by the twelfth article of amendment.

Section 2. The Congress shall have power to enforce this article by appropriate legislation.

Amendment 24

(Ratified January 23, 1964)

Section 1. The right of citizens of the United States to vote in any primary or other election for President or Vice President, for electors for President or Vice President, or for Senator or Representative in Congress, shall not be denied or abridged by the United States or any State by reason of failure to pay any poll tax or other tax.

Section 2. The Congress shall have power to enforce this article by appropriate legislation.

Amendment 25

(Ratified February 10, 1967)

Section 1. In case of the removal of the President from office or of his death or resignation, the Vice President shall become President.

Section 2. Whenever there is a vacancy in the office of the Vice President, the President shall nominate a Vice President who shall take office upon confirmation by a majority vote of both Houses of Congress.

Section 3. Whenever the President transmits to the President pro tempore of the Senate and the Speaker of the House of Representatives his written declaration that he is unable to discharge the powers and duties of his office, and until he transmits to them a written declaration to the contrary, such powers and duties shall be discharged by the Vice President as Acting President.

Section 4. Whenever the Vice President and a majority of either the principal officers of the executive departments or of such other body as Congress may by law provide, transmit to the President pro tempore of the Senate and the Speaker of the House of Representatives their written declaration that the President is unable to discharge the powers and duties of his office, the Vice President shall immediately assume the powers and duties of the office as Acting President.

Thereafter, when the President transmits to the President pro tempore of the Senate and the Speaker of the House of Representatives his written declaration that no inability exists, he shall resume the powers and duties of his office unless the Vice President and a majority of either the principal officers of the executive department or of such other body as Congress may by law provide, transmit within four days to the President pro tempore of the Senate and the Speaker of the House of Representatives their written declaration that the President is unable to discharge the powers and duties of his office. Thereupon Congress shall decide the issue, assembling within forty-eight hours for that purpose if not in session. If the Congress, within twenty-one days after receipt of the latter written declaration, or, if Congress is not in session, within twenty-one days after Congress is required to assemble, determines by two-thirds vote of both Houses that the President is unable to discharge the powers and duties of his office, the Vice President shall continue to discharge the same as Acting President; otherwise, the President shall resume the powers and duties of his office.

Amendment 26

(Ratified July 1, 1971)

Section 1. The right of citizens of the United States, who are eighteen years of age or older, to vote shall not be denied or abridged by the United States or by any State on account of age.

Section 2. The Congress shall have the power to enforce this article by appropriate legislation.

Amendment 27

(Ratified May 7, 1992)

No law, varying the compensation for the services of the Senators and Representatives, shall take effect, until an election of Representatives shall have intervened.

THE GOVERNMENT OF THE UNITED STATES

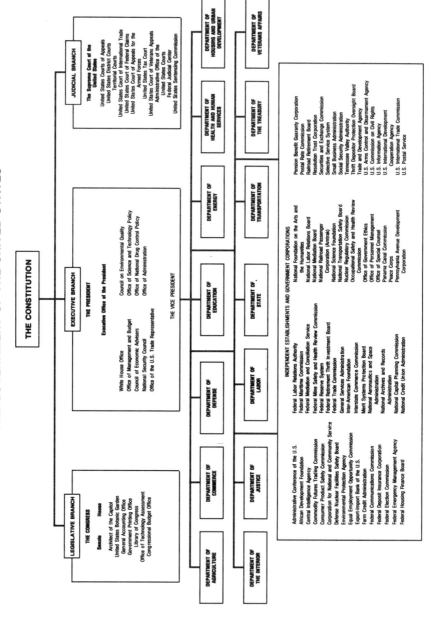

THE CONSTITUTION

LEGISLATIVE BRANCH

THE CONGRESS

Senate   House

Architect of the Capitol
United States Botanic Garden
General Accounting Office
Government Printing Office
Library of Congress
Office of Technology Assessment
Congressional Budget Office

EXECUTIVE BRANCH

THE PRESIDENT

Executive Office of the President

White House Office
Office of Management and Budget
Council of Economic Advisers
National Security Council
Office of the U.S. Trade Representative

Council on Environmental Quality
Office of Science and Technology Policy
Office of National Drug Control Policy
Office of Administration

THE VICE PRESIDENT

JUDICIAL BRANCH

The Supreme Court of the United States

United States Courts of Appeals
United States District Courts
Territorial Courts
United States Court of International Trade
United States Court of Federal Claims
United States Court of Appeals for the Armed Forces
United States Tax Court
United States Court of Veterans Appeals
Administrative Office of the United States Courts
Federal Judicial Center
United States Sentencing Commission

DEPARTMENT OF AGRICULTURE

DEPARTMENT OF COMMERCE

DEPARTMENT OF DEFENSE

DEPARTMENT OF EDUCATION

DEPARTMENT OF ENERGY

DEPARTMENT OF HEALTH AND HUMAN SERVICES

DEPARTMENT OF HOUSING AND URBAN DEVELOPMENT

DEPARTMENT OF THE INTERIOR

DEPARTMENT OF JUSTICE

DEPARTMENT OF LABOR

DEPARTMENT OF STATE

DEPARTMENT OF TRANSPORTATION

DEPARTMENT OF THE TREASURY

DEPARTMENT OF VETERANS AFFAIRS

INDEPENDENT ESTABLISHMENTS AND GOVERNMENT CORPORATIONS

Administrative Conference of the U.S.
African Development Foundation
Central Intelligence Agency
Commodity Futures Trading Commission
Consumer Product Safety Commission
Corporation for National and Community Service
Defense Nuclear Facilities Safety Board
Environmental Protection Agency
Equal Employment Opportunity Commission
Export-Import Bank of the U.S.
Farm Credit Administration
Federal Communications Commission
Federal Deposit Insurance Corporation
Federal Election Commission
Federal Emergency Management Agency
Federal Housing Finance Board

Federal Labor Relations Authority
Federal Maritime Commission
Federal Mediation and Conciliation Service
Federal Mine Safety and Health Review Commission
Federal Reserve System
Federal Retirement Thrift Investment Board
Federal Trade Commission
General Services Administration
Inter-American Foundation
Interstate Commerce Commission
Merit Systems Protection Board
National Aeronautics and Space Administration
National Archives and Records Administration
National Capital Planning Commission
National Credit Union Administration

National Foundation on the Arts and the Humanities
National Labor Relations Board
National Mediation Board
National Railroad Passenger Corporation (Amtrak)
National Science Foundation
National Transportation Safety Board
Nuclear Regulatory Commission
Occupational Safety and Health Review Commission
Office of Government Ethics
Office of Personnel Management
Office of Special Counsel
Panama Canal Commission
Peace Corps
Pennsylvania Avenue Development Corporation

Pension Benefit Guaranty Corporation
Postal Rate Commission
Railroad Retirement Board
Resolution Trust Corporation
Securities and Exchange Commission
Selective Service System
Small Business Administration
Social Security Administration
Tennessee Valley Authority
Thrift Depositor Protection Oversight Board
Trade and Development Agency
U.S. Arms Control and Disarmament Agency
U.S. Commission on Civil Rights
U.S. Information Agency
U.S. International Development Cooperation Agency
U.S. International Trade Commission
U.S. Postal Service

Legislative Branch

LEGISLATIVE BRANCH

CONGRESS
One Hundred and Fourth Congress, First Session

The Senate
The Capitol, Washington, DC 20510
Phone, 202–224–3121

President of the Senate (Vice President of the United States)	ALBERT GORE, JR.
President pro tempore	STROM THURMOND
Majority Leader	BOB DOLE
Minority Leader	THOMAS DASCHLE
Secretary of the Senate	KELLY D. JOHNSTON
Sergeant at Arms	HOWARD O. GREENE, JR.
Secretary for the Majority	ELIZABETH B. GREENE
Secretary for the Minority	C. ABBOTT SAFFOLD
Chaplain	LLOYD OGILVIE

The House of Representatives
The Capitol, Washington, DC 20515
Phone, 202–224–3121

The Speaker	NEWT GINGRICH
Clerk	ROBIN H. CARLE
Sergeant at Arms	WILSON L. LIVINGOOD
Chief Administrative Officer	SCOT M. FAULKNER
Chaplain	REV. JAMES DAVID FORD

The Congress of the United States was created by Article I, section 1, of the Constitution, adopted by the Constitutional Convention on September 17, 1787, providing that "All legislative Powers herein granted shall be vested in a Congress of the United States, which shall consist of a Senate and House of Representatives."

25

163-239 95 – 2

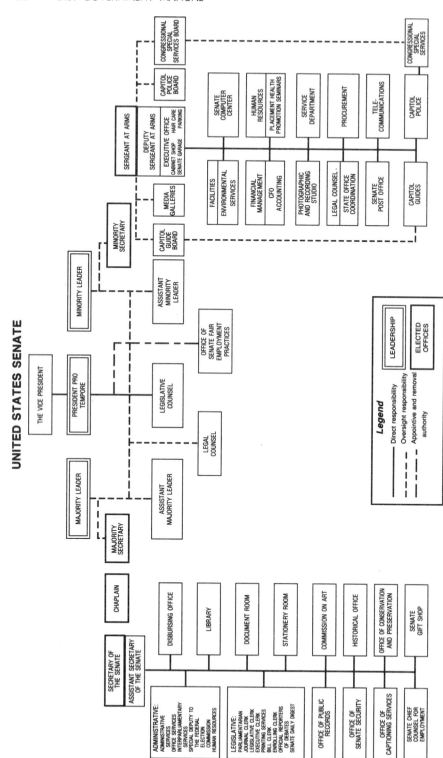

HOUSE OF REPRESENTATIVES

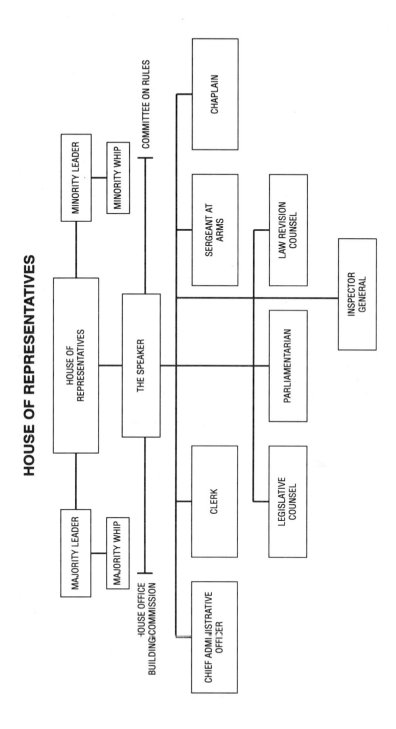

The first Congress under the Constitution met on March 4, 1789, in the Federal Hall in New York City. The membership then consisted of 20 [1] Senators and 59 Representatives.

The Senate is composed of 100 Members, 2 from each State, who are elected to serve for a term of 6 years. Senators were originally chosen by the State legislatures. This procedure was changed by the seventeenth amendment to the Constitution, adopted in 1913, which made the election of Senators a function of the people. There are three classes of Senators, and a new class is elected every 2 years.

The House of Representatives comprises 435 Representatives. The number representing each State is determined by population, but every State is entitled to at least one Representative. Members are elected by the people for 2-year terms, all terms running for the same period.

Both the Senators and the Representatives must be residents of the State from which they are chosen. In addition, a Senator must be at least 30 years of age and must have been a citizen of the United States for at least 9 years; a Representative must be at least 25 years of age and must have been a citizen for at least 7 years.

A Resident Commissioner from Puerto Rico (elected for a 4-year term) and Delegates from American Samoa, the District of Columbia, Guam, and the Virgin Islands complete the composition of the Congress of the United States. Delegates are elected for a term of 2 years. The Resident Commissioner and Delegates may take part in the floor discussions but have no vote in the full House or in the Committee of the Whole House on the State of the Union. They do, however, vote in the committees to which they are assigned.

Officers   The Vice President of the United States is the Presiding Officer of the Senate; in his absence the duties are taken over by a President pro tempore, elected by that body, or someone designated by him. The Presiding Officer of the House of Representatives, the Speaker, is elected by the House; he may designate any Member of the House to act in his absence.

The positions of Senate majority and minority leader have been in existence only since the early years of the 20th century. Leaders are elected at the beginning of each new Congress by a majority vote of the Senators in their political party. In cooperation with their party organizations, leaders are responsible for the design and achievement of a legislative program. This involves managing the flow of legislation, expediting noncontroversial measures, and keeping Members informed regarding proposed action on pending business. Each leader serves as an *ex officio* member of his party's policymaking and organizational bodies and is aided by an assistant floor leader (whip) and a party secretary.

The House leadership is structured essentially the same as the Senate, with the Members in the political parties responsible for the election of their respective leader and whips.

The Secretary of the Senate, elected by vote of the Senate, performs the duties of the Presiding Officer of the Senate in the absence of the Vice President and pending the election of a President pro tempore. The Secretary is the custodian of the seal of the Senate, draws requisitions on the Secretary of the Treasury for moneys appropriated for the compensation of Senators, officers, and employees, and for the contingent expenses of the Senate, and is empowered to administer oaths to any officer of the Senate and to any witness produced before it. The Secretary's executive duties include certification of extracts from the Journal of the Senate; the attestation of bills and joint,

---

[1] New York ratified the Constitution on July 26, 1788, but did not elect its Senators until July 15 and 16, 1789. North Carolina did not ratify the Constitution until November 21, 1789; Rhode Island on May 29, 1790.

concurrent, and Senate resolutions; in impeachment trials, issuance, under the authority of the Presiding Officer, of all orders, mandates, writs, and precepts authorized by the Senate; and certification to the President of the United States of the advice and consent of the Senate to ratification of treaties and the names of persons confirmed or rejected upon the nomination of the President.

The Sergeant at Arms of the Senate is elected by and serves as the Executive Officer of that body. She directs and supervises the various departments and facilities under her jurisdiction. She is also the Law Enforcement and Protocol Officer. As Law Enforcement Officer, she has statutory power to make arrests; to locate absentee Senators for a quorum; to enforce Senate rules and regulations as they pertain to the Senate Chamber, the Senate wing of the Capitol, and the Senate Office Buildings. She serves as a member of the Capitol Police Board and as its chairman each odd year; and, subject to the Presiding Officer, maintains order in the Senate Chamber. As Protocol Officer, she is responsible for many aspects of ceremonial functions, including the inauguration of the President of the United States; arranging funerals of Senators who die in office; escorting the President when he addresses a Joint Session of Congress or attends any function in the Senate; and escorting heads of state when they visit the Senate.

The elected officers of the House of Representatives include the Clerk, the Sergeant at Arms, the Doorkeeper, and the Chaplain.

The clerk is custodian of the seal of the House and administers the primary legislative activities of the House. These duties include: accepting the credentials of the Members-elect and calling the Members to order at the commencement of the first session of each Congress; keeping the Journal; taking all votes and certifying the passage of bills; and processing all legislation. Through various departments, the Clerk also provides floor and committee reporting services; legislative information and reference services; the administration of

House reports pursuant to certain legislation including the Ethics in Government Act, the Federal Election Campaign Act, and the Federal Regulation of Lobbying Act; is responsible for the distribution of House documents and supervises the operations of the House Document Room; and administers the House Page Program. The Clerk is also charged with supervision of the offices vacated by Members due to death, resignation, or expulsion.

The Sergeant at Arms maintains the order of the House under the direction of the Speaker and is the keeper of the Mace. As a member of the U.S. Capitol Police Board, the Sergeant at Arms is the chief law enforcement officer for the House and serves as Board Chairman each even year. The ceremonial and protocol duties parallel those of the Senate Sergeant at Arms and include arranging the inauguration of the President of the United States, Joint Sessions of Congress, visits to the House of heads of state, and funerals of Members of Congress.

The Sergeant at Arms enforces the rules relating to the privileges of the Hall of the House, including admission to the galleries.

The Chief Administrative Officer is charged with the administration of other House support services, including: payroll, benefits, postal operations and internal mail distribution, office furnishings, office equipment, office supplies, and the administration of the House televised floor proceedings.

Committees   The work of preparing and considering legislation is done largely by committees of both Houses of Congress. There are 16 standing committees in the Senate and 19 in the House of Representatives. The standing committees of the Senate and the House of Representatives are shown in the list below. In addition, there are select committees in each House (one in the House of Representatives for the One Hundred and Fourth Congress), and various congressional commissions and joint committees composed of Members of both Houses. Each House may also appoint special investigating committees.

The membership of the standing committees of each House is chosen by a vote of the entire body; members of other committees are appointed under the provisions of the measure establishing them.

Each bill and resolution is usually referred to the appropriate committee, which may report a bill out in its original form, favorably or unfavorably, recommend amendments, or allow the proposed legislation to die in committee without action.

Standing Committees of the Congress

House Committee	Room[1]	Senate Committee	Room[2]
Agriculture	1301	Agriculture, Nutrition, and Forestry	SR–328A
Appropriations	H218	Appropriations	S–128
Banking and Financial Services	2129	Armed Services	SR–228
Budget	309	Banking, Housing, and Urban Affairs	SD–534
Commerce	2125	Budget	SD–621
Economic and Educational Opportunities	2181	Commerce, Science, and Transportation	SD–508
Government Reform and Oversight	2157	Energy and Natural Resources	SD–364
House Oversight	1309	Environment and Public Works	SD–458
Commission on Congressional Mailing Standards:			
Majority	1307		
Minority	1339		
International Relations	2170	Finance	SD–217
Judiciary	2138	Foreign Relations	SD–450
Publications	B29		
National Security	2120	Governmental Affairs	SD–340
Resources	1324	Judiciary	SD–224
Rules	H312	Labor and Human Resources	SD–428
Minority	234		
Science	2320	Rules and Administration	SR–305
Small Business	2361	Small Business	SR–428A
Standards of Official Conduct	HT2	Veterans' Affairs	SR–414
Office of Advice and Education	HT2		
Transportation and Infrastructure	2165		
Veterans' Affairs	335		
Ways and Means	1102		

[1] Room numbers with three digits are in the Cannon House Office Building, four digits beginning with 1 are in the Longworth House Office Building, and four digits beginning with 2 are in the Rayburn House Office Building.
[2] Room numbers preceded by S are in the main Capitol building; those preceded by SD are in the Dirksen Office Building; and those preceded by SR are in the Russell Office Building.
[3] O'Neill House Office Building.

Congressional Record   Proceedings of Congress are published in the *Congressional Record,* which is issued when Congress is in session. Publication of the *Record* began March 4, 1873; it was the first record of debate officially reported, printed, and published directly by the Federal Government. The Daily Digest of the *Congressional Record,* printed in the back of each issue of the *Record,* summarizes the proceedings of that day in each House, and before each of their committees and subcommittees, respectively. The Digest also presents the legislative program for each day and, at the end of the week, gives the program for the following week. Its publication was begun March 17, 1947.
Sessions   Section 4 of Article I of the Constitution makes it mandatory that "The Congress shall assemble at least once in every Year. . . ." Under this

provision, also, the date for convening Congress was designated originally as the first Monday in December, "unless they shall by Law appoint a different Day." Eighteen acts were passed, up to 1820, providing for the meeting of Congress on other days of the year. From 1820 to 1934, however, Congress met regularly on the first Monday in December. In 1934 the Twentieth Amendment changed the convening of Congress to January 3, unless Congress "shall by law appoint a different day." In addition, the President, according to Article II, section 3, of the Constitution "may, on extraordinary Occasions, convene both Houses, or either of them, and in Case of Disagreement between them, with Respect to the Time of Adjournment, he may adjourn them to such Time as he shall think proper. . . ."

Powers of Congress Article I, section 8, of the Constitution defines the powers of Congress. Included are the powers to assess and collect taxes—called the chief power; to regulate commerce, both interstate and foreign; to coin money; to establish post offices and post roads; to establish courts inferior to the Supreme Court; to declare war; and to raise and maintain an army and navy. Congress is further empowered "To provide for calling forth the Militia to execute the Laws of the Union, suppress Insurrections and repel Invasions;" and "To make all Laws which shall be necessary and proper for carrying into Execution the foregoing Powers, and all other Powers vested by this Constitution in the Government of the United States, or in any Department or Officer thereof."

Amendments to the Constitution Another power vested in the Congress is the right to propose amendments to the Constitution, whenever two-thirds of both Houses shall deem it necessary. Should two-thirds of the State legislatures demand changes in the Constitution, it is the duty of Congress to call a constitutional convention. Proposed amendments shall be valid as part of the Constitution when ratified by the legislatures or by conventions of three-fourths of the States, as one or the other mode of ratification may be proposed by Congress.

Special Powers of the Senate Under the Constitution, the Senate is granted certain powers not accorded to the House of Representatives. The Senate approves or disapproves certain Presidential appointments by majority vote, and treaties must be concurred in by a two-thirds vote.

Special Powers of the House of Representatives The House of Representatives is granted the power of originating all bills for the raising of revenue.

Both Houses of Congress act in impeachment proceedings, which, according to the Constitution, may be instituted against the President, Vice President, and all civil officers of the United States. The House of Representatives has the sole power of impeachment, and the Senate has the sole power to try impeachments.

Prohibitions upon Congress Section 9 of Article I of the Constitution also imposes prohibitions upon Congress. "The Privilege of the Writ of Habeas Corpus shall not be suspended, unless when in Cases of Rebellion or Invasion the public Safety may require it." A bill of attainder or an ex post facto law cannot be passed. No export duty can be imposed. Ports of one State cannot be given preference over those of another State. "No money shall be drawn from the Treasury, but in Consequence of Appropriations made by Law. . . ." No title of nobility may be granted.

Rights of Members According to section 6 of Article I, Members of Congress are granted certain privileges. In no case, except in treason, felony, and breach of the peace, can Members be arrested while attending sessions of Congress "and in going to and returning from the same. . . ." Furthermore, the Members cannot be questioned in any other place for remarks made in Congress. Each House may expel a Member of its body by a two-thirds vote.

Enactment of Laws All bills and joint resolutions must pass both the House of Representatives and the Senate and must be signed by the President, except those proposing a constitutional amendment, in order to become law, or be passed over the President's veto by a two-thirds vote of both Houses of Congress. Section 7 of Article I states: "If any Bill shall not be returned by the President within ten Days (Sundays excepted) after it shall have been presented to him, the Same shall be a Law, in like Manner as if he had signed it, unless the Congress by their Adjournment prevent its Return, in which Case it shall not be a Law."

When a bill or joint resolution is introduced in the House, the usual procedure for its enactment into law is as follows:

—assignment to House committee having jurisdiction;

If favorably considered, it is reported to the House either in its original form or with recommended amendments;

—if the bill or resolution is passed by the House, it is messaged to the Senate and referred to the committee having jurisdiction;

—in the Senate committee the bill, if favorably considered, may be reported in the form as received from the House, or with recommended amendments;

—the approved bill or resolution is reported to the Senate, and if passed by that body, is returned to the House;

—if one body does not accept the amendments to a bill by the other body, a conference committee comprised of Members of both bodies is usually appointed to effect a compromise;

—when the bill or joint resolution is finally approved by both Houses, it is signed by the Speaker (or Speaker pro tempore) and the Vice President (or President pro tempore or acting President pro tempore) and is presented to the President; and

—once the President's signature is affixed, the measure becomes a law. If the President vetoes the bill, it cannot become a law unless it is re-passed by a two-thirds vote of both Houses.

Publications The *Congressional Directory,* the *Senate Manual,* and the *House Rules* and *Manual* may be obtained from the Superintendent of Documents, Government Printing Office, Washington, DC 20402.

Senators

[Republicans in roman (56); Democrats in italic (44); total, 100]

Room numbers preceded by SR are in the Russell Office Building (Delaware and Constitution Avenues); those preceded by SD are in the Dirksen Office Building (First Street and Constitution Avenue); and those preceded by SH are in the Hart Office Building (Second and C Streets). Members' offices may be reached by phone at 202–224–3121.

Name	State	Room
Abraham, Spencer	Michigan	SD–241
Akaka, Daniel K	Hawaii	SH–720
Ashcroft, John	Missouri	SR–170
Baucus, Max	Montana	SH–511
Bennett, Robert F	Utah	SD–431
Biden, Joseph R., Jr	Delaware	SR–221
Bingaman, Jeff	New Mexico	SH–703
Bond, Christopher S	Missouri	SR–293
Boxer, Barbara	California	SH–112
Bradley, Bill	New Jersey	SH–731
Breaux, John B	Louisiana	SH–516
Brown, Hank	Colorado	SH–716
Bryan, Richard H	Nevada	SR–364
Bumpers, Dale	Arkansas	SD–229
Burns, Conrad R	Montana	SD–183
Byrd, Robert C	West Virginia	SH–311
Campbell, Ben Nighthorse	Colorado	SR–380
Chafee, John H	Rhode Island	SD–505
Coats, Dan	Indiana	SR–404
Cochran, Thad	Mississippi	SR–326
Cohen, William S	Maine	SH–322
Conrad, Kent	North Dakota	SH–724
Coverdell, Paul	Georgia	SR–200
Craig, Larry E	Idaho	SH–313
D'Amato, Alfonse	New York	SH–520
Daschle, Thomas A	South Dakota	SH–509
DeWine, Mike	Ohio	SR–140
Dodd, Christopher J	Connecticut	SR–444
Dole, Bob	Kansas	SH–141
Domenici, Pete V	New Mexico	SH–328
Dorgan, Byron L	North Dakota	SH–713
Exon, J. James	Nebraska	SH–528
Faircloth, Lauch	North Carolina	SH–708

Senators—Continued

[Republicans in roman (56); Democrats in italic (44); total, 100]
Room numbers preceded by SR are in the Russell Office Building (Delaware and Constitution Avenues); those preceded by SD are in the Dirksen Office Building (First Street and Constitution Avenue); and those preceded by SH are in the Hart Office Building (Second and C Streets). Members' offices may be reached by phone at 202–224–3121.

Name	State	Room
Feingold, Russell D	Wisconsin	SH–502
Feinstein, Dianne	California	SH–331
Ford, Wendell H	Kentucky	SR–173A
Frist, Bill	Tennessee	SD–565
Glenn, John	Ohio	SH–503
Gorton, Slade	Washington	SH–730
Graham, Bob	Florida	SH–524
Gramm, Phil	Texas	SR–370
Grams, Rod	Minnesota	SD–261
Grassley, Chuck	Iowa	SH–135
Gregg, Judd	New Hampshire	SR–393
Harkin, Tom	Iowa	SH–531
Hatch, Orrin G	Utah	SR–135
Hatfield, Mark O	Oregon	SH–711
Heflin, Howell	Alabama	SH–728
Helms, Jesse	North Carolina	SD–403
Hollings, Ernest F	South Carolina	SR–125
Hutchison, Kay Bailey	Texas	SR–283
Inhofe, James	Oklahoma	SR–453
Inouye, Daniel K	Hawaii	SH–722
Jeffords, James M	Vermont	SH–513
Johnston, J. Bennett	Louisiana	SH–136
Kassebaum, Nancy Landon	Kansas	SR–302
Kempthorne, Dirk	Idaho	SD–367
Kennedy, Edward M	Massachusetts	SR–315
Kerrey, J. Robert	Nebraska	SH–303
Kerry, John F	Massachusetts	SR–421
Kohl, Herb	Wisconsin	SH–330
Kyl, Jon	Arizona	SH–702
Lautenberg, Frank R	New Jersey	SH–506
Leahy, Patrick J	Vermont	SR–433
Levin, Carl	Michigan	SR–459
Lieberman, Joseph I	Connecticut	SH–316
Lott, Trent	Mississippi	SR–487
Lugar, Richard G	Indiana	SH–306
Mack, Connie	Florida	SH–517
McCain, John	Arizona	SR–241
McConnell, Mitch	Kentucky	SR–361A
Mikulski, Barbara A	Maryland	SH–709
Moseley-Braun, Carol	Illinois	SH–320
Moynihan, Daniel Patrick	New York	SR–464
Murkowski, Frank H	Alaska	SH–706
Murray, Patty	Washington	SR–111
Nickles, Don	Oklahoma	SH 133
Nunn, Sam	Georgia	SD–303
Packwood, Bob	Oregon	SR–259
Pell, Claiborne	Rhode Island	SR–335
Pressler, Larry	South Dakota	SR–243
Pryor, David H	Arkansas	SR–267
Reid, Harry	Nevada	SH–324
Robb, Charles S	Virginia	SR–154
Rockefeller, John D., IV	West Virginia	SH–109
Roth, William V., Jr	Delaware	SH–104

Senators—Continued

[Republicans in roman (56); Democrats in italic (44); total, 100]

Room numbers preceded by SR are in the Russell Office Building (Delaware and Constitution Avenues); those preceded by SD are in the Dirksen Office Building (First Street and Constitution Avenue); and those preceded by SH are in the Hart Office Building (Second and C Streets). Members' offices may be reached by phone at 202–224–3121.

Name	State	Room
Santorum, Rick	Pennsylvania	SR–120
Sarbanes, Paul S	Maryland	SH–309
Shelby, Richard C	Alabama	SH–110
Simon, Paul	Illinois	SD–462
Simpson, Alan K	Wyoming	SD–105
Smith, Bob	New Hampshire	SD–332
Snowe, Olympia J	Maine	SR–495
Specter, Arlen	Pennsylvania	SH–530
Stevens, Ted	Arkansas	SH–522
Thomas, Craig	Wyoming	SH–302
Thompson, Fred	Tennessee	SD–523
Thurmond, Strom	South Carolina	SR–217
Warner, John	Virginia	SR–225
Wellstone, Paul D	Minnesota	SH–717

Representatives

[Republicans in roman (231); Democrats in italic (203); Independents in bold (1); total (435)]

Room numbers with three digits are in the Cannon House Office Building (New Jersey and Independence Avenues), four digits beginning with 1 are in the Longworth House Office Building (between South Capitol Street and New Jersey Avenue on Independence Avenue), and four digits beginning with 2 are in the Rayburn House Office Building (between First and South Capitol Streets on Independence Avenue). Members' offices may be reached by phone at 202–224–3121.

Name	State (District)	Room
Abercrombie, Neil	Hawaii (1)	1233
Ackerman, Gary L	New York (5)	2243
Allard, Wayne	Colorado (4)	422
Andrews, Robert E	New Jersey (1)	2439
Archer, Bill	Texas (7)	1236
Armey, Richard K	Texas (26)	301
Bachus, Spencer	Alabama (6)	127
Baesler, Scotty	Kentucky (6)	113
Baker, Bill	California (10)	1724
Baker, Richard H	Louisiana (6)	434
Baldacci, John Elias	Maine (2)	1740
Ballenger, Cass	North Carolina (10)	2238
Barcia, James A	Michigan (5)	1410
Barr, Bob	Georgia (7)	1607
Barrett, Bill	Nebraska (3)	1213
Barrett, Thomas M	Wisconsin (5)	1224
Bartlett, Roscoe G.	Maryland (6)	322
Barton, Joe	Texas (6)	2264
Bass, Charles F.	New Hampshire (2)	1728
Bateman, Herbert H	Virginia (1)	2350
Becerra, Xavier	California (30)	1119
Beilenson, Anthony C	California (24)	2465
Bentsen, Ken	Texas (25)	128
Bereuter, Doug	Nebraska (1)	2348
Berman, Howard L	California (26)	2231
Bevill, Tom	Alabama (4)	2302
Bilbray, Brian P	California (49)	1004
Bilirakis, Michael	Florida (9)	2240

Representatives—Continued

[Republicans in roman (231); Democrats in italic (203); Independents in bold (1); total (435)]
Room numbers with three digits are in the Cannon House Office Building (New Jersey and Independence Avenues), four digits beginning with 1 are in the Longworth House Office Building (between South Capitol Street and New Jersey Avenue on Independence Avenue), and four digits beginning with 2 are in the Rayburn House Office Building (between First and South Capitol Streets on Independence Avenue). Members' offices may be reached by phone at 202–224–3121.

Name	State (District)	Room
Bishop, Sanford D., Jr	Georgia (2)	1632
Bliley, Thomas J., Jr	Virginia (7)	2241
Blute, Peter	Massachusetts (3)	1029
Boehlert, Sherwood L	New York (23)	2246
Boehner, John A	Ohio (8)	1011
Bonilla, Henry	Texas (23)	1427
Bonior, David E	Michigan (10)	2207
Bono, Sonny	California (44)	512
Borski, Robert A	Pennsylvania (3)	2182
Boucher, Rick	Virginia (9)	2245
Brewster, Bill K	Oklahoma (3)	1727
Browder, Glen	Alabama (3)	2344
Brown, Corrine	Florida (3)	1610
Brown, George E., Jr	California (42)	2300
Brown, Sherrod	Ohio (13)	1019
Brownback, Sam	Kansas (2)	1313
Bryant, Ed	Tennessee (7)	1516
Bryant, John	Texas (5)	2330
Bunn, Jim	Oregon (5)	1517
Bunning, Jim	Kentucky (4)	2437
Burr, Richard	North Carolina (5)	1431
Burton, Dan	Indiana (6)	2411
Buyer, Stephen E	Indiana (5)	326
Callahan, Sonny	Alabama (1)	2418
Calvert, Ken	California (43)	1523
Camp, Dave	Michigan (4)	137
Canady, Charles T	Florida (12)	1222
Cardin, Benjamin L	Maryland (3)	104
Castle, Michael N	Delaware (At Large)	1207
Chabot, Steve	Ohio (1)	1641
Chambliss, Saxby	Georgia (8)	1708
Chapman, Jim	Texas (1)	2417
Chenoweth, Helen	Idaho (1)	1719
Christensen, Jon	Nebraska (2)	1020
Chrysler, Dick	Michigan (8)	327
Clay, William (Bill)	Missouri (1)	2306
Clayton, Eva M	North Carolina (1)	222
Clement, Bob	Tennessee (5)	2229
Clinger, William F., Jr	Pennsylvania (5)	2160
Clyburn, James E	South Carolina (6)	319
Coble, Howard	North Carolina (6)	403
Coburn, Tom A.	Oklahoma (2)	511
Coleman, Ronald D	Texas (16)	2312
Collins, Barbara-Rose	Michigan (15)	401
Collins, Cardiss	Illinois (7)	2308
Collins, Mac	Georgia (3)	1130
Combest, Larry	Texas (19)	1511
Condit, Gary A	California (18)	2444
Conyers, John, Jr	Michigan (14)	2426
Cooley, Wes	Oregon (2)	1609
Costello, Jerry F	Illinois (12)	2454
Cox, Christopher	California (47)	2402

Representatives—Continued

[Republicans in roman (231); Democrats in italic (203); Independents in bold (1); total (435)]

Room numbers with three digits are in the Cannon House Office Building (New Jersey and Independence Avenues), four digits beginning with 1 are in the Longworth House Office Building (between South Capitol Street and New Jersey Avenue on Independence Avenue), and four digits beginning with 2 are in the Rayburn House Office Building (between First and South Capitol Streets on Independence Avenue). Members' offices may be reached by phone at 202–224–3121.

Name	State (District)	Room
Coyne, William J	Pennsylvania (14)	2455
Cramer, Robert E. (Bud), Jr	Alabama (5)	236
Crane, Philip M	Illinois (8)	233
Crapo, Michael D	Idaho (2)	437
Cremeans, Frank A.	Ohio (6)	1107
Cubin, Barbara	Wyoming (At Large)	1114
Cunningham, Randy (Duke)	California (51)	227
Danner, Pat	Missouri (6)	1323
Davis, Thomas M.	Virginia (11)	415
Deal, Nathan	Georgia (9)	1406
DeFazio, Peter A	Oregon (4)	2134
de la Garza, E	Texas (15)	1401
DeLauro, Rosa L	Connecticut (3)	436
DeLay, Tom	Texas (22)	203
Dellums, Ronald V	California (9)	2108
Deutsch, Peter	Florida (20)	204
Diaz-Balart, Lincoln	Florida (21)	431
Dickey, Jay	Arkansas (4)	230
Dicks, Norman D	Washington (6)	2467
Dingell, John D	Michigan (16)	2328
Dixon, Julian C	California (32)	2252
Doggett, Lloyd	Texas (10)	126
Dooley, Calvin M	California (20)	1227
Doolittle, John T	California (4)	1526
Dornan, Robert K	California (46)	1201
Doyle, Michael F	Pennsylvania (18)	1218
Dreier, David	California (28)	411
Duncan, John J., Jr	Tennessee (2)	2400
Dunn, Jennifer	Washington (8)	432
Durbin, Richard J	Illinois (20)	2463
Edwards, Chet	Texas (11)	328
Ehlers, Vernon J	Michigan (3)	1717
Ehrlich, Robert L., Jr	Maryland (2)	315
Emerson, Bill	Missouri (8)	2268
Engel, Eliot L	New York (17)	1433
English, Phil	Pennsylvania (21)	1721
Ensign, John E	Nevada (1)	414
Eshoo, Anna G	California (14)	308
Evans, Lane	Illinois (17)	2335
Everett, Terry	Alabama (2)	208
Ewing, Thomas W	Illinois (15)	1317
Farr, Sam	California (17)	1117
Fattah, Chaka	Pennsylvania (2)	1205
Fawell, Harris W	Illinois (13)	2159
Fazio, Vic	California (3)	2113
Fields, Cleo	Louisiana (4)	218
Fields, Jack	Texas (8)	2228
Filner, Bob	California (50)	504
Flake, Floyd H	New York (6)	1035
Flanagan, Michael Patrick	Illinois (5)	1407
Foglietta, Thomas M	Pennsylvania (1)	341
Foley, Mark Adam	Florida (16)	506

Representatives—Continued

[Republicans in roman (231); Democrats in italic (203); Independents in bold (1); total (435)]
Room numbers with three digits are in the Cannon House Office Building (New Jersey and Independence Avenues), four digits beginning with 1 are in the Longworth House Office Building (between South Capitol Street and New Jersey Avenue on Independence Avenue), and four digits beginning with 2 are in the Rayburn House Office Building (between First and South Capitol Streets on Independence Avenue). Members' offices may be reached by phone at 202–224–3121.

Name	State (District)	Room
Forbes, Michael P	New York (1)	502
Ford, Harold E	Tennessee (9)	2111
Fowler, Tillie K	Florida (4)	413
Fox, Jon D	Pennsylvania (13)	510
Frank, Barney	Massachusetts (4)	2210
Franks, Bob	New Jersey (7)	429
Franks, Gary A	Connecticut (5)	133
Frelinghuysen, Rodney P	New Jersey (11)	514
Frisa, Dan	New York (4)	1529
Frost, Martin	Texas (24)	2459
Funderburk, David	North Carolina (2)	427
Furse, Elizabeth	Oregon (1)	316
Gallegly, Elton	California (23)	2441
Ganske, Greg	Iowa (4)	1108
Gejdenson, Sam	Connecticut (2)	2416
Gekas, George W	Pennsylvania (17)	2410
Gephardt, Richard A	Missouri (3)	1226
Geren, Pete	Texas (12)	2448
Gibbons, Sam	Florida (11)	2204
Gilchrest, Wayne T	Maryland (1)	332
Gillmor, Paul E	Ohio (5)	1203
Gilman, Benjamin A	New York (20)	2449
Gingrich, Newt	Georgia (6)	2428
Gonzalez, Henry B	Texas (20)	2413
Goodlatte, Bob	Virginia (6)	123
Goodling, William F	Pennsylvania (19)	2263
Gordon, Bart	Tennessee (6)	2201
Goss, Porter J	Florida (14)	108
Graham, Lindsey O	South Carolina (3)	1429
Green, Gene	Texas (29)	1024
Greenwood, James C	Pennsylvania (8)	430
Gunderson, Steve	Wisconsin (3)	2185
Gutierrez, Luis V	Illinois (4)	408
Gutknecht, Gil	Minnesota (4)	425
Hall, Ralph M	Texas (4)	2236
Hall, Tony P	Ohio (3)	1432
Hamilton, Lee H	Indiana (9)	2314
Hancock, Mel	Missouri (7)	438
Hansen, James V	Utah (1)	2466
Harman, Jane	California (36)	325
Hastert, J. Dennis	Illinois (14)	2453
Hastings, Alcee L	Florida (23)	1039
Hastings, Richard (Doc)	Washington (4)	1229
Hayes, James A	Louisiana (7)	2432
Hayworth, J.D.	Arizona (6)	1023
Hefley, Joel	Colorado (5)	2351
Hefner, W.G. (Bill)	North Carolina (8)	2470
Heineman, Fred	North Carolina (4)	1440
Herger, Wally	California (2)	2433
Hilleary, Van	Tennessee (4)	114
Hilliard, Earl F	Alabama (7)	1007
Hinchey, Maurice D	New York (26)	1524

Representatives—Continued

[Republicans in roman (231); Democrats in italic (203); Independents in bold (1); total (435)]
Room numbers with three digits are in the Cannon House Office Building (New Jersey and Independence Avenues), four digits beginning with 1 are in the Longworth House Office Building (between South Capitol Street and New Jersey Avenue on Independence Avenue), and four digits beginning with 2 are in the Rayburn House Office Building (between First and South Capitol Streets on Independence Avenue). Members' offices may be reached by phone at 202–224–3121.

Name	State (District)	Room
Hobson, David L	Ohio (7)	1514
Hoekstra, Peter	Michigan (2)	1122
Hoke, Martin R	Ohio (10)	212
Holden, Tim	Pennsylvania (6)	1421
Horn, Stephen	California (38)	129
Hostettler, John N	Indiana (8)	1404
Houghton, Amo	New York (31)	1110
Hoyer, Steny H	Maryland (5)	1705
Hunter, Duncan	California (52)	2265
Hutchinson, Y. Tim	Arkansas (3)	1005
Hyde, Henry J	Illinois (6)	2110
Inglis, Bob	South Carolina (4)	1237
Istook, Ernest J., Jr	Oklahoma (5)	119
Jackson-Lee, Sheila	Texas (18)	1520
Jacobs, Andrew, Jr	Indiana (10)	2313
Jefferson, William J	Louisiana (2)	240
Johnson, Eddie Bernice	Texas (30)	1123
Johnson, Nancy L	Connecticut (6)	343
Johnson, Sam	Texas (3)	1030
Johnson, Tim	South Dakota (At Large)	2438
Johnston, Harry	Florida (19)	2458
Jones, Walter B., Jr	North Carolina (3)	214
Kanjorski, Paul E	Pennsylvania (11)	2429
Kaptur, Marcy	Ohio (9)	2104
Kasich, John R	Ohio (12)	1131
Kelly, Sue W	New York (19)	1037
Kennedy, Joseph P., II	Massachusetts (8)	2242
Kennedy, Patrick J	Rhode Island (1)	1505
Kennelly, Barbara B	Connecticut (1)	201
Kildee, Dale E	Michigan (9)	2187
Kim, Jay	California (41)	435
King, Peter T	New York (3)	224
Kingston, Jack	Georgia (1)	1507
Kleczka, Gerald D	Wisconsin (4)	2301
Klink, Ron	Pennsylvania (4)	125
Klug, Scott L	Wisconsin (2)	1113
Knollenberg, Joe	Michigan (11)	1221
Kolbe, Jim	Arizona (5)	205
LaFalce, John J	New York (29)	2310
LaHood, Ray	Illinois (18)	329
Lantos, Tom	California (12)	2217
Largent, Steve	Oklahoma (1)	410
Latham, Tom	Iowa (5)	516
LaTourette, Steven C	Ohio (19)	1508
Laughlin, Greg	Texas (14)	442
Lazio, Rick	New York (2)	314
Leach, James A	Iowa (1)	2186
Levin, Sander M	Michigan (12)	2230
Lewis, Jerry	California (40)	2112
Lewis, John	Georgia (5)	229
Lewis, Ron	Kentucky (2)	412
Lightfoot, Jim	Iowa (3)	2161

Representatives—Continued

[Republicans in roman (231); Democrats in italic (203); Independents in bold (1); total (435)]
Room numbers with three digits are in the Cannon House Office Building (New Jersey and Independence Avenues), four digits beginning with 1 are in the Longworth House Office Building (between South Capitol Street and New Jersey Avenue on Independence Avenue), and four digits beginning with 2 are in the Rayburn House Office Building (between First and South Capitol Streets on Independence Avenue). Members' offices may be reached by phone at 202–224–3121.

Name	State (District)	Room
Lincoln, Blanche Lambert	Arizona (1)	1204
Linder, John	Georgia (4)	1318
Lipinski, William O	Illinois (3)	1501
Livingston, Bob	Louisiana (1)	2406
LoBiondo, Frank A	New Jersey (2)	513
Lofgren, Zoe	California (16)	118
Longley, James B., Jr	Maine (1)	226
Lowey, Nita M	New York (18)	2421
Lucas, Frank D	Oklahoma (6)	107
Luther, William P	Minnesota (6)	1419
McCarthy, Karen	Missouri (5)	1232
McCollum, Bill	Florida (8)	2266
McCrery, Jim	Louisiana (5)	225
McDade, Joseph M	Pennsylvania (10)	2107
McDermott, Jim	Washington (7)	2349
McHale, Paul	Pennsylvania (15)	217
McHugh, John M	New York (24)	416
McInnis, Scott	Colorado (3)	215
McIntosh, David M	Indiana (2)	1208
McKeon, Howard P. (Buck)	California (25)	307
McKinney, Cynthia A.	Georgia (11)	124
McNulty, Michael R	New York (21)	2442
Maloney, Carolyn B	New York (14)	1504
Manton, Thomas J	New York (7)	2235
Manzullo, Donald A	Illinois (16)	426
Markey, Edward J	Massachusetts (7)	2133
Martinez, Matthew G	California (31)	2239
Martini, William J	New Jersey (8)	1513
Mascara, Frank	Pennsylvania (20)	1531
Matsui, Robert T	California (5)	2311
Meehan, Martin T	Massachusetts (5)	318
Meek, Carrie P	Florida (17)	404
Menendez, Robert	New Jersey (13)	1730
Metcalf, Jack	Washington (2)	507
Meyers, Jan	Kansas (3)	2303
Mfume, Kweisi	Maryland (7)	2419
Mica, John L	Florida (7)	336
Miller, Dan	Florida (13)	117
Miller, George	California (7)	2205
Mineta, Norman Y	California (15)	2221
Minge, David	Minnesota (2)	1415
Mink, Patsy T	Hawaii (2)	2135
Moakley, John Joseph	Massachusetts (9)	235
Molinari, Susan	New York (13)	2435
Mollohan, Alan B	West Virginia (1)	2427
Montgomery, G.V. (Sonny)	Mississippi (3)	2184
Moorhead, Carlos J	California (27)	2346
Moran, James P	Virginia (8)	405
Morella, Constance A	Maryland (8)	106
Murtha, John P	Pennsylvania (12)	2423
Myers, John T	Indiana (7)	2372
Myrick, Sue	North Carolina (9)	509

Representatives—Continued

[Republicans in roman (231); Democrats in italic (203); Independents in bold (1); total (435)]
Room numbers with three digits are in the Cannon House Office Building (New Jersey and Independence Avenues), four digits beginning with 1 are in the Longworth House Office Building (between South Capitol Street and New Jersey Avenue on Independence Avenue), and four digits beginning with 2 are in the Rayburn House Office Building (between First and South Capitol Streets on Independence Avenue). Members' offices may be reached by phone at 202–224–3121.

Name	State (District)	Room
Nadler, Jerrold	New York (8)	109
Neal, Richard E	Massachusetts (2)	2431
Nethercutt, George R., Jr	Washington (5)	1527
Neumann, Mark W	Wisconsin (1)	1725
Ney, Robert W	Ohio (18)	1605
Norwood, Charlie	Georgia (10)	1707
Nussle, Jim	Iowa (2)	303
Oberstar, James L	Minnesota (8)	2366
Obey, David R	Wisconsin (7)	2462
Olver, John W	Massachusetts (1)	1027
Ortiz, Solomon P	Texas (27)	2136
Orton, Bill	Utah (3)	440
Owens, Major R	New York (11)	2305
Oxley, Michael G	Ohio (4)	2233
Packard, Ron	California (48)	2162
Pallone, Frank, Jr	New Jersey (6)	420
Parker, Mike	Mississippi (4)	2445
Pastor, Ed	Arizona (2)	223
Paxon, Bill	New York (27)	2436
Payne, Donald M	New Jersey (10)	2244
Payne, L.F	Virginia (5)	2412
Pelosi, Nancy	California (8)	2457
Peterson, Collin C	Minnesota (7)	1314
Peterson, Douglas (Pete)	Florida (2)	306
Petri, Thomas E	Wisconsin (6)	2262
Pickett, Owen B	Virginia (2)	2430
Pombo, Richard W	California (11)	1519
Pomeroy, Earl	North Dakota (At Large)	1533
Porter, John Edward	Illinois (10)	2373
Portman, Rob	Ohio (2)	238
Poshard, Glenn	Illinois (19)	2334
Pryce, Deborah	Ohio (15)	221
Quillen, James H. (Jimmy)	Tennessee (1)	102
Quinn, Jack	New York (30)	331
Rahall, Nick J., II	West Virginia (3)	2269
Ramstad, Jim	Minnesota (3)	103
Rangel, Charles B	New York (15)	2354
Reed, Jack	Rhode Island (2)	1510
Regula, Ralph	Ohio (16)	2309
Reynolds, Mel	Illinois (2)	312
Richardson, Bill	New Mexico (3)	2209
Riggs, Frank	California (1)	1714
Rivers, Lynn N	Michigan (13)	1116
Roberts, Pat	Kansas (1)	1126
Roemer, Tim	Indiana (3)	407
Rogers, Harold	Kentucky (5)	2468
Rohrabacher, Dana	California (45)	2338
Ros-Lehtinen, Ileana	Florida (18)	2440
Rose, Charlie	North Carolina (7)	242
Roth, Toby	Wisconsin (8)	2234
Roukema, Marge	New Jersey (5)	2469
Roybal-Allard, Lucille	California (33)	324

Representatives—Continued

[Republicans in roman (231); Democrats in italic (203); Independents in bold (1); total (435)]

Room numbers with three digits are in the Cannon House Office Building (New Jersey and Independence Avenues), four digits beginning with 1 are in the Longworth House Office Building (between South Capitol Street and New Jersey Avenue on Independence Avenue), and four digits beginning with 2 are in the Rayburn House Office Building (between First and South Capitol Streets on Independence Avenue). Members' offices may be reached by phone at 202–224–3121.

Name	State (District)	Room
Royce, Edward R	California (39)	1133
Rush, Bobby L	Illinois (1)	131
Sabo, Martin Olav	Minnesota (5)	2336
Salmon, Matt	Arizona (1)	115
Sanders, Bernard	Vermont (At Large)	213
Sanford, Marshall (Mark)	South Carolina (1)	1223
Sawyer, Thomas C	Ohio (14)	1414
Saxton, Jim	New Jersey (3)	339
Scarborough, Joe	Florida (1)	1523
Schaefer, Dan	Colorado (6)	2353
Schiff, Steven	New Mexico (1)	2404
Schroeder, Patricia	Colorado (1)	2307
Schumer, Charles E	New York (9)	2211
Scott, Robert C	Virginia (3)	501
Seastrand, Andrea H	California (22)	1216
Sensenbrenner, F. James, Jr	Wisconsin (9)	2332
Serrano, José E	New York (16)	2342
Shadegg, John B	Arizona (4)	503
Shaw, E. Clay, Jr	Florida (22)	2267
Shays, Christopher	Connecticut (4)	1502
Shuster, Bud	Pennsylvania (9)	2188
Sisisky, Norman	Virginia (4)	2371
Skaggs, David E	Colorado (2)	1124
Skeen, Joe	New Mexico (2)	2367
Skelton, Ike	Missouri (4)	2227
Slaughter, Louise McIntosh	New York (28)	2347
Smith, Christopher H	New Jersey (4)	2370
Smith, Lamar S	Texas (21)	2443
Smith, Linda	Washington (3)	1217
Smith, Nick	Michigan (7)	1530
Solomon, Gerald B.H	New York (22)	2206
Souder, Mark E	Indiana (4)	508
Spence, Floyd	South Carolina (2)	2405
Spratt, John M., Jr	South Carolina (5)	1536
Stark, Fortney Pete	California (13)	239
Stearns, Cliff	Florida (6)	2352
Stenholm, Charles W	Texas (17)	1211
Stockman, Steve	Texas (9)	417
Stokes, Louis	Ohio (11)	2365
Studds, Gerry E	Massachusetts (10)	237
Stump, Bob	Arizona (3)	211
Stupak, Bart	Michigan (1)	317
Talent, James M	Missouri (2)	1020
Tanner, John S	Tennessee (8)	127
Tate, Randy	Washington (9)	1118
Tauzin, W.J. (Billy)	Louisiana (3)	2183
Taylor, Charles H	North Carolina (11)	231
Taylor, Gene	Mississippi (5)	2447
Tejeda, Frank	Texas (28)	323
Thomas, William M	California (21)	2208
Thompson, Bennie G	Mississippi (2)	1408
Thornberry, William M. (Mac)	Texas (13)	1535

Representatives—Continued

[Republicans in roman (231); Democrats in italic (203); Independents in bold (1); total (435)]
Room numbers with three digits are in the Cannon House Office Building (New Jersey and Independence Avenues), four digits beginning with 1 are in the Longworth House Office Building (between South Capitol Street and New Jersey Avenue on Independence Avenue), and four digits beginning with 2 are in the Rayburn House Office Building (between First and South Capitol Streets on Independence Avenue). Members' offices may be reached by phone at 202–224–3121.

Name	State (District)	Room
Thornton, Ray	Arkansas (2)	1214
Thurman, Karen L	Florida (5)	130
Tiahrt, Todd	Kansas (4)	1319
Torkildsen, Peter G	Massachusetts (6)	120
Torres, Esteban Edward	California (34)	2368
Torricelli, Robert G	New Jersey (9)	1026
Towns, Edolphus	New York (10)	2232
Traficant, James A., Jr	Ohio (17)	2446
Tucker, Walter R., III	California (37)	419
Upton, Fred	Michigan (6)	2333
Velázquez, Nydia M	New York (12)	132
Vento, Bruce F	Minnesota (4)	2304
Visclosky, Peter J	Indiana (1)	2464
Volkmer, Harold L	Missouri (9)	2409
Vucanovich, Barbara F	Nevada (2)	2202
Waldholtz, Enid G	Utah (2)	515
Walker, Robert S	Pennsylvania (16)	2369
Walsh, James T	New York (25)	1330
Wamp, Zach	Tennessee (3)	423
Ward, Mike	Kentucky (3)	1032
Waters, Maxine	California (35)	330
Watt, Melvin L	North Carolina (12)	1230
Watts, J.C., Jr	Oklahoma (4)	1713
Waxman, Henry A	California (29)	2408
Weldon, Curt	Pennsylvania (7)	2452
Weldon, Dave	Florida (15)	216
Weller, Jerry	Illinois (11)	1710
White, Rick	Washington (1)	116
Whitfield, Ed	Kentucky (1)	1541
Wicker, Roger F	Mississippi (1)	206
Williams, Pat	Montana (At Large)	2329
Wilson, Charles	Texas (2)	2256
Wise, Robert E., Jr	West Virginia (2)	2434
Wolf, Frank R	Virginia (10)	241
Woolsey, Lynn C	California (6)	439
Wyden, Ron	Oregon (3)	1111
Wynn, Albert Russell	Maryland (4)	418
Yates, Sidney R	Illinois (9)	2109
Young, C.W. Bill	Florida (10)	2407
Young, Don	Alaska (At Large)	2331
Zeliff, William H., Jr	New Hampshire (1)	1210
Zimmer, Dick	New Jersey (12)	228

Delegates

Faleomavaega, Eni F.H	American Samoa	2422
Norton, Eleanor Holmes	District of Columbia	1424
Underwood, Robert A	Guam	424

Resident Commissioner

Romero-Barceló, Carlos A	Puerto Rico	428

For further information concerning the United States Senate, contact the Secretary of the Senate, The Capitol, Washington, DC 20510. Phone, 202–224–2115. For further information concerning the House of Representatives, contact the Clerk, The Capitol, Washington, DC 20515. Phone, 202–225–7000.

Telephone directories for the United States Senate and the House of Representatives are available for sale by the Superintendent of Documents, Government Printing Office, Washington, DC 20402.

ARCHITECT OF THE CAPITOL

U.S. Capitol Building, Washington, DC 20515
Phone, 202–228–1793

Architect of the Capitol	GEORGE M. WHITE

The Architect of the Capitol is responsible for the care and maintenance of the U.S. Capitol and nearby buildings and grounds while implementing reconstruction and landscape improvement projects according to the original intent of the Capitol's designers.

The Architect of the Capitol is charged with operating and maintaining the buildings of the Capitol committed to his care by Congress. Permanent authority for these functions was established by the act of August 15, 1876 (40 U.S.C. 162, 163). The Architect's duties include the mechanical and structural maintenance of the Capitol, the conservation and care of works of art in the building, the upkeep and improvement of the Capitol grounds, and the arrangement of inaugural and other ceremonies held in the building or on the grounds. Legislation is enacted from time to time providing for additional buildings and grounds to be placed under the jurisdiction of the Architect of the Capitol.

In addition to the Capitol, the Architect is responsible for the upkeep of all of the congressional office buildings, the Library of Congress buildings, the United States Supreme Court building, the Thurgood Marshall Federal Judiciary Building, the Capitol Power Plant, the Capitol Police headquarters, and the Robert A. Taft Memorial. The Architect performs his duties in connection with the Senate side of the Capitol, the Senate office buildings, and the operation of the Senate restaurants subject to the approval of the Senate Committee on Rules and Administration. In matters of general policy in connection with the House office buildings and the Capitol Power Plant, his activities are subject to the approval and direction of the House Office Building Commission. The Architect is under the direction of the Speaker in matters concerning the House side of the Capitol. Also, the Architect of the Capitol serves as the Acting Director of the United States Botanic Garden under the Joint Committee on the Library.

Until 1989 the position of Architect of the Capitol was filled by Presidential appointment for an indefinite term. Legislation enacted in 1989 provided that the Architect be appointed by the President for a 10-year term, with the advice and consent of the Senate, from a list of 3 candidates recommended by a congressional commission. Upon confirmation by the Senate, the Architect becomes an official of the legislative branch as an officer and agent of Congress and is eligible for reappointment after completion of his term.

The Architect, whose original duties were limited to designing and supervising the construction of the Capitol, has assumed additional responsibilities for activities that have been assigned to the office by Congress. Today, in light of the widespread activities under the jurisdiction of the Architect of the Capitol, the administrative function challenges the architectural and engineering functions of the office.

Projects carried out by the Architect of the Capitol in recent years include renovation and restoration of the Statue of Freedom, the Rotunda and other areas in the Capitol, and the Library of Congress; procurement and installation of television and broadcasting facilities for the House and Senate chambers and hearing rooms; improvement to building utility, energy-management, and security systems; installation of a Senate subway system; development and implementation of the Legislative Branch Telecommunications Network; plans for the complete renovation of the U.S. Botanic Garden Conservatory; the design of a National Garden adjacent to the Conservatory; and plans for a new Capitol Visitor Center. The Architect also oversaw the design and construction of the Thurgood Marshall Federal Judiciary Building for the U.S. courts. Ongoing conservation/renovation projects include the Brumidi corridors in the Capitol, a substantial barrier-removal program throughout the Capitol Complex, and the east monumental stairs on the Capitol's House wing.

The Architect of the Capitol also serves as a member of numerous governing or advisory bodies, including: Capitol Police Board, Capitol Guide Board, House of Representatives Page Board, District of Columbia Zoning Commission, Board of Directors of the Pennsylvania Avenue Development Corporation, Advisory Council on Historic Preservation, National Capital Memorial Commission, Art Advisory Committee to the Washington Metropolitan Area Transit Authority, and the National Institute for Conservation of Cultural Property. He is also an *ex officio* member of the United States Capitol Preservation Commission and the Commission on the Bicentennial of the United States Capitol. In addition, he serves as the Coordinator of Civil Defense for the Capitol complex.

For further information, contact the Office of the Architect of the Capitol, U.S. Capitol Building, Washington, DC 20515. Phone, 202–228–1793.

UNITED STATES BOTANIC GARDEN

Office of Executive Director, 245 First Street SW., Washington, DC 20024
Phone, 202–225–8333

Conservatory, Maryland Avenue, First to Second Streets SW., Washington, DC 20024
Phone, 202–225–6646

Production Facility, 4700 Shepherd Parkway SW., Washington, DC 20032
Phone, 202–563–2220

Director (Architect of the Capitol)	GEORGE M. WHITE, *Acting*
Executive Director	JEFFREY P. COOPER-SMITH

The United States Botanic Garden is an educational and scientific display garden. It informs and educates visitors about the importance, and irreplaceable value, of plants to the well-being of humankind and to the fragile ecosystems that support all life.

The Botanic Garden's indoor and outdoor displays convey information on the aesthetic, cultural, economic, therapeutic, and ecological value of plants worldwide.

The Conservatory, one of the largest structures of its kind in this country, features both indoor exhibits and two outdoor courtyard gardens. Collections in this facility attract many visitors annually, including botanists, horticulturists, ecologists, students, and garden club members. The permanent collections include: orchids, epiphytes, bromeliads, carnivorous plants, ferns, cycads, cacti, succulents, medicinal plants, rare and endangered plants, and plants valued as sources of food, beverages, fibers, and other industrial products. Specialty exhibits range from artwork inspired by plants to seasonal flower shows highlighting the beauty of chrysanthemums, poinsettias, spring flowers, and attractive summer terrace arrangements.

Outdoor plantings are showcased in Bartholdi Park. Also located in this park is Bartholdi Fountain, created by Frederic-Auguste Bartholdi (1834–1904), sculptor of the Statue of Liberty. To the west of the Conservatory, a rose garden marks the border of a 3-acre tract that is the future site of the National Garden.

The Garden offers educational facilities by making available for study to students, botanists, and floriculturists many rare and interesting botanical specimens. Every year botanical specimens are received from all over the world with requests for identification, and one of the services rendered by the Garden to the public is the identification of such specimens and the furnishing of information relating to the proper methods of growing them.

The United States Botanic Garden was founded in 1820 under the auspices of the Columbian Institute for the Promotion of Arts and Sciences, an organization that was the outgrowth of an association known as the Metropolitan Society and that received its charter from Congress on April 20, 1818. The Garden continued under the direction of this Institute until 1837, when the Institute ceased to exist as an active organization.

It remained abandoned until 1842, when it became necessary for the Government to provide accommodations for the botanical collections brought to Washington, DC, from the South Seas by the United States Exploring Expedition of 1838–42, under the leadership of Capt. Charles Wilkes. The collections were placed temporarily on exhibition at the Patent Office upon return of the expedition in June 1842. The first greenhouse for this purpose was constructed in 1842 on a lot behind the Patent Office Building under the direction and control of the Joint Committee of Congress on the Library, from funds appropriated by Congress.

The act of May 15, 1850 (9 Stat. 427), provided for the relocation of the Botanic Garden under the direction of the Joint Committee on the Library. The site selected was on the Mall at the west end of the Capitol Grounds, practically the same site the Botanic Garden occupied during the period it functioned under the Columbia Institute. This site was later enlarged, and the main area continued to serve as the principal Botanic Garden site from 1850 to 1933, when the Garden was relocated to its present site.

Although the Botanic Garden began functioning as a Government-owned institution in 1842, the records indicate that it was not until 1856 that the maintenance of the Garden was specifically placed under the direction of the Joint Committee on the Library and a regular, annual appropriation was provided by Congress (11 Stat. 104).

At the present time the Joint Committee exercises its supervision through the Architect of the Capitol, who has been serving as Acting Director since 1934.

The Botanic Garden is open to the public from 9 a.m. to 5 p.m. daily.

For further information concerning the United States Botanic Garden, contact the Office of the Architect of the Capitol, U.S. Capitol Building, Washington, DC 20515. Phone, 202–225–1200.

GENERAL ACCOUNTING OFFICE

441 G Street NW., Washington, DC 20548
Phone, 202–512–3000

Comptroller General of the United States	CHARLES A. BOWSHER
Deputy Comptroller General of the United States	(VACANCY)
Special Assistant to the Comptroller General	JAMES F. HINCHMAN
Assistant Comptroller General for Planning and Reporting	J. DEXTER PEACH
Assistant Comptroller General for Operations	JAMES L. HOWARD
Assistant Comptroller General for Policy	BRIAN P. CROWLEY
Assistant Comptroller General for Quality Management	RICHARD L. FOGEL
Assistant Comptroller General, General Government Division	JOHNNY C. FINCH
Assistant Comptroller General, Health, Education, and Human Services Division	JANET L. SHIKLES
Assistant Comptroller General, Office of Information Management and Communications	F. KEVIN BOLAND
Assistant Comptroller General, National Security and International Affairs Division	HENRY L. HINTON, JR.
Assistant Comptroller General, Resources, Community, and Economic Development Division	KEITH O. FULTZ
Assistant Comptroller General, Accounting and Information Management Division	GENE L. DODARO
Assistant Comptroller General, Program Evaluation and Methodology Division	TERRY E. HEDRICK
General Counsel	ROBERT P. MURPHY

Support Functions:

Director, Office of the Chief Economist	JAMES R. WHITE
Director, Civil Rights Office/Office of Affirmative Action Plans	NILDA I. APONTE
Director, Office of Congressional Relations	M. THOMAS HAGENSTAD
Director, Office of Counseling and Career Development	HOWARD N. JOHNSON
Director, General Services and Controller	JOSEPH L. DWYER, JR.
Director, Office of Internal Evaluation	FRANCES GARCIA
Director, Office of International Audit Organization Liaison	PETER V. ALIFERIS
Director, Personnel	PATRICIA M. RODGERS
Director, Office of Program Planning	PAUL L. JONES
Director, Office of Public Affairs	CLEVE E. CORLETT
Director, Office of Recruitment	FRANCES GARCIA
Director, Office of Special Investigations	RICHARD STIENER
Director, Training Institute	ANNE K. KLEIN
Chair, Personnel Appeals Board	NANCY A. MCBRIDE

GENERAL ACCOUNTING OFFICE

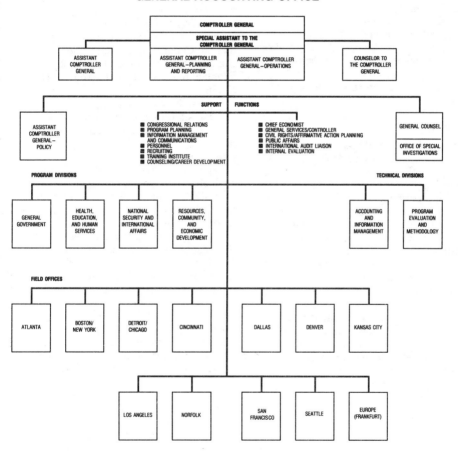

The General Accounting Office is the investigative arm of the Congress and is charged with examining all matters relating to the receipt and disbursement of public funds.

The General Accounting Office (GAO) was established by the Budget and Accounting Act of 1921 (31 U.S.C. 702), to independently audit Government agencies. Over the years, the Congress has expanded GAO's audit authority, added new responsibilities and duties, and strengthened GAO's ability to perform independently.

The Office is under the control and direction of the Comptroller General of the United States, who is appointed by the President with the advice and consent of the Senate for a term of 15 years.

Activities

Audits and Evaluations Supporting the Congress is GAO's fundamental responsibility. In meeting this objective, GAO performs a variety of services, the most prominent of which are audits and evaluations of Government programs and activities. The majority of these reviews are made in response to specific congressional requests. The Office is required to perform work requested by committee chairpersons and, as a matter of policy, assigns equal status to requests from Ranking Minority Members. GAO also responds to individual Member requests, as possible. Other assignments are initiated pursuant to standing commitments to congressional committees, and some reviews are specifically required by law. Finally, some assignments are independently undertaken in accordance with GAO's basic legislative responsibilities.

The ability to review practically any Government function requires a multidisciplined staff able to conduct assignments wherever needed. GAO's staff has expertise in a variety of disciplines—accounting, law, public and business administration, economics, the social and physical sciences, and others. The Office is organized so that staff members concentrate on specific subject areas, enabling them to develop a detailed level of knowledge. When an assignment requires specialized experience not available within GAO, outside experts assist the permanent staff. GAO's staff goes wherever necessary on assignments, working onsite to gather data, test transactions, and observe firsthand how Government programs and activities are carried out.

Accounting and Information Management Policy The Office ensures that the Congress has available for its use current, accurate, and complete financial management data. To do this, GAO:

—prescribes accounting principles and standards for the executive branch;

—advises other Federal agencies on fiscal and related policies and procedures; and

—prescribes standards for auditing and evaluating Government programs.

In addition, the Comptroller General, the Secretary of the Treasury, and the Director of the Office of Management and Budget develop standardized information and data processing systems. This includes standard terminology, definitions, classifications, and codes for fiscal, budgetary, and program-related data and information.

Legal Services The Office provides various legal services to the Congress. In response to inquiries from committees and Members, the Comptroller General provides advice on legal issues involving Government programs and activities. GAO is also available to assist in drafting legislation and reviewing legislative proposals before the Congress. In addition, GAO reviews and reports to the Congress on proposed rescissions and deferrals of Government funds.

Other legal services include resolving bid protests that challenge Government contract awards, assisting Government agencies in interpreting the laws governing the expenditure of public funds, and adjudicating claims for and against the Government.

In addition, GAO's staff of trained investigators conducts special investigations and assists auditors and evaluators when they encounter possible criminal and civil misconduct. When warranted, GAO refers the results of its investigations to the Department of Justice and other law enforcement authorities.

Reporting Authorities The Office offers a range of products to communicate the results of its work. The type of product depends on the assignment's objectives and the needs of the intended user. Product types include testimony, oral briefings, and written reports. Virtually all of GAO's reports are available to the public.

A list of GAO reports issued or released during the previous month is furnished monthly to the Congress, its Members, and committees. Copies of GAO reports are also furnished to interested congressional parties; Federal, State, local, and foreign governments; members of the press; college faculty, students, and libraries; and nonprofit organizations.

Copies of unclassified reports are available from the U.S. General Accounting Office, P.O. Box 6015, Gaithersburg, MD 20884–6015. Phone, 202–512–6000. The first copy of each report is free; additional copies are $2 each. There is a 25-percent discount on orders of 100 or more copies mailed to a single address. Orders must be prepaid by cash, check, or money order addressed to the Superintendent of Documents.

For further information, contact the Office of Public Affairs, General Accounting Office, 441 G Street NW., Washington, DC 20548. Phone, 202–512–4800.

GOVERNMENT PRINTING OFFICE

North Capitol and H Streets NW., Washington, DC 20401
Phone, 202–512–0000

Public Printer	MICHAEL F. DIMARIO
Deputy Public Printer	JAMES N. JOYNER
Director, Equal Employment Opportunity	CLAUDETTE BOULDIN
Director, Labor and Employee Relations	NEAL FINE
Director, Materials Management	THOMAS L. HUGHES
Manager, Printing Procurement Department	MEREDITH L. ARNESON
Manager, Quality Control and Technical Department	GEORGE J. COLLINS
Administrative Law Judge	STUART M. FOSS
General Counsel	ANTHONY J. ZAGAMI
Inspector General	LEWIS L. SMALL
Director, Office of Budget	WILLIAM M. GUY
Director, Office of Congressional, Legislative, and Public Affairs	FRANCIS W. BIDEN
Director, Policy Coordination Staff	VINCENT F. ARENDES
Director, Office of Administration	(VACANCY)
Comptroller	ROBERT B. HOLSTEIN
Director, Engineering Service	JOSEPH A. PALANK
Director, Information Resources Management	PATRICIA R. GARDNER
Director, Occupational Health and Environmental Services	WILLIAM T. HARRIS
Director, Office of Administrative Support	RAYMOND J. GARVEY

Director, Office of Planning	THOMAS J. MULDOON
Director, Office of Personnel	EDWARD J. BLATT
Director, Customer Services	(VACANCY)
Director, Institute for Federal Printing and Publishing	LOIS SCHUTTE
Superintendent, Congressional Printing Management Division	CHARLES C. COOK, SR.
Superintendent, Departmental Account Representative Division	ROBERT G. COX
Superintendent, Typography and Design Division	JOHN W. SAPP
Director, Production Services	GLENN H. ROTTMANN
Manager, Production Department	(VACANCY)
Superintendent of Documents	WAYNE P. KELLEY
Director, Documents Sales Service	JAMES D. YOUNG
Director, Library Programs Service	JAMES D. YOUNG, *Acting*
Director, Electronic Information Dissemination Services	JUDITH C. RUSSELL, *Acting*
Chief, Technical Support Group	MITCHELL E. PHELAN

The Government Printing Office produces, procures, and disseminates printed and electronic publications of the Congress as well as the executive departments and establishments of the Federal Government.

The Government Printing Office (GPO) began operations in accordance with Congressional Joint Resolution 25 of June 23, 1860. The activities of the Government Printing Office are outlined and defined in the public printing and documents chapters of Title 44 of the U.S. Code.

The congressional Joint Committee on Printing serves in an oversight capacity for the Government Printing Office. The Public Printer, who serves as the head of the agency, is appointed by the President with the advice and consent of the Senate.

Activities

The Government Printing Office produces and procures printed and electronic publications for Congress and the departments and establishments of the Federal Government. It furnishes blank paper, inks, and similar supplies to all governmental activities on order. It prepares catalogs and distributes and sells Government publications in printed and electronic formats.

The Office invites bids from commercial suppliers on a wide variety of printing and reproduction services, awards and administers contracts, and maintains liaison between ordering agencies and contractors.

Printing and binding processes used are electronic photocomposition; offset photography, stripping, platemaking, and press; and manual and machine bookbinding. Electronic databases prepared for printing are premastered for CD–ROM replication and are used to provide online access.

The Office sells through mail orders and Government bookstores approximately 20,000 different printed and electronic publications that originate in various Government agencies, and administers the depository library program through which selected Government publications are made available in libraries throughout the country. The Office also provides online access to key publications of the Federal Government, including the *Congressional Record* and the *Federal Register.*

Sources of Information

Congressional, Legislative, and Public Affairs General inquiries about GPO should be directed to the Office of Congressional, Legislative, and Public

GOVERNMENT PRINTING OFFICE

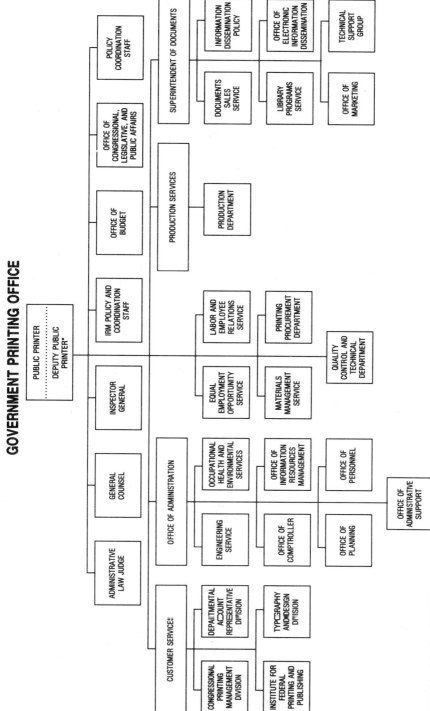

*OIRM designated senior official (DSO).

Affairs. Phone, 202–512–1991; or e-mail, [gpo5@access.digex.net].

Contracts Commercial printers interested in government printing contract opportunities should direct inquiries to the Manager, Printing Procurement Department, Government Printing Office, Washington, DC 20401 (phone, 202–512–0327), or contact the GPO Regional Printing Procurement Office in the following cities: Atlanta, GA; Boston, MA; Chicago, IL; Columbus, OH; Dallas, TX; Denver, CO; Hampton, VA; Los Angeles, CA; New York, NY; Philadelphia, PA; St. Louis, MO; San Francisco, CA; Seattle, WA; Oklahoma City, OK; San Antonio, TX; San Diego, CA; Pittsburgh, PA; New Orleans, LA; or Charleston, SC.

Suppliers of paper and related products; printing and binding equipment, related parts, and supplies; purchasers of scrap or surplus printing and binding equipment, waste, and salvage materials; and freight carriers should contact the Director of Materials Management, Government Printing Office, Washington, DC 20401. Phone, 202–512–0935.

The booklet *How To Do Business with the Government Printing Office, A Guide for Contractors* is available upon request from any regional GPO procurement office.

Employment Office of Personnel Management registers are used in filling administrative, technical, crafts, and clerical positions. Inquiries should be directed to the Chief, Employment Branch, Government Printing Office, Washington, DC 20401. Phone, 202–512–1198.

Publications Orders and inquiries concerning publications and subscriptions for sale by the Government Printing Office should be directed to the Superintendent of Documents, Government Printing Office, Washington, DC 20402. Phone, 202–512–1800.

To keep abreast of Government publications, the public is offered listings of varying scope.

The *GPO Sales Publications Reference File (PRF)* provides author, title, and subject access to Government publications available for sale through the Superintendent of Documents. It is available for purchase from the Superintendent of Documents.

The *Monthly Catalog of U.S. Government Publications* is the most comprehensive listing of Government publications issued by Federal departments and agencies. It is available for purchase from the Superintendent of Documents.

There also are two free catalogs of new or popular publications available: *U.S. Government Books,* which lists hundreds of best selling titles, and *New Books,* a bimonthly list of all Government publications placed on sale in the preceding 2 months. These publications can be obtained by calling the Superintendent of Documents at 202–512–1800.

Remittance for all publications ordered from the Superintendent of Documents must be received in advance of shipment by check or money order payable to the Superintendent of Documents. Orders also may be charged to MasterCard or VISA accounts or a GPO deposit account.

Online Access The GPO access service provides online access to key Government publications via the Internet. For information about this service, contact the GPO access support team at 202–512–1530, or e-mail at help@eids05.eids.gpo.gov.

Depository Libraries GPO distributes printed and electronic publications to approximately 1,400 depository libraries nationwide where they may be used free of charge to the public. A list of depository libraries is available from the Superintendent of Documents. Phone, 202–512–1119. Popular Government publications may be purchased at the GPO bookstores listed on page 53.

Bookstores—Government Printing Office

City	Address	Telephone
Washington, DC, area:		
Main Bookstore	710 N. Capitol St. NW.	202–512–0132
McPherson Square	1510 H St. NW.	202–653–5075
Retail Sales Outlet	8660 Cherry Ln., Laurel, MD	301–953–7974
Atlanta, GA	Suite 120, 1st Union Plz., 999 Peachtree St. NE.	404–347–1900
Birmingham, AL	2021 3d Ave. N.	205–731–1056
Boston, MA	Rm. 169, 10 Causeway St.	617–720–4180
Chicago, IL	Rm. 124, 401 S. State St.	312–353–5133
Cleveland, OH	Rm. 1653, 1240 E. 9th St.	216–522–4922
Columbus, OH	Rm. 207, 200 N. High St.	614–469–6956
Dallas, TX	Rm. 1C50, 1100 Commerce St.	214–767–0076
Denver, CO	Rm. 117, 1961 Stout St.	303–844–3964
Detroit, MI	Suite 160, 477 Michigan Ave.	313–226–7816
Houston, TX	801 Travis St.	713–228–1187
Jacksonville, FL	Rm. 100, 100 W. Bay St.	904–353–0569
Kansas City, MO	120 Bannister Mall, 5600 E. Bannister Rd.	816–767–8225
Los Angeles, CA	C–Level, ARCO Plz., 505 S. Flower St.	213–239–9844
Milwaukee, WI	Rm. 150, 310 W. Wisconsin Ave.	414–297–1304
New York, NY	Rm. 110, 26 Federal Plz.	212–264–3825
Philadelphia, PA	100 N. 17th St.	215–636–1900
Pittsburgh, PA	Rm. 118, 1000 Liberty Ave.	412–644–2721
Portland, OR	1305 SW. 1st Ave.	503–221–6217
Pueblo, CO	Norwest Banks Bldg., 201 W. 8th St.	719–544–3142
San Francisco, CA	Marathon Plz., Rm. 141–S, 303 2d St.	415–512–2770
Seattle, WA	Rm. 194, 915 2d Ave.	206–553–4271

For further information, contact the Office of Congressional, Legislative, and Public Affairs, Government Printing Office, North Capitol and H Streets NW., Washington, DC 20401. Phone, 202–512–1991, or e-mail at [gpo5@access.digex.net].

LIBRARY OF CONGRESS

101 Independence Avenue SE., Washington, DC 20540
Phone, 202–707–5000

Librarian of Congress	JAMES H. BILLINGTON
Deputy Librarian of Congress	HIRAM L. DAVIS
Chief of Staff	SUZANNE THORIN
Associate Librarian for Collections Services	WINSTON TABB
Associate Librarian for Constituent Services	DONALD C. CURRAN
Associate Librarian for Cultural Affairs	CAROLYN THOMPSON BROWN
Associate Librarian for Human Resources Services	LLOYD A. PAULS
Director, Congressional Research Service	DANIEL MULHOLLAN
Register of Copyrights and Associate Librarian for Copyright Services	MARYBETH PETERS
Law Librarian	RUBENS MEDINA
General Counsel	JOHN J. KOMINSKI
Inspector General	JOHN W. RENSBARGER
Chief, Loan Division	L. CHRISTOPHER WRIGHT

Library of Congress Trust Fund Board

Chairman (Librarian of Congress)	JAMES H. BILLINGTON
(Secretary of the Treasury)	ROBERT E. RUBIN

(U.S. Senator from Oregon and Chairman, Joint Committee on the Library)	MARK O. HATFIELD
Appointive Members	EDWIN L. COX, ADELE HALL, JOHN KLUGE, ARTHUR ORTENBERG, PETER LYNCH, LAURENCE TISCH, THOMAS S. FOLEY

The Library of Congress is the national library of the United States, offering diverse materials for research including the world's most extensive collections in many areas such as American history, music, and law.

The Library of Congress was established by act of April 24, 1800 (2 Stat. 56), appropriating $5,000 ''for the purchase of such books as may be necessary for the use of Congress....'' The Library's scope of responsibility has been widened by subsequent legislation (2 U.S.C. 131–168d). The Librarian, appointed by the President with the advice and consent of the Senate, directs the Library.

Supported mainly by the appropriations of Congress, the Library also uses income from funds received from foundations and other private sources and administered by the Library of Congress Trust Fund Board, as well as monetary gifts presented for direct application (2 U.S.C. 154–163).

Under the organic law, the Library's first responsibility is service to Congress. As the Library has developed, its range of service has come to include the entire governmental establishment and the public at large, making it a national library for the United States.

Activities

Collections The Library's extensive collections are universal in scope. They include books, serials, and pamphlets on every subject and in a multitude of languages and research materials, in many formats, including maps, photographs, manuscripts, motion pictures, and sound recordings. Among them are the most comprehensive collections of Chinese, Japanese, and Russian language books outside Asia and the former Soviet Union; volumes relating to science and legal materials outstanding for American and foreign law; the world's largest collection of published aeronautical literature; and the most extensive collection in the Western Hemisphere of books printed before 1501 A.D.

The manuscript collections relate to manifold aspects of American history and civilization, and include the personal papers of most of the Presidents from George Washington through Calvin Coolidge. The music collections contain volumes and pieces—manuscript and published—from classic works to the newest popular compositions. Other materials available for research include maps and views; photographic records from the daguerreotype to the latest news photo; recordings, including folksongs and other music, speeches, and poetry readings; prints, drawings, and posters; government documents, newspapers, and periodicals from all over the world; and motion pictures, microforms, and audio and video tapes.

Reference Resources Admission to the various research facilities of the Library is free. No introduction or credentials are required for persons over high school age. Readers must submit appropriate photo identification with a current address and, for certain collections, like those of the Manuscript, Rare Book and Special Collections, and Motion Picture, Broadcasting and Recorded Sound Divisions, there are additional requirements. As demands for service to Congress and Federal Government agencies increase, reference service available through correspondence has become limited. The Library must decline some requests and refer correspondents to a library within their area that can provide satisfactory assistance. While priority is given to inquiries pertaining to its holdings of special materials or to subjects in which its resources are unique, the Library does

LIBRARY OF CONGRESS

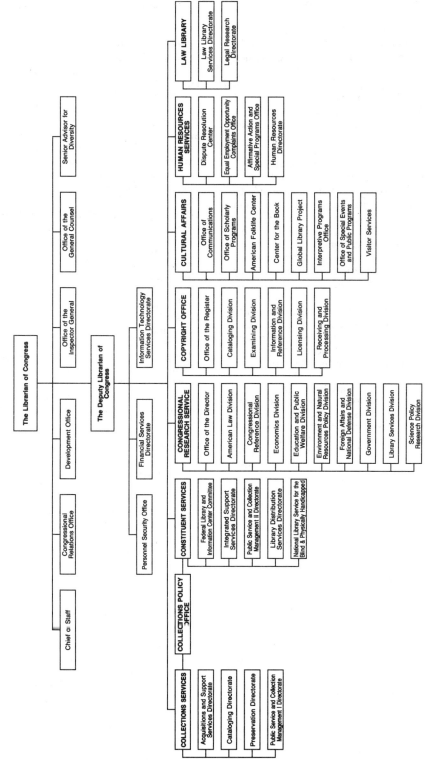

attempt to provide helpful responses to all inquirers.

Copyrights   Since 1870 the Library has been responsible for copyrights, which are registered by the Copyright Office (acts of July 8, 1870 (16 Stat. 212–217), February 19, 1897 (29 Stat. 545), March 4, 1909, as amended and codified (35 Stat. 1075), and October 19, 1976, as amended and codified (90 Stat. 2541)). All copyrightable works, whether published or unpublished, are subject to a system of statutory protection that gives the copyright owner certain exclusive rights, including the right to reproduce the copyrighted work and distribute it to the public by sale, rental, lease, or lending. Works of authorship include books, periodicals, and other literary works, including computer programs, musical compositions, song lyrics, dramas and dramatico-musical compositions, pictorial, graphic, and sculptural works, architectural works, pantomimes and choreographic works, motion pictures and other audiovisual works, and sound recordings.

Extension of Service   The Library extends its service through:

—an interlibrary loan system;

—the photoduplication, at reasonable cost, of books, manuscripts, maps, newspapers, and prints in its collections;

—the sale of sound recordings, which are released by its Recording Laboratory;

—the exchange of duplicates with other institutions;

—the sale of printed catalog cards and magnetic tapes and the publication in book format or microform of cumulative catalogs, which make available the results of the expert bibliographical and cataloging work of its technical personnel;

—a centralized cataloging program whereby the Library of Congress acquires material published all over the world, catalogs it promptly, and distributes cataloging information in machine-readable form as well as by printed cards and other means to the Nation's libraries;

—a cooperative cataloging program whereby the cataloging of data, by name authority and bibliographic records, prepared by other libraries becomes part of the Library of Congress data base and is distributed through the MARC Distribution Service;

—a cataloging-in-publication program in cooperation with American publishers for printing cataloging information in current books;

—the National Serials Data Program, a national center that maintains a record of serial titles to which International Standard Serial Numbers have been assigned and serves, with this file, as the United States Register; and

—the development of general schemes of classification (Library of Congress and Dewey Decimal), subject headings, and cataloging, embracing the entire field of printed matter.

Furthermore, the Library provides for:

—the preparation of bibliographical lists responsive to the needs of Government and research;

—the maintenance and the publication of *The National Union Catalogs* and other cooperative publications;

—the publication of catalogs, bibliographical guides, and lists, and of texts of original manuscripts and rare books in the Library of Congress;

—the circulation in traveling exhibitions of items from the Library's collections;

—the provision of books in braille and "talking book" records, as well as books on tape, for the blind and the physically handicapped through 142 cooperating libraries throughout the United States;

—the distribution of its electronic materials via the Internet, including more than 40 million bilbiographic records, summaries of congressional bills, copyright registrations, bibliographies and research guides, summaries of foreign laws, an index of Southeast Asian POW/MIA documents, and selections from the Library's unique historical collections—the Library's major contribution to the National Digital Library— via *LC WEB* (http://www.loc.gov); online public legislative information through *Thomas* (http://thomas.loc.gov); major exhibits from the past 3 years using either file transfer protocol (ftp.loc.gov), *LC Marvel* (marvel.loc.gov), or *LC Web;* pointers to external Internet resources including extensive international, national, State, and local government information and an international electronic library of resources arranged by "LC" subject headings; and

—the provision of research and analytical services on a fee-for-service basis to agencies in the executive and judicial branches.

Congressional Research Service   The Congressional Research Service (CRS) serves the Congress. The Service provides objective, nonpartisan research, analysis, and informational support to assist Congress in its legislative, oversight, and representative functions.

CRS evolved from the Legislative Reference Service, whose statutory authority dates back to the Legislative Reorganization Act of 1946, as amended (2 U.S.C. 72a note), and the Legislative Reorganization Act of 1970, as amended (2 U.S.C. 166), authorizing increased emphasis on in-depth research and analysis. Its mandate has grown over the years in response to the increasing scope of public policy issues on the congressional agenda. The Service's staff anticipates and responds to congressional information and policy analysis needs in an interdisciplinary manner. For the last several years, the Service has answered more than one-half million requests annually.

CRS provides timely and objective information and analysis in response to congressional inquiries at every stage of the legislative process concerning subject areas relevant to policy issues before Congress. The CRS director, assisted by a management team, oversees and coordinates the work of seven research divisions, which span a range of public policy subjects and disciplines. These divisions contain scholars and experts in the following broad areas: American law, economics, environment and natural resources policy, foreign affairs and national defense, government, and science policy. The highest level researchers are senior specialists, with national and international recognition in their fields. CRS contains two reference divisions— the Congressional Reference Division

and the Library Services Division. These divisions provide reference, bibliographic, and other informational services to Congress and CRS staff using both traditional and techniques and sophisticated computerized systems. CRS creates and maintains a number of specialized reading lists for Members of Congress and their staffs, and disseminates other materials of interest.

The Service maintains those parts of the Library of Congress' automated information system that cover legislative matters, including digests of all public bills and briefing papers on major legislative issues. CRS administrative offices include Special Programs, Operations, Policy, Research Coordination, and the Director's office.

In addition to responding to individual requests for information and analysis, CRS anticipates congressional needs for research and develops and presents seminars that provide a forum for discussion among Members of Congress and their staffs, CRS specialists, and nationally recognized experts on important legislative issues. Audio and visual materials on a variety of topics of congressional interest are also produced and aired on the congressional cable television system. A language service section provides a variety of foreign language services, including translations.

For further information, call 202–707–7904.

American Folklife Center   The Center, which was established in the Library of Congress by act of January 2, 1976 (20 U.S.C. 2102 *et seq.*), has a coordinative function both in and outside the Federal Establishment to carry out appropriate programs to support, preserve, and present American folklife through such activities as receiving and maintaining folklife collections, scholarly research, field projects, performances, exhibitions, festivals, workshops, publications, and audiovisual presentations. The Center is directed by a Board of Trustees consisting of four members appointed by the President from Federal agencies; four each appointed by the President pro tempore of the Senate and the Speaker of the House from private life; and five *ex officio* members, including: the

Librarian of Congress, the Secretary of the Smithsonian Institution, the Chairmen of the National Endowment for the Arts and the National Endowment for the Humanities, and the Director of the Center.

The Center has conducted projects in many locations across the country, such as the ethnic communities of Chicago, IL; southern Georgia; a ranching community in northern Nevada; the Blue Ridge Parkway in southern Virginia and northern North Carolina; and the States of New Jersey, Rhode Island, and Montana. The projects have provided large collections of recordings and photographs, for the Archive of Folk Culture. The Center administers the Federal Cylinder Project, which is charged with preserving and disseminating music and oral traditions recorded on wax cylinders dating from the late 1800's to the early 1940's. A cultural conservation study was developed at the Center, in cooperation with the Department of the Interior, pursuant to a congressional mandate. Various conferences, workshops, and symposia are given throughout the year. A series of outdoor concerts of traditional music are scheduled monthly at the Library, April through September.

The *Folklife Center News*, a quarterly newsletter, and other informational publications are available upon request. The Government Printing Office sells additional Center publications.

The American Folklife Center maintains and administers the Archive of Folk Culture, an extensive collection of ethnographic materials from this country and around the world. It is the national repository for folk-related recordings, manuscripts, and other unpublished materials. The Center's reading room contains over 3,500 books and periodicals; a sizable collection of magazines, newsletters, unpublished theses, and dissertations; field notes; and many textual and some musical transcriptions and recordings.

For further information, call 202–707–6590.

Center for the Book   The Center was established in the Library of Congress by act of October 13, 1977 (2 U.S.C. 171

et seq.), to stimulate public interest in books, reading, and libraries, and to encourage the study of books and print culture. The Center is a catalyst for promoting and exploring the vital role of books, reading, and libraries—nationally and internationally. As a partnership between the Government and the private sector, the Center for the Book depends on tax-deductible contributions from individuals and corporations to support its programs.

The Center's activities are directed toward the general public and scholars. The overall program includes reading and promotion projects with television and radio networks, symposia, lectures, exhibitions, special events, and publications. The 1995–96 national reading promotion theme is *Shape Your Future—READ!* More than 120 national educational and civic organizations are participating in the campaign.

Since 1984, 29 States have established statewide book centers that are affiliated with the Center for the Book in the Library of Congress. State centers plan and fund their own projects, involving members of the State's "community of the book," including authors, readers, prominent citizens, and public officials who serve as honorary advisors.

For further information, call 202–707–5221.

National Preservation Program   The Library provides technical information related to the preservation of library and archival material. A series of leaflets on various preservation and conservation topics has been prepared by the Preservation Office. Information and publications are available from the Library of Congress, National Preservation Program Office, Washington, DC 20540–4540.. Phone, 202–707–1840.

National Film Preservation Board   The National Film Preservation Board, established by the National Film Preservation Act of 1992 (2 U.S.C. 179b), serves as a public advisory group to the Librarian of Congress. The Board consists of 36 members and alternates representing the many parts of the diverse American film industry, film archives, scholars, and others. As its primary mission, the Board works to ensure the survival, conservation, and increased public availability of America's film heritage, including: advising the Librarian on the annual selection of films to the National Film Registry and, counseling the Librarian on development and implementation of the national film preservation plan. Key publications are *Film Preservation 1993: A Study of the Current State of American Film Preservation* (4 volumes, 748 pages) and *Redefining Film Preservation: A National Plan* (79 pages). Phone, 202–707–6240.

Sources of Information

Books for the Blind and Physically Handicapped Talking and braille books and magazines are distributed through 142 regional and subregional libraries to blind and physically handicapped residents of the United States and its territories. Information is available at public libraries throughout the United States and from the headquarters office, Library of Congress, National Library Service for the Blind and Physically Handicapped, 1291 Taylor Street NW., Washington, DC 20542–5300. Phone, 202–707–5100.

Cataloging Data Distribution Cataloging and bibliographic information in the form of printed catalog cards, microfiche catalogs, book catalogs, magnetic tapes, CD–ROM databases, bibliographies, and other technical publications is distributed to libraries and other institutions. Information about ordering materials is available from the Library of Congress, Cataloging Distribution Service, Washington, DC 20541–5210. Phone, 202–707–6100. TDD, 202–707–0012. Fax, 202–707–1334. Internet: cdsinfo@mail.loc.gov.

Library of Congress card numbers for new publications are assigned by the Cataloging in Publication Division. Direct inquiries to Library of Congress, CIP Division, Washington, DC 20540–4320. Phone, 202–707–6372.

Contracts Persons seeking to do business with the Library of Congress should contact the Library of Congress, Contracts and Logistics Services,

Landover Center Annex, 1701 Brightseat Road, Landover, MD 20785. Phone, 202–707–8717.

Copyright Services Information about the copyright law (title 17 of the United States Code), the method of securing copyright, and registration procedures may be obtained by writing to the Library of Congress, Copyright Office, Washington, DC 20559–6000. Phone, 202–707–3000. Copyright information is also available over Internet: Telnet to marvel.loc.gov and login as "marvel" to access system. Registration application forms may be ordered by calling the forms hotline at 202–707–9100. Reports on copyright facts found in the records of the Copyright Office may be obtained for a fee of $20 an hour; any member of the public, however, may use without charge the Copyright Card Catalog in the Copyright Office. Copyright Office records in machine-readable form cataloged from January 1, 1978, to the present are available over Internet. Telnet to locis.loc.gov or gain access through LC MARVEL by telnetting marvel.loc.gov and login as "marvel" to access system. The Copyright Information Office is located in Room LM–401, James Madison Memorial Building, 101 Independence Avenue SE., Washington, DC 20559–6000, and is open to the public Monday–Friday, 8:30 a.m. to 5:00 p.m. eastern time, except Federal holidays.

Employment Employment inquiries and applications (on Standard Form 171, Application for Federal Employment) should be directed to the Library of Congress, Human Resources Services Operations Office, Washington, DC 20540–2200. Potential applicants are encouraged to visit the Employment Office, Room LM–107, 101 Independence Avenue SE., where current vacancy announcements and application forms are available. The Human Resources hotline provides recorded information on career opportunities. Phone, 202–707–4315.

Photoduplication Service Copies of manuscripts, prints, photographs, maps, and book material not subject to copyright and other restrictions are available for a fee. Order forms for photoreproduction and price schedules are available from the Library of Congress, Photoduplication Service, Washington, DC 20540–5230. Phone, 202–707–5640.

Publications A list of *Library of Congress Publications in Print,* many of which are of interest to the general public, is available free upon request to Library of Congress, Office Systems Services, Washington, DC 20540–5440. A monthly *Calendar of Events,* listing programs and exhibitions at the Library of Congress, can be mailed regularly to persons within 100 miles of Washington, DC 20540–5440. Make requests to Library of Congress, Office Systems Services, Washington, DC 20540–5441.

Reference and Bibliographic Services Guidance is offered to readers in the identification and use of the material in the Library's collections, and reference service in answer to inquiries is offered to those who have exhausted local, State, and regional resources. Persons requiring services that cannot be performed by the Library staff can be supplied with names of private researchers who work on a fee basis. Requests for information should be directed to the Library of Congress, National Reference Service, Washington, DC 20540–5570. Phone, 202–707–5522. Fax, 202–707–1389.

Research and Reference Services in Science and Technology Reference specialists in the Science and

Technology Division answer without charge brief technical inquiries entailing a bibliographic response. Of special interest is a technical report collection exceeding 3.4 million titles. Most of these are in microform and are readily accessible for viewing in the Science Reading Room. Requests for reference service should be directed to the Library of Congress, Science and Technology Division, Washington, DC 20540–5580. Phone, 202–707–5522.

An informal series of reference guides is issued by the Science and Technology Division under the general title *LC Science Tracer Bullet.* These guides are designed to help a reader locate published material on a subject about which he or she has only general knowledge. For a list of available titles, write to the Library of Congress, Science and Technology Division, Reference Section, Washington, DC 20540–5580. Phone, 202–707–5522.

Research Services in General Topics Federal Government agencies can procure directed research and analytical products using the collections of the Library of Congress through the Federal Research Division. Science and social science topics of research are conducted by staff specialists exclusively on behalf of Federal agencies on a fee-for-service basis. Requests for service should be directed to Library of Congress, Federal Research Division, Marketing Office, Washington, DC 20540–5220. Phone, 202–707–9904. Fax, 202–245–5290.

For further information, contact the Public Affairs Office, Library of Congress, 101 Independence Avenue SE., Washington, DC 20540–8610. Phone, 202–707–2905. Fax, 202–707–9199.

OFFICE OF TECHNOLOGY ASSESSMENT [1]

600 Pennsylvania Avenue SE., Washington, DC 20510–8025
Phone, 202–224–8713

Director	ROGER C. HERDMAN
Executive Assistant to the Director	BARBARA LINKINS
Director, Congressional Affairs	JAMES JENSEN
Director, Press Affairs	JEAN K. MCDONALD

[1] This Office will become inactive on September 30, 1995.

Assistant Director, Industry, Commerce, and International Security Division	PETER BLAIR
Program Director, Energy, Transportation, and Infrastructure	EMILIA GOVAN
Program Director, International Security and Space	ALAN SHAW
Program Director, Industry Telecommunications and Commerce	ANDY WYCKOFF
Assistant Director, Health, Education, and Environment Division	CLYDE BEHNEY
Program Director, Education and Human Resources	DENISE DOUGHERTY
Program Director, Environment	ROBERT NIBLOCK
Program Director, Health	SEAN TUNIS

Congressional Board

Chairman	(VACANCY)
Vice Chairman	SEN. EDWARD M. KENNEDY
Senate Members	ORRIN G. HATCH, ERNEST F. HOLLINGS, EDWARD M. KENNEDY, CLAIBORNE PELL, (VACANCY)
House of Representatives Members	GEORGE E. BROWN, JR., JOHN D. DINGELL, AMO HOUGHTON, JIM MCDERMOTT, MICHAEL OXLEY, (VACANCY)
OTA Member (nonvoting)	ROGER C. HERDMAN

Advisory Council

Chairman	JAMES C. HUNT
Vice Chairman	MAX LENNON
Members	CHARLES BOWSHER, LEWIS BRANSCOMB, HERBERT DOAN, NEIL HARL, JAMES C. HUNT, JOSHUA LEDERBERG, MAX LENNON, DANIEL MULHOLLAN, THOMAS PERKINS, CHASE N. PETERSON, JOHN F.M. SIMS, MARINA VON NEUMANN WHITMAN

The Office of Technology Assessment reports to the Congress on the scientific and technical impact of government policies and proposed legislative initiatives.

The Office of Technology Assessment (OTA) was created by the Technology Assessment Act of 1972 (2 U.S.C. 472) to serve the United States Congress by providing objective analyses of major public policy issues related to scientific and technological change. The Office began operations in January 1974.

The bipartisan 13-member Board includes 6 Senators appointed by the President pro tempore, 6 Members of the House of Representatives appointed by the Speaker, and the Director of OTA, who is a nonvoting member.

The Technology Assessment Advisory Council comprises 10 public members eminent in science and technology. The Council is appointed by the Board and advises the Board and OTA on assessments and other matters.

The Office's assessments explore complex issues involving science and technology, helping Congress resolve uncertainties and conflicting claims,

OFFICE OF TECHNOLOGY ASSESSMENT

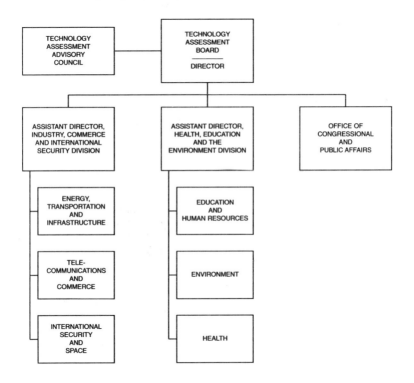

identifying alternative policy options, and providing foresight or early alert to new developments that could have important implications for future Federal policy. Requests for assessments may be made by the chairman of any congressional committee acting for himself or on behalf of a ranking minority member, or a majority of committee members; by the OTA Board; or by the OTA Director, in consultation with the Board.

The Office's work centers on comprehensive assessments that may take 1 to 2 years to complete. It also draws upon its past and current work to provide a variety of responses to meet immediate congressional needs, such as briefings, testimony, and special reports.

Office assessment teams work closely with congressional staff and support agencies to ensure that major committee concerns are addressed, and to stay in touch with the published work and current activities of analysts and researchers in the executive branch and throughout the public and private interest sectors. Each project is guided by an advisory panel of experts on a particular subject to ensure that reports are objective, fair, and authoritative.

After approval for release by the Board, OTA assessment reports are distributed to the requesting committees, with summaries provided to all Members of Congress. The reports are available to the public through the Government Printing Office.

Sources of Information

Information may be obtained from the following sources:

Congressional and Public Affairs Office (documents for congressional use and general information about OTA). Phone, 202–224–9241.

Publications Request Department (OTA documents for general public use). Phone, 202–224–8996.

Internet. OTA.GOV.

Press. Phone, 202–228–6204.

Fax. Phone, 202–228–6098.

CONGRESSIONAL BUDGET OFFICE

Second and D Streets SW., Washington, DC 20515
Phone, 202–226–2621

Director	JUNE E. O'NEILL
Deputy Director	JAMES L. BLUM
General Counsel	GAIL DEL BALZO
Director, Office of Intergovernmental Relations	STANLEY L. GREIGG
Assistant Director for Budget Analysis	PAUL N. VAN DE WATER
Assistant Director for Macroeconomic Analysis	ROBERT A. DENNIS
Assistant Director for Tax Analysis	ROSEMARY MARCUSS
Assistant Director for Natural Resources and Commerce	JAN PAUL ACTON
Assistant Director for Health and Human Resources	JOSEPH R. ANTOS
Assistant Director for National Security	CINDY WILLIAMS
Assistant Director for Special Studies	ROBERT W. HARTMAN

The Congressional Budget Office provides the Congress with assessments of the economic impact of the Federal budget.

The Congressional Budget Office (CBO) was established by the Congressional Budget Act of 1974 (2 U.S.C. 601), which also created a procedure by which the United States Congress considers and acts upon the annual

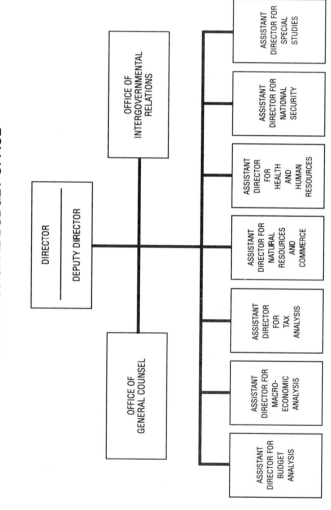

CONGRESSIONAL BUDGET OFFICE

DIRECTOR

DEPUTY DIRECTOR

OFFICE OF INTERGOVERNMENTAL RELATIONS

OFFICE OF GENERAL COUNSEL

ASSISTANT DIRECTOR FOR SPECIAL STUDIES

ASSISTANT DIRECTOR FOR NATIONAL SECURITY

ASSISTANT DIRECTOR FOR HEALTH AND HUMAN RESOURCES

ASSISTANT DIRECTOR FOR NATURAL RESOURCES AND COMMERCE

ASSISTANT DIRECTOR FOR TAX ANALYSIS

ASSISTANT DIRECTOR FOR MACRO-ECONOMIC ANALYSIS

ASSISTANT DIRECTOR FOR BUDGET ANALYSIS

Federal budget. This process enables the Congress to have an overview of the Federal budget and to make overall decisions regarding spending and taxing levels and the deficit or surplus these levels incur.

The Congressional Budget Office provides Congress with basic budget data and with analyses of alternative fiscal, budgetary, and programmatic policy issues.

Activities

Economic Forecasting and Fiscal Policy Analysis The Federal budget affects and is affected by the national economy. The Congressional Budget Office provides Congress with biannual forecasts of the economy and analyses of economic trends and alternative fiscal policies.

Scorekeeping Under the budget process the Congress establishes, by concurrent resolution, targets (or ceilings) for overall expenditures, budget authority and budget outlays, and for broad functional categories. The Congress also establishes targets (or ceilings) for the levels of revenues, the deficit, and the public debt. CBO "keeps score" for the Congress by monitoring the results of congressional action on individual authorization, appropriation, and revenue bills against the targets (or ceilings) specified in the concurrent resolution.

Cost Projections The Congressional Budget Office prepares 5-year cost estimates for carrying out any public bill or resolution reported by congressional committees. As soon as practicable after the beginning of each fiscal year, CBO also provides 5-year projections on the costs of continuing current Federal spending and taxation policies.

Annual Report on the Budget The Congressional Budget Office is responsible for furnishing the House and Senate Budget Committees by February 15 of each year with a report that includes a discussion of alternative spending and revenue levels and alternative allocations among major programs and functional categories, all in the light of major national needs and the effect on the balanced growth and development of the United States.

Budget-Related Studies The Congressional Budget Office undertakes studies requested by the Congress on budget-related areas. This service is provided in the following order of priority to: the House and Senate Budget Committees; the House and Senate Appropriations Committees; the Senate Finance and the House Ways and Means Committees; and all other congressional committees.

Sequestration Reports These advisory reports are mandated by the Balanced Budget and Emergency Deficit Control Act of 1985, as amended (2 U.S.C. 901). These reports estimate whether proposed spending levels breach categorical spending limits or cause a deficit in excess of the target and, if so, it estimates the amount and percentage of budget resources that should be sequestered to eliminate any excesses.

Pay-As-You-Go The Balanced Budget and Emergency Deficit Control Act of 1985, as amended (2 U.S.C. 901), requires CBO to provide the Office of Management and Budget with an estimate of the amount of change in outlays or receipts for each fiscal year for any direct spending or receipts legislation as soon as practicable after Congress completes action on that legislation.

For further information, contact the Office of Intergovernmental Relations, Congressional Budget Office, Second and D Streets SW., Washington, DC 20515. Phone, 202–226–2600.

Judicial Branch

JUDICIAL BRANCH

THE SUPREME COURT OF THE UNITED STATES

United States Supreme Court Building
1 First Street NE., Washington, DC 20543
Phone, 202–479–3000

Members:

Chief Justice of the United States	WILLIAM H. REHNQUIST
Associate Justices	JOHN PAUL STEVENS, SANDRA DAY O'CONNOR, ANTONIN SCALIA, ANTHONY M. KENNEDY, DAVID H. SOUTER, CLARENCE THOMAS, RUTH BADER GINSBURG, STEPHEN G. BREYER

Officers:

Clerk	WILLIAM K. SUTER
Reporter of Decisions	FRANK D. WAGNER
Librarian	SHELLEY L. DOWLING
Marshal	DALE E. BOSLEY

Article III, section 1, of the Constitution of the United States provides that "[t]he judicial Power of the United States, shall be vested in one supreme Court, and in such inferior Courts as the Congress may from time to time ordain and establish." The Supreme Court of the United States was created in accordance with this provision and by authority of the Judiciary Act of September 24, 1789 (1 Stat. 73). It was organized on February 2, 1790.

The Supreme Court comprises the Chief Justice of the United States and such number of Associate Justices as may be fixed by Congress. Under that authority, and by virtue of act of June 25, 1948 (28 U.S.C. 1), the number of Associate Justices is eight. Power to nominate the Justices is vested in the President of the United States, and appointments are made with the advice and consent of the Senate. Article III, section 1, of the Constitution further provides that "[t]he Judges, both of the supreme and inferior Courts, shall hold their Offices during good Behaviour, and shall, at stated Times, receive for their Services, a Compensation, which shall not be diminished during their Continuance in Office." A Justice may, if so desired, retire at the age of 70 after serving for 10 years as a Federal judge or at age 65 after 15 years of service.

The Clerk, the Reporter of Decisions, the Librarian, and the Marshal are appointed by the Court to assist in the performance of its functions. Other Court officers, including the Administrative Assistant, the Court Counsel, the Curator, the Director of Data Systems, and the Public Information Officer, are appointed by the Chief Justice to assist him with the administrative aspects of his position.

69

The library is open to members of the bar of the Court, attorneys for the various Federal departments and agencies, and Members of Congress. Only members of the bar of the Court may practice before the Supreme Court.

The term of the Court begins, by law, the first Monday in October of each year and continues as long as the business before the Court requires, usually until about the end of June. Six members constitute a quorum. Approximately 7,000 cases are passed upon in the course of a term. In addition, some 1,200 applications of various kinds are filed each year that can be acted upon by a single Justice.

Jurisdiction   According to the Constitution (art. III, sec. 2), "[t]he judicial Power shall extend to all Cases, in Law and Equity, arising under this Constitution, the Laws of the United States, and Treaties made, or which shall be made, under their Authority;—to all Cases affecting Ambassadors, other public Ministers and Consuls;—to all Cases of admiralty and maritime Jurisdiction;—to Controversies to which the United States shall be a Party;—to Controversies between two or more States;—between a State and Citizens of another State;—between Citizens of different States;—between Citizens of the same State claiming Lands under Grants of different States, and between a State, or the Citizens thereof, and foreign States, Citizens or Subjects.

"In all Cases affecting Ambassadors, other public Ministers and Consuls, and those in which a State shall be Party, the supreme Court shall have original Jurisdiction. In all the other Cases before mentioned, the supreme Court shall have appellate Jurisdiction, both as to Law and Fact, with such Exceptions, and under such Regulations as the Congress shall make."

Appellate jurisdiction has been conferred upon the Supreme Court by various statutes, under the authority given Congress by the Constitution. The basic statute effective at this time in conferring and controlling jurisdiction of the Supreme Court may be found in 28 U.S.C. 1251, 1253, 1254, 1257–1259, and various special statutes. Congress has no authority to change the original jurisdiction of this Court.

Rulemaking Power   Congress has from time to time conferred upon the Supreme Court power to prescribe rules of procedure to be followed by the lower courts of the United States. Pursuant to these statutes there are now in force rules promulgated by the Court to govern civil and criminal cases in the district courts, bankruptcy proceedings, admiralty cases, appellate proceedings, and the trial of misdemeanors before U.S. magistrate judges.

For further information concerning the Supreme Court, contact the Public Information Office, United States Supreme Court Building, 1 First Street NE., Washington, DC 20543. Phone, 202–479–3211.

Lower Courts

Article III of the Constitution declares, in section 1, that the judicial power of the United States shall be invested in one Supreme Court and in "such inferior Courts as the Congress may from time to time ordain and establish." The Supreme Court has held that these constitutional courts " . . . share in the exercise of the judicial power defined in that section, can be invested with no other jurisdiction, and have judges who hold office during good behavior, with no power in Congress to provide otherwise."

United States Courts of Appeals   The courts of appeals are intermediate appellate courts created by act of March 3, 1891 (28 U.S.C. ch. 3), to relieve the Supreme Court of considering all appeals in cases originally decided by the Federal trial courts. They are empowered to review all final decisions and certain interlocutory decisions (18 U.S.C. 3731, 3734; 28 U.S.C. 1291, 1292) of district courts. They also are empowered to review and enforce orders of many Federal administrative bodies. The decisions of the courts of appeals are final except as they are subject to discretionary review or appeal in the Supreme Court.

The United States is divided geographically into 12 judicial circuits, including the District of Columbia. Each circuit has a court of appeals (28 U.S.C. 41, 1294). Each of the 50 States is assigned to one of the circuits, and the Territories are assigned variously to the first, third, and ninth circuits. There is also a Court of Appeals for the Federal Circuit, which has nationwide jurisdiction defined by subject matter. At present each court of appeals has from 6 to 28 permanent circuit judgeships (179 in all), depending upon the amount of judicial work in the circuit. Circuit judges hold their offices during good behavior as provided by Article III, section 1, of the Constitution. The judge senior in commission who is under 70 years of age (65 at inception of term), has been in office at least 1 year, and has not previously been chief judge, serves as the chief judge of the circuit for a 7-year term. One of the justices of the Supreme Court is assigned as circuit justice for each of the 13 judicial circuits. Each court of appeals normally hears cases in panels consisting of three judges but may sit *en banc* with all judges present.

The judges of each circuit by vote determine the size of the judicial council for the circuit, which consists of the chief judge and an equal number of circuit and district judges. The council considers the state of Federal judicial business in the circuit and may "make all necessary and appropriate orders for [its] effective and expeditious administration . . ." (28 U.S.C. 332). The chief judge of each circuit summons annually a judicial conference of all circuit and district judges in the circuit, and sometimes members of the bar, to discuss the business of the Federal courts of the circuit (28 U.S.C. 333). The chief judge of each circuit and a district judge elected from each of the 12 geographical circuits, together with the chief judge of the Court of International Trade, serve as members of the Judicial Conference of the United States, over which the Chief Justice of the United States presides. This is the governing body for the administration of the Federal judicial system as a whole (28 U.S.C. 331).

United States Court of Appeals for the Federal Circuit   This court was established under Article III of the Constitution pursuant to the Federal Courts Improvement Act of 1982 (28 U.S.C. 1 note), as successor to the former United States Court of Customs and Patent Appeals and the United States Court of Claims. The jurisdiction of the court is nationwide (as provided by 28 U.S.C. 1295) and includes appeals from the district courts in patent cases; appeals from the district courts in contract, and certain other civil actions in which the United States is a defendant; and appeals from final decisions of the U.S. Court of International Trade, the U.S. Court of Federal Claims, and the U.S. Court of Veterans Appeals. The jurisdiction of the court also includes the review of administrative rulings by the Patent and Trademark Office, U.S. International Trade Commission, Secretary of Commerce, agency boards of contract appeals, and the Merit Systems Protection Board, as well as rulemaking of the Department of Veterans Affairs; review of decisions of the U.S. Senate Select Committee on Ethics concerning discrimination claims of Senate employees; and review of a final order of an entity to be designated by the President concerning discrimination claims of Presidential appointees.

The court consists of 12 circuit judges. It sits in panels of three or more on each case and may also hear or rehear a case *en banc*. The court sits principally in Washington, DC, and may hold court wherever any court of appeals sits (28 U.S.C. 48).

Judicial Circuits—United States Courts of Appeals

Circuit	Judges	Official Station
	District of Columbia Circuit	
(*Clerk:* Mark J. Langer; *Circuit Executive:* Linda Ferren; Washington, DC)	*Circuit Justice* Chief Justice William H. Rehnquist	
	Circuit Judges Harry T. Edwards, *Chief Judge*	Washington, DC
	Patricia M. Wald	Do.
		Do.
	Laurence H. Silberman	Do.
	James L. Buckley	Do.
	Stephen F. Williams	Do.
	Douglas H. Ginsburg	Do.
	David Bryan Sentelle	Do.
	Karen LeCraft Henderson	Do.
	A. Raymond Randolph	Do.
	Judith W. Rogers	Do.
	David S. Tatel	Do.
	(Vacancy)	
	First Circuit	
Districts of Maine, New Hampshire, Massachusetts, Rhode Island, and Puerto Rico (*Clerk:* Francis P. Scigliano; *Circuit Executive:* Vincent F. Flanagan; Boston, MA)	*Circuit Justice* Justice David H. Souter	
	Circuit Judges Juan R. Torruella, *Chief Judge*	San Juan, PR
	Bruce M. Selya	Providence, RI
	Conrad K. Cyr	Bangor, ME
	Michael Boudin	Boston, MA
	Norman H. Stahl	Concord, NH
	Sandra L. Lynch	Boston, MA
	Second Circuit	
Districts of Vermont, Connecticut, northern New York, southern New York, eastern New York, and western New York (*Clerk:* George Lange III; *Circuit Executive:* Steven Flanders; New York, NY)	*Circuit Justice* Justice Ruth Bader Ginsburg	
	Circuit Judges Jon O. Newman, *Chief Judge*	Hartford, CT
	Amalya Lyle Kearse	New York, NY
	Ralph K. Winter, Jr.	New Haven, CT
	Roger J. Miner	Albany, NY
	Frank X. Altimari	Uniondale, NY
	J. Daniel Mahoney	Milford, CT
	John M. Walker, Jr.	New York, NY
	Joseph M. McLaughlin	Do.
	Dennis G. Jacobs	Do.
	Pierre N. Leval	Do.
	Guido Calabresi	New Haven, CT
	Jose A. Cabranes	Do.
	Fred I. Parker	Burlington, VT
	Third Circuit	
Districts of New Jersey, eastern Pennsylvania, middle Pennsylvania, western Pennsylvania, Delaware, and the Virgin Islands (*Clerk:* P. Douglas Sisk; *Circuit Executive:* Toby D. Slawsky; Philadelphia, PA)	*Circuit Justice* Justice David H. Souter	
	Circuit Judges Dolores Korman Sloviter, *Chief Judge*	Philadelphia, PA
	Edward R. Becker	Philadelphia, PA
	Walter K. Stapleton	Wilmington, DE
	Carol Los Mansmann	Pittsburgh, PA
	Morton I. Greenberg	Trenton, NJ
	Anthony J. Scirica	Philadelphia, PA
	William D. Hutchinson	Pottsville, PA
	Robert E. Cowen	Trenton, NJ
	Richard Lowell Nygaard	Erie, PA
	Samuel A. Alito, Jr.	Newark, NJ
	Jane R. Roth	Wilmington, DE
	Timothy K. Lewis	Pittsburgh, PA
	Theodore A. McKee	Philadelphia, PA
	H. Lee Sarokin	Newark, NJ

Judicial Circuits—United States Courts of Appeals—Continued

Circuit	Judges	Official Station
Fourth Circuit		
Districts of Maryland, northern West Virginia, southern West Virginia, eastern Virginia, western Virginia, eastern North Carolina, middle North Carolina, western North Carolina, and South Carolina (*Clerk:* Bert M. Montague; *Circuit Executive:* Samuel W. Phillips; Richmond, VA)	*Circuit Justice* Chief Justice William H. Rehnquist *Circuit Judges* Sam J. Ervin III, *Chief Judge* Donald S. Russell H. Emory Widener, Jr. Kenneth K. Hall Francis D. Murnaghan, Jr. James Harvie Wilkinson III William W. Wilkins, Jr. Paul V. Niemeyer J. Michael Luttig Clyde H. Hamilton Karen J. Williams M. Blane Michael Diana Gribbon Motz (2 vacancies)	Morganton, NC Spartanburg, SC Abingdon, VA Charleston, WV Baltimore, MD Charlottesville, VA Greenville, SC Baltimore, MD Alexandria, VA Columbia, SC Orangeburg, SC Charleston, WV Baltimore, MD
Fifth Circuit		
Districts of northern Mississippi, southern Mississippi, eastern Louisiana, middle Louisiana, western Louisiana, northern Texas, southern Texas, eastern Texas, and western Texas (*Clerk:* Charles R. Fulbruge III; *Circuit Executive:* Lydia Comberrel; New Orleans, LA)	*Circuit Justice* Justice Antonin Scalia *Circuit Judges* Henry A. Politz, *Chief Judge* Carolyn Dineen King William L. Garwood E. Grady Jolly Patrick E. Higginbotham W. Eugene Davis Edith H. Jones Jerry Edwin Smith John M. Duhe, Jr. Rhesa H. Barksdale Jacques L. Wiener, Jr. Emilio M. Garza Harold R. Demoss, Jr. Fortunado P. Benavides Carl E. Stewart Robert M. Parker (Vacancy)	Shreveport, LA Houston, TX Austin, TX Jackson, MS Dallas, TX Lafayette, LA Houston, TX Houston, TX Lafayette, LA Jackson, MS Shreveport, LA San Antonio, TX Houston, TX Austin, TX Shreveport, LA Tyler, TX
Sixth Circuit		
Districts of northern Ohio, southern Ohio, eastern Michigan, western Michigan, eastern Kentucky, western Kentucky, eastern Tennessee, middle Tennessee, and western Tennessee (*Clerk:* Leonard Green; *Circuit Executive:* James A. Higgins; Cincinnati, OH)	*Circuit Justice* Justice John Paul Stevens *Circuit Judges* Gilbert S. Merritt, *Chief Judge* Damon J. Keith Cornelia G. Kennedy Boyce F. Martin, Jr. Nathaniel R. Jones H. Ted Milburn David A. Nelson James L. Ryan Danny J. Boggs Alan E. Norris Richard F. Suhrheinrich Eugene E. Siler, Jr. Alice M. Batchelder Martha Craig Daughtrey Karen Nelson Moore (Vacancy)	Nashville, TN Detroit, MI Detroit, MI Louisville, KY Cincinnati, OH Chattanooga, TN Cincinnati, OH Detroit, MI Louisville, KY Columbus, OH Lansing, MI London, KY Medina, OH Nashville, TN Cleveland, OH
Seventh Circuit		
Districts of northern Indiana, southern Indiana, northern Illinois, central Illinois,	*Circuit Justice* Justice John Paul Stevens	

Judicial Circuits—United States Courts of Appeals—Continued

Circuit	Judges	Official Station
southern Illinois, eastern Wisconsin, and western Wisconsin (*Clerk:* Thomas F. Strubbe; *Circuit Executive:* Collins T. Fitzpatrick; Chicago, IL)	*Circuit Judges* Richard A. Posner, *Chief Judge* Walter J. Cummings John L. Coffey Joel M. Flaum Frank H. Easterbrook Kenneth F. Ripple Daniel A. Manion Michael S. Kanne Ilana Diamond Rovner (2 vacancies)	Chicago, IL Do. Milwaukee, WI Chicago, IL Chicago, IL South Bend, IN South Bend, IN Lafayette, IN Chicago, IL

Eighth Circuit

Circuit	Judges	Official Station
Districts of Minnesota, northern Iowa, southern Iowa, eastern Missouri, western Missouri, eastern Arkansas, western Arkansas, Nebraska, North Dakota, and South Dakota (*Clerk:* Michael Ellis Gans; *Circuit Executive:* June L. Boadwine; St. Louis, MO, and St. Paul, MN)	*Circuit Justice* Justice Clarence Thomas *Circuit Judges* Richard S. Arnold, *Chief Judge* Theodore McMillian George G. Fagg Pasco M. Bowman II Roger L. Wollman Frank J. Magill Clarence Arlen Beam James B. Loken David R. Hansen Morris S. Arnold Diana E. Murphy	Little Rock, AR St. Louis, MO Des Moines, IA Kansas City, MO Sioux Falls, SD Fargo, ND Lincoln, NE St. Paul, MN Cedar Rapids, IA Little Rock, AR Minneapolis, MN

Ninth Circuit

Circuit	Judges	Official Station
Districts of northern California, eastern California, central California, southern California, Oregon, Nevada, Montana, eastern Washington, western Washington, Idaho, Arizona, Alaska, Hawaii, Territory of Guam, and District Court for the Northern Mariana Islands (*Clerk:* Cathy Catterson; *Circuit Executive:* Gregory B. Walters; San Francisco, CA)	*Circuit Justice* Justice Sandra Day O'Connor *Circuit Judges* J. Clifford Wallace, *Chief Judge* James R. Browning Proctor Hug, Jr. Mary M. Schroeder Betty B. Fletcher Harry Pregerson Cecil F. Poole William C. Canby, Jr. Stephen Reinhardt Robert R. Beezer Cynthia Holcomb Hall Charles E. Wiggins Melvin Brunetti Alex Kozinski John T. Noonan, Jr. David R. Thompson Diarmuid F. O'Scannlain Edward Leavy Stephen S. Trott Ferdinand F. Fernandez Pamela A. Rymer Thomas G. Nelson Andrew J. Kleinfeld Michael D. Hawkins (4 vacancies)	San Diego, CA San Francisco, CA Reno, NV Phoenix, AZ Seattle, WA Woodland Hills, CA San Francisco, CA Phoenix, AZ Los Angeles, CA Seattle, WA Pasadena, CA Reno, NV Reno, NV Pasadena, CA San Francisco, CA San Diego, CA Portland, OR Portland, OR Boise, ID Pasadena, CA Pasadena, CA Boise, ID Fairbanks, AK Phoenix, AZ

Tenth Circuit

Circuit	Judges	Official Station
Districts of Colorado, Wyoming, Utah, Kansas, eastern Oklahoma, northern Oklahoma, western Oklahoma, and New Mexico (*Clerk:* Patrick J. Fisher; *Circuit Executive:* Robert L. Hoecker;	*Circuit Justice* Justice Stephen G. Breyer *Circuit Judges* Stephanie K. Seymour, *Chief Judge* John P. Moore Stephen H. Anderson Deanell Reece Tacha Bobby R. Baldock	Tulsa, OK Denver, CO Salt Lake City, UT Lawrence, KS Roswell, NM

Judicial Circuits—United States Courts of Appeals—Continued

Circuit	Judges	Official Station
Denver, CO)	Wade Brorby	Cheyenne, WY
	David M. Ebel	Denver, CO
	Paul J. Kelly, Jr.	Santa Fe, NM
	Robert H. Henry	Oklahoma City, OK
	Mary Beck Briscoe	Topeka, KS
	(2 vacancies)	

Eleventh Circuit		
Districts of northern Georgia, middle Georgia, southern Georgia, northern Florida, middle Florida, southern Florida, northern Alabama, middle Alabama, southern Alabama (*Clerk:* Miguel J. Cortez, Jr.; *Circuit Executive:* Norman E. Zoller; Atlanta, GA)	*Circuit Justice* Justice Anthony M. Kennedy	
	Circuit Judges Gerald B. Tjoflat, *Chief Judge*	Jacksonville, FL
	Phyllis A. Kravitch	Atlanta, GA
	Joseph Woodrow Hatchett	Tallahassee, FL
	R. Lanier Anderson III	Macon, GA
	J.L. Edmondson	Atlanta, GA
	Emmett Ripley Cox	Mobile, AL
	Stanley F. Birch, Jr.	Atlanta, GA
	Joel F. Dubina	Montgomery, AL
	Susan H. Black	Jacksonville, FL
	Edward E. Carnes	Montgomery, AL
	Rosemary Barkett	Miami, FL
	(Vacancy)	

Federal Circuit—Washington, DC

Circuit Justice
Chief Justice William H. Rehnquist

Chief Judge
Glenn L. Archer, Jr.

Judges
Helen Wilson Nies
Giles S. Rich
Pauline Newman
Haldane Robert Mayer
Paul R. Michel
S. Jay Plager
Alan D. Lourie
Raymond C. Clevenger III
Randall R. Rader
Alvin A. Schall
William C. Bryson

Clerk: Francis X. Gindhart
Administrative Services Officer: Ruth A. Butler

United States District Courts   The district courts are the trial courts of general Federal jurisdiction. Each State has at least one district court, while the larger States have as many as four. Altogether there are 89 district courts in the 50 States, plus the one in the District of Columbia. In addition, the Commonwealth of Puerto Rico has a district court with jurisdiction corresponding to that of district courts in the various States.

At present, each district court has from 2 to 28 Federal district judgeships, depending upon the amount of judicial work within its territory. Only one judge is usually required to hear and decide a case in a district court, but in some limited cases it is required that three judges be called together to comprise the court (28 U.S.C. 2284). The judge senior in commission who is under 70 years of age (65 at inception of term), has been in office for at least 1 year, and has not previously been chief judge, serves as chief judge for a 7-year term. There are altogether 610 permanent district judgeships in the 50 States and 15 in the District of Columbia. There are 7 district judgeships in Puerto Rico. District judges hold their offices during good behavior as provided by Article III, section 1, of the Constitution. However, Congress may create temporary judgeships for a court with the provision that when a vacancy occurs in that district, such vacancy shall not be filled. Each district court has one or more United States magistrate judges and bankruptcy judges, a clerk, a United States attorney, a United States marshal, probation officers, court reporters, and their staffs. The jurisdiction of the district courts is set forth in title 28, chapter 85, of the United States Code and at 18 U.S.C. 3231.

Cases from the district courts are reviewable on appeal by the applicable court of appeals.

Territorial Courts   Pursuant to its authority to govern the Territories (art. IV, sec. 3, clause 2, of the Constitution),

Congress has established district courts in the territories of Guam and the Virgin Islands. The District Court of the Canal Zone was abolished on April 1, 1982, pursuant to the Panama Canal Act of 1979 (22 U.S.C. 3601 note). Congress has also established a district court in the Northern Mariana Islands, which presently is administered by the United States under a trusteeship agreement with the United Nations. These Territorial courts have jurisdiction not only over the subjects described in the judicial article of the Constitution but also over many local matters that, within the States, are decided in State courts. The district court of Puerto Rico, by contrast, is established under Article III, is classified like other "district courts," and is called a "court of the United States" (28 U.S.C. 451). There is one judge each in Guam and the Northern Mariana Islands, and two in the Virgin Islands. The judges in these courts are appointed for terms of 10 years.

For further information concerning the lower courts, contact the Administrative Office of the United States Courts, Thurgood Marshall Federal Judiciary Building, One Columbus Circle NE., Washington, DC 20544.

United States Court of International Trade This court was originally established as the Board of United States General Appraisers by act of June 10, 1890, which conferred upon it jurisdiction theretofore held by the district and circuit courts in actions arising under the tariff acts (19 U.S.C. ch. 4). The act of May 28, 1926 (19 U.S.C. 405a), created the United States Customs Court to supersede the Board; by acts of August 7, 1939, and June 25, 1948 (28 U.S.C. 1582, 1583), the court was integrated into the United States court structure, organization, and procedure. The act of July 14, 1956 (28 U.S.C. 251), established the court as a court of record of the United States under Article III of the Constitution.

The Customs Courts Act of 1980 (28 U.S.C. 251) constituted the court as the United States Court of International Trade and revised provisions relating to its jurisdiction. The Court of International

Trade has all the powers in law and equity of a district court.

The Court of International Trade has jurisdiction over any civil action against the United States arising from Federal laws governing import transactions. This includes classification and valuation cases, as well as authority to review certain agency determinations under the Trade Agreements Act of 1979 (19 U.S.C. 2501) involving antidumping and countervailing duty matters. In addition, it has exclusive jurisdiction of civil actions to review determinations as to the eligibility of workers, firms, and communities for adjustment assistance under the Trade Act of 1974 (19 U.S.C. 2101). Civil actions commenced by the United States to recover customs duties, to recover on a customs bond, or for certain civil penalties alleging fraud or negligence are also within the exclusive jurisdiction of the court.

The court is composed of a chief judge and eight judges, not more than five of whom may belong to any one political party. Any of its judges may be temporarily designated and assigned by the Chief Justice of the United States to sit as a court of appeals or district court judge in any circuit or district. The court has a clerk and deputy clerks, a librarian, court reporters, and other supporting personnel. Cases before the court may be tried before a jury. Under the Federal Courts Improvement Act of 1982 (28 U.S.C. 1295), appeals are taken to the U.S. Court of Appeals for the Federal Circuit, and ultimately review may be sought in appropriate cases in the Supreme Court of the United States.

The principal offices are located in New York, NY, but the court is empowered to hear and determine cases arising at any port or place within the jurisdiction of the United States.

For further information, contact the Clerk, United States Court of International Trade, One Federal Plaza, New York, NY 10007. Phone, 212–264–2814.

Judicial Panel on Multidistrict Litigation The Panel, created by act of April 29, 1968 (28 U.S.C. 1407), and consisting of seven Federal judges designated by the

Chief Justice from the courts of appeals and district courts, is authorized to temporarily transfer to a single district, for coordinated or consolidated pretrial proceedings, civil actions pending in different districts that involve one or more common questions of fact.

For further information, contact the Clerk, Judicial Panel on Multidistrict Litigation, Room G–255, Thurgood Marshall Federal Judiciary Building, One Columbus Circle NE., Washington, DC 20002. Phone, 202–273–2800.

Special Courts

The Supreme Court has held that ". . . Article III [of the Constitution] does not express the full authority of Congress to create courts, and that other Articles invest Congress with powers in the exertion of which it may create inferior courts and clothe them with functions deemed essential or helpful in carrying those powers into execution." Such courts, known as legislative courts, have functions which ". . . are directed to the execution of one or more of such powers and are prescribed by Congress independently of section 2 of Article III; and their judges hold office for such term as Congress prescribes, whether it be a fixed period of years or during good behavior." Appeals from the decisions of these courts, with the exception of the U.S. Tax Court and the U.S. Court of Military Appeals, may be taken to the U.S. Court of Appeals for the Federal Circuit. Appeals from the decisions of the Tax Court may be taken to the court of appeals in which judicial circuit the case was initially heard. Certain decisions of the U.S. Court of Military Appeals are reviewable by writ of certiorari in the Supreme Court.

United States Court of Federal Claims The Claims Court was established on October 1, 1982, as an Article I court (28 U.S.C. 171, Article I, U.S. Constitution). The Claims Court succeeds to the original jurisdiction of the former Court of Claims, as provided for in 20 U.S.C. 1491 *et seq.* Its name was changed to the United States Court of Federal Claims by the Federal Courts Administration Act of 1992 (28 U.S.C. 1 note, 106 Stat. 4516). The Court is composed of a chief judge, designated by the President, and 15 associate judges. All judges are appointed for 15-year terms by the President with the advice and consent of the Senate.

The court has jurisdiction over claims seeking money judgments against the United States. A claim must be founded upon either: the United States Constitution; an act of Congress; the regulation of an executive department; an express or implied-in-fact contract with the United States; or damages, liquidated or unliquidated, in cases not sounding in tort.

If a bidder files a claim with the Court before the award of a Government contract, it has jurisdiction to grant declaratory judgments and equitable relief. Under the Contract Disputes Act (41 U.S.C. 601 *et seq.*), the Court may render judgments upon a claim by or against a contractor, or any dispute between a contractor and the United States Government arising under the act.

The Congress, from time to time, also grants the Court jurisdiction over specific types of claims against the United States. The National Vaccine Injury Compensation Program, established by 42 U.S.C. 300aa–10 (the Vaccine Act), is an example of such special jurisdiction.

The Court also reports to Congress on bills referred by either the House of Representatives or the Senate.

Judgments of the Court are final and conclusive on both the claimant and the United States. All judgments are subject to appeal to the United States Court of Appeals for the Federal Circuit. Collateral to any judgment, the Court may issue orders directing the restoration to office or status of any claimant or the correction of applicable records.

The Court's jurisdiction is nationwide. Trials are conducted before individual judges at locations most convenient and least expensive to citizens.

For further information, contact the Clerk of Court, United States Court of Federal Claims, 717 Madison Place NW., Washington, DC 20005. Phone, 202–219–9657.

United States Court of Appeals for the Armed Forces   This court was established under Article I of the Constitution of the United States pursuant to act of May 5, 1950, as amended (10 U.S.C. 867). Subject only to certiorari review by the Supreme Court of the United States in a limited number of cases, the court serves as the final appellate tribunal to review court-martial convictions of all the armed services. It is exclusively an appellate criminal court, consisting of five civilian judges who are appointed for 15-year terms by the President with the advice and consent of the Senate. The court is called upon to exercise jurisdiction to review the record in all cases:

—extending to death;

—certified to the court by a Judge Advocate General of an armed service or by the General Counsel of the Department of Transportation, acting for the Coast Guard; or

—petitioned by accused who have received a sentence of confinement for 1 year or more, and/or a punitive discharge.

The court also exercises authority under the All Writs Act (28 U.S.C. 1651 (a)).

In addition, the judges of the court are required by law to work jointly with the senior uniformed lawyer from each Armed Force, the Chief Counsel of the Coast Guard, and two members of the public appointed by the Secretary of Defense, to make an annual comprehensive survey and to report annually to the Congress on the operation and progress of the military justice system under the Uniform Code of Military Justice, and to recommend improvements wherever necessary.

For further information, contact the Clerk, United States Court of Appeals for the Armed Forces, 450 E Street NW., Washington, DC 20442–0001. Phone, 202–272–1448. Fax, 202–504–4672.

United States Tax Court   This is a court of record under Article I of the Constitution of the United States (26 U.S.C. 7441). Currently an independent judicial body in the legislative branch, the court was originally created as the United States Board of Tax Appeals, an independent agency in the executive branch, by the Revenue Act of 1924 (43 Stat. 336) and continued by the Revenue Act of 1926 (44 Stat. 105), the Internal Revenue Codes of 1939, 1954, and 1986. The name was changed to the Tax Court of the United States by the Revenue Act of 1942 (56 Stat. 957), and the Article I status and change in name to United States Tax Court were effected by the Tax Reform Act of 1969 (83 Stat. 730).

The court is composed of 19 judges. Its strength is augmented by senior judges who may be recalled by the chief judge to perform further judicial duties and by 14 special trial judges who are appointed by the chief judge and serve at the pleasure of the court. The chief judge is elected biennially from among the 19 judges of the court.

The Tax Court tries and adjudicates controversies involving the existence of deficiencies or overpayments in income, estate, gift, and generation-skipping transfer taxes in cases where deficiencies have been determined by the Commissioner of Internal Revenue. It also hears cases commenced by transferees and fiduciaries who have been issued notices of liability by the Commissioner.

The Tax Court has jurisdiction to redetermine excise taxes and penalties imposed on private foundations. Similar jurisdiction over excise taxes has been conferred with regard to public charities, qualified pension plans, and real estate investment trusts.

At the option of the individual taxpayer, simplified procedures may be utilized for the trials of small tax cases, provided that in a case conducted under these procedures the decision of the court would be final and not subject to review by any court. The jurisdictional maximum for such cases is $10,000 for any disputed year.

In disputes relating to public inspection of written determinations by the Internal Revenue Service, the Tax Court has jurisdiction to restrain disclosure or to obtain additional disclosure of written determinations or background file documents and, at the request of any person, to order disclosure of the identity of any person to whom the written determination pertains, if there has been a third party contact noted on the determination made public.

The Tax Court has jurisdiction to render declaratory judgments relating to the qualification of retirement plans, including pension, profit-sharing, stock bonus, annuity, and bond purchase plans; the tax-exempt status of a charitable organization, qualified charitable donee, private foundation, or private operating foundation; and the status of interest on certain governmental obligations. Additional jurisdiction was conferred on the Tax Court by the Technical and Miscellaneous Revenue Act of 1988 (102 Stat. 3342). Such jurisdiction includes injunctive authority over certain procedure assessments, authority to review certain jeopardy assessments and jeopardy levies, and authority to hear and decide appeals by taxpayers from the denial of administrative costs by the Internal Revenue Service.

All decisions, other than small tax case decisions, are subject to review by the courts of appeals and thereafter by the Supreme Court of the United States upon the granting of a writ of certiorari.

The office of the court and all of its judges are located in Washington, DC, with the exception of a field office located in Los Angeles, CA. The court conducts trial sessions at various locations within the United States as reasonably convenient to taxpayers as practicable. Each trial session is conducted by a single judge or a special trial judge. All proceedings are public and are conducted judicially in accordance with the court's Rules of Practice and the rules of evidence applicable in trials without a jury in the U.S. District Court for the District of Columbia. A fee of $60 is prescribed for the filing of a petition. Practice before the court is limited to practitioners admitted under the court's Rules.

For further information, contact the Administrative Office, United States Tax Court, 400 Second Street NW., Washington, DC 20217. Phone, 202–606–8751.

United States Court of Veterans Appeals The United States Court of Veterans Appeals was established on November 18, 1988 (102 Stat. 4105, 38 U.S.C. 4051) pursuant to Article I of the Constitution, and given exclusive jurisdiction to review decisions of the Board of Veterans Appeals. However, the Court may not review the schedule of ratings for disabilities or actions of the Secretary in adopting or revising that schedule. Decisions of the Court of Veterans Appeals may be appealed to the United States Court of Appeals for the Federal Circuit.

The Court consists of a chief judge and at least two, but not more than six, associate judges. All judges are appointed by the President with the advice and consent of the Senate for terms of 15 years.

The court's principal office is in the District of Columbia, but the Court can also act at any place within the United States.

For further information, contact the Clerk, United States Court of Veterans Appeals, Suite 900, 625 Indiana Avenue NW., Washington, DC 20004–2950. Phone, 202–501–5970.

Other Courts There have also been created two courts of local jurisdiction for the District of Columbia: the District of Columbia Court of Appeals and the Superior Court.

Business of the Federal Courts

The business of all the Federal courts described here, except the Court of Military Appeals, the Tax Court, the Court of Veterans Appeals, and the District of Columbia courts, is discussed in detail in the text and tables of the *Annual Report of the Director of the Administrative Office of the United States Courts (1940–93).*

ADMINISTRATIVE OFFICE OF THE UNITED STATES COURTS

Washington, DC 20544
Phone: See "Sources of Information" section at end of statement.

Director	L. RALPH MECHAM
Deputy Director	(VACANCY)
Associate Director for Management and Operations	CLARENCE A. LEE, JR.
Chief, Office of Audit	DAVID L. GELLMAN
Chief, Office of Management Coordination	CATHY A. MCCARTHY
Chief, Office of Program Assessment	DUANE R. LEE
Associate Director and General Counsel	WILLIAM R. BURCHILL, JR.
Assistant Director, Judicial Conference Executive Secretariat	KAREN K. SIEGEL
Assistant Director, Congressional, External and Public Affairs	MICHAEL W. BLOMMER
Assistant Director for Automation and Technology	ROY L. CARTER
Deputy Assistant Director	JAMES S. LAMB
Chief, Automation Planning and Policy Formulation Office	KATHRYN C. HOGAN
Chief, Technology Enhancement Office	RICHARD D. FENNELL
Assistant Director for Court Programs	NOEL J. AUGUSTYN
Chief, Court Administration Policy Staff	ABEL J. MATTOS
Assistant Director for Facilities, Security and Administrative Services	P. GERALD THACKER
Deputy Assistant Director	WILLIAM J. LEHMAN
Court Security Officer	DONALD W. TUCKER
Chief, Relocation and Travel Management Office	ROBERT E. MORELAND
Assistant Director for Finance and Budget	RICHARD A. AMES
Deputy Assistant Director	NANCY A. POTOK
Chief, Economy Subcommittee Support Office	DIANE V. MARGESON, *Acting*
Financial Liaison Officers	PENNY G. JACOBS
	GEORGE H. SCHAFER
Chief, Judicial Impact Office	NANCY A. POTOK
Assistant Director for Human Resources and Statistics	MYRA HOWZE SHIPLETT
Deputy Assistant Director	R. TOWNSEND ROBINSON
Chief, Analytical Services Office	DAVID L. COOK
Chief, Education and Training Office	ROSEMARY M. MALCOLM
Chief, Equal Employment Opportunity and Special Projects Office	MAURICE E. WHITE
Assistant Director for Judges Programs	PETER G. MCCABE
Chief, Long Range Planning Office	PETER G. MCCABE
Chief, Rules Committee Support Office	JOHN K. RABIEJ
Chief, Accounting and Financial Systems Division	PHILIP L. MCKINNEY
Chief, Administrative Office Internal Services Division	CHARLES F. MCBRIDE
Chief, Appellate and Circuit Court Administration Division	JOHN P. HEHMAN

Chief, Article III Judges Division	JOHN E. HOWELL
Chief, Bankruptcy Court Administration Division	GLEN K. PALMAN
Chief, Bankruptcy Judges Division	FRANCIS F. SZCZEBAK
Chief, Budget Division	JOSEPH J. BOBEK
Chief, Court Systems Division	STEPHEN M. BECKMAN
Chief, Contracts and Services Division	RALPH J. SIMMONS
Chief, Defender Services Division	THEODORE J. LIDZ
Chief, District Court Administration Division	LYDIA PELEGRIN
Chief, Human Resources Division	CHARLOTTE G. PEDDICORD
Chief, Information Resources Management Services Division	DENNIS E. MOREY
Chief, Integrated Technology Division	PAMELA B. WHITE
Chief, Judiciary Data Center	DAVID S. CLAYTON
Chief, Magistrate Judges Division	THOMAS C. HNATOWSKI
Chief, Probation and Pretrial Services Division	EUNICE HOLT JONES
Chief, Space and Facilities Division	WILLIAM J. LEHMAN
Chief, Statistics Division	STEVEN R. SCHLESINGER
Chief, Systems Technology Division	FRANK S. DOZIER

The Administrative Office of the United States Courts is charged with the nonjudicial, administrative business of the United States Courts, including the maintenance of workload statistics and the disbursement of funds appropriated for the maintenance of the U.S. judicial system.

The Administrative Office of the United States Courts was created by act of August 7, 1939 (28 U.S.C. 601). The Office was established November 6, 1939. Its Director and Deputy Director are appointed by the Chief Justice of the United States after consultation with the Judicial Conference.

Administering the Courts   The Director is the administrative officer of the courts of the United States (except the Supreme Court). Under the guidance of the Judicial Conference of the United States the Director is required, among other things, to:

—supervise all administrative matters relating to the offices of clerks and other clerical and administrative personnel of the courts;

—examine the state of the dockets of the courts, secure information as to the courts' need of assistance, and prepare and transmit quarterly to the chief judges of the circuits statistical data and reports as to the business of the courts;

—submit to the annual meeting of the Judicial Conference of the United States, at least 2 weeks prior thereto, a report of the activities of the Administrative Office

and the state of the business of the courts;

—fix the compensation of employees of the courts whose compensation is not otherwise fixed by law;

—regulate and pay annuities to widows and surviving dependent children of judges;

—disburse moneys appropriated for the maintenance and operation of the courts;

—examine accounts of court officers;

—regulate travel of judicial personnel;

—provide accommodations and supplies for the courts and their clerical and administrative personnel;

—establish and maintain programs for the certification and utilization of court interpreters and the provision of special interpretation services in the courts; and

—perform such other duties as may be assigned to him by the Supreme Court or the Judicial Conference of the United States.

The Director is also responsible for the preparation and submission of the budget of the courts, except the budget of the Supreme Court.

Probation Officers   The Administrative Office exercises general supervision of

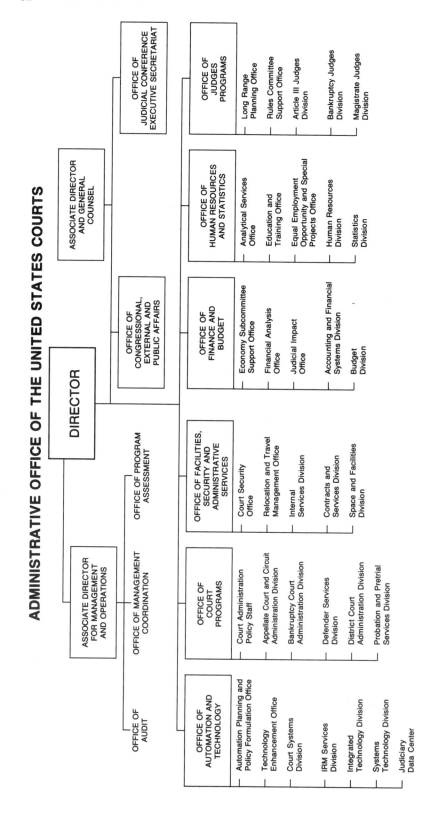

ADMINISTRATIVE OFFICE OF THE UNITED STATES COURTS

the accounts and practices of the Federal probation offices, subject to primary control by the respective district courts that they serve. The Office publishes quarterly, in cooperation with the Bureau of Prisons of the Department of Justice, a magazine entitled *Federal Probation,* which is a journal "of correctional philosophy and practice."

The Director also has responsibility with respect to the establishment of pretrial services in the district courts under the Pretrial Services Act of 1982 (18 U.S.C. 3152). These offices report to their respective courts information concerning pretrial release of persons charged with Federal offenses and supervise such persons who are released to their custody.

Bankruptcy The Bankruptcy Amendments and Federal Judgeship Act of 1984 (28 U.S.C. 151) provided that the bankruptcy judges for each judicial district shall constitute a unit of the district court to be known as the bankruptcy court. Bankruptcy judges are appointed by the courts of appeals in such numbers as authorized by Congress and serve for a term of 14 years as judicial officers of the district courts.

This act placed jurisdiction in the district courts over all cases under title 11, United States Code, and all proceedings arising in or related to cases under that title (28 U.S.C. 1334). The district court may provide for such cases and proceedings to be referred to its bankruptcy judges (as authorized by 28 U.S.C. 157).

The Director of the Administrative Office recommends to the Judicial Conference the official duty stations and places of holding court of bankruptcy judges, surveys the need for additional bankruptcy judgeships to be recommended to Congress, and determines the staff needs of bankruptcy judges and the clerks of the bankruptcy courts.

Federal Magistrate Judges Under the Federal Magistrates Act, as amended (28 U.S.C. 631), the Director of the Administrative Office, under the supervision and direction of the Judicial Conference, exercises general supervision over administrative matters in offices of United States magistrate judges, compiles and evaluates statistical data relating to such offices, and submits reports thereon to the Conference. The Director reports annually to Congress on the business that has come before United States magistrate judges and also prepares legal and administrative manuals for the use of the magistrate judges. The act provides for surveys to be conducted by the Administrative Office of the conditions in the judicial districts in order to make recommendations as to the number, location, and salaries of magistrate judges, which are determined by the Conference subject to the availability of appropriated funds.

Federal Defenders The Criminal Justice Act (18 U.S.C. 3006A) establishes the procedure for the appointment of counsel in Federal criminal cases for individuals who are unable to afford adequate representation under plans adopted by each district court. The act also permits the establishment of Federal public defender or Federal community defender organizations by the district courts in districts where at least 200 persons annually require the appointment of counsel. Two adjacent districts may be combined to reach this total.

Each defender organization submits to the Director of the Administrative Office an annual report of its activities along with a proposed budget or, in the case of community defender organizations, a proposed grant for the coming year. The Director is responsible for the submission of the proposed budgets and grants to the Judicial Conference for approval. The Director also makes payments to the defender organizations out of appropriations in accordance with the approved budgets and grants, as well as compensating private counsel appointed to defend criminal cases in the United States courts.

Sources of Information

Information may be obtained from the following offices:

Bankruptcy Judges Division. Phone, 202–273–1900.

Budget Division. Phone, 202–273–2100.

Defender Services Division. Phone, 202–273–1670.

General Counsel. Phone, 202–273–1100.

Human Resources Division. Phone, 202–273–1270.

Judicial Conference Executive Secretariat. Phone, 202–273–1140.

Legislative, External and Public Affairs Office. Phone, 202–273–1120.

Magistrate Judges Division. Phone, 202–273–1830.

Probation and Pretrial Services Division. Phone, 202–273–1600.

Statistics Division. Phone, 202–273–2240.

For further information, contact one of the offices listed above, Administrative Office of the United States Courts, Thurgood Marshall Federal Judiciary Building, One Columbus Circle NE., Washington, DC 20544.

FEDERAL JUDICIAL CENTER

Thurgood Marshall Federal Judiciary Building,
One Columbus Circle NE., Washington, DC 20002
Phone: See "Sources of Information" section at end of statement

Director	Rya W. Zobel
Deputy Director	Russell R. Wheeler
Director of Research	William B. Eldridge
Director of Planning and Technology	Gordon Bermant
Director of Judicial Education	Robb M. Jones
Director of Court Education	Emily Z. Huebner
Director of Publications and Media	Sylvan A. Sobel

The Federal Judicial Center is the judicial branch's agency for planning and policy research, systems development, and continuing education.

The Federal Judicial Center was created by act of December 20, 1967 (28 U.S.C. 620), to further the development and adoption of improved judicial administration in the courts of the United States.

The Center's basic policies and activities are determined by its Board, which is composed of the Chief Justice of the United States, who is, by statute, permanent Chairman of the Board, and two judges of the United States courts of appeals, three judges of the United States district courts, and one bankruptcy judge, all of whom are elected for 4-year terms by the Judicial Conference of the United States. The Director of the Administrative Office of the United States Courts is also a permanent member of the Board.

Congress assigned the Center the following basic functions:

—to conduct research on the operation of the United States courts and

to stimulate and coordinate such research on the part of other public and private persons and agencies;

—to stimulate, create, develop, and conduct programs of continuing education and training for judges and support personnel of the judicial branch;

—to study and determine ways in which automatic data processing and systems procedures may be applied to the administration of the courts;

—to provide staff, research, and planning assistance to the Judicial Conference and its committees, consistent with the performance of the other functions set forth above;

—to develop recommendations for improvement in the administration and management of the courts and to submit recommendations to the Judicial Conference of the United States;

—to submit to government agencies recommendations for improvement of their programs or activities that relate to the administration of justice;

—to conduct, coordinate, and encourage programs relating to the history of the judicial branch; and

—to cooperate with and assist other agencies and organizations in providing advice to further improvement in the administration of justice in the courts of foreign countries.

Sources of Information

Employment Employment inquiries and applications may be directed to the Office of Personnel. Phone, 202–273–4165.

Publications Single copies of most Federal Judicial Center publications are available free of charge. Phone, 202–273–4153.

For further information, contact the Federal Judicial Center, Thurgood Marshall Federal Judiciary Building, One Columbus Circle NE., Washington, DC 20002. For a recorded message and office directory, dial 202–273–4000 on a touch-tone phone.

UNITED STATES SENTENCING COMMISSION

Suite 2–500, South Lobby, One Columbus Circle NE., Washington, DC 20002–8002
Phone, 202–273–4500

Chairman	RICHARD P. CONABOY
Vice Chairmen	MICHAEL S. GELACEK
	A. DAVID MAZZONE
Commissioners	WAYNE A. BUDD, JULIE E. CARNES, MICHAEL GOLDSMITH, DEANELL R. TACHA
Commissioners (*ex officio*)	JO ANN HARRIS
	EDWARD F. REILLY, JR.
Staff Director	PHYLLIS J. NEWTON
Deputy Staff Director	PAUL K. MARTIN
General Counsel	JOHN R. STEER
Director of Training and Technical Assistance	SHARON O. HENEGAN
Special Projects Director	PAUL HOFER
Principal Technical Advisor	PETER B. HOFFMAN
Director of Administration	MARY G. HOGYA
Director of Policy Analysis	SUSAN KATZENELSON
Director of Communications	KENT S. LARSEN
Director of Monitoring	ELIZABETH A. MCGRATH
Executive Assistant to the Chairman	TIMOTHY B. MCGRATH
Chief Deputy General Counsel	DONALD A. PURDY, JR.
Legislative Counsel	WINTHROP M. SWENSON
Deputy Director of Training and Technical Assistance	SUSAN WINARSKY

The United States Sentencing Commission develops sentencing policies and practices for the Federal criminal justice system.

The United States Sentencing Commission was established as an independent commission in the judicial branch of the Federal Government by the Sentencing Reform Act of 1984 (28 U.S.C. 991 *et seq.* and 18 U.S.C. 3551 *et seq.*). The Commission establishes sentencing policies and practices for the Federal courts, including guidelines prescribing the appropriate form and

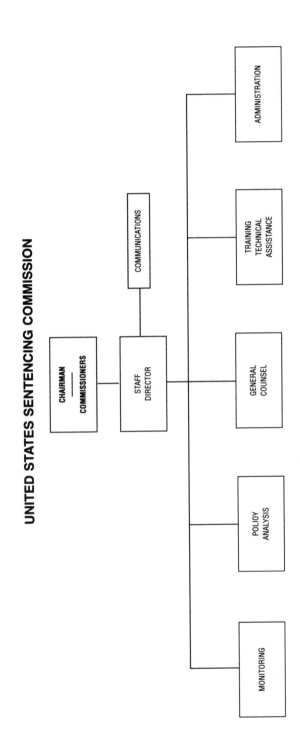

UNITED STATES SENTENCING COMMISSION

severity of punishment for offenders convicted of Federal crimes.

The Commission is composed of seven voting members appointed by the President with the advice and consent of the Senate for 6-year terms, and two nonvoting members. One of the voting members is appointed Chairman.

The Commission evaluates the effects of the sentencing guidelines on the criminal justice system, advises Congress regarding the modification or enactment of statutes relating to criminal law and sentencing matters, establishes a research and development program on sentencing issues, and performs other related duties.

In executing its duties, the Commission promulgates and distributes to Federal courts and to the U.S. Probation System guidelines to be used in determining sentences to be imposed in criminal cases, general policy statements regarding the application of guidelines, and policy statements on the appropriate use of probation and supervised release revocation provisions. These sentencing guidelines and policy statements are designed to further the purposes of just punishment, deterrence, incapacitation, and rehabilitation; provide fairness in meeting the purposes of sentencing; avoid unwarranted disparity; and reflect advancement in the knowledge of human behavior as it relates to the criminal justice process.

In addition, the Commission provides training, conducts research on sentencing-related issues, and serves as an information resource for Congress, criminal justice practitioners, and the public.

Sources of Information

Public Information   Information concerning the Commission's activities is available from the Office of Communications. Phone, 202–273–4590.

Judges and Probation Officers Technical Assistance Service   Phone, 202–273–4545 (hotline).

Prosecuting and Defense Attorneys   Phone, 202–273–4527 (hotline).

For further information, contact the Office of Communications, United States Sentencing Commission, Suite 2–500, South Lobby, One Columbus Circle NE., Washington, DC 20002–8002. Phone, 202–273–4590.

Executive Branch

EXECUTIVE BRANCH

THE PRESIDENT OF THE UNITED STATES

THE PRESIDENT OF THE UNITED STATES   WILLIAM J. CLINTON

Article II, section 1, of the Constitution provides that "the executive Power shall be vested in a President of the United States of America. He shall hold his Office during the Term of four Years, * * * together with the Vice President, chosen for the same Term * * *." In addition to the powers set forth in the Constitution, the statutes have conferred upon the President specific authority and responsibility covering a wide range of matters (United States Code Index).

The President is the administrative head of the executive branch of the Government, which includes numerous agencies, both temporary and permanent, as well as the 14 executive departments.

THE CABINET

The Cabinet, a creation of custom and tradition dating back to George Washington's administration, functions at the pleasure of the President. Its purpose is to advise the President upon any subject, relating to the duties of the respective offices, on which he requests information (pursuant to Article II, section 2, of the Constitution).

The Cabinet is composed of the heads of the 14 executive departments—the Secretaries of Agriculture, Commerce, Defense, Education, Energy, Health and Human Services, Housing and Urban Development, Interior, Labor, State, Transportation, Treasury, and Veterans Affairs, and the Attorney General. Additionally, in the Clinton administration, Cabinet-level rank has been accorded to: the Chief of Staff to the President; the Chairman, Council of Economic Advisers; the Administrator, Environmental Protection Agency; the Director, Office of Management and Budget; the U.S. Representative to the United Nations; and the U.S. Trade Representative. The Vice President also participates in Cabinet meetings, and from time to time, other individuals are invited to participate in discussions of particular subjects. A Secretary to the Cabinet is designated to provide for the orderly handling and followup of matters brought before the Cabinet.

EXECUTIVE OFFICE OF THE PRESIDENT

Under authority of the Reorganization Act of 1939 (5 U.S.C. 133–133r, 133t note), various agencies were transferred to the Executive Office of the President by the President's Reorganization Plans I and II of 1939 (5 U.S.C. app.), effective July 1, 1939. Executive Order 8248 of September 8, 1939, established the divisions of the Executive Office and defined their functions. Subsequently, Presidents have used Executive orders, reorganization plans, and legislative initiatives to reorganize the

91

Executive Office to make its composition compatible with the goals of their administrations.

The White House Office

1600 Pennsylvania Avenue NW., Washington, DC 20500
Phone, 202–456–1111

Chief of Staff	LEON E. PANETTA
Advisor to the President for Policy and Strategy and Executive Assistant to the Chief of Staff for Policy	GEORGE R. STEPHANOPOULOS
Counselor to the President for Business Affairs	THOMAS F. MCLARTY III
Counsel to the President	ABNER J. MIKVA
Deputy Counsel to the President	JAMES COSTELLO
Chair, Counsel of Economic Advisors	JOE STIGLITZ
Assistant to the President and Deputy Chief of Staff for Policy and Political Activity	HAROLD ICKES
Assistant to the President and Deputy Chief of Staff for White House Operations	ERSKINE BOWLES
Assistant to the President and Director of Political Affairs	DOUGLAS SOSNIK
Assistant to the President and Director for Special Projects	RAHM I. EMANUEL
Assistant to the President and Coordinator for Strategic Planning and Communications	MARK D. GEARAN
Assistant to the President for Science and Technology and Director, Office of Science and Technology Policy	JOHN H. GIBBONS
Assistant to the President and Director of Legislative Affairs	PATRICK GRIFFIN
Assistant to the President and Director of Intergovernmental Affairs	MARCIA L. HALE
Assistant to the President and Director of Public Liaison	ALEXIS M. HERMAN
Assistant to the President and Press Secretary	MIKE MCCURRY
Assistant to the President for National Security Affairs	ANTHONY LAKE
Assistant to the President and Deputy Counsel to the President	BRUCE LINDSEY
Assistant to the President and Staff Secretary	TODD STERN
Assistant to the President, and Chief of Staff and Counselor to the Vice President	JOHN M. QUINN
Assistant to the President for Domestic Policy	CAROL H. RASCO
Assistant to the President and Director of the National Economic Council	LAURA D. TYSON
Assistant to the President for National Service	ELI J. SEGAL
Assistant to the President and Chief of Staff to the First Lady	MARGARET A. WILLIAMS
Assistant to the President for Management and Administration	JODIE TORKELSON
Assistant to the President for Speechwriting and Research	DONALD BAER
Assistant to the President and Director of Presidential Personnel	BOB NASH

Assistant to the President and Cabinet Secretary	KITTY HIGGINS
Deputy Assistant to the President and Director of Scheduling and Advance	WILLIAM WEBSTER
Deputy Assistant to the President for National Security Affairs	SAMUEL R. BERGER
Deputy Assistant to the President and Deputy Director of Legislative Affairs	SUSAN A. BROPHY
Deputy Assistant to the President and Press Secretary to the First Lady	LISA M. CAPUTO
Deputy Assistant to the President for Economic Policy	W. BOWMAN CUTTER
Deputy Assistant to the President and Deputy Director of Intergovernmental Affairs	JOHN B. EMERSON
Deputy Assistant to the President and Deputy Director of Intergovernmental Affairs	JOHN P. HART
Deputy Assistant to the President for Scheduling and Appointments and Director of Oval Office Operations	NANCY HERNREICH
Deputy Assistant to the President and Director, White House Military Office	ALAN SULLIVAN
Deputy Assistant to the President for Public Liaison	DORIS O. MATSUI
Deputy Assistant to the President for Legislative Affairs (House)	LORRAINE MILLER
Deputy Assistant to the President and Deputy Press Secretary for Operations	EVELYN LIEBERMAN
Deputy Assistant to the President and Deputy Director of Political Affairs	KAREN HANCOX
Deputy Assistant to the President and Deputy Director of Intergovernmental Affairs	KEVIN M. O'KEEFE
Deputy Assistant to the President and Deputy Cabinet Secretary	STEPHEN B. SILVERMAN
Deputy Assistant to the President for National Security Affairs and Staff Director of the National Security Council	NANCY E. SODERBERG
Deputy Assistant to the President for Domestic Policy	BRUCE N. REED
Deputy Assistant to the President for Legislative Affairs (Senate)	STEVEN J. RICCHETTI
Deputy Assistants to the President for Political Affairs	MARSHA SCOTT, CRAIG SMITH
Deputy Assistant to the President for Legislative Affairs	ALPHONSO MALDON
Deputy Assistant to the President for Presidential Personnel	PATSY L. THOMASSON
Deputy Assistant to the President for Economic Policy	GENE SPERLING
Deputy Assistant to the President and Deputy Director of Advance	PAIGE REFFE
Deputy Assistant to the President and Deputy Chief of Staff to the First Lady	MELANNE VERVEER
Deputy Assistant to the President	IRA FISHMAN

Deputy Assistant to the President and Deputy Director and Chief of Staff for Presidential Personnel	ANTONELLA PIANALTO
Deputy Assistant to the President for Domestic Policy	JEREMY BEN-AMI
Deputy Assistant to the President for Women's Initiatives and Outreach	BETSY MYERS
Deputy Assistant to the President for Intergovernmental Affairs	LORETTA T. AVENT
Special Assistant to the President and Senior Director for Defense Policy and Arms Control	ROBERT G. BELL
Special Assistant to the President for and Senior Director of Speechwriting	ROBERT O. BOORSTIN
Special Assistant to the President and Senior Director for Russian, Ukrainian and Eurasian Affairs	COIT BLACKER
Special Assistants to the President for Legislative Affairs (Senate)	PAUL CAREY
	TRACEY THORNTON
Special Assistants to the President for Legislative Affairs	BARBARA CHOW, JANET MURGUIA, DANIEL TATE
Special Assistant to the President and Senior Director for Global Issues and Multilateral Affairs	RICHARD CLARKE
Special Assistant to the President and Senior Director for Environmental Affairs	EILEEN B. CLAUSSEN
Special Assistant to the President for Economic Policy	MICHAEL D. DEICH
Special Assistant to the President for Economic Policy and Director to the National Economic Council	PAUL R. DIMOND
Special Assistant to the President for Health Policy Development	CHRISTOPHER JENNINGS
Special Assistant to the President and Senior Director for Inter-American Affairs	RICHARD E. FEINBERG
Special Assistant to the President and Senior Director for Democracy	MORTON HALPERIN
Special Assistant to the President for Economic Policy and Director to the National Economic Council	ELWOOD J. HOLSTEIN
Special Assistant to the President and Senior Director for Near East and South Asian Affairs	MARK PARRIS
Special Assistant to the President and Senior Director, National Security Affairs	DANIEL FRIED
Special Assistant to the President for Legislative Affairs and Staff Director	TIMOTHY J. KEATING
Special Assistant to the President and Trip Director	ANDREW FRIENDLY
Special Assistant to the President and Associate Director of Presidential Personnel	PEGGY A. CLARK
Special Assistant to the President and Trip Director for the First Lady	KELLY CRAIGHEAD

Special Assistant to the President and Director of Correspondence and Presidential Messages	JAMES A. DORSKIND
Special Assistants to the President and Associate Directors of Presidential Personnel	CHARLES DUNCAN
	ELIZABETH MONTOYA
Special Assistants to the President	JENNIFER O'CONNOR
	WENDY SMITH
Special Assistant to the President and Legal Advisor	ALAN J. KRECZKO
Special Assistant to the President for Economic Policy and Senior Director to the National Economic Council	ROBERT KYLE
Special Assistants to the President for Political Affairs	ERIC EVES, THOMAS S. EPSTEIN, RAY MARTINEZ, LINDA L. MOORE
Special Assistant to the President and Assistant to the Chief of Staff	MARK MIDDLETON
Special Assistant to the President and Deputy Staff Secretary	PHIL CAPLAN
Special Assistant to the President and Senior Director for Nonproliferation and Export Controls	DANIEL B. PONEMAN
Special Assistant to the President for Economic Policy	DOROTHY L. ROBYN
Special Assistant to the President and Senior Director for Asian Affairs	STANLEY OWEN ROTH
Special Assistant to the President and Deputy Director of Scheduling	LEE SATTERFIELD
Special Assistant to the President and Counselor	RICHARD SCHIFTER
Special Assistant to the President for Economic Policy and Director to the National Economic Council	ELLEN SHAPIRO SEIDMAN
Special Assistant to the President and Director of Scheduling for the First Lady	PATRICIA SOLLS
Special Assistant to the President for the National Security Council	HEATHER ROSS
Special Assistant to the President and Senior Director of Legislative Affairs	WILLIAM DANVERS
Special Assistant to the President for Cabinet Affairs	LEEANN INADOMI
Special Assistant to the President and Senior Director for African Affairs	SUSAN RICE
Special Assistant to the President and Social Secretary	ANN STOCK
Special Assistant to the President and Deputy Director of Scheduling	STEPHANIE STREETT
Special Assistant to the President and Senior Director for Intelligence Programs	GEORGE J. TENET
Special Assistant to the President for Management and Administration and Director of the Office of Administration	(VACANCY)
Special Assistant to the President for Policy Coordination	MICHAEL A. WALDMAN

Special Assistant to the President and Director of Research	ANNE F. WALKER
Special Assistant to the President and Senior Director for European Affairs	ALEXANDER VERSHBOW
Special Assistant to the President and Deputy Director of Scheduling	ANNE WALLEY
Special Assistants to the President for Public Liaison	MARILYN YAGER
	KATHLEEN SMITH CARR
Counsel to the Vice President	KUMIKI GIBSON
National Security Advisor for the Vice President	LEON S. FUERTH
Special Advisor for Policy Development	IRA MAGAZINER
Associate Counsels to the President	CHRISTOPHER CERF, DAVID FEIN, MARVIN KRISLOV, CHERYL MILLS, MIRIAM NEMETZ, STEPHEN R. NEUWIRTH, VICTORIA RADD, CLIFFORD M. SLOAN, KATHLEEN WHALEN

The White House Office serves the President in the performance of the many detailed activities incident to his immediate office.

The staff of the President facilitates and maintains communication with the Congress, the individual Members of the Congress, the heads of executive agencies, the press and other information media, and the general public.

The various Assistants to the President assist the President in such matters as he may direct.

Office of Management and Budget
Executive Office Building, Washington, DC 20503
Phone, 202–395–3080

Director	ALICE M. RIVLIN
Deputy Director	(VACANCY)
Deputy Director for Management	JOHN KOSKINEN
Executive Associate Director	JACOB J. LEW
Associate Director for Legislative Affairs	(VACANCY)
Associate Director for Administration	JOHN B. ARTHUR
Senior Advisors to the Director	JILL BLICKSTEIN, WILLIAM HALTER, CHANTALE WONG
General Counsel	ROBERT DAMUS
Associate Director for Communications	LARRY HAAS
Associate Director for Economic Policy	JOSEPH MINARIK
Assistant Director for Budget	BARRY ANDERSON
Deputy Assistant Director for Budget Analysis and Systems	PHIL DAME
Deputy Assistant Director for Budget Review and Concepts	DICK EMERY
Assistant Director for Legislative Reference	JAMES C. MURR
Associate Director for National Security and International Affairs	GORDON ADAMS

Deputy Associate Director, National Security Division	PHEBE VICKERS
Deputy Associate Director, International Affairs Division	PHILIP DUSAULT
Associate Director for Human Resources	KENNETH APFEL
Deputy Associate Director for Human Resources	BARRY WHITE
Associate Director for Health and Personnel	NANCY-ANN MIN
Deputy Associate Director for Health	BARRY CLENDENIN
Deputy Associate Director for VA/Personnel	(VACANCY)
Associate Director for General Government	ROBERT LITAN
Deputy Associate Director, Transportation, Commerce, Justice, and Federal Services Division	KENNETH SCHWARTZ
Deputy Associate Director, Housing, Treasury, and Finance Division	ALAN RHINESMITH
Associate Director for Natural Resources, Energy, and Science	T.J. GLAUTHIER
Deputy Associate Director, Natural Resources Division	RONALD COGSWELL
Deputy Associate Director, Energy and Science Division	KATHY PEROFF
Administrator, Office of Information and Regulatory Affairs	SALLY KATZEN
Deputy Administrator for Information and Regulatory Management	JAMES MACRAE
Controller	EDWARD DESEVE
Deputy Controller	NORWOOD JACKSON
Administrator, Office of Federal Procurement Policy	STEVEN KELMAN
Deputy Administrator for Federal Procurement Policy	WILLIAM COLEMAN

The Office of Management and Budget evaluates, formulates, and coordinates management procedures and program objectives within and among Federal departments and agencies. It also controls the administration of the Federal budget, while routinely providing the President with recommendations regarding budget proposals and relevant legislative enactments.

The Office of Management and Budget (OMB), formerly the Bureau of the Budget, was established in the Executive Office of the President pursuant to Reorganization Plan No. 1 of 1939 (5 U.S.C. app.), effective July 1, 1939.

By Executive Order 11541 of July 1, 1970, all functions transferred to the President of the United States by part I of Reorganization Plan No. 2 of 1970 (5 U.S.C. app.) were delegated to the Director of the Office of Management and Budget. Such functions are to be carried out by the Director under the direction of the President. Reorganization Plan No. 1 of 1977 (5

U.S.C. app.) and Executive orders issued pursuant to that plan further amended the functions of OMB. The Office's primary functions are:

—to assist the President in developing and maintaining effective government by reviewing the organizational structure and management procedures of the executive branch to ensure that the intended results are achieved;

—to assist in developing efficient coordinating mechanisms to implement Government activities and to expand interagency cooperation;

OFFICE OF MANAGEMENT AND BUDGET

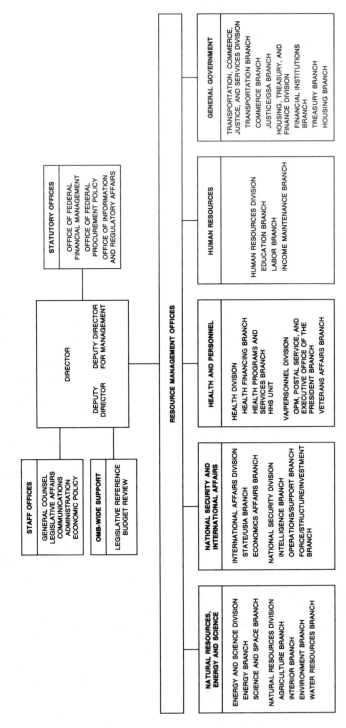

STAFF OFFICES

GENERAL COUNSEL
LEGISLATIVE AFFAIRS
COMMUNICATIONS
ADMINISTRATION
ECONOMIC POLICY

OMB-WIDE SUPPORT

LEGISLATIVE REFERENCE
BUDGET REVIEW

DIRECTOR

DEPUTY DIRECTOR

DEPUTY DIRECTOR
FOR MANAGEMENT

STATUTORY OFFICES

OFFICE OF FEDERAL
FINANCIAL MANAGEMENT
OFFICE OF FEDERAL
PROCUREMENT POLICY
OFFICE OF INFORMATION
AND REGULATORY AFFAIRS

RESOURCE MANAGEMENT OFFICES

**NATURAL RESOURCES,
ENERGY AND SCIENCE**

ENERGY AND SCIENCE DIVISION
ENERGY BRANCH
SCIENCE AND SPACE BRANCH
NATURAL RESOURCES DIVISION
AGRICULTURE BRANCH
INTERIOR BRANCH
ENVIRONMENT BRANCH
WATER RESOURCES BRANCH

**NATIONAL SECURITY AND
INTERNATIONAL AFFAIRS**

INTERNATIONAL AFFAIRS DIVISION
STATE/USIA BRANCH
ECONOMICS AFFAIRS BRANCH
NATIONAL SECURITY DIVISION
INTELLIGENCE BRANCH
OPERATIONS/SUPPORT BRANCH
FORCE/STRUCTURE/INVESTMENT
BRANCH

HEALTH AND PERSONNEL

HEALTH DIVISION
HEALTH FINANCING BRANCH
HEALTH PROGRAMS AND
SERVICES BRANCH
HHS UNIT
VA/PERSONNEL DIVISION
OPM, POSTAL SERVICE, AND
EXECUTIVE OFFICE OF THE
PRESIDENT BRANCH
VETERANS AFFAIRS BRANCH

HUMAN RESOURCES

HUMAN RESOURCES DIVISION
EDUCATION BRANCH
LABOR BRANCH
INCOME MAINTENANCE BRANCH

GENERAL GOVERNMENT

TRANSPORTATION, COMMERCE,
JUSTICE, AND SERVICES DIVISION
TRANSPORTATION BRANCH
COMMERCE BRANCH
JUSTICE/GSA BRANCH
HOUSING, TREASURY, AND
FINANCE DIVISION
FINANCIAL INSTITUTIONS
BRANCH
TREASURY BRANCH
HOUSING BRANCH

—to assist the President in preparing the budget and in formulating the Government's fiscal program;

—to supervise and control the administration of the budget;

—to assist the President by clearing and coordinating departmental advice on proposed legislation and by making recommendations effecting Presidential action on legislative enactments, in accordance with past practice;

—to assist in developing regulatory reform proposals and programs for paperwork reduction, especially reporting burdens of the public;

—to assist in considering, clearing, and, where necessary, preparing proposed Executive orders and proclamations;

—to plan and develop information systems that provide the President with program performance data;

—to plan, conduct, and promote evaluation efforts that assist the President in assessing program objectives, performance, and efficiency;

—to keep the President informed of the progress of activities by Government agencies with respect to work proposed, initiated, and completed, together with the relative timing of work between the several agencies of the Government, all to the end that the work programs of the several agencies of the executive branch of the Government may be coordinated and that the moneys appropriated by the Congress may be expended in the most economical manner, barring overlapping and duplication of effort; and

—to improve the economy, efficiency, and effectiveness of the procurement processes by providing overall direction of procurement policies, regulations, procedures, and forms.

Sources of Information

Employment Various civil service examinations and registers are used for filling positions, such as economist, budget examiner, and management analyst. Inquiries on employment should be directed to the Personnel Division, Office of Administration, Washington, DC 20500. Phone, 202–395–1088.

Inquiries Contact the Office of Administration, Office of Management and Budget, New Executive Office Building, Washington, DC 20503. Phone, 202–395–3080.

Publications *The Budget of the U.S. Government, The Budget System and Concepts,* and *Catalog of Federal Domestic Assistance* are for sale by the Superintendent of Documents, Government Printing Office, Washington, DC 20402.

Council of Economic Advisers

Old Executive Office Building, Washington, DC 20500
Phone, 202–395–5084

Chairman	LAURA D. TYSON
Members	JOSEPH E. STIGLITZ
	(VACANCY)
Special Assistant to the Chairman	THOMAS P. O'DONNELL

The Council of Economic Advisers primarily performs an analysis and appraisal of the national economy for the purpose of providing policy recommendations to the President.

The Council of Economic Advisers was established in the Executive Office of the President by the Employment Act of 1946 (15 U.S.C. 1023). It now functions under that statute and Reorganization

Plan No. 9 of 1953 (5 U.S.C. app.), effective August 1, 1953.

The Council consists of three members appointed by the President with the advice and consent of the Senate, and one of the members is designated by the President as Chairman.

The Council analyzes the national economy and its various segments; advises the President on economic developments; appraises the economic programs and policies of the Federal Government; recommends to the President policies for economic growth and stability; assists in the preparation of the economic reports of the President to the Congress; and prepares the Annual Report of the Council of Economic Advisers.

For further information, contact the Council of Economic Advisers, Old Executive Office Building, Washington, DC 20500. Phone, 202–395–5084.

National Security Council

Old Executive Office Building, Washington, DC 20506
Phone, 202–456–1414

Members:

The President	WILLIAM J. CLINTON
The Vice President	ALBERT GORE, JR.
The Secretary of State	WARREN M. CHRISTOPHER
The Secretary of Defense	WILLIAM J. PERRY

Statutory Advisers:

Director of Central Intelligence	JOHN M. DEUTCH
Chairman, Joint Chiefs of Staff	GEN. JOHN M. SHALIKASHVILI, USA

Standing Participants:

The Secretary of the Treasury	ROBERT E. RUBIN
U.S. Representative to the United Nations	MADELEINE K. ALBRIGHT
Chief of Staff to the President	LEON E. PANETTA
Assistant to the President for National Security Affairs	ANTHONY LAKE
Assistant to the President for Economic Policy	LAURA D. TYSON

Officials:

Assistant to the President for National Security Affairs	ANTHONY LAKE
Deputy Assistants to the President for National Security Affairs	SAMUEL R. BERGER
	NANCY E. SODERBERG
Executive Secretary	ANDREW D. SENS

The National Security Council was established by the National Security Act of 1947, as amended (50 U.S.C. 402). The Council was placed in the Executive Office of the President by Reorganization Plan No. 4 of 1949 (5 U.S.C. app.).

The National Security Council is chaired by the President. Its statutory members, in addition to the President, are the Vice President and the Secretaries of State and Defense. The Chairman of the Joint Chiefs of Staff is the statutory military adviser to the

Council, and the Director of Central Intelligence is its intelligence adviser. The Secretary of the Treasury, the U.S. Representative to the United Nations, the Assistant to the President for National Security Affairs, the Assistant to the President for Economic Policy, and the Chief of Staff to the President are invited to all meetings of the Council. The Attorney General is invited to attend meetings pertaining to her jurisdiction; other officials are invited, as appropriate.

The Council advises and assists the President in integrating all aspects of national security policy as it affects the United States—domestic, foreign, military, intelligence, and economic—in conjunction with the National Economic Council.

Office of the United States Trade Representative

600 Seventeenth Street NW., Washington, DC 20506
Phone, 202–395–3230

United States Trade Representative	MICHAEL KANTOR
Deputy U.S. Trade Representatives (Washington)	JEFFREY LANG
	CHARLENE BARSHEFSKY
Deputy U.S. Trade Representative (Geneva)	BOOTH GARDNER
Chief of Staff	PETER SCHER
Senior Counsel and Negotiator	IRA SHAPIRO
General Counsel	IRA SHAPIRO, *Acting*
Chief Textiles Negotiator	JENNIFER HILLMAN
Assistant U.S. Trade Representative for Intergovernmental Affairs and Public Liaison	PHYLLIS JONES
Assistant U.S. Trade Representative for Public Affairs	ANNE LUZZATTO
Assistant U.S. Trade Representative for Congressional Affairs	NANCY LEAMOND
Assistant U.S. Trade Representative for Economic Affairs	DAVID WALTERS
Assistant U.S. Trade Representative for Policy Coordination	FRED MONTGOMERY
Special Counsel for Finance and Investment Policy	HOWARD REED
Assistant U.S. Trade Representative for Agricultural Affairs	SUZANNE EARLY
Assistant U.S. Trade Representative for Trade and Development	JON ROSENBAUM
Assistant U.S. Trade Representative for World Trade Organization (WTO)	DOROTHY DWOSKIN
Assistant U.S. Trade Representative for Industry	DONALD PHILLIPS
Assistant U.S. Trade Representative for Japan and China	LEE SANDS
Assistant U.S. Trade Representative for Asia and the Pacific	BOB CASSIDY
Assistant U.S. Trade Representative for APEC Affairs	NANCY ADAMS

Assistant U.S. Trade Representative for Europe and the Mediterranean	CHRIS MARCH
Assistant U.S. Trade Representative for Environment	JENNIFER HAVERKAMP, *Acting*
Associate U.S. Trade Representative for Western Hemisphere	PETER ALLGEIER
Assistant U.S. Trade Representative for North American Affairs	DAVID WEISS
Assistant U.S. Trade Representative for Services, Investment and Intellectual Property	DON ABLESON
Assistant U.S. Trade Representative for Administration	JOHN HOPKINS

The United States Trade Representative is responsible for directing all trade negotiations of and formulating trade policy for the United States.

The Office of the United States Trade Representative was created as the Office of the Special Representative for Trade Negotiations by Executive Order 11075 of January 15, 1963. The Trade Act of 1974 (19 U.S.C. 2171) established the Office as an agency of the Executive Office of the President charged with administering the trade agreements program under the Tariff Act of 1930 (19 U.S.C. 1654), the Trade Expansion Act of 1962 (19 U.S.C. 1801), and the Trade Act of 1974 (19 U.S.C. 2101). Other powers and responsibilities for coordinating trade policy were assigned to the Office by the Trade Act of 1974 and by the President in Executive Order 11846 of March 27, 1975, as amended.

Reorganization Plan No. 3 of 1979 (5 U.S.C. app.), implemented by Executive Order 12188 of January 4, 1980, charged the Office with responsibility for setting and administering overall trade policy. It also provides that the United States Trade Representative shall be chief representative of the United States for:

—all activities concerning the General Agreement on Tariffs and Trade;

—discussions, meetings, and negotiations in the Organization for Economic Cooperation and Development when such activities deal primarily with trade and commodity issues;

—negotiations in the United Nations Conference on Trade and Development and other multilateral institutions when such negotiations deal primarily with trade and commodity issues;

—other bilateral and multilateral negotiations when trade, including East-West trade, or commodities is the primary issue;

—negotiations under sections 704 and 734 of the Tariff Act of 1930 (19 U.S.C. 1671c and 1673c); and

—negotiations concerning direct investment incentives and disincentives and bilateral investment issues concerning barriers to investment.

The Omnibus Trade and Competitiveness Act of 1988 codified these prior authorities and added additional authority, including the implementation of section 301 actions (regarding enforcement of U.S. rights under international trade agreements).

The Office is headed by the United States Trade Representative, a Cabinet-level official with the rank of Ambassador, who is directly responsible to the President. There are three Deputy United States Trade Representatives, who also hold the rank of Ambassador, two located in Washington and one in Geneva. The Chief Textile Negotiator and the Uruguay Round Coordinator also hold the rank of Ambassador.

The United States Trade Representative serves as an *ex officio* member of the Boards of Directors of the Export-Import Bank and the Overseas Private Investment Corporation, and serves on the National Advisory Council for International Monetary and Financial Policy.

For further information, contact the Office of Public Affairs, Office of the United States Trade Representative, 600 Seventeenth Street NW., Washington, DC 20506. Phone, 202–395–3230.

Council on Environmental Quality

360 Old Executive Office Building (OEOB), Washington, DC 20501
202–456–6224

722 Jackson Place NW., Washington, DC 20503
Phone, 202–395–5750

Chair	KATHLEEN A. MCGINTY
Chief of Staff	SHELLEY N. FIDLER
General Counsel	DINAH BEAR
Associate General Counsel	ELISABETH BLAUG
Associate Director for International Trade and Development	JANE BRADLEY
Associate Director for Toxics and Environmental Protection	BRAD CAMPBELL
Associate Director for NEPA Oversight	RAY CLARK
Associate Director for Congressional Affairs	MICHELLE DENTON
Confidential Assistant	KATHLEEN GALLAGHER
Assistant to the Chair for Policy and Administration	MATT GENTILE
Associate Director for Natural Resources	TOM JENSEN
Associate Director for Communications	BRIAN JOHNSON
Associate Director for Sustainable Development	KEITH LAUGHLIN
Associate Director for Global Environment	DAVID SANDALOW
Policy Analyst	WENDELL STILLS
Assistant to the Chair for Strategic Planning and Outreach	BETH VIOLA
Special Assistant to the Chair	ROBERT VANDERMARK
Associate Director for Air, Transportation, and Energy	WESLEY WARREN

The Council on Environmental Quality was established within the Executive Office of the President by the National Environmental Policy Act of 1969 (42 U.S.C. 4341 *et seq.*) to formulate and recommend national policies to promote the improvement of the quality of the environment. Additional responsibilities were provided by the Environmental Quality Improvement Act of 1970 (42 U.S.C. 4371 *et seq.*).

The Council consists of three members appointed by the President with the advice and consent of the Senate, and one of the members is designated by the President as Chairman.

The Council develops and recommends to the President national policies that further environmental quality; performs a continuing analysis of changes or trends in the national environment; reviews and appraises programs of the Federal Government to determine their contributions to sound environmental policy; conducts studies, research, and analyses relating to ecological systems and environmental quality; assists the President in the preparation of the annual environmental quality report to the Congress; and oversees implementation of the National Environmental Policy Act. The Chairman of the Council also serves as Chair of the President's Commission on

Environmental Quality.

For further information, contact the Information Office, Council on Environmental Quality, 722 Jackson Place NW., Washington, DC 20503. Phone, 202–395–5754.

Office of Science and Technology Policy
Old Executive Office Building, Washington, DC 20500
Phone, 202–395–7347; Fax, 202–456–6022

Assistant to the President for Science and Technology, and Director	JOHN H. GIBBONS
Associate Director for Environment	ROBERT WATSON
Associate Director for National Security and International Affairs	JANE WALES
Associate Director for Science	M.R.C. GREENWOOD
Associate Director for Technology	LIONEL S. JOHNS
Assistant Director for Environment	MARK SCHAEFER
Executive Secretary for the National Science and Technology Council	ANGELA PHILLIPS DIAZ

The Office of Science and Technology Policy was established within the Executive Office of the President by the National Science and Technology Policy, Organization, and Priorities Act of 1976 (42 U.S.C. 6611).

The Office serves as a source of scientific, engineering, and technological analysis and judgment for the President with respect to major policies, plans, and programs of the Federal Government. In carrying out this mission, the act provides that the Office shall advise the President of scientific and technological considerations involved in areas of national concern, including the economy, national

security, health, foreign relations, and the environment; evaluate the scale, quality, and effectiveness of the Federal effort in science and technology; provide advice and assistance to the President, the Office of Management and Budget, and Federal agencies throughout the Federal budget development process; and assist the President in providing leadership and coordination for the research and development programs of the Federal Government.

Sources of Information

Electronic access through the World Wide Web: http://www.whitehouse.gov/ OSTP.html

For further information, contact the Office of Science and Technology Policy, Old Executive Office Building, Washington, DC 20500. Phone, 202–395–7347.

Office of National Drug Control Policy

Executive Office of the President, Washington, DC 20500
Phone, 202–395–6700

Director	LEE PATRICK BROWN
Chief of Staff	ROBERT WASSERMAN
Director of Public and Legislative Affairs	CHARLOTTE HAYES
Director of Planning, Budget and Research	JOHN CARNEVALE
General Counsel	EDWARD H. JURITH
Deputy Director for Demand Reduction	FRED W. GARCIA
Deputy Director for Supply Reduction	HENRY MARSDEN, *Acting*
Associate Director for State and Local Affairs	GEORGE KOSNIK, *Acting*
Director, Counter-Drug Technology Assessment Center	ALBERT BRANDENSTEIN

The Office of National Drug Control Policy coordinates Federal, State, and local efforts to control illegal drug abuse and devises national strategies to effectively carry out antidrug activities.

The Office of National Drug Control Policy was established by the National Narcotics Leadership Act of 1988 (21 U.S.C. 1501 et seq.), effective January 29, 1989, as amended by the Violent Crime Control and Law Enforcement Act of 1994 (21 U.S.C. 1502, 1506, 1508).

The Office is headed by the Director of National Drug Control Policy, who is appointed by the President with the advice and consent of the Senate. The Director is assisted by the Deputy Director for Demand Reduction and the Deputy Director for Supply Reduction. The Bureau of State and Local Affairs is a separate division of the Office, headed by an Associate Director for National Drug Control Policy.

The Director of National Drug Control Policy is responsible for establishing policies, objectives, and priorities for the National Drug Control Program, and for annually promulgating a National Drug Control Strategy to be submitted to the Congress by the President. The Director advises the President regarding necessary changes in the organization, management, budgeting, and personnel allocation of Federal agencies involved in drug enforcement activities, and is also responsible for notifying Federal agencies if their policies are not in compliance with their responsibilities under the National Drug Control Strategy.

For further information, contact the Office of National Drug Control Policy, Executive Office of the President, Washington, DC 20500. Phone, 202–395–6700.

Office of Administration

Old Executive Office Building
725 Seventeenth Street NW., Washington, DC 20503
Phone, 202–395–6963

Special Assistant to the President for Management and Administration and Director, Office of Administration	PATSY L. THOMASSON

OFFICE OF NATIONAL DRUG CONTROL POLICY

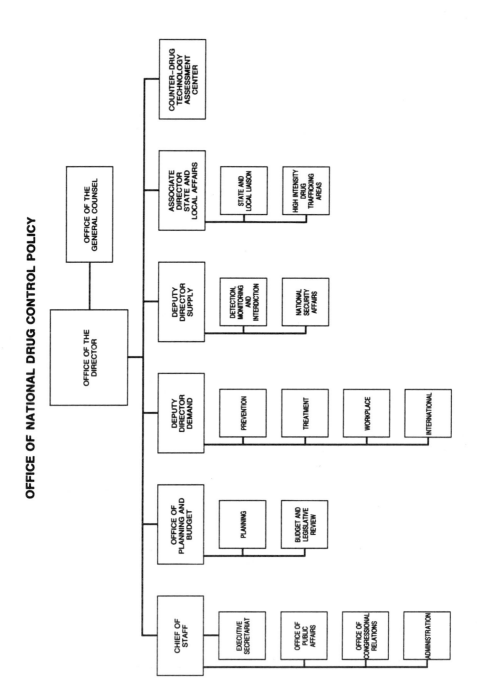

Deputy Director	JOHN W. CRESSMAN
General Counsel	NELSON CUNNINGHAM
Customer Advocacy Coordinator	ASHLEY RAINES
Director, Financial Management Division	JURG HOCHULI
Assistant to the Deputy Director for Administrative Operations	ADA L. POSEY
Director, Information Systems and Technology Division	JAMES MACDONALD
Director, Library and Research Services Division	MARY ANN NOWELL
Director, Personnel Management Division	MARY COUTTS BECK

The Office of Administration was established within the Executive Office of the President by Reorganization Plan No. 1 of 1977 (5 U.S.C. app.). The Office was activated, effective December 4, 1977, by Executive Order 12028 of December 12, 1977.

The Office of Administration provides administrative support services to all units within the Executive Office of the President. The services provided include information, personnel, and financial management; data processing; library services; records maintenance; and general office operations, such as mail, messenger, printing, procurement, and supply services.

For further information, contact the Office of the Deputy Director, Office of Administration, Washington, DC 20503. Phone, 202–395–6963.

OFFICE OF THE VICE PRESIDENT OF THE UNITED STATES

Old Executive Office Building, Washington, DC 20501
Phone, 202–456–2326

THE VICE PRESIDENT	ALBERT GORE, JR.
Chief of Staff and Counselor to the Vice President	JOHN M. QUINN
Deputy Chief of Staff	DAVID M. STRAUSS
Director of Communications for the Vice President	LORRAINE A. VOLES
Counsel to the Vice President	KUMIKI GIBSON
National Security Advisor for the Vice President	LEON S. FUERTH
Deputy Counsel and Director of Legislative Affairs for the Vice President	THURGOOD MARSHALL, JR.
Executive Assistant to the Vice President	HEATHER MARABELI
Special Assistant to the Vice President and Chief of Staff to Mrs. Gore	SKILA S. HARRIS
Chief Domestic Policy Advisor for the Vice President	GREG C. SIMON
Senior Policy Advisor for the Vice President	ELAINE C. KAMARCK
Director of Correspondence for the Vice President	BILL MASON

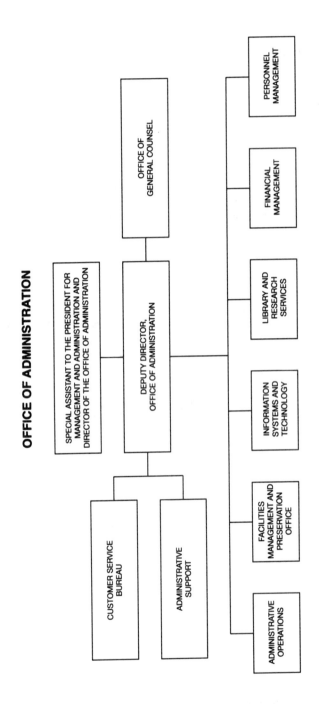

OFFICE OF ADMINISTRATION

Director of Scheduling for the Vice President	KIMBERLY H. TILLEY
Director of Advance and Deputy Director of Scheduling for the Vice President	DENNIS W. ALPERT

Article II, section I, of the Constitution provides that the President "shall hold his Office during the Term of four Years * * * together with the Vice President * * *." In addition to his role as President of the Senate, the Vice President is empowered to succeed to the Presidency, pursuant to Article II and the 20th and 25th amendments to the Constitution.

The executive functions of the Vice President include participation in Cabinet meetings and, by statute, membership on the National Security Council and the Board of Regents of the Smithsonian Institution.

Departments

DEPARTMENT OF AGRICULTURE
Fourteenth Street and Independence Avenue SW., Washington, DC 20250
Phone, 202–720–2791

SECRETARY OF AGRICULTURE	DAN GLICKMAN
Deputy Secretary	RICHARD ROMINGER
Under Secretary for Farm and Foreign Agricultural Services	GENE MOOS
Deputy Under Secretaries	DALLAS SMITH
	JAMES SCHROEDER
Administrator, Consolidated Farm Service Agency	GRANT BUNTROCK, *Acting*
Administrator, Foreign Agricultural Service	GUS SCHUMACHER
Under Secretary for Food, Nutrition, and Consumer Services	ELLEN HAAS
Deputy Under Secretary	SHIRLEY WATKINS
Administrator, Food and Consumer Service	BILL LUDWIG
Under Secretary for Food Safety	MIKE TAYLOR, *Acting*
Administrator, Food Safety and Inspection Service	MIKE TAYLOR
Under Secretary for Natural Resources and Environment	JAMES LYONS
Deputy Under Secretary for Forestry	ADELA BACKIEL
Deputy Under Secretary for Conservation	TOM HEBERT
Chief, Forest Service	JACK THOMAS
Chief, Natural Resources Conservation Service	PAUL W. JOHNSON
Under Secretary for Research, Education, and Economics	KARL STAUBER
Deputy Under Secretary	FLOYD HORN
Administrator, Agricultural Research Service	R.D. PLOWMAN
Administrator, Cooperative State Research, Education, and Extension Service	WILLIAM CARLSON, *Acting*
Administrator, Economic Research Service	JOHN DUNMORE, *Acting*
Administrator, National Agricultural Statistics Service	DONALD BAY
Under Secretary for Rural Economic and Community Development	MICHAEL DUNN, *Acting*
Deputy Under Secretaries	MICHAEL DUNN
	KARL STAUBER

111

Administrator, Rural Housing and Cooperative Development Service	DAYTON WATKINS, *Acting*
Administrator, Rural Housing and Community Development Service	MAUREEN KENNEDY, *Acting*
Administrator, Rural Utilities Service	WALLY BEYER
Assistant Secretary for Marketing and Regulatory Programs	PAT JENSEN, *Acting*
Deputy Assistant Secretary	(VACANCY)
Administrator, Agricultural Marketing Service	LON HATAMIYA
Administrator, Animal and Plant Health Inspection Service	LONNIE KING, *Acting*
Administrator, Grain Inspection, Packers and Stockyards Administration	JAMES R. BAKER
Assistant Secretary for Administration	WARDELL TOWNSEND, JR.
Deputy Assistant Secretary	ANNE REED
Chairman, Board of Contract Appeals	EDWARD HOURY
Judicial Officer	DONALD A. CAMPBELL
Chief Judge, Administrative Law Judges	VICTOR PALMER
Director, Office of Civil Rights Enforcement	DAVID MONTOYA
Director, Office of Information Resources Management	JOHN OKAY
Director, Office of Operations	IRA L. HOBBS
Director, Office of Personnel	EVELYN WHITE
Assistant Secretary for Congressional Relations	SCOTT SHEARER, *Acting*
Chief Financial Officer	ANTHONY WILLIAMS
Deputy Chief Financial Officer	TED DAVID
Director, Office of Finance and Management	ALLEN JOHNSON
General Counsel	JAMES GILLILAND
Deputy General Counsel	BONNIE LUKEN
Inspector General	ROGER VIADERO
Deputy Inspector General	CHARLES GILLUM
Director, Office of Communications	ALI WEBB
Chief Economist	KEITH COLLINS
Director, Office of Budget and Program Analysis	STEPHEN B. DEWHURST
Director, National Appeals Division	FRED YOUNG, *Acting*

[For the Department of Agriculture statement of organization, see the *Code of Federal Regulations*, Title 7, Part 2]

The Department of Agriculture works to improve and maintain farm income and to develop and expand markets abroad for agricultural products. The Department helps to curb and to cure poverty, hunger, and malnutrition. It works to enhance the environment and to maintain our production capacity by helping landowners protect the soil, water, forests, and other natural resources. Rural development, credit, and conservation programs are key resources for carrying out national growth policies. Department research findings directly or indirectly benefit all Americans. The Department, through inspection and grading services, safeguards and ensures standards of quality in the daily food supply.

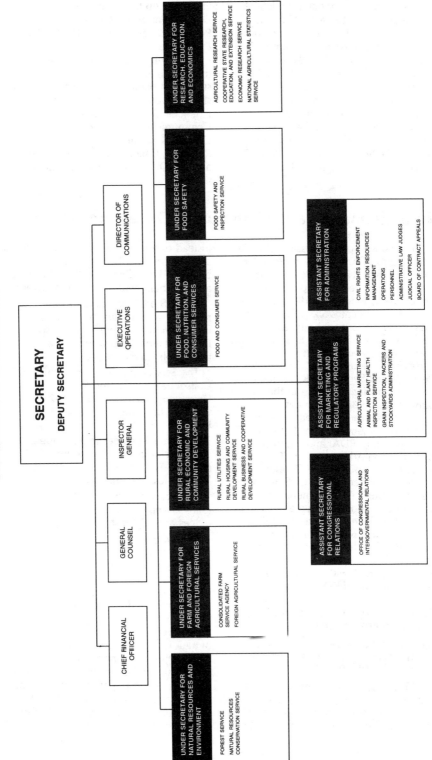

DEPARTMENT OF AGRICULTURE

SECRETARY

DEPUTY SECRETARY

- CHIEF FINANCIAL OFFICER
- GENERAL COUNSEL
- INSPECTOR GENERAL
- EXECUTIVE OPERATIONS
- DIRECTOR OF COMMUNICATIONS

UNDER SECRETARY FOR NATURAL RESOURCES AND ENVIRONMENT
- FOREST SERVICE
- NATURAL RESOURCES CONSERVATION SERVICE

UNDER SECRETARY FOR FARM AND FOREIGN AGRICULTURAL SERVICES
- CONSOLIDATED FARM SERVICE AGENCY
- FOREIGN AGRICULTURAL SERVICE

UNDER SECRETARY FOR RURAL ECONOMIC AND COMMUNITY DEVELOPMENT
- RURAL UTILITIES SERVICE
- RURAL HOUSING AND COMMUNITY DEVELOPMENT SERVICE
- RURAL BUSINESS AND COOPERATIVE DEVELOPMENT SERVICE

UNDER SECRETARY FOR FOOD, NUTRITION, AND CONSUMER SERVICES
- FOOD AND CONSUMER SERVICE

UNDER SECRETARY FOR FOOD SAFETY
- FOOD SAFETY AND INSPECTION SERVICE

UNDER SECRETARY FOR RESEARCH, EDUCATION, AND ECONOMICS
- AGRICULTURAL RESEARCH SERVICE
- COOPERATIVE STATE RESEARCH, EDUCATION, AND EXTENSION SERVICE
- ECONOMIC RESEARCH SERVICE
- NATIONAL AGRICULTURAL STATISTICS SERVICE

ASSISTANT SECRETARY FOR CONGRESSIONAL RELATIONS
- OFFICE OF CONGRESSIONAL AND INTERGOVERNMENTAL RELATIONS

ASSISTANT SECRETARY FOR MARKETING AND REGULATORY PROGRAMS
- AGRICULTURAL MARKETING SERVICE
- ANIMAL AND PLANT HEALTH INSPECTION SERVICE
- GRAIN INSPECTION, PACKERS AND STOCKYARDS ADMINISTRATION

ASSISTANT SECRETARY FOR ADMINISTRATION
- CIVIL RIGHTS ENFORCEMENT
- INFORMATION RESOURCES MANAGEMENT
- OPERATIONS
- PERSONNEL
- ADMINISTRATIVE LAW JUDGES
- JUDICIAL OFFICER
- BOARD OF CONTRACT APPEALS

The Department of Agriculture (USDA) was created by act of May 15, 1862 (7 U.S.C. 2201), and was administered by a Commissioner of Agriculture until 1889 (5 U.S.C. 511, 514, 516). By act of February 9, 1889 (7 U.S.C. 2202, 2208, 2212), the powers and duties of the Department were enlarged. The Department was made the eighth executive department in the Federal Government, and the Commissioner became the Secretary of Agriculture. The Department was reorganized under the Federal Crop Insurance Reform and Department of Agriculture Reorganization Act of 1994 (7 U.S.C. 6901 note).

In carrying out its work in the program mission areas, USDA relies on the support of departmental administration staff, as well as the Office of the Chief Financial Officer, Office of Communications, Office of Congressional and Intergovernmental Relations, Office of Inspector General, and the Office of the General Counsel.

Rural Economic and Community Development

The rural development mission of USDA is to help rural Americans improve the quality of their lives. To do so, it has fostered a new relationship among Government, industry, and communities. Rural development work is focused in three organizations reporting to the Under Secretary for Rural Economic and Community Development:

The Rural Housing and Community Development Service (RHCDS) includes the rural housing programs of the Farmers Home Administration (FmHA), as well as the rural community loan programs of the Rural Development Administration (RDA) and the Rural Electrification Administration (REA).

The Rural Business and Cooperative Development Service (RBCDS) includes the Agricultural Development Service, business development programs of RDA and REA and the Alternate Agriculture Research and Commercialization Center.

The Rural Utilities Service (RUS) combines the telephone and electric programs of REA with the water and sewer programs of RDA.

Rural Housing and Community Development Service

[For the Rural Housing and Community Development Service statement of organization, see the *Code of Federal Regulations*, Title 7, Part 2003]

In 1994, the Rural Housing and Community Development Service redefined the way it does business. It became the lender of first opportunity instead of a lender of last resort. RHCDS also streamlined the way it does business, both directly with its borrowers and internally with its own employees.

RHCDS provides loans to rural residents who are unable to get credit from commercial sources at reasonable rates and terms and who have a reasonable chance for success.

The Service operates under the Consolidated Farm and Rural Development Act (7 U.S.C. 1921) and title V of the Housing Act of 1949 (42 U.S.C. 1471).

RHCDS guarantees loans made by commercial lenders for modest rural housing. The agency also makes direct loans to low-income rural residents.

Rural residents may apply for these loans at approximately 1,750 local offices and 258 district offices.

RHCDS provides financial and management assistance through the following types of loans:

Operating Loans   RHCDS guarantees loans made by commercial lenders and provides some direct loans. Operating loan funds may be used to acquire needed resources, to make improved use of their land and labor resources, and to make adjustments necessary for successful rural enterprises. Funds may be advanced to pay for equipment and home operating needs; refinance chattel debts; provide operating credit to fish farmers; carry out forestry purposes; and develop income-producing, nonfarm enterprises.

For loans made directly by the Administration, the interest rate is set periodically, based on the Federal Government's cost of borrowing. For loans made by other lenders and guaranteed by the Administration, the interest rate is negotiated between the lender and the borrower. Loans may be repaid over 1 to 7 years. RHCDS also provides interest assistance by subsidizing the rate on guaranteed loans up to 4 percent, depending on borrower needs. Other reliable agricultural credit sources are encouraged to support as much of the essential needs of loan applicants as possible with the balance supplied from operating loan funds of the agency. Operating loan borrowers are expected to refinance their operating loans and return to conventional credit when able to do so.

Youth Project Loans   The Service makes loans to individual rural residents who are at least 10 but not more than 20 years old to establish and operate income-producing enterprises of modest size, either on the farm or in other locations. The interest rate is determined by formula, periodically, based on the cost of Government borrowing. Repayment terms depend upon the type of project for which the loan is made. This program is designed to help 4–H Clubs, Future Farmers of America, and other youth group members finance their agricultural or nonagricultural projects.

Emergency Loans   Emergency loans are made to eligible rural residents/ enterprises for losses arising from natural disasters.

Each loan is scheduled for repayment as rapidly as feasible, in annual installments, consistent with the borrower's reasonable ability to pay. The schedule varies according to the purpose of the loan.

The interest rate for emergency loans offsetting actual losses is 4.5 percent. Loans are limited to $500,000 or 80 percent of actual losses, less any insurance protection.

Loans to Indian Tribes   Loans to Indian tribes and tribal corporations are made for the acquisition of lands within the reservation. Loans are made for up to 40 years. The interest rate is set periodically, based on the cost of Government borrowing.

Guaranteed Rural Housing Loan Program   Under the Guaranteed Rural Housing Loan Program, RHCDS guarantees loans made by commercial lenders to moderate-income rural residents. Eligible applicants have sufficient income and acceptable credit, but lack the downpayment to secure a loan without help. RHCDS provides up to 100-percent financing for eligible borrowers and guarantees participating lenders against most losses.

Direct Rural Housing Loans   Section 502 loans are made to low-income families for housing in rural areas. Loans can be made to build, purchase, repair, and refinance homes. The maximum term can be 38 years, and the loan may be for 100 percent of the appraised value. The basic interest rate is determined periodically, based on the cost of money. Borrowers may qualify for annual subsidy on the loan, which can reduce the interest rate to as low as 1 percent. Cosigners on promissory notes may be permitted for applicants who are deficient in repayment ability.

Builders may obtain from the Service "conditional commitments" that are assurances to a builder or seller that if their houses meet agency lending requirements, then the agency may make loans to qualified applicants to buy the houses.

An owner-occupant may obtain a section 504 loan of up to $15,000, or, in the case of senior citizens, a grant of up to $5,000 to remove hazards to the health and safety of the family. These loans, available to very low-income families, are made at 1-percent interest.

Loans are made to private, nonprofit corporations, consumer cooperatives, State or local public agencies, and individuals or organizations operating on a profit or limited profit basis to provide rental or cooperative housing in rural areas for persons of low and moderate income. Maximum term is 50 years. Rental assistance may be available to help defray rent paid by low-income families.

Loans repayable in 2 years are authorized to nonprofit organizations to purchase and develop land for resale as homesites for persons of low-to-moderate income.

Loans and grants are also authorized for housing for farm laborers.

Housing the Homeless RHCDS offers single-family housing inventory property to nonprofit organizations or public bodies for transitional housing for the homeless. Qualifying organizations may lease nonprogram property if they can show a documented need in the community for the type of housing use proposed and the financial ability to meet proposed housing costs.

Community Program Loans Direct and guaranteed loans are authorized to public and quasi-public bodies, nonprofit associations, and certain Indian tribes for essential community facilities, such as fire and rescue and health care. Necessary related equipment may also be purchased.

The interest rate is set quarterly for direct loans and is based on yields of municipal bonds. Guaranteed loans bear an interest rate negotiated by the lender and the borrower. Rural Housing guarantees a lender against losses up to 90 percent of principal and interest.

Community facility loans may be made in towns populated up to 20,000.

Nondiscrimination in employment and occupancy is required.

For further information, contact the Information Staff, Rural Housing and Community Development Service, Department of Agriculture, Washington, DC 20250. Phone, 202–720–4323.

Rural Business and Cooperative Development Service

The Rural Business and Cooperative Development Service (RBCDS) was created to direct financial and technical assistance to areas of special needs in rural America. It will focus on underdeveloped communities, the Northwest Timber Initiative and water in Alaskan villages. Through its community and business loan and grant programs it extends financial assistance for water and waste disposal loans.

RBCDS promotes economic development in rural communities by financing needed facilities, assisting business development and rural cooperatives, and developing effective national strategies for rural economic development.

RBCDS was authorized by title XXIII of the Food, Agriculture, Conservation, and Trade Act of 1990, as amended (7 U.S.C. 2006f et seq.), and was officially established within the Department of Agriculture by Secretary's Memorandum 1020–34 dated December 31, 1991. RBCDS operates its loan and grant programs principally under the Consolidated Farm and Rural Development Act (7 U.S.C. 1921 et seq.).

The Service provides financial assistance through the following types of loans and grants:

Business and Industry Loans The Service is authorized to make or guarantee loans to public, private, or cooperative associations organized for profit or nonprofit; to certain Indian tribes or tribal groups; or to individuals for the purpose of improving, developing, or financing business, industry, and employment and improving the economic and environmental climate in rural communities.

The purpose is to develop business enterprises in rural areas and cities with populations of less than 50,000, with priority to applications for projects in open country and rural communities and towns with populations of 25,000 and smaller.

Private lenders initiate, process, close, service, and supervise guaranteed loans; the Rural Business and Cooperative Development Service guarantees a lender against loss up to 90 percent of principal and interest. Interest rates are determined between borrower and lender.

Intermediary Relending Program Loans Loans are made to nonprofit corporations, public agencies, Indian tribes, or cooperatives to establish revolving loan funds from which the borrower, in turn, makes loans to finance businesses or community development projects. Entities that receive loans from RBCDS are referred to as "intermediaries" and entities that receive loans from intermediaries are referred to as "ultimate recipients." Loans to intermediaries may be up to $2,000,000, to be repaid over a 30-year period at 1-percent interest. Loans to ultimate recipients must not exceed $150,000. The term and interest rate to ultimate recipients are set by the intermediary. Ultimate recipients must not be located in a city with a population of 25,000 or more.

Empowerment Program The Program develops and maintains programs to identify Empowerment Zones, Enterprise Communities, AmeriCorps, and other Presidential initiatives to support rural development through the selection of areas of greatest need. The Program works with other USDA agencies, other Federal agencies, State and local governments, and private organizations and universities in a combined effort to develop and promote comprehensive community and economic development in rural America.

Industrial Development Grants Grants are available to finance and facilitate development of small and emerging private business enterprises in rural areas or cities populated up to 50,000, with priority to applications for projects in open country, rural communities and towns of 25,000 and smaller, and economically distressed communities. Industrial Development Grants include grants made to third-party lenders to establish revolving loan programs.

Eligibility is limited to public bodies and private, nonprofit corporations. Public bodies include incorporated towns and villages, boroughs, townships, counties, States, authorities, districts, and Indian tribal groups in rural areas.

Funds may be used to finance and develop small and emerging private business enterprises. Costs that may be paid from grant funds include the acquisition and development of land and the construction of buildings, plants, equipment, access streets and roads, parking areas, utility and service extensions, refinancing, fees, technical assistance, startup operating costs, and working capital.

Rural Development Strategy Assistance RBCDS provides assistance to rural communities in developing effective, long-term strategies for community and economic development. RBCDS staff works on a national and local basis to develop and implement creative strategies that involve partnerships between RBCDS and other agencies, both public and private, to enhance the economic competitiveness of rural communities. This assures that RBCDS and other public programs work closely in creating sustainable development over the long term.

In addition to its other programs, RBCDS provides administrative services to the State Rural Development Councils (SRDC's). This service is a secretarial support function only.

The SRDC's operate under the authority of 7 U.S.C. 2204b. The goals are to improve rural development program coordination among Federal agencies; to undertake active partnerships with States, localities, and the private sector; and to improve the effectiveness of Federal rural development efforts by adopting a strategic and comprehensive approach to rural development.

SRDC's review rural development needs and available resources and develop a strategic plan to execute their goals. The Executive Director, who serves at the pleasure of SRDC leadership, supports the membership in implementing the SRDC strategic State plan. Typical implementation efforts involve the resolution of intergovernmental and intragovernmental barriers for effective rural programs. Issues identified by the SRDC's which cannot be solved at the State level are advanced to the national level for consideration.

Federal members from 11 executive departments, 5 independent agencies, and 2 White House bodies are represented on the national and State levels. At the State level, SRDC members include representatives from Federal, State, local, and tribal governments, along with the private sector— both profit and nonprofit.

Cooperative Services   Under provisions of Public Law 103–211, Agricultural Cooperative Service programs were united with the RBCDS. The new Cooperative Services Program helps farmers and rural communities to become self-reliant through the use of cooperative organizations. Studies are conducted to support cooperatives that market farm products, purchase production supplies, and perform related business services. These studies concentrate on the financial, organizational, legal, social, and economic aspects of cooperative activity.

Technical assistance and research is provided to improve cooperative performance in organizing new cooperatives, merging existing cooperatives, changing the business structure, and developing strategies for growth. Applied research is conducted to give farmers and rural communities expert assistance pertaining to their cooperatives.

Cooperative Services also collects and publishes statistics regarding the role and scope of cooperative activity in U.S. agriculture. Its monthly magazine, *Farmer Cooperatives*, reports current developments and research for cooperative management and leadership.

Alternative Agricultural Research and Commercialization Center   The Center provides and monitors financial assistance for the development and commercialization of new nonfood and nonfeed products from agricultural/forestry commodities. The Center promotes new and alternative uses for agricultural materials. It also expands market opportunities through development of value-added industrial products and promotes environmentally friendly products.

For further information, contact the Rural Business and Cooperative Development Service, Room 5405–S, Department of Agriculture, Fourteenth Street and Independence Avenue SW., Washington, DC 20250–0320. Phone, 202–690–2394.

Rural Utilities Service

[For the Rural Utilities Service statement of organization, see the *Code of Federal Regulations,* Title 7, Part 1700]

The Rural Utilities Service (RUS) is involved in providing access to the information superhighway in rural America, awarding grants to electric and telephone utilities in 10 states to create local revolving loan funds for rural economic development projects. The funds provide rural water and sewer projects, community facilities, and industrial parks to spur economic development and job opportunities.

RUS is a credit agency of the U.S. Department of Agriculture that assists rural electric and telephone utilities in obtaining financing. The assistance includes direct and Federal Financing Bank (FFB) funded loans and shared security arrangements that permit the borrowers to obtain financing from other lenders without a guarantee.

A total of 1,098 rural electric and 1,029 rural telephone utilities in 47 States, Puerto Rico, the Virgin Islands, Guam, the Republic of the Marshall Islands, the Northern Mariana Islands, and the Federated States of Micronesia have received these loans, loan guarantees, or other assistance to construct, expand, and improve rural electric and telephone systems.

RUS was established by Executive Order 7037 of May 11, 1935, as part of a general program of unemployment relief. It was given statutory authority by the Rural Electrification Act of 1936, as amended (7 U.S.C. 901–950b). Its Administrator is appointed by the President with the advice and consent of the Senate.

Electric Program   The Rural Electrification Act of 1936, as amended (7 U.S.C. 901–950b), authorized RUS, then the Rural Electrification Administration (REA), as a lending agency with responsibility for developing a program to provide and improve electric service to persons in rural areas, as defined by the Bureau of the Census.

The act requires that preference be given to nonprofit and cooperative associations and to public bodies. With RUS' assistance, rural electric utilities have obtained financing to construct electric generating plants and transmission and distribution lines to provide initial and continued reliable electric service.

Telephone Program In 1949, RUS (then REA) was authorized to make loans to provide telephone service in rural areas. Congress directed that the rural telephone program be conducted to "assure the availability of adequate telephone service to the widest practicable number of rural users of such service." About 75 percent of the telephone systems financed by the agency are commercial companies, and about 25 percent are subscriber-owned cooperatives.

Loans Loans are made in accordance with the act and are subject to the provisions of the Federal Credit Reform Act of 1991. By law, RUS direct loans are made or insured at a municipal rate, but not greater than 7 percent. In cases of hardship, the Administrator may approve loans at an interest rate of 5 percent.

RUS also obtains funds from the Federal Financing Bank (FFB), which it lends to borrowers, mostly for large-scale electric and telephone facilities at an interest rate equal to the cost of money paid by FFB, plus one-eighth of 1 percent. FFB is located within the Department of the Treasury.

Supplemental Financing A 1973 statement of congressional policy—not part of the law—said, in part, "...that rural electric and telephone systems should be encouraged and assisted in developing their resources and ability to achieve the financial strength needed to enable them to satisfy their credit needs from their own financial organizations and other sources at reasonable rates and terms consistent with the loan applicant's ability to pay and achievement of the act's objectives."

When RUS approves electric loans, it requires most borrowers to obtain 30 percent of their loan needs from nonagency sources without an agency guarantee. These nonagency sources include the National Rural Utilities Cooperative Finance Corporation, which is owned by electric cooperatives and the National Bank for Cooperatives.

Telephone borrowers obtain supplemental financing from the Rural Telephone Bank (RTB), an agency of the United States that was established in 1971. Loans are made to telephone systems able to meet RTB's requirements. Bank loans are made for the same purposes as loans made by RUS but bear interest at a rate consistent with the Bank's cost of money. Effective in fiscal year 1988, the budget act changed the method of determining Bank interest rates.

The Rural Telephone Bank is managed by a 13-member board of directors. The Administrator serves as Governor of the Bank until conversion to private ownership, control, and operation. This will take place when 51 percent of the Class A stock issued to the United States and outstanding at any time after September 30, 1995, has been fully redeemed and retired. The Bank board holds at least four regularly scheduled meetings a year. Activities of RTB are carried out by RUS employees and the Office of the General Counsel of the U.S. Department of Agriculture.

Emergency Community Water Assistance Grants Grants may be made for 100 percent of project costs to assist rural communities experiencing a significant decline in quantity or quality of drinking water. Grants can be made to rural cities or towns with populations not exceeding the State's nonmetropolitan median household income requirement. The maximum grant is $500,000 when the significant decline in quantity or quality of water occurred within 2 years, or $75,000, to make emergency repairs and replacement of facilities on existing systems.

Technical Assistance and Training Grants Grants are available for nonprofit organizations to provide rural water and waste system officials with technical assistance and training on a wide range of issues relating to the delivery of water and waste service to rural residents. Legislation requires that at least 1 percent and not more than 2 percent of the funds appropriated for water and waste disposal grants be set aside for these grants.

Solid Waste Management Grants
Grants are available for nonprofit organizations and public bodies to provide technical assistance and training to rural areas and towns populated up to 10,000 to reduce or eliminate pollution of water resources and improve planning and management of solid waste facilities.

Rural Water Circuit Rider Technical Assistance Program   Since 1980, the National Rural Water Association (NRWA) has provided, by contract, technical assistance to rural water systems. Circuit riders assist rural water systems with day-to-day operational, financial, and management problems. Currently there are 52 circuit riders that cover the 48 continental United States. The assistance may be requested by rural water systems or by RUS. When circuit riders are not working on specific requests, they call on rural water systems to offer assistance. The Association reports monthly to the national office. The program complements loan "supervision" responsibilities.

Rural Development   Effective in fiscal year 1988, the Omnibus Budget Reconciliation Act established a rural development program to provide interest-free loans and grants to electric and telephone borrowers to promote rural economic development and job creation projects. The program has financed such projects as business incubators, startups and expansions, community development, studies, and a variety of initiatives at the local level.

The Rural Economic Development Act of 1990 established other programs to promote economic and community development, including a Distance Learning and Medical Link Grant Program, and gave borrowers authority to defer RUS loan payments to make investments in rural development. Borrowers previously had been given authority to invest their own funds in rural development projects.

For further information, contact the Legislative and Public Affairs Staff, Rural Utilities Service, Department of Agriculture, Washington, DC 20250. Phone, 202–720–1255.

Marketing and Regulatory Programs

This mission area—formerly composed of the Agricultural Marketing Service (AMS), Animal and Plant Health Inspection Service (APHIS), Federal Grain Inspection Service (FGIS), Food Safety and Inspection Service (FSIS) and Packers and Stockyards Administration (P&SA)— was divided into two mission areas:

Food safety is now managed by the Under Secretary for Food Safety. Included in the 1994 reorganization are the entire operational and support structure of FSIS, plus those units from AMS and APHIS with responsibility for assuring the safety of food products.

The remaining units of AMS and APHIS report to the Assistant Secretary for Marketing and Regulatory Programs. In addition, two areas of responsibility delegated to FGIS and P&SA comprise the Grain Inspection, Packers and Stockyards Administration (GIPSA). This unit reports to the Assistant Secretary for Marketing and Regulatory Programs.

Agricultural Marketing Service

The Agricultural Marketing Service was established by the Secretary of Agriculture on April 2, 1972, under the authority of Reorganization Plan No. 2 of 1953 (5 U.S.C. app.) and other authorities. The Service administers standardization, grading, inspection, certification, market news, marketing orders, and research, promotion, and regulatory programs.

Market News   The Service provides current, unbiased information to producers, processors, distributors, and others to assist them in the orderly marketing and distribution of farm commodities. Information is collected on supplies, demand, prices, movement, location, quality, condition, and other market data on farm products in specific markets and marketing areas. The data is disseminated nationally via a modern satellite system and is shared with several countries. The Service also assists countries in developing their own marketing information systems.

Standardization, Grading, and Classing Grade standards have been established for nearly 240 agricultural commodities to help buyers and sellers trade on agreed-upon quality levels. Standards are developed with the benefit of views from those in the industries directly affected and others interested. The Service also participates in developing international standards to facilitate trade.

Grading and classing services are provided to certify the grade and quality of products. These grading services are provided to buyers and sellers of live cattle, swine, sheep, meat, poultry, eggs, rabbits, fruits, vegetables, tree nuts, peanuts, dairy products, and tobacco. Classing services are provided to buyers and sellers of cotton and cotton products. These services are mainly voluntary and are provided upon request and for a fee. The Service also is responsible for the certification of turpentine and other naval stores products, and the testing of seed.

Laboratory Testing The Service provides scientific and laboratory support to its commodity programs relating to testing of microbiological and chemical factors in food products through grading, certification, acceptance, and regulatory programs; processing and finishing tests for cotton fiber and yarn; testing of peanuts for aflatoxin, and testing of imported flue-cured and burley tobacco for pesticide residues, and testing seeds for germination and purity. The agency also carries out quality assurance and safety oversight activities with respect to the Service's commodity division laboratory and testing activities relating to milk market administrators, resident grading programs, and State and private laboratory programs.

The Service also administers the Pesticide Data Program which, in cooperation with States, samples and analyzes fresh fruits and vegetables for pesticide residues. It shares residue test results with the Environmental Protection Agency and other public agencies.

Food Quality Assurance Under a Governmentwide quality assurance program, AMS is responsible for the development and revision of specifications used by Federal agencies in procuring food for military and civilian uses. The Service coordinates and approves certification programs designed to ensure that purchased products conform to the specification requirements.

Section 32 Programs Under section 32 of the act of August 24, 1935, as amended (7 U.S.C. 612c), 30 percent of customs receipts collected during each calendar year are automatically appropriated for expanding outlets for various commodities. Portions of these funds are transferred to the Food and Nutrition Service of USDA and to the Department of Commerce. Remaining funds are used to purchase commodities for the National School Lunch Program and other feeding programs, for diversion to other outlets, and for administering agreement and order programs.

Regulatory Programs The Service administers several regulatory programs designed collectively to protect producers, handlers, and consumers of agricultural commodities from financial loss or personal injury resulting from careless, deceptive, or fraudulent marketing practices. Such regulatory programs encourage fair trading practices in the marketing of fruits and vegetables, require truth in seed labeling and in advertising.

Under the Egg Products Inspection Act (21 U.S.C. 1031–1056), the Service provides mandatory inspection for wholesomeness in all plants processing liquid, dried, or frozen egg products, and controls the disposition of restricted shell eggs—eggs that are a potential health hazard.

Marketing Agreements and Orders These programs, under authority of the Agricultural Marketing Agreement Act of 1937 (7 U.S.C. 601 *et seq.*), help to establish and maintain orderly marketing conditions for certain commodities. Milk marketing orders establish minimum prices that handlers or distributors are required to pay producers. Programs for fruits, vegetables, and related specialty crops like nuts and spearmint oil help stabilize supplies and market prices. In some cases, they also authorize research and market development activities, including advertising supported by assessments that handlers pay. Through orderly marketing, adjusting the supply to demand, and avoiding unreasonable fluctuations during the marketing season, the income of producers is increased by normal market forces, and consumer interests are protected through quality and quantity control.

Federal marketing orders originate with a request from a producer group to the Secretary of Agriculture. The Secretary can conduct hearings and referenda based on the producer group's proposal for a marketing order. Producer and handler assessments finance their operations.

In carrying out the Government role, the Service ensures that persons interested in the development and operation of the programs have a fair hearing and that each marketing order works according to Federal law and established rules and guidelines.

Plant Variety Protection Program Under authority of the Plant Variety Protection Act (7 U.S.C. 2321 *et seq.*), the Service administers a program that provides for the issuance of "certificates of plant variety protection." These certificates afford developers of novel varieties of sexually reproduced plants exclusive rights to sell, reproduce, import, or export such varieties, or use them in the production of hybrids or different varieties for a period of 18 years.

Research and Promotion Programs The Service monitors certain industry-sponsored research, promotion, and information programs authorized by Federal laws. These programs provide farmers with a means to finance and operate various research, promotion, and information activities for cotton, potatoes, eggs, milk and dairy products,

beef, pork, wool, mohair, honey, watermelon, limes, mushrooms, soybeans, and fresh cut flowers.

Transportation Programs The Service is also responsible for the development of an efficient transportation system for rural America that begins at the farm gate, moves agricultural and other rural products through the Nation's highways, railroads, airports, and waterways, and into the domestic and international marketplace. To accomplish this, AMS conducts economic studies and analyses of these systems, and represents agricultural and rural transportation interests in policy and regulatory forums. To provide direct assistance to the transportation community, AMS supplies research and technical information to producers, producer groups, shippers, exporters, rural communities, carriers, governmental agencies, and universities.

The Service carries out responsibilities of USDA's former Office of Transportation under the Agricultural Adjustment Act of 1938 (7 U.S.C. 1281), the Agricultural Marketing Act of 1946 (7 U.S.C. 1621), the Agricultural Trade Development and Assistance Act of 1954 (7 U.S.C. 1691), the Rural Development Act of 1972 (7 U.S.C. 1921 note), the International Carriage of Perishable Foodstuffs Act (7 U.S.C. 4401), and the Cooperative Marketing Act of 1926 (7 U.S.C. 451–457).

Organic Standards Under the Organic Foods Production Act of 1990 (7 U.S.C. 501–522), the Service assists a National Organic Standards Board in developing national organic standards.

Other Programs Other marketing service activities include financial grants to States for marketing improvement projects. The agency also has responsibility for the conduct of studies of the facilities and methods used in the physical distribution of food and other farm products; for research designed to improve the handling of all agricultural products as they move from farm to consumers; and for increasing marketing efficiency by developing improved operating methods, facilities, and equipment for processing, handling, and distributing dairy, poultry, and meat products.

The Agricultural Marketing Service manages the Pesticide Recordkeeping Program in coordination with the National Agricultural Statistics Service and the Environmental Protection Agency. The Service has developed educational programs and assists State agencies in inspecting applicator records.

Field Organization   Programs and activities in the field are carried out through a variety of different types of organizations reporting to their respective Washington components.

For further information, contact the Information Staff, Agricultural Marketing Service, Department of Agriculture, P.O. Box 96456, Washington, DC 20250. Phone, 202–720–8999.

Animal and Plant Health Inspection Service

[For the Animal and Plant Health Inspection Service statement of organization, see the *Code of Federal Regulations*, Title 7, Part 371]

The Animal and Plant Health Inspection Service was reestablished by the Secretary of Agriculture on March 14, 1977, pursuant to authority contained in 5 U.S.C. 301 and Reorganization Plan No. 2 of 1953 (5 U.S.C. app.).

The Service was established to conduct regulatory and control programs to protect and improve animal and plant health for the benefit of man and the environment. In cooperation with State governments, the agency administers Federal laws and regulations pertaining to animal and plant health and quarantine, humane treatment of animals, and the control and eradication of pests and diseases. Regulations to prevent the introduction or interstate spread of certain animal or plant pests or diseases are also enforced by the Service. It also carries out research and operational activities to reduce crop and livestock depredations caused by birds, rodents, and predators.

Plant Protection and Quarantine Programs   Plant protection officials are responsible for programs to control or eradicate plant pests and diseases. These programs are carried out in cooperation with the States involved, other Federal agencies, farmers, and private organizations. Pest control programs use a single tool or a combination of pest control techniques, both chemical and nonchemical, which are both effective and safe.

Agricultural quarantine inspection officials administer Federal regulations that prohibit or restrict the entry of foreign pests and plants, plant products, animal products and byproducts, and other materials that may harbor pests or diseases. Inspection service is maintained at all major ocean, air, border, and interior ports of entry in the continental United States and in Hawaii, Alaska, Puerto Rico, U.S. Virgin Islands, Bahamas, and Bermuda. Services also are provided on a regular or on-call basis at some 500 outlying ports and military installations throughout the country.

Other responsibilities include the inspection and certification of domestic commodities for export, regulation of the import and export of endangered plant species, and ensuring that imported seed is free of noxious weeds.

Veterinary Services   Animal health officials are responsible for determining the existence and extent of outbreaks of communicable diseases and pests affecting livestock and poultry. They organize and conduct control eradication and certification programs in cooperation with industry and State officials.

Service officials assess risk relating to animal diseases and preharvest food safety. They maintain food inspection and quarantine service at designated ports of entry for imported animals and birds and are responsible for the health certification of livestock and poultry exported to other countries.

Regulatory Enforcement and Animal Care   The Service administers Federal laws concerned with the humane care and handling of all warm-blooded animals bought, sold, and transported— including common carriers—in commerce and used or intended for use as pets at the wholesale level, or used or intended for use in exhibitions or for research purposes. The agency also enforces the Horse Protection Act of 1970 (15 U.S.C. 1821 note), which prohibits the soring of horses at shows and sales.

International Services Service officials represent the APHIS agenda in the international arena. This includes conduct of cooperative plant and animal pest and disease control, eradication, and surveillance programs in foreign countries. These programs provide a first line of defense for the United States against threats such as screwworm, medfly, foot-and-mouth disease, and other exotic diseases and pests. Service officials provide international representation concerning sanitary and phytosanitary technical trade issues, and manage programs for overseas preclearance of commodities, passengers, and U.S. military activities.

Biotechnology, Biologics, and Environmental Protection Service officials are responsible for the regulation of genetically engineered organisms and products that present a plant pest risk. Regulation is carried out through a permit system. The Service also administers a Federal law intended to ensure that all veterinary biological products, whether developed by conventional or new biotechnological procedures, used in the diagnosis, prevention, and treatment of animal disease are safe, pure, potent, and effective. This responsibility is met by regulating firms that manufacture veterinary biological products subject to the act. This includes licensing the manufacturing establishment and its products; inspecting production facilities and production methods; and testing products under a surveillance program.

Animal Damage Control Animal damage control officials cooperate with States, counties, local communities, and agricultural producer groups to reduce crop and livestock depredations caused by birds, rodents, and predators. The officials conduct research into predator-prey relationships, new control methods, and more efficient and safe uses of present methods such as toxicants, repellants and attractants, biological controls, scare devices, and habitat

alteration. Using methods and techniques that are biologically sound, environmentally acceptable, and economically feasible, they participate in efforts to educate and advise farmers and ranchers on proper uses of control methods and techniques; they suppress serious nuisances and threats to public health and safety caused by birds, rodents, and other wildlife in urban and rural communities; and they work with airport managers to reduce risks of bird strikes.

For further information, contact Legislative and Public Affairs, Animal and Plant Health Inspection Service, Department of Agriculture, Washington, DC 20250. Phone, 202–720–2511.

Grain Inspection, Packers and Stockyards Administration

The Grain Inspection, Packers and Stockyards Administration (GIPSA) comprises the former Federal Grain Inspection Service and the former Packers and Stockyards Administration. The primary task of GIPSA is to carry out the provisions of the United States Grain Standards Act (7 U.S.C. 71 et seq.), the Packers and Stockyards Act of 1921, as amended (7 U.S.C. 181–229), the Truth in Lending and Fair Credit Billing Acts (15 U.S.C. 1601 et seq.), and the Equal Credit Opportunity Act (15 U.S.C. 1691 et seq.) with respect to firms subject to GIPSA. GIPSA also administers the provisions of section 1324 of the Food Security Act of 1985 (7 U.S.C. 1631), certifying State central filing systems for notification of liens against farm products and ensures integrity in the inspection, weighing, and handling of U.S. grain. An Administrator, appointed by the President with the advice and consent of the Senate, heads the agency.

GIPSA is responsible for establishing official U.S. standards for grain and other assigned commodities, and for administrating a nationwide official inspection and weighing system. GIPSA may, in response to formal application, authorize private and State agencies to perform official services under the authority contained in the act.

Three of GIPSA's four grain inspection divisions are located in Washington, DC;

the fourth is located in Kansas City, MO. Most employees work in field offices around the Nation.

Inspection   The United States Grain Standards Act requires, with some exceptions, all U.S. export grain be officially inspected. At export port locations, inspection is performed by GIPSA or by State agencies that have been delegated export inspection authority by the Administrator. For domestic grain, marketed at inland locations, the Administrator designates private and State agencies to provide official inspection services upon request. Both export and domestic services are provided on a fee basis.

To ensure that the official U.S. grain standards are applied uniformly nationwide, GIPSA's field offices provide oversight, guidance, and assistance to non-Federal agencies performing inspection activities, both at export and inland inspection points.

Buyers and sellers may request appeal inspections of original inspection results, first from a field office and then, if desired, from GIPSA's Board of Appeals and Review. GIPSA maintains a quality control program to monitor the national inspection system and to ensure that all field locations accurately and uniformly apply the U.S. grain standards.

Weighing   Official weighing of U.S. export grain is performed at port locations by GIPSA or by State agencies that have been delegated export weighing authority by the Administrator. For domestic grain marketed at inland locations, the weighing services may be provided by GIPSA or by designated private or State agencies. Weighing services are provided on a fee basis, upon request.

As with inspection activities, GIPSA field offices provide oversight, guidance, and assistance to non-Federal agencies performing official weighing services. With the support of the Association of American Railroads and user fees, it conducts a railroad track scale-testing program which includes an annual testing service for all State and railroad company-owned master scales. GIPSA is the only entity, public or private, which connects all railroad track scales to the national standards.

Standardization   GIPSA is responsible for establishing, maintaining, and, as needed, revising official U.S. standards. Such standards exist for corn, wheat, rye, oats, barley, flaxseed, sorghum, soybeans, triticale, sunflower seed, canola, and mixed grain. GIPSA is authorized to perform applied research to develop methods of improving accuracy and uniformity in grading grain.

It is also responsible for standardization and inspection activities for rice, dry beans, peas, lentils, hay, straw, hops, and related processed grain commodities under the Agricultural Marketing Act of 1946, as amended (7 U.S.C. 1621). Although standards no longer exist for hay, straw, and hops, GIPSA maintains inspection procedures for and retains authority to inspect these commodities.

Compliance   GIPSA's compliance activities ensure accurate and uniform implementation of the act, applicable provisions of the Agricultural Marketing Act of 1946, and related regulations—including designating States and private agencies to carry out official inspection and weighing functions and monitoring, and overseeing and reviewing the operations of such agencies to ensure adequate performance.

GIPSA administers a registration program for all firms that export grain from the United States. In conjunction with the Office of the Inspector General, it carries out a program for investigating reported violations, and initiates followup and corrective actions when appropriate. The total compliance program ensures the integrity of the national inspection and weighing system.

Packers and Stockyards Activities   The Packers and Stockyards Act is an antitrust, trade practice, and financial protection law. Its principal purpose is to maintain effective competition and fair trade practices in the marketing of livestock, meat, and poultry for the protection of livestock and poultry producers. Members of the livestock, poultry, and meat industries are also protected against unfair or monopolistic practices of competitors. The act also protects consumers against unfair business practices in the marketing of meats and poultry and against restrictions of competition that could unduly affect meat and poultry prices. The provisions of the Packers and Stockyards Act are enforced by investigations of violations of the act with emphasis on payment protection; detecting instances of commercial bribery, fraud in livestock marketing, and false weighing; requiring adequate bond coverage for commission firms, dealers, and packers; and the surveillance of marketing methods at public markets and in geographical market areas of the country.

For further information, contact the Grain Inspection, Packers and Stockyards Administration, Department of Agriculture, Washington, DC 20250. Phone, 202–720–0219.

Food Safety and Inspection Service

The Food Safety and Inspection Service (FSIS) was established by the Secretary of Agriculture on June 17, 1981, pursuant to authority contained in 5 U.S.C. 301 and Reorganization Plan No. 2 of 1953 (5 U.S.C. app.). At that time, the Service was delegated authority for regulating the meat and poultry industry to ensure that meat and poultry, and meat and poultry products moving in interstate and foreign commerce were safe, wholesome, and accurately labeled. Under the Secretary's Memorandum No. 1010–1, dated October 23, 1994, the Service's authority was extended to include the inspection of egg products.

Meat, Poultry, and Egg Products Inspection   Federal meat and poultry inspection is mandatory for the following animals and birds used for human food: cattle, calves, swine, goats, sheep, lambs, horses (and other equines), chickens, turkeys, ducks, geese, and guineas. The work includes inspection of each animal or bird at slaughter, and inspection of processed products during various stages of production. Under the Egg Products Inspection Act (21 U.S.C. 1031–1056), the Service conducts

mandatory, continuous inspection of the production of liquid, dried, and frozen egg products, to ensure that egg products are safe, wholesome, unadulterated, and accurately labeled. The Service tests samples of egg products, and meat and poultry products for microbial and chemical contaminants to monitor trends for enforcement purposes.

Facilities and equipment are approved by FSIS before inspection is granted, and each product label must be approved by the agency before products can be sold. The agency monitors meat and poultry products in storage, distribution, and retail channels; and takes necessary compliance actions to perfect the public, including detention of products, voluntary product recalls, court-sized seizures of products, administrative withdrawal of inspection, and referral for criminal prosecution. The Service also conducts State programs for the inspection of meat and poultry products sold in intrastate commerce.

The Service monitors livestock upon arrival at federally inspected facilities to ensure compliance with the Humane Slaughter Act (7 U.S.C. 1901–1906); conducts voluntary reimbursed inspection for rabbits, other domestic food animals, and certain egg products not covered by the inspection law (7 U.S.C. 1621–1627); and ensures that inedible egg products and inedible products from meat or poultry, such as offal rendered for animal feed, are properly identified and isolated from edible products (21 U.S.C. 1031–1056 and 7 U.S.C. 1624, respectively).

The Service conducts a toll-free Meat and Poultry Hotline (800–535–4555; in the Washington metropolitan area, 202–720–3333) to answer questions about labeling and safe handling of meat and poultry, meat and poultry products, and egg products. The hotline is also accessible (on the same extension) by TDD.

For further information, contact the Director of Information and Legislative Affairs, Food Safety and Inspection Service, Department of Agriculture, Washington, DC 20250. Phone, 202–720–7943.

Food, Nutrition, and Consumer Services

This mission area of USDA ensures access to nutritious, healthful diets for all Americans. It coordinates USDA's consumer education and outreach activities, encourage consumer involvement in USDA policymaking, and ensures that USDA adequately addresses consumer concerns and interests.

It concentrates on the Electronic Benefits Transfer (EBT), eliminating the use of paper coupons while providing the recipient with a plastic card and personal identification number that functions like money. At the grocery check-out counter, no money and no Food Stamps change hands. All accounting is done electronically.

Under the USDA reorganization legislation, a center for nutrition policy and education was created underscoring the Department's commitment to nutrition and nutrition education.

Food and Consumer Service

[For the Food and Consumer Service statement of organization, see the *Federal Register* of June 6, 1970, 35 FR 8835]

The Food and Consumer Service is the agency of the Department that administers the programs to make food assistance available to people who need it. These programs are operated in cooperation with States and local governments.

The Service, formerly the Food and Nutrition Service, was established on August 8, 1969, by the Secretary of Agriculture, under authority of 5 U.S.C. 301 and Reorganization Plan No. 2 of 1953 (5 U.S.C. app.).

Food Stamps   The Food Stamp Program provides food coupons through State and local welfare agencies to needy persons to increase their food purchasing power. The coupons are used by program participants to buy food in any retail store that has been approved by the Food and Consumer Service to accept and redeem the food coupons.

Special Nutrition Programs   The Service administers several programs designed to improve the nutrition of children, particularly those from low-income families. Principal among these is the National School Lunch Program, which provides financial assistance to public and nonprofit private schools of high school grade and under, in operating nonprofit school lunch programs.

The School Breakfast Program provides cash assistance to State educational agencies to help schools in operating nonprofit breakfast programs meeting established nutritional standards. It is especially important in improving the diets of needy children who may receive breakfast free or at reduced prices.

The Summer Food Service Program for Children helps various organizations get nutritious meals to needy preschool and school-aged children during the summer months or during vacations in areas operating under a continuous school calendar.

The Child and Adult Care Food Program is a companion activity that helps to get nutritious meals to preschool and school-age children in child care facilities and to functionally impaired adults in facilities that provide nonresidential care for such individuals.

The Special Milk Program for Children, which is administered in schools, institutions, and split-session kindergartens that do not participate in any other Federal food program, is designed to help child nutrition by paying a share of the cost of increased servings of fluid milk made to children.

Food Distribution   The Food Distribution Program makes foods available to eligible recipients. Foods purchased by the Department are made available principally to children in school lunch and breakfast programs, in summer camps and child care centers, and to the nutrition program for the elderly. Also, commodities are distributed to needy families through food banks, charitable institutions, and local government agencies.

The program on Indian reservations provides Indians on or near reservations with access to a wide range of donated foods, including meat, fruit, vegetables, and dairy and grain products.

Supplemental Food Programs The Special Supplemental Food Program for Women, Infants and Children—the WIC Program—provides specified nutritious food supplements, nutrition education, and health care referrals to pregnant women, breastfeeding women up to 12 months post partum, non-breastfeeding women up to 6 months post partum, and children up to 5 years of age. Participants are determined by competent professionals (physicians, nutritionists, nurses, and other health officials) to be at nutritional risk because of nutritionally related medical conditions or inadequate nutrition.

Cash grants are made available to participating State health departments or comparable State agencies, or recognized Indian tribes, bands, or groups. The State agencies distribute funds to the local agencies, and the funds are used to provide foods for WIC recipients and to pay specified administrative and clinical costs.

Commodity Supplemental Food Program This program provides supplemental foods and nutrition education to low-income infants and children; pregnant, post partum, and breastfeeding women; and elderly persons who are vulnerable to malnutrition and reside in approved project areas. The Department purchases foods for distribution through State agencies.

Nutrition Education and Training Under this program funds are granted to the States for the development and dissemination of nutrition information and materials to children and for in-service training of food service and teaching personnel.

No person may be discriminated against—in the operation of any of the programs administered by the Food and Nutrition Service—because of race, color, sex, creed, national origin, or handicap.

For further information, contact the Public Information Officer, Food and Consumer Service, Department of Agriculture, Alexandria, VA 22302. Phone, 703–305–2276.

Farm and Foreign Agricultural Services

Through the Consolidated Farm Service Agency (CFSA), this mission area administers farm commodity, crop insurance, and resource conservation programs for farmers, and makes loans through a network of State and county offices. CFSA programs are directed at agricultural producers or, in the case of loans, at those with farming experience.

On October 13, 1994, the Federal Crop Insurance Reform and Department of Agriculture Reorganization Act of 1994 was enacted to streamline USDA and deliver programs and services to the public more efficiently. The new CFSA unifies most of the Agricultural Stabilization and Conservation Service, most of the Federal Crop Insurance Corporation, the farm loan section of the Farmers Home Administration, and the administrative service section of the Foreign Agricultural Service.

Consolidated Farm Service Agency
CFSA administers commodity and related land use programs designed for voluntary production adjustment, resource protection, and price, market, and farm income stabilization.

In each State, operations are supervised by a State committee of three or five members appointed by the Secretary. A State Executive Director, appointed by the Secretary, and staff carry on day-to-day operations of the State office. The State Director of the Agricultural Extension Service is an *ex officio* member of the State committee.

In each of approximately 3,000 agricultural counties, a county committee of three farmer members is responsible for local administration. A county executive director, with other necessary staff, is employed to carry on day-to-day operations of the county office.

Commodity Programs CFSA administers the Commodity Credit Corporation's commodity stabilization programs for wheat, corn, cotton (upland and extra long staple), seed cotton, soybeans and minor oilseeds, peanuts, rice, tobacco, milk, wool, mohair, barley, oats, sugarbeets, sugarcane, grain sorghum, rye, and honey. Commodity stabilization is achieved through commodity loans, purchases, and payments to eligible producers.

For most commodities, loans and payments are made directly to producers on the unprocessed commodity through CFSA's county offices. Some commodities are also purchased from producers. Price support loans, payments, and purchases also can be made available through cooperative marketing associations. The price of milk is stabilized through purchases of processed dairy products: butter, American-type cheese, and nonfat dry milk. Price stabilization programs for tobacco and peanuts are carried out through loans to producer associations that, in turn, make program benefits available to producers. Tobacco producers must contribute to a fund to assure that the tobacco program operates at no net cost to taxpayers, other than administrative costs. For burley and flue-cured tobaccos, purchasers contribute equally with producers. These contributions are in addition to budget deficit assessments also being paid by producers and purchasers. Stabilization of sugarbeet and sugarcane prices is carried out through loans to sugar processors, who in turn make program benefits available to producers.

Loans to producers can either be "recourse" —allowing producers to repay their loans at principal plus interest—or "nonrecourse". Nonrecourse loans enable the producer to forfeit or deliver the commodity to the Commodity Credit Corporation with settlement based on the quantity and quality of goods delivered if the market price falls below the loan rate.

Loan deficiency payments are available to producers who agree to forgo a nonrecourse loan. The loan rate, as determined by the Commodity Credit Corporation, is higher than the market rate.

Eligibility for commodity loans, purchases, and payments is, in most cases, conditional upon participation in acreage reduction, paid-land diversion, payment-in-kind, allotment, or quota programs in effect for the particular crop.

Under the Food, Agriculture, Conservation, and Trade Act of 1990, payments are limited to an annual ceiling of $125,000 per person on the total payments of upland cotton, extra long staple cotton, wheat, rice, and feed grain programs for the 1991 through 1995 crops.

The act greatly expanded flexibility for participating farmers to shift program crop plantings, as well as options for oilseeds and industrial and experimental crops.

Emergency Assistance Such programs offered to farmers in emergency-designated areas may include any or all of the following:

—furnishing cost-sharing assistance for feed purchases, purchasing fuel to burn spines off prickly pear cactus, or making available Corporation-owned feed grains at reduced prices to eligible producers who have suffered a substancial loss of their normal livestock feed production due to a natural disaster, and in some instances, donations of feed grains;

—cost-sharing with farmers who carry out emergency conservation practices to rehabilitate farmland damaged by natural disaster; and

—allowing haying and grazing on acreage diverted to conserving uses under the commodity programs or long-term land retirement program on a county-by-county basis, as needed, in the event of a natural disaster.

Grain Reserve Program The Food, Agriculture, Conservation, and Trade Act of 1990 reauthorized the Grain Reserve Program for farmer-owned wheat, corn, grain sorghum, oats, and barley. When entry into the Reserve is authorized by the Secretary of Agriculture, producers may enter into a contract extending their 9-month loan for an additional 27 months and receive quarterly storage payments.

Loans may be repaid at any time. Interest may be charged when prices exceed 105 percent of the target; however, storage payments cease when prices exceed 95 percent of the target price.

Dairy Refund Payment Program   The Dairy Refund Payment Program provides producers refunds of the reductions in the price received for milk during a calendar year. Reductions in price are required by law for all milk produced in the United States and marketed commercially in calendar years 1991 to 1995.

Indemnity Program   The Dairy Indemnity Payment Program provides indemnity payments to dairy farmers whose milk has been removed from the commercial market because it contained residues of chemicals or toxic substances, including nuclear radiation or fallout.

National Security   CFSA is responsible for national security emergency preparedness plans and programs relating to food production, conservation, and stabilization; food processing, storage, and wholesale distribution; livestock and poultry feed, seed, and the domestic distribution of fertilizer; and farm equipment and repair parts.

CFSA also provides services relating to expansion of productive capacity, materials, and facilities under the Defense Production Act of 1950, as amended (50 U.S.C. 2061); plans for management, control, and allocation of water to be used for agricultural production and food processing; consolidates all claims for material, labor, equipment, supplies, and services needed to support the national security emergency responsibilities of USDA; and guarantees payments or makes loans, as needed, for the continuation of food and agriculture activities in a national security emergency.

Financial management and budget support, and financial risk assessments and analyses are provided by CFSA for the General Sales Manager of the Foreign Agricultural Service in administering Commodity Credit Corporation export credit sales and guarantee programs and Food for Peace programs.

To carry out the Agricultural Foreign Investment Disclosure Act of 1978 (7 U.S.C. 3501), the Department assigned CFSA the primary responsibility of collecting information through a reporting system involving all States and most counties. The agency assesses penalties on late filed information and refusals to file. The Administrator rules on appeals resulting from penalties assessed for violations of the act.

Conservation Programs   CFSA conservation programs help preserve and improve the wealth and promise of America's farmlands.

The Conservation Reserve Program (CRP) targets the most fragile farmland by encouraging farmers to stop growing crops on cropland designated by soil conservationists and plant a permanent vegetative cover instead. In return, the farmer receives an annual rental payment.

The Agricultural Conservation Program (ACP) is a joint effort by agricultural producers, Federal and State agencies, and other groups to restorw and protect the Nation's land and water resources and preserve the environment. Cost-sharing is provided to ranchers/farmers to encourage them to carry out conservation and environmental protection practices on agricultural land that result in long-term public benefits.

Producers who plant agricultural commodities on highly erodible land without an approved conservation plan or system, or wetland converted after December 23, 1985, will be considered ineligible for USDA program benefits. In addition, producers who convert wetland after December 28, 1990, will be ineligible for USDA benefits until the wetland is restored. Other provisions of the 1990 law are designed to discourage farming practices that may have adverse environmental impacts.

For further information, contact the Public Affairs Staff, Consolidated Farm Service Agency, Department of Agriculture, P.O. Box 2415, Washington, DC 20013. Phone, 202–720–5237.

Commodity Credit Corporation

The Commodity Credit Corporation was organized October 17, 1933, pursuant to Executive Order 6340 of October 16, 1933, under the laws of the State of Delaware, as an agency of the United States. From October 17, 1933, to July 1, 1939, the Corporation was managed and operated in close affiliation with the Reconstruction Finance Corporation. On July 1, 1939, the agency was transferred to the Department of Agriculture by the President's Reorganization Plan No. I of 1939 (5 U.S.C. app.). Approval of the Commodity Credit Corporation Charter Act on June 29, 1948 (15 U.S.C. 714), subsequently amended, established the Corporation, effective July 1, 1948, as an agency and instrumentality of the United States under a permanent Federal charter.

The Corporation stabilizes, supports, and protects farm income and prices, assists in maintaining balanced and adequate supplies of agricultural commodities and their products, and facilitates the orderly distribution of commodities.

The Corporation is managed by a Board of Directors, subject to the general supervision and direction of the Secretary of Agriculture, who is an *ex officio* Director and Chairman of the Board. The Board consists of seven members (in addition to the Secretary of Agriculture), who are appointed by the President of the United States.

The Corporation is capitalized at $100 million and has statutory authority to borrow up to $30 billion from the U.S. Treasury. It utilizes the personnel and facilities of the Consolidated Farm Service Agency and, in certain foreign assistance operations, the Foreign Agricultural Service to carry out its activities.

A commodity office in Kansas City, MO, has specific responsibilities for the acquisition, handling, storage, and disposal of commodities and products held by the Corporation.

Commodity Stabilization Loan, purchase, and/or payment programs of the Corporation are administered by CFSA for wheat, corn, upland and extra-long staple cotton, peanuts, rice, tobacco, milk, honey, barley, oats, grain sorghum, rye, soybeans and minor oilseeds, sugarbeets, and sugarcane.

Commodities acquired under the stabilization program are disposed of through domestic and export sales, commodity certificate exchanges, transfers to other Government agencies, and donations for domestic and foreign welfare use. The Corporation also is authorized to exchange surplus agricultural commodities it has acquired by the Corporation for strategic and other materials and services produced abroad.

Foreign Assistance Under Public Law 480, the Agricultural Trade Development and Assistance Act of 1954, as amended (7 U.S.C. 1691), the Corporation carries out assigned foreign assistance activities, such as guaranteeing the credit sale of U.S. agricultural commodities abroad. Major emphasis is also being directed toward meeting the needs of developing nations under the Food for Peace Act of 1966 (7 U.S.C. 1691), which further amends the Agricultural Trade Development and Assistance Act of 1954. Under these authorities, agricultural commodities are supplied and exported to combat hunger and malnutrition and to encourage economic development in the developing countries. In addition, the Corporation supplies commodities under the Food for Progress Program to provide assistance to developing democracies.

The Corporation encourages U.S. financial institutions to provide financing to developing countries under the Export Credit Guarantee Programs administered by the Foreign Agricultural Service.

For further information, contact the Public Affairs Staff, Commodity Credit Corporation, Department of Agriculture, P.O. Box 2415, Washington, DC 20013. Phone, 202–720–5237. For information about Commodity Credit Corporation export programs, contact the Information Division, Foreign Agricultural Service, Department of Agriculture. Phone, 202–720–3448.

Federal Crop Insurance Corporation

The Federal Crop Insurance Corporation (FCIC) is a Government-owned corporation within the Consolidated

Farm Service Agency (CFSA). The purpose of FCIC is to promote the national welfare by improving the economic stability of agriculture through a sound system of crop insurance.

The manager of FCIC is also the Deputy Administrator for Risk Management, Consolidated Farm Service Agency. The manager is responsible for directing a widely used and actuarially sound crop insurance program; providing an alternate form of coverage for crops that are currently not insurable and evaluating new insurance products. The manager also serves as a member of the FCIC Board of Directors and acts as facilitator for board activities.

Federal crop insurance protects against unavoidable production losses due to adverse weather and other named perils. The protection does not extend to crop losses resulting from neglect, poor farming prices, or theft, and does not insure against financial losses resulting from low prices.

FCIC was established on February 16, 1938 (7 U.S.C. 1501). On October 13, 1994, the Federal Crop Insurance Reform Act of 1994 (7 U.S.C. 1501 note) significantly changed the way in which government assists producers suffering a major crop loss. A major objective of the reform was to replace the uncertainty of previous ad hoc disaster assistance with the predictability of crop insurance protection.

Under the new insurance program, producers must purchase at least the catastrophic level (CAT) of crop insurance of economic significance to participate in USDA price support and production adjustment programs, certain USDA farm loans and the Conservation Reserve Program. CAT coverage provides pre-acre return similar to the coverage under most previous ad hoc disaster programs. The coverage is fully subsidized by the Federal Government apart from a nominal processing fee paid by the producer. In order to give producers more service options, catastrophic insurance coverage may be obtained from either commercial insurance agents or local USDA offices.

Producers may purchase additional insurance coverage providing greater protection. This additional coverage is only available through commercial insurance companies and agents. To participate at higher levels of coverage, FCIC has provided additional money and policy incentives.

For crops that are not yet insurable, a provision of the Crop Insurance Act establishes a Noninsured Crop Disaster Assistance Program (NAP). In the event of a catastrophic crop loss, NAP provides benefits that are similar to those provided by catastrophic crop insurance. Payments are triggered when area losses for the crop exceed 35 percent, and individual crop losses exceed 50 percent of the expected yield. Producers do not have to participate in the NAP program in order to be eligible for other USDA farm programs or loans. The NAP program is administered through local USDA offices.

FCIC's mission is carried out by employees of the Consolidated Farm Service Agency and commercial insurance companies and their agents.

Farm Loans

The Consolidated Farm Service Agency has direct and guaranteed loan programs to help farmers who are temporarily unable to obtain private, commercial credit. In many cases, these are beginning farmers who have insufficient net worth to qualify for commercial credit. In other cases, these are farmers who have suffered financial setbacks from natural disasters, or who have limited resources with which to establish and maintain profitable farming operations.

Farmers who qualify obtain their credit needs through the use of loan guarantees, where a local agricultural lender makes and services the loan, and CFSA guarantees the loan up to a maximum of 90 percent. CFSA also has the responsibility of approving all loan guarantees and providing monitoring and oeversight of lenders' activities.

For those unable to qualify for a loan guarantee from a commercial lender, CFSA also makes direct loans. These loans are made and serviced by a CFSA official, who provides credit counseling and supervision to its direct borrowers by assessing and evaluating all aspects of the farming operation.

Unlike the commodity loans, CFSA administers several types of loans which can only be approved for those who have repayment ability, and the loans must be fully secured and are not "nonrecourse." These include farm ownership loans, farm ownership downpayment loans, farm operating loans, emergency loss loans, and rural youth loans.

CFSA's mission is to provide supervised credit. This means that CFSA should be identifying each individual borrower's specific strengths and weaknesses in farm production and management, then providing information on alternatives and other options to address the weaknesses and achieve maximum productivity. Supervised credit makes the difference between success and failure for many farm credit customers.

To help them retain ownership of their farms, CFSA provides certain loan servicing benefits to borrowers whose accounts are delinquent due to circumstances beyond their control, such as:

—reamortization, restructuring, and/or deferral of loans;

—rescheduling at the limited resource (lower interest) rate;

—acceptance of conservation easements on environmentally sensitive land in exchange for writedown of debt; and

—writing down the debt to its net recovery value.

If none of these options results in a feasible farming operation, customers are offered the opportunity to purchase their debt at its net recovery value. If this is not possible, other options include the following:

—conveyance of the property to CFSA and then leasing it back with an option to purchase;

—debt settlement based on ability to pay; (The collateral securing the loan may be retained if its market value is paid.) and

—in extreme cases, where a successful operation cannot be developed, CFSA helps the borrower to retain the homestead and up to 10 acres of land.

If not leased or purchased by their former owners, farms that come into CFSA ownership are sold at market value, with a preference to beginning and minority farmers. Beginning farmers must have been in the business less than 10 years and meet certain other requirements concerning land ownership and management ability.

The eventual goal of CFSA's farm credit programs is to graduate its customers to commercial credit. Once a farmer is able to obtain credit from the commercial lending sector, the Agency's mission of providing temporary, supervised credit is successfully completed.

For further information, contact the Manager, Federal Crop Insurance Corporation, Department of Agriculture, Washington, DC 20250. Phone, 202–254–8460.

Foreign Agricultural Service

The Foreign Agricultural Service (FAS) has primary responsibility for USDA's overseas market information, access, and development programs. It also administers USDA's export assistance and foreign food assistance programs. The Service carries out its tasks through its network of agricultural counselors, attachés, and trade officers stationed overseas and its U.S.-based team of analysts, marketing specialists, negotiators, and other professionals.

The Foreign Agricultural Service maintains a worldwide agricultural intelligence and reporting system through its attache service. This service consists of a team of professional agriculturalists posted in more than 75 countries around the world. They represent the Department of Agriculture and provide information and data on foreign government agricultural policies, analyses of supply and demand conditions, commercial trade relationships, and market opportunities.

They report on more than 100 farm commodities, weather, economic factors, and related subjects that affect agriculture and agricultural trade.

At FAS in Washington, DC, agricultural economists and marketing specialists analyze these and other reports. These analyses are supplemented by accumulated background information and by the Crop Condition Assessment system, which analyzes Landsat satellite, weather, and other data.

To improve access for U.S. farm products abroad, FAS' international trade policy specialists coordinate and direct USDA's responsibilities in international trade agreement programs and negotiations. They maintain an ongoing effort to reduce foreign trade barriers and practices that discourage the export of U.S. farm products.

To follow foreign governmental actions that affect the market for U.S. agricultural commodities, FAS relies on its agricultural counselors and attachés. In Washington, a staff of international trade specialists analyzes the trade policies and practices of foreign governments to ensure conduct in conformance with international treaty obligations. During international negotiations, FAS provides staff and support for U.S. agricultural representation.

The Service has a continuing market development program to create, service, and expand commercial export markets for U.S. agricultural products. It carries out programs with nonprofit commodity groups called Cooperators, trade associations, and State agriculture departments and their regional associations. It manages market opportunity referral services and organizes trade fairs and sales teams.

The Service's Office of the General Sales Manager also oversees agricultural functions under the Public Law 480 Food for Peace Program, title I (7 U.S.C. 1701); section 416(b) of the Agricultural Act of 1949 (7 U.S.C. 1431); the Commodity Credit Corporation's (CCC) Export Credit Guarantee Programs; several other export assistance programs; and direct sales of Corporation-owned surplus commodities.

The Commodity Credit Corporation Export Credit Guarantee (GSM-102) and the Intermediate Export Credit Guarantee (GSM-103) Programs encourage the development or expansion of overseas markets for U.S. agricultural commodities by providing guarantees on private financing of U.S. exports to foreign buyers purchasing on credit terms.

The foreign buyer contracts for the purchase of U.S. commodities on a deferred-payment basis of 3 years or less under GSM–102, or between 3 and 10 years under GSM–103. The foreign buyer's bank issues a letter of credit to guarantee payment to the U.S. exporter or an assignee U.S. lending institution. To receive the payment guarantee, the exporter registers the sale with CCC prior to export and pays a guarantee fee. The payment guarantee is implemented only if the foreign bank fails to pay the exporter or the assignee U.S. lending institution.

The Corporation considers coverage on sales of any U.S. agricultural commodity that has the potential of expanding U.S. export markets. A U.S. exporter, private foreign buyer, or foreign government may submit requests that may result in authorized guarantee coverage.

Several export assistance programs are designed to counter or offset the adverse effects from competitors' unfair trade practices on U.S. agriculture. These programs include the Export Enhancement Program (EEP) and the Dairy Export Incentive Program (DEIP).

Under EEP, USDA provides Corporation-owned commodities or cash as export bonuses to make U.S. commodities more competitive in the world marketplace. The DEIP and EEP programs are similar, but DEIP is restricted to dairy products.

The Foreign Agricultural Service is also responsible for sales of Corporation-owned surplus commodities to private trade, foreign government, and nonprofit organizations. Direct sales may be negotiated on a case-by-case basis and on a cash or credit basis. The only criteria for financing direct sales are a 3-year maximum credit plan and the arrangement of suitable payment terms.

Another program authorized by the Food, Agriculture, Conservation, and Trade Act of 1990 is the Market Promotion Program, formerly known as Targeted Export Assistance (TEA). The Market Promotion Program provides assistance in the form of cash or commodities to trade promotion organizations to help fund their market development activities overseas, particularly in those markets where the United States encounters unfair trade practices by foreign competitors or importers.

The Service helps other USDA agencies, U.S. universities, and others enhance America's agricultural competitiveness globally; and increases income and food availability in developing nations by mobilizing expertise for agriculturally led economic growth.

The Service's programs enhance U.S. agriculture's competitiveness by providing U.S. agriculturalists and scientists with linkages to world resources. These linkages often produce new germplasm and technologies that can be vital to improving our current agricultural base and producing new and alternative products. They also foster relationships and understandings that result in trade opportunities and strengthened strategic and political ties.

The Service is a link between the technical expertise of the U.S. agricultural community and Third World nations. By sharing agricultural knowledge with less-developed nations, the United States provides tools to help build stable economies and a more prosperous world. In the process, less-developed nations overcome the barriers of hunger and poverty and gain the economic means to buy needed goods and services in the world marketplace.

Also, it manages programs to exchange visits, germplasm, and technologies between U.S. and international scientists; supports collaborative research projects of mutual interest to the United States and other nations; taps the U.S. agricultural community to provide technical assistance and professional development and training programs to assist economic development in lower income nations; serves as U.S. liaison with international organizations; and organizes overseas trade and investment missions.

These activities serve the needs of other USDA agencies, the Agency for International Development, other public and private institutions, foreign nations, development banks, and the U.S. university and agricultural communities.

For further information, contact the Information Division, Foreign Agricultural Service, Deparment of Agriculture, Washington, DC 20250–1000. Phone, 202–720–7115.

Research, Education, and Economics

This mission area's main focus is to create, apply, and transfer knowledge and technology to provide affordable food and fiber, ensure foods safety and nutrition, and support rural development and natural resource needs of people by conducting integrated national and international research, information, education, and statistical programs and services that are in the national interest.

Agricultural Research Service

The Agricultural Research Service (ARS) provides access to agricultural information and develops new knowledge and technology needed to solve technical agricultural problems of broad scope and high national priority. The goal is to ensure adequate availability of high quality, safe food, and other agricultural products—to meet the nutritional needs of the American consumer, sustain a viable and competitive food and agricultural economy, enhance the quality of life and economic opportunity for rural citizens and society as a whole, and maintain a quality environment and natural resource base.

All administrative and management responsibilities of the four Research, Education, and Economic agencies— Agricultural Research Service (ARS), Cooperative State Research, Education, and Extension Service (CSREES), Economic Research Service (ERS), and National Agricultural Statistics Service (NASS)—are administered by the ARS Administrative and Financial

Management Unit headquartered in Washington, DC.

Research activities are carried out at 114 domestic locations (including Puerto Rico) and 2 overseas locations. Much of this research is conducted in cooperation with partners in State universities and experiment stations, other Federal agencies, and private organizations. A national program staff, headquartered in Beltsville, MD, is the focal point in the overall planning and coordination of ARS' research programs. Day-to-day management of the respective programs for specific field locations is assigned to eight area offices.

Area Offices—Agricultural Research Service

Office	Address
BELTSVILLE AREA—Beltsville Agricultural Research Center, National Arboretum, Washington, DC	Bldg. 003, Beltsville Agricultural Research Ctr. W., Beltsville, MD 20705
MIDSOUTH AREA—Alabama, Kentucky, Louisiana, Mississippi, Tennessee	P.O. Box 225, Stoneville, MS 38776
MIDWEST AREA—Illinois, Indiana, Iowa, Michigan, Minnesota, Missouri, Ohio, Wisconsin	1815 N. University St., Peoria, IL 61804
NORTHERN PLAINS AREA—Colorado, Kansas, Montana, Nebraska, North Dakota, South Dakota, Utah, Wyoming	Suite 150, 1201 Oakridge Rd., Fort Collins, CO 80525–5562
NORTH ATLANTIC AREA—Connecticut, Delaware, Maine, Maryland, Massachusetts, New Hampshire, New Jersey, New York, Pennsylvania, Rhode Island, Vermont, West Virginia	600 E. Mermaid Ln., Philadelphia, PA 19118
PACIFIC WEST AREA—Alaska, Arizona, California, Hawaii, Idaho, Nevada, Oregon, Washington	800 Buchanan St., Albany, CA 94710
SOUTH ATLANTIC AREA—Florida, Georgia, North Carolina, Puerto Rico, South Carolina, Virgin Islands, Virginia	P.O. Box 5677, Athens, GA 30613
SOUTHERN PLAINS AREA—Arkansas, New Mexico, Oklahoma, Texas	Suite 230, 7607 Eastmark Dr., College Station, TX 77840

The National Agricultural Library (NAL), administered by ARS, provides information services over a broad range of agricultural interests to a wide cross-section of users, from research scientists to the general public. The Library assists its users through a variety of specialized information centers. Its staff utilizes advanced information technologies to generate new information products, creating an electronic library as it improves access to the knowledge stored in its multimedia collection of more than 2 million items.

Information is made available through loans, photocopies, reference services,

and literature searches. A subject profiling system for selective searches of agricultural data bases is available for USDA scientists. Citations to the agricultural literature are stored in the AGRICultural OnLine Access (AGRICOLA) data base, available through online computer systems and on compact disc. The Library also distributes in the United States the AGRIS data base of citations to the agricultural literature prepared by centers in various parts of the world and coordinated by the Food and Agriculture Organization of the United Nations.

For further information, contact the Information Staff, Agricultural Research Service, Department of Agriculture, 6303 Ivy Lane, Room 450, Greenbelt, MD 20770. Phone, 301–344–2340.

Cooperative State Research, Education, and Extension Service

The Cooperative State Research, Education, and Extension Service (CSREES) expands the research and higher education functions of the former Cooperative State Research Service and the education and outreach functions of the former Extension Service. The result is better customer service and an enhanced ability to respond to national priorities.

CSREES links the research and education resources and activities of the U.S. Department of Agriculture and works with the following institutions: land-grant institutions in each State, territory, and the District of Columbia; more than 130 colleges of agriculture; 59 agricultural experiment stations; 57 cooperative extension services; 63 schools of forestry; sixteen 1890 historically Black land-grant institutions and Tuskegee University; 27 colleges of veterinary medicine; 42 schools and colleges of family and consumer services; twenty-nine 1994 Native American land-grant institutions; and 127 Hispanic-serving institutions, including 81 members and 45 associate members of the Hispanic Association of Colleges and Universities.

In cooperation with its partners and customers, CSREES provides the focus to advance a global system of research, extension, and higher education in the food and agricultural sciences and related environmental and human sciences to benefit people, communities, and the Nation.

The CSREES mission emphasizes partnerships with the public and private sectors to maximize the effectiveness of limited resources. CSREES programs increase and provide access to scientific knowledge; strengthen the capabilities of land-grant and other institutions in research, extension, and higher education; increase access to and use of improved communication and network systems; and promote informed decisionmaking by producers, families, and social conditions in the United States and globally. These conditions include improved agricultural and other economic enterprises; safer, cleaner water, food, and air; enhanced stewardship and management of natural resources; healthier, more responsible and more productive individuals, families, and communities; and a stable, secure, diverse, and affordable national food supply.

CSREES' research, extension, and education leadership is provided through programs in Plant and Animal Production, Protection, and Processing; Natural Resources and Environment; Rural, Economic, and Social Development; Families, 4–H, and Nutrition; Partnerships; Competitive Research Grants and Awards Management; Science and Education Resources Development; and Communications, Technology, and Distance Education.

The CSREES partnership with the land-grant universities and their representatives is critical to the effective shared planning, delivery, and accountability for research, higher education, and extension programs.

CSREES is a recognized leader in the design, organization, and application of advanced communication technologies and in meeting the growing demand for enhanced distance education capabilities. CSREES provides essential community access to research and education knowledge and connects the private citizen to other Federal Government information.

CSREES also provides support and assistance for the Joint Council on Food and Agricultural Sciences, the National Agricultural Research and Extension Users Advisory Board, and the Committee of Nine (for regional programs).

For further information, contact the Communications Information, and Distance Education Office, Cooperative State Research, Education, and Extension Service, Department of Agriculture, Washington, DC 20250–0906. Internet: CSREES@reeusda.gov. Phone, 202–720–3029. Fax, 202–690–0289. TDD, 702–690–1899.

Economic Research Service

The mission of the Economic Research Service (ERS) is to provide economic and other social science information and analysis for public and private decisions on agriculture, food natural resources, and rural America. ERS produces such information for use by the general public and to help the executive and legislative branches develop, administer, and evaluate agricultural and rural policies and programs. ERS produces economic information through a program of research and analysis on: domestic and international agricultural developments; statistical indicators of food and consumer issues and concerns, including nutrition education and food assistance, food safety regulation, determinants of consumer demand for quality and safety, and food marketing trends and developments; agricultural resource and environmental issues; and the effect of public and private actions and policies on national rural and agricultural conditions, including the transformation of the rural economy, the financial performance of the farm sector, and the implications of changing farm credit and financial market structures.

For further information, contact the Information Services Division, Economics Research Service, Department of Agriculture, Washington, DC 20005–4788. Phone, 202–219–0515.

Office of Energy and New Uses   The Office of Energy and New Uses serves as the focal point for all energy-related matters within the Department. The Office is responsible for developing and coordinating all USDA energy policies; reviewing and evaluating all USDA energy and energy-related programs; evaluating the economics of new non-food uses for agricultural crops; serving as economic liaison on new uses issues; and providing liaison with the Department of Energy and other Federal agencies and departments on energy activities that may affect agriculture and rural America. A major component of this responsibility for the coordination and evaluation of the departmental Biofuels Program. The Office also represents the Department in meetings with agriculture, industry, and consumer groups to discuss effects of departmental energy policies, programs, and proposals on the agricultural sector and rural economy.

For further information, contact the Information Services Division, Economic Research Service, Department of Agriculture, Washington, DC 20005–4788. Phone, 202–219–0515.

National Agricultural Statistics Service

The National Agricultural Statistics Service prepares estimates and reports on production, supply, price, and other items necessary for the orderly operation of the U.S. agricultural economy.

The reports include statistics on field crops, fruits and vegetables, dairy, cattle, hogs, sheep, poultry, aquaculture, and related commodities or processed products. Other estimates concern farm numbers, farm production expenditures, agricultural chemical use, prices received by farmers for products sold, prices paid for commodities and services, indexes of prices received and paid, parity prices, farm employment, and farm wage rates.

The Service prepares these estimates through a complex system of sample surveys of producers, processors, buyers, and others associated with agriculture. Information is gathered by mail, telephone, personal interviews, and field visits.

The 45 State-Federal offices, serving all 50 States, and the national office prepare weekly, monthly, annual, and other periodic reports for free distribution to the news media, Congress, and survey respondents. The reports are available to others on a subscription basis. Information on crop and livestock products appears in about 400 reports issued annually. Cooperative agreements with State agencies also permit preparation and publication of estimates of individual crops and livestock by counties in most States.

The Service performs reimbursable survey work and statistical consulting services for other Federal and State agencies and provides technical assistance for developing agricultural data systems in other countries.

Economics Management Staff

The Economics Management Staff provides management services to the National Agricultural Statistics Service, the Economic Research Service, the World Agricultural Outlook Board, the Economic Analysis Staff, and the Office of Energy. These services include budget, financial management, personnel and related programs, administrative services,

information, equal opportunity and civil rights, and general management assistance.

For further information, contact the Information Division, Economics Management Staff, Department of Agriculture, Washington, DC 20005–4789. Phone, 202–219–0504.

Natural Resources and Environment

This mission area is responsible for fostering sound stewardship of 75 percent of the Nation's total land area. Ecosystems underpin the operating philosophy of the service in order to maximize stewardship of our natural resources. The ecosystem approach ensures that products, values, services, and uses desired by people are produced in ways that sustain healthy, productive ecosystems.

Forest Service

[For the Forest Service statement of organization, see the *Code of Federal Regulations,* Title 36, Part 200.1]

The Forest Service was created by the Transfer Act of February 1, 1905 (16 U.S.C. 472), which transferred the Federal forest reserves and the responsibility for their management from the Department of the Interior to the Department of Agriculture. The forest reserves were established by the President from the public domain under authority of the Creative Act of March 3, 1891 (26 Stat. 1103). The protection and development of the reserves (which became the national forests in 1907) are governed by the Organic Act of June 4, 1897, as amended (16 U.S.C. 473–478); the Multiple Use-Sustained Yield Act of June 12, 1960 (16 U.S.C. 528–531); the Forest and Rangeland Renewable Resources Planning Act of 1974 (16 U.S.C. 1601–1610); and the National Forest Management Act of 1976 (90 Stat. 2947). The Weeks Law of March 1, 1911, as amended (16 U.S.C. 480), allowed the Government to purchase and exchange land for national forests. **Objectives** The Forest Service has the Federal responsibility for national

leadership in forestry. As set forth in law, its mission is to achieve quality land management under the sustainable, multiple-use management concept to meet the diverse needs of people. To accomplish this goal, it has adopted objectives which include:

—advocating a conservation ethic in promoting the health, productivity, diversity, and beauty of forests and associated lands;

—listening to people and responding to their diverse needs in making decisions;

—protecting and managing the national forests and grasslands to best demonstrate the sustainable, multiple-use management concept;

—providing technical and financial assistance to State and private forest landowners, encouraging them toward active stewardship and quality land management in meeting their specific objectives;

—providing technical and financial assistance to cities and communities to improve their natural environment by planting trees and caring for their forests;

—providing international technical assistance and scientific exchanges to sustain and enhance global resources and to encourage quality land management;

—assisting States and communities in using the forests wisely to promote rural economic development and a quality rural environment;

—developing and providing scientific and technical knowledge, improving our capability to protect, manage, and use forests and rangelands; and

—providing work, training, and education to the unemployed,

underemployed, elderly, youth, and the disadvantaged.

National Forest System The Service manages 155 national forests, 20 national grasslands, and 8 land utilization projects on over 191 million acres in 44 States, the Virgin Islands, and Puerto Rico under the principles of multiple-use and sustained yield. The Nation's tremendous need for wood and paper products is balanced with the other vital, renewable resources or benefits that the national forests and grasslands provide: recreation and natural beauty, wildlife habitat, livestock forage, and water supplies. The guiding principle is the greatest good to the greatest number in the long run.

These lands are protected as much as possible from wildfire, epidemics of disease and insect pests, erosion, floods, and water and air pollution. Burned areas get emergency seeding treatment to prevent massive erosion and stream siltation. Roads and trails are built where needed to allow for closely regulated timber harvesting and to give the public access to outdoor recreation areas and provide scenic drives and hikes. Picnic, camping, water-sport, skiing, and other areas are provided with facilities for public convenience and enjoyment. Timber harvesting methods are used that will protect the land and streams, assure rapid renewal of the forest, provide food and cover for wildlife and fish, and have minimum impact on scenic and recreation values. Local communities benefit from the logging and milling activities. These lands also provide needed oil, gas, and minerals. Rangelands are improved for millions of livestock and game animals. The national forests provide a refuge for many species of endangered birds, animals, and fish. Some 34.6 million acres are set aside as wilderness and 175,000 acres as primitive areas where timber will not be harvested.

Cooperation With the States The Service provides national leadership and financial and technical assistance to non-Federal forest landowners, operators, processors of forest products, and urban forestry interests. Through its cooperative State and private forestry

programs, the Service protects and improves the quality of air, water, soil, and open space and encourages uses of natural resources on non-Federal lands that best meet the needs of the Nation, while protecting the environment.

Cooperative programs are carried out through the State foresters or equivalent State officials, who receive grant funding under the Cooperative Forestry Assistance Act of 1978 (16 U.S.C. 2101). Cooperators at the State and local levels provide the delivery system for most State and private forestry programs.

Grant funds and technical assistance are available for rural forestry assistance, forestry incentives, insect and disease control, urban forestry assistance, rural fire prevention and control, organization management assistance, State forest resource planning, and technology implementation.

The Service also cooperates with the Soil Conservation Service, the Agricultural Stabilization and Conservation Service, and other USDA agencies in providing leadership and technical assistance for the forestry aspects of conservation programs.

State and private forestry also is responsible for ensuring that the Service and its cooperators keep abreast of the best knowledge and technology in carrying out its programs, and helping to develop technology transfer plans for implementing research results for a broad range of potential users.

Forest Research The Service performs basic and applied research to develop the scientific information and technology needed to protect, manage, use, and sustain the natural resources of the Nation's 1.6 billion acres of forests and rangelands. This research is conducted through a network of eight forest experiment stations, a Forest Products Laboratory, and the International Institute of Tropical Forestry, including research work units at 77 project locations throughout the United States, Puerto Rico, and the Pacific Trust Islands. Under the authority of the McSweeny-McNary Act of May 22, 1928, as amended and supplemented (45 Stat. 699), research is often performed in cooperation with many of the State agricultural colleges. The Forest Research Service's strategy focuses on three major program components: understanding the structure and functions of forest and range ecosystems; understanding how people perceive and value the protection, management, and use of natural resources; and determining which protection, management, and utilization practices are most suitable for sustainable production and use of the world's natural resources.

International Forestry In response to the U.S. commitment to support natural resource conservation around the world, Congress established the International Forestry Division within the USDA's Forest Service. Its mandate is to provide assistance that promotes sustainable development and global environmental stability, particularly in key countries important in global climate change. This mandate includes a national goal for sustainable management of all forests by the year 2000, investigating research topics with implications for global forest management, or actually sharing resource management experience with colleagues around the world.

Responsibility for global stewardship is shared by the entire Forest Service. The Forest Service's Office of International Forestry mobilizes support of all Forest Service units—Research, National Forest System, State and Private Forestry, Administration, and Programs and Legislation—to work with other governmental agencies, nongovernmental groups, and international organizations in four major international areas: strategic planning and policy development, training and technical assistance, research and scientific exchange, and disaster relief.

Human Resource Programs The Service operates the Youth Conservation Corps and the Volunteers in the National Forests programs and participates with the Department of Labor on several human resource programs that involve the Nation's citizens, both young and old, in forestry-related activities. Included in these programs are the Job Corps and the Senior Community Service

Employment Program. These programs annually accomplish millions of dollars worth of conservation work, while providing participants with such benefits as training, paid employment, and meaningful outdoor experience.

Field Offices—Forest Service

Address
National Forest System Regions [1]—Regional Forester
1. Northern — Federal Bldg. (P.O. Box 7669), Missoula, MT 59807
2. Rocky Mountain — 740 Simms St. (P.O. Box 25127), Lakewood, CO 80225
3. Southwestern — 517 Gold Ave. SW., Albuquerque, NM 87102
4. Intermountain — 324 25th St., Ogden, UT 84401
5. Pacific Southwest — 630 Sansome St., San Francisco, CA 94111
6. Pacific Northwest — 333 SW. 1st Ave. (P.O. Box 3623), Portland, OR 97208
8. Southern — 1720 Peachtree Rd. NW., Atlanta, GA 30367
9. Eastern — 310 W. Wisconsin Ave., Milwaukee, WI 53203
10. Alaska — Federal Office Bldg. (P.O. Box 21628), Juneau, AK 99802
Forest and Range Experiment Stations—Director
Intermountain — 324 25th St., Ogden, UT 84401
North Central — 1992 Folwell Ave., St. Paul, MN 55108
Northeastern — Suite 200, 100 Matson Ford Rd. (P.O. Box 6775), Radnor, PA 19087–4585
Pacific Northwest — 333 SW. 1st Ave. (P.O. Box 3890), Portland, OR 97208
Pacific Southwest — 1960 Addison St. (P.O. Box 245), Berkeley, CA 94701
Rocky Mountain — 240 W. Prospect Ave., Fort Collins, CO 80526
Southeastern — 200 Weaver Blvd. (P.O. Box 2860), Asheville, NC 28804
Southern — 701 Loyola Ave., U.S. Postal Service Bldg., New Orleans, LA 70113
Forest Products Laboratory — 1 Gifford Pinchot Dr., Madison, WI 53705
State and Private Forestry Areas [2]—Director
Northeastern — 370 Reed Rd., Broomall, PA 19008
International Institute of Tropical Forestry — Guadecanal St. (Call Box 25000), Rio Piedras, PR 00928

[1] There is no Region 7.
[2] In Regions 1 through 6, 8, and 10, State and private forestry activities are directed from regional headquarters.

For further information, contact the Public Affairs Office, Forest Service, Department of Agriculture, P.O. Box 96090, Washington, DC 20090–6090. Phone, 202–720–3760.

Natural Resources Conservation Service

[For the Natural Resources Conservation Service statement of organization, see the *Code of Federal Regulations,* Title 7, Parts 600 and 601]

The Natural Resources Conservation Service (NRCS), formerly the Soil Conservation Service, has national responsibility for helping America's farmers, ranchers, and other private landowners develop and carry out voluntary efforts to conserve and protect our natural resources. NRCS is the technical delivery arm for conservation of the United States Department of Agriculture.

NRCS key programs are as follows:

Conservation Technical Assistance This is the foundation program of NRCS. Under this program, the agency provides technical assistance to land users and units of government for the purpose of sustaining agricultural productivity and protecting and enhancing the natural resource base. This assistance is based on the voluntary cooperation of private landowners and involves comprehensive approaches to reduce soil erosion, improve soil and water quantity and quality, improve and conserve wetlands, enhance fish and wildlife habitat, improve air quality, improve pasture and range condition, reduce upstream flooding, and improve woodlands. Every year, more than 1 million land users receive these technical services, which are channeled through nearly 3,000 conservation districts across the United States and its territories.

Natural Resources Inventory The Natural Resources Inventory (NRI) is a report issued every 5 years on how well the Nation is sustaining natural resources on non-Federal land. This report contains the most comprehensive and statistically reliable data of its kind in the world. The NRI provides data on the kind and amount of soil, water, vegetation, and related resources; the effects of current land use and management practices on the present and future supply and condition of soil, water, and vegetation; and the changes and trends in the use, extent, and condition of these resources. NRI data and analytical software are available to the public on CD–ROM.

National Cooperative Soil Survey The National Cooperative Soil Survey provides the public with local information on the uses and capabilities of their soils. The published soil survey for a county or other designated area includes maps and interpretations that

are the foundation for farm planning and other private land use decisions as well as for resource planning and policy by local, State, and Federal Governments. The surveys are conducted cooperatively with other Federal, State, and local agencies and land grant universities. NRCS is the national and world leader in soil classification and soil mapping, and is now expanding its work in soil quality.

Snow Survey and Water Supply Forecasting Program This program collects snowpack moisture data and forecasts seasonal water supplies for streams that derive most of their water from snowmelt. It helps farm operators, rural communities, and municipalities manage water resources through water supply forecasts. It also provides hydrometeorological data for regulating reservoir storage and managing streamflow. The Snow Supply Program is conducted in 11 Western States and Alaska.

Plant Materials Program At 26 plant materials centers across the country, NRCS tests, selects, and ensures the commercial availability of new and improved conservation plants for erosion reduction, wetland restoration, water quality improvement, streambank and riparian area protection, coastal dune stabilization, biomass production, carbon sequestration, and other needs. The Plant Materials Program is a cooperative effort with conservation districts, other Federal and State agencies, commercial businesses, and seed and nursery associations.

River Basin Surveys and Investigations This program involves NRCS with Federal, State, and local agencies in river basin surveys and investigations, flood hazard analysis, and floodplain management assistance. It addresses a variety of natural resource concerns— water quality, water conservation, wetlands protection, agricultural drought, rural development, municipal and industrial water needs, and fish and wildlife habitat.

Public Law 83–566 Small Watersheds Program The Small Watersheds Program helps local sponsoring groups to voluntarily plan and install watershed protection projects on private lands. These projects include flood prevention, water quality improvement, soil erosion and sediment reduction, rural and municipal water supply, irrigation water management, fish and wildlife habitat enhancement, and wetlands restoration. NRCS helps local community groups, government entities, and private landowners working together using an integrated, comprehensive watershed approach to natural resource planning.

Public Law 78–534 Flood Prevention Program This program applies to 11 specific flood prevention projects covering about 35 million acres in 11 States. It provides help in flood prevention, water management, and reduction and erosion sedimentation. It also can help in developing recreational facilities and improving fish and wildlife habitat.

Emergency Watershed Protection Program This program provides emergency assistance to safeguard lives and property in jeopardy due to sudden watershed impairment by natural disasters. Emergency work includes quickly establishing a protective plant cover on denuded land and stream banks; opening dangerously restricted channels; and repairing diversions and levees. An emergency area need not be declared a national disaster area to be eligible for help under this program.

Great Plains Conservation Program This program (GPCP) helps bring about long-term solutions to natural resource problems in the 10 Great Plains States. It is aimed at total conservation treatment of entire farms or ranches. Program participation is voluntary and provides technical assistance and a long-term cost-share contract between the participant and NRCS. GPCP has been effective in addressing the needs of socially disadvantaged farmers and ranchers and the needs of American Indian farmers and ranchers. In addition to providing significant erosion and sediment reduction benefits, the program addresses problems related to water quality, wildlife habitat protection, and other environmental concerns.

Resource Conservation and Development Program This program (RC&D) is a locally driven program—an opportunity for civic-oriented groups to work together sharing knowledge and resources in solving common problems facing their region. The program offers aid in balancing the environmental, economic, and social needs of an area. A USDA coordinator helps each designated RC&D council plan, develop, and carry out programs for resource conservation, water management, community development, and environmental enhancement.

Rural Abandoned Mine Program This program (RAMP) helps protect people and the environment from the adverse effects of past coal-mining practices and promotes the development of the soil and water resources on unreclaimed mine land. It provides technical and financial assistance to land users who voluntarily enter into 5-to-10-year contracts for the reclamation of eligible land and water.

Wetlands Reserve Program Under this program, USDA purchases easements from agricultural land owners who voluntarily agree to restore and protect wetlands. NRCS employees help these owners develop plans to retire critical wetland habitat for crop production. The primary objectives are to preserve and restore wetlands, improve wildlife habitat, and protect migratory waterfowl.

Water Bank Program NRCS helps landowners protect, improve, or restore wetlands by identifying eligible lands, helping owners develop conservation plans, and implementing necessary land treatments. Through 10-year rental agreements between USDA and landowners, the Water Bank Program protects important nesting, breeding, and feeding areas for migratory waterfowl. Other benefits of the program include water conservation, erosion control, flood control, and landscape beautification.

Colorado River Basin Salinity Control Program This voluntary incentive program supports the Nation's commitment to water quality in the Colorado River, which provides water to more than 18 million people in parts of seven Western States and Mexico. NRCS provides financial and technical assistance to control salt loading in the Colorado River from both natural and human-caused sources. Among the remedies used are management practices to prevent irrigation-induced erosion.

Forestry Incentives Program   This program helps to increase the Nation's supply of products from nonindustrial private forest lands. This also ensures more effective use of existing forest lands and, over time, helps to prevent shortages and price increases for forest products. The program shares the cost incurred by landowners for tree planting and timberstand improvement.

Farms-For-The-Future Program   This program guarantees USDA loans and subsidizes interest on State loans to purchase agricultural land or development rights to preserve vital farmland resources for future generations. The money also can be reinvested by the States to generate earnings for future farmland protection efforts.

For further information, contact the Office of Public Affairs, Natural Resources Conservation Service, Department of Agriculture, P.O. Box 2890, Washington, DC 20013. Phone, 202–720–3210.

Graduate School, U.S. Department of Agriculture

Fourteenth Street and Independence Avenue SW., Washington, DC 20250
Phone, 202–401–9129

Director	PHILIP H. HUDSON
Deputy Director	LYNN EDWARDS
Program Director, Center for Applied Technology	NAT HOPKINS
Program Director, Correspondence Study	NORMA HARWOOD
Director of Information and Public Affairs	BRIAN GRAY
Program Director, Evening and Saturday	RONALD MACNAB
Program Director, Government Audit Training Institute	DONALD SMULAND
Program Director, International Training	JANE BURKE
Program Director, International Visitor and Exchange	LILY PARSONS
Director of Administration	WILLIAM CAPEZIO
Registrar	CAROLYN NELSON

The Graduate School, U.S. Department of Agriculture, is a continuing education school offering career-related training to adults. It is self-supporting and does not receive direct appropriated funds from Congress or the Department of Agriculture. Fees charged individuals and Government agencies are nominal. Courses are planned with the assistance of Government professionals and specialists. The faculty is mostly part-time and is drawn from throughout Government and the community at large. They are selected because of their professional and specialized knowledge and experience and thus bring a practicality and experience to their classrooms. Faculty holding regular Government positions take annual leave or leave without pay when teaching during their normal work hours. The school does not grant degrees but does provide planned sequences of courses leading to certificates of accomplishment in a number of occupational and career fields important to government. Training areas include management, auditing, computer science, communications, foreign language, procurement, financial management, and others.

The Graduate School's objective is to improve Government services by providing needed continuing education and training opportunities for Government employees and agencies. The Graduate School, administered by a Director and governed by a General Administration Board appointed by the Secretary of Agriculture, was established by the Secretary of Agriculture on September 2, 1921, pursuant to act of May 15, 1862 (7 U.S.C. 2201); joint resolution of April 12, 1892 (27 Stat. 395); and the Deficiencies Appropriation Act of March 3, 1901 (20 U.S.C. 91).

For further information, contact the Information Office, Graduate School, U.S. Department of Agriculture, Room 129, 600 Maryland Avenue SW., Washington, DC 20024. Phone, 202–401–9129.

Sources of Information

Consumer Activities Educational, organizational, and financial assistance is offered to consumers and their families in such fields as rural housing and farm operating programs, improved nutrition, family living and recreation, food stamp, school lunch, donated foods, and other food programs. Phone, 202–447–2791.
Contracts and Small Business Activities Contact the Office of Small and Disadvantaged Business Utilization, Department of Agriculture, Washington, DC 20250. Phone, 202–720–7117.
Employment Most jobs in the Department are in the competitive service and are filled by applicants who have established eligibility under an appropriate examination administered by the Office of Personnel Management or Department Special Examining Units.

General employment inquiries may be sent to the Recruitment and Employment Division, Office of Personnel, Department of Agriculture, Washington, DC 20250. Phone, 202–720–5626.

Persons interested in employment in the Food and Nutrition Service should contact the Regional Offices located in Atlanta, Boston, Chicago, Dallas, Denver, San Francisco, and Robbinsville, NJ, or the national headquarters in Alexandria, VA. Phone, 703–305–2351.

Persons interested in employment in the Office of the Inspector General should contact the USDA Office of Personnel, Room 31–W, Administration Building, Washington, DC 20250. Phone, 202–720–5781.

In addition, all Forest Service field units listed on page 141 will accept employment applications.
Environment Educational, organizational, technical, and financial assistance is offered to local citizens, their organizations and communities in such fields as watershed protection, flood prevention, soil and water conservation practices to reduce erosion and sedimentation, community water and waste disposal systems, safe use of pesticides, and the development of pesticide alternatives.

Contact the nearest county Extension agent or USDA office, or write to the Office of Public Affairs, Department of Agriculture, Washington, DC 20250, for information on consumer activities and the environment, as previously described. Phone, 202–720–2791.
Films Motion pictures on a variety of agricultural subjects are available for loan through various State Extension Service film libraries. Contact the Video and Teleconference Division, Office of Public Affairs, Department of Agriculture, Washington, DC 20250, for a listing of cooperating film libraries. Phone, 202–720–6072.

Color filmstrips and slide sets on a variety of subjects are available for purchase. For a listing of titles and prices, contact the Photography Division, Office of Public Affairs, Department of Agriculture, Washington, DC 20250. Phone, 202–720–6633.
Whistleblower Hotline Persons wishing to register complaints of alleged improprieties concerning the Department

should contact one of the Regional
Offices or the Inspector General's
"Whistleblower Hotline"—outside
Washington, DC, phone toll-free, 800–
424–9121; within the Washington, DC,
metropolitan area, phone, 202–690–
1622, or 202–690–1202 (TDD).

Reading Rooms   Located at each USDA
agency; addresses indicated in text.
Speakers   Contact the nearest
Department of Agriculture office or
county Extension agent. In the District of
Columbia, contact the Office of Public
Liaison, Office of Public Affairs,
Department of Agriculture, Washington,
DC 20250. Phone, 202–720–2798.

For further information concerning the Department of Agriculture, contact the Office of Public Affairs,
Department of Agriculture, Washington, DC 20250. Phone, 202–720–2791.

DEPARTMENT OF COMMERCE

Fourteenth Street between Constitution and Pennsylvania Avenues NW.,
Washington, DC 20230
Phone, 202–482–2000

SECRETARY OF COMMERCE	RONALD H. BROWN
Chief of Staff	WILLIAM W. GINSBERG
Counsellor to the Secretary	WILLIAM J. TAYLOR III
Assistant to the Secretary and Director, Office of Policy and Strategic Planning	JONATHAN SALLET
Executive Assistant to the Secretary	BARBARA J. SCHMITZ
Director, Office of White House Liaison	MARIANNE SMITH
Executive Secretary	(VACANCY)
Deputy Executive Secretary	CHERYL CARTER
Deputy Secretary of Commerce	DAVID J. BARRAM
Associate Deputy Secretary	KENT HUGHES
Assistant Deputy Secretary	MARTHA JOHNSON
Director, Office of Space Commerce	KEITH CALHOUN-SENGHOR
Director, Office of Small and Disadvantaged Business Utilization	JAMES MARUCA
General Counsel	GINGER E. LEW
Deputy General Counsel	KATHLEEN A. AMBROSE
Counselor to the General Counsel	GLENN T. PIERCY
Assistant General Counsel for Administration	BARBARA S. FREDERICKS
Assistant General Counsel for Legislation and Regulation	MICHAEL A. LEVITT
Assistant General Counsel for Finance and Litigation	ALDEN F. ABBOTT
Chief Counsel for Economics and Statistics Administration	JAMES K. WHITE
Chief Counsel for Export Administration	HOYT H. ZIA
Chief Counsel for Import Administration	STEPHEN J. POWELL
Chief Counsel for International Commerce	ELEANOR ROBERTS LEWIS
Chief Counsel for Minority Business Development	PERCY ROBINSON, *Acting*
Chief Counsel for Technology Administration	MARK BOHANNON
Assistant Secretary for Legislative and Intergovernmental Affairs	(VACANCY)
Deputy Assistant Secretary for Legislative and Intergovernmental Affairs	CARMEN GUZMAN LOWREY
Deputy Assistant Secretary for Intergovernmental Affairs	MICHAEL FRAZIER
Inspector General	FRANK DEGEORGE
Deputy Inspector General	MICHAEL ZIMMERMAN
Counsel to the Inspector General	K. WAYNE WEAVER
Assistant Inspector General for Auditing	JOHN D. NEWELL
Assistant Inspector General for Investigations	DAMON L. BARBAT
Assistant Inspector General for Systems Evaluation	JUDITH J. GORDON

147

Assistant Inspector General for Inspections and Resource Management	JOHNNIE E. FRAZIER
Assistant Inspector General for Compliance and Audit Resolution	GEORGE E. ROSS
Director, Office of Public Affairs	JILL SCHUKER
Press Secretary, Office of the Press Secretary	CAROL L. HAMILTON
Director, Office of Business Liaison	MELISSA MOSS
Director, Office of Consumer Affairs	LAJUAN JOHNSON
Chief Financial Officer and Assistant Secretary for Administration	THOMAS R. BLOOM
Deputy Assistant Secretary for Administration	GLORIA GUTIÉRREZ
Director for Budget, Management and Information and Chief Information Officer	ALAN P. BALUTIS
Director, Office of Budget	MARK E. BROWN
Director, Office of Management and Organization	STEPHEN C. BROWNING
Director, Office of Information Policy and Technology	JAMES MCNAMEE
Director, Office of Information Planning and Review	THOMAS SCOTT
Manager, Decision Analysis Center	CHARLES F. TREAT
Director, Office of Civil Rights	COURTLAND COX, *Acting*
Director for Executive Budgeting and Assistance Management	SONYA G. STEWART
Director, Office of Executive Assistance Management	JOHN J. PHELAN III
Working Capital Fund Administrator	THOMAS D. JONES
Director for Financial Management and Deputy Chief Financial Officer	CLYDE G. MCSHAN II
Deputy Director	DOUGLAS K. DAY
Director, Office of Financial Policy and Assistance	THEODORE A. JOHNSON
Director, Office of Financial Planning and Reporting	LEONARD L. SWEENEY, *Acting*
Director, Office of Financial Management Systems	JOSEPH A. SCLAFANI
Director, Office of Computer Services	PATRICK F. SMITH, *Acting*
Director for Human Resources Management	ELIZABETH W. STROUD
Deputy Director	CAROLYN P. ACREE
Director, Office of Personnel Operations	SANDRA RICHARDSON
Director, Office of Workforce Effectiveness and Executive Resources	H. JAMES REESE
Director, Office of Labor and Employee Relations	RUSS FORRESTER
Director, Office of Automated Systems and Pay Policy	LYNN M. EDDY
Director for Administrative Services	HARRY E. BRADLEY, JR., *Acting*
Director, Office of Federal Property Programs	HARRY E. BRADLEY, JR.
Director for Security	STEVEN E. GARMON
Director for Acquisition Management	SHIRL G. KINNEY
Director for Systems and Telecommunications Management	RONALD P. HACK

Director, Office of Telecommunications Management	THOMAS W. ZETTY
Director, Office of Information Systems	JAMES E. SQUIER
Director, Office of Technical Support and Networks Services	GEORGE H. IMBER
Under Secretary for Economic Affairs and Administrator	EVERETT M. EHRLICH
Deputy Under Secretary	PAUL A. LONDON
Associate Under Secretary	SALLY C. ERICSSON
Director, Office of Policy Development	JEFFREY L. MAYER
Director, STAT—U.S.A.	KENNETH ROGERS
Executive Director	(VACANCY)
Director of Administration	B. JEROME JACKSON
Chief Economist	LEWIS A. ALEXANDER
Director, Office of International Macroeconomic Analysis	SUMIYE OKUBO
Director, Office of Economic Conditions and Forecasting	CARL E. COX
Director, Bureau of the Census	MARTHA FARNSWORTH RICHE
Deputy Director	HARRY A. SCARR
Assistant Director for Communications	JANE A. CALLEN
Principal Associate Director and Chief Financial Officer	FREDERICK T. ALT
Principal Associate Director for Programs	PAULA J. SCHNEIDER
Associate Director for Administration	CHARLES V. ST. LAWRENCE
Associate Director for Information Technology	ARNOLD A. JACKSON
Associate Director for Planning and Organization Development	STANLEY D. MATCHETT
Comptroller	STANLEY D. MATCHETT, *Acting*
Associate Director for Field Operations	BRYANT BENTON
Associate Director for Economic Programs	FREDERICK T. KNICKERBOCKER
Assistant Director for Economic Programs	THOMAS L. MESENBOURG
Associate Director for Decennial Census	ROBERT W. MARX
Assistant Director for Decennial Census	SUSAN M. MISKURA
Associate Director for Demographic Programs	WILLIAM P. BUTZ
Associate Director for Statistical Design, Methodology and Standards	ROBERT D. TORTORA
Director, Bureau of Economic Analysis	(VACANCY)
Deputy Director	J. STEVEN LANDEFELD
Associate Director for National Economic Accounts	GERALD F. DONAHOE
Associate Director for Regional Economics	HUGH W. KNOX
Associate Director for International Economics	GERALD A. POLLACK
Associate Director for Industry Accounts	(VACANCY)
Chief Economist	JACK E. TRIPLETT
Chief Statistician	ROBERT P. PARKER
Under Secretary for Export Administration	WILLIAM A. REINSCH
Deputy Under Secretary	BARRY CARTER
Director of Administration	ROBERT F. KUGELMAN
Director of Congressional and Public Affairs	SHARON YANAGI
Assistant Secretary for Export Administration	SUE E. ECKERT
Deputy Assistant Secretary	IAIN S. BAIRD

Assistant Secretary for Export Enforcement	JOHN DESPRES
Deputy Assistant Secretary	FRANK DELIBERTI
Assistant Secretary for Economic Development	(VACANCY)
Deputy Assistant Secretary	WILBUR F. HAWKINS
Deputy Assistant Secretary for Program Operations	PEDRO R. GARZA
Deputy Assistant Secretary for Program Support	CHESTER J. STRAUB JR.
Chief Counsel	AWILDA MARQUET
Under Secretary for International Trade	JEFFREY E. GARTEN
Deputy Under Secretary	TIMOTHY J. HAUSER
Deputy Under Secretary for International Trade Policy Development	DAVID J. ROTHKOPF
Counselor to the Department	JAN H. KALICKI
Director of Administration	ALAN NEUSCHATZ
Assistant Secretary for International Economic Policy	CHARLES F. MEISSNER
Deputy Assistant Secretary for International Economic Policy	JOHN HUANG
Deputy Assistant Secretary for the Western Hemisphere	ANN HUGHES
Deputy Assistant Secretary for Europe	FRANKLIN J. VARGO
Deputy Assistant Secretary for Africa and the Near East	JOHN WALKER
Deputy Assistant Secretary for Asia and the Pacific	NANCY LINN PATTON
Deputy Assistant Secretary for Japan	MARJORY SEARING
Assistant Secretary for Import Administration	SUSAN G. ESSERMAN
Deputy Assistant Secretary for Import Administration	PAUL L. JOFFE
Deputy Assistant Secretary for Compliance	JOSEPH A. SPETRINI
Deputy Assistant Secretary for Investigations	BARBARA STAFFORD
Assistant Secretary for Trade Development	RAYMOND E. VICKERY
Deputy Assistant Secretary for Trade Development	CLYDE W. ROBINSON
Deputy Assistant Secretary for Basic Industries	MICHAEL J. COPPS
Deputy Assistant Secretary for Technology and Aerospace Industries	ELLIS R. MOTTUR
Deputy Assistant Secretary for Service Industries and Finance	JUDE KEARNEY
Deputy Assistant Secretary for Textiles, Apparel and Consumer Goods Industries	RITA D. HAYES
Deputy Assistant Secretary for Environmental Technologies Exports	ANNE L. ALONZO
Assistant Secretary and Director General of the U.S. and Foreign Commercial Service	LAURI FITZ-PEGADO
Deputy Assistant Secretary for the U.S. and Foreign Commercial Service	ROBERT S. LARUSSA
Deputy Assistant Secretary for Domestic Operations	DANIEL J. MCLAUGHLIN
Deputy Assistant Secretary for International Operations	ROBERT TAFT

Deputy Assistant Secretary for Export Promotion Services — MARY FRAN KIRCHNER
Director, Minority Business Development Agency — JOAN PARROTT-FONSECA
Chief Counsel — PERCY ROBINSON, *Acting*
Assistant Director for External Affairs — BETTIE BACA
Associate Director for Finance and Administration — RAFAEL BORRAS
Associate Director for Strategic Planning — ELIO MULLER
Assistant Director for Operations — PAUL R. WEBBER IV
Assistant Director for Program and Policy Development — C. HOWIE HODGES
Under Secretary for Oceans and Atmosphere and Administrator — D. JAMES BAKER
Counselor to the Under Secretary — SUSAN B. FRUCHTER
Assistant Secretary for Oceans and Atmosphere and Deputy Administrator — DOUGLAS K. HALL
Deputy Under Secretary for Oceans and Atmosphere — DIANA H. JOSEPHSON
Associate Deputy Under Secretary — JOHN J. CAREY
Chief Scientist — KATHRYN D. SULLIVAN
Deputy Assistant Secretary for International Affairs — WILLIAM E. MARTIN
Deputy Assistant Secretary for Oceans and Atmosphere — KATHARINE W. KIMBALL
Assistant Administrator for Fisheries — ROLLAND A. SCHMITTEN
Assistant Administrator for Ocean Services and Coastal Zone Management — W. STANLEY WILSON
Assistant Administrator for Oceanic and Atmospheric Research — NED A. OSTENSO
Assistant Administrator for Weather Service — ELBERT W. FRIDAY, JR.
Assistant Administrator for Environmental Satellites, Data, and Information Services — ROBERT S. WINOKUR
Director, Global Programs — J. MICHAEL HALL
Director, Coastal Ocean Program — DONALD SCAVIA
Director, Public and Constituent Affairs — LORI ANN ARGUELLES
Director, Sustainable Development and Intergovernmental Affairs — JOHN K. BULLARD
Director, Policy and Strategic Planning — SUSAN B. FRUCHTER
Director, Legislative Affairs — SALLY J. YOZELL
Director, Education Affairs — (VACANCY)
Director, International Affairs — WILLIAM E. MARTIN, *Acting*
General Counsel — TERRY D. GARCIA
Director, National Oceanic and Atmospheric Administration Corps Operations — SIGMUND R. PETERSEN
Director of Administration — DONALD E. HUMPHRIES, *Acting*
Director, High Performance Computing Communications — THOMAS N. PYKE, JR.
Director, System Acquisition — THOMAS E. MCGUNIGAL
Comptroller — ANDREW H. MOXAM
Director, Program Coordination — STEPHEN H. MANZO
Assistant Secretary for Communications and Information — LARRY IRVING
Deputy Assistant Secretary — THOMAS J. SUGRUE

Chief Counsel	BARBARA WELLBERY
Director, Policy Coordination and Management	MICHELE C. FARQUHAR
Associate Administrator for Spectrum Management	RICHARD D. PARLOW
Associate Administrator for Policy Analysis and Development	JOE GATTUSO, *Acting*
Associate Administrator for Telecommunication Sciences	WILLIAM F. UTLAUT
Associate Administrator for International Affairs	CAROL DARR
Associate Administrator for Telecommunications and Information Applications	BERNADETTE A. MCGUIRE-RIVERA
Assistant Secretary and Commissioner of Patents and Trademarks	BRUCE A. LEHMAN
Deputy Assistant Secretary and Deputy Commissioner	LAWRENCE J. GOFNEY, JR., *Acting*
Assistant Commissioner for Patents	LAWRENCE J. GOFNEY, JR.
Assistant Commissioner for Trademarks	PHILIP G. HAMPTON
Associate Commissioner and Chief Financial Officer	BRADFORD R. HUTHER
Chief Information Officer	DENNIS SHAW
Under Secretary for Technology	MARY L. GOOD
Deputy Under Secretary	GARY R. BACHULA
Staff Director for Technology	JOYCE S. HASTY
Chief Counsel	MARK BOHANNON
Assistant Secretary for Technology Policy	GRAHAM R. MITCHELL
Deputy Assistant Secretary for Technology Policy	KELLY H. CARNES
Director, Office of International Policy	ELLIOT MAXWELL
Director, Office of Manufacturing Competitiveness	CARY GRAVATT
Director, Office of Technology Competitiveness	JON PAUGH
Director, National Institute of Standards and Technology	ARATI PRABHAKAR
Deputy Director	RAYMOND G. KAMMER
Associate Director	SAMUEL KRAMER
Director of Administration	JORGE R. URRUTIA
Director, Technology Services	PETER L.M. HEYDEMANN
Director, Electronics and Electrical Engineering Laboratory	JUDSON C. FRENCH
Director, Chemical Science and Technology Laboratory	HRATCH G. SEMERJIAN
Director, Physics Laboratory	KATHERINE B. GEBBIE
Director, Materials Science and Engineering Laboratory	LYLE H. SCHWARTZ
Director, Building and Fire Research Laboratory	RICHARD N. WRIGHT
Director, Computer Systems Laboratory	JAMES H. BURROWS
Director, Computing and Applied Mathematics Laboratory	JOAN R. ROSENBLATT
Director, Advanced Technology Program	BRIAN C. BELANGER, *Acting*

Director, Manufacturing Extension Partnership Program	KEVIN M. CARR, *Acting*
Director, Office of Quality Programs	CURT W. REIMANN
Director, National Technical Information Service	DONALD R. JOHNSON
Deputy Director	DONALD W. CORRIGAN
Under Secretary for Travel and Tourism	GREG FARMER
Deputy Under Secretary	LESLIE R. DOGGETT
Assistant Secretary for Tourism Marketing	(VACANCY)
Deputy Assistant Secretary for Tourism Marketing	W. DON WYNEGAR
Director, Office of Policy and Planning	HELEN MARANO, *Acting*
Director, Office of Research	RON ERDMANN, *Acting*
Director, Office of Strategic Planning and Administration	LEE J. WELLS

The Department of Commerce encourages, serves, and promotes the Nation's international trade, economic growth, and technological advancement. The Department provides a wide variety of programs through the competitive free enterprise system. It offers assistance and information to increase America's competitiveness in the world economy; administers programs to prevent unfair foreign trade competition; provides social and economic statistics and analyses for business and government planners; provides research and support for the increased use of scientific, engineering, and technological development; works to improve our understanding and benefits of the Earth's physical environment and oceanic resources; grants patents and registers trademarks; develops policies and conducts research on telecommunications; provides assistance to promote domestic economic development; promotes travel to the United States by residents of foreign countries; and assists in the growth of minority businesses.

The Department was designated as such by act of March 4, 1913 (15 U.S.C. 1501), which reorganized the Department of Commerce and Labor, created by act of February 14, 1903 (15 U.S.C. 1501), by transferring all labor activities into a new, separate Department of Labor. The Department of Commerce (DOC) is composed of the Office of the Secretary and the operating units.

Office of the Secretary

Secretary   The Secretary is responsible for the administration of all functions and authorities assigned to the Department of Commerce and for advising the President on Federal policy and programs affecting the industrial and commercial segments of the national economy. The Secretary is served by the offices of Deputy Secretary, Inspector General, and General Counsel and the Assistant Secretaries of Administration,

Legislative and Intergovernmental Affairs, and Public Affairs. Other offices whose public purposes are widely administered are detailed below and on the following pages.

Office of the Press Secretary   The Office of the Press Secretary serves as the Secretary's official liaison to the news media in the United States and the world. The Office handles all media inquiries related to the Secretary, provides the press with information and support on events and trips involving the Secretary, researches and compiles press information for the Department of Commerce, and is in constant communication with all forms of media regarding Department of Commerce and administration initiatives.

Business Liaison   This office develops and promotes a cooperative working relationship and ensures effective communication between the Department of Commerce and the business community. The Office's objectives are

DEPARTMENT OF COMMERCE

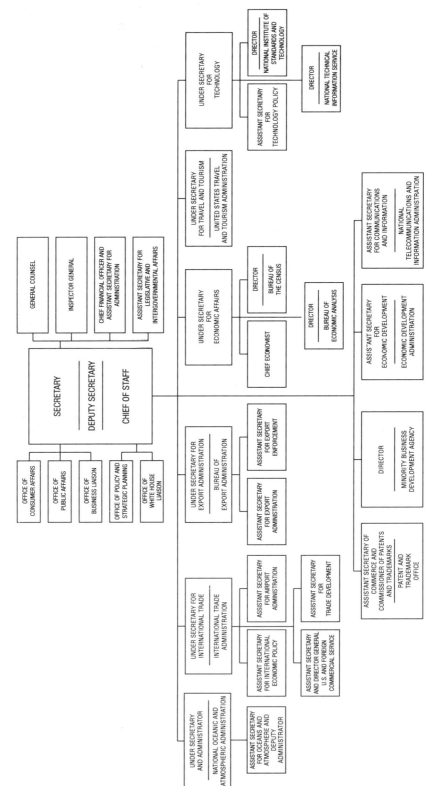

to keep the business community aware of Department and administration resources, policies, and programs, and to keep Department and administration officials aware of issues of concern to business. The Office also promotes business involvement in departmental policymaking and program development, and provides technical assistance to businesses that desire help in dealing with the Government.

For further information, call 202–482–3942.

Consumer Affairs This office encourages and assists the business community in being responsive to consumer interests in a global marketplace; assists and educates consumers with marketplace problems and informs them about resources and programs within the Department; and coordinates and represents the Department's consumer affairs activities with consumer groups and other Federal, State, county, and municipal government agencies, and international organizations.

For further information, call 202–482–5001; or fax, 202–482–6007; or fax on demand, 202–501–1191.

Small and Disadvantaged Business Utilization The Office of Small and Disadvantaged Business Utilization (OSDBU) serves as the principal departmental advocate for small, minority, and women business owners. OSDBU assures that small firms fully participate in Commerce programs and receive the maximum amount of Commerce contract and subcontract dollars.

OSDBU is the focal point of Commerce's constant efforts to increase awards to small firms by searching for opportunities to match with the capabilities of small, minority, and women-owned firms.

OSDBU informs the small business community about Commerce opportunities by publishing the *Annual Forecast of Contracts,* by individual counseling, and by participating with other Federal agencies and trade associations at procurement fairs.

OSDBU was established by the Small Business Act, as amended (15 U.S.C. 644).

For further information, call 202–482–3387.

Economics and Statistics Administration

The Under Secretary for Economic Affairs advises the Secretary and other Government officials on matters relating to economic developments and forecasts and on the development of macroeconomic and microeconomic policy. The Under Secretary, as Administrator of the Economics and Statistics Administration, exercises general supervision over the Bureau of the Census and the Bureau of Economic Analysis.

Current economic data are available to the public through the National Trade Data Bank and the Economic Bulletin Board.

For further information, call 202–482–1986.

Bureau of the Census

[For the Bureau of the Census statement of organization, see the *Federal Register* of Sept. 16, 1975, 40 FR 42765]

The Bureau of the Census was established as a permanent office by act of March 6, 1902 (32 Stat. 51). The major functions of the Bureau are authorized by the Constitution, which provides that a census of population shall be taken every 10 years, and by laws codified as title 13 of the United States Code. The law also provides that the information collected by the Bureau from individual persons, households, or establishments be kept strictly confidential and be used only for statistical purposes.

The principal functions of the Bureau include:

—decennial censuses of population and housing;

—quinquennial censuses of agriculture, State and local governments, manufacturers, mineral industries, distributive trades, construction industries, and transportation;

—current surveys that provide information on many of the subjects covered in the censuses at monthly, quarterly, annual, or other intervals;

—compilation of current statistics on U.S. foreign trade, including data on imports, exports, and shipping;

—special censuses at the request and expense of States and local government units;

—publication of estimates and projections of the population;

—current data on population and housing characteristics; and

—current reports on manufacturing, retail and wholesale trade, services, construction, imports and exports, State and local government finances and employment, and other subjects.

The Bureau makes available statistical results of its censuses, surveys, and other programs to the public through printed reports, computer tape, CD–ROM's, microfiche, and other media and prepares special tabulations sponsored and paid for by data users. It also produces statistical compendia, catalogs, guides, and directories that are useful in locating information on specific subjects. Upon request, the Bureau makes searches of decennial census records and furnishes certificates to individuals for use as evidence of age, relationship, or place of birth. A fee is charged for such searches.

Field Organization—Bureau of the Census

Office	Address
REGIONAL OFFICES:	
ATLANTA—Alabama, Florida, Georgia (all counties), South Carolina (counties of Aiken and Edgefield), Tennessee (all counties except Fayette, Hardeman, Mcnairy, Shelby, and Tipton), and Virginia (counties of Bristol City, Scott, and Washington)	Suite 3200, 101 Marietta St. NW., Atlanta, GA 30303–2700
BOSTON—Connecticut, Maine, Massachusetts, New Hampshire, New York (counties of Albany, Allegany, Broome, Cattaraugus, Cayuga, Chautauqua, Chemung, Chanango, Clinton, Erie, Essex, Franklin, Fulton, Genesse, Greene, Hamilton, Herkimer, Jefferson, Lewis, Livingston, Madison, Monroe, Montgomery, Niagara, Oneida, Onondaga, Orleans, Oswego, Otsego, Rensselaer, St. Lawrence, Saratoga, Schenectady, Schoharie, Schuyler, Seneca, Steuben, Tioga, Tompkins, Warren, Washington, Wayne, Wyoming, and Yates), Rhode Island, and Vermont (all counties)	Suite 310, 2 Copley Pl., P.O. Box 9108, Boston, MA 02117–9108
CHARLOTTE—District of Columbia, Indiana (counties of Clark, Floyd, Harrison, and Scott), Kentucky (all counties except Boone, Bracken, Campbell, Gallatin, Grant, Harrison, Henderson, Pendleton, and Robertson), Maryland (counties of Calvert, Charles, Frederick, Montgomery, Prince Georges, and St. Mary's), North Carolina (all counties), Ohio (Lawrence County), South Carolina (all counties except Aiken and Edgefield), Virginia (all counties except Bristol City, Scott, and Washington), and West Virginia (counties of Boone, Cabell, Lincoln, Logan, McDowell, Mercer, Mingo, Wayne, and Wyoming)	Suite 106, 901 Center Park Dr., Charlotte, NC 28217–2935
CHICAGO—Illinois (all counties except Clinton, Jersey, Madison, Monroe, and St. Claire), Indiana (all counties except Clark, Dearborn, Floyd, Harrison, Ohio, and Scott), Iowa (Scott County), and Kentucky (Henderson County)	Suite 5501, 2255 Enterprise Dr., Westchester, IL 60154–5800
DALLAS—Arkansas, Louisiana, Mississippi, New Mexico, Oklahoma (counties of Bryan, Le Flore, McCurtain, and Sequoyah), Tennessee (counties of Fayette, Hardeman, Mcnairy, Shelby, and Tipton), and Texas	Suite 210, 6303 Harry Hines Blvd., Dallas, TX 75235–5269

Field Organization—Bureau of the Census—Continued

Office	Address
DENVER—Arizona, Colorado, Iowa (Pottawattamie County), Kansas (all counties except Allen, Atchison, Bourbon, Crawford, Douglas, Franklin, Jackson, Jefferson, Johnson, Leavenworth, Linn, Miami, Neosho, Osage, Shawnee, and Wyandotte), Nebraska (all counties except Dakota), North Dakota (all counties except Cass), Oklahoma (all counties except Bryan, LeFlore, McCurtain, and Sequoyah), South Dakota, Utah (all counties except Washington), and Wyoming	P.O. Box 272020, 6900 W. Jefferson Ave., Denver, CO 80227–9020
DETROIT—Indiana (county of Dearborn and Ohio), Kentucky (counties of Boone, Bracken, Campbell, Gallatin, Grant, Harrison, Kenton, Pendleton, and Robertson), Michigan, Ohio (all counties except Lawrence), Pennsylvania (Mercer County), and West Virginia (counties of Brooke, Hancock, Marshall, and Ohio)	P.O. Box 33405, 1395 Brewery Park Blvd., Detroit, MI 48232–5405
KANSAS CITY—Illinois (counties of Clinton, Jersey, Madison, Monroe, and St. Clair), Iowa (all counties except Pottawattamie and Scott), Kansas (counties of Allen, Atchison, Bourbon, Crawford, Douglas, Franklin, Jackson, Jefferson, Johnson, Leavenworth, Linn, Miami, Neosho, Osage, Shawnee, and Wyandotte), Minnesota, Missouri, Nebraska (Dakota County), North Dakota (Cass County), and Wisconsin	Suite 600, Gateway Tower II, 400 State Ave., Kansas City, KS 66101–2410
LOS ANGELES—California (counties of Fresno, Imperial, Inyo, Kern, Kings, Los Angeles, Madera, Mariposa, Merced, Monterey, Orange, Riverside, San Benito, San Bernardino, San Diego, San Luis Obispo, Santa Barbara, Tulare, and Ventura), Hawaii, Nevada (counties of Clark and Nye), and Utah (Washington County)	Suite 300, 15350 Sherman Way, Van Nuys, CA 91406–4224
NEW YORK—New Jersey (counties of Bergen, Essex, Hudson, Middlesex, Morris, Passaic, Somerset, and Union) and New York (counties of Bronx, Columbia, Delaware, Dutchess, Kings, Nassau, New York, Orange, Putnam, Queens, Richmond, Rockland, Suffolk, Sullivan, Ulster, and Westchester)	Rm. 37–130, 26 Federal Plz., New York, NY 10278–0044
PHILADELPHIA—Delaware, Maryland (counties of Allegany, Anne Arundel, Baltimore, Baltimore City, Caroline, Carroll, Cecil, Dorchester, Garrett, Harford, Howard, Kent, Queen Annes, Somerset, Talbot, Washington, Wicomico, and Worcester), New Jersey (counties of Atlantic, Burlington, Camden, Cape May, Cumberland, Gloucester, Hunterdon, Mercer, Monmouth, Ocean, Salem, Sussex, and Warren), Pennsylvania (all counties except Mercer), West Virginia (all counties except Boone, Brooke, Cabell, Hancock, Lincoln, Logan, Marshall, McDowell, Mercer, Mingo, Ohio, Wayne, and Wyoming)	105 S. 7th St., Philadelphia, PA 19106–3395
SEATTLE—Alaska, California (counties of Alameda, Alpine, Amadore, Butte, Calaveras, Colusa, Contra Costa, Del Norte, El Dorado, Glenn, Humboldt, Lake, Lassen, Marin, Mendocino, Modoc, Mono, Napa, Nevada, Placer, Plumas, Sacramento, San Francisco, San Joaquin, San Mateo, Santa Clara, Santa Cruz, Shasta, Sierra, Siskiyou, Solano, Sonoma, Stanislaus, Sutter, Tehama, Trinity, Tuolumne, Yolo, Yuba), Idaho, Nevada (all counties except Clark and Nye), Oregon, and Washington	Suite 500, 101 Stewart St., Seattle, WA 98101–1098
DATA PREPARATION DIVISION	1202 E. 10th St., Jeffersonville, IN 47132
PERSONAL CENSUS SEARCH UNIT	P.O. Box 1545, Jeffersonville, IN 47131
HAGERSTOWN COMPUTER–ASSISTED TELEPHONE INTERVIEWING CENTER	319 E. Antietam St., Hagerstown, MD 21740–5789
TUCSON COMPUTER–ASSISTED TELEPHONE INTERVIEWING CENTER	Suite 151, 6363 S. Country Club Rd., Tucson, AZ 85706–5906

For further information, contact the Public Information Office, Bureau of the Census, Department of Commerce, Washington, DC 20233. Phone, 301–457–2794.

Bureau of Economic Analysis

[For the Bureau of Economic Analysis statement of organization, see the *Federal Register* of Dec. 29, 1980, 45 FR 85496]

The Bureau of Economic Analysis (BEA) is the Nation's economic accountant—integrating and interpreting a variety of source data to draw a complete and consistent picture of the U.S. economy. BEA's economic accounts provide information on such key issues as economic growth, regional development, and the Nation's position in the world economy.

The national income and product accounts—featuring gross domestic product—provide a quantitative view of the production, distribution, and use of the Nation's output. BEA also prepares estimates of the Nation's tangible wealth and input-output tables that show how industries interact. In addition, BEA maintains a system of leading, coincident, and lagging indicators to track business cycles.

The regional economic accounts provide estimates of personal income, population, and employment for regions, States, and metropolitan areas. BEA prepares estimates of gross state product and projections of regional economic activity.

The international economic accounts encompass U.S. international transactions (balance of payments) with foreign countries and the international investment position of the United States. BEA provides survey-based data on foreign direct investment in the United States and U.S. direct investment abroad.

For further information, contact the Public Information Office, Bureau of Economic Analysis, Department of Commerce, Washington, DC 20230. Phone, 202–606–9900. Fax, 202–606–5310.

Bureau of Export Administration

[For the Bureau of Export Administration statement of organization, see the *Federal Register* of June 7, 1988, 53 FR 20881]

The Bureau of Export Administration was established as a separate agency within the Department of Commerce on October 1, 1987, to separate the functions of export promotion and export control as mandated by the Export Administration Act, as amended (50 U.S.C. app. 2401 *et seq.*).

The Bureau directs the Nation's export control policy. Major functions include processing license applications, conducting foreign availability studies to determine when products should be decontrolled, and enforcing U.S. export control laws.

Export Administration   This office oversees export licensing, technology and policy analysis, economic security and nonproliferation issues, and foreign availability determinations. These activities are instrumental in reducing processing time for granting export licenses and in keeping the list of controlled technology consistent with

current risks. This office also works with our allies in seeking stronger, more uniform ways of controlling strategic exports.

Export Enforcement   This office investigates breaches of U.S. export control laws and analyzes export intelligence to assess diversion risks. In addition, this office administers and enforces the antiboycott provisions of the Export Administration Act.

Field Offices—Bureau of Export Administration

Field Area	Address
Boston, MA	Rm. 350, 10 Causeway St., 02222
Dallas, TX	Rm. 622, 525 Griffin St., 75202
Des Plaines, IL	Suite 300, 2400 E. Devon St., 60018
Fort Lauderdale, FL ...	Suite 1260, 200 E. Lasolas Blvd., 33301
Irvine, CA	Suite 310, 2601 Main St., 92714
Newport Beach, CA ...	Suite 345, 3300 Irvine Ave., 92660
Portland, OR	Rm. 241, 121 SW. Salmon St., 97204
San Jose, CA	Suite 250, 96 N. 3d St., 95112–5519
Santa Clara, CA	Suite 226, 5201 Great America Pky., 95054
Springfield, VA	Rm. 201, 8001 Forbes Pl., 22161
Staten Island, NY	Teleport II, 2 Teleport Dr., 10311

For further information, contact the Bureau of Export Administration, Office of Public Affairs, Room 3895, Fourteenth Street and Constitution Avenue NW., Washington, DC 20230. Phone, 202–482–2721.

Economic Development Administration

The Economic Development Administration (EDA) was created in 1965 under the Public Works and Economic Development Act (42 U.S.C. 3121) as part of an effort to target Federal resources to economically distressed areas and to help develop local economies in the United States. EDA was mandated to assist rural and urban communities that were outside the mainstream economy and that, as a result, lagged in economic development, industrial growth, and personal income.

EDA's economic development assistance programs (EDAP's) are carried out through a network of headquarters and regional personnel. EDA provides grants for public works and development facilities, planning and coordination, defense conversion, and other financial assistance that help to reduce substantial and persistent unemployment in economically distressed areas.

Public works and development facilities grants support infrastructure projects that foster the establishment or expansion of industrial and commercial businesses, supporting the retention and creation of jobs.

Planning grants support the design and implementation of effective economic development policies and programs, by local development organizations, in States and communities.

Technical assistance grants provide for local feasibility and industry studies, management and operational assistance, natural resource development, and export promotion. In addition, EDA funds a network of university centers that provides technical assistance.

Research, evaluation, and demonstration funds are used to support studies about the causes of economic distress and to seek solutions to counteract and prevent such problems.

Economic readjustment grants help communities adjust to a gradual erosion or sudden dislocation of their local economic structure.

Defense conversion grants assist communities adversely affected by Department of Defense base closures and defense contract cutbacks, as well as Department of Energy realignments, by providing development tools that can be effectively and easily implemented.

The Trade Adjustment Assistance Program provides technical assistance to certified firms and industries which have been economically injured by the impact of decreased imports. Comprehensive technical assistance is provided through the Department's wide-ranging network of assistance centers.

Regional Offices—Economic Development Administration

Region	Address
ATLANTA, GA	Suite 1820, 401 W. Peachtree St. NW., 30308–3510
Alabama	Rm. 134, 474 S. Court St., Montgomery, AL 36104
Florida	Rm. 423, 80 N. Hughey Ave., Orlando, FL 32801
Georgia	Suite 1820, 401 W. Peachtree St. NW., Atlanta, GA 30308–3510
Kentucky	Rm. 200, 771 Corporate Dr., Lexington, KY 40503–5477
Mississippi	Rm. 221, 100 W. Capitol St., Jackson, MS 39269
North Carolina	Rm. 128, 300 Fayetteville St. Mall, P.O. Box 2522, Raleigh, NC 27601
South Carolina	Rm. 840, Strom Thurmond Federal Bldg., Columbia, SC 29201
Tennessee	261 Cumberland Bend Dr., Nashville, TN 37228
AUSTIN, TX	Suite 201, 611 E. 6th St., 78701
Arkansas	Rm. 2500, 700 W. Capitol St., Little Rock, AR 72201
Louisiana	Rm. 104, 412 N. 4th St., Baton Rouge, LA 70802–5523
New Mexico	P.O. Box 2662, 120 S. Federal Pl., Santa Fe, NM 87501
Oklahoma	Suite 148, 5500 N. Western, Oklahoma City, OK 73118–4011
Texas	Suite 201, 611 E. 6th St., Austin, TX 78701
CHICAGO, IL	Suite 855, 111 N. Canal, 60606–7204
Illinois	Suite 204, 509 W. Capitol St., Springfield, IL 62704
Indiana	Rm. 402, 46 E. Ohio St., Indianapolis, IN 46204
Michigan	Rm. 1018, 100 N. Warren Ave., Saginaw, MI 48606–0667
Minnesota	Rm. 104, 515 W. 1st St., Duluth, MN 55802
Ohio	Rm. 607, 200 N. High St., Columbus, OH 43214
Wisconsin	Rm. 202, 505 S. Dewey St., Eau Claire, WI 54701
DENVER, CO	Suite 670, 1244 Speer Blvd., 80204

Regional Offices—Economic Development Administration—Continued

Region	Address
Colorado and Kansas	Rm. 632, 1244 Speer Blvd., Denver, CO 80204
Iowa	Rm. 593A, 210 Walnut St., Des Moines, IA 50309
Missouri	Rm. 8308H, 1222 Spruce St., St. Louis, MO 63103
Montana	Rm. 196, Federal Bldg., Helena, MT 59626
North Dakota	P.O. Box 1911, Bismarck, ND 58501
South Dakota and Nebraska	Rm. 219, Federal Bldg., Pierre, SD 57501
Utah and Wyoming	125 S. State St., Salt Lake City, UT 84138
PHILADELPHIA, PA	105 S. 7th St., 19106
Connecticut and Rhode Island	450 Main St., Hartford, CT 06103
Maine	Rm. 410–D, 40 Western Ave., Augusta, ME 04330
Maryland, Delaware, and District of Columbia.	2d Fl., 2568 Riva Rd., Annapolis, MD 21401
Massachusetts	Rm. 420, 10 Causeway St., Boston, MA 02222–1036
New Hampshire and Vermont	Suite 209, 143 N. Main St., Concord, NH 03301
New Jersey	Rm. 703, 44 S. Clinton Ave., Trenton, NJ 08609
New York	Suite 104, 620 Erie Blvd. W., Syracuse, NY 13204
Pennsylvania	1933A New Bernick Hwy., Bloomsburg, PA 17815
Puerto Rico and Virgin Islands	Rm. 620, Federal Office Bldg., 150 Carlos Chardon, Hato Rey, PR 00918–1738
Virginia	Rm. 8002, 400 N. 8th St., Richmond, VA 23240
West Virginia	Rm. 305, 550 Eagan St., Charleston, WV 25301
SEATTLE, WA	Rm. 1856, 915 2d Ave., 98174
Alaska	Rm. G–80, 605 W. 4th Ave., Anchorage, AK 99501–7594
Arizona	Rm. 3406, 230 N. 1st Ave., Phoenix, AZ 85025
California	Rm. 11105, 11000 Wilshire Blvd., Los Angeles, CA 90024
	Suite A, 1345 J St., Sacramento, CA 95814
	Suite B, 1345 J St., Sacramento, CA 95814
Hawaii, Guam, American Samoa, Marshall Islands, Micronesia, and Northern Marianas.	P.O. Box 50264, Honolulu, HI 96850
Idaho	Rm. 441, 304 N. 8th St., Boise, ID 83702
Oregon	Suite 244, 121 SW. Salmon St., Portland, OR 97204
Washington	Rm. 1856, 915 2d Ave., Seattle, WA 98174

For further information, contact the Economic Development Administration, Department of Commerce, Washington, DC 20230. Phone, 202–482–5112. Fax, 202–482–0995.

International Trade Administration

[For the International Trade Administration statement of organization, see the *Federal Register* of Jan. 25, 1980, 45 FR 6148]

The International Trade Administration was established on January 2, 1980, by the Secretary of Commerce to promote world trade and to strengthen the international trade and investment position of the United States.

The Administration is headed by the Under Secretary for International Trade, who coordinates all issues concerning import administration, international economic policy and programs, and trade development. It is responsible for nonagricultural trade operations of the U.S. Government and supports the trade policy negotiation efforts of the U.S. Trade Representative.

International Economic Policy The Assistant Secretary for International

Economic Policy advises on the analysis, formulation, and implementation of international economic policies of a bilateral, multilateral, or regional nature. Reporting to the Assistant Secretary are five Deputy Assistant Secretaries (for Europe; the Western Hemisphere; Asia and the Pacific; Africa and the Near East; and Japan) who have responsibility for trade and investment issues with particular countries and regions of the world. In addition, there is a Deputy Assistant Secretary for International Economic Policy who has responsibility for multilateral affairs and for overall policy coordination.

Import Administration The Assistant Secretary for Import Administration defends American industry against injurious and unfair trade practices by administering efficiently, fairly, and in a manner consistent with U.S. international trade obligations the antidumping and countervailing duty laws of the United States; the machine tool arrangements with Japan and Taiwan under the President's Machine Tool Program; and the U.S.-Japan Semiconductor Agreement. The Assistant Secretary ensures the proper administration of foreign trade zones and advises the Secretary on establishment of new zones; and administers programs governing watch assemblies, and other statutory import programs.

Trade Development The Assistant Secretary for Trade Development advises on international trade and investment policies pertaining to U.S. industrial sectors, carries out programs to strengthen domestic export competitiveness, and promotes U.S. industry's increased participation in international markets. The Assistant Secretary manages an integrated Trade Development Program that includes industry analysis and trade promotion organized by industry sectors. Deputy Assistant Secretaries for Technology and Aerospace Industries; Basic Industries; Service Industries and Finance; Textiles, Apparel and Consumer Goods Industries; and Environmental Technologies Exports report to the Assistant Secretary.

U.S. and Foreign Commercial Service The Assistant Secretary and Director General of the U.S. and Foreign Commercial Service develops, produces, markets, and manages an effective line of high-quality products and services geared to the marketing information needs of the U.S. exporting and international business community and manages the delivery of Administration programs through 47 domestic offices and U.S. export assistance centers located in the United States and 132 posts located in 68 countries throughout the world. The Assistant Secretary and Director General supports overseas trade promotion events; manages a variety of export promotion services and products; promotes U.S. products and services throughout the world market; conducts conferences and seminars in the United States; assists State and private-sector organizations on export financing; and promotes the export of U.S. fish by working with the domestic fishing industry and the National Oceanic and Atmospheric Administration.

Domestic Offices—International Trade Administration

Location	Address	Director	Telephone
Anchorage, AK	World Trade Ctr., 421 W. 1st St., 99501	Charles Becker	907–271–6237
Atlanta, GA	4360 Chamblee-Dunwoody Rd., 30341	George T. Norton, Jr.	404–452–9101
Baltimore, MD	Suite 2432, World Trade Ctr., 401 Pratt St., 21202	Roger Fortner	410–962–4539
Birmingham, AL	950 22d St. N., 35203	Patrick Wall	205–731–1331
Boston, MA	Suite 307, World Trade Ctr., Commonwealth Pier Area, 02210.	Francis J. O'Connor	617–565–8563
Buffalo, NY	Rm. 1312, 111 W. Huron St., 14202	George Buchanan	716–846–4191
Charleston, WV	Suite 807, 405 Capitol St., 25301	W. Davis Coale	312–353–8040
Chicago, IL	Suite 2440, Xerox Ctr., 55 W. Monroe St., 60603	Brad Dunderman	312–353–4450
Cincinnati, OH	9504 Federal Office Bldg., 550 Main St., 45202	John M. McCasli	513–684–2944
Cleveland, OH	Suite 700, Bank One Ctr., 600 Superior Ave., 44114	Toby T. Zettler	216–522–4750
Columbia, SC	Suite 172, 1835 Assembly St., 29201	Ann H. Watts	803–765–5345
Dallas, TX	2050 N. Stemmons Fwy., S. 170, 75258	(Vacancy)	214–767–0542
Denver, CO	Suite 680, 1625 Broadway, 80202	Neil Hesse	303–844–6622
Des Moines, IA	Rm. 817, 210 Walnut St., 50309	Randall J. LaBounty	515–284–4222
Detroit, MI	1140 McNamara Bldg., 477 Michigan Ave., 48226	Dean Peterson	313–226–3650
Greensboro, NC	Suite 400, 400 W. Market St., 27401	Samuel P. Troy	910–333–5345
Hartford, CT	Rm. 610–B, 450 Main St., 06103	Carl Jacobsen	203–240–3530
Honolulu, HI	P.O. Box 50026, 300 Ala Moana Blvd., 96850	George Dolan	808–541–1782
Houston, TX	Suite 1160, 1 Allen Ctr., 500 Dallas St., 77002	James Cook	713–229–2578
Indianapolis, IN	Suite 106, Pennwood One, 11405 N. Pennsylvania St., 46302.	Andrew W. Thress	317–582–2300
Jackson, MS	Suite 310, 201 W. Capitol St., 39201–2005	Mark E. Spinney	601–965–4388
Kansas City, MO	Rm. 635, 601 E. 12th St., 64106	Rick Villalobos	816–426–3141
Little Rock, AR	Suite 700, 425 W. Capitol Ave., 72201	Lon J. Hardin	501–324–5794
Los Angeles, CA	Rm. 9200, 11000 Wilshire Blvd., 90024	Steve Morrison	310–235–7104
Louisville, KY	Rm. 634B, 601 E. Broadway, 40202	John Autin	502–582–5066
Miami, FL	Suite 617, P.O. Box 590570, 5600 NW. 38th St., 33166	Peter B. Alois	305–526–7425
Milwaukee, WI	Rm. 596, 517 E. Wisconsin Ave., 53202	Paul D. Churchill	414–297–3473
Minneapolis, MN	Rm. 108, 110 S. 4th St., 55401	Ronald E. Kramer	612–348–1638

Domestic Offices—International Trade Administration—Continued

Location	Address	Director	Telephone
Nashville, TN	Suite 1114, Parkway Towers, 404 James Robertson Pky., 37219.	James Charlet	615–736–5161
New Orleans, LA	Rm. 1043, Hale Boggs Federal Bldg., 501 Magazine St., 70130.	Paul K. Rees	504–589–6546
New York, NY	Rm. 3718, 26 Federal Plz., 10278	Joel Barkan	212–264–0634
Oklahoma City, OK	6601 Broadway Extension, 73116	Ronald L. Wilson	405–231–5302
Omaha, NE	11133 O St., 68137	(Vacancy)	402–221–3664
Philadelphia, PA	Suite 201, 600 Americas Ave., King of Prussia, 19406 .	Robert Kistler	610–962–4980
Phoenix, AZ	9th Fl., 2901 N. Central Ave., 85025	Frank Woods	602–640–2513
Pittsburgh, PA	Rm. 2002, 1000 Liberty Ave., 15222	John McCartney	412–644–2850
Portland, OR	Suite 242, 1 World Trade Ctr., 121 SW. Salmon St., 97204.	Denny Barnes	503–326–3001
Reno, NV	1755 E. Plumb Lane, No. 152, 89502	James K. Hellwig	702–784–5203
Richmond, VA	Suite 550, 700 Centre, 704 E. Franklin St., 23219	Philip A. Ouzts	804–771–2246
Salt Lake City, UT	Suite 105, 324 S. State St., 84111	Stephen P. Smoot	801–524–5116
San Diego, CA	Suite 230, 6363 Greenwich Dr., 92122	Mary Delmege	619–557–5395
San Francisco, CA	14th Fl., 250 Montgomery St., 94104	Betty D. Neuhart	415–705–2300
San Juan, PR	Rm. G–55, Federal Bldg., Hato Rey, 00918	J. Enrique Vilella	809–766–5555
Savannah, GA	Rm. A–107, 120 Barnard St., 31401	Barbara Prieto	912–652–4204
Seattle, WA	Suite 290, 3131 Elliott Ave., 98121	Lisa Kjaer-Schade	206–553–5615
St. Louis, MO	Suite 303, 8182 Maryland Ave., 63105	Sandra Gerley	314–425–3302
Trenton, NJ	Suite 100, Bldg. 6, 3131 Princeton Pike, 08648	Rod Stuart	609–989–2100

For further information, contact the International Trade Administration, Department of Commerce, Washington, DC 20230. Phone, 202–482–3809.

Minority Business Development Agency

[For the Minority Business Development Agency statement of organization, see the *Federal Register* of Mar. 17, 1972, 37 FR 5650, as amended]

The Minority Business Development Agency, formerly the Office of Minority Business Enterprise, was established by the Secretary of Commerce on November 1, 1979, and operates under the authority of Executive Order 11625 of October 13, 1971. The Agency develops and coordinates a national program for minority business enterprise.

The Agency was created to assist minority businesses in achieving effective and equitable participation in the American free enterprise system and in overcoming social and economic disadvantages that have limited their participation in the past. The Agency provides national policies and leadership in forming and strengthening a partnership of business, industry, and government with the Nation's minority businesses.

Management and technical assistance is provided to minority firms on request, primarily through a network of Minority Business Development Centers funded by the Agency, as well as Minority Enterprise Growth Assistance (MEGA) Centers. Specialized business assistance is available to minority firms or potential entrepreneurs.

The Agency promotes and coordinates the efforts of other Federal agencies in assisting or providing market opportunities for minority business. It coordinates opportunities for minority firms in the private sector. Through such public and private cooperative activities, the Agency promotes the participation of Federal, State, and local governments, and business and industry in directing resources for the development of strong minority businesses.

Regional Offices—Minority Business Development Agency

Region	Address	Director	Telephone
Atlanta, GA	Suite 1930, 401 W. Peachtree St. NW., 30308–3516 ...	Robert Henderson	404–730–3300
Chicago, IL	Suite 1440, 55 E. Monroe St., 60603	David Vega	312–353–0182
Dallas, TX	Suite 7B23, 1100 Commerce St., 75242	John Iglehart	214–767–8001

Regional Offices—Minority Business Development Agency—Continued

Region	Address	Director	Telephone
New York, NY	Suite 37–20, 26 Federal Plz., 10278	Heyward Davenport ...	212–264–3262
San Francisco, CA	Rm. 1280, 221 Main St., 94105	Melda Cabrera	415–974–9597

District Offices—Minority Business Development Agency

District	Address	Officer	Telephone
Boston, MA	Rm. 418, 10 Causeway St., 02222–1041	Rochelle K. Schwartz ..	617–565–6850
El Monte, CA	Suite 455, 9660 Flair Dr., 91713	Joseph Galindo	818–453–8636
Miami, FL	Rm. 928, 51 SW. 1st Ave., 33130	Rodolfo Suarez	305–536–5054
Philadelphia, PA	Rm. 10128, 600 Arch St., 19106	Alfonso C. Jackson	215–597–9236

For further information, contact the Office of External Affairs, Minority Business Development Agency, Department of Commerce, Washington, DC 20230. Phone, 202–482–4547.

National Oceanic and Atmospheric Administration

U.S. Department of Commerce, Washington, DC 20230
Phone, 202–482–2985

[For the National Oceanic and Atmospheric Administration statement of organization, see the *Federal Register* of Feb. 13, 1978, 43 FR 6128]

The National Oceanic and Atmospheric Administration was formed on October 3, 1970, by Reorganization Plan No. 4 of 1970 (5 U.S.C. app.). Its principal functions are authorized by title 15, chapter 9, United States Code (National Weather Service); title 33, chapter 17, United States Code (National Ocean Survey); and title 16, chapter 9, United States Code (National Marine Fisheries Service).

The Administration's mission is to explore, map, and chart the global ocean and its living resources and to manage, use, and conserve those resources; to describe, monitor, and predict conditions in the atmosphere, ocean, Sun, and space environment; to issue warnings against impending destructive natural events; to assess the consequences of inadvertent environmental modification over several scales of time; and to manage and disseminate long-term environmental information.

Among its principal activities, the Administration reports the weather of the United States and its possessions and provides weather forecasts to the general public; issues warnings against such destructive natural events as hurricanes, tornadoes, floods, and tsunamis; and provides services in support of aviation, marine activities, agriculture, forestry, urban air-quality control, and other weather-sensitive activities. The Administration also monitors and reports all non-Federal weather modification activities conducted in the United States.

The Administration conducts an integrated program of management, research, and services related to the protection and rational use of living marine resources and their habitats, and protects marine mammals and endangered marine species. It prepares and issues nautical and aeronautical charts, provides the Nation's precise geodetic surveys, and conducts broad research programs in marine and atmospheric sciences, solar-terrestrial physics, and experimental meteorology, including weather modification. The Administration also predicts tides, currents, and the state of the oceans; conducts research and development aimed at providing alternatives to ocean dumping; and develops sound national policies in the areas of ocean mining and energy. It provides Federal leadership in promoting wise and balanced management of the Nation's coastal zone.

In addition, the Administration provides satellite observations of the environment by operating a national environmental satellite system; and conducts an integrated program of research and services relating to the oceans and inland waters, the lower and upper atmosphere, space environment, and the Earth to increase understanding of the geophysical environment. It acquires, stores, and disseminates worldwide environmental data through a system of meteorological, oceanographic, geodetic, and seismological data centers.

The Administration also administers and directs the oceanic research programs by providing grants to institutions for marine research, education, and advisory services; develops a system of data buoys for automatically obtaining and disseminating marine environmental data; and promotes the development of technology to meet future needs of the marine community.

Field Organization—National Oceanic and Atmospheric Administration

Organization	Address	Director	Telephone
NATIONAL WEATHER SERVICE			
Alaska region	Rm. 507, No. 23, 222 W. 7th Ave., Anchorage, AK 99513–7575.	Richard J. Hutcheon	907–271–5136
Central region	Rm. 1836, 601 E. 12th St., Kansas City, MO 64106–2897.	Richard P. Augulis	816–426–5400
Eastern region	Airport Corporate Ctr., 630 Johnson Ave., Bohemia, NY 11716.	John T. Forsing, *Acting*	516–244–0100
National Meteorological Center.	5200 Auth Rd., Camp Springs, MD 20746.	Ronald D. McPherson	301–763–8016
Pacific region	P.O. Box 50027, Honolulu, HI 96850	Richard H. Hagermeyer	808–541–1641
Southern region	Rm. 10A26, 819 Taylor St., Fort Worth, TX 76102.	Harry S. Hassel	817–334–2651
Western region	P.O. Box 11188, Federal Bldg., Salt Lake City, UT 84147–0188.	Thomas D. Potter	801–524–5122
NATIONAL MARINE FISHERIES SERVICE			
Alaska region	P.O. Box 21668, Juneau, AK 99802–1668.	Steven Pennoyer	907–586–7221
Northwest region	7600 Sand Point Way NE., BIN C15700, Bldg. 1, Seattle, WA 98115–0070.	William W. Stelle, Jr.	206–526–6150
Northeast region	1 Blackburn Dr., Gloucester, MA 01930	Allen Peterson, *Acting*	508–281–9250
Southeast region	9721 Executive Center Dr. N., St. Petersburg, FL 33702.	Andrew J. Kemmerer	813–570–5301
Southwest region	Suite 4200, 501 W. Ocean Blvd., Long Beach, CA 90802.	Hilda Diaz-Soltero	310–980–4001
NATIONAL ENVIRONMENTAL SATELLITE, DATA, AND INFORMATION SERVICE			
National Climatic Data Center	Federal Bldg., Asheville, NC 28801–2696.	Kenneth D. Hadeen	704–259–0476
National Geophysical Data Center.	RL–3, 325 Broadway, Boulder, CO 80303–3328.	Michael Chinnery	303–497–6215
National Oceanographic Data Center.	1825 Connecticut Ave. NW., Washington, DC 20235.	Bruce C. Douglas	202–606–4594
NATIONAL OCEAN SERVICE			
Pacific office	7600 Sandy Point Way NE., Seattle, WA 98115–0070.	David M. Kennedy	206–526–6317
Marine sanctuaries and reserves.	1305 East-West Hwy., Silver Spring, MD 20910.	James P. Lawless, *Acting*	301–713–3125
OFFICE OF OCEANIC AND ATMOSPHERIC RESEARCH			
Forecast Systems Laboratory	325 Broadway, Boulder, CO 80303	Alexander E. MacDonald	303–497–6378
Space Environmental Laboratory.	325 Broadway, Boulder, CO 80303	Ernest Hildner	303–497–3311
Aeronomy Laboratory	325 Broadway, Boulder, CO 80303	Daniel L. Albritton	303–497–5785
Environmental Technology Laboratory.	325 Broadway, Boulder, CO 80303	Steven F. Clifford	303–497–6291
Climate Monitoring and Diagnostics Laboratory.	325 Broadway, Boulder, CO 80303	E. Ferguson	303–497–6966
Air Resources Laboratories ..	1335 East-West Hwy., Silver Spring, MD 20910.	Bruce Hicks	301–713–0684
Atlantic Oceanographic and Meteorological Laboratories.	4301 Rickenbacher Causeway, Virginia Key, Miami, FL 33149.	Hugo F. Bezdek	305–361–4300

Field Organization—National Oceanic and Atmospheric Administration—Continued

Organization	Address	Director	Telephone
Great Lakes Environmental Research Laboratory.	2205 Commonwealth Blvd., Ann Arbor, MI 48105–1593.	Alfred M. Beeton	313–741–2244
Pacific Marine Environmental Laboratory.	7600 Sand Point Way NE., Seattle, WA 98115–0070.	Eddie N. Bernard	206–526–6800
Geophysical Fluid Dynamics Laboratory.	P.O. Box 308, Princeton, NJ 08542	J.D. Mahlman	609–452–6502
National Severe Storms Laboratory.	1313 Halley Cir., Norman, OK 73069	Robert A. Maddox	405–366–0427
ADMINISTRATIVE SUPPORT CENTERS			
Central Administrative Support Center.	601 E. 12th St., Kansas City, MO 64106–2897.	Martha R. Lumpkin	816–426–2050
Eastern Administrative Support Center.	200 World Trade Ctr., Suite 201, Norfolk, VA 23510–1624.	Gerald R. Lucas	804–441–6864
Mountain Administrative Support Center.	325 Broadway, Boulder, CO 80303–3328.	Helen M. Crown, *Acting*	303–497–6370
Western Administrative Support Center.	7600 Sand Point Way NE., Seattle, WA 98115–0070.	Kelly C. Sandy	206–526–6026
NOAA CORPS OPERATIONS CENTERS			
Atlantic Marine Center	439 W. York St., Norfolk, VA 23510–1114.	Rear Adm. Freddie Jefferies	804–441–6776
Commissioned Personnel Center.	1315 East-West Hwy., Silver Spring, MD 20910.	Capt. Theodore Wyzewski	301–713–3475
Pacific Marine Center	1801 Fairview Ave. E., Seattle, WA 98102–3767.	Rear Adm. John C. Albright	206–442–7656

For further information, contact the Office of Public Affairs, National Oceanic and Atmospheric Administration, Department of Commerce, Washington, DC 20230. Phone, 202–482–4190.

National Telecommunications and Information Administration

[For the National Telecommunications and Information Administration statement of organization, see the *Federal Register* of June 5, 1978, 43 FR 24348]

The National Telecommunications and Information Administration (NTIA) was established in 1978 pursuant to Reorganization Plan No. 1 of 1977 (5 U.S.C. app.) and Executive Order 12046 of March 27, 1978 (3 CFR, 1978 Comp., p. 158), by combining the Office of Telecommunications Policy, Executive Office of the President, and the Department of Commerce's Office of Telecommunications to form a new agency reporting to the Secretary of Commerce. NTIA's functions are detailed in the National Telecommunications and Information Administration Organization Act (47 U.S.C. 901 *et. seq.*).

The Public Telecommunications Facilities Program (PTFP) was transferred to NTIA in 1979 from the Department of Health, Education, and Welfare pursuant to the Public Telecommunications Financing Act of 1978 (47 U.S.C. 390 *et seq.*), to take advantage of NTIA's technical and policy expertise. Also, NTIA is administering the National Endowment for Children's Educational Television under title 47 United States Code, section 394.

NTIA's principal responsibilities and functions include:

—serving as the principal executive branch adviser to the President on telecommunications and information policy;

—developing and presenting U.S. plans and policies at international communications conferences and related meetings;

—prescribing policies for and managing Federal use of the radio frequency spectrum, in accordance with Executive Order 12046, issued under section 305 of the Communications Act of 1934, as amended (47 U.S.C. 305);

—serving as the principal Federal telecommunications research and engineering laboratory, through NTIA's Institute for Telecommunication Sciences (ITS), headquartered in Boulder, Colorado;

—providing grants through the Telecommunications and Information Infrastructure Assistance Program for planning and demonstration projects to promote the goals of the development and widespread availability of advanced telecommunications technologies, to enhance the delivery of social services and generally serve the public interest, to promote access to government information and increase civic participation, and to support the development of an advanced nationwide telecommunications and information infrastructure;

—providing grants through the Public Telecommunications Facilities Program to extend delivery of public telecommunications services to U.S. citizens, to increase ownership and management by women and minorities, and to strengthen the capabilities of existing public broadcasting stations to provide telecommunications services; and

—providing grants through the National Endowment for Children's Educational Television to enhance the creation and production of educational television programming for children to develop fundamental intellectual skills.

For further information, contact the National Telecommunications and Information Administration, Department of Commerce, Washington, DC 20230. Phone, 202–482–1551.

Patent and Trademark Office

[For the Patent and Trademark Office statement of organization, see the *Federal Register* of Apr. 14, 1975, 40 FR 16707]

The patent system was established by Congress ". . . to promote the progress of . . . the useful arts. . ." under Article I, section 8, U.S. Constitution (title 35, United States Code: Patents). The registration of trademarks is based on the commerce clause of the U.S. Constitution (title 15 United States Code, chapter 22: Trademarks). The Patent and Trademark Office grants patents and registers trademarks to qualified applicants.

The Office examines applications for three kinds of patents: design patents (issued for 14 years), plant patents, and utility patents (issued for 17 years). Also, the Office issues Statutory Invention Registrations, which have the defensive but not the enforceable attributes of a patent. It also processes international applications for patents under the provisions of the Patent Cooperation Treaty, including, as of July 1, 1986, the examination provisions of chapter II of the Treaty.

About 107,000 patents were issued for fiscal year 1993 that provide inventors with exclusive rights to the results of their creative efforts. Patents and trademarks may be reviewed and searched in the Office and in over 78 patent and trademark depository libraries around the country. The patent system fosters innovation, investment in developing and marketing inventions, and prompt disclosure of technological information.

About 86,122 trademarks were registered for fiscal year 1993, and 6,182 trademark registrations were renewed. A trademark includes any distinctive word, name, symbol, device, or any combination thereof adopted and used, or intended to be used, by a manufacturer or merchant to identify his goods or services and distinguish them from those manufactured or sold by others. Trademarks, registered for 10 years, with renewal rights of equal term, are examined by the Office for compliance with various statutory requirements to prevent unfair competition and consumer deception.

In addition to the examination of patent and trademark applications, issuance of patents, and registration of trademarks, the Patent and Trademark Office:

—sells printed copies of issued patents and trademark registrations;

—records and indexes documents transferring ownership;

—maintains a scientific library and search files containing over 30 million documents, including U.S. and foreign patents and U.S. trademarks;

—provides search rooms for the public to research their applications;

—hears and decides appeals from prospective inventors and trademark applicants;

—participates in legal proceedings involving the issue of patents or registration of trademarks;

—advocates strengthening intellectual property protection worldwide;

—compiles the *Official Gazettes*, a weekly notice of patents issued and trademarks registered by the Office, including other information; and

—maintains a roster of patent agents and attorneys qualified and recognized to practice before the Office.

For further information, contact the Office of Public Affairs, Patent and Trademark Office, Washington, DC 20231. Phone, 703–305–8341. The Office's operations are located at 2121 Crystal Drive, Arlington, VA 22202.

Technology Administration

The Technology Administration was established by Congress in 1988 (15 U.S.C. 3704) and consists of the Office of Technology Policy (OTP), the National Institute of Standards and Technology (NIST), and the National Technical Information Service (NTIS). The Technology Administration is headed by the Under Secretary for Technology who serves as a principal advisor to the Secretary of Commerce and as the Department's spokesperson for science and technology issues.

The Technology Administration serves as the premier technology agency working with U.S. industry in addressing competitiveness, and in exercising leadership both within the Department of Commerce and governmentwide. It discharges this role through OTP by advocating coherent policies for maximizing the impact of technology on economic growth, through NIST by carrying out technology programs with U.S. industry, and through NTIS by disseminating technology information.

For further information, call 202–482–1575.

Office of Technology Policy

The primary role of the Office of Technology Policy is to offer assistance to private sector and government communities in advocating and pursuing policies that maximize the impact of technology on economic growth, and by exercising leadership to define the role of government in supporting U.S. industrial competitiveness in the post-cold war environment. OTP serves as a liaison to the private sector to identify barriers to the rapid commercialization of technology, elicits support for Administration civilian technology policies, and ensures that industry's interests are reflected in standards and technology agreements and civilian technology policy. OTP also assists Federal, State, and local officials, industry, and academic institutions in promoting the technological growth and competitiveness of the U.S. economy.

For further information, call 202–482–5687.

National Institute of Standards and Technology

The National Institute of Standards and Technology (NIST) assists industry in developing technology to improve product quality; modernizes manufacturing processes; ensures product reliability; and facilitates rapid commercialization of products based on new scientific discoveries.

NIST's primary mission is to promote U.S. economic growth by working with industry to develop and apply technology, measurements, and standards. It carries out this mission through four major programs:

—an Advanced Technology Program (ATP) that provides cost-shared awards to industry to develop high-risk technologies that can enable significant commercial advances;

—a grassroots Manufacturing Extension Partnership (MEP) that helps small and medium-sized companies to access regional and national sources of information, knowledge, and insight into the use of modern manufacturing and production technologies;

—a strong laboratory effort planned and implemented in cooperation with industry that focuses on infrastructural technologies such as measurements, standards, evaluated data, and test methods. Research is mainly performed in the areas of: electronics and electrical engineering, manufacturing engineering, chemical science and technology, physics, materials science and engineering, building and fire research, computer systems, and computing and applied mathematics; and

— a quality improvement program that is associated with the Malcolm Baldrige National Quality Award. The award recognizes quality achievements in the areas of manufacturing, service, and small business.

For further information, call 301–975–3058.

National Technical Information Service

The National Technical Information Service (NTIS) is the Nation's largest central clearinghouse and Governmentwide resource for scientific, technical, engineering, and other business-related information. NTIS acquires its information from U.S. government agencies and their contractors and grantees, as well as from foreign, primarily governmental, sources. NTIS is a self-supporting Federal agency

within the Technology Administration of the Department of Commerce.

NTIS' collection of information, exceeding 2.5 million works, covers current events, business and management studies, research and development, manufacturing, standards, translations of foreign works, foreign and domestic trade, general statistics, and more. Since the implementation of the American Technology Preeminence Act (ATPA), NTIS is able to offer an even more diverse and practical range of information. ATPA requires all Federal agencies to transfer, in a timely manner, unclassified scientific, technical, and engineering information resulting from federally funded research and development activities to NTIS. NTIS' multimedia products range from paper copy technical reports and periodicals to CD–ROM's, audiovisual products, computer software and electronic databases, and on-line services.

FedWorld® NTIS' electronic marketplace provides public access to thousands of government documents; connects to several hundred Federal on-line systems; and offers instant electronic delivery of selected products from NTIS. FedWorld® provides both dial-up and Internet access to information from numerous Government agencies and programs, at no charge to the public.

The *NTIS Preview Database* on FedWorld® contains titles entered into the NTIS collection within the last 30 days (approximately 7,000 new products each month). The database is a 30-day rolling window of citations updated semimonthly. Half of the citations are removed midmonth, and newer citations are added.

To connect to FedWorld®, set modem parity to none, data bits to 8, and stop bit to 1. Set terminal emulation to ANSI. Set duplex to full. Then set your communications software to dial FedWorld® at 703–321–FEDW. By Internet, telnet to fedworld.gov or file transfer protocol to ftp.fedWorld.gov. For World Wide Web services, point your Web browser to open the URL http://www.fedworld.gov. For more information or technical assistance, please call the FedWorld® help desk at 703–487–4608.

NTIS Database   The *NTIS Bibliographic Database* is available on CD–ROM or on line through commercial vendors listed in the free *NTIS Products and Services Catalog* (PR–827NEB). The database is also available to research and development organizations and agencies on direct lease. For more information, call 703–487–4929.

Subject Area Selections   NTIS has a large collection of information on the environment—including handbooks and guides, regulations and updates, economic studies, and applied technology. NTIS is the exclusive distributor of Superfund documents. For the free catalog *Environment Highlights,* ask for PR–868NEB.

NTIS distributes health care materials such as the National Library of Medicine's *Grateful Med* and *MeSH* search tools, as well as an extensive range of other technical reports in the health field. Request your free catalog on health-related products, *Health Care Highlights* (PR–745NEB).

Business Highlights catalog (PR–985NEB) provides product listings for data necessary for decisionmaking in today's business market. As part of its expansion in the business subject area, NTIS is rapidly increasing its collection of overseas business information.

NTIS Alerts are published twice each month and contain summaries of the latest Government-sponsored projects and their findings and are available in more than 30 broad subject areas. NTIS also prints customized *Alerts* from over 150 available subtopics to suit recipients' needs. For a free catalog, call 703–487–4650 and request PR–797NEB.

Published Searches are exclusively prepared bibliographies containing 50–250 of the latest abstracts of research reports and studies available from a preselected individual database. With each order, a completely new and updated bibliography is produced. For more information on *Published Searches,* call 703–487–4650 and request PR–186NEB.

Government Reports Announcements & Index Journal announces approximately 80,000 research and development and engineering results annually. Its comprehensive coverage provides thousands of entries within each issue making it a valuable, multidisciplinary current awareness resource. This item is available by subscription and is published twice a month. Call 703–487–4630 to receive answers to your inquiries on this product.

Technology Transfer   NTIS provides technology transfer services such as patent licensing and publishes the *Directory of Federal Laboratory and Technology Resources.* This valuable directory guides you to hundreds of Federal agencies, laboratories, and engineering centers willing to share their expertise to aid in your research. Request flyer PR–746NEB for more details on this product.

NTIS also produces the *Federal Research in Progress (FEDRIP) Database* that summarizes more than 150,000 ongoing U.S. government research and development and engineering project summaries. FEDRIP is available for lease by calling 703–487–4929; it is also available online through commercial vendors. For a free search guide, call the NTIS Sales Desk at 703–487–4650 and request PR–847NEB.

Global Competitive Intelligence   As part of its expansion in the business subject area, NTIS is rapidly increasing its collection of information from international sources. The new *Foreign Technology Update,* a twice-monthly publication, tracks scientific and technical developments from around the world. To receive information on this subscription product, please call 703–487–4630. A publication such as the *International Trade Administration Bibliography* (PB93–218360NEB), with more than 1,000 competitive intelligence-related reports and studies, is also available. Call the NTIS Sales Desk at 703–487–4650 for price quotes and more information.

NTIS makes available the Japanese Online Information System (JOIS) through an agreement with the Japan Center of Science and Technology. To receive information on searching JOIS, call 703–487–4819. To help you keep up with technical information from Japan, NTIS, in conjunction with the Department's Japan Technology Program, has updated popular Japanese directories: request PR–825NEB for more information.

Continuous Acquisition and Life-Cycle Support Information Center NTIS operates the Continuous Acquisition and Life-Cycle Support (CALS) Information Center with support of the Office of the Secretary of Defense to promote the widespread understanding, acceptance, and use of CALS principles through an effective flow of CALS-related technical information. The Center provides a public source of CALS, Electronic Commerce, Electronic Data Interchange, and related information including standards and specifications, technical reports, training materials, computer datafiles, and the CALS Electronic Bulletin Board system (available on FedWorld®). To receive the free brochure *CALS Information Services from NTIS,* request PR–898NEB.

Federal Computer Products Center NTIS provides computer software and datafiles on tape, diskette, and CD–ROM, as well as video tapes. Call the NTIS Sales Desk at 703–487–4650; or fax your requests to 703–321–8547 to receive free product information on the *Directory of U.S. Government Software for Mainframes and Microcomputers* (PR–261NEB) and the *Directory of U.S. Government Datafiles* (PR–629NEB).

National Audiovisual Center The National Audiovisual Center (NAC) consolidates most of the U.S. Government's activity in the duplication and distribution of audio, visual, and multimedia products. The collection contains more than 9,000 Government-produced audiovisual products in a wide range of formats. The range of subject areas includes foreign language training, occupational safety and health, law enforcement training, fire service training, history, science, medical training, business and economics, agriculture, and natural resources. For the free *Media Resource Catalog* that lists NAC's most popular titles, call the NTIS Sales Desk at 703–487–4650 and ask for PR–1001NEB.

Joint Ventures NTIS works with private industry to build strategic alliances. These include the use of contracts or cooperative agreements with the private sector, individuals, or other organizations. The objective is to create new information products for U.S. Government-produced data and software. NTIS is seeking partnerships to open new channels of sales and distribution. Call 703–487–4785 for more information about joint ventures.

Free NTIS Catalogs To obtain copies of the catalogs or brochures listed above, or to receive a free copy of the *NTIS Catalog of Products and Services* (PR–827NEB), call the NTIS Sales Desk at 703–487–4650, or send your request by fax to 703–321–8547.

United States Travel and Tourism Administration

[For the United States Travel and Tourism Administration statement of organization, see the *Federal Register* of June 25, 1982, 47 FR 27594]

The United States Travel and Tourism Administration was established by the National Tourism Policy Act of 1981, as amended (22 U.S.C. 2121 note).

The Administration is headed by the Under Secretary of Commerce for Travel and Tourism who advises the Secretary of Commerce on the formulation and execution of policy affecting the American tourism industry and its contribution to the Nation's economic development and international trade objectives. The Administration also maintains trade development, trade policy, and statistical research programs designed to increase the American travel industry's awareness of the export market, facilitate the entry of medium- and small-sized American travel companies into the market, and eliminate barriers to market entry for those companies. The Administration maintains eight regional offices located in Frankfurt, London, Mexico City, Milan, Paris, Sydney, Tokyo, and Toronto; and an office servicing five South American markets located in Miami.

For further information, contact the United States Travel and Tourism Administration, Department of Commerce, Washington, DC 20230. Phone, 202–482–3811.

Sources of Information

Age and Citizenship Age search and citizenship information is available from the Personal Census Search Unit, Data Preparation Division, P.O. Box 1545, Jeffersonville, IN 47131. Phone, 812–285–5314.

Consumer Affairs Information is available to businesses and consumers regarding good business practices and complaint handling. Fact sheets on complaint handling are available in English and Spanish. Consumer bulletins describe consumer-related programs in the Commerce Department as well as in the Office's customer service plan. Write to the Office of Consumer Affairs, U.S. Department of Commerce, Washington, DC 20230. Phone, 202–482–5001; fax, 202–482–6007; and fax on demand, 202–501–1191.

Office of Economic Conversion Information The Office of Economic Conversion Information (OECI) is a clearinghouse for communities, businesses, and workers seeking to obtain information regarding defense adjustment and economic development. The OECI database contains descriptions and contact numbers of Federal, State, and local programs; guides and models for economic development; and many other related items.

OECI information can be accessed in six different ways: via phone, mail, Internet, electronic bulletin board, flash fax, and through CD–ROM at Federal depository libraries. For more information, write to: Office of Economic Conversion Information, Economic Development Administration, Department of Commerce, Washington, DC 20230. Phone, 1–800–345–1222; Internet address: ecix.doc.gov; electronic bulletin board, 1–800–352–2949.

Environment The National Oceanic and Atmospheric Administration monitors the conditions in the ocean, atmosphere, and Earth-Sun environment; prepares and issues weather warnings and forecasts; provides Federal leadership in managing the living resources of the sea and the Nation's coastal zone; ensures that marine mammals and endangered marine species are protected under the law; and provides worldwide environmental data and information products and services in the atmospheric, marine, solid earth, and solar terrestrial sciences. It also conducts research aimed at remote sensing of the physical environment and provides a variety of environmental quality control services, including those for urban airborne pollution control, estuarine water movement, and water resources management. Write to the Office of Public and Constituent Affairs, National Oceanic and Atmospheric Administration, Washington, DC 20230. Phone, 202–482–6090.

The Patent and Trademark Office has priority programs for the processing of applications for patents that could aid in materially enhancing the environment. Write to the Assistant Secretary and Commissioner of Patents and Trademarks, Office of Special Program Examination, Washington, DC 20231. Phone, 703–305–9282.

Field Employment
National Oceanic and Atmospheric Administration The Department of Commerce has field employment offices at the Western Administrative Support Center, Bin C15700, 7600 Sand Point Way NE., Seattle, WA 98115 (phone, 206–526–6053); the Mountain

Administrative Support Center, 325 Broadway, Boulder, CO 80303 (phone, 303–497–6305); the Central Administrative Support Center, 601 East Twelfth Street, Kansas City, MO 64106 (phone, 816–426–2056); and the Eastern Administrative Support Center, 200 World Trade Center, Norfolk, VA 23510–1624. Phone, 804–441–6516.

Office of Public Affairs

Publications   The titles of selected publications are printed below with the operating units responsible for their issuance. These and other publications dealing with a wide range of business, economic, environmental, scientific, and technical matters are announced in the weekly *Business Service Checklist,* which may be purchased from the Superintendent of Documents, Government Printing Office, Washington, DC 20402. Phone, 202–783–3238.

The Secretary's *Annual Report to Congress* and *Serving the Nation,* two publications which describe the missions, functions, and accomplishments of Commerce agencies and offices, are available by writing the Department of Commerce, Office of Public Affairs, Pennsylvania Avenue and 14th Street NW., Room 5610, Washington, DC, or by calling 202–219–3605 for the *Annual Report* and 202–482–4901 for *Serving the Nation.*

Further information on Commerce publications is available at any of the Department's International Trade Administration district offices.

Lists of Other Documents   Individuals with access to fax machines can dial 202–501–1191 *(Flash Facts)* to obtain lists of other publication contacts, Secretarial speeches and biographies, press releases, audiovisuals, Commerce bureau public affairs contacts, and Department programs by subject.

Bureau of the Census   *Census Catalog and Guide; Statistical Abstract of the U.S.; Historical Statistics of the United States, Colonial Times to 1970; County and City Data Book, 1988;* and *State and Metropolitan Area Data Book, 1991.*

Available from the Government Printing Office.

Bureau of Economic Analysis   Publications available from the Government Printing Office include the following:*Survey of Current Business; National Income and Product Accounts of the United States, 1929–88; Benchmark Input-Output Accounts of the United States, 1987; Local Area Personal Income, 1969–92;* and*Foreign Direct Investment in the United States: Establishment Data for Manufacturing, 1991.* Online access is available through the Commerce Department's Economic Bulletin Board and via Internet. For information, call STAT–USA on 202–482–1986. Additional information on BEA's programs, products, and services is found in the *User's Guide to BEA Information.* For a copy, write to BEA's Public Information Office, BE–53, Bureau of Economic Analysis, Department of Commerce, Washington, DC 20230; or call 202–606–9900.

International Trade Administration   *Business America* (published biweekly). Available from the Government Printing Office and at ITA District Offices.

Minority Business Development Agency   *Minority Business Today, Federal Resource Guide, BDC Directory, MBDA Annual Business Assistance Report (ABAR),* and *Federal Agency Performance for Minority Business Development.* Available from MBDA, Communications Division, Department of Commerce, Washington, DC 20230. Phone, 202–482–1936.

National Institute of Standards and Technology   *Journal of Research; Publications of the National Institute of Standards and Technology; Handbook of Mathematical Functions; Experimental Statistics; International System of Units (SI); Standard Reference Materials Catalog; Specifications, Tolerances, and Other Technical Requirements for Weighing and Measuring Devices Handbook;* and *Uniform Laws and Regulations Handbook.* Available from the Government Printing Office.

National Technical Information Service   Customer assistance telephone numbers: NTIS Sales Desk, 703–487–4650;

Research services for product identification, 703–487–4780; Subscription Section, 703–487–4630; technical support for computer products, 703–487–4763; and Customer services (for help in tracing an order), 703–487–4660. Orders for NTIS products may be sent by fax to 703–321–8547 or through the Internet address: orders@ntis.fedworld.gov.

An information center and bookstore is located at NTIS headquarters, 5285 Port Royal Road, Springfield, VA 22161. The bookstore is open to the public for walk-in service from 8:30 a.m.–5:00 p.m., eastern time, Monday through Friday.

The NTIS Fax Direct Central Information Service can be reached by dialing 703–487–4142. This fax-on-demand service provides an information center for current NTIS information available by fax. Using this service, guides and descriptions of other NTIS fax information services may be sent to the fax machine of your choice. Current NTIS Fax Direct services include a title list of the most popular titles in various subject categories and NTIS product information.

To connect to the FedWorld® On-Line Information Network: Set modem parity to none, data bits to 8, and stop bit to 1. Set terminal emulation to ANSI. Set duplex to full. Then set your communications software to dial FedWorld® at 703–321–FEDW. By Internet, telnet to fedworld.gov or file transfer protocol to ftp.fedworld.gov. For World Wide Web services, point your Web browser to open URL http://www.fedworld.gov. For more information or technical assistance, please call the FedWorld® help desk at 703–487–4608.

National Oceanic and Atmospheric Administration *Floods, Flash Floods and Warnings* and *Tornado Safety.* Available from the Government Printing Office. Also available from NOAA's Office of Public and Constituent Affairs are technical memoranda, technical reports, and monographs, nautical and aeronautical charts, coastal zone maps, magnetic tape, and a wide variety of raw and processed environmental data.

Phone, 202–482–6090. Schools should contact the Office of Public and Constituent Affairs, 14th Street and Constitution Avenue NW., Washington, DC 20230.

National Telecommunications and Information Administration Several hundred Technical Reports, Technical Memoranda, Special Publications, Contractor Reports, and other information products have been published by NTIA or its predecessor agency since 1970. The publications are available from the National Telecommunications and Information Administration, Department of Commerce, Washington, DC 20230 (phone, 202–482–1551); or the National Telecommunications and Information Administration, Institute for Telecommunication Sciences, Department of Commerce, Boulder, CO 80302 (phone, 303–497–3572). Electronic information can be obtained from the NTIA General Bulletin Board (phone, 202–482–1199); or the Information Infrastructure Task Force Bulletin Board (phone, 202–501–1920).

Office of Acquisition Management Acquisition Management has available an Electronic Bulletin Board System (BBS) for providing miscellaneous procurement information to the public. In order to access the OCS/Procurement BBS, the following modem setting is recommended: 8 bits, no parity, 1 stop bit, up to 9600 baud for speed, full duplex, and ANSI terminal emulation. To connect the system, call 703–487–4166. After configuring your communications software for the settings above, dial into the BBS. When the connection is completed, enter your user ID or enter "NEW". If you do not have an account established on this system, type "NEW". You will then be prompted to answer several questions to establish an account and to select a password. This system uses your name as your user ID. When prompted for an address and telephone number, please use your business information. After completing this process, the system will assign an ID code. You will have access to all public areas on the BBS. You will receive a message from the system operator that will contain the documentation for using this system as an attachment or the documentation can be read online through the Information Center. This is a menu-driven system and is easy to navigate. If you experience any technical problems using the BBS, please contact the Office of Computer Services, Department of Commerce, on 703–487–4790. If you have general questions concerning the system, please contact the Office of Acquisition Management, Department of Commerce, on 202–482–5755.

Patent and Trademark Office *General Information Concerning Patents, Basic*

Facts About Trademarks, Official Gazette of the United States Patent and Trademark Office, and *Attorneys and Agents Registered to Practice Before the U.S. Patent and Trademark Office.* Available from the Government Printing Office.

Reading Rooms See address of specific operating unit.

Small Business and Minority Business Activities See statement on page 155.

Telephone Directory The Department of Commerce telephone directory is available for sale by the Superintendent of Documents, Government Printing Office, Washington, DC 20402. Phone, 202–783–3238.

For further information concerning the Department of Commerce, contact the Office of Public Affairs, Department of Commerce, Fourteenth Street between Constitution and Pennsylvania Avenues NW., Washington, DC 20230. Phone, 202–219–3605.

DEPARTMENT OF DEFENSE

Office of the Secretary, The Pentagon, Washington, DC 20301–1155
Phone, 703–545–6700

SECRETARY OF DEFENSE	WILLIAM J. PERRY
Deputy Secretary of Defense	(VACANCY)
Special Assistants to the Secretary and Deputy Secretaries of Defense	LAWRENCE J. CAVAIOLA, ROBERT B. HALL, MARGARET C. SULLIVAN
Counselor to the Secretary and Deputy Secretary of Defense	LARRY K. SMITH
Executive Secretary	COL. ROBERT P. MCALEER, USMC
Under Secretary of Defense for Acquisition and Technology	PAUL G. KAMINSKI
Principal Deputy Under Secretary of Defense for Acquisition and Technology	NOEL LONGUEMARE, JR.
Director, Defense Research and Engineering	ANITA K. JONES
Assistant Secretary of Defense (Economic Security)	JOSHUA GOTBAUM
Assistant to the Secretary of Defense for Atomic Energy	HAROLD P. SMITH, JR.
Deputy Under Secretary of Defense (Space)	GIL KLINGER, *Acting*
Deputy Under Secretary of Defense (Advanced Technology)	V. LARRY LYNN
Deputy Under Secretary of Defense (Environmental Security)	SHERRI W. GOODMAN
Deputy Under Secretary of Defense (Logistics)	JAMES R. KLUGH
Deputy Under Secretary of Defense (Acquisition Reform)	COLLEEN A. PRESTON
Director, Small and Disadvantaged Business Utilization	L.C. ALDERMAN
Under Secretary of Defense for Policy	WALTER B. SLOCOMBE
Principal Deputy Under Secretary of Defense for Policy	JAN M. LODAL
Assistant Secretary of Defense (International Security Affairs)	JOSEPH S. NYE, JR.
Assistant Secretary of Defense (International Security Policy)	ASHTON B. CARTER
Assistant Secretary of Defense (Strategy, Requirements, and Assessments)	EDWARD L. WARNER III
Director of Net Assessment	ANDREW W. MARSHALL
Assistant Secretary of Defense (Special Operations and Low-Intensity Conflict)	H. ALLEN HOLMES
Defense Advisor, U.S. Mission NATO	CATHERINE KELLERHER
Deputy for Policy Liaison	KATHLEEN M. DELASKI
Deputy for Policy Support	LINTON WELLS II
Under Secretary of Defense for Personnel and Readiness	EDWIN DORN

175

Assistant Secretary of Defense (Force Management Policy)	FREDERICK F.Y. PANG
Assistant Secretary of Defense (Health Affairs)	STEPHEN C. JOSEPH, M.D.
Assistant Secretary of Defense (Reserve Affairs)	DEBORAH R. LEE
Deputy Under Secretary of Defense (Readiness)	L. FINCH
Deputy Under Secretary of Defense (Requirements and Resources)	JEANNE FITES
Under Secretary of Defense (Comptroller)/Chief Financial Officer	JOHN J. HAMRE
Principal Deputy Under Secretary (Comptroller)	ALICE C. MARONI
Director, Program Analysis and Evaluation	WILLIAM J. LYNN III
Assistant Secretary of Defense (Command, Control, Communications, and Intelligence)	EMMETT PAIGE, JR.
Assistant Secretary of Defense (Legislative Affairs)	SANDRA K. STUART
General Counsel	JUDITH A. MILLER
Director, Operational Test and Evaluation	PHILIP E. COYLE III
Inspector General	ELEANOR HILL
Assistant to the Secretary of Defense (Intelligence Oversight)	WALTER JAJKO
Assistant to the Secretary of Defense (Public Affairs)	KENNETH H. BACON
Director of Administration and Management	D.O. COOKE

Joint Chiefs of Staff

Chairman	GEN. JOHN M. SHALIKASHVILI, USA
Vice Chairman	ADM. WILLIAM A. OWENS, USN
Chief of Staff, Army	GEN. GORDON R. SULLIVAN, USA
Chief of Naval Operations	ADM. J.M. BOORDA, USN
Chief of Staff, Air Force	GEN. RONALD R. FOGLEMAN, USAF
Commandant, Marine Corps	GEN. C.E. MUNDY, JR., USMC

Joint Staff

Director	LT. GEN. WALTER KROSS, USAF
Vice Director	MAJ. GEN. CHARLES T. ROBERTSON, USAF
Director for Manpower and Personnel—J–1	REAR ADM. P.A. TRACEY, USN
Director, Intelligence—J–2	MAJ. GEN. PATRICK M. HUGHES, USA
Director for Operations—J–3	LT. GEN. HOWELL M. ESTES III, USAF
Director for Logistics—J–4	VICE ADM. JOHN B. LAPLANTE, USN
Director for Strategic Plans and Policy—J–5	LT. GEN. WESLEY K. CLARK, USA
Director for Command, Control, Communications and Computer System—J–6	VICE ADM. ARTHUR K. CEBROWSKI, USN

Director for Operational Plans and
Interoperability—J–7
Director for Force Structure, Resources and
Assessment—J–8

MAJ. GEN. STEPHEN SILVASY, JR.,
USA
MAJ. GEN. RALPH E. EBERHART,
USAF

[For the Department of Defense statement of organization, see the *Code of Federal Regulations*, Title 32, Chapter I, Subchapter R]

The Department of Defense is responsible for providing the military forces needed to deter war and protect the security of our country.

The major elements of these forces are the Army, Navy, Marine Corps, and Air Force, consisting of about 1.5 million men and women on active duty. They are backed, in case of emergency, by the 1 million members of the reserve components. In addition, there are about 900,000 civilian employees in the Defense Department.

Under the President, who is also Commander in Chief, the Secretary of Defense exercises authority, direction, and control over the Department, which includes the separately organized military departments of Army, Navy, and Air Force, the Joint Chiefs of Staff providing military advice, the unified combatant commands, and various defense agencies established for specific purposes.

The National Security Act Amendments of 1949 redesignated the National Military Establishment as the Department of Defense and established it as an executive department (10 U.S.C. 111), with the Secretary of Defense as its head. Since that time, many legislative and administrative changes have occurred, evolving the Department into the structure under which it currently operates.

Structure

The Department of Defense is composed of the Office of the Secretary of Defense; the military departments and the military services within those departments; the Chairman of the Joint Chiefs of Staff and the Joint Staff; the unified combatant commands; the Defense agencies; DOD field activities; and such other offices, agencies, activities, and commands as may be established or designated by law, or by the President or the Secretary of Defense.

In providing immediate staff assistance and advice to the Secretary of Defense, the Office of the Secretary of Defense and the Chairman of the Joint Chiefs of Staff, and the Joint Staff, though separately identified and organized, function in full coordination and cooperation.

The Office of the Secretary of Defense includes the offices of the Deputy Secretary of Defense; the Under Secretary of Defense for Acquisition and Technology; the Under Secretary of Defense for Policy; the Under Secretary of Defense (Comptroller)/Chief Financial Officer; the Under Secretary of Defense for Personnel and Readiness; the Director of Defense Research and Engineering; Assistant Secretaries of Defense; the General Counsel; the Inspector General; the Director of Operational Test and Evaluation; and such other staff offices as the Secretary of Defense establishes to assist him in carrying out his duties and responsibilities. The heads of these offices are staff advisers to the Secretary and perform such functions as he assigns to them.

The Joint Chiefs of Staff consist of the Chairman; the Vice Chairman; the Chief of Staff, U.S. Army; the Chief of Naval Operations; the Chief of Staff, U.S. Air Force; and the Commandant of the Marine Corps. Supported, subject to the authority of the Chairman, by the Joint Staff, they constitute the immediate military staff of the Secretary of Defense. The Chairman is the principal military adviser to the President, the National Security Council, and the Secretary of Defense. The other members of the Joint

DEPARTMENT OF DEFENSE

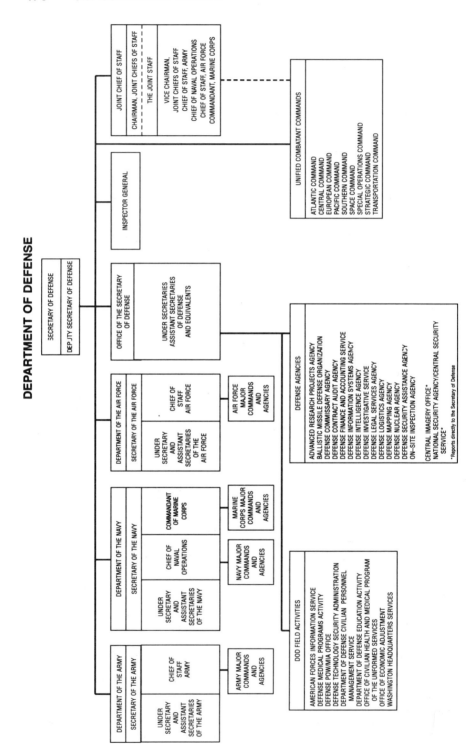

SECRETARY OF DEFENSE

DEPUTY SECRETARY OF DEFENSE

INSPECTOR GENERAL

JOINT CHIEF OF STAFF
- CHAIRMAN, JOINT CHIEFS OF STAFF
- THE JOINT STAFF
- VICE CHAIRMAN, JOINT CHIEFS OF STAFF
- CHIEF OF STAFF, ARMY
- CHIEF OF NAVAL OPERATIONS
- CHIEF OF STAFF, AIR FORCE
- COMMANDANT, MARINE CORPS

UNIFIED COMBATANT COMMANDS
- ATLANTIC COMMAND
- CENTRAL COMMAND
- EUROPEAN COMMAND
- PACIFIC COMMAND
- SOUTHERN COMMAND
- SPACE COMMAND
- SPECIAL OPERATIONS COMMAND
- STRATEGIC COMMAND
- TRANSPORTATION COMMAND

OFFICE OF THE SECRETARY OF DEFENSE

UNDER SECRETARIES ASSISTANT SECRETARIES OF DEFENSE AND EQUIVALENTS

DEPARTMENT OF THE ARMY

SECRETARY OF THE ARMY

UNDER SECRETARY AND ASSISTANT SECRETARIES OF THE ARMY

CHIEF OF STAFF ARMY

ARMY MAJOR COMMANDS AND AGENCIES

DEPARTMENT OF THE NAVY

SECRETARY OF THE NAVY

UNDER SECRETARY AND ASSISTANT SECRETARIES OF THE NAVY

CHIEF OF NAVAL OPERATIONS

COMMANDANT OF MARINE CORPS

NAVY MAJOR COMMANDS AND AGENCIES

MARINE CORPS MAJOR COMMANDS AND AGENCIES

DEPARTMENT OF THE AIR FORCE

SECRETARY OF THE AIR FORCE

UNDER SECRETARY AND ASSISTANT SECRETARIES OF THE AIR FORCE

CHIEF OF STAFF AIR FORCE

AIR FORCE MAJOR COMMANDS AND AGENCIES

DEFENSE AGENCIES
- ADVANCED RESEARCH PROJECTS AGENCY
- BALLISTIC MISSILE DEFENSE ORGANIZATION
- DEFENSE COMMISSARY AGENCY
- DEFENSE CONTRACT AUDIT AGENCY
- DEFENSE FINANCE AND ACCOUNTING SERVICE
- DEFENSE INFORMATION SYSTEMS AGENCY
- DEFENSE INTELLIGENCE AGENCY
- DEFENSE INVESTIGATIVE SERVICE
- DEFENSE LEGAL SERVICES AGENCY
- DEFENSE LOGISTICS AGENCY
- DEFENSE MAPPING AGENCY
- DEFENSE NUCLEAR AGENCY
- DEFENSE SECURITY ASSISTANCE AGENCY
- ON-SITE INSPECTION AGENCY

CENTRAL IMAGERY OFFICE*
NATIONAL SECURITY AGENCY/CENTRAL SECURITY SERVICE*

*Reports directly to the Secretary of Defense

DOD FIELD ACTIVITIES
- AMERICAN FORCES INFORMATION SERVICE
- DEFENSE MEDICAL PROGRAMS ACTIVITY
- DEFENSE POW/MIA OFFICE
- DEFENSE TECHNOLOGY SECURITY ADMINISTRATION
- DEPARTMENT OF DEFENSE CIVILIAN PERSONNEL MANAGEMENT SERVICE
- DEPARTMENT OF DEFENSE EDUCATION ACTIVITY
- OFFICE OF CIVILIAN HEALTH AND MEDICAL PROGRAM OF THE UNIFORMED SERVICES
- OFFICE OF ECONOMIC ADJUSTMENT
- WASHINGTON HEADQUARTERS SERVICES

Chiefs of Staff are the senior military officers of their respective services and are military advisers to the President, the National Security Council, and the Secretary of Defense. The Vice Chairman of the Joint Chiefs acts as Chairman in the absence of the Chairman.

Each military department (the Department of the Navy includes naval aviation and the United States Marine Corps) is separately organized under its own Secretary and functions under the authority, direction, and control of the Secretary of Defense. The Secretary of each military department is responsible to the Secretary of Defense for the operation and efficiency of his department. Orders to the military departments are issued through the Secretaries of these departments, or their designees, by the Secretary of Defense or under authority specifically delegated in writing by the Secretary of Defense or provided by law.

The commanders of unified combatant commands are responsible to the President and the Secretary of Defense for accomplishing the military missions assigned to them and exercising command authority over forces assigned to them. The operational chain of command runs from the President to the Secretary of Defense to the commanders of the unified combatant commands. The Chairman of the Joint Chiefs of Staff functions within the chain of command by transmitting the orders of the President or the Secretary of Defense to the commanders of the unified combatant commands.

Office of the Secretary of Defense

Secretary of Defense The Secretary of Defense is the principal defense policy adviser to the President and is responsible for the formulation of general defense policy and policy related to DOD, and for the execution of approved policy. Under the direction of the President, the Secretary exercises authority, direction, and control over the Department of Defense.

Deputy Secretary of Defense The Deputy Secretary of Defense is delegated full power and authority to act for the Secretary of Defense and to exercise the powers of the Secretary on any and all matters for which the Secretary is authorized to act pursuant to law.

Acquisition and Technology The Under Secretary of Defense for Acquisition and Technology is the principal staff assistant and adviser to the Secretary of Defense for all matters relating to the acquisition system, research and development, test and evaluation, production, logistics, military construction, procurement, and economic affairs. The Under Secretary serves as the Defense acquisition executive with responsibility for supervising the performance of the entire Department acquisition system and chairing the Defense Acquisition Board.

Policy The Under Secretary of Defense for Policy is the principal staff assistant to the Secretary of Defense for policy matters relating to overall international security policy and political-military affairs. Functional areas include NATO affairs; net assessments; foreign military sales; arms limitation agreements; international trade and technology; regional security affairs; special operations and low-intensity conflict; integration of departmental plans and policies with overall national security objectives; drug control policy, requirements, priorities, systems, resources, and programs; and issuance of policy guidance affecting departmental programs.

Personnel and Readiness The Under Secretary of Defense for Personnel and Readiness is the principal staff assistant and adviser to the Secretary of Defense for policy matter relating to the structure and readiness of the Total Force. Functional areas include: readiness; civilian and military personnel policies, programs, and systems; civilian and military equal opportunity programs;

health policies, programs, and activities; Reserve Component programs, policies, and activities; family policy, dependent's education, and personnel support programs; and mobilization planning and requirements.

Operational Test and Evaluation   The Director of Operational Test and Evaluation serves as the principal staff assistant and adviser to the Secretary of Defense on operational test and evaluation in the Department of Defense and is the principal test and evaluation official within the senior management of the Department. The Director prescribes policies and procedures for the conduct of operational test and evaluation within the Department; provides advice and makes recommendations to the Secretary of Defense and issues guidance to and consults with the heads of Defense Components with respect to such activities and specific programs to be conducted in connection with a major defense acquisition program; monitors and reviews all test and evaluation programs to ensure adherence to approved policies and standards; and reviews and makes recommendations to the Secretary of Defense on all

budgetary and financial matters relating to such activities, including operational test facilities and equipment. In addition, the Secretary and Deputy Secretary of Defense are assisted by a special staff of assistants to include the Assistant Secretary of Defense for Legislative Affairs; the General Counsel; the Inspector General; the Assistant to the Secretary of Defense for Intelligence Oversight; the Assistant to the Secretary of Defense for Public Affairs; the Director for Administration and Management; and such other offices as the Secretary of Defense establishes to assist him in carrying out his duties and responsibilities.

Command, Control, Communications and Intelligence   The Assistant Secretary of Defense (Command, Control, Communications and Intelligence (C^3I)) is the principal staff assistant and adviser to the Secretary and Deputy Secretary of Defense for C^3I, information management, counterintelligence, and security countermeasures matters, including warning reconnaissance and intelligence and intelligence-related activities conducted by the Department of Defense.

Joint Chiefs of Staff

Joint Chiefs of Staff

The Joint Chiefs of Staff consists of the Chairman of the Joint Chiefs of Staff; the Vice Chairman; the Chief of Staff of the Army; the Chief of Naval Operations; the Chief of Staff of the Air Force; and the Commandant of the Marine Corps.

The Chairman of the Joint Chiefs of Staff is the principal military adviser to the President, the National Security Council, and the Secretary of Defense. The other members of the Joint Chiefs of Staff are military advisers who may provide additional information upon request from the President, the National Security Council, or the Secretary of Defense. They may also submit their advice when it does not agree with that of the Chairman.

Subject to the authority of the President and the Secretary of Defense, the Chairman of the Joint Chiefs of Staff is responsible for:

—assisting the President and the Secretary of Defense in providing for the strategic direction and planning of the Armed Forces;

—allocating resources to fulfill strategic plans;

—making recommendations for the assignment of responsibilities within the Armed Forces in accordance with and in support of those logistic and mobility plans;

—comparing the capabilities of American and allied Armed Forces with those of potential adversaries;

—preparing and reviewing contingency plans that conform to policy guidance from the President and the Secretary of Defense;

—preparing joint logistic and mobility plans to support contingency plans; and

—recommending assignment of logistic and mobility responsibilities to the Armed Forces to fulfill logistic and mobility plans.

The Chairman advises the Secretary of Defense on critical deficiencies and strengths in force capabilities (including manpower, logistic, and mobility support) and assesses the effect of such deficiencies and strengths on meeting national security objectives and policy and on strategic plans. He establishes and maintains a uniform system for evaluating the preparedness of each unified combatant command to carry out assigned missions.

The Chairman advises the Secretary of Defense on the priorities of the requirements identified by the commanders of the unified combatant commands and on the extent to which program recommendations and budget proposals of the military departments and other DOD components for a fiscal year conform with priorities established in requirements of the unified combatant commands. He is responsible for submitting to the Secretary alternative program recommendations and budget proposals with guidance provided by the Secretary, in order to achieve greater conformance with priorities established by the unified combatant commands. The Chairman also advises the Secretary on the extent to which major programs and policies of the Armed Forces in the area of manpower conform with strategic plans and assesses military requirements for defense acquisition programs.

Additionally, the Chairman:

—formulates doctrine and training policies and coordinates military education and training;

—represents the United States on the Military Staff Committee of the United Nations;

—performs such other duties as may be prescribed by law or by the President and the Secretary of Defense;

—convenes and presides over regular meetings of the Joint Chiefs of Staff;

—assists the Joint Chiefs in carrying on their business as promptly as practicable; and

—schedules issues for consideration by the Joint Chiefs.

The Chairman, while so serving, holds the grade of general or admiral and outranks all other officers of the Armed Forces.

The Vice Chairman of the Joint Chiefs performs duties assigned by the Chairman, with the approval of the Secretary of Defense. The Vice Chairman acts as Chairman when there is a vacancy in the office of the Chairman, or in the absence or disability of the Chairman. The Vice Chairman, while so serving, holds the grade of general or admiral and outranks all other officers of the Armed Forces except the Chairman of the Joint Chiefs of Staff.

Joint Staff

The Joint Staff under the Chairman of the Joint Chiefs of Staff assists the Chairman and, subject to the authority of the Chairman, the other members of the Joint Chiefs of Staff, in carrying out their responsibilities.

The Joint Staff is headed by a Director who is selected by the Chairman in consultation with the other members of the Joint Chiefs of Staff, and with the approval of the Secretary of Defense. Officers assigned to serve on the Joint Staff are selected by the Chairman in approximate equal numbers from the Army, Navy, Marine Corps, and Air Force. The Joint Staff is composed of all members of the Armed Forces and civilian employees assigned or detailed to permanent duty to perform the functions assigned to the Chairman of the Joint Chiefs of Staff.

Sources of Information

Contracts and Small Business Activities Contact the Director, Small and Disadvantaged Business Utilization, Office of the Secretary of Defense, Room 2A340, The Pentagon, Washington, DC 20301–3061. Phone, 703–697–9383.

DOD Directives and Instructions Correspondence and Directives Directorate, Washington Headquarters Services, Room 2A286, The Pentagon, Washington, DC 20301–1155. Phone, 703–697–4111.

Employment Almost all positions are in the competitive service and are filled from civil service registers. College recruiting requirements are limited primarily to management intern positions at the B.S. and M.S. levels. For additional information, inquiries should be addressed to the Chief, Staffing Division, Directorate for Personnel and Security, Washington Headquarters Services, Room 2E148, The Pentagon, Washington, DC 20301–1155. Phone, 703–614–4066.

Films The Department of Defense has certain motion pictures and videotapes available for public, nonprofit exhibition. These are productions required to support training and internal information objectives. There is a catalog of productions available to the public for sale from the National Technical Information Service, 5285 Port Royal Road, Springfield, VA 22161. Each Service has its own catalog for internal use. Interested persons should contact the nearest installation of each Service to obtain the appropriate address of the film/videotape distribution center serving that area. Additionally, the Public Affairs Office of each Service at its headquarters in Washington, DC, should be contacted. There is no charge for listings of films. No admission or any other fees may be charged for viewing of films and each film must be shown in its entirety,

including all titles at beginning and end; no portion of the film may be reproduced, edited, or cut in any manner; and qualified operators must be provided by the borrower. Interested purchasers of Department of Defense films may also contact the Sales Branch, National Audio-Visual Center, 8750 Edgeworth Drive, Capitol Heights, MD 20743–3701. Phone, 301–763–1896.

Pentagon Tours Guided tours of the Pentagon are available Monday through Friday, excluding Federal holidays. The 1-hour tours start at the Concourse. For further information or reservations, call 703–695–1776; or write: Pentagon Tour Director, Room 3C1054, Washington, DC 20301–1400.

Speakers Scheduling of speaking engagements for civilian and military representatives of the Department of Defense is a responsibility of the Director for Programs, Office of the Assistant to the Secretary of Defense (Public Affairs). Speakers on a variety of defense subjects are available in response to invitations at no cost to the local sponsor. However, any speaker can accept transportation, meals, and lodging, if offered by the sponsor of the public event in which he is to participate.

Written requests for speakers should be forwarded to the Director for Community Relations, Office of the Assistant to the Secretary of Defense (Public Affairs), The Pentagon, Washington, DC 20301–1400 (phone, 703–695–2113); or to the Public Affairs Officer of the nearest military installation.

Telephone Directory The Department of Defense telephone directory is available for sale by the Superintendent of Documents, Government Printing Office, Washington, DC 20402. Phone, 202–512–1800.

For further information concerning the Department of Defense, contact the Director, Directorate for Public Communication, Office of the Assistant to the Secretary of Defense (Public Affairs), The Pentagon, Washington, DC 20301–1400. Phone, 703–697–5737.

DOD FIELD ACTIVITIES

American Forces Information Service

The American Forces Information Service, established in 1977 under the supervision of the Assistant to the Secretary of Defense (Public Affairs), is responsible for the Department's internal information program, visual information policy, and visual information and public affairs training. The Armed Forces Radio and Television Service, the Print Media Directorate (which includes among its many products the *Current News Early Bird*), the Armed Forces Radio and Television Service Broadcast Center, the Television-Audio Support Activity, the Defense Information Schools, and the Defense Visual Information Center function under the Director of American Forces Information Service. In addition, the Service provides policy guidance and oversight for departmental periodicals and pamphlets, *Stars and Stripes* newspapers, military command newspapers, the broadcast elements of the military departments, and departmental audiovisual matters.

(American Forces Information Service, Department of Defense, Suite 311, 601 North Fairfax Street, Alexandria, VA 22314–2007. Phone, 703–274–4839.)

Department of Defense Civilian Personnel Management Service

The Department of Defense Civilian Personnel Management Service (CPMS) was established August 30, 1993. It is under the authority, direction, and control of the Under Secretary of Defense for Personnel and Readiness, and provides civilian personnel policy support, functional information management, and civilian personnel administrative services to DOD components and their activities.

(Department of Defense Civilian Personnel Management Service, 1400 Key Boulevard, B200, Arlington, VA 22209–5144. Phone, 703–696–2720.)

Department of Defense Education Activity

The Department of Defense Education Activity (DODEA) was established in 1992 under the authority, direction, and control of the Under Secretary of Defense for Personnel and Readiness. It consists of three subordinate organizational entities: the Department of Defense Dependents Schools, the Department of Defense Domestic Dependent Elementary and Secondary Schools, and the Continuing Adult and Post-Secondary Education Office. The mission of DODEA is to serve as the principal staff adviser to the Under Secretary of Defense for Personnel and Readiness on all Defense education matters relative to overseas, stateside, and continuing adult and post-secondary education activities and programs; formulate, develop, and implement policies, technical guidance, and standards for the effective management of Defense education activities and programs; plan, direct, coordinate, and manage the education programs for eligible dependents of U.S. military and civilian personnel stationed overseas and stateside, including those enrolled in continuing adult and post-secondary education programs; evaluate the programmatic and operational policies and procedures for the DOD Dependent Schools, DOD Domestic Dependent Elementary and Secondary Schools, and the Continuing Adult and Post-Secondary Education Programs; and provide education activity representation at meetings and deliberations of educational panels and advisory groups.

(Department of Defense Education Activity, 4040 North Fairfax Drive, Arlington, VA 22203–1635. Phone, 703–696–4236.)

Office of Civilian Health and Medical Program of the Uniformed Services

The Office of Civilian Health and Medical Program of the Uniformed Services (OCHAMPUS) was established as a field activity in 1974. The Office contracts for and administers, in concert with military officials, regional managed care support contracts for medical care provided in military treatment facilities and by civilian sources for active duty and retired service members and their dependents and survivors. A regional structure, called TRICARE, combines two formerly separate components of the

Military Health Services System: care in military facilities; and, under OCHAMPUS oversight, a civilian medical care program to supplement the care available from the military facilities.

(Office of Civilian Health and Medical Program of the Uniformed Services, Department of Defense, Aurora, CO 80045. Phone, 303–361–1313.)

Defense Medical Programs Activity The Activity develops and maintains the Department of Defense Unified Medical Program to provide resources for all medical activities; develops, maintains, and provides guidance for an integrated system for planning, programming, and budgeting for medical facility military construction projects throughout DOD and for managing the allocation of the financial resources approved for such projects; develops, maintains, and oversees the design, enhancement, operation, procurement, and management of information systems and related communications and automated systems in support of the activities of the DOD Military Health Services System (MHSS); manages the DOD-wide automated MHSS information systems; provides other support for DOD military medical programs, as directed by the Assistant Secretary of Defense (Health Affairs).

(Defense Medical Programs Activity, Department of Defense, Skyline 5, Suite 810, 5111 Leesburg Pike, Falls Church, VA 22041–3201. Phone, 703–756–8707. Fax, 703–756–8706.)

Defense Prisoner of War/Missing in Action Office The Defense Prisoner of War/Missing in Action Office (DPMO) was established July 16, 1993, under the authority, direction, and control of the Assistant Secretary of Defense for International Security Affairs, and provides centralized management of prisoner of war/missing in action (POW/MIA) affairs with the Department of Defense. The Office provides DOD participation in the conduct of negotiations with officials of foreign governments in efforts to achieve the fullest possible accounting of missing American service men and women; assembles and analyzes information and maintains data bases on U.S. military

and civilian personnel who are, or were, prisoners of war or missing in action; declassifies DOD documents for disclosure and release in accordance with section 1082 of Public Law 102–190 (50 U.S.C. 401 note) and Executive Order 12812 of July 22, 1992; and maintains open channels of communication on POW/MIA matters between the Department and the Congress, POW/MIA families, and veteran organizations through periodic consultations and other appropriate methods.

(Defense Prisoner of War/Missing in Action Office, Department of Defense, OASD/ISA, The Pentagon, Washington, DC 20301–2400. Phone, 703–602–2102. Fax, 703–602–1891)

Defense Technology Security Administration The Defense Technology Security Administration was established by the Deputy Secretary of Defense on May 10, 1985, under the policy and overall management of the Under Secretary of Defense for Policy. The Administration is responsible for reviewing the international transfer of defense-related technology, goods, services, and munitions consistent with U.S. foreign policy and national security objectives.

(Defense Technology Security Administration, Department of Defense, Suite 300, 400 Army Navy Drive, Arlington, VA 22202. Phone, 703–604–5215.)

Office of Economic Adjustment The Office of Economic Adjustment is responsible for planning and managing the Department's economic adjustment programs and for assisting Federal, State, and local officials in cooperative efforts to alleviate any serious social and economic side effects resulting from major departmental realignments or other actions.

(Office of Economic Adjustment, Department of Defense, 400 Army Navy Drive, Suite 200, Arlington, VA 22202–2884. Phone, 703–604–6020.)

Washington Headquarters Services The Director of Administration and Management serves in a dual capacity as the Director of Washington Headquarters Services. The agency's mission is to provide administrative and operational support to certain Department of Defense activities in the National Capital region. Such support includes budget and accounting, personnel management, office services, security, correspondence, directives and records management, travel, building administration, information and data systems, voting assistance program, and other administrative support as required.

(Washington Headquarters Services, Department of Defense, Room 3D972, The Pentagon, Washington, DC 20301–1155. Phone, 703–695–4436.)

DEPARTMENT OF THE AIR FORCE

1670 Air Force Pentagon, Washington, DC 20330-1670

SECRETARY OF THE AIR FORCE	SHEILA E. WIDNALL
Confidential Assistant	NORMA J. PEARCE
Staff Assistant	S. SGT. FRANK D. GILROY
Deputy Military Assistant	LT. COL. JANET A. THERIANOS
Executive Assistant	LT. COL. DENNIS M. KAAN
Executive Officer	PATRICIA RYDER
Under Secretary of the Air Force	RUDY F. DELEON
Special Assistant	CLARK A. MURDOCK
Military Assistant	COL. ERIK L. WINBORN
Executive Officer	LT. COL. TIMOTHY MILBRATH
Executive Noncommissioned Officer	S. SGT. KIMALA RICHE
Administrative Assistant	BRIAN MCHUGH
Deputy Under Secretary (International Affairs)	ROBERT D. BAUERLEIN
Assistant Deputy Under Secretary (International Affairs)	MAJ. GEN. H. HALE BURR, JR.
Executive Officer	LT. COL. JOSEPH A. SPANN
Director, Small and Disadvantaged Business Utilization	ANTHONY J. DELUCA
Assistant Secretary (Manpower, Reserve Affairs, Installations, and Environment)	RODNEY A. COLEMAN
Principal Deputy Assistant Secretary (Manpower, Reserve Affairs, Installations, and Environment)	PHILLIP P. UPSCHULTE
Military Assistant	LT. COL. TERRILL W. RILEY
Executive Officer	CAPT. SHELIA O. UPHOFF
Deputy Assistant Secretary (Force Management and Personnel)	RUBY B. DEMESME
Deputy Assistant Secretary (Reserve Affairs)	BRYAN E. SHARRATT
Deputy Assistant Secretary (Installations)	JIMMY G. DISHNER
Director, Air Force Real Estate Agency	ANTHONY R. JONKERS
Deputy Assistant Secretry (Environment, Safety and Occupational Health)	THOMAS W. L. MCCALL, JR.
Deputy, Air Force Review Boards	JOE G. LINEBERGER
Executive Director, Air Force Board, Correction of Military Records	MACK M. BURTON, *Acting*
Director, Air Force Base Conversion Agency	ALAN K. OLSEN
Director, Air Force Personnel Council	COL. TERRANCE L. MURTAUGH
Director, Air Force Civilian Appellate Review Office	SOPHIE A. CLARK, *Acting*
Deputy (Equal Opportunity)	DENNIS M. COLLINS
Assistant Secretary (Financial Management and Comptroller of the Air Force)	ROBERT F. HALE
Principal Deputy Assistant Secretary (Financial Management)	JOHN W. BEACH
Deputy Assistant Secretary (Budget)	MAJ. GEN. A.D. BUNGER

186

Director, Budget and Appropriations Liaison	COL. JOHN R. TARASCIO
Director, Budget Management and Execution	ROBERT W. ZOOK
Director, Budget Investment	CATHLYNN B. SPARKS
Director, Budget Operations	BRIG. GEN. GEORGE T. STRINGER
Director, Budget Programs	COL. RODNEY W. WOOD
Deputy Assistant Secretary (Cost and Economics)	LEROY T. BASEMAN
Deputy (Management Systems)	A. ERNEST FITZGERALD
Deputy Assistant Secretary (Plans, Systems and Analysis)	JOHN J. NETHERY
Assistant Secretary (Acquisition)	CLARK G. FIESTER
Principal Deputy Assistant Secretary (Acquisition)	LT. GEN. RICHARD E. HAWLEY
Deputy Assistant Secretary (Acquisition and Management)	DARLEEN A. DRUYUN
Deputy Assistant Secretary (Research and Engineering)	JAMES J. MATTICE
Deputy Assistant Secretary (Communications, Computers, and Logistics)	LLOYD K. MOSEMANN II
Deputy Assistant Secretary (Contracting)	MAJ. GEN. ROBERT W. DREWES
Deputy Assistant Secretary (Management Policy and Program Integration)	BLAISE J. DURANTE
Director, Long Range Power Projection, Special Operations Forces, Airlift and Training Programs	BRIG. GEN. JAMES M. RICHARDS III
Director, Electronics and Special Programs	COL. MICHAEL W. SCHOENFELD
Director, Fighter, Communications, Computers, and Weapons Programs	BRIG. GEN. JOHN W. HAWLEY
Director, Space Programs	MAJ. GEN. ROBERT S. DICKMAN
Director, Science and Technology	COL. AUBIN A. HIGGINS, *Acting*
Director, Air Force Program Executive Office	CLARK G. FIESTER
Assistant Secretary (Space)	JEFFREY K. HARRIS
Principal Deputy Assistant Secretary (Space)	JIMMIE D. HILL
Deputy Assistant Secretary (Space Plans and Policy)	RICHARD M. MCCORMICK
Director, Space Systems	BRIG. GEN. THOMAS J. SCANLAN, JR.
Director, Special Projects	BRIG. GEN. DONALD R. WALKER
General Counsel	SHEILA C. CHESTON, *Acting*
The Inspector General	LT. GEN. MARCUS A. ANDERSON
Deputy Inspector General	MAJ. GEN. BRUCE J. LOTZBIRE
Administrative Assistant to the Secretary	WILLIAM A. DAVIDSON
Chief, Civilian Personnel	(VACANCY)
Director, Information Management	COL. KEVIN A. COLLINS
Facility Manager, Air Force Executive Dining Room	ALFONSO C. SISNEROS
Director, Plans, Programs and Budget	COL. DAVID C. WALKER
Chief, Personnel Division	MAJ. EDWARD G. PATRICK
Director, Security and Investigative Programs	LT. COL. ERIC E. PATTERSON
The Auditor General of the Air Force	JACKIE R. CRAWFORD
Director, Legislative Liaison	MAJ. GEN. NORMAND G. LEZY

Deputy Director, Legislative Liaison	COL. CHARLES FOX
Chief, Congressional Inquiry Division	COL. JOHN WILSON
Director, Public Affairs	BRIG. GEN. RONALD T. SCONYERS
Deputy Director, Public Affairs	COL. HAL SMARKOLA
Chief, Public Affairs Staff Group	COL. ALAN DEFEND
Chief, Community Relations	WALT WERNER
Chief, Media Relations	COL. TOM BOYD
Chief, Resources	COL. MIKE CONLEY
Chief, Security Review	JUNE FORTE
Chief, Air Force News Agency Liaison Office	MAJ. WILL HUMMISTON

Air Staff

Chief of Staff	GEN. RONALD R. FOGLEMAN
Vice Chief of Staff	GEN. THOMAS S. MOORMAN, JR.
Assistant Vice Chief of Staff	(VACANCY)
Special Assistant to the Secretary and Chief of Staff Air Force for Base Realignment and Transition	MAJ. GEN. JAY D. BLUME, JR.
Special Assistant, Theater Air Defense	MAJ. GEN. W. THOMAS WEST
Chief, Safety	BRIG. GEN. ORIN L. GODSEY
Chief, Security Police	BRIG. GEN. STEPHEN C. MANNELL
Chairman, Scientific Advisory Board	GENE H. MCCALL
Director, Services	COL. STEVAN B. RICHARDS
Director, Programs and Evaluation	(VACANCY)
Director, Test and Evaluation	LT. GEN. HOWARD W. LEAF, USAF (RET.)
The Civil Engineer	MAJ. GEN. JAMES E. MCCARTHY
Air Force Historian	RICHARD P. HALLION
Chief Scientist of the Air Force	EDWARD A. FEIGENBAUM
Chief, Air Force Reserve	MAJ. GEN. ROBERT A. MCINTOSH
Chief, National Guard Bureau	LT. GEN. EDWARD D. BACA
Surgeon General of the Air Force	LT. GEN. EDGAR R. ANDERSON, JR.
Chief, Chaplains	MAJ. GEN. DONALD J. HARLIN
The Judge Advocate General	MAJ. GEN. NOLAN SKLUTE
Commander, Air Force Legal Services Agency	BRIG. GEN. OLAN G. WALDROP, JR.
Deputy Chief of Staff (Personnel)	LT. GEN. EUGENE E. HABIGER
Deputy Chief of Staff (Plans and Operations)	LT. GEN. JOSEPH W. RALSTON
Deputy Chief of Staff (Logistics)	MAJ. GEN. GEORGE T. BABBITT, JR.
Deputy Chief of Staff (Command, Control, Communications, and Computers)	LT. GEN. CARL G. O'BERRY
Assistant Chief of Staff (Intelligence)	MAJ. GEN. KENNETH A. MINIHAN
Commander, 497th Intelligence Group	COL. JAMES M. SULLIVAN
Director of Assessments, National Air Intelligence Center	ROBERT S. BOYD

Major Commands:

Air Combat Command (Langley Air Force Base, VA 23665–2788)	GEN. JOHN M. LOH
Air Force Materiel Command (Wright-Patterson Air Force Base, OH 45433–5001)	GEN. RONALD W. YATES
Air Mobility Command (Scott Air Force Base, IL 62225–5363)	GEN. ROBERT L. RUTHERFORD
Air Force Space Command (Peterson Air Force Base, CO 80914–4020)	GEN. JOSEPH W. ASHY

Air Force Special Operations Command (Hurlburt Field, FL 32544–5273)

MAJ. GEN. JAMES L. HOBSON, JR.

Air Education and Training Command (Randolph Air Force Base, TX 78150–4324)

GEN. HENRY VICCELLIO, JR.

Overseas Commands:

Pacific Air Forces (Hickam Air Force Base, HI 96853–5420)

GEN. JOHN G. LORBER

United States Air Forces in Europe (APO AE 09094–0501)

GEN. JAMES L. JAMERSON

Named Activities:

Air Force Office of Colonel Matters (Washington, DC 20330–1040)

BRIG. GEN. LARRY W. NORTHINGTON

Air Force Office of General Officer Matters (Washington, DC 20330–1040)

COL. T. MICHAEL MOSELEY

Air Force Office of Senior Executive Matters (Washington, DC 20330–1040)

KAREN L. BINGO

Field Operating Agencies:

Air Force Audit Agency (Washington, DC 20330–1125)

JACKIE CRAWFORD

Air Force Base Conversion Agency (Arlington, VA 22209–2808)

ALAN OLSEN

Air Force Center for Environmental Excellence (Brooks Air Force Base, TX 78235–5318)

J.B. COLE

Air Force Civil Engineer Support Agency (Tyndall Air Force Base, FL 32403–5319)

COL. DONALD J. THOMAS

Air Force Civilian Personnel Management Center (Randolph Air Force Base, TX 78150–4530)

JOHN R. GRAHAM

Air Force Combat Operations Staff (Washington, DC 20330–1480)

COL. ALFRED P. MCCRACKEN

Air Force Command, Control, Communications and Computer Agency (Scott Air Force Base, IL 62225–5222)

BRIG. GEN. HARRY D. RADUEGE, JR.

Air Force Cost Analysis Agency (Arlington, VA 22202–4306)

COL. GORDON D. KAGE

Air Force Doctrine Center (Langley Air Force Base, VA 23622–2722)

COL. ROBERT D. COFFMAN

Air Force Flight Standards Agency (Washington, DC 20330–1480)

COL. DENNIS TRAYNOR

Air Force Frequency Management Agency (Arlington, VA 22203–1613)

LT. COL. WILLIAM A. BELOTE

Air Force Historical Research Agency (Maxwell Air Force Base, AL 36112–6424)

COL. RICHARD RAUSCHKOLB

Air Force Inspection Agency (Kirtland Air Force Base, NM 87117–5670)

COL. ROBERT M. MURDOCK

Air Force Legal Services Agency (Bolling Air Force Base, Washington, DC 20332

BRIG. GEN. OLAN G. WALDROP, JR.

Air Force Logistics Management Agency (Maxwell Air Force Base, Gunter Annex, AL 36114–3236)

COL. RUSSELL G. STAFFORD

Air Force Management Engineering Agency (Randolph Air Force Base, TX 78150–4451)	COL. CHARLES F. DIBRELL
Air Force Medical Operations Agency (Bolling Air Force Base, Washington, DC 20332–5113)	MAJ. GEN. CHARLES H. ROADMAN II
Air Force Medical Support Agency (Brooks Air Force Base, TX 78235–5121)	COL. RICHARD RUSHMORE
Air Force Military Personnel Center (Randolph Air Force Base, TX 78150–4703)	MAJ. GEN. WILLIAM B. DAVITTE
Air Force News Agency (Kelly Air Force Base, TX 78241–5601)	COL. TEDDY G. TILMA
Air Force Office of Special Investigations (Bolling Air Force Base, Washington, DC 20332–0001)	BRIG. GEN. ROBERT A. HOFFMANN
Air Force Personnel Operations Agency (Washington, DC 20330–1040)	STEVE N. SMITH
Air Force Program Executive Office (Washington, DC 20330–1060)	CLARK G. FIESTER
Air Force Real Estate Agency (Bolling Air Force Base, Washington, DC 20332–5107)	ANTHONY R. YONKERS
Air Force Reserve (Robins Air Force Base, GA 31098–1635)	MAJ. GEN. JAMES E. SHERRARD
Air Force Review Boards Agency (Washington, DC 20330–1661)	JOE G. LINEBERGER
Air Force Safety Agency (Norton Air Force Base, CA 92409–7001)	COL. JOHN R. CLAPPER
Air Force Security Police Agency (Kirtland Air Force Base, NM 87117–5664)	COL. JOHN E. KILLEN
Air Force Services Agency (Randolph Air Force Base, TX 78150–4755)	COL. DAVID F. HONEYCUTT
Air Force Studies and Analyses Agency (Washington, DC 20330–1570)	COL. THOMAS A. CARDWELL III
Air Force Technical Applications Center (Patrick Air Force Base, FL 32925–3002)	COL. GLEN E. SHAFFER
Air Intelligence Agency (San Antonio, TX 78243–7009)	BRIG. GEN. ROBERT T. OSTERTHALER
Air National Guard Readiness Center (Andrews Air Force Base, MD 20331–5157)	BRIG. GEN. LARRY K. ARNOLD
Air Reserve Personnel Center (Denver, CO 80280–5400)	COL. JAMES WHITE, JR.
Air Weather Service (Scott Air Force Base, IL 62225–5206)	COL. FRANK MISCIASCI
Center for Air Force History (Bolling Air Force Base, Washington, DC 20332–4113)	JACOB NEUFELD
Joint Services Survival, Evasion, Resistance and Escape Agency (Fort Belvoir, VA 22060–5788)	COL. ROBERT C. BONN, JR.
Air Force Pentagon Communications Agency (Washington, DC 20330–1600)	COL. STEPHEN E. ANNO

Direct Reporting Units:

11th Support Wing (Bolling Air Force Base, Washington, DC 20332–5100)	COL. STEVEN A. ROSER

Air Force Operational Test and Evaluation Center (Kirtland Air Force Base, NM 87117–5558)

MAJ. GEN. GEORGE B. HARRISON

U.S. Air Force Academy (USAFA, CO 80840–5001)

LT. GEN. PAUL E. STEIN

The Department of the Air Force is responsible for defending the peace and security of the United States through control and exploitation of air and space.

The Department of the Air Force (USAF) was established as part of the National Military Establishment by the National Security Act of 1947 (61 Stat. 502) and came into being on September 18, 1947. The National Security Act Amendments of 1949 redesignated the National Military Establishment as the Department of Defense, established it as an executive department, and made the Department of the Air Force a military department within the Department of Defense (63 Stat. 578). The Department of the Air Force is separately organized under the Secretary of the Air Force. It operates under the authority, direction, and control of the Secretary of Defense (10 U.S.C. 8010). The Department consists of the Office of the Secretary of the Air Force, the Air Staff, and field organizations.

OFFICE OF THE SECRETARY

The Office of the Secretary consists of the offices of the Under Secretary, four Assistant Secretaries, the General Counsel, the Administrative Assistant, Legislative Liaison, Public Affairs, International Affairs, Small and Disadvantaged Business Utilization, the Auditor General, and the Inspector General of the Air Force. The heads of these offices are staff advisors to the Secretary for functions the Secretary assigns to them.

The Department of the Air Force is administered by the Secretary of the Air Force, who is responsible for and has the authority to conduct all affairs of the Department. The Secretary's responsibilities include matters pertaining to organization, training, logistical support, maintenance, welfare of personnel, administrative, recruiting, research and development, and other activities prescribed by the President or the Secretary of Defense. The principal assistant to the Secretary is the Under Secretary, who acts with the full authority of the Secretary on all affairs of the Department.

AIR STAFF

The mission of the Air Staff is to furnish professional assistance to the Secretary, Under Secretary, and Assistant Secretaries of the Air Force and to the Chief of Staff in executing their responsibilities.

Structure The Air Staff is a management headquarters functional organization under the Chief of Staff, United States Air Force. Titles throughout all organizational levels reflect functions involved.

Functions and Activities All Staff functions are specialized into well-defined areas to effect the management principles of functionality, integration, flexibility, simplicity, and decentralization. The Air Staff retains those management functions that legally cannot be delegated or decentralized, are needed by the Secretary and Chief of

DEPARTMENT OF THE AIR FORCE

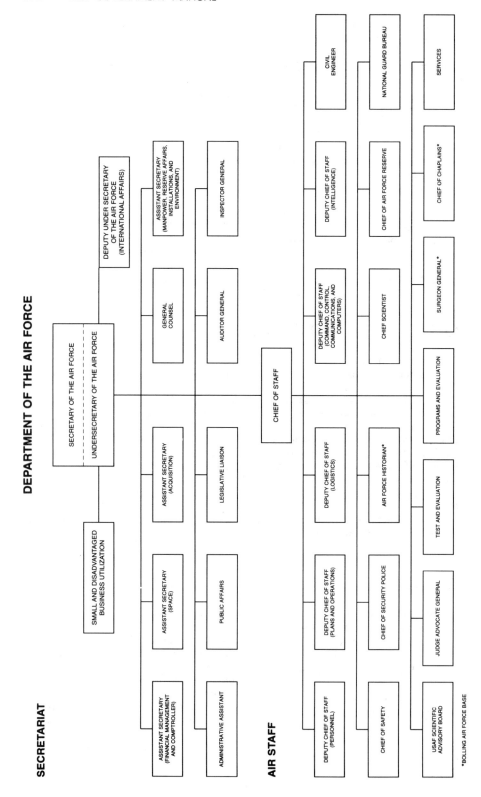

SECRETARIAT

AIR STAFF

*BOLLING AIR FORCE BASE

Staff, are essential to respond promptly to the Secretary of Defense, or are required to determine the design and structure of the Air Force in the future.

Chief of Staff   The Chief of Staff is directly responsible to the Secretary of the Air Force for the efficiency and operational readiness of the U.S. Air Force. He is a member of the Joint Chiefs of Staff (JCS) of the Department of Defense. The Chief of Staff is assisted by the Vice Chief of Staff in all areas of responsibility except JCS. The Assistant Vice Chief of Staff assists the Chief and Vice Chief in the discharge of their duties.

Special Staff   The Special Staff is an adjunct to the Chief of Staff, independent of the basic staff structure, and provides advisory and support services to both the Chief of Staff and the Air Staff. The Special Staff consists of: the Assistant Chief of Staff, Intelligence; the Civil Engineer; the Chief of Safety; the Chief of Security Police; the Air Force Historian; the USAF Scientist; the Chief of Air Force Reserve; the National Guard Bureau; the Scientific Advisory Board; the Judge Advocate General; the Director, Test and Evaluation; the Director, Programs and Evaluation; the Surgeon General; the Chief of Chaplains; Services; and the Chief Master Sergeant of the Air Force.

Deputy Chiefs of Staff   The Deputy Chiefs of Staff (DCS's) function primarily as a coordinating level on policy matters and represent the corporate structure. Substantive functions are organized under the DCS's in homogenous groups called directorates. Under the directorates, functions are further broken down into divisions and branches. The DCS's are Personnel; Plans and Operations; Logistics; and Command, Control, Communications and Computers.

FIELD ORGANIZATIONS

The major commands, field operating agencies, and direct reporting units together represent the field organizations of the U.S. Air Force. These are organized primarily on a functional basis in the United States and on an area basis overseas. These commands are responsible for accomplishing certain phases of the worldwide activities of the U.S. Air Force. They also are responsible for organizing, administering, equipping, and training their subordinate elements for the accomplishment of assigned missions.

Major Commands

The Continental U.S. Commands

Air Combat Command   This Command is responsible for CONUS-based fighters, bombers, ICBM's, reconnaissance aircraft, C3I platforms, and some theater airlifts and tankers. It provides forces directly to Unified Commands or augments theater air forces already forward deployed. Air Combat Command was formed in June 1992 from elements of the former Strategic Air Command and the Tactical Air Command.

Air Force Materiel Command   This Command researches, develops, tests, acquires, delivers, and logistically supports every Air Force weapon system. It has responsibilities from inception of a weapon system on the drawing board, support through its operational life, and its final disposition. Air Force Materiel Command operates major product centers, logistics centers, test centers, and laboratories. It was created in July 1992 from integration of Air Force Logistics Command and Air Force Systems Command.

Air Mobility Command   This Command is responsible for all intertheater airlift assets and most of the tanker and theater airlift force. It was formed in June 1992 from elements of Strategic Air Command and Military Airlift Command.

Air Force Space Command   This Command provides resource management and operation of assigned assets for space control, space force application, force enhancement, space support, and strategic aerospace defense. It operates space and ballistic missile systems. The Command provides a close link between its space activities and, through the U.S. Space Command, the unified command structure.

Air Force Special Operations Command   This Command organizes, trains, and equips Air Force special operations forces. It is the USAF component of the United States Special Operations Command (USSOCOM).

Air Education and Training Command   This Command recruits, commissions, and trains Air Force enlisted and officer personnel. It provides basic military training, initial and advanced technical training, undergraduate and graduate flying training, and professional military and degree-granting professional education. The Command also conducts joint, medical service, readiness and Air Force security assistance training.

Overseas Commands

Pacific Air Forces   The Pacific Air Forces is a major command of the U.S. Air Force and is the Air Force component of the U.S. Pacific Command. Its primary mission is to organize, train, equip, administer, and prepare assigned forces for combat, including: fighter, reconnaissance, air control, close air support, and defense suppression units to conduct defensive and offensive air operations. It provides combat-ready air elements to the U.S. European Command and participates in joint and combined air operations.

United States Air Forces in Europe   The United States Air Forces in Europe is a major command of the U.S. Air Force and is the Air Force component of the U.S. European Command. Its primary mission is to organize, train, equip, administer, and prepare assigned forces for combat, including: fighter, reconnaissance, air control, close air support, and defense suppression units to conduct defensive and offensive air operations. It provides combat-ready air elements to the U.S. European Command and participates in joint and combined air operations.

Field Operating Agencies

Air Force Audit Agency   The Agency provides independent, internal audit and appraisal of financial, operational, management, and support activities as a service to all levels of management.

Air Force Base Conversion Agency   The Agency serves as the Federal real property disposal agent and provides integrated execution management for Air Force bases in the United States as they are closed under the authorities of the Base Closure and Realignment Act of 1988 and the Defense Base Closure and Realignment Act of 1990. The major air commands are responsible for operating their installations and terminating or shifting military missions to other units, until the base closure date. Thereafter, installations are transferred to the Air Force Base Conversion Agency for final disposition.

Air Force Center for Environmental Excellence   The Center provides the Air Force with an in-house capability to manage all aspects of environmental cleanup, planning, and compliance.

Air Force Civil Engineer Support Agency   The Agency provides civil engineering technical assistance and operating support to Air Force bases and organizations. This includes engineering design, operations and maintenance, fire protection, explosive ordnance disposal, disaster preparedness, and air base operability.

Air Force Civilian Personnel Management Center The Center directs, develops, manages, and evaluates the wide range of Federal and internal programs affecting Air Force civilians, including foreign nationals, worldwide.

Air Force Combat Operations Staff The Staff provides readiness-oriented, combat-related support to the Chief of Staff, U.S. Air Force. The Staff serves as the permanent nucleus of a centralized, highly responsive, and integrated combat support structure. It includes the combat-related activities of functions such as operations, operations plans, intelligence, logistics, and personnel.

Air Force Command, Control, Communications and Computers Agency The Agency provides base and point-to-point communications, computer facilities, and automated data processing services, primarily to the U.S. Air Force, but also to other governmental, civil, national, and foreign agencies.

Air Force Cost Analysis Agency The Agency develops cost analysis tools, methods, data bases, models, and automated systems which are used in resource allocation and cost management decisions throughout Air Force.

Air Force Doctrine Center The Center develops and publishes basic and operational level doctrine for the Air Force and provides Air Force inputs into joint and combined doctrine development.

Air Force Flight Standards Agency The Agency manages the interoperability of civil and military airspace and air traffic control systems to ensure worldwide combat and peacetime capabilities. Through its various components, the Agency develops and maintains standards and procedures for flight operations, air traffic control aeronautical information, flight planning, notice to airmen, and navigation and landing systems worldwide. In addition, the Agency facilitates the development of common civil and military airspace.

Air Force Frequency Management Agency The Agency implements the USAF's use of the radio frequency electromagnetic spectrum. It develops procedures on a national, international, and government-to-government basis within the scope of international agreements.

Air Force Historical Research Agency The Agency provides Air Force commanders historical assistance in carrying out their assigned missions and responsibilities and implements the USAF history program. Its responsibilities include serving as a repository for Air Force historical records, determining lineage and honors of Air Force units, and preparing books and other historical works on Air Force and military aviation.

Air Force Inspection Agency The Agency directs the Air Force inspection programs, evaluating operational readiness, accident prevention, and management systems.

Air Force Legal Services Agency The Agency provides Air Force-wide legal services in the functional areas of military justice, patents, claims and tort litigation, general litigation, labor law, preventive law, and legal aid. It also administers the Federal Legal Information Through Electronics Program for the Air Force as executive agent for the Department of Defense.

Air Force Logistics Management Agency The Agency conducts studies and develops, analyzes, tests, evaluates, and recommends new or improved concepts, methods, systems, or procedures that enhance logistics efficiency and effectiveness.

Air Force Management Engineering Agency The Agency develops and maintains Air Force manpower determinants to improve manpower utilization and implements the Air Force Management Engineering and Productivity Programs.

Air Force Medical Operations Agency The Agency assists the USAF Surgeon General in developing plans, programs, and practices for the Air Force Medical Service, aerospace medicine, clinical investigations, quality assurance, health promotion, family advocacy, bioenvironmental engineering, military public health, and radioactive material management.

Air Force Medical Support Agency The Agency assists the USAF Surgeon General in developing plans, programs, and practices relating to Air Force health care in peace and war in the areas of patient administration, health facilities, medical service information systems, and medical logistics.

Air Force Military Personnel Center The Center executes personnel plans and programs and supervises procedures applicable to the worldwide management and administration of Air Force military personnel.

Air Force News Agency The Agency plans and executes the U.S. Air Force's internal information program for all military and civilian personnel. It develops, produces, and distributes materials in support of information, orientation, motivation, and unit morale goals and provides information about Air Force people and missions to hometown news media and national commercial magazines.

Air Force Office of Special Investigations The Office provides criminal, counterintelligence, personnel security, and special investigative services to Air Force activities. It collects, analyzes, and reports significant information about these matters.

Air Force Personnel Operations Agency The Agency performs operational programs located in the Washington, DC, area because of proximity to other Federal personnel activities or Headquarters U.S. Air Force. This includes operation of personnel models and data bases for force structure management; Air Force Relocation; Injury and Unemployment Compensation Programs; awards programs; employee and labor relations support; and Air Force Quality Assessments.

Air Force Program Executive Office The Office oversees major USAF acquisition programs in selected weapons systems and other categories. An outgrowth of the Defense Management Review, it is headed by the USAF Service Acquisition Executive and includes the Program Executive Officers who oversee Program Managers in the major commands.

Air Force Real Estate Agency The Agency acquires, manages, and disposes of land for the Air Force worldwide and maintains a complete land and facilities inventory.

Air Force Reserve The Air Force Reserve performs the U.S. Air Force's Chief of Staff field responsibilities of command of the Air Force Reserve, and is responsible for participation in the formulation of plans for the management, administration, and execution of programs affecting Air Force Reserve units and mobilization of these reserves, when needed.

Air Force Review Boards Agency The Agency consists of the Air Force Board for Correction of Military Records (AFBCMR), the Air Force Civilian Appellate Review Agency (AFCARA), and the Air Force Personnel Council. AFBCMR and AFCARA ensure compliance with appropriate legal and policy guidelines in correcting military records and in resolving civilian employee complaints. The Personnel Council advises the Air Force Secretariat on matters relating to various personnel policies and the effective management of active and reserve components of the Air Force. Boards under the Council examine such matters as discharges, physical disability cases, and decorations.

Air Force Safety Agency The Agency is responsible for implementing and executing Air Force safety and nuclear surety policies, plans, and programs USAF-wide, as directed by the Chief of Safety.

Air Force Security Police Agency The Agency develops operational practices in peacetime and wartime environments to carry out programs for the security of Air Force resources and information and the delivery of law enforcement services. The office implements plans, policies, and programs for base defense; maintenance of security police personnel, training, systems and equipment programs, and the physical security of Air Force resources; information, personnel, and industrial security programs and the wartime information security program; maintenance of law and order; prisoner rehabilitation and corrections programs; vehicle traffic management, and the military working dog program.

Air Force Services Agency   The Agency manages worldwide Air Force operations of Air Force members and their families to improve USAF readiness.

Air Force Studies and Analyses Agency The Agency performs studies to assist and support the decisionmaking process of the Air Force. It performs independent studies and evaluations of Air Force requirements, proposals, plans, and programs, while providing comparisons and trade-off analyses. The Agency also evaluates critical technical and operational issues and monitors applicable tests and evaluations that address such issues.

Air Force Technical Applications Center The Center operates and maintains the U.S. Atomic Energy Detection System. Its specific responsibilities include monitoring compliance with various nuclear test ban treaties; installing and operating equipment for detection and indentification of foreign nuclear weapons tests; and identifying whether events are produced by humans or by nature. In addition, the Air Force Technical Applications Center conducts research to improve atomic energy detection systems.

Air Intelligence Agency   The Agency provides intelligence service in support of USAF operations through the conduct of comprehensive research, direction of collection activities, processing and dissemination of intelligence information and intelligence, and the exercise of management and control of intelligence systems and special security systems.

Air National Guard Readiness Center The Center performs the operational and technical tasks associated with manning, equipping, and training Air National Guard units to required preparedness levels.

Air Reserve Personnel Center   The Center develops management policies, plans, and programs pertaining to Air Force Reserve personnel when they are not on extended active duty, and provides personnel management for reserve forces of the Air Force and personnel support for mobilization of these forces.

Air Weather Service   The Air Weather Service is the USAF technical center of weather expertise for all levels of the Air Force and Army.

Center for Air Force History   The Center operates under the policy guidance of the Air Force Historian. The Center has two basic missions: to research, write, and publish books and other studies on the history of the Air Force; and to provide historical support through the Air Force Historian to Headquarters U.S. Air Force.

Joint Services Survival, Evasion, Resistance and Escape Agency   The Agency serves as DOD's executive agent for three areas: JCS Operational Evasion and Escape matters; Department of Defense Code of Conduct/Survival, Evasion, Resistance, and Escape training; and the POW/MIA program.

Air Force Pentagon Communications Agency   The Agency provides the Secretary of Defense, Joint Chiefs of Staff, Secretary of the Air Force, and Chief of Staff of the Air Force with command, control, communications, and computer systems (C4) to satisfy critical national defense requirements, automated systems for preparing and submitting the President's budget, and decisionmaking aides for top DOD officials. The Air Force Pentagon Communications Agency also secures C4 for the National Command Authority to evaluate global events and respond to crises.

Direct Reporting Units

11th Support Wing   The 11th Support Wing provides logistical and administrative support to Air Force activities in the Washington, DC, area that do not have their own internal support, including Headquarters U.S. Air Force and the Air Force Secretariat. In addition, it represents the Air Force in matters pertaining to the National Capital Region.

Air Force Operational Test and Evaluation Center The Center manages the Air Force Operational Test and Evaluation (OPT) Program; assesses the operational utility of all major and selected non-major Air Force systems with using, implementing, and supporting commands, as required; and is responsible for recommending policy and planning, directing, evaluating, and reporting on the Air Force OPT Program.

U.S. Air Force Academy The Academy provides instruction and experience to cadets so that they graduate with the essential tools for leadership and motivation to become career officers in the U.S. Air Force.

For further information concerning the Department of the Air Force, contact the Office of the Director of Public Affairs, Department of the Air Force, 1670 Air Force Pentagon, Washington, DC 20330–1670. Phone, 703–697–6061.

DEPARTMENT OF THE ARMY

The Pentagon, Washington, DC 20310
Phone, 202-545-6700

SECRETARY OF THE ARMY	TOGO D. WEST, JR.
Senior Military Assistant	COL. T. MICHAEL CREWS
Military Assistants	COL. ILONA E. PREWITT
	LT. COL. R. MARK BROWN
Aides-de-Camp	COL. RANDALL D. BOOKOUT
	CAPT. CHERYL H. KELLER
Assistant to the Secretary	PAM JENOFF
Under Secretary of the Army	JOSEPH R. REEDER
Executive to the Under Secretary	COL. ROBERT D. GLACEL
Military Assistants	LT. COL. RALPH BALL, CAPT. RAY
	BINGHAM, LT. COL. JOHN M. CAL
Assistant to the Under Secretary	WILLIAM K. TAKAKOSHI
Deputy Under Secretary of the Army	WALTER W. HOLLIS
(Operations Research)	
Assistant Secretary of the Army (Civil Works)	JOHN H. ZIRSCHKY, *Acting*
Principal Deputy Assistant Secretary	JOHN H. ZIRSCHKY
Executive Officer	COL. JOHN A. MILLS
Deputy Assistant Secretary for Planning,	(VACANCY)
Policy and Legislation	
Deputy Assistant Secretary for Management	STEVEN DOLA
and Budget	
Deputy Assistant Secretary for Project	ROBERT N. STEARNS
Management	
Assistant for Regulatory Affairs	MICHAEL L. DAVIS
Assistant for Interagency and International	KEVIN V. COOK
Affairs	
Assistant for Water Resources	ROBERT J. KAIGHN
Assistant Secretary of the Army (Financial	HELEN T. MCCOY
Management and Comptroller)	
Principal Deputy Assistant Secretary	NEIL R. GINNETTI
Executive Officer	COL. ROLAND A. ARTEAGA
Military Assistant	LT. COL. EARL NICKS
Deputy Assistant Secretary for Resource	ROBERT RAYNSFORD
Analysis and Business Practice	
Deputy Assistant Secretary for Financial	ERNEST J. GREGORY
Operations	
Deputy Assistant Secretary for Army Budget	MAJ. GEN. ROBERT T. HOWARD
Director, US Army Cost and Economic	ROBERT W. YOUNG
Analysis Center	
Assistant Secretary of the Army (Installations,	ROBERT M. WALKER
Logistics and Environment)	
Principal Deputy Assistant Secretary	ALMA BOYD MOORE
Executive Officer	COL. PAUL T. HUMPHREY
Military Assistant	LT. COL. DOUGLAS S. WATSON

Deputy Assistant Secretary for Environment, Safety and Occupational Health	LEWIS D. WALKER
Deputy Assistant Secretary for Installations and Housing	PAUL W. JOHNSON
Deputy Assistant Secretary for Logistics	ERIC A. ORSINI
Deputy for Chemical Demilitarization	COL. JAMES M. COVERSTONE
Assistant Secretary of the Army (Manpower and Reserve Affairs)	SARA E. LISTER
Principal Deputy Assistant Secretary	ARCHIE D. BARRETT
Executive Officer	COL. EVERETT I. MADDEN
Deputy Assistant Secretary for Civilian Personnel Policy	CAROL D. SMITH
Deputy Assistant Secretary for Force Management, Manpower, and Resources	JASON L. SPIEGEL
Deputy Assistant Secretary for Military Personnel and Equal Opportunity	ROBERT M. EMMERICHS
Deputy Assistant Secretary for Reserve Affairs, Training and Mobilization	TODD A. WEILER
Deputy Assistant Secretary for Review Boards and Equal Employment Opportunity Compliance and Complaints Review	JOHN W. MATTHEWS
Assistant Secretary of the Army (Research, Development and Acquisition)	GILBERT F. DECKER
Military Deputy to the Assistant Secretary	LT. GEN. WILLIAM H. FORSTER
Executive Officer	COL. JOHN P. GEIS
Executive to the Military Deputy	LT. COL. MICHAEL HAMILTON
Deputy Assistant Secretary for Procurement	KENNETH J. OSCAR
Deputy Assistant Secretary for Research and Technology	GEORGE T. SINGLEY
Deputy Assistant Secretary for Plans, Programs and Policy	KEITH CHARLES
Deputy for Systems Management and International Cooperation	MAJ. GEN. RONALD V. HITE
Director for Assessment and Evaluation	HERBERT K. FALLIN, JR.
General Counsel	LAWRENCE M. BASKIR
Principal Deputy General Counsel	LAWRENCE M. BASKIR
Executive Officer	COL. CHARLES BEARDALL
Deputy General Counsel for Acquisition	ANTHONY H. GAMBOA
Deputy General Counsel for Operations and Personnel	THOMAS W. TAYLOR
Deputy General Counsel for Ethics and Fiscal	MATT RERES
Deputy General Counsel for Civil Works and Environment	EARL H. STOCKDALE, JR.
Administrative Assistant to the Secretary of the Army	(VACANCY)
Deputy Administrative Assistant	(VACANCY)
Director of Policy and Plans	JOEL B. HUDSON

Headquarters Services—Washington:

Coordinator	(VACANCY)
Director of Equal Employment Opportunity	DEBRA A. MUSE
Director of Information Management Support Center	ROBERT L. LAYCHAK

Director of Defense Supply Service (Washington)	COL. LARRY STEWART
Director of Defense Telecommunications Service (Washington)	MICHAEL A. NEWTON
Director of Personnel and Employment Services (Washington)	PETER B. HORN
Director of Safety, Security and Support Services (Washington)	JOEL B. HUDSON
Director of Space and Building Management Service (Washington)	EDWARD E. PAVLICK
Director for Information Systems for Command, Control, Communications and Computers	LT. GEN. OTTO J. GUENTHER
Vice Director	DAVID BORLAND
Executive Officer	COL. BILLY BURSE
Director of Modernization and Integration	(VACANCY)
Director of Plans and Program	MAJ. GEN. DAVID E. WHITE
Director of Spectrum Management	FRANK M. HOLDERNESS
Director of Architecture	COL. JEREMIAH GARRETSON
Director of Army Information	COL. ALBERT ARNOLD, *Acting*
The Inspector General	LT. GEN. RONALD H. GRIFFITH
Deputy Inspector General	MAJ. GEN. RICHARD SIEGFRIED
Auditor General	FRANCIS E. REARDON
Deputy Auditor General	THOMAS DRUZGAL
Chief of Public Affairs	MAJ. GEN. CHARLES W. MCCLAIN
Deputy Chief	COL. STEVE F. RAUSCH
Executive Officer	COL. JAMES D. MOUDY
Chief of Command Information and Production	TANSILL R. JOHNSON
Chief of Public Communications	COL. DONALD P. MAPLE
Chief of Leadership Support	COL. BARRY E. WILLEY
Chief of Legislative Liaison	MAJ. GEN. JERRY C. HARRISON
Deputy Chief	COL. WILLIAM D. MCGILL
Special Assistant for Legislative Affairs	ROBERT J. WINCHESTER
Executive Officer	WILSON A. SHATZER
Chief of Congressional Inquiry	COL. JAMES M. JONES
Chief of House Liaison	COL. JOHN MCNULTY
Chief of Senate Liaison	COL. FRANK HURD
Chief of Investigation and Legislative	COL. MICHAEL CHAPMAN
Chief of Programs	LT. COL. STEVE CURRY, *Acting*
Chairman, Armed Reserve Forces Policy Committee	MAJ. GEN. N.A. TRUDEAU
Deputy Chairman	MAJ. GEN. JOHN E. SCULLY
Director of Small and Disadvantaged Business Utilization	SUSAN E. HALEY, *Acting*
Deputy Director	JOHN R. NELSON, *Acting*

Office of the Chief of Staff:

Chief of Staff, United States Army	GEN. GORDON R. SULLIVAN
Vice Chief of Staff	GEN. JOHN H. TILELLI
Director of the Army Staff	LT. GEN. CHARLES E. DOMINY
Director of Management	BRIG. GEN. JAMES E. SHANE
Director of Program Analysis and Evaluation	BRIG. GEN. DAVID K. HEEBNER

Army Staff:

| Deputy Chief of Staff for Intelligence | MAJ. GEN. PAUL E. MENOHER |

Deputy Chief of Staff for Logistics	LT. GEN. JOHNNIE E. WILSON
Deputy Chief of Staff for Operations and Plans	LT. GEN. PAUL E. BLACKWELL
Deputy Chief of Staff for Personnel	LT. GEN. THEODORE G. STROUP
Assistant Chief of Staff for Installation Management	MAJ. GEN. JOHN H. LITTLE
Chief, Army Reserve	MAJ. GEN. MAX BARATZ
The Judge Advocate General	MAJ. GEN. MICHAEL J. NARDOTTI
The Surgeon General	LT. GEN. ALCIDE M. LANOUE
Chief of Chaplains	MAJ. GEN. DONALD W. SHEA
Chief of Engineers	LT. GEN. ARTHUR E. WILLIAMS
Chief, National Guard Bureau	LT. GEN. EDWARD D. BACA

Major Army Commands:

Commanding General, U.S. Army Material Command	GEN. LEON E. SALOMON
Commanding General, U.S. Army Corps of Engineers	LT. GEN. ARTHUR E. WILLIAMS
Commanding General, U.S. Army Criminal Investigation Command	MAJ. GEN. PETER T. BERRY
Commanding General, U.S. Army Forces Command	GEN. DENNIS J. REIMER
Commanding General, U.S. Army Information Systems Command	MAJ. GEN. SAMUEL A. LEFFLER
Commanding General, U.S. Army Intelligence and Security Command	BRIG. GEN. TRENT N. THOMAS
Commanding General, U.S. Army Medical Command	MAJ. GEN. RICHARD D. CAMERON
Commanding General, U.S. Army Military District of Washington	MAJ. GEN. FRED A. GORDAN
Commanding General, U.S. Army Military Traffic Management Command	MAJ. GEN. ROGER G. THOMPSON
Commanding General, U.S. Army Special Operations Command	LT. GEN. JAMES T. SCOTT
Commanding General, U.S. Army Training and Doctrine Command	GEN. WILLIAM W. HARTZOG
Commanding General, U.S. Army South	MAJ. GEN. LAWSON W. MAGRUDER
Commanding General, Eighth U.S. Army	GEN. GARY E. LUCK
Commanding General, U.S. Army Pacific	LT. GEN. ROBERT L. ORD III
Commanding General, U.S. Army Europe	GEN. WILLIAM W. CROUCH

DEPARTMENT OF THE ARMY

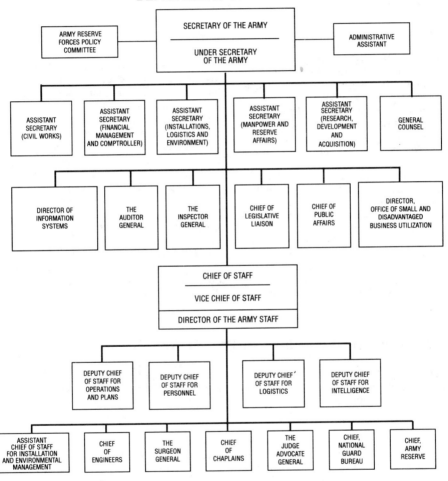

The mission of the Department of the Army is to organize, train, and equip active duty and reserve forces for the preservation of peace, security, and the defense of our nation. It serves as part of our national military team, whose members include the Navy, Air Force, Marines, and Coast Guard. The Army's mission focuses on land operations; its soldiers must be trained with modern arms and equipment and be ready to respond quickly.

The Army also administers programs aimed at protecting the environment, improving waterway navigation, flood and beach erosion control, and water resource development. It provides military assistance to Federal, State, and local government agencies, including natural disaster relief assistance.

The American Continental Army, now called the United States Army, was established by the Continental Congress on June 14, 1775, more than a year before the Declaration of Independence.

The Department of War was established as an executive department at the seat of government by act approved August 7, 1789 (1 Stat. 49). The Secretary of War was established as its head.

The National Security Act of 1947 (50 U.S.C. 401) created the National Military Establishment, and the Department of War was designated the Department of the Army. The title of its Secretary became Secretary of the Army (5 U.S.C. 171).

The National Security Act Amendments of 1949 (63 Stat. 578) provided that the Department of the Army be a military department within the Department of Defense.

The Army Organization Act of 1950 (64 Stat. 263) provided the statutory basis for the internal organization of the Army and the Department of the Army. The act consolidated and revised the numerous earlier laws, incorporated various adjustments made necessary by the National Security Act of 1947 and other postwar enactments, and provided for the organization of the Department of the Army in a single comprehensive statute, with certain minor exceptions. In general, the act followed the policy of vesting broad organizational powers in the Secretary of the Army, subject to delegation by him, rather than specifying duties of subordinate officers (10 U.S.C. 3012, 3062).

Office of the Secretary of the Army

Secretary   The Secretary of the Army is the head of the Department of the Army. Subject to the direction, authority, and control of the President as Commander in Chief and of the Secretary of Defense, the Secretary of the Army is responsible for and has the authority to conduct all affairs of the Department of the Army, including its organization, administration, operation, efficiency, and such other activities as may be prescribed by the President or the Secretary of Defense as authorized by law.

Certain civilian functions, such as comptroller, acquisition, inspector general, auditing and information management, are also under the authority of the Office of the Secretary of the Army. Additionally, the Secretary is responsible for civil functions, such as oversight of the Panama Canal Commission and execution of the Panama Canal Treaty; the civil works program of the Corps of Engineers; Arlington and Soldiers' Home National Cemeteries; and such other activities of a civil nature as may be prescribed by higher authority or authorized by law.

Principal Assistants   The Under Secretary of the Army is the primary assistant to the Secretary. Other principal assistants include: the Assistant Secretaries, General Counsel, Administrative Assistant, the several Directors and Chiefs, the Auditor

General, and the Chairman of the Army Reserve Forces Policy Committee.

Army Policy Council The Council is the senior policy advisory council of the Department of the Army. It provides the Secretary of the Army and his principal civilian and military assistants with a forum for the discussion of Army subjects of significant policy interest and an opportunity for members to consult with other members on matters arising within their specific areas of responsibility.

For further information, call 703–695–7922.

Army Staff

The Army Staff, presided over by the Chief of Staff, is the military staff of the Secretary of the Army. The Army Staff renders professional advice and assistance to the Secretary of the Army, the Under Secretary of the Army, the Assistant Secretaries of the Army, and other officials of the Army Secretariat.

It is the duty of the Army Staff to:

—prepare for employment of the Army and for such recruiting, organizing, supplying, equipping, training, mobilizing, and demobilizing of the Army as will assist the execution of any power, duty, or function of the Secretary or the Chief of Staff;

—investigate and report upon the efficiency of the Army and its preparation for military operations;

—act as the agent of the Secretary of the Army and the Chief of Staff in coordinating the action of all organizations of the Department of the Army; and

—perform such other duties not otherwise assigned by law as may be prescribed by the Secretary of the Army.

Chief of Staff The Chief of Staff is the principal military adviser to the Secretary of the Army and is charged by him with the planning, development, execution, review, and analysis of the Army programs. The Chief of Staff, under the direction of the Secretary of the Army, supervises the members and organization of the Army and performs the duties prescribed for him by the National Security Act of 1947 (50 U.S.C. 401) and other laws. He is directly responsible to the Secretary of the Army for the efficiency of the Army, its state of preparation for military operations, and plans therefor.

Department of the Army Program Areas

Military Operations and Plans Determination of requirements and priorities for, and the employment of, Army forces strategy formation; mid-range, long-range, and regional strategy application; arms control, negotiation and disarmament; national security affairs; joint service matters; net assessment; politico-military affairs; force mobilization and demobilization; force planning, programming structuring, development, analysis and management; operational readiness; overall roles and missions; collective security; individual and unit training; psychological operations; unconventional warfare; counterterrorism; operations security; signal security; military aspects of space and sea; special plans; table of equipment development and approval; electronic warfare; nuclear and chemical matters; civil affairs; military support of civil defense; civil disturbance; domestic actions; audiovisual activities; command and control; automation and communications programs and activities; management of the program for law enforcement, correction and crime prevention for military members of the Army; and physical security.

Personnel Management of military and civilian personnel for overall integrated support of the Army, including policies and programs for manpower utilization standards, allocation and documentation, career development, equal opportunity, leadership, alcohol and drug abuse control, welfare and morale, promotion, retention, and separation; military compensation, transportation and travel entitlements; the personnel aspects of military construction and housing management; research and development related to training personnel, manpower systems, and human factors; and management of civilian personnel training.

Reserve Components Management of individual and unit readiness and mobilization for Reserve Components, comprised of the Army National Guard and the U.S. Army Reserve.

Intelligence Management of Army intelligence and counterintelligence activities, personnel, equipment, systems, and organizations; Army cryptology, topography, and meteorology; coordination of Army requirements for mapping, charting, and geodesy; and Army industrial security.

Management-Comptrollership Review and analysis of Army programs and major Army commands; management information systems in the financial area, progress and statistical reporting, and reports control; financial management, budgeting, finance and accounting, cost analysis, economic analysis, military pay and allowances, resource management, and productivity and value improvement; regulatory policies and programs pertaining to the overall management of the Army; and legislative policies and programs pertaining to appropriation acts affecting the Army.

Research, Development, and Materiel Acquisition Management of Army research, development and materiel acquistion; planning, programming, budgeting and execution for the acquisition of materiel obtained by the procurement appropriations for the Army; materiel life cycle management from concept phase through acquisition; and international acquisition programs.

Information Management Automation, communications, audiovisual, records management, publications, and information management.

Logistics Management of Department of the Army logistical activities for the movement and maintenance of forces; logistical planning and support of Army and joint service operations; materiel and supply management and maintenance; security assistance; transportation; and Army interservice supply operations.

Engineering Management of Army engineering, construction, installations, family housing, real estate, facilities requirements and stationing, and real property maintenance activities; environmental preservation and improvement activities; applicable research and development activities for engineer missions to include environmental sciences; Army topographic and military geographic information activities; and engineer aspects of Army strategic and operational plans.

Civil Functions Civil functions of the Department of the Army include the Civil Works Program, the administration of Arlington and Soldiers' Home National Cemeteries, and other related matters. The Army's Civil Works Program, a responsibility of the Corps of Engineers under the direction and supervision of the Secretary of the Army, dates back to 1824 and is the Nation's major Federal water resources development activity and involves engineering works such as major dams, reservoirs, levees, harbors, waterways, locks, and many other types of structures. These works provide flood protection for cities and major river valleys, reduce the cost of transportation, supply water for municipal and industrial use, generate hydroelectric power, provide recreational opportunities for vast numbers of people, regulate the rivers for many purposes including the improvement of water quality, protect the shores of oceans and lakes, and provide other types of benefits. Planning assistance is also provided to States and other non-Federal entities for the comprehensive management of water resources, including pollution abatement works. In addition, through the Civil Works Program the Federal Government protects the navigable waters of the United States under legislation empowering the Secretary of the Army to prohibit activities that would reduce the value of such waters to the Nation.

Medical Management of health services for the Army and, as directed for other services, agencies, and organizations; health standards for Army personnel; health professional education and training; career management authority over commissioned and warrant officer personnel of the Army Medical Department; medical research, materiel development, testing and evaluation; policies concerning health aspects of Army environmental programs and prevention of disease; and planning, programming, and budgeting for Army-wide health services.

Inspection Management of inquiries, inspections, and reports on matters affecting the performance of mission and the state of discipline, efficiency, economy, and morale of the Department of the Army.

Religious Management of religious and moral leadership and chaplain support activities Armywide; religious ministrations, religious education, pastoral care, and counseling for Army military personnel; liaison with the ecclesiastical agencies; chapel construction requirements and design approval; and career management of clergymen serving in the Chaplains Branch.

Legal Legal advisory services provided for all military personnel and agencies of the Army; review and take final action as designee of the Secretary of the Army on complaints of wrongs by service personnel submitted under the Uniform Code of Military Justice; administration of military justice and civil law matters pertaining to the Army; administration of Army claims and legal assistance services; operation of the legal system of appellate reviews of court-martial records as provided by the Uniform Code of Military Justice; general court-martial and real property records custodianship; records administration of proceedings of courts of inquiry and military commissions; liaison service with the Department of Justice and other Federal and State agencies on matters connected with litigation and legal proceedings concerning the Army; and career management of Judge Advocate General's Corps officers.

Public Affairs Public information, command information, and community relations services and preparation of information plans and programs in support of Army basic plans and programs.

History Advisory and coordination service provided on historical matters, including historical properties; formulation and execution of the Army Historical Program; and preparation and publication of histories required by the Army.

Major Army Commands

United States Army Forces Command The Commanding General, United States Army Forces Command, commands all assigned active Army forces in the continental United States and the Continental United States Armies, and assigned United States Army Reserve Troop Program Units in the continental United States and Puerto Rico. He also commands those subordinate commands, installations, and activities assigned by Headquarters, Department of the Army, and, as directed, provides administrative and logistical support through his subordinate installation commanders to other Department of the Army, Department of Defense, or other Government agencies. He also serves as the Commander in Chief, Forces Command, a specified command, and as the Commander in Chief, Army Forces Atlantic Command, the Army component of the United States Atlantic Command, a unified command.

The Commanding General of each of the Continental United States Armies has the primary mission, under the Commanding General, United States Army Forces Command, to command the United States Army Reserve, plan for mobilization, coordinate domestic emergencies, and exercise training supervision over the Army National Guard. The five Army areas are as follows:

First United States Army (Headquarters, Fort George G. Meade, MD)—Connecticut, Delaware, the District of Columbia, Maine, Maryland, Massachusetts, New Hampshire, New Jersey, New York, Pennsylvania, Rhode Island, Vermont, Virginia, and West Virginia.

Second United States Army (Headquarters, Fort Gillem, GA)—Alabama, Florida, Georgia, Kentucky, Mississippi, North Carolina, Puerto Rico, South Carolina, and Tennessee.

Third United States Army (Headquarters, Fort McPherson, GA).

Fifth United States Army (Headquarters, Fort Sam Houston, TX)—Arkansas, Kansas, Louisiana, Missouri, Nebraska, New Mexico, Oklahoma, and Texas.

Sixth United States Army (Headquarters, Presidio of San Francisco, CA)—Arizona, California, Colorado, Idaho, Montana, Nevada, North Dakota, Oregon, South Dakota, Utah, Washington, and Wyoming.

For further information, call 404–669–5607.

United States Army Training and Doctrine Command   The Commanding General, United States Army Training and Doctrine Command, prepares the Army for war and acts as its architect for the future. The Commanding General accomplishes his duty through six related mission domains—doctrine, force design, materiel requirements, leader development, training, and mission support. He is responsible for conducting all concept and doctrine development not assigned by HQDA to other commands and agencies and integrates the Army's total doctrine development. He is further responsible for conducting all combat developments not assigned by HQDA to other commands and agencies. As the Army's principal combat developer, the Commanding General guides, coordinates, and integrates the Army's total combat

development effort. Additionally, he develops, maintains, and supervises the training system by which the total Army trains to fight.

The Commanding General commands installations and activities as assigned by Headquarters, Department of the Army; and, as directed, provides administrative and logistical support through his assigned installation commanders to elements and agencies of the Department of the Army, the Department of Defense, or other Federal agencies that are tenants or satellites of the installation.

For further information, call 804–727–4465.

United States Army Materiel Command   The Commanding General, United States Army Materiel Command, develops and provides materiel and related services to the Army, to Army elements of unified commands and specified commands, to Department of Defense agencies, and to other United States and foreign agencies as directed. His principal missions are to equip and sustain a trained, ready Army; to provide equipment and services to other nations through the security assistance program; to develop and acquire non-major systems and equipment; to provide development and acquisition support to program managers; to define, develop, and acquire superior technologies; to maintain the mobilization capabilities necessary to support the Army in emergencies; and to continue to improve productivity and quality of life.

For further information, call 703–274–9625.

United States Army Information Systems Command   The Commanding General, United States Army Information Systems Command, is responsible for providing information systems and services to the Army and to other Department of Defense agencies and Government organizations as directed.

For further information, call 602–538–6161.

United States Army Intelligence and Security Command   The Commanding General, United States Army Intelligence and Security Command, is responsible for worldwide support of the Army at echelons above corps through electronic warfare, intelligence collection, counterintelligence, and operations security.

For further information, call 703–706–1232.

United States Army Health Services Command The Commanding General, United States Army Health Services Command, performs health services for the Army within the United States and, as directed, for other governmental agencies and activities. He commands the Army hospital system within the United States and other organizations, units, and facilities as may be directed. He is responsible for the conduct of medical professional education for Army personnel. He is further responsible for the development of medical doctrine, concepts, organizations, materiel requirements, and systems in support of the Army.

For further information, call 512–221–6313.

United States Army Criminal Investigation Command The Commanding General, USACIC, centrally commands and controls worldwide Army investigation of serious crime, provides the full range of investigative support to all Army elements, conducts sensitive and special interest investigations, and provides personal security for selected Army and DOD officials. To support these missions, the Commanding General operates a forensic laboratory system and a crime records center. The investigative mission inherently includes devising investigative standards, procedures, and doctrinal policies; special agent accreditation/certification; collection/analysis of criminal intelligence; assisting the legal community (and the Department of Justice) in fraud-related actions; and operating a polygraph program.

For further information, call 703–756–1232.

Military Traffic Management Command The Commanding General, Military Traffic Management Command, is the Executive Director for military traffic

management, land transportation, and common-user ocean terminal service within the continental United States, and for worldwide traffic management of the Department of Defense personal property moving and storage program. He provides transportation engineering services and support to all Department of Defense components. He administers Department of Defense activities pertaining to Highways for National Defense and Railroads for National Defense.

For further information, call 703–756–1724.

United States Army Military District of Washington The Commanding General, United States Army Military District of Washington, commands units, activities, and installations in the National Capital area as may be assigned by Headquarters Department of the Army (HQDA); provides base operation and other support to the Department of the Army, Department of Defense, or other Government activities that are tenants of or are located on their installations for such support; plans for and executes those missions peculiar to the needs of the seat of government as assigned by HQDA; and provides an organized and responsive defense of designated Department of Defense facilities.

For further information, call 202–475–0565.

United States Army Corps of Engineers The Commanding General, United States Army Corps of Engineers, serves as the Army's Real Property Manager, performing the full cycle of real property activities (requirements, programming, acquisition, operation, maintenance, and disposal); manages and executes engineering, construction, and real estate programs for the Army and the United States Air Force; and performs research and development in support of these programs. He manages and executes Civil Works Programs. These programs include research and development, planning, design, construction, operation and maintenance, and real estate activities related to rivers, harbors, and waterways; administration of laws for protection and preservation of navigable waters and related resources such as wetlands. He also assists in recovery from natural disasters.

For further information, call 202–272–0001.

Army Components of Unified Commands   The missions of the commanding generals of the Army components of unified commands are set forth in directives of the Department of Defense. The Army components of unified commands are major commands of the Department of the Army and consist of such subordinate commands, units, activities, and installations as may be assigned to them by Headquarters, Department of the Army. In certain

unified command areas—such as United States Atlantic Command—where the Army does not have a separate, single, and distinct component headquarters or commander, a designated Army commander in the area will be responsible for certain Army "component" functions that must be performed at his location.

COMMANDS:

United States Army Europe. Phone, 011–49–6221–57–8831.
United States Army Japan. Phone, 011–81–0462–51–1520.
Eighth United States Army (Pentagon Korean Liaison Office). Phone, 703–694–3475.
United States Army Western Command. Phone, 808–471–7471.
United States Army Special Operations Command. Phone, 919–432–7587.

United States Military Academy
West Point, NY 10996

Superintendent	LT. GEN. HOWARD D. GRAVES
Commandant of Cadets	MAJ. GEN. THOMAS C. FOLEY
Dean of the Academic Board	BRIG. GEN. GERALD E. GALLOWAY

The United States Military Academy is located at West Point, NY. The course is of 4 years' duration, during which the cadets receive, besides a general education, theoretical and practical

training as junior officers. Cadets who complete the course satisfactorily receive the degree of Bachelor of Science and a commission as second lieutenant in the Army.

For further general information concerning the United States Military Academy, contact the Public Affairs Office, United States Military Academy, West Point, NY 10996. Phone, 914–938–4261. For information about Military Academy admission criteria and policies, contact the Office of the Registrar, United States Military Academy, West Point, NY 10996.

Sources of Information

Arlington and Soldiers' Home National Cemeteries   For information write to the Superintendent, Arlington National Cemetery, Arlington, VA 22211–5003. Phone, 703–695–3175.
Army Historical Program   For information concerning the Army Historical Program, write to the U.S. Army Center of Military History, HQDA (DAMH), Pulaski Building, Washington,

DC 20314–0200. Phone, 202–272–0291.
Civilian Employment   Employment inquiries and applications should be directed to the following: (1) For employment in the Washington, DC, metropolitan area—Personnel and Employment Service—Washington, Room 3D727, The Pentagon, Washington, DC 20310–6800 (phone,

703–695–3383); (2) For employment outside the Washington, DC, metropolitan area—address or apply directly to the Army installation where employment is desired, Attn: Civilian Personnel Office; (3) For employment overseas—U.S. Army Civilian Personnel Center, Attn: PECC–CSS, Hoffman II Building, 200 Stovall Street, Alexandria, VA 22332–0300 (phone, 703–325–8712).

Contracts Contract procurement policies and procedures are the responsibility of the Deputy for Procurement, Office of the Assistant Secretary of the Army (Research, Development and Acquisition), Room 2E661, The Pentagon, Washington, DC 20310–0103. Phone, 703–695–2488.

Environment Contact the Public Affairs Office, Office of the Chief of Engineers, Washington, DC 20314–1000, phone, 202–272–0010; or the nearest Corps of Engineers Division or District Office located in most major cities throughout the United States.

Films, Videotapes, and Videodiscs Requests for loan of Army-produced films, videotapes, and videodiscs should be addressed to the Visual Information Support Centers of Army installations. Army productions are available for sale from the National Audiovisual Center (NAC), Washington, DC 20409–3701. Department of the Army pamphlet 25–90, *Visual Information Products Catalog,* lists the products that have been cleared for public release.

Freedom of Information and Privacy Act Requests Requests should be addressed to the Information Management Officer of the Army installation or activity responsible for the requested information. If it is uncertain which Army activity has the information, requests may be submitted to the Army Freedom of Information and Privacy Act Division, Information Systems Command-Pentagon, Attn: ASQNS-OP-F, Room 1146, 2461 Eisenhower Avenue, Alexandria, VA 22331–0301. Phone, 703–325–6163.

Publications Requests should be addressed to the Information Management Officer of the Army activity

that publishes the requested publication. Official publications published by Headquarters, Department of the Army, are available from the National Technical Information Service, Department of Commerce, Attn: Order Preprocessing Section, 5285 Port Royal Road, Springfield, VA 22161–2171. Phone, 703–487–4600. If it is uncertain which Army activity published the publication, requests should be addressed to the Publishing Division, U.S. Army Publications and Printing Command, Room 1050, 2461 Eisenhower Avenue, Alexandria, VA 22331–0301. Phone, 202–325–6292.

Reading Rooms The Pentagon Library is located in Room 1A518, The Pentagon, Washington, DC 20310–6000. Phone, 703–697–4301. The Discharge Review/Correction Boards Reading Room is located in Room 2E165, The Pentagon, Washington, DC 20319–1803. Phone, 703–695–3973. The Army Freedom of Information Act Reading Room is located in Room 1146, 2461 Eisenhower Avenue, Alexandria, VA 22331–0301. Phone, 703–325–6163.

Military Career and Training Opportunities

Information on all phases of Army enlistments and specialized training are available by writing the United States Army Recruiting Command, Fort Sheridan, IL 60037. Phone, 312–926–3322.

Army Health Professions For information concerning career opportunities in Army Health Professions, write to HQDA (SGPS-PD), Skyline No. 5, 5100 Leesburg Pike, Falls Church, VA 22041–3258. Phone, 703–756–8114.

Army ROTC The Army Reserve Officers' Training Corps is an educational program designed to develop college-educated officers for the Active Army, the Army National Guard, and the Army Reserve. For information, write or contact the Professor of Military Science at the nearest college or university offering the program, or the Army ROTC Regional Headquarters in your area.

Army National Guard For information concerning individual training opportunities in the National Guard, contact the Army National Guard, ARO–OAC–ME, Edgewood, MD 21010–5420. Phone, 301–671–4789.

Chaplains Corps For information concerning career opportunities as a chaplain, write to the Chief of Chaplains, HQDA (DACH–ZA), Washington, DC 20310. Phone, 703–695–1133.

Commissioning Opportunities for Women All commissioning sources available to men are available to women.

Judge Advocate General's Corps For information concerning career opportunities as a lawyer, military and civilian, write to the Personnel, Plans, and Training Office, Office of the Judge Advocate General, Department of the Army, HQDA (DAJA–PT), Washington, DC 20310–2206. Phone, 703–695–1353.

Officer Candidate Schools Members of the Active Army may attend the 14-week course at Fort Benning, GA. Members of the Reserve Components may attend a short course at Fort Benning, GA.

United States Military Academy For information write to Director of Admissions, United States Military Academy, West Point, NY 10996. Phone, 914–938–4041.

Public Affairs and Community Relations For official Army information and community relations, contact the Office of the Chief of Public Affairs, Department of the Army, Washington, DC 20310–1508. Phone, 703–694– 0741. During nonoffice hours, call 202–695–0441.

Research Industry may obtain information on long-range research and development plans concerning future materiel requirements and objectives from Commander, U.S. Army Materiel Command, Attn: AMCPA, 5001 Eisenhower Ave., Alexandria, VA 22333–0001. Phone, 703–274–8010.

Small Business Activities Aids to assist small businesses in obtaining defense procurement contracts are available through the Office of Small and Disadvantaged Business Utilization, Office of the Secretary of the Army, Room 2A712, The Pentagon, Washington, DC 20310–0106. Phone, 703–695–9800.

Speakers Civilian organizations desiring an Army speaker may contact a nearby Army installation or write or call the Community Relations Division, Office of the Chief of Public Affairs, Department of the Army, Washington, DC 20310– 1508. Phone, 703–697–5720. Requests for Army Reserve speakers may be addressed to HQDA (DAAR–PA), Washington, DC 20310–2423, or the local Army Reserve Center. Organizations in the Washington, DC, area desiring chaplain speakers may contact the Chief of Chaplains, Department of the Army, Washington, DC 20310–2700. Phone, 703–695– 1137. Information on speakers may be obtained by contacting the Public Affairs Office, Office of the Chief of Engineers, Washington, DC 20314, or the nearest Corps of Engineer Division or District Office.

For further information concerning the Department of the Army, contact the Office of the Chief of Public Affairs, Headquarters, Department of the Army, Washington, DC 20310–1508. Phone, 703–694–0741.

DEPARTMENT OF THE NAVY

The Pentagon, Washington, DC 20350
Phone, 703–545–6700

SECRETARY OF THE NAVY	JOHN H. DALTON
Executive Assistant and Naval Aide	CAPT. W.B. SCHMIDT
Special Assistant and Marine Corps Aide	COL. G. NEWBOLD, USMC
Administrative Aide	COMDR. M. SEGLEM
Director, Office of Program Appraisal	REAR ADM. W. PUTNAM
Deputy Director	COL. R. APPLETON
Executive Assistant	LT. COMDR. S. JORDAN
Under Secretary of the Navy	RICHARD DANZIG
Executive Assistant and Naval Aide	CAPT. KEVIN J. COSGRIFF, USN
Special Assistant and Marine Corps Aide	COL. ROBERT E. LEE, USMC
Assistant for Administration	(VACANCY)
Director, Small and Disadvantaged Business Utilization	D.L. HATHAWAY
Director, Total Quality Leadership Office	LINDA DOHERTY
Auditor General of the Navy	RICHARD L. SHAFFER
Director, Naval Criminal Investigative Service	R.D. NEDROW
Chief of Information	REAR ADM. K. PEASE, USN
Deputy Chief of Information	CAPT. CHARLES D. CONNOR, USN
Chief of Legislative Affairs	REAR ADM. ROBERT J. NATTER, USN
Deputy Chief of Legislative Affairs	CAPT. JAY M. COHEN, USN
General Counsel	STEVEN S. HONIGMAN
Executive Assistant and Special Counsel	CAPT. J.B. MONTGOMERY, USN
Principal Deputy General Counsel	LEIGH A. BRADLEY
Deputy General Counsel	EUGENE P. ANGRIST
Associate General Counsel (Management)	FRED A. PHELPS
Associate General Counsel (Litigation)	ARTHUR H. HILDEBRANDT
Assistant General Counsel (Research, Development, and Acquisition)	HARVEY J. NATHAN
Assistant General Counsel (Manpower and Reserve Affairs)	JOSEPH G. LYNCH
Assistant General Counsel (Installation and Environment)	C. JOHN TURNQUIST
Counsel, Comptroller of the Navy	MARGARET A. OLSEN
Counsel, Commandant of the Marine Corps	P.M. MURPHY
Counsel, Naval Air Systems Command	CHARLES J. MCMANUS
Counsel, Space and Naval Warfare Systems Command	SOPHIE A. KRASIK
Counsel, Naval Facilities Engineering Command	CHRISTINE C. MUTH
Counsel, Naval Sea Systems Command	WILLIAM P. MOLZAHN
Counsel, Naval Supply Systems Command	DOUGLAS P. LARSEN, JR.
Counsel, Military Sealift Command	RICHARD S. HAYNES
Counsel, Office of the Chief of Naval Research	ELWARD L. SAUL

213

Naval Inspector General	VICE ADM. D.M. BENNETT, USN
Deputy Naval Inspector General	PATRICIA S. KOTZEN
Judge Advocate General of the Navy	REAR ADM. H.E. GRANT, JAGC, USN
Deputy Judge Advocate General	REAR ADM. C.M. LEGRAND, JAGC, USN
Assistant Secretary of the Navy (Financial Management)/Comptroller of the Navy	DEBORAH P. CHRISTIE
Principal Deputy	GLADYS J. COMMONS
Executive Assistant and Naval Aide	CAPT. RICHARD J. PARISH, USN
Special Assistant and Marine Corps Aide	LT. COL. DEBRA WOODWARD, USMC
Director, Office of Budget and Reports	REAR ADM. WILLIAM J. HANCOCK, USN
Director, Office of Finance and Accounting	FREDERICK E. WYANT
Assistant Secretary of the Navy (Manpower and Reserve Affairs)	BERNARD S. ROSTKER
Executive Assistant and Naval Aide	CAPT. EUGENE F. URICOLI, USN
Military Assistant and Marine Corps Aide	COL. J.M. EICHER, USMC
Deputy Assistant Secretary (Manpower)	KAREN S. HEATH
Deputy Assistant Secretary (Reserve Affairs)	WADE R. SANDERS
Deputy Assistant Secretary (Personnel Programs)	CHARLES L. TOMPKINS
Deputy Assistant Secretary (Force Support and Families)	YVONNE M. HARRISON
Deputy Assistant Secretary (Civilian Personnel Policy/Equal Employment Opportunity)	DOROTHY M. MELETZKE
Director, Naval Council of Personnel Boards	COL. E.M. ALBERTSON
Deputy Director	(VACANCY)
Executive Director, Board for Correction of Naval Records	W. DEAN PFEIFFER
Deputy Executive Director	ROBERT D. ZSALMAN
Assistant Secretary of the Navy (Installation and Environment)	ROBERT B. PIRIE, JR.
Executive Assistant and Naval Aide	CAPT. ANDREW D. BRUNHART
Special Assistant and Marine Aide	LT. COL. LARRY JOHNSON
Principal Deputy	CHERYL KANDARAS
Deputy Assistant Secretary (Environment and Safety)	ELSIE L. MUNSELL
Deputy Assistant Secretary (Installation and Facilities)	DUNCAN HOLADAY
Deputy Assistant Secretary (Shore Resources)	RICHARD O. THOMAS
Deputy Assistant Secretary (Conversion and Redevelopment)	WILLIAM J. CASSIDY, JR.
Deputy Assistant Secretary (Force Basing and Infracture Requirements Analysis)	CHARLES P. NEMFAKOS
Assistant Secretary of the Navy (Research, Development and Acquisition)	NORA SLATKIN
Executive Assistant/Naval Aide	CAPT. LARRY PFITZENMAIER, USN
Special Assistant/Marine Corps Aide	COL. DAVID SADDLER, USMC
Principal Deputy	VICE ADM. W.C. BOWES, USN
Deputy Assistant Secretary (ASW Programs)	EDWARD ZDANKIEWICZ
Deputy Assistant Secretary (Air Programs)	WILLIAM J. SCHAEFER

Deputy Assistant Secretary (Command, Control, Communications, Computers, Intelligence/Electronic Warfare/Space (C⁴I/EW/Space))	MARVIN LANGSTON
Deputy Assistant Secretary (Ship Programs)	RONALD K. KISS
Deputy for Acquisition Policy, Integrity Accountability/Competition Advocate General	REAR ADM. MICHAEL SULLIVAN, USN
Deputy for Expeditionary Forces Programs	MAJ. GEN. DAVID RICHWINE, USMC
Director, Navy International Programs Office	(VACANCY)
Director, Acquisition Career Management	W.H. HAUENSTEIN
Director, Resources and Evaluation	(VACANCY)
Chief, Naval Research	REAR ADM. MARC PELAEZ
Executive Assistant	COMDR. MARK TOMB
Program Executive Officers/Direct Reporting Program Managers	REAR ADM. B.D. STRONG, USN; D.P. CZELUSNIAK; REAR ADM. W.A. STUSSIE, *Acting;* REAR ADM. G.P. NANOS, JR.; TIM DOUGLAS; REAR ADM. R.D. WILLIAMS III, USN; REAR ADM. J.T. HOOD, USN; REAR ADM. G.A. HUCHTING, USN; REAR ADM. R.E. FRICK, USN; J. DESALME, JR.; COL. J.M. FEIGLEY, USMC; BRIG. GEN. G.K. MUELLNER, USAF

U.S. Navy

Chief of Naval Operations	ADM. J.M. BOORDA, USN
Vice Chief of Naval Operations	ADM. J.W. PRUEHER, USN
Deputy Chief, Manpower and Personnel	VICE ADM. F.L. BOWMAN, USN
Director of Naval Intelligence	REAR ADM. M.W. CRAMER, USN
Deputy Chief, Logistics	VICE ADM. W.A. EARNER, USN
Deputy Chief, Plans, Policy and Operations	VICE ADM. J.P. REASON, USN
Director of Space and Electronic Warfare	VICE ADM. W.J. DAVIS, JR., USN
Director of Naval Training	VICE ADM. T.W. WRIGHT, USN
Deputy Chief, Resources, Warfare Requirements and Assessments	VICE ADM. T.J. LOPEZ, USN
Assistant Vice Chief of Naval Operations	CAPT. R.J. HORNE, USN
Director of Naval Nuclear Propulsion Program	ADM. B. DEMARS, USN
Director of Test and Evaluation and Technology Requirements	REAR ADM. T.D. RYAN, USN
Surgeon General of the Navy	VICE ADM. H.M. KOENIG, MC, USN
Director of Naval Reserve	REAR ADM. T.F. HALL, USN
Oceanographer of the Navy	REAR ADM. G.W. DAVIS VI, USN
Chief of Chaplains of the Navy/Director of Religious Ministries	REAR ADM. D.K. MUCHOW, CHC, USN
Special Assistant for Public Affairs Support	REAR ADM. K. PEASE, USN
Special Assistant for Safety Matters	REAR ADM. J. MOBLEY, USN
Special Assistant for Inspection Support	VICE ADM. D.M. BENNETT, USN
Special Assistant for Legal Services	REAR ADM. H.E. GRANT, JAGC, USN

Special Assistant for Legislative Support	REAR ADM. R.J. NATTER, USN
Special Assistant for Naval Investigative Matters and Security	R.D. NEDROW
Special Assistant for Material Inspections and Surveys	REAR ADM. P.R. OLSON, USN

Major Shore Commands:

Director, Strategic Systems Program	REAR ADM. G.P. NANOS, JR., USN
Commander, Naval Air Systems Command	VICE ADM. J.A. LOCKARD, USN
Commander, Space and Naval Warfare Systems Command	REAR ADM. G.F.A. WAGNER, USN
Commander, Naval Facilities Engineering Command	REAR ADM. J.E. BUFFINGTON, CEC, USN
Commander, Naval Sea Systems Command	VICE ADM. G.R. STERNER, USN
Commander, Naval Supply Systems Command	REAR ADM. R.M. MOORE, SC, USN
Chief, Bureau of Medicine and Surgery	VICE ADM. H.M. KOENIG, MC, USN
Chief of Naval Personnel	VICE ADM. F.L. BOWMAN, USN
Commander, Naval Meteorology and Oceanography Command	REAR ADM. P.G. GAFFNEY II, USN
Commander, Naval Computer and Telecommunications Command	CAPT. T.A. STARK, USN
Director, Office of Naval Intelligence	REAR ADM. M.W. CRAMER, USN
Commander, Naval Security Group Command	REAR ADM. T.F. STEVENS, USN
Chief of Naval Education and Training	VICE ADM. T.W. WRIGHT, USN
Commander, Naval Legal Service Command	REAR ADM. C.M. LEGRAND, JAGC, USN
Commander, Naval Doctrine Command	REAR ADM. F.L. LEWIS, USN
Commander, Naval Space Command	REAR ADM. P.S. ANSELMO, USN

Major Fleet Commands:

Commander in Chief, U.S. Atlantic Fleet	ADM. W.J. FLANAGAN, JR., USN
Commander in Chief, U.S. Pacific Fleet	ADM. R.J. ZLATOPER, USN
Commander in Chief, U.S. Naval Forces Europe	ADM. L.W. SMITH, JR., USN
Commander, Military Sealift Command	VICE ADM. P.W. QUAST, USN
Commander, U.S. Naval Forces Central Command	VICE ADM. J.S. REDD, USN
Commander, Naval Special Warfare Command	REAR ADM. R.C. SMITH, JR., USN
Commander, Naval Reserve Force	REAR ADM. T.F. HALL, USN
Commander, Operational Test and Evaluation Force	REAR ADM. J.J. ZERR, USN

U.S. Marine Corps

Commandant of the Marine Corps	GEN. C.E. MUNDY, JR., USMC
Military Secretary to the Commandant	COL. J.C. FLYNN, USMC
Sergeant Major of the Marine Corps	SGT. MAJ. H.G. OVERSTREET, USMC
Assistant Commandant of the Marine Corps	GEN. R.D. HEARNEY, USMC
Aide-de-Camp	MAJ. T.M. RILEY, USMC
Secretary of the General Staff	COL. M.E. LOWE, USMC
Director, Special Projects Directorate	COL. D.T. SWAN, USMC
Counsel for the Commandant	P.M. MURPHY
Deputy Chief of Staff for Plans, Policies, and Operations	LT. GEN. A.C. BLADES, USMC
Director, Operations Division	MAJ. GEN. J.H. ADMIRE, USMC
Director, Plans Division	MAJ. GEN. T.L. WILKERSON, USMC

Deputy Chief of Staff for Aviation	LT. GEN. H.W. BLOT, USMC
Assistant Deputy Chief of Staff for Aviation and Director, Aviation Plans, Policy and Requirements Division	BRIG. GEN. R. MAGNUS, USMC
Deputy Chief of Staff for Manpower and Reserve Affairs	LT. GEN. G.R. CHRISTMAS, USMC
Assistant Deputy Chief of Staff for Manpower and Reserve Affairs for Reserve Affairs	MAJ. GEN. R.G. RICHARD, USMC
Assistant Deputy Chief of Staff for Manpower and Reserve Affairs	D.S. HOWELL
Director, Personnel Management Division	MAJ. GEN. P.G. HOWARD, USMC
Director, Manpower Plans and Policy Division	BRIG. GEN. C.L. STANLEY, USMC
Director, Morale, Welfare, and Recreation Support Activity	J.R. JOY
Director, Human Resources Division	COL. K.W. HILLMAN, USMC
Deputy Chief of Staff for Installations and Logistics	LT. GEN. J.A. BRABHAM, USMC
Special Assistant	(VACANCY)
Director, Facilities and Services Division	BRIG. GEN. T.A. BRAATEN, USMC
Director, Contracts Division	P.E. ZANFAGNA
Director, Logistics Plans, Policies, and Strategic Mobility Division	BRIG. GEN. G.S. MCKISSOCK, USMC
Director, Programs and Financial Management Division	COL. R.W. HANSEN, USMC
Deputy Chief of Staff for Programs and Resources	MAJ. GEN. J.W. OSTER, USMC
Director, Programs Division	J.R. MASCIARELLI
Director, Fiscal Division	H.L. DIXSON
Assistant Chief of Staff for Command, Control, Communications, Computer, and Intelligence	MAJ. GEN. J.P. VANRIPER, USMC
Deputy Assistant Chief of Staff	M.H. DECKER
Director of Intelligence	MAJ. GEN. J.P. VANRIPER, USMC
Legislative Assistant to the Commandant	MAJ. GEN. M.D. RYAN, USMC
Director of Public Affairs	BRIG. GEN. T.P. MURRAY, USMC
Staff Judge Advocate to the Commandant of the Marine Corps	BRIG. GEN. M.C. WHOLLEY, USMC
Director of Administration and Resource Management	L.J. KELLY
Director of Marine Corps History and Museums and President, Permanent Marine Corps Uniform Board	BRIG. GEN. E.H. SIMMONS, USMC (RET.)
The Medical Officer, U.S. Marine Corps	REAR ADM. D.I. WRIGHT, USN
The Dental Officer, U.S. Marine Corps	REAR ADM. J.K. JOHNSON, USN
The Chaplain, U.S. Marine Corps	CAPT. G.W. PUCCIARELLI, USN
Commanding General, Marine Corps Recruiting Command	MAJ. GEN. J.R. DAVIS, USMC
Commanding General, Marine Corps Combat Development Command	LT. GEN. C.E. WHILHELM
Commander, Marine Corps System Command	MAJ. GEN. C.A. MUTTER, USMC
Commanding General, Marine Corps Base, Quantico	BRIG. GEN. M.R. STEELE, USMC

[For the Department of the Navy statement of organization, see the *Code of Federal Regulations,* Title 32, Part 700]

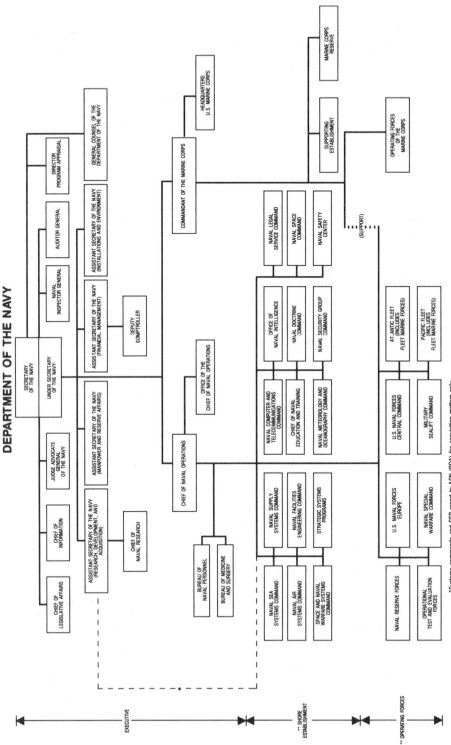

DEPARTMENT OF THE NAVY

*Systems commands and SSP report to ASN (RDA) for acquisition matters only.
**Also includes other Echelon 2 commands and subordinate activities under the command or supervision of the designated organizations.

The primary mission of the Department of the Navy is to protect the United States, as directed by the President or the Secretary of Defense, by the effective prosecution of war at sea including, with its Marine Corps component, the seizure or defense of advanced naval bases; to support, as required, the forces of all military departments of the United States; and to maintain freedom of the seas.

The United States Navy was founded on October 13, 1775, when Congress enacted the first legislation creating the Continental Navy of the American Revolution. The Department of the Navy and the Office of Secretary of the Navy were established by act of April 30, 1798 (10 U.S.C. 5011, 5031). For 9 years prior to that date, by act of August 7, 1789 (1 Stat. 49), the conduct of naval affairs was under the Secretary of War.

The National Security Act Amendments of 1949 provided that the Department of the Navy be a military department within the Department of Defense (63 Stat. 578).

The Secretary of the Navy is appointed by the President as the head of the Department of the Navy and is responsible to the Secretary of Defense for the operation and efficiency of the Navy (10 U.S.C. 5031).

The organization of the Department of the Navy is reflected in the organization chart and personnel listing. The Department of the Navy includes the U.S. Coast Guard when it is operating as a Service in the Navy.

Office of the Secretary of the Navy

Secretary of the Navy

The Secretary of the Navy is the head of the Department of the Navy. Under the direction, authority, and control of the Secretary of Defense, the Secretary of the Navy is responsible for the policies and control of the Department of the Navy, including its organization, administration, functioning, and efficiency. The members of the Secretary's executive administration assist in the discharge of the responsibilities of the Secretary of the Navy.

During the temporary absence of the Secretary of the Navy, the Under Secretary of the Navy is next in succession to act as the Secretary of the Navy. The Under Secretary functions as deputy and principal assistant to the Secretary, and acts with full authority of the Secretary in the general management of the Department.

Civilian Executive Assistants

The Civilian Executive Assistants to the Secretary are the principal advisers and assistants to the Secretary of the Navy on the administration of the affairs of the Department of the Navy as a whole and are assigned Departmentwide responsibilities for areas essential to the efficient administration of the Department of the Navy.

The Civilian Executive Assistants to the Secretary of the Navy are the Under Secretary of the Navy, the Assistant Secretaries of the Navy, and the General Counsel of the Navy. It is the policy of the Secretary to assign Departmentwide responsibilities essential to the efficient administration of the Department of the Navy to the Civilian Executive Assistants.

Each Civilian Executive Assistant, within an assigned area of responsibility, is the principal adviser and assistant to the Secretary on the administration of the affairs of the Department of the Navy. The Civilian Executive Assistants carry out the duties in harmony with the statutory positions of the Chief of Naval Operations, who is the principal military adviser and executive to the Secretary regarding naval matters, and the Commandant of the Marine Corps, who is the principal military adviser and executive regarding Marine Corps matters. Each is authorized and directed

to act for the Secretary within his
assigned area of responsibility.

The Staff Assistants

The Staff Assistants to the Secretary of
the Navy are the Naval Inspector
General, the Comptroller of the Navy,
the Auditor General of the Navy, and the
Chief of Information. The heads of such
other offices and boards established by
law or by the Secretary for the purpose
of assisting the Secretary or one or more
of the Civilian Executive Assistants in the
administration of the Department of the
Navy are detailed as follows.

Judge Advocate General   The Judge
Advocate General is the senior officer
and head of the Judge Advocate
General's Corps, and the Office of the
Judge Advocate General. The Judge
Advocate General provides or supervises
the provision of all legal advice and
related services throughout the
Department of the Navy, except for the
advice and services provided by the
General Counsel. He also performs
functions required or authorized by law;
provides legal and policy advice to the
Secretary of the Navy on military justice,
ethics, administrative law, claims,
environmental law, operational and
international law and treaty
interpretation, and litigation involving
these issues; and acts on other matters as
directed by the Secretary.

The Judge Advocate General also
supervises the administration of military
justice throughout the Department of the
Navy, performs functions required or
authorized by the Uniform Code of
Military Justice, and provides technical
supervision for the Naval Justice School
at Newport, RI.

The Judge Advocate General maintains
a close working relationship with the
General Counsel on all matters of
common interest and liaisons with other
departments and agencies of the
Government as appropriate.

The Deputy Judge Advocate General
performs the duties of the Judge
Advocate General when there is a
vacancy in that office, or during the
absence or disability of the Judge
Advocate General. The Deputy Judge

Advocate General is also Commander of
the Naval Legal Service Command
which includes Naval Legal Service
Offices, their detachments, and the
Naval Justice School.

Officers of the Judge Advocate
General's Corps and judge advocates of
the Marine Corps provide a variety of
legal services to both individual
servicemembers and naval commands
and activities. Legal assistance service to
qualified servicemembers and their
dependents includes advice on tax,
adoption, divorce, contracts, and
landlord/tenant matters. Individual
servicemembers are provided personal
representation for courts-martial, and
may be provided assistance for
nonjudicial punishment, complaints
pursuant to Article 138 of the Uniform
Code of Military Justice, and petitions to
the Board for Correction of Naval
Records.

Unified, specified, and naval
commands are provided legal service on
such diverse matters as investigations,
claims, environmental law, admiralty,
operational and international law and
treaty interpretation, courts-martial,
nonjudicial punishment, civilian
personnel law at field activities (under
the overall coordination and policy
guidance of the Office of Civilian
Personnel Management), military
personnel law, Freedom of Information
Act/Privacy Act, service of process, and
the authority of installation commanders.

**(Public Affairs Officer, Office of the Judge
Advocate General, Department of the Navy, 200
Stovall Street, Alexandria, VA 22332–2400. Phone,
703–614–7420.)**

Naval Criminal Investigative Service

The Director, Naval Criminal
Investigative Service, commands a
worldwide organization with
representation in more than 160
geographic locations to provide criminal
investigative, counterintelligence, law
enforcement and physical security, and
information and personnel security
support to the Navy and Marine Corps,
both ashore and afloat. The Naval
Criminal Investigative Service is
comprised of law enforcement
professionals who are investigators,

crime laboratory technicians, technical investigative specialists, security specialists, and administrative support personnel.

(Director, Naval Criminal Investigative Service, Department of the Navy, Washington, DC 20388–5000. For general information, call 202–433–8800, or contact the Operations Control Center/ Headquarters Duty Officer, 202–433–9323.)

Research and Technology The Office of Naval Research, established by act of Congress on August 1, 1946 (10 U.S.C. 5150–5153), is headed by the Chief of Naval Research, who is authorized to act for the Secretary of the Navy on all assigned matters.

The Office is integrated headquarters of the Navy for science and technology investment. Within the science and technology structure, funding for basic research, exploratory development, advanced technology development, manufacturing technologies, and small business support is merged under the management of the Chief of Naval Research. The Office of Naval Research integrates the Navy's science and technology investments, and accelerates research results into technology development and manufacturing processes on U.S. production lines.

(Office of Naval Research, Ballston Tower 1, 800 North Quincy Street, Arlington, VA 22217–5660. Phone, 703–696–5031.)

Personnel Boards The Naval Council of Personnel Boards, comprised of the Naval Discharge Review Board, Naval Complaints Review Board, Naval Clemency and Parole Board, and the Physical Evaluation Board administers, under the Assistant Secretary of the Navy (Manpower and Reserve Affairs), personnel services and support as indicated by each component board's title.

The Naval Discharge Review Board reviews, pursuant to 10 U.S.C. 1553, upon its own motion or upon request by or on behalf of former Navy and Marine Corps members, the type and reason for discharge or dismissal received by that former member, except a discharge or dismissal by reason of the sentence of general court-martial. It determines whether, under reasonable standards of

naval law and discipline, a discharge or dismissal should be changed and, if so, what change should be made.

The Naval Complaints Review Board reviews, upon request, decisional documents and/or index entries created by the Naval Discharge Review Board after April 1, 1977. The Naval Complaints Review Board determines whether decisional documents conform to those applicable regulations of the Department of Defense and the Department of the Navy.

The Naval Clemency and Parole Board reviews, pursuant to 10 U.S.C. 953–954, Navy and Marine Corps court-martial cases referred to it and grants or denies clemency; and, pursuant to 10 U.S.C. 952, reviews and directs that parole be granted or denied in cases referred to it for review.

The Physical Evaluation Board organizes and administers disability evaluations within the Department of the Navy, pursuant to 10 U.S.C., chapter 61, and other applicable provisions of law and regulation. It is comprised of the Record Review Panel, regional hearing panels at Bethesda, MD, and San Diego, CA, and disability evaluation system counselors located at major medical centers. The system considers evidence concerning disabilities of personnel and determines the appropriate disposition in each case.

(Naval Council of Personnel Boards, Department of the Navy, Room 905, 801 North Randolph Street, Arlington, VA 22203. Phone, 703–696–4356.)

Naval Records The Board for Correction of Naval Records is a statutory civilian board established, pursuant to the provisions of 10 U.S.C. 1552, to relieve the Congress of the burden and necessity of considering private relief legislation for the correction of errors and injustices suffered by members and former members of the Navy and Marine Corps. The Secretary of the Navy, acting through this board of civilians of the executive part of the Department, is authorized to take action consistent with law and regulation to correct naval or military records of the Department of the Navy where such action is necessary or appropriate to correct an error or to remove an injustice. The Board represents the highest echelon of review of administrative errors and injustices. The Board reviews, on application,

actions taken by various boards and officials in the Department.

(Board for Correction of Naval Records, Department of the Navy, Room 2432, Navy Annex, Washington, DC 20370–5100. Phone, 703–614–1402.)

United States Navy

Chief of Naval Operations

In the performance of his duties within the Department of the Navy, the Chief of Naval Operations takes precedence above all other officers of the naval service. He is the Navy member of the Joint Chiefs of Staff.

The Chief of Naval Operations, under the Secretary of the Navy, exercises command over certain central executive organizations, assigned shore activities, and the Operating Forces of the Navy.

The Chief of Naval Operations plans for and provides the manpower, material, weapons, facilities, and services to support the needs of the Navy, with the exception of the Fleet Marine Forces; maintains water transportation services, including sea transportation services for the Department of Defense; directs the Naval Reserve; and exercises authority for matters of naval administration, including matters related to customs and traditions of the naval service, security, intelligence, discipline, naval communications, and naval operations.

The Chief of Naval Operations exercises area coordination authority over all shore activities of the Department of the Navy to ensure that total efforts afford adequate support to the combatant forces and are coordinated among themselves to assure economy and efficiency of operation.

Operating Forces of the Navy

The Operating Forces of the Navy are responsible for naval operations necessary to carry out the Department of the Navy's role in upholding and advancing the national policies and interests of the United States. The Operating Forces of the Navy include

the several fleets, seagoing forces, Fleet Marine Forces and other assigned Marine Corps forces, the Military Sealift Command, and other forces and activities as may be assigned by the President or the Secretary of the Navy. The Chief of Naval Operations is responsible for the command and administration of the Operating Forces of the Navy.

The Pacific Fleet is composed of ships, submarines, and aircraft operating throughout the Pacific and Indian Oceans.

The Atlantic Fleet is composed of ships, submarines, and aircraft that operate throughout the Atlantic Ocean and Mediterranean Sea.

The Naval Forces, Europe, includes forces assigned by the Chief of Naval Operations or made available from either the Pacific or Atlantic Fleet to operate in the European theater.

The Military Sealift Command provides ocean transportation (by Government-owned or commercial vessels) for personnel and cargo of all components of the Department of Defense and as authorized for other Federal agencies; operates and maintains underway replenishment ships and other vessels providing mobile logistic support to elements of the combatant fleets; and operates ships in support of scientific projects and other programs for Federal agencies.

Other major commands of the Operating Forces of the Navy are the Commander, U.S. Naval Forces Central Command; Commander, Operational Test and Evaluation Force; Commander, Naval Special Warfare Command; and Commander, Naval Reserve Force.

Navy Command Structure

The Chief of Naval Operations manages and supports the Operating Forces of the Navy through the following executive and functional organization structure.

Chief of Naval Operations The Office of the Chief of Naval Operations is the headquarters of the Navy which advises and assists the Secretary, the Under Secretary, the Assistant Secretaries, and the Chief of Naval Operations in the discharge of their responsibilities. The Office of the Chief of Naval Operations was established basically in its present structure by Executive Order 9635 of September 29, 1945, and later by act of March 5, 1948 (10 U.S.C. 141, 171, 5036(b), 5081–5088); and by act of October 1, 1986 (10 U.S.C. 111 note).

Sea Systems The Commander, Naval Sea Systems Command, provides material support to the Navy and Marine Corps, and for mobilization purposes to the Department of Defense and Department of Transportation, for ships, submarines, and other sea platforms, shipboard combat systems and components, other surface and undersea warfare and weapons systems, and ordnance expendables not specifically assigned to other system commands.

(Commander, Naval Sea Systems Command, Washington, DC 20362–5101. Phone, 703–602–3328.)

Air Systems The Commander, Naval Air Systems Command, provides for the material support to the Navy and Marine Corps for aircraft, airborne weapon systems, avionics, related photographic and support equipment, ranges, and targets.

(Commander, Naval Air Systems Command, Washington, DC 20361–0001. Phone, 703–692–2260.)

Space and Naval Warfare Systems The Commander, Space and Naval Warfare Systems Command, provides technical and material support to the Department of the Navy for space systems; command, control, communications, and intelligence systems; and electronic warfare and undersea surveillance.

(Commander, Space and Naval Warfare Systems Command, Washington, DC 20363–5100. Phone, 703–602–8768.)

Supply Systems The Commander, Naval Supply Systems Command, provides for the material support to the Navy and Marine Corps for materials, supplies, and supporting services by providing supply management policies and methods and administering related support service systems.

(Commander, Naval Supply Systems Command, Washington, DC 20376–5000. Phone, 703–695–4009.)

Naval Facilities The Commander, Naval Facilities Engineering Command, provides for material and technical support to the Navy and Marine Corps for shore facilities, real property and utilities, fixed ocean systems and structures, transportation and construction equipment, energy, environmental and natural resources management, and support of the Naval Construction Forces.

(Commander, Naval Facilities Engineering Command, 200 Stovall Street, Alexandria, VA 22332–2300. Phone, 703–325–0589.)

Strategic Systems The Director, Strategic Systems Programs, provides for the development, production, and material support to the Navy for fleet ballistic missile and strategic weapon systems, including the missiles, platforms, and associated equipment; security, training of personnel, and the installation and direction of necessary supporting facilities.

(Director, Strategic Systems Programs, Department of the Navy, Washington, DC 20376–5002. Phone, 703–695–2158.)

Naval Personnel The Chief of Naval Personnel directs the procurement, distribution, administration, and career motivation of the military personnel of the regular and reserve components of the United States Navy to meet the quantitative and qualitative manpower requirements determined by the Chief of Naval Operations. He also directs the management and administration of the

Navy Civilian Personnel/Equal Employment Opportunity Programs and develops servicewide programs for improved human resources management.

(Bureau of Naval Personnel, Department of the Navy, Federal Office Building No. 2, Washington, DC 20370–5000. Phone, 703–614–1271.)

Naval Medicine The Chief, Bureau of Medicine and Surgery:

—directs the provision of medical and dental services for Navy and Marine Corps personnel and other persons authorized by law;

—ensures that health care program policies are optimally executed through the acquisition and effective utilization of financial and manpower resources;

—maintains all assigned activities in a proper state of material and personnel readiness to fulfill assigned peacetime and contingency mission taskings;

—administers the execution and implementation of contingency support plans and programs that provide for an effective medical and dental readiness capability;

—acquires, trains, and maintains a force of professional and technical personnel;

—provides professional and technical medical and dental service to the Fleet, Fleet Marine Force, and shore activities of the Navy;

—ensures that assigned activities are able to achieve successful accreditation and recognition by appropriate governmental and civilian agencies and commissions; and

—ensures cooperation with civil authorities in matters pertaining to public health disasters and other emergencies, in conjunction with maintaining and safeguarding the health of Navy and Marine Corps personnel.

(Bureau of Medicine and Surgery, Department of the Navy, Twenty-third and E Streets NW., Washington, DC 20372–5120. Phone, 202–653–1327.)

Oceanography The Commander, Naval Meteorology and Oceanography Command, and the Superintendent, U.S. Naval Observatory, are responsible for the science, technology, engineering, operations, and those personnel and facilities associated with each, which are essential to explore the ocean and the atmosphere and to provide astronomical data and time for naval and related national objectives. Oceanography examines how naval operations are influenced by the physical environment and applies its findings to the development of technology and methods for improving naval operations.

The Naval Oceanographic Program embraces five major disciplines of physical science to investigate the nature and behavior of the ocean environment in which the Navy operates. They are:

Hydrography—to collect data for the charting of the oceans and to establish geodetic references for navigation;

Oceanography—to define the characteristics of the water volume for use in ocean reporting and prediction, and studies of underwater acoustics, water dynamics, corrosion, and other factors influencing the performance of naval systems;

Meteorology—to define the characteristics of the atmosphere for use in weather reporting and prediction, and studies of upper atmosphere winds and currents, refractive indices for radar performance, and similar factors;

Astrometry—to determine the position and motions of celestial bodies required for accurate navigation, operational support, and use in calculating precise geodetic positions and azimuth references on Earth; and

Precise Time—to determine, provide, and manage the distribution of precise time and time interval (frequency), both atomic and astronomical, for use in electronic navigation and command, control, and communications.

(Oceanographer of the Navy, U.S. Naval Observatory, Washington, DC 20392–1800. Phone, 202–653–1295. Commander, Naval Meteorology and Oceanography Command, Stennis Space Center, Bay St. Louis, MS 39529–5002. Phone, 601–688–4726. Superintendent, Naval Observatory, Washington, DC 20392–5100. Phone, 202–653–1541.)

Space Command The Commander, Naval Space Command, provides operational space systems support to naval forces worldwide and helps prepare the naval service for extended future involvement in space. The

Command has operational responsibility for all Navy space-related systems, plus coordination responsibility with other operational activities so that the space capabilities are integrated into the Navy's operational plans. The Command identifies fleet operational requirements for space systems, which will be translated into specific program planning and budgeting. The Command has operational responsibility for the Navy Navigation Satellite System, the Naval Space Surveillance System, and elements supporting the Fleet Satellite Communications System.

The Command has administrative responsibility for the Fleet Surveillance Support Command and the Relocatable Over-the-Horizon Radar System, a broad area surveillance high-frequency radar that will have the capability to be relocated to prepared global sites to support naval forces.

(Commander, Naval Space Command, Department of the Navy, Dahlgren, VA 22448–5170. Phone, 703–663–7841.)

Legal Services   The Commander, Naval Legal Service Command, under the command of the Chief of Naval Operations, is responsible for administering the legal services program within the Navy and providing command direction for all Naval Legal Service Command activities and resources.

(Commander, Naval Legal Service Command, 200 Stovall Street, Alexandria, VA 22332–2400. Phone, 703–325–9820.)

Computers and Telecommunications   The Commander, Naval Computer and Telecommunications Command, performs functions to provide, operate, and maintain all Navy ashore communications resources and all non-tactical information and resources for command, control, and administration of the Navy and those elements of the Defense Communications System assigned to the Navy.

(Commander, Naval Computer and Telecommunications Command, 4401 Massachusetts Avenue NW., Washington, DC 20390–5290. Phone, 202–282–0357.)

Cryptology   The Commander, Naval Security Group Command, performs cryptologic functions; provides, operates, and maintains an adequate Naval Security Group; approves requirements for the use of existing Naval Security Group capabilities and resources; and coordinates the execution of approved cryptologic programs.

(Commander, Naval Security Group Command, 3801 Nebraska Avenue NW., Washington, DC 20393–5210. Phone, 202–282–0272.)

Intelligence   The Director, Office of Naval Intelligence, ensures the fulfillment of the intelligence requirements and responsibilities of the Department of the Navy.

(Director, Office of Naval Intelligence, Department of the Navy, 4600 Silver Hill Road, Washington, DC 20389–5000. Phone, 202–763–3552; hotline, 301–763–3557.)

Education and Training   The mission of the Chief of Naval Education and Training is to:
  —provide assigned shore-based education and training for Navy, certain Marine Corps, and other personnel in support of the Fleet, Naval Shore Establishment, Naval Reserve, Interservice Training Program, and Security Assistance Program;
  —develop specifically designated education and training afloat programs for the Fleet;
  —execute the Navy's responsibility for voluntary education and dependents education;
  —participate with research and development activities in the development and implementation of the most effective teaching and training systems and devices for optimal education and training; and
  —perform such other functions as directed.

(Chief of Naval Education and Training, Naval Air Station, Department of the Navy, Pensacola, FL 32508–5100. Phone, 904–452–4858.)

Naval Doctrine Command   The Commander, Naval Doctrine Command, is the primary authority for the development of naval concepts and integrated naval doctrine and is charged to:

—serve as coordinating authority for the development and evaluation of Navy service-specific doctrine;

—provide a coordinated Navy/Marine Corps naval voice in joint and combined doctrine development; and

—ensure that Navy, naval, and joint doctrine are addressed in training and education curricula and in operations, exercises, and wargames.

(Commander, Naval Doctrine Command, Suite 200, 8952 First Street, Norfolk, VA 23511–3790. Phone, 804–445–0555.)

United States Marine Corps

Commandant of the Marine Corps,
Headquarters, U.S. Marine Corps, Washington, DC 20380–0001
Phone, 703–614–2344

The United States Marine Corps was established on November 10, 1775, by resolution of the Continental Congress. Marine Corps' composition and functions are detailed in 10 U.S.C. 5063, and functions are performed as follows:

—The Marine Corps, within the Department of the Navy, is organized to include not less than three combat divisions and three aircraft wings, and such other land combat, aviation, and other services as may be organic therein.

—The Marine Corps is organized, trained, and equipped to provide Fleet Marine Forces of combined arms, together with supporting air components, for service with the fleet in the seizure or defense of advanced naval bases and for the conduct of such land operations as may be essential to the prosecution of a naval campaign.

—In addition, the Marine Corps provides detachments and organizations for service on armed vessels of the Navy, provides security detachments for the protection of naval property at naval stations and bases, and performs such other duties as the President may direct. However, these additional duties may not detract from or interfere with the operations for which the Marine Corps is primarily organized.

—The Marine Corps develops, in coordination with the Army and the Air Force, those phases of amphibious operations that pertain to the tactics, techniques, and equipment used by landing forces.

—The Marine Corps is responsible, in accordance with integrated joint

mobilization plans, for the expansion of peacetime components of the Marine Corps to meet the needs of war.

Organization   The Marine Corps is composed of Headquarters, U.S. Marine Corps; the Operating Forces; and the Supporting Establishment. The Operating Forces consist of Fleet Marine Force Atlantic, Fleet Marine Force Pacific, Marine Corps Reserve, Marine Security Forces, and Marine Detachments Afloat. The supporting establishment includes recruiting activities, training installations, reserve support activities, ground and aviation installations, and logistics bases.

The Marine Corps deploys and employs for combat as Marine Air Ground Task Forces (MAGTF's). There are four types of MAGTF's: the Marine Expeditionary Force, the Marine Expeditionary Brigade, the Marine Expeditionary Unit, and the Special Purpose MAGTF. Each of these MAGTF's has a command element, a ground combat element, an aviation combat element, and a combat service support element. The size and specific organization of the MAGTF is determined by the task to be accomplished—task organization. For instance, Marine Expeditionary Units are routinely deployed on amphibious ships to the Mediterranean Sea, Persian Gulf, and Pacific Ocean providing deterrence to aggressors and reassurance to our allies through their forward presence and unique crisis response capabilities. Larger MAGTF's can rapidly deploy by air, sea, or any combination of means from both coasts of the United States and forward bases in the Western Pacific to respond to contingencies worldwide.

Marine Corps Districts

District/Address	Telephone
1. 605 Stewart Ave., Garden City, NY 11530–4761	516–228–5652
4. Bldg. 75, Naval Base, Philadelphia, PA 19112–5000	215–897–6301

Marine Corps Districts—Continued

District/Address	Telephone
6. 1655 Peachtree St. NE., Atlanta, GA 30309–3117	404–347–7561
8. Bldg. 10, Naval Support Activity, New Orleans, LA 70142–5100	504–361–2619
9. 10000 W. 75th St., Shawnee Mission, KS 66204–2265	913–236–3302
12. 3704 Hochmuth Ave., San Diego, CA 92140	619–542–5570

United States Naval Academy

Annapolis, MD 21402–5018
Phone, 1–800–638–9156 (Office of the Dean of Admissions—Candidate Guidance)

The United States Naval Academy is the undergraduate college of the naval service. Through its comprehensive 4-year program, which stresses excellence in academics, physical education, professional training, conduct, and honor, the Academy prepares young men and women morally, mentally, and physically to be professional officers in the Navy and Marine Corps. All graduates receive a bachelor of science degree in 1 of 18 majors.

For further information concerning the United States Naval Academy, contact the Superintendent, United States Naval Academy, Annapolis, MD 21402–5018.

Sources of Information

Astronomy   The United States Naval Observatory provides the astronomical data and precise time required by the Navy and other components of the Department of Defense for navigation, precise positioning, and command, control, and communications. These data also are made available to other Government agencies and to the general public. To broaden the understanding of the mission, functions, and programs of the Naval Observatory, regular night tours and special group day tours are conducted. The night tours are open to the general public and are given every Monday night, except on Federal holidays. Information concerning activities of the observatory and public tours may be obtained by writing to the Superintendent, Naval Observatory, Washington, DC 20392–5100. Phone, 202–653–1543.

Civilian Employment   Information about civilian employment opportunities within the Department of the Navy in the Washington, DC, metropolitan area can be obtained from the Office of Civilian Personnel Management, Northeast Region, Washington Detachment, 801 North Randolph Street, Arlington, VA 22203–1927 (phone, 703–696–4567); or the Commandant of the Marine Corps (ARCA), Headquarters, U.S. Marine Corps, Washington, DC 20380 (phone, 703–697–7474).

Consumer Activities   Research programs of the Office of the Chief of Naval Research cover a broad spectrum of scientific fields, primarily for the needs of the Navy, but much information is of interest to the public. Inquiries on specific research programs should be directed to the Office of Naval Research, ONR (Code 10), 800 North Quincy Street, Arlington, VA 22217–5660. Phone, 703–696–5031. Inquiries on specific technology programs should be directed to the Director, Office of Naval Technology, ONT (Code 20), 800

North Quincy Street, Arlington, VA 22217–5000. Phone, 202–696–5115.

Contracts and Small Business Activities Information in these areas can be obtained from the Assistant Secretary of the Navy (Research, Engineering, and Systems), Department of the Navy, 2211 Jefferson Davis Highway, Arlington, VA 22244–5120 (phone, 703–602–2700). Information pertaining specifically to the Marine Corps in the areas of small businesses, minority-owned businesses, and labor surplus activities can be obtained from the Marine Corps Small Business Specialist (LS), Installations and Logistics Department, Headquarters, U.S. Marine Corps, Washington, DC 20380. Phone, 703–696–1022.

Environment The Assistant Secretary of the Navy (Installations and Environment) is responsible for the conduct of the environmental protection and natural resources management programs of the Navy and Marine Corps, and serves as the focal point for the Department in establishing policy in environmental affairs. This is the contact for liaison at the highest level with other Federal and State agencies in addition to private agencies organized on a national level. All environmental impact statements that originate within the Navy and Marine Corps for submission to the Environmental Protection Agency, in compliance with the National Environmental Policy Act, are processed by the Assistant Secretary of the Navy (Installation and Environment). This Office maintains close liaison with the Council on Environmental Quality, the Environmental Protection Agency, and the Deputy Assistant Secretary of Defense (Environmental Security) in the implementation of the environmental protection and natural resources management programs. Other responsible offices within the Department of the Navy are the Environmental Protection, Occupational Safety and Health Division in the Office of the Chief of Naval Operations, and the Office of the Deputy Chief of Staff for Installations and Logistics, Headquarters, U.S. Marine Corps.

General Inquiries Navy and Marine Corps recruiting offices, installation commanders, and Commanding Officers of Marine Corps Districts (table on page 227) can answer general inquiries concerning the Navy and Marine Corps and their community and public information programs.

Also, the Chief of Information makes accurate and timely information about the Navy available so that the general public, the press, and Congress may understand and assess the Navy's programs, operations, and needs; coordinating Navy participation in community events; and supervising the Navy's internal information programs. Phone, 703–697–5342.

Military Career and Training Opportunities
Marine Corps The Marine Corps conducts enlisted and officer training programs requiring various lengths of service and provides the assurance of specialized skill training and other benefits.

The Marine Corps provides opportunities for training in a variety of technical skills that are necessary in support of ground and aviation combat operations. Radar operation and repair, meteorology, engineer equipment and automotive mechanics, artillery and armor repair, data processing, communications-electronics, jet aircraft repair, avionics, and air control are but a few specialized fields available.

The Marine Corps participates in the Naval Reserve Officers Training Corps Program for commissioning officers in the Marine Corps.

Platoon Leaders Class is a Marine Corps program for commissioning officers in the Marine Corps Reserve. Freshmen, sophomores, or juniors in an accredited college may apply. The Program provides financial assistance to undergraduates.

The Officer Candidate Class is another program for commissioning officers in the Marine Corps Reserve. Applicants must be college graduates or in their senior year.

Information on the above programs is available at most civilian educational institutions and Navy and Marine Corps recruiting stations. Local telephone directories list the address and telephone number of the Recruiting Station and Officer Selection Officer under U.S. Government. Interested persons also may write directly to the Commandant of the Marine Corps (M&RA), Washington, DC 20380–0001. Phone, 703–614–2914.

Information concerning Marine Corps Reserve opportunities can be obtained from local Marine Corps recruiting stations or Marine Corps Reserve Drill Centers. Interested persons may also write directly to the Commandant of the Marine Corps (M&RA, RA), Washington, DC 20380–0001.

Speakers and Films Information can be obtained on the following: speakers (phone, 703–697–8711); films (phone, 703–697–5342); and the Naval Recruiting Exhibit Center (phone, 904–452–5348). Information concerning the Navy can be obtained by writing the Office of Information, Department of the Navy, Washington, DC 20350 (phone, 202–695–0965). Information on how to obtain Marine Corps speakers can be obtained by writing to the Director of Public Affairs, Headquarters, U.S. Marine Corps, Washington, DC 20380–0001; or by contacting the Director of any Marine Corps District.

For further information concerning the Navy and Marine Corps, contact the Office of Information, Department of the Navy, Washington, DC 20350 (phone, 703–697–7391); or the Legislative Assistant to the Commandant and Director of Public Affairs, Headquarters, U.S. Marine Corps, Washington, DC 20380 (phone, 703–614–1492).

DEFENSE AGENCIES

Advanced Research Projects Agency
3701 North Fairfax Drive, Arlington, VA 22203–1714
Phone, 703–696–2444

Director	LARRY LYNN, *Acting*
Deputy Director	DUANE A. ADAMS
Deputy Director for Management	RON H. REGISTER

The Advanced Research Projects Agency is a separately organized agency within the Department of Defense under a Director appointed by the Secretary of Defense. The Agency, under the authority, direction, and control of the Director of Defense Research and Engineering (DDR&E), engages in advanced basic and applied research and development projects essential to the Department of Defense, and conducts prototype projects that embody technology that may be incorporated into joint programs, programs in support of deployed U.S. forces, selected Military Department programs, or dual-use programs and, on request, assists the Military Departments in their research and development efforts.

In this regard, the Agency arranges, manages, and directs the performance of work connected with assigned advanced projects by the Military Departments, other government agencies, individuals, private business entities, and educational or research institutions, as appropriate; recommends through the DDR&E to the Secretary of Defense assignment of advanced projects to the Agency; keeps the DDR&E, the Chairman of the Joint Chiefs of Staff, the Military Departments, and other Department of Defense agencies informed on significant new developments and technological advances within assigned projects; and performs other such functions as the Secretary of Defense or the DDR&E may assign.

For further information, contact the Advanced Research Projects Agency, 3701 North Fairfax Drive, Arlington, VA 22203–1714. Phone, 703–696–2444.

Ballistic Missile Defense Organization
The Pentagon, Washington, DC 20301–7100
Phone, 703–697–4040

Director	LT. GEN. MALCOLM O'NEILL, USA

Deputy Director   WILLIAM EVERS
Chief of Staff   COL. P. MCKELUY, USAF

[For the Ballistic Missile Defense Organization statement of organization, see the *Code of Federal Regulations,* Title 32, Part 388]

The Ballistic Missile Defense Organization (formerly the Strategic Defense Initiative Organization) was established as a separate agency of the Department of Defense and is Presidentially chartered and mandated by Congress to develop ballistic missile defense systems that are capable of providing highly effective defense of the United States, forward-deployed and expeditionary elements of the U.S. Armed Forces, and allies of the United States.

The agency's mission is to manage and direct DOD's Ballistic Missile Defense acquisition programs, which include theater missile defense and a national missile defense for the U.S. The agency also is responsible for the continuing research and development of follow-on technologies that are relevant for long-term ballistic missile defense. These programs will build a technical foundation for evolutionary growth in future ballistic missile defenses. In developing these acquisition and technology programs, the agency utilizes the services of the Military Departments, the Department of Energy, private industries, and educational and research institutions.

For further information, contact Management Operations, Ballistic Missile Defense Organization, Washington, DC 20301–7100. Phone, 703–693–1532.

Central Imagery Office
Suite 300, 8401 Old Courthouse Road, Vienna, VA 22182

Director   ANNETTE J. KRYGIEL
Deputy Director   MAJ. GEN. BRETT M. DULA, USAF

The Central Imagery Office (CIO) was established on May 6, 1992, and operates under DOD Directive 5105.56. The Office ensures that Government intelligence, mapping, charting and geodesy, and other needs for imagery are met effectively and efficiently in a manner conducive to national security, consistent with the authorities and duties of the Secretary of Defense and the Director of Central Intelligence. CIO provides support functions to the Department of Defense, the Central Intelligence Agency, and other Federal departments and agencies on matters concerning imagery relating to national security.

For further information, contact the Office of the Director, Administration, Suite 300, 8401 Old Courthouse Road, Vienna, VA 22182–3820. Phone, 703–275–5810.

Defense Commissary Agency

Fort Lee, VA 23801–6300
Phone, 804–734–8721

Director	MAJ. GEN. RICHARD E. BEALE, JR.
Chief Executive Officer	CHARLES M. WIKER
Chief of Staff	COL. RONALD P. MCCOY, USAF

The Defense Commissary Agency was established by direction of the Secretary of Defense on November 9, 1990, and operates under DOD Directive 5105.55.

The Agency is responsible for providing an efficient and effective worldwide system of commissaries for reselling groceries and household supplies at low, practical prices (consistent with quality) to members of the Military Services, their families, and other authorized patrons, while maintaining high standards of quality, facilities, products, and service. In addition, DeCA provides a peacetime training environment for troop support logisticians needed in wartime and, as circumstances dictate, troop issue subsistence support to military dining facilities consistent with Service needs.

Sources of Information

Employment General employment inquiries should be addressed to Headquarters, Defense Commissary Agency, Attn: Personnel Management Support Office, Fort Lee, VA 23801–6300. Phone, 804–734–8684.
Procurement and Small Business Activities For information, contact the Director, Small and Disadvantaged Business Utilization, Headquarters, Defense Commissary Agency, Fort Lee, VA 23801–6300. Phone, 804–734–8828.
Publication *How To Do Business with DeCA* is available free of charge from the Director, Small and Disadvantaged Business Utilization, above address.

For further information, contact the Director of Corporate Communications, Fort Lee, VA 23801–6300. Phone, 804–734–8134.

Defense Contract Audit Agency

Building 4, Cameron Station, Alexandria, VA 22304–6178
Phone, 703–274–6785

Director	WILLIAM H. REED
Deputy Director	MICHAEL J. THIBAULT

The Defense Contract Audit Agency was established in 1965 and operates under Department of Defense Directive 5105.36.

The Agency performs all necessary contract audit functions for the Department of Defense and provides accounting and financial advisory services to all Defense components

responsible for procurement and contract administration. These services are provided in connection with the negotiation, administration, and settlement of contracts and subcontracts. They include evaluating the acceptability of costs claimed or proposed by contractors and reviewing the efficiency and economy of contractor operations.

Other Government agencies may request the Agency's services under appropriate arrangements.

The Agency manages its operations through 5 regional offices responsible for approximately 131 field audit offices throughout the United States and overseas. Each region is responsible for the contract auditing function in its assigned area.

Regional Offices—Defense Contract Audit Agency

Region	Address	Director	Telephone
CENTRAL	Suite 300, 106 Decker Ct., Irving, TX 75062–2795	C.T. Cherry	214–650–4800
EASTERN	Suite 300, 2400 Lake Park Dr., Smyrna, GA 30080–7644	Richard R. Buhre	404–319–4400
MID–ATLANTIC	Suite 1000, 615 Chestnut St., Philadelphia, PA 19106–4498.	William H. Kraft	215–597–7451
NORTHEASTERN	83 Hartwell Ave., Lexington, MA 02173–3163	Francis Summers, Jr.	617–377–9710
WESTERN	Suite 300, 16700 Valley View Ave., La Mirada, CA 90638–5830.	Robert W. Matter	714–228–7001

For further information, contact the Executive Officer, Defense Contract Audit Agency, Cameron Station, Alexandria, VA 22304–6178. Phone, 703–274–7319. Information regarding employment may be obtained from the regional offices.

Defense Finance and Accounting Service

Room 425, Crystal Mall 3, Arlington, VA 22240–5291
Phone, 703–607–2616

Director	RICHARD F. KEEVEY
Principal Deputy Director	GARY W. AMLIN

The Defense Finance and Accounting Service was established by direction of the Secretary of Defense on November 26, 1990, and operates under DOD Directive 5118.5.

The Service is responsible for making all payments, including payroll and contracts, and for maintaining all finance and accounting records for the Department of Defense. The Service is responsible for preparing annual financial statements for DOD in accordance with the Chief Financial Officers Act of 1990. The Service is also responsible for the consolidation, standardization, upgrading, and integration of finance and accounting requirements, functions, processes, operations, and systems in the Department.

For further information, contact the Public Affairs Office, Room 416, Crystal Mall 3, Arlington, VA 22240–5219. Phone, 703–607–2821.

Defense Information Systems Agency

701 South Court House Road, Arlington, VA 22204–2199
Phone, 703–607–6020

Director	LT. GEN. ALBERT J. EDMONDS, USAF

Deputy Director   (VACANCY)
Chief of Staff   MICHAEL F. SLAWSON, *Acting*

The Defense Information Systems Agency (DISA), originally established as the Defense Communications Agency, is a combat support agency of the Department of Defense.

The Agency is organized into a headquarters and field activities acting for the Director in assigned areas of responsibilty. The field organizations include the White House Communications Agency; the Joint Tactical Command, Control, and Communications Agency; and the Defense Commercial Communications Office.

DISA is responsible for planning, developing, and supporting command, control, communications, and information systems that serve the needs of the National Command Authorities under all conditions of peace and war. It provides guidance and support on technical and operational C^3 and information systems issues affecting the Office of the Secretary of Defense, the Military Departments, the Chairman of the Joint Chiefs of Staff, the Unified Combatant Commands, and the Defense Agencies. It ensures the interoperability of the Worldwide Military Command and Control System (WWMCCS), the Defense Communications System (DCS), theater and tactical command and control systems, North Atlantic Treaty Organization and/or allied C^3 systems, and those national and/or international commercial systems that affect the DISA mission. It supports national security emergency preparedness telecommunications functions of the National Communications System (NCS), as prescribed by Executive Order 12472 of April 3, 1984.

For further information, contact the Chief, Corporate Public Affairs, Defense Information Systems Agency, 701 South Courthouse Road, Arlington, VA 22204–2199. Phone, 703–692–9270.

Defense Intelligence Agency
The Pentagon, Washington, DC 20340–2033
Phone, 703–695–0071

Director   LT. GEN. JAMES R. CLAPPER, JR., USAF
Deputy Director   MICHAEL F. MUNSON
Chief of Staff   JOHN T. BERBRICH

The Defense Intelligence Agency (DIA) was established by DOD Directive 5105.21, effective October 1, 1961, under provisions of the National Security Act of 1947, as amended (50 U.S.C. 401 et seq.).

DIA is a combat support agency. The Agency's intelligence activities support military operations in peacetime, crisis, contingency, and combat; weapons systems acquisition and planning; and defense policymaking. To accomplish the assigned mission, DIA produces military intelligence for national foreign intelligence and counterintelligence products; coordinates all DOD intelligence collection requirements; operates the Central Measurement and Signals Intelligence (MASINT) Office; manages the Defense Human Intelligence (HUMINT) Service and the Defense Attache System; and provides foreign intelligence and couterintelligence support to the Secretary of Defense and the Chairman of the Joint Chiefs of Staff. The Director of DIA coordinates the Defense General Intelligence and Applications Program, an element of the DOD Joint Military Intelligence Program, and manages the General Defense Intelligence Program within the National Foreign Intelligence Program.

For further information, contact the Defense Intelligence Agency, The Pentagon, Washington, DC 20340–2033. Phone, 703–695–0071.

Defense Investigative Service

1340 Braddock Place, Alexandria, VA 22314–1651
Phone, 703–325–5324

Director   JOHN F. DONNELLY

The Defense Investigative Service was established by the Secretary of Defense, effective January 1, 1972. The Service is chartered by Department of Defense Directive 5105.42.

The Service consists of a Headquarters, three Operations Centers, the Capital Area, and four regional offices with subordinate field offices and resident agencies located in the 50 States and Puerto Rico, the Office of Industrial Security International—Europe, in Brussels, Belgium, and Mannheim, Federal Republic of Germany; and the Office of Industrial Security International—Far East, in Camp Zama, Japan.

The Service conducts all personnel security investigations for Department components and, when authorized, also conducts investigations for other U.S. Government activities. These include investigation of allegations of subversive affiliations, adverse suitability

information, or any other situation that requires resolution to complete the personnel security investigation.

The Service is responsible for the three major programs involving industrial security: the Defense Industrial Security Program; the Key Assets Protection Program; and the Arms, Ammunition and Explosives Security Program.

The Service also manages the Defense Clearance and Investigations Index, a centralized listing of all Defense components investigative files, and security clearance information pertaining to Department of Defense personnel.

Regional Offices—Defense Investigative Service

City	Director
Alexandria, VA 22331–1000	Willard J. Isaacs, Jr.
Cherry Hill, NJ 08034–1908	James B. Witkowski, Jr.
Irving, TX 75062	James S. Rogner
Long Beach, CA 90807–4013	William H. Williams
Smyrna, GA 30080–7606	John S. Benson

For further information, contact the Chief, Office of Information and Public Affairs, Defense Investigative Service, 1340 Braddock Place, Alexandria, VA 22314–1651. Phone, 703–325–5324.

Defense Legal Services Agency

The Pentagon, Washington, DC 20301-1600
Phone, 703-695-3341

Director (General Counsel, Department of Defense)	JUDITH A. MILLER
Principal Deputy Director (Principal Deputy General Counsel)	STEPHEN W. PRESTON

The Defense Legal Services Agency was established by Department of Defense Directive 5145.4, dated August 12, 1981. The Agency is under the authority, direction, and control of the General Counsel of the Department of Defense, who also serves as its Director.

The Agency provides legal advice and services for the Office of the Secretary of Defense, its field activities, and the Defense agencies. It provides technical support and assistance for development of the Department's Legislative program; coordinates positions on legislation and Presidential Executive orders; provides a centralized legislative and congressional document reference and distribution point for the Department; and maintains the Department's historical legislative files. The Agency administers the Defense Industrial Security Clearance Review program and the Standards of Conduct Ethics program.

For further information, contact the Administrative Officer, Defense Legal Services Agency, The Pentagon, Washington, DC 20301-1600. Phone, 703-697-8343.

Defense Logistics Agency

Cameron Station, Alexandria, VA 22304-6100
Phone, 703-274-6000 or 6001

Director	VICE ADM. E.M. STRAW, SC, USN
Principal Deputy Director	MAJ. GEN. L.P. FARRELL, JR., USAF

The Defense Logistics Agency was established by the Secretary of Defense and operates under Department of Defense Directive 5105.22.

The Agency consists of a Headquarters and 17 primary level field activities and their subordinate activities. Some of the subordinate activities—the Defense Fuel Supply Center, the Defense Contract Management Command, the Defense Reutilization and Marketing Service, and the Defense Personnel Support Center—operate in overseas areas. There are also some Headquarters management support offices that perform field support on a centralized basis.

The mission of the Agency, as a combat support agency, is to provide effective and efficient worldwide logistics support to the Military Departments and the Unified Commands under conditions of peace or war, as well as to other Department of Defense components, Federal civilian agencies, foreign governments, and international organizations, as assigned.

The Agency provides logistics services directly associated with furnishing materiel commodities and items of supply that have been determined to be appropriate for integrated management by a single agency on behalf of all

Defense components or that have been otherwise specifically assigned. It administers Departmentwide logistics management systems, programs, and activities, as assigned, including the provision of technical assistance, support services, and information.

Defense Contract Management Command The Defense Contract Management Command (DCMC) was established as a Defense Logistics Agency major subordinate Command reporting to the Director of the Agency, effective February 6, 1990. The Commander of DCMC is responsible for contract administration services currently performed worldwide by the Agency. Those services include contract management support, program and technical support, and quality assurance. Also, the Commander is authorized to organize, direct, manage, and control all functions and resources assigned to DCMC.

Primary Level Field Activities

Inventory Control There are six inventory control points (ICP's) which are responsible for materiel management of assigned commodities and items of supply relating to food, clothing, textiles, medical, chemical, petroleum, industrial, construction, electronics, and general items. The Defense Fuel Supply Center is also responsible for the contracting of commercial petroleum services and coal, as well as all crude oil and petroleum products for the Strategic Petroleum Reserve.

For further information, call 703–274–6000 or 6001.

Service Centers The five service centers furnish varied support services as follows:

The Defense Logistics Services Center is responsible for maintenance of the Federal Cataloging System records including the development and dissemination of cataloging and item intelligence data to the Military Departments and other authorized customers.

The Agency's Administrative Support Center provides administrative support

and common service functions to Agency activities within the Washington, DC, metropolitan area.

The Defense Reutilization and Marketing Service is responsible for the integrated management of worldwide personal property disposal operations, including reutilization of serviceable assets, in support of the Military Departments and other authorized customers.

The DLA Systems Design Center is responsible for the operational execution of the Agency's Automated Data Processing and Telecommunications Programs.

The Defense National Stockpile Center is responsible for acquiring, upgrading, rotating, and disposing of stockpile materials. The Center conducts operations, including storage, security, testing, contracting and quality studies, maintenance, and replacement of materials in the Defense National Stockpile. The Center directs the development of new or revised specifications and special instructions for existing and proposed strategic and critical materials to be stockpiled.

For further information, call 703–274–6000 or 6001.

Distribution Regions/Depots The two Defense Distribution Regions—East and West—operate the CONUS-wide supply distribution systems directed by DMRD 902, Consolidation of DOD Distribution Functions. The consolidation included the transfer of material distribution and related functions. Distribution is defined as all actions involving the receipt of new procurement, redistributions, and field returns; storage of materials, including care of material and supplies in storage; issue materials; consolidation and containerization of material; preservation, packaging, packing, and marking; physical inventory; quality control; traffic management; other transportation services; unit material fielding and set assembly/disassembly; and transshipment and minor repair.

Districts The five Defense Contract Management districts provide contract administration services including the performance of contract administration, production, quality assurance, and data and financial management activities, and small business/labor surplus programs, within the United States and such external areas as specifically authorized. A sixth organization, Defense Contract Management Command International, is

located in Dayton, OH, and performs the contract management function worldwide. These districts report to the Defense Contract Management Command.

For further information, call 703–274–6000 or 6001.

Primary Level Field Activities—Defense Logistics Agency

Activity	Commander
DEFENSE SUPPLY CENTERS:	
Defense Construction Supply Center	Rear Adm. E.A. Elliot, SC, USN
Defense Electronics Supply Center	Brig. Gen. L.T. Garrett, USMC
Defense Fuel Supply Center	Brig. Gen. L. Wilson, Jr., USAF
Defense General Supply Center	Rear Adm. K.W. Lippert, SC, USN
Defense Industrial Supply Center	Brig. Gen. R.E. Beauchamp, USA
Defense Personnel Support Center	Brig. Gen. C.H. Freeman, USA
DEFENSE SERVICE CENTERS:	
Defense Logistics Services Center	Col. L.E. Simpson, USMC
Defense Reutilization and Marketing Service	Capt. D.A. Hempson, SC, USN
DLA Administrative Support Center	R.A. Martinez
DLA Systems Design Center	P.K. Anderson, SC, USN
Defense National Stockpile Center	R.J. Connelly
DEFENSE DISTRIBUTION REGIONS/DEPOTS:	
Defense Distribution Region East	Col. J.C. Hinebaugh, USA
Defense Distribution Region West	Col. J.W. LaBounty, USA
DEFENSE CONTRACT MANAGEMENT DISTRICTS:	
South	Col. L.T. Watts, Jr., USAF
Northeast	Capt. J.P. Gould, SC, USN
West	Capt. R.L. Ketts, SC, USN
Defense Contract Management Command International	Capt. L.D. Harder, SC, USN

Sources of Information

Consumer Activities Questions concerning this program or placement on the Department of Defense bidders list should be addressed to DOD Surplus Sales, P.O. Box 1370, Battle Creek, MI 49016. Phone, 616–962–6511, extension 6736 or 6737.

Employment For the Washington, DC, metropolitan area, inquiries and applications should be addressed to Defense Logistics Agency, DLA Administrative Support Center, Attn: DASC–KS, Room 6–214, Cameron Station, Alexandria, VA 22304–6100. Phone, 703–274–7087. For other areas, contact the local DLA field activity.

The Agency has a college recruitment program. Schools interested in participating should direct inquiries to Defense Logistics Agency, Attn: CAHS, Room 3D224, Cameron Station, Alexandria, VA 22304–6100. Phone, 703–274–6040.

Environment For information concerning the Agency's program,

contact Defense Logistics Agency, Attn: CAAE, Room 4D489, Cameron Station, Alexandria, VA 22304–6100. Phone, 703–274–6967.

Films For information on films available for public showing, contact Defense Logistics Agency, Attn: DASC–T, Room 3C547, Cameron Station, Alexandria, VA 22304–6100. Phone, 703–274–6130.

Procurement and Small Business Activities For information, contact Director, Small and Disadvantaged Business Utilization (AQAU), Building 6–170, Cameron Station, Alexandria, VA 22304–6100. Phone, 703–274–6471.

Publications *An Identification of Commodities Purchased by the Defense Logistics Agency* is available free of charge from the Director, Small and Disadvantaged Business Utilization (AQAU), above address.

Reading Room Defense Logistics Agency Library, Building 5, Door 10, Cameron Station, Alexandria, VA 22304–6100. Phone, 703–274–6056.

For further information, contact the Defense Logistics Agency, Cameron Station, Alexandria, VA 22304–6100. Phone, 703–274–6115.

Defense Mapping Agency
8613 Lee Highway, Fairfax, VA 22031–2139
Phone, 703–285–9368

Director	MAJ. GEN. PHILIP W. NUBER, USAF
Deputy Director	W. DOUGLAS SMITH
Chief of Staff	CAPT. LAWRENCE W. URBIK, USN

The Defense Mapping Agency (DMA) was established in 1972, when mapping, charting, and geodesy functions of the Defense Community were combined into this joint Department of Defense agency. The Agency operates as a combat support agency of DOD.

The mission of the Agency is to enhance national security and support the Office of the Secretary of Defense, the Chairman of the Joint Chiefs of Staff, Unified Combatant Commands, Military Departments, and other users, by producing and distributing mapping, charting, and geodetic products and services.

The Defense Mapping Agency has some 7,500 employees in more than 50 locations around the world.

Agency Components

The mapping, charting, and geodesy functions of the Agency are principally conducted by its three major production centers: the DMA Aerospace Center, which is located in St. Louis, MO; the DMA Hydrographic/Topographic Center, located in Bethesda, MD; and the DMA Reston Center, which is located in Reston, VA.

The DMA Systems Center, located in Bethesda, MD, is responsible for advancing the capability of producing Agency products using softcopy or computerized production techniques.

The DMA Combat Support Center is primarily responsible for the distribution of Agency products to the military and civilian users. Its headquarters is located in Bethesda, MD.

The Agency also operates the Defense Mapping School at Fort Belvoir, VA, under the Human Resources Directorate. The school provides training in aspects of mapping, charting, and geodesy.

Components—Defense Mapping Agency

Activity	Address	Director
DMA Aerospace Center	3200 S. 2d St., St. Louis, MO 63118–3399	William Brown
DMA Combat Support Center	6001 MacArthur Blvd., Bethesda, MD 20816–5001.	Col. Robert Kirby, USA
DMA Hydrographic/Topographic Center	4600 Sangamore Rd., Bethesda, MD 20816–5003.	William N. Hogan
DMA Reston Center	12310 Sunrise Valley Dr., Reston, VA 22091–3414	Paul L. Peeler, Jr.
DMA Systems Center	4600 Sangamore Rd., Bethesda, MD 20816	Earl W. Phillips

Sources of Information

Contracts and Small Business Activities
For information, contact the Small and Disadvantaged Business Utilization Office, Director of Acquisition, Defense Mapping Agency, 8613 Lee Highway, Fairfax, VA 22031–2137.

Employment General employment applications and inquiries should be addressed to the following:

Central Recruiting Branch, ST L–12, Attn: DMA (HRSAX), Defense Mapping Agency, St. Louis, MO 63118–3399. Phone, 800–777–6104 (toll-free). Central Recruitment/Intake Branch, Stop D–73, Attn: DMA (HRAR), Defense Mapping Agency, 8613 Lee Highway, Fairfax, VA 22031–2137. Phone, 800–526–3379 (toll-free).

Public Sale of Maps and Charts Defense Mapping Agency nautical, aeronautical, and Flight Information Publication (FLIP) products are sold by the National Ocean Service (NOS). Nautical charts of coastal waterways of the continental United States, Hawaii, Alaska, and the U.S. territories may also be purchased from NOS. For information on ordering products, contact the NOS Distribution Branch, N/CG33, 6501

Lafayette Avenue, Riverdale, MD 20737. Phone, 301–436–6990.

To apply for sales agent status within the Agency, contact the Agents Service Unit, NOS Distribution Branch, 6501 Lafayette Avenue, Riverdale, MD 20737. Phone, 301–436–8726.

DMA topographic maps, gazetteers, and other publications are sold by the U.S. Geological Survey (USGS), Department of the Interior. Topographic maps of the continental United States and Hawaii may also be purchased from USGS. For domestic and international DMA topographic products, contact the Distribution Branch, United States Geological Survey, Department of the Interior, Box 25286, Denver, CO 80225. Phone, 303–236–7477.

Defense Nuclear Agency

Washington, DC 20305–1000
Phone, 202–325–7095

Director	Maj. Gen. Kenneth L. Hagemann, USAF
Deputy Director	George W. Ullrich
Chief of Staff	Col. Robert P. Summers, USAF

The Defense Nuclear Agency (DNA) was established in 1971 and operates under DOD Directive 5105.31. Under authority, direction, and control of the Assistant to the Secretary of Defense (Atomic Energy), DNA serves as DOD's center for nuclear expertise.

The Agency is organized into a headquarters and a field command. The DNA field command operates the Interservice Nuclear Weapons School and manages the Johnston Atoll in the Pacific, the site of the Army's Chemical Agent Demilitarization System.

The Agency's mission includes nuclear weapons stockpile management, Cooperative Threat Reduction Program support, nuclear weapon effects research, and arms control and counterproliferation support. DNA

research helps ensure U.S. forces are prepared to operate on future battlefields in which opponents may possess conventional, nuclear, biological, or chemical capabilities.

DNA maintains the Department of Defense nuclear weapons stockpile and its associated reporting system, ensuring its reliability, safety, and security through training, inspections, and research. Additionally, DNA provides emergency response support and planning assistance for nuclear weapons accidents or improvised nuclear device incidents.

The Agency manages and implements the Cooperative Threat Reduction Program to assist the Newly Independent States of the Former Soviet Union in the safe, secure dismantlement of nuclear, chemical, and other weapons.

Through the use of simulators and computer models, DNA retains the scientific expertise and develops data necessary to ensure advanced conventional systems, nuclear systems, and command and control assets will continue to operate in potential nuclear environments. This expertise is also used to provide commanders options for effective targeting against underground or hardened structures as well as enhanced battle damage assessment capabilities.

DNA develops arms control treaty verification technologies that might be used in on-site inspections. Agency counterproliferation efforts are concentrated on technology base

development and acquisition strategy development.

Sources of Information

Employment Inquiries should be directed as follows:

Headquarters—Defense Nuclear Agency, Attn: CVHR, 6801 Telegraph Road, Alexandria, VA 22310–2298. Phone, 703–325–7591.

Field Command—1680 Texas Street SE., Kirtland Air Force Base, NM 87117–5669. Phone, 505–846–9561.

Procurement and Small Business Activities Contact the Defense Nuclear Agency, Attn: AM, 6801 Telegraph Road, Alexandria, VA 22310–3398. Phone, 703–325–5021.

For further information, contact the Public Affairs Office, Defense Nuclear Agency, 6801 Telegraph Road, Alexandria, VA 22310–3398. Phone, 703–325–7095.

Defense Security Assistance Agency
The Pentagon, Washington, DC 22202
Phone, 703–604–6513

Director — LT. GEN. THOMAS G. RHAME, USA
Deputy Director — H. DIEHL MCKALIP

The Defense Security Assistance Agency was established on September 1, 1971, by DOD Directive 5105.38, dated August 11, 1971.

The Agency directs, administers, and supervises the execution of approved

security assistance plans and programs, such as military assistance, international military education and training, and foreign military sales. In so doing, it works closely with the U.S. Security Assistance offices worldwide.

For further information, contact the Defense Security Assistance Agency, The Pentagon, Washington, DC 22202. Phone, 703–604–6513.

National Security Agency/Central Security Service
Fort George G. Meade, MD 20755–6000
Phone, 301–688–6311

Director — VICE ADM. JOHN M. MCCONNELL, USN
Deputy Director — WILLIAM P. CROWELL

The National Security Agency/Central Security Service is responsible for the centralized coordination, direction, and performance of highly specialized technical functions in support of U.S. Government activities to protect U.S. communications and produce foreign intelligence information. The National Security Agency was established by Presidential directive in 1952 as a separately organized Agency within the Department of Defense. In this directive, the President designated the Secretary of Defense as Executive Agent for the signals intelligence and communications security activities of the Government. The Agency was charged with an additional mission, computer security, in a 1984 Presidential directive, and with an operations security training mission in a 1988 Presidential directive.

In 1972 the Central Security Service was established, in accordance with a Presidential memorandum, to provide a more unified cryptologic organization within the Department of Defense and appointed the Director, National Security Agency, as Chief of the Central Security Service.

The Agency has two primary missions: an information systems security mission and a foreign intelligence information mission. To accomplish these missions, the Director has been assigned the following responsibilities:

—prescribing certain security principles, doctrines, and procedures for the U.S. Government;

—organizing, operating, and managing certain activities and facilities for the production of foreign intelligence information;

—organizing and coordinating the research and engineering activities of the U.S. Government that are in support of the Agency's assigned functions;

—regulating certain communications in support of Agency missions; and

—operating the National Computer Security Center in support of the Director's role as national manager for telecommunications security and automated information systems security.

Executive Order 12333 of December 4, 1981, describes in more detail the responsibilities of the National Security Agency.

On-Site Inspection Agency
Washington, DC 20041–0498
Phone, 703–742–4326

Director	BRIG. GEN. GREGORY G. GOVAN, USA
Principal Deputy Director	JOERG H. MENZEL

The On-Site Inspection Agency was established as a separate Department of Defense agency on January 26, 1988, to implement the 13-year inspection regime of the Intermediate-Range Nuclear Forces (INF) Treaty. The Agency's mission has since expanded to include implementation of onsite inspection and escort requirements of the Threshold Test Ban Treaty (TTBT); implementation of like requirements of the Conventional Armed Forces in Europe (CFE) Treaty;

implementation of the inspection regime of the Vienna Document of 1990; and planning for the Strategic Arms Reduction Treaty (START), Peaceful Nuclear Explosion Treaty (PNET), and Chemical Weapons (CW) agreements. The Agency also serves as the Defense Department's executive agent to the United Nations' Special Commission on Iraq and to the State Department for Operation Provide Hope.

The Agency is manned by military personnel from all of the armed services, as well as civilian technical experts and support personnel. It maintains liaison with various government agencies interested in arms control and draws its three civilian deputy directors from the U.S. Arms Control and Disarmament Agency, State Department, and Federal Bureau of Investigation.

For further information, contact the Public Affairs Office, On-Site Inspection Agency, Washington, DC 20041–0498. Phone, 703–742–4326.

JOINT SERVICE SCHOOLS

Defense Acquisition University
Alexandria, VA 22311–1772
Phone, 703–845–6766

President	THOMAS M. CREAN

The Defense Acquisition University (DAU), established pursuant to the Defense Acquisition Workforce Improvement Act of 1990 (10 U.S.C. 1701 note), serves as the DOD center for acquisition education, training, research, and publication. DAU is structured as an educational consortium, with centralized planning and management of the acquisition education and training activities of 16 Army, Navy, Air Force, and DOD component schools.

DAU's mission is to educate and train military and civilian professionals for effective service in defense acquisition, to centrally manage resources for course development delivery, research, and publications.

For further information, contact the Director for University Operations, Defense Acquisition University, 2001 North Beauregard Street, Alexandria, VA 22311–1772. Phone, 703–845–6763.

Defense Systems Management College
Fort Belvoir, VA 22060–5565
Phone, 703–805–3363; 800–845–7606 (toll free)

Commandant	BRIG. GEN. CLAUDE M. BOLTON, JR., USAF
Provost	BRIG GEN. EDWARD HIRSCH, USA (RET.)

The Defense Systems Management College (DSMC), established July 1, 1971, is a joint service educational institution, and is the largest school in the Defense Acquisition University. The mission of the College is to promote and support the adoption and practice of sound systems management principles by the acquisition workforce through education, research, and information dissemination.

In addition to a 14-week Advanced Program Management Course, DSMC's academic program consists of 25 other courses of 3 days to 4 weeks in duration; all with the purpose of educating DOD acquisition professionals, military and civilian, in a broad spectrum of management activities through formal studies, simulation exercises, and case studies. Many of these courses are mandatory for certification in various career fields within Service acquisition corps. Individuals from Defense industry and other Federal agencies may attend DSMC courses on a space-available basis. In addition to the main campus located at Fort Belvoir, VA, courses are taught at the four regions of Boston, MA; Huntsville, AL; St. Louis, MO; and Los Angeles, CA; and at selected on-site locations on an as-requested basis.

For further information, contact the Office of the Registrar, Defense Systems Management College, Fort Belvoir, VA 22060. Phone, 703–805–2227.

Joint Military Intelligence College

Defense Intelligence Analysis Center, Washington, DC 20340–5100
Phone, 202–373–3299

President	A. DENIS CLIFT
Deputy to the President	COL. JOHN A. WAHLQUIST, USAF

The Joint Military Intelligence College (JMIC), previously the Defense Intelligence College, was established January 1, 1963. It is a joint service, educational institution operating under the authority of the Director of the Defense Intelligence Agency. The College's mission is to assist in the career development of military and civilian personnel who are assigned to intelligence functions or who are pursuing broad careers in intelligence.

The College offers the master of science of strategic intelligence (MSSI) degree program and two diploma programs: the Postgraduate Intelligence Program (PGIP) and the Undergraduate Intelligence Program (UGIP). Students may enroll for full- or part-time study at the main campus located on Bolling Air Force Base. Part-time programs are also offered at JMIC's three satellite campuses at the National Air Intelligence Center, the National Security Agency, and the State Department. Two weekend programs are available as well; one is specifically for reservists and is taught by reserve faculty.

The Joint Military Intelligence College is accredited by the Middle States Association of Colleges and Schools.

For further information, contact the Admissions Office, MCA–2, Joint Military Intelligence College, Defense Intelligence Analysis Center, Washington, DC 20340–5100. Phone, 202–373–3299.

National Defense University

Fort Lesley J. McNair, Fourth and P Streets SW., Washington, DC 20319–6000
Phone, 202–287–9401

President	LT. GEN. ERVIN J. ROKKE, USAF
Vice President	WILLIAM G. WALKER
Chief of Staff	COL. ROBERT B. CLARKE, USA

The National Defense University was established by the Department of Defense on January 16, 1976, thereby merging the Industrial College of the Armed Forces and the National War College to form a university. Because the two senior service colleges are located at Fort Lesley J. McNair, Washington, DC, their close affiliation reduces administrative costs, provides for the sharing of faculty expertise and educational resources, and promotes a constructive dialog, which benefits both colleges. On August 16, 1981, the Armed Forces Staff College in Norfolk, VA, an institution educating mid-career officers, was incorporated into the National Defense University. This action united the Department of Defense's three joint colleges under one university and allowed coordination of the curricula and professional development of its students and the sharing of its resources.

The mission of the National Defense University is to ensure excellence in professional military education and research in the essential elements of national security.

For further information, contact the Administrative Office, National Defense University, Fort Lesley J. McNair, Fourth and P Streets SW., Washington, DC 20319–6000. Phone, 202–287–9460.

The National War College
Fort Lesley J. McNair, Fourth and P Streets SW., Washington, DC 20319–6000
Phone, 202–475–1776

Commandant	REAR ADM. MICHAEL A. MCDEVITT, USN

The National War College provides education in national security policy to selected military officers and career civil service employees of Federal departments and agencies concerned with national security. It is the only senior service college with the primary mission of offering a course of study that emphasizes national security policy formulation and the planning and implementation of national strategy.

Its 10-month academic program is an issue-centered study in U.S. national security. The elective program is designed to permit each student to tailor his academic experience to meet individual professional development needs.

For further information, contact the Department of Administration, The National War College, Fort Lesley J. McNair, Fourth and P Streets SW., Washington, DC 20319–6000. Phone, 202–475–1776.

Industrial College of the Armed Forces
Fort Lesley J. McNair, Fourth and P Streets SW., Washington, DC 20319–6000
Phone, 202–475–1832

Commandant	REAR ADM. JEROME F. SMITH, JR., USN

The Industrial College of the Armed Forces is the Nation's leading educational institution for the study of the resources component of national power and its integration into national security strategy. The College prepares selected military and civilians for senior leadership positions by conducting postgraduate executive-level courses of study and associated research. Its 10-month academic program is organized into two semesters: focusing on national security strategy and management of natural resources, respectively.

For further information, contact the Director of Administration, Industrial College of the Armed Forces, Fort Lesley J. McNair, Fourth and P Streets, SW., Washington, DC 20319–6000. Phone, 202–475–1832.

Armed Forces Staff College

Norfolk, VA 23511–1702
Phone, 804–444–5302

Commandant	BRIG. GEN. ROGER E. CARLTON, USAF
Chief of Staff	COL. LEONARD L. WALLS, USAF

The Armed Forces Staff College (AFSC), a major component of the National Defense University, is an intermediate- and senior-level joint college in the professional military education system dedicated to the study of the principles, perspectives, and techniques of joint and combined operational planning and warfighting.

The mission of AFSC is to educate staff officers and other leaders in joint and combined operational planning and warfighting to instill a primary commitment of joint teamwork, attitudes, and perspectives. The College accomplishes this mission through three schools: the Joint and Combined Warfighting School (JCWS), the Joint and Combined Staff Officer School (JCSOS), and the Joint Command, Control, and Electronic Warfare School (JCEWS).

For further information, contact the Department of Academic Affairs, Armed Forces Staff College, 7800 Hampton Blvd., Norfolk, VA 23511–1702. Phone, 804–444–5074. Fax, 804–444–5422.

Information Resources Management College

Fort Leslie J. McNair, Building 62, Washington, DC 20319–6000
Phone, 202–287–9321

Dean	JOHN M. CARABELLO

The Information Resources Management College (IRMC) was established on March 1, 1990, as a full college of the National Defense University. It provides graduate-level courses in information resources management. The College prepares senior DOD officials for joint management of the information resources component of national power and its integration with, and support to, national strategy.

The IRMC curriculum is designed to provide a forum where senior Defense professionals—interacting with the faculty—not only gain knowledge, qualifications, and competencies for Defense IRM leadership, but contribute to the growth and excellence of the field itself. The premier offering of the college is the 16-week Advanced Management Program (AMP). AMP is supplemented by a number of advanced studies courses available to students in all colleges of the National Defense University. Additionally, the College offers a series of intensive courses related to specific problematic areas and emerging concepts of IRM, and special symposia, seminars, and workshops focusing on critical IRM issues and directions.

For further information, contact the Registrar, Information Resources Management College, Fort Leslie J. McNair, Building 62, Washington, DC 20319–6000. Phone, 202–287–9321.

Uniformed Services University of the Health Sciences

4301 Jones Bridge Road, Bethesda, MD 20814–4799
Phone, 301–295–3030

President	JAMES A. ZIMBLE, M.D.
Dean, School of Medicine	VAL G. HEMMING, M.D., *Acting*

Authorized by act of September 21, 1972 (10 U.S.C. 2112), the Uniformed Services University of the Health Sciences was established to educate career-oriented medical officers for the Military Departments and the Public Health Service.

The University currently incorporates the F. Edward Hébert School of Medicine and graduate and continuing education programs. It is located on the National Naval Medical Center (NNMC) reservation in Bethesda, MD.

Students are selected by procedures recommended by the Board of Regents and prescribed by the Secretary of Defense. The actual selection is carried out by a faculty committee on admissions and is based upon motivation and dedication to a career in the uniformed services and an overall appraisal of the personal and intellectual characteristics of the candidates without regard to sex, race, religion, or national origin. Applicants must be U.S. citizens. Matriculants will be commissioned officers in one of the uniformed services. They must meet the physical and personal qualifications for such a commission and must give evidence of a strong commitment to serving as a uniformed medical officer. The graduating medical student is required to serve a period of obligation of not less than 7 years, excluding graduate medical education.

For further information, contact the President, Uniformed Services University of the Health Sciences, 4301 Jones Bridge Road, Bethesda, MD 20814–4799. Phone, 301–295–3030.

DEPARTMENT OF EDUCATION

600 Independence Avenue SW., Washington, DC 20202
Phone, 202–708–5366

SECRETARY OF EDUCATION	RICHARD W. RILEY
Chief of Staff	FRANK S. HOLLEMAN
Director, Office of Public Affairs	KATHRYN KAHLER
Deputy Secretary	MADELEINE KUNIN
Under Secretary	MARSHALL C. SMITH
Director, Planning and Evaluation Service	ALAN GINSBURG
Director, Budget Service	SALLY CHRISTENSEN
Assistant Secretary for Management	RODNEY M. MCCOWAN
Director, Information Resources Group	GLORIA PARKER
Director, Office of Hearings and Appeals	FRANK J. FUREY
Director, Human Resources Group	VERONICA D. TRIETSCH
Director, Quality Workplace Group	TONY CONQUES
Assistant Secretary for Intergovernmental and Interagency Affairs	GILBERTO MARIO MORENO
Director, White House Initiatives on Hispanic Education	ALFRED RAMIREZ
Director, Office of Non-Public Education	MICHELLE L. DOYLE
Director, Operations Support Staff	GLORIA MOUNTS
Inspector General	JOHN P. HIGGINS, JR., *Acting*
Assistant Inspector General for Investigation Services	DIANNE VAN RIPER
Assistant Inspector General for Policy, Planning and Management Services	JOHN P. HIGGINS, JR.
Assistant Inspector General for Audit Services	STEVEN MCNAMARA
Assistant Secretary for Legislation and Congressional Affairs	KAY CASSTEVENS
Director, Legislation Staff	THOMAS WOLANIN, *Acting*
Director, Congressional Affairs Staff	(VACANCY)
General Counsel	JUDITH A. WINSTON
Deputy General Counsel for Postsecondary and Departmental Service	FELIX BAXTER
Deputy General Counsel for Program Service	STEVEN Y. WINNICK
Deputy General Counsel for Regulations and Legislation Service	JAMIENNE S. STUDLEY
Assistant Secretary for Civil Rights	NORMA CANTÚ
Deputy Assistant Secretary	RAYMOND C. PIERCE
Director, Planning, Analysis and Systems Service	ALLEN JACKSON
Director, Policy, Enforcement and Program Service	JEANNETTE LIM
Assistant Secretary for Educational Research and Improvement	SHARON P. ROBINSON
Deputy Assistant Secretary for Operations	DICK W. HAYS
Director, Library Programs	RAY FRY

249

Director, Programs for the Improvement of Practice	EVE BITHER
Director, Office of Research	JOSEPH CONATY, *Acting*
Commissioner, National Center for Education Statistics	EMERSON J. ELLIOTT
Assistant Secretary for Special Education and Rehabilitative Services	JUDITH HEUMANN
Director, Special Education Programs	THOMAS HEHIR
Director, National Institute on Disability and Rehabilitation Research	KATHERINE D. SEELMAN
Commissioner, Rehabilitation Services Administration	FREDRIC K. SCHROEDER
Director, Office of Bilingual Education and Minority Languages Affairs	EUGENE GARCIA
Assistant Secretary for Elementary and Secondary Education	THOMAS W. PAYZANT
Director, Compensatory Education Programs	MARY JEAN LETENDRE
Director, Impact Aid Programs	CATHERINE SCHAGH, *Acting*
Director, School Improvement Programs	ALICIA CORO
Director, Office of Indian Education	JAMES KOHLMOOS, *Acting*
Director, Office of Migrant Education	BAYLA F. WHITE
Assistant Secretary for Vocational and Adult Education	AUGUSTA S. KAPPNER
Assistant Secretary for Postsecondary Education	DAVID A. LONGANECKER
Deputy Assistant Secretary for Higher Education Programs	CLAUDIO R. PRIETO
Director, Center for International Education	RICHARD D. SCARFO, *Acting*
Deputy Assistant Secretary for Student Financial Assistance Programs	DAVID LONGANECKER, *Acting*
Service Director, Policy, Training and Analysis Service	DEBORAH BROWN, *Acting*
Service Director, Accounting and Financial Management Service	LINDA PAULSEN
Director, Program Systems Service	CARL O'RILEY
Director, Institutional Participation and Oversight Service	WILLIAM MORAN, *Acting*
Director, Regional Operations Division	BONNIE LEBOLD
Director, Fund for the Improvement of Postsecondary Education	CHARLES KARELIS
Service Director, Debt Collection Service	JOHN HAINES
Chief Financial Officer	DONALD R. WURTZ
Director, Accounting and Financial Management Service	MITCHELL L. LAINE
Director, Grants and Contracts Service	GARY J. RASMUSSEN

The Department of Education is the Cabinet-level department that establishes policy for, administers, and coordinates most Federal assistance to education. Its mission is to ensure access to education and to promote educational excellence throughtout the Nation.

The Department of Education was created by the Department of Education Organization Act (20 U.S.C. 3411). The Department is administered under the supervision and direction of the Secretary of Education.

DEPARTMENT OF EDUCATION

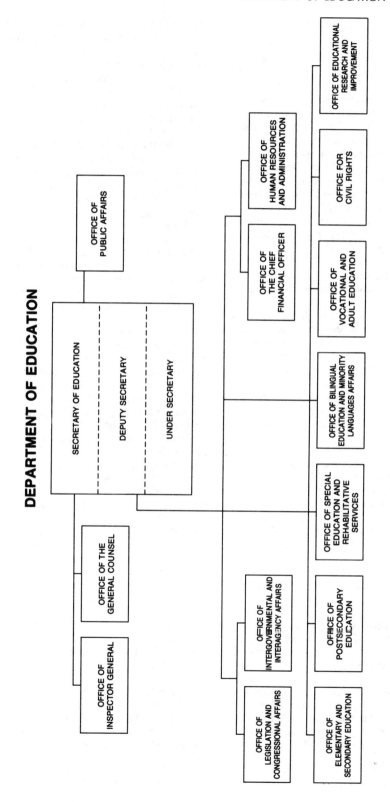

OFFICE OF PUBLIC AFFAIRS

SECRETARY OF EDUCATION
DEPUTY SECRETARY
UNDER SECRETARY

OFFICE OF INSPECTOR GENERAL

OFFICE OF THE GENERAL COUNSEL

OFFICE OF LEGISLATION AND CONGRESSIONAL AFFAIRS

OFFICE OF INTERGOVERNMENTAL AND INTERAGENCY AFFAIRS

OFFICE OF ELEMENTARY AND SECONDARY EDUCATION

OFFICE OF POSTSECONDARY EDUCATION

OFFICE OF SPECIAL EDUCATION AND REHABILITATIVE SERVICES

OFFICE OF BILINGUAL EDUCATION AND MINORITY LANGUAGES AFFAIRS

OFFICE OF VOCATIONAL AND ADULT EDUCATION

OFFICE OF THE CHIEF FINANCIAL OFFICER

OFFICE OF HUMAN RESOURCES AND ADMINISTRATION

OFFICE FOR CIVIL RIGHTS

OFFICE OF EDUCATIONAL RESEARCH AND IMPROVEMENT

Office of the Secretary

Secretary   The Secretary of Education advises the President on education plans, policies, and programs of the Federal Government. The Secretary also carries out certain Federal responsibilities for four federally aided corporations: the American Printing House for the Blind, Gallaudet University, Howard University, and the National Technical Institute for the Deaf. The Deputy Secretary, the Assistant Secretaries, the Inspector General, the General Counsel, the Chief Financial Officer, and the Under Secretary are the principal officers and aid the Secretary in the overall management of the Department.

Bilingual Education   The Office of Bilingual Education and Minority Languages Affairs administers programs designed to fund activities that assist students with limited English proficiency. The Office administers the discretionary grant competition for 14 grant programs established by law and 1 formula grant program under the Immigrant Education Program. The Office also administers contracts for research and evaluation, technical assistance, and clearinghouse activities to meet the special educational needs of populations with limited English proficiency.

Civil Rights   The Assistant Secretary for Civil Rights is responsible for ensuring that institutional recipients of Federal financial assistance do not discriminate against American students, faculty, or other individuals on the basis of race, color, national origin, sex, handicap, or age.

Elementary and Secondary Education   The Assistant Secretary for Elementary and Secondary Education formulates policy for, directs, and coordinates the activities relating to preschool, elementary, and secondary education in the Department. Included are grants and contracts to State educational agencies and local school districts, postsecondary schools and nonprofit organizations for State and local reform, compensatory, migrant, and Indian education; drug-free schools; other school improvement programs; and impact aid.

Educational Research and Improvement   The Assistant Secretary for Educational Research and Improvement provides national leadership in expanding fundamental knowledge and improving the quality of education. This Office is responsible for conducting and supporting education-related research activities; monitoring the state of education through the collection and analysis of statistical data; promoting the use and application of research and development to improve instructional practices in the classroom; and, disseminating these findings and providing technical assistance to specific problems at school sites.

Vocational and Adult Education   The Assistant Secretary for Vocational and Adult Education administers grant, contract, and technical assistance programs for vocational-technical education and for adult education and literacy. The Office is also responsible for coordinating these programs with other Education Department and Federal programs supporting services and research for adult education, literacy, and occupational training.

Special Education and Rehabilitative Services   The Assistant Secretary for Special Education and Rehabilitative Services is responsible for special education programs and services expressly designed to meet the needs and develop the full potential of children with disabilities; and comprehensive rehabilitation service programs specifically designed to reduce human dependency, to increase self-reliance, and to fully utilize the productive capabilities of all persons with disabilities. Programs include support for training of teachers and other professional personnel; grants for research; financial aid to help States initiate, expand, and improve their resources; and media services and captioned films for hearing-impaired persons.

Postsecondary Education   The Assistant Secretary for Postsecondary Education formulates policy and directs and coordinates programs for assistance to postsecondary educational institutions and students pursuing a postsecondary education. Programs include assistance for the improvement and expansion of American educational resources for international studies and services, grants to improve instruction in crucial academic subjects, and construction assistance for academic facilities. Also included are programs of student financial assistance, including Pell Grants, Supplemental Educational Opportunity Grants, Grants to States for State Student Incentives, Work-Study,Federal Direct Student Loans, Stafford Loans, Parent Loans for Undergraduate Students (PLUS), Supplemental Loans for Students (SLS), Consolidation Loans, and Perkins Loans.

The administration and implementation of the Federal Director Loan Program is under the authority of the Senior Advisor to the Secretary through September 30, 1996.

Regional Offices   Each regional office serves as a center for the dissemination of information and provides technical assistance to State and local educational agencies and other institutions and individuals interested in Federal education activities. At present, offices are located in 10 cities: Atlanta, GA; Boston, MA; Chicago, IL; Dallas, TX; Denver, CO; Kansas City, MO; New York, NY; Philadelphia, PA; San Francisco, CA; and Seattle, WA.

Federally Aided Corporations

(These Corporations are supported in part by Federal funds appropriated in the budget of the Department of Education.)

American Printing House for the Blind

P.O. Box 6085, Louisville, KY 40206
Phone, 502–895–2405

President	TUCK TINSLEY
Chairman of the Board	JOHN BARR

The American Printing House for the Blind was incorporated by the Kentucky Legislature in 1858 to assist in the education of the blind by distributing Braille books, talking books, and educational aids without cost to educational institutions educating blind children pursuant to the act "To Promote the Education of the Blind," as amended (20 Stat. 467), adopted by Congress in 1879.

Gallaudet University

800 Florida Avenue NE., Washington, DC 20002
Phone, 202–651–5000

Chairman, Board of Trustees	PHIL BRAVIN
President, Gallaudet University	I. KING JORDAN
Dean of Graduate Studies and Research	MICHAEL KARCHMER
Vice President for Administration and Business	PAUL KELLY

Dean of College for Continuing Education	PATTI E. SINGLETON, *Acting*
Vice President, Pre-College Programs	HARVEY CORSON

The Columbia Institution for the Instruction of the Deaf and Dumb, and the Blind was incorporated by act of February 16, 1857 (11 Stat. 161). An amendatory act of February 23, 1865 (13 Stat. 436), changed the name to the Columbia Institution for the Instruction of the Deaf and Dumb. The name was subsequently changed to Columbia Institution for the Deaf by act of March 4, 1911 (36 Stat. 1422). The act of June 18, 1954 (20 U.S.C. 691 *et seq.*), changed its name to Gallaudet College. The Education of the Deaf Act of 1986 (20 U.S.C. 4301) changed the name to Gallaudet University.

Gallaudet University was established to provide a liberal higher education for deaf persons who need special facilities to compensate for their loss of hearing. The primary purpose of the university is to afford its students the intellectual and spiritual development that can be acquired through a study of the liberal arts and sciences.

In addition to its undergraduate program, Gallaudet University operates a graduate program at the master's level for preparing teachers and other professional personnel to work with persons who are deaf, a research program focusing on problems related to deafness, and a preschool for young deaf children.

Accreditation   Gallaudet University is accredited by the Middle States Association of Colleges and Secondary Schools, the National Council for Accreditation of Teacher Education, and the Council on Social Work Education.

Model Secondary School for the Deaf   The school was established by act of

October 15, 1966 (20 U.S.C. 693), when the Department of Health, Education, and Welfare entered into an agreement with Gallaudet College for the establishment and operation, including construction, of such a facility. It was established as an exemplary educational facility for deaf students of high school age from the District of Columbia, Maryland, Virginia, West Virginia, Pennsylvania, and Delaware. The school's mission is to provide maximum flexibility in curricula and to encourage originality, imagination, and innovation needed to satisfy deaf students' high levels of aspirations.

The objectives of the school are to provide day and residential facilities for deaf youth of high school age, in order to prepare some for college and other advanced study and to provide terminal education for others; to prepare all students to the maximum extent possible to be independent, contributing members of society; and to stimulate the development of similar programs throughout the Nation.

Kendall Demonstration Elementary School   The school, which is located on the campus of Gallaudet University and now serves approximately 200 students, became the Nation's first demonstration elementary school for the deaf by act of December 24, 1970 (20 U.S.C. 695), which authorized Gallaudet College to operate and maintain the school as a model that will experiment in techniques and materials, and to disseminate information from these and future projects to educational facilities for deaf children throughout the country.

For further information, contact the Division of Public Service, Gallaudet University, 800 Florida Avenue NE., Washington, DC 20002. Phone, 202–651–5505.

Howard University

2400 Sixth Street NW., Washington, DC 20059
Phone, 202–806–6100

Interim President   JOYCE A. LADNER

Howard University was established by act of March 2, 1867 (14 Stat. 438). It is governed by a 27-member self-perpetuating board of trustees. The University maintains a special relationship with the Federal Government through the Department of Education.

Howard University, jointly supported by congressional appropriations and private funds, is a comprehensive university organization offering instruction in 17 schools and colleges as follows: the college of liberal arts, the school of engineering, the school of architecture and planning, the school of business and public administration, the college of fine arts, the college of medicine, the college of dentistry, the college of pharmacy and pharmaceutical

science, the school of law, the school of religion, the graduate school, the school of social work, the school of communications, the school of education, the college of nursing, the school of human ecology, the college of allied health sciences, and a summer school. In addition, Howard University has research institutes in the following areas: the arts and the humanities, urban affairs and research, drug abuse and addiction, minority business education, and the study of educational policy.

The University is coeducational and admits students of every race, creed, color, and national origin, but it accepts and discharges a special responsibility for the admission and training of black students.

For further information, contact the Office of University Communications, Howard University, 2400 Sixth Street NW., Washington, DC 20001. Phone, 202–806–0970.

National Institute for Literacy

Suite 200, 800 Connecticut Avenue NW., Washington, DC 20006
Phone, 202–632–1500

Director   ANDREW HARTMAN

The National Institute for Literacy is administered under an interagency agreement among the Secretaries of Education, Labor, and Health and Human Services. The Institute's mission

is to enhance the national effort to eliminate illiteracy by the year 2000 by creating a national network and serving as a focal point for coordination and dissemination of information.

National Technical Institute for the Deaf

Rochester Institute of Technology

2 Lomb Memorial Drive, Rochester, NY 14623
Phone, 716–475–6400 (voice only)

President of Rochester Institute of Technology	ALBERT J. SIMONE
Interim Director of the National Technical Institute for the Deaf	JAMES DECARO

The National Technical Institute for the Deaf (NTID) was established by act of June 8, 1965 (20 U.S.C. 681), and after several years of planning, programs began in 1968. Funded through the Department of Education, it is an integral part of a larger institution known as the Rochester Institute of Technology (RIT).

NTID's presence at RIT is the first effort to educate large numbers of deaf students within a college campus planned primarily for hearing students. Unique in the world, NTID is a vital part of RIT's main 1,300-acre campus in suburban Rochester, NY. It provides educational opportunities for qualified students from every State in the Nation and, through educational outreach, publications, and related service, serves deaf persons throughout the world. In addition, NTID conducts research to better understand the role of deafness in education and employment, and to develop innovative teaching techniques. It develops training activities for its faculty and staff, as well as for other professionals working with deaf persons across the country.

One of the major reasons for NTID's success in helping deaf students join the mainstream of American life is its close working relationship with other RIT colleges in developing career-oriented programs of study. One of RIT's main strengths over the years has been its ability to adapt its educational programs to technological and social change. NTID helps keep that RIT tradition alive and has served more than 5,362 deaf students since 1968.

Deaf graduates from RIT have found employment throughout the Nation or have moved on to advanced academic studies. Of those who pursued employment, more than 90 percent have been placed in jobs; 93 percent in jobs commensurate with their educational preparation. Of those employed, 80 percent work in business and industry, more than 11 percent in government, and the remainder in education.

An applicant for NTID at RIT must be a U.S. resident. An overall eighth grade achievement level or above is required, and, except under special circumstances, an applicant must have completed a secondary program. An applicant also must show evidence of need for special services because of hearing loss and have an unaided better ear average of 70dB ISO. References are requested.

Both Institutes are accredited by the Middle States Association of Colleges and Secondary Schools. RIT also has been accredited by the Engineers' Council for Professional Development; National Association of Schools of Art; Committee on Professional Training of American Chemical Society; Council on Social Work Education; and the National Accrediting Agency for Clinical Laboratory Sciences.

For further information, contact the Public Information Office, National Technical Institute for the Deaf, 2 Lomb Memorial Drive, Rochester, NY 14623. Phone, 716–475–6283.

Sources of Information

Office of the Secretary
Inquiries on the following information may be directed to the specified office, Department of Education, 600 Independence Avenue SW., Washington, DC 20202.

Contracts and Small Business Activities
Call or write the Office of Small and Disadvantaged Business Utilization. Phone, 202–708–9820.

Employment Inquiries and applications for employment, and inquiries regarding the college recruitment program, should be directed to the Human Resources Group. Phone, 202–401–0553.

Organization and Internal Procedures
Call or write the Director, Strategy and Management Consulting Group. Phone, 202–260–0875.

For further information concerning the Department of Education, contact the Information Center, Department of Education, Room 4608 (ROB3), 600 Independence Avenue SW., Washington, DC 20202. Phone, 202–708–5366.

DEPARTMENT OF ENERGY

1000 Independence Avenue SW., Washington, DC 20585
Phone, 202–586–5000

SECRETARY OF ENERGY	HAZEL R. O'LEARY
Deputy Secretary	WILLIAM H. WHITE
Associate Deputy Secretary for Field Management	DONALD W. PEARMAN, JR.
Under Secretary	CHARLES B. CURTIS
Deputy Under Secretary for Technology Partnerships and Economic Competitiveness	ALEXANDER MACLACHLAN
General Counsel	ROBERT R. NORDHAUS
Inspector General	JOHN C. LAYTON
Assistant Secretary, Congressional and Intergovernmental Affairs	CAROLYN HERR WATTS, *Acting*
Assistant Secretary, Policy	SUSAN F. TIERNEY
Assistant Secretary, Environment, Safety and Health	TARA J. O'TOOLE
Assistant Secretary, Human Resources and Administration	ARCHER L. DURHAM
Assistant Secretary, Fossil Energy	PATRICIA F. GODLEY
Assistant Secretary, Defense Programs	VICTOR H. REIS
Assistant Secretary, Energy Efficiency and Renewable Energy	CHRISTINE A. ERVIN
Assistant Secretary, Environmental Management	THOMAS P. GRUMBLY
Administrator, Energy Information Administration	JAY E. HAKES
Director, Fissile Materials Disposition	GREGORY P. RUDY, *Acting*
Director, Worker and Community Transition	ROBERT W. DEGRASSE, JR.
Director of Public and Consumer Affairs	MICHAEL G. GAULDIN
Director of Energy Research	MARTHA A. KREBS
Director of Civilian Radioactive Waste Management	DANIEL A. DREYFUS
Director of Hearings and Appeals	GEORGE B. BREZNAY
Director of Nonproliferation and National Security	KENNETH E. BAKER, *Acting*
Chief Financial Officer	JOSEPH F. VIVONA
Director of Nuclear Energy, Science and Technology	TERRY R. LASH
Director of Science Education and Technical Information	TERRY CORNWELL RUMSEY
Director of Economic Impact and Diversity	CORLISS S. MOODY
Director of Quality Management	NANCY WEIDENFELLER
Director of Secretary of Energy Advisory Board	PETER F. DIDISHEIM, *Acting*
Chairman, Federal Energy Regulatory Commission	ELIZABETH ANNE MOLER

258

DEPARTMENT OF ENERGY

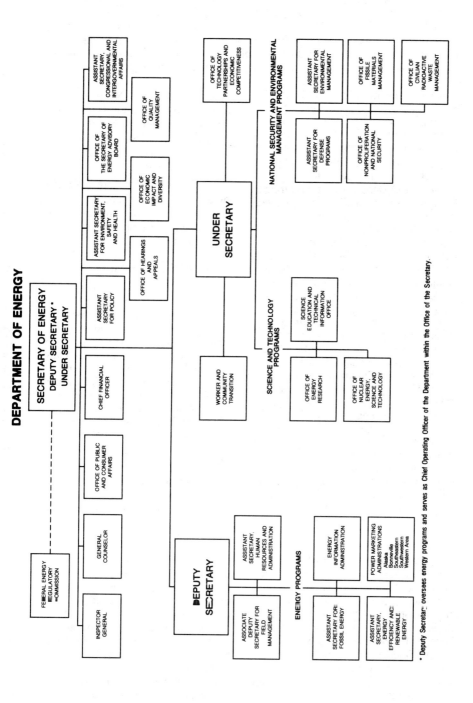

* Deputy Secretary oversees energy programs and serves as Chief Operating Officer of the Department within the Office of the Secretary.

The Department of Energy provides the framework for a comprehensive and balanced national energy plan through the coordination and administration of the energy functions of the Federal Government. The Department is responsible for long-term, high-risk research and development of energy technology; the marketing of Federal power; energy conservation; the nuclear weapons program; energy regulatory programs; and a central energy data collection and analysis program.

The Department of Energy (DOE) was established by the Department of Energy Organization Act (42 U.S.C. 7131), effective October 1, 1977, pursuant to Executive Order 12009 of September 13, 1977. The act consolidated the major Federal energy functions into one Cabinet-level Department, transferring to DOE all the responsibilities of the Energy Research and Development Administration; the Federal Energy Administration; the Federal Power Commission; and the Alaska, Bonneville, Southeastern, and Southwestern Power Administrations, formerly components of the Department of the Interior, as well as the power-marketing functions of the Department of the Interior's Bureau of Reclamation. Also transferred to DOE were certain functions of the Interstate Commerce Commission and the Departments of Commerce, Housing and Urban Development, the Navy, and the Interior (42 U.S.C. 7152–7156).

Offices managing programs which require large budget outlays or provide technical direction and support are structured to reflect the principal programmatic missions of the Department: Energy Programs, National Security and Environmental Management Programs, and Science and Technology Programs. The Energy Programs area includes the Offices of the Assistant Secretaries for Energy Efficiency and Renewable Energy and Fossil Energy; the Power Marketing Administrations; and the Energy Information Administration. The Science and Technology Programs area includes the Offices of Energy Research, Science Education and Technical Information, and Nuclear Energy, Science and Techology. The National Security and Environmental Management Programs area includes the Offices of the Assistant Secretaries for Defense Programs and Environmental Management; the Offices of

Nonproliferation and National Security; Worker and Community Transition; Technology Partnerships and Economic Compeititveness; Fissile Materials Disposition; and Civilian Radioactive Waste Management.

The Department's organization also includes the Federal Energy Regulatory Commission, which is an independent regulatory organization within the Department.

Office of the Secretary

Secretary The Secretary, as Chief Executive Officer, provides the overall vision, programmatic leadership, management direction, and administration of the Department. The principal offices serving the Secretary include the Deputy Secretary, Under Secretary, General Counsel, Inspector General, Chief Financial Officer, and the Assistant Secretaries. The following units, whose public purposes are broadly applied, are detailed further.

Staff Offices

Field Management The Associate Deputy Secretary for Field Management provides centralized responsibility for strategic planning, management coordination, and oversight of the Department's field operations, in general; and, specifically, for executing programs and projects accomplished through the Department's eight multipurpose operations offices. This office is also responsible for establishing and managing procedures for receiving, tracking, and conducting investigations related to "whistleblower" reprisal complaints; preparing cases for adjudication; and establishing procedures for processing appeals to the Secretary of Energy for appropriate action.

Policy The Assistant Secretary for Policy formulates, recommends, and manages national and international policy development, strategic plans, and integration of departmental policy and program and budget goals; conducts integrated policy analyses; conducts systematic evaluations of the Department's programs to ensure that each maximizes its contributions to the national energy strategy and the Department's goals and objectives; ensures that U.S. international energy policies and programs conform to national goals, legislation, and treaty obligations; coordinates cooperative international energy programs with foreign governments and international organizations, such as the International Energy Agency and the International Atomic Energy Agency; and develops and tests energy emergency plans and analyzes departmental energy emergency capabilities and vulnerabilities.

Environment, Safety and Health The Assistant Secretary for Environment, Safety and Health provides independent oversight of departmental execution of environmental, occupational safety and health, nuclear/nonnuclear safety and security laws, regulations, and policies; ensures that departmental programs are in compliance with environmental, health, and nuclear/nonnuclear safety protection plans, regulations, and procedures; provides an independent overview and assessment of Department-controlled activities to ensure that safety-impacted programs receive management review; and carries out the legal functions of the nuclear safety civil penalty and criminal referral activities mandated by the Price-Anderson Amendments Act.

Hearings and Appeals The Office of Hearings and Appeals reviews and issues all final DOE orders of an adjudicatory nature, other than those involving matters over which the Federal Energy Regulatory Commission exercises final jurisdiction. The Office is responsible for considering and issuing decisions on appeals from orders of a regulatory nature issued by DOE components and requests for exception or exemption from any regulatory or mandatory requirements.

The Board of Contract Appeals hears and resolves appeals pertaining to contract-related matters. The Board may act as the Department's Contract Adjustment Board, the Financial Assistance Appeal Board, or the Invention Licensing Appeal Board.

Economic Impact and Diversity The Office of Economic Impact and Diversity advises the Secretary on the effects of energy policies, regulations, and other actions of the Department and its components on minorities, minority business enterprises and minority educational institutions, and on ways to ensure that minorities are afforded an opportunity to participate in energy programs of the Department; carries out policy, plan, and oversight functions under sections 8 and 15 of the Small Business Act relating to preferred programs for small businesses, disadvantaged business, labor surplus area concerns, and women-owned businesses; and administers the policy, procedures, plans, and systems of the Department's equal opportunity and civil rights activities.

Office of Worker and Community Transition This Office develops policies and programs necessary to plan for and mitigate the impacts of changing conditions on the workers and communities affected by the Department's mission changes; assures that those policies and programs are carried out in a way that guarantees fair treatment of all concerned, while at the same time recognizing the unique conditions at each site and in each contract; and assists those communities most affected by the changing missions at Department sites by using the Department's resources to stimulate economic development.

The primary functions of the Office include:

—serving as the focal point for the Department on matters of worker and community transition;

—developing the policies and guidelines for all aspects of work force restructuring;

—developing the policies and guidelines necessary for community transition;

—providing necessary analytical capabilities to develop profiles and trend analyses of current contractor work force capabilities, needed work force skills, and traning or acquisition needs and developing strategies for addressing those needs through retraining or recruitment;

—providing oversight and assistance to sites in conducting cost-benefit and other analyses arising out of contract reform, section 3161 of the 1993 national defense authorization act, and related work force issues or initiatives;

—reviewing and coordinating policies of other Energy Department organizations that affect worker or community transition, including policies in Environment, Safety and Health, Facility Management, Procurement, Contract Reform, and Facility Transition;

—providing assistance and review of field activities to assure fairness in the policy toward workers and communities across the Department of Energy complex and monitoring performance to assure plan objectives and agreements are carried out; and

—serving as the point of contact for national labor organizations and oversee the collective bargaining process of the Department to assure compatibility with contract reform initiatives and compliance with section 3161 of the National Defense Authorization Act for Fiscal Year 1993; and assisting sites, where necessary, by providing technical, legal, or other assistance with labor relations.

Office of Quality Management This Office assists and supports Department of Energy executives and managers in their charge to implement the principles and culture of quality management within the Department. Through Total Quality Management, the Office supports the implementation of performance measures throughout the Department.

The primary functions of the Office are:

—developing and implementing the Department's quality initiative strategy and promoting and guiding the use of total quality principles;

—providing information and technical assistance to departmental officials on customer identification, performance measures, measurement of service quality, process improvement methods and tools, and statistical analysis;

—designing, coordinating, and providing leadership and Total Quality Management training for senior staff and managers and staffers Departmentwide;

—facilitating and providing technical advice and staff support to the Department Leadership Group and Quality Council which are responsible for championing the Secretary's Quality Initiative;

—coordinating and supporting the implementation of performance measures throughout the Department; and

—serving as the point of contact and liaison for quality management activities within the Department and with the Federal Quality Institute, other Federal agencies, and external entities.

Energy Programs

Energy Efficiency and Renewable Energy The Assistant Secretary for Energy Efficiency and Renewable Energy is responsible for formulating and directing programs designed to increase the production and utilization of renewable energy (solar, biomass, wind, geothermal, alcohol fuels, etc.) and improving the energy efficiency of transportation, buildings, industrial systems, and related processes through support of long-term, high-risk research and development activities. The Assistant Secretary also has responsibility for administering statutorily mandated assistance programs that provide financial assistance for State energy planning, weatherization of housing owned by the poor and disadvantaged, and the implementation of energy conservation measures by schools and hospitals, local units of government, and public care institutions.

For further information, contact the Director of Management and Resources. Phone, 202–586–6768.

Fossil Energy   The Assistant Secretary for Fossil Energy is responsible for research and development programs involving fossil fuels—coal, petroleum, and gas. The fossil energy program involves applied research, exploratory development, and limited proof-of-concept testing targeted to high-risk and high-payoff endeavors. The objective of the program is to provide the general technology and knowledge base that the private sector can use to complete development and initiate commercialization of advanced processes and energy systems. The program is principally executed through two Energy Technology Centers located in the field.

The Assistant Secretary also manages the Clean Coal Technology Program, the Strategic Petroleum Reserve, the Naval Petroleum and Oil Shale Reserves, and the Liquefied Gaseous Fuels Spill Test Facility.

For further information, contact the Deputy Assistant Secretary for Management. Phone, 301–903–2617.

Energy Information Administration   The Energy Information Administration is responsible for the timely and accurate collection, processing, and publication of data in the areas of energy resource reserves, energy production, demand, consumption, distribution, and technology.

The Administration performs analyses of energy data to assist government and nongovernment users in understanding energy trends. Analyses are prepared on complex, long-term energy trends and the microeconomic and macroeconomic impacts of energy trends on regional and industrial sectors. Special purpose analyses are prepared involving competition within the energy industries, the capital/financial structure of energy companies, and interfuel substitution. Audits are conducted to ensure the validity of regulatory and other energy data.

The Administration provides data publication and distribution services within DOE, throughout the Government, and for the public. It is a clearinghouse for general information on energy and coordinates its activities with the Department's Technical Information Center.

For further information, contact the Director, National Energy Information Center. Phone, 202–586–1185; (TDD) 202–586–1181.

National Security and Environmental Management Programs

Civilian Radioactive Waste Management   The Office of Civilian Radioactive Waste Management was established by the Nuclear Waste Policy Act of 1982 (42 U.S.C. 10224). The Office has responsibility for the Nuclear Waste Fund and for the management of Federal programs for recommending, constructing, and operating repositories for disposal of high-level radioactive waste and spent nuclear fuel; interim storage of spent nuclear fuel; monitored retrievable storage; and research, development, and demonstration regarding disposal of high-level radioactive waste and spent nuclear fuel.

For further information, contact the Associate Director for Program and Resources Management. Phone, 202–586–9116.

Defense Programs   The Assistant Secretary for Defense Programs directs the Nation's nuclear weapons research, development, testing, production, and surveillance program, as well as the production of the special nuclear materials used by the weapons program within the Department, and management of defense nuclear waste and byproducts. The Office also manages research in inertial confinement fusion.

For further information, contact the Deputy Assistant Secretary for Resource Management. Phone, 202–586–2295.

Environmental Management   The Office of Environmental Management provides program policy guidance and manages the assessment and cleanup of inactive waste sites and facilities, continues safe and effective waste management operations, and develops and implements an aggressively applied waste research and development program to provide innovative environmental technologies that yield permanent disposal solutions at reduced costs. The Office provides centralized management for the Department for waste management operations, environmental restoration, and applied research and development programs and activities, including environmental restoration and waste management program policy and guidance to DOE field offices in these areas.

For further information, contact the Office of Administrative Management. Phone, 202–586–2661.

Nonproliferation and National Security The Office of Nonproliferation and National Security ensures that intelligence information requirements of the Secretary and senior departmental policymakers are met and that the Department's technical, analytical, and research expertise is made available to the intelligence community in accordance with Executive Order 12333 of December 4, 1981. The Office directs the development of the Department's policy, plans, and procedures relating to arms control, nonproliferation, export controls and safeguard activities; safeguards and secures classified information and protects departmental and Department of Energy contractor facilities and installations; manages the Department's Emergency Management System, which responds to and mitigates the consequences resulting from operational, energy, and continuity of Government emergencies; manages the Department's research and development program for verifying and monitoring arms implementation and compliance activities; manages the Department's international safeguards research and development program and physical security responsibilities in support of the Federal Government's nonproliferation policies and agreements; manages a personnel security program for sensitive positions within the Department; and

provides threat assessments and support to headquarters and field offices.

Office of Fissile Materials Disposition The Office reports to the Under Secretary and is responsible for all activities of the Department relating to the management, storage, and disposition of fissile materials from weapons and weapon systems that are excess to national security needs of the United States. Key responsibilities include coordinating the development of Department of Energy policy regarding these fissile materials; overseeing the development of technical and economic analyses and related research and development for this effort; preparing a Programmatic Environmental Impact Statement on the long-term storage and disposition of surplus fissile materials; carrying out an extensive program of outreach and public communications necessary to develop a sustainable consensus on storage and dispostion efforts; and providing technical support to the President's Interagency Working Group addressing surplus plutonium control and disposition.

—The primary functions of the Office include:

—managing the development of policy and directs implementation of departmental efforts regarding long-term storage of all weapons usable fissile materials and the disposition of those weapons-usable fissile materials declared excess to the national security needs;

—representing the Under Secretary in meetings, discussions, and decision-making forums within the Department, as well as with other agencies, Congress, and the public;

—serving as the Department's principal point of contact for matters involving Energy Headquarters and field office management in issues and problems associated with the long-term storage and disposition of surplus weapons-usable fissile materials;

—serving as the Program's point of contact for the Offices of Congressional Affairs, Public Affairs, and the Controller on matters relevant to the Program's involvement with Congress, State and local government, media communications, and the budget;

—assuring consistency, proper coordination within the Programs, reflection of current policy, and timeliness of the Program's responses;

—overseeing preparation of a Programmatic Environmental Impact Statement (PEIS) for the storage of all weapons-usable fissile materials and the disposition of surplus fissile materials;

—serving as the Department's primary communications channel with the public and affected stakeholders on surplus fissile materials matters;

—coordinating the Department's participation on the President's Interagency Working Group for the matters involving surplus plutonium control and disposition; and

—controlling funds authorized and appropriated for the program.

Science and Technology Programs

Energy Research   The Office of Energy Research advises the Secretary on the physical and energy research and development programs of the Department, and financial assistance and budgetary priorities for these activities.

The Office manages the basic energy sciences, high energy physics, and fusion energy research programs; administers DOE programs supporting university researchers; funds research in mathematical and computational sciences critical to the use and development of supercomputers; and administers a financial support program for research and development projects not funded elsewhere in the Department. The Office also manages a research program directed at determining the generic environmental, health, and safety aspects of energy technologies and programs.

The Office monitors DOE research and development programs for deficiencies or duplications and, in conjunction with the Assistant Secretary for Congressional and Intergovernmental Affairs, monitors the international exchange of scientific and technical personnel.

For further information, contact the Director of Management. Phone, 301–903–4944.

Nuclear Energy, Science and Technology   The Office of Nuclear Energy, Science and Technology administers the Department's research and development programs associated with fission energy. This includes programs relating to nuclear reactor development, both civilian and naval; nuclear fuel cycle; and space nuclear applications. The Office also manages the Department's Remedial Action Program to treat or stabilize radioactive wastes and perform decontamination and decommissioning at DOE surplus sites. In addition, the Office conducts technical analyses and provides advice concerning nonproliferation; assesses alternative nuclear systems and new reactor and fuel cycle concepts; and evaluates proposed advanced nuclear fission energy concepts and technical improvements for possible application to nuclear powerplant systems.

For further information, contact the Director of Policy and Management. Phone, 202–586–6630.

Science Education and Technical Information   The Office of Science Education and Technical Information provides centralized responsibility for developing and implementing departmental policy for university and science education programs, and manages coordination and oversight of the collection and dissemination of information resulting from the Department's research and development activities. The Office coordinates the establishment, communication, and implementation of policy, procedures, and standards for the handling of scientific and technical information; advises the Secretary of Energy with respect to science, math, and engineering precollege and university education programs; represents the United States in multilateral information exchange activities of the International Atomic Energy Agency, International Energy Agency, and international exchange agreements; disseminates scientific and technical information received from international agreements; and manages and executes agreements for the dissemination of Department of Energy scientific and technical information products.

Independent Commission

Federal Energy Regulatory Commission An independent, five-member commission within the Department of Energy, the Federal Energy Regulatory Commission has retained many of the functions of the Federal Power Commission, such as setting rates and charges for the transportation and sale of natural gas and for the transmission and sale of electricity and the licensing of hydroelectric power projects. In addition, the Commission establishes rates or charges for the transportation of oil by pipeline, as well as the valuation of such pipelines.

For further information, contact the Executive Director. Phone, 202–208–0300.

Field Structure

DOE Operations Offices and Contractor-Operated Field Installations

The vast majority of the Department's energy research and development, nuclear weapons research and development, and testing and production activities are carried out by contractors who operate Government-owned facilities. Management and administration of Government-owned, contractor-operated facility contracts are the major responsibility of the Department's eight operations offices.

DOE operations offices provide a formal link between Department headquarters and the field laboratories and other operating facilities. They also manage programs and projects as assigned from headquarters. Routine management guidance, coordination, and oversight of the operations offices is provided by the Office of the Associate Deputy Secretary for Field Management. Daily specific program direction for the operations offices is provided by the cognizant Assistant Secretaries and the Director or program officer.

Operations Offices—Department of Energy

Office/Address	Telephone
Albuquerque, NM (P.O. Box 5400, 87185)	505–845–6049
Chicago, IL (9800 S. Cass Ave., Argonne, IL 60439)	708–252–2110
Idaho Falls, ID (785 Doe Pl., 83401)	208–526–1322
Las Vegas, NV (P.O. Box 98518, 89193–8518)	702–295–3211

Operations Offices—Department of Energy—Continued

Office/Address	Telephone
Oak Ridge, TN (P.O. Box 2001, 37831)	615–576–4444
Oakland, CA (1301 Clay St., 94612)	510–637–1800
Richland, WA (P.O. Box 550, 825 Jadwin Ave., 99352)	509–376–7395
Savannah River, SC (P.O. Box A, Aiken, SC 29802)	803–725–2277

Other Field Offices The Department also has several field offices concerned primarily with specific programs, such as the Strategic Petroleum Reserve Project Office, two offices involved with the development of nuclear reactors for the Navy, and several offices devoted to the management of the Naval Petroleum and Oil Shale Reserves.

Power Administrations

The marketing and transmission of electric power produced at Federal hydroelectric projects and reservoirs is carried out by the Department's five Power Administrations. Management oversight of the Power Administrations is the responsibility of the Deputy Secretary.

Bonneville Power Administration The Administration was created pursuant to the Bonneville Project Act of August 20, 1937, as amended (16 U.S.C. 832 *et seq.*). Through a regionwide, interconnecting transmission system it markets electric power and energy from Federal hydroelectric projects in the Pacific Northwest constructed and operated by the Army Corps of Engineers and the Department of the Interior's Bureau of Reclamation. Through interregional connections, it sells surplus power to areas outside the Pacific Northwest region and participates in exchanges of power.

The Administration markets power produced by the Federal Columbia River Power System at the lowest rates, consistent with sound business practices. Preference is given to public entities.

Power is sold at wholesale to utilities and directly to electroprocess industries and other Federal agencies. The Administration also exchanges electric power; prepares wholesale rates and repayment schedules; and constructs, operates, and maintains a transmission system that integrates Federal power projects and interconnects with non-Federal utility systems.

In addition, the Administration is responsible for energy conservation, renewable resource development, and fish and wildlife enhancement under the provisions of the Pacific Northwest Electric Power Planning and Conservation Act of 1980 (16 U.S.C. 839 note).

The Administration, in cooperation with the Corps of Engineers, represents the United States in implementing the provisions of the Columbia River Treaty with Canada.

By act of October 18, 1974 (16 U.S.C. 838), the Bonneville Power Administration has the authority, in lieu of appropriations, to use its revenues and to sell revenue bonds to the U.S. Treasury to finance its programs.

For further information, contact the Bonneville Power Administration, P.O. Box 3621, 1002 NE. Holladay Street, Portland, OR 97208. Phone, 503–230–5101.

Southeastern Power Administration

The Administration was created by the Secretary of the Interior in 1950 to carry out functions assigned to the Secretary by the Flood Control Act of 1944 (58 Stat. 890), which pertain to the transmission and disposition of surplus electric power and energy generated at reservoir projects that are or may be under the control of the Department of the Army in the States of West Virginia, Virginia, North Carolina, South Carolina, Georgia, Florida, Alabama, Mississippi, Tennessee, and Kentucky. The Southeastern Power Administration was transferred from the Department of the Interior to the Department of Energy by the Department of Energy Organization Act (42 U.S.C. 7152), effective October 1, 1977.

The Administration transmits and disposes of the surplus electric power and energy generated at the Federal reservoir projects in such manner as to encourage the most widespread use. The Administration sets the lowest possible rates to consumers, consistent with sound business principles, and gives preference in the sale of such power and energy to public bodies and cooperatives.

The program of the Administration includes the negotiation, preparation, execution, and administration of contracts for the disposition of electric power; the preparation of wholesale rates and repayment schedules; the provision by construction, contract, or otherwise, of transmission and related facilities to interconnect reservoir projects and to serve contractual loads; and activities pertaining to the planning and operation of power facilities.

For further information, contact the Southeastern Power Administration, Elberton, GA 30635. Phone, 706–283–9911.

Alaska Power Administration The Administration is responsible for operating and marketing power for two Federal hydroelectric projects in Alaska. Legislative authorities for this work include the Eklutna Project Act (64 Stat. 382); the Snettisham Project authorization in the Flood Control Act of 1962 (76 Stat. 1193); the power-marketing provision of the Flood Control Act of 1944 (58 Stat. 890); the act of August 9, 1955, Investigation of Water Resources, Alaska; and section 201 of the Water Resources Development Act of 1976 (90 Stat. 2944).

Power operations and marketing functions involving the Eklutna and Snettisham Hydroelectric Projects include the projects' transmission systems serving the Anchorage and Juneau areas.

For further information, contact the Alaska Power Administration, Suite 2B, 2770 Sherwood Lane, Juneau, AK 99801. Phone, 907–586–7405.

Southwestern Power Administration

The Administration was created by the Secretary of the Interior in 1943 to carry out the Secretary's responsibility for the sale and disposition of electric power and energy generated at certain projects constructed and operated by the Department of the Army. For these projects, the Administration carries out the functions assigned to the Secretary by the Flood Control Act of 1944 (16 U.S.C. 825s) in the States of Arkansas, Kansas, Louisiana, Missouri, Oklahoma, and Texas. Since October 1, 1977, the Southwestern Power Administration has been functioning under the direction of the Secretary of Energy, pursuant to section 302(a)(1) of the Department of Energy Organization Act (42 U.S.C. 7152).

The headquarters office is located at Tulsa, OK, and there are three area offices—Springfield, MO; Muskogee, OK; and Jonesboro, AR—four maintenance units, and two dispatching offices.

The Southwestern Power Administration transmits and disposes of the electric power and energy generated at Federal reservoir projects, supplemented by power purchased from public and private utilities, in such a manner as to encourage the most widespread and economical use. The Administration sets the lowest possible rates to consumers, consistent with sound business principles, and gives preference in the sale of power and energy to public bodies and cooperatives.

The Administration:

—develops, negotiates, and administers contracts for the sale and interchange of electric power and energy on a wholesale basis;

—prepares rate and repayment studies;

—designs and constructs transmission lines and related facilities to interconnect hydroelectric projects of the Administration's system and other systems, both public and private;

—operates and maintains the high-voltage transmission system to serve contractual loads, maintain reliable interconnections, and utilize excess capacity to provide transmission service to others;

—develops long-range marketing programs for maximum utilization of power from existing and proposed hydroelectric projects; and

—conducts and participates in the comprehensive planning of water resource development in the Southwest.

For further information, contact the Southwestern Power Administration, P.O. Box 1619, Tulsa, OK 74101. Phone, 918–581–7474.

Western Area Power Administration

The Administration was established on December 21, 1977, pursuant to section 302 of the Department of Energy Organization Act (42 U.S.C. 7152). The Administration is responsible for the Federal electric power-marketing and transmission functions in 15 central and western States, encompassing a geographic area of 1.3 million square miles. The Administration sells power to 532 customers, consisting of cooperatives, municipalities, public utility districts, private utilities, Federal and State agencies, and irrigation districts. The wholesale power customers, in turn, provide service to millions of retail consumers in the States of Arizona, California, Colorado, Iowa, Kansas, Minnesota, Montana, Nebraska, Nevada, New Mexico, North Dakota, South Dakota, Texas, Utah, and Wyoming.

The Administration is responsible for the operation and maintenance of 16,178 miles of transmission lines, 228 substations, and various auxiliary power facilities in the aforementioned geographic areas and also for planning, construction, and operation and maintenance of additional Federal transmission facilities that may be authorized in the future. Electric power marketed by the Administration is generated by the Bureau of Reclamation, the U.S. Army Corps of Engineers, and the International Boundary and Water

Commission, which operates 47 hydropower generating plants in its service area. In addition, it markets the United States entitlement from the Navajo coal-fired plant near Page, AZ. The Administration's current installed generating capacity is 8,321 megawatts.

In carrying out the Federal power-marketing program, the Administration's organization consists of the Headquarters Office located in Golden, CO; five area offices—Billings, MT; Boulder City, NV; Loveland, CO; Sacramento, CA; and Salt Lake City, UT—five district offices, and one power systems operations office.

For further information, contact the Western Area Power Administration, P.O. Box 3402, Golden, CO 80401. Phone, 303–231–1513.

For further information concerning the Department of Energy, contact the Office of Public and Consumer Affairs, Department of Energy, 1000 Independence Avenue SW., Washington, DC 20585. Phone, 202–586–4940.

DEPARTMENT OF HEALTH AND HUMAN SERVICES

200 Independence Avenue SW., Washington, DC 20201
Phone, 202–619–0257

SECRETARY OF HEALTH AND HUMAN SERVICES	DONNA E. SHALALA
Counselor to the Secretary	PETER B. EDELMAN
Confidential Assistant to the Secretary	JOLINDA GAITHER
Deputy Secretary	WALTER BROADNAX
Chief of Staff	KEVIN THURM
Executive Secretary	CLAUDIA COOLEY
Inspector General	JUNE GIBBS BROWN
Principal Deputy Inspector General	MICHAEL F. MANGANO
Deputy Inspector General for Management and Policy	DENNIS J. DUQUETTE
Deputy Inspector General for Audit Services	THOMAS D. ROSLEWICZ
Deputy Inspector General for Investigations	(VACANCY)
Assistant Inspector General for Criminal Investigations	JOHN E. HARTWIG
Deputy Inspector General for Evaluation and Inspections	GEORGE F. GROB
Assistant Inspector General for Civil Fraud and Administrative Adjudication	EILEEN T. BOYD
Director, Office for Civil Rights	DENNIS HAYASHI
Deputy Director	OMAR V. GUERRERO
Associate Deputy Director, Management Planning and Evaluation	PAUL R. KRETCHMAR
Deputy to the Associate Director, Management Planning and Evaluation	(VACANCY)
Associate Deputy Director, Program Operations	RONALD COPELAND
Deputy to the Associate Deputy Director, Program Operations	PATRICIA MACKEY
Director, Policy and Special Projects Staff	MARCELLA HAYNES
Director, U.S. Office of Consumer Affairs and Special Assistant to the President	BERNICE FRIEDLANDER
Director, U.S. Office of Consumer Affairs and Special Assistant to the President	POLLY BACA
Assistant Secretary (Public Affairs)	AVIS LAVELLE
Deputy Assistant Secretary for Public Affairs (Policy and Communications)	MELISSA SKOLFIELD
Deputy Assistant Secretary for Public Affairs (Media)	VICTOR ZONANA
Director, News Division	P. CAMPBELL GARDETT
Assistant Secretary (Legislation)	JERRY D. KLEPNER
Special Assistant	IRENE BUENO
Principal Deputy Assistant Secretary	RICHARD J. TARPLIN
Deputy Assistant Secretary (Congressional Liaison)	KIMBERLY C. PARKER

Deputy Assistant Secretary (Health)	KAREN L. POLLITZ
Deputy Assistant Secretary (Human Services)	MARY M. BOURDETTE
Assistant Secretary for Planning and Evaluation	DAVID T. ELLWOOD
Executive Assistant	NAOMI GOLDSTEIN
Deputy Assistant Secretary for Health Policy	KENNETH THORPE
Deputy Assistant Secretary for Program Systems	GERALD H. BRITTEN
Deputy Assistant Secretary for Human Services Policy	WENDELL E. PRIMUS
Deputy Assistant Secretary for Disability Aging and Long-Term Care Policy	ROBYN STONE
General Counsel	HARRIET S. RABB
Deputy General Counsel	BEVERLY DENNIS III
Deputy General Counsel (Legal Counsel)	NAN HUNTER
Special Assistant to the General Counsel	ANDREW HYMAN
Executive Officer	(VACANCY)
Associate General Counsel, Business and Administrative Law Division	(VACANCY)
Associate General Counsel, Civil Rights Division	GEORGE LYON
Associate General Counsel, Children, Families and Aging	(VACANCY)
Associate General Counsel, Food and Drug Division	MARGARET PORTER
Associate General Counsel, Health Care Financing Division	DARREL GRINSTEAD
Associate General Counsel, Inspector General Counsel	D. MCCARTY THORNTON
Associate General Counsel, Legislation	(VACANCY)
Deputy General Counsel, Program Review	ANNA L. DURAND
Associate General Counsel, Public Health Division	RICHARD RISEBERG
Deputy General Counsel, Regulation	MICHAEL S. WALD
Assistant Secretary for Management and Budget	ELIZABETH M. JAMES, *Acting*
Principal Deputy Assistant Secretary for Management and Budget	ELIZABETH M. JAMES
Senior Advisor	LAVARNE BURTON
Deputy Assistant Secretary, Budget	DENNIS P. WILLIAMS
Deputy Assistant Secretary, Finance	GEORGE STRADER
Deputy Assistant Secretary for Information Resources Management	NEIL STILLMAN
Deputy Assistant Secretary for Grants and Acquisition Management	TERRENCE J. TYCHAN
Director, Administrative Services Center	PEGGY I. DODD
Assistant Secretary for Personnel Administration and Director, Equal Employment Opportunity	THOMAS S. MCFEE
Deputy Assistant Secretary for Personnel Administration and Deputy Director, Equal Employment Opportunity	EUGENE KINLOW
Director, Center for Human Resource Strategic Planning and Policy	CHARLES J. MCCARTY
Chairman, Departmental Appeals Board	NORVAL (JOHN) D. SETTLE

Director, Office of Human Resource   THOMAS M. KING
    Information Management
Director, Office of Personnel Services   (VACANCY)
Director, Office of Human Relations   (VACANCY)

ADMINISTRATION ON AGING

330 Independence Avenue SW., Washington, DC 20201
Phone, 202–619–0556

Assistant Secretary for Aging   FERNANDO M. TORRES-GIL
Principal Deputy Assistant Secretary   PORTIA P. MITTELMAN
Deputy Assistant Secretary for Program   JOHN F. MCCARTHY
    Development and Elder Rights Programs
Deputy Assistant Secretary for Program   WILLIAM F. BENSON
    Operations and Intergovernmental Affairs
Director, Office of State and Community   EDWIN L. WALKER
    Programs
Director, Office of American Indian, Alaskan M. YVONNE JACKSON
    Native, and Native Hawaiian Programs
Director, Office of Policy Coordination and (VACANCY)
    Analysis
Director, Office of Administration and   DONALD D. SMITH
    Management
Director, Office of Field Operations   ALICIA V. ORS

ADMINISTRATION FOR CHILDREN AND FAMILIES

370 L'Enfant Promenade SW., Washington, DC 20447
Phone, 202–401–9200

Assistant Secretary   MARY JO BANE
Principal Deputy Assistant Secretary   (VACANCY)
Deputy Assistant Secretary for Program   LAURENCE J. LOVE
    Operations
Deputy Assistant Secretary for Policy and   ANN ROSEWATER
    External Affairs
Commissioner, Administration on Children,   OLIVIA GOLDEN
    Youth and Families
Commissioner, Administration on   BOB WILLIAMS
    Developmental Disabilities
Commissioner, Administration for Native   GARY KIMBLE
    Americans
Director, Office of Child Support Enforcement MARY JO BANE
Deputy Director, Office of Child Support   DAVID GRAY ROSS
    Enforcement
Director, Office of Community Services   DONALD SYKES
Director, Office of Information Systems   MARK RAGAN, Acting
    Management/Child Support Information
    Systems
Director, Office of Financial Management   NORMAN THOMPSON
Director, Office of Management   NORMAN THOMPSON, Acting
Director, Office of Policy and Evaluation   HOWARD ROLSTON
Director, Office of Public Affairs   MICHAEL KHARFEN
Director, Office of Refugee Resettlement   LAVINIA LIMON
Director, Office of Family Assistance   LAVINIA LIMON, Acting

PUBLIC HEALTH SERVICE
Office of the Assistant Secretary for Health

200 Independence Avenue SW., Washington, DC 20201
Phone, 202–690–7694

5600 Fishers Lane, Rockville, MD 20857
Phone, 301–443–2403

Assistant Secretary for Health	PHILIP R. LEE
Principal Deputy Assistant Secretary for Health	JO IVEY BOUFFORD
Deputy Assistant Secretary for Health	WILLIAM CORR
Surgeon General of the Public Health Service	AUDREY F. MANLEY, *Acting*
Deputy Assistant Secretary for Health Disease Prevention and Health Promotion and Health Planning and Evaluation	SUSANNE STOIBER, *Acting*
Deputy Assistant Secretary for Health (Management and Budget)	ANTHONY L. ITTEILAG
Deputy Assistant Secretary for Health (Communications)	MARTIS J. DAVIS
Deputy Assistant Secretary for Health (Interagency Liaison)	ROBERT O. VALDEZ, *Acting*
Deputy Assistant Secretary for International and Refugee Health	(VACANCY)
Deputy Assistant Secretary for Legislation (Health)	KAREN L. POLLITZ
Deputy Assistant Secretary for Minority Health	CLAY E. SIMPSON, *Acting*
Deputy Assistant Secretary for Population Affairs	FELICIA H. STEWART
Director, Office of Adolescent Pregnancy Programs	PATRICK J. SHEERAN, *Acting*
Director, Office of Family Planning	SAMUEL S. TAYLOR, *Acting*
Deputy Assistant Secretary for Health (Policy Development)	ROZ LASKER
Deputy Assistant Secretary for Women's Health	SUSAN J. BLUMENTHAL
Executive Director, President's Council on Physical Fitness and Sports	SANDRA PERLMUTTER
Director, Office of HIV/AIDS Policy	ARTHUR J. LAWRENCE, *Acting*
Director, National Vaccine Program Office	(VACANCY)
Director, Office of Emergency Preparedness	FRANK E. YOUNG
Director, Office of Equal Employment Opportunity	PEDRO J. MORALES
Director, Office of Disease Prevention and Health Promotion and Health Planning and Evaluation	JAMES A. HARRELL, *Acting*
Director, Office of Intergovernmental Affairs	ANTHONY F. FITZPATRICK
Director, Office of International Health	LINDA VOGEL
Director, Office of Refugee Health	JOANNE LUUIU
Director, Office of Research Integrity	LYLE W. BIVENS
Director, PHS Executive Secretariat	ROBERT A. RICKARD

Agency for Health Care Policy and Research
2101 E. Jefferson Street, Rockville, MD 20852
Phone, 301–227–8364

Administrator	CLIFTON R. GOUS

Deputy Administrator (VACANCY)
Director, Office of Planning and Resource CLIFTON R. GOUS, *Acting*
Management
Director, Office of Science and Data J. MICHAEL FITZMAURICE
Development
Director, Office of the Forum for Quality and DOUGLAS B. KAMEROW
Effectiveness in Health Care
Director, Office of Health Technology THOMAS V. HOLOHAN
Assessment
Director, Center for Medical Effectiveness RICHARD J. GREENE
Research
Director, Center for General Health Services DONALD E. GOLDSTONE
Intramural Research
Director, Center for General Health Services LINDA K. DEMLO, *Acting*
Extramural Research
Director, Center for Research Dissemination CHRISTINE WILLIAMS, *Acting*
and Liaison

Centers for Disease Control and Prevention

1600 Clifton Road NE., Atlanta, GA 30333
Phone, 404–639–3311

Director DAVID SATCHER
Deputy Director CLAIRE V. BROOME
Associate Director, HIV/AIDS JAMES W. CURRAN
Associate Director, International Health JOE H. DAVIS
Associate Director, Management and ARTHUR C. JACKSON
Operations
Associate Director, Minority Health RUEBEN C. WARREN
Associate Director, Policy, Planning, and MARTHA F. KATZ
Evaluation
Associate Director, Science DIXIE SNIDER, *Acting*
Associate Director, Washington HELENE GAYLE
Deputy Director, Washington Office FRANCES L. DEPEYSTER
Special Assistant to the Associate Director, ROBERT C. IRWIN
Washington
Office of Equal Employment Opportunity SUE J. PORTER
Director, Office of Program Support ARTHUR C. JACKSON
Director, Office of Health and Safety JONATHAN Y. RICHMOND
Director, Office of Program Planning and MARTHA F. KATZ
Evaluation
Director, Office of Public Affairs ANN M. SIMS, *Acting*
Director, Epidemiology Program Office STEPHEN B. THACKER
Director, International Health Program Office JOE H. DAVIS
Director, National Immunization Program WALTER A. ORENSTEIN
Director, Public Health Practice Program EDWARD L. BAKER
Office
Director, National Center for Environmental RICHARD J. JACKSON
Health
Director, National Center for Chronic Disease JIM MARKS, *Acting*
Prevention and Health Promotion
Director, National Center for Infectious JAMES M. HUGHES
Diseases
Director, National Center for Injury Prevention MARK L. ROSENBERG
and Control

Director, National Center for Prevention Services	HELENE GAYLE, *Acting*
Director, National Institute for Occupational Safety and Health	LINDA ROSENSTOCK
Director, National Center for Health Statistics	JOHN ANDERSON, *Acting*

Agency for Toxic Substances and Disease Registry
1600 Clifton Road NE., Atlanta, GA 30333
Phone, 404–452–4111

Administrator	DAVID SATCHER
Deputy Administrator	CLAIRE V. BROOME
Assistant Administrator	BARRY L. JOHNSON
Deputy Assistant Administrator	WILLIAM D. ADAMS

Food and Drug Administration
5600 Fishers Lane, Rockville, MD 20857
Phone, 301–443–1544

Commissioner of Food and Drugs	DAVID A. KESSLER
Advisor to the Commissioner	MARY PENDERGAST
Chief Mediator and Ombudsman	AMANDA PEDERSEN
Chief Counsel	MARGARET J. PORTER
Special Assistant for Investigations	JOHN H. MITCHELL, *Acting*
Special Agent in Charge, Office of Special Investigations	TOMMY L. HAMPTON
Senior Advisor for Science	ELKAN BLOUT
Deputy Commissioner for Operations	LINDA SUYDAM, *Acting*
Associate Commissioner for Regulatory Affairs	RONALD G. CHESEMORE
Director, Center for Biologics Evaluation and Research	KATHRYN C. ZOON
Director, Center for Drug Evaluation and Research	JANET WOODCOCK
Director, Center for Devices and Radiological Health	D. BRUCE BURLINGTON
Director, Center for Food Safety and Applied Nutrition	FRED R. SHANK
Director, Center for Veterinary Medicine	STEPHEN F. SUNDLOF
Director, National Center for Toxicological Research	BERNARD A. SCHWETZ
Director, Office of AIDS and Special Health Issues	RANDY WYKOFF
Director, Office of Orphan Products Development	MARLENE E. HAFFNER
Deputy Commissioner for Policy	WILLIAM SCHULTZ
Director, Policy Development and Coordination Staff	CATHERINE C. LORRAINE, *Acting*
Director, Policy Research Staff	JURIAN STROBOS
Director, Regulations Policy and Management Staff	EDWIN V. DUTRA, JR.
Deputy Commissioner for External Affairs	SHARON SMITH HOLSTON
Associate Commissioner for Consumer Affairs	R. ALEXANDER GRANT

Associate Commissioner for Health Affairs	STUART L. NIGHTINGALE
Associate Commissioner for Legislative Affairs	DIANE THOMPSON
Associate Commissioner for Public Affairs	JAMES O'HARA III
Director, Office of Women's Health	RUTH MERKATZ
Deputy Commissioner for Management and Systems	MARY JO VEVERKA
Associate Commissioner for Management	ROBERT J. BYRD
Associate Commissioner for Planning and Evaluation	PAUL COPPINGER
Associate Commissioner for Information Resources Management	JAMES T. MCMAHON

Health Resources and Services Administration
5600 Fishers Lane, Rockville, MD 20857
Phone, 301–443–2086

Administrator	CIRO V. SUMAYA
Deputy Administrator	JOHN D. MAHONEY
Chief Medical Officer	WILLIAM A. ROBINSON, M.D.
Associate Administrator for AIDS	G. STEPHEN BOWEN
Associate Administrator for Operations and Management	JAMES P. PURVIS, *Acting*
Associate Administrator for Planning, Evaluation, and Legislation	RONALD H. CARLSON
Associate Administrator for Communications	SYLVIA SHAFFER
Associate Administrator for Policy Coordination	CHERRY TSUTSUMIDA, *Acting*
Associate Administrator for International Health	GEORGE B. DINES
Associate Administrator for Minority Health	ILEANA C. HERRELL
Associate Administrator for Equal Opportunity and Civil Rights	J. CALVIN ADAMS
Associate Administrator for Public Health Practice	DOUGLAS S. LLOYD
Associate Administrator for Information Resources Management	JAMES E. LARSON
Director, Office of Rural Health Policy	JEFFREY HUMAN
Director, Bureau of Health Professions	FITZHUGH M. MULLAN
Director, Maternal and Child Health Bureau	AUDREY H. NORA
Director, Bureau of Health Resources Development	G. STEPHEN BOWEN
Director, Bureau of Primary Health Care	MARILYN H. GASTON

Indian Health Service
5600 Fishers Lane, Rockville, MD 20857
Phone, 301–443–1083

Director	MICHAEL H. TRUJILLO, M.D.
Deputy Director	MICHEL LINCOLN
Director of Headquarters Operations	LUANA L. REYES, *Acting*
Director, Communications Staff	TONY KENDRICKS
Director, Policy Review and Coordination Staff	JOSEPH DEFFENBAUGH, *Acting*
Director, Executive Secretariat	DARRELL GALPIN

Director, Equal Employment Opportunity and Civil Rights Staff	CECELIA HEFTEL
Associate Director, Office of Administration and Management	GEORGE BUZZARD
Associate Director, Office of Planning, Evaluation, and Legislation	ED SIMERMEYER, *Acting*
Associate Director, Office of Tribal Activities	DOUGLAS BLACK
Associate Director, Office of Environmental Health and Engineering	GARY HARTZ, *Acting*
Associate Director, Office of Information Resource Management	RICHARD CHURCH
Associate Director, Office of Health Programs	PHILLIP SMITH, M.D.
Associate Director, Office of Human Resources	ROBERT MCSWAIN, *Acting*
Associate Director, Office of Health Program Research and Development	ELEANORE ROBERTSON

National Institutes of Health

9000 Rockville Pike, Bethesda, MD 20892
Phone, 301–496–4000

Director	HAROLD E. VARMUS
Deputy Director	RUTH L. KIRSCHSTEIN
Deputy Director for Intramural Research	MICHAEL M. GOTTESMAN
Deputy Director for Extramural Research	WENDY BALDWIN
Deputy Director for Science Policy and Technology Transfer	DARYL A. CHAMBLEE, *Acting*
Assistant Director for Program Coordination	VIDA H. BEAVEN
Associate Director for Research on Women's Health	VIVIAN W. PINN
Associate Director for Research on Minority Health	JOHN RUFFIN
Associate Director for Administration	LEAMON M. LEE
Associate Director for AIDS Research	WILLIAM E. PAUL
Associate Director for Clinical Research	JOHN I. GALLIN
Associate Director for Communications	R. ANNE THOMAS
Associate Director for Disease Prevention	WILLIAM R. HARLAN
Associate Director for Extramural Affairs	GEORGE J. GALASSO
Associate Director for Intramural Affairs	PHILIP S. CHEN, JR.
Associate Director for Research Services	STEPHEN A. FICCA
Director, Office of Equal Employment Opportunity	NAOMI CHURCHILL
Director, National Cancer Institute	EDWARD J. SONDIK, *Acting*
Director, National Heart, Lung, and Blood Institute	CLAUDE J.M. LENFANT
Director, National Institute of Diabetes and Digestive and Kidney Diseases	PHILLIP GORDEN
Director, National Library of Medicine	DONALD A.B. LINDBERG
Director, National Institute of Allergy and Infectious Diseases	ANTHONY S. FAUCI
Director, National Institute on Deafness and Other Communication Disorders	JAMES B. SNOW, JR.
Director, National Institute of Dental Research	DUSHANKA V. KLEINMAN
Director, National Institute of Neurological Disorders and Stroke	ZACH W. HALL

Director, National Institute of General Medical Sciences	MARVIN CASSMAN, *Acting*
Director, National Institute of Child Health and Human Development	DUANE F. ALEXANDER
Director, National Institute of Environmental Health Sciences	KENNETH OLDEN
Director, National Eye Institute	CARL KUPFER
Director, National Institute on Aging	RICHARD HODES
Director, National Institute of Arthritis and Musculoskeletal and Skin Diseases	MICHAEL D. LOCKSHIN, *Acting*
Director, National Institute on Alcohol Abuse and Alcoholism	ENOCH GORDIS
Director, National Institute on Drug Abuse	ALAN I. LESHNER
Director, National Institute of Mental Health	REX WILLIAM COWDRY, *Acting*
Director, Division of Research Grants	DONAL H. LUECKE, *Acting*
Director, Clinical Center	JOHN I. GALLIN
Director, National Center for Research Resources	JUDITH L. VAITUKAITIS
Director, Fogarty International Center	PHILIP E. SCHAMBRA
Director, Division of Computer Research and Technology	DAVID RODBARD
Director, National Institute of Nursing Research	PATRICIA A. GRADY
Director, National Center for Human Genome Research	FRANCIS S. COLLINS

SUBSTANCE ABUSE AND MENTAL HEALTH SERVICES ADMINISTRATION

5600 Fishers Lane, Rockville, MD 20857
Phone, 301–443–4797

Administrator	NELBA CHAVEZ
Deputy Administrator	MICHELE W. APPLEGATE, *Acting*
Associate Administrator for Management	RICHARD KOPANDA, *Acting*
Associate Administrator for Communications	JAMES FRIEDMAN, *Acting*
Associate Administrator for Extramural Programs	JOEL GOLDSTEIN, *Acting*
Associate Administrator for Policy and Program Coordination	FRANK J. SULLIVAN
Associate Administrator for Alcohol Prevention and Treatment Policy	BETTINA M. SCOTT, *Acting*
Director, Office on AIDS	CYNTHIA PRATHER, *Acting*
Associate Administrator for Women's Services	MARY C. KNIPMEYER
Director, Office of Applied Studies	DANIEL MELNICK, *Acting*
Director, Center for Substance Abuse Prevention	ELAINE M. JOHNSON
Director, Center for Substance Abuse Treatment	DAVID J. MACTAS
Director, Center for Mental Health Services	BERNARD S. ARONS
Director, Office of Management, Planning, and Communications	MICHELE W. APPLEGATE, *Acting*

HEALTH CARE FINANCING ADMINISTRATION

200 Independence Avenue SW., Washington, DC 20201
Phone, 202-245-6113

Administrator	BRUCE C. VLADECK
Deputy Administrator	HELEN SMITS, M.D.
Executive Associate Administrator	(VACANCY)
Chairman, Provider Reimbursement Review Board	IRVIN W. KUES
Director, Equal Employment Opportunity Staff	JOANNE HITCHCOCK, M.D.
Director, Executive Secretariat	JOYCE SOMSAK
Director, Office of Legislative and Inter-Governmental Affairs	DEBORAH CHANG
Deputy Director	THOMAS GUSTAFSON
Director, Medicaid Bureau	SALLY RICHARDSON
Deputy Director	ROZANN ABATO
Director, Office of Managed Care	RODNEY ARMSTEAD, M.D.
Deputy Director	GALE DRAPALA
Associate Administrator for Customer Relations and Communication	PAMELA GENTRY, *Acting*
Director, Office of Beneficiary Services	ROGER GOODACRE
Director, Office of Public Affairs	ANNE MARIE HUMMEL
Director, Office of Public Liaison	MARTHA DISARIO
Associate Administrator for Policy	KATHLEEN BUTO
Deputy Associate Administrator	BARBARA COOPER
Director, Bureau of Policy Development	THOMAS AULT
Deputy Director	BARBARA WYNN
Director, Office of Research and Demonstrations	(VACANCY)
Deputy Director	THOMAS KICKHAM
Director, Office of the Actuary	RICHARD FOSTER
Deputy Director	(VACANCY)
Associate Administrator for Operations and Resource Management	STEVEN PELOVITZ
Deputy Associate Administrator	DAVID BUTLER
Director, Office of the Attorney Advisor	MARION SILVA
Director, Office of Financial and Human Resources	WILLIAM BROGLIE
Deputy Director	RONALD GWYN
Director, Bureau of Program Operations	CAROL WALTON
Deputy Director	GARY KAVANAGH
Director, Bureau of Data Management and Strategy	REGINA MCPHILLIPS
Deputy Director	MICHAEL ODACHOWSKI
Director, Health Standards and Quality Bureau	BARBARA GAGEL
Deputy Director	DAVID CLARK

The Department of Health and Human Services is the Cabinet-level department of the Federal executive branch most concerned with people and most involved with the Nation's human concerns. In one way or another—whether it is mailing out Social Security checks or making health services more widely available—HHS touches the lives of more Americans than any other Federal agency. It is literally a department of people serving people, from newborn infants to our most elderly citizens.

DEPARTMENT OF HEALTH AND HUMAN SERVICES

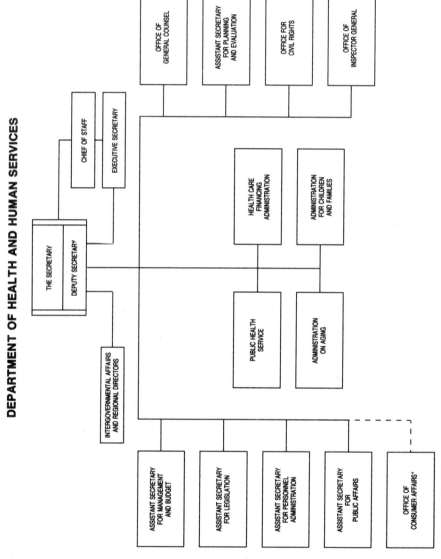

THE SECRETARY / DEPUTY SECRETARY

CHIEF OF STAFF

EXECUTIVE SECRETARY

INTERGOVERNMENTAL AFFAIRS AND REGIONAL DIRECTORS

OFFICE OF GENERAL COUNSEL

ASSISTANT SECRETARY FOR PLANNING AND EVALUATION

OFFICE FOR CIVIL RIGHTS

OFFICE OF INSPECTOR GENERAL

HEALTH CARE FINANCING ADMINISTRATION

ADMINISTRATION FOR CHILDREN AND FAMILIES

PUBLIC HEALTH SERVICE

ADMINISTRATION ON AGING

ASSISTANT SECRETARY FOR MANAGEMENT AND BUDGET

ASSISTANT SECRETARY FOR LEGISLATION

ASSISTANT SECRETARY FOR PERSONNEL ADMINISTRATION

ASSISTANT SECRETARY FOR PUBLIC AFFAIRS

OFFICE OF CONSUMER AFFAIRS*

* Located administratively in HHS; reports to the President.

The Department of Health, Education, and Welfare was created on April 11, 1953 (5 U.S.C. app.). The Department was redesignated as the Department of Health and Human Services (HHS), effective May 4, 1980, by the Department of Education Organization Act (20 U.S.C. 3508).

Office of the Secretary

The Secretary of Health and Human Services advises the President on health, welfare, and income security plans, policies, and programs of the Federal Government. The Secretary directs Department staff in carrying out the approved programs and activities of the Department and promotes general public understanding of the Department's goals, programs, and objectives. The Secretary administers these functions through the Office of the Secretary and the five Operating Divisions, which include: the Administration on Aging, the Substance Abuse and Mental Health Services Administration, the Health Care Financing Administration, the Administration for Children and Families, and the Public Health Service. The Office of the Secretary includes the offices of Deputy Secretary, the Assistant Secretaries, Inspector General, and General Counsel. Some offices whose public purposes are broadly applied are detailed further.

Civil Rights   The Office for Civil Rights is responsible for the administration and enforcement of the following laws that prohibit discrimination in federally assisted health and human services programs:
  —title VI of the Civil Rights Act of 1964;
  —section 504 of the Rehabilitation Act of 1973, as amended;
  —the Age Discrimination Act of 1975;
  —title IX of the Education Amendments of 1972;
  —section 407 of the Drug Abuse Offense and Treatment Act of 1972;

  —section 321 of the Comprehensive Alcohol Abuse and Alcoholism Prevention, Treatment and Rehabilitation Act of 1970;
  —the Equal Employment Opportunity provisions of the Communications Finance Act of 1934, as amended;
  —titles VI and XVI of the Public Health Service Act;
  —the nondiscrimination provisions of the Omnibus Budget Reconciliation Act of 1981;
  —section 307(a) of the Family Violence Prevention and Services Act;
  —titles VII and VIII of the Public Health Service Act; and
  —subtitle A, title II, of the Americans with Disabilities Act of 1990.

Consumer Affairs   The U.S. Office of Consumer Affairs advises the White House and the Secretary of HHS on consumer-related policy and programs and is responsible for handling consumer matters; analyzes and coordinates implementation of all Federal activities in the area of consumer protection; and recommends ways in which governmental consumer programs can be made more effective. The Director of the Office also chairs the U.S. Consumer Affairs Council.

Regional Offices

The 10 Regional Directors of the Department of Health and Human Services are the Secretary's representatives in direct, official dealings with State and local government organizations. They provide a central focus in each region for departmental relations with Congress and promote general understanding of Department programs, policies, and objectives. They also advise the Secretary on the potential effects of decisions and provide administrative services and support to Department programs and activities in the regions.

Regional Offices—Department of Health and Human Services
(Areas included within each region are indicated on the map in Appendix A.)

Region/Address	Director	Telephone
1. John F. Kennedy Federal Bldg., Boston, MA 02203	Philip Johnston	617–565–1500

Regional Offices—Department of Health and Human Services—Continued
(Areas included within each region are indicated on the map in Appendix A.)

Region/Address	Director	Telephone
2. 26 Federal Plz., New York, NY 10278	Alison E. Greene	212–264–4600
3. 3535 Market St., Philadelphia, PA 19104	Lynn Yeakel	215–596–6492
4. 101 Marietta Twr., Atlanta, GA 30323	Patricia Ford-Roegner	404–331–2442
5. 105 W. Adams St., Chicago, IL 60603	Elaine Weiss	312–353–5160
6. 1200 Main Twr., Dallas, TX 75202	Patricia Montoya	214–767–3301
7. 601 E. 12th St., Kansas City, MO 64106	Kathleen Steele	816–426–2821
8. 1961 Stout St., Denver, CO 80294–3538	Margaret Cary	303–844–3372
9. Federal Office Bldg., San Francisco, CA 94102	Grantland Johnson	415–556–1961
10. Blanchard Plz. Bldg., 2201 6th Ave., Seattle, WA 98121	Patrick McBride, *Acting*	206–615–2010

Administration on Aging

The Administration on Aging is the principal agency designated to carry out the provisions of the Older Americans Act of 1965, as amended (42 U.S.C. 3001 *et seq*). As the lead agency within HHS on all issues concerning aging, it:

—advises the Secretary, Department components, and other Federal departments and agencies on the characteristics, circumstances, and needs of older people;

—develops policies, plans, and programs designed to promote their welfare and advocates for their needs in HHS program planning and policy development;

—administers a program of formula grants to States to establish State and community programs for older persons under the title III of the act (45 CFR 1321);

—administers a program of grants to American Indians, Alaskan Natives, and Native Hawaiians to establish programs for older Native Americans under title VI of the act (45 CFR 1328);

—provides policy, procedural direction, and technical assistance to States and Native American grantees to promote the development of community-based systems of comprehensive social, nutrition, and support services for older persons;

—administers programs of training, research, and demonstration under title IV of the act; and

—administers ombudsman and legal services oversight and protective services for older people under title VII of the act.

For further information, contact the Assistant Secretary for Aging. Phone, 202–401–4541.

Administration for Children and Families

The Administration for Children and Families (ACF) was created on April 15, 1991, under authority of section 6 of Reorganization Plan No. 1 of 1953 and pursuant to the authority vested in the Secretary of Health and Human Services.

The Administration is headed by the Assistant Secretary for Children and Families, who reports to the Secretary of HHS. The Assistant Secretary also serves as the Director of Child Support Enforcement. The Administration provides executive direction, leadership,

and guidance to all ACF components; advises the Secretary and Deputy Secretary on ACF programs; and recommends actions and strategies to improve coordination of ACF efforts with other programs, agencies, and governmental levels or jurisdictions.

Administration on Children, Youth and Families   The Administration on Children, Youth and Families (ACYF) advises the Secretary, through the Assistant Secretary for Children and Families, on matters relating to the sound development of children, youth, and families. ACYF administers State grant programs under titles IV–B and IV–E of the Social Security Act to assist States in providing child welfare services and foster care and adoption assistance; child care programs authorized under title IV–A of the Social Security Act and the Child Care and Development Block Grant; and State grant programs to improve and increase child abuse prevention and treatment activities and develop family preservation and family support services. ACYF also administers the Head Start Program; services for runaway and homeless youth and their families; the Youth Gang Drug Prevention Program; child welfare services research, demonstration and training programs, the Adoption Opportunities Program, and other discretionary child welfare services programs; child abuse and neglect research and demonstration programs; and the Community Schools Youth Services and Supervision Grant Program. ACYF also supports and encourages initiatives to involve the private and voluntary sectors in the areas of children, youth, and families.

In concert with other components of ACF, ACYF develops and implements research, demonstration, and evaluation strategies for the discretionary funding of activities designed to improve and enrich the lives of children and youth and to strengthen families.

For further information, contact the Commissioner, Administration on Children, Youth and Families, Administration for Children and Families, Department of Health and Human Services, 370 L'Enfant Promenade SW., Washington DC 20447. Phone, 202–205–8347 or 202–401–2337.

Administration on Developmental Disabilities   The Administration on Developmental Disabilities (ADD) advises the Secretary, through the Assistant Secretary for Children and Families, on matters relating to persons with developmental disabilities and their families. ADD serves as the focal point in the Department for supporting and encouraging the provision of quality services to persons with developmental disabilities; assists States, through the

design and implementation of a comprehensive and continuing State plan, in increasing independence, productivity, and community inclusion of persons with developmental disabilities; administers the Basic State Grant Program, the Protection and Advocacy Grant Program, and other discretionary programs; and serves as a resource in developing policies and programs to reduce or eliminate barriers experienced by persons with developmental disabilities.

In concert with other components of ACF, ADD develops and implements research, demonstration, and evaluation strategies for discretionary funding of activities to improve lives of persons with developmental disabilities.

For further information, contact the Commissioner, Administration on Developmental Disabilities, Administration for Children and Families, Department of Health and Human Services, 370 L'Enfant Promenade SW., Washington, DC 20447. Phone, 202–690–6590.

Native Americans   The Administration for Native Americans (ANA) advises the Secretary, through the Assistant Secretary for Children and Families, on matters relating to American Indians, Alaskan Natives, Native American Pacific Islanders, and Native Hawaiians—hereinafter referred to as Native Americans. ANA represents the concerns of Native Americans and serves as the focal point in the Department on the full range of developmental, social, and economic strategies that support Native American self-determination and self-sufficiency.

ANA administers grant programs to eligible Indian tribes and Native American organizations in urban and rural areas; provides departmental liaison with other Federal agencies on Native American affairs, in conjunction with the Office of the Assistant Secretary for Children and Families; develops and implements research, demonstration, and evaluation strategies for discretionary funding of activities; and explores new program concepts and methods for increasing the social and economic development of Native Americans.

For further information, contact the Commissioner, Administration for Native Americans, Administration for Children and Families, Department of Health and Human Services, 370 L'Enfant Promenade SW., Washington, DC 20447. Phone, 202–690–7776.

Child Support Enforcement   The Office of Child Support Enforcement (OCSE) advises the Secretary on matters relating to child support enforcement. The Office provides direction, guidance, and oversight to State Child Support Enforcement (CSE) program offices and on activities authorized and directed by title IV, part D of the Social Security Act, and other pertinent legislation. The general purpose of CSE legislation is to require States to develop programs for establishing and enforcing support obligations by locating absent parents, establishing paternity when necessary, and obtaining child support. The Office assists States in establishing adequate reporting procedures and maintaining records for operating CSE programs and of amounts collected and disbursed under such programs, as well as costs incurred in collecting such amounts. The Office validates applications from States for permission to utilize U.S. courts to enforce orders for support against absent parents, and operates the Federal Parent Locator Service. It certifies to the Secretary of the Treasury the amounts of child support obligations that require collection in specific instances.

For further information, contact the Child Support Information Officer, Office of Child Support Enforcement, Administration for Children and Families, Department of Health and Human Services, 370 L'Enfant Promenade SW., Washington, DC 20447. Phone, 202–401–9373.

Community Services   The Office of Community Services (OCS) advises the Secretary, through the Assistant Secretary for Children and Families, on matters relating to community programs that promote economic self-sufficiency. The Office is responsible for administering programs that serve low-income and needy individuals and addresses the overall goal of personal responsibility in achieving and maintaining self-sufficiency. It administers the

Community Services Block Grant, Social Services Block Grant, and the Low-Income Energy Assistance Program and a variety of discretionary grant programs that foster family stability, economic security, responsibility, and self-support. Also, it promotes and provides services to homeless and low-income individuals and develops new and innovative approaches to reduce welfare dependency.

For further information, contact the Director, Office of Community Services, Administration for Children and Families, Department of Health and Human Services, 370 L'Enfant Promenade SW., Washington, DC 20447. Phone, 202–401–9333.

Office of Information Systems Management/Child Support Information Systems   The Office of Information Systems Management/Child Support Information Systems advises the Assistant Secretary for Children and Families/ Director of Child Support Enforcement on issues and policies pertaining to information management. It oversees the utilization of information resources throughout ACF. It directs ACF's information systems, computer centers, and communications network activities. The Office approves, monitors, and certifies State information system projects for ACF programs funded under title IV, parts A, B, E, and F of the Social Security Act. The Office establishes departmental policy and coordinates with other Federal agencies regarding State computer-related projects for computer matching and integrated systems. The Office of Child Support Information Systems is a separate organizational unit which reports to the Director of Child Support Enforcement, and which approves, monitors, and certifies State information systems projects as specified under title IV, part D of the Social Security Act.

For further information, contact the Director, Office of Information Systems Management/Child Support Information Systems, Administration for Children and Families, Department of Health and Human Services, 370 L'Enfant Promenade SW., Washington, DC 20447. Phone, 202–401–6960.

Financial Management   The Office of Financial Management advises the Assistant Secretary for Children and

Families on financial management matters. It provides leadership and direction on budget development and budget execution, financial and grants policy, oversight and administration of formula, entitlement, and block and discretionary grants; and resolution of audit findings, disallowances, and appeals.

For further information, contact the Director, Office of Financial Management, Administration for Children and Families, Department of Health and Human Services, 370 L'Enfant Promenade SW., Washington, DC 20447. Phone, 202–401–9238.

Office of Management   The Office of Management advises and assists the Assistant Secretary for Children and Families in the areas of human resource management, organizational analysis, facilities and telecommunications management, and acquisitions management. It provides service to all ACF components on such administration and management activities as personnel, staff development, labor relations, support services, management analysis, internal controls, and organizational studies.

For further information, contact the Director, Office of Management, Administration for Children and Families, Department of Health and Human Services, 370 L'Enfant Promenade SW., Washington, DC 20447. Phone, 202–401–9260.

Policy and Evaluation   The Office of Policy and Evaluation recommends to and advises the Assistant Secretary for Children and Families on all policy and programmatic matters having substantial impact on program direction in areas such as program content and objectives, program evaluation and results, and the costs and benefits of carrying out the programs. It oversees policy and congressional and legislative affairs, and manages ACF's regulatory, legislative, research, demonstration, and evaluation agendas and oversees special initiatives within ACF. The Office plans, develops, and monitors strategies for promoting ACF policy and analyzes the impact of

programmatic alternatives, including the fiscal impact.

For further information, contact the Director, Office of Policy and Evaluation, Administration for Children and Families, Department of Health and Human Services, 370 L'Enfant Promenade SW., Washington, DC 20447. Phone, 202–401–9220.

Public Affairs   The Office of Public Affairs (OPA) coordinates public affairs and communication services for the Assistant Secretary for Children and Families and for all ACF components. OPA provides leadership, direction, and oversight in promoting ACF's public affairs policies, programs, and initiatives. It strategically coordinates ACF's relationship with the public and private news media and responds to all media inquiries concerning ACF programs and related issues; directs the audiovisual and publication management systems for ACF; and serves as the focal point for intergovernmental coordination activities with State and local officials, special interest groups, professional and business organizations, private and voluntary groups, and other Federal agencies.

For further information, contact the Director, Office of Public Affairs, Administration for Children and Families, Department of Health and Human Services, 370 L'Enfant Promenade SW., Washington, DC 20447. Phone, 202–401–9215.

Refugee Resettlement   The Office of Refugee Resettlement (ORR) advises the Secretary, through the Assistant Secretary for Children and Families, on policies and programs regarding refugee resettlement, legalized aliens, and repatriation matters. ORR plans, develops, and directs implementation of a comprehensive program for domestic refugee and entrant resettlement assistance. The Office provides direction and technical guidance to the nationwide administration of programs including Refugee and Entrant Resettlement, State Legislation Impact

Assistance Grants, and the U.S. Repatriate Program.

For further information, contact the Director, Office of Refugee Resettlement, Administration for Children and Families, Department of Health and Human Services, 370 L'Enfant Promenade SW., Washington, DC 20447. Phone, 202–401–9246.

Office of Family Assistance   The Office of Family Assistance (OFA) advises the Secretary, through the Assistant Secretary for Children and Families, on matters relating to public assistance and economic self-sufficiency programs. The Office provides leadership, direction, and technical guidance in administering the following programs nationwide: Aid to Families with Dependent Children; Aid to the Aged, Blind, and Disabled in Guam, Puerto Rico, and the Virgin Islands; the Emergency Assistance Program; the Job Opportunities and Basic Skills Training Program; and child care under title IV, part A of the Social Security Act. OFA develops,

recommends, and issues policies, procedures, and interpretations to provide direction to these programs. It develops and implements standards and policies for regulating integrated quality control activities of the Department and the operating divisions. The Office provides technical assistance to States and assesses their performance in administering these programs; reviews State planning for administrative and operational improvements; and recommends actions to improve effectiveness. It directs reviews, provides consultations, and conducts necessary negotiations to achieve adherence to Federal laws and regulations in State plans for public assistance program administration. Also, it coordinates with ACYF on child care programs.

For further information, contact the Director, Office of Family Assistance, Administration for Children and Families, Department of Health and Human Services, 370 L'Enfant Promenade SW., Washington, DC 20447. Phone, 202–401–9275.

Regional Offices—Administration for Children and Families

Region/Address	Administrator	Telephone
I. Boston, MA (Rm. 2000, John F. Kennedy Federal Bldg., 02203)	Hugh Galligan	617–565–1020
II. New York, NY (Rm. 4049, 26 Federal Plz., 10278)	Mary Ann Higgins	212–264–2890
III. Philadelphia, PA (Rm. 5450, Gateway Bldg., 3535 Market St., 19104).	Ralph E. Douglas	215–596–0352
IV. Atlanta, GA (Suite 821, 101 Marietta Twr., 30323)	Patricia S. Brooks	404–331–5733
V. Chicago, IL (20th Fl., 105 W. Adams St., 60603)	Marion Steffy	312–353–4237
VI. Dallas, TX (1200 Main Twr. Bldg., 75202)	Leon McCowan	214–767–9648
VII. Kansas City, MO (Rm. 384, Federal Bldg., 601 E. 12th St., 64106).	Linda Carson	816–426–3981
VIII. Denver, CO (Rm. 1185, Federal Bldg., 1961 Stout St., 80294–3538).	Frank Fajardo	303–844–2622
IX. San Francisco, CA (Rm. 450, 50 United Nations Plz., 94102)	Sharon Fujii	415–556–7800
X. Seattle, WA (Blanchard Plz., 2201 6th Ave., 98121)	Stephen Henigson	206–553–2775

Public Health Service

[For the Public Health Service statement of organization, see the *Federal Register* of Dec. 2, 1977, 42 FR 61317]

The Public Health Service was established by act of July 16, 1798 (ch. 77, 1 Stat. 605), authorizing marine hospitals for the care of American merchant seamen. Subsequent legislation has vastly broadened the scope of its activities.

The Public Health Service Act of July 1, 1944 (42 U.S.C. 201), consolidated

and revised substantially all existing legislation relating to the Public Health Service. The basic Public Health Service legal responsibilities have been broadened and expanded many times since 1944. Major organizational changes have occurred within the Public Health Service to support its mission to promote the protection and advancement of the Nation's physical and mental health. This is accomplished by:

—coordinating with the States to set and implement national health policy and pursue effective intergovernmental relations;

—generating and upholding cooperative international health-related agreements, policies, and programs;

—conducting medical and biomedical research;

—sponsoring and administering programs for the development of health resources, prevention and control of diseases, and alcohol and drug abuse;

—providing resources and expertise to the States and other public and private institutions in the planning, direction, and delivery of physical and mental health care services; and

—enforcing laws to assure the safety and efficacy of drugs and protection against impure and unsafe foods, cosmetics, medical devices, and radiation-producing projects.

The Office of the Assistant Secretary for Health consists of general and special staff offices that support the Assistant Secretary for Health and the Surgeon General plan and direct the activities of the Public Health Service.

Agency for Health Care Policy and Research The Agency was established by the Omnibus Budget Reconciliation Act of 1989 (42 U.S.C. 299) as the successor to the National Center for Health Services Research and Health Care Technology Assessment. The Agency is the Federal Government's focal point for health services research. The Agency for Health Care Policy and Research is the only Federal agency charged with producing and disseminating scientific and policy-relevant information about the quality, medical effectiveness, and cost of health care. The Agency's programs focus on maximizing the value of our national health care investment by analyzing the costs and improving the outcomes of health care. Its priorities include:

—reducing health care costs, through studies on the interaction of cost, quality, and access; microsimulation modeling, to understand the effect of proposed health care reform; and analyzing health care costs effected by

acute, ambulatory, and long-term care and AIDS;

—expanding clinical practice guideline activities by increasing production of important guidelines and evaluating their effect on the cost and quality of health care; and

—enhancing the scientific evidence base for cost-effective clinical practices, by expanding research to improve clinical decisionmaking and strengthening clinical information systems for effectiveness research.

The Agency supports and conducts research integral to understanding the design and performance of the health care delivery system, and undertakes widespread dissemination of the results of its research and clinical guidelines it supports. The emphasis on widespread and rapid dissemination and research on more effective dissemination methods reflects the goal of the Agency to enhance the value of our national investment in health care.

The Agency plays an important role in increasing possibilities for future health services research, including medical effectiveness research through its support for methodological studies; data development and research training particularly, related to primary care; and minority and rural health. The Agency also has an active program in medical liability.

For further information, call 301–594–8364.

Centers for Disease Control and Prevention

The Centers for Disease Control and Prevention (CDC), established as an operating health agency within the Public Health Service by the Secretary of Health, Education, and Welfare on July 1, 1973, is the Federal agency charged with protecting the public health of the Nation by providing leadership and direction in the prevention and control of diseases and other preventable conditions and responding to public health emergencies. It is composed of 11 major operating components: Epidemiology Program Office, International Health Program Office, National Immunization Program Office,

Public Health Practice Program Office, National Center for Prevention Services, National Center for Environmental Health, National Center for Injury Prevention and Control, National Institute for Occupational Safety and Health, National Center for Chronic Disease Prevention and Health Promotion, National Center for Infectious Diseases, and the National Center for Health Statistics.

The Agency administers national programs for the prevention and control of communicable and vector-borne diseases, injury, and other preventable conditions. It develops and implements programs in chronic disease prevention and control, including consultation with State and local health departments. It develops and implements programs to deal with environmental health problems, including responding to environmental, chemical, and radiation emergencies.

The Agency directs and enforces foreign quarantine activities and regulations; provides consultation and assistance in upgrading the performance of public health and clinical laboratories; organizes and implements a National Health Promotion Program, including a nationwide program of research, information, and education in the field of smoking and health. It also collects, maintains, analyzes, and disseminates national data on health status and health services.

To ensure safe and healthful working conditions for all working people, occupational safety and health standards are developed, and research and other activities are carried out, through the National Institute for Occupational Safety and Health.

The Agency also provides consultation to other nations in the control of preventable diseases, and participates with national and international agencies in the eradication or control of communicable diseases and other preventable conditions.

For further information, call 404–639–3286.

Agency for Toxic Substances and Disease Registry

The Agency for Toxic Substances and Disease Registry was established as an operating agency within the Public Health Service by the Secretary of Health and Human Services on April 19, 1983. The Agency's mission is to carry out the health-related responsibilities of the Comprehensive Environmental Response, Compensation, and Liability Act of 1980 (42 U.S.C. 9601 et seq.), as amended by the Superfund Amendments and Reauthorization Act of 1986, the Resource Conservation and Recovery Act (42 U.S.C. 6901 et seq.), and provisions of the Solid Waste Disposal Act relating to sites and substances found at those sites and other forms of uncontrolled releases of toxic substances into the environment. The Agency provides leadership and direction to programs and activities designed to protect both the public and workers from exposure and/or the adverse health effects of hazardous substances in storage sites or released in fires, explosions, or transportation accidents.

To carry out this mission, the Agency, in cooperation with States and other Federal and local agencies:

—collects, maintains, analyzes, and disseminates information relating to serious diseases, mortality, and human exposure to toxic or hazardous substances;

—establishes appropriate registries necessary for long-term followup or specific scientific studies;

—establishes and maintains a complete listing of areas closed to the public or otherwise restricted in use because of toxic substance contamination;

—assists, consults, and coordinates with private or public health care providers in the provision of medical care and testing of exposed individuals;

—assists the Environmental Protection Agency in identifying hazardous waste substances to be regulated;

—develops scientific and technical procedures for evaluating public health risks from hazardous substance incidents and for developing recommendations to

protect public health and worker safety and health in instances of exposure or potential exposure to hazardous substances; and
—arranges for program support to ensure adequate response to public health emergencies.

For further information, call 404–639–0727.

Food and Drug Administration

The name "Food and Drug Administration" was first provided by the Agriculture Appropriation Act of 1931 (46 Stat. 392), although similar law enforcement functions had been in existence under different organizational titles since January 1, 1907, when the Food and Drug Act of 1906 (21 U.S.C. 1–15) became effective.

The Food and Drug Administration's activities are directed toward protecting the health of the Nation against impure and unsafe foods, drugs and cosmetics, and other potential hazards.

Office of Operations   The Office:
—advises and assists the Commissioner and other key officials on compliance-oriented matters;
—develops and administers all agency field operations and provides direction and counsel to regional Food and Drug Directors;
—administers regulation of biological products under the biological product control provisions of the Public Health Service Act and applicable provisions of the Federal Food, Drug, and Cosmetic Act;
—works to develop an AIDS vaccine and AIDS diagnostic tests, and conducts other AIDS-related activities;
—develops and administers programs with regard to the safety, effectiveness, and labeling of all drug products for human use;
—develops and administers programs with regard to the safety, composition, quality (including nutrition), and labeling of foods, food additives, colors, and cosmetics;
—develops and administers programs for controlling unnecessary exposure of humans to, and assures the safe and efficacious use of, ionizing and non-

ionizing radiation-emitting electronic products;
—develops and administers programs with regard to the safety, effectiveness, and labeling of medical devices for human use; and
—develops and administers programs with regard to the safety and effectiveness of animal drugs, feeds, feed additives, veterinary medical devices (medical devices for animal use), and other veterinary medical products.

The Office of Operations includes the Office of Regulatory Affairs, the regional field offices, the Center for Biologics Evaluation and Research, the Center for Drug Evaluation and Research, the Center for Food Safety and Applied Nutrition, the Center for Devices and Radiological Health, the Center for Veterinary Medicine, the National Center for Toxicological Research, the Office of AIDS Coordination, the Office of Orphan Products Development, and the Office of Biotechnology.

Center for Drug Evaluation and Research   The Center develops Administration policy with regard to the safety, effectiveness, and labeling of all drug products for human use and reviews and evaluates new drug applications and investigational new drug applications. It develops and implements standards for the safety and effectiveness of all over-the-counter drugs and monitors the quality of marketed drug products through product testing, surveillance, and compliance programs.

The Center coordinates with the Center for Biologics Evaluation and Research regarding activities for biological drug products, including research, compliance, and product review and approval, and develops and promulgates guidelines on Current Good Manufacturing Practices for use by the drug industry. It develops and disseminates information and educational material dealing with drug products to the medical community and the public in coordination with the Office of the Commissioner. It conducts research and develops scientific standards on the composition, quality, safety, and effectiveness of human drugs; collects and evaluates information on the effects and use trends of marketed drug products; monitors prescription drug advertising and promotional labeling to assure their accuracy and integrity; and analyzes data on accidental poisonings and disseminates toxicity and treatment information on household products and medicines.

In carrying out these functions, the Center cooperates with other components of the Administration, other Public Health Service organizations, governmental and international agencies, volunteer health organizations, universities, individual scientists, nongovernmental laboratories, and manufacturers of drug products.

For further information, call 301–443–2894.

Center for Biologics Evaluation and Research   The Center administers regulation of biological products under the biological product control provisions of the Public Health Service Act and applicable provisions of the Federal Food, Drug, and Cosmetic Act. It provides dominant focus in the Administration for coordination of the Acquired Immune Deficiency Syndrome (AIDS) program, works to develop an AIDS vaccine and AIDS diagnostic tests, and conducts other AIDS-related activities. It inspects manufacturers' facilities for compliance with standards, tests products submitted for release, establishes written and physical standards, and approves licensing of manufacturers to produce biological products.

The Center plans and conducts research related to the development, manufacture, testing, and use of both new and old biological products to develop a scientific base for establishing standards designed to ensure the continued safety, purity, potency, and efficacy of biological products and coordinates with the Center for Drug Evaluation and Research regarding activities for biological drug products, including research, compliance, and product review and approval.

The Center plans and conducts research on the preparation,

preservation, and safety of blood and blood products, the methods of testing safety, purity, potency, and efficacy of such products for therapeutic use, and the immunological problems concerned with products, testing, and use of diagnostic reagents employed in grouping and typing blood.

In carrying out these functions, the Center cooperates with other components of the Administration, other Public Health Service organizations, governmental and international agencies, volunteer health organizations, universities, individual scientists, nongovernmental laboratories, and manufacturers of biological products.

For further information, call 301–295–9000.

Center for Food Safety and Applied Nutrition   The Center conducts research and develops standards on the composition, quality, nutrition, and safety of food and food additives, colors, and cosmetics. It conducts research designed to improve the detection, prevention, and control of contamination that may be responsible for illness or injury conveyed by foods, colors, and cosmetics and coordinates and evaluates the Administration's surveillance and compliance programs relating to foods, colors, and cosmetics.

The Center also reviews industry petitions and develops regulations for food standards to permit the safe use of color additives and food additives; collects and interprets data on nutrition, food additives, and environmental factors affecting the total chemical result posed by food additives; and maintains a nutritional data bank.

For further information, call 202–205–4943.

Center for Veterinary Medicine   The Center develops and conducts programs with respect to the safety and efficacy of veterinary preparations and devices; evaluates proposed use of veterinary preparations for animal safety and efficacy; and evaluates the Administration's surveillance and compliance programs relating to veterinary drugs and other veterinary medical matters.

For further information, call 301–295–8752.

Center for Devices and Radiological Health The Center develops and carries out a national program designed to control unnecessary exposure of humans to, and ensure the safe and efficacious use of, potentially hazardous ionizing and non-ionizing radiation. It develops policy and priorities regarding Administration programs relating to the safety, effectiveness, and labeling of medical devices for human use; conducts an electronic product radiation control program, including the development and administration of performance standards.

The Center plans, conducts, and supports research and testing relating to medical devices and to the health effects of radiation exposure; and reviews and evaluates medical devices premarket approval applications, product development protocols, and exemption requests for investigational devices. It develops, promulgates, and enforces performance standards for appropriate categories of medical devices and Good Manufacturing Practice regulations for manufacturers; and provides technical and other nonfinancial assistance to small manufacturers of medical devices.

The Center develops regulations, standards, and criteria and recommends changes in Administration legislative authority necessary to protect the public health; provides scientific and technical support to other components within the Administration and other agencies on matters relating to radiological health and medical devices; and maintains appropriate liaison with other Federal, State, and international agencies, with industry, and with consumer and professional organizations.

For further information, call 301–443–4690.

National Center for Toxicological Research The Center conducts research programs to study the biological effects of potentially toxic chemical substances found in the environment, emphasizing the determination of the health effects resulting from long-term, low-level

exposure to chemical toxicants and the basic biological processes for chemical toxicants in animal organisms; develops improved methodologies and test protocols for evaluating the safety of chemical toxicants and the data that will facilitate the extrapolation of toxicological data from laboratory animals to man; and develops Center programs as a natural resource under the National Toxicology Program.

For further information, call 501–543–7304.

Regional Operations Field operations for the enforcement of the laws under the jurisdiction of the Food and Drug Administration are carried out by 6 Regional Field Offices located in the cities of the Department's Regional Offices, through 21 District Offices and 135 Resident Inspection Posts located throughout the United States and Puerto Rico.

For further information, call 301–443–1594. For a listing of Public Affairs Offices, see page 305.

Office of Policy The Office directs and coordinates the agency's rulemaking activities and regulations development system; initiates new and more efficient systems or procedures to accomplish agency goals in the rulemaking process and plans regulatory reform steps; and serves as the agency's focal point for developing and maintaining communications, policies, and programs with regard to regulations development and international harmonization, including international standard setting and bilateral agreements on inspections.

The Office of Policy includes the Policy Development and Coordination Staff, Policy Research Staff, and Regulations Policy and Management Staff.

Office of External Affairs The Office:

—advises and assists the Commissioner concerning legislative needs;

—serves as the focal point for overall legislative liaison activities;

—advises and assists the Commissioner and other key officials on all public information programs;

—acts as the focal point for disseminating news on FDA activities;
—advises and assists the Commissioner on health issues which have an impact on policy, direction, and long-range program goals;
—coordinates agency relations with health professional groups and represents the agency on issues involving technology assessment and medical insurance coverage decisions regarding FDA-regulated products;
—advises and assists the Commissioner on consumer affairs issues;
—serves as the agency's focal point for coordinating information from appropriate agency components about significant consumer affairs issues;
—advises and assists the Commissioner and other agency officials on industry-related issues which have an impact on policy, direction, and goals; and
—serves as the agency's focal point on small business, scientific, and trade affairs.

The Office of External Affairs includes the Office of Consumer Affairs, the Office of Health Affairs, the Office of Legislative Affairs, the Office of Public Affairs, the Office of AIDS and Special Health Issues, and the Office of Women's Health.

Office of Management and Systems
The Office:
—advises and assists the Commissioner regarding the performance of FDA resource planning, development, and evaluation activities;
—develops program and planning strategy through analysis and evaluation of issues affecting policies and program performance;
—assures that the conduct of agency administrative and financial management activities, including budget, finance, personnel, organization, methods, grants and contracts, procurement and property, records, and similar support activities effectively supports program operations;
—coordinates the integration and development of management information systems; and

—advises the Commissioner on management information systems policies.

The Office of Management and Systems includes the Office of Planning and Evaluation, the Office of Information Resources Management, and the Office of Management.

Health Resources and Services Administration The Administration has leadership responsibility in the Public Health Service for general health services and resource issues relating to access, equity, quality, and cost of care.

To accomplish this goal, the Administration:
—supports States and communities in their efforts to plan, organize, and deliver health care, especially to underserved area residents, migrant workers, mothers and children, the homeless, and other groups with special needs;
—participates in the Federal campaign against AIDS by administering provisions of the Ryan White Comprehensive AIDS Research Emergency (CARE) Act, funding service demonstration projects in major cities, establishing centers to train health professionals serving AIDS patients, supporting renovation of health facilities for AIDS patients, and awarding pediatric health care grants;
—provides leadership in improving the education, distribution, quality, and use of the health professionals needed to staff the Nation's health care system;
—works to determine impact of managed health care on the medical and health workforce, with promoted emphasis on primary and preventitive health care;
—tracks the supply of and requirements for health professionals and addresses their competence through the operation of a health practitioner data bank;
—monitors developments affecting health facilities and ensures that previously aided institutions honor their commitments to provide uncompensated care;
—administers the National Organ Transplant Act by serving as an information resource on donation,

procurement, and transplantation and by promoting other activities designed to increase the availability of donor organs and bone marrow;
—provides direct, personal health services for Hansen's disease patients and other designated beneficiaries;
—assists Federal managers to assure that employees and workplace health factors that increase the Government's productivity are raised to the highest practical level;
—monitors rural health issues; helps coordinate government and private efforts on behalf of rural health facilities; and promotes adaption of telecommunications and other technology to meet health needs of underserved rural areas;
—processes claims submitted under the National Vaccine Injury Compensation Program;
—strengthens the public health system by working with State and local public health agencies;
—works to address special health needs of populations in U.S. border regions and within immigrant populations;
—oversees management of the Federal initiative to combat infant mortality through grants to hard-hit communities working to overcome social and non-financial barriers to prenatal care; and
—coordinates health program activities that address the special needs and problems of minority populations.

For further information, contact the Associate Administrator for Communications. Phone, 301–443–2086.

Major Components

Bureau of Primary Health Care   The Bureau serves as a national focus for efforts to ensure the availability and delivery of health care services in health-professional shortage areas, to medically underserved populations, and to those with special needs.
    To accomplish this goal, the Bureau:
—provides, through project grants to community-based organizations, funds to meet the health needs of populations in medically underserved areas by supporting the development of primary health care delivery capacity;

—provides, through project grants to State, local, voluntary, public, and private entities, funds to help them meet the health needs of special populations such as migrants, Alzheimer's disease patients, the homeless, AIDS victims, Pacific Basin inhabitants, Native Hawaiians, residents of public housing projects, and victims of black lung disease;
—administers the National Health Service Corps Program, which recruits and places highly trained health care practitioners for health-professional shortage areas and populations;
—administers the National Health Service Corps Scholarship and Loan Repayment Programs, which provide financial assistance to medical, dental, and nursing students or former students in return for service in health-professional shortage areas;
—designates health-professional shortage and medically underserved areas and populations;
—provides leadership and direction for the Bureau of Prisons Medical Program, the National Hansen's Disease Program;
—provides on a reimbursable basis comprehensive occupational health consultation and assistance to Federal agencies to enhance productivity and limit employment-related liability through the Federal Employee Occupational Health Program; and
—administers the Veterans Health Care Act of 1992 (38 U.S.C. 101 note), which provides that participating manufacturers sell Medicaid-covered outpatient drugs to eligible entities at discount prices.

For further information, contact the Public Affairs Officer. Phone, 301–443–4814.

Bureau of Health Professions   The Bureau provides national leadership in coordinating, evaluating, and supporting the development and utilization of the Nation's health personnel.
    To accomplish this goal, the Bureau:
—serves as a focus for health care quality assurance activities, issues related to malpractice, and operation of the National Practitioner Data Bank and the Vaccine Injury Compensation Program;

—supports through grants health professions and nurse training institutions, targeting resources to areas of high national priority such as disease prevention, health promotion, bedside nursing, care of the elderly, and HIV/AIDS;
—funds regional centers that provide educational services and multidisciplinary training for health professions faculty and practitioners in geriatric health care;
—supports programs to increase the supply of primary care practitioners and to improve the distribution of health professionals;
—develops, tests, and demonstrates new and improved approaches to the development and utilization of health personnel within various patterns of health care delivery and financing systems;
—provides leadership for promoting equity in access to health services and health careers for the disadvantaged;
—administers several loan programs supporting students training for careers in the health professions and nursing;
—funds regional centers to train faculty and practicing health professionals in the counseling, diagnosis, and management of HIV/AIDS-infected individuals;
—collects and analyzes data and disseminates information on the characteristics and capacities of U.S. health training systems;
—assesses the Nation's health personnel force and forecasts supply and requirements; and
—serves as a focus for technical assistance activities in the international projects relevant to domestic health personnel problems in coordination with the Office of the Administrator, Health Resources and Services Administration.

For further information, contact the Information Officer. Phone, 301–443–2060.

Bureau of Health Resources Development   The Bureau of Health Resources Development (BHRD) has four major programs: Health Facilities, Organ Transplantation, HIV Services, and Trauma and Emergency Medical Systems.

The Health Facilities Program monitors compliance by health care facilities with assurances and/or obligations resulting from Hill-Burton grants and loans, and health professions and nurse training construction grants and determines the operational, financial, and engineering condition of applicants and recipients of Federal House Administration mortgages for hospital construction.

The Organ Transplantation Program supports the National Organ Procurement and Transplantation Network, designed to ensure equitable distribution of available organs to patients and transplant centers, and a Scientific Registry of demographic and clinical information on transplant recipients. The program also awards and manages a program of grants and contracts to organ procurement organizations (OPO's) and other nonprofit entities to increase the number of organ donors in the United States. As of October 1994, the Division of Organ Transplantation assumed oversight of the National Marrow Donor Program, a volunteer registry of potential, unrelated bone marrow donors.

BHRD's Division of HIV Services administers programs which provide health care and support services for people living with HIV disease. The Division is responsible for awarding and monitoring the grant programs established by titles I and II of the Ryan White Comprehensive AIDS Resources Emergency (CARE) Act of 1990. These programs provide resources to eligible metropolitan with the highest levels of reported AIDs cases and to States and territories to improve the quality and availability of health care and support services for individuals and families with HIV disease.

In addition, the Bureau's Office of Science and Epidemiology (OSE) administers the Special Projects of National Significance (SPNS), programs whose goals are to advance knowledge and skills in the delivery of health and support services to persons with HIV infection. Overall objectives of the SPNS program are to assess the effectiveness of difference models of care; support innovative program design; and promote replication of effective models.

BHRD's Division of Trauma and Emergency Medical Systems provides grants to States for developing and implementing trauma care systems, and to public and nonprofit entities to improve availability and quality of emergency medical services in rural areas.

Maternal and Child Health Bureau   The Bureau develops, administers, directs, coordinates, monitors, and supports Federal policy and programs pertaining to health and related-care systems for the Nation's mothers and children. Programs administered by the Bureau address the full spectrum of primary, secondary, and tertiary care services and related activities conducted in the public and private sector which impact upon maternal and child health.

To accomplish this goal, the Bureau:
—provides national leadership in supporting, identifying, and interpreting national trends and issues relating to the health needs of mothers, infants, children (both normal and with special health care needs), and administers State block and discretionary grants, contracts, and funding arrangements designed to address these issues;
—administers grant, contracts, and other funding arrangements and programs under title V of the Social Security Act, as amended, relating to implementation of State maternal and child health (MCH) service programs, research, training, and education programs located in institutions of higher learning and State and local health agencies and organizations involved in the care of mothers and children;
—administers grants, contracts, and other funding arrangements under section 2671 of the Public Health Service Act for research and services pertaining to the health status of pediatric AIDS patients;
—administers grants, contracts, and other funding arrangements under title V of the Social Security Act, as amended, relating to the care of persons affected by hemophilia (regardless of age);
—administers grants and contracts under title XIX of the Public Health

Service Act relating to pediatric emergency medical systems development and care improvement;
—develops, promotes, and directs efforts to improve the management, financing, operational effectiveness and efficiency of health care systems and the Healthy Start Initiative to reduce infant mortality, organizations, and providers of maternal and child health and related care;
—serves as the principal adviser to and coordinates activities with other Administration organizational elements, other Federal organizations within and outside the Department, and with State and local agencies and professional and scientific organizations;
—provides technical assistance and consultation to the full spectrum of primary, secondary, and tertiary MCH agencies and organizations in both the public and private sector; and
—maintains liaison and coordinates with non-Federal public and private entities to accomplish the Bureau's mission and objectives.

For further information, contact the Information Officer. Phone, 301–443–3376.

Indian Health Service

The goal of the Indian Health Service is to raise the health status of American Indians and Alaska Natives to the highest possible level. The Indian Health Service provides a comprehensive health services delivery system for American Indians and Alaska Natives, with opportunity for maximum tribal involvement, in developing and managing programs to meet their health needs.

To carry out its mission and attain its goal, the Service:
—assists Indian tribes in developing their health programs through activities such as health management training, technical assistance, and human resource development;
—facilitates and assists Indian tribes in coordinating health planning; in obtaining and utilizing health resources available through Federal, State, and local programs; in operating comprehensive health programs; and in health program evaluation;

—provides comprehensive health care services, including hospital and ambulatory medical care, preventive and rehabilitative services, and development of community sanitation facilities; and —serves as the principal Federal advocate in the health care field for Indians to ensure comprehensive health services for American Indian and Alaska Native people.

For further information, contact the Indian Health Service Communications Office. Phone, 301–443–3593.

National Institutes of Health

The National Institutes of Health (NIH) is the principal biomedical research agency of the Federal Government. Its mission is to employ science in the pursuit of knowledge to improve human health conditions. To accomplish this goal, the Institute seeks to expand fundamental knowledge about the nature and behavior of living systems, to apply that knowledge to extend the health of human lives, and to reduce the burdens resulting from disease and disability. In the quest of this mission, NIH supports biomedical and behavorial research domestically and abroad, conducts research in its own laboratories and clinics, trains promising young researchers, and promotes acquiring and distributing medical knowledge. Focal points have been established to assist in developing NIH-wide goals for health research and research training programs related to women and minorities, coordinating program direction, and ensuring that research pertaining to women's and minority health is identified and addressed through research activities conducted and supported by NIH. Research activities conducted by NIH will determine much of the quality of health care for the future and reinforce the quality of health care currently available.

Major Components

National Cancer Institute   Research on cancer is a high priority program as a result of the National Cancer Act, which made the conquest of cancer a national goal. The Institute developed a National Cancer Program to expand existing scientific knowledge on cancer cause and prevention as well as on the diagnosis, treatment, and rehabilitation of cancer patients.

Research activities conducted in the Institute's laboratories or supported through grants or contracts include many investigative approaches to cancer, including chemistry, biochemistry, biology, molecular biology, immunology, radiation physics, experimental chemotherapy, epidemiology, biometry, radiotherapy, and pharmacology. Cancer research facilities are constructed with Institute support, and training is provided under university-based programs. The Institute, through its cancer control element, applies research findings as rapidly as possible in preventing and controlling human cancer.

For further information, call 301–496–5737.

National Heart, Lung, and Blood Institute   The Institute conducts studies and research into the clinical use of blood and all aspects of the management of blood resources, and supports training of personnel in fundamental science and clinical disciplines for participation in basic and clinical research programs relating to heart, blood vessel, blood, and lung diseases.

It coordinates with other research institutes and with all Federal agency programs relating to the above diseases, including programs in hypertension, stroke, respiratory distress, and sickle cell anemia.

The Institute plans, conducts, fosters, and supports an integrated and coordinated program of research, investigations, clinical trials and demonstrations relating to the causes, prevention, methods of diagnosis and treatment (including emergency medical treatment) of heart, blood vessel, lung, and blood diseases through research performed in its own laboratories and through contracts and research grants to scientific institutions and to individual scientists.

The Institute also conducts educational activities, including the collection and dissemination of educational materials about these diseases, with emphasis on the prevention thereof, for health professionals and the lay public, and maintains continuing relationships with institutions and professional associations and with international, national, and State and local officials, and voluntary agencies and organizations working in these areas.

For further information, call 301–496–2411.

National Library of Medicine   The Library, which serves as the Nation's chief medical information source, is authorized to provide medical library services and on-line bibliographic searching capabilities, such as MEDLINE, TOXLINE, and others, to public and private agencies and organizations, institutions, and individuals. It is responsible for the development and management of a Biomedical Communications Network, applying advanced technology to the improvement of biomedical communications, and operates a computer-based toxicology information system for the scientific community, industry, and other Federal agencies. Through its National Center for Biotechnology Information, the Library has a leadership role in developing new information technologies to aid in the understanding of the molecular processes that control health and disease. In addition, the Library acquires and makes available for distribution audiovisual instructional material, and develops prototype audiovisual communication programs for the health educational community. Through grants and contracts, the Library administers programs of assistance to the Nation's medical libraries that include support of a Regional Medical Library network, research in the field of medical library science, establishment and improvement of the basic library resources, and supporting biomedical scientific publications of a nonprofit nature.

For further information, call 301–496–6308.

National Institute of Diabetes and Digestive and Kidney Diseases   The Institute conducts, fosters, and supports basic and clinical research into the causes, prevention, diagnosis, and treatment of the various metabolic and digestive diseases. It covers the broad areas of diabetes, blood, endocrine, and metabolic diseases; digestive diseases and nutrition; and kidney and urologic diseases, joined with the Artificial Kidney/Chronic Uremia Program, through research performed in its own laboratories and clinics, research grants, individual and institutional research training awards, applied research and development programs through the contract mechanisms, field epidemiologic and clinical investigation studies on selected populations in the United States, and collection and dissemination of information on Institute programs.

For further information, call 301–496–5741.

National Institute of Allergy and Infectious Diseases   The Institute conducts and supports broadly based research and research training on the causes, characteristics, prevention, control, and treatment of a wide variety of diseases believed to be attributable to infectious agents, including bacteria, viruses, and parasites, to allergies, or to other deficiencies or disorders in the responses of the body's immune mechanisms. Among areas of special emphasis are: asthma and allergic disease, clinical immunology, including organ transplantation, venereal diseases, hepatitis, influenza and other viral respiratory infections, disease control measures, research and development, antiviral substances, and hospital-associated infections.

For further information, call 301–496–5717.

National Institute of Child Health and Human Development   The Institute conducts and supports biomedical and behavioral research on child and maternal health; on problems of human development, with special reference to mental retardation; and on family structure, the dynamics of human population, and the reproductive process. Specific areas of research include pediatric and maternal AIDS, genetic diseases, short stature, premature puberty, infertility, minority health, learning disabilities such as dyslexia, sexually transmitted diseases, and the causes of infant morbidity and mortality—including low birth weight, premature birth, and sudden infant death syndrome. The Institute recently added a National Center for Medical Rehabilitation Research, which conducts and supports research and research training related to the rehabilitation of people with physical disabilities. Research-related findings are disseminated to other researchers, medical practitioners, and the general public to improve the health of children and families.

For further information, call 301–496–5133.

National Institute on Deafness and Other Communication Disorders   The Institute conducts and supports research and training with respect to disorders of hearing and other communication processes, including diseases affecting hearing, balance, voice, speech, language, taste, and smell through a diversity of research performed in its own laboratories; a program of research grants, individual and institutional research training awards, career development awards, center grants, and contracts to public and private research institutions and organizations.

For further information, call 301–496–7243.

National Institute of Dental Research The Institute supports and conducts clinical and laboratory research directed toward the ultimate eradication of tooth decay and of a broad array of oral-facial disorders.

For further information, call 301–496–6621.

National Institute of Environmental Health Sciences   The Institute, located in Research Triangle Park, NC, conducts and supports fundamental research concerned with defining, measuring, and understanding the effects of chemical, biological, and physical factors in the environment on the health and well-being of man.

For further information, call 919–541–3211.

National Institute of General Medical Sciences   The emphasis of the Institute's programs for support of research and research training is basic biomedical science. The activities range from cell biology to genetics to pharmacology and systemic response to trauma and anesthesia.

For further information, call 301–594–7811.

National Institute of Neurological Disorders and Stroke   The Institute conducts and supports fundamental and applied research on human neurological disorders such as Parkinson's disease, epilepsy, multiple sclerosis, muscular dystrophy, head and spinal cord injuries, and stroke. The Institute also conducts and supports research on the development and function of the normal brain and nervous system in order to better understand normal processes relating to disease states.

For further information, call 301–496–5751.

National Eye Institute   The Institute conducts and supports fundamental studies on the eye and visual system, and on the causes, prevention, diagnosis, and treatment of visual disorders.

For further information, call 301–496–4274.

National Institute on Aging   The Institute conducts and supports biomedical and behavioral research to increase the knowledge of the aging process and associated physical, psychological, and social factors, resulting from advanced age. Incontinence, menopause, susceptibility to diseases, and memory loss are among the areas of special concern.

For further information, call 301–496–5345.

National Institute of Alcohol Abuse and Alcoholism   The Institute conducts and supports biomedical and behavioral research, health services research, research training, and health information dissemination with respect to the prevention and treatment of alcohol abuse and alcoholism, and provides a national focus for the Federal effort to increase knowledge and promote effective strategies to deal with health problems and issues associated with alcohol abuse and alcoholism.

For further information, call 301–443–3885.

National Institute of Arthritis and Musculoskeletal and Skin Diseases The Institute conducts and supports fundamental research in the major disease categories of arthritis and musculoskeletal and skin diseases through research performed in its own laboratories and clinics, epidemiologic studies, research contracts and grants, and cooperative agreements to scientific institutions and to individuals. It supports training of personnel in fundamental sciences and clinical disciplines, conducts educational activities, including the collection and dissemination of health educational materials on these diseases, and coordinates with the other research institutes and with all Federal health programs relevant activities in the categorical diseases.

For further information, call 301–496–4353.

National Institute on Drug Abuse The Institute provides national leadership and conducts and supports biomedical and behavioral research, health services research, research training, and health information dissemination with respect to the prevention of drug abuse and the treatment of drug abusers.

For further information, call 301–443–6480.

National Institute of Mental Health The Institute provides leadership for a national program to increase knowledge and advance effective strategies to deal with problems and issues in the promotion of mental health, and the prevention and treatment of mental illness.

For further information, call 301–443–3673.

Clinical Center The Center is designed to bring scientists working in the Center's laboratories into proximity with clinicians caring for patients, so that they may collaborate on problems of mutual concern. The research institutes select patients, referred to the National Institutes of Health by physicians throughout the United States and overseas, for clinical studies of specific diseases and disorders. A certain percentage of the patients are "normal volunteers," healthy persons who provide an index of normal body functions against which to measure the abnormal. Normal volunteers come under varied sponsorship, such as colleges, civic groups, and religious organizations.

For further information, call 301–496–3227.

Fogarty International Center The Center promotes discussion, study, and research on the development of science internationally as it relates to health and administers a number of international programs for advanced study in the health sciences.

For further information, call 301–496–4625.

National Center for Human Genome Research The Center provides leadership for and formulates research goals and long-range plans to accomplish the mission of the Human Genome Project, including the study of ethical, legal, and social implications of human genome research. Through grants, contracts, cooperative agreements, and individual and institutional research training awards, the Center supports and administers research and research training programs in human genome research and the systematic, targeted effort to create detailed maps of the genomes of organisms. It provides coordination of genome research, both nationally and internationally; serves as a focal point within NIH and the Department for Federal interagency coordination and collaboration with industry and academia; and sponsors scientific meetings and symposia to promote progress through information sharing. Through its Division of Intramural Research (DIR), the Center plans and conducts a program of laboratory and clinical research related to the application of genome research to the understanding of human genetic disease and the development of DNA diagnostics and gene therapies.

For further information, call 301–496–0844.

National Institute of Nursing Research The Institute provides leadership for nursing research, supports and conducts research and training, and disseminates information to build a scientific base for nursing practice and patient care, and to promote health and improve the effects of illness on the American people.

For further information, call 301–496–0523.

Division of Computer Research and Technology The Division conducts an integrated research, developmental, and service program in computer-related physical and life sciences in support of Institute biomedical research programs.

For further information, call 301–496–5206.

National Center for Research Resources The Center administers, fosters, and supports research for the development and support of various research resources needed on an institutional,

regional, or national basis for health-related research. Programs are carried out through research grants and individual and institutional research training awards; cooperation and collaboration with organizations and institutions engaged in multicategorical research resource activities; and collection and dissemination of information on research and findings in these areas. The Center oversees a centralized program of intramural research resources through the planning, performance, and reporting of research projects.

For further information, call 301–496–5605.

Division of Research Grants The Division provides staff support to the Office of the Director, National Institutes of Health, in the formulation of grant and award policies and procedures, central receipt of all Public Health Service applications for research and research training support, and makes initial referral to Service components.

For further information, call 301–594–7333.

Substance Abuse and Mental Health Services Administration

The Substance Abuse and Mental Health Services Administration (SAMHSA) provides national leadership to ensure that knowledge, based on science and state-of-the-art practice, is effectively used for the prevention and treatment of addictive and mental disorders. SAMHSA strives to improve access and reduce barriers to high-quality, effective programs and services for individuals who suffer from or are at risk for these disorders, as well as for their families and communities.

Major Components

Center for Substance Abuse Prevention The Center for Substance Abuse Prevention (CSAP) provides a national focus for the Federal effort to prevent

alcohol and other drug abuse. In carrying out its responsibility, the Center:

—develops, implements, and reviews prevention and health promotion policy related to alcohol and other drug abuse, analyzing the impact of Federal activities on State and local governments and private program activities;

—provides a national focus for the Federal effort to demonstrate and promote effective strategies to prevent the abuse of alcohol and other drugs;

—supports innovative comprehensive, collaborative, community-based prevention demonstration programs;

—operates grant programs for projects to demonstrate effective models for the prevention and early intervention of alcohol and drug use/abuse among high-risk youth, and other specific target populations, including those within the workplace;

—sponsors regional and national workshops and conferences on the prevention of alcohol and other drug abuse;

—supports training for substance abuse practitioners and other health professionals involved in alcohol and drug abuse education, prevention, and early intervention;

—provides technical assistance to States and local authorities and other national organizations and groups in the planning, establishment, and maintenance of substance abuse prevention efforts;

—reviews and approves or disapproves the State Prevention Plans developed under the Substance Abuse Prevention and Treatment Block Grant Program authority;

—serves as a national authority and resource for the development and analysis of information relating to the prevention of abuse of alcohol and other drugs;

—participates in the dissemination and implementation of research findings by PHS agencies on the prevention of the abuse of alcohol and other drugs;

—collaborates with and encourages other Federal agencies and national, State, and local organizations to promote substance abuse prevention activities; and

—provides and promotes the evaluation of individual projects, as well as overall programs.

Center for Substance Abuse Treatment
The principal function of the Center for Substance Abuse Treatment (CSAT) is to provide national leadership for the Federal effort to enhance approaches and expand programs focusing on the treatment of substance abusers, as well as associated problems of physical illness and co morbidity. In carrying out its responsibility, the Center:

—collaborates with States, communities, health care providers, and national organizations to upgrade the quality of addiction treatment, to improve the effectiveness of substance abuse treatment programs, and to expand addiction treatment capacity;

—provides financial assistance to targeted geographic areas to increase treatment programs for substance abuse and other related disorders, and to strengthen the collaboration among the members of the substance abuse treatment community;

—provides a focus for addressing the treatment needs of individuals with multiple drug, alcohol, physical, and co-morbidity problems;

—administers a demonstration grant for projects that will implement and evaluate the Comprehensive Residential Drug Prevention and Treatment Program for substance-abusing women and their children;

—coordinates the evaluation of the Center's drug treatment programs, such as the Comprehensive Residential Drug Prevention and Treatment Program for substance-abusing women and their children;

—collaborates with the National Institute on Drug Abuse and the States to promote the development of treatment outcome standards;

—collaborates with the Office of the Administrator and other SAMHSA components in treatment data collection;

—administers programs for the training of health and allied health care providers;

—promotes mainstreaming of alcohol, drug abuse, and mental health treatment into the health care system; and

—administers the Substance Abuse Prevention and Treatment Block Grant Program, including compliance reviews, technical assistance to States, Territories, and Indian tribes, and the application and reporting requirements related to the block grant programs.

Center for Mental Health Services The Center for Mental Health Services (CMHS) provides national leadership to ensure the application of scientifically established findings and practice-based knowledge in the prevention and treatment of mental disorders; to improve access, reduce barriers, and promote high-quality, effective programs and services for people with or at risk for such disorders, as well as for their families and communities; and to promote the rehabilitation of people with

mental disorders. To accomplish its mission, the Center:
—supports service and demonstration programs designed to improve access to care, quality of treatment, rehabilitation, prevention, and related services, especially for those traditionally underserved or inadequately served;
—identifies national mental health goals and develops strategies to meet them;
—designs and supports evaluations, assessments, and service research activities to assist States, communities, and providers;
—supports activities to improve the administration, availability, organization, and financing of mental health care;
—supports technical assistance activities to educate professionals, consumers, family members, and communities, and promotes training efforts to enhance the human resources necessary to support mental health services;
—collects data on the various forms of mental illness, including data on treatment programs, type of care provided, characteristics of those treated, prevalence, and such other useful data;
—administers Community Mental Health Services block grants and other programs providing direct assistance to States;
—collects, synthesizes, and disseminates mental health information and research findings to States and other governmental and mental health-related organizations, and the public;
—collaborates with other Federal, State, and sub-State units of government and the private sector to improve the system of treatment and social welfare supports for seriously mentally ill adults and severely emotionally disturbed children and adolescents;
—conducts activities to promote advocacy, self-help, and mutual support and to ensure the legal rights of mentally ill persons, including those in jails and prisons; and
—collaborates with the alcohol, drug abuse, and mental health institutes of NIH on service research issues, as well as on other programmatic issues.

Office of Management, Planning, and Communications The Office of Management, Planning, and Communications (OMPC) serves as the focal point for management, planning, and communications functions in support of SAMHSA components. In carrying out its responsibility, the Office:
—develops policies, guidelines, and procedures concerning SAMHSA-wide administrative management;
—conducts SAMHSA's activities in the areas of: financial management; management analysis and services; grants and contracts management and services, including cost advisory services; information systems, including computer support and ADP systems; personnel management; and general administrative services, including procurement and material management;
—conducts studies and analyses of SAMHSA-wide policies and programs;
—provides SAMHSA-wide correspondence control services;
—analyzes legislative issues, develops policy- and position-related papers, and maintains liaison with congressional committees;
—manages SAMHSA-wide intergovernmental and international activities and constituent relations;
—organizes and administers SAMHSA's communications and public affairs activities;
—conducts outreach to the media and related organizations to facilitate coverage and interpretation of SAMHSA's programs and objectives;
—provides a mechanism for clearance and review of SAMHSA-wide communications, education, and information projects and related activities;
—collects and compiles alcohol and other drug abuse prevention literature and other materials, and supports the CSAP National Clearinghouse for Alcohol and Drug Information and the Regional Alcohol and Drug Awareness Resource Network to disseminate such materials among States, political subdivisions, educational agencies and institutions, health and drug treatment and rehabilitation networks, and the general public; and

—supports a clearinghouse to serve as a focal point for information

dissemination that will meet the mental health service needs of professionals.

Health Care Financing Administration

[For the Health Care Financing Administration statement of organization, see the *Federal Register* of March 29, 1994, 59 FR 14628]

The Health Care Financing Administration (HCFA) was created as a principal operating component of the Department by the Secretary on March 8, 1977, to combine under one administration the oversight of the Medicare program, the Federal portion of the Medicaid program, and related quality assurance activities. Today, HCFA serves 68 million elderly, disabled, and poor Americans through Medicare and Medicaid—approximately one-quarter of the United States population.

Medicare The Medicare Program provides health insurance coverage for people age 65 and over, younger people who are receiving social security disability benefits, and persons who need dialysis or kidney transplants for treatment of end-stage renal disease. As a Medicare beneficiary, one can choose how to receive hospital, doctor, and other health care services covered by Medicare. Beneficiaries can receive care either through the traditional fee-for-service delivery system or through coordinated care plans, such as health

maintenance organizations and competitive medical plans, which have contracts with Medicare.

Medicaid The Medicaid Program is a medical assistance program jointly financed by State and Federal governments for eligible low-income individuals. Medicaid covers health care expenses for all recipients of Aid to Families with Dependent Children, and most States also cover the needy elderly, blind, and disabled who receive cash assistance under the Supplemental Security Income Program. Coverage also is extended to certain infants and low-income pregnant women and, at the option of the State, other low-income individuals with medical bills that qualify them as categorically or medically needy.

Quality Assurance The Medicare/Medicaid programs include a quality assurance focal point to carry out the quality assurance provisions of the Medicare and Medicaid programs; the development and implementation of health and safety standards of care providers in Federal health programs; and the implementation of the end stage renal disease and the peer review provisions.

For further information, contact the Administrator, Health Care Financing Administration, Department of Health and Human Services, 200 Independence Avenue SW., Washington, DC 20201. Phone, 410–966–3000.

Sources of Information

Office of the Secretary

Inquiries on the following information may be directed to the specified office, Department of Health and Human Services, Humphrey Building, 200 Independence Avenue SW., Washington, DC 20201.

Civil Rights For information on enforcement of civil rights laws, call or write the Office for Civil Rights, Cohen Building, Washington, DC 20201. Phone: Washington, DC, metropolitan area (202–863–0100 or TDD, 202–863–0101). Outside Washington, DC,

metropolitan area (800–368–1019 or TDD, 800–537–7697).
Consumer Activities   Call or write the U.S. Office of Consumer Affairs. Phone, 202–395–7900.
Contracts and Small Business Activities For information concerning programs, call or write the Director, Office of Small and Disadvantaged Business Utilization. Phone, 202–690–7300.
Employment   Inquiries regarding applications for employment and the college recruitment program should be directed to the Office of Personnel Services. Phone, 202–619–2560.
Locator   Inquiries about the location and telephone numbers of HHS offices should be directed to the HHS locator, Room G–174, Wilbert H. Cohen Building, 330 Independence Avenue SW., Washington, DC 20201. Phone, 202–619–0257.
Telephone Directory   The Department of Health and Human Services telephone directory is available for sale by the Superintendent of Documents, Government Printing Office, Washington, DC 20402. Phone, 202–783–3238.

Office of Inspector General

General inquiries may be directed to the Office of Inspector General, Department of Health and Human Services, 330 Independence Avenue SW., Washington, DC 20201.
Hotline   Individuals wishing to report fraud, waste, or abuse against Department programs should write to: OIG Hotline, P.O. Box 17303, Baltimore, MD 21203–7303. Phone, 800–368–5779 (toll-free).
Publications   Single copies of most Office of Inspector General publications are available free of charge. Phone, 202–619–1142.

Administration for Children and Families

General inquiries may be directed to the Administration for Children and Families, Department of Health and Human Services, Washington, DC 20447. Phone, 202–401–9200.

Contracts   Contact the Division of Acquisition Management, Office of Management. Phone, 202–401–9306.
Information Center   Office of Public Affairs, 7th Floor, Aerospace Building, 370 L'Enfant Promenade SW., Washington, DC 20744. Phone, 202–401–9215.
Mental Retardation   Call or write the President's Committee on Mental Retardation for information on HHS' mental retardation programs. Phone, 202–619–0634.

Public Health Service

Office of the Assistant Secretary for Health   Inquiries on the following subjects should be directed to the specified office, Office of the Assistant Secretary for Health, 5600 Fishers Lane, Rockville, MD 20857.
Employment   The majority of positions are in the Federal civil service. Employment inquiries should be addressed to the Division of Personnel Operations, Room 17–34. Phone, 301–443–6900.

Many medical, scientific, and technical positions are filled through the Commissioned Corps of the Public Health Service, a uniformed service of the U.S. Government. Inquiries should be directed to the Division of Commissioned Personnel, Office of the Surgeon General, Room 4A–07. Phone, 1–800–279–1606 or 301–594–3483.
Films, Publications, and Other Information   Information concerning films, publications, and other specific information should be directed to the several health agencies that follow. All other inquiries about the Public Health Service should be directed to the Office of Health Communications, Room 721–H, Hubert H. Humphrey Building. Phone, 202–690–6867.

Agency for Health Care Policy and Research

Inquiries on the following subjects may be directed to the appropriate office at the Agency for Health Care Policy and Research, 2101 E. Jefferson St., Rockville, MD 20852.

Grants Write to the Chief, Grants Management Branch. Phone, 301–594–1447.

Contracts Write to the Chief, Contracts Management Branch. Phone, 301–594–2441.

Employment Inquiries should be addressed to the Chief, Organization and Management Systems Staff. Phone, 301–594–1445.

Publications Single copies of most publications produced by the Agency are available free of charge from the AHCPR Publications Clearinghouse, P.O. Box 8547, Silver Spring, MD 20907. Phone, 800–358–9295 (toll-free).

Alcohol, Drug Abuse, and Mental Health Administration

Inquiries on the following subjects may be directed to the specified office, Alcohol, Drug Abuse, and Mental Health Administration, 5600 Fishers Lane, Rockville, MD 20857.

Contracts Write to the Director, Division of Grants and Contracts Management. Phone, 301–443–4147.

Employment Inquiries should be addressed to the Director, Division of Personnel Management. Phone, 301–443–3408.

Publications Write to the Associate Administrator for Communications and External Affairs. Phone, 301–443–3783.

Centers for Disease Control and Prevention

Inquiries on the following information may be directed to the office indicated at the Centers for Disease Control and Prevention, 1600 Clifton Road NE., Atlanta, GA 30333.

Employment The majority of positions are in the Federal civil service. For information about positions, inquiries may be addressed to the Personnel Management Office.

Many medical, scientific, and technical positions are filled through the Commissioned Corps of the Public Health Service, a uniformed service of the U.S. Government. Inquiries may be addressed to Centers for Disease Control and Prevention Personnel Management Office (phone, 404–639–3276); or to Division of Commissioned Personnel, Office of the Surgeon General, Public Health Service, Department of Health and Human Services, 5600 Fishers Lane, Rockville, MD 20857.

Films Information concerning availability of audiovisual materials related to program activities may be obtained from the Office of Public Affairs. Phone, 404–639–3286.

Publications Single copies of most publications are available free of charge from the Management Analysis and Services Office, Centers for Disease Control and Prevention. Phone, 404–639–3534.

Bulk quantities of publications may be purchased from the Superintendent of Documents, Government Printing Office, Washington, DC 20402.

Food and Drug Administration

Inquiries on the following subjects may be directed to the specified office, Food and Drug Administration, 5600 Fishers Lane, Rockville, MD 20857.

Consumer Activities FDA Public Affairs Offices are located in 32 cities across the country. Consumer phones in these same cities provide recorded messages of interest to the consumer. Phone, 301–443–5006.

Public Affairs Offices—Food and Drug Administration

Office	Address	Telephone
Atlanta, GA	60 8th St. NE., 30309	404–347–7355
Baltimore, MD	900 Madison Ave., 21201	301–962–3731
Boston, MA	1 Montvale Ave., Stoneham, MA 02180	617–279–1479
Brooklyn, NY	850 3d Ave., 11232	718–965–5043
Buffalo, NY	599 Delaware Ave., 14202	716–846–4483
Chicago, IL	Suite 550, 300 S. Riverside Plz., S. Chicago, IL 60606	312–353–7126
Cincinnati, OH	1141 Central Pkwy., 45202–1097	513–684–3501
Cleveland, OH	P.O. Box 838, 3820 Center Rd., Brunswick, OH 44212	216–273–1038
Dallas, TX	3032 Bryan St., 75204	214–655–5315
Denver, CO	P.O. Box 25087, Bldg. 20, Denver Federal Ctr., 80225–0087	303–236–3018
Detroit, MI	1560 E. Jefferson Ave., 48207	313–226–6274

Public Affairs Offices—Food and Drug Administration—Continued

Office	Address	Telephone
Houston, TX	Suite 420, 1445 N. Loop West, 77008	713–229–2322
Indianapolis, IN	Rm. 693, 575 N. Pennsylvania St., 46204	317–269–6500
Irvine, CA	14900 MacArthur Blvd., Suite 300	714–798–7600
Kansas City, MO	1009 Cherry St., 64106	816–374–6366
Minneapolis, MN	240 Hennepin Ave., 55401	612–334–4103
Nashville, TN	297 Plus Park Blvd., 37217	615–736–7277
New Orleans, LA	4298 Elysian Fields Ave., 70122	504–589–2420
Omaha, NE	200 S. 16th St., 68102	402–221–4676
Orlando, FL	Suite 120, 7200 Lake Ellenor Dr., 32809	305–855–0900
Parsippany, NJ	10 Waterview Blvd., 3d Fl., 07054	201–645–3265
Philadelphia, PA	Rm. 900, 2d and Chestnut Sts., 19106	215–597–4390
San Antonio, TX	Rm. B–406, 727 E. Durango, 78206	512–229–6737
San Francisco, CA	Rm. 526, 50 United Nations Plz., 94102	415–556–1457
San Juan, PR	466 Fernandez Juncos Ave., 00901–3223	809–729–6852
Seattle, WA	22201 23d Dr. SE., Bothell, WA 98021–4421	206–483–4953
St. Louis, MO	808 N. Collins Alley, 63102	314–425–5021

Contracts   Contact the Director, Division of Contracts and Grants Management (HFA–500). Phone, 301–443–6890.

Employment   The Administration uses various civil service examinations and registers in its recruitment for positions such as consumer safety officers, pharmacologists, microbiologists, physiologists, chemists, mathematical statisticians, physicians, dentists, animal caretakers, etc. Inquiries for positions in the Washington, DC, metropolitan area should be directed to the Personnel Officer (HFA–400). Phone, 301–443–2234.

Inquiries for positions outside the Washington, DC, area should be directed to the appropriate local FDA office.

Schools interested in the college recruitment program should write to the Personnel Officer (HFA–400). Phone, 301–443–2234.

Publications   *FDA Consumer,* FDA's official magazine, is available from the Superintendent of Documents, Government Printing Office, Washington, DC 20402. Phone, 301–443–3220.

Reading Rooms   Freedom of Information, Room 12A–30, phone, 301–443–1813; Hearing Clerk, Room 123, 12420 Parklawn Drive, Rockville, MD 20852, phone, 301–443–1751; and Press Office, Room 15–05 (or Room 3807, FB–8, 200 C Street SW., Washington, DC 20204), phone, 301–443–3285.

Speakers   Available for presentations to private organizations and community groups. Requests should be directed to the local FDA office.

Health Resources and Services Administration

Inquiries on the following should be directed to the specified office, Health Resources and Services Administration, 5600 Fishers Lane, Rockville, MD 20857.

Employment   The majority of positions are in the Federal civil service. For positions in the Washington, DC, metropolitan area, employment inquiries may be addressed to the Division of Personnel, Room 14A46. Phone, 301–443–5460 or TDD, 301–443–5278. For information on vacant positions, call 301–443–1230.

Hiring in other areas is decentralized to the Regional Health Administrators in each of the 10 HHS regional offices. The U.S. Government listings in the appropriate commercial telephone directories will provide specific addresses.

Some health professional positions are filled through the Commissioned Corps of the Public Health Service, a uniformed service of the U.S. Government. Inquiries may be addressed to Division of Commissioned Personnel, Office of the Surgeon General, Public Health Service, Parklawn Building, 5600 Fishers Lane, Rockville, MD 20857.

Films   Information concerning the availability of audiovisual materials related to program activities, including films for recruiting minorities into health professions and women into dentistry, is available from the Office of Communications.

Publications Single copies of most publications are available free of charge from the Office of Communications, Room 14–45. Bulk quantities of publications may be purchased from the Superintendent of Documents, Government Printing Office, Washington, DC 20402. Certain technical publications may be purchased from the National Technical Information Service, Department of Commerce, Springfield, VA 22151.

Indian Health Service

Inquiries on the following subjects should be directed to the specified office, Indian Health Service, 5600 Fishers Lane, Rockville, MD 20857.

Employment The majority of positions are in the Federal civil service. For positions in the Washington, DC, metropolitan area, employment inquiries may be addressed to the Division of Personnel Management, Office of Human Resources, Room 4B–44. Phone, 301–443–6520.

Hiring in other parts of the country is decentralized to the 12 area offices. The U.S. Government listings are in the commercial telephone directories for: Aberdeen, SD; Albuquerque, NM; Anchorage, AK; Bemidji, MN; Billings, MT; Nashville, TN; Oklahoma City, OK; Phoenix, AZ; Portland, OR; Sacramento, CA; Tucson, AZ; and Window Rock, AZ.

The area offices can be referenced for specific addresses. Some health professional positions are filled through the Commissioned Corps of the Public Health Service, a uniformed service of the U.S. Government. Inquiries may be addressed to the Commissioned Personnel Management Branch, Room 4B–19. Phone, 301–443–3464.

Publications Single copies of publications describing the Indian Health Service and the health status of American Indians and Alaska Natives are available free of charge from the Communications Office, Room 6–35. Phone, 301–443–3593.

National Institutes of Health

Inquiries on the following subjects may be directed to the office indicated at the National Institutes of Health, Bethesda, MD 20892, or the address given.

Contracts For information on research and development contracts, contact the Division of Contracts and Grants. Phone, 301–496–6431. For all other contracts, contact the Division of Procurement. Phone, 301–496–7488.

Employment A wide range of civil service examinations and registers are used; staff fellowships are available to recent doctorates in biomedical sciences; college recruitment is conducted as necessary to meet requirements. Write to the Office of Information Resources Management. Phone, 301–496–4197.

PHS Commissioned Officer Program For information on the Commissioned Officer programs at NIH and the program for early commissioning of senior medical students in the Reserve Corps of the Public Health Service, contact the Division of Personnel Management. Phone, 301–496–4212.

Environment Research on the biological effects of chemical, physical, and biological substances present in the environment are conducted and supported by the National Institute of Environmental Health Sciences, Research Triangle Park, NC 22709. Phone, 919–541–3211.

Films Research and health-related films are available for loan from the National Library of Medicine, Collection Access Section, Bethesda, MD 20984. Films are available for purchase from the National Audiovisual Center (General Services Administration), Washington, DC 20409.

Publications Publications, brochures, and reports on health and disease problems, medical research, and biomedical communications are available from the Division of Public Information, Office of Communications, National Institutes of Health, Bethesda, MD 20892 (phone, 301–496–4143); or Government Printing Office, Washington, DC 20402. Publications include: *Journal of National Cancer Institute; Environmental Health Perspectives; Scientific Directory and*

Annual Bibliography; NLM—Medline (brochure); and *NIH Publications List.* Single copies of these publications are available from NIH. *Index Medicus, Cumulated Index Medicus Annual,* and *Research Grants Index* may be ordered from the Government Printing Office.

Substance Abuse and Mental Health Services Administration

Inquiries on the following subjects may be directed to the specified office, Substance Abuse and Mental Health Services Administration, 5600 Fishers Lane, Rockville, MD 20857.
Contracts Write to the Director, Division of Grants and Contracts Management. Phone, 301–443–3334.
Employment Inquiries should be addressed to the Director, Division of Personnel Management. Phone, 301–443–3408.
Publications Write to the Associate Administrator for Communications. Phone, 301–443–8956.

Health Care Financing Administration

Inquiries on the following subjects may be directed to the Health Care Financing Administration, Department of Health and Human Services, 7500 Security Boulevard, Baltimore, MD 21244–1850.
Contracts and Small Business Activities Contact the Director, Research Contracts and Grants Division. Phone, 410–786–5157.
Employment Inquiries should be addressed to the Office of Human Resources, Division of Staffing and Employee Services. Phone, 410–786–5501. For information on employment in a regional office, contact the Regional Personnel Officer in the Office of the Regional Director for that region.
Publications For information on publications, write to the Distribution Management Branch, Division of Printing and Distribution Services. Phone, 410–786–7892.

For further information concerning the Department of Health and Human Services, contact the Information Center, Department of Health and Human Services, 200 Independence Avenue SW., Washington, DC 20201. Phone, 202–619–0257.

DEPARTMENT OF HOUSING AND URBAN DEVELOPMENT

451 Seventh Street SW., Washington, DC 20410
Phone, 202–708–1422

SECRETARY OF HOUSING AND URBAN DEVELOPMENT	HENRY G. CISNEROS
Chief of Staff	BRUCE J. KATZ
Senior Advisor to the Secretary	FRANK D. WING, JR.
Special Advisor to the Secretary for Labor Management	MARI BARR
Deputy Secretary	DWIGHT P. ROBINSON, *Acting*
Assistant to the Deputy Secretary for Management Planning and Operations	ALBERT M. MILLER, *Acting*
Director, Office of the Assistant to the Deputy Secretary for Field Management	JOHN E. WILSON
Assistant to the Secretary for Labor Relations	(VACANCY)
Director, Office of Small and Disadvantaged Business Utilization	(VACANCY)
Chief Administrative Law Judge	ALAN W. HEIFETZ
Chair, HUD Board of Contract Appeals and Chief Administrative Judge	DAVID T. ANDERSON
Director, Office of Executive Scheduling	PAULETTE D. PORTER
Special Assistant, Office of HUD CARES (Constituent Action Response)	PATRICIA A. NEWTON
Director, Special Actions Office	GEORGE LATIMER
Director, Executive Secretariat	THOMAS J. HYDE
Director, Office of Departmental Equal Employment Opportunity	MARI BARR, *Acting*
Deputy Director	(VACANCY)
Assistant Secretary, Office of Administration	MARILYNN A. DAVIS
General Counsel	NELSON DÍAZ
Assistant Secretary, Office of Community Planning and Development	ANDREW M. CUOMO
General Deputy Assistant Secretary	MARK C. GORDON
Assistant Secretary, Office of Fair Housing and Equal Opportunity	(VACANCY)
Chief Financial Officer	(VACANCY)
Inspector General	SUSAN GAFFNEY
Assistant Secretary for Housing—Federal Housing Commissioner	NICOLAS P. RETSINAS
General Deputy Assistant Secretary	JEANNE K. ENGEL
Associate General Deputy Assistant Secretary	JAMES E. SCHOENBERGER
Office of the Housing-FHA Comptroller, Housing—FHA Comptroller	CHRIS PETERSON, *Acting*
Assistant Secretary, Office of Congressional and Intergovernmental Relations	(VACANCY)

Deputy Assistant Secretary, Office of Federal-Relief, South Dade County, FL	(VACANCY)
Director, Office of Lead-Based Paint Abatement and Poisoning Prevention	(VACANCY)
Director, Office of Federal Housing Enterprise Oversight	AIDA ALVAREZ
Assistant Secretary, Office of Public and Indian Housing	JOSEPH SHULDINER
General Deputy Assistant Secretary	MICHAEL B. JANIS
Director, Office of Construction, Rehabilitation, and Maintenance	(VACANCY)
Assistant Secretary, Office of Policy Development and Research	MICHAEL A. STEGMAN
General Deputy Assistant Secretary	LAWRENCE L. THOMPSON
President, Government National Mortgage Association	DWIGHT P. ROBINSON
Executive Vice President	ROBERT P. KALISH
Assistant Secretary, Office of Public Affairs	JEAN NOLAN

The Department of Housing and Urban Development is the principal Federal agency responsible for programs concerned with the Nation's housing needs, fair housing opportunities, and improvement and development of the Nation's communities.

The Department of Housing and Urban Development (HUD) was established by the Department of Housing and Urban Development Act (42 U.S.C. 3532–3537), effective November 9, 1965. It was created to:

—administer the principal programs that provide assistance for housing and for the development of the Nation's communities;

—encourage the solution of housing and community development problems through States and localities; and

—encourage the maximum contributions that may be made by vigorous private homebuilding and mortgage lending industries, both primary and secondary, to housing, community development, and the national economy.

Although HUD administers many programs, its major functions may be grouped into six categories, which include:

—insuring mortgages for single-family and multifamily dwellings, and extending loans for home improvement and for purchasing mobile homes;

—channeling funds from investors into the mortgage industry through the Government National Mortgage Association;

—making direct loans for construction or rehabilitation of housing projects for the elderly and the handicapped;

—providing Federal housing subsidies for low- and moderate-income families;

—providing grants to States and communities for community development activities; and

—promoting and enforcing fair housing and equal housing opportunity.

Office of the Secretary

Secretary   The Department is administered under the supervision and direction of a Cabinet-level Secretary who:

—formulates recommendations for basic policies in the fields of housing and community development;

—works with the Executive Office of the President and other Federal agencies to ensure that economic and fiscal policies in housing and community development are consistent with other economic and fiscal policies of the Government;

—encourages private enterprise to serve as large a part of the Nation's total housing and community development needs as possible;

—promotes the growth of cities and States and the efficient and effective use

DEPARTMENT OF HOUSING AND URBAN DEVELOPMENT

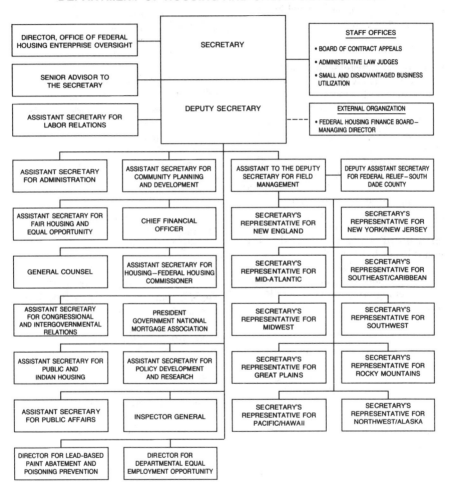

of housing and community and economic development resources by stimulating private sector initiatives, public/private sector partnerships, and public entrepreneurship;

—ensures equal access to housing and affirmatively prevents discrimination in housing; and

—provides general oversight, as required by law, of the Federal National Mortgage Association.

Staff Offices

Small and Disadvantaged Business Utilization　The Office of Small and Disadvantaged Business Utilization oversees HUD's small and disadvantaged set-aside contracting activities and the Minority Business Enterprise Programs.

Administrative Law Judges　The Office of Administrative Law Judges hears and decides Federal Housing discrimination cases under the Administrative Procedure Act, as well as those arising under departmental regulations.

HUD Board of Contract Appeals　The Board issues binding decisions on all appeals of HUD actions in contracting, awarding grants, disciplining mortgagees, and offsetting tax refunds of people indebted to HUD.

External Organizations

Federal Housing Finance Board　The Board, established as an independent agency in the executive branch by the Financial Institutions Reform, Recovery, and Enforcement Act of 1989, oversees the Federal Home Loan Banks. Its function is to ensure that the Federal Home Loan Banks carry out their housing finance mission, remain adequately capitalized, and operate in a safe and sound manner.

Deputy Assistant Secretary for Federal Relief—South Dade County　The Office of Federal Relief—South Dade County was established as part of President Clinton's seven-point plan for helping South Dade County recover from Hurricane Andrew. The role of this Office is to help local, county, and State officials and community groups organize to address their problems, and to coordinate the work of the various Federal agencies having a role in the relief project.

The temporary South Dade County HUD Office is staffed with technical experts in HUD's programs. This is not a servicing HUD Field Office. The Jacksonville and Coral Gable offices will continue to process and control all HUD funds and approvals for the South Dade County area.

Director for Federal Housing Enterprise Oversight　The mission of this office, as defined by the Federal Housing Enterprises Financial Safety and Soundness Act of 1992, is to oversee the financial safety and soundness of the Federal National Mortgage Association and the Federal Home Loan Mortgage Corporation.

Departmental Offices　Other departmental offices include Office of Administration, Office of Chief Financial Officer, Office of General Counsel, Office of Congressional and Intergovernmental Relations, Office of Public Affairs, Office of Inspector General, and Office of Departmental Equal Employment Opportunity.

Program Areas

Assistant Secretary for Housing— Federal Housing Commissioner　This office underwrites single family, multifamily, property improvement, and manufactured home loans; administers special purpose programs designed specifically for the elderly, the handicapped, and the chronically mentally ill; administers assisted housing programs for low-income families who are experiencing difficulties affording standard housing; administers grants to fund resident ownership of multifamily house properties development; and protects consumers against fraudulent practices of land developers and promoters.

For further information, contact the Assistant Secretary for Housing—Federal Housing Commissioner. Phone, 202–708–3600.

Assistant Secretary for Community Planning and Development The Assistant Secretary for Community Planning and Development advises the Secretary regarding community and economic development programs and functions, including the promulgation of policies, standards, procedures, and technical assistance. In addition, the Assistant Secretary is responsible for implementing:

—Community Development Block Grant (CDBG) programs for entitlement communities and State- and HUD-administered small cities; Section 108 Community Development Loan Guarantees; Special Purpose Grants for insular areas and historically black colleges and universities; Community Development Work-Study and Technical Assistance; and Appalachian Regional Commission grants;

—Hope for Ownership of Single Family Homes (HOPE 3), which provides homeownership opportunities to lower income persons by providing Federal assistance to carry out or finance the acquisition and rehabilitation of single family properties for sale and occupancy by families at affordable prices;

—Home Investment in Affordable Housing (HOME), which provides Federal assistance for use by participating jurisdictions or Indian tribes for housing rehabilitation, tenant-based assistance, assistance to first-time homebuyers, and new construction when a jurisdiction is determined to need new rental housing;

—the homelessness programs: including the Supportive Housing Demonstration Program (transitional housing and permanent housing components), Supplemental Assistance for Facilities to Assist the Homeless (SAFAH), Shelter Plus Care, Surplus Property for Use To Assist the Homeless, Section 8 Moderate Rehabilitation Single Room Occupancy (SRO) Program,

Housing Opportunities for Persons With AIDS, and Emergency Shelter Grants and Safe Havens;

—the Neighborhood Development Demonstration Program;

—the Uniform Relocation Assistance and Real Property Acquisition Policies Act of 1970;

—the Comprehensive Housing Affordability Strategy (CHAS);

—statutes and Executive orders that set forth efforts to improve the environment, pursuant to the National Environmental Policy Act of 1969;

—community planning and development efforts with other departments and agencies, public and private organizations, private industry, financial markets, and international organizations;

—the Revolving Fund (liquidation programs), to assist in the efficient liquidation of assets acquired under various housing and urban development programs; and

—the closeout of terminated Community Planning and Development programs.

For further information, contact the Assistant Secretary for Community Planning and Development. Phone, 202–708–2690.

Assistant Secretary for Policy Development and Research This office:

—evaluates and analyzes existing and proposed programs and policies;

—undertakes research, studies, testing, and demonstrations related to the Department's mission;

—provides the Secretary and program administrators with information for use in formulating policy, assessing alternative policies, and measuring their impact;

—develops a research agenda to reflect the overall policy needs of the Department;

—conducts field studies and evaluates all major programs to determine their effectiveness and to analyze their costs and benefits;

—provides the Secretary with economic, legal, and policy analyses of all issues related to the Department's oversight responsibilities over major housing finance institutions; and

—administers the Office of University Partnerships and oversees grants awarded for the Community Development Work Study, Joint Community Development, and Community Outreach Programs.

For further information, contact the Assistant Secretary for Policy Development and Research. Phone, 202–708–1600.

Lead-Based Paint Abatement and Poisoning Prevention   This office is responsible to the Secretary for all lead-based paint abatement and poisoning prevention activities in the Department, including, but not limited to, policy development, abatement, training, regulations, research, and policies applicable to other HUD programs. Some specific activities include:
—increasing awareness by the public and the building industry of the dangers of lead-based paint poisoning and the options for detection, risk reduction, and abatement;
—encouraging the development of safer, more effective, and less-costly methods for detection, risk reduction, and abatement; and
—encouraging State and local governments to develop lead-based paint programs covering primary prevention, including public education, contractor certification, hazard reduction, financing, and enforcement.

For further information, contact the Director, Office of Lead-Based Paint Abatement and Poisoning Prevention. Phone, 202–755–1785.

Assistant Secretary for Fair Housing and Equal Opportunity   This office administers:
—fair housing laws and regulations prohibiting discrimination in public and private housing on the basis of race, color, religion, sex, national origin, handicap, or familial status;
—equal opportunity laws and regulations prohibiting discrimination in HUD-assisted housing and community development programs on the basis of race, handicap, sex, age, or national origin; and
—equal employment opportunity laws and regulations prohibiting discrimination on the basis of race, color, religion, sex, national origin, handicap, or age.

For further information, contact the Assistant Secretary for Fair Housing and Equal Opportunity. Phone, 202–708–4252.

Assistant Secretary for Public and Indian Housing   This office:
—administers public and Indian housing programs, including rental and homeownership programs, and provides technical and financial assistance in planning, developing, and managing low-income projects;
—provides operating subsidies for public housing agencies (PHA's) and Indian housing authorities (IHA's), including procedures for reviewing the management of public housing agencies;
—administers the Comprehensive Improvement Assistance Grant Programs for modernization of low-income housing projects to upgrade living conditions, correct physical deficiencies, and achieve operating efficiency and economy;
—administers the Resident Initiatives Program for resident participation, resident management, homeownership, economic development and supportive services and drug-free neighbor programs;
—protects tenants from the hazards of lead-based paint poisoning by requiring PHA's and IHA's to comply with HUD regulations for the testing and removal of lead-based paint from low-income housing units;
—implements and monitors program requirements related to program eligibility and admission of families to public and assisted housing, and tenant income and rent requirements pertaining to continued occupancy;
—administers the Section 8 Voucher and Certificate Programs and the Moderate Rehabilitation Program; and
—coordinates all departmental housing and community development programs for Indian and Alaskan Natives.

For further information, contact the Office of Public and Indian Housing. Phone, 202–708–0950.

Government National Mortgage Association   This office, also known as

Ginnie Mae (GNMA), is a Government corporation. GNMA's purpose is to support the Government's housing objectives by establishing secondary market facilities for residential mortgages; guaranteeing mortgage-backed securities composed of FHA-insured or VA-guaranteed mortgage loans that are issued by private lenders and guaranteed by GNMA with the full faith and credit of the United States; and through its mortgage-backed securities programs, increases the overall supply of credit available for housing by providing a vehicle for channeling funds from the securities market into the mortgage market.

For further information, contact the Government National Mortgage Association. Phone, 202–708–0926.

Field Structure

The field offices of the Department have boundaries prescribed by the Secretary. Each field office is headed by a Secretary's Representative, who is responsible to the Secretary for the management of the offices within the prescribed area.

For information concerning the detailed jurisdiction of an office, contact the nearest area office.

The field activities of the Office of the Inspector General are carried out through the field offices listed in the following table.

Area/State Offices—Department of Housing and Urban Development

(Areas included within each region are indicated on the map in Appendix A.)

(SR: Secretary's Representative; A: District Inspector General for Audit; SA: Special Agent in Charge)

	Area Office	Address	Officer in Charge	Telephone
1.	NEW ENGLAND—Massachusetts	Rm. 375, 10 Causeway St., Thomas P. O'Neill Federal Bldg., Boston, 02222–1092	Mary Lou K. Crane (SR)	617–565–5234
			William D. Hartnett (A)	617–565–5259
			Raymond A. Carolan (SA)	617–565–5293
2.	NEW YORK/NEW JERSEY—New York	26 Federal Plz., New York, 10278–0068	José Cintrón (SR)	212–264–6500
			A. Paul Kane (A)	212–264–4174
			(Vacancy) (SA)	212–264–8062
3.	MID-ATLANTIC—Pennsylvania	1000 Penn Sq. E., Wanamaker Bldg., Philadelphia, 19107–3390	Karen A. Miller (SR)	215–656–0501
			Edward F. Momorella (A)	215–656–3401
			Robert J. Brickley (SA)	215–656–3410
	OIG CAPITAL DISTRICT OFFICE—Department of Housing and Urban Development	Office of Inspector General/Capital District Office, 451 7th St. SW., Rm. 3154, Washington, DC 20410	Janice LeRoy (A) Kenneth J. Darnall (SA)	202–708–0351 202–708–0387
4.	SOUTHEAST/CARIBBEAN—Georgia	Richard B. Russell Federal Bldg., 75 Spring St. SW., Atlanta, 30303–3388	Davey L. Gibson (SR)	404–331–5136
			Kathryn M. Kuhl-Inclan (A)	404–331–3369
			Emil J. Schuster (SA)	404–331–5155
5.	MIDWEST—Illinois	Ralph H. Metcalfe Federal Bldg., 77 W. Jackson Blvd., Chicago, 60604–3507	Edwin W. Eisendrath (SR)	312–353–5680
			Dale L. Chouteau (A) Robert C. Groves (SA)	312–353–7832 312–353–4196
6.	SOUTHWEST—Texas	P.O. Box 2905, 1600 Throckmorton, Fort Worth, 76113–2905	Stephen R. Weatherford (SR)	817–885–5401
			D. Michael Beard (A)	817–885–5551

Area/State Offices—Department of Housing and Urban Development—Continued
(Areas included within each region are indicated on the map in Appendix A.)
(SR: Secretary's Representative; A: District Inspector General for Audit; SA: Special Agent in Charge)

Area Office	Address	Officer in Charge	Telephone
		Larry D. Chapman (SA)	817–885–5561
7. GREAT PLAINS—Kansas/Missouri	Gateway Twr. II, 400 State Ave., Kansas City, KS 66101–2406	Joseph J. O'Hern (SR)	913–551–5462
		Joseph R. Aguirre (A)	913–551–5870
		Nancy S. Brown (SA)	913–551–5866
8. ROCKY MOUNTAINS—Colorado	1st Interstate Twr. N., 633 17th St., Denver, 80202–3607	Anthony J. Hernandez (SR)	303–672–5440
		Warren Anderson (A)	303–672–5452
		Winn F. Williams (SA)	303–672–5449
9. PACIFIC/HAWAII—California	P.O. Box 36003, 450 Golden Gate Ave., San Francisco, 94102–3448	Arthur C. Agnos (SR)	415–556–4752
		Gary E. Albright (A)	415–556–6895
		Daniel G. Pifer (SA)	415–556–5490
10. NORTHWEST/ALASKA—Washington	Suite 200, Seattle Federal Office Bldg., 909 1st Ave., 98104–1000	Robert N. Santos (SR)	206–220–5101
		A. George Tilley (A)	206–220–5360
		Noel A. Tognazzini (SA)	206–220–5380

Sources of Information

Inquiries on the following subjects should be directed to the nearest field office or to the Department of Housing and Urban Development, (specific headquarters office), 451 Seventh Street SW., Washington, DC 20410. Phone, 202–708–1112 (voice); and 202–708–1455 (TDD). Telephone numbers are not toll-free.

Directory Locator   Phone, 202–708–1112 (voice); and 202–708–1455 (TDD).

Contracts   Contact the headquarters' Office of Procurement and Contracts (phone, 202–708–1290); or the nearest field office's Regional Contracting Division.

Property Disposition   Single family properties: Contact the headquarters' Property Disposition Division (phone, 202–708–0740); or the local Chief Property Officer at the nearest HUD field office. Multifamily Properties: Contact the headquarters' Property Disposition Division (phone, 202–708–3343); or the Field Housing Director at the nearest

HUD field office.

Employment   Inquiries and applications should be directed to the headquarters' Office of Personnel (phone, 202–708–0408); or the nearest field office's Personnel Division.

Program Information Center   The Center provides viewing facilities for information regarding departmental activities and functions and publications and other literature to headquarters visitors. Phone, 202–708–1420.

Freedom of Information Act (FOIA) Requests   Persons interested in inspecting documents or records under the Freedom of Information Act should contact the Freedom of Information Officer. Phone, 202–708–3054.

Written requests should be directed to U.S. Department of Housing and Urban Development, Director, Executive Secretariat, Room 10139, 451 Seventh Street SW., Washington, DC 20410.

HUD Hotline The Hotline is maintained by the Office of the Inspector General as a means for individuals to report activities involving fraud, waste, or mismanagement. Phone, 202–708–4200 (headquarters); 800–347–3735 (toll-free); or 202–708–2451 (TDD).

For further information concerning the Department of Housing and Urban Development, contact the Office of Public Affairs, 451 Seventh Street SW., Washington, DC 20410. Phone, 202–708–0980.

DEPARTMENT OF THE INTERIOR

1849 C Street NW., Washington, DC 20240
Phone, 202–208–3171

SECRETARY OF THE INTERIOR	BRUCE BABBITT
Deputy Secretary	(VACANCY)
Associate Deputy Secretary	(VACANCY)
Chief of Staff	(VACANCY)
Deputy Chief of Staff	B.J. THORNBERRY
Director of Congressional Affairs	MELANIE BELLER
Special Assistants and Counselors to the Secretary	JAMES H. PIPKIN, JOHN J. DUFFY, EDWARD B. COHEN
Special Assistant to the Secretary and White House Liaison	ROBERT K. HATTOY
Assistant to the Secretary and Director, Office of Communications	(VACANCY)
Director of External Affairs	LUCIA A. WYMAN
Special Assistant to the Secretary and Director, Executive Secretariat	NANCY K. HAYES
Assistant to the Secretary	MOLLY POAG
Director, Office of Regulatory Affairs	JULIE FALKNER
Executive Director (President's Commission on Sustainable Development)	MOLLY H. OLSON
Special Assistant to the Secretary for Alaska	DEBORAH L. WILLIAMS
Special Assistant to the Secretary	FAITH R. ROESSEL
Solicitor	JOHN D. LESHY
Deputy Solicitor	ANNE H. SHIELDS
Associate Solicitor (General Law)	(VACANCY)
Associate Solicitor (Conservation and Wildlife)	ROBERT L. BAUM
Associate Solicitor (Indian Affairs)	(VACANCY)
Associate Solicitor (Energy and Resources)	PATRICIA J. BENEKE
Associate Solicitor (Surface Mining)	KAY HENRY
Inspector General	WILMA A. LEWIS
Deputy Inspector General	JOYCE N. FLEISCHMAN
Assistant Inspector General (Administration)	SHIRLEY E. LLOYD
Assistant Inspector General (Investigations)	THOMAS I. SHEEHAN
Deputy Assistant Inspector General (Audits)	MARVIN E. PIERCE
General Counsel	THOMAS E. ROBINSON
Assistant Secretary—Water and Science	(VACANCY)
Deputy Assistant Secretary	(VACANCY)
Director, U.S. Bureau of Mines	RHEA GRAHAM
Director, U.S. Geological Survey	GORDON P. EATON
Commissioner, Bureau of Reclamation	DANIEL P. BEARD
Assistant Secretary for Fish and Wildlife and Parks	GEORGE T. FRAMPTON, JR.
Deputy Assistant Secretary	ROBERT P. DAVISON
Director, U.S. Fish and Wildlife Service	MOLLIE BEATTIE
Director, National Biological Survey	H. RONALD PULLIAM

318

Director, National Park Service	ROGER G. KENNEDY
Assistant Secretary—Indian Affairs	ADA E. DEER
Deputy Assistant Secretary	MICHAEL J. ANDERSON
Commissioner of Indian Affairs	(VACANCY)
Deputy Commissioner of Indian Affairs	HILDA MANUEL
Assistant Secretary—Land and Minerals Management	ROBERT L. ARMSTRONG
Deputy Assistant Secretary	SYLVIA V. BACA
Director, Minerals Management Service	CYNTHIA L. QUATERMAN
Director, Bureau of Land Management	(VACANCY)
Director, Office of Surface Mining Reclamation and Enforcement	ROBERT URAM
Assistant Secretary—Territorial and International Affairs	LESLIE M. TURNER
Deputy Assistant Secretary	ALLEN P. STAYMAN
Assistant Secretary—Policy, Management and Budget	BONNIE R. COHEN
Director, Office of Hearings and Appeals	BARRY E. HILL
Director, Office of Small and Disadvantaged Business Utilization	(VACANCY)
Deputy Assistant Secretary for Human Resources	THERESA TRUJEQUE
Director, Office of Equal Opportunity	E. MELODEE STITH
Director, Office of National Service and Educational Partnerships	DELORES L. CHACON
Director, Office of Personnel	WOODROW W. HOPPER, JR.
Director, Ethics Staff	GABRIELE J. PAONE
Director, Drug Program Coordination Staff	KATHLEEN M. MEALY
Chief, Personnel Services Division	SHARON ELLER
Counselor to the Secretary and Deputy Assistant Secretary for Policy	JOSEPH L. SAX
Director, Office of Environmental Policy and Compliance	WILLIE R. TAYLOR
Director, Office of Policy Analysis	BROOKS B. YEAGER
Director of Fiscal Resources	ROBERT J. LAMB
Director, Office of Acquisition and Property Management	PAUL A. DENETT
Director, Office of Budget	MARY ANN LAWLER
Director, Office of Financial Management	R. SCHUYLER LESHER
Director, Office of Information Resources Management	(VACANCY)
Director of Operations	CLAUDIA P. SCHECHTER
Director, Office of Construction Management	OSCAR W. MUELLER, JR.
Director, Office of Administrative Services	ALBERT C. CAMACHO
Director, Office of Aircraft Services	ELMER J. HURD
Director, Office of Enforcement and Security Management	JOHN J. GANNON
Director, Office of Occupational Safety and Health	(VACANCY)
Director, Office of Hazard and Fire Programs Coordination	JAMES C. DOUGLAS

As the Nation's principal conservation agency, the Department of the Interior has responsibility for most of our nationally owned public lands and natural resources.

DEPARTMENT OF THE INTERIOR

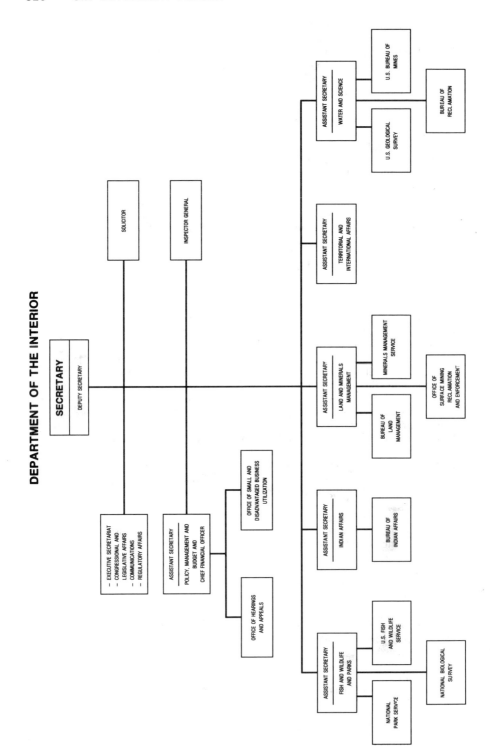

This includes fostering sound use of our land and water resources; assessing and protecting our fish, wildlife, and biological diversity; preserving the environmental and cultural values of our national parks and historical places; and providing for the enjoyment of life through outdoor recreation. The Department assesses our mineral resources and works to ensure that their development is in the best interests of all our people by encouraging stewardship and citizen participation in their care. The Department also has a major responsibility for American Indian reservation communities and for people who live in island territories under United States administration.

The Department of the Interior was created by act of March 3, 1849 (43 U.S.C. 1451), which transferred to it the General Land Office, the Office of Indian Affairs, the Pension Office, and the Patent Office. It was reorganized by Reorganization Plan No. 3 of 1950, as amended (5 U.S.C. app.).

Over the years, other functions have been added and removed, so that its role has changed from that of general housekeeper for the Federal Government to that of custodian of the Nation's natural resources.

Office of the Secretary

Secretary The Secretary of the Interior reports directly to the President and is responsible for the direction and supervision of all operations and activities of the Department. The Office of the Secretary includes the offices of Deputy Secretary, the Assistant Secretaries, and Inspector General. Some areas where public purposes are broadly applied include:

Fish and Wildlife and Parks The Assistant Secretary for Fish and Wildlife and Parks discharges the duties of the Secretary with the authority and direct responsibility for programs associated with conservation in the use of natural and cultural resources; and the enhancement, protection, and monitoring of fish, wildlife, vegetation, and habitat. The Assistant Secretary represents the Department in the coordination of marine environmental quality and biological resources programs with other Federal agencies. The Assistant Secretary also exercises Secretarial direction and supervision over the United States Fish and Wildlife Service, the National Biological Service, and the National Park Service.

Water and Science The Assistant Secretary (Water and Science) discharges the duties of the Secretary with the authority and direct responsibility to carry out the statutory mandate to manage and direct programs that support the development and implementation of water, mineral, and science policies and assist the development of economically and environmentally sound resource activities. The Assistant Secretary oversees the programs of the Bureau of Reclamation, the United States Bureau of Mines, and the United States Geological Survey.

The Office of the Assistant Secretary provides advice on Earth science matters to the Secretary and represents the Department of the Interior in interagency efforts on a range of scientific issues.

Land and Minerals Management The Assistant Secretary (Land and Minerals Management) discharges the duties of the Secretary with the authority and direct responsibility for programs associated with public land management; operations management and leasing for minerals on public lands, including the Outer Continental Shelf to the outer limits of the United States economic jurisdiction; minerals operations management on Indian lands; surface mining reclamation and enforcement functions; and management of revenues from Federal and Indian mineral leases.

The Assistant Secretary exercises Secretarial direction and supervision over the Bureau of Land Management, the Minerals Management Service, and the Office of Surface Mining Reclamation and Enforcement.

Indian Affairs The Assistant Secretary (Indian Affairs) discharges the authority and responsibility of the Secretary for

activities pertaining to Indians and Indian affairs. The Assistant Secretary is responsible for exercising Secretarial direction and supervision over the Bureau of Indian Affairs by:
—providing the Secretary with detailed and objective advice on matters involving Indians and Indian affairs;
—identifying and acting on issues affecting Indian policy and programs;
—establishing policy on Indian affairs;
—maintaining liaison and coordination between the Department of the Interior and other Federal agencies that provide services or funding to Indians;
—representing the Department in transactions with Congress;
—monitoring and evaluating ongoing activities related to Indian affairs; and
—undertaking or providing leadership in special assignments and projects for the Secretary.

Territorial and International Affairs
The Office of the Assistant Secretary (Territorial and International Affairs) was established by Secretarial Order 3046 of February 14, 1980. The Assistant Secretary discharges the authority and responsibility of the Secretary for activities pertaining to U.S. insular areas and the Freely Associated States (Republic of the Marshall Islands and Federated States of Micronesia) and for the coordination of international affairs of the Department.

The Assistant Secretary is responsible for building mutually beneficial partnerships to facilitate locally determined economic, social, and political development in the U.S. insular areas of Guam, American Samoa, the Virgin Islands, the Commonwealth of the Northern Mariana Islands, and the Trust Territory of the Pacific Islands (Republic of Palau). The degree to which the Office conducts activities to further these objectives in a specific insular area depends on the status of the local government, its relationship to the Secretary of the Interior, and the extent of development already achieved within the insular area.

In consultation with the Assistant Secretary of State for East Asian and Pacific Affairs, who is responsible for

government-to-government relations with the Freely Associated States, the Assistant Secretary for Territorial and International Affairs is responsible for general oversight of all Federal programs provided to the Freely Associated States of the Republic of the Marshall Islands and the Federated States of Micronesia under the Compact of Free Association.

The Assistant Secretary also serves as the Department's focal point for analysis, development, and review of the Department's policy and programs pertaining to international activities and the opportunities for support of U.S. foreign policy through the use of the Department's natural resource and environmental expertise.

For further information, contact the Office of Territorial and International Affairs, Department of the Interior, Washington, DC 20240. Phone, 202–208–4822.

Policy, Management and Budget The Assistant Secretary (Policy, Management and Budget) discharges the authority of the Secretary for all phases of management and administrative activities, serves as the principal policy adviser to the Secretary, and is the Department's Chief Financial Officer.

Office of the Solicitor

The Office of the Solicitor performs all of the legal work of the Department with the exception of that performed by the Office of Hearings and Appeals, the Office of Congressional and Legislative Affairs, and the Office of Inspector General. The Solicitor is the principal legal advisor to the Secretary and the chief law officer of the Department.

The headquarters office, located in Washington, DC, consists of five Divisions. The Division of Conservation and Wildlife is responsible for legal matters involving the programs of the Assistant Secretary for Fish and Wildlife and Parks, the National Park Service, the National Biological Service, and the U.S. Fish and Wildlife Service. The Division of Energy and Resources is responsible for legal matters involving the programs of the Assistant Secretary (Water and Science), the Assistant Secretary (Land and Minerals Management), the Bureau of Land Management, the United States Bureau of Mines, the United States Geological Survey, the Bureau of Reclamation, and the Minerals Management Service. The Division of Indian Affairs is responsible for legal matters involving the programs of the Assistant Secretary (Indian Affairs) and the Bureau of Indian Affairs. The Division of Surface Mining provides legal advice to the Assistant Secretary (Land and Minerals Management) on surface mining matters and to the Office of Surface Mining Reclamation and Enforcement. The Division of General Law is responsible for general administrative law and legal matters involving programs under the jurisdiction of the Office of the Secretary, the Assistant Secretary (Policy, Management and Budget), and the Office for Equal Opportunity. Administrative and support services for the Office of the Solicitor are provided by the Division of Administration.

The field organization of the Office is divided into seven regions, each headed by a Regional Solicitor.

Regional Offices—Office of the Solicitor

Region	Address	Telephone
ALASKA—Alaska	Suite 300, 4230 University Dr., Anchorage, AK 95508–4626	907–271–4131
NORTHEAST—Connecticut, Delaware, Illinois, Indiana, Maine, Maryland, Massachusetts, Michigan, Minnesota, New Hampshire, New Jersey, New York, North Dakota, Ohio, Pennsylvania, Rhode Island, South Dakota, Vermont, Virginia, West Virginia, Wisconsin	Suite 612, 1 Gateway Ctr., Newton Corner, MA 02158–2802	617–527–3400
PACIFIC NORTHWEST—Idaho, Montana, Oregon, Washington	Suite 60, 500 NE. Multnomah St., Portland, OR 197232	503–231–2125
PACIFIC SOUTHWEST—Arizona, California, Hawaii, Nevada, Pacific Territories, Utah	Rm. E–2753, 2800 Cottage Way, Sacramento, CA 95825–1890	916–976–2141
ROCKY MOUNTAIN—Colorado, Iowa, Kansas, Missouri, Nebraska, Wyoming	Rm. D–105, P.O. Box 25007, Denver, CO 80225	303–231–5353
SOUTHEAST—Alabama, Florida, Georgia, Kentucky, Mississippi, North Carolina, Puerto Rico, South Carolina, Tennessee, Virgin Islands	Suite 304, 75 Spring St. SW., Atlanta, GA 30303	404–331–5504
SOUTHWEST—Arkansas, Louisiana, New Mexico, Oklahoma, Texas	Suite 200, 2400 Louisiana Blvd. NE., Albuquerque, NM 87110–4316	505–883–6700

For further information, contact the Associate Solicitor for Administration, Office of the Solicitor, Department of the Interior, Washington, DC 20240. Phone, 202–208–6115.

Office of Inspector General

The Office of Inspector General provides policy direction and conducts, supervises, and coordinates all audits, investigations, and other activities in the Department designed to promote economy and efficiency or prevent and detect fraud and abuse.

In the insular areas of Guam, American Samoa, the Virgin Islands, and the Commonwealth of the Northern Mariana Islands, the Office performs the functions of government comptroller through audit of revenues and receipts and expenditure of funds and property pursuant to the Insular Areas Act of 1982 (48 U.S.C. 1422).

Regional Offices—Office of Inspector General
(A: Audits; I: Investigations)

Region/Headquarters	Address	Telephone
EASTERN:		
Arlington, VA (A)	Suite 425, 1550 Wilson Blvd., 22209	703–235–9231
Arlington, VA (I)	Suite 410, 1550 Wilson Blvd., 22209	703–235–9221
CENTRAL:		
Lakewood, CO (A)	Suite 510, 134 Union Blvd., 80228	303–236–9243
WESTERN:		
Sacramento, CA (A)	Rm. W2400, 2800 Cottage Way, 95825	916–978–4891
Lakewood, CO (I)	Suite 540, 134 Union Blvd., 80228	303–236–8296
CARIBBEAN:		

Regional Offices—Office of Inspector General—Continued
(A: Audits; I: Investigations)

Region/Headquarters	Address	Telephone
St. Thomas, VI (A)	Rm. 207, Federal Bldg., 00802	809–774–8300
NORTH PACIFIC:		
Agana, GU (A)	Suite 807, 238 Archbishop F.C. Flores St., 96910	700–550–7279

For further information, contact the Office of Inspector General, Department of the Interior, Washington, DC 20240. Phone, 202–208–4356.

Office of Hearings and Appeals

The Office of Hearings and Appeals is a unit of the Office of the Secretary and is headed by a Director, who reports administratively to the Assistant Secretary (Policy, Management and Budget).

The Office of Hearings and Appeals is responsible for departmental quasi-judicial and related functions. Administrative law judges and three formal boards of appeal render decisions in cases pertaining to contract disputes; Indian probate and administrative appeals; public and acquired lands and their resources; submerged offshore lands of the Outer Continental Shelf; surface coal mining control and reclamation; claims under the Alaska Native Claims Settlement Act; and enforcement of the importation and transportation of rare and endangered species. The Director of the Office of Hearings and Appeals may assign administrative law judges or other officials from the Office of Hearings and Appeals for the purpose of holding rulemaking hearings and may also assign administrative law judges or establish ad hoc boards of appeal to meet special requirements of disputes not falling under one of the previously listed categories. Board decisions are final for the Department.

The Office includes the headquarters organization and nine field offices for administrative law judges.

For further information, contact the Office of Hearings and Appeals, Department of the Interior, 4015 Wilson Boulevard, Arlington, VA 22203. Phone, 703–235–3810.

Bureaus

United States Fish and Wildlife Service

[For the United States Fish and Wildlife Service statement of organization, see the *Code of Federal Regulations*, Title 50, Subchapter A, Part 2]

The United States Fish and Wildlife Service's national responsibility in the service of fish, wildlife, and people spans more than 120 years to the establishment in 1871 of a predecessor agency, the Bureau of Fisheries. First created as an independent agency, the Bureau of Fisheries was later placed in the Department of Commerce. A second predecessor agency, the Bureau of Biological Survey, was established in 1885 in the Department of Agriculture.

In 1939 the two Bureaus and their functions were transferred to the Department of the Interior. They were consolidated into one agency and redesignated the Fish and Wildlife Service in 1940 by Reorganization Plan III (5 U.S.C. app.).

Further reorganization came in 1956 when the Fish and Wildlife Act (16 U.S.C. 742a) created the United States Fish and Wildlife Service and provided for it to replace and succeed the former Fish and Wildlife Service. The Act established two Bureaus within the new Service: the Bureau of Commercial Fisheries and the Bureau of Sport Fisheries and Wildlife.

In 1970, under Reorganization Plans 3 and 4 (5 U.S.C. app.), the Bureau of Commercial Fisheries was transferred to the Department of Commerce. The Bureau of Sport Fisheries and Wildlife, which remained in Interior, was renamed by an act of Congress in April 1974 (16 U.S.C. 742b) as the United States Fish and Wildlife Service.

The Service is composed of a headquarters office in Washington, DC, 7 regional offices, and a variety of field units and installations. These include more than 500 national wildlife refuges and 166 waterfowl production areas totaling more than 92 million acres; 78 national fish hatcheries; and a nationwide network of wildlife law enforcement agents.

The United States Fish and Wildlife Service is responsible for migratory birds, endangered species, certain marine mammals, and inland sport fisheries. Its mission is to conserve, protect, and enhance fish and wildlife and their habitats for the continuing benefit of the American people. Within this framework, the Service strives to foster an environmental stewardship ethic based on ecological principles and scientific knowledge of wildlife; works with the States to improve the conservation and management of the Nation's fish and wildlife resources; and administers a national program providing opportunities to the American public to understand, appreciate, and wisely use these resources.

In the area of resource management, the Service provides leadership for the protection and improvement of land and water environments (habitat preservation), which directly benefits the living natural resources and adds quality to human life. Activities include:
—surveillance of pesticides, heavy metals, and other contaminants;
—studies of fish and wildlife populations;
—ecological studies;
—environmental impact assessment, including hydroelectric dams, nuclear power sites, stream channelization, and dredge-and-fill permits; and
—environmental impact statement review.

The Service is responsible for improving and maintaining fish and wildlife resources by proper management of wildlife and habitat. It also helps fulfilling the public demand for recreational fishing while maintaining the Nation's fisheries at a level and in a condition that will ensure their continued survival. Specific wildlife and fishery resources programs include:
—migratory birds: wildlife refuge management for production, migration, and wintering; law enforcement; game, bird population, production, and harvest surveys;
—mammals and nonmigratory birds: refuge management of resident species, law enforcement, protection of certain marine mammals, and technical assistance;
—coastal anadromous fish: hatchery production and stocking;
—Great Lakes fisheries: hatchery production of lake trout and fishery management in cooperation with Canada and the States; and
—other inland fisheries: hatchery production and stocking of Indian lands, and technical assistance.

The Service provides national and international leadership in identifying, protecting, and restoring endangered species of fish, wildlife, and plants. This program includes:
—developing the Federal Endangered and Threatened Species List, conducting of status surveys, preparing recovery plans, and coordinating efforts nationally and internationally;
—operating national wildlife refuges;
—law enforcement;
—foreign importation enforcement; and
—consultation with foreign countries.

Public use and information programs include preparing leaflets and brochures; operating environmental study areas on Service lands for use by school groups and teachers; operating visitor centers, self-guided nature trails, observation towers, and display ponds; and providing recreational activities, such as hunting, fishing, and wildlife photography.

The Service's Federal aid programs apportion funds generated by excise taxes on sporting arms and equipment to the States and territories for projects designed to conserve and enhance the Nation's fish and wildlife resources.

Regional Offices—United States Fish and Wildlife Service

Region	Address	Telephone
ALBUQUERQUE—Arizona, New Mexico, Oklahoma, Texas	P.O. Box 1306, Albuquerque, NM 87103	505–766–2321
ANCHORAGE—Alaska	1011 E. Tudor Rd., Anchorage, AK 99503	907–786–3542
ATLANTA—Alabama, Arkansas, Florida, Georgia, Kentucky, Louisiana, Mississippi, North Carolina, Puerto Rico, South Carolina, Tennessee, Virgin Islands	1875 Century Blvd., Atlanta, GA 30345	404–679–4000
HADLEY—Connecticut, Delaware, Maine, Maryland, Massachusetts, New Hampshire, New Jersey, New York, Pennsylvania, Rhode Island, Vermont, Virginia, West Virginia	300 Westgate Ctr. Dr., Hadley, MA 01035–9589	413–253–8200
DENVER—Colorado, Kansas, Montana, Nebraska, North Dakota, South Dakota, Utah, Wyoming	P.O. Box 25486, Denver, CO 80225	303–236–7920
PORTLAND—California, Hawaii, Idaho, Nevada, Oregon, Washington, Pacific Islands	911 NE. 11th Ave., Portland, OR 97232–4181	503–231–6118
TWIN CITIES—Illinois, Indiana, Iowa, Michigan, Minnesota, Missouri, Ohio, Wisconsin	Federal Bldg., Fort Snelling, Twin Cities, MN 55111	612–725–3500

For further information, contact the Office of Public Affairs, United States Fish and Wildlife Service, Department of the Interior, Washington, DC 20240. Phone, 202–208–5634.

National Park Service

The National Park Service was established in the Department of the Interior on August 25, 1916 (16 U.S.C. 1).

The National Park Service is dedicated to conserving unimpaired the natural and cultural resources and values of the National Park System for the enjoyment, education, and inspiration of this and future generations. The Service is also responsible for managing a great variety of national and international programs designed to help extend the benefits of natural and cultural resource conservation and outdoor recreation throughout this country and the world.

The National Park Service has a Service Center in Denver that provides planning, architectural, engineering, and other professional services. There are more than 365 units in the National Park System, including national parks and monuments; scenic parkways, preserves, trails, riverways, seashores, lakeshores, and recreation areas; and historic sites associated with important movements, events, and personalities of the American past.

Activities   The National Park Service develops and implements park management plans and staffs the areas under its administration. It relates the natural values and historical significance of these areas to the public through talks, tours, films, exhibits, publications, and other interpretive media. It operates campgrounds and other visitor facilities and provides—usually through concessions—lodging, food, and transportation services in many areas.

The National Park Service also administers the following programs: the State portion of the Land and Water Conservation Fund, Nationwide Outdoor Recreation coordination and information and State comprehensive outdoor recreation planning, planning and technical assistance for the National Wild and Scenic Rivers System, and the National Trails System, natural area programs, the National Register of Historic Places, national historic landmarks, historic preservation, technical preservation services, Historic American Buildings Survey, Historic American Engineering Record, and interagency archeological services.

Field Area Offices—National Park Service

Field Area	Address	Telephone
ALASKA—Alaska	2525 Gambell St., Anchorage, AK 99503–2892	907–257–2690
INTERMOUNTAIN—Arizona, Colorado, Montana, New Mexico, Oklahoma, Texas, Utah, Wyoming	P.O. Box 25287, 12795 W. Alameda Pky., Denver, CO 80225–0287	303–969–2500

Field Area Offices—National Park Service—Continued

Field Area	Address	Telephone
MIDWEST—Arkansas, Illinois, Indiana, Iowa, Kansas, Michigan, Minnesota, Missouri, Nebraska, North Dakota, Ohio, South Dakota, Wisconsin	1709 Jackson St., Omaha, NE 68102	402–221–3431
NATIONAL CAPITAL—Washington, DC, and nearby Maryland and Virginia	1100 Ohio Dr. SW., Washington, DC 20242	202–619–7005
NORTHEAST—Connecticut, Delaware, Maine, Maryland, Massachusetts, New Hampshire, New Jersey, New York, Pennyslvania, Rhode Island, Vermont, Virginia, West Virginia	U.S. Custom House, 200 Chestnut St., Philadelphia, PA 19106	215–597–7013
PACIFIC WEST—California, Guam, Hawaii, Idaho, Nevada, Northern Mariana Islands, Oregon, Washington	Suite 600, 600 Harrison St., San Francisco, CA 94107–1372	415–744–3876
SOUTHEAST—Alabama, Florida, Georgia, Kentucky, Louisiana, Mississippi, North Carolina, Puerto Rico, South Carolina, Tennessee, Virgin Islands	75 Spring St. SW., Atlanta, GA 30303	404–331–5185

For further information, contact the Chief, Office of Public Affairs, National Park Service, Department of the Interior, P.O. Box 37127, Washington, DC 20013–7127. Phone, 202–208–6843.

National Biological Service

The National Biological Service (NBS) became operational on November 11, 1993, through the transfer of certain functions of the following Interior bureaus: U.S. Fish and Wildlife Service, National Park Service, Bureau of Land Management, Minerals Management Service, Office of Surface Mining Reclamation and Enforcement, U.S. Geological Survey, and Bureau of Reclamation.

The mission of NBS is to work with others to provide the scientific understanding and technologies needed to support the sound management and conservation of our Nation's biological resources. To accomplish this mission, NBS undertakes research, inventory, monitoring information sharing, and technology transfer activities to foster an understanding of biological systems and their benefits to society. Through these activities, NBS provides essential scientific support, technical assistance, and information required for sound management and policy decisions regarding the Nation's biological resources. NBS establishes partnerships with other Federal, State, and local agencies; with museums and universities; and with private organizations in order to bring coherence to largely uncoordinated efforts and to further fulfill its mission.

NBS consists of a Headquarters Office, located in Washington, DC; 4 regions, located in Lafayette, LA; Denver, CO; Seattle, WA; and Leetown, WV; 16 science centers; 88 field stations; and 54 cooperative research units, all located at colleges and universities.

For further information, contact the Public Affairs Office, National Biological Service, Department of the Interior, 1849 C Street NW., Washington, DC 20240. Phone, 202–482–3048.

United States Bureau of Mines

The United States Bureau of Mines was established July 1, 1910, in the Department of the Interior by the Organic Act of May 16, 1910, as amended (30 U.S.C. 1, 3, 5–7). The 1910 act has been supplemented by several statutes, including those authorizing production and sale of helium, and research on environmental problems associated with minerals.

The Bureau is primarily a research and factfinding agency. Its goal is to help ensure that the Nation has adequate supplies of nonfuel minerals for security and other needs. Research is conducted to provide the technology for the extraction, processing, use, and recycling of the Nation's nonfuel mineral resources at a reasonable cost without harm to the environment or the workers involved.

The Bureau also collects, compiles, analyzes, and publishes statistical and economic information on all phases of nonfuel mineral resource development, including exploration, production, shipments, demand, stocks, prices, imports, and exports. Special studies are frequently made on subjects of particular national interest, such as the effects of potential economic, technologic, or legal developments on resource availability. The effects of policy alternatives on mineral supply and demand are also analyzed.

For further information, contact the Office of Public Information, United States Bureau of Mines, Department of the Interior, 810 Seventh Street NW., Washington, DC 20241. Phone, 202–501–9649.

United States Geological Survey

The United States Geological Survey (USGS) was established by act of March 3, 1879 (43 U.S.C. 31), which provided for "the classification of the public lands and the examination of the geological structure, mineral resources, and products of the national domain." The act of September 5, 1962 (43 U.S.C. 31(b)), expanded this authorization to include such examinations outside the national domain. Topographic mapping and chemical and physical research were recognized as an essential part of the investigations and studies authorized by act of March 3, 1879, and specific provision was made for them through subsequent legislation.

Provision was made in 1894 for gauging the streams and determining the water supply of the United States. Authorizations for publication, sale, and distribution of material prepared by USGS are contained in several statutes (43 U.S.C. 41–45; 44 U.S.C. 1318–1320).

USGS is also authorized to maintain an archive of land-remote sensing data for historical, scientific, and technical purposes, including long-term global environmental monitoring; establish a National Geologic Mapping Program; expedite the production of a geologic-map data base; establish and support the Federal Geographic Data Committee, which is chaired by the Secretary of the

Interior; and serve as the designated lead agency for the Federal Water Information Coordination Program.

The Geological Survey's primary responsibilities are: investigating and assessing the Nation's land, water, energy, and mineral resources; conducting research on global change; and investigating natural hazards such as earthquakes, volcanoes, landslides, floods, and droughts. To attain these objectives, USGS prepares maps and digital and cartographic data; collects and interprets data on energy and mineral resources; conducts nationwide assessments of the quality, quantity, and use of the Nation's water resources; performs fundamental and applied research in the sciences and techniques involved; and publishes and disseminates the results of its investigations in thousands of new maps and reports each year.

For further information, contact the Public Affairs Office, United States Geological Survey, Department of the Interior, 119 National Center, Reston, VA 22092. Phone, 703–648–4460.

Office of Surface Mining Reclamation and Enforcement

The Office of Surface Mining Reclamation and Enforcement (OSM) was established in the Department of the Interior by the Surface Mining Control and Reclamation Act of 1977 (30 U.S.C. 1211).

The Office's primary goal is to assist States in operating a nationwide program that protects society and the environment from the adverse effects of coal mining, while ensuring that surface coal mining can be done without permanent damage to land and water resources. The main objectives, now that most coal-mining States have assumed primary responsibility for regulating coal mining and reclamation activities within their borders, are to oversee mining regulatory and abandoned mine reclamation programs in States with primary responsibility, to assist States in meeting the objectives of the act, and to regulate mining and reclamation activities in those States choosing not to assume primary responsibility.

The Office's headquarters is located in Washington, DC. In addition, regional coordinating centers, located in Pittsburgh, PA; Alton, IL; and Denver, CO; provide technical support to the States and to OSM's 13 field offices and 8 area offices. The field offices interact with State, tribal and Federal agencies, assisting the States in implementing their regulatory and reclamation programs. The regional coordinating centers also review mine plans and permit applications on Federal lands.

Activities The Office establishes national policy for the conduct of the surface mining control and reclamation program provided for in the act, reviews and approves amendments to previously approved State programs, and reviews and recommends approval of new State program submissions. Other activities include:

—managing the collection, disbursement, and accounting for abandoned mine land fees;

—administering civil penalties programs;

—establishing technical standards and regulatory policy for reclamation and enforcement efforts;

—providing guidance for environmental considerations, research, training, and technology transfer for State, tribal and Federal regulatory and abandoned mine land reclamation programs; and

—monitoring and evaluating State and tribal regulatory programs, cooperative agreements, and abandoned mine land reclamation programs.

For further information, contact the Office of Public Affairs, Office of Surface Mining Reclamation and Enforcement, Department of the Interior, Washington, DC 20240. Phone, 202–208–2719. TDD, 202–208–2737

Bureau of Indian Affairs

The Bureau of Indian Affairs was created as part of the War Department in 1824 and transferred to the Department of the Interior when the latter was established in 1849. The Snyder Act of 1921 (25 U.S.C. 13) provided substantive law for appropriations covering the conduct of activities by the Bureau of Indian Affairs. The scope and character of the authorizations contained in this act were broadened by the Indian Reorganization Act of 1934 (25 U.S.C. 461 *et seq.*), the Indian Self-Determination and Education Assistance Act of 1975, as amended (25 U.S.C. 450), title XI of the Education Amendments of 1978 (20 U.S.C. 2701 note), and the Hawkins-Stafford Elementary and Secondary School Improvement Amendments of 1988 (20 U.S.C. 2701).

The principal objectives of the Bureau are to encourage and assist Indian and Alaska Native people to manage their own affairs under the trust relationship to the Federal Government; to facilitate, with maximum involvement of Indian and Alaska Native people, full development of their human and natural resource potential; to mobilize all public and private aids to the advancement of Indian and Alaska Native people for use by them; and to promote self-determination by utilizing the skill and capabilities of Indian and Alaska Native people in the direction and management of programs for their benefit.

Activities In carrying out these objectives, the Bureau works with Indian and Alaska Native people, tribal governments, Native American organizations, other Federal agencies, State and local governments, and other interested groups in the development and implementation of effective programs for their advancement.

The Bureau also acts as trustee for their lands and moneys held in trust by the United States, assisting them to realize maximum benefits from such resources.

Area Offices—Bureau of Indian Affairs

Area	Address	Telephone
Aberdeen, SD	115 4th Ave. SE., 57401–4382	605–226–7343
Albuquerque, NM	P.O. Box 26567, 615 1st St. NW., 87125–6567	505–766–3170
Anadarko, OK	P.O. Box 368, WCD Office Complex, Hwy. 8, 75003	405–247–6673
Billings, MT	316 N. 26th St., 59101–1397	406–657–6315

Area Offices—Bureau of Indian Affairs—Continued

Area	Address	Telephone
Eastern Area	Suite 260, 3701 N. Fairfax Dr., Arlington, VA 22203	703–235–2571
Juneau, AK	Suite 5, 9109 Mendenhall Rd., 99802–5520	907–586–7177
Minneapolis, MN	331 S. 2d Ave., 55401–2241	612–349–3631
Muskogee, OK	Old Federal Bldg., 5th and W. Okmulgee, 74401–4898	918–687–2296
Navajo Area	P.O. Box M, WR–1, BIA Bldg., Window Rock Blvd., Window Rock, AZ 86515–0714.	602–871–5151
	P.O. Box 1060, Gallup, NM 87305	505–863–8314
Phoenix, AZ	P.O. Box 10, 1 N. 1st St., 85001–0010	602–379–6600
Portland, OR	911 NE. 11th Ave., 97232–4169	503–231–6702
Sacramento, CA	2800 Cottage Way, 95825–1884	916–484–4682

For further information, contact the Public Affairs Office, Bureau of Indian Affairs, Department of the Interior, Washington, DC 20240. Phone, 202–208–3710.

Minerals Management Service

The Minerals Management Service was established on January 19, 1982, by Secretarial Order 3071, under the authority provided by section 2 of Reorganization Plan No. 3 of 1950 (5 U.S.C. app.), and further amended on May 10 and May 26, 1982.

Secretarial Order 3087, dated December 3, 1982, and amendment 1, dated February 7, 1983, provided for the transfer of royalty and mineral revenue management functions, including collection and distribution, to the Minerals Management Service and transferred all onshore minerals management functions on Federal and Indian lands to the Bureau of Land Management.

The Service assesses the nature, extent, recoverability, and value of leasable minerals on the Outer Continental Shelf. It ensures the orderly and timely inventory and development, as well as the efficient recovery, of mineral resources; encourages utilization of the best available and safest technology; provides for fair, full, and accurate returns to the Federal Treasury for produced commodities; and safeguards against fraud, waste, and abuse.

Offshore Minerals Management   The Service is responsible for resource evaluation, environmental review, leasing activities (including public liaison and planning functions), lease management, and inspection and enforcement programs for Outer Continental Shelf lands.

Five-year oil and gas leasing programs are developed for leasing on the Outer Continental Shelf in consultation with the Congress, the 23 coastal States, local governments, environmental groups, industry, and the public.

The Service conducts extensive environmental studies and consultations with State officials prior to issuing leases. Once leases have been issued, inspectors conduct frequent inspections of offshore operations, and environmental studies personnel collect more data to ensure that marine environments are kept free of pollutants.

Royalty Management   The Service is responsible for the collection and distribution of all royalty payments, rentals, bonus payments, fines, penalties, assessments, and other revenues due the Federal Government and Indian lessors as monies or royalties-in-kind from the extraction of mineral resources from Federal and Indian lands onshore and from the leasing and extraction of mineral resources on the Outer Continental Shelf.

The revenues generated by minerals leasing are one of the largest nontax sources of income to the Federal Government. As specified by law, these revenues are distributed to the States, to the general fund of the Treasury, and to Indian tribes and allottees.

The basic organization of the Service consists of a headquarters in Washington, DC, with program components located in Herndon, VA; the Royalty Management Program, headquartered in Lakewood, CO; three Outer Continental Shelf regional offices; and two administrative service centers.

Field Offices—Minerals Management Service

Office	Address	Telephone
ROYALTY MANAGEMENT PROGRAM ...	P.O. Box 25165, Denver, CO 80225–0165	303–231–3058
OCS Regional Offices		
ALASKA REGION	Rm. 110, 949 E. 36th Ave., Anchorage, AK 99508–4302	907–271–6010
GULF OF MEXICO REGION	1201 Elmwood Park Blvd., New Orleans, LA 70123–2394	504–736–2589
PACIFIC REGION	770 Paseo Camarillo, Camarillo, CA 93010–6064	805–389–7502
Administrative Service Centers		
WESTERN SERVICE CENTER	P.O. Box 25165, Denver, CO 80225–0165	303–275–7300
SOUTHERN SERVICE CENTER	1201 Elmwood Park Blvd., New Orleans, LA 70123–2394	504–736–2616

For further information, contact the Office of Communications and Governmental Affairs, Room 4260, (MS 4013), 1849 C Street NW., Washington, DC 20240–7000. Phone, 202–208–3985.

Bureau of Land Management

The Bureau of Land Management (BLM) was established July 16, 1946, by the consolidation of the General Land Office (created in 1812) and the Grazing Service (formed in 1934).

The Federal Land Policy and Management Act of 1976 (90 Stat. 2743) repealed and replaced many obsolete or overlapping statutes. It provides a basic mission statement for the Bureau and establishes policy guidelines and criteria for the management of public lands and resources administered by the Bureau.

The Bureau's basic organization consists of a headquarters in Washington, DC, a Service Center in Denver, CO, a Fire Center in Boise, ID, and a Training Center in Phoenix, AZ, which have BLM-wide support responsibilities; and a field organization of State, district, and resource area offices. The Bureau also utilizes a system of advisory councils to assist in the development of management plans and policies.

The Bureau is responsible for the total management of more than 270 million acres of public lands. These lands are located primarily in the West and Alaska; however, small scattered parcels are located in other States. In addition to minerals management responsibilities on the public lands, BLM is also responsible for subsurface resource management of an additional 300 million acres where mineral rights are owned by the Federal Government.

Resources managed by the Bureau include timber, solid minerals, oil and gas, geothermal energy, wildlife habitat, endangered plant and animal species, rangeland vegetation, recreation and cultural values, wild and scenic rivers, designated conservation and wilderness areas, and open space. Bureau programs provide for the protection (including fire suppression), orderly development, and use of the public lands and resources under principles of multiple use and sustained yield. Land use plans are developed with public involvement to provide orderly use and development while maintaining and enhancing the quality of the environment. The Bureau also manages watersheds to protect soil and enhance water quality; develops recreational opportunities on public lands; administers programs to protect and manage wild horses and burros; and, under certain conditions, makes land available for sale to individuals, organizations, local governments, and other Federal agencies when such transfer is in the public interest. Lands may be leased to State and local government agencies and to nonprofit organizations for certain purposes.

The Bureau oversees and manages the development of energy and mineral leases and ensures compliance with applicable regulations governing the extraction of these resources.

The Bureau has responsibility to issue rights-of-way, in certain instances, for crossing Federal lands under other agencies' jurisdiction. It also has general enforcement authority.

The Bureau is responsible for the survey of Federal lands and establishes and maintains public land records and records of mining claims. It administers a program of payments in lieu of taxes based on the amount of federally owned

lands in counties and other units of local government.

Field Offices—Bureau of Land Management

State Office	Address	Telephone
ALASKA—Alaska	No. 13, 222 W. 7th Ave., Anchorage, AK 99513–7599	907–271–5076
ARIZONA—Arizona	P.O. Box 16563, 3707 N. 7th St., Phoenix, AZ 85011	602–650–0500
CALIFORNIA—California	Rm. E–2841, 2800 Cottage Way, Sacramento, CA 95825	916–979–2845
COLORADO—Colorado	2850 Youngfield St., Lakewood, CO 80215–7076	303–239–3700
EASTERN STATES—All States bordering on and east of the Mississippi River.	7450 Boston Blvd., Springfield, VA 22153	703–440–1700
IDAHO—Idaho	3380 Americana Ter., Boise, ID 83706	208–384–3001
MONTANA—Montana, North Dakota, South Dakota.	P.O. Box 36800, 222 N. 32d St., Billings, MT 59107–6800	406–255–2904
NEVADA—Nevada	P.O. Box 12000, 850 Harvard Way, Reno, NV 89520–0006	702–785–6590
NEW MEXICO—Kansas, New Mexico, Oklahoma, Texas.	P.O. Box 27115, 1474 Rodeo Rd., Santa Fe, NM 87502–0115.	505–438–7501
OREGON—Oregon, Washington	P.O. Box 2965, 1515 SW. 5th Ave, Portland, OR 97208–2965.	503–952–6024
UTAH—Utah	P.O. Box 45155, 324 S. State St., Salt Lake City, UT 84145–1550.	801–539–4010
WYOMING—Nebraska, Wyoming	P.O. Box 1828, 2515 Warren Ave., Cheyenne, WY 82003	307–775–6001
Service and Support Offices		
NATIONAL INTERAGENCY FIRE CENTER	3833 South Development Ave., Boise, ID 83705–5354	208–387–5446
DENVER SERVICE CENTER	Denver Federal Center Bldg. 50, P.O. Box 25047, Denver, CO 80225–0047.	303–236–6452

For further information, contact the Office of Public Affairs, Bureau of Land Management, Department of the Interior, Washington, DC 20240. Phone, 202–208–3435.

Bureau of Reclamation

The mission of the Bureau of Reclamation is to manage, develop, and protect, for the public welfare, water and related resources in an environmentally and economically sound manner.

The Reclamation Act of 1902 (43 U.S.C. 371 *et seq.*) authorized the Secretary of the Interior to administer a reclamation program that would provide the arid and semiarid lands of the 17 contiguous Western States a secure, year-round water supply for irrigation. To perform the mission, the Reclamation Service was created within the United States Geological Survey. In 1907 the Reclamation Service was separated from the Survey, and in 1923 was renamed the Bureau of Reclamation.

The Reclamation program has helped to settle and develop the West by providing for sustained economic growth, an improved environment, and an enhanced quality of life through the development of a water storage and delivery infrastructure, which provides safe and dependable water supplies and hydroelectric power for agricultural, municipal, and industrial users; protects and improves water quality; provides recreational and fish and wildlife

benefits; enhances river regulations; and helps control damaging floods.

With this infrastructure largely in place, the Reclamation program is now focusing greater emphasis on resource management and protection than on development. Following a balanced approach to the stewardship of the West's water and related land and energy resources, the Bureau:

—works in partnership with others to develop water conservation plans, provide for the efficient and effective use of water and related resources, and improve the management of existing water resources;

—designs and constructs water resources projects, as authorized by the Congress;

—helps to develop and supports or enhances recreational uses at Reclamation projects;

—conducts research and encourages technology transfer to improve resource management, development, and protection;

—ensures that the lands it manages are free from hazardous and toxic waste and assists other Federal and State agencies in protecting and restoring surface water and ground water resources from hazardous waste contamination;

—operates and maintains its facilities to ensure reliability, safety, and economic operation to protect the public, property, and the Nation's investment in the facilities, and to preserve and enhance environmental resources; and

—provides engineering and technical support to Federal and State agencies, to Native American tribes, and to other nations to help accomplish national, regional, and international resource

management, development, and protection objectives.

Through contracts with project beneficiaries, the Bureau arranges repayment to the Federal Treasury for construction, operation, and maintenance costs. Approximately 80 percent of all direct project costs are repaid to the Government.

Reclamation project facilities in operation include 355 storage reservoirs, 69,400 miles of canals and other water conveyances and distribution facilities, and 52 hydroelectric powerplants.

Major Offices—Bureau of Reclamation

Office/Region	Address	Telephone
COMMISSIONER	Rm. 7654, Department of the Interior, Washington, DC 20240–0001.	202–208–4157
RECLAMATION SERVICE CENTER	Bldg. 67, Box 25007, Denver, CO 80225	303–236–7000
GREAT PLAINS REGION	Box 36900, 316 N. 26th St., Billings, MT 59107	406–247–7608
LOWER COLORADO REGION	Box 61470, Nevada Hwy. and Park St., Boulder City, NV 89005.	702–293–8420
MID–PACIFIC REGION	2800 Cottage Way, Sacramento, CA 95825	916–979–2837
PACIFIC NORTHWEST REGION	1150 N. Curtis Rd., Boise, ID 83706	208–378–5020
UPPER COLORADO REGION	Box 11568, 125 S. State St., Salt Lake City, UT 84147	801–524–6477

For further information, contact the Public Affairs Division, Bureau of Reclamation, Department of the Interior, Washington, DC 20240–0001. Phone, 202–208–4662.

Sources of Information

Inquiries on the following subjects should be directed to the specified office, Department of the Interior, Washington, DC 20240.

Contracts Contact the Office of Acquisition and Property Management, Room 5526. Phone, 202–208–6431.

Departmental Museum Provides information regarding departmental activities. Publications and other literature are available to the public free of charge. Located in Room 1238 (Museum), Main Interior Building. Phone, 202–208–4743.

Employment Direct general inquiries to the Office of Personnel or visit any of the field personnel offices.

Publications Most departmental publications are available from the Superintendent of Documents, Government Printing Office, Washington, DC 20402. All other inquiries regarding publications should be directed to the individual bureau or

office's publications or public affairs office.

Information regarding bibliographies on select subjects is available from the Information Services Branch of the Natural Resources Library. Phone, 202–208–5815.

Reading Room Natural Resources Library, Main Interior Building. Phone, 202–208–5815.

Telephone Directory The Department of the Interior telephone directory is available for sale by the Superintendent of Documents, Government Printing Office, Washington, DC 20402,

United States Fish and Wildlife Service

Inquiries on the following subjects should be directed to the specified office, U.S. Fish and Wildlife Service, Department of the Interior, Washington, DC 20240.

Contracts Contact the Washington, DC, headquarters Division of

Contracting and General Services (phone, 703–358–1728); or any of the regional offices.

Employment   For information regarding employment opportunities with the U.S. Fish and Wildlife Service, contact the Headquarters Personnel Office (phone, 703–358–1743); or the regional office within the area you are seeking employment.

Import/Export Permits   To obtain CITES permits for the import and export of wildlife, contact the Office of Management Authority. Phone, 703–358–2104.

Public and News Media Inquiries Specific information about the U.S. Fish and Wildlife Service and its activities is available from the Office of Current Information (phone, 202–208–5634); or the public affairs officer in each of the Service's regional offices.

Publications   The U.S. Fish and Wildlife Service has publications available on subjects ranging from the National Wildlife Refuge System to endangered species. Some publications are only available as sales items from the Superintendent of Documents, Government Printing Office, Washington, DC 20402. Further information is available from the Publications Unit, U.S. Fish and Wildlife Service, Washington, DC 20240. Phone, 703–358–1711.

National Park Service

Contracts   Contact the nearest regional office, Administrative Services Division, National Park Service, P.O. Box 37127, Washington, DC 20013–7127 (phone, 202–523–5133); or the Denver Service Center, P.O. Box 25287, 12795 West Alameda Parkway, Denver, CO 80225 (phone, 303–969–2110).

Employment   Employment inquiries and applications may be sent to the Personnel Office, National Park Service, Department of the Interior, Washington, DC, and to the field area offices and individual parks. Applications for seasonal employment (which must be received between September 1 and January 15) should be sent to the Division of Personnel Management,

National Park Service, P.O. Box 37127, Washington, DC 20013–7127. Phone, 202–208–5074. Schools interested in the recruitment program should write to: Chief Personnel Officer, National Park Service, P.O. Box 37127, Department of the Interior, Washington, DC 20013–7127. Phone, 202–208–5093

Films   The National Park Service has many films on environmental and historical themes. For a list of these films and sales and for information on how to obtain them, write: National Technical Information Center, Springfield, VA 22161. Phone, 703–487–4650.

Grants-in-Aid   For information on grants authorized under the Land and Water Conservation Fund, the Urban Park and Recreation Recovery Program, and the Historic Preservation Fund, write the National Park Service, P.O. Box 37127, Washington, DC 20013–7127. Phone, 202–343–3700 or 202–343–9564.

Publications   Items related to the National Park Service are available from the Superintendent of Documents, Government Printing Office, Washington, DC 20402. Items include *The National Park System Map & Guide, The National Parks: Index 1993, National Parks: Lesser Known Areas,* and *The Civil War at a Glance,* an official handbook series highlighting specific parks, publications in archaeology, several commemorative posters, and thematic brochures. Contact the Consumer Information Center, Pueblo, CO 81009, for other publications about the National Park Service. For general park and camping information, write to the National Park Service, Office of Public Inquiries, P.O. Box 37127, Room 3424, Washington, DC 20013–7127.

United States Bureau of Mines

Contracts   Contact the Branch of Procurement, United States Bureau of Mines, Department of the Interior, 810 Seventh Street NW., Washington, DC 20241. Phone, 202–501–9259.

Employment   For information on employment opportunities throughout the United States, contact the Chief, Division of Personnel, United States Bureau of Mines, Department of the

Interior, 810 Seventh Street NW., Washington, DC 20241. Phone, 202–501–9600.

Films Requests for film loans should be directed to: Motion Pictures, United States Bureau of Mines, P.O. Box 18070, Cochrans Mill Road, Pittsburgh, PA 15236. Phone, 412–892–6845.

Publications *Mineral Industry Surveys* (monthly, quarterly and annual), *Metal Industry Indicators* (economic newsletter), bimonthly list of *New Publications of the Bureau of Mines* and *Technology News* (periodic fact sheet) can be obtained without charge from the U.S. Bureau of Mines, Branch of Production and Distribution, P.O. Box 18070, Cochrans Mill Road, Pittsburgh, PA 15236. *Commodity and State Annual Reports, Mineral Yearbooks* in three volumes (Vol. I—Metals and Minerals, Vol. II—Domestic, and Vol. III—International), *U.S. Bureau of Mines Publications and Articles* (listing), and *Special Publications* (e.g, *Mineral Commodity Summaries*, *CD-ROM's*, etc.) can be purchased from the Superintendent of Documents, U.S. Government Printing Office, P.O. Box 371954, Pittsburgh, PA 15250–7954.

Information on other Bureau of Mines publications is available from the Superintendent of Documents, U.S. Government Printing Office, Mail Stop SSOM, Washington, DC 20402. Paper and microfiche copies of most publications, such as reports of investigations, bulletins, information circulars, U.S. Bureau of Mines publications and articles (listing), and special publications, etc., issued after 1970 are available from the National Technical Information Service, 5285 Port Royal Road, Springfield, VA 22161. Phone, 703–487–4650.

Electronic Information Commodity statistics, abstracts of publications, bimonthly lists of publications, and other information are available through the following three systems:

Internet Access: To use the U.S.

Bureau of Mines Gopher server on Internet, connect to: **gopher.usbm.gov** port 70, using gopher client software; or contact the Systems Administrator for technical questions on 412–892–6499, or **klevemmc@miner.usbm.gov**

Mines Data: Computer bulletin board. Log on via modem through 202–501–0373, or call 202–501–0406 for technical assistance.

Mines FaxBack: Return fax service. Use the touch-tone handset attached to your fax machine's telephone jack. (ISDN [digital] telephones cannot be used with fax machines.) Dial 202–219–3644. Listen to the menu options and punch in the number of your selection, using the touch-tone telephone. After completing your selection, press the start button on your fax machine.

United States Geological Survey

Contracts, Grants, and Cooperative Agreements Write to the Administrative Division, Office of Procurement and Contracts, 205 National Center, 12201 Sunrise Valley Drive, Reston, VA 22092. Phone, 703–648–7373.

Employment Inquiries should be directed to one of the following Personnel Offices:

Recruitment and Placement, 215 National Center, 12201 Sunrise Valley Dr., Reston, VA 22092. Phone, 703–648–6131.

Personnel Office, United States Geological Survey, Suite 160, 3850 Holcomb Bridge Rd., Norcross, GA 30092. Phone, 404–409–7750.

Personnel Office, United States Geological Survey, 1400 Independence Rd., Rolla, MO 65401. Phone, 314–341–0810.

Personnel Office, United States Geological Survey, Denver Federal Ctr., Bldg. 25, Denver, CO 80225. Phone, 303–236–5900.

Personnel Office, United States Geological Survey, 345 Middlefield Rd., Menlo Park, CA 94025. Phone, 415–329–4104.

General Inquiries A network of 10 earth science Information Centers (ESIC's) responds to requests for Earth science information that are made in person, by mail, or by telephone and assists in the selection and ordering of all U.S. Geological Survey products:

Rm. 101, 4230 University Dr., Anchorage, AK 99508–4664. Phone, 907–786–7011.

Rm. 3128, Bldg. 3 (MS 532), 345 Middlefield Rd., Menlo Park, CA 94025. Phone, 415–329–4309.

Box 25046, (MS 504), Denver Federal Ctr., Denver, CO 80225. Phone, 303–236–5829.

Rm. 2650, Dept. of the Interior Bldg., 1849 C St. NW., Washington, DC 20240. Phone, 202–208–4047.

Bldg. 3101, Stennis Space Ctr., Bay St. Louis, MS 39529. Phone, 601–688–3544.

(MS 231), 1400 Independence Rd., Rolla, MO 65401. Phone, 314–341–0851.

2d Fl., 2222 W. 2300 S., Salt Lake City, UT 84119. Phone, 801–975–3742.

Rm. 1C402, 507 National Ctr., 12201 Sunrise Valley Dr., Reston, VA 22092. Phone, 703–648–6045.

Rm. 135, U.S. Post Office Bldg., W. 904 Riverside Ave., Spokane, WA 99201. Phone, 509–353–2524.

EROS Data Center, Sioux Falls, SD 57198. Phone, 605–594–6151.

Maps Maps are sold by the Branch of Distribution, United States Geological Survey, Box 25286, Denver Federal Center, Denver, CO 80225 (phone, 303–236–7477); and the Earth Science Information Centers (*see* General Inquiries). Information about the status of U.S. Geological Survey mapping in any State and availability of maps by other Federal and State agencies can be obtained from the Earth Science Information Center, 507 National Center, 12201 Sunrise Valley Drive, Reston, VA 22092. Phone, 800–USA–MAPS; or in Virginia, 703–648–6045.

Outreach/External and Media Affairs The Public Affairs Office of the U.S. Geological Survey coordinates external contacts and special events, responds to news media inquiries, arranges interviews, and prepares news and releases and other informational products pertaining to Survey programs and activities. The headquarters office is located at 119 National Center, 12201 Sunrise Valley Drive, Reston, VA 22092. Phone, 703–648–4460. News media service also is available in Menlo Park—San Francisco. Phone, 415–329–4000.

Publications The U.S. Geological Survey publishes technical and scientific reports and maps, described in the monthly periodical *New Publications of the U.S. Geological Survey*, with yearly supplements; *Publications of the U.S. Geological Survey, 1879–1961*; *Publications of the Geological Survey, 1962–1970*; and a variety of nontechnical publications described in *General Interest Publications of the United States Geological Survey*.

Book and Digital Data Series (CD–ROM) publications are sold by the U.S. Geological Survey's Branch of Distribution, Denver Federal Center, Box 25286, Denver, CO 80225 (phone, 303–236–7477), and by the U.S. Geological Survey's Earth Science Information Centers (*see* General Inquiries).

Open-file reports, in the form of microfiche and/or black and white paper copies, diskettes, and CD–ROM's are sold by the United States Geological Survey, Open File Reports—ESIC, Denver Federal Center, Box 25425, Denver, CO 80225. Phone, 303–236–7476.

Single copies of a variety of nontechnical leaflets, technical reports, books, and special interest publications on Earth science subjects and U.S. Geological Survey activities are available to the public upon request from the United States Geological Survey, Branch of Distribution, Denver Federal Center, Box 25286, Denver, CO 80225. Phone, 303–236–7477. Bulk quantities may be purchased from the Superintendent of Documents, Government Printing Office, Washington, DC 20402.

Reading Rooms Facilities for examination of reports, maps, publications of the U.S. Geological Survey, and a wide selection of general Earth science information resources and historical documents are located at the U.S. Geological Survey's libraries at the National Center, 12201 Sunrise Valley Drive, Reston, VA 22092; Denver Federal Center, Building 20, Box 25046, Denver, CO 80225; 345 Middlefield Road, Menlo Park, CA 94025; and 2255 North Gemini Drive, Flagstaff, AZ 86001; and Earth Science Information Centers (*see* General Inquiries). Maps, aerial photographs, geodetic control data or index material, and cartographic data in digital form may be examined at the following Earth Science Information Centers:

Rm. 1C402, 507 National Center, 12201 Sunrise Valley Dr., Reston, VA 22092. 1400 Independence Rd., Rolla, MO 65401. Bldg. 3101, Stennis Space Ctr., MS 39529. Box 25046, Bldg. 25, (MS 504), Lakewood Center, Denver Federal Ctr., Denver, CO 80225. 345 Middlefield Rd., Menlo Park, CA 94025. 4230 University Dr., Anchorage, AK 99508–4664.

Spacecraft and aircraft remote sensor data may be examined at the EROS Data Center, Sioux Falls, SD 57198. Phone, 605–594–6151.

Water Data   Information on the availability of and access to water data acquired by the U.S. Geological Survey and other local, State, and Federal agencies may be obtained from the National Water Data Exchange, 421 National Center, 12201 Sunrise Valley Drive, Reston, VA 22092. Phone, 703–648–5663.

Office of Surface Mining Reclamation and Enforcement

Contracts   Contact the Procurement Branch, Office of Surface Mining, Department of the Interior, 1951 Constitution Avenue NW., Washington, DC 20240. Phone, 202–343–4685. TDD, 202–208–2737.

Employment   For information on employment opportunities throughout the United States, contact the Chief, Division of Personnel, Office of Surface Mining, Department of the Interior, 1951 Constitution Avenue NW., Washington, DC 20240. Phone, 202–208–2965. TDD, 202–208–2737.

Bureau of Indian Affairs

Inquiries regarding the Bureau of Indian Affairs may be obtained by calling the Office of Public Affairs at 202–208–3710, or writing to the Chief, Office of Public Affairs, 1849 C Street, NW., Mailstop 1340 MIB, Washington, DC 20240,

Minerals Management Service

Inquiries on specific subjects should be directed to the appropriate headquarters office at 1849 C Street NW., Washington, DC 20240, or to the appropriate Minerals Management Service field office.

Public and News Media Inquiries   Specific information about the Minerals Management Service and its activities is available from the Chief, Office of Communications and Governmental Affairs, Room 4260, (MS 4013), 1849 C Street NW., Washington, DC 20240.

Bureau of Land Management

Contracts   Contracts in excess of $25,000 for public land projects are awarded by the Contracting Office of the Denver Service Center. Phone, 303–969–6502. Contracts for Federal information processing are awarded by the Information Resources Acquisition Branch of the Denver Service Center. Phone, 303–236–6498. Contracts for public land projects in the States of Oregon and Washington are awarded by the Contracting Office in Portland, OR. Phone, 503–952–6216.

Employment   Initial appointments to the Bureau are made from registers established by the Office of Personnel Management as a result of examination announcements issued by area offices of the Office of Personnel Management throughout the country. The following Office of Personnel Management announcements are applicable to most professional positions within the Bureau. Announcement No. 421, Biological and Agricultural Sciences; Announcement No. 424, Engineering, Physical Sciences and Related Professions. The Mid-Level and Senior-Level registers are also used in a limited number of cases for social sciences professionals and other positions.

Inquiries should be directed to the Service Center, any Bureau of Land Management State Office, or to the Personnel Officer, Bureau of Land Management, Department of the Interior, Washington, DC, from whom the booklet *Career Opportunities in the BLM* is available.

General Inquiries   The Bureau occasionally sells tracts of land, but generally by public auction and never for less than fair market value. It acts as the leasing agent for mineral rights on public and other federally administered lands. Information may be obtained from any of the State offices or from the Bureau of Land Management, Office of Public Affairs, Department of the Interior, Washington, DC 20240. Phone, 202–208–3435.

Publications   The annual publication *Public Land Statistics,* which relates to public lands, is available from the Superintendent of Documents, Government Printing Office, Washington, DC 20402.

Reading Rooms   All State offices provide facilities for individuals who wish to examine status records, tract books, or other records relating to the public lands and their resources.

Small Business Activities   The Bureau has four major buying offices that provide contacts for small business activities. The Service Center Branches of Procurement (phone, 303–969–6502) and Information Resources Acquisition (phone, 303–236–6498) are responsible for the western States' activities, except for Oregon (phone, 503–952–6218), which is a major buying office. All other small business contacts may be made to the small business specialist at the Eastern States office (phone, 703–440–1596); or the Washington office of the Bureau (phone, 202–452–5170).

Speakers   Local Bureau offices will arrange for speakers to explain Bureau programs upon request from organizations within their areas of jurisdiction.

Bureau of Reclamation

Contracts   The Advance Construction Bulletin and Advance Equipment Bulletin give information to contractors, manufacturers, and suppliers. Available from the Acquisition and Assistance Division, Building 67, Denver Federal Center, Denver, CO 80225. Phone, 303–236–8040 (ext. 227).

Employment   Information on engineering and other positions is available from the Personnel Office, Denver (phone, 303–236–3834); or from the nearest regional office.

Publications   Publications for sale are available through the National Technical Information Service. Phone, 1–800–553–6847.

Speakers and Films   A volunteer speaker service provides engineers and scientists for schools and civic groups in the Denver area. Films are available on free loan. For speakers or films, contact the Reclamation Service Center in Denver, CO (phone, 303–236–7000).

DEPARTMENT OF JUSTICE

Tenth Street and Constitution Avenue NW., Washington, DC 20530
Phone, 202–514–2000

THE ATTORNEY GENERAL	JANET RENO
Chief of Staff	JOHN M. HOGAN
Confidential Assistant to the Attorney General	BESSIE L. MEADOWS
Assistants to the Attorney General	ROXIE LOPEZ, DONNA F. TEMPLETON
Special Assistant to the Attorney General	ELIZABETH HYMAN
White House Fellow	YVONNE CAMPOS
Deputy Attorney General	JAMIE S. GORELICK
Confidential Assistant	PATRICIA A. BINNINGER
Principal Associate Deputy Attorney General	MERRICK B. GARLAND
Executive Assistant and Counsel	DENNIS M. CORRIGAN
Associate Deputy Attorneys General	ANDREW FOIS, DAVID MARGOLIS, MARK R. STEINBERG, SETH WAXMAN
Special Counsel, Financial Institution Fraud	GERALD M. STERN
Counsels to the Attorney General	ROGER C. ADAMS, ELIZABETH R. FINE, PAUL J. FISHMAN, BETH A. WILKINSON, GERRI LYNN RATLIFF
Special Assistants to the Deputy Attorney General	CASEY COOPER, AMY JEFFRESS, GEOFFREY KLINEBERG, CHARLES S. SGRO
Director, Executive Office for National Security	MARK R. STEINBERG
Counsel, International Programs	DREW C. ARENA
Associate Attorney General	JOHN R. SCHMIDT
Confidential Assistant	CATHERINE E. GALLAGHER
Principal Deputy Associate Attorney General	NANCY E. MCFADDEN
Deputy Associate Attorneys General	PAUL R. FRIEDMAN, JOHN C. DWYER, FRANCIS M. ALLEGRA
Assistant Associate Attorneys General	JOAN SILVERSTEIN, JAMES VIGIL, JR., KEVIN HYNES
Special Assistants to the Associate Attorney General	ERIK REID
Director, Office of Violence Against Women	BONNIE CAMPBELL
Solicitor General	DREW S. DAYS III
Inspector General	MICHAEL BROMWICH
Assistant Attorney General, Office of Legal Counsel	WALTER E. DELLINGER
Assistant Attorney General, Office of Legislative Affairs	KENT MARKUS, *Acting*
Assistant Attorney General, Office of Policy Development	ELEANOR D. ACHESON
Assistant Attorney General for Administration	STEPHEN R. COLGATE
Assistant Attorney General, Antitrust Division	ANNE K. BINGAMAN

339

Assistant Attorney General, Civil Division	FRANK W. HUNGER
Assistant Attorney General, Civil Rights Division	DEVAL L. PATRICK
Assistant Attorney General, Criminal Division	JO ANN HARRIS
Assistant Attorney General, Environment and Natural Resources Division	LOIS J. SCHIFFER
Assistant Attorney General, Tax Division	LORETTA C. ARGRETT
Assistant Attorney General, Office of Justice Programs	LAURIE ROBINSON
Director, Office of Public Affairs	CARL L. STERN
Directors, Office of Information and Privacy	RICHARD L. HUFF
	DANIEL J. METCALFE
Director, Executive Office for U.S. Attorneys	CAROL DIBATTISTE
Director, Bureau of Prisons	KATHLEEN M. HAWK
Director, Federal Bureau of Investigation	LOUIS J. FREEH
Director, United States Marshals Service	EDUARDO GONZALEZ
Director, Executive Office for Immigration Review	ANTHONY C. MOSCATO
Director, Executive Office for United States Trustees	JOSEPH PATCHAN
Director, Community Relations Service	JEFFREY L. WEISS, *Acting*
Director, Community Orienting Policing Services	JOSEPH BRANN
Administrator, Drug Enforcement Administration	THOMAS A. CONSTANTINE
Commissioner, Immigration and Naturalization Service	DORIS MEISSNER
Chairman, United States Parole Commission	EDWARD F. REILLY, JR.
Chairman, Foreign Claims Settlement Commission	DELISSA A. RIDGWAY
Chief, INTERPOL–U.S. National Central Bureau	SHELLEY G. ALTENSTADTER
Counsel, Office of Intelligence Policy and Review	RICHARD SCRUGGS
Counsel, Office of Professional Responsibility	MICHAEL E. SHAHEEN, JR.
Pardon Attorney	MARGARET C. LOVE

[For the Department of Justice statement of organization, see the *Code of Federal Regulations,* Title 28, Chapter I, Part 0]

As the largest law firm in the Nation, the Department of Justice serves as counsel for its citizens. It represents them in enforcing the law in the public interest. Through its thousands of lawyers, investigators, and agents, the Department plays the key role in protection against criminals and subversion, in ensuring healthy competition of business in our free enterprise system, in safeguarding the consumer, and in enforcing drug, immigration, and naturalization laws. The Department also plays a significant role in protecting citizens through its efforts for effective law enforcement, crime prevention, crime detection, and prosecution and rehabilitation of offenders.

Moreover, the Department conducts all suits in the Supreme Court in which the United States is concerned. It represents the Government in legal matters generally, rendering legal advice and opinions, upon request, to the President and to the heads of the executive departments. The Attorney General supervises and directs these activities, as well as those of the U.S. attorneys and U.S. marshals in the various judicial districts around the country.

DEPARTMENT OF JUSTICE

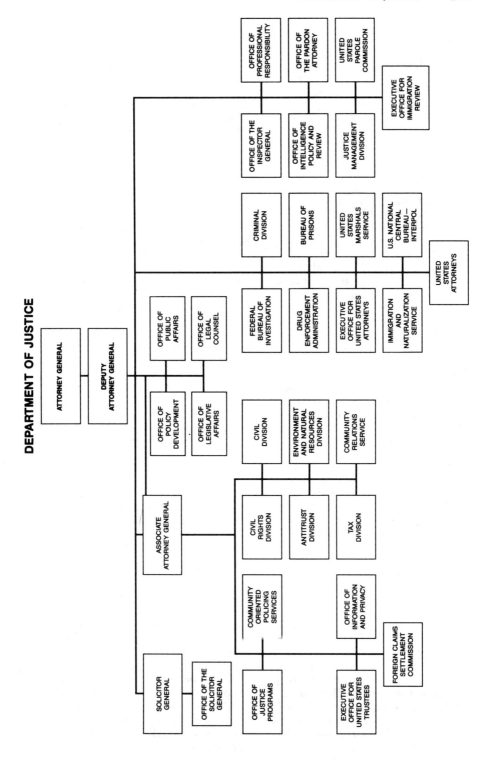

- ATTORNEY GENERAL
- DEPUTY ATTORNEY GENERAL
- OFFICE OF PUBLIC AFFAIRS
- OFFICE OF LEGAL COUNSEL
- OFFICE OF POLICY DEVELOPMENT
- OFFICE OF LEGISLATIVE AFFAIRS
- ASSOCIATE ATTORNEY GENERAL
- SOLICITOR GENERAL
- OFFICE OF THE SOLICITOR GENERAL
- OFFICE OF PROFESSIONAL RESPONSIBILITY
- OFFICE OF THE PARDON ATTORNEY
- UNITED STATES PAROLE COMMISSION
- EXECUTIVE OFFICE FOR IMMIGRATION REVIEW
- OFFICE OF THE INSPECTOR GENERAL
- OFFICE OF INTELLIGENCE POLICY AND REVIEW
- JUSTICE MANAGEMENT DIVISION
- CRIMINAL DIVISION
- BUREAU OF PRISONS
- UNITED STATES MARSHALS SERVICE
- U.S. NATIONAL CENTRAL BUREAU—INTERPOL
- UNITED STATES ATTORNEYS
- FEDERAL BUREAU OF INVESTIGATION
- DRUG ENFORCEMENT ADMINISTRATION
- EXECUTIVE OFFICE FOR UNITED STATES ATTORNEYS
- IMMIGRATION AND NATURALIZATION SERVICE
- CIVIL DIVISION
- ENVIRONMENT AND NATURAL RESOURCES DIVISION
- COMMUNITY RELATIONS SERVICE
- CIVIL RIGHTS DIVISION
- ANTITRUST DIVISION
- TAX DIVISION
- COMMUNITY ORIENTED POLICING SERVICES
- OFFICE OF INFORMATION AND PRIVACY
- FOREIGN CLAIMS SETTLEMENT COMMISSION
- OFFICE OF JUSTICE PROGRAMS
- EXECUTIVE OFFICE FOR UNITED STATES TRUSTEES

The Department of Justice was established by act of June 22, 1870, as amended (28 U.S.C. 501, 503, 509 note), with the Attorney General as its head. Prior to 1870 the Attorney General was a member of the President's Cabinet, but not the head of a department, the office having been created under authority of act of September 24, 1789, as amended (28 U.S.C. 503).

The affairs and activities of the Department of Justice are generally directed by the Attorney General. The offices, divisions, bureaus, and boards of the Department follow.

Offices

Attorney General   The Attorney General, as head of the Department of Justice and chief law enforcement officer of the Federal Government, represents the United States in legal matters generally and gives advice and opinions to the President and to the heads of the executive departments of the Government when so requested. The Attorney General appears in person to represent the Government before the U.S. Supreme Court in cases of exceptional gravity or importance. The Office of the Attorney General oversees the Offices of Deputy Attorney General, Associate Attorneys General, Legal Counsel, and Inspector General, as well as the following offices whose public purposes are widely applied.

Solicitor General   The Solicitor General represents the U.S. Government in cases before the Supreme Court. He decides what cases the Government should ask the Supreme Court to review and what position the Government should take in cases before the Court. Also, he supervises the preparation of the Government's Supreme Court briefs and other legal documents and the conduct of the oral arguments in the Court. He or his staff argue most of the Government's cases in the Supreme Court. The Solicitor General's duties also include deciding whether the United States should appeal in all cases it loses before the lower courts.

Legal Counsel   The Assistant Attorney General in charge of the Office of Legal Counsel assists the Attorney General in fulfilling the Attorney General's function as legal adviser to the President and all the executive branch agencies. The Office drafts legal opinions of the Attorney General rendered in response to requests from the President and heads of the executive departments. It also provides its own written opinions and informal advice in response to requests from the various agencies of the Government, as well as offices within the Department and from Presidential staff and advisers, typically dealing with legal issues involving agency disagreements or with pending legislation. The Office also is responsible for providing legal advice to the executive branch on all constitutional questions.

All Executive orders and proclamations proposed to be issued by the President are reviewed by the Office of Legal Counsel for form and legality, as are various other matters that require the President's formal approval. In addition, the Office of Legal Counsel functions as general counsel for the Department. It reviews all proposed orders of the Attorney General and all regulations requiring the Attorney General's approval.

The Office coordinates the work of the Department with respect to treaties, executive agreements, and international organizations. It performs a variety of special assignments referred by the Attorney General or the Deputy Attorney General. However, it is not authorized to give legal advice to private persons.

Information and Privacy   The Office of Information and Privacy (OIP) operates under the supervision of a Director, who manages the Department's responsibilities related to the Freedom of Information Act (FOIA) and the Privacy

Act. These responsibilities include coordinating policy development and compliance Governmentwide for FOIA, and by the Department for the Privacy Act; and adjudicating all appeals from denials by any Department component of access to information under those acts. OIP also processes all initial requests under those acts for access to the records of the Offices of the Attorney General, Deputy Attorney General, Associate Attorney General, and other senior management offices of the Department.

Pardon Attorney   The Office of the Pardon Attorney, in consultation with the Attorney General or his designee, assists the President in the exercise of executive clemency as authorized under Article II, section 2, of the Constitution. Generally, all requests for executive clemency are directed to the Pardon Attorney for investigation and review. Executive clemency may take several forms, including pardon, commutation, remission of fine, and reprieve.

Community Relations Service   The Service was created by title X of the Civil Rights Act of 1964 (42 U.S.C. 2000g *et seq.*). Pursuant to Executive Order No. 12341 of January 21, 1982, the Attorney General expanded the Service's mandate to include responsibility for the Cuban/Haitian Entrant Program (CHEP), as authorized by subsection 501(c)(1)(A) of the Refugee Education Assistance Act of 1980 (8 U.S.C. 1522). The Community Relations Service is under the general authority of the Attorney General and is headed by a Director, appointed by the President with the advice and consent of the Senate.

The mission of the Service is to prevent and resolve community conflicts and reduce community tensions arising from actions, policies, and practices perceived to be discriminatory on the basis of race, color, or national origin. The Service offers assistance to communities in resolving disputes relating to race, color, or national origin and facilitates the development of viable agreements as alternatives to coercion, violence, or litigation. It also assists and supports communities in developing local mechanisms as proactive measures to prevent or reduce racial/ethnic tensions.

The services provided include conciliation, mediation, technical assistance, and training, and involve specialized procedures for preventing and resolving racial and ethnic conflicts. The Service provides assistance directly to people and their communities. It shows no partiality among disputing parties and, in promoting the principles and ideals of nondiscrimination, applies skills that allow parties to mediate their own disputes. The Service's conciliators, who are located in 10 regional offices and 3 field offices around the country, assist people of diverse racial and cultural backgrounds.

The Service offers its assistance either on its own motion, when in its judgment peaceful relations among the citizens of a community are threatened, or upon request of State or local officials or other interested persons. The Service seeks the cooperation of appropriate State and local, and public and private agencies in carrying out the agency's mission.

Under the Refugee Education and Assistance Act, the Community Relations Service provides assistance for the processing, care, and placement within the United States of Cuban and Haitian entrants. Working with voluntary and governmental agencies, the Service's headquarters and Miami field offices provide humanitarian relief for the successful resettlement of Cuban and Haitian entrants. These services include shelter care, child welfare, and family reunification for these individuals following their release from Immigration and Naturalization Service custody.

The Community Relations Service's Primary Resettlement Program provides transitional community-based refugee resettlement services to recently apprehended Haitian nationals paroled from detention at Immigration and Naturalization Service Processing Centers—primarily the Krome Service Processing Center in South Florida and the U.S. Naval Base at Guantanamo, Cuba—and to recently encountered and paroled Cuban nationals from ports throughout Florida, mostly the Key West coast guard station.

The Secondary Resettlement Program provides resettlement services, emphasizing employment placement and retention at specialized sites outside of Florida, to Cubans and Haitians whose initial resettlement in South Florida did not lead to self-sufficiency.

Under the Unaccompanied Minors Program, the Service has extensive experience in providing services to Cuban and Haitian minors apprehended by the Immigration and Naturalization Service (INS). Since 1986, under a memorandum of agreement with INS, the Community Relations Service has provided similar services to other alien minors detained at the Krome Service Processing Center in Miami, FL, and other detention facilities in Houston and Harlingen, TX.

The Community Relations Service provides residential shelter care; health services; and counseling, educational, recreational, and family reunification services to unaccompanied alien minors through grants to voluntary agencies. These services are provided in compliance with existing State child welfare standards and regulations. The Service's involvement ensures that alien children apprehended by INS are placed in safe and suitable environments.

Regional Offices—Community Relations Service

(Areas included within each region are indicated on the map in Appendix A.)

Region/Address	Director	Phone/FTS
1. Boston, MA (99 Summer St., 02110)	Martin A. Walsh	617–424–5715
2. New York, NY (26 Federal Plz., 10278)	Patricia Glenn	212–264–0700
3. Philadelphia, PA (2d and Chestnut Sts., 19106)	Jonathan Chace	215–597–2344
4. Atlanta, GA (75 Piedmont Ave. NE., 30303)	Ozell Sutton	404–331–6883
5. Chicago, IL (55 W. Monroe St., 60603)	Jesse Taylor	312–353–4391
6. Dallas, TX (1420 W. Mockingbird Ln., 75247)	Gilbert J. Chavez	214–655–8175
7. Kansas City, MO (323 W. 8th St., 64105)	Atkins Warren	816–374–6522
8. Denver, CO (1244 Speer Blvd., 80204–3584)	Leo Cardenas	303–844–2973
9. San Francisco, CA (33 New Montgomery St., 94105–4511)	Julian Klugman	415–744–6565
10. Seattle, WA (915 2d Ave., 98101)	Robert Lamb, Jr.	206–220–6700

For further information, contact any regional office or the Director, Community Relations Service, Department of Justice, Suite 330, 5550 Friendship Boulevard, Chevy Chase, MD 20815. Phone, 301–492–5929.

Justice Management Division Under the direction of the Assistant Attorney General for Administration, the Division provides assistance to senior management officials relating to basic Department policy for evaluation, budget and financial management, personnel management and training, equal opportunity programs, automatic data processing and telecommunications, security, records management, procurement, real property and materiel management, and for all other matters pertaining to organization, management, and administration.

The Division provides direct administrative support services, such as personnel, accounting, payroll, procurement, budget, and facilities and property management to the offices, boards, and divisions of the Department; and operates several central services, such as automated data processing and payroll. The Division supplies automated litigation support as required to the Department of Justice and to other Federal agencies involved in litigation.

The Division develops and promulgates Departmentwide policies, standards, and procedures for the management of automated information processing resources and for the directive system and reviews their implementation. The Division collects, organizes, and disseminates recorded information that is necessary for the Department to carry out its statutory mandate and provides general research and reference assistance regarding information to Department staff, other Government attorneys, and members of the public.

Professional Responsibility The Office of Professional Responsibility, which reports directly to the Attorney General, is responsible for investigating allegations of criminal or ethical misconduct by employees of the Justice Department. The Counsel on Professional Responsibility heads the Office, the role of which is to ensure that departmental employees continue to perform their duties in accordance with the high professional standards expected of the Nation's principal law enforcement agency.

All allegations against Department employees in attorney, criminal investigative, or law enforcement positions involving violations of law, departmental regulations, or departmental applicable standards of conduct, are reported to the Office of Professional Responsibility. At the Counsel's discretion, the Office frequently conducts its own investigations into those allegations.

The Office may also participate in or direct an investigation conducted by another component of the Department, or may simply monitor an investigation conducted by an appropriate agency having jurisdiction over the matter. In addition, the Office oversees the internal inspection operations of the Federal Bureau of Investigation and Drug Enforcement Administration.

The Counsel submits an annual report to the Attorney General that reviews and evaluates the Department's internal inspection units. The Counsel makes recommendations to the Attorney General on the need for changes in policies or procedures that become evident during the course of internal inquiries reviewed or initiated by the Office.

Intelligence Policy and Review The Office of Intelligence Policy and Review, under the direction of the Counsel to the Attorney General for Intelligence Policy, is responsible for advising the Attorney General on all matters relating to the national security activities of the United States. The Office also serves as adviser to the Attorney General and various client agencies, including the Central Intelligence Agency, the Federal Bureau of Investigation, the National Security Agency, and the Defense and State Departments, concerning questions of law, regulation, and guidelines as well as the legality of domestic and overseas intelligence operations.

The Office prepares and files all applications for surveillances and searches under the Foreign Intelligence Surveillance Act of 1978, assists Government agencies by providing legal advice on matters of national security law and policy and represents the Department of Justice on a variety of interagency committees. The Office also comments on and coordinates other agencies' views regarding proposed legislation affecting national security and intelligence matters.

The Office serves as adviser to the Attorney General and various client agencies, including the Central Intelligence Agency, the Federal Bureau of Investigation, the National Security Agency, and the Defense and State Departments, concerning questions of law, regulation, and guidelines as well as the legality of domestic and overseas intelligence operations.

Executive Office for United States Attorneys Under the supervision of the Deputy Attorney General and the direction of a Director, the Executive Office for United States Attorneys provides general executive assistance and nonlitigative oversight to the 94 offices of United States attorneys, including evaluating the performance of the offices of United States attorneys, making appropriate reports and taking corrective action where indicated, and coordinating and directing the relationships of the offices of the United States attorneys with other organizational units of the Department of Justice.

The Office supervises the operation of the Office of Legal Education, including the Attorney General's Advocacy Institute and the Legal Education Institute, which develops, conducts, and authorizes the training of Federal executive branch legal personnel and support staff. Administrative and logistic services, including the allocation of personnel, financial resources, and office automation equipment, are furnished to the offices of the United States attorneys. The Office supervises the implementation and administration of the Law Enforcement Coordination Program and of the Victim and Witness Protection Act. Direction and administrative support are provided to the Debt Collection Program and Debt Collection Criminal Fines.

The Office manages the appointment process of United States attorneys, assistant United States attorneys, and special assistant United States attorneys. The *United States Attorneys' Manual* and the *United States Attorneys' Bulletin* are published and maintained for the internal guidance of the United States attorneys' offices and those other organizational units of the Department concerned with litigation. The Office also provides legal opinions, interpretations, and advice to United States attorneys on topics such as budget, legislation, ethics, and Department guidelines.

U.S. Trustee Program   The U.S. Trustee Program acts in the public interest to promote the efficiency and to protect and preserve the integrity of the bankruptcy system. It works to secure the just, speedy, and economical resolution of bankruptcy cases; monitors the conduct of parties, takes action to ensure compliance with applicable laws and procedures, and identifies and investigates bankruptcy fraud and abuse; and oversees administrative functions in bankruptcy cases. The Program is funded by the U.S. Trustee System Fund, which consists mainly of filing fees paid by debtors invoking the protections of the bankruptcy laws.

The U.S. Trustees supervise the administration of four of the five types of bankruptcy proceedings defined under the Bankruptcy Code. These are:

—proceedings under chapter 7 in which the assets of the debtor are liquidated;

—reorganization proceedings under chapter 11 for rehabilitation of the business debtor;

—adjustments of debts of a family farmer with regular income under chapter 12; and

—adjustment of debts of an individual with regular income under chapter 13, pursuant to which an individual can discharge debts by arranging for payments over a period of time. The U.S. Trustee does not have a significant role in proceedings under chapter 9, which relates to the adjustment of debts of a municipality.

Specific responsibilities of the U.S. Trustees include:

—appointing and supervising the performance of private trustees in individual cases;

—appointing and convening creditors' committees in chapter 11 corporate reorganization cases;

—reviewing applications for the retention of professionals and the payment of fees;

—reviewing disclosure statements and submitting statements to the court regarding their adequacy;

—appointing trustees or examiners in such cases as needed;

—ensuring that the assets involved in bankruptcy cases are protected during the administration of cases;

—serving as trustees in chapters 7, 12, and 13 cases where private trustees are unwilling to serve; and

—presenting matters relating to the Bankruptcy Code in court.

Executive Office for U.S. Trustees   The Attorney General is charged with the appointment, supervision, and coordination of the U.S. Trustees and Assistant U.S. Trustees. Day-to-day policy and legal direction, coordination, and control are provided by the Director of the Executive Office for U.S. Trustees who is appointed by the Attorney General. The Executive Office also provides administrative and management support to individual U.S. Trustee Offices.

For further information, contact the Executive Office for U.S. Trustees, Department of Justice, Suite 700, 901 E Street NW., Washington, DC 20530. Phone, 202-307-1391.

Divisions

Antitrust Division

The Assistant Attorney General in charge of the Antitrust Division is responsible for promoting and maintaining competitive markets by enforcing the Federal antitrust laws. Such enforcement, which is the principal function of the Division, involves investigating possible antitrust violations, conducting grand jury proceedings, preparing and trying antitrust cases, prosecuting appeals, and negotiating and enforcing final judgments. The antitrust laws affect virtually all industries and apply to every phase of business, including manufacturing, transportation, distribution, and marketing. They prohibit a variety of practices that restrain trade, such as price-fixing conspiracies, corporate mergers likely to reduce the competitive vigor of particular markets, and predatory acts designed to achieve or maintain monopoly power. The Division prosecutes serious and willful violations of the antitrust laws by filing criminal suits that can lead to large fines and jail sentences. Where criminal prosecution is not appropriate, the Division seeks a court order forbidding future violations of the law and requiring steps by the defendant to remedy the anticompetitive effects of past violations.

The Division also is responsible for acting as an advocate of competition within the Federal Government. This involves formal appearances in Federal administrative agency proceedings, development of legislative initiatives to promote deregulation and eliminate unjustifiable exemptions from the antitrust laws, participation on executive branch policy task forces, and publication of reports on regulated industry performance. The Division provides formal advice to other agencies on the competitive implications of proposed transactions requiring Federal approval, such as construction of nuclear powerplants and mergers of financial institutions. It also consults with Federal agencies on a variety of other matters, including the issuance of Federal coal and oil drilling leases and the disposition of surplus Government property.

In addition, the Antitrust Division represents the United States in judicial proceedings to review certain orders of the Interstate Commerce Commission, Federal Maritime Commission, Federal Communications Commission, and Nuclear Regulatory Commission, and provides direct court representation for the Secretary of the Treasury in certain Bureau of Alcohol, Tobacco and Firearms cases. It also participates in Federal Trade Commission cases before the Supreme Court.

In the international law area, the Division represents the United States on the Committee on Competition Law and Policy of the Organization for Economic Cooperation and Development, participates in the United Nations Conference on Trade and Development, and, through the Department of State, maintains liaison with foreign governments on antimonopoly laws and policies.

For further information, contact the FOIA Unit, Antitrust Division, Department of Justice, Tenth Street and Pennsylvania Avenue NW., Washington, DC 20530. Phone, 202–514–2692.

Civil Division

The Civil Division represents the United States, its departments and agencies, Members of Congress, Cabinet officers, and other Federal employees. Its litigation reflects the diversity of Government activities, involving, for example, the defense of challenges to Presidential actions; national security issues; benefit programs; energy policies; commercial issues such as contract disputes, banking, insurance, patents, fraud, and debt collection; all manner of accident and liability claims; and violations of the immigration and consumer protection laws. Each year, Division attorneys handle thousands of cases that collectively involve billions of dollars in claims and recoveries. The Division confronts significant policy issues, which often rise to constitutional dimensions, in defending and enforcing various Federal programs and actions.

The Civil Division litigates cases in all Federal district courts, the U.S. Courts of Appeals, the U.S. Court of Federal Claims, other Federal and State courts, and the courts of foreign nations. Division attorneys either conduct this litigation personally or they supervise or assist the U.S. attorneys and foreign counsel to whom the Division refers the cases. The Division is composed of seven major groups: the Torts Branch, the Commercial Litigation Branch, the Federal Programs Branch, the Appellate Staff, the Office of Consumer Litigation, the Office of Immigration Litigation, and an Office of Management Programs.

Torts   The Torts Branch is responsible for suits under the Federal Tort Claims Act, including medical malpractice, aviation disasters, environmental and occupational disease, and radiation and toxic substance exposure. It also handles maritime litigation and suits that seek personal monetary judgments against individual officers or employees.

Tort litigation more specifically includes the defense of all Federal Tort Claims Act suits against the United States, and the prosecution of suits in tort on behalf of the United States. Suits and administrative claims for death, personal injury, and property damage brought under the Tort Claims Act allege negligence on the part of Government employees acting within the scope of their employment and involve matters such as the operation of Government vehicles, the maintenance of Government premises, and the performance of Federal services and regulatory functions such as medical treatment, hospital care, and the control of civilian, military, and commercial air traffic. In addition, the Torts Branch defends petitions filed pursuant to the Vaccine Injury Compensation Program and is responsible for administering the Radiation Exposure Compensation Act.

Tort litigation also includes all legal proceedings involving the United States related to ships, shipping, navigable waters, and workmen's compensation. The Division's admiralty litigation includes suits for personal injury and property damage involving vessels, shore installations, and maritime personnel, equipment, and cargoes; suits arising out of contracts involving shipping, chartering of vessels, and the construction, repair, and salvaging of vessels; proceedings to enforce navigation and shipping laws; and litigation based on international maritime agreements.

Commercial Litigation   The Commercial Litigation Branch is responsible for litigation associated with the Government's diverse financial involvements.

This litigation includes all monetary suits involving contracts, express or implied; actions to foreclose on Government mortgages and liens; bankruptcy and insolvency proceedings; and suits against guarantors and sureties.

Branch attorneys bring suit under the False Claims Act (31 U.S.C. 3729) for the recovery of treble damages and civil penalties, and alternative remedies, upon proof of loss to the Government sustained through fraud in the award or performance of Government contracts, false claims presented in connection with Federal programs, the submission of false statements and vouchers to Government agencies, and the use of other fraudulent devices in transactions with the Government. These suits include those filed pursuant to the *qui tam* provisions of the False Claims Act, in which private citizens with knowledge of fraud against the Government may file a lawsuit against the perpetrators on behalf of the United States and share in a percentage of any monetary recovery. Branch attorneys also bring suits to recover sums paid to bribe Government officials and kickbacks in Government procurement.

The Branch is responsible for all cases in the U.S. Court of International Trade, including suits brought by importers of merchandise to challenge the appraisement or classification of imported goods or other decisions of the U.S. Customs Service in its administration of the tariff laws and schedules.

The Branch has responsibility for all litigation in the U.S. Court of Federal

Claims except for those cases assigned to the Environment and Natural Resources Division and the Tax Division. Included are:

—patent cases and suits arising out of construction, procurement, service contracts, and claims associated with contract terminations;

—claims involving freight rate disputes arising out of the transportation of Government property;

—claims for just compensation under the fifth amendment;

—claims for salary or retirement by civilian and military personnel; and

—cases assigned by congressional reference or special legislation.

Likewise, Branch attorneys handle the majority of cases before the Court of Appeals for the Federal Circuit. This litigation involves appeals of decisions made by the U.S. Court of Federal Claims, the U.S. Court of Veterans Appeals, Boards of Contract Appeals, the Merit Systems Protection Board, and Federal district courts.

The Branch handles all litigation involving the rights, liabilities, and administrative functions of the Government with respect to patent, copyright, and trademark matters. This includes:

—defense of patent infringement suits based on the liability of the United States for infringements in connection with the performance of Government contracts;

—legal proceedings to establish Government priority of invention;

—suits for specific performance to require transfer of rights and title and payment of royalties;

—suits to cancel patents acquired by fraud upon the Patent Office;

—defense of administrative acts of the Register of Copyrights; and

—actions on behalf of the Government involving the use of trademarks.

The Branch is also responsible for the supervision of litigation in foreign courts involving the United States as a party and suits against U.S. employees stationed abroad who are being sued in the course of their Government service. Additionally, the Branch renders international judicial assistance to foreign and international tribunals.

Federal Programs   The Federal Programs Branch defends and asserts the programs, policies, and decisions of virtually all Federal departments and agencies, the President, Cabinet officers, Members of Congress, and other Government officials. It defends against constitutional challenges to statutes, suits to overturn Government policies and programs, and challenges to the legality of Government decisions. These suits typically seek injunctive and declaratory relief and range from objections to the way that the Government deals with its employees to allegations that the President has violated the Constitution or Federal law. The Branch also initiates suits to enforce regulatory statutes and to remedy or prevent statutory or regulatory violations.

The areas of litigation include:

—defense of suits against the heads of Federal departments and agencies and other government officials to enjoin official actions, as well as suits for judicial review of administrative decisions, orders, and regulations;

—defense and prosecution of suits involving national security, including suits to protect sensitive intelligence sources and materials;

—prosecution of suits to prevent interference with Government operations;

—litigation concerning the constitutionality of Federal legislation; and

—defense of suits involving specialized statutes, such as the Freedom of Information Act, the Federal Advisory Committee Act, and the Privacy Act.

Appellate Staff   The Appellate Staff has primary responsibility for the litigation of Civil Division cases in the appellate courts. The Staff prepares Government briefs and presents oral argument for the cases. Additionally, the Appellate Staff participates in drafting all documents filed for these cases in the United States Supreme Court, including briefs on the merits, petitions for certiorari, and jurisdictional statements.

Consumer Litigation   The Office of Consumer Litigation is responsible for civil and criminal litigation and related matters arising under various consumer protection and public health statutes, including the Federal Food, Drug, and Cosmetic Act, the Federal Trade Commission Act, the Consumer Product Safety Act, the Hazardous Substances Act, and the Truth in Lending Act. The Office also serves as a liaison with other Federal agencies and with local enforcement agencies for the referral of consumer complaints outside the jurisdiction of the Department of Justice.

Immigration Litigation The Office of Immigration Litigation is responsible for conducting civil litigation under the Immigration and Nationality Act (8 U.S.C. 1101) and related laws and for representing the United States in civil litigation brought against employees of the Immigration and Naturalization Service. In addition, this Office handles district court litigation, deportation review proceedings, habeas corpus review and general advice, and immigration-related appellate matters. The Office is also responsible for cases pertaining to the issuance of visas and passports, and for litigation arising under the amnesty and employer sanctions provisions of the Immigration Reform and Control Act of 1986 (8 U.S.C. 1255a, 1324a) and 1990 immigration reforms.

Management Programs The Office of Management Programs provides management and administrative services to the Division, including policy analysis and planning, administrative management, budget formulation and execution, management information systems, office automation, and automated litigation support.

For further information, contact the Office of the Assistant Attorney General, Civil Division, Department of Justice, Tenth Street and Pennsylvania Avenue NW., Washington, DC 20530. Phone, 202–514–3301.

Civil Rights Division

The Civil Rights Division, headed by an Assistant Attorney General, was established in 1957 to secure effective Federal enforcement of civil rights. The Division is the primary institution within the Federal Government responsible for enforcing Federal statutes prohibiting discrimination on the basis of race, sex, disability, religion, and national origin. The Division is composed of the following Sections:

Appellate Section The Appellate Section handles civil rights cases in the courts of appeals and, in cooperation with the Solicitor General, in the Supreme Court. The Section frequently participates in *amicus curiae* cases that affect the Division, and provides counsel to the Department on civil rights and appellate litigation. It handles all appeals from both favorable and adverse judgments in which the Government participates.

Coordination and Review Section This Section coordinates the enforcement by Federal agencies of various civil rights statutes that prohibit discrimination on the basis of race, color, national origin, sex, and religion in programs and activities that receive Federal financial assistance. The Section also conducts compliance reviews and investigates complaints of discrimination on the basis of race, color, national origin, sex, age, and religion in the services and activities of recipients of Federal financial assistance from the Department of Justice.

Criminal Section Under the Federal criminal civil rights statutes, the Criminal Section prosecutes conduct involving conspiracies to interfere with federally protected rights, deprivation of rights under color of law, the use of force or threat of force to injure or intimidate someone in their enjoyment of specific rights (such as voting, housing, employment, education, public facilities, and accommodations), interference with the free excercise of religious beliefs or damage to religious property, and the holding of a worker in a condition of slavery or involuntary servitude. More recently, the Section began enforcing the criminal aspects of the new Freedom of Access to Clinic Entrances Act (FACE). This statute prohibits conduct intended to injure, intimidate, or interfere with persons seeking to obtain or provide reproductive services. Also, a task force staffed by attorneys from both the Criminal and Civil Rights Divisions was created by the Attorney General to determine if there is any organized criminal effort to commit violence upon abortion providers.

Educational Opportunities Section   The Educational Opportunities Section enforces title IV of the Civil Rights Act of 1964 and the Equal Educational Opportunities Act of 1974. In addition, it represents the Department of Education in certain suits filed against and on behalf of the Secretary of Education. The Section closely monitors approximately 400 school districts operating under desegregation court orders.

Employment Litigation Section   The Employment Litigation Section enforces the provisions of title VII of the Civil Rights Act of 1964, as amended, and other Federal laws prohibiting employment practices that discriminate on the grounds of race, sex, religion, and national origin, as they apply to State and local government employers.

Housing and Civil Enforcement Section The Housing and Civil Enforcement Section has principal responsibility for enforcing the Fair Housing Act of 1968, as amended, which prohibits discrimination in housing on the basis of race, color, religion, sex, national origin, disability, and familial status. The act allows the Section to bring cases on behalf of individuals where a complaint is filed with the Department of Housing and Urban Development (HUD). Additionally, the Section enforces the Equal Credit Opportunity Act, which prohibits discrimination in credit transactions; and title II of the Civil Rights Act of 1964, which prohibits discrimination in places of public accommodations, such as hotels, restaurants, and places of entertainment.

Office of Special Counsel for Immigration Related Unfair Employment Practices   The Office of Special Counsel for Immigration Related Unfair Employment Practices was established pursuant to section 102 of the Immigration Reform and Control Act of 1986 (8 U.S.C. 1324b). The Special Counsel is responsible for investigating and prosecuting charges of national origin and citizenship status discrimination in hiring, firing, or recruitment. Jurisdiction over national origin charges is limited to those not covered by the Equal Employment Opportunity Commission. Jurisdiction over citizenship status is exclusive.

The Special Counsel files complaints before an administrative law judge based on charges filed with this Office or on its own independent investigations. Appeals of administrative decisions are to the U.S. Courts of Appeals.

In addition, the Special Counsel coordinates with the Immigration and Naturalization Service, the Equal Employment Opportunity Commission, and other Federal agencies in promoting public awareness of the antidiscrimination provisions of the act, through employer and public interest conferences, public service announcements, and nationwide distribution of enforcement information.

Disability Rights Section   This Section (previously the Public Access Section) enforces Titles I, II, and III of the Americans with Disabilities Act of 1990 (ADA) and Department of Justice regulations implementing these provisions, provides technical assistance to entities covered by the ADA and to persons protected by the ADA, and coordinates the technical assistance efforts of all Federal agencies with technical assistance responsibilities under the ADA. The Section also certifies that State or local building codes meet or exceed the requirements of the ADA. The Section is also responsible for carrying out the Department's responsibilities under section 504 of the Rehabilitation Act of 1973.

Special Litigation Section   The Special Litigation Section is responsible for protecting the constitutional and statutory rights of persons confined in certain institutions owned or operated by State or local governments, including facilities for individuals with mental and developmental disabilities, nursing homes, prisons, jails, and juvenile detention facilities where a pattern or practice of violations exist. This authority is granted by the Civil Rights of Institutionalized Persons Act. The Section is also responsible for civil enforcement provisions of the Freedom of Access to Clinic Entrances Act (FACE) which prohibits force or the threat of force for the purpose of interfering with the provision of reproductive services; and the police misconduct provision of the Violent Crime Control and Law Enforcement Act of 1994, which gives the Attorney General authority to remedy patterns and practices of misconduct by certain law enforcement authorities.

Voting Section The Voting Section is responsible for the enforcement of the Voting Rights Act of 1965, the Voting Accessibility for the Elderly and Handicapped Act, the Uniformed and Overseas Citizens Absentee Voting Act, the National Voter Registration Act of 1993, and other statutory provisions designed to safeguard the right to vote of racial and language minorities, illiterate persons, individuals with disabilities, overseas citizens, persons who change their residence shortly before a Presidential election, and persons 18 to 20 years of age.

Under section 2 of the Voting Rights Act, the Section brings lawsuits to remedy discriminatory election practices. Under section 5 of the Voting Rights Act, the Section reviews voting changes submitted to the Attorney General and defends section 5 litigation in court to assure that redistricting plans and other changes in voting practices and procedures do not abridge the right to vote of racial or language minorities. Under section 8 of the Voting Rights Act, the Attorney General requests the assignment of Federal observers—who generally are employees of the Office of Personnel Management—to monitor polling place activities on election day to document and deter discriminatory practices.

Administrative Management Section This Section supports the Division by providing a diverse array of management and technical services, including personnel administration, budget formulation and execution, facilities services, mail and file operations, and automated systems. This Section also contains the Freedom of Information/ Privacy Act Branch, which ensures that the Division complies with all aspects of the Freedom of Information and Privacy Acts.

Another component of the Administrative Management Section is the Office of Redress Administration, which implements the responsibilities given to the Attorney General under section 105 of the Civil Liberties Act of 1988. The Act provides for redress to American citizens and permanent resident aliens of Japanese ancestry who were evacuated, relocated, and interned by the United States during World War II.

For further information, contact the Executive Officer, Civil Rights Division, Department of Justice, P.O. Box 65310, Washington, DC 20035– 5310. Phone, 202–514–4224.

Criminal Division

The Criminal Division develops, enforces, and supervises the application of all Federal criminal laws, except those specifically assigned to other divisions. The Division and the 93 U.S. attorneys are responsible for overseeing criminal matters under more than 900 statutes, as well as certain civil litigation. In addition to its direct litigation responsibilities, the Division formulates and implements criminal enforcement policy and provides advice and assistance. The Division approves or monitors sensitive areas of law enforcement such as participation in the Witness Security Program and the use of electronic surveillance; advises the Attorney General, Congress, the Office of Management and Budget, and the White House of matters of criminal law; provides legal advice and assistance to Federal prosecutors and investigative agencies; and provides leadership for coordinating international as well as Federal, State, and local law enforcement matters.

Office of Administration   The Office of Administration performs a wide range of administrative and managerial functions for the components of the Criminal Division, including budget preparation and execution, personnel actions, computer support services, mail and records services, procurement, and security.

Appellate Section   The Appellate Section prepares draft briefs and certiorari petitions for the Solicitor General to be filed in the U.S. Supreme Court; makes recommendations to the Solicitor General as to whether further review on adverse decisions in the district courts and courts of appeals is necessary; and prepares briefs and argues cases in the courts of appeals.

The Section assists U.S. attorneys and Division prosecutors in preparing briefs for the courts of appeals and provides advice on Speedy Trial Act [of 1974] problems and a variety of other legal issues.

Asset Forfeiture   The Asset Forfeiture Office provides centralized management of the Department's Asset Forfeiture Program to ensure its integrity and to maximize its full law enforcement potential. The Office provides oversight, management, and direction to the various Federal participating components. It initiates, coordinates, and reviews legislative and policy proposals impacting on the program and serves as the Department's contact for Congress, other executive branch agencies, and State and local law enforcement agencies. The Office develops, promulgates, and oversees uniform forfeiture policies of the Department. It assists in the litigation of both civil and criminal asset forfeiture cases, either by conducting the litigation itself or providing legal and practical advice to the U.S. attorneys or their assistants. The Office oversees asset forfeiture training seminars for Federal prosecutors, investigating agents, and contract personnel. It also adjudicates all petitions for remission or mitigation of forfeited assets in judicial forfeiture cases. The Office administers the program for sharing federally forfeited property with State and local enforcement agencies, as well as other nations, and oversees the approval of the placement of such property into official use by the Federal agencies.

Child Exploitation and Obscenity   The Child Exploitation and Obscenity Section (CEOS) prosecutes violators of Federal criminal statutes relating to sexual exploitation of minors, child support, and obscenity. Under these statutes, the Section prosecutes those who possess, manufacture, or distribute child pornography, those who sell, buy, or transport children interstate or internationally to engage in sexually explicit conduct; those who travel interstate or internationally to sexually abuse children; those who sexually abuse children on Federal and Indian lands; those who do not pay certain court-ordered child support payments; and those who transport obscene material in interstate or foreign commerce either by the mails, common carrier, cable television lines, telephone lines, or satellite transmission. Section attorneys also assist U.S. attorneys in investigations, trials, and appeals related to these statutes. Finally, Section attorneys provide advice on victim-witness issues and develop and refine proposals for prosecution policies, legislation, governmental practices, and agency regulations in the areas of child sexual exploitation of minors, child support, and obscenity.

Fraud   The Fraud Section, the largest component of the Criminal Division, directs and coordinates the Federal effort against fraud and white-collar crime, focusing primarily on complex frauds that involve: multidistrict and international activities; financial institutions; the insurance industry; Government programs and procurement procedures, including health care providers, defense procurement fraud, and Housing and Urban Development fraud; the securities and commodities exchanges; and multidistrict schemes that involve consumer victimization, such as telemarketing. The Section conducts investigations and prosecutes on its own about 100 fraud cases of national significance or great complexity annually. It also assists U.S. attorneys with cases, where requested. The Section maintains a regional Bank Fraud Task Force field office in Dallas, TX, and Boston, MA, and provides staffing for the San Diego Bank Fraud Task Force. The Section also trains Federal agents and prosecutors through its conferences and participation in other Federal conferences.

General Litigation and Legal Advice The General Litigation and Legal Advice Section investigates and prosecutes cases involving violations of approximately two-thirds of all Federal criminal statutes. Its Computer Crime Unit enforces the Computer Fraud and Abuse Act. Other Section jurisdiction includes crimes against the public and crimes against government operations and offenses involving criminally enforceable regulations in the areas of health, safety, and welfare. Examples of areas handled by the Section include wiretapping violations, information technology crimes and customs fraud, theft, or destruction of Government property, obstruction of justice, perjury and offenses on Federal or Indian reservations or on the high seas. The Section also handles certain civil matters and provides extensive legal advice to officials of the Department, U.S. attorneys' offices, and investigative agencies relating to its broad spectrum of responsibilities.

Internal Security The Internal Security Section supervises the investigation and prosecution of cases affecting national security, foreign relations, and the export of military and strategic commodities and technology. The Section has exclusive responsibility for authorizing the prosecution of cases under criminal statutes relating to espionage, sabotage, neutrality, and atomic energy. It provides legal advice to U.S. attorneys' offices and investigative agencies on all matters within its area of responsibility, which includes 88 Federal statutes affecting national security. It also coordinates criminal cases involving the application of the Classified Information Procedures Act. The Section also administers and

enforces the Foreign Agents Registration Act of 1938 and related disclosure statutes.

Money Laundering The Money Laundering Section works with the entire spectrum of law enforcement and regulatory agencies using an interagency, interdisciplinary, and international approach. The Section is mandated to: coordinate multidistrict investigations and prosecutions; provide guidance, legal advice, and assistance with respect to money laundering investigations and prosecutions to U.S. attorneys' offices and investigative agencies; develop regulatory and legislative initiatives; ensure, through implementation of the money laundering prosecution guidelines, the uniform application of the money laundering statutes; litigate complex, sensitive, and multidistrict money laundering cases and provide litigation assistance to U.S. attorneys' offices and Criminal Division components; participate in international efforts to combat money laundering; develop, use, and teach cutting-edge investigative and prosecutive methodologies; identify new trends and typologies in money laundering; develop national strategy with respect to new and emerging trends, and coordinate responses among appropriate agencies; and provide training, materials, and conferences for attorneys and law enforcement personnel in conjunction with the Department's Office of Legal Education. The Money Laundering Section carries its own litigation caseload and, at the same time, works with other law enforcement agencies throughout the country to promote innovative, yet uniform development of the law in money laundering and money laundering-related forfeiture matters.

Narcotic and Dangerous Drugs The Narcotic and Dangerous Drug Section investigates and prosecutes complex, multidefendant narcotics and related money-laundering cases. The Section coordinates complex multidistrict cases and provides direct litigation support to the Organized Crime Drug Enforcement Task Forces, the High Intensity Drug Trafficking Areas programs, and other multiagency initiatives. The Section litigates appeals from cases prosecuted by its attorneys and appeals of denials or revocations of licenses and registrations by the Administrator of the Drug Enforcement Administration.

Section attorneys actively participate in various working groups formed to assist the Department in fulfilling its responsibilities in the development and implementation of domestic and international narcotics law enforcement programs and policies.

The Section includes a Drug Intelligence Unit which serves as a point of contact when information gathering efforts of the intelligence community overlap with domestic investigations and prosecutions.

Enforcement Operations The Office of Enforcement Operations oversees the use of the most sophisticated investigative tools at the Department's disposal, including electronic surveillance and the Federal Witness Protection Program. The Office provides U.S. attorneys' offices and the various Criminal Division components with a wide range of prosecutorial support services in these and other areas. These areas include reviewing all Federal electronic surveillance requests; reviewing and authorizing requests to apply for court orders permitting the use of video surveillance; authorizing or denying the entry of all applicants into the Federal Witness Security Program, coordinating and administering all Program components and matters relating to all aspects of the Witness Security Program; approving or denying requests by Federal agencies to utilize Federal prisoners for investigative purposes; administering the International Prisoner Transfer Program; coordinating requests for U.S. prisoners to testify in foreign countries; and supervising the mechanism by which persons who are not Federal law enforcement officers or agents may become Special Deputy United States Marshals. The Office provides legal advice to Federal, State, and local law enforcement agencies on the use of Federal electronic surveillance statutes, and assists in developing

Department policy on emerging technologies and telecommunications issues. It also assists, upon request, in the drafting of reply briefs involving electronic surveillance issues.

The Office responds to requests for disclosure of information under the Freedom of Information Act and the Privacy Act.

International Affairs The Office of International Affairs supports the Department's legal divisions, the U.S. attorneys, and State and local prosecutors regarding questions of foreign and international law, including issues related to extradition and mutual legal assistance treaties. The Office also coordinates all international evidence gathering. In conjunction with the State Department, the Office engages in the negotiation of new extradition and mutual legal assistance treaties and executive agreements throughout the world. Office attorneys also participate on a number of committees established under the auspices of the United Nations and other international organizations that are directed at resolving a variety of international law enforcement problems, such as narcotics trafficking and money laundering. The Office maintains a permanent field office in Rome.

Legislation The Office of Legislation develops legislative proposals, legal memoranda, and congressional testimony. The Office also prepares comments on pending and proposed legislation affecting the Federal criminal justice system. It works closely with the U.S. Sentencing Commission and provides legal support to the Advisory Committee on Criminal Rules and the Federal Rules of Evidence of the Judicial Conference regarding the Federal Rules of Criminal Procedure.

Professional Development and Training The Office of Professional Development and Training furthers the goals of the Criminal Division relating to its initiatives in international training. In this regard, the Office coordinates the training of judges and prosecutors abroad through various Government agencies and U.S. embassies. The Office coordinates such training programs in

South and Central America and in Central and Eastern Europe.

The Office also serves as the Department's liaison between various private and public agencies that sponsor visits to the United States for foreign officials who are interested in the U.S. legal system. The Office makes presentations explaining the U.S. criminal system process to hundreds of international visitors each year.

Another responsibility of this Office is the revision and publication of Criminal Division manuals and monographs. The Office also has a small in-house video library to afford Criminal Division attorneys easy access to quick updates in important areas of the law, such as sentencing guidelines and the admissibility of DNA (deoxyribonucleic acid) identification evidence.

Policy and Management Analysis The Office of Policy and Management Analysis analyzes policy and management issues relating to criminal justice enforcement and makes recommendations to senior managers in the Criminal Division and the Department. The Office is involved in projects that may require contact with U.S. attorneys, Federal investigators, and other law enforcement officials.

Special Investigations The Office of Special Investigations detects and investigates individuals who took part in Nazi-sponsored acts of persecution abroad before and during World War II, and who subsequently entered, or seek to enter, the United States illegally and/ or fraudulently. It then takes appropriate legal action seeking their exclusion, denaturalization, and/or deportation.

Organized Crime and Racketeering The Organized Crime and Racketeering Section coordinated the Department's program to combat organized crime. The principal enforcement efforts are currently directed against traditional groups—such as La Cosa Nostra families, and emerging groups from Asia and Europe—such as Chinese Triads, the Sicilian Mafia, and Russian organized crime. The Section supervises the investigation and prosecution of these cases by Strike Force Units within U.S.

attorneys' offices in 21 Federal districts having a significant organized crime presence. These cases involve a broad spectrum of criminal statutes, including extortion, murder, bribery, fraud, narcotics, and labor racketeering.

The Section is involved in setting national priorities for the organized crime program by coordinating with investigative agencies such as the Federal Bureau of Investigation, the Drug Enforcement Administration, and others; and by working with the Attorney General's Organized Crime Council, which is ultimately responsible for the Federal Government's policy in this area.

In addition to its close supervision of all Federal organized crime cases, the Section maintains close control over all Government uses of the RICO statute, and provides extensive advice to prosecutors about the use of this powerful tool for cases involving patterns of serious criminal conduct.

In a more specialized context, the Section provides support for criminal prosecutions, which may not include organized criminal groups. These cases involve labor-management disputes, the internal affairs of labor unions in the private sector, and the operation of employee pension and welfare benefit plans.

Public Integrity The Public Integrity Section oversees the Federal effort to combat corruption through the prosecution of elected and appointed public officials at all levels of Government. The Section has exclusive jurisdiction over allegations of criminal misconduct by Federal judges, and also monitors the investigation and prosecution of election and conflict of interest crimes. Section attorneys prosecute selected cases against Federal, State, and local officials, and are available as a source of advice and expertise to other prosecutors and to investigators. Since 1978, the Section has supervised the administration of the Independent Counsel provisions of the Ethics in Government Act.

Terrorism and Violent Crime The Terrorism and Violent Crime Section investigates and prosecutes Federal offenses relating to international terrorism incidents which impact on U.S. interests. The Section also oversees the prosecution of domestic violent crime offenses over which Federal jurisdiction exists, as well as the prosecution of firearms and explosives violations. In appropriate instances, Section attorneys assume direct responsibility for the prosecution of violent crime cases. The Section assists in the implementation of an initiative designed to deter criminals from possessing firearms by using Federal firearms laws, which generally provide longer and often mandatory sentences for gun offenses. Additionally, the Section administers the national anti-violent crime strategy which is being carried out in every Federal judicial district. The strategy focuses particular attention on the investigation and prosecution of gang-related crimes. Section attorneys provide legal advice to Federal prosecutors concerning Federal statutes relating to murder, assault, kidnapping, threats, robbery, weapons and explosives control, malicious destruction of property, and aircraft and sea piracy. The Section also formulates legislative initiatives and Department policies relating to international terrorism and violent crime, and coordinates such initiatives and strategies with other Government agencies.

Executive Office for the Organized Crime Drug Enforcement Task Forces Since 1982, the Organized Crime Drug Enforcement Task Forces (OCDETF) Program has been the principal coordinating mechanism for Federal, State, and local enforcement investigations and prosecutions aimed at high-level drug trafficking and related enterprises. The OCDETF goal is to dismantle and/or significantly disrupt the operations of those enterprises by investigating, prosecuting, and convicting the organizational leadership.

The Executive Office for OCDFTF supports the work of over 4,000 Federal agents and prosecutors and an annual average of 6,000 State and local personnel in OCDETF activities through the coordination of legal and administrative services provided to the Task Forces; the collection, analyses, and reporting on caseload and other statistical data for the Task Forces; the coordination of multiagency research reports for the Attorney General, the Under Secretary of the Treasury, the U.S. attorneys, the President, the Congress, and others; and the policy formulation and management of the fiscal aspects of the program.

For further information, contact the Office of the Assistant Attorney General, Criminal Division, Department of Justice, Tenth Street and Pennsylvania Avenue NW., Washington, DC 20530. Phone, 202–514–2601.

Environment and Natural Resources Division

The Environment and Natural Resources Division, formerly known as the Land and Natural Resources Division, is the Nation's environmental lawyer. It is responsible for litigating significant cases—ranging from protection of endangered species, to global climate change, to cleaning up the Nation's hazardous waste sites. A key Division responsibility is enforcing civil and criminal environmental laws in order to protect its citizens' health and environment. The Division also defends environmental challenges to Government programs and activities. It represents the United States in all matters concerning the protection, use, and development of the Nation's natural resources and public lands, wildlife protection, Indian rights and claims, and the acquisition of Federal property.

Environmental Crimes The Environmental Crimes Section is responsible for prosecuting individuals and industries which have violated laws designed to protect the environment. The Section works closely with the Federal Bureau of Investigation and criminal investigators for the Environmental Protection Agency (EPA) in dealing with violations of such statutes as the Clean Air Act; the Comprehensive Environmental Response, Compensation and Liability Act (Superfund); and the Resource Conservation and Recovery Act (RCRA), among others.

Environmental Enforcement The Environmental Enforcement Section is responsible for handling most of the affirmative civil litigation brought on behalf of the United States Environmental Protection Agency; claims for damages to our natural resources on behalf of the Departments of Interior, Commerce, and Agriculture; claims for contribution against private parties for contamination of public land; and recoupment of money spent to clean up certain oil spills on behalf of the United States Coast Guard. The Section supports the regulatory programs of its client agencies through litigation to obtain compliance with environmental statutes, establishes a credible deterrent against violation of those statutes, recoups Federal funds spent to abate environmental contamination, and obtains money to restore or replace natural resources damaged through oil spills or the release of hazardous substances into the environment. The primary statutes within the Section's responsibility are: the Comprehensive Environmental Response, Compensation and Liability Act (Superfund); the Clean Air Act; the Clean Water Act; the Resource Conservation and Recovery Act; the Safe Drinking Water Act; and the Oil Pollution Act of 1990.

Environmental Defense The Environmental Defense Section represents the United States, principally EPA, in suits challenging the Government's administration of Federal environmental laws. The goal of the Section's litigation is to assure that environmental laws are implemented in a fair and consistent manner nationwide. The lawsuits arise in Federal district and appellate courts, and include challenges by industries, environmental groups, and citizens that Federal agencies are not meeting environmental standards. The Section also protects the Nation's wetlands from unauthorized development and destruction, through both enforcement actions against illegal activities and actions defending Corps of Engineer decisions on permit applications.

Wildlife and Marine Resources The Wildlife and Marine Resources Section tries both civil and criminal cases under Federal wildlife laws and laws concerning the protection of marine fish and mammals. Prosecutions focus on illegal hunting, smuggling, and black-market dealers of protected fish and wildlife. Civil litigation, particularly under the Endangered Species Act, often focuses on conflicts between the needs of protected species versus pressures for development by both the Federal Government and private enterprise.

General Litigation The General Litigation Section is responsible for ensuring compliance with over 80 different statutes dealing with land management issues of federally owned properties and natural resources. This includes litigation under the National Environmental Policy Act, the Federal Land Policy Management Act, and the National Historic Preservation Act. Important sources of Federal revenue such as offshore oil leasing and coal slurry pipeline cases are examples of the varied matters handled by the Section. In addition, the Section represents the United States in all legal and equitable claims asserted by Indian tribes on the grounds that the United States has failed to honor its obligations to the tribes.

Indian Resources The Indian Resources Section represents the United States in its trust capacity for individual Indians or Indian tribes. These suits include establishing water rights, establishing and protecting hunting and fishing rights, collecting damages for trespass on Indian lands, and establishing reservation boundaries and rights to land. The litigation is often complex but of vital interest to the Indians.

Land Acquisition The Land Acquisition Section is responsible for acquiring land, through condemnation proceedings, for use by the Federal Government for purposes ranging from establishing public parks to creating missile sites, and for approving title to lands being acquired by the United States by direct purchase. The Section seeks to implement the just compensation clause of the Fifth Amendment in a way that is fair both to property owners and taxpayers. The legal and factual issues involved can include the power of the

United States to condemn under specific acts of Congress; ascertainment of the fair market value of property; applicability of zoning regulations and problems related to subdivisions; capitalization of income; and the admissibility of evidence.

Policy, Legislation and Special Litigation
The Policy, Legislation and Special Litigation Section advises and assists the Assistant Attorney General on specific policy matters and particular litigation. It coordinates and directs the Division's legislative program, including appearances of Division witnesses before congressional committees. Other duties include responding to citizens' requests and serving as the Division's ethics officer. Attorneys in the Section also litigate *amicus curiae* cases and undertake other special litigation projects.

Appeals   The Appellate Section is responsible for conducting all appeals in cases initially tried in lower courts by any of the sections within the Division. In addition, the Section drafts briefs for all Division cases which reach the level of the U.S. Supreme Court, and formulates recommendations to the Solicitor General that seek authority to appeal unfavorable decisions. The Section deals with the full range and complexity of the new and challenging issues presented by environmental law.

Executive Office   The Executive Office serves as administrator to the Division on financial management, personnel, automated systems, procurement, and automated litigation support issues.

For further information, contact the Office of the Assistant Attorney General, Environment and Natural Resources Division, Department of Justice, Tenth Street and Pennsylvania Avenue NW., Washington, DC 20530. Phone, 202–514–2701.

Tax Division

The Tax Division represents the United States and its officers in all civil and criminal litigation arising under the internal revenue laws, other than proceedings in the United States Tax Court. While the Division's primary client is the Internal Revenue Service, it also represents Federal officials and employees in actions arising out of the performance of their official duties, as well as representing other Federal departments and agencies in their dealings with State and local tax authorities. In civil tax litigation the Division's responsibility involves cases in the United States District Courts, the United States Court of Federal Claims, the United States Courts of Appeals, and the U. S. Supreme Court, as well as cases in the State courts.

The Division represents the United States in many different types of disputes, both civil and criminal, dealing with the interpretation of Federal tax laws. For example, when the Internal Revenue Service challenges a tax return and determines a deficiency, the taxpayer may pay the full amount of tax assessed and then bring a suit against the Government for refund. The Division defends the Government in these refund actions.

Other areas of civil litigation in which the Tax Division is involved on behalf of the Federal Government include:

—suits brought by individuals to foreclose mortgages or to quiet title to property in which the United States is named as a party defendant because of the existence of a Federal tax lien on the property;

—suits brought by the United States to collect unpaid assessments, to foreclose Federal tax liens or determine the priority of such liens, to obtain judgments against delinquent taxpayers, to enforce summonses, and to establish tax claims in bankruptcy, receivership, or probate proceedings;

—proceedings involving mandamus, injunctions, and other specific writs arising in connection with internal revenue matters;

—suits against Internal Revenue Service employees for damages claimed because of alleged injuries caused in the performance of their official duties;

—suits against the Secretary of the Treasury, the Commissioner of Internal Revenue, or similar officials to test the validity of regulations or rulings not in the context of a specific refund action;

—suits brought by the United States to enjoin the promotion of abusive tax

shelters and to enjoin activities relating to aiding and abetting the understatement of tax liabilities of others;
—suits brought by taxpayers for a judicial determination of the reasonableness of a jeopardy or termination assessment and the appropriateness of the amount;
—proceedings brought against the Tax Division and the Internal Revenue Service for disclosure of information under the Freedom of Information Act; and
—intergovernmental immunity suits in which the United States resists attempts to apply a State or local tax to some activity or property of the United States.

The Division also collects judgments in tax cases. To this end, the Division directs collection efforts and coordinates with, monitors the efforts of, and provides assistance to the various United States attorneys' offices in collecting outstanding judgments in tax cases.

With respect to criminal tax litigation, the Division prosecutes or supervises the prosecution of all criminal offenses committed under the internal revenue laws, including attempts to evade and defeat taxes, willful failures to file returns and to pay taxes, filing false returns and other deceptive documents, making false statements to revenue officials, and other miscellaneous offenses involving internal revenue matters. These duties include the institution of criminal proceedings and collaboration with U.S. attorneys in the conduct of litigation in the trial and appellate courts. Further, Tax Division attorneys frequently conduct grand jury investigations and actual trials of criminal tax cases, often as a result of

requests for assistance by the appropriate U.S. attorney. In its efforts to deter willful deception through prosecution of criminal offenders, the Tax Division also plays a significant role in curbing organized crime, public corruption, narcotics trafficking, and financial institution fraud.

The primary functions of the Division are to aid the Internal Revenue Service in collecting the Federal revenue and to establish principles of law that will serve as guidelines to taxpayers and their representatives, as well as to the Internal Revenue Service, in the administration of the Internal Revenue Code. As a result, coordination with the Internal Revenue Service's administrative policies and the Treasury Department's legislative tax concerns in developing litigating postures is essential.

The Division also provides input into the preparation of reports to the Congress, the Office of Management and Budget, and the Office of Legislative Affairs on pending or proposed legislation and monitors congressional activities with respect to matters of interest to the Division.

In accordance with the Attorney General's program to enhance the litigating skills of Department attorneys, the Division conducts training programs for its attorneys, with special emphasis on matters unique to tax litigation and the development of advocacy skills.

For further information, contact the Office of the Assistant Attorney General, Tax Division, Department of Justice, Tenth Street and Pennsylvania Avenue NW., Washington, DC 20530. Phone, 202–514–2901.

Bureaus

Federal Bureau of Investigation

Ninth Street and Pennsylvania Avenue NW., Washington, DC 20535. Phone, 202–324–3000

The Federal Bureau of Investigation (FBI) is the principal investigative arm of the United States Department of Justice. It is

charged with gathering and reporting facts, locating witnesses, and compiling evidence in cases involving Federal jurisdiction.

The Federal Bureau of Investigation was established in 1908 by the Attorney General, who directed that Department of Justice investigations be handled by its own staff. The Bureau is charged with investigating all violations of Federal law except those that have been assigned by legislative enactment or otherwise to another Federal agency. Its jurisdiction includes a wide range of responsibilities in the criminal, civil, and security fields. Priority has been assigned to the five areas that affect society the most: organized crime/drugs, counterterrorism, white-collar crime, foreign counterintelligence, and violent crime.

On January 28, 1982, the Attorney General assigned concurrent jurisdiction for the enforcement of the Controlled Substances Act (21 U.S.C. 801) to the Bureau and the Drug Enforcement Administration (DEA). The DEA Administrator reports to the Attorney General through the FBI Director.

The Bureau also offers cooperative services such as fingerprint identification, laboratory examination, police training, and the National Crime Information Center to duly authorized law enforcement agencies.

The Bureau headquarters in Washington, DC, consists of nine separate divisions, a Deputy Director, an Office of Public and Congressional Affairs, an Office of Equal Employment Opportunity Affairs, and a Director's staff.

The Bureau's investigations are conducted through 56 field offices. Most of its investigative personnel are trained at the FBI Academy in Quantico, VA.

For further information, contact the Office of Public and Congressional Affairs, Federal Bureau of Investigation, J. Edgar Hoover F.B.I. Building, Ninth Street and Pennsylvania Avenue NW., Washington, DC 20535. Phone, 202–324–2727.

Bureau of Prisons

320 First Street NW., Washington, DC 20534. Phone, 202–307–3198

The mission of the Bureau of Prisons is to protect society by confining offenders in the controlled environments of prisons and community-based facilities that are safe, humane, and appropriately secure, and which provide work and other self-improvement opportunities to assist offenders in becoming law-abiding citizens.

The Executive Office of the Director provides overall direction for agency operations. In addition to typical administrative functions performed by an agency head, the Offices of General Counsel and Internal Affairs are within the Office and report to the Director.

The Administration Division develops plans, programs, and policies concerning the acquisition, construction, and staffing of new facilities, as well as budget development, financial management, procurement, and contracting.

The Correctional Programs Division is responsible for managing the correctional services (security) operations in Bureau institutions and case and unit management, as well as religious and psychological services, drug treatment programs, and inmate systems.

Federal Prison Industries (trade name UNICOR) is a wholly owned Government corporation whose mission is to provide employment and training opportunities for inmates confined in Federal correctional facilities. UNICOR manufactures a wide range of items— from executive and systems furniture to electronics, textiles, and graphics/signage. Services performed by UNICOR's inmates include data entry, printing, and furniture refinishing. The corporation funds selected preindustrial, vocational, and experimental training programs.

The Health Services Division has oversight responsibility for all medical and psychiatric programs; environmental and occupational health services; food and nutrition services; and farm operations.

The Human Resource Management Division provides personnel, training, and labor management within the agency. Its functions also include pay and position management and recruitment.

The National Institute of Corrections provides technical assistance and training for State and local correctional agencies throughout the country. It also provides grants for research, evaluation, and program development. The Institute's administrative offices, Prison Division, and Community Corrections Division are located in Washington, DC;

and the Jails Division, Training Academy, and Information Center are located in Longmont, CO. The Institute receives logistical support from the Bureau of Prisons but is a separate budget entity.

The Program Review Division oversees agency review functions, ensures internal controls, and coordinates the year-end assurance statement to the Attorney General. This division also conducts in-depth analyses of review outcomes, and tracks and monitors management changes made in accord with those findings.

The Information, Policy and Public Affairs Division encompasses the Bureau's Information Systems; Policy Review; Information Resources Management; Research and Evaluation; Security Technology; Documents Control; External Liaison; Archives; and Office of Public Affairs.

The Community Corrections and Detention Division is responsible for the Bureau's Community Corrections and Detention Programs, Contract Services, Administration, and Program Development.

The Bureau is subdivided into six geographic regions, each staffed with field-qualified personnel who are responsible for policy development and oversight, providing operational guidance to field locations, and providing support functions in areas such as auditing, technical assistance, budget, and personnel. Each regional office is headed by an experienced career Bureau manager who is a full member of the Bureau's executive staff.

For further information, contact the Public Information Officer, Bureau of Prisons, Department of Justice, Washington, DC 20534. Phone, 202–307–3198.

United States Marshals Service

600 Army Navy Drive, Arlington, VA 22202–4210. Phone, 202–307–9065

The United States Marshals Service is the Nation's oldest Federal law enforcement agency, having served as a vital link between the executive and judicial branches of the Government since 1789. Today, the Presidentially appointed marshals and their support staff of approximately 3,500 deputy marshals and administrative personnel operate from 427 office locations in all 94 Federal judicial districts nationwide, from Guam to Puerto Rico, and from Alaska to Florida.

The Marshals Service performs tasks that are essential to the operation of virtually every aspect of the Federal justice system. The Service is responsible for:

—providing support and protection for the Federal courts, including security for over 700 judicial facilities and nearly 2,000 judges and magistrates, as well as countless other trial participants such as jurors and attorneys;

—apprehending most Federal fugitives;

—operating the Federal Witness Security program, ensuring the safety of endangered government witnesses;

—maintaining custody of and transporting thousands of Federal prisoners annually;

—executing court orders and arrest warrants;

—seizing, managing, and selling property forfeited to the Government by drug traffickers and other criminals, and assisting the Justice Department's Seizure and Forfeiture Program; and

—responding to emergency circumstances, including civil disturbances, terrorist incidents, and other crisis situations, through its Special Operations Group, and restoring order in riot and mob-violence situations.

The Director of the U.S. Marshals Service, who is appointed by the President, supervises the operations of the Service throughout the United States and its territories. The Deputy Director for Operations oversees the Service's enforcement, court security, witness protection, prisoner transportation, and asset seizure and forfeiture activities. The Deputy Director for Administration is responsible for personnel management; procurement and property management; space, transportation, and communications; information systems;

and the U.S. Marshals Service Training Academy.

For further information, contact the Office of Congressional and Public Affairs, U.S. Marshals Service, Department of Justice, Suite 1260, 600 Army Navy Drive, Arlington, VA 22202. Phone, 202–307–9065.

United States National Central Bureau–International Criminal Police Organization

Washington, DC 20530. Phone, 202–272–8383

The U.S. National Central Bureau (USNCB) represents the United States in INTERPOL, the International Criminal Police Organization. Also known as INTERPOL—Washington, USNCB provides an essential communications link between the U.S. police community and their counterparts in the foreign member countries.

INTERPOL is an association of 169 countries dedicated to promoting mutual assistance among law enforcement authorities in the prevention and suppression of international crime. With no police force of its own, INTERPOL has no powers of arrest or search and seizure. Instead, INTERPOL serves as a channel of communication among the police of the member countries, and provides a forum for discussions, working group meetings, and symposia to enable police to focus on specific areas of criminal activity affecting their countries.

United States participation in INTERPOL began in 1938 by congressional authorization, designating the Attorney General as the official representative to the organization. INTERPOL operations were interrupted during World War II, but resumed in 1947.

The Attorney General officially designated the Secretary of the Treasury as the U.S. representative to INTERPOL in 1958, and the U.S. National Central Bureau was established within the Treasury Department in 1969. In 1977, an arrangement was effected between Justice and Treasury officials establishing dual authority in administering USNCB. This Memorandum of Understanding

designates the Attorney General as the permanent representative to INTERPOL and the Secretary of the Treasury as the alternate representative.

The Bureau operates through cooperative efforts with Federal, State, and local law enforcement agencies. Programs and initiatives, such as the State Liaison Program and the Canadian Interface Project, broaden the scope of U.S. investigative resources to include the international community, thus forming an integral part of the United States efforts to confront the problem of international crime.

Federal and State law enforcement agencies represented at the USNCB include the Federal Bureau of Investigation; U.S. Marshals Service; Drug Enforcement Administration; Immigration and Naturalization Service; Criminal Division, U.S. Customs Service; U.S. Secret Service; Internal Revenue Service; Bureau of Alcohol, Tobacco and Firearms; Office of the Comptroller of the Currency; Office of the Inspector General, Department of Agriculture; U.S. Postal Inspection Service; Bureau of Diplomatic Security, Department of State; Naval Investigative Service; Federal Law Enforcement Training Center; Financial Crimes Enforcement Network; and the Massachusetts State Police.

Under the State Liaison Program, States establish an office within their own law enforcement community to serve as liaison to USNCB. International leads developed in criminal investigations being conducted by a State or local police entity can be pursued through their Liaison Office, and criminal investigative requests from abroad are funneled through the relevant State liaison office for action by the appropriate State or local agency. All 50 States now participate in the liaison program, which is currently coordinated by a representative from the Massachusetts State Police.

USNCB has two sub-bureaus which serve to more effectively address the law enforcement needs of U.S. territories. The sub-bureaus are located in San Juan,

Puerto Rico; and Pago Pago, American Samoa.

For further information, contact the U.S. National Central Bureau–INTERPOL, Washington, DC 20530. Phone, 202–272–8383.

Immigration and Naturalization Service

425 I Street NW., Washington, DC 20536. Phone, 202–514–4316, 4330, or 4354

[For the Immigration and Naturalization Service statement of organization, see the *Code of Federal Regulations*, Title 8, Aliens and Nationality]

The Immigration and Naturalization Service (INS) was created by act of March 3, 1891 (8 U.S.C. 1551 note), and its purpose and responsibilities were further specified by the Immigration and Nationality Act, as amended (8 U.S.C. 1101 note), which charges the Attorney General with the administration and enforcement of its provisions. The Attorney General has delegated authority to the Commissioner of the Immigration and Naturalization service to carry out these provisions of immigraion law.

Overall policy and executive direction flow from the Washington, DC, headquarters office through 3 regional offices to 33 district offices and 21 border patrol sectors throughout the United States. INS also maintains three district offices in Bangkok, Thailand; Mexico City, Mexico; and Rome, Italy.

INS carries out its mission through operational programs in adjudications and naturalization, inspections, investigations, and detention and deportation, as well as the U.S. Border Patrol. These programs are divided into the following mission responsibilities:

—facilitating the entry of persons legally admissible as immigrants or as visitors to the United States;

—granting benefits under the Immigration and Nationality Act, as amended, including providing assistance to those seeking asylum, temporary or permanent resident status, or naturalization;

—preventing unlawful entry, employment, or receipt of benefits by those who are not entitled to them; and

—apprehending or removing those aliens who enter or remain illegally in the United States and/or whose stay is not in the public interest.

The Service also has a firm commitment to strengthen criminal investigations and seek the most effective deterrents to illegal immigration.

For further information, contact the Office of Information, Immigration and Naturalization Service, Department of Justice, 425 I Street NW., Washington, DC 20536. Phone, 202–514–4316, 4330, or 4354.

Drug Enforcement Administration

600–700 Army Navy Drive, Arlington, VA 22202. Phone, 202–307–1000; FTS, 367–1000

The Drug Enforcement Administration (DEA) is the lead Federal agency in enforcing narcotics and controlled substances laws and regulations. It was created in July 1973, by Reorganization Plan No. 2 of 1973 (5 U.S.C. app.), which merged four separate drug law enforcement agencies.

DEA enforces the provisions of the controlled substances and chemical diversion and trafficking laws and regulations of the United States, and operates on a worldwide basis. It presents cases to the criminal and civil justice systems of the United States—or any other competent jurisdiction—on those significant organizations and their members involved in cultivation, production, smuggling, distribution, or diversion of controlled substances appearing in or destined for illegal traffic in the United States. DEA immobilizes these organizations by arresting their members, confiscating their drugs, and seizing their assets; and creates, manages, and supports enforcement-related programs—domestically and internationally—aimed at reducing the availability of and demand for controlled substances.

DEA's responsibilities include:

—investigation of major narcotic violators who operate at interstate and international levels;

—seizure and forfeiture of assets derived from, traceable to, or intended to be used for illicit drug trafficking;

—enforcement of regulations governing the legal manufacture, distribution, and dispensing of controlled substances;

—management of a national narcotics intelligence system;

—coordination with Federal, State, and local law enforcement authorities and cooperation with counterpart agencies abroad; and

—training, scientific research, and information exchange in support of drug traffic prevention and control.

DEA manages the El Paso Intelligence Center (EPIC), a 24-hour tactical drug intelligence center, which utilizes DEA and Federal personnel from 13 other agencies.

The Administration concentrates its efforts on high-level narcotics smuggling and distribution organizations in the United States and abroad, working closely with such agencies as the Customs Service, the Internal Revenue Service, and the Coast Guard. It also chairs the 11-agency National Narcotics Intelligence Consumers Committee, which develops an annual report on drug production, trafficking, and abuse trends.

Approximately 400 Administration compliance investigators enforce regulation of the legal manufacture and distribution of prescription drugs. The agency also maintains an active training program for narcotics officers in other Federal, State, and local agencies—as well as foreign police.

The Administration maintains liaison with the United Nations, INTERPOL, and other organizations on matters relating to international narcotics control programs. It has offices throughout the United States and in 50 foreign countries.

For further information, contact the Public Affairs Section, Drug Enforcement Administration, Department of Justice, Washington, DC 20537. Phone, 202–307–7977.

Office of Justice Programs

633 Indiana Avenue NW., Washington, DC 20531. Phone, 202–307–0781

The Office of Justice Programs (OJP) was established by the Justice Assistance Act of 1984 and reauthorized in 1994 to provide Federal leadership, coordination, and assistance needed to make the Nation's justice system more efficient and effective in preventing and controlling crime. OJP and its five program bureaus are responsible for collecting statistical data and conducting analyses; identifying emerging criminal justice issues; developing and testing promising approaches to address these issues; evaluating program results, and disseminating these findings and other information to State and local governments.

The Office is headed by an Assistant Attorney General who, by statute and delegation of authority from the Attorney General, establishes, guides, promotes, and coordinates policy; focuses efforts on the priorities established by the President and the Attorney General; and promotes coordination among the five major bureaus or offices within OJP. These are: Bureau of Justice Assistance, Bureau of Justice Statistics, National Institute of Justice, Office of Juvenile Justice and Delinquency Prevention, and Office for Victims of Crime.

Through the programs developed and financed by its bureaus and offices, OJP works to form partnerships among Federal, State, and local government officials to control drug abuse and trafficking, rehabilitate crime-ridden neighborhoods, improve the administration of justice in America, meet the needs of crime victims, and find innovative ways to address problems such as gang violence, prison crowding, juvenile crime, and white-collar crime. The functions of each bureau or office are interrelated. For example, the statistics generated by the Bureau of Justice Statistics may drive the research that is conducted through the National Institute of Justice and the Office of Juvenile Justice and Delinquency Prevention. Research results may generate new programs that receive support from the Bureau of Justice Assistance and the Office of Juvenile Justice and Delinquency Prevention.

Although some research and technical assistance is provided directly by OJP's bureaus and offices, most of the work is accomplished through Federal financial assistance to scholars, practitioners, and State and local governments.

Program bureaus and offices award formula grants to State agencies, which, in turn, subgrant funds to units of State and local government. Formula grant programs—drug control and system improvement, juvenile justice, victims compensation, and victims assistance—are administered by State agencies designated by each State's Governor. Discretionary grant programs usually are announced in the *Federal Register,* and applications are made directly to the sponsoring Office of Justice Programs bureau or office.

Bureau of Justice Assistance   The Bureau provides financial and technical assistance to State and local units of government to control drug abuse, drug trafficking, and violent crime and to improve the criminal justice system.

The Anti-Drug Abuse Act of 1988 (42 U.S.C. 3750), which established the Edward Byrne Memorial State and Local Law Enforcement Assistance Programs, authorizes the Bureau to make grants for the purpose of enforcing State and local laws that establish offenses similar to those designated in the Controlled Substances Act and to improve the functioning of the criminal justice system, with emphasis on violent crime and serious offenders. The States are required to prepare a statewide anti-drug and violent crime strategy as part of their applications for Formula Grant funds. Federal funds may be used for up to 75 percent of the total project costs.

The Bureau uses the Discretionary Grant Program to provide State and local criminal justice agencies with state-of-the-art information on innovative and effective programs, practices, and techniques through demonstration projects, training, and technical assistance. For example, the Bureau is developing and implementing comprehensive crime control and crime prevention strategies for communities faced with high rates of violence and drug-related crime through the Comprehensive Communities Program. BJA also supports violence reduction initiatives, such as homicide investigations and firearms control programs. Criminal justice agencies are provided assistance in addressing new issues and problems, such as the spread of drug-trafficking gangs; intermediate punishment, such as bootcamps; and drug testing of criminal offenders. The Bureau also supports programs that are national or multistate in scope, such as Operation Weed and Seed, the Regional Information Sharing Systems, the National White Collar Crime Center, and the National Crime Prevention (McGruff) Campaign. Discretionary Grant funds are awarded directly by the Bureau and do not require matching funds.

Direct assistance is also provided by the Bureau through the Emergency Federal Law Enforcement Assistance, Federal Surplus Property Transfer, Prison Industry Certification, Public Safety Officers' Death and Disability Benefits, and the State Criminal Alien Assistance Programs.

Bureau of Justice Statistics   The Bureau is responsible for collecting, analyzing, publishing, and disseminating statistical information on crime, its perpetrators and victims, and the operation of justice systems at all levels of government and internationally.

The Bureau also assists State governments in developing capabilities in criminal justice statistics and improving their criminal justice records and information systems.

The Bureau provides the President, the Congress, other officials, and the public with timely and accurate data about crime and the administration of justice. The Bureau publishes concise *Special Reports* and periodic *Bulletins* that provide up-to-date statistical information on various aspects of criminal justice. In addition, lengthier volumes present detailed analyses of specific topics.

The National Crime Victimization Survey is the largest ongoing statistical series currently conducted by the Bureau. Using interviews from a large sample of U.S. households, the Survey measures the rates at which the Nation's population is victimized by crimes of violence and theft.

Other statistical series cover civil justice, prison and jail inmates, probation and parole, adjudication, processing offenders as they move through the criminal justice system, criminal justice expenditure and employment, law enforcement management and administration, and the Federal justice system.

The Bureau supports a statistical component in the National Criminal Justice Reference Service. The Bureau of Justice Statistics Clearinghouse provides reference services for people requesting information, maintains a mailing list, and distributes Bureau publications. The Bureau may be contacted on 800–732–3277 (toll-free).

The Bureau also manages the Drugs and Crime Data Center and Clearinghouse, funded by the Office of National Drug Control Policy, which gathers and evaluates existing data on drugs and the justice system; identifies drug enforcement data gaps; operates a clearinghouse/reference center that serves as a single source for those in need of drug statistics; and prepares special reports and tabulations of existing drug data. The Drugs and Crime Data Center and Clearinghouse may be contacted on 800–666–3332 (toll-free).

National Institute of Justice   The National Institute of Justice (NIJ) sponsors special projects and research and development programs designed to improve and strengthen the criminal justice system and reduce or prevent crime. It also conducts national demonstration projects that employ innovative or promising approaches for improving criminal justice, and develops new technologies to fight crime and improve criminal justice.

NIJ conducts evaluations to determine the effectiveness of criminal justice programs, particularly programs funded by the Bureau of Justice Assistance, and identifies programs that promise to be successful if continued or replicated in other jurisdictions. For example, it has evaluated the effectiveness of innovative drug control programs, including neighborhood-oriented policing, community anti-drug initiatives, multijurisdictional task forces, and drug testing programs.

NIJ's evaluations of new approaches for holding offenders accountable for their crimes has provided invaluable information regarding such programs as bootcamps, youth challenge camps, intensive community supervision, specialized probation, and prison work-release programs. The corrections information sharing system at NIJ assists State and local officials in exchanging information on innovative and cost-effective concepts and techniques for planning, financing, and constructing new prisons and jails.

In addition, NIJ works to fulfill the information needs of the criminal justice system by publishing and disseminating reports and other materials from its research, demonstration, evaluation, and other programs; provides training and technical assistance to justice officials on innovations developed through its programs; and serves as the national and international clearinghouse of justice information for Federal, State, and local governments.

For further information, contact the National Criminal Justice Reference Service. Phone, 1–800–851–3420.

Office of Juvenile Justice and Delinquency Prevention   The Office was created by the Juvenile Justice and Delinquency Prevention Act of 1974 (42 U.S.C. 5601) in response to national concern about juvenile crime. It is the primary Federal agency for addressing juvenile crime and delinquency and the problem of missing and exploited children. The Office is comprised of five divisions.

The State Relations and Assistance Division oversees the Formula Grants Program. States can receive formula grants to help implement delinquency prevention, control, and system improvement programs, including the core requirements of the Juvenile Justice and Deliquency Prevention Act. These core requirements include deinstitutionalizing status offenders, separating juveniles from adult offenders in institutions, removing juveniles from adult jails and lockups, and addressing the disproportionate confinement of minority youth. Technical assistance is provided to States and communities to enhance their programs. The Division also administers the Title V Prevention Incentive Grants Program.

The Special Emphasis Division provides funds directly to public and private nonprofit agencies and individuals to foster new approaches to deliquency prevention and control and the improvement of the juvenile justice system. The Division focuses on such areas as serious, violent, and chronic juvenile offenders; gangs; at-risk female juvenile offenders; and school dropouts.

The Research and Program Development Division sponsors research and studies about national trends in juvenile deliquency and drug use, serious juvenile crime, the causes of deliquency, prevention strategies, program evaluation, and improvement of the juvenile justice system. It is also responsible for program evaluation, statistics, and demonstration programs.

The Training and Technical Assistance Division sponsors training for juvenile justice practitioners, policymakers, and organizations and provides technical assistance in planning, funding, establishing, operating, and evaluating juvenile delinquency programs. In addition, the Division administers juvenile court and prosecutor training, court-appointed special advocates, and children's advocacy center programs under the Victims of Child Abuse Act of 1990 (42 U.S.C. 13001).

The Information Dissemination Unit conducts a wide variety of information dissemination activities for the Office in support of its statutory mandate to serve as a clearinghouse and information center for the preparation, publication, and dissemination of information on juvenile delinquency and missing children. The Unit also monitors the operations of the juvenile justice clearinghouse, which collects, stores, and disseminates the Office's and other juvenile justice-related publications. The toll-free telephone number is 1–800–638–8736.

Programs   The Concentration of Federal Efforts Program and the Missing Children's Program are also under the Office's direction. The Concentration of Federal Efforts Program coordinates Federal programs dealing with juvenile delinquency and assists Federal agencies that have responsibility for delinquency prevention and treatment. It also promotes interagency cooperation in eliminating duplicate efforts and provides direction for the use of Federal resources in facilitating a comprehensive, unified Federal juvenile justice policy.

The Missing Children's Program was created in 1984 by the Missing Children's Assistance Act to provide Federal leadership in ensuring that every practical step is taken in recovering missing children, reuniting them with their families, and prosecuting abductors. The Program serves as a central focus for research, data collection, policy development, training professionals in the field, and providing information about missing and exploited children. It also funds the National Center for Missing and Exploited Children, which operates a national toll-free telephone line and serves as a national information clearinghouse.

Office for Victims of Crime   The Office for Victims of Crime (OVC) serves as the Federal focal point for addressing the needs and improving the treatment of crime victims. This includes carrying out the activities mandated by the Victims of Crime Act of 1984 (VOCA), as amended (42 U.S.C. 10601 note); monitoring compliance with the provisions regarding assistance for Federal crime victims of the Victim and Witness Protection Act of 1982; and implementing the recommendations of the President's Task Force on Victims of Crime, the Attorney General's Task Force on Family Violence, and the President's Child Safety Partnership.

VOCA created a Crime Victims Fund in the U.S. Treasury to provide Federal financial assistance to State governments to compensate and assist victims of crime. Monies in the fund come from fines and penalties assessed on convicted Federal defendants. The Office awards grants to States to compensate crime victims for expenses, such as medical costs, resulting from their victimization. Grants also are awarded to State governments to support State and local programs that provide direct assistance to crime victims and their families. Priority for victim assistance funds is given to programs providing direct services to victims of sexual assualt, spouse abuse, and child abuse. States also must use grant funds to assist previously underserved victim populations, such as victims of drunk drivers or the families of homicide victims.

A small portion of the Crime Victims Fund is available to support services for victims of Federal crimes. Programs under this initiative have focused on developing victim assistance services for Federal crime victims in Indian country, creating an emergency fund for use by U.S. attorneys offices to pay for emergency services for Federal crime victims, and assisting Native American child abuse victims.

In collaboration with other agencies and groups, OVC administers numerous projects serving the victims of drug-related crimes. The Office also supports national programs to improve and coordinate services to crime victims and sponsors conferences and training for criminal justice practitioners, medical and mental health personnel, the clergy, and others who work with crime victims and their families. In addition, each year OVC sponsors National Crime Victims' Rights Week to increase public awareness of crime victims' special needs and to honor those who work on behalf of victims. The OVC Resource Center, which provides information concerning victims issues to victims advocates, criminal justice practitioners, and the public, is funded by OVC. The Center may be reached toll-free on 1–800–627–6872.

Violence Against Women Program Office The Violence Against Women Program Office coordinates the activities of the Bureaus within OJP relating to violence against women. It also establishes the policy for and administers the Department's formula and

discretionary grant programs authorized by the Violence Against Women Act of 1994.

The program assists the Nation's criminal justice system to respond to the needs and concerns of women who have been, or potentially could be, victimized by violence. The program emphasizes enhanced delivery of services to women victimized by violence, and will work to strengthen outreach efforts to minorities and disabled women. The Office provides technical assistance to State and tribal government officials in plannimg innovative and effective criminal justice responses to violent crimes committed against women. The Office provides Indian tribal governments with funds to develop and strengthen the tribal justice system's response to violent crimes committed against Native American women through a discretionary grant program.

States that receive Violence Against Women Program formula grant funds are required to engage in a multidisciplinary planning process involving law enforcement; prosecution; nonprofit, nongovernmental victim service providers including domestic violence and sexual assault coalitions; key criminal justice practitioners; and community leaders to develop a coordinated and integrated strategy to address to address violence against women. Funds may be used to support seven broad purpose areas including training for law enforcement officers and prosecutors to identify and respond more effectively to violent crimes against women; developing, training, or expanding special units of law enforcement officers and prosecutors to respond to violent crimes against women; developing, training, or expanding special units of law enforcement officers and prosecutors to respond to violent crimes against women; developing and improving data collection and communications systems linking police, prosecutors, and courts, or to identify and track arrests, protection orders, violations of protection orders; creating or enhancing victim services programs and programs addressing stalking; and developing and enhancing programs which focus on the special needs of Indian tribes in addressing violent crimes.

Drug Court Program Office   The Drug Court Program Office was established to support the development and implementation of effective Drug Court programming at the State, local, and tribal level. The Office coordinates the Drug Court activities of OJP's five component bureaus and administers the Drug Court Grant Program as authorized by Title V of the Violent Crime Control and Law Enforcement Act of 1994.

This discretionary grant program assists local units of government in the planning, implementation, and improvement of Drug Courts which target non-violent, drug-involved offenders. The Office strives to strengthen existing Drug Courts and develop new Drug Courts, encouraging them to provide continuing judicial supervision, mandatory periodic testing for substance abuse among clients, substance abuse treatment, offender supervision, management and aftercare, combined with appropriate sanctions for failure to comply with program requirements. The Office will work closely with agencies and organizations involved in the areas of justice and recovery. The Office also will develop and deliver appropriate technical assistance, training, and research findings in order to enhance the effectiveness and operation of both existing and new Drug Courts.

Corrections Program Office   The Corrections Program Office provides policy direction, coordination, and administration for the corrections programs authorized by the Violent Crime Control and Law Enforcement Act of 1994. In particular, the Office is responsible for the following grant programs: Violent Offender Incarceration; Truth in Sentencing; Punishment of Young Offenders Formula Grants; Family Unity Demonstration Projects; and Residential Substance Abuse Treatment for State Prisoners.

The largest grant programs--the Violent Offender and Truth in Sentencing Incentive Grants--provide assistance through formula grants to States, and States organized as multi-State compacts, for adult and juvenile correctional systems. The program recognizes that States and local jurisdictions have experienced substantial increases in jail, prison, and juvenile confinement populations in recent years, resulting in escalating costs and serious difficulties in managing overcapacity correctional populations. This program provides funds for States to construct, expand, modify, operate, and improve correctional facilities, including boot camp facilities and other alternative correctional programs that will free secure prison space for the confinement of violent offenders.

The Corrections Program Office emphasizes comprehensive correctional planning and State/local coordination in the provision of correctional services to offenders. States participating in the grant program will receive technical assistance and training and be expected to participate in a comprehensive national evaluation.

For further information, contact the Office of Congressional and Public Affairs, Office of Justice Programs, Department of Justice, 633 Indiana Avenue NW., Washington, DC 20531. Phone, 202–307–0781.

Boards

Executive Office for Immigration Review

Falls Church, VA 22041

The Attorney General is responsible for the administration and enforcement of the Immigration and Nationality Act of 1952 (8 U.S.C. 1101) and all other laws relating to the immigration and naturalization of aliens. Certain powers and authorities of the Attorney General for the administration and interpretation of the immigration laws are delegated to the Executive Office for Immigration Review. The Executive Office for Immigration Review is completely independent of the Immigration and Naturalization Service, the body charged with the enforcement of the immigration laws. It includes the Board of Immigration Appeals, the Office of the Chief Immigration Judge, and the Office of the Chief Administrative Hearing Officer. It operates under the supervision of the Deputy Attorney General and is headed by a Director, who is responsible for the immediate supervision of the Board of Immigration Appeals, the Office of the Chief Immigration Judge, and the Office of the Chief Administrative Hearing Officer.

Board of Immigration Appeals The Board of Immigration Appeals is a quasi-judicial body composed of a Chairman, Vice Chairman, and seven members, and a Chief Attorney-Examiner, who is also an alternate Board member.

Located in Falls Church, VA, the Board hears oral argument in that location. The Board is authorized a staff of attorney-advisers who assist the Board in the preparation of decisions.

The Board has been given nationwide jurisdiction to hear appeals from decisions entered by district and center directors of the Immigration and Naturalization Service and by immigration judges. In addition, the Board is responsible for hearing appeals involving the suspension or barring from practice of attorneys and representatives before the Service and the Board.

Decisions of the Board are binding on all Service officers and immigration judges unless modified or overruled by the Attorney General, and are subject to judicial review in the Federal courts. The majority of appeals reaching the Board involves orders of deportation and applications for relief from deportation. Other cases before the Board include the exclusion of aliens applying for admission to the United States, petitions to classify the status of alien relatives for the issuance of preference immigrant visas, fines imposed upon carriers for the violation of the immigration laws, and motions for reopening and reconsideration of decisions previously rendered.

Following a review of the record and research into questions of law raised by the parties, the attorney-adviser drafts a proposed order for consideration of the Board members. He or she frequently confers with individual Board members concerning the proposed order. Attorney-advisers also assist in various administrative and support functions. In addition to developing expertise in the field of immigration law, the attorney-adviser is often called upon to analyze questions of constitutional law, State, Federal, and foreign civil and criminal law.

Office of the Chief Immigration Judge The Office of the Chief Immigration Judge is responsible for the general supervision and direction of the immigration judges in the performance of their duties. It establishes operational policies for the offices of the immigration judges and evaluates the performance of those offices.

Located in Falls Church, VA, the Office of the Chief Immigration Judge includes a headquarters staff of management and legal personnel.

Office of the Immigration Judge The offices of the immigration judges are responsible for presiding at formal, quasi-judicial deportation and exclusion proceedings. The immigration judges act independently in their decisionmaking capacity, and their decisions are administratively final unless appealed or certified to the Board of Immigration Appeals.

In exclusion proceedings, an immigration judge determines whether an individual arriving from a foreign country should be allowed to enter the United States or should be excluded and deported. Located throughout the United States, each judge has jurisdiction to consider various forms of relief available in exclusion proceedings, including applications for asylum and relief under section 243(h) of the Immigration and Nationality Act of 1952 (8 U.S.C. 1158, 1253).

In deportation proceedings, the immigration judge determines whether an individual who has already entered the United States is deportable from this country. In such proceedings the judge also adjudicates applications for the various forms of relief available under this country's immigration laws. These include applications for adjustment of status, suspension of deportation, voluntary departure, relief under section 212(c) of the act (8 U.S.C. 1182), and applications for asylum and withholding of deportation.

Office of the Chief Administrative Hearing Officer   The Office of the Chief Administrative Hearing Officer is responsible for the general supervision of administrative law judges in the performance of their duties under 8 U.S.C. 1324a–1324c. Administrative law judge proceedings are mandated by the Immigration and Nationality Act and concern allegations of unlawful employment of aliens, unfair immigration-related employment discrimination, and immigration document fraud.

For further information, contact the Counsel to the Director, Executive Office for Immigration Review, Department of Justice, Falls Church, VA 22041. Phone, 703–305–0470.

United States Parole Commission

5550 Friendship Boulevard, Chevy Chase, MD 20815. Phone, 301–492–5990

The granting, denying, or revocation of parole for eligible Federal offenders rests in the discretion of the U.S. Parole Commission. The Commission will be abolished on November 1, 1997, 10 years after the implementation of the U.S. Sentencing Guidelines. (The Comprehensive Crime Control Act of 1984 abolished the U.S. Parole Commission and instituted mandatory sentencing for all offenders whose crimes were committed after November 1, 1987.) The Commission is also responsible for the supervision of paroled or otherwise released offenders until expiration of their terms and may discharge parolees early from supervision. Under the Labor Management Reporting and Disclosure Act of 1959 (29 U.S.C. 401 note), the Commission determines whether or not persons convicted of certain crimes may

serve as officials in the field of organized labor or in labor-oriented management positions; likewise, under the Employment Retirement Income and Security Act of 1974, the Commission determines whether or not such persons may provide services to or be employed by employment benefit plans.

The Parole Commission presently consists of six members, appointed by the President with the advice and consent of the Senate. It has sole authority to grant, modify, or revoke paroles of eligible U.S. prisoners serving sentences of more than 1 year and D.C. Code prisoners housed in Federal institutions. It is responsible for the supervision of parolees and prisoners released upon the expiration of their sentences with allowances for statutory good time, and the determination of supervisory conditions and terms. U.S. probation officers supervise parolees and mandatory releasees under the direction of the Commission.

The Anti-Drug Abuse Act of 1988 gave the Commission jurisdiction over all foreign transfer treaty cases beginning January 1, 1989. For offenses committed after November 1, 1987, the Commission is to apply the guidelines of the U.S. Sentencing Commission.

For further information, contact the Office of the Chairman, United States Parole Commission, Department of Justice, 5550 Friendship Boulevard, Chevy Chase, MD 20815. Phone, 301–492–5990.

Office of Community Oriented Policing Services

The Office of Community Oriented Policing Services (COPS) was created with the passage of the Violent Crime Control and Law Enforcement Act of 1994 to achieve several goals: to advance the philosophy of community policing as a national law enforcement strategy; to deploy 100,000 new police officers in community policing roles; to reinforce partnerships that will sustain community policing; and to evaluate and demonstrate the effectiveness of community policing to improve the quality of life by reducing the levels of disorder, violence, and crime in our communities.

The primary activity of the COPS Office is the awarding of competitive, discretionary grants directly to law enforcement agencies across the United States and its territories. Over the life of the COPS Office, approximately $8 billion in grant funding will be made available to achieve these goals.

The COPS Office is headed by a Director, appointed by the Attorney General, and is organized into several divisions. The Grants Administration Division is responsible for developing and designing new programs to provide resources for the hiring of new officers and to further the adoption and implementation of community policing, reviewing grant applications, maintaining liaison with the Office of Justice Programs for financial review of applications, monitoring grant awards, developing and maintaining databases to support policymaking, participating in the evaluation of the grant programs, and coordination of the Office's research agenda. Within the Grants Administration Division are the Police Hiring section and the Program Planning, Research and Evaluation section.

The Training and Technical Assistance Division is responsible for coordinating the provision of training and technical assistance to advance the adoption, implementation and sustaining of community policing in the thousands of communities served by the COPS Office.

The Legal Division is responsible for providing legal advice to the Director and other functional areas of the COPS Office, and for ensuring compliance with the legal requirements applicable to the activities of the COPS Office.

The Congressional Relations Division assists Members of Congress in serving their constituents, thereby facilitating greater dissemination of information about COPS programs and activities, and provides input in program design and development and policy formulation so that programs and policies reflect legislative intent and address congressional needs.

The Communications Division provides ongoing information about community policing and COPS programs

through every available channel of communication, including timely and accurate responses to media inquiries, interviews, public events, publications and related materials produced by and for any telecommunication format.

The Intergovernmental and Public Liaison Division maintains channels for communication and feedback regarding COPS programs with representatives of interested local, State, and national organizations and with local elected officials.

Finally, the Administrative Division provides support services to the COPS Office, including resource management to recruit, train, and maintain a professional workforce; fiscal resource management to perform the accounting and budget formulation and execution functions necessary to administer the COPS appropriation; facilities management to acquire and maintain space, provide security, and procure supplies, equipment, telephones, and other services; and information resource management.

Foreign Claims Settlement Commission of the United States

The Foreign Claims Settlement Commission of the United States is a quasi-judicial, independent agency within the Department of Justice which adjudicates claims of U.S. nationals against foreign governments, either under specific jurisdiction conferred by Congress or pursuant to international claims settlement agreements. Funds for payment of the Commission's awards are derived from congressional appropriations, international claims settlements, or the liquidation of foreign assets in the United States by the Departments of Justice and the Treasury.

The Commission recently started an Albanian Claims Program, to adjudicate claims and make awards compensating U.S. nationals for losses resulting from nationalization, expropriation, intervention and other property-taking by the Albanian regime which took power at the end of World War II.

The Commission recently completed the adjudication of more than 3,100 claims against the Government of Iran, which arose out of the 1979 Islamic Revolution. The Iran Claims Program resulted in total awards in excess of $86 million between 1991 and February 1995, pursuant to the June 1990 Iran-U.S. Settlement Agreement and the Iran Claims Settlement Act (50 U.S.C. 1701 note).

The Commission also has authority under the War Claims Act of 1948, as amended (50 U.S.C. app. 2001 *et seq.*), to receive, determine the validity and amount, and provide for the payment of claims by U.S. servicemen and civilians held as prisoners of war or interned by a hostile force in Southeast Asia during the Vietnam conflict, or by the survivors of such servicemen and civilians.

In addition, the Commission furnishes technical assistance and advice to other Federal agencies and offices in planning new claims adjudication programs, and negotiating international claims settlement agreements. In addition, the Commission is responsible for maintaining records and responding to inquiries related to the various claims programs it has conducted under the International Claims Settlement Act of 1949, as amended, involving the Governments of Yugoslavia, Panama, Poland, Bulgaria, Hungary, Romania, Italy, the Soviet Union, Czechoslovakia, Cuba, the German Democratic Republic, the People's Republic of China, Vietnam, Ethiopia, and Egypt, as well as those authorized under the War Claims Act of 1948, and other statutes.

The Commission's organization and functions are defined in the International Claims Settlement Act of 1949, as amended (22 U.S.C. 1621 *et seq.*), the War Claims Act of 1948, as amended (50 U.S.C. app. 2001 *et seq.*), and the Iran Claims Settlement Act (50 U.S.C. 1701 note).

For further information, contact the Office of the Chair, Foreign Claims Settlement Commission of the United States, Department of Justice, Suite 6002, 600 E Street NW., Washington, DC 20579. Phone, 202–616–6975; or fax, 202–616–6993.

Sources of Information

Controlled Substances Act Registration Information about registration under the Controlled Substances Act may be obtained from the Registration Section of the Drug Enforcement Administration, P.O. Box 28083, Central Station, Washington, DC 20038. Phone, 202–307–7255.

Employment The Department maintains an agencywide job line. Phone, 202–514–3397.

Attorneys' applications: Director, Office of Attorney Personnel Management, Department of Justice, Room 6150, Tenth Street and Constitution Avenue NW., Washington, DC 20530. Phone, 202–514–1432. Assistant U.S. attorney applicants should apply to individual U.S. attorneys.

United States Marshals Service: Field Staffing Branch, United States Marshals Service, Department of Justice, 600 Army Navy Drive, Arlington, VA 22202–4210.

Federal Bureau of Investigation: Director, Washington, DC 20535, or any of the field offices or resident agencies whose addresses are listed in the front of most local telephone directories.

Immigration and Naturalization Service: Central Office, 425 I Street NW., Washington, DC 20536 (phone, 202–514–2530); or any regional or district office.

Drug Enforcement Administration: regional offices, laboratories, or Washington Headquarters Office of Personnel.

Bureau of Prisons: Central Office, 320 First Street NW., Washington, DC 20534 (phone, 202–307–3082); or any regional or field office.

Office of Justice Programs, 633 Indiana Avenue NW., Washington, DC 20531. Phone, 202–307–0730.

United States Trustee Program, Room 770, 901 E Street NW., Washington, DC 20530. Phone, 202–616–1000.

Foreign Claims Settlement Commission: Attorneys: Office of the Chief Counsel, Suite 6002, 600 E Street NW., Washington, DC 20579 (phone, 202–616–6975); Other: Administrative Officer, same address and phone.
Reading Rooms Located in Washington, DC, at: U.S. Department of Justice, Room 6505, Tenth Street and Constitution Avenue NW., Washington, DC 20530 (phone, 202–514–3775). Bureau of Prisons, 320 First Street NW., 20534 (phone, 202–307–3029); Immigration and Naturalization Service, 425 I Street NW., 20536 (phone, 202–514–2837); Foreign Claims Settlement Commission, 600 E Street NW., 20579 (phone, 202–616–6975). Also at the U.S. Parole Commission, 5550 Friendship Boulevard, Chevy Chase, MD 20815 (phone, 301–492–5959); Board of Immigration Appeals, Suite 2400, 5107 Leesburg Pike, Falls Church, VA 22041 (phone, 703–305–0168); some of the Immigration and Naturalization Service district offices; and the National Institute of Justice, 9th Floor, 633 Indiana Avenue NW., Washington, DC 20531 (phone, 202–307–5883).
Publications and Films The *FBI Law Enforcement Bulletin* and *Uniform Crime Reports—Crime in the United States* are available from the Superintendent of Documents, Government Printing Office, Washington, DC 20402.

The Annual Report of the Attorney General of the United States is published each year by the Department of Justice, Washington, DC 20530.

Approximately nine textbooks on citizenship, consisting of teachers manuals and student textbooks at various reading levels, are distributed free to public schools for applicants for citizenship and are on sale to all others from the Superintendent of Documents, Government Printing Office, Washington, DC 20402. Public schools or organizations under the supervision of public schools which are entitled to free textbooks should make their requests to the appropriate Immigration and Naturalization Service Regional Office (See appropriate section of this manual for mailing addresses.). For general information, call 202–514–3946.

The Freedom of Information Act Guide and Privacy Act Overview and the *Freedom of Information Case List,* both published annually, are available from the Superintendent of Documents, Government Printing Office, Washington, DC 20530; and in electronic format through INTERNET–Library of Congress. ISBN 0–16–042921–8.

FOIA Update (Stock No. 727–002–00000–6), published quarterly, is available free of charge to FOIA offices and other interested offices Governmentwide. This publication is also available from the Superintendent of Documents, Government Printing Office, Washington, DC 20402; and in electronic format through INTERNET–Library of Congress.

Guidelines for Effective Human Relations Commissions, Annual Report of the Community Relations Service, Community Relations Service Brochure, CRS Hotline Brochure, Police Use of Deadly Force: A Conciliation Handbook for Citizens and Police, Principles of Good Policing: Avoiding Violence Between Police and Citizens, Resolving Racial Conflict: A Guide for Municipalities, and *Viewpoints and Guidelines on Court-Appointed Citizens Monitoring Commissions in School Desegregation* are available upon request from the Public Information Office, Community Relations Service, Department of Justice, Washington, DC 20530.

A limited number of drug educational films are available, free of charge, to civic, educational, private, and religious groups.

A limited selection of pamphlets and brochures is available. The most widely requested publication is *Drugs of Abuse,* an identification manual intended for professional use. Single copies are free.

Copies of the Foreign Claims Settlement Commission's semiannual (through December 1966) and annual (from January 1967) reports to the Congress concerning its activities are available at the Commission in limited quantities.
Reference Service In 1972, the National Institute of Justice established

the National Criminal Justice Reference Service (NCJRS). All five OJP bureaus now support NCJRS, a clearinghouse of information and publications concerning OJP programs and other information of interest to the criminal justice community. The Office's National Institute of Justice, which has supported the clearinghouse for almost 20 years, provides most of the funding for the National Criminal Justice Reference Service. Police, corrections agencies, courts, criminal justice planners, juvenile justice practitioners, community crime prevention groups, and others needing information for planning and problem solving in criminal justice can refer to this international information service specially designed to assist the justice community.

The National Criminal Justice Reference Service provides information from its computerized data base system free or at a minimal cost to users through a variety of products and services including the bimonthly *NIJ Catalog*, which contains abstracts of significant additions to the data base and pertinent information and a Calendar of Events announcing upcoming training courses and conferences; selected hardcopy documents upon request; three types of data base search packages; various microfiche products; and referrals to other information sources. Under contracts with OJP bureaus, the National Criminal Justice Reference Service also operates the Drugs and Crime Data Center and Clearinghouse, the Bureau of Justice Assistance Clearinghouse, the Justice Statistics Clearinghouse, the Juvenile Justice Clearinghouse, the National Victims Resource Center, and the Construction Information Exchange. All the Service's clearinghouses may be contacted on 800–851–3420 (toll-free); or in the Washington, DC, metropolitan area on 301–251–5500.

The NCJRS Electronic Bulletin Board, with 3,000 registered users, makes NCJRS' services available online. The Bulletin Board may be accessed by modem on 301–738–8895.

Organizations and individuals may register to receive information from the National Criminal Justice Reference Service by writing NCJRS, Box 6000, 1600 Research Boulevard, Rockville, MD 20850.

Small Business Activities Contract information for small businesses can be obtained from the Office of Small and Disadvantaged Business Utilization, Department of Justice, Tenth Street and Pennsylvania Avenue NW., Washington, DC 20530. Phone, 202–616–0521.

For further information concerning the Department of Justice, contact the Office of Public Affairs, Department of Justice, Tenth Street and Constitution Avenue NW., Washington, DC 20530. Phone, 202–514–2007 (voice); 202–786–5731 (TDD).

DEPARTMENT OF LABOR

200 Constitution Avenue NW., Washington, DC 20210
Phone, 202–219–5000

SECRETARY OF LABOR	ROBERT B. REICH
Chief of Staff	LESLIE LOBLE
Confidential Assistant to the Secretary	ANN DELORY
Counselor to the Secretary	JOHN D. DONAHUE
Executive Secretary	T. MICHAEL KERR
Deputy Secretary	THOMAS P. GLYNN
Associate Deputy Secretary	STEPHEN ROSENTHAL
Chief Economist	ALAN KRUEGER
Director, Office of Small Business and Minority Affairs	JUNE M. ROBINSON
Executive Director, Administrative Appeals	DAVID A. O'BRIAN
Chief Administrative Law Judge	JOHN VITTRONE, *Acting*
Chief Administrative Appeals Judge, Benefits Review Board	BETTY J. HALL
Chairman, Employees Compensation Appeals Board	MICHAEL J. WALSH
Chairman, Wage Appeals Board	CHARLES E. SHEARER, JR.
Director, Women's Bureau	KAREN BETH NUSSBAUM
Deputy Director	DELORES L. CROCKETT, *Acting*
Inspector General	CHARLES C. MASTEN
Deputy Inspector General	I.A. BASSETT, JR.
Assistant Inspector General for Audit	GERALD W. PETERSON
Deputy Assistant Inspector General for Audit	JOSEPH E. FISCH
Assistant Inspector General for Investigation	F.M. BROADWAY
Assistant Inspector General for Resource Management and Legislative Assessment	E.J. GERMAN
Assistant Inspector General for Labor Racketeering	GUSTAVE A. SCHICK
Legal Counsel to Inspector General	SYLVIA HOROWITZ
Assistant Secretary for Public Affairs	ANNE LEWIS
Deputy Assistant Secretary	MARY MEAGHER
Solicitor of Labor	THOMAS S. WILLIAMSON, JR.
Deputy Solicitor, National Operations	OLIVER B. QUINN
Deputy Solicitor, Regional Operations	RONALD G. WHITING
Deputy Solicitor, Planning and Coordination	JUDITH F. KRAMER
Director, Office of Management	LYDIA G. LEEDS
Associate Solicitor, Employment and Training Legal Services	CHARLES D. RAYMOND
Associate Solicitor, Fair Labor Standards	MONICA GALLAGHER
Associate Solicitor, Legislation and Legal Counsel	ROBERT A. SHAPIRO
Associate Solicitor, Labor-Management Laws	JOHN F. DEPENBROCK
Associate Solicitor, Black Lung Benefits	DONALD S. SHIRE
Associate Solicitor, Employee Benefits	CAROL DEDEO

377

Associate Solicitor, Occupational Safety and Health	JOSEPH M. WOODWARD
Associate Solicitor, Civil Rights	JAMES D. HENRY
Associate Solicitor, Plan Benefits Security	MARC I. MACHIZ
Associate Solicitor, Mine Safety and Health	EDWARD P. CLAIR
Associate Solicitor, Special Appellate and Supreme Court Litigation	ALLEN H. FELDMAN
Assistant Secretary for Congressional and Intergovernmental Affairs	GERI D. PALAST
Deputy Assistant Secretaries	MARY ANN RICHARDSON
	DARLA J. LETOURNEAU
Deputy Under Secretary for International Affairs	JOAQUIN F. OTERO
Associate Deputy Under Secretary for Policy	ANDREW J. SAMET
Director, Office of Management, Administration and Planning	MARION F. HOUSTOUN
Assistant Secretary for Policy	TIM BARNICLE
Deputy Assistant Secretaries	ROLAND G. DROITSCH
	LESLIE LOBLE
Assistant Secretary for Administration and Management	CYNTHIA A. METZLER
Deputy Assistant Secretary	CECILIA J. BANKINS
Comptroller for the Department	WILLIAM R. REISE
Director, National Capital Service Center	THOMAS K. DELANEY
Director, Information Resources Management	JOHN DINNEEN
Director, Civil Rights	ANNABELLE T. LOCKHART
Director, Administrative and Procurement Programs	JANICE SAWYER
Director, Personnel Management	LARRY GOODWIN
Director, Office of Safety and Health	FREDERICK DRAYTON
Assistant Secretary for Veterans' Employment and Training	PRESTON M. TAYLOR, JR.
Deputy Assistant Secretary	ESPIRIDION A. BORREGO
Assistant Secretary for Employment and Training	DOUG ROSS
Deputy Assistant Secretaries	CAROLYN GOLDING, JOHN ROBINSON, RAYMOND J. UHALDE
Administrator, Office of Financial and Administrative Management	BRYAN T. KEILTY
Administrator, Office of Job Training Programs	DOLORES BATTLE
Administrator, Office of Strategic Planning and Policy Development	(VACANCY)
Administrator, Office of Regional Management	BARBARA ANN FARMER
Administrator, Office of Work-Based Learning	JAMES VAN ERDEN
Director, Unemployment Insurance Service	MARY ANN WYRSCH
Director, United States Employment Service	ROBERT A. SCHAERFI
Director, Public and Intergovernmental Affairs	BONNIE FRIEDMAN
Assistant Secretary for the Office of the American Workplace	CHARLES L. SMITH

Deputy Assistant Secretary for Workplace Programs — ROBERT PORTMAN

Deputy Assistant Secretary for Labor-Management Programs — CHARLES RICHARDS

Deputy Assistant Secretary for Labor-Management Standards — EDMUNDO GONZALES

Director, Public Affairs Team — MEG INGOLD

Director, Administrative Management and Technology Team — JOAN RIND

Assistant Secretary, Pension and Welfare Benefits Administration — OLENA BERG

Deputy Assistant Secretaries — ALAN D. LEBOWITZ
MEREDITH MILLER

Director, Office of Enforcement — CHARLES LERNER

Director, Office of Regulations and Interpretations — ROBERT DOYLE

Chief Accountant — IAN DINGWALD

Director, Program Services — JUNE PATRON

Director, Exemption Determinations — IVAN STRASFELD

Director, Information Management — MERVYN SCHWEDT

Director, Program Planning and Evaluation — BRIAN MCDONNELL

Director, Office of Policy and Legislative Analysis — GERALD LINDREW

Director, Office of Research and Economic Analysis — RICHARD HINZ

Assistant Secretary, Employment Standards Administration — BERNARD E. ANDERSON

Deputy Assistant Secretary — MARIA ECHAVESTE

Director, Equal Employment Opportunity Unit — CARVIN COOK

Administrator, Wage and Hour Division — MARIA ECHAVESTE

Deputy Administrator — JOHN R. FRASER

Deputy Assistant Secretary for Federal Contract Compliance Programs — SHIRLEY J. WILCHER

Deputy Director — LEONARD J. BIERMANN

Director, Division of Policy, Planning and Program Development — ANNIE A. BLACKWELL

Director, Division of Program Operation — ROBERT B. GREAUX

Deputy Assistant Secretary for Office of Workers' Compensation Programs — IDA L. CASTRO

Deputy Director — SHELBY HALLMARK

Director, Office of Management, Administration and Planning — DONNA G. COPSON

Deputy Director — ELEANOR H. SMITH

Director, Office of Public Affairs — ROBERT A. CUCCIA

Chief, Branch of Legislative and Regulatory Analysis — PATRICK J. MOWRY

Assistant Secretary for Occupational Safety and Health — JOSEPH A. DEAR

Deputy Assistant Secretaries — RICHARD L. HAYES
JAMES W. STANLEY

Director, Office of Information and Consumer Affairs — JAMES F. FOSTER

Director, Office of Special Management Programs — FRED HAWKINS

Director, Office of Construction and Engineering	CHARLES CULVER
Director, Office of Statistics	STEPHEN NEWELL
Director, Policy	MICHAEL SILVERSTEIN
Director, Administrative Programs	DAVID C. ZEIGLER
Director, Federal/State Operations	PAULA WHITE
Director, Field Programs	LEO CAREY
Director, Technical Support	STEVE MALLINGER, *Acting*
Director, Compliance Programs	JOHN MILES
Director, Health Standards Programs	CHARLES ADKINS
Director, Safety Standards Programs	THOMAS SHEPICH
Commissioner of Labor Statistics	KATHARINE G. ABRAHAM
Deputy Commissioner for Administration and Internal Operations	WILLIAM G. BARRON, JR.
Assistant Commissioner for Technology and Survey Processing	CARL J. LOWE
Director for Survey Processing	JOHN D. SINKS
Director for Technology and Computing Services	ARNOLD BRESNICK
Assistant Commissioner for Administration	DANIEL J. LACEY
Director, Quality and Information Management	JOHN M. GALVIN
Associate Commissioner for Employment and Unemployment Statistics	THOMAS J. PLEWES
Deputy Associate Commissioner for Employment and Unemployment Statistics	(VACANCY)
Assistant Commissioner for Federal/State Programs	(VACANCY)
Assistant Commissioner for Current Employment Analysis	JOHN E. BREGGER
Associate Commissioner for Prices and Living Conditions	KENNETH V. DALTON
Deputy Associate Commissioner for Prices and Living Conditions	(VACANCY)
Assistant Commissioner for Consumer Prices and Price Indexes	PAUL A. ARMKNECHT
Assistant Commissioner for Industrial Prices and Price Indexes	JOHN M. GALVIN
Assistant Commissioner for International Prices	KATRINA W. REUT
Associate Commissioner for Compensation and Working Conditions	KIMBERLY D. ZIESCHANG
Deputy Associate Commissioner for Compensation and Working Conditions	(VACANCY)
Assistant Commissioner for Safety, Health, and Working Conditions	WILLIAM M. EISENBERG
Assistant Commissioner for Compensation Levels and Trends	KATHLEEN M. MACDONALD
Associate Commissioner for Productivity and Technology	EDWIN R. DEAN
Associate Commissioner for Employment Projections	RONALD E. KUTSCHER
Associate Commissioner for Publications and Special Studies	DEBORAH P. KLEIN

Associate Commissioner for Field Operations	LAURA B. KING
Associate Commissioner for Research and Evaluation	WESLEY L. SCHAIBLE
Assistant Commissioner for Survey Methods Research	CATHRYN S. DIPPO
Assistant Commissioner for Economic Research	MARILYN E. MANSER
Assistant Secretary for Mine Safety and Health	J. DAVITT MCATEER
Deputy Assistant Secretary for Policy	ANDREA HRICKO
Deputy Assistant Secretary for Operations	EDWARD C. HUGLER
Administrator for Coal Mine Safety and Health	MARVIN W. NICHOLS, JR.
Administrator for Metal and Nonmetal Mine Safety and Health	VERNON R. GOMEZ
Director of Technical Support	KENNETH T. HOWARD
Director of Educational Policy and Development	FRANK SCHWAMBERGER, *Acting*
Director, Office of Standards, Regulations and Variances	PATRICIA W. SILVEY
Director, Office of Assessments	RICHARD G. HIGH, JR.
Director of Administration and Management	RICHARD L. BRECHBIEL
Director of Program Policy Evaluation	GEORGE M. FESAK, JR.
Director, Office of Information and Public Affairs	WAYNE E. VENEMAN
Chief, Office of Congressional and Legislative Affairs	(VACANCY)
Legislative Affairs Specialist	SYLVIA MILANESE

The purpose of the Department of Labor is to foster, promote, and develop the welfare of the wage earners of the United States, to improve their working conditions, and to advance their opportunities for profitable employment. In carrying out this mission, the Department administers a variety of Federal labor laws guaranteeing workers' rights to safe and healthful working conditions, a minimum hourly wage and overtime pay, freedom from employment discrimination, unemployment insurance, and workers' compensation. The Department also protects workers' pension rights; provides for job training programs; helps workers find jobs; works to strengthen free collective bargaining; and keeps track of changes in employment, prices, and other national economic measurements. As the Department seeks to assist all Americans who need and want to work, special efforts are made to meet the unique job market problems of older workers, youths, minority group members, women, the handicapped, and other groups.

The Department of Labor (DOL), the ninth executive department, was created by act of March 4, 1913 (29 U.S.C. 551). A Bureau of Labor was first created by Congress in 1884 under the Interior Department. The Bureau of Labor later became independent as a Department of Labor without executive rank. It again returned to bureau status in the Department of Commerce and Labor, which was created by act of February 14, 1903 (15 U.S.C. 1501).

Office of the Secretary of Labor

Secretary The Secretary is the head of the Department of Labor and the principal adviser to the President on the development and execution of policies and the administration and enforcement of laws relating to wage earners, their working conditions, and their employment opportunities. The Office of the Secretary includes the Offices of Deputy Secretary, Inspector General, the Assistant Secretaries, and the Solicitor of

DEPARTMENT OF LABOR

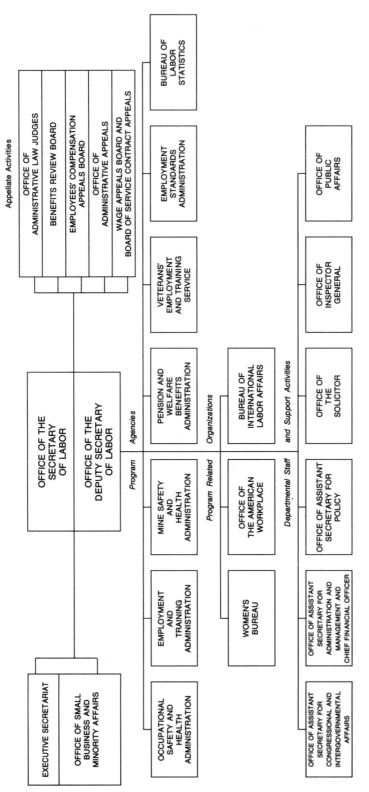

Labor. Other offices whose public purposes are widely applied are detailed below and on the following pages.

Office of the Deputy Secretary of Labor

Deputy Secretary The Deputy Secretary of Labor is the principal adviser to the Secretary and serves as Acting Secretary in the Secretary's absence.

Employees' Compensation Appeals Board The Employees' Compensation Appeals Board consists of three members and three alternate members appointed by the Secretary of Labor, one of whom is designated as Chairman. The function of the Board is to consider and decide appeals from final decisions in cases arising under the Federal Employees' Compensation Act (5 U.S.C. 8101). The decisions of the Board are final and not subject to court review.

For further information, call 202–401–8600.

Administrative Appeals The Office of Administrative Appeals assists the Deputy Secretary in reviewing appeals from decisions of Administrative Law Judges under certain laws and programs. These appeals arise under the Job Training Partnership Act, the Trade Act, the Surface Transportation Assistance Act, the Energy Reorganization Act, and several environmental laws, unemployment insurance conformity proceedings, and cases brought by the Office of Federal Contract Compliance Programs.

For further information, contact the Director, Office of Administrative Appeals. Phone, 202–219– 9728.

Women's Bureau The Women's Bureau is responsible for formulating standards and policies that promote the welfare of wage earning women, improve their working conditions, increase their efficiency, and advance their opportunities for profitable employment.

Regional Offices—Women's Bureau
(Areas included within each region are indicated on the map in Appendix A.)

Region/Address	Administrator
I. Boston, MA (1 Congress St., 02114)	Jacqueline Cooke
II. New York, NY (201 Varick St., 10014)	Mary Murphree
III. Philadelphia, PA (3535 Market St., 19104)	(Vacancy)
IV. Atlanta, GA (1371 Peachtree St. NE., 30367)	Dorris Muscadoo, Acting
V. Chicago, IL (230 S. Dearborn St., 60604)	Sandra K. Frank
VI. Dallas, TX (525 Griffin Sq., 75202)	Evelyn F. Smith
VII. Kansas City, MO (911 Walnut St., 64106)	Rose A. Kemp
VIII. Denver, CO (Suite 905, 1801 California St., 80202–2614)	Oleta Crain
IX. San Francisco, CA (71 Stevenson St., 94105)	Madeline Mixer
X. Seattle, WA (1111 3d Ave., 98101)	Karen Furia

For further information, call 202–219–6611.

Office of Small Business and Minority Affairs This office, reporting to the Deputy Secretary of Labor, administers the Department's small and disadvantaged business utilization program; Executive Order 12876, to promote and increase participation of historically black colleges and universities in Federal programs, and similar initiatives for Hispanic and other minority colleges and universities; and the Federal Advisory Committee Act, to provide administrative support and guidance to DOL advisory, interagency, and intradepartmental committees.

For further information, call 202–219–9148.

Office of Administrative Law Judges
Administrative law judges preside over formal hearings to determine violations of minimum wage requirements, overtime payments, compensation benefits, employee discrimination, grant performance, alien certification, employee protection, and health and safety regulations set forth under numerous statutes, Executive orders, and regulations. With few exceptions, hearings are required to be conducted in

accordance with the Administrative Procedure Act (5 U.S.C. note prec. 551).

For further information, contact the Office of the Chief Administrative Law Judge. Phone, 202–565–5330.

Benefits Review   The Benefits Review Board is a five-member quasi-judicial body with exclusive jurisdiction to consider and decide appeals raising substantial questions of law or fact from decisions of Administrative Law Judges with respect to cases arising under the Longshoremen's and Harbor Workers' Compensation Act (33 U.S.C. 901) and its extensions and the Black Lung Benefits Act of 1972 (30 U.S.C. 801). The Board exercises the same review authority that the United States District Courts formerly held in these areas of the law prior to the 1972 amendments to both acts.

For further information, contact the Administrative Officer. Phone, 202–633–7500.

Wage Appeals/Service Contract Appeals The Wage Appeals Board and the Board of Service Contract Appeals act on behalf of the Secretary of Labor in deciding appeals on questions of law and fact, taken in the discretion of the Boards from wage determinations issued under the Davis-Bacon Act (and its related Federal construction contract prevailing wage statutes) and the McNamara-O'Hara Service Contract Act; debarments under the Department's regulations (29 CFR, Part 5), which implement Reorganization Plan No. 14 of 1950 (5 U.S.C. app.), effective May 24, 1950, and debarments under the Department's regulations (29 CFR, Part 4), which implement the Service Contract Act; under the Department's regulations, disputes concerning the payment of prevailing wage rates or proper classifications that involve significant sums of money, large groups of employees, or novel or unusual situations; questions relating to coverage of the various acts; and recommendations by Federal agencies for appropriate adjustments of liquidated

damages that are assessed under the Contract Work Hours and Safety Standards Act.

For further information, contact the Executive Secretary. Phone, 202–219–9039.

The Solicitor of Labor

The Office of the Solicitor (SOL) provides the Secretary of Labor and departmental officials with the legal services required to accomplish the mission of the Department of Labor and the priority goals established by the Secretary. Through attorney staff in Washington and 15 field offices, the Solicitor directs a broad-scale litigation effort in the Federal courts pertaining to the statutes administered by the Department, including institution and prosecution of Civil Court actions under the Fair Labor Standards Act, the Employment Retirement Income Security Act of 1971, and the Migrant Seasonal Agricultural Worker Protection Act. The attorney staff also represents the Department in hearings under various laws including the Occupational Safety and Health Act of 1970, the Black Lung Benefits Reform Act, Federal Mine Safety and Health Act of 1977, and various Government contract labor standards laws. Appellate litigation is conducted by attorneys in the national headquarters, and trial litigation is carried out by attorneys under the direction of regional solicitors.

The Solicitor of Labor also coordinates the Department's legislative program; prepares testimony and reports on proposed legislation; provides legal advice to interagency groups responsible for U.S. trade matters; participates in international organizations including the International Labor Organization; and reviews rules, orders, and regulations.

For further information, contact the Office of Administration, Management and Litigation Support, Office of the Solicitor, Department of Labor, 200 Constitution Avenue NW., Washington, DC 20210. Phone, 202–219–6863.

Regional Offices—Office of the Solicitor

(RS: Regional Solicitor; ARS: Associate Regional Solicitor)

Region	Address	Solicitor
1. Connecticut, Maine, Massachusetts, New Hampshire, Rhode Island, Vermont	1 Congress St., Boston, MA 02114	Albert H. Ross (RS)
2. New Jersey, New York, Puerto Rico, Virgin Islands	201 Varick St., New York, NY 10014	Patricia M. Rodenhausen (RS)
3. Delaware, District of Columbia, Maryland, Pennsylvania, Virginia, West Virginia	3535 Market St., Philadelphia, PA 19104	Deborah Pierce-Shields
Branch Office	Rm. 516, 4015 Wilson Blvd., Arlington, VA 22203	(Vacancy)
4. Alabama, Florida, Georgia, Kentucky, Mississippi, North Carolina, South Carolina, Tennessee	1371 Peachtree St. NE., Atlanta, GA 30367	Jaylynn K. Fortney (RS)
Branch Offices	2015 2d Ave. N., Birmingham, AL 35203	Cynthia W. Brown (RS)
	2002 Richard Jones Rd., Nashville, TN 37215	Ralph D. York (ARS)
5. Illinois, Indiana, Michigan, Minnesota, Ohio, Wisconsin	230 S. Dearborn St., Chicago, IL 60604	Richard J. Fiore (RS)
Branch Office	1240 E. 9th St., Cleveland, OH 44199	Benjamin Chinni (ARS)
6. Arkansas, Louisiana, New Mexico, Oklahoma, Texas	525 S. Griffin St., Dallas, TX 75202	James E. White (RS)
7. Colorado, Iowa, Kansas, Missouri, Montana, Nebraska, North Dakota, South Dakota, Utah, Wyoming	911 Walnut St., Kansas City, MO 64106	Tedrick A. Housh (RS)
Branch Office	1961 Stout St., Denver, CO 80294	Henry C. Mahlman (ARS)
8. Alaska, Arizona, California, Hawaii, Idaho, Nevada, Oregon, Washington	71 Stevenson St., San Francisco, CA 94119	Daniel W. Teehan (RS)
Branch Offices	300 N. Los Angeles St., Los Angeles, CA 90012	John C. Nangle (ARS)
	1111 3d Ave., Seattle, WA 98101	(Vacancy)

International Affairs

The Bureau of International Labor Affairs (ILAB) carries out the Department of Labor's international responsibilities under the direction of the Deputy Under Secretary for International Affairs, and assists in formulating international economic, trade, and immigration policies affecting American workers.

The Bureau represents the United States on delegations to multilateral and bilateral trade negotiations, and on such international bodies as the General Agreement on Tariffs and Trade (GATT), the International Labor Organization (ILO), the Organization for Economic Cooperation and Development (OECD), and other U.N. organizations. It also helps administer the U.S. labor attache program at embassies abroad; carries out overseas technical assistance projects; monitors internationally recognized worker rights; and conducts labor study programs for foreign visitors to the United States.

The Deputy Under Secretary serves as U.S. Government Representative to the ILO Governing Body, a Presidential appointment, and as head of the tripartite U.S. delegation to the annual ILO Conference.

ILAB established, in 1993, a congressionally mandated project to gather information on child labor practices worldwide. Specifically, Congress directed the Secretary of Labor to undertake a review identifying any foreign industry and its host country that utilize child labor in the export of manufactured products from industry or mining to the United States. ILAB published its first report, entitled *By The Sweat and Toil of Children: The Use of Child Labor in American Imports,* in September 1994.

Effective January 1, 1994, the Secretary of Labor established, within the Bureau, the U.S. National Administrative Office of the North American Agreement on Labor Cooperation.

Employment and Training Administration

The Employment and Training Administration, through a variety of programs, fulfills responsibilities assigned to the Secretary of Labor that relate to employment services, job training, and unemployment insurance. Component offices and services of the Administration administer a Federal-State employment security system; fund and oversee programs to provide work experience and training for groups having difficulty entering or returning to the work force; formulate and promote apprenticeship standards and programs; and conduct continuing programs of research, development, and evaluation.

The Assistant Secretary for Employment and Training directs the administration of agency programs and is responsible for ensuring that programs funded through the agency are free from unlawful discrimination, fraud, and abuse, and that they comply with constitutional, statutory, and regulatory provisions. It is the policy of the Administration to promote equal opportunity, affirmative action, and integrity in programs to which the Administration extends financial assistance.

The Administration has five major components that cover employment security, job training, planning and policy development, financial and administrative management, and regional management.

Federal Unemployment Insurance Service The Federal-State Unemployment Compensation Program, under provisions of the Social Security Act of 1935 (42 U.S.C. 1305), is the basic program of income support for the Nation's unemployed workers. With limited Federal intervention, unemployment insurance benefits are payable under laws of individual States. The Federal Unemployment Insurance Service provides leadership and policy guidance to State employment security agencies for the development, improvement, and operation of the Federal-State unemployment insurance system and of related wage-loss, worker

dislocation, and adjustment assistance compensation programs, including to ex-service personnel and Federal civilian workers, and supplemental or extended benefits programs.

The Service reviews State unemployment insurance laws and their administration by the States to determine whether they are in conformity with Federal requirements; supervises the development of programs and methods for benefit, adjudication, appeals, tax collection, and trust fund management activities implemented by the State agencies; oversees the actuarial soundness of the level and relationship of State expenditures, revenues, and reserves, and of Federal appropriations for payment of benefits; and is implementing a quality control program to provide a diagnostic tool for States to identify and correct errors in benefit payments and tax collections and to raise program quality and integrity.

The Service also provides national leadership and direction in implementing its responsibilities under trade adjustment assistance, redwood park expansion, airline deregulation, and disaster unemployment assistance legislation.

For further information, call 202–219–0600.

United States Employment Service The Service, under the provisions of the Wagner-Peyser Act (29 U.S.C. 49 *et seq.*), provides assistance to States in establishing and maintaining a system of local public employment offices in the States and territories and interstate clearance of Labor. The State public employment service is responsible for providing unemployed individuals and other jobseekers with job placement, and other employment services and for providing employers with recruitment services and referrals of job-seeking applicants.

The Service administers the Work Incentive (WIN) program, which was authorized by the Social Security Amendments of 1967 (42 U.S.C. 1305 note) and 1971 (85 Stat. 802). WIN is jointly administered by the Departments of Labor and Health and Human Services and is designed to help persons receiving Aid to Families with Dependent Children (AFDC) become self-supporting.

The Service, through the State public employment service system, also provides subsidiary services which include:

—certifying aliens who seek to enter the United States for permanent employment as immigrants or as temporary workers;

—providing specialized recruitment assistance to employers;

—determining classifications of labor surplus area annually and for exceptional circumstance petitions;

—providing labor surplus area information to the general public and to other Federal or State agencies to meet various program responsibilities;

—disseminating labor market information;

—providing individuals with guidance, counseling, testing referral, and job opportunities;

—reviewing rural industrialization loan and grant certification applications under the Rural Development Act of 1972 (7 U.S.C. 1921);

—distributing airline job opening information for rehiring under the Airline Deregulation Act (49 U.S.C. app. 1301); and

—providing supportive services to employers and applicants through the Federal bonding program.

For further information, call 202–219–0157.

Office of Work-Based Learning The Office administers activities under several Federal laws regarding worker training and retraining. These include the dislocated worker program under the Economic Dislocation and Worker Adjustment Assistance Act (EDWAA) (Title III of the Job Training Partnership Act (JTPA)); Federal activities under the Worker Adjustment and Retraining Notification Act (WARN); Federal activities under the Apprenticeship Act; and the Trade Adjustment Assistance Program under the Trade Act. In

addition, the Office carries out research and demonstration programs.

For further information, call 202–219–0540.

Office of Worker Retraining and Adjustment Programs The Office performs dislocated worker programs functions under the the Economic Dislocation and Worker Adjustment Assistance Act (Title III of JTPA), and Federal activities under the Worker Adjustment and Retraining Notification Act.

For further information, call 202–219–0525.

Office of Trade Adjustment Assistance The Office administers the Trade Adjustment Assistance program provisions of the Trade Act of 1974, as amended (19 U.S.C. 2101 *et seq.*), through agreements with the States. The program provides reemployment services such as training, job search and relocation allowances, and weekly cash payments to U.S. workers who are separated from employment because of foreign imports.

The Office receives petitions for adjustment assistance from either adversely affected workers, a duly recognized union, or an authorized representative of the workers and conducts factfinding investigations to develop necessary data on which certification determinations can be based. Determinations may involve approval, denial, or termination of worker groups' eligibility for trade adjustment assistance benefits.

The Office develops policies and prepares program directives to regional offices and State agencies on the administration and funding of reemployment services, and develops and maintains a system for allocating funds to those offices and agencies for reemployment services. It also directs and conducts industry studies of the number of workers in a domestic industry likely to be certified as eligible for adjustment assistance and of the extent to which existing training and employment programs may facilitate the workers' adjustment to import competition when an industry petitions the Federal Government that it is being injured because of import competition.

For further information, call 202–219–0555.

Bureau of Apprenticeship and Training
The National Apprenticeship Act (29 U.S.C. 50) was passed in 1937 to enable the Department of Labor to formulate and promote the furtherance of labor standards necessary to safeguard the welfare of apprentices and cooperate with the States in the promotion of such standards, and to bring together employers and labor for the formulation of programs of apprenticeship.

Sponsors and potential sponsors are encouraged and assisted in the development, expansion, and improvement of apprenticeship and other forms of allied industrial training. Technical information on training methods, public training facilities, and successfully executed systems are made available to industry. Through field representatives in States, the Bureau works closely with employers, labor unions, vocational schools, community planning groups, and others concerned with apprenticeship.

Programs must meet standards established by the Bureau or a recognized State Apprenticeship Council to be registered. Field compliance reviews are conducted to determine conformity with Federal equal employment opportunity and other standards for apprenticeship and training.

For further information, call 202–219–0540.

Job Training Partnership Act
The Office of Job Training Programs is responsible for the development and issuance of Federal procedures and policies pertaining to the operation of the Job Training Partnership Act (29 U.S.C. 1501 note) programs.

Under the act, the Secretary of Labor makes block grants to the 50 States, Guam, the Virgin Islands, Puerto Rico, the Commonwealth of the Northern Marianas, American Samoa, Republic of the Marshall Islands, Republic of Palau, Federated States of Micronesia, and the District of Columbia.

The goal of the act is to train or retrain and place eligible individuals in permanent, unsubsidized employment, preferably in the private sector. Eligible individuals are primarily economically disadvantaged individuals, in particular economically disadvantaged youth, dislocated workers, and others who face significant barriers to employment. The act also provides that a fixed percentage of the block grant be used for programs for older individuals.

The Job Training Partnership Act may be used for a variety of purposes including classroom instruction in occupational skills and other job-related training; on-the-job training; recruitment; orientation; counseling; testing; and placements and supportive services. In addition to the block grants, the act provides for national programs for special target groups such as Native Americans and migrant and seasonal farmworkers. It also provides authority for the Job Corps, a residential training program for disadvantaged youth.

The act is open-ended legislation and was signed into law on October 13, 1982. Implementing regulations for the act issued by the Department of Labor are contained in title 20 of the *Code of Federal Regulations,* parts 626–636 and 675–684.

For further information, call 202–219–0236.

Senior Community Service Employment Program   Authorized by title V of the Older Americans Act (42 U.S.C. 3056), the program makes subsidized, part-time job opportunities in community service activities available to low-income persons aged 55 and above. Project grants are made to national-level public and private nonprofit agencies and to units of State governments. The distribution of funds among the States is governed by a statutory apportionment formula.

For further information, call 202–219–0500.

Regional Management
The Office of Regional Management provides leadership to the Employment and Training Administration's regional offices that are located in 10 areas

throughout the United States. The Office executes direct-line authority over Administration field activities (except the Bureau of Apprenticeship and Training and Job Corps) and provides a central point of contact at the headquarters level in connection with national office component dealings with regional staff.

Within its area of jurisdiction, each regional office is responsible for the oversight and grant administration of employment and training programs operated by State governments. Other public interest responsibilities include the coordination of Administration activities with Federal assistance programs of other agencies within the region; the implementation of employment training administrative policies on equal employment opportunity; and assistance to the States in carrying out operational responsibilities for employment and training programs at the State and local levels.

Regional Offices—Employment and Training Administration

(Areas included within each region are indicated on the map in Appendix A.)

Region/Address	Administrator
I. Boston, MA (John F. Kennedy Federal Bldg., 02203)	Robert Semler
II. New York, NY (201 Varick St., 10014)	Thomas E. Hill
III. Philadelphia, PA (P.O. Box 8796, 19101)	William J. Haltigan
IV. Atlanta, GA (1371 Peachtree St. NE., 30367)	Dan Lowry
V. Chicago, IL (230 S. Dearborn St., 60604)	Joseph C. Juarez
VI. Dallas, TX (525 Griffin Sq. Bldg., 75202)	Norma B. Selvera, Acting
VII. Kansas City, MO (911 Walnut St., 64106)	William H. Hood, Acting
VIII. Denver, CO (1961 Stout St., 80294)	Luis Sepulveda
IX. San Francisco, CA (71 Stevenson St., 94102)	Don A. Balcer
X. Seattle, WA (909 1st Ave., 98174)	Armando Quiroz

For further information, call 202-219-0585.

Office of the American Workplace

The Office of the American Workplace was created by Secretary's Order No 2–93, dated July 21, 1993. The Assistant Secretary for the American Workplace is responsible for administering and directing workplace programs which: encourage the development of work organization, human resource practices, technology, and performance measurements that enhance business competitiveness and the skills, involvement, and commitment of front-line workers; promote innovative relations among managers, labor unions, and professional organizations and workers; administer statutory programs to certify employee protection provisions of various federally sponsored transportation programs; and safeguard the financial integrity and internal democracy of American labor unions, while assisting the unions in improving their organizational and administrative effectiveness.

Office of Work and Technology Policy This office provides advice and assistance on the creation and implementation of high-performance workplace programs; fosters programs which encourage the development of work organizations, technology, and performance measures that enhance the skill, involvement, and commitment of managers and front-line workers; coordinates contact with the Secretary and business and industry leaders on the transformation of the American workplace; helps define and promote the new American workplace and encourages joint ventures with industry organizations to promote effective workplace practices; and generates national-scale interest in developing new work systems to increase America's competitive performance, while developing American workers to their maximum potential.

Office of Labor-Management Programs This office develops policy on all aspects of labor-management relations, related legislation, and Federal programs affecting collective bargaining and other labor relations matters; provides technical assistance and information resources to employers and unions in developing and implementing cooperative labor-management programs; builds and promotes a labor-management network to encourage the dissemination of cooperative labor-management relations and high-performance workplace practices among employers and workers and coordinates Federal, State, and local government programs in conjunction with government organizations; and administers worker protection provisions of the Federal Transit Act, the Rail Passenger Service Act, the Redwood National Park Expansion Act, and the Airline Deregulation Act.

Office of Labor-Management Standards This office administers provisions of the Labor-Management Reporting and Disclosure Act of 1959 (29 U.S.C. 401) and section 1209 of the Postal Reorganization Act (39 U.S.C. 1209), which affect labor organizations in the private sector and labor organizations composed of Postal Service employees; as well as section 701 of the Civil Service Reform Act (5 U.S.C. 7120) and section 1017 of the Foreign Service Act (22 U.S.C. 4117), which affect labor organizations composed of employees of most agencies of the executive branch of the Federal Government. These provisions regulate certain internal union

procedures, protect the rights of members in approximately 36,000 unions; govern the handling of union funds; provide for reporting and public disclosure of certain financial transactions and administrative practices of unions, union officers and employees, surety companies, employers, and labor relations consultants; establish requirements for the election of union officers; and establish requirements for the imposition and administration of trusteeships.

This office conducts criminal and civil investigations to safeguard the financial integrity of unions and to ensure union democracy; and conducts investigative audits of labor unions to uncover and remedy criminal and civil violations of the Labor-Management Reporting and Disclosure Act and related statutes. Enforcement through the Federal courts also is available under the reporting and disclosure act procedures, while the standards of conduct are enforced by administrative action with a final decision by the Assistant Secretary.

The Office also administers a public disclosure program for financial and other reports filed by unions and others and provides compliance assistance to help unions and others comply with the statutes.

For further information, contact the Public Affairs Team, Office of the American Workplace, Department of Labor, Room N5402, 200 Constitution Avenue NW., Washington, DC 20210. Phone, 202–219–6098.

Area Offices—Office of Labor-Management Standards

Area	Address	Administrator
ATLANTA—Alabama, Florida, Georgia, South Carolina	Suite 600, 1365 Peachtree St. NE., Atlanta, GA 30367	Ronald Lehman
BOSTON—Connecticut, Maine, Massachusetts, New Hampshire, New York (northern and western), Rhode Island, Vermont	Suite 302, 121 High St., Boston, MA 02110	Eric Feldman, *Acting*
CHICAGO—Illinois (northern), Indiana (northern), Michigan, Minnesota, North Dakota, South Dakota, Wisconsin	Suite 774, 230 S. Dearborn St., Chicago, IL 60604–2773	Kamil Bishara, *Acting*
CLEVELAND—Indiana (southern), Kentucky, Ohio	Suite 831, 1240 E. 9th St., Cleveland, OH 44199	James Gearhart, *Acting*
DALLAS—Arkansas, Louisiana, Mississippi, Oklahoma, Texas	Suite 300, 525 Griffin Sq. Bldg., Dallas, TX 75202	David Seifert, *Acting*
KANSAS CITY—Colorado, Illinois (southern), Iowa, Kansas, Missouri, Montana, Nebraska, New Mexico, Utah, Wyoming	Suite 950, 1100 Main St., Kansas City, MO 64105	Kamil Bishara
NEW YORK—New Jersey, New York (southeastern and metropolitan areas)	Suite 878, 201 Varick St., New York, NY 10014	Eric Feldman, Acting

Area Offices—Office of Labor-Management Standards—Continued

Area	Address	Administrator
PHILADELPHIA—Delaware, Pennsylvania, West Virginia	Suite 9452, 600 Arch St., Philadelphia, PA 19106	Eric Feldman
SAN FRANCISCO—Alaska, Arizona, California, Hawaii, Idaho, Nevada, Oregon, Washington	Suite 725, 71 Stevenson St., San Francisco, CA 94105	C. Russell Rock
WASHINGTON, DC—District of Columbia, Maryland, North Carolina, Puerto Rico, Tennessee, Virginia	Suite 558, 1730 K St. NW., Washington, DC 20006	Robert L. Merriner

Pension and Welfare Benefits Administration

The Pension and Welfare Benefits Administration (PWBA) helps to protect the economic future and retirement security of working Americans, as required under the Employment Retirement Income Security Act of 1974 (ERISA) (29 U.S.C. 1001).

The act requires administrators of private pension and welfare plans to provide plan participants with easily understandable summaries of plans; to file those summaries with the agency; and to report annually on the financial operation of the plans and bonding of persons charged with handling plan funds and assets. Plan administrators must also meet strict fiduciary responsibility standards that are enforced by PWBA.

The Administration is charged with assuring responsible management of nearly 1 million pension plans and 4½ million health and welfare plans, and is the national guardian of a vast private retirement and welfare benefit system. Its major activities include: formulating current and future policy; conducting research; issuing regulations and technical guidance concerning ERISA requirements; enforcing ERISA requirements; and assisting and educating the public and the employee benefits community about ERISA. The Administration is enforced through its 15 field offices nationwide and the national office in Washington, DC.

Vesting, participation, and funding standards are primarily administered by the Internal Revenue Service.

Field Offices—Pension and Welfare Benefits Administration

Area/Address	Director
Atlanta, GA (Rm. 205, 1371 Peachtree St. NE., 30367)	Howard Marsh
Miami, Fl (Suite 504, 111 NW. 183d St., 33169)	Jesse Day
Boston, MA (7th Fl., One Bowdoin Sq., 02114)	James Benages
Chicago, IL (Suite 840, 401 S. State St., 60605)	Kenneth Bazar
Cincinnati, OH (Suite 210, 1885 Dixie Hwy., Fort Wright, KY 41011)	Joseph Menez
Detroit, MI (Rm. 619, 231 W. Lafayette Blvd., 48226)	Robert Jogan
Dallas, TX (Rm. 707, 525 S. Griffin St., 75202)	Bruce Rudd
Kansas City, MO (Suite 1200, City Center Sq., 1100 Main, 64105	Gregory Egan
St. Louis, MO (Rm. 338, 815 Olive St., 63101)	Roger Schlueter
Los Angeles, CA (Suite 514, 790 E. Colorado Blvd., Pasadena, CA 91101)	David Ganz
New York, NY (Rm. 226, 1633 Broadway, 10019)	John Wehrum, Jr.
Philadelphia, PA (Rm. M300, Gateway Bldg., 3535 Market St., 19104)	Gerard Gumpertz
Washington, DC (Suite 556, 1730 K St. NW., 20006)	Robin Pearl
San Francisco, CA (Suite 915, P.O. Box 190250, 71 Stevenson St., 94119–0250)	Leonard Garofolo
Seattle, WA (Rm. 000, 1111 3d Ave., 98101–3212)	John Daanlan

For further information, call 202–219–8921.

Employment Standards Administration

The Assistant Secretary for Employment Standards has responsibility for administering and directing employment standards programs dealing with: minimum wage and overtime standards; registration of farm labor contractors; determining prevailing wage rates to be paid on Government contracts and subcontracts; nondiscrimination and affirmative action for minorities, women, veterans, and handicapped Government contract and subcontract workers; and workers' compensation programs for Federal and certain private employers and employees.

For further information, call 202–219–7320.

Wage and Hour Division

The Wage and Hour Administrator is responsible for planning, directing, and administering programs dealing with a variety of Federal labor legislation. These programs are designed to:
 —protect low-wage incomes as provided by the minimum wage provisions of the Fair Labor Standards Act (29 U.S.C. 201);
 —safeguard the health and welfare of workers by discouraging excessively long hours of work through enforcement of the overtime provisions of the Fair Labor Standards Act;
 —safeguard the health and well-being of minors;
 —prevent curtailment of employment and earnings for students, trainees, and handicapped workers;
 —minimize losses of income and job rights caused by indebtedness; and
 —direct a program of farm labor contractor registration designed to protect the health, safety, and welfare of migrant and seasonal agricultural workers; and
 —administer and enforce a number of immigration-related programs (with INS) designed to safeguard the rights of both American and foreign workers and to prevent American workers similarly employed from being adversely affected by employment of alien workers.
 The Wage and Hour Division is also responsible for predetermination of prevailing wage rates for Federal construction contracts and federally assisted programs for construction, alteration and repair of public works subject to the Davis-Bacon (40 U.S.C. 276a) and related acts, and a continuing program for determining wage rates under the Service Contract Act (41 U.S.C. 351). The Division also has enforcement responsibility in ensuring that prevailing wages and overtime standards are paid in accordance with the provisions of the Davis-Bacon and related acts: Service Contract Act, Public Contracts Act, and Contract Work Hours and Safety Standards Act.

For further information, contact the Office of the Administrator, Wage and Hour Division, Department of Labor, Room S–3502, 200 Constitution Avenue NW., Washington, DC 20210. Phone, 202–219–8305.

Office of Workers' Compensation Programs

The Office of Workers' Compensation Programs is responsible for the administration of the three basic Federal workers' compensation laws: the Federal Employees Compensation Act, which provides workers' compensation for Federal employees and others; the Longshore and Harbor Workers' Compensation Act and its various extensions (the Defense Base Act, Outer Continental Shelf Lands Act, Nonappropriated Fund Instrumentalities Act, the District of Columbia Compensation Act, the War Hazards Compensation Act, and the War Claims Act), which provide benefits to employees in private enterprise while engaged in maritime employment on navigable waters in the United States, as well as employees of certain government contractors and to private employers in the District of Columbia for injuries that occurred prior to July 27, 1982; and the Black Lung Benefits Act, as amended, which extends benefits to coal miners who are totally disabled due to pneumoconiosis, a respiratory disease contracted after prolonged inhalation of coal mine dust, and to their survivors when the miner's death is due to pneumoconiosis.

Regional Administrators/Directors—Employment Standards Administration

(Areas included within each region are indicated on the map in Appendix A.)

Region Office/Address	Wage and Hour Regional Administrator	Federal Contract Compliance Regional Director	Workers' Compensation Programs Regional Director
1. Boston, MA (1 Congress St., 02203)	Walter P. Parker	Brenda J. Joyce	Charity Benz
2. New York, NY (201 Varick St., 10014)	Doris Wooten	Carmen McCulloch	Kenneth Hamlett
3. Philadelphia, PA (3535 Market St., 19104)	James W. Kight	Joseph J. Dubray, Jr.	Robert D. Lotz
4. Atlanta, GA (1375 Peachtree St. NE., 30367).	Alfred H. Perry	Carol A. Gaudin	
5. Jacksonville, FL (214 N. Hogan St., 32202)			Nancy L. Ricker
6. Chicago, IL (230 S. Dearborn St., 60604)	Everett P. Jennings, *Acting.*	Halcolm Holliman	Phyllis Crane
7. Dallas, TX (525 Griffin St., 75202)	Manuel J. Villareal	Joe C. Garcia	(Vacancy)
8. Kansas City, MO (Center City Sq., 1100 Main St., 64105).	Everett P. Jennings	(Vacancy)	Charles O. Ketcham, Jr.
9. Denver, CO (1801 California St., 80294)	(Vacancy)	Irene N. Mee	Robert J. Mansanares
10. San Francisco, CA (71 Stevenson St., 94105).	William C. Buhl	Helene Haase	Donna Onodera
11. Seattle, WA (1111 3d Ave., 98101)	(Vacancy)	John Checkett	Thomas K. Morgan

District Offices—Workers' Compensation Programs

District/Address	FECA District Director	DLHWC District Director	DCMWC District Director
1. Boston, MA (1 Congress St., 02203)	Robert M. Sullivan	Randolph L. Regula	
2. New York, NY (201 Varick St., 10014)	Jonathan A. Lawrence	Richard V. Robilotti	
3. Philadelphia, PA (3535 Market St., 19104)	Alonza Hart	John McTaggart	
4. Baltimore, MD (31 Hopkins Plz., 21201)		Bruno DiSimone	
5. Norfolk, VA (200 Granby Mall, 23510)		Basil E. Voultsides	
6. Johnstown, PA (Rm. 201, 319 Washington St., 15901).			Stuart Glassman
7. Greensburg, PA (1225 S. Main St., 15601)			John Ciszek
8. Wilkes-Barre, PA (116 S. Main St., 18701)			Jack Geller
9. Charleston, WV (2 Hale St., 25301)			Robert Hardesty
10. Pikeville, KY (334 Main St., 41501)			Harry Skidmore
11. Jacksonville, FL (214 N. Hogan St., 32202)	William C. Franson	(Vacancy)	
12. New Orleans, LA (701 Loyola St., 70113)		Marilyn Felkner	
13. Houston, TX (12600 Featherwood Dr., 77004).		Chris John Gleasman	
14. Dallas, TX (525 Griffin St., 75202)	E. Martin Walker		
15. Chicago, IL (230 S. Dearborn St., 60604)	Richard Kadus	Thomas C. Hunter	
16. Cleveland, OH (1240 E. 9th St., 44199)	Deborah Sanford		
17. Columbus, OH (274 Marconi Blvd., 43215)			Don Dopps
18. Kansas City, MO (911 Walnut St., 64106)	Charles O. Ketcham, Jr.		
19. Denver, CO (1801 California St., 80294)	Robert Mitchell		John Martin
20. San Francisco, CA (71 Stevenson St., 94102).	Ed Bouros	Ed Orozco	
21. Honolulu, HI (300 Ala Moana Blvd., 96850)		(Vacancy)	
22. Seattle, WA (1111 3d Ave., 98101–3212)	William Howard	Karen Goodwin	
23. Long Beach, CA (401 E. Ocean Blvd., 90807).		Joyce Terry	
24. Washington, DC (800 N. Capitol St. NW., 20210).	Ora T. Wright		

For further information, contact the Office of the Director, Office of Workers' Compensation Programs, Department of Labor, Room S–3524, 200 Constitution Avenue NW., Washington, DC 20210. Phone, 202–219–7503.

Occupational Safety and Health Administration

The Assistant Secretary for Occupational Safety and Health has responsibility for occupational safety and health activities. The Occupational Safety and Health Administration, established pursuant to the Occupational Safety and Health Act of 1970 (29 U.S.C. 651 et seq.), develops and promulgates occupational safety and health standards; develops and issues regulations; conducts investigations and inspections to determine the status of compliance with safety and health standards and regulations; and issues citations and proposes penalties for noncompliance with safety and health standards and regulations.

Regional Offices—Occupational Safety and Health Administration
(Areas included within each region are indicated on the map in Appendix A.)

Region/Address	Administrator	Telephone
1. Boston, MA (133 Portland St., 02114)	John T. Phillips	617–565–7159
2. New York, NY (201 Varick St., 10014)	Patricia Clark	212–337–2378
3. Philadelphia, PA (3535 Market St., 19104)	Linda R. Anku	215–596–1201
4. Atlanta, GA (1375 Peachtree St. NE., 30367)	R. Davis Layne	404–347–3573
5. Chicago, IL (230 S. Dearborn St., 60604)	Michael Connors	312–353–2220
6. Dallas, TX (555 Griffin St., 75202)	E.B. Blanton	214–767–4731
7. Kansas City, MO (1100 Main St., 64105)	Marcia Drumm, Acting	816–426–5861
8. Denver, CO (1999 Broadway, 80202)	Byron R. Chadwick	303–391–5858
9. San Francisco, CA (71 Stevenson St., 94105)	Frank Strasheim	415–744–6670
10. Seattle, WA (1111 3d Ave., 98101)	Richard Terrill, Acting	206–553–5930

For further information, contact the Occupational Safety and Health Administration, Department of Labor, 200 Constitution Avenue NW., Washington, DC 20210. Phone, 202–219–8151.

Mine Safety and Health Administration

The Assistant Secretary of Labor for Mine Safety and Health has responsibility for safety and health in the Nation's mines.

The Federal Coal Mine Health and Safety Act of 1969 (30 U.S.C. 801 et seq.) gave the Administration strong enforcement provisions to protect the Nation's coal miners and, in 1977, the Congress passed amendments which strengthened the act, expanding its protections and extending its provisions to the noncoal mining industry.

The Administration develops and promulgates mandatory safety and health standards, ensures compliance with such standards, assesses civil penalties for violations, and investigates accidents. It cooperates with and provides assistance to the States in the development of effective State mine safety and health programs, improves and expands training programs in cooperation with the States and the mining industry, and, in coordination with the Department of Health and Human Services and the Department of the Interior, contributes to the improvement and expansion of mine safety and health research and development. All of these activities are aimed at preventing and reducing mine accidents and occupational diseases in the mining industry.

The statutory responsibilities of the Administration are administered by a headquarters staff located at Arlington, VA, reporting to the Assistant Secretary for Mine Safety and Health and by a field network of district, subdistrict, and field offices, technology centers, and the Approval and Certification Center.

For further information, contact the Office of Information and Public Affairs, Mine Safety and Health Administration, Department of Labor, Room 601, 4015 Wilson Boulevard, Arlington, VA 22203. Phone, 703–235–1452.

District Offices—Mine Safety and Health Administration

District/Address	Telephone
Coal Mine Safety and Health	
I. Wilkes-Barre, PA (20 N. Pennsylvania Ave., 18701)	717–826–6321
II. Hunker, PA (R 1, Box 736, 15639)	412–925–5150
III. Morgantown, WV (5012 Mountaineer Mall, 26505)	304–291–4277
IV. Mt. Hope, WV (100 Bluestone Rd., 25880)	304–877–3900
V. Norton, VA (P.O. Box 560, 24273)	703–679–0230
VI. Pikeville, KY (100 Ratliff Creek Rd., 41501)	606–432–0943
VII. Barbourville, KY (HC 66, Box 1762, 40906)	606–546–5123
VIII. Vincennes, IN (P.O. Box 418, 47591)	812–882–7617
IX. Denver, CO (P.O. Box 25367, 80225–0367)	303–231–5458
X. Madisonville, KY (100 YMCA Dr., 42431–9019)	502–821–4180
Metal/Nonmetal Mine Safety and Health	
Northeastern District (230 Executive Dr., Cranberry Township, PA 16066–6415)	412–772–2333
Southeastern District (135 Gemini Cir., Birmingham, AL 35209–4896)	205–290–7294
North Central District (515 W. 1st St., Duluth, MN 55802–1302)	218–720–5448
South Central District (1100 Commerce St., Dallas, TX 75242–0499)	214–767–8401
Rocky Mountain District (P.O. Box 25367, Denver, CO 80225–0367)	303–231–5465
Western District (3333 Vaca Valley Pky., Vacaville, CA 95688)	707–447–9844

Labor Statistics

The Bureau of Labor Statistics is the principal data-gathering agency of the Federal Government in the broad field of labor economics. It has no enforcement or regulatory functions. The Bureau collects, processes, analyzes, and disseminates data relating to employment, unemployment, and other characteristics of the labor force; prices and consumer expenditures; wages, other worker compensation, and industrial relations; productivity and technological change; economic growth and employment projections; and occupational safety and health. Most of the data are collected in surveys conducted by the Bureau, the Bureau of the Census (on a contract basis), or on a cooperative basis with State agencies.

The Bureau strives to have its data satisfy a number of criteria, including:

relevance to current social and economic issues, timeliness in reflecting today's rapidly changing economic conditions, accuracy and consistently high statistical quality, and impartiality in both subject matter and presentation.

The basic data—practically all supplied voluntarily by business establishments and members of private households—are issued in monthly, quarterly, and annual news releases; bulletins, reports, and special publications; and periodicals. Data are also made available through an electronic news service, magnetic tape, diskettes, and microfiche, as well as on Internet. Regional offices issue additional reports and releases usually presenting locality or regional detail.

Regional Offices—Bureau of Labor Statistics

Region/Address	Address	Commissioner
ATLANTA—Alabama, Florida, Georgia, Kentucky, Mississippi, North Carolina, South Carolina, Tennessee	1371 Peachtree St. NE., Atlanta, GA 30367	Janet S. Rankin
BOSTON—Connecticut, Maine, Massachusetts, New Hampshire, Rhode Island, Vermont	1603–B Federal Bldg., Boston, MA 02203	Anthony J. Ferrara
CHICAGO—Illinois, Indiana, Michigan, Minnesota, Ohio, Wisconsin	230 S. Dearborn St., Chicago, IL 60604	Lois Orr
DALLAS—Arkansas, Louisiana, New Mexico, Oklahoma, Texas	525 Griffin Sq. Bldg., Dallas, TX 75202	Robert A. Goddie
KANSAS CITY—Colorado, Iowa, Kansas, Missouri, Montana, Nebraska, North Dakota, South Dakota, Utah, Wyoming	Suite 600, City Center Sq., 1100 Main St., 64106)	Gunnan Engen

Regional Offices—Bureau of Labor Statistics—Continued

Region/Address	Address	Commissioner
NEW YORK—New Jersey, New York, Puerto Rico, Virgin Islands, Canal Zone	201 Varick St., New York, NY 10014	(Vacancy)
PHILADELPHIA—Delaware, District of Columbia, Maryland, Pennsylvania, Virginia, West Virginia	3535 Market St., Philadelphia, PA 19104	Alan M. Paisner
SAN FRANCISCO—Alaska, American Samoa, Arizona, California, Guam, Hawaii, Idaho, Nevada, Oregon, Trust Territory of the Pacific Islands, Washington	71 Stevenson St., San Francisco, CA 94119–3766	Sam M. Hirabayashi

For further information, contact the Associate Commissioner, Office of Publications, Bureau of Labor Statistics, Department of Labor, Room 4110, 2 Massachusetts Ave. NW., Washington, DC 20212. Phone, 202–606–5900.

Veterans' Employment and Training Service

The Veterans' Employment and Training Service is the component of the Department of Labor administered by the Assistant Secretary for Veterans' Employment and Training. The Assistant Secretary is the principal advisor to the Secretary of Labor in the formulation and implementation of all departmental policies, procedures, and regulations affecting veterans and is responsible for administering veterans' employment and training programs and activities through the Service to ensure that legislative and regulatory mandates are accomplished.

The Service carries out its responsibilities for directing the Department's veterans' employment and training programs through a nationwide network that includes Regional Administrators, Directors (in each State) and Assistant Directors (one for each 250,000 veterans in each State) for Veterans' Employment and Training, Assistant Regional Administrators and Area Agents for Veterans' Reemployment Rights, Veterans' Program Specialists, and program support staff.

The Service field staff works closely with and provides technical assistance to State Employment Security Agencies and Job Training Partnership Act grant recipients to ensure that veterans are provided the priority services required by law. They also coordinate with employers, labor unions, veterans service organizations, and community organizations through planned public information and outreach activities. Federal contractors are provided management assistance in complying with their veterans affirmative action and reporting obligations.

Also administered by the Assistant Secretary through the Service is the Job Training Partnership Act, title IV, part C grant program designed to meet the employment and training needs of service-connected disabled veterans, Vietnam-era veterans, and veterans recently separated from military service. IV–C grants are awarded and monitored through the Service's national office and field staff.

Certain other Service staff also administer the veterans reemployment rights program. They provide assistance to help restore job, seniority, and pension rights to veterans following absences from work for active military service and to protect employment and retention rights of members of the Reserve or National Guard.

Regional Administrators/State Directors—Veterans' Employment and Training Service
(RA: Regional Administrator; D: Director)
(Areas included within each region are indicated on the map in Appendix A.)

Region/Address	Director	Telephone
REGION I		

Regional Administrators/State Directors—Veterans' Employment and Training Service—Continued

(RA: Regional Administrator; D: Director)
(Areas included within each region are indicated on the map in Appendix A.)

Region/Address	Director	Telephone
Boston, MA (c/o Commonwealth of Massachusetts, 2d Fl., 19 Staniford St., 02114).	Travis Dixon (D)	617–626–6690
Boston, MA (11th Fl., 1 Congress St., 02114)	Norman M. Ahlquist (RA)	617–565–2080
Wethersford, CT (200 Follybrook Blvd., 16601)	Robert B. Inman (D)	203–566–3326
Concord, NH (Rm. 208, 143 N. Main St., 03301)	David Houle (D)	603–225–1424
Lewiston, ME (522 Lisbon St., 04243)	Jon Guay (D)	207–783–5352
Montpelier, VT (Rm. 303, 87 State St., 05602)	Ronald R. Benoit	802–828–4441
Providence, RI (507 U.S. Courthouse, N. Federal Bldg., 02903)	John Dunn (D)	401–528–5134
REGION II		
Albany, NY (Rm. 518, Bldg. 12, Harriman State Campus, 12240)	James H. Hartman (D)	518–472–4415
Hato Rey, PR (No. 198, Calle Guayama, 03918)	Angel Mojica (D)	809–754–5391
New York, NY (Rm. 766, 201 Varick St., 10014)	H. Miles Sisson (RA)	212–337–2211
Trenton, NJ (11th Fl., 28 Yard Ave., CN–058, 08625)	Alan E. Grohs (D)	609–292–2930
REGION III		
Baltimore, MD (Rm. 210, 1100 N. Eutaw St., 21201)	Stanley Seidel (D)	410–767–2110
Charleston, WV (Rm. 205, 112 California Ave., 25305)	David L. Bush (D)	304–558–4001
Harrisburg, PA (Rm. 625, Labor and Industry Bldg., 17121)	Larry Babbitts (D)	717–787–5834
Newark, DE (Suite 105, Stockton Bldg., University Plz., 19702)	Joseph Hortiz (D)	302–368–6898
Philadelphia, PA (Rm. 802, U.S. Customs House, 2d & Chestnut Sts., 19106).	Ervin Pope (RA)	215–597–1664
Richmond, VA (Suite 1409, 701 E. Franklin St., 23219)	(Vacancy) (D)	804–786–6599
Washington, DC (Rm. 108, 500 C St. NW., 20001)	(Vacancy) (D)	202–727–3342
REGION IV		
Atlanta, GA (Rm. 326, 1371 Peachtree St. NE., 30367–2312)	William Bolls (RA)	404–347–3673
Atlanta, GA (Suite 504, Sussex Pl., 148 International Blvd. NE., 30303) .	Hartwell H. Morris (D)	404–331–3893
Columbia, SC (Suite 101–A, 914 Richland St., 29201)	William C. Plowden, Jr. (D)	803–765–5195
Frankfort, KY (c/o Department for Employment Services, 275 E. Main St., 40621).	Charles R. Netherton (D)	502–564–7062
Jackson, MS (1520 W. Capitol St., 39215–1699)	(Vacancy) (D)	601–965–4204
Montgomery, AL (Rm. 543, 649 Monroe St., 36131–4220)	Thomas M. Karrh (D)	205–223–7677
Nashville, TN (Rm. 317, 301 James Robertson Pky., 37245–4000)	Richard E. Ritchie (D)	615–741–2437
Raleigh, NC (Bldg. M, 700 Wade Ave., 27605)	Steven Guess (D)	919–856–4742
Tallahassee, FL (Suite 205, 2574 Seagate Dr., 32399–0676)	LaMont P. Davis (D)	904–877–4164
REGION V		
Chicago, IL (Rm. 1064, 230 S. Dearborn St., 60604)	Milo Guarnero (RA)	312–353–0970
Chicago, IL (2 North, 401 S. State St., 60605)	Samuel L. Parks (D)	312–793–3433
Columbus, OH (Rm. 523, 145 S. Front St., 43215)	Wesley Leggett (D)	614–466–2768
Detroit, MI (Suite 407, 7310 Woodward Ave., 48202)	Maurice Wallingford (D)	313–872–2383
Indianapolis, IN (Rm. 103, 10 N. Senate Ave., 46204)	Bruce Redman (D)	317–232–6804
Madison, WI (Rm. 250, 201 E. Washington Ave., 53703)	James R. Gutowski (D)	608–266–3110
St. Paul, MN (3rd Fl., 390 N. Robert, 55101)	Michael D. Graham (D)	612–290–3028
REGION VI		
Albuquerque, NM (401 Broadway NE., 87102)	Jacob Castillo (D)	505–766–2113
Austin, TX (Suite 516–T, TEC Bldg., 1117 Trinity St., 78701)	John McKinny (D)	512–463–2207
Baton Rouge, LA (Rm. 184,, Admin. Bldg. 1001 N. 23d St., 70804)	Lester Parmenter (D)	504–389–0339
Dallas, TX (Rm. 205, 525 Griffin Sq. Bldg., Griffin and Young Sts., 75202).	Lester L. Williams, Jr. (RA)	214–767–4987
Little Rock, AR (Rm. G–12, Employment Security Bldg., State Capitol Mall, 72201).	Billy R. Threlkeld (D)	501–682–3786
Oklahoma City, OK (Rm. 301, Will Rogers Memorial Office Bldg., 73105).	Darrell H. Hill (D)	405–557–7189
REGION VII		
Des Moines, IA (150 Des Moines St., 50309)	Leonard E. Shaw, Jr. (D)	515–281–4061
Jefferson City, MO (421 E. Dunklin St., 65104)	Mickey J. Jones (D)	314–751–3921
Kansas City, MO (Rm. 803, 1100 Main St., 64105)	(Vacancy) (RA)	816–426–7151
Lincoln, NE (550 S. 16th St., 68509)	Richard Nelson (D)	402–437–5289
Topeka, KS (1309 Topeka Blvd., 66612)	Gayle A. Gibson (D)	913–296–5032
REGION VIII		
Aberdeen, SD (420 S. Roosevelt St., 57402–4730)	Earl R. Schultz (D)	605–226–7289
Bismarck, ND (1000 Divide Ave., 58502–1632)	Richard Ryan (D)	701–250–4337
Casper, WY (100 W. Midwest Ave., 82602)	David McNulty (D)	307–261–5454
Denver, CO (Suite 910, 1801 California St., 80202–2614)	Ronald G. Bachman (RA)	303–844–2151
Denver, CO (Tower II, Sic 400, 1515 Arabahoe St. 80202-2117)	Mark A. McGinty (D)	303–844–2151
Helena, MT (111 N. Last Chance Gulch, 59601–4144)	H. Polly LaTray-Holmes (D)	406–449–5431
Salt Lake City, UT (140 E. 300 South St., 84111–2305)	Dale Brockbank (D)	801–524–5703
REGION IX		
Carson City, NV (Rm. 205, 1923 N. Carson St., 89702)	Claude U. Shipley (D)	702–687–4632
Honolulu, HI (Rm. 232A, 830 Punch Bowl St., 96813)	Gilbert Hough (D)	808–522–8216
Phoenix, AZ (1400 W. Washington St., 85005)	Marco A. Valenzuela (D)	602–379–4961

Regional Administrators/State Directors—Veterans' Employment and Training Service—Continued
(RA: Regional Administrator; D: Director)
(Areas included within each region are indicated on the map in Appendix A.)

Region/Address	Director	Telephone
Sacramento, CA (Rm. W1142, 800 Capitol Mall, 94280–0001)	Charles Martinez (D)	916–654–8178
San Francisco, CA (Suite 705, 71 Stevenson St., 94105)	John E. Giannelli, Jr. (RA) .	415–744–6677
REGION X		
Boise, ID (Rm. 303, 317 Main St., 83735)	Robert M. Wilson (D)	208–334–6163
Juneau, AK (1111 W. 8th St., 99802–5509)	Daniel Travis (D)	907–465–2723
Olympia, WA (605 Woodview Dr. SE., 98503)	Donald J. Hutt (D)	206–438–4600
Salem, OR (875 Union St. NE., 97311)	Rex A. Newell (D)	503–378–3338
Seattle, WA (Suite 800, 1111 3d Ave., 98101–3212)	(Vacancy) (RA)	206–553–4831

For further information, contact the Assistant Secretary for Veterans' Employment and Training, Department of Labor, 200 Constitution Avenue NW., Washington, DC 20210. Phone, 202–219–9116.

Sources of Information

Contracts General inquiries may be directed to the Office of Acquisition Integrity, OASAM, Room S–1522, 200 Constitution Avenue NW., Washington, DC 20210. Phone, 202–219–8904.

Inquiries on doing business with the Job Corps should be directed to the appropriate Job Corps Regional Director in the Employment and Training Administration regional office.

Employment Personnel offices use lists of eligibles from the clerical, scientific, technical, and general examinations of the Office of Personnel Management.

Inquiries and applications may be directed to any of the eight personnel offices at: Department of Labor, 200 Constitution Avenue NW., Washington, DC 20210, or the nearest regional office. Information on specific vacancies may be obtained by calling the Department's Job Opportunity Bank System. Phone, 800–366–2753.

Publications The Office of Public Affairs distributes a brochure entitled *Department of Labor,* which describes the activities of the major agencies within the Department, and *Publications of the Department of Labor,* a subject listing of publications available from the Department.

The Employment and Training Administration issues periodicals such as *Area Trends in Employment and Unemployment* available by subscription through the Superintendent of Documents, Government Printing Office,

Washington, DC 20402. Information about publications may be obtained from the Administration's Information Office. Phone, 202–219–6871.

The Office of Labor-Management Standards publishes the text of the Labor-Management Reporting and Disclosure Act (29 U.S.C. 401) and pamphlets that explain the reporting, election, bonding, and trusteeship provisions of the act. The pamphlets and reporting forms used by persons covered by the act are available free in limited quantities from the OLMS National Office at Room N–5616, 200 Constitution Avenue NW., Washington, DC 20210, and from OLMS field offices listed in the telephone directory under United States Government, Department of Labor.

The Pension and Welfare Benefits Administration distributes fact sheets, pamphlets, and booklets on employer obligations and employee rights under ERISA. A list of publications is available by writing: PWBA, Division of Public Information, Room N–5666, 200 Constitution Avenue NW., Washington, DC 20210. Phone, 202–219–8921.

The Bureau of Labor Statistics has an Information Office in the General Accounting Office Building, 441 G Street NW., Washington, DC 20212, phone, 202–219–1221. Periodicals include the *Monthly Labor Review, Consumer Price Index, Producer Prices and Price Indexes, Employment and Earnings,*

Current Wage Developments, Occupational Outlook Handbook, and *Occupational Outlook Quarterly.* Publications are both free and for sale, but for-sale items must be obtained from the Superintendent of Documents, Government Printing Office. Inquiries may be directed to the Washington Information Office or to the Bureau's regional offices.

Publications of the Employment Standards Administration, such as *Handy Reference Guide to the Fair Labor Standards Act,* and *OFCCP, Making Affirmative Action Work,* are available from the nearest area office. Single copies are free.

Reading Rooms Department of Labor Library, Room N2439, Frances Perkins Building, 200 Constitution Avenue NW., Washington, DC 20210. Phone, 202–219–6988.

The Office of Labor-Management Standards maintains a Public Disclosure Room at Room N–5616, 200 Constitution Avenue NW., Washington, DC 20210. Reports filed under the Labor-Management Reporting and Disclosure Act may be examined there and purchased for 15 cents per page. Reports also may be obtained by calling the Public Disclosure Room at 202–219–7393, or by contacting an Office field office listed in the telephone directory under United States Government, Department of Labor.

The Pension and Welfare Benefits Administration maintains a Public Disclosure Room at Room N–5507, 200 Constitution Avenue NW., Washington, DC 20210. Reports filed under the Employee Retirement Income Security Act may be examined there and purchased for 10 cents per page or by calling the Public Disclosure Room at 202–219–8771.

For further information concerning the Department of Labor, contact the Office of Public Affairs, Department of Labor, Room S–1032, 200 Constitution Avenue NW., Washington, DC 20210. Phone, 202–219–7316.

DEPARTMENT OF STATE

2201 C Street NW., Washington, DC 20520
Phone, 202–647–4000

SECRETARY OF STATE	WARREN M. CHRISTOPHER
Chief of Staff	THOMAS E. DONILON
Executive Assistant to the Secretary	ROBERT BRADTKE
Special Assistant to the Secretary and Executive Secretary of the Department	KENNETH C. BRILL
Deputy Assistant Secretary for Equal Employment Opportunity and Civil Rights	DEIDRE A. DAVIS
Chief of Protocol	MOLLY M. RAISER
Chairman, Foreign Service Grievance Board	JAMES OLDHAM
Civil Service Ombudsman	CATHERINE W. BROWN
Deputy Secretary of State	STROBE TALBOTT
Under Secretary for Political Affairs	PETER TARNOFF
Under Secretary for Economic and Agricultural Affairs	JOAN E. SPERO
Under Secretary for Global Affairs	TIMOTHY E. WIRTH
Under Secretary for Arms Control and International Security Affairs	LYNN E. DAVIS
Under Secretary for Management	RICHARD M. MOOSE
Assistant Secretary for Administration	PATRICK F. KENNEDY
Assistant Secretary for Consular Affairs	MARY A. RYAN
Assistant Secretary for Diplomatic Security	ANTHONY C.E. QUAINTON
Chief Financial Officer	RICHARD L. GREENE
Director General of the Foreign Service and Director of Personnel	GENTA HAWKINS HOLMES
Medical Director, Department of State and the Foreign Service	ELMER F. RIGAMER, M.D.
Executive Secretary, Board of the Foreign Service	LEWIS A. LUKENS
Director of the Foreign Service Institute	(VACANCY)
Director, Office of Foreign Missions	ERIC JAMES BOSWELL
Assistant Secretary for Population, Refugee, and Migration Affairs	PHYLLIS E. OAKLEY
Inspector General	JACQUELINE L. WILLIAMS-BRIDGER
Director, Policy Planning Staff	JAMES B. STEINBERG
Assistant Secretary for Legislative Affairs	WENDY RUTH SHERMAN
Assistant Secretary for Democracy, Human Rights and Labor	JOHN SHATTUCK
Legal Adviser	CONRAD K. HARPER
Assistant Secretary for African Affairs	GEORGE MOOSE
Assistant Secretary for East Asian and Pacific Affairs	WINSTON LORD
Assistant Secretary for European and Canadian Affairs	RICHARD HOLBROOKE
Assistant Secretary for Inter-American Affairs	ALEXANDER F. WATSON

400

Permanent Representative of the United States of America to the Organization of American States	HARRIET C. BABBITT
Assistant Secretary for Near Eastern Affairs	ROBERT H. PELLETREAU
Assistant Secretary for South Asian Affairs	ROBIN L. RAPHEL
Assistant Secretary for Economic and Business Affairs	DANIEL K. TARULLO
Assistant Secretary for Intelligence and Research	TOBY TRISTER GATI
Assistant Secretary for International Organization Affairs	(VACANCY)
Assistant Secretary for Oceans and International Environmental and Scientific Affairs	ELINOR G. CONSTABLE
Assistant Secretary for Public Affairs	THOMAS E. DONILON
Assistant Secretary, Bureau of Politico-Military Affairs	THOMAS E. MCNAMARA
Assistant Secretary for International Narcotics and Law Enforcement Affairs	ROBERT S. GELBARD
U.S. Coordinator, International Communications and Information Policy	VONYA B. MCCANN

United States Mission to the United Nations [1]

799 United Nations Plaza, New York, NY 10017

United States Representative to the United Nations and Representative in the Security Council	MADELEINE K. ALBRIGHT
Deputy United States Representative to the United Nations	EDWARD GNEHM, JR.
Deputy United States Representative in the Security Council	DAVID E. BIRENBAUM
United States Representative on the Economic and Social Council	VICTOR MARRERO
Alternate Representative for Special Political Affairs in the United Nations	KARL F. INDERFURTH

[For the Department of State statement of organization, see the *Code of Federal Regulations*, Title 22, Part 5]

The Department of State advises the President in the formulation and execution of foreign policy. As Chief Executive, the President has overall responsibility for the foreign policy of the United States. The Department of State's primary objective in the conduct of foreign relations is to promote the long-range security and well-being of the United States. The Department determines and analyzes the facts relating to American overseas interests, makes recommendations on policy and future action, and takes the necessary steps to carry out established policy. In so doing, the Department engages in continuous consultations with the American public, the

---

[1] For a description of the organization and functions of the United Nations, see page 775.

DEPARTMENT OF STATE

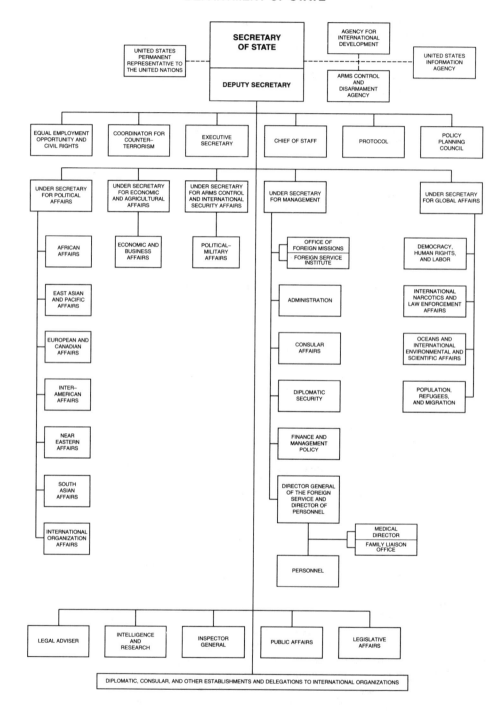

Congress, other U.S. departments and agencies, and foreign governments; negotiates treaties and agreements with foreign nations; speaks for the United States in the United Nations and in more than 50 major international organizations in which the United States participates; and represents the United States at more than 800 international conferences annually.

The Department of State, the senior executive department of the U.S. Government, was established by act of July 27, 1789, as the Department of Foreign Affairs and was renamed Department of State by act of September 15, 1789 (22 U.S.C. 2651 note).

Office of the Secretary

Secretary of State The Secretary of State, the principal foreign policy adviser to the President, is responsible for the overall direction, coordination, and supervision of U.S. foreign relations and for the interdepartmental activities of the U.S. Government overseas. The Secretary is the first-ranking member of the Cabinet, is a member of the National Security Council, and is in charge of the operations of the Department, including the Foreign Service. The Office of the Secretary includes the offices of the Deputy Secretary, Under Secretaries, Assistant Secretaries, Counselor, Legal Adviser, and Inspector General. Some areas where public purposes are widely applied are detailed below and on the following pages.

Economic and Agricultural Affairs The Under Secretary for Economic and Agricultural Affairs is principal adviser to the Secretary and Deputy Secretary in the formulation and conduct of foreign economic policy. Specific areas for which the Under Secretary is responsible include international trade, agriculture, energy, finance, transportation, and relations with developing countries.

International Security Affairs The Under Secretary for International Security Affairs is responsible for assuring the integration of all elements of the Foreign Assistance Program as an effective instrument of U.S. foreign policy and serves as Chairman of the Arms Transfer Management Group. The Under Secretary is also responsible for international scientific and technological issues, communications and information policy, and technology transfers.

Regional Bureaus

Six Assistant Secretaries direct the activities of the geographic bureaus, which are responsible for our foreign affairs activities throughout the world. These are the Bureaus of African Affairs, European and Canadian Affairs, East Asian and Pacific Affairs, Inter-American Affairs, and Near Eastern Affairs, and South Asian Affairs.

The regional Assistant Secretaries also serve as Chairmen of Interdepartmental Groups in the National Security Council system. These groups discuss and decide issues that can be settled at the Assistant Secretary level, including those arising out of the implementation of National Security Council decisions. They prepare policy papers for consideration by the Council and contingency papers on potential crisis areas for Council review.

Functional Areas

Diplomatic Security The Bureau of Diplomatic Security, established under the Omnibus Diplomatic Security and Antiterrorism Act of 1986, as amended

(22 U.S.C. 4803 *et seq.*), provides a secure environment for conducting American diplomacy and promoting American interests worldwide.

The Assistant Secretary of State for Diplomatic Security is responsible for:
—security and protective operations abroad and in the United States;
—counter-terrorism planning and coordination;
—security technology development;
—foreign government security training; and
—personnel training.

The *Security Awareness Staff* directs the development and execution of Bureauwide security and information awareness policies and programs, press and media relations, and public awareness. The Security Awareness Program provides information on diplomatic security concerns and is a focal point for responding to public inquiries and maintaining media relations on diplomatic security issues and events. The Training Support Division provides publications and training videotapes on diplomatic security concerns.

The *Private Sector Liaison Staff* maintains daily contact with and actively supports the U.S. private sector by disseminating timely, unclassified security information concerning the safety of U.S. private sector personnel, facilities, and operations abroad. The Staff operates the Electronic Bulletin Board, a computerized, unclassified security information data base accessible to U.S. private sector enterprises. It also provides direct consultation services to the private sector concerning security threats abroad.

The *Overseas Security Advisory Council* promotes cooperation on security-related issues between the American private sector interests worldwide and the Department of State, as provided in 22 U.S.C. 2656 and the Federal Advisory Committee Act, as amended (5 U.S.C. app.). The Council establishes continuing liaison and provides for operational security cooperation between Department security functions and the private sector. The Council also provides for regular and timely exchange of information between the private sector and the Department concerning developments in protective security. Additionally, it recommends methods and provides material for coordinating security planning and implementation of security programs.

The *Office of Policy, Planning, and Budget* assists in developing and coordinating Department and interagency security policy issues and standards through participation in committees, councils, and working groups and in providing assistance to Diplomatic Security program offices by resolving policy inconsistencies.

For further information, call 703–204–6217.

Economic and Business Affairs The Bureau of Economic and Business Affairs has overall responsibility for formulating and implementing policy regarding foreign economic matters, including resource and food policy, international energy issues, trade, economic sanctions, international finance and development, and aviation and maritime affairs.

For further information, call 202–647–2720.

Finance and Management Policy The Bureau of Finance and Management Policy is directed by the Chief Financial Officer (CFO), who serves as the Department's Budget Officer and Management Control Officer and assists in managing the Department and its posts. The CFO, assisted by well-qualified and well-trained financial management personnel, establishes effective management policies and internal controls; ensures adequate systems to produce useful, reliable, and timely financial and related programmatic information; develops useful financial analysis and performance reports; and integrates budget execution and accounting functions.

For further information, call 202–647–6778.

Foreign Service Institute The Foreign Service Institute of the Department of State is the Federal Government's primary training institution for officers and support personnel of the foreign affairs community. In addition to the Department of State, the Institute provides training for more than 40 other governmental agencies. The Institute's more than 300 courses, including 60 language courses, range in length from several days to 2 years. The courses are designed to promote successful performance in each professional assignment, to ease the adjustment to other countries and cultures, and to enhance the leadership and management capabilities of the foreign affairs community.

For further information, call 703–302–6729.

Intelligence and Research The Bureau of Intelligence and Research coordinates programs of intelligence, analysis, and research for the Department and other Federal agencies, and produces intelligence studies and current intelligence analyses essential to foreign policy determination and execution. Through its Office of Research, the Bureau maintains liaison with cultural and educational institutions and oversees contract research and conferences on foreign affairs subjects.

For further information, call 202–647–1080.

International Communications and Information Policy The Bureau of International Communications and Information Policy is the principal adviser to the Secretary of State on international telecommunications policy issues affecting U.S. foreign policy and national security. The Bureau acts as coordinator with other U.S. Government agencies and the private sector in the formulation and implementation of international policies relating to a wide range of rapidly evolving communications and information technologies. The Bureau promotes U.S. telecommunications interests bilaterally and multilaterally.

For further information, call 202–647–5832.

International Narcotics and Law Enforcement Affairs The Bureau of International Narcotics and Law Enforcement Affairs is responsible for

developing, coordinating, and implementing international narcotics control assistance activities of the Department of State as authorized under sections 481 and 482 of the Foreign Assistance Act of 1961, as amended (22 U.S.C. 2291, 2292). It is the principal point of contact and provides advice on international narcotics control matters for the Office of Management and Budget, the National Security Council, and the White House Office of National Drug Control Policy in ensuring implementation of U.S. policy in international narcotics matters.

The Bureau provides guidance on narcotics control matters to chiefs of missions and directs narcotics control coordinators at posts abroad; communicates or authorizes communication, as appropriate with foreign governments, on drug control matters including negotiating, concluding, and terminating agreements relating to international narcotics control programs as authorized by section 1(g)(3) of State Department Delegation of Authority No. 145 of February 4, 1980.

For further information, call 202–647–3450.

International Organization Affairs The Bureau of International Organization Affairs provides guidance and support for United States participation in international organizations and conferences. It leads in the development, coordination, and implementation of United States multilateral policy. The Bureau formulates and implements United States policy toward international organizations, with particular emphasis on those organizations which make up the United Nations system.

For further information, call 202–647–6400

Legal Adviser The Legal Adviser is the principal adviser to the Secretary and, through the Secretary, to the President on all matters of international law arising in the conduct of United States foreign relations. The Legal Adviser also provides general legal advice and services to the Secretary and other officials of the Department on matters with which the Department and overseas posts are concerned.

Medical Services The Office of Medical Services develops, manages, and staffs a worldwide primary health care system for U.S. citizen employees, and their eligible dependents, residing abroad. Agencies which participate in this medical program include the Department of State, the U.S. Information Agency, the U.S. Agency for International Development, and over 48 other foreign affairs agencies and offices. In support of its overseas operations, the Office approves and monitors the medical evacuation of patients, conducts pre-employment and in-service physical examinations, and provides clinical referral and advisory services. Domestically, the Office offers occupational health care, as well as numerous health education and health maintenance programs.

For further information, call 202-647-3617.

Consular Affairs The Bureau of Consular Affairs, under the direction of the Assistant Secretary, is responsible for the administration and enforcement of the provisions of the immigration and nationality laws, insofar as they concern the Department and the Foreign Service, for the issuance of passports and visas and related services, and for the protection and welfare of American citizens and interests abroad. Approximately 4 million passports a year are issued by the Passport Office of the Bureau, which has agencies in Boston, Chicago, Honolulu, Houston, Los Angeles, Miami, New Orleans, New York, Philadelphia, San Francisco, Seattle, Stamford, and Washington, DC.

For further information, see Sources of Information on page 409.

Political-Military Affairs The Bureau of Political-Military Affairs provides guidance and coordinates policy formulation on national security issues, including: nonproliferation of weapons of mass destruction and missile technology; nuclear and conventional arms control; defense relations and security assistance; and export controls.

It acts as the Department's primary liaison with the Department of Defense. The Bureau also participates in all major arms control, nonproliferation, and other security-related negotiations.

The Bureau's major activities are designed to further U.S. national security objectives by: stabilizing regional military balances through negotiations and security assistance; negotiating reductions in global inventories of weapons of mass destruction and curbing their proliferation; maintaining global access for U.S. military forces; inhibiting adversaries' access to militarily significant technologies; and promoting responsible U.S. defense trade.

For further information, call 202-647-6968.

Protocol The Chief of Protocol is the principal adviser to the U.S. Government, the President, the Vice President, and the Secretary of State on matters of diplomatic procedure governed by law or international custom and practice. The Office is responsible for:

—visits of foreign chiefs of state, heads of government, and other high officials to the United States;

—operation of the President's guest house, Blair House;

—delegations representing the President at official ceremonies abroad;

—conduct of official ceremonial functions and public events;

—accreditation of over 100,000 embassy, consular, international organization, and other foreign government personnel and members of their families throughout the United States;

—determining entitlement to diplomatic or consular immunity;

—publication of diplomatic, mission employee, and consular lists;

—resolution of problems arising out of diplomatic or consular immunity such as legal and police matters;

—approving the opening of consular offices in conjunction with the Office of Foreign Missions;

—official interpretation of the Order of Precedence;

—conducting an outreach program of cultural enrichment and substantive briefings of the Diplomatic Corps; and

—organizing credential presentations of newly arrived Ambassadors to the President and to the Secretary of State.

For further information, call 202-647-2663.

Foreign Service

To a great extent the future of our country depends on the relations we have with other countries, and those relations are conducted principally by the United States Foreign Service. Presently, representatives at 164 Embassies, 10 missions, 3 U.S. liaison offices, 1 U.S. interests section, 70 consulates general, 20 consulates, 4 branch offices, and 46 consular agencies throughout the world report to the State Department on the multitude of foreign developments that have a bearing on the welfare and security of the American people. These trained representatives provide the President and the Secretary of State with much of the raw material from which foreign policy is made and with the recommendations that help shape it.

The Ambassador is the personal representative of the President and reports to the President through the Secretary of State. Ambassadors have full responsibility for implementing the U.S. foreign policy by any and all U.S. Government personnel within their country of assignment, except those under military commands. Their responsibilities include negotiating agreements between the United States and the host country, explaining and disseminating official U.S. policy, and maintaining cordial relations with that country's government and people.

A listing of Foreign Service posts, together with addresses and telephone numbers and key personnel, appears in *Key Officers of Foreign Service Posts—Guide for Business Representatives,* which is for sale by the Superintendent of Documents, Government Printing Office, Washington, DC 20402.

United States Diplomatic Offices— Foreign Service

(C: Consular Office; N: No Embassy or Consular Office)

Country/Embassy	Ambassador
Albania/Tirana	Joseph E. Lake
Algeria/Algiers	Ronald E. Neumann
Angola/Luanda (N)	Edmond De Jarnette, Jr. (Director)
Antigua and Barbuda/St. Johns	Jeanette W. Hyde
Argentina/Buenos Aires	James R. Cheek
Armenia/Yerevan	Harry J. Gilmore
Australia/Canberra	Edward J. Perkins
Austria/Vienna	Swanee G. Hunt
Azerbaijan/Baku	Richard D. Kauzlarich
Bahamas/Nassau	Sidney Williams
Bahrain/Manama	David M. Ransom
Bangladesh/Dhaka	David N. Merrill
Barbados/Bridgetown	Jeanette W. Hyde
Belarus/Minsk	Kenneth S. Yalowitz
Belgium/Brussels	Alan J. Blinken
Belize/Belize City	George C. Bruno
Benin/Cotonou	Ruth A. Davis
Bolivia/La Paz	Curt W. Kamman
Bosnia and Herzegovina/Sarajevo.	Victor Jackovich
Botswana/Gaborone	Howard F. Jeter
Brazil/Brasilia	Melvyn Levitsky
Brunei Darussalam/Bandar Seri Begawan.	Theresa A. Tull
Bulgaria/Sofia	William D. Montgomery
Burkina Faso/Ouagadougou	Donald J. McConnell
Burundi/Bujumbura	Robert Krueger
Cambodia/Phnom Penh	Charles H. Twining, Jr.
Cameroon/Yaoundé	Harriet W. Isom
Canada/Ottawa	James J. Blanchard
Cape Verde/Praia	Joseph M. Segars
Central African Republic/Bangui	Robert E. Gribbin III
Chad/N'Djamena	Laurence E. Pope II
Chile/Santiago	Gabriel Guerra-Mondragon
China, People's Republic of/ Beijing.	J. Stapleton Roy
Colombia/Bogotá	Myles R.R. Frechette
Comoros, Federal and Islamic Republic of the/Moroni (N).	Leslie M. Alexander
Congo/Brazzaville	William C. Ramsay
Costa Rica/San Jose	Peter J. de Vos
Cote d'Ivoire/Abidjan	Hume A. Horan
Croatia/Zagreb	Peter W. Galbraith
Cuba/Havana (U.S. Interest Section).	Joseph G. Sullivan
Cyprus/Nicosia	Robert A. Boucher
Czech Republic/Prague	Adrian A. Basora
Denmark/Copenhagen	Edward E. Elson
Djibouti, Republic of/Djibouti	Martin L. Cheshes
Dominica/Roseau (N)	Jeanette W. Hyde
Dominican Republic/Santo Domingo.	Donna J. Hrinak
Ecuador/Quito	Peter F. Romero
Egypt/Cairo	Edward S. Walker
El Salvador/San Salvador	Alan H. Flanigan
Equatorial Guinea/Malabo	John E. Bennett
Eritrea/Asmara	Robert G. Houdek

United States Diplomatic Offices—
Foreign Service—Continued
(C: Consular Office; N: No Embassy or Consular Office)

Country/Embassy	Ambassador
Estonia/Tallinn	(Vacancy)
Ethiopia/Addis Ababa	Irvin Hicks
Fiji/Suva	(Vacancy)
Finland/Helsinki	Derek Shearer
France/Paris	Pamela Harriman
Gabonese Republic (Resident Libreville)/Libreville.	Joseph C. Wilson IV
Gambia/Banjul	Andrew J. Winter
Georgia/Tbilisi	Kent N. Brown
Germany, Federal Republic of/ Bonn.	Charles E. Redman
Ghana/Accra	Kenneth L. Brown
Greece/Athens	Thomas M.T. Niles
Grenada/St. George	Jeanette W. Hyde
Guatemala/Guatemala	Marilyn McAfee
Guinea/Conakry	Joseph A. Saloom III
Guinea-Bissau/Bissau	Roger A. McGuire
Guyana, Cooperative Republic of/Georgetown.	George F. Jones
Haiti/Port-au-Prince	William L. Swing
Holy See/Vatican City	Raymond L. Flynn
Honduras/Tegucigalpa	William T. Pryce
Hong Kong/Hong Kong (C)	Richard W. Mueller
Hungary/Budapest	Donald M. Blinken
Iceland/Reykjavik	Parker W. Borg
India/New Delhi	Frank G. Wisner
Indonesia/Jakarta	Robert L. Barry
Ireland/Dublin	Jean K. Smith
Israel/Tel Aviv	Martin S. Indyk
Italy/Rome	Reginald Bartholomew
Jamaica/Kingston	Jerome G. Cooper
Japan/Tokyo	Walter F. Mondale
Jerusalem	Edward G. Abington
Jordan, Hashemite Kingdom of/ Amman.	Wesley W. Egan
Kazakhstan/Almaty	William H. Courtney
Kenya/Nairobi	Aurelia E. Brazeal
Kiribati/Parawa (N)	(Vacancy)
Korea/Seoul	James T. Laney
Kuwait/Kuwait	Ryan C. Crocker
Kyrgyz Republic/Bishkek	Eileen A. Malloy
Lao People's Democratic Republic/Vientiane.	Victor L. Tomseth
Latvia/Riga	Ints M. Silins
Lebanon/Beirut	Mark G. Hambley
Lesotho/Maseru	Bismarck Myrick
Liberia/Monrovia	William P. Twaddell
Lithuania/Vilnius	James W. Swihart, Jr.
Luxembourg/Luxembourg	Clay Constantinou
Madagascar/Antananarivo	Dennis P. Barrett
Malawi/Lilongwe	Peter R. Chaveas
Malaysia/Kuala Lampur	John S. Wolf
Maldives/Malé (N)	Teresita C. Schaffer
Mali/Bamako	(Vacancy)
Malta/Valletta	Joseph R. Paolino, Jr.
Marshall Islands/Majuro	David C. Fields
Mauritania/Nouakchott	Dorothy M. Sampas
Mauritius/Port Louis	Leslie M. Alexander
Mexico/Mexico City	James R. Jones
Micronesia/Kolonia	March Fong Eu
Moldova/Chisinau	Mary C. Pendleton
Mongolia/Ulaanbaatar/	Donald C. Johnson
Morocco/Rabat	Marc C. Ginsberg
Mozambique/Maputo	Dennis C. Jett
Namibia/Windhoek	Marshall F. McCallie
Nauru/Yaren (N)	(Vacancy)
Nepal/Kathmandu	Sandra L. Vogelgesang
Netherlands/The Hague	K. Terry Dornbush

United States Diplomatic Offices—
Foreign Service—Continued
(C: Consular Office; N: No Embassy or Consular Office)

Country/Embassy	Ambassador
New Zealand/Wellington	Josiah H. Beeman
Nicaragua/Managua	John F. Maisto
Niger/Niamey	John S. Davison
Nigeria/Abuja	Walter C. Carrington
Norway/Oslo	Thomas A. Loftus
Oman/Muscat	David J. Dunford
Pakistan/Islamabad	John C. Monjo
Panama/Panama	(Vacancy)
Papua New Guinea/Port Moresby.	Richard W. Teare
Paraguay/Asunción	Robert E. Service
Peru/Lima	Alvin P. Adams, Jr.
Philippines/Manila	John D. Negroponte
Poland/Warsaw	Nicholas A. Rey
Portugal/Lisbon	Elizabeth F. Bagley
Qatar/Doha	Kenton W. Keith
Romania/Bucharest	Alfred H. Moses
Russian Federation/Moscow	Thomas R. Pickering
Rwanda/Kigali	David P. Rawson
St. Kitts and Nevis	Jeanette W. Hyde
St. Lucia/Castries (N)	Jeanette W. Hyde
St. Vincent and the Grenadines	Jeanette W. Hyde
Sao Tomé and Principe/Sao Tomé (N).	Joseph C. Wilson IV
Saudi Arabia/Riyadh	Raymond E. Mabus, Jr.
Senegal/Dakar	Mark Johnson
Seychelles, Republic of/Victoria	Carlton B. Stokes
Sierra Leone/Freetown	Lauralee M. Peters
Singapore/Singapore	Timothy A. Chorba
Slovak Republic/Bratislava	Theodore E. Russell
Slovenia/Ljubljana	E. Allan Wendt
Solomon Islands/Honiara	Richard W. Teare
Somali Democratic Republic/ Mogadishu.	Daniel H. Simpson
South Africa	Princeton N. Lyman
Spain/Madrid	Richard N. Gardner
Sri Lanka/Colombo	Teresita C. Schaeffer
Sudan/Khartoum	Donald K. Petterson
Suriname/Paramaribo	Roger R. Gamble
Swaziland/Mbabane	John T. Sprott
Sweden/Stockholm	Thomas L. Siebert
Switzerland/Bern	M. Larry Lawrence
Syrian Arab Republic/Damascus	Christopher W.S. Ross
Tajikistan/Dushanbe	Stanley T. Escudero
Tanzania/Dar es Salaam	Brady Anderson
Thailand/Bangkok	David F. Lambertson
Togo/Lomé	Johnny Young
Tonga	(Vacancy)
Trinidad and Tobago/Port-of-Spain.	Brian J. Donnelly
Tunisia/Tunis	Mary Ann Casey
Turkey/Ankara	Marc Grossman
Turkmenistan/Ashgabat	Joseph S. Hulings III
Tuvalu/Funafuti	(Vacancy)
Uganda/Kampala	E. Michael Southwick
Ukraine/Kiev	William G. Miller
United Arab Emirates/Abu Dhabi	William A. Rugh
United Kingdom of Great Britain and Northern Ireland/London.	William J. Crowe, Jr.
Uruguay, Oriental Republic of/ Montevideo.	Thomas J. Dodd
Uzbekistan/Tashkent	Henry L. Clarke
Vanuatu	Richard W. Teare
Venezuela/Caracas	Jeffrey Davidow
Western Samoa/Apia	Josiah H. Beeman
Yemen/Sanaa	David G. Newton
Zambia/Lusaka	Roland K. Kuchel
Zimbabwe/Harare	Johnny Carson

Sources of Information

Audiovisual Materials The Bureau of Consular Affairs has a 12-minute videotape on the safety of international travel. "Traveling Abroad More Safely" provides general practical advice to U.S. citizen travelers on avoiding the hazards of foreign travel. It includes steps to take prior to departure, ways to protect against theft and legal problems, and ways U.S. embassies and consulates can assist U.S. citizens who encounter difficulty abroad. The tape is available for $9 in VHS and Beta and $12.50 in 3/4-inch format, plus a $3 mailing and handling fee from Video Transfer, Inc., 5710 Arundel Avenue, Rockville, MD 20552. Phone, 301–881–0270.

Contracts General inquiries may be directed to the Office of Acquisitions (A/OPR/ACQ), Department of State, Washington, DC 20520. Phone, 703–875–6000.

Diplomatic and Official Passports Department employees may use diplomatic and official passports only as long as they are retained in the position or status for which originally issued. Section 51.4 of title 22 of the *Code of Federal Regulations* states that such passports must be returned upon termination of the bearer's diplomatic or official status.

In accordance with the Department's *Foreign Affairs Manual* (3 FAM 784), it is the responsibility of administrative officers to ensure that Form DS–8A includes a record of the disposition of passports issued to separating or retiring employees and their dependents. This includes all diplomatic and official passports, as well as any tourist passports for which the employee has been reimbursed by the Department.

Because of the possibility of misuse of these documents, it is important that all offices establish and maintain effective control over passport use. These passports are normally destroyed by passport services; however, they may be cancelled and returned as mementos if requested.

Diplomatic passports may not be used by employees for strictly personal travel.

Regulations permit their use for incidental personal travel related to an official assignment if the host government does not object. However, if employees or their dependents prefer to travel on a regular tourist passport in connection with official travel, they may apply by paying the regular passport fees and claiming reimbursement on their travel voucher.

Inquiries on these matters should be directed to Passport Services, Diplomatic and Congressional Travel Branch. Phone, 202–326–6234.

Employment Inquiries about employment in the Foreign Service should be directed to: PER/REE/REC, P.O. Box 9317, Arlington, VA 22210. Phone, 703–875–7490. Inquiries about civil service positions in the Department of State should be directed to: PER/CSP/POD, P.O. Box 18657, Washington, DC 20036–8657. The Department's Civil Service Employment Information Office is located inside the D Street north lobby entrance of the Department of State building, Washington, DC. The Civil Service Personnel Office provides a 24-hour job information line. Phone, 202–647–7284.

Freedom of Information Act and Privacy Act Requests Requests from the public for Department of State records should be addressed to the Director, Office of Freedom of Information Privacy and Classification Review, Department of State, 2201 C Street NW., Washington, DC 20520–1512. Phone, 202–647–8484. Individuals are requested to indicate on the outside of the envelope the statute under which they are requesting access: FOIA REQUEST or PRIVACY REQUEST.

Any identifiable Department of State document can be requested under the Freedom of Information Act (5 U.S.C. 552). Requesters should provide as much identifying information as possible about the document to assist the Department in locating it. Include subject matter, timeframe, originator of the information, or any other helpful data.

Only persons who are U.S. citizens or aliens who are lawfully admitted to the United States for permanent residence can request information under the Privacy Act (5 U.S.C. 552a). Under this act, individuals may request access to records that are maintained under the individual's name or some other personally identifiable symbol. Descriptions of record systems from which documents can be retrieved by the individual's name are published in the *Federal Register,* copies of which are available from the Director, Office of Freedom of Information, Privacy and Classification Review. To expedite processing of requests, individuals should specify the system of records they wish to have searched and should provide the following identifying information: full name; aliases (if any); date and place of birth; and circumstances, including approximate time period, which would have led to the creation of the record.

A public reading room, where unclassified and declassified documents may be inspected, is located in the Department of State, 2201 C Street NW., Washington, DC. Phone, 202–647–8484. Directions to the reading room may be obtained from receptionists at public entrances to the Department.

Missing Persons, Emergencies, Deaths of Americans Abroad   For information concerning missing persons, emergencies, travel advisories, and arrests or deaths of Americans abroad, contact the Citizens Emergency Center, Department of State. Phone, 202–647–5225. Correspondence should be directed to: Overseas Citizens Services, Bureau of Consular Affairs, Department of State, Washington, DC 20520.

Inquiries regarding citizenship, international parental child abduction, judicial assistance, overseas voting, and adoption of foreign children by private U.S. citizens should be directed to: Citizens Consular Service, Bureau of Consular Affairs, Room 4817, Department of State, Washington, DC 20520. Phone, 202–647–3666.

Passports   For information concerning the issuance of U.S. passports, contact Passport Services, Bureau of Consular Affairs, 1111 19th Street NW., Washington, DC 20522–1705 (phone, 202–647–0518), or any of the field offices. Additional information concerning passport applications is available for sale by the Superintendent of Documents, Government Printing Office, Washington, DC 20402.

Field Offices—Passport Office

City	Address	Telephone
Boston, MA	Thomas P. O'Neill Federal Bldg., 02222	617–565–6998
Chicago, IL	Federal Bldg., 60604	312–353–7155
Honolulu, HI	Federal Bldg., 96850	808–541–1919
Houston, TX	1919 Smith St., 77002	713–653–3153
Los Angeles, CA	11000 Wilshire Blvd., 90024–3615	310–575–7070
Miami, FL	Federal Office Bldg., 33130	305–536–4681
New Orleans, LA	701 Loyola Ave., 70113	504–589–6728
New York, NY	Rockefeller Ctr., 10111–0031	212–399–5290
Philadelphia, PA	Federal Bldg., 19106	215–597–7480
San Francisco, CA	525 Market St., 94105–2773	415–744–4010
Seattle, WA	Federal Bldg., 98174	206–220–7777
Stamford, CT	1 Landmark Sq., 06901	203–325–4401
Washington, DC	1425 K St. NW., 20522–1705	202–647–0518

Publications   The Department's Bureau of Public Affairs produces a variety of publications on the Department and foreign policy, including two official documentary series, *Foreign Relations of the United States* and *American Foreign Policy: Current Documents,* and two publications on U.S. foreign policy, *Dispatch* and *Background Notes.*

The series *Foreign Relations of the United States,* published since 1861 in over 300 volumes, constitutes the official documentary record of U.S. foreign policy. It is the most extensive and most near-current publication of diplomatic papers in the world. The Office of the Historian will soon complete the 75 print volumes and microfiche supplements documenting the foreign policy of the Eisenhower administration (1953–1960). Publication of 32 print volumes and supplements on the foreign policy of the Kennedy administration (1961–1963) will be completed by 1996.

The *American Foreign Policy* annual volumes contain current official public expressions of policy that best convey the objectives of U.S. foreign policy. The series includes texts of major official messages, addresses, statements, reports, and communications by the White House, Department of State, and other Federal agencies involved in the foreign affairs process. Microfiche supplements, which include additional public documents, accompany the 1981 and subsequent annual volumes.

The Department's weekly magazine, *Dispatch*, offers a diverse compilation of speeches, congressional testimony, policy statements, fact sheets, and other foreign policy information.

Background Notes provide brief, factual summaries concerning the people, history, government, economy, and foreign relations of about 180 countries (excluding the United States) and of selected international organizations. A free index is available.

Dispatches, Background Notes, and other materials—including reports to Congress—are carried over the Government Printing Office's (GPO) Federal Bulletin Board Service. This information can also be accessed through the Department of Commerce's National Technical Information Service's FedWorld® network, as well as through other data base services. A GPO deposit account may be opened by calling 202–512–0822.

For information on these and other Department publications, write to Public Information, Bureau of Public Affairs, Department of State, Room 5831, Washington, DC 20520. Phone, 202–647–6575.

Reading Room   To review declassified Department documents, contact the receptionists at the public entrance to the Department of State, 2201 C Street

NW., Washington, DC, for the specific location. Phone, 202–647–8484.

Telephone Directory   The Department's telephone directory is available for sale by the Superintendent of Documents, Government Printing Office, Washington, DC 20402.

Tips for U.S. Travelers Abroad   The following pamphlets from the Bureau of Consular Affairs are for sale for $1 by the Superintendent of Documents, U.S. Government Printing Office, Washington, DC 20402:

Travel Tips for Older Americans contains basic information on passports, currency, health, aid for serious problems, and other useful travel tips for senior citizens.

Your Trip Abroad contains basic information on passports, vaccinations, unusual travel requirements, dual nationality, drugs, modes of travel, customs, legal requirements, and many other topics for the American tourist, business representative, or student traveling overseas.

A Safe Trip Abroad contains helpful precautions to minimize one's chances of becoming a victim of terrorism and also provides other safety tips.

Tips for Americans Residing Abroad contains advice for more than 2 million Americans living in foreign countries.

Travel Warning on Drugs Abroad contains important facts on the potential dangers of being arrested for illegal drugs abroad and the type of assistance that U.S. consular officers can and cannot provide. This booklet is free from the Department of State, Consular Affairs/Public Affairs Staff, Room 5807, Washington, DC 20520.

The Bureau of Consular Affairs also publishes a series of brochures on travel to specific areas of the world. Depending on the region, the brochures cover topics such as currency and customs regulations, entry requirements, dual nationality, and restrictions on the use of photography. Copies are available from the Government Printing Office for $1. Currently available are: *Tips for Travelers to the Caribbean; Tips for Travelers to Eastern Europe; Tips for Travelers to Mexico; Tips for Travelers to the Middle East and North Africa; Tips* for *Travelers to the People's Republic of China; Tips for Travelers to South Asia; Tips for Travelers to the USSR; Tips for Travelers to Central and South America,* and *Tips for Travelers to Sub-Saharan Africa.*

Foreign Entry Requirements contains visa and other entry requirements of foreign countries. Order for 50 cents from the Consumer Information Center, Pueblo, CO 81009.

Visas   To obtain information on visas for foreigners wishing to enter the United States, call 202–663–1225.

For further information concerning the Department of State, contact the Office of Public Communication, Public Information Service, Bureau of Public Affairs, Department of State, Washington, DC 20520. Phone, 202–647–6575.

DEPARTMENT OF TRANSPORTATION

400 Seventh Street SW., Washington, DC 20590
Phone, 202–366–4000

SECRETARY OF TRANSPORTATION — FEDERICO PEÑA
Chief of Staff — ANN M. BORMOLINI
  Deputy Chief of Staff — KATHERINE L. ARCHULETA
  White House Liaison — ANITA PEREZ FURGUSON
  Special Assistants to the Secretary — JUDITH A. BURRELL
    JEFFREY P. MORALES
Deputy Secretary — MORTIMER L. DOWNEY
  Director for Drug Enforcement and Program Compliance — ALBERT ALVAREZ
Associate Deputy Secretary and Director, Office of Intermodalism — MICHAEL P. HUERTA
  Deputy Director — FRANK PENTTI
Director, Executive Secretariat — MARGARITA ROQUE
Chairman, Board of Contract Appeals — THADDEUS V. WARE
Director of Civil Rights — ANTONIO J. CALIFA
Director of Small and Disadvantaged Business Utilization — LUZ A. HOPEWELL
Director of Commercial Space Transportation — FRANK C. WEAVER
  Associate Managing Director — PATTI GRACE SMITH
  Associate Director for Licensing and Safety — BOBBY R. QUISENBERRY
  Associate Director for Commercial Space Policy and International Affairs — RICHARD W. SCOTT, JR.
Director of Intelligence and Security — REAR ADM. PAUL E. BUSICK, USCG
  Deputy Director of Intelligence and Security — (VACANCY)
  Deputy Director of Intermodalism — FRANK PENTTI
Inspector General — A. MARY SCHIAVO
  Deputy Inspector General — MARIO A. LAURO, JR.
  Senior Counsel to the Inspector General — ROGER P. WILLIAMS
  Assistant Inspector General for Auditing — RAYMOND J. DECARLI
  Deputy Assistant Inspector General for Auditing — LAWRENCE H. WEINTROB
  Assistant Inspector General for Inspections and Evaluations — WILBUR L. DANIELS
  Deputy Assistant Inspector General for Inspections and Evaluations — (VACANCY)
  Assistant Inspector General for Investigations — (VACANCY)
  Deputy Assistant Inspector General for Investigations — (VACANCY)
  Director of Administration — PATRICIA J. THOMPSON
General Counsel — STEPHEN H. KAPLAN
  Deputy General Counsel — ROSALIND A. KNAPP
  Special Counsel — DIANE R. LIFF
  Assistant General Counsel for Environmental, Civil Rights and General Law — ROBERTA D. GABEL
    Deputy Assistants — JAMES R. DANN

413

	DAVID K. TOCHEN
Patent Counsel	OTTO M. WILDENSTEINER
Chief, Freedom of Information Act Division	ROBERT R. MEEKS, *Acting*
Assistant General Counsel for International Law	DONALD H. HORN
Deputy Assistant	JOSEPH A. BROOKS
Assistant General Counsel for Litigation	PAUL M. GEIER
Deputy Assistant	DALE C. ANDREWS
Assistant General Counsel for Legislation	THOMAS W. HERLIHY
Deputy Assistant	CLARE R. DONELAN
Assistant General Counsel for Regulation and Enforcement	NEIL R. EISNER
Deputy Assistant	ROBERT C. ASHBY
Chief, Documentary Services Division	PAULETTE V. TWINE
Chairman, Board for Correction of Military Records	ROBERT H. JOOST
Deputy Chairman	NANCY BATTAGLIA
Assistant General Counsel for Aviation Enforcement and Proceedings	SAMUEL PODBERESKY
Deputy Assistant	DAYTON LEHMAN, JR.
Assistant Secretary for Transportation Policy	FRANK E. KRUESI
Deputy Assistant Secretaries	JOSEPH F. CANNY
	JOHN N. LIEBER
Director of Environment, Energy, and Safety	DONALD R. TRILLING
Director of Economics	(VACANCY)
Assistant Secretary for Aviation and International Affairs	(VACANCY)
Deputy Assistant Secretaries	PATRICK V. MURPHY, JR.
	MARK L. GERCHICK
Director of International Transportation and Trade	ARNOLD LEVINE
Director of International Aviation	PAUL GRETCH
Director of Aviation Analysis	JOHN COLEMAN
Assistant Secretary for Budget and Programs	LOUISE FRANKEL STOLL
Deputy Assistant Secretary	EUGENE A. CONTI, JR.
Deputy Chief Financial Officer	DAVID K. KLEINBURG
Director of Programs and Evaluation	GEORGE W. MCDONALD
Director of Budget	KATHERINE E. COLLINS
Director of Financial Management	EILEEN T. POWELL
Assistant Secretary for Administration	MELISSA J. SPILLENKOTHEN
Director of Personnel	GLENDA M. TATE
Director of Management Planning	PATRICIA D. PARRISH
Director of Information Resource Management	EUGENE K. TAYLOR, JR.
Director of Administrative Services and Property Management	RONALD D. KEEFER
Director, Office of Hearings	JOHN J. MATHIAS
Director of Acquisition and Grant Management	(VACANCY)
Director of Security	JOHN J. TAYLOR
Assistant Secretary for Governmental Affairs	STEVEN O. PALMER
Deputy Assistant Secretary	JOHN C. HORSLEY
Director of Congressional Affairs	REGINA SULLIVAN
Director of Intergovernmental Affairs	(VACANCY)

Assistant to the Secretary and Director of Public Affairs	STEVEN J. AKEY
Deputy Director of Public Affairs	(VACANCY)

UNITED STATES COAST GUARD

2100 Second Street SW., Washington, DC 20593–0001
Phone, 202–267–2229

Commandant	ADM. ROBERT E. KRAMEK, USCG
Vice Commandant	VICE ADM. ARTHUR E. HENN, USCG
Chaplain	CAPT. THOMAS K. CHADWICK, USCG
International Affairs Director/Foreign Policy Advisor	GERARD P. YOEST
Chief Administrative Law Judge	JOSEPH N. INGOLIA
Chairman, Marine Safety Council	REAR ADM. JOHN E. SHKOR, USCG
Chief, Congressional Affairs Staff	CAPT. GUY T. GOODWIN, USCG
Chief, Public Affairs Staff	(VACANCY)
Chief of Staff	VICE ADM. KENT H. WILLIAMS, USCG
Deputy Chief of Staff	CAPT. JOHN F. MCGOWAN, USCG
Director of Resources	REAR ADM. TIMOTHY W. JOSIAH, USCG
Director of Finance and Procurement	WILLIAM H. CAMPBELL
Chief, Office of Acquisition	REAR ADM. THOMAS H. COLLINS, USCG
Chief, Office of Engineering, Logistics and Development	REAR ADM. EDWARD J. BARRETT, USCG
Chief, Office of Civil Rights	WALTER R. SOMERVILLE
Chief, Office of Health and Safety	REAR ADM. ALAN M. STEINMAN, USPHS
Chief Counsel	REAR ADM. JOHN E. SHKOR, USCG
Chief, Office of Marine Safety, Security and Environmental Protection	REAR ADM. JAMES C. CARD, USCG
Chief, Office of Law Enforcement and Defense Operations	REAR ADM. NORMAN T. SAUNDERS, USCG
Chief, Office of Navigation Safety and Waterway Services	REAR ADM. RUDY K. PESCHEL, USCG
Chief, Office of Personnel and Training	REAR ADM. WILLIAM C. DONNELL, USCG
Chief, Office of Readiness and Reserve	REAR ADM. RICHARD M. LARRABEE III, USCG
Chief, Office of Command, Control and Communications	REAR ADM. DAVID E. CIANCAGLINI, USCG

FEDERAL AVIATION ADMINISTRATION

800 Independence Avenue SW., Washington, DC 20591
Phone, 202–366–4000

Administrator	DAVID R. HINSON
Deputy Administrator	LINDA HALL DASCHLE
Associate Administrator for Airports	CYNTHIA D. RICH
Deputy Associate Administrator for Airports	QUENTIN S. TAYLOR

Director of Airport Planning and Programming	PAUL L. GALIS
Director of Airport Safety and Standards	LEONARD E. MUDD
Chief Counsel	JOHN H. CASSADY, *Acting*
Associate Administrator for Civil Aviation Security	CATHAL L. FLYNN
Director of Civil Aviation Security Intelligence	PATRICK MCDONNELL
Director of Civil Aviation Security Operations	LYNNE A. OSMUS
Director of Civil Aviation Security Policy and Planning	BRUCE R. BUTTERWORTH
Assistant Administrator for Civil Rights	LEON C. WATKINS
Assistant Administrator for Government and Industry Affairs	BRADLEY MIMS
Assistant Administrator for Policy, Planning, and International Aviation	BARRY L. VALENTINE
Deputy Assistant Administrator for Policy Planning and International Aviation	LOUISE E. MAILLETT
Director of Aviation Policy and Plans	JOHN M. RODGERS
Director of Environment and Energy	JAMES B. ERICKSON
Director of International Aviation	JOAN W. BAUERLEIN
Assistant Administrator for Public Affairs	SANDRA ALLEN
Assistant Administrator for Systems Safety	CHRISTOPER A. HART
Associate Administrator for Administration	DALE E. MCDANIEL, *Acting*
Director of Financial Services	RUTH A. LEVERENZ
Director of Business Information	LAWRENCE COVINGTON, *Acting*
Director of Human Resource Management	KAY FRANCES DOLAN, *Acting*
Associate Administrator for Regulation and Certification	ANTHONY J. BRODERICK, JR.
Deputy Associate Administrator for Regulation and Certification	DANIEL C. BEAUDETTE
Federal Air Surgeon	JON L. JORDAN, M.D.
Director of Accident Investigation	DAVID F. THOMAS
Director, Aircraft Certification Service	THOMAS E. MCSWEENEY
Director, Flight Standards Service	THOMAS C. ACCARDI
Director of Rulemaking	CHRIS A. CHRISTIE
Associate Administrator for Air Traffic Services	MONTE BELGER
	DARLENE M. FREEMAN
Director, Air Traffic Service	BILL JEFFERS
Director, Airway Facilities Service	JOAQUIN ARCHILLA
Director of System Capacity and Requirements	CARL SCHELLENBERG
Director of Independent Operational Test and Evaluation	A. MARTIN PHILLIPS
Associate Administrator for Research and Acquisitions	GEORGE L. DONOHUE
Director of Acquisitions	DENNIS DEGAETANO
Director of Air Traffic Systems Development	ROBERT VALONE
Director of Aviation Research	ANDRES ZELLWEGER
Director of Communication, Navigation, and Surveillance Systems	LONI CZEKALSKI
Director of System Architecture and Program Evaluation	RONALD MORGAN
Director of Information Technology	THERON A. GRAY

FEDERAL HIGHWAY ADMINISTRATION
400 Seventh Street SW., Washington, DC 20590
Phone, 202–366–0660

Administrator	RODNEY E. SLATER
Deputy Administrator	JANE F. GARVEY
Executive Director	ANTHONY R. KANE
Chief Counsel	THEODORE A. MCCONNELL
Deputy Chief Counsel	EDWARD V.A. KUSSY
Director of External Communications	ANDREW M. PAVEN
Director of Civil Rights	EDWARD W. MORRIS, JR.
Director of Program Review	EMIL ELINSKY
Director of Intelligent Transportation Systems Joint Program Office	CHRISTINE M. JOHNSON
Associate Administrator for Policy	GLORIA J. JEFF
Director of Policy Development	MADELEINE S. BLOOM
Director of Highway Information Management	DAVID R. MCELHANEY
Director of International Programs	(VACANCY)
Associate Administrator for Research and Development	JOHN A. CLEMENTS
Deputy Associate Administrator for Research and Development	ROBERT J. BETSOLD
Director of the National Highway Institute	MOGES AYELE
Director of Engineering and Highway Operations Research and Development	CHARLES J. NEMMERS
Director of Safety and Traffic Operations Research and Development	LYLE G. SAXTON
Director of Research and Development Operations and Support	ROBERT J. KREKLAU
Director of Advanced Research	THOMAS J. PASKO
Associate Administrator for Program Development	THOMAS J. PTAK
Director of Engineering	WILLIAM A. WESEMAN
Director of Environment and Planning	KEVIN E. HEANUE
Director of Right-of-Way	BARBARA K. ORSKI
Associate Administrator for Safety and System Applications	DENNIS C. JUDYCKI
Director of Highway Safety	FREDERICK G. WRIGHT
Director of Traffic Management and Intelligent Transportation Systems Applications	SUSAN B. LAUFFER
Director of Technology Applications	JOSEPH S. TOOLE
Associate Administrator for Motor Carriers	GEORGE L. REAGLE
Director of Motor Carrier Research and Standards	JAMES E. SCAPELLATOR
Director of Motor Carrier Information Analysis	JOHN F. GRIMM
Director of Planning and Customer Liaison	MICHAEL F. TRENTACOSTE
Director of Motor Carrier Field Operations	CLINTON O. MAGBY
Director of Motor Carrier Safety and Technology	(VACANCY)
Associate Administrator for Administration	GEORGE S. MOORE, JR.
Deputy Associate Administrator for Administration	DIANA L. ZEIDEL

Director of Personnel and Training — JERRY A. HAWKINS
Director of Information and Management Services — MICHAEL J. VECCHIETTI
Director of Fiscal Services — PETER J. BASSO
Director of Contracts and Procurement — (VACANCY)
Federal Lands Highway Program Administrator — THOMAS O. EDICK

FEDERAL RAILROAD ADMINISTRATION

400 Seventh Street SW., Washington, DC 20590
Phone, 202–366–4000

Administrator — JOLENE M. MOLITORIS
Deputy Administrator — DONALD M. ITZKOFF
  Chief of Staff — FRANCES T. GREENBERG
  Director, Office of Civil Rights — MILES S. WASHINGTON, JR.
  Director, Office of Public Affairs — DAVID BOLGER
  Director, Office of Budget — KATHRYN B. MURPHY
Chief Counsel — S. MARK LINDSEY
  Deputy Chief Counsel — MICHAEL T. HALEY
  Assistant Chief Counsel, General Law Division — ROBERT S. VERMUT
  Assistant Chief Counsel, Safety Law Division — DAN SMITH
Associate Administrator for Administration — RAY ROGERS
  Deputy Associate Administrator for Administration — THOMAS F. PROCTOR
  Director, Office of Human Resources — THOMAS F. PROCTOR, *Acting*
  Director, Office of Information Technology and Productivity Improvement — MANNIE A. DUNCAN
  Director, Office of Acquisition and Grants Services — JOSEPH KERNER
  Director, Office of Financial Services — GERALD SCHOENAUER
Associate Administrator for Policy — SALLY HILL COOPER
  Deputy Associate Administrator for Industry and Intermodal Policy — JANE H. BACHNER, *Acting*
  Deputy Associate Administrator for Policy Systems — RAPHAEL KEDAR
Associate Administrator for Safety — BRUCE FINE
  Deputy Associate Administrators for Safety, Standards and Program Development — GRADY C. COTHEN
  Deputy Associate Administrator for Safety Compliance and Program Implementation — PHILIP OLEKSZYK
  Director, Office of Safety Enforcement — EDWARD R. ENGLISH
  Director, Office of Safety Analysis — JOHN G. LEEDS
Associate Administrator for Railroad Development — JAMES T. MCQUEEN
  Deputy Associate Administrator for Railroad Development — ARRIGO MONGINI
  Director, Office of Passenger and Freight Services — ROBERT C. HUNTER
  Director, Northeast Corridor Program — MICHAEL SAUNDERS
  Director, Office of Research and Development — CLAIRE L. ORTH
  DOT Contact, Transportation Test Center, Pueblo, CO — GUNARS SPONS

NATIONAL HIGHWAY TRAFFIC SAFETY ADMINISTRATION
400 Seventh Street SW., Washington, DC 20590
Phone, 202–366–9550

Administrator	RICARDO MARTINEZ
Deputy Administrator	PHILIP R. RECHT
Executive Director	HOWARD M. SMOLKIN
Director, Executive Correspondence	LINDA DIVELBISS
Director, Office of Civil Rights	GEORGE B. QUICK
Chief Counsel	JOHN G. WOMACK, JR., *Acting*
Director, Office of Public and Consumer Affairs	BARRY MCCAHILL, *Acting*
Associate Administrator for Plans and Policy	DONALD C. BISCHOFF
Director, Office of Strategic Planning and Evaluation	CARL E. NASH
Director, Office of Regulatory Analysis	L. ROBERT SHELTON
Director, Office of Budget and Policy Development	L. ROBERT SHELTON, *Acting*
Associate Administrator for Safety Performance Standards	BARRY FELRICE
Director, Office of Vehicle Safety Standards	PATRICIA BRESLIN
Director, Office of Market Incentives	JAMES HACKNEY, *Acting*
Associate Administrator for Research and Development	GEORGE L. PARKER
Director, Office of Crash Avoidance Research	WILLIAM A. LEASURE
Director, Office of Crashworthiness Research	RALPH HITCHCOCK
Director, Vehicle Research and Test Center	MICHAEL MONK
Director, National Center for Statistics and Analysis	WILLIAM H. WALSH, JR.
Associate Administrator for Safety Assurance	WILLIAM A. BOEHLY
Director, Office of Defects Investigation	KATHLEEN DEMETER
Director, Office of Vehicle Safety Compliance	MARILYNNE E. JACOBS
Associate Administrator for Traffic Safety Programs	MICHAEL B. BROWNLEE
Director, Office of Occupant Protection	JAMES NICHOLS
Director, Office of Alcohol and State Programs	JAMES HEDLUND
Director, Office of Enforcement and Emergency Services	MARILENA AMONI
Director, Office of Program Development and Evaluation	TED ANDERSON
Associate Administrator for State and Community Services	ADELE DERBY
Chief, Program Implementation Staff	RITA WEISS
Chief, Program Support Staff	MARLENE MARKINSON
Associate Administrator for Administration	HERMAN L. SIMMS, *Acting*
Director, Office of Personnel	HERMAN SIMMS
Director, Office of Contracts and Procurement	(VACANCY)
Director, Office of Information Resource Management	(VACANCY)
Director, Office of Administrative Operations	(VACANCY)
Director, Office of Financial Management	CHARLES H. KENT

FEDERAL TRANSIT ADMINISTRATION
400 Seventh Street SW., Washington, DC 20590
Phone, 202–366–4043

Administrator	GORDON J. LINTON
Deputy Administrator	GRACE CRUNICAN
Chief Counsel	BERLE M. SHILLER
Director, Communications and External Affairs	PETER G. HALPIN
Director, Executive Secretariat	MARY F. KNAPP
Director, Office of Civil Rights	SUSAN E. SCHRUTH, *Acting*
Director, Office of Public Affairs	(VACANCY)
Associate Administrator for Budget and Policy	JANETTE I. SADIK-KHAN
Associate Administrator for Grants Management	ROBERT H. MCMANUS
Associate Administrator for Technical Assistance and Safety	LAWRENCE L. SCHULMAN
Associate Administrator for Administration	THOMAS R. HUNT

MARITIME ADMINISTRATION
400 Seventh Street SW., Washington, DC 20590
Phone, 202–366–5807

Administrator	ALBERT J. HERBERGER
Deputy Administrator	JOAN B. YIM
Deputy Administrator for Inland Waterways and Great Lakes	JOHN E. GRAYKOWSKI
Director of Congressional and Public Affairs	SHARON K. BROOKS
Chief Counsel	JOAN M. BONDAREFF
Deputy Chief Counsel	ROBERT J. PATTON, JR.
Secretary, Maritime Administration/Maritime Subsidy Board	JOEL C. RICHARD
Coordinator of Research and Development	PAUL B. MENTZ
Director, Office of Maritime Labor, Training, and Safety	TAYLOR E. JONES II
Associate Administrator for Administration	JOHN L. MANN, JR.
Director, Office of Management Services	RALPH W. FERGUSON
Director, Office of Budget	TAYLOR E. JONES II, *Acting*
Director, Office of Accounting	JOHN G. HOBAN
Director, Office of Information Resources Management	LESLIE E. HEARN
Director, Office of Personnel	SHERRY D. GILSON
Director, Office of Acquisition	TIMOTHY P. ROARK
Associate Administrator for Policy, International Trade, and Marketing	BRUCE J. CARLTON
Director, Office of Policy and Plans	BRUCE J. CARLTON, *Acting*
Director, Office of International Activities	JAMES A. TREICHEL
Director, Office of Marketing	THOMAS W. HARRELSON
Director, Office of Statistical and Economic Analysis	WILLIAM B. EBERSOLD
Associate Administrator for Ship Financial Assistance and Cargo Preference	JAMES J. ZOK
Director, Office of Ship Financing	MITCHELL D. LAX
Director, Office of Costs and Rates	MICHAEL P. FERRIS
Director, Office of Subsidy and Insurance	EDMOND J. FITZGERALD
Director, Office of Financial Approvals	RICHARD J. MCDONNELL

Director, Office of Cargo Preference	(VACANCY)
Associate Administrator for National Security	MICHAEL DELPERCIO, JR., *Acting*
Director, Office of Ship Operations	MICHAEL DELPERCIO, JR.
Director, Office of National Security Plans	THOMAS M.P. CHRISTENSEN
Director, Office of Sealift Support	JAMES F. CAPONITI
Associate Administrator for Shipbuilding and Technology Development	EDWIN B. SCHIMLER, *Acting*
Director, Office of Ship Construction	EDWIN B. SCHIMLER, *Acting*
Director, Office of Shipyard Revitalization	JOSEPH A. BYRNE
Associate Administrator for Port, Intermodal, and Environmental Activities	MARGARET D. BLUM
Deputy Associate Administrator for Port, Intermodal, and Environmental Activities	CARMINE P. GERACE
Director, Office of Intermodal Development	JOHN W. CARNES, *Acting*
Director, Office of Environmental Activities	ZELVIN LEVINE, *Acting*
Director, Office of Ports and Domestic Shipping	JOHN M. PISANI
Director, North Atlantic Region	ROBERT MCKEON
Director, Great Lakes Region	ALPHA H. AMES, JR.
Director, Central Region	DEEPAK VARSHNEY, *Acting*
Director, South Atlantic Region	MAYANK JAIN
Director, Western Region	FRANCIS X. JOHNSTON
Superintendent, United States Merchant Marine Academy	THOMAS T. MATTESON

SAINT LAWRENCE SEAWAY DEVELOPMENT CORPORATION

Washington Office: 400 Seventh Street SW., Washington, DC 20590
Phone, 202–366–0091; 1–800–785–2779

Massena Office: 180 Andrews Street, Massena, NY 13662
Phone, 315–764–3200

Administrator	STANFORD E. PARRIS
Chief of Staff	DAVID G. SANDERS
Assistant Resident Manager	ERMAN J. COCCI
Associate Administrator	THEODORE J. BRUE
Comptroller	EDWARD MARGOSIAN
Chief Counsel	MARC C. OWEN
Director of Communications	DENNIS E. DEUSCHL
Director of Operations and Maintenance	STEPHEN C. HUNG
Director of Human Resources	MARY ANN HAZEL
Director of Marketing	STEPHEN J. RYBICKI
Director of Development and Logistics	ROBERT J. LEWIS

RESEARCH AND SPECIAL PROGRAMS ADMINISTRATION

400 Seventh Street SW., Washington, DC 20590
Phone, 202–366–4433

Administrator	D.K. SHARMA
Deputy Administrator	ANA SOL GUTIERREZ
Special Assistant	WILLIAM VINCENT
Chief Counsel	JUDITH S. KALETA
Director, Office of Civil Rights	JUDITH FOIST
Director, Office of Policy and Program Support	KELLEY S. COYNER

Director, Office of Emergency Transportation	LLOYD E. MILBURN
Director, Volpe National Transportation Systems Center	RICHARD R. JOHN
Associate Administrator for Management and Administration	ROSE A. MCMURRAY
Associate Administrator for Pipeline Safety	(VACANCY)
Associate Administrator for Hazardous Materials Safety	ALAN I. ROBERTS
Associate Administrator for Research, Technology, and Analysis	(VACANCY)
Director, Office of Research Policy and Technology Transfer	(VACANCY)
Director, Office of Airline Statistics	JAMES W. MITCHELL
Director, Office of Automated Tariffs	DONALD W. BRIGHT
Director, Office of University Research and Education	ELAINE E. JOOST, *Acting*
Director, Transportation Safety Institute	H. ALDRIDGE GILLESPIE

BUREAU OF TRANSPORTATION STATISTICS

400 Seventh Street SW., Washington, DC 20590
Phone, 202–366–DATA

Director	T.R. LAKSHMANAN
Deputy Director	ROBERT A. KNISELY
Associate Director, Analysis and Data Development	ROLF R. SCHMITT
Associate Director, Data User Services	PHILIP N. FULTON
Assistant Director, Geography Information Services	BRUCE D. SPEAR
Assistant Director, Information Technology Center	ROBERT C. ZARNETSKE
Administrative Officer	LORELEI S. EVANS

[For the Department of Transportation statement of organization, see the *Code of Federal Regulations,* Title 49, Part 1, Subpart A]

The U.S. Department of Transportation establishes the Nation's overall transportation policy. Under its umbrella there are 10 administrations whose jurisdictions include highway planning, development, and construction; urban mass transit; railroads; aviation; and the safety of waterways, ports, highways, and oil and gas pipelines. Decisions made by the Department in conjunction with the appropriate State and local officials strongly affect other programs such as land planning, energy conservation, scarce resource utilization, and technological change.

The Department of Transportation (DOT) was established by act of October 15, 1966, as amended (49 U.S.C. 102 and 102 note), "to assure the coordinated, effective administration of the transportation programs of the Federal Government" and to develop "national transportation policies and programs conducive to the provision of fast, safe, efficient, and convenient transportation

at the lowest cost consistent therewith." It became operational in April 1967 and was comprised of elements transferred from eight other major departments and agencies. It presently consists of the Office of the Secretary and 10 operating administrations whose heads report directly to the Secretary and who have highly decentralized authority.

DEPARTMENT OF TRANSPORTATION

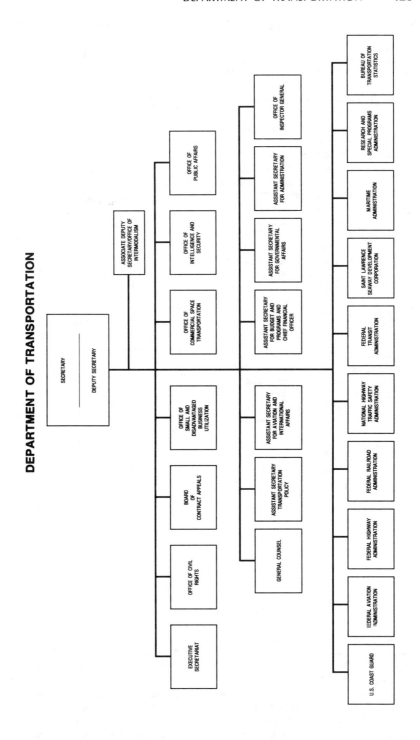

SECRETARY

DEPUTY SECRETARY

ASSOCIATE DEPUTY SECRETARY/OFFICE OF INTERMODALISM

EXECUTIVE SECRETARIAT

OFFICE OF CIVIL RIGHTS

BOARD OF CONTRACT APPEALS

OFFICE OF SMALL AND DISADVANTAGED BUSINESS UTILIZATION

OFFICE OF COMMERCIAL SPACE TRANSPORTATION

OFFICE OF INTELLIGENCE AND SECURITY

OFFICE OF PUBLIC AFFAIRS

GENERAL COUNSEL

ASSISTANT SECRETARY TRANSPORTATION POLICY

ASSISTANT SECRETARY FOR AVIATION AND INTERNATIONAL AFFAIRS

ASSISTANT SECRETARY FOR BUDGET AND PROGRAMS AND CHIEF FINANCIAL OFFICER

ASSISTANT SECRETARY FOR GOVERNMENTAL AFFAIRS

ASSISTANT SECRETARY FOR ADMINISTRATION

OFFICE OF INSPECTOR GENERAL

U.S. COAST GUARD

FEDERAL AVIATION ADMINISTRATION

FEDERAL HIGHWAY ADMINISTRATION

FEDERAL RAILROAD ADMINISTRATION

NATIONAL HIGHWAY TRAFFIC SAFETY ADMINISTRATION

FEDERAL TRANSIT ADMINISTRATION

SAINT LAWRENCE SEAWAY DEVELOPMENT CORPORATION

MARITIME ADMINISTRATION

RESEARCH AND SPECIAL PROGRAMS ADMINISTRATION

BUREAU OF TRANSPORTATION STATISTICS

Office of the Secretary of Transportation

[For the Office of the Secretary of Transportation statement of organization, see the *Code of Federal Regulations,* Title 49, Part 1, Subpart B]

The Department of Transportation is administered by the Secretary of Transportation, who is the principal adviser to the President in all matters relating to Federal transportation programs. The Secretary is assisted in the administration of the Department by a Deputy Secretary of Transportation, a Associate Deputy Secretary, the Assistant Secretaries, a General Counsel, the Inspector General, and several Directors and Chairmen. Areas where public purposes are widely served are detailed below and on the following pages.

Office of Intermodalism   The mission of the Office of Intermodalism is to provide departmental leadership and coordination in developing an intermodal transportation system to move people and goods in an energy-efficient, economic manner that obtains the optimum yield from the Nation's transportation resources. The Office:

—serves as the Department's principal advisor and advocate for intermodal transportation;

—coordinates Federal intermodal transportation policy and initiates policies to promote more efficient intermodal transportation;

—develops, maintains, and disseminates intermodal transportation data through the Bureau of Transportation Statistics and coordinates collection of data for that data base with the State departments of transportation and metropolitan planning organizations (MPO's);

—provides technical assistance to State departments of transportation and MPO's in large metropolitan areas to facilitate the collection of intermodal data to assist and evaluate intermodal planning;

—coordinates Federal research on intermodal transportation in accordance with the plan developed pursuant to section 6009(b) of the Intermodal Surface Transportation Efficiency Act of 1991 (ISTEA), and carries out additional research needs identified by the Director of the Office;

—reviews State-generated intermodal management systems annually as required under section 1034 of ISTEA, to assure continued progress towards improvement and integration of all associated transportation systems; and

—advances intermodal initiatives supported by State and local governments and the private sector through regionally based staff assignments.

Aviation and International Affairs   The Assistant Secretary for Aviation and International Affairs is the principal official for the development, review, and coordination of policy for international transportation. The Assistant Secretary:

—develops policies to support the Department in aviation and maritime multilateral and bilateral negotiations with foreign governments and participates on the U.S. negotiating delegations;

—develops policies on a wide range of international transportation and trade matters;

—furnishes guidance to the United States Trade Representative's Trade Policy Committee in efforts to improve the U.S. balance of payments;

—coordinates efforts to combat transport-related terrorist acts and drug smuggling;

—arranges and coordinates cooperative agreements with foreign governments for the exchange of state-of-the-art scientific and technical information;

—provides assistance to the Agency for International Development's transportation programs in developing countries; and

—participates on the U.S.-Saudi Arabian Joint Commission for Economic Cooperation.

The Assistant Secretary also:

—develops, coordinates, and carries out U.S. Government policy relating to the economic regulation of the airline industry, including licensing of U.S. and foreign carriers to serve in international air transportation and carrier fitness determinations;

—processes and resolves complaints concerning unfair competitive practices in international fares and rates;
—establishes international and intra-Alaska mail rates; and
—determines the disposition of requests for approval and immunization from the antitrust laws of international aviation agreements.

The Assistant Secretary also administers the essential air service program, which involves:
—establishing appropriate subsidy levels for subsidized carriers;
—processing applications to terminate, suspend, or reduce air service below the defined essential level;
—determining which carrier among various applicants should be selected to provide subsidized service; and
—continuously reviewing essential air service definitions for each community.

For further information, call 202–366–4551.

Civil Rights The Director of the Office of Civil Rights is the principal adviser to the Secretary on civil rights and equal opportunity matters. The Director acts for and represents the Secretary to assure full and affirmative implementation of civil rights and equal opportunity precepts within the Department in all its official actions, including departmental employment practices, services rendered to the public, operation of federally assisted activities, and other programs and efforts involving departmental assistance, participation, or endorsement. This Office is also responsible for the implementation of Executive Order 12677 of April 28, 1989, on aid to historically black colleges and universities.

For further information, call 202–366–4648.

Small and Disadvantaged Business Utilization The Office of Small and Disadvantaged Business Utilization, established in July 1980, is responsible for the Department's implementation and execution of the functions and duties under sections 8 and 15 of the Small Business Act (15 U.S.C. 637, 644) for developing policies and procedures consistent with Federal statutes to provide policy direction for minority,

women-owned, and small and disadvantaged business participation in the Department's procurement and Federal financial assistance activities. The Office is also responsible for setting the Department's goals for minority, women-owned, and small disadvantaged businesses, which includes monitoring and evaluating the accomplishments of these goals.

The Minority Business Resource Center, a division of the Office, is authorized under Public Law 97–449 (49 U.S.C. 332) to develop and implement program activities directed at stimulating, promoting, and actively assisting small and minority-owned business participation in departmental procurement and Federal financial assistance activities. The Center's program consists of a Short Term Lending Program, under which lines of credit up to $500,000 are available at prime interest rates to finance accounts receivable, and a Bonding Assistance Program which enables firms to obtain bid, performance, and payment bonds of up to $100,000 per contract in support of transportation-related contracts. The Center also operates several other program initiatives which provide technical and educational assistance, outreach, and information dissemination involving minority chambers of commerce and trade associations, historically black colleges and universities, and Hispanic-serving institutions. The Center also operates a National Information Clearinghouse.

For further information, call 202–366–1930 or 800–532–1169 (toll-free).

Contract Appeals The Board of Contract Appeals conducts hearings and issues final decisions in appeals from contracting officer decisions under contracts awarded by the Department and its constituent administrations in accordance with the Contract Disputes Act of 1978 (41 U.S.C. 601); sits as the Contract Adjustment Board with plenary authority to grant extraordinary contractual relief under Public Law 85–804 (50 U.S.C. 1431); and hears and decides all contractor debarment cases pursuant to 41 CFR 12–1.604–1 (1984).

Judges are designated as hearing officers to hear cases arising as a result of suspensions and debarments of participants in DOT financial assistance programs and perform such other adjudicatory functions assigned by the Secretary not inconsistent with the duties and responsibilities of the Board as set forth in the Contract Disputes Act of 1978.

For further information, contact the Board of Contract Appeals, Department of Transportation, 400 Seventh Street SW., Washington, DC 20590. Phone, 202–366–4305.

Commercial Space Transportation The Office of Commercial Space Transportation is the Government agency responsible for regulating and promoting the U.S. commercial space transportation

industry. The Office licenses the private sector launching of space payloads on expendable launch vehicles and commercial space launch facilities. It also sets insurance requirements for the protection of persons and property and assures that space transportation activities are in compliance with U.S. domestic and foreign policy. In addition, the Office is charged with promoting and facilitating the industry and provides a focal point in the Federal Government for formulating and implementing consistent policies that enable the American space transportation industry to compete in domestic and international markets.

For further information, call 202–366–5770; fax, 202–366–7256.

United States Coast Guard

The Coast Guard, established by act of January 28, 1915 (14 U.S.C. 1), became a component of the Department of Transportation on April 1, 1967, pursuant to the Department of Transportation Act of October 15, 1966 (49 U.S.C. app. 1651 note). The Coast Guard is a branch of the Armed Forces of the United States at all times and is a service within the Department of Transportation except when operating as part of the Navy in time of war or when the President directs.

The predecessor of the Coast Guard, the Revenue Marine, was established in 1790 as a Federal maritime law enforcement agency. Many other major responsibilities have since been added.

Activities

Search and Rescue The Coast Guard maintains a system of rescue vessels, aircraft, and communications facilities to carry out its function of saving life and property in and over the high seas and the navigable waters of the United States. This function includes flood relief and removing hazards to navigation.

For further information, call 202–267–1948.

Maritime Law Enforcement The Coast Guard is the primary maritime law enforcement agency for the United States. It enforces or assists in the enforcement of applicable Federal laws and treaties and other international agreements to which the United States is party, on, over, and under the high seas and waters subject to the jurisdiction of the United States, and may conduct investigations into suspected violations of such laws and international agreements. The Coast Guard works with other Federal agencies in the enforcement of such laws as they pertain to the protection of living and nonliving resources and in the suppression of smuggling and illicit drug trafficking.

For further information, call 202–267–1890.

Marine Inspection The Coast Guard is charged with formulating, administering, and enforcing various safety standards for the design, construction, equipment, and maintenance of commercial vessels of the United States and offshore structures on the Outer Continental Shelf. The program includes enforcement of safety standards on foreign vessels subject to U.S. jurisdiction.

Investigations are conducted of reported marine accidents, casualties, violations of law and regulations, misconduct, negligence, and incompetence occurring on commercial vessels subject to U.S. jurisdiction. Surveillance operations and boardings are conducted to detect violations of law and regulations. The program also functions to facilitate marine transportation by admeasuring and administering the vessel documentation laws.

For further information, call 202–267–1464.

Marine Licensing The Coast Guard administers a system for evaluating and licensing of U.S. Merchant Marine personnel. This program develops safe manning standards for commercial vessels. The Coast Guard also maintains oversight and approval authority for the numerous mariner training programs.

For further information, call 202–267–0218.

Great Lakes Pilotage The Coast Guard administers the Great Lakes Pilotage Act of 1960 (46 U.S.C. 216), which regulates pilotage services on the Great Lakes.

For further information, call 202–267–0214.

Marine Environmental Response The Coast Guard is responsible for enforcing the Federal Water Pollution Control Act (33 U.S.C. 1251) and various other laws relating to the protection of the marine environment. Program objectives are to ensure that public health and welfare and the environment are protected when spills occur. Under these laws, U.S. and foreign vessels are prohibited from using U.S. waters unless they have insurance or other guarantees that potential pollution liability for cleanup and damages will be met.

Other functions include providing a National Response Center to receive reports of oil and hazardous substance spills, investigating spills, initiating subsequent civil penalty actions when warranted, encouraging and monitoring responsible party cleanups, and when necessary, coordinating federally funded spill response operations. The program also provides a National Strike Force to

assist Federal On-Scene Coordinators in responding to pollution incidents.

For further information, call 202–267–0518.

Port Safety and Security This program is administered by the Coast Guard Captains of the Port. The Coast Guard is authorized to enforce rules and regulations governing the safety and security of ports and anchorages, and the movement of vessels and prevention of pollution in U.S. waters. Port safety and security functions include supervising cargo transfer operations, both storage and stowage, conducting harbor patrols and waterfront facility inspections, establishing security zones as required, and the control of vessel movement.

For further information, call 202–267–0489.

Waterways Management The Coast Guard has a significant role in the safe and orderly passage of cargo, people, and vessels on our nation's waterways. It has established Vessel Traffic Services in six major ports to provide for the safe movement of vessels at all times, but particularly during hazardous conditions, restricted visibility, or bad weather. The program's goal is to ensure the safe, efficient flow of commerce. The Coast Guard also regulates the installation of equipment necessary for vessel safety.

For further information, call 202–267–0980.

Aids to Navigation The Coast Guard establishes and maintains the U.S. aids to navigation system that includes lights, buoys, daybeacons, fog signals, marine radiobeacons, racons, and long-range radionavigation aids. Long-range radionavigation aids include loran-C, OMEGA, and the Global Positioning System (GPS). Aids are established in or adjacent to waters subject to the jurisdiction of the United States, although OMEGA provides global coverage, and loran-C coverage has been established in parts of the Western Pacific, Europe, and the Mediterranean to meet Department of Defense requirements. These aids are intended to assist a navigator to determine a position or plot a safe course or to warn the navigator of dangers or obstructions to navigation. Other functions related to navigation aids include broadcasting marine information and publishing Local Notice to Mariners and Light Lists.

For further information, call 202–267–1965.

Bridge Administration   The Coast Guard administers the statutes regulating the construction, maintenance, and operation of bridges and causeways across the navigable waters of the United States to provide for safe navigation through and under bridges.

For further information, call 202–267–0368.

Ice Operations   The Coast Guard operates the Nation's icebreaking vessels (icebreakers and ice-capable cutters), supported by aircraft, for ice reconnaissance, to facilitate maritime transportation and aid in prevention of flooding in domestic waters. Additionally, icebreakers support logistics to U.S. polar installations and also support scientific research in Arctic and Antarctic waters.

For further information, call 202–267–1450.

Deepwater Ports   Under the provisions of the Deepwater Port Act of 1974 (33 U.S.C. 1501), the Coast Guard administers a licensing and regulatory program governing the construction, ownership (international aspects), and operation of deepwater ports on the high seas to transfer oil from tankers to shore.

For further information, call 202–267–0495.

Boating Safety   The Coast Guard develops and directs a national boating safety program aimed at making the operation of small craft in U.S. waters both pleasurable and safe. This is accomplished by establishing uniform safety standards for recreational boats and associated equipment; encouraging State efforts through a grant-in-aid and liaison program; coordinating public education and information programs; administering the Coast Guard Auxiliary;

and enforcing compliance with Federal laws and regulations relative to safe use and safety equipment requirements for small boats.

For further information, call 202–267–1077.

Coast Guard Auxiliary   The Auxiliary is a nonmilitary volunteer organization of private citizens who own small boats, aircraft, or radio stations. Auxiliary members assist the Coast Guard by conducting boating education programs, patrolling marine regattas, participating in search and rescue operations, and conducting courtesy marine examinations.

For further information, call 202–267–1001.

Military Readiness   As required by law, the Coast Guard maintains a state of readiness to function as a specialized service in the Navy in time of war, or as directed by the President. Coastal and harbor defense, including port security, are the most important military tasks assigned to the Coast Guard in times of national crisis.

For further information, call 202–267–2039.

Reserve Training   The Coast Guard Reserve provides qualified individuals and trained units for active duty in time of war or national emergency and at such other times as the national security requires. In addition to its role in national defense, the Reserve augments the active service in the performance of peacetime missions during domestic emergencies and during routine and peak operations.

For further information, call 202–267–1240.

Marine Safety Council   The Marine Safety Council acts as a deliberative body to consider proposed Coast Guard regulations and to provide a forum for the consideration of related problems.

For further information, call 202–267–1477.

District and Field Organizations—United States Coast Guard

Organization	Address	Commander	Telephone
ATLANTIC AREA	Governors Island, New York, NY 10004–5098	Vice Adm. James M. Loy, USCG	212–668–7196

District and Field Organizations—United States Coast Guard—Continued

Organization	Address	Commander	Telephone
Maintenance and Logistics Command—Atlantic	Governors Island, New York, NY 10004–5098	Rear Adm. Douglas H. Teeson II, USCG	212–668–7197
1st District—Connecticut, Maine, Massachusetts, New Hampshire, northern New Jersey, eastern New York, Rhode Island, Vermont	408 Atlantic Ave., Boston, MA 02210–2209	Rear Adm. John L. Linnon, USCG	617–223–8480
2d District—Arkansas, Colorado, Illinois, Indiana, Iowa, Kansas, Kentucky, Minnesota, Missouri, Nebraska, North Dakota, Ohio, Oklahoma, western Pennsylvania, South Dakota, Tennessee, West Virginia, Wisconsin, Wyoming	1222 Spruce St., St. Louis, MO 63103–2832	Rear Adm. Paul M. Blayney, USCG	314–539–7601
5th District—Delaware, District of Columbia, Maryland, southern New Jersey, North Carolina, eastern Pennsylvania, Virginia	431 Crawford St., Portsmouth, VA 23704–5004	Rear Adm. Roger T. Rufe, USCG	804–398–6287
7th District—Florida, Georgia, Puerto Rico, South Carolina, Virgin Islands	909 SE. 1st Ave., Miami, FL 33131–3050	Rear Adm. William P. Leahy, USCG	305–536–5654
8th District—Alabama, Louisiana, Mississippi, New Mexico, Texas	500 Camp St., New Orleans, LA 70130–3396	Rear Adm. Robert C. North, USCG	504–589–6298
9th District—Great Lakes area	1240 E. 9th St., Cleveland, OH 44199–2060	Rear Adm. Gerald F. Woolever, USCG	216–522–3910
PACIFIC AREA	Coast Guard Island, Alameda, CA 94501–5100	Vice Adm. Richard D. Herr, USCG	510–437–3196
Maintenance and Logistics Command—Pacific	Coast Guard Island, Alameda, CA 94501–5100	Rear Adm. Gordon G. Piche, USCG	415–437–3939
11th District—Arizona, California, Nevada, Utah	400 Oceangate Blvd., Long Beach, CA 90822–5399	Rear Adm. Richard A. Appelbaum, USCG	310–980–4300
13th District—Idaho, Montana, Oregon, Washington	915 2d Ave., Seattle, WA 98174–1067	Rear Adm. Joseph W. Lockwood, USCG	206–220–7090
14th District—American Samoa, Guam, Hawaii, Pacific Islands	9th Fl., 300 Ala Moana Blvd., Honolulu, HI 96850–4982	Rear Adm. Howard B. Gehring, USCG	808–541–2051
17th District—Alaska	P.O. Box 3–5000, Juneau, AK 99802–1217	Rear Adm. Ernest R. Riutta, USCG	907–463–2025
U.S. COAST GUARD ACADEMY, SUPERINTENDENT	New London, CT 06320–4195	Rear Adm. Paul E. Versaw, USCG	203–444–8285
NATIONAL POLLUTION FUNDS CENTER, DIRECTOR	Suite 1000, 4200 Wilson Blvd., Arlington, VA 22203–1804	Daniel F. Sheehan	703–235–4700
MILITARY PERSONNEL COMMAND, COMMANDER	2100 2d St. SW., Washington, DC 20593	Rear Adm. Fred L. Ames, USCG	202–267–2321

For further information, contact the Information Office, United States Coast Guard, Department of Transportation, 2100 Second Street SW., Washington, DC 20593. Phone, 202–267–2229.

Federal Aviation Administration

The Federal Aviation Administration, formerly the Federal Aviation Agency, was established by the Federal Aviation Act of 1958 (49 U.S.C. 106) and became a component of the Department of Transportation in 1967 pursuant to the Department of Transportation Act (49 U.S.C. app. 1651 note).

The Administration is charged with:

—regulating air commerce in ways that best promote its development and safety and fulfill the requirements of national defense;

controlling the use of navigable airspace of the United States and regulating both civil and military operations in such airspace in the interest of safety and efficiency;

—promoting, encouraging, and developing civil aeronautics;

—consolidating research and development with respect to air navigation facilities;

—installing and operating air navigation facilities;

—developing and operating a common system of air traffic control and navigation for both civil and military aircraft; and

—developing and implementing programs and regulations to control aircraft noise, sonic boom, and other environmental effects of civil aviation.

Activities

Safety Regulation The Administrator issues and enforces rules, regulations, and minimum standards relating to the manufacture, operation, and maintenance of aircraft, as well as the rating and certification (including medical) of airmen and the certification of airports serving air carriers.

The agency performs flight inspection of air navigation facilities in the U.S. and, as required, abroad. It also enforces regulations under the Hazardous Materials Transportation Act (49 U.S.C. app. 1801 note) applicable to shipments by air.

Airspace and Air Traffic Management The safe and efficient utilization of the navigable airspace is a primary objective of the agency. To meet this objective, it operates a network of airport traffic control towers, air route traffic control centers, and flight service stations. It develops air traffic rules and regulations and allocates the use of the airspace. It also provides for the security control of air traffic to meet national defense requirements.

Air Navigation Facilities The agency is responsible for the location, construction or installation, maintenance, operation, and quality assurance of Federal visual and electronic aids to air navigation. The agency operates and maintains voice/data communications equipment, radar facilities, computer systems, and visual display equipment at flight service stations, airport traffic control towers, and air route traffic control centers.

Research, Engineering, and Development The research, engineering, and development activities of the agency are directed toward providing the systems, procedures,

facilities, and devices needed for a safe and efficient system of air navigation and air traffic control to meet the needs of civil aviation and the air defense system. The agency also performs an aeromedical research function to apply knowledge gained from its research program and the work of others to the safety and promotion of civil aviation and the health, safety, and efficiency of agency employees. The agency also supports development and testing of improved aircraft, engines, propellers, and appliances.

Test and Evaluation The agency conducts tests and evaluations of specified items such as aviation systems, subsystems, equipment, devices, materials, concepts, or procedures at any phase in the cycle of their development from conception to acceptance and implementation, as well as assigned independent testing at key decision points.

Airport Programs The agency maintains a national plan of airport requirements, administers a grant program for development of public use airports to assure and improve safety and to meet current and future airport capacity needs, evaluates the environmental impacts of airport development, and administers an airport noise compatibility program with the goal of reducing noncompatible uses around airports. It also develops standards and technical guidance on airport planning, design, safety, and operations and provides grants to assist public agencies in airport system and master planning and airport development and improvement.

Registration and Recordation The agency provides a system for the registration of aircraft and recording of documents affecting title or interest in the aircraft, aircraft engines, propellers, appliances, and spare parts.

Civil Aviation Abroad Under the Federal Aviation Act of 1958 and the International Aviation Facilities Act (49 U.S.C. app. 1151), the agency promotes aviation safety and civil aviation abroad by exchanging aeronautical information with foreign aviation authorities;

certifying foreign repair stations, airmen, and mechanics; negotiating bilateral airworthiness agreements to facilitate the import and export of aircraft and components; and providing technical assistance and training in all areas of the agency's expertise. It provides technical representation at international conferences, including participation in the International Civil Aviation Organization and other international organizations.

Other Programs The agency administers the aviation insurance and aircraft loan guarantee programs. It is an allotting agency under the Defense Materials System with respect to priorities and allocation for civil aircraft and civil aviation operations. The agency develops specifications for the preparation of aeronautical charts. It publishes current information on airways and airport service and issues technical publications for the improvement of safety in flight, airport planning and design, and other aeronautical activities. It serves as the executive administration for the operation and maintenance of the Department of Transportation automated payroll and personnel systems.

Major Field Organizations—Federal Aviation Administration

Region/Field Office	Address	Administrator/Director
ALASKAN—Alaska	P.O. Box 14, 701 C St., Anchorage, AK 99513	Jacqueline L. Smith
CENTRAL—Iowa, Kansas, Missouri, Nebraska	601 E. 12th St., Kansas City, MO 64106	John E. Turner
EASTERN—Delaware, Maryland, New Jersey, New York, Pennsylvania, Virginia, West Virginia	Federal Bldg., JFK International Airport, Jamaica, NY 11430	Arlene B. Feldman
GREAT LAKES—Illinois, Indiana, Michigan, Minnesota, North Dakota, Ohio, South Dakota, Wisconsin	2300 E. Devon Ave., Des Plaines, IL 60018	Jerry Franklin
NEW ENGLAND—Connecticut, Maine, Massachusetts, New Hampshire, Rhode Island, Vermont	12 New England Executive Park, Burlington, MA 01803	Robert Bartanowicz, *Acting*
NORTHWEST MOUNTAIN—Colorado, Idaho, Montana, Oregon, Utah, Washington, Wyoming	1601 Lind Ave. SW., Renton, WA 98055	Frederick M. Isaac
SOUTHERN—Alabama, Georgia, Florida, Kentucky, Mississippi, North Carolina, Puerto Rico, South Carolina, Tennessee	P.O. Box 20636, Atlanta, GA 30320	Carolyn C. Blum
SOUTHWEST—Arkansas, Louisiana, New Mexico, Oklahoma, Texas	Fort Worth, TX 76193–0001	Clyde M. DeHart
WESTERN–PACIFIC—Arizona, California, Hawaii, Nevada	P.O. Box 92007, Los Angeles, CA 90009	Lynore C. Brekke, *Acting*
EUROPE, AFRICA, and MIDDLE EAST OFFICE	15, Rue de la Loi B–1040, Brussels, Belgium	Patrick N. Poe
ASIA–PACIFIC OFFICE	U.S. Embassy, FAA, Singapore	M. Craig Beard
LATIN AMERICA–CARIBBEAN OFFICE	Miami International Airport, Miami FL	Raymond A. Salazar
FAA TECHNICAL CENTER	Atlantic City, NJ 08405	Frank Elbertson
MIKE MONRONEY AERONAUTICAL CENTER	P.O. Box 25082, Oklahoma City, OK 73125	Homer C. McClure

For further information, contact the Office of Public Affairs (Public Inquiry Center, APA–230), Federal Aviation Administration, Department of Transportation, 800 Independence Avenue SW., Washington, DC 20591. Phone, 202–267–3484. Fax, 202–267–5039.

Federal Highway Administration

The Federal Highway Administration became a component of the Department of Transportation in 1967 pursuant to the Department of Transportation Act (49 U.S.C. app. 1651 note). It administers the highway transportation programs of the Department of Transportation under pertinent legislation and the provisions of law cited in section 6(a) of the act (49 U.S.C. 104).

The Administration encompasses highway transportation in its broadest scope, seeking to coordinate highways with other modes of transportation to achieve the most effective balance of transportation systems and facilities under cohesive Federal transportation policies pursuant to the act.

Activities

Federal-Aid Highway Program The Administration administers the Federal-aid highway program of financial assistance to the States for highway construction and improvement of efficiency in highway and traffic operations. This program provides for the improvement of approximately 155,000 miles of the National Highway System, which includes the approximately 42,795-mile Dwight D. Eisenhower System of Interstate and Defense Highways and other public roads (except those classified as local or rural minor collectors). The Interstate System's construction and preservation is financed generally on a 90-percent Federal, 10-percent State basis. However, National Highway System projects not on the Interstate System and most projects on other roads are funded on an 80-percent Federal, 20-percent State basis.

The Administration is also responsible for the Highway Bridge Replacement and Rehabilitation Program to assist in the inspection, analysis, and rehabilitation or replacement of bridges on public roads. In addition, it administers an emergency program to assist in the repair or reconstruction of Federal-aid highways and certain Federal roads that have suffered serious damage by natural disasters over a wide area or catastrophic failures.

The Federal-aid highway program also involves improving access for the handicapped, encouraging the joint use and development of highway corridors, acquiring real property for right-of-way, and providing relocation assistance to those displaced by highway construction, encouraging disadvantaged business enterprises to participate in highway construction, and preserving along highways the natural beauty of the countryside, public parks and recreation lands, wildlife and waterfowl refuges, and historic sites. The agency is responsible for developing and

maintaining standards for traffic control devices used on all public streets and highways.

FHWA funds are also available to State revenue agencies for enforcement of highway use taxes, and to State and local governments and public authorities for congestion pricing pilot projects. For the highway use tax evasion program, projects are funded at 100-percent Federal share with funds allocated to the States annually at the discretion of the Secretary of Transportation. The congestion pricing pilot program provides support at 80-percent Federal share for the study and implementation of projects involving market-based approaches to congestion management. A new block grant-type program, the Surface Transportation Program, has been implemented. It may be used by the States and localities for any roads (including NHS) that are not functionally classified referred to as local or rural minor collectors. These roads are now collectively referred to as "Federal-aid roads." Bridge projects paid for with STP funds are not restricted to Federal-aid roads but may be on any public road. Transit capital projects are also eligible under this program.

Highway Safety Programs The Administration is responsible for several highway-related safety programs, including a State and community safety program jointly administered with NHTSA and a highway safety construction program to eliminate road hazards and improve rail/highway crossing safety. These safety construction programs fund activities that remove, relocate, or shield roadside obstacles, identify and correct hazardous locations, eliminate or reduce hazards at railroad crossings, and improve signing, pavement markings, and signalization.

Motor Carrier Programs Under the provisions of the Surface Transportation Assistance Act of 1982 (23 U.S.C. 101), the Administration was authorized to establish and maintain a National Network for trucks, review State truck size and weight enforcement programs, and assist in obtaining uniformity among the States in the area of commercial motor carrier registration and taxation reporting.

The Administration works cooperatively with States and private industry to achieve uniform motor carrier requirements in safety regulations, inspections and fines, licensing, registration and taxation requirements, and accident data. It provides grants to States for technical assistance, training, and equipment associated with participation in the International Registration Plan and the International Fuel Tax Agreement.

Under the authority of the motor carrier safety provisions of title 49 of the United States Code, the agency exercises Federal regulatory jurisdiction over the safety performance of all commercial motor carriers engaged in interstate or foreign commerce. It deals with more than 330,000 carriers and approximately 36,000 shippers of hazardous materials. Reviews are conducted at the carrier's facilities to determine the safety performance of the carrier's over-the-road operations. These reviews may lead to prosecution or other sanctions against violators of the Federal motor carrier safety regulations or the hazardous materials transportation regulations.

The Commercial Motor Vehicle Safety Act of 1986 (49 U.S.C. app. 2701 note) authorizes the Administration to establish national standards for a single commercial vehicle driver license for State issuance; a national information system clearinghouse for commercial driver license information; knowledge and skills tests for licensing commercial vehicle drivers; and disqualification of drivers for serious traffic offenses, including alcohol and drug abuse. The agency has responsibility for administering the Motor Carrier Safety Assistance Program, a partnership agreement between the Federal Government and the States, under the provisions of sections 401–404 of the Surface Transportation Assistance Act of 1982 (49 U.S.C. app. 2301–2304).

In fiscal year 1994, States performed 2 million roadside inspections and decommissioned over 500,000 vehicles and 129,000 drivers for safety regulation violations.

Federal Lands Highway Program The Administration, through cooperative agreements with Federal land managing agencies, administers a coordinated Federal lands program relating to forest highways, public lands highways, park roads and parkways, and defense access and Indian reservation roads. This program provides for the funding of more than 80,000 miles of federally owned roads or public authority-owned roads that are open for public travel and serve Federal lands. The agency's Federal Lands Highway Office and three field divisions provide for program coordination and administration, and conduct transportation planning, engineering studies, design, construction engineering assistance, and construction contract administration.

Research and Technology The Administration coordinates varied research, development, and technology transfer activities consisting of six principal programs: Intelligent Transportation Systems, Highway Research and Development, Long-Term Pavement Performance, Technology Applications, Local Technical Assistance, and the National Highway Institute.

Through its National Highway Institute (NHI), the Administration develops and administers, in cooperation with State highway agencies, instructional training programs designed for public sector employees, private citizens, and foreign nationals engaged in highway work of interest to the United States. NHI is headquarters for the Pan American Institute of Highways, which is a program designed to provide training and technology transfer to Latin American countries. NHI works closely with universities through the Dwight David Eisenhower Transportation Fellowship Program and the University Transportation Centers Program.

International Programs The Administration supports and participates in efforts to find research and technology abroad which can be applied in the United States and will provide a better quality, more cost-effective highway system. Such activities include coordination and assistance for U.S.

study teams abroad, cosponsoring international technology centers, and technical committee deliberations and studies. Other efforts include support for export promotion and trade advocacy; a technical assistance program for Russia; and, technical cooperation on border issues affecting the United States, Mexico, and Canada.

Additional Programs The Administration also administers a highway planning program, the highway construction phase of the Appalachian Regional Development Program, and the Territorial Highway Program; provides highway program support and technical assistance on an allocation/transfer basis for other Federal agencies. It administers civil rights programs pursuant to a variety of statutes. The programs have the aims of preventing discrimination in the impacts of programs and activities of

recipients and subrecipients; providing equal employment opportunities and promoting diversity in public employment (Federal/State transportation agencies' motor carrier safety program and commercial driver's license program recipients and subrecipients) and private employment (contractors, subcontractors, material suppliers, vendors, and consultants) related to agency-funded projects; providing training opportunities for minorities and women in highway construction crafts; ensuring contracting opportunities for disadvantaged business enterprises and other historically underutilized businesses; increasing opportunities for historically black colleges and universities, members of the Hispanic Association of Colleges and Universities, and Indian community colleges and universities.

Major Field Organizations—Federal Highway Administration
(Areas included within each region are indicated on the map in Appendix A.)

Region [1]	Address	Administrator	Telephone
1. Connecticut, Maine, Massachusetts, New Hampshire, New Jersey, New York, Puerto Rico, Rhode Island, Vermont	Rm. 719, Leo W. O'Brien Federal Bldg., Albany, NY 12207	(vacancy)	518–431–4236
3. Delaware, District of Columbia, Maryland, Pennsylvania, Virginia, West Virginia	Suite 4000, 10 S. Howard St., Baltimore, MD 21201	David S. Gendell	410–962–0093
4. Alabama, Florida, Georgia, Kentucky, Mississippi, North Carolina, South Carolina, Tennessee	Suite 200, 1720 Peachtree Rd. NW., Atlanta, GA 30367	Leon N. Larson	404–347–4078
5. Illinois, Indiana, Michigan, Minnesota, Ohio, Wisconsin	Suite 301, 19900 Governors Hwy., Olympia Fields, IL 60461–1021	(Vacancy)	708–283–3510
6. Arkansas, Louisiana, New Mexico, Oklahoma, Texas	Rm. 8A00, 819 Taylor St., Fort Worth, TX 76102	Edward A. Wueste	817–334–4393
7. Iowa, Kansas, Missouri, Nebraska	6301 Rockhill Rd., Kansas City, MO 64141	Arthur E. Hamilton	816–276–2700
8. Colorado, Montana, North Dakota, South Dakota, Utah, Wyoming	Rm. 400, 555 Zang St., Lakewood, CO 80228	Vincent F. Schimmeller	303–969–6722
9. Arizona, California, Hawaii, Nevada	Suite 2100, 201 Mission St., San Francisco, CA 94105	(Vacancy)	415–744–2639
10. Alaska, Idaho, Oregon, Washington	Suite 600, 222 SW. Columbia St., Portland, OR 97201	Leon J. Whitman, Jr.	503–326–2048

[1] Region 1 conforms to Standard Regions 1 and 2.

For further information, contact the Office of Information and Management Services, Federal Highway Administration, Department of Transportation, 400 Seventh Street SW., Washington, DC 20590. Phone, 202–366–0534.

Federal Railroad Administration

The purpose of the Federal Railroad Administration is to promulgate and enforce rail safety regulations, administer railroad financial assistance programs, conduct research and development in support of improved railroad safety and national rail transportation policy, provide for the rehabilitation of Northeast Corridor rail passenger service, and consolidate government support of rail transportation activities.

The Federal Railroad Administration was created pursuant to section 3(e)(1) of the Department of Transportation Act of 1966 (49 U.S.C. app. 1652).

Activities

Railroad Safety   The Administration administers and enforces the Federal laws and related regulations designed to promote safety on railroads; exercises jurisdiction over all areas of rail safety under the Rail Safety Act of 1970, such as track maintenance, inspection standards, equipment standards, and operating practices. It also administers and enforces regulations resulting from railroad safety legislation for locomotives, signals, safety appliances, power brakes, hours of service, transportation of explosives and other dangerous articles, and reporting and investigation of railroad accidents. Railroad and related industry equipment, facilities, and records are inspected and required reports reviewed.

Research and Development   A ground transportation research and development program is administered to advance all aspects of intercity ground transportation and railroad safety pertaining to the physical sciences and engineering, in order to improve railroad safety and ensure that railroads continue to be a viable national transportation resource.

Transportation Test Center   This 50-square-mile facility, located near Pueblo, CO, provides testing for advanced and conventional systems and techniques designed to improve ground transportation. The facility has been managed and staffed for the

Administration by the Association of American Railroads since October 1, 1982. The United States and Canadian Governments and private industry use this facility to explore, under controlled conditions, the operation of both conventional and advanced systems. It is used by the Federal Transit Administration for testing of urban rapid transit vehicles.

For further information, contact the Transportation Test Center, Pueblo, CO 81001. Phone, 303–545–5660, ext. 5000.

Policy   Program management for new and revised policies, plans, and projects related to railroad transportation economics, finance, system planning, and operations is provided; appropriate studies and analyses are performed; relevant tests, demonstrations, and evaluations are conducted; and labor/management programs are evaluated. Analyses of issues before regulatory agencies are carried out and recommendations are made to the Secretary as to the positions to be taken by DOT.

Passenger and Freight Services   The Administration administers a program of Federal assistance for national, regional, and local rail services. Programs include rail freight service assistance programs; rail service continuation programs and State rail planning; and rail passenger service on a national, regional, and local basis.

The agency also administers programs to develop, implement, and administer rail system policies, plans, and programs for the Northeast Corridor in support of applicable provisions of the Railroad Revitalization and Regulatory Reform Act of 1976 (45 U.S.C. 801), the Rail Passenger Service Act (45 U.S.C. 501), and related legislation.

Major Field Organizations—Federal Railroad Administration

Region	Address	Regional Director of Railroad Safety
1. NORTHEASTERN—Connecticut, Maine, Massachusetts, New Hampshire, New Jersey, New York, Rhode Island, Vermont	10th Fl., 55 Broadway, Cambridge, MA 02142	Mark H. McKeon
2. EASTERN—Delaware, District of Columbia, Maryland, Ohio, Pennsylvania, Virginia, West Virginia	Suite 712, 841 Chestnut St., Philadelphia, PA 19107–4407	John F. Megary

Major Field Organizations—Federal Railroad Administration—Continued

Region	Address	Regional Director of Railroad Safety
3. SOUTHERN—Alabama, Florida, Georgia, Kentucky, Mississippi, North Carolina, South Carolina, Tennessee	Suite 440, 1720 Peachtree Rd. NW., North Tower, Atlanta, GA 30309	Christopher G. Clune
4. CENTRAL—Illinois, Indiana, Michigan, Minnesota, Wisconsin	Suite 655, 111 N. Canel St., Chicago, IL 60606	Richard M. McCord
5. SOUTHWESTERN—Arkansas, Louisiana, New Mexico, Oklahoma, Texas	Suite 425, 8701 Bedford Euless Rd., Hurst, TX 76053	Shafter H. Stotts, Jr.
6. MIDWESTERN—Colorado, Iowa, Kansas, Missouri, Nebraska	Rm. 1807, 911 Walnut St., Kansas City, MO 64106–2095	Darrell J. Tisor
7. WESTERN—Arizona, California, Nevada, Utah	Rm. 7007, 650 Capital Mall, Sacramento, CA 95812–1139	Harry T. Paton
8. NORTHWESTERN—Alaska, Idaho, Montana, North Dakota, Oregon, South Dakota, Washington, Wyoming	Suite 650, Murdock Bldg., 703 Broadway, Vancouver, WA 98660	Chester Southern

For further information, contact the Public Affairs Officer, Federal Railroad Administration, Department of Transportation, 400 Seventh Street SW., Washington, DC 20590. Phone, 202–366–0881.

National Highway Traffic Safety Administration

[For the National Highway Traffic Safety Administration statement of organization, see the *Code of Federal Regulations,* Title 49, Part 501]

The National Highway Traffic Safety Administration was established by the Highway Safety Act of 1970 (23 U.S.C. 401 note). The Administration carries out programs relating to the safety performance of motor vehicles and related equipment, motor vehicle drivers, occupants, and pedestrians, and a uniform nationwide speed limit under title 49 U.S. Code, chapter 301, and the Highway Safety Act of 1966, as amended (23 U.S.C. 401 *et seq.*). Under the authority of title 49 U.S. Code, chapters 321, 323, 325, 327, 329, and 331, the Administration carries out programs and studies aimed at reducing economic losses in motor vehicle crashes and repairs through general motor vehicle programs; administers the Federal odometer law; issues theft prevention standards; and promulgates average fuel economy standards for passenger and nonpassenger motor vehicles.

Under the authority of the Clean Air Amendments of 1970 (42 U.S.C. 7544(2)), the Administration certifies as to the consistency of Environmental Protection Agency State grants with any highway safety program developed

pursuant to section 402 of title 23 of the United States Code.

The National Highway Traffic Safety Administration was established to carry out a congressional mandate to reduce the mounting number of deaths, injuries, and economic losses resulting from motor vehicle crashes on the Nation's highways and to provide motor vehicle damage susceptibility and ease of repair information, motor vehicle inspection demonstrations, and protection of purchasers of motor vehicles having altered odometers, and to provide average standards for greater vehicle mileage per gallon of fuel for vehicles under 10,000 pounds (gross vehicle weight).

Activities

Safety Performance Standards The Administration administers motor vehicle safety programs to:

—reduce the occurrence of highway crashes and the severity of resulting injuries;

—improve survivability and injury recovery by better post-crash measures;

—reduce the economic losses in crashes;

—provide consumer information in the areas of tire grading for treadwear, temperature resistance, and traction; and

—establish safeguards for the protection of purchasers of motor vehicles having altered or reset odometers.

Under the Administration's program, Federal Motor Vehicle Safety Standards are issued that prescribe safety features and levels of safety-related performance for vehicles and items of motor vehicle equipment. Damage susceptibility, crashworthiness, and theft prevention are to be studied and reported to the Congress and the public.

The Energy Policy and Conservation Act, as amended (42 U.S.C. 6201 note), sets automotive fuel economy standards for passenger cars for model years 1985 and thereafter. The Administration has the option of altering the standards for the post-1985 period.

The Administration develops and promulgates mandatory fuel economy standards for light trucks for each model year and administers the fuel economy regulatory program. The Administration establishes rules for the collection and reporting of information required concerning manufacturers' technological alternatives and corporate economic capabilities in meeting fuel economy standards.

Traffic Safety Programs   The Administration leads the national traffic safety and emergency services efforts in order to save lives, reduce injuries, and lessen medical and other costs. In accomplishing these tasks, it utilizes behavioral research, demonstration, and evaluation, in addition to developing safety programs and strategies, for use by a variety of public and private agencies and organizations.

The Administration maintains a national register of information on individuals whose licenses to operate a motor vehicle have been revoked, suspended, cancelled, or denied; or who have been convicted of certain traffic-related violations such as driving while impaired by alcohol or other drugs. The information obtained from the register assists State driver licensing officials in determining whether or not to issue a license.

State and Community Services   The law provides for Federal matching funds for States and local communities to assist them with their highway safety programs. Areas of primary emphasis include: impaired driving, occupant protection, motorcycle safety, police traffic services, pedestrian and bicycle safety, emergency medical services, speed control, and traffic records. The Agency provides guidance and technical assistance in all of these areas.

The law also provides incentive funds to encourage States to implement effective impaired-driving programs and to encourage the use of safety belts and motorcycle helmets.

Research and Development   To provide a foundation for the development of motor vehicle and highway safety program standards, the Agency administers a broad-scale program of research, development, testing, demonstration, and evaluation of motor vehicles, motor vehicle equipment, advanced technologies, and accident data collection and analysis.

The research program covers numerous areas affecting safety problems and includes provision for appropriate laboratory testing facilities to obtain necessary basic data. In this connection, research in both light and heavy vehicle crashworthiness and crash avoidance is being pursued. The objectives are to encourage industry to adopt advanced motor vehicle safety designs, stimulate public awareness of safety potentials, and provide a base for vehicle safety information.

The Administration maintains a collection of scientific and technical information related to motor vehicle safety, and operates the National Center for Statistics and Analysis, whose activities include the development and maintenance of highway accident data collection systems and related analysis efforts. These comprehensive motor vehicle safety information resources serve as documentary reference points for Federal, State, and local agencies, as well as industry, universities, and the public.

Regional Offices—National Highway Traffic Safety Administration

(Areas included within each region are indicated on the map in Appendix A.)

	Headquarters/Address	Administrator
I.	Cambridge, MA (Kendall Sq., Code 903, 02142)	George A. Luciano
II.	White Plains, NY (222 Mamaroneck Ave., 10605)	Tom Louizou
III.	Hanover, MD (Suite L, 7526 Connelley Dr., 21076–1699)	Eugene Peterson
IV.	Atlanta, GA (1720 Peachtree Rd. NW., 30309)	Tom Enright
V.	Homewood Heights, IL (18209 Dixie Hwy., 60430)	Donald J. McNamara

Regional Offices—National Highway Traffic Safety Administration—Continued

(Areas included within each region are indicated on the map in Appendix A.)

	Headquarters/Address	Administrator
VI.	Fort Worth, TX (819 Taylor St., 76102–6177)	Georgia Chakiris
VII.	Kansas City, MO (P.O. Box 412515, 64141)	Norman B. McPherson
VIII.	Denver, CO (4th Fl., 555 Zang St., 80228)	Louis R. De Carolis
IX.	San Francisco, CA (201 Mission St., 94105)	Joseph M. Cindrich
X.	Seattle, WA 98174 (915 2d Ave.)	Curtis A. Winston

For further information concerning the National Highway Traffic Safety Administration, contact the Office of Public and Consumer Affairs, National Highway Traffic Safety Administration, Department of Transportation, 400 Seventh Street SW., Washington, DC 20590. Phone, 202–366–9550. Additional information may be obtained by calling the Technical Reference Division, Office of Administrative Operations. Phone, 202–366–2768.

Federal Transit Administration

[For the Federal Transit Administration statement of organization, see the *Code of Federal Regulations*, Title 49, Part 601]

The Federal Transit Administration was established as a component of the Department of Transportation by section 3 of Reorganization Plan No. 2 of 1968 (5 U.S.C. app.), effective July 1, 1968. The Administration (formerly the Urban Mass Transportation Administration) previously operated under authority of the Federal Transit Act, as amended (49 U.S.C. app. 1601 *et seq.*). The Federal Transit Act was repealed on July 5, 1994, and the Federal transit laws were codified and re-enacted as chapter 53 of title 49, United States Code.

The missions of the Administration are:

—to assist in the development of improved mass transportation facilities, equipment, techniques, and methods, with the cooperation of mass transportation companies both public and private;

—to encourage the planning and establishment of areawide urban mass transportation systems needed for economical and desirable urban development, with the cooperation of mass transportation companies both public and private;

—to provide assistance to State and local governments and their instrumentalities in financing such systems, to be operated by public or private mass transportation companies as determined by local needs; and

—to provide financial assistance to State and local governments to help implement national goals relating to mobility for elderly persons, persons with disabilities, and economically disadvantaged persons.

Programs

Section 5309, Capital Program These grants are authorized to assist in financing the acquisition, construction, reconstruction, and improvement of facilities and equipment for use—by operation, lease, or otherwise—in mass transportation service in urban areas. Only public agencies are eligible as applicants. Private transit operators may be assisted under the program through arrangements with an eligible public body.

The Federal grant is 80 percent of the net project cost. If the project is in an urbanized area, it must be part of a program for a unified or officially coordinated urban transportation system as a part of the comprehensive planned development of the area.

Annual funding is allocated in three categories: 40-percent funding for fixed guideway modernization in which funds are apportioned by a statutory formula; 40-percent funding for construction of new, fixed guideway systems and their extensions; and 20-percent funding for replacement, rehabilitation, and purchase of buses and related equipment and the construction of bus-related facilities.

Urbanized Area Formula Program Section 5307 is a formula-apportioned resource that has been available for capital, operating, and planning assistance since fiscal year 1984. Section 9 replaced an earlier formula assistance program, section 5, which was phased out with the passage of the Federal Public Transportation Act of 1982.

Recipients of funds in urbanized areas of over 200,000 population are jointly designated by the Governors of the respective States, local officials, and public transit operators. The Governor acts as recipient for urbanized areas with populations from 50,000 up to 200,000. Recipients must be State, regional, or local governmental bodies or public agencies. Private transit operators may be assisted under the program through arrangements with an eligible public entity.

Grants may be made for 80 percent of the project cost for capital and planning activities and up to 50 percent for operating subsidies. Each year, potential grantees submit a proposed program of projects for funding based on the State Transportation Improvement Program. This program contains all of the highway and transit projects endorsed at the metropolitan and State levels for Federal funding, resulting from the State and local transportation planning process.

For further information, contact the Regional Office for the area concerned.

Nonurbanized Area Formula Program
The section 5311 program provides capital and operating assistance for public transportation in nonurbanized areas (under 50,000 population). Funds are allocated by formula to the Governor and the program is administered at the State level by the designated transportation agency. Eligible activities are operating assistance, planning, administrative and program development activities, coordination of public transportation programs, vehicle acquisition, and other capital investments in support of general or special transit services, including services provided for the elderly and handicapped and other transit-dependent persons. A fixed percentage of a State's annual apportionment must be spent to carry out a program for the development and support of inner-city bus transportation, unless the State Governor certifies that such needs are adequately met. A Rural Transit Assistance Program authorized under section 18(h) provides funding for training and technical assistance for transit operators in nonurbanized areas. Capital assistance is funded up to an 80-percent Federal share and operating assistance is funded with up to a 50-percent Federal share.

Elderly and Persons with Disabilities Program The Section 5310 Program provides capital assistance to private nonprofit organizations for transportation of elderly persons and persons with disabilities where services provided by public operators are unavailable, insufficient, or inappropriate; to public bodies approved by the State to coordinate services for elderly persons or persons with disabilities; or to public bodies which certify to the Governor that no nonprofit corporation or association is readily available in an area to provide the service. Funds are allocated by formula to the States; local organizations apply for funding through a designated State agency.

Technical Assistance The Administration provides funds for research, development, and demonstration projects in urban transportation for the purpose of increasing productivity and efficiency in urban and nonurban area transportation systems, improving mass transportation service and equipment, and assisting State and local governments in providing total urban transportation services in a cost-effective, safe manner, and expanding private-sector participation in all facets of urban transportation.

The Administration conducts a program of research, development, and demonstration addressing the following principal areas: advanced public transportation systems, clean air, finance, information, human resources and productivity, regional mobility, rural transportation, safety and security, technology development, and transit accessibility.

Major project areas include developing and demonstrating new approaches to involve employers, developers, local governments, and transportation providers in finding solutions to the problems of regional mobility, with special emphasis on the following:

—promoting institutional changes required to improve mobility in suburban areas and between suburbs and central city locations;

—encouraging management and organized labor to jointly seek opportunities for improving performance through upgrading of skills for nonmanagerial personnel;

—identifying, evaluating, and documenting significant cost-effective approaches to modernizing existing rail transit systems;

—encouraging participation by the private sector in the provision of transportation services and encouragement of joint public/private financing of transit capital investments;

—providing guidance and training concerning long-term financial planning and leasing of capital assets;

—implementing a program of new model bus testing and test facility improvements;

—promoting the delivery of safe and effective public transportation in nonurbanized areas;

—assisting new safety and security initiatives, including safety training; and

—compiling information on costs, benefits, financial feasibility, and

performance of new energy sources including nonpolluting fuels.

Projects are conducted under grants and cooperative agreements with public bodies, including State and local governments, or contracts with private organizations, both profit and nonprofit.

For further information, contact the Regional Office for the area concerned.

University Research and Training Grants Grants may be awarded to public and private nonprofit institutions of higher learning to assist in conducting research and training activities that address urban and rural transit issues and needs and in providing training for students and working professionals in the field of urban transportation analysis and operations. The objective is to encourage and support university research, education, and training that addresses and is responsive to Federal, State, and local transportation concerns, and advances the understanding and resolution of critical transportation problems.

Rural The Rural Transportation Assistance Program provides assistance for transit research, technical assistance, training, and related support activities in non-urbanized areas (less than 50,000 population). A portion of this is used at the national level for development of training materials, development and maintenance of a national clearing house on rural activities, and technical assistance through peer practitioners to promote exemplary techniques and practices.

For further information, call 202–366–4052.

Managerial Training Program Grants to governmental bodies and agencies and operators of public transportation services provide fellowships for training in public or private training institutions for personnel employed in managerial, technical, and professional positions in the public transportation field. The assistance provided under this section is provided on a 50–50 funding match basis. Available funds will be used exclusively for single agency grants or for States submitting comprehensive applications on behalf of agencies within the State. A "block" type grant is awarded on the basis of comprehensive, agencywide training plans to support training activities for periods of up to 24 months. The Administration will allow 50 percent of the costs incurred by grantees for training and educational expenses which may include tuition, fees, books, or other training materials, excluding any equipment items.

For further information, call 202–366–4052.

Safety The Federal Transit Administration Safety Program is designed to support State and local agencies in fulfilling their responsibility for the safety and security of urban mass transportation facilities and services. The program accomplishes its objectives through the encouragement and sponsorship of safety and security planning, training, information collection and analysis, drug control programs, system/safety assurance reviews, generic

research, and other cooperative government/industry activities.

For further information, call 202–366–2896.

Field Organization—Federal Transit Administration

(Regions included within each area are indicated on the map in Appendix A.)

Region/Address	Telephone
I. Cambridge, MA (Transportation Systems Ctr., Suite 920, Kendall Sq., 55 Broadway, 02142) .	617–494–2055
II. New York, NY (Suite 2940, 26 Federal Plz., 10278)	212–264–8162
III. Philadelphia, PA (Suite 500, 1760 Market St., 19103)	215–656–6900
IV. Atlanta, GA (Suite 400, 1720 Peachtree Rd. NW., 30309)	404–347–3948
V. Chicago, IL (Rm. 1415, 55 E. Monroe St., 60603)	312–353–2789
VI. Arlington, TX (Suite 175, 524 E. Lamar Blvd., 76011–3900)	817–860–9663
VII. Kansas City, MO (Suite 303, 6301 Rockhill Rd., 64131)	816–523–0204
VIII. Denver, CO (Suite 650, 216 16th St., 80202)	303–844–3242
IX. San Francisco, CA (Suite 2210, 201 Mission St., San Francisco, CA 94105)	415–744–3133
X. Seattle, WA (Suite 3142, 915 2d Ave., 98174)	206–220–7954

For further information, contact the area/regional office for the area concerned or contact the Office of Public Affairs, Federal Transit Administration, Department of Transportation, 400 Seventh Street SW., Washington, DC 20590. Phone, 202–366–4043. Technical information may be obtained by contacting the Transit Research Information Center. Phone, 202–366–9157.

Maritime Administration

The Maritime Administration was established by Reorganization Plan No. 21 of 1950 (5 U.S.C. app.), effective May 24, 1950. The Maritime Act of 1981 (46 U.S.C. 1601) transferred the Maritime Administration to the Department of Transportation, effective August 6, 1981.

The Maritime Administration administers programs to aid in the development, promotion, and operation of the U.S. merchant marine. It is also charged with organizing and directing emergency merchant ship operations.

The Maritime Administration administers subsidy programs, through the Maritime Subsidy Board, under which the Federal Government, subject to statutory limitations, pays the

difference between certain costs of operating ships under the U.S. flag and foreign competitive flags on essential services, and the difference between the costs of constructing ships in U.S. and foreign shipyards. It provides financing guarantees for the construction, reconstruction, and reconditioning of ships; and enters into capital construction fund agreements that grant tax deferrals on moneys to be used for the acquisition, construction, or reconstruction of ships.

The Administration constructs or supervises the construction of merchant type ships for the Federal Government. It helps industry generate increased business for U.S. ships and conducts programs to develop ports, facilities, and intermodal transport, and to promote domestic shipping.

The Administration conducts program and technical studies and administers a War Risk Insurance Program that insures operators and seamen against losses caused by hostile action if domestic commercial insurance is not available.

Under emergency conditions the Maritime Administration charters Government-owned ships to U.S. operators, requisitions or procures ships owned by U.S. citizens, and allocates them to meet defense needs.

It maintains a National Defense Reserve Fleet of Government-owned ships that it operates through ship managers and general agents when required in national defense interests. An element of this activity is the Ready Reserve Force consisting of a number of ships available for quick-response activation.

It regulates sales to aliens and transfers to foreign registry of ships that are fully or partially owned by U.S. citizens. It also disposes of Government-owned ships found nonessential for national defense.

The Administration operates the U.S. Merchant Marine Academy, Kings Point, NY, where young people are trained to become merchant marine officers, and conducts training in shipboard firefighting at Earle, NJ, and Toledo, OH. It also administers a Federal assistance program for the maritime academies operated by California, Maine, Massachusetts, Michigan, New York, and Texas.

Field Organization—Maritime Administration

Region	Address	Telephone
CENTRAL REGION	Suite 2590, 365 Canal St., New Orleans, LA 70130–1137	504–589–6556
GREAT LAKES REGION	Suite 185, 2860 South River Rd., Des Plaines, IL 60018–2413	708–298–4535
NORTH ATLANTIC REGION	Rm. 3737, 26 Federal Plz., New York, NY 10278	212–264–1300
SOUTH ATLANTIC REGION	Rm. 211, Bldg. 4D, 7737 Hampton Blvd., Norfolk, VA 23505	804–441–6393
U.S. MERCHANT MARINE ACADEMY	Kings Point, NY 11024–1699	516–773–5000
WESTERN REGION	Suite 2200, 201 Mission St., San Francisco, CA 94105–1905	415–744–3125

For further information, contact the Office of Congressional and Public Affairs, Maritime Administration, Department of Transportation, 400 Seventh Street SW., Washington, DC 20590. Phone, 202–366–5807.

Saint Lawrence Seaway Development Corporation

The Saint Lawrence Seaway Development Corporation was established by act of May 13, 1954 (33 U.S.C. 981–990), as an operating administration of the Department of Transportation.

The Corporation, a wholly Government-owned enterprise, is responsible for the development, operation, and maintenance of that part of the St. Lawrence Seaway between the port of Montreal and Lake Erie, within the territorial limits of the United States.

It is the function of the Seaway Corporation to provide a safe, efficient, and effective water artery for maritime commerce, both in peacetime and in time of national emergency. Effective October 1, 1994, the collection of U.S. tolls for transit of Seaway facilities was waived. However, in accordance with existing binational memoranda of agreement, the Seaway Corporation negotiates Canadian toll rates for users of the Seaway System with the Saint Lawrence Seaway Authority of Canada.

The Corporation coordinates its activities with its Canadian counterpart, particularly with respect to overall operations, traffic control, navigation aids, safety, navigation dates, and related programs designed to fully develop the Seaway System. The Corporation encourages the development of traffic through the Great Lakes/Seaway system so as to contribute significantly to the comprehensive economic and environmental development of the entire region.

For further information, contact the Director of Communications, Saint Lawrence Seaway Development Corporation, Department of Transportation, 400 Seventh Street SW., Washington, DC 20590. Phone, 202–366–0091.

Research and Special Programs Administration

The Research and Special Programs Administration (RSPA) was established formally on September 23, 1977. It is responsible for hazardous materials transportation and pipeline safety, transportation emergency preparedness, safety training, multimodal transportation research and development activities, and collection and dissemination of air carrier economic data.

Office of Hazardous Materials Safety

400 Seventh Street SW., Washington, DC 20590. Phone, 202–366–0656

The Office of Hazardous Materials Safety develops and issues regulations for the safe transportation of hazardous materials by all modes, excluding bulk transportation by water. The regulations cover shipper and carrier operations, packaging and container specifications, and hazardous materials definitions. The Office is also responsible for the enforcement of regulations other than those applicable to a single mode of transportation. The Office manages a user-fee funded grant program to assist States in planning for hazardous materials emergencies and to assist States and Indian tribes with training for hazardous materials emergencies. Additionally, the Office executes a national safety program to safeguard food and certain other products from contamination during motor or rail transportation. A computer bulletin board, in conjunction with the Federal Emergency Management Agency, offers nationwide access to topics related to hazardous materials transportation safety and can be accessed by dialing 1–800–PLANFOR (752–6367). The Office is the national focal point for coordination and control of the Department's multimodal hazardous materials regulatory program, ensuring uniformity of approach and action by all modal administrations.

Regional Offices—Office of Hazardous Materials Safety

Region	Address	Chief
EASTERN—Connecticut, Delaware, District of Columbia, Florida, Georgia, Maine, Maryland, Massachusetts, New Hampshire, New Jersey, New York, North Carolina, Pennsylvania, Puerto Rico, Rhode Island, South Carolina, Vermont, Virginia, West Virginia	Suite 550, 10 Park Pl., Newark, NJ 07102	(Vacancy)
CENTRAL—Illinois, Indiana, Iowa, Kansas, Kentucky, Michigan, Minnesota, Missouri, Nebraska, North Dakota, Ohio, South Dakota, Wisconsin	Suite 136, 2350 E. Devon Ave., Des Plaines, IL 60018	Colleen Abbenhaus
WESTERN—Alaska, Arizona, California, Colorado, Hawaii, Idaho, Montana, Nevada, Oregon, Utah, Washington, Wyoming	Suite 230, 3200 Inland Empire Blvd., Ontario, CA 91764	Anthony Smialek
SOUTHWESTERN—Alabama, Arkansas, Louisiana, Mississippi, New Mexico, Oklahoma, Tennessee, Texas	Rm. 2224B, 2320 LaBranch St., Houston, TX 77004	Jesse Hughes

Office of Pipeline Safety

400 Seventh Street SW., Washington, DC 20590. Phone, 202–366–4595

The Office of Pipeline Safety establishes and provides for compliance with standards that assure public safety and environmental protection in the transportation of gas and hazardous liquids by pipeline. The Office administers a program whereby a State agency can voluntarily assert safety regulatory jurisdiction over all or some intrastate pipeline facilities. The Federal Government is authorized to pay a State agency grant-in-aid funds of up to 50 percent of the actual cost for carrying out its pipeline safety program. The

Office under the Oil Pollution Act of 1990 established regulations requiring petroleum pipeline operators to prepare and submit plans to respond to oil spills for Federal review and approval.

Regional Offices—Office of Pipeline Safety

Region	Address	Chief
CENTRAL—Illinois, Indiana, Iowa, Kansas, Michigan, Minnesota, Missouri, Nebraska, North Dakota, Ohio, South Dakota, Wisconsin	Rm. 1811, 911 Walnut St., Kansas City, MO 64106	Ivan Huntoon
EASTERN—Connecticut, Delaware, District of Columbia, Maine, Maryland, Massachusetts, New Hampshire, New Jersey, New York, Pennsylvania, Rhode Island, Vermont, Virginia, West Virginia	Rm. 2108, 400 7th St. SW., Washington, DC 20590	William Gute
SOUTHERN—Alabama, Arkansas, Florida, Georgia, Kentucky, Mississippi, North Carolina, Puerto Rico, South Carolina, Tennessee	Suite 446 N., 1720 Peachtree Rd. NW., Atlanta, GA 30309	Frederick Joyner
SOUTHWEST—Arizona, Louisiana, New Mexico, Oklahoma, Texas	2320 LaBranch, Houston, TX 77004	James Thomas
WESTERN—Alaska, California, Colorado, Hawaii, Idaho, Montana, Nevada, Oregon, Utah, Washington, Wyoming	Suite 230, 12600 W. Colfax Ave., Lakewood, CO 80215	Edward Ondak

Office of Research, Technology, and Analysis

400 Seventh Street SW., Washington, DC 20590. Phone, 202–366–4434

The Office of Research, Technology, and Analysis serves as the principal adviser to the Administrator of RSPA on all research, technology, and analysis program activities as they relate to RSPA's mission, programs, and objectives; conduct of the airline statistical data technology transfer; and scientific and technological activities within RPSA. The Office oversees and directs the activities of the Transportation Safety Institute (TSI).

Office of Airline Statistics

400 Seventh Street SW., Washington, DC 20590. Phone, 202–366–9059

The Office of Airline Statistics fulfills the Secretary's statutory responsibility to collect and disseminate economic aviation data. The data shows the financial and statistical results of air carrier operations in providing air transportation. The Office identifies the DOT program requirements for aviation data and arranges access. Where data collections are needed, the Office prescribes rules for air carrier accounting and reporting. It also receives the reports, validates and processes the data, and generates a variety of end-product publications and data banks. Aviation data may be viewed in the Office's public reports facility or accessed through a variety of Government and private-sector services. Certain restrictions apply to public access to some of the data.

For information about access to public reports and information about Office functions, call 202–366–9059, DAI–1.

Office of University Research and Education

400 Seventh Street SW., Washington, DC 20590. Phone, 202–366–5442

The Office of University Research and Education acts as principal adviser to RSPA and the Department on university research and education activities; provides a point of contact with the academic community; stimulates broad-based university involvement with intermodal transportation problems and issues; and manages a national grant program to establish and operate university transportation centers and university research institutes.

Office of Automated Tariffs

400 Seventh Street SW., Washington, DC 20590. Phone, 202–366–2414

The Office of Automated Tariffs is responsible for administering the Department's programs of air carrier tariff filings. Tariffs are filed in accordance with the Federal Aviation

Act of 1958, as amended (49 U.S.C. app. 1301 *et seq.*), and title 14, part 221 of the *Code of Federal Regulations.* These provisions require that U.S. and foreign air carriers file the tariffs setting passenger fares, cargo rates, additional charges, and the rules related to the application of the fares and rates where the tariffs are applicable to international air transportation.

Office of Research Policy and Technology Transfer

400 Seventh Street SW., Washington, DC 20590. Phone, 202–366–4208

The Office of Research Policy and Technology Transfer oversees the Department's entire research and development programs, and those technical assistance and technology sharing activities which bring the results of research and development to its users and establishes needs for future research. This responsibility includes coordination and oversight of the Department's technology transfer activities under the Stevenson-Wydler Technology Innovation Act of 1980, as amended (15 U.S.C. 3701 *et seq.*), relating to the transfer of federally funded technology to the marketplace.

Transportation Safety Institute

Department of Transportation, 6500 South McArthur Boulevard, Oklahoma City, OK 73125. Phone, 405–954–3153

The Institute was established in 1971 by the Secretary of Transportation to support the Department's efforts to reduce the number and cost of transportation accidents by promoting safety and security management through education. The Institute is a primary source of transportation safety and security training and technical assistance on domestic and international levels for Department of Transportation elements, as well as other Federal, State, and local government agencies.

Office of Emergency Transportation

400 Seventh Street SW., Washington, DC 20590. Phone, 202–366–5270

The Office of Emergency Transportation provides the staff to administer and execute the Secretary of Transportation's statutory and administrative responsibilities in the area of transportation civil emergency preparedness. It is the primary element of the Department engaged in the development, coordination, and review of policies, plans, and programs for attaining and maintaining a high state of Federal transportation emergency preparedness. This Office oversees the effective discharge of the Secretary's responsibilities in all emergencies affecting the national defense and in national or regional emergencies, including those caused by natural disasters and other crisis situations.

Volpe National Transportation Systems Center

Kendall Square, Cambridge, MA 02142. Phone, 617–494–2224

The Volpe National Transportation Systems Center (Volpe Center), as part of RSPA, provides research, analysis, and systems capability to the Department of Transportation (DOT) and other agencies requiring expertise in national transportation and logistics programs.

Integrated systems approaches are developed by Volpe Center to address Federal transportation issues of national importance. It does not appear as a line item in the Federal budget, but is funded directly by its sponsors. Volpe Center projects are therefore responsive to customer needs. The Center has come to be increasingly recognized by government, industry, and academia as a focal point for the assimilation, generation, and interchange of knowledge and understanding concerning national and international transportation and logistics systems. The Volpe Center is widely valued as a vital national resource for solving complex transportation and logistics problems.

Based on shifting national priorities and availability of its resources, Volpe Center programmatic activities for DOT and other agencies vary from year to year.

Volpe Center programs emphasize policy support and analysis, cost-effective Government procurement, environmental protection and remediation, transportation safety and security, and infrastructure modernization.

For further information, contact the Office of Program and Policy Support, Research and Special Programs Administration, Department of Transportation, 400 Seventh Street SW., Washington, DC 20590. Phone, 202–366–4831.

Bureau of Transportation Statistics

The Bureau of Transportation Statistics (BTS) was organized pursuant to section 6006 of the Intermodal Surface Transportation Efficiency Act of 1991 (ISTEA) (49 U.S.C. 111), and was formally established by the Secretary of Transportation on December 16, 1992. BTS has an intermodal transportation focus whose missions are to compile, analyze, and make accessible information on the Nation's transportation systems; to collect information on intermodal transportation and other areas; and to enhance the quality and effectiveness of DOT's statistical programs through research, the development of guidelines, and the promotion of improvements in data acquisition and use.

The programs of BTS are organized in six functional areas and are mandated by ISTEA to:
—compile, analyze, and publish statistics;
—develop a long-term data collection program;
—develop guidelines to improve the credibility and effectiveness of the Department's statistics;
—represent transportation interests in the statistical community;
—make statistics accessible and understandable; and
—identify data needs.

For further information, call 202–366–DATA; or via Internet: bts@phantom.dot.gov. Fax, 202–366–3640.

Sources of Information

Inquiries for information on the following subjects should be directed to the specified office, Department of Transportation, Washington, DC 20590, or to the address indicated.

Coast Guard Career and Training Opportunities Inquiries for information on the U.S. Coast Guard Academy should be directed to the Director of Admissions, U.S. Coast Guard Academy, New London, CT 06320. Phone, 203–444–8444.

Information on the enlistment program and the Officer Candidate School may be obtained from the local recruiting offices or the Commandant (G–PRJ), U.S.

Coast Guard, Washington, DC 20593. Phone, 202–267–1726.

Persons interested in joining the Coast Guard Auxiliary may obtain information from the Commandant (G–NAB), U.S. Coast Guard, Washington, DC 20593. Phone, 202–267–1077.

Consumer Activities For information about air travelers' rights or for assistance in resolving consumer problems with providers of commercial air transportation services, contact the Consumer Affairs Division (phone, 202–366–2220); for consumer assistance, to report possible boat safety defects, and to obtain information on boats and associated equipment involved in safety defect (recall) campaigns, call the U.S. Coast Guard's Boating Safety Hotline. Residents of Washington, DC, call 267–0780. Other residents nationwide, call 800–368–5647 (toll-free).

To report vehicle safety problems, obtain information on motor vehicle and highway safety, or to request consumer information publications, call the National Highway Traffic Safety Administration's 24-hour Auto Safety Hotline. Residents of Washington, DC, call 366–0123. Other residents nationwide (except Alaska and Hawaii) call, 800–424–9393 (toll-free).

Contracts Contact the Office of Acquisition and Grant Management. Phone, 202–366–4285.

Employment Principal occupations in the Department are covered in the civil service examinations for air traffic controller, electronics maintenance technician, engineer (civil, aeronautical, automotive, electronic, highway, general), administrative/management, and clerical. For positions in Washington, DC, inquiries should be directed to the Central Employment Information Office, Office of Personnel, Room 9113, 400 Seventh Street SW., Washington, DC 20590 (phone, 202–366–9391). For employment outside of Washington, DC, inquiries may be directed to regional and district offices of the various administrations.

Schools interested in participating in the college recruitment program should address inquiries to the regional and district offices of the various administrations.

Environment Inquiries on environmental activities and programs should be directed to the Assistant Secretary for Transportation Policy, Office of Environment, Energy, and Safety, Washington, DC 20590. Phone, 202–366–4366.

Films Many films on transportation subjects are available for use by educational institutions, community groups, private organizations, etc. Requests for specific films relating to a particular mode of transportation may be directed to the appropriate operating administration.

Fraud, Waste, and Abuse To report, contact the Office of Inspector General Hotline, P.O. Box 23178, Washington, DC 20024. Phone, 202–366–1461 or 800–424–9071 (toll-free).

Publications The Department and its operating agencies issue publications on a wide variety of subjects. Many of these publications are available from the issuing agency or for sale from the Government Printing Office and the National Technical Information Service, 5285 Port Royal Road, Springfield, VA 22151. Contact the Department or the specific agency at the addresses indicated in the text.

Reading Rooms Contact the Office of the General Counsel, Room 4107, Public Docket, Department of Transportation, 400 Seventh Street SW., Washington, DC 20590. Phone, 202–366–9322. Administrations and their regional offices maintain reading rooms for public use. Contact the specific administration at the address indicated in the text.

Other reading rooms include: Department of Transportation Library, Room 2200, 400 Seventh Street SW., Washington, DC 20590 (phone, 202–366–0746); Department of Transportation Law Library, Room 2215, 400 Seventh Street SW., Washington, DC 20590 (phone, 202–366–0749); Department of Transportation Library, FOB–10A Services Section, Room 930, 800 Independence Avenue SW., Washington, DC 20591 (phone, 202–267–3115); and U.S. Coast Guard Law Library, Room 4407, 2100 Second Street SW., Washington, DC 20593 (phone, 202–267–2536).

Speakers The Department of Transportation and its operating administrations and regional offices make speakers available for civic, labor, and community groups. Contact the specific agency or the nearest regional office at the address indicated in the text.

Telephone Directory The Department of Transportation telephone directory is available for sale by the Superintendent of Documents, Government Printing Office, Washington, DC 20402.

For further information concerning the Department of Transportation, contact the Office of the Assistant Secretary for Public Affairs, Department of Transportation, 400 Seventh Street SW., Washington, DC 20590. Phone, 202–366–5580

DEPARTMENT OF THE TREASURY

1500 Pennsylvania Avenue NW., Washington, DC 20220
Phone, 202–622–2000

SECRETARY OF THE TREASURY	ROBERT E. RUBIN
Deputy Secretary	FRANK N. NEWMAN
Chief of Staff	SYLVIA M. MATHEWS
Executive Secretary and Senior Adviser to the Secretary	BENJAMIN H. NYE
Under Secretary (International Affairs)	LAWRENCE H. SUMMERS
Under Secretary (Domestic Finance)	(VACANCY)
Deputy Assistant Secretary for Federal Finance	DARCY E. BRADBURY
Director, Office of Market Finance	JILL K. OUSELEY
Director, Office of Federal Finance Policy Analysis	NORMAN K. CARLETON
Deputy Assistant Secretary for Government Finance Policy Analysis	MOZELLE W. THOMPSON
Director, Office of Corporate Finance	(VACANCY)
Director, Office of Government Financing	CHARLES D. HAWORTH
Director, Office of Synthetic Fuels	RALPH L. BAYRER
Under Secretary (Enforcement)	RONALD K. NOBLE
Assistant Secretary (Enforcement)	(VACANCY)
Deputy Assistant Secretary (Law Enforcement)	REBECCA HEDLUND, *Acting*
Director, Office of Law Enforcement	CHARLES BRISBIN
Director, Project Outreach	HERBERT JONES
Director, Office of Financial Crimes Enforcement Network (FinCEN)	STANLEY E. MORRIS
Director, Office of Foreign Assets Control	R. RICHARD NEWCOMB
Deputy Assistant Secretary (Regulatory, Tariff and Trade Enforcement)	JOHN P. SIMPSON
Director, Office of Trade and Tariff Affairs	DENNIS M. O'CONNELL
Assistant Secretary (Financial Institutions)	RICHARD S. CARNELL
Deputy Assistant Secretary for Financial Institutions Policy	FE MORALES MARKS
Director, Office of Financial Institutions	GORDON EASTBURN
Director, Office of Financial Institutions, Oversight and Policy	JOAN AFFLECK-SMITH
Assistant Secretary (Economic Policy)	ALICIA H. MUNNELL
Deputy Assistant Secretary for Macroeconomics Analysis	JAMES BRADFORD DE LONG
Director, Office of Financial Analysis	JOHN H. AUTEN
Deputy Assistant Secretary for Policy Coordination	ROBERT F. GILLINGHAM
Director, Office of Economic Analysis	JOHN S. GREENLEES
Director, Office of Policy Analysis	JOHN C. HAMBOR
Director, Office of Data Management	THOMAS A. MCCOWAN, JR.

Director, Office of Foreign Portfolio Investment Survey	WILLIAM L. GRIEVER
Fiscal Assistant Secretary	GERALD MURPHY
Deputy Fiscal Assistant Secretary	MARCUS W. PAGE
Assistant Fiscal Assistant Secretary	JOHN A. KILCOYNE
Director, Office of Cash and Debt Management	DONALD A. CHIODO
Senior Advisor for Fiscal Management	ROGER A. BEZDEK
General Counsel	EDWARD S. KNIGHT
Deputy General Counsel	NEAL WOLIN
Associate General Counsel (Legislation, Litigation, and Regulation)	RICHARD S. CARRO
Assistant General Counsel (Banking and Finance)	JOHN E. BOWMAN
Assistant General Counsel (Enforcement)	ROBERT M. MCNAMARA, JR.
Assistant General Counsel (Administrative and General Law)	KENNETH R. SCHMALZBACH
Assistant General Counsel (International Affairs)	RUSSELL L. MUNK
Tax Legislative Counsel	GLEN A. KOHL
Benefits Tax Counsel	RANDOLF H. HARDOCK
Counsel to the Inspector General	FRANCINE J. KERNER
Assistant Secretary (International Affairs)	JEFFREY SHAFER
Director of Program Services	DANIEL A. O'BRIEN, *Acting*
Deputy Assistant Secretary for International Monetary and Financial Policy	TIMOTHY F. GEITHNER
Director, Office of Foreign Exchange Operations	JOHN D. LANGE, JR.
Director, Office of International Banking and Portfolio Investment	JOHN L. WEEKS
Director, Office of Industrial Nations and Global Analyses	ROBERT HARLOW, *Acting*
Director, Office of International Monetary Policy	JAMES M. LISTER
Deputy Assistant Secretary for Middle East and Energy Policy	CHARLES SCHOTTA
Director, Office of Middle East and Energy	DAVID S. CURRY
Director, U.S.-Saudi Arabian Joint Commission Program Office	JON M. GAASERUD
Deputy Assistant Secretary for International Development and Debt Policy	SUSAN B. LEVINE
Director, Office of Multilateral Development Banks	JOSEPH EICHENBERGER
Director, Office of International Debt Policy	MARY E. CHAVES
Deputy Assistant Secretary for Developing Nations	JAMES H. FALL III
Director, Office of Latin American and Caribbean Nations	BRUCE M. JUBA
Director, Office of Asian and Near East Nations	MARGRETHE LUNDSAGER
Director, Office of African Nations and Paris Club	EDWIN L. BARBER III
Deputy Assistant Secretary for Trade and Investment Policy	WILLIAM E. BARREDA

Director, Office of International Trade	T. WHITTIER WARTHIN
Director, Office of International Investment	DONALD CRAFTS
Director, Office of Trade Finance	STEVEN F. TVARDEK
Director, Office of Financial Services Negotiations	TODD CRAWFORD
Deputy Assistant Secretary for Eastern Europe and Former Soviet Union	DAVID LIPTON
Director, Office of Eastern European Nations	(VACANCY)
Director, Office of Former Soviet Union Nations	MARK SOBEL
Director, Office of Technical Assistance	DANIEL ZELIKOW
Assistant Secretary (Legislative Affairs)	MICHAEL A. LEVY
Director, Office of Legislative Affairs	GAIL E. PETERSON
Deputy Assistant Secretary (Tax and Budget)	LINDA ROBERTSON
Deputy Assistant Secretary (International)	GEORGE R. TYLER
Deputy Executive Assistant Secretary for Public Liaison	JOYCE H. CARRIER
Assistant Secretary for Management/Chief Financial Officer	GEORGE MUÑOZ
Deputy Chief Financial Officer	EDWIN A. VERBURG
Director, Office of Security	RICHARD P. KILEY
Deputy Assistant Secretary for Departmental Finance and Management	W. SCOTT GOULD
Director, Office of Small Business and Disadvantaged Utilization	T.J. GARCIA, *Acting*
Director, Office of Procurement	ROBERT A. WELCH
Director, Office of Real and Personal Property Management	ROBERT T. HARPER
Director, Office of Personnel Policy	ROBERT BREVIS, *Acting*
Director, Office of Equal Opportunity Program	RONALD A. GLASER
Director, Treasury Integrated Management Information Systems	EDWARD B. POWELL III
Director, Office of Organizational Improvement	JUDY OCHS, *Acting*
Director, Office of Budget	CARL MORAVITZ
Director, Treasury Reinvention	ANTHONY A. FLEMING, *Acting*
Director, Office of Strategic Planning	JOHN MURPHY
Director, Treasury Executive Institute	SUELLEN HAMBY
Deputy Assistant Secretary for Administration	ALEX RODRIGUEZ
Director, Office of Management Advisory Services	WILLIAM H. GILLERS
Director, Automated Systems Division	G. DALE SEWARD
Director, Office of Printing and Graphics Division	KIRK B. MARKLAND
Director, Facilities Management Division	JAMES R. HAULSEY
Director, Office of Financial Management Division	MARY BETH SHAW
Director, Procurement Services Division	WESLEY L. HAWLEY
Director, Administrative Operations Division	IDA HERNANDEZ
Director, Personnel Resources Division	ROSEMARY DOWNING

Deputy Assistant Secretary for Information Systems	WUSHOW CHOU
Director, Office of Information Resources Management	JANE L. SULLIVAN
Director, Office of Telecommunications Management	JAMES J. FLYZIK
Assistant Secretary (Public Affairs)	JOAN LOGUE-KINDER
Deputy Assistant Secretary for Public Affairs	HOWARD M. SCHLOSS
Director, Public Affairs	CHRIS PEACOCK
Assistant Secretary (Tax Policy)	LESLIE SAMUELS
Deputy Assistant Secretary (Tax Policy)	CYNTHIA BEERBOWER
Tax Legislative Counsel	GLEN A. KOHL
International Tax Counsel	(VACANCY)
Benefits Tax Counsel	RANDOLF HARDOCK
Deputy Assistant Secretary (Tax Analysis)	ERIC TODER
Director, Office of Tax Analysis	LOWELL DWORIN
Treasurer of the United States	MARY ELLEN WITHROW
Inspector General	VALERIE LAU
Special Assistants to the Inspector General	BARRY SAVILL
	RAISA OTERO-CESARIO
Director, Inspectors General Auditor Training Institute	ANDREW J. PASDEN
Counsel to the Inspector General	(VACANCY)
Deputy Inspector General	ROBERT P. CESCA
Assistant Inspector General for Investigations	JAMES M. COTTOS
Deputy Assistant Inspector General for Investigations	CHESTER W. WHITE
Assistant Inspector General for Audit	RICHARD B. CALAHAN
Deputy Assistant Inspector General for Audit (Operations)	DENNIS S. SCHINDEL
Deputy Assistant Inspector General for Audit (Program Services)	(VACANCY)
Assistant Inspector General for Policy, Planning, and Resources/Chief Financial Officer	JOHN N. BALAKOS
Deputy Assistant Inspector General for Policy, Planning and Resources/Deputy Chief Financial Officer	CLIFFORD JENNINGS
Assistant Inspector General for Oversight and Quality Assurance	GARY L. WHITTINGTON

BUREAU OF ALCOHOL, TOBACCO AND FIREARMS

650 Massachusetts Avenue NW., Washington, DC 20226
Phone, 202-927-8500

Director	JOHN W. MAGAW
Deputy Director	DANIEL R. BLACK
Ombudsman	PETER MASTIN
Equal Opportunity Executive Assistant	MARJORIE R. KORNEGAY
Legislative Affairs Executive Assistant	PETER GAGLIARDI
Liaison and Public Information Executive Assistant	JOHN KILLORIN
Strategic Planning Office	WAYNE MILLER
Chief Counsel	BRADLEY BUCKLES, *Acting*
Assistant Director (Inspection)	RICHARD J. HANKINSON

Associate Director (Enforcement)	CHARLES THOMSON
Assistant Director (Management)	RICHARD J. WATKINS
Assistant Director (Science and Information Technology)	ARTHUR J. LIBERTUCCI
Assistant Director (Training and Professional Development)	GALE D. ROSSIDES

OFFICE OF THE COMPTROLLER OF THE CURRENCY
250 E Street SW., Washington, DC 20219
Phone, 202–874–5000

Comptroller	EUGENE A. LUDWIG
Executive Assistant	BALLARD C. GILMORE
Senior Deputy Comptroller for Economic Analysis	KONRAD S. ALT
Deputy Comptroller, Public Affairs	LEONORA S. CROSS
Director, Communications	ELLEN STOCKDALE
Director, Press Relations	NAOMI SALUS
Director, Congressional Liaison	CAROLYN Z. MCFARLANE
Director, Banking Relations	WILLIAM F. GRANT III
Director, Community Development	JANICE A. BOOKER
Senior Deputy Comptroller for Bank Supervision Policy	SUSAN F. KRAUSE
Deputy Comptroller for Special Supervision	(VACANCY)
Deputy Comptroller for International Banking and Finance	JON HARTZELL
Chief National Bank Examiner	JIMMY F. BARTON
Deputy Comptroller for Information Resources Management	ALLAN B. GUERRINA
Deputy Comptroller for Compliance Management	STEPHEN M. CROSS
Senior Deputy Comptroller for Bank Supervision Operations	STEPHEN R. STEINBRINK
District Liaison	FRED E. FINKE
Deputy Comptroller for Multinational Banking	RALPH E. SHARPE
Deputy Comptroller for Capital Markets	DOUGLAS E. HARRIS
Senior Deputy Comptroller for Corporate Activities and Policy Analysis	FRANK MAGUIRE, JR.
Deputy Comptroller for Bank Organization and Structure	STEVEN J. WEISS
Deputy Comptroller for Economic and Policy Analysis	JAMES KAMIHACHI
Senior Deputy Comptroller for Administration	JUDITH A. WALTER
Deputy Comptroller for Resource Management	GARY W. NORTON
Chief Financial Officer	RONALD P. PASSERO
Chief Counsel	JULIE L. WILLIAMS
Deputy Chief Counsels	ROBERT B. SERINO
	RAYMOND NATTER

UNITED STATES CUSTOMS SERVICE
1301 Constitution Avenue NW., Washington, DC 20229
Phone, 202–927–2095

Commissioner of Customs	GEORGE WEISE

Confidential Assistant   PAM JOHNSTON
Special Assistant to the Commissioner   ROBERT MITCHELL
Deputy Commissioner   MICHAEL LANE
Associate Commissioner (Organizational Effectiveness)   DEBORAH SPERO, *Acting*
Assistant Commissioner (International Affairs)   DOUGLAS BROWNING
Assistant Commissioner (Management)   CARLTON BRAINARD
Comptroller   C. WAYNE HAMILTON, *Acting*
Assistant Commissioner (Information Management)   WILLIAM RILEY
Assistant Commissioner (Enforcement)   JOHN LUKSIC, *Acting*
Assistant Commissioner (Inspection and Control)   CHARLES W. WINWOOD
Assistant Commissioner (Commercial Operations)   SAMUEL BANKS
Assistant Commissioner (Internal Affairs)   WALTER BIONDI
Assistant Commissioner (Congressional and Public Affairs)   JOSE PADILLA
Chief Counsel   MICHAEL T. SCHMITZ
Special Assistant to the Commissioner (Equal Opportunity)   LINDA BATTS

BUREAU OF ENGRAVING AND PRINTING

Fourteenth and C Streets SW., Washington, DC 20228
Phone, 202–874–3019

Director   PETER H. DALY
Associate Director (Chief Operating Officer)   CARLA F. KIDWELL
Associate Director (Chief Financial Officer)   L. PAUL BLACKMER, JR.
Assistant Director (Management)   TIMOTHY G. VIGOTSKY
Assistant Director (Technology)   MILTON J. SEIDEL
Assistant Director (Research and Development)   THOMAS A. FERGUSON
Deputy Associate Director (Fort Worth Operations)   RAY E. LAVAN
Chief Counsel   CARROL H. KINSEY

FEDERAL LAW ENFORCEMENT TRAINING CENTER

Glynco, GA 31524
Phone, 912–267–2100; Washington, DC, 202–927–8940; FLETC-Tucson, AZ, Operations, 602–750–4075; Artesia, NM, Operations, 505–748–8000

Director   CHARLES F. RINKEVICH
Deputy Director   R.J. MILLER
Associate Director   JOHN C. DOOHER
Director (Administration)   KENNETH A. HALL
Director (General Training)   DONALD PARKURST, *Acting*
Director (Special Training)   RAY M. RICE
Director (State and Local Training)   HOBART M. HENSON
Director (Artesia, NM, Operations)   JEFFERY HESSER
Director (Washington, DC, Office)   JOHN C. DOOHER

FINANCIAL MANAGEMENT SERVICE
401 Fourteenth Street SW., Washington, DC 20227
Phone, 202–874–6740

Commissioner	RUSSELL D. MORRIS
Deputy Commissioner	MICHAEL T. SMOKOVICH
Director, Legislative and Public Affairs	JIM L. HAGEDORN
Director, Planning Office	JOHN LEWIN, *Acting*
Chief Counsel	DAVID A. INGOLD
Assistant Commissioner, Agency Services	WALTER L. JORDAN
Assistant Commissioner, Federal Finance	LARRY D. STOUT
Assistant Commissioner, Financial Information	DIANE E. CLARK
Assistant Commissioner, Information Resources	CONSTANCE E. CRAIG
Assistant Commissioner, Management (CFO)	MITCHELL A. LEVINE
Assistant Commissioner, Regional Operations	BLAND T. BROCKENBOROUGH

INTERNAL REVENUE SERVICE
1111 Constitution Avenue NW., Washington, DC 20224
Phone, 202–622–5000

Commissioner of Internal Revenue	MARGARET MILNER RICHARDSON
Assistants to the Commissioner	MICHAEL DANILACK, BETH-ANN GENTILE, HEATHER MALLOY, J. PAUL WHITEHEAD III
Special Assistant to the Commissioner	HELEN BOLTON
Chief, Commissioner's Staff	JIM NELSON
Director, Scheduling and Advance Office	BARBARA NICHOLS
Taxpayer Ombudsman	LEE MONKS
Deputy Commissioner	MICHAEL P. DOLAN
Assistant to the Deputy Commissioner	JAMES E. ROGERS, JR.
Chief Counsel	STUART BROWN
Deputy Chief Counsel	MARLENE GROSS
Associate Chief Counsel (Domestic)	JUDY DUNN
Associate Chief Counsel (Employee Benefits/Exempt Organizations)	SARAH HALL INGRAM
Associate Chief Counsel (Enforcement Litigation)	ELIOT FIELDING
Associate Chief Counsel (Finance/ Management)	RICHARD MIHELCIC
Associate Chief Counsel (International)	ROBERT CULBERTSON
National Director of Appeals	JAMES DOUGHERTY
Chief Compliance Officer	PHIL BRAND
Executive Assistant	MARIE DUFORE
Assistant Commissioner (Collection)	STEVEN E. TAYLOR, *Acting*
Assistant Commissioner (Criminal Investigation)	DON VOGEL
Deputy Assistant Commissioner (Criminal Investigation)	PAUL M. MIYAHARA
Assistant Commissioner (Examination)	JOHN MONACO
Asssitant Commissioner (Employee Plans/ Exempt Organizations)	JIM MCGOVERN
Assistant Commissioner (International)	REGINA DEANEHAN

Deputy Assistant Commissioner (International)	LOU CARLOW
Chief Financial Officer	C. MORGAN KINGHORN
Executive Assistant	PAM LARUE, *Acting*
Controller	JOE DONLON
Chief Information Officer	HANK PHILCOX
Executive Assistant	KAREN DENEROFF
Deputy Chief Information Officer	DAVE GAUGLER
Privacy Advocate Officer	ROBERT VEEDER
Chief Inspector	GARY BELL
Deputy Chief Inspector	DOUG CROUCH
Assistant Chief Inspector (Internal Audit)	BILLY MORRISON
Assistant Chief Inspector (Internal Security)	SEBASTIAN LORIGO
Chief, Management and Administration	DAVID MADER
Executive Assistant	JOANN BUCK
Assistant Commissioner (Procurement)	GREG ROTHWELL
Deputy Assistant Commissioner (Procurement)	JIM WILLIAMS
Assistant to the Commissioner (Equal Opportunity)	ED CHAVEZ
Chief, Strategic Planning and Communications	ROBERT E. WENZEL
Executive Assistant	FRANK SPIEGELBERG
Director of Communications	ANTHONY CIOTOLA
Director, Legislative Affairs Division	ANNE RAFFAELLI
Chief, Taxpayer Services	JUDY K. VAN ALFEN
Executive Assistant	BLANCA ZAYAS
Assistant Commissioner (Taxpayer Service)	GWEN KRAUSS
Chief, Headquarters Operations	ROGER BURGESS
Executive Assistant	BEN DADD
Modernization Executive	LARRY WESTFALL
Executive Assistant	CAROL A. BARNETT

UNITED STATES MINT

633 Third Street NW., Washington, DC 20220
Phone, 202–874–6000

Director of the Mint	PHILIP N. DIEHL
Deputy Director	JOHN P. MITCHELL
Special Assistant to the Director	ERIC HALLERBERG
Chief Counsel	KENNETH B. GUBIN
Chief, Security/Internal Review	WILLIAM F. DADDIO
Associate Director for Policy and Management	JAY WEINSTEIN, *Acting*
Deputy Associate Director for Finance/Deputy Chief Financial Officer	(VACANCY)
Associate Director/Chief Operating Officer	ANDREW COSGAREA, JR.
Associate Director for Marketing	DAVID PICKENS

BUREAU OF THE PUBLIC DEBT

999 E Street NW., Washington, DC 20239–0001
Phone, 202–219–3300

Commissioner	RICHARD L. GREGG
Deputy Commissioner	VAN ZECK
Director, Government Securities Regulation Staff	KENNETH R. PAPAJ

Chief Counsel	CYNTHIA REESE, *Acting*
Assistant Commissioner (Financing)	CARL M. LOCKEN, JR.
Assistant Commissioner (Securities and Accounting Services)	JANE O'BRIEN, ACTING
Assistant Commissioner (Administration)	THOMAS W. HARRISON
Assistant Commissioner (Automated Information Systems)	NOEL E. KEESOR
Assistant Commissioner (Savings Bond Operations)	ARTHUR A. KLASS
Assistant Commissioner (Public Debt Accounting)	DEBRA HINES, *Acting*
Executive Director (Savings Bonds Marketing Office)	DINO DECONCINI

UNITED STATES SECRET SERVICE

1800 G Street NW., Washington, DC 20223
Phone, 202–435–5708

Director	ELJAY B. BOWRON
Deputy Director	RICHARD J. GRIFFIN
Assistant Director (Administration)	W. RALPH BASHAM
Assistant Director (Inspection)	JAMES G. HUSE
Assistant Director (Protective Research)	DAVID C. LEE
Assistant Director (Protective Operations)	RICHARD S. MILLER
Assistant Director (Investigations)	PAUL A. HACKENBERRY
Assistant Director (Government Liaison and Public Affairs)	H. TERRENCE SAMWAY
Assistant Director (Training)	K. DAVID HOLMES
Chief Counsel	JOHN J. KELLEHER

OFFICE OF THRIFT SUPERVISION

1700 G Street NW., Washington, DC 20552
Phone, 202–906–6000

Director	JONATHAN L. FIECHTER, *Acting*
Director for Minority Affairs	NADINE ELZY
Director for Research and Analysis	KENNETH F. RYDER
Director for Chief Counsel	CAROLYN J. BUCK
Director for Supervision	JOHN F. DOWNEY
Director for Administration	CORA P. BEEBE
Director for Congressional Affairs	JOHN L. VON SEGGREN, *Acting*
Director for Press Relations	WILLIAM E. FULWIDER, *Acting*
Associate Director for FDIC Operations	WALTER B. MASON
Resolution Trust Corporation Liaison	LEE LASSITER

The Department of the Treasury performs four basic functions: formulating and recommending economic, financial, tax, and fiscal policies; serving as financial agent for the U.S. Government; enforcing the law; and manufacturing coins and currency.

The Treasury Department was created by act of September 2, 1789 (31 U.S.C. 301 and 301 note). Many subsequent acts have figured in the development of the Department, delegating new duties to its charge and establishing the numerous bureaus and divisions that now comprise the Treasury.

DEPARTMENT OF THE TREASURY

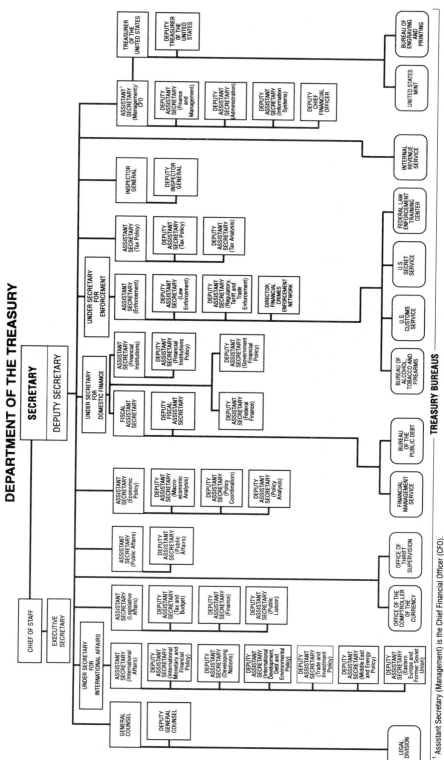

TREASURY BUREAUS

¹ Assistant Secretary (Management) is the Chief Financial Officer (CFO).

Secretary

As a major policy adviser to the President, the Secretary has primary responsibility for formulating and recommending domestic and international financial, economic, and tax policy; participating in the formulation of broad fiscal policies that have general significance for the economy; and managing the public debt. The Secretary also oversees the activities of the Department in carrying out its major law enforcement responsibility; in serving as the financial agent for the U.S. Government; and in manufacturing coins, currency, and other products for customer agencies.

In addition, the Secretary has many responsibilities as chief financial officer of the Government. The Secretary serves as Chairman pro tempore of the Economic Policy Council and as U.S. Governor of the International Monetary Fund, the International Bank for Reconstruction and Development, the Inter-American Development Bank, and the African Development Bank. The Office of the Secretary includes the offices of Deputy Secretary, General Counsel, Inspector General, the Under Secretaries, the Assistant Secretaries, and Treasurer. Some areas where public purposes are widely applied are detailed below and on the following pages.

Deputy Secretary

The Deputy Secretary assists the Secretary in the supervision and direction of the Department and its assigned programs, and acts for the Secretary in his absence.

Under Secretary for International Affairs

The Under Secretary for International Affairs advises and assists the Secretary and Deputy Secretary of the Treasury in the formulation and execution of U.S. international policy. These responsibilities include the development of policies and guidance of Department activities in the areas of international monetary affairs, trade and investment policy, international debt strategy, and U.S. participation in international financial institutions. The Under Secretary acts as the U.S. G-7 Deputy with responsibility for coordinating economic policies with finance ministers from seven industrial nations and preparing the President for the annual economic summits.

Under Secretary for Domestic Finance

The Under Secretary for Domestic Finance advises and assists the Secretary and Deputy Secretary of the Treasury in the areas of domestic finance, banking, and other related economic matters. These responsibilities include the development of policies and guidance for Treasury Department activities in the areas of financial institutions, Federal debt finance, financial regulation, and capital markets.

Under Secretary for Enforcement

The Office of the Under Secretary for Enforcement was established in fiscal year 1994 to promote and protect the Treasury Department's enforcement interest, to effect an equalization across other departmental secretariats as they deal on enforcement issues.

Assistant Secretaries

Financial Institutions The Assistant Secretary (Domestic Finance) advises and assists the Secretary, Deputy Secretary, and Under Secretary for Finance on matters of Federal, State, and local finance, financial institutions policy, and synthetic fuels projects.

In the area of Federal finance, the Office is responsible for Government financing and debt management; determining interest rates for various Federal borrowing, lending, and investment purposes under pertinent statutes; and developing legislative and administrative principles and standards for Federal credit programs, loan asset sales, and the Federal Financing Bank.

The Office is also responsible for:
—issues involving the financing of State and local governments;
—oversight of the Office of Revenue Sharing, which returns specified amounts

of federally collected funds to eligible units of general-purpose governments;

—coordinating the Treasury Department's legislative efforts with regard to financial institutions legislation and legislation affecting the Federal agencies that regulate financial institutions; and

—providing support to carry out the Department's responsibilities regarding the Securities Investor Protection Corporation, the Pension Benefit Guaranty Corporation, and synthetic fuels projects taken over from the Synthetic Fuels Corporation.

Economic Policy   The Assistant Secretary (Economic Policy) informs the Secretary and other senior Treasury officials of current and prospective economic developments and assists in the determination of appropriate economic policies. The Assistant Secretary:

—reviews and analyzes both domestic and international economic issues, as well as developments in the financial markets;

—participates with the Secretary in the Economic Policy Council and the Troika Forecasting Group, which develops official economic projections and advises the President on choices among alternative courses of economic policy; and

—works closely with officials of the Office of Management and Budget, the Council of Economic Advisers, and other Government agencies on the economic forecasts underlying the yearly budget process, and advises the Secretary on the economic effects of tax and budget policy.

Within the Office of Economic Policy, staff support is provided by the Office of Financial Analysis, the Office of Special Studies, the Office of Monetary Policy Analysis, and the Applied Econometric Staff.

Enforcement   The Assistant Secretary (Enforcement) supervises the following operating bureaus: U.S. Secret Service; U.S. Customs Service; Federal Law Enforcement Training Center; and Alcohol, Tobacco and Firearms. In addition, the Assistant Secretary is responsible for the Office of Financial

Enforcement, and the Office of Foreign Assets Control.

The Assistant Secretary coordinates Treasury law enforcement matters, including the formulation of policies for Treasury enforcement activities, and cooperates on law enforcement matters with other Federal agencies.

The important missions of protecting the President and other high Government officials and preventing counterfeiting of U.S. currency and theft and forgery of Government securities and checks are entrusted to the United States Secret Service. The U.S. Customs Service collects revenue from imports and enforces the customs laws. In addition, it interdicts contraband, including narcotics, along the land and sea borders of the United States. The Bureau of Alcohol, Tobacco and Firearms is charged with collecting excise taxes on alcoholic beverages and tobacco products; suppressing traffic in illicit distilled spirits and illegal use of explosives; and controlling the sale and registration of firearms. The Federal Law Enforcement Training Center provides law enforcement training for personnel of Federal agencies. The Office of Financial Enforcement assists in implementing the Bank Secrecy Act and administering related Treasury regulations. The Office of Foreign Assets Control assists U.S. foreign policy aims by controlling assets in the United States of "blocked" countries and the flow of funds and trade to them.

Fiscal Affairs   The Office of the Fiscal Assistant Secretary was established pursuant to Reorganization Plan No. III of 1940 (5 U.S.C. app.). The Office supervises the administration of the Government's fiscal affairs. This includes the administration of Treasury financing operations; management of Treasury's cash balances in tax and loan investment accounts in commercial financial institutions and operating balances with Federal Reserve Banks; and the Department's participation in the Joint Financial Management Improvement Program for improvement of accounting in the Federal Government. Supervision and oversight over the functions and activities of the Financial Management

Service and the Bureau of the Public Debt are also provided. The Fiscal Assistant Secretary is responsible for improved cash management, debt collection, and credit administration on a Governmentwide basis under the umbrella of the Administration's Reform '88 initiative.

The Office:

—acts as liaison between the Secretary and other Government agencies with respect to their financial operations;by the reality that the dynamic was played

—manages the cash position of the Treasury and projects and monitors "debt subject-to-limit";

—directs the performance of the fiscal agency functions of the Federal Reserve Banks;

—conducts Governmentwide accounting and cash management activities;

—exercises supervision over depositories of the United States; and

—provides management overview of investment practices for Government trust and other accounts.

International Affairs   The Office of the Assistant Secretary (International Affairs) advises and assists the Secretary, Deputy Secretary, and Under Secretary for International Affairs in the formulation and execution of policies dealing with international monetary, financial, commercial, energy, and trade policies and programs. The work of the Office is organized into groups responsible for monetary affairs, developing nations, trade and investment policy, and Arabian Peninsula affairs.

These functions are performed by supporting staff offices, which:

—conduct financial diplomacy with industrial and developing nations and regions;

—work toward improving the structure and operations of the International monetary system;

—monitor developments in foreign exchange and other markets and official operations affecting those markets;

—facilitate structural monetary cooperation through the International Monetary Fund and other channels;

—oversee U.S. participation in the multilateral development banks and coordinate U.S. policies and operations relating to bilateral and multilateral development lending programs and institutions;

—formulate policy concerning financing of trade;

—coordinate policies toward foreign investments in the United States and U.S. investments abroad; and

—analyze balance of payments and other basic financial and economic data, including data on petroleum, affecting world payment patterns and the world economic outlook.

As part of those functions, the Office supports the Secretary in his role as co-Chairman of the U.S.-Saudi Arabian Joint Commission on Economic Cooperation, co-Chairman of the U.S.-Israel Joint Committee for Investment and Trade, co-Chairman of the U.S.-China Joint Economic Committee, and Chairman of the National Advisory Council on International Monetary and Financial Policies.

Treasurer of the United States   The Office of the Treasurer of the United States was established on September 6, 1777. The Treasurer was originally charged with the receipt and custody of Government funds, but many of these functions have been assumed by different bureaus of the Department of the Treasury. In 1981, the Treasurer was assigned responsibility for oversight of the Bureau of Engraving and Printing and the United States Mint. The Treasurer reports to the Secretary through the Assistant Secretary (Management)/Chief Financial Officer.

Tax Policy   The Office of the Assistant Secretary (Tax Policy) advises and assists the Secretary and the Deputy Secretary in the formulation and execution of domestic and international tax policies and programs.

These functions, carried out by supporting staff offices, include:

—analysis of proposed tax legislation and tax programs;

—projections of economic trends affecting tax bases;

—studies of effects of alternative tax measures;

—preparation of official estimates of Government receipts for the President's annual budget messages;
—legal advice and analysis on domestic and international tax matters;
—assistance in the development and review of tax legislation and domestic and international tax regulations and rulings; and
—participation in international tax treaty negotiations and in maintenance of relations with international organizations on tax matters.

For further information concerning the Departmental Offices, contact the Public Affairs Office, Department of the Treasury, 1500 Pennsylvania Avenue NW., Washington, DC 20220. Phone, 202–622–2960.

Bureau of Alcohol, Tobacco and Firearms

The Bureau of Alcohol, Tobacco and Firearms was established by Treasury Department Order No. 221, effective July 1, 1972. The order transferred the functions, powers, and duties arising under laws relating to alcohol, tobacco, firearms, and explosives from the Internal Revenue Service to the Bureau. On December 5, 1978, Treasury Department Order No. 120–1 assigned to the Bureau responsibility for enforcing chapter 114 of title 18 of the United States Code (18 U.S.C. 2341 et seq.) relating to interstate trafficking in contraband cigarettes. With passage of the Anti-Arson Act of 1982, the Bureau was given the additional responsibility of addressing commercial arson nationwide.

Bureau Headquarters is located in Washington, DC, but since the Bureau is decentralized, most of its personnel are stationed throughout the country where many of its operational functions are performed.

The Bureau is responsible for enforcing and administering firearms and explosives laws, as well as those covering the production, taxation, and distribution of alcohol and tobacco products. The Bureau's objectives are to maximize compliance with and investigate violations of these laws. To achieve these goals, the Bureau is divided into two basic functions: criminal enforcement and regulatory enforcement.

The objectives of criminal enforcement activities are to:

—suppress illegal trafficking, possession and use of firearms, destructive devices, and explosives;
—impact arson-for-profit schemes;
—suppress the traffic in illicit distilled spirits;
—suppress interstate trafficking in contraband cigarettes;
—assist Federal, State, and local law enforcement agencies in reducing crime and violence; and
—investigate narcotics traffickers who use firearms and explosives as tools of their trade, especially violent gangs.

The objectives of regulatory enforcement activities are to:

—determine and ensure full collection of revenue due from legal alcohol, tobacco, firearms, and ammunition manufacturing industries;
—fulfill the Bureau's responsibility in ensuring product integrity and health warning statements, and in preventing commercial bribery, consumer deception, and other improper trade practices in the beverage alcohol industry;
—assist other Federal, State, and local governmental agencies in the resolution of problems relating to revenue protection;
—ensure that persons prohibited by law from manufacturing, importing, or dealing in alcohol, tobacco, firearms, and explosives do not obtain a license or permit;
—ensure that storage facilities for explosives are safe, secure, and properly stored to avoid presenting a hazard to the public; and

—ensure that an audit trail is preserved to permit the tracing of firearms used in the commission of crimes and full accountability for explosive materials.

Regional Offices—Compliance Operations

Region	Address	Director
MIDWEST—Illinois, Indiana, Kentucky, Michigan, Minnesota, North Dakota, Ohio, South Dakota, West Virginia, Wisconsin	15th Fl., 230 S. Dearborn St., Chicago, IL 60604	Wayne P. Moran
NORTH ATLANTIC— Connecticut, Delaware, District of Columbia, Maine, Maryland, Massachusetts, New Hampshire, New Jersey, New York, Pennsylvania, Rhode Island, Vermont	Rm. 620, 6 World Trade Ctr., New York, NY 10048	Bruce L. Weininger
SOUTHEAST—Alabama, Florida, Georgia, Mississippi, North Carolina, Puerto Rico, South Carolina, Tennessee, Virginia, Virgin Islands	Suite 300, 2600 Century Pky., Atlanta, GA 30345	Larry Moore
SOUTHWEST—Arkansas, Colorado, Iowa, Louisiana, New Mexico, Oklahoma, Texas, Nebraska, Kansas, Missouri, Arizona	7th Fl., 1114 Commerce St., Dallas, TX 75242	Dave Royalty
WESTERN—Alaska, American Samoa, California, Guam, Idaho, Montana, Nevada, Oregon, Pacific Islands, Utah, Washington, Hawaii, Wyoming	11th Fl., 221 Main St., San Francisco, CA 94105	Victoria J. Renneckar

Field Division Offices—Office of Enforcement

Field Division	Address	Special Agent in Charge
Atlanta, GA	Suite 406, 101 Marietta St. NW., 30303	Richard C. Fox
Baltimore, MD	Suite 210, 103 S. Gay St., 21202	Margaret Moore
Birmingham, AL	Rm. 725, 2121 8th Ave. N., 35203	James Cavanaugh
Boston, MA	Rm. 701, 10 Causeway St., 02222–1081	Terence J. McArdle
Charlotte, NC	Suite 400, 4530 Park Rd., 28209	Paul J. Lyon
Chicago, IL	Suite 350 S., 300 S. Riverside Plz., 60606–6616	Richard Rawlins
Cleveland, OH	Rm. 301, 7251 Engle Rd., Middleburg Heights, OH 44130	Charles E. Wallace
Dallas, TX	P.O. Box 50906, 75250–0906	Lester Martz
Detroit, MI	Suite 300, 1155 Brewery Park Blvd., 48207–2602	Stanley Zimmerman
Houston, TX	Suite 210, 15355 Vantage Pky. W., 77032	Donnie A. Carter
Kansas City, MO	Suite 200, 2600 Grand Ave., 64108	Richard Cook
Los Angeles, CA	Suite 800, 350 S. Figueroa St., 90071	George Rodriguez
Louisville, KY	Suite 807, 510 W. Broadway, 40202	William A. Curley
New Orleans, LA	Suite 1050, 111 Veterans Memorial Hwy., Heritage Plaza Bldg., Metairie, LA 70005.	Robert Stellingworth
Miami, FL	Suite 120, 8420 NW. 52d St., 33166	Robert Creighton
Nashville, TN	Suite 215, 215 Centerview Dr., Brentwood, TN 37027	Richard Garner
New York, NY	Rm. 1016, 90 Church St., 10007	Henry J. Ballas
Philadelphia, PA	Rm. 504, 2d and Chestnut Sts., 19106	Robert H. Wall
Phoenix, AZ	Suite 1010, 3003 N. Central Ave., 85012	Bernard LaForest
San Francisco, CA	Suite 1250, 221 Main St., 94105	Paul M. Snabel
Seattle, WA	Rm. 806, 915 2d Ave., 98174	Nels C. Nelson
St. Louis, MO	Suite 550, 100 S. 4th St., 63102	Daniel B. Hoggatt
St. Paul, MN	1870 Minnesota World Trade Ctr., 30 E. 7th St., 55101	James R. Switzer
Washington, DC	Suite 620, 607 14th St. NW., 20005	Patrick D. Hynes

Office of the Comptroller of the Currency

[For the Office of the Comptroller of the Currency statement of organization, see the *Code of Federal Regulations,* Title 12, Part 4]

The Office of the Comptroller of the Currency (OCC) was created February 25, 1863 (12 Stat. 665), as a bureau of the Department of the Treasury. Its primary mission is to regulate national banks. OCC is headed by the Comptroller, who is appointed for a 5-year term by the President with the advice and consent of the Senate. By statute, the Comptroller also serves a concurrent term as Director of the Federal Deposit Insurance Corporation (FDIC).

OCC regulates national banks by its power to examine banks; approve or deny applications for new bank charters, branches, or mergers; take enforcement action—such as bank closures—against banks that are not in compliance with laws and regulations; and issue rules, regulations, and interpretations on banking practices.

OCC supervises approximately 3,300 national banks, including their trust activities and overseas operations. Each bank is examined annually through a nationwide staff of approximately 2,400 bank examiners supervised in 6 district offices. OCC is independently funded through assessments of the assets of national banks.

For further information, contact the Communications Division, Office of the Comptroller of the Currency, Department of the Treasury, 250 E Street SW., Washington, DC 20219. Phone, 202–874–4700.

United States Customs Service

The fifth act of the first Congress, passed on July 31, 1789 (1 Stat. 29), established customs districts and authorized customs officers to collect duties on goods, wares, and merchandise imposed by the second act of the first Congress, dated July 4, 1789 (1 Stat. 24). The Bureau of Customs was established as a separate agency under the Treasury Department on March 3, 1927 (19 U.S.C. 2071) and, effective August 1, 1973, was redesignated the United States Customs Service by Treasury Department Order 165–23 of April 4, 1973.

The Customs Service collects the revenue from imports and enforces customs and related laws. Customs also administers the Tariff Act of 1930, as amended (19 U.S.C. 1654), and other customs laws. Some of the responsibilities that Customs is specifically charged with are:

—assessing and collecting customs duties, excise taxes, fees, and penalties due on imported merchandise;

—interdicting and seizing contraband, including narcotics and illegal drugs;

—processing persons, carriers, cargo, and mail into and out of the United States;

—administering certain navigation laws; and

—detecting and apprehending persons engaged in fraudulent practices designed to circumvent customs and related laws; copyright, patent, and trademark provisions; quotas; and marking requirements for imported merchandise.

As the principal border enforcement agency, Customs' mission has been extended over the years to assisting in the administration and enforcement of some 400 provisions of law on behalf of more than 40 Government agencies. Today, in addition to enforcing the Tariff Act of 1930 and other customs statutes, the Customs Service:

—enforces export control laws and intercepts illegal high-technology and weapons exports;

—cooperates with other Federal agencies and foreign governments in suppressing the traffic of illegal narcotics and pornography;

—enforces reporting requirements of the Bank Secrecy Act; and

—collects international trade statistics.

Also, Customs enforces a wide range of requirements to protect the public, such as auto safety and emission control standards, radiation and radioactive material standards; counterfeit monetary instruments; flammable fabric restrictions; animal and plant quarantine requirements; and food, drug, and hazardous substance prohibitions.

Customs is extensively involved with outside commercial and policy organizations and trade associations, and with international organizations and foreign customs services. Customs is a member of the multinational Customs Cooperation Council, the Cabinet Committee to Combat Terrorism, and the International Narcotics Control Program. In addition, Customs participates in and supports the activities and programs of various international organizations and agreements, including the General Agreement on Tariffs and Trade (GATT), the International Civil Aviation Organization, and the Organization of American States (OAS). Headquarters of the U.S. Customs Service is located in Washington, DC, under the supervision of the Commissioner of Customs, who is appointed by the Secretary of the Treasury.

The 50 States, plus the Virgin Islands and Puerto Rico, are divided into seven Customs Regions. Contained within these regions are 44 subordinate district or area offices under which there are approximately 240 ports of entry.

The foreign field offices of the Customs Service are located in Bangkok, Bonn, Dublin, Hermosillo, Hong Kong, London, Mexico City, Milan, Monterrey, Ottawa, Panama City, Paris, Rome, Seoul, Singapore, Tokyo, Vienna, and The Hague. An attaché represents U.S. Customs in the U.S. Mission to the European Communities in Brussels.

The Customs Service also operates a Canine Enforcement Training Center at Front Royal, VA.

Regional Offices—U.S. Customs Service

(C: Commissioner; DC: Deputy Commissioner; RC: Regional Commissioner; DD: District Director; AD: Area Director)

Regional Headquarters/ District Offices	Address	Officer	Telephone
MAIN HEADQUARTERS:			
Washington, DC	1301 Constitution Ave. NW., 20229	George Weise (C)	202–927–1000
		Michael Lane (DC)	202–927–1010
NEW YORK:			
New York, NY	6 World Trade Ctr., 10048	Anthony M. Liberta (RC)	212–466–4444
		Jean F. Maguire (AD)	212–466–5817
	Kennedy Airport, 11430	Thomas Mattina (AD)	718–553–1542
NORTH CENTRAL:			
Chicago, IL	55 E. Monroe St., 60603	Garnet Fee (RC)	312–353–4733
	610 S. Canal St., 60607	Richard Roster (DD)	312–353–6100
Cleveland, OH	55 Erie View Plz., 44114	John Regan (DD)	216–891–3800
Detroit, MI	477 Michigan Ave., 48226	William L. Morandini (DD)	313–226–3177
Duluth, MN	209 Federal Bldg., 55802	Barbara Lanbus (DD)	218–720–5201
Great Falls, MT	300 2d Ave. S., 59401	Eugene Kerven (DD)	406–453–7631
Milwaukee, WI	6269 Ace Industrial Dr., 53237	Valerie Torgerson (DD)	414–571–2860
Minneapolis, MN	110 S. 4th St., 55401	Peter Gonzalez (AD)	612–348–1690
Pembina, ND	Post Office Bldg., 58271	Raymond Hagerty, Jr. (DD).	701–825–6201
St. Louis, MO	7911 Forsyth Bldg., 63105	Theodore Galantowicz (DD).	314–428–2662
NORTHEAST:			
Baltimore, MD	40 S. Gay St., 21202	Carole Graves (DD)	410–962–2666
Boston, MA	10 Causeway St., 02222	Philip Spayd (RC)	617–565–6210
		(vacancy) (DD)	617–565–6147
Buffalo, NY	111 W. Huron St., 14202	Richard McMullen (DD)	716–846–4373
Ogdensburg, NY	127 N. Water St., 13669	William Dietzel (DD)	315–393–0660
Philadelphia, PA	2d & Chestnut Sts., 19106	William Luebkert (DD)	215–597–4606
Portland, ME	312 Fore St., 04112	Emery W. Ingalls (DD)	207–780–3326
Providence, RI	49 Pavilion Ave., 02905	Richard Barrette (DD)	401–528–5081
St. Albans, VT	Main & Stebbins Sts., 05478	Michael D'Ambrosio (DD) .	802–524–7352
SOUTH CENTRAL:			
Mobile, AL	150 N. Royal, 36602	(Vacancy) (DD)	334–441–6061
New Orleans, LA	423 Canal St., 70130	J. Robert Grimes (RC)	589–589–6324
		Joanne Comelison (DD)	504–589–6353
SOUTHEAST:			
Charleston, SC	200 E. Bay St., 29401	Mamie Pollock (DD)	803–727–4312
Charlotte, NC	1801–R Crossbeam Dr., 28217	John R. Babb (DD)	704–329–6100
Miami, FL	909 SE. 1st Ave., 33131	Robert McNamara, *Acting* (RC).	305–536–5952
	77 SE. 5th St., 33131	D. Lynn Gordon (DD)	305–869–2800
Norfolk, VA	101 E. Main St., 23510	Dennis H. Murphy (DD)	804–441–3400
St. Thomas, VI	U.S. Federal Bldg., Veterans Dr., 60801	Michael G. Murphy (DD)	809–774–2510
San Juan, PR	U.S. Customhouse (P.O. Box 2112), 00903.	Alphonso Robles (DD)	809–729–6950
Savannah, GA	1 E. Bay St., 31401	Robert Richter (DD)	912–652–4256
Tampa, FL	4430 E. Adams Dr., 33605	Diane Zwicker (DD)	813–228–2381
Washington, DC	P.O. Box 17423, 20041	William Green (DD)	703–318–5900

Regional Offices—U.S. Customs Service—Continued

(C: Commissioner; DC: Deputy Commissioner; RC: Regional Commissioner; DD: District Director; AD: Area Director)

Regional Headquarters/ District Offices	Address	Officer	Telephone
SOUTHWEST:			
Dallas/Fort Worth, TX	1205 Royal Ln., Dallas/Fort Worth Airport, 75261.	David Greenleaf (DD)	214–574–2170
El Paso, TX	Bridge of the Americas (P.O. Box 9516), 79985.	Gurdit Dhillon (DD)	915–540–5800
Houston, TX	5850 San Felipe St., 77057	Robert Trotter (RC)	713–942–6843
	1717 E. Loep, 77019	Patricia McCauley (DD)	713–671–1000
Laredo, TX	Lincoln-Juarez Bridge, 78044	Audrey Adams (DD)	210–726–2267
Nogales, AZ	International and Terrace Sts., 85621 ...	(Vacancy) (DD)	520–287–1410
Port Arthur, TX	4550 75th Ave., 77642	John Jumper (DD)	409–724–0087
PACIFIC:			
Anchorage, AK	605 W. 4th Ave., 99501	Dan Holland (DD)	907–271–2675
Columbia Snake, OR	511 NW. Broadway, 97209	Lois Fields (DD)	503–326–2865
Honolulu, HI	335 Merchant St., 96806	George Roberts (DD)	808–522–8060
Los Angeles, CA	Suite 705, 1 World Trade Ctr., Long Beach, CA 90831.	Rudy Camacho (RC)	310–980–3100
Los Angeles/Long Beach, CA	300 S. Ferry St., San Pedro, CA 90731	John Heinrich (DD)	310–514–6001
San Diego, CA	880 Front St., 92188	Rex Applegate (DD)	619–557–5455
San Francisco, CA	555 Battery St., 94718	Paul Andrews (DD)	415–744–7700
Seattle, WA	1000 2d Ave., 97104	Thomas Hardy (DD)	206–553–0554

For further information, contact the U.S. Customs Service, Department of the Treasury, 1301 Constitution Avenue NW., Washington, DC 20229. Phone, 202–927–2095.

Bureau of Engraving and Printing

The Bureau of Engraving and Printing operates on basic authorities conferred by act of July 11, 1862 (31 U.S.C. 303) and additional authorities contained in past appropriations made to the Bureau that are still in force.

A working capital fund was established in accordance with the provisions of section 2 of act of August 4, 1950, as amended (31 U.S.C. 5142), which placed the Bureau on a completely reimbursable basis. The Bureau is headed by a Director, who is appointed by the Secretary of the Treasury.

The Bureau of Engraving and Printing designs, prints, and finishes a large variety of security products including Federal Reserve notes, U.S. postage stamps, Treasury securities, identification cards, and certificates. It also is responsible for advising and assisting Federal agencies in the design and production of other government documents that, because of their innate value or some other reason, require security or counterfeit-deterrence characteristics.

The Bureau is the largest printer of security documents in the world; over 40 billion security documents are printed annually. The Bureau's headquarters is located in Washington, DC. A second currency plant, located in Fort Worth, TX, is operational and will have the capacity to produce approximately 5 billion notes annually by 1996.

For further information, contact the Office of Public Affairs, Bureau of Engraving and Printing, Department of the Treasury, Room 104–18M, Fourteenth and C Streets SW., Washington, DC 20228. Phone, 202–874–3019.

Federal Law Enforcement Training Center

The Federal Law Enforcement Training Center was established by Treasury Department Order No. 217, effective March 2, 1970; and reaffirmed by Treasury Department Order No. 140–01 of September 20, 1994.

The Federal Law Enforcement Training Center is headed by a Director, who is appointed by the Secretary of the Treasury. The Center conducts operations at its training facility located at Glynco, GA. The Center also maintains a Washington, DC, office at 650 Massachusetts Avenue NW., Washington, DC 20226. Phone, 202–927–8940. In addition, the Center has a satellite operation located at Artesia, NM 88210 (phone, 505–748–8000).

The Center is an interagency training facility serving over 70 Federal law enforcement organizations. The major training effort is in the area of basic programs to teach common areas of law enforcement skills to police and investigative personnel. The Center also conducts advanced programs in areas of common need, such as white-collar crime, the use of microcomputers as an investigative tool, advanced law enforcement photography, international banking/money laundering, marine law enforcement, and several instructor training courses. In addition to the basic and common advanced programs, the Center provides the facilities and support services for participating organizations to conduct advanced training for their own law enforcement personnel. The Center offers selective, highly specialized training programs to State and local officers as an aid in deterring crime. These programs include a variety of areas such as fraud and financial investigations, marine law enforcement, arson for profit, international banking/money laundering, and criminal intelligence analyst training.

The Center develops the curriculum content and training techniques for recruit training, and advises and assists the participating organizations in producing, formulating, and operating specialized training materials and equipment.

Administrative and financial activities are supervised by the Department of the Treasury. However, training policy, programs, criteria, and standards are governed by the interagency Board of Directors, comprised of senior officials from eight departments and independent agencies.

For further information, contact the Public Affairs Office, Federal Law Enforcement Training Center, Department of the Treasury, Glynco, GA 31524. Phone, 912–267–2447.

Financial Management Service

The mission of the Financial Management Service (FMS) is to improve the quality of Government financial management. Its commitment and responsibility is to help its Government customers achieve success. It does this by linking program and financial management objectives and by providing financial services, information, and advice to its customers. FMS serves taxpayers, the Treasury Department, Federal program agencies, and Government policymakers.

Working Capital Management The Service is responsible for programs to improve cash management, credit management, debt collection, and financial management systems Governmentwide. For cash management, the Service issues guidelines and regulations and assists other agencies in managing financial transactions to maximize investment earnings and reduce the interest costs of borrowed funds. For credit management, the Service issues guidelines and regulations and assists program agencies with management of credit activities, including loan programs, to improve all parts of the credit cycle, such as credit extension, loan servicing, debt collection, and write-off procedures. The Service is presently working with other agencies to improve financial management systems and the way Government handles its payments, collections, and receivables, and to take advantage of new automation technology.

Payments   The Service issues approximately 426 million Treasury checks and close to 407 million electronic fund transfer payments annually for Federal salaries and wages, payments to suppliers of goods and services to the Federal Government, income tax refunds, and payments under major Government programs such as social security and veterans' benefits. The Service pays all Treasury checks and reconciles them against the accounts of Government disbursing officers, receives and examines claims for checks that are cashed under forged endorsements or that are lost, stolen, or destroyed; and issues new checks on approved claims. The Service uses two electronic funds-transfer methods: the automated clearinghouses—for recurring payments such as Government benefits and salaries—and wire transfers through the Fedline System. The latter is a computer-to-computer link with the Federal Reserve System that allows for the electronic transfer of funds to virtually any financial institution in the United States.

Collections   The Service supervises the collection of Government receipts and

operates and maintains the systems for collecting these receipts. The Service is working with all Federal agencies to improve the availability of collected funds and the reporting of collection information to Treasury. Current collection systems include the Treasury General Account System, the Treasury Tax and Loan System for withholding and other Federal tax deposits, and the Treasury National Automated Lockbox System for accelerating the processing of agency receipts.

Central Accounting and Reporting   The Service maintains a central system that accounts for the monetary assets and liabilities of the Treasury and tracks Government collection and payment operations. Periodic reports are prepared to show budget results, the Government's overall financial status, and other financial operations. These reports include the *Daily Treasury Statement,* the *Monthly Treasury Statement,* the *Quarterly Treasury Bulletin,* the annual *Treasury Report,* and the annual *Treasury Consolidated Financial Statement.*

Disbursing Centers—Financial Management Service

Center/Address	Director
Austin, TX (1619 Woodward St., 78741)	Gordon Hickam
Birmingham, AL (190 Vulcan Rd., 35209)	Andy Wilson
Chicago, IL (356 S. Clark St., 60605)	Ollice C. Holden
Kansas City, KS (2100 W. 36th Ave., 66103)	John H. Adams
Philadelphia, PA (5000 Wissahickon Ave., 19144)	Michael Colerruso, *Acting*
San Francisco, CA (390 Main St., 94105)	Philip Belisle

For further information, contact the Office of Legislative and Public Affairs, Financial Management Service, Department of the Treasury, Room 555, 401 Fourteenth Street SW., Washington, DC 20227. Phone, 202–874–6740.

Internal Revenue Service

The Office of the Commissioner of Internal Revenue was established by act of July 1, 1862 (26 U.S.C. 7802).

The Internal Revenue Service is responsible for administering and enforcing the internal revenue laws and

in accordance with the tax laws and regulations;
—advises the public of their rights and responsibilities;
—determines the extent of compliance and the causes of noncompliance;
—properly administers and enforces the tax laws; and
—continually searches for and implements new, more efficient ways of accomplishing its mission.
Basic activities include:
—ensuring satisfactory resolution of taxpayer complaints, providing taxpayer service and education;
—determining, assessing, and collecting internal revenue taxes;
—determining pension plan qualifications and exempt organization status; and
—preparing and issuing rulings and regulations to supplement the provisions of the Internal Revenue Code.

The source of most revenues collected is the individual income tax and the social insurance and retirement taxes, with other major sources being the corporation income, excise, estate, and gift taxes. Congress first received authority to levy taxes on the income of individuals and corporations in 1913, pursuant to the 16th amendment of the Constitution.

Organization

Service organization is designed for maximum decentralization, consistent with the need for uniform interpretation of the tax laws and efficient utilization of resources. There are three organizational levels: the National Office; the Regional Offices; and the District Offices, Service Centers, and the Austin Compliance Center (in the Southwest Region). Districts may have local offices, the number and location of which are determined by taxpayer and agency needs.

Headquarters Organization The National Office, located in Washington, DC, develops nationwide policies and programs for the administration of the internal revenue laws and provides overall direction to the field organization. The Martinsburg Computing Center in Martinsburg, WV, and the Detroit Computing Center in Detroit, MI, also are assigned to the National Office.

Field Organization

As a decentralized organization, most agency personnel and activities are assigned to field installations.
Regional Offices There are seven Regional Offices, each headed by a Regional Commissioner, which supervise and evaluate the operations of District Offices, Service Centers, and the Austin Compliance Center.

Regional Offices—Internal Revenue Service

Region	Address	Commissioner
CENTRAL—Indiana, Kentucky, Michigan, Ohio, West Virginia	550 Main St., Cincinnati, OH 45202	Leon Moore
MID–ATLANTIC—Delaware, Maryland, New Jersey, Pennsylvania, Virginia	841 Chestnut St., Philadelphia, PA 19107	Charles H. Brennan
MIDWEST—Illinois, Iowa, Minnesota, Missouri, Montana, Nebraska, North Dakota, South Dakota, Wisconsin	Gateway IV Bldg., 300 S. Riverside Plz., Chicago, IL 60606	David Blattner
NORTH ATLANTIC—Connecticut, Maine, Massachusetts, New Hampshire, New York, Rhode Island, Vermont	90 Church St., New York, NY 10007	Herma Hightower
SOUTHEAST—Alabama, Arkansas, Georgia, Florida, Louisiana, Mississippi, North Carolina, South Carolina, Tennessee	401 W Peachtree St NE, Atlanta, GA 30365	John D Johnson
SOUTHWEST—Arizona, Colorado, Kansas, New Mexico, Oklahoma, Texas, Utah, Wyoming	4050 Alpha Rd., Dallas, TX 75244–4203	Richard C. Voskuil
WESTERN—Alaska, California, Hawaii, Idaho, Nevada, Oregon, Washington	1650 Mission St., San Francisco, CA 94103	Thomas Coleman

District Offices   There are 62 Internal Revenue districts, each administered by a District Director. Districts may encompass an entire State, or a certain number of counties within a State, depending on population. Programs of the District include taxpayer service, examination, collection, criminal investigation, resources management, and, in some districts, pension plans and exempt organizations. Functions performed are: assistance and service to taxpayers, determination of tax liability by examination of tax returns, determination of pension plan

qualification, collection of delinquent returns and taxes, and investigation of criminal and civil violations of internal revenue laws (except those relating to alcohol, tobacco, firearms, and explosives). Directors are responsible for the deposit of taxes collected by the District and for initial processing of original applications for admission to practice before the Internal Revenue Service and renewal issuances for those practitioners already enrolled. Local offices may be established to meet taxpayer needs and agency workload requirements.

Internal Revenue Districts—Internal Revenue Service

District	Address	Director
ALABAMA	500 22d St. S., Birmingham, 35233	Richard F. Moran
ALASKA	949 E. 36th Ave., Anchorage, 99508	Michael R. Allen
ARIZONA	210 E. Earl Dr., Phoenix, 85012	Mark Cox
ARKANSAS	700 W. Capitol Ave., Little Rock, 72201	James Donelson
CALIFORNIA:		
Laguna Niguel	24000 Avila Rd., 92677	Jesse Cota
Los Angeles	300 N. Los Angeles St., 90012	Richard Orosco
Sacramento	4330 Watt Ave., North Highland, CA 95660	Gerald F. Swanson
San Francisco	Suite 16005, 1301 Clay St., Oakland, 94612	Calvin Esselstrom
San Jose	55 S. Market St., 95113	Billy J. Brown
COLORADO	600 17th St., Denver, 80202	Walter A. Hutton, Jr.
CONNECTICUT	135 High St., Hartford, 06103	James E. Quinn
DELAWARE	409 Silverside Rd., Wilmington, 19809	John F. Devlin
DISTRICT OF COLUMBIA	(part of Baltimore District)	
FLORIDA:		
Fort Lauderdale	3d Fl., Bldg. B, 1 University Dr., 33324	Merlin W. Heye
Jacksonville	400 W. Bay St., 32202	Dale Hart
GEORGIA	401 W. Peachtree St., Atlanta, 30365	Nelson A. Brooke
HAWAII	300 Ala Moana Blvd., Honolulu, 96850	Robert Ah Nee
IDAHO	550 W. Fort St., Boise, 83724	Jerald Heschel
ILLINOIS:		
Chicago	230 S. Dearborn St., 60604	Marilyn Day
Springfield	320 W. Washington St., 62701	John Wendorff
INDIANA	575 N. Pennsylvania St., Indianapolis, 46204	David B. Palmer
IOWA	210 Walnut St., Des Moines, 50309	Stephen J. Stalcup
KANSAS	271 W. 3d St. N., Wichita, 67232	Bruce R. Thomas
KENTUCKY	601 W. Broadway, Louisville, 40202	Alvin Kolak
LOUISIANA	600 S. Maestri Pl., New Orleans, 70130	Thomas Grace
MAINE	68 Sewall St., Augusta, 04330	Ray F. Howard
MARYLAND	31 Hopkins Plz., Baltimore, 21201	Paul Harrington
MASSACHUSETTS	John F. Kennedy Federal Bldg., Boston, 02203	Francine Crowley
MICHIGAN	477 Michigan Ave., Detroit, 48226	Arlene G. Kay
MINNESOTA	316 N. Robert St., St. Paul, 55101	Inar Morics
MISSISSIPPI	100 W. Capitol St., Jackson, 39269	Robert Douthitt
MISSOURI	1222 Spruce St., St. Louis, 63101	Ronald Lamert
MONTANA	301 S. Park Ave., Helena, 59626	Thomas Kuniz
NEBRASKA	106 S. 15th St., Omaha, 68102	James A. Grant
NEVADA	4750 W. Oakey Blvd., Las Vegas, 89102	Brian McMahon
NEW HAMPSHIRE	80 Daniel St., Portsmouth, 03801	James Helm
NEW JERSEY	970 Broad St., Newark, 07102	John J. Jennings
NEW MEXICO	538 Montgomery NE., Albuquerque, 87109	Bernard Barela
NEW YORK:		
Albany	Clinton Ave. and N. Pearl St., 12207	Joseph Rusek
Brooklyn	625 Fulton St., 11201	Herbert Huff
Buffalo	111 W. Huron St., 14202	Steven Jenson
Manhattan	120 Church St., New York, 10007	Eugene Alexander
NORTH CAROLINA	320 Federal Pl., Greensboro, 27401	J.R. Starkey
NORTH DAKOTA	653 2d Ave. N., Fargo, 58102	Thomas L. Eastwood
OHIO:		
Cincinnati	550 Main St., 45202	C. Ashley Bullard
Cleveland	1240 E. 9th St., 44199	Henry O. Lamar, Jr.
OKLAHOMA	55 N. Robinson St., Oklahoma City, 73102	Kenneth J. Sawyer
OREGON	1220 SW. 3d Ave., Portland, 97204	Carolyn Leonard

Internal Revenue Districts—Internal Revenue Service—Continued

District	Address	Director
PENNSYLVANIA:		
Philadelphia	600 Arch St., 19106	Richard McCleary
Pittsburgh	1000 Liberty Ave., 15222	Deborah S. Decker
PUERTO RICO	Stop 27½, Ponce de Leon Ave., Hato Rey, 00917	Ramon Rivera [1]
RHODE ISLAND	380 Westminster Mall, Providence, 02903	William Caine
SOUTH CAROLINA	1835 Assembly St., Columbia, 29201	Donald L. Breihan
SOUTH DAKOTA	115 4th Ave. SE., Aberdeen, 57401	Barbara Olberding
TENNESSEE	801 Broadway, Nashville, 37203	John C. Stocker
TEXAS:		
Austin	300 E. 8th St., 78701	Jean K. Pope
Dallas	1100 Commerce St., 75242	Bobby Scott
Houston	1919 Smith St., 77002	James Kopidlansky
UTAH	465 S. 4th East, Salt Lake City, 84111	Carol M. Fay
VERMONT	199 Main St., Burlington, 05402	Michael M. Greenspan
VIRGINIA	400 N. 8th St., Richmond, 23240	Maggie Lullo
WASHINGTON	915 2d Ave., Seattle, 98174	J. Paul Beene
WEST VIRGINIA	425 Juliana St., Parkersburg, 26101	Edward J. Weiler
WISCONSIN	310 W. Wisconsin Ave., Milwaukee, 53203	John Ader
WYOMING	308 W. 21st St., Cheyenne, 82001	Stephen Taylor

Overseas Taxpayers

Office	Address
DISTRICT OF COLUMBIA	Office of Taxpayer Service and Compliance, 950 L'Enfant Plaza SW. (IN:C), 20024

[1] Director's Representative

Service Centers   Under the supervision of the Regional Commissioner having jurisdiction over the area of their location are 10 service centers, located at Andover, MA; Austin, TX; Brookhaven, NY; Chamblee, GA; Covington, KY; Fresno, CA; Kansas City, MO; Memphis, TN; Ogden, UT; and Philadelphia, PA. Each service center processes tax returns and related documents and maintains accountability records for taxes collected. Programs include the processing, verification, and accounting control of tax returns; the assessment and certification of refunds of taxes; and administering assigned examination, criminal investigation, and collection functions.

The Austin Compliance Center, located in Austin, TX, administers the examination, criminal investigation, and collection functions formerly assigned to the Austin Service Center.

For further information, contact any District Office or the Internal Revenue Service Headquarters, Department of the Treasury, 1111 Constitution Avenue NW., Washington, DC 20224. Phone, 202–622–5000.

United States Mint

The establishment of a mint was authorized by act of April 2, 1792 (1 Stat. 246). The Bureau of the Mint was established by act of February 12, 1873 (17 Stat. 424) and recodified on September 13, 1982 (31 U.S.C. 304, 5131). The name was changed to United States Mint by Secretarial order dated January 9, 1984.

The primary mission of the Mint is to produce an adequate volume of circulating coinage for the Nation to conduct its trade and commerce. The Mint also produces and sells numismatic coins, American Eagle gold and silver bullion coins, and national medals. Further, the Fort Knox Bullion Depository is the storage facility for the Nation's gold bullion.

The U.S. Mint maintains sales centers at the Philadelphia and Denver Mints, and at Union Station in Washington,

DC. Public tours are conducted, with free admission, at the Philadelphia and Denver Mints.

Field Facilities
(S: Superintendent; O: Officer in Charge)

Facility/Address	Facility Head
United States Mint, Philadelphia, PA 19106	Augustine A. Albino, *Acting* (S)
United States Mint, Denver, CO 80204	Raymond J. DeBroekert, *Acting* (S)
United States Mint, San Francisco, CA 94102 and the Old Mint, San Francisco, CA 94103	Donald T. Butler, *Acting* (S)
United States Mint, West Point, NY 10996	Harry J. Edwards, *Acting* (S)
United States Bullion Depository, Fort Knox, KY 40121	James M. Curtis (O)

For further information, contact the United States Mint, Department of the Treasury, Judiciary Square Building, 633 Third Street NW., Washington, DC 20220. Phone, 202–874–6450.

Bureau of the Public Debt

The Bureau of the Public Debt was established on June 30, 1940, pursuant to the Reorganization Act of 1939 (31 U.S.C. 306).

Its mission is to borrow the money needed to operate the Federal Government; account for the resulting public debt; and to issue Treasury securities to refund maturing debt and raise new money.

The Bureau fulfills its mission through six programs: commercial book-entry securities, direct access securities, savings securities, Government securities, market regulation, and public debt accounting.

The Bureau auctions and issues Treasury bills, notes, and bonds and manages the U.S. Savings Bond Program. It issues, services, and redeems bonds through a nationwide network of issuing and paying agents. The Bureau also promotes the sale and retention of savings bonds through payroll savings plans and financial institutions and is supported by a network of volunteers. It provides daily and other periodic reports to account for the composition and size of the debt. In addition, the Bureau implements the regulations for the Government securities market. These regulations provide for investor protection while maintaining a fair and liquid market for Government securities.

The Bureau of the Public Debt was established on June 30, 1940, pursuant to the Reorganization Act of 1939 (31 U.S.C. 306). Principal offices of the Bureau are located in Washington, DC, and Parkersburg, WV.

For more information, contact the Public Affairs Officer, Office of the Commissioner, Bureau of the Public Debt, Washington, DC 20239–0001. Phone, 202–219–3302.

United States Secret Service

Pursuant to certain sections of titles 3 and 18 of the United States Code, the mission of the Secret Service includes the authority and responsibility:
—to protect the President, the Vice President, the President-elect, the Vice-President-elect, and members of their immediate families; major Presidential and Vice Presidential candidates; former Presidents and their spouses, except that protection of a spouse shall terminate in the event of remarriage; minor children

of a former President until the age of 16; visiting heads of foreign states or governments; other distinguished foreign visitors to the United States; and official representatives of the United States performing special missions abroad, as directed by the President;

—to provide security at the White House complex and other Presidential offices, the temporary official residence of the Vice President in the District of Columbia, and foreign diplomatic missions in the Washington, DC, metropolitan area and throughout the United States, its territories and possessions, as prescribed by statute;

—to detect and arrest any person committing any offense against the laws of the United States relating to currency,

coins, obligations, and securities of the United States or of foreign governments;

—to suppress the forgery and fraudulent negotiation or redemption of Federal Government checks, bonds, and other obligations or securities of the United States;

—to conduct investigations relating to certain criminal violations of the Federal Deposit Insurance Act, the Federal Land Bank Act, and the Government Losses in Shipment Act; and

—to detect and arrest offenders of laws pertaining to electronic funds transfer frauds, credit and debit card frauds, false identification documents or devices, computer access fraud, and U.S. Department of Agriculture food coupons, including authority to participate cards.

District Offices—United States Secret Service

District	Address	Telephone
Albany GA	Suite 221, 235 Roosevelt Ave., 31701–2374	518–431–0205
Albany, NY	Rm. 244, 445 Broadway, 12207	518–472–2884
Albuquerque, NM	Suite 1700, 505 Marquette St. NW., 87102	505–766–3336
Anchorage, AK	Rm. 526, 222 W. 7th Ave., 99513–7592	907–271–5148
Atlanta, GA	Suite 2906, 401 W. Peachtree St., 30308–3516	404–331–6111
Atlantic City, NJ	Rm. 200, 1701 Pacific Ave., 08401	609–347–0772
Austin, TX	Suite 972, 300 E. 8th St., 78701	512–482–5103
Bakersfield, CA	Suite 190, 5701 Truxton Ave., 93309	805–861–4112
Baltimore, MD	Suite 1124, 100 S. Charles St., 21201	410–962–2200
Baton Rouge, LA	Rm. 1502, 1 American Pl., 70825	504–389–0763
Birmingham, AL	Suite 203, 500 S. 22d St., 35233	205–731–1144
Bismarck, ND	Rm. 432, Federal Bldg., 58501	701–255–3294
Boise, ID	Rm. 730, 550 W. Fort St., 83724	208–334–1403
Boston, MA	Suite 791, 10 Causeway St., 02222	617–565–5640
Buffalo, NY	Rm. 1208, 111 W. Huron St., 14202	716–846–4401
Canton, OH	Rm. 211, 201 Cleveland Ave. SW., 44702	216–489–4400
Charleston, SC	Suite 630, 334 Meeting St., 29403	803–727–4691
Charleston, WV	Suite 910, 1 Valley Sq., 25301	304–347–5188
Charlotte, NC	Suite 226, Parkwood Bldg., 4350 Park Rd., 28209	704–523–9583
Chattanooga, TN	Rm. 204, Martin Luther King Blvd. and Georgia Ave., 37401	615–752–5125
Cheyenne, WY	Suite 3026, 2120 Capitol Ave., 82001	307–772–2380
Chicago, IL	Suite 1200 N., 300 S. Riverside Plz., 60606	312–353–5431
Cincinnati, OH	Rm. 6118, 550 Main St., 45202	513–684–3585
Cleveland, OH	Rm. 440, 6100 Rockside Woods Blvd., 44131–2334	216–522–4365
Colorado Springs, CO	P.O. Box 666, 80901	719–632–3325
Columbia, SC	Suite 1425, Strom Thurmond Federal Bldg., 1835 Assembly St., 29201 ..	803–765–5446
Columbus, OH	Suite 800, 500 S. Front St., 43215	614–469–7370
Concord, NH	Suite 250, 197 Loudon Rd., 03301	603–228–3428
Dallas, TX	Suite 300, Caltex House, 125 E. John W. Carpenter Fwy., Irving, TX 75062–2752.	214–655–2500
Dayton, OH	P.O. Box 743, 200 W. 2d St., 45402	513–222–2013
Denver, CO	Suite 1430, 1660 Lincoln St., 80264	303–866–1010
Des Moines, IA	637 Federal Bldg., 210 Walnut St., 50309	515–284–4565
Detroit, MI	Suite 1000, Patrick V. McNamara Bldg., 477 Michigan Ave. 48226	313 226 6100
El Paso, TX	Suite 210, 4849 N. Mesa, 79912	915–533–6950
Fresno, CA	Suite 207, 5200 N. Palm Ave., 93704	209–487–5204
Grand Rapids, MI	Rm. 326, 110 Michigan Ave. NW., 49503	616–456–2276
Great Falls, MT	No. 11, 3d St. N., 59401	406–452–8515
Greenville, SC	P.O. Box 10676, 29603	803–233–1490
Harrisburg, PA	P.O. Box 1244, 17108	717–782–4811
Honolulu, HI	P.O. Box 50046, Rm. 6309, 300 Ala Moana Blvd., 96850	808–541–1912
Houston, TX	Suite 500, 602 Sawyer St., 77007	713–868–2299
Indianapolis, IN	Suite 211, 575 N. Pennsylvania St., 46204	317–226–6444
Jackson, MS	Suite 840, 100 W. Capitol St., 39269	601–965–4436
Jacksonville, FL	Suite 500, 7820 Arlington Expy., 32211	904–232–2777
Jamaica, NY	2d Fl., Bldg. 80, John F. Kennedy International Airport, 11430	718–553–0911
Kansas City, MO	Suite 510, 1150 Grand Ave., 64106	816–374–6102

District Offices—United States Secret Service—Continued

District	Address	Telephone
Knoxville, TN	Rm. 517, 710 Locust St., 37902	615–545–4627
Las Vegas, NV	P.O. Box 16027, 89101	702–388–6446
Lexington, KY	P.O. Box 13310, 40583	606–233–2453
Little Rock, AR	Suite 1700, 111 Center St., 72201–3529	501–324–6241
Los Angeles, CA	17th Fl., Roybal Federal Bldg., 255 E. Temple St., 90012	213–894–4830
Louisville, KY	Rm. 377, 600 Dr. Martin Luther King, Jr., Pl., 40202	502–582–5171
Lubbock, TX	P.O. Box 2975, 79048	806–743–7347
Madison, WI	P.O. Box 2154, 53701	608–264–5191
McAllen, TX	Suite 1107, 200 S. 10th St., 78501	210–630–5811
Melville, NY	Suite 216E, 35 Pinelawn Rd., 11747–3154	516–249–0984
Memphis, TN	Suite 204, 5350 Poplar Ave., 38119	901–766–7632
Miami, FL	Suite 100, 8375 NW. 53d St., 33166	305–591–3660
Milwaukee, WI	Rm. 572, 517 E. Wisconsin Ave., 53202	414–297–3587
Minneapolis, MN	Rm. 218, 110 S. 4th St., 55401	612–348–1800
Mobile, AL	Suite 200, 182d and Francis Sts., 36602–3501	205–441–5851
Montgomery, AL	Suite 605, 1 Commerce St., 36104	205–223–7601
Morristown, NJ	34 Headquarters Plz., 07960–3990	201–645–2334
Nashville, TN	658 U.S. Courthouse, 801 Broadway St., 37203	615–736–5841
New Haven, CT	P.O. Box 45, 06501	203–865–2449
New Orleans, LA	Rm. 807, 501 Magazine St., 70130	504–589–4041
New York, NY	9th Fl., 7 World Trade Ctr., New York City, 10048–1901	212–637–4500
Norfolk, VA	Rm. 400, Federal Bldg., 23510	804–441–3200
Oklahoma City, OK	Suite 926, 200 NW. 5th St., 73102	405–231–4476
Omaha, NE	Rm. 905, Old Federal Bldg., 106 S. 15th St., 68102	402–221–4671
Orlando, FL	Suite 670, 135 W. Central Blvd., 32801	407–648–6333
Philadelphia, PA	7236 Federal Bldg., 600 Arch St., 19106	215–597–0600
Phoenix, AZ	Suite 2180, 3200 N. Central Ave., 85012	602–640–5580
Pittsburgh, PA	Rm. 835, 1000 Liberty Ave., 15222	412–644–3384
Portland, ME	2d Fl., Tower B, 100 Middle St., 04104	207–780–3493
Portland, OR	Suite 1330, 121 SW. Salmon St., 97204	503–326–2162
Providence, RI	Suite 343, 380 Westminster St., 02903	401–331–6456
Raleigh, NC	Suite 210, 4407 Bland Rd., 27609–6296	919–790–2834
Reno, NV	Suite 850, 100 W. Liberty St., 89501	702–784–5354
Richmond, VA	Suite 1910, Main St. Ctr., 23219	804–771–2274
Riverside, CA	P.O. Box 1525, 92502	909–276–6781
Roanoke, VA	Suite 2, 105 Franklin Rd. SW., 24011	703–857–2208
Rochester, NY	Rm. 606, 100 State St., 14614	716–263–6830
Sacramento, CA	Suite 530, 501 J St., 95814	916–498–5141
Saginaw, MI	Suite 200, 301 E. Genesee Ave., Saginaw, MI 48607	517–752–8076
St. Louis, MO	Rm. 924, 1114 Market St., 63101	314–539–2238
Salt Lake City, UT	Suite 450, American Plz. II, 57 W. 200 S., 84101	801–524–5910
San Antonio, TX	Rm. B410, 727 E. Durango Blvd., 78206	210–229–6175
San Diego, CA	Suite 660, 550 W. C St., 92101–8811	619–557–5640
San Francisco, CA	Suite 530, 345 Spear St., 94105	415–744–9026
San Jose, CA	Suite 2050, 280 S. 1st St., 95113	408–291–7233
San Juan, PR	Rm. 539, Carlos E. Chardon Ave., Hato Rey, PR 00917–1717	809–766–5539
Santa Ana, CA	Suite 500, 200 W. Santa Ana Blvd., 92701	714–836–2805
Savannah, GA	Suite 570, 23 Bull St., 31401	912–652–4401
Scranton, PA	Rm. 304, Washington and Linden Sts., 18501	717–346–5781
Seattle, WA	Rm. 890, 915 2d Ave., 98174	206–220–6800
Shreveport, LA	Suite 525, 401 Edwards St., 71101	318–676–3500
Sioux Falls, SD	Suite 405, 230 S. Phillips Ave., 57102	605–330–4565
Spokane, WA	Suite 1340, 601 W. Riverside Ave., 99201–0611	509–353–2532
Springfield, IL	Suite 301, 400 W. Monroe St., 62704	217–492–4033
Springfield, MO	Suite 306, 901 E. St. Louis St., 65806	417–864–8340
Syracuse, NY	Post Box 7006, Federal Station, 13261	315–448–0304
Tampa, FL	Rm. 1101, 501 E. Polk St., 33602	813–228–2636
Toledo, OH	Rm. 305, 234 Summit St., 43604	419–259–6434
Trenton, NJ	Suite 202, 101 Carnegie Ctr., Princeton, NJ, 08540–6231	609–989–2008
Tucson, AZ	Box FB–56, 300 W. Congress St., 85701	520–670–4730
Tulsa, OK	Suite 400, 125 W. 15 St., 74119	918–581–7272
Tyler, TX	Suite 395, 6101 S. Broadway, 75703	903–534–2933
Ventura, CA	Suite 161, 5500 Telegraph Rd., 93003	805–339–9180
Washington, DC	Suite 1000, 1050 Connecticut Ave. NW., 20036–5305	202–435–5100
West Palm Beach, FL	Suite 800, 505 S. Flagler Dr., 33401	407–659–0184
White Plains, NY	Suite 300, 140 Grand St., 10601	914–682–6300
Wichita, KS	Rm. 225, 225 N. Market, 67202	316–267–1452
Wilmington, DE	Rm. 414, 920 King St., 19801	302–573–6188
Wilmington, NC	P.O. Box 120, 28402	910–343–4411

District Offices Overseas—United States Secret Service

District	Address	Telephone
Bangkok, Thailand	American Embassy, Box 64/Bangkok, APO AP 96546	011–662–252–5040, ext. 2651

District Offices Overseas—United States Secret Service—Continued

District	Address	Telephone
Bonn, West Germany .	American Embassy/Bonn, Unit 21701, Box 300, APO New York, NY 09080.	011–49–228–339–2587
London, England	American Embassy/USSS, PSC 801, Box 64, FPO AE, 09498–4064.	011–44–71–499–9000, ext. 2846
Manila, Philippines	American Embassy/Manila APO AP 96440	011–632–521–1838
Paris, France	Paris Embassy/USSS, Unit 21551, Box D306, APO AE, 09777.	9–011–331–4289–0330
Rome, Italy	American Embassy/Rome, PSC 59, Box 100, USSS, APO AE, 09624.	011–39–6–4674–1, ext. 2736

For further information, contact any District Office or the Office of Government Liaison and Public Affairs, United States Secret Service, Department of the Treasury, 1800 G Street NW., Washington, DC 20223. Phone, 202–435–5708.

Office of Thrift Supervision

The Office of Thrift Supervision (OTS) was established as a bureau of the Treasury Department in August 1989 and became operational in October 1989 as part of a major reorganization of the thrift regulatory structure mandated by the Financial Institutions Reform, Recovery and Enforcement Act. In that act, Congress gave OTS authority to charter Federal thrift institutions and serve as the primary regulator of approximately 1,700 Federal- and State-chartered thrifts belonging to the Savings Association Insurance Fund (SAIF). OTS' mission is to regulate savings associations to maintain the safety, soundness, and viability of the industry; and to support the industry's efforts to meet housing and other financial services needs. OTS carries out this responsibility through risk-focused supervision that includes adopting regulations governing the savings and loan industry, examining and supervising thrift institutions and their affiliates, and taking appropriate action to enforce their compliance with Federal law and regulations. In addition to overseeing thrift institutions, OTS also regulates, examines, and supervises companies that own thrifts and controls the acquisition of thrifts by such holding companies.

OTS is headed by a Director appointed by the President and confirmed by the Senate to serve a 5-year term. The Director also serves on the boards of the Federal Deposit Insurance Corporation, the Resolution Trust Corporation, the Thrift Depositor Protection Oversight Board, and the Neighborhood Reinvestment Corporation.

To carry out its mission, OTS is organized into five main divisions:

Washington Operations develops national policy guidelines to clarify and implement statutes and regulations; establishes programs to implement new policies and laws; and develops and maintains surveillance systems that monitor the condition of the industry and assist in identifying emerging supervisory problem areas. It also develops and maintains financial management and information systems; maintains human resources programs; and performs other related functions.

Regional Operations examines and supervises thrift institutions through five regional offices to ensure the safety and soundness of the industry, and to promote housing and other financial services in areas with the greatest need. It also oversees the training and development of Federal thrift regulators through accredited programs. The regional offices are headquartered in Jersey City, NJ; Atlanta, GA; Chicago, IL; Dallas, TX; and San Francisco, CA.

Chief Counsel provides a full range of legal services to the agency, including drafting regulations, representing the agency in court, and taking enforcement actions against savings institutions that violate laws or regulations. This office also acts on corporate filings required by the Securities and Exchange Act of 1934.

Congressional Affairs interacts with members of Congress, congressional staff, and committee members on behalf of OTS to accomplish the legislative objectives of the Office. This division disseminates information to the Congress pertaining to OTS' supervisory, regulatory, and enforcement activities and policies, and manages congressional-liaison programs.

Public Affairs oversees dissemination of information concerning OTS regulations, policies, and key developments within the Office by establishing and maintaining effective liaisons with the media, the general public, the thrift industry, Government agencies, and other key constituencies. It convenes press conferences and distributes news releases.

The division also maintains an archive of business records and documented actions of OTS and its predecessor, the Federal Home Loan Bank Board; responds to Freedom of Information requests; and maintains a public reference room for viewing securities filing and other public documents.

OTS is a nonappropriated agency and, thus, uses no tax money to fund its operations. Its expenses are met by fees and assessments on the thrift institutions it regulates.

For further information, contact the Communications Division, Office of Thrift Supervision, 1700 G Street NW., Washington, DC 20552. Phone, 202–906–6913.

Sources of Information

Departmental Offices

Contracts Write to the Director, Office of Procurement, Room 6101, Main Treasury Annex, Washington, DC 20220. Phone, 202–622–0520.

Environment Environmental statements prepared by the Department are available for review in the Departmental Library. Information on Treasury environmental matters may be obtained from the Office of the Assistant Secretary of the Treasury (Management), Treasury Department, Washington, DC 20220. Phone, 202–622–0043.

General Inquiries For general information about the Treasury Department, including copies of news releases and texts of speeches by high Treasury officials, write to the Office of the Assistant Secretary (Public Affairs and Public Liaison), Room 3430, Departmental Offices, Treasury Department, Washington, DC 20220. Phone, 202–622–2920.

Reading Room The Reading Room is located in the Treasury Library, Room 5030, Main Treasury Building, 1500 Pennsylvania Avenue NW., Washington, DC 20220. Phone, 202–622–0990.

Small and Disadvantaged Business Activities Write to the Director, Office of Small and Disadvantaged Business Utilization, Room 6101, Main Treasury Annex, Washington, DC 20220. Phone, 202–622–0530.

Tax Legislation Information on tax legislation may be obtained from the Assistant Secretary (Tax Policy), Departmental Offices, Treasury Department, Washington, DC 20220. Phone, 202–622–0050.

Telephone Directory The Treasury Department telephone directory is available for sale by the Superintendent of Documents, Government Printing Office, Washington, DC 20402.

Office of Inspector General

Employment Contact the Human Resources Division, Office of Inspector General, Room 7116, 1201 Constitution Avenue NW., Washington, DC 20220. Phone, 202–927–5230.

Freedom of Information Act/Privacy Act Requests Inquiries should be directed to Freedom of Information Act Request, Department of the Treasury, Room 1054, 1500 Pennsylvania Avenue NW., Washington, DC 20220.

General Inquiries   Write to the Office of Inspector General, 1500 Pennsylvania Avenue NW., Washington, DC 20220.

Publications   Semiannual reports to the Congress on the Office of Inspector General are available from the Office of Inspector General, 1500 Pennsylvania Avenue NW., Washington, DC 20220.

Office of the Comptroller of the Currency

Publications   Write or call the Communications Division, 250 E Street SW., Washington, DC 20219. Phone, 202–874–4700; or fax, 202–874–5263.

Freedom of Information Act Requests Write or call the disclosure officer, Communications Division, 250 E Street SW., Washington, DC 20219. Phone, 202–874–4700; or fax, 202–874–5263.

Employment   The primary occupation is national bank examiner. Examiners are hired generally at the entry level through a college recruitment program. Descriptive literature and information are available from the Director for Human Resources, 250 E Street SW., Washington, DC 20219. Phone, 202–874–5000; or fax, 202–874–5447.

Contracts   Contact the procurement officer at 250 E Street SW., Washington, DC 20219. Phone, 202–874–5000; or fax, 202–874–5625.

United States Customs Service

Address inquiries on the following subjects to the specified office, U.S. Customs Service, 1301 Constitution Avenue NW., Washington, DC 20229. Phone, 202–927–2095.

Contracts   Write to the National Logistics Center, 6026 Lakeside Boulevard, Indianapolis, IN 46278.

Employment   The U.S. Customs Service recruits from the Treasury Enforcement Agent examination. Employment inquiries may be addressed to the Director, Office of Human Resources in Washington, DC.

Forms   Available from any district director's office. (There is a nominal charge for large quantities of certain forms.)

General Inquiries   Contact the nearest district director's office for information

regarding customs regulations and procedures for all persons entering the United States and the entry and clearance of imported merchandise.

Publications   The U.S. Customs Service issues publications of interest to the general, importing, and traveling public that can be obtained from any of the District Directors' offices, or by writing to the Public Services and Information Materials Division in Washington, DC. Single copies of many of these publications are available at no charge to the public.

Reading Rooms   Located at the headquarters library and in each of the seven regional offices.

Speakers   Speakers are available for private organizations or community groups throughout the country. Contact any local customs officer or the Public Affairs Office in Washington, DC.

Bureau of Engraving and Printing

Address inquiries on the following subjects to the specified office, Bureau of Engraving and Printing, Fourteenth and C Streets SW., Washington, DC 20228.

Contracts and Small Business Activities Information relating to contracts and small business activity may be obtained by contacting the Office of Procurement. Phone, 202–874–2534.

Employment   The Bureau, as the world's largest security printer, employs personnel in a multitude of different craft, administrative, and professional fields. Competitive job opportunities may be available in the printing crafts, maintenance trades/crafts, engineering, electro-machinists, research, chemistry, data processing/computers, quality assurance, personnel, procurement, financial management, and other administrative fields. Due to the high level of security required, the Bureau also employs its own police force and a range of security specialists.

The Bureau participates in co-op and stay-in-school programs that enable students to gain work experience while pursuing their education. Periodically, apprenticeship programs may be announced in selected crafts.

Information regarding employment opportunities and required qualifications is available from the Staffing and Classification Division, Office of Personnel. Phone, 202–874–3747.

Freedom of Information Act Requests Inquiries should be directed to the Bureau Disclosure Officer, Office of Management Services, Room 321–12A. Phone, 202–874–2687.

General Inquiries Requests for information about the Bureau, its products, or numismatic and philatelic interests should be addressed to the Office of Communications, Room 109M. Phone, 202–874–3019.

Product Sales Uncut sheets of currency, engraved Presidential portraits, historical engravings of national landmarks, and other similar products are available for purchase in the Visitors' Center or through the mail. The Visitors' Center sales area, located in the Fifteenth Street Lobby of the main building, is open from 8:30 a.m. to 3:30 p.m. on the same days as tours. Information and order forms for sales items may be obtained by writing to the Office of Communications, Room 109M, or by calling 202–874–3019.

Financial Management Service

Inquiries on the following subjects should be directed to the specified office, 401 Fourteenth Street SW., Washington, DC 20227.

Contracts Write to the Director, Acquisition Management Division, Room 112 LC. Phone, 202–874–6910.

Employment Inquiries may be directed to the Personnel Management Division, Room 120 LC. Phone, 202–874–7080.

Fax Facsimile transmittal services are available by dialing 202–874–6743.

Internal Revenue Service

Audiovisual Materials Films, some of which are available in Spanish, provide information on the American tax system, examination and appeal rights, and the tax responsibilities of running a small business. The films can be obtained by contacting any District Office.

Also available are audio and video cassette tapes that provide step-by-step

instructions for preparing basic individual income tax forms. These tapes are available in many local libraries.

Contracts Write to Internal Revenue Service, 1111 Constitution Avenue NW. (HR: C), Washington, DC 20224 (phone, 202–535–4804); or Chief, Facilities Management Branch, at any of the Internal Revenue regional offices.

Educational Programs The Service provides, free of charge, general tax information publications and booklets on specific tax topics. Taxpayer information materials also are distributed to major television networks and many radio and television stations, daily and weekly newspapers, magazines, and specialized publications. Special educational materials and films are provided for use in high schools and colleges. Individuals starting a new business are given specialized materials and information at small business workshops, and community colleges provide classes based on material provided by the Service. The Community Outreach Tax Assistance program provides agency employees to assist community groups at mutually convenient times and locations.

Through the Volunteer Income Tax Assistance program and the Tax Counseling for the Elderly program, the Service recruits, trains, and supports volunteers who offer free tax assistance to low-income, elderly, military, and non-English-speaking taxpayers.

Materials, films, and information on the educational programs can be obtained by contacting any District Office.

Employment Almost every major field of study has some application to the work of the Service. A substantial number of positions are filled by persons whose major educational preparation was accounting, business administration, finance, economics, criminology, and law. There are, however, a great number of positions that are filled by persons whose college major was political science, public administration, education, liberal arts, or other fields not directly related to business or law. Extensive use is made of competitive registers and examinations in selecting employees. Schools interested in participating in the extensive recruitment program, or anyone considering employment with the Service, may direct inquiries to the Recruitment Coordinator at any of the Regional or District Offices.

Problem Resolution Program   Each District has a Problem Resolution Officer who attempts to resolve taxpayers' complaints not satisfied through regular channels.

Publications   *The Annual Report—Commissioner of Internal Revenue* (Pub. 55), as well as periodic reports of Statistics of Incomes, which present statistical tabulations concerning various tax returns filed, are available from the Superintendent of Documents, Government Printing Office, Washington, DC 20402. *Audit of Returns, Appeal Rights, and Claims for Refund* (Pub. 556), *Your Federal Income Tax* (Pub. 17), *Farmers Tax Guide* (Pub. 225), *Tax Guide for Small Business* (Pub. 334), and other publications are available at Internal Revenue Service offices free of charge.

Reading Rooms   Public reading rooms are located in the National Office and in each Regional Office or, in some cases, a District Office located in a Regional Office building.

Speakers   Speakers on provisions of the tax law and operations of the Internal Revenue Service for professional and community groups may be obtained by writing to the District Directors or, for national organizations only, to the Public Affairs Division at the IRS National Headquarters in Washington, DC.

Taxpayer Service   The Internal Revenue Service provides year-round tax information and assistance to taxpayers, primarily through its toll-free telephone system. Taxpayers requesting information about the tax system, their rights and obligations under it, and the tax benefits available to them can call the number listed in their local telephone directory and in the tax form packages mailed to them annually. This service allows taxpayers anywhere in the United States to call the service without paying a long-distance charge. Special toll-free telephone assistance also is available to deaf and hearing-impaired taxpayers who have access to a teletypewriter or television/phone. These special numbers are included in the annual tax form packages and also are available from any agency office.

Taxpayers may also visit agency offices for help with their tax problems. The Service provides return preparation assistance to taxpayers by guiding groups of individuals line by line on the preparation of their returns. Individual preparation is available for handicapped or other individuals unable to use the group preparation method.

Foreign language tax assistance also is available at many locations.

United States Mint

Contracts and Employment   Inquiries should be directed to the facility head of the appropriate field office or to the Director of the Mint.

Numismatic Services   The United States Mint maintains public exhibit and sales areas at the Philadelphia and Denver Mints, and at Union Station in Washington, DC. Brochures and order forms for official coins, medals, and other numismatic items may also be obtained by writing to the United States Mint, 10001 Aerospace Road, Lanham, MD 20706. Phone, 202–283–COIN.

Publications   *The Annual Report of the Director of the Mint* and *World Coinage Report* are available from the United States Mint, Washington, DC, and the Superintendent of Documents, Government Printing Office, Washington, DC 20402.

Bureau of the Public Debt

Employment   General employment inquiries should be addressed to the Bureau of the Public Debt, Division of Personnel Management, Employment and Classification Branch, Parkersburg, WV 26106–1328. Phone, 304–480–6144.

Savings Bonds   Savings bonds are continuously on sale at more than 40,000 financial institutions and their branches in virtually every locality in the United States. Information about bonds is provided by such issuing agents.

Free informational materials are available from the Bureau of the Public Debt, Savings Bonds Marketing Office, Department of the Treasury, Washington, DC 20226. Phone, 202–377–7715. Current rate information is available toll-free by calling 1–800–4US–BOND.

Requests for information relating to holdings of all series of savings bonds, savings notes, and retirement plan or individual retirement bonds should be addressed to the Bureau of the Public Debt, Department of the Treasury, 200 Third Street, Parkersburg, WV 26106–1328. Phone, 304–480–6112.

Treasury Securities   Information inquiries regarding the purchase of Treasury bills, bonds, and notes should be addressed to your local Federal Reserve Bank or branch, or to the Bureau of the Public Debt, Department F, Washington, DC 20239–1200. Phone, 202–874–4060.

Office of Thrift Supervision

Fax   Facsimile transmittal services are available by dialing 202–906–5748.

United States Secret Service

Information about employment opportunities and publications and general public information may be obtained by contacting the nearest Secret Service field office or the Office of Government Liaison and Public Affairs, 1800 G Street NW., Washington, DC 20223. Phone, 202–435–5708.

For further information concerning the Department of the Treasury, contact the Public Affairs Office, Department of the Treasury, 1500 Pennsylvania Avenue NW., Washington, DC 20220. Phone, 202–622–2960.

DEPARTMENT OF VETERANS AFFAIRS

810 Vermont Avenue NW., Washington, DC 20420
Phone, 202–273–4900

SECRETARY OF VETERANS AFFAIRS	JESSE BROWN
Executive Assistant to the Secretary	ROY SPICER
Special Assistant to the Secretary	PATRICIA CARRINGTON
Deputy Secretary	HERSHEL GOBER
Assistant to the Deputy Secretary	DEWEY SPENCER
Chief of Staff	HAROLD F. GRACEY, JR.
Veterans' Service Organization Liaison	PHILIP RIGGIN
White House Liaison	HEYWARD BANNISTER
Executive Secretary	LINDA KAUFMAN
Inspector General	STEPHEN A. TRODDEN
Chairman, Board of Contract Appeals	GUY H. MCMICHAEL III
Director, Office of Small and Disadvantaged Business Utilization	SCOTT F. DENNISTON
General Counsel	MARY LOU KEENER
Special Assistant to the General Counsel	NEIL RICHMAN
Deputy General Counsel	ROBERT E. COY
Assistant General Counsels	JOHN H. THOMPSON, NEAL C. LAWSON, WILLIAM E. THOMAS, JR., HOWARD C. LEM, NORMAN G. COOPER
Chairman, Board of Veterans' Appeals	CHARLES L. CRAGIN
Executive Assistant to the Chairman	MARJORIE A. AUER
Director, Management and Administration	RONALD R. AUMENT
Chief Counsel	STEVEN L. KELLER
Counsel to the Chairman, Litigation Support	RICHARD C. THRASHER, *Acting*
Counsel to the Chairman, Legal Affairs	THOMAS D. ROBERTS, *Acting*
Vice Chairman	ROGER K. BAUER
Deputy Vice Chairman	RICHARD B. STANDEFER
Director, Administrative Service	NANCY D. STACKHOUSE
Under Secretary for Health, Veterans Health Administration	KENNETH W. KIZER, M.D.
Chief of Staff	MICHAEL HUGHES
Director, Executive Correspondence	PAMELA GALYEAN
Medical Inspector	CHARLES KOERBER, *Acting*
Staff Director	(VACANCY)
Deputy Under Secretary for Health	THOMAS GARTHWAITE, M.D.
Executive Assistant	(VACANCY)
Associate Chief Medical Director for Operations	JULE MOREVAC
Regional Director (Region 1—Eastern)	BARBARA GALLAGHER
Regional Director (Region 2—Central)	DAVID WHATLEY
Director, Field Support	ALAN T. MAURER
Regional Director (Region 3—Southern)	JOHN HIGGINS, M.D.
Regional Director (Region 4—Western)	SHEILA CULLEN, *Acting*

481

Associate Deputy Chief Medical Director for Clinical Programs	DAVID H. LAW, M.D., *Acting*
Deputy Associate Deputy Chief Medical Director for Hospital-Based Services	GABRIEL MANASSE, M.D., *Acting*
Deputy Associate Deputy Chief Medical Director for Ambulatory Care	ROBERT GEBHART, M.D.
Assistant Chief Medical Director, Dentistry	CHESTER P. PACZKOWSKI, D.D.S.
Assistant Chief Medical Director for Geriatrics and Extended Care	THOMAS T. YOSHIKAWA, M.D.
Director, Readjustment Counseling Service	ALFONSO A. BATRES, M.D.
Assistant Chief Medical Director for Environmental Medicine and Public Health	SUSAN H. MATHER, M.D.
Deputy Associate Deputy Chief Medical Director for Rehabilitation and Prosthetics	CONNER HIGGINS, M.D., *Acting*
Assistant Chief Medical Director for Nursing Programs	NANCY VALENTINE
Associate Chief Medical Director for Research and Development	RAYMOND SPHAR, M.D., *Acting*
Director, Medical Research Service	MARTIN ALBERT, M.D.
Director, Health Services Research and Development Service	DANIEL DEYKIN, M.D.
Associate Chief Medical Director for Academic Affairs	ELIZABETH M. SHORT, M.D.
Director, Affiliated Residency Programs	VICTOR S. WAHBY, M.D., *Acting*
Director, Learning Resources Service	DIANE WIESENTHAL, *Acting*
Director, Associated Health Professions Education Programs Service	CHARLOTTE BEASON
Director, Administrative Operations Staff	EVERT H. MELANDER, *Acting*
Director, Continuing Education Service	(VACANCY)
Associate Chief Medical Director for Quality Management	GALEN BARBOUR, M.D.
Director, Quality Management Systems Office	JAY HALPERN
Director, Quality Management Planning and Evaluation	SCOTT BECK
Director, Risk Management	DEBBY WALDER
Associate Chief Medical Director for Administration	LYDIA B. MAVRIDIS
Director, Administrative Services	(VACANCY)
Director, Medical Information Resources Management Office	ROBERT KOLODER, M.D.
Director, Management Support Office	THOMAS J. HOGAN
Director, Health Care Staff Development and Retention Office	HUBERT B. PALMER
Director, Medical Care Cost Recovery Office	WALTER BESECKER
Director, Medical Sharing Office	ARTHUR S. HAMERSCHLAG
Chief Financial Officer	TODD GRAMS
Director, Medical Programs Budget Office	C.R. WICHLACZ
Director, Strategic Planning and Policy Office	JAMES M. GREGG
Director, Management Review and Evaluation Office	MAUREEN S. BALTAY

Director, Construction Project Coordination and Budget Office — LINDA KURZ

Director, Construction Policy, Criteria and Facility Development Plan Office — BRUCE PLECINSKI

Associate Chief Medical Director for Construction Management — C.V. YARBROUGH

Deputy Associate Chief — ROBERT L. NEARY, JR.

Director, Program and Financial Management Office — PAMELA P. DIX

Director, Information Management Office — MICHAEL J. WILLIAMS

Director, Real Property Management Office — LAWRENCE J. HILL

Director, Eastern Area Project Office — HAROLD M. GOODE

Director, Western Area Project Office — JAMES W. LAWSON

Director, Facilities Quality Office — LLOYD H. SIEGEL

Director, Consulting Support Office — JOHN P. HORNAK

Director, Asset and Enterprise Development Office — ANATOLIJ KUSHNIR

Under Secretary for Benefits, Veterans Benefits Administration — R.J. VOGEL

Deputy Under Secretary for Benefits — RAYMOND H. AVENT

Chief Information Officer — WILLIAM STINGER

Director, Office of Executive Management and Communications — PATRICIA GRYSAVAGE

Director, Office of Human Resources — VENTRIS GIBSON

Director, Debt Management Staff — DANIEL D. OSENDORF

Director, Office of Information Technology — GEORGE VAVERIS

Director, Eastern Area — DAVID A. BRIGHAM

Director, Central Area — STEPHEN L. LEMONS

Director, Southern Area — LEO C. WURSCHMIDT

Director, Western Area — JACK MCREYNOLDS

Director, Compensation and Pension Service — J. GARY HICKMAN

Director, Education Service — CELIA DOLLARHIDE

Director, Office of Resource Management — ROBERT GARDNER

Director, Loan Guaranty Service — KEITH PEDIGO

Director, Veterans Assistance Service — NEWELL QUINTON

Director, Vocational Rehabilitation Service — LARRY WOODARD

Director, Insurance Service — THOMAS LASTOWKA

Director, National Cemetery System — JERRY W. BOWEN

Special Assistant — DINA C. WOOD

Director, Office of Field Operations — ROGER R. RAPP

Director, Field Programs Service — FRED L. WATSON

Director, Technical Support Service — ROBERT B. HOLBROOK

Director, State Cemetery Grants Service — HAROLD F. GRABER

Director, Office of Operations Support — VINCENT L. BARILE

Director, Administration Service — (VACANCY)

Director, Budget and Planning Service — DOROTHY M. MACKAY

Director, Executive Communications and Public Affairs Service — ALEXANDER HAVAS

Director, Information Systems Service — MARK P. DUROCHER

Director, Office of Memorial Programs — DONNELL S. MOHR

Director, Claims Evaluation Service — CHRISTINE FARRELL

Director, Acquisitions Service — JOSEPH C. KEPPLE

Directors, National Cemetery System Area Offices:

Philadelphia, PA — PATRICK J. GARTLAND

Atlanta, GA	ROBERT WILK
Denver, CO	THOMAS G. BALSANEK
Assistant Secretary for Management	D. MARK CATLETT
Deputy to the Assistant Secretary	STANLEY R. SINCLAIR
Deputy Assistant Secretary for Budget	SHIRLEY C. CAROZZA
Deputy Assistant Secretary for Financial Management	FRANK W. SULLIVAN
Deputy Assistant Secretary for Information Resources Management	NADA D. HARRIS
Deputy Assistant Secretary for Acquisition and Materiel Management	GARY J. KRUMP
Assistant Secretary for Policy and Planning	DENNIS DUFFY
Executive Assistant	NANCY TACKETT
Deputy Assistant Secretary for Policy	EDWARD CHOW, JR.
Associate Deputy Assistant Secretary for Policy	IRWIN PERNICK
Deputy Assistant Secretary for Planning	NORA E. EGAN
Director, National Center for Veterans Analysis and Statistics	H. DAVID BURGE
Assistant Secretary for Human Resources and Administration	EUGENE A. BRICKHOUSE
Deputy Assistant Secretary for Human Resources Management	RONALD E. COWLES
Deputy Assistant Secretary for Equal Opportunity	GERALD K. HINCH
Deputy Assistant Secretary for Administration	ROBERT W. SCHULTZ
Deputy Assistant Secretary for Security and Law Enforcement	JOHN H. BAFFA
Assistant Secretary for Public and Intergovernmental Affairs	KATHY ELENA JURADO
Executive Assistant	MARTI MCALISTER GALLO
Deputy Assistant Secretary for Public Affairs	JAMES H. HOLLEY
Deputy Assistant Secretary for Intergovernmental Affairs	DALE L. RENAUD
Director, Veterans Canteen Service	JAMES B. DONAHOE
Assistant Secretary for Congressional Affairs	EDWARD P. SCOTT
Deputy Assistant Secretary for Congressional Liaison	(VACANCY)
Deputy Assistant Secretary for Legislative Affairs	(VACANCY)

The Department of Veterans Affairs operates programs to benefit veterans and members of their families. Benefits include compensation payments for disabilities or death related to military service; pensions; education and rehabilitation; home loan guaranty; burial; and a medical care program incorporating nursing homes, clinics, and medical centers.

The Department of Veterans Affairs (VA) was established as an executive department by the Department of Veterans Affairs Act (38 U.S.C. 201 note). The Department's predecessor, the Veterans Administration, had been established as an independent agency under the President by Executive Order 5398 of July 21, 1930, in accordance with the act of July 3, 1930 (46 Stat. 1016). This act authorized the President to consolidate and coordinate the U.S. Veterans Bureau, the Bureau of Pensions, and the National Home for Volunteer Soldiers.

DEPARTMENT OF VETERANS AFFAIRS

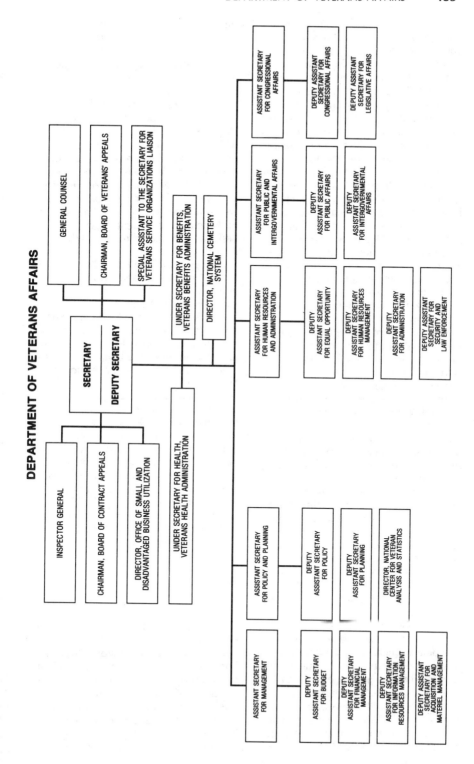

INSPECTOR GENERAL

GENERAL COUNSEL

CHAIRMAN, BOARD OF CONTRACT APPEALS

CHAIRMAN, BOARD OF VETERANS' APPEALS

DIRECTOR, OFFICE OF SMALL AND DISADVANTAGED BUSINESS UTILIZATION

SPECIAL ASSISTANT TO THE SECRETARY FOR VETERANS SERVICE ORGANIZATIONS LIAISON

SECRETARY

DEPUTY SECRETARY

UNDER SECRETARY FOR HEALTH, VETERANS HEALTH ADMINISTRATION

UNDER SECRETARY FOR BENEFITS, VETERANS BENEFITS ADMINISTRATION

DIRECTOR, NATIONAL CEMETERY SYSTEM

ASSISTANT SECRETARY FOR HUMAN RESOURCES AND ADMINISTRATION

DEPUTY ASSISTANT SECRETARY FOR EQUAL OPPORTUNITY

DEPUTY ASSISTANT SECRETARY FOR HUMAN RESOURCES MANAGEMENT

DEPUTY ASSISTANT SECRETARY FOR ADMINISTRATION

DEPUTY ASSISTANT SECRETARY FOR SECURITY AND LAW ENFORCEMENT

ASSISTANT SECRETARY FOR PUBLIC AND INTERGOVERNMENTAL AFFAIRS

DEPUTY ASSISTANT SECRETARY FOR PUBLIC AFFAIRS

DEPUTY ASSISTANT SECRETARY FOR INTERGOVERNMENTAL AFFAIRS

ASSISTANT SECRETARY FOR CONGRESSIONAL AFFAIRS

DEPUTY ASSISTANT SECRETARY FOR CONGRESSIONAL AFFAIRS

DEPUTY ASSISTANT SECRETARY FOR LEGISLATIVE AFFAIRS

ASSISTANT SECRETARY FOR POLICY AND PLANNING

DEPUTY ASSISTANT SECRETARY FOR POLICY

DEPUTY ASSISTANT SECRETARY FOR PLANNING

DIRECTOR, NATIONAL CENTER FOR VETERAN ANALYSIS AND STATISTICS

ASSISTANT SECRETARY FOR MANAGEMENT

DEPUTY ASSISTANT SECRETARY FOR BUDGET

DEPUTY ASSISTANT SECRETARY FOR FINANCIAL MANAGEMENT

DEPUTY ASSISTANT SECRETARY FOR INFORMATION RESOURCES MANAGEMENT

DEPUTY ASSISTANT SECRETARY FOR ACQUISITION AND MATERIEL MANAGEMENT

The Department of Veterans Affairs comprises three organizations that administer veterans programs: the Veterans Health Administration, the Veterans Benefits Administration, and the National Cemetery System. Each organization has field facilities and a Central Office component. The Central Office also includes separate offices that provide support to the top organizations' operations as well as to top VA executives. Top Central Office managers, including the Inspector General and General Counsel, report to the highest level of Department management, which consists of the Secretary of Veterans Affairs and the Deputy Secretary.

Assistant Secretaries Five Assistant Secretaries provide policy guidance, operational support, and managerial oversight to the Secretary and Deputy Secretary, the administrations, and other top offices. They include the Assistant Secretaries of Finance and Information Resources Management, Policy and Planning, Human Resources and Administration, Public and Intergovernmental Affairs, and Congressional Affairs. Other central management offices are detailed as follows.

Board of Veterans' Appeals The Board of Veterans' Appeals (BVA) is responsible, on behalf of the Secretary of Veterans Affairs, for entering the final appellate decisions in claims of entitlement to veterans' benefits. The Board is also responsible for deciding matters concerning fees charged by attorneys and agents for representation of veterans before VA. The mission of the Board, set forth in title 38 of the United States Code, sections 7101–7109, is to conduct hearings, consider and dispose of appeals properly before the Board in a timely manner, and issue quality decisions in compliance with the law. The Board is headed by a Chairman, who is appointed by the President and confirmed by the Senate, and who is directly responsible to the Secretary of Veterans Affairs. Members of the Board are appointed by the Secretary with the approval of the President and are under the administrative control and

supervision of the Chairman. Each BVA decision is signed by a Board member acting as an agent of the Secretary. Final BVA decisions are appealable to the United States Court of Veterans Appeals.

Board of Contract Appeals The Board of Contract Appeals was established on March 1, 1979, pursuant to the Contract Disputes Act of 1978 (41 U.S.C. 601–613). The Board is a statutory, quasi-judicial tribunal that hears and decides appeals from decisions of Contracting Officers on claims relating to contracts awarded by VA, or by any other agency when such agency or the Administrator for Federal Procurement Policy has designated the Board to decide the appeal.

In August 1985, the Board's jurisdiction was expanded to include applications for attorney fees and expenses under the Equal Access to Justice Act, as amended (5 U.S.C. 504 note). Board decisions are final within VA, but may be appealed, either by the Government or by the contractor, to the United States Court of Appeals for the Federal Circuit.

The Board also acts as a trier of disputed material facts in debarment/suspension proceedings. Additionally, the Chairman of the Board is the senior official within the Department to promote alternate dispute resolution pursuant to the Administrative Dispute Resolution Act (5 U.S.C. 581 note). Finally, the Board is charged with resolving any disputes between drug manufacturers and the Secretary with regard to pharmaceutical pricing agreements provisions of the Veterans Health Care Act of 1992 (38 U.S.C. 101 note).

Health Services

The Veterans Health Administration, formerly the Veterans Health Services and Research Administration, provides hospital, nursing home, and domiciliary care, and outpatient medical and dental care to eligible veterans of military service in the Armed Forces. It operates 171 medical centers, 35 domiciliaries, 340 outpatient clinics, 127 nursing home care units, and 196 Vietnam Veteran

Outreach Centers in the United States, the Commonwealth of Puerto Rico, and the Republic of the Philippines, and provides for similar care under VA auspices in non-VA hospitals and community nursing homes and for visits by veterans to non-VA physicians and dentists for outpatient treatment. It also supports veterans under care in hospitals, nursing homes, and domiciliaries operated by 35 States. Under the Civilian Health and Medical Program, dependents of certain veterans are provided with medical care supplied by non-VA institutions and physicians.

The Administration conducts both individual medical and health-care delivery research projects and multihospital research programs. It assists in the education of physicians and dentists, and with training of many other health care professionals through affiliations with educational institutions and organizations. These programs are all conducted as prescribed by the Secretary of Veterans Affairs pursuant to sections 4101–4115 of title 38 of the United States Code and other statutory authority and regulations.

Veterans Benefits

The Veterans Benefits Administration, formerly the Department of Veterans Benefits, conducts an integrated program of veterans benefits.

Compensation and Pension The Compensation and Pension Service has responsibility for:
—claims for disability compensation and pension;
—automobile allowances and special adaptive equipment;
—claims for specially adapted housing;
—special clothing allowances;
—emergency officers' retirement pay;
—eligibility determinations based on military service for other VA benefits and services or those of other Government agencies;
—survivors' claims for death compensation, dependency and indemnity compensation, death pension, burial and plot allowance claims;
—claims for accrued benefits;

—forfeiture determinations;
—claims for adjusted compensation in death cases; and
—claims for reimbursement for headstone or marker.

Education The Education Service has responsibility for: the Montgomery GI Bill—Active Duty and Selected Reserve (chapters 30 and 106); the Post Vietnam Era Veterans' Educational Assistance Program (chapter 32); the Survivors' and Dependents' Educational Assistance Program (chapter 35); the Section 901 Test Program; and school approvals and compliance surveys.

Vocational Rehabilitation The Vocational Rehabilitation Service has responsibility for: outreach, motivation, evaluation, counseling, training, employment, and other rehabilitation services to disabled veterans (chapters 31 and 15); evaluation, counseling, and miscellaneous services to veterans and servicepersons (chapter 30) and other VA education programs; evaluation, counseling, education, and miscellaneous services to sons, daughters, and spouses of totally and permanently disabled veterans and to surviving orphans, widows, or widowers of certain deceased veterans, including rehabilitation services to certain handicapped dependents (chapter 35); and affirmative action activities.

Loan Guaranty Loan guaranty operations include: appraising properties to establish their values; supervising the construction of new residential properties; establishing the eligibility of veterans for the program; passing on the ability of a veteran to repay a loan and the credit risk; servicing and liquidating defaulted loans; and disposing of real estate acquired as the consequence of defaulted loans.

Insurance Life insurance operations are for the benefit of service members, veterans, and their beneficiaries. The day-to-day processing of all matters related to individual insurance accounts is handled by the Regional Office and Insurance Centers in Philadelphia, PA, and St. Paul, MN. These two centers provide the full range of functional activities necessary for a national life insurance program. Activities include the complete maintenance of individual accounts, underwriting functions, and life and death insurance claims awards, as well as any other insurance-related transactions.

The agency is also responsible for the administration of the Veterans Mortgage Life Insurance program for those disabled veterans who receive a VA grant for specially adapted housing. Accounts are maintained at the Regional Office and Insurance Center in St. Paul, MN.

In addition, the agency is responsible for supervising the Servicemen's Group Life Insurance (SGLI) and Veterans Group Life Insurance (VGLI) programs. Both programs are handled through the Office of Servicemen's Group Life Insurance, 231 Washington Street, Newark, NJ 07102.

Veterans Assistance   Through the Veterans Assistance Service, information, advice, and assistance are provided to veterans, their dependents and beneficiaries, representatives, and others in applying for benefits administered by the Department of Veterans Affairs. In addition, the Veterans Assistance Service cooperates with the Department of Labor and other Federal, State, and local agencies in developing employment opportunities for veterans, and referral for assistance in resolving socioeconomic, housing, and other related problems.

The Service is responsible for maintaining a benefits protection program (fiduciary activities) for minors and incompetent adult beneficiaries. It also provides field investigative services for other VA components. It ensures compliance by schools and training institutions with VA directives. It also ensures compliance with title VI of the Civil Rights Act of 1964 (42 U.S.C. 2000d); title IX of the Education Amendments of 1972 (20 U.S.C. 1681); section 504 of the Rehabilitation Act of 1973 (29 U.S.C. 794); and the Age Discrimination Act of 1975, as amended (42 U.S.C. 6101). The programs of the Service are provided through VA regional offices, VA medical centers, itinerant visits to communities, and a

special toll-free telephone service available in all 50 States, the District of Columbia, and Puerto Rico.

The Veterans Assistance Service also has the responsibility of providing information regarding veterans benefits to the various branches of the Armed Forces here and abroad and to veterans residing in foreign countries through United States embassies and consular offices, and of coordinating veterans' activities with foreign governments.

National Cemetery System

The National Cemetery System (NCS) provides services to veterans, reservists, and National Guard members with 20 years' qualifying service and their families by operating national cemeteries; furnishing headstones and markers for the graves of U.S. veterans, reservists, and National Guard members with 20 years' qualifying service worldwide; awarding grants to aid States in developing, improving, and expanding veterans cemeteries; and serving as the operations element for the Presidential Memorial Certificate Program.

The mission of the National Cemetery System is:

—to provide, upon request, the interment of eligible servicemembers, veterans, reservists, National Guard members with 20 years' qualifying service, their spouses, and certain children in VA national cemeteries and to maintain their graves;

—to mark, upon application, the graves of eligible veterans, reservists, and National Guard members with 20 years' qualifying service worldwide who are buried in national, State, or private cemeteries;

—to administer the State Cemetery Grants Program, which provides financial assistance to States for establishing, improving, and expanding State veterans cemeteries; and

—to provide Presidential Memorial Certificates to the loved ones of honorably discharged, deceased servicemembers or veterans.

The National Cemetery area offices, located in Atlanta, GA; Philadelphia, PA; and Denver, CO; provide direct support to the 114 national cemeteries located throughout the United States and Puerto Rico.

Field Facilities

Insurance Centers Two field sites house all individual insurance records covering service members and veterans under the Government–administered programs: WW I United States Government Life Insurance; WW II National Service Life Insurance; Post-Korean Conflict; Veterans Reopened Insurance for the disabled of WW II and Korea; and Service-Disabled Veterans Insurance, the only Government–administered program open for new issues to disabled veterans only.

The two field locations are the VA Regional Office and Insurance Centers in Philadelphia, PA, and St. Paul, MN. All World War I insurance accounts, .accounts for which the premium is paid by allotment from military service pay, and those paid by deduction from VA compensation or preauthorized debit are located at Philadelphia. All remaining insurance accounts are geographically distributed between the two VA Centers—with the Mississippi River serving as the approximate line of division. The Philadelphia Veterans Affairs Center is also responsible for formulating policy for the veterans insurance programs.

The insurance functions performed by the two field stations include the total range of insurance operations to provide individual policy, underwriting, and life and death insurance claims service for service members, veterans, and their beneficiaries.

Regional Office Department of Veterans Affairs regional offices:

—grant benefits and services provided by law for veterans, their dependents, and beneficiaries within an assigned territory;

—furnish information regarding VA benefits and services;

—adjudicate claims and makes awards for disability compensation and pension;

—supervise the payment of VA benefits to incompetent beneficiaries;

—aid, guide, and prescribe vocational rehabilitation training and administer educational benefits;

—guarantee loans for purchase of manufactured homes and lots and condominium units, purchase or construction or alteration of homes and farm residences, and under certain conditions, guarantee refinancing loans;

—process grants for specially adapted housing;

—process death claims;

—assist the veteran in exercising rights to benefits and services; and

—supervise VA offices under their jurisdiction.

The offices are also responsible for veterans assistance activities, including coordination of efforts of participating agencies in an "outreach" program to assist returning service members, particularly those who are educationally disadvantaged.

Services to U.S. veterans in most foreign countries normally are provided by the VA Regional Office, District of Columbia. The Honolulu Regional Office serves the Islands of American Samoa, the Commonwealth of the Northern Mariana Islands, Guam, Wake, and Midway and the Trust Territory of the Pacific Islands. U.S. veterans in the Virgin Islands and Mexico are served by the San Juan and Houston offices, respectively. Service is provided in cooperation with embassy staffs of the Department of State.

Department of Veterans Affairs Regional Office, District of Columbia The Department of Veterans Affairs Regional Office, District of Columbia, is a typical regional office with additional functions. It has global jurisdiction and grants benefits and services provided by law for veterans and their beneficiaries and dependents residing outside the territorial limits of the United States, and it adjudicates certain unusual claims and actions not common to all regional offices, such as WW I adjusted compensation death cases, forfeiture cases, and benefits under special enactments provided by the Congress. It also maintains liaison with the Treasury Department on types and methods of payments to recipients in foreign countries.

VA Office The VA office provides veterans assistance and such other services as cannot be conveniently provided to veterans, their dependents and beneficiaries, and others in a given locality by a regional office or center.

Medical Center Veterans Affairs Medical Centers provide eligible beneficiaries with medical and other health care services equivalent to those provided by private-sector institutions, augmented in many instances by services to meet the special requirements of veterans. One hundred and thirty-three VA medical facilities are affiliated with 104 medical facilities for residency training; 72 VA medical facilities are affiliated with 59 dental schools; and all centers cooperate with one or more educational institutions in programs of nursing, associated health professions and occupations, and administrative training and related research, both in individual projects and in association with other VA medical centers in broad cooperative studies. There are 106 nursing home care units associated with VA medical centers to provide skilled nursing care and related medical services to patients who are no longer in need of hospital care.

VA Regional Office and Insurance Center Veterans Affairs Regional Office and Insurance Centers combine a

regional office and an insurance center under the jurisdiction of one director.

VA Medical and Regional Office Center Veterans Affairs Medical and Regional Office Centers combine a regional office and a medical center or a regional office, medical center, and domiciliary under the jurisdiction of one director.

Domiciliary Veterans Affairs Domiciliaries provide the least intensive level of inpatient medical care. This includes necessary ambulatory medical treatment, rehabilitation, and support services in a structured environment to veterans who are unable because of their disabilities to provide adequately for themselves in the community.

Outpatient Clinic Veterans Affairs Outpatient Clinics provide eligible beneficiaries with ambulatory care.

VA National Cemetery Veterans Affairs national cemeteries are the final resting places for burial of the remains of veterans, reservists, and National Guard members with 20 years' qualifying service, their spouses, and certain eligible dependents. Memorial markers for veterans, reservists, and National Guard members with 20 years' qualifying service, whose remains are not available for burial, may also be placed in a national cemetery. These cemeteries are designated as national shrines created in tribute to the sacrifices of all Americans who have served in the U.S. Armed Forces.

National Facilities—Department of Veterans Affairs

Address	Type of facility	Director
National Facilities Under the Veterans Health Administration, Veterans Benefits Administration, and National Cemetery System—Centers, Domiciliaries, Medical Centers, Medical and Regional Office Centers, Outpatient Clinics, Insurance Centers, Regional Offices, Supply Activities, and National Cemeteries		
ALABAMA:		
Birmingham, 35233 (700 S. 19th St.)	Medical Center	William Mountcastle
Mobile, 36604 (1202 Virginia St.) (Mail: Barrancas National Cemetery, FL).	National Cemetery	Sandra Beckley
Montgomery, 36109–3798 (215 Perry Hill Rd.)	Medical Center	John R. Rowan
Montgomery, 36109 (345 Perry Hill Rd.)	Regional Office	Sam Maraman
Seale, 36875 (553 Hwy. 165) (Fort Mitchell National Cemetery).	National Cemetery	William Trower
Tuscaloosa, 35404	Medical Center	Kenneth W. Ruyle
Tuskegee, 36083	Medical Center	Jimmie L. Clay
ALASKA:		
Anchorage, 99508 (2925 Debarr Rd.)	Outpatient Clinic and Regional Office .	Al Poteet
Fort Richardson, 99505 (P.O. Box 5–498)	National Cemetery	James L. Fitzgerald
Sitka, 99835 (803 Sawmill Creek Rd.) (Mail: Fort Richardson National Cemetery, AK).	......do	James L. Fitzgerald
ARIZONA:		
Phoenix, 85012 (7th St. and Indian School Rd.) ..	Medical Center	John Fears
Phoenix, 85012 (3225 N. Central Ave.)	Regional Office	David W. Walls

National Facilities—Department of Veterans Affairs—Continued

Address	Type of facility	Director
Phoenix, 85024 (23029 N. Cave Creek Rd.) (National Memorial Cemetery of Arizona).	National Cemetery	Arthur D. Smith
Prescott, 86313	Medical Center (medical and domiciliary).	Patricia McClem
Prescott, 86313 (VA Medical Center) (Mail: National Memorial Cemetery of Arizona).	National Cemetery	Arthur D. Smith
Tucson, 85723	Medical Center	Jonathan Gartner
ARKANSAS:		
Fayetteville, 72703	Medical Center	Richard F. Robinson
Fayetteville, 72701 (700 Government Ave.)	National Cemetery	Lawrence E. Bibbs
Fort Smith, 72901 (522 Garland Ave.)	....do	Karen Browne
Little Rock, 72206 (2523 Confederate Blvd.)	....do	Mary Ann Fisher
Little Rock, 72205 (300 Roosevelt Rd.) (John L. McClellan Memorial Veterans Hospital). Little Rock Division North Little Rock Division (Mail: Little Rock)	Medical Center	George Gray
North Little Rock, 72115, (P.O. Box 1280, Bldg. 65, Fort Root).	Regional Office	Samuel L. Holmes
CALIFORNIA:		
Benicia, 94523 (150 Muir Rd.)	Medical Center	Sheila Collen
Fresno, 93703 (2615 Clinton Ave.)	....do	James DeNiro
Gustine, 95322 (32053 W. McCabe Rd.) (San Joaquin Valley National Cemetery).	National Cemetery	Dennis Kuehl
Livermore, 94550	Medical Center	James Groff
Loma Linda, 92357 (11201 Benton St.) (Jerry L. Pettis Memorial Veterans Hospital).	....do	Dean R. Stordahl
Long Beach, 90822 (5901 E. 7th St.)	Medical Center	Jerry Boyd
Los Angeles, 90013 (425 S. Hill St.)	Outpatient Clinic	Lee Nackman
Los Angeles, 90024 (11000 Wilshire Blvd.)	Regional Office	Stewart F. Liff
Los Angeles, 90049 (950 S. Sepulveda Blvd.)	National Cemetery	Gertrude Devenney
Oakland, 94612–5209 (Oakland Federal Bldg., 1301 Clay St.).	Regional Office	Donald E. Stout
Palo Alto, 94304 (3801 Miranda Ave.) Menlo Park Division Palo Alto Division	Medical Center	James Groff
Riverside, 92508 (22495 Van Buren Blvd.)	National Cemetery	Steve Jorgensen
San Bruno, 94066 (1300 Sneath Lane) (Golden Gate National Cemetery).	....do	Cynthia Nunez
San Diego, 92161 (3350 La Jolla Village Dr.)	Medical Center	Leonard C. Rogers
San Diego, 92108 (2022 Camino Del Rio N.)	Regional Office	Patrick Nappi
San Diego, 92166 (Point Loma, P.O. Box 6237) (Fort Rosecrans National Cemetery).	National Cemetery	Helen B. Szumylo
San Francisco, 94121 (4150 Clement St.)	Medical Center	Lawrence C. Stewart
San Francisco, 94129 (P.O. Box 29012, Presidio of San Francisco) (Mail: Golden Gate National Cemetery, CA).	National Cemetery	Cynthia Nunez
Sepulveda, 91343	Medical Center	Perey C. Norman
West Los Angeles, 90073	....do (medical and domiciliary)	Kenneth J. Clark
COLORADO:		
Denver, 80225 (P.O. Box 25126, 44 Union Blvd.)	Regional Office	(Vacancy)
Denver, 80220 (1055 Clermont St.)	Medical Center	Thomas A. Trujillo
Denver, 80225 (Denver Federal Center)	Prosthetics Distribution Center	Robert A. Shields
Denver, 80235 (3698 S. Sheridan Blvd.) (Fort Logan National Cemetery).	National Cemetery	Robert McCollum
Fort Lyon, 81038	Denver Distribution Center	Robert E. Lee, D.P.M.
Fort Lyon, 81838 (VA Medical Center) (Mail: Fort Logan National Cemetery, CO).	National Cemetery	Robert McCollum
Fort Lyon, 81038	Medical Center	David W. Smith
Grand Junction, 81501	Prosthetics Distribution Center	(Vacancy)
Grand Junction, 81501	Medical Center	Robert R. Rhyne, D.D.S.
CONNECTICUT:		
Hartford, 06103 (150 Main St.)	Regional Office	Catherine Smith
Newington, 06111 (555 Willard Ave.)	Medical Center	Vincent Ngr
West Haven, 06516 (W. Spring St.)	....do	(Vacancy)
DELAWARE:		
Wilmington, 19805 (1601 Kirkwood Hwy.)	Medical and Regional Office Center	Dexter Dix
DISTRICT OF COLUMBIA:		
Washington, 20422 (50 Irving St. NW.)	Medical Center	Sanford M. Garfunkel
Washington, 20421 (1120 Vermont Ave. NW.)	Regional Office	C. Faye Norred
FLORIDA:		
Bay Pines, 33504 (1000 Bay Pines Blvd. N.)	Medical Center (medical and domiciliary).	Thomas Weaver
Bay Pines, 33504–0477 (P.O. Box 477)	National Cemetery	Ronald R. Pemberton
Bushnell, 33513 (Florida National Cemetery) (Mail: Florida National Cemetery, FL).	....do	Ronald R. Pemberton

National Facilities—Department of Veterans Affairs—Continued

Address	Type of facility	Director
Gainesville, 32608–1197 (1601 SW. Archer Rd.) .	Medical Center	J. Malcom Randall
Lake City, 32055–5898 (801 S. Marion St.)	Medical Center	Alline Norman
Miami, 33125 (1201 NW. 16th St.)	.....do	Thomas C. Doherty
Pensacola, 32508–1099 (Naval Air Station) (Barrancas National Cemetery).	National Cemetery	Sandra Beckley
St. Augustine, 32084 (104 Marine St.) (Mail: Florida National Cemetery, FL).	.....do	Ronald R. Pemberton
St. Petersburg, 33731 (P.O. Box 1437)	Regional Office	Carlos Rainwater
Tampa, 33612 (13000 Bruce B. Downs Blvd.) (James A. Haley Veterans Hospital).	Medical Center	Richard A. Silver
GEORGIA:		
Atlanta, 30365 (730 Peachtree St. NE.)	Regional Office	R. Stedman Sloan, *Acting*
Augusta, 30904–6285 (2460 Wrightsboro Rd. (10)). Forest Hills Division Lenwood Division	Medical Center	Thomas L. Ayres
Decatur, 30033 (1670 Clairmont Rd.)	.....do	Larry Deal
Dublin, 31021	Medical Center (medical and domiciliary).	William O. Edgar
Marietta, 30060 (500 Washington Ave.)	National Cemetery	George Vaughn
HAWAII:		
Honolulu, 96850 (P.O. Box 50188)	Medical and Regional Office Center ...	Barry Raff
Honolulu, 96813–1729 (2177 Puowaina Dr.) (National Memorial Cemetery of the Pacific).	National Cemetery	Gene E. Castagnetti
IDAHO:		
Boise, 83702 (805 W. Franklin St.)	Regional Office	(Vacancy)
Boise, 83702–4598 (5th and Fort Sts.)	Medical Center	Wayne Tippets
ILLINOIS:		
Alton, 62003 (600 Pearl St.) (Mail: Jefferson Barracks National Cemetery, MO).	National Cemetery	Ralph E. Church
Chicago, 60611 (333 E. Huron St.)	Medical Center	Joseph L. Moore
Chicago, 60612 (820 S. Damen Ave.)	.....do	John Denardo
Chicago, 60680 (P.O. Box 8136)	Regional Office	Montgomery D. Watson
Danville, 61832	Medical Center	James S. Jones
Danville, 61832 (1900 E. Main St.)	National Cemetery	Richard J. Pless
Hines, 60666–0303 (Lock Box 66303, AMF O'Hare, IL).	Finance Center	James Burkett
Hines, 60141 (Edward Hines, Jr. Hospital)	Medical Center	Joan E. Cummings, M.D.
Hines, 60141 (P.O. Box 76)	VA National Acquisition Center	Nancy L. Darn
Hines, 60141 (P.O. Box 27)	Service and Distribution Center	David Garcia
Marion, 62959 (2401 W. Main St.)	Medical Center	Linda Kurz
Mound City, 62963 (P.O. Box 38, Highway 37) (Mail: Jefferson Barracks National Cemetery, MO).	National Cemetery	Ralph E. Church
North Chicago, 60064	Medical Center	Alfred S. Pete
Quincy, 63201 (36th and Maine Sts.) (Mail: Keokuk National Cemetery, Rock Island, IL).	National Cemetery	Mary Dill
Rock Island, 61299 (P.O. Box 737, Rock Island Arsenal).	.....do	Mary Dill
Springfield, 62707 (5063 Camp Butler Rd., R #1) (Camp Butler National Cemetery).	National Cemetery	Kurt Rotar
INDIANA:		
Fort Wayne, 46805 (1600 Randalia Dr.)	Medical Center	Jonathan D. Hawk
Indianapolis, 46202 (1481 W. 10th St.) Cold Spring Road Division Tenth Street Division (Mail: 1481 W. 10th St., Indianapolis)	.....do	Alice Wood
Indianapolis, 46204 (575 N. Pennsylvania St.)	Regional Office	Dennis R. Wyant
Indianapolis, 46208 (700 W. 38th St.) (Crown Hill National Cemetery) (Mail: Marion National Cemetery, IN).	National Cemetery	Bobby A. Moton
Marion, 46952–4589	Medical Center	Jon E. Crisman
Marion, 46952 (1700 E. 38th St.)	National Cemetery	Bobby A. Moton
New Albany, 47150 (1943 Elkin Ave.) (Mail: Zachary Taylor National Cemetery, KY).	.....do	Gary D. Peak
IOWA:		
Des Moines, 50309 (210 Walnut St.)	Regional Office	Norman W. Bauer
Des Moines, 50310–5774 (30th and Euclid Ave.)	Medical Center	Ellen DeGeorge-Smith
Iowa City, 52246–5774 (Highway 6 W.)	.....do	Gary L. Wilkinson
Keokuk, 52632 (1701 J St.) (Mail: Rock Island National Cemetery, IL).	National Cemetery	Mary Dill
Knoxville, 50138	Medical Center	Donald D. Ziska
KANSAS:		
Fort Leavenworth, 66048 (Mail: Leavenworth National Cemetery, KS).	National Cemetery	Gerald T. Vitela

National Facilities—Department of Veterans Affairs—Continued

Address	Type of facility	Director
Fort Scott, 66701 (P.O. Box 917)	...do	Gerald T. Vitela
Leavenworth, 66048	Medical Center (medical and domiciliary).	Carole B. Smith
Leavenworth, 66048 (P.O. Box 1694)	National Cemetery	Gerald T. Vitela
Topeka, 66622 (2200 Gage Blvd.)	Medical Center	Edgar Tucker
Wichita, 67218 (5500 E. Kellogg)	...do	Jerry E. Mayhall
Wichita, 67216 (5500 E. Kellogg)	Regional Office	Gary L. Campbell
KENTUCKY:		
Danville, 40204 (277 N. 1st St.) (Mail: Camp Nelson National Cemetery, KY).	National Cemetery	Jeffrey Teas
Lebanon, 40033 (20 HWY. 208E) (Mail: Zachary Taylor National Cemetery, KY).	...do	Gary D. Peak
Lexington, 40511	Medical Center	Helen Cornish
Cooper Drive Division		
Leestown Division		
Lexington, 40508 (833 W. Main St.) (Mail: Camp Nelson National Cemetery, KY).	National Cemetery	Jeffrey Teas
Louisville, 40202 (545 S. 3d St.)	Regional Office	Henry W. Gresham
Louisville, 40202 (800 Zorn Ave.)	Medical Center	Larry J. Sander
Louisville, 40204 (701 Baxter Ave.) (Cave Hill National Cemetery) (Mail: Zachary Taylor National Cemetery, KY).	National Cemetery	Gary D. Peak
Louisville, 40207 (4701 Brownsboro Rd.) (Zachary Taylor National Cemetery).	...do	Gary D. Peak
Nancy, 42544 (Mill Springs National Cemetery) (Mail: Camp Nelson National Cemetery, KY).	...do	Jeffrey Teas
Nicholasville, 40356 (6980 Danville Rd.) (Camp Nelson National Cemetery).	...do	Jeffrey Teas
LOUISIANA:		
Alexandria, 71301	Medical Center	Billy M. Valentine
Baton Rouge, 70806 (220 N. 19th St.) (Mail: Port Hudson National Cemetery, LA).	National Cemetery	Virgil M. Wertenberger
New Orleans, 70146 (1601 Peridido St.)	Medical Center	John D. Church, Jr.
New Orleans, 70113 (701 Loyola Ave.)	Regional Office	William D. Fillman
Pineville, 71360 (209 E. Shamrock Ave.) (Alexandria National Cemetery).	National Cemetery	Lavern Nunnally
Shreveport, 71130 (510 E. Stoner Ave.)	Medical Center	Michael Hamilton
Zachary, 70791 (20978 Port Hickey Rd.) (Port Hudson National Cemetery).	National Cemetery	Virgil M. Wertenberger
MAINE:		
Togus, 04330	Medical and Regional Office Center	Jack Sims
Togus, 04330 (VA Medical and Regional Office Center) (Mail: Massachusetts National Cemetery, MA).	National Cemetery	David Wells
MARYLAND:		
Annapolis, 21401 (800 West St.) (Mail: Baltimore National Cemetery, MD).	National Cemetery	Robin Pohlman
Baltimore, 21201 (31 Hopkins Plz.)	Regional Office	(Vacancy)
Baltimore, 21218 (3900 Loch Raven Blvd.)	Medical Center	Dennis Smith
Baltimore, 21228 (5501 Frederick Ave.)	National Cemetery	Robin Pohlman
Baltimore, 21229 (3445 Frederick Ave.) (Loudon Park National Cemetery) (Mail: Baltimore National Cemetery, MD).	National Cemetery	Robin Pohlman
Fort Howard, 21052	Medical Center	Charles Clark
Perry Point, 21902	...do	Allan Gross
MASSACHUSETTS:		
Bedford, 01730 (200 Springs Rd.) (Edith Nourse Rogers Memorial Veterans Hospital).	...do	Bill Conte
Boston, 02130 (150 S. Huntington Ave.)	...do	Smith Jenkins, Jr.
Boston, 02203 (John F. Kennedy Federal Bldg.)	Regional Office	Michael D. Olson
Boston, 02108 (17 Court St.)	Outpatient Clinic	combined VA Boston
Bourne, 02532 (Connery Ave.) (Massachusetts National Cemetery).	National Cemetery	David Wells
Northampton, 01060	Medical Center	Gary Rossio
West Roxbury, 02132 (1400 Veterans of Foreign Wars Pky.).	...do	Michael Lawson
MICHIGAN:		
Allen Park, 48101	Medical Center	(Vacancy)
Ann Arbor, 48105 (2215 Fuller Rd.)	...do	Edward Gamache
Augusta, 49012 (15501 Dickman Rd.) (Fort Custer National Cemetery).	National Cemetery	Robert Poe
Battle Creek, 49106	Medical Center	(Vacancy)
Detroit, 48226 (477 Michigan Ave.)	Regional Office	Robert J. Epley
Iron Mountain, 49801	Medical Center	Glen Grippen
Saginaw, 48602 (1500 Weiss St.)	...do	Robert Sabini

National Facilities—Department of Veterans Affairs—Continued

Address	Type of facility	Director
MINNESOTA:		
Minneapolis, 55417 (1 Veterans Dr.)	......do	Charles Milbrandt
Minneapolis, 55950–1199 (7601 34th Ave., S.) (Fort Snelling National Cemetery).	National Cemetery	William D. Napton
St. Cloud, 56301 (4801 8th St. N.)	Medical Center	Thomas A. Holthaus
St. Paul, 55111 (Bishop Henry Whipple Federal Bldg., Fort Snelling). Remittances: P.O. Box 1820.	Regional Office and Insurance Center	Ronald J. Henke
MISSISSIPPI:		
Biloxi, 39531	Medical Center (medical and domiciliary).	George Rodman
Biloxi Hospital and Domiciliary Division		
Gulfport Hospital Division		
(Mail: Biloxi, MS)		
Biloxi, 39535–4968 (P.O. Box 4968)	National Cemetery	Jeffrey S. Barnes
Corinth, 38834 (1551 Horton St.) (Mail: Memphis National Cemetery, TN).	......do	Mark E. Maynard
Jackson, 39216 (1500 E. Woodrow Wilson Ave.)	Medical Center	Richard P. Miller
Jackson, 39269 (100 W. Capitol St.)	Regional Office	Mary F. Layland
Natchez, 39120 (41 Cemetery Rd.)	National Cemetery	John Bacon
MISSOURI:		
Columbia, 65201 (800 Hospital Dr.) (Harry S. Truman Memorial Veterans Hospital).	Medical Center	John T. Carson
Jefferson City, 65101 (1024 E. McCarthy) (Mail: Jefferson Barracks National Cemetery, MO).	National Cemetery	Ralph E. Church
Kansas City, 64128 (4801 Linwood Blvd.)	Medical Center	Hugh Doran
Poplar Bluff, 63901	......do	A. Alexander, M.D.
Springfield, 65804 (1702 E. Seminole St.)	National Cemetery	Dane Freeman
St. Louis, 63125	Medical Center	Donald Ziegenhorn
John J. Cochran Division		
Jefferson Barracks Division		
St. Louis, 63115 (P.O. Box 5020)	Records Processing Center	George T. Burns, *Acting*
St. Louis, 63103 (400 S. 18th St.)	Regional Office	Donald R. Ramsey
St. Louis, 63125 (2100 Sheridan Dr.) (Jefferson Barracks National Cemetery).	National Cemetery	Ralph E. Church
MONTANA:		
Fort Harrison, 59636	Medical and Regional Office Center ...	Joseph Underkofler
Miles City, 59301	Medical Center	Richard Stanley
NEBRASKA:		
Grand Island, 68801	......do	Michael Murphy
Lincoln, 68510 (600 S. 70th St.)	......do	David A. Asper
Lincoln, 68516 (5631 S. 48th St.)	Regional Office	David Barrett
Maxwell, 69151 (HCO 1, Box 67) (Fort McPherson National Cemetery).	National Cemetery	Shirley Milenski
Omaha, 68105 (4101 Woolworth Ave.)	Medical Center	John Phillips
NEVADA:		
Las Vegas, 89015 (102 Lake Mead Dr.)	Outpatient Clinic	Raymond J. Reeves
Reno, 89520 (1000 Locust St.)	Medical Center	Gary Whitfield
Reno, 89520 (1201 Terminal Way)	Regional Office	Eileen Straub
NEW HAMPSHIRE:		
Manchester, 03104 (718 Smyth Rd.)	Medical Center	(Vacancy)
Manchester, 03103 (275 Chestnut St.)	Regional Office	Edward Hubbard
NEW JERSEY:		
Beverly, 08010 (R #1, Bridgeboro Rd.)	National Cemetery	Delores T. Blake
East Orange, 07019	Medical Center	Kenneth Mizrach
Lyons, 07939	......do	A. Paul Kidd
Newark, 07102 (20 Washington Pl.)	Regional Office	Robert P. Van Sprang
Salem, 08079 (R.F.D. 3, Fort Mott Rd., Box 542) (Finn's Point National Cemetery) (Mail: Beverly National Cemetery, NJ).	National Cemetery	Delores T. Blake
Somerville, 08876	Asset Management Service	Robert Nelson
NEW MEXICO:		
Albuquerque, 87108 (2100 Ridgecrest Dr. SE.) ...	Medical Center	Norman Brown
Albuquerque, 87102 (500 Gold Ave. SW.)	Regional Office	Ray W. Hall
Fort Bayard, 88036 (P.O. Box 189) (Fort Bayard National Cemetery) (Mail: Fort Bliss National Cemetery, TX).	National Cemetery	Eileen Harrison
Santa Fe, 87501 (P.O. Box 88, 501 N. Guadalupe St.).	......do	Gloria C. Gamez
NEW YORK:		
Albany, 12208 (113 Holland Ave.)	Medical Center	Fred Malphurs
Batavia, 14020	......do	Paul J. McCool
Bath, 14810	Medical Center (medical and domiciliary).	Michael Sullivan
Bath, 14810 (VA Medical Center)	National Cemetery	David G. Dimmick

National Facilities—Department of Veterans Affairs—Continued

Address	Type of facility	Director
Bronx, 10468 (130 W. Kingsbridge Rd.)	Medical Center	Mary Ann Musumecii
Brooklyn, 11209 (800 Poly Pl.)	......do	James J. Farsetta
Brooklyn Division		
St. Albans Division		
Brooklyn, 11205 (35 Ryerson St.)	Outpatient Clinic	James J. Farsetta
Brooklyn, 11208 (625 Jamaica Ave.) (Cypress Hills National Cemetery) (Mail: Long Island National Cemetery, NY).	National Cemetery	Mike Cariota
Buffalo, 14202 (111 W. Huron St.)	Regional Office	(Vacancy)
Buffalo, 14215 (3495 Bailey Ave.)	Medical Center	Richard S. Droske
Calverton, 11933 (210 Princeton Blvd.)	National Cemetery	Patrick Hallinan
Canandaigua, 14424	Medical Center	Stuart Collyer
Castle Point, 12511	......do	Ronald F. Lipp
Elmira, 14901 (1825 Davis St.) (Woodlawn National Cemetery) (Mail: Bath National Cemetery, NY).	National Cemetery	David G. Dimmick
Farmingdale, 11735–1211 (2040 Wellwood Ave.) (Long Island National Cemetery).	......do	Mike Cariota
Montrose, 10548 (Franklin Delano Roosevelt Hospital).	Medical Center	(Vacancy)
New York, 10001 (252 7th Ave. at 24th St.)	Regional Office	Joseph Thompson
New York, 10001 (1st Ave. at E. 24th St.)	Medical Center	John Donnellan, Jr.
Northport, Long Island, 11768	......do	Eleanor Travers, M.D.
Syracuse, 13210 (Irving Ave. and University Pl.) .	......do	Phillip Thomas
NORTH CAROLINA:		
Asheville, 28805	......do	James A. Christian
Durham, 27705 (508 Fulton St. and Erwin Rd.) ...	......do	Michael Phaup
Fayetteville, 28301 (2300 Ramsey St.)	......do	Jerome Calhoun
New Bern, 28560 (1711 National Ave.)	National Cemetery	Margaret S. Yarborough
Raleigh, 27610 (501 Rock Quarry Rd.)	......do	Walter Gray, Jr.
Salisbury, 28144 (1601 Brenner Ave.)	Medical Center	R. Eugene Konik
Salisbury, 28144 (202 Government Rd.)	National Cemetery	Abraham G. Stice
Wilmington, 28403 (2011 Market St.) (Mail: New Bern National Cemetery, NC).	......do	Margaret S. Yarborough
Winston-Salem, 27102 (251 N. Main St.)	Regional Office	John Montgomery
NORTH DAKOTA:		
Fargo, 58102 (2101 Elm St.)	Medical and Regional Office Center ...	Douglas Kenyon
OHIO:		
Chillicothe, 45601	Medical Center	Michael Walton
Cincinnati, 45220 (3200 Vine St.)	......do	Gary Nugent
Cleveland, 44106–3800 (10701 East Blvd.)	......do	Krista Ludenia
Becksville Division		
Wade Park Division		
Cleveland, 44199 (1240 E. 9th St.)	Regional Office	Phillip J. Ross
Columbus, 43221 (2090 Kenny Rd.)	Outpatient Clinic	Lilian T. Thome, M.D.
Dayton, 45428 (VA Medical Center, 4100 W. 3d St.).	Medical Center (medical and domiciliary).	Edgar Thorsland
Dayton, 45428	National Cemetery	Karen J. DuHart
OKLAHOMA:		
Fort Gibson, 74434 (1423 Cemetery Rd.)	......do	Candice Underwood
Muskogee, 74401 (Memorial Station, Honor Heights Dr.).	Medical Center	(Vacancy)
Muskogee, 74401 (125 S. Main St.)	Regional Office	Jerry G. McRae
Oklahoma City, 73104 (921 NE. 13th St.)	Medical Center	Steve J. Gentling
OREGON:		
Eagle Point, 97524 (2763 Riley Rd.)	National Cemetery	Darryl Ferrell
Portland, 97207 (3710 SW. U.S. Veterans Hospital Rd.).	Medical Center	Barry L. Bell
Portland, 97204 (1220 SW. 3d Ave.)	Regional Office	Joseph Williams
Portland, 97266–6937 (11800 SE. Mt. Scott Blvd., P.O. Box 66147) (Willamette National Cemetery).	National Cemetery	Billy D. Murphy
Roseburg, 07470 0810	Medical Center	Alan Perry
Roseburg, 97470 (VA Medical Center) (Mail: Willamette National Cemetery, OR).	National Cemetery	Maintained by VAMC
White City, 97503	Domiciliary	George Ardries, Jr.
PENNSYLVANIA:		
Altoona, 16602–4377	Medical Center	Gerald Williams
Annville, 17003–9618 (R 2, Box 484) (Indiantown Gap National Cemetery).	National Cemetery	Charlene R. Lewis
Aspinwall (see Pittsburgh, 15240)		
Butler, 16001–2480	Medical Center	Peter Stajduhar, M.D.
Coatesville, 19320	......do	Gary Devansky
Erie, 16501 (135 E. 38th St. Blvd.)	......do	Stephen M. Lucas
Lebanon, 17042	......do	Leonard Washington, Jr.

National Facilities—Department of Veterans Affairs—Continued

Address	Type of facility	Director
Philadelphia, 19101 (5000 Wissahickon Ave.) (Insurance remittances: P.O. Box 7787). (Mail: P.O. Box 8079).	Regional Office and Insurance Center	Thomas M. Lastowka
Philadelphia, 19104 (University and Woodland Aves.).	Medical Center	Earl Falast
Philadelphia, 19138 (Haines St. and Limekiln Pike) (Mail: Beverly National Cemetery, NJ).	National Cemetery	Delores T. Blake
Pittsburgh, 15222 (1000 Liberty Ave.)	Regional Office	Harold T. Bushey
Pittsburgh, 15206 (Highland Dr.)	Medical Center	Laurn Miller
Pittsburgh, 15240 (University Dr. C) Aspinwall Division Pittsburgh Division (Mail: University Drive, Pittsburgh)	......do	Thomas A. Cappello
Wilkes-Barre, 18711 (1111 East End Blvd.)	......do	Reedes Hurt
PHILIPPINE REPUBLIC:		
Manila (1131 Roxas Blvd.) (AP 96440)	Regional Office and Outpatient Clinic .	Robert F. Moakley
PUERTO RICO:		
Bayamon, 00960 (P.O. Box 1298) (Puerto Rico National Cemetery).	National Cemetery	(Vacancy)
Hato Rey, 00918 (U.S. Courthouse and Federal Bldg., Carlos E. Chardon St.).		
San Juan, 00927–5800 (Barrio Monacillos G.P.O., Box 4867).	Medical Center	Edward Valenzuela
San Juan, 00936 (U.S. Courthouse and Federal Bldg., Carlos E. Chardon St., Hato Rey, G.P.O. Box 4867).	Regional Office	Gary L. Cole
RHODE ISLAND:		
Providence, 02903 (380 Westminster Mall)	Regional Office	(Vacancy)
Providence, 02908 (Davis Park)	Medical Center	Edward H. Seiler
SOUTH CAROLINA:		
Beaufort, 29902 (1601 Boundary St.)	National Cemetery	Rafael M. Rodriguez
Charleston, 29401–5799 (109 Bee St.)	Medical Center	Dean Billik
Columbia, 29201 (William Jennings Bryan Dorn Veterans Hospital).	......do	Robert M. Athey
Columbia, 29201 (1801 Assembly St.)	Regional Office	R. Stedman Sloan, Jr.
Florence, 29501 (803 E. National Cemetery Rd.)	National Cemetery	Kenneth LaFevor
SOUTH DAKOTA:		
Fort Meade, 57741	Medical Center	Peter Henry
Fort Meade, 57785 (Mail: Black Hills National Cemetery, SD).	National Cemetery	Douglas D. Miner
Hot Springs, 57747	Medical Center (medical and domiciliary).	Daniel Marsh
Hot Springs, 57747 (VA Medical Center) (Mail: Black Hills National Cemetery, SD).	National Cemetery	Douglas D. Miner
Sioux Falls, 57117 (Royal C. Johnson Veterans Memorial Hospital).	Medical Center and Regional Office ...	R. Vincent Crawford
Sturgis, 57785 (P.O. Box 640) (Black Hills National Cemetery).	National Cemetery	Daniel Nelson
TENNESSEE:		
Chattanooga, 37404 (1200 Bailey Ave.)	......do	James Wallace
Knoxville, 37917 (939 Tyson St. NW.) (Mail: Mountain Home).	......do	Rodney Dunn
Madison, 37115–4619 (1420 Gallatin Rd. S.) (Nashville National Cemetery).	......do	Sandy L. Noguez
Memphis, 38104 (1030 Jefferson Ave.)	Medical Center	Kenneth L. Mulholland
Memphis, 38122 (3568 Townes Ave.)	National Cemetery	Mark E. Maynard
Mountain Home, 37684 (Johnson City)	Medical Center (medical and domiciliary).	Carl Gerber, M.D.
Mountain Home, 37684 (P.O. Box 8)	National Cemetery	Rodney Dunn
Murfreesboro, 37129–1236	Medical Center	Brian Heckert
Nashville, 37212–2637 (1310 24th Ave. S.)	......do	Larry E. Deters
Nashville, 37203 (110 9th Ave. S.)	Regional Office	Thomas Jensen
TEXAS:		
Amarillo, 79106 (6010 Amarillo Blvd. W.)	Medical Center	Y.C. Parris
Austin, 78772 (1615 E. Woodward St.)	Automation Center	Robert Evans
Austin, 78714–9575 (P.O. Box 149975)	Finance Center	Harlan R. Hively
Big Spring, 79720	Medical Center	Gary Brown
Bonham, 75418 (Sam Rayburn Memorial Veterans Center).	Medical Center (medical and domiciliary).	Charles Freeman
Dallas, 75216 (4500 S. Lancaster Rd.)	Medical Center	Alan Harper
El Paso, 79925 (5919 Brook Hollow Dr.)	Outpatient Clinic	Frank Caldwell
Fort Bliss, 79906 (5200 Fred Wilson Rd., P.O. Box 6342).	National Cemetery	Eileen Harrison
Houston, 77030 (2002 Holcombe Blvd.)	Medical Center	Robert Stott
Houston, 77054 (8900 Lakes at 610 Dr.)	Regional Office	(Vacancy)

National Facilities—Department of Veterans Affairs—Continued

Address	Type of facility	Director
Houston, 77038 (10410 Veterans Memorial Dr.) ..	National Cemetery	Clyde Rowney
Kerrville, 78028	Medical Center	Arnold E. Mouish
Kerrville, 78028 (VA Medical Center, 3600 Memorial Blvd.) (Mail: Fort Sam Houston, TX).	National Cemetery	Joe A. Ramos
Marlin, 76661	Medical Center	Melvin Baker
San Antonio, 78285 (7400 Merton Minter Blvd.) (Audi L. Murphy Memorial Veterans Hospital).	......do	Jose R. Coronado
San Antonio, 98202 (517 Paso Hondo St.) (Mail: Fort Sam Houston National Cemetery, TX).	National Cemetery	Joe A. Ramos
San Antonio, 78209 (1520 Harry Wurzbach Rd.) (Fort Sam Houston National Cemetery).	National Cemetery	Joe A. Ramos
Temple, 76504 (Olin E. Teague Veterans Center)	Medical Center (medical and domiciliary).	Michael R. Harwell
Waco, 76711 (4800 Memorial Dr.)	Medical Center	Wallace M. Hopkins
Waco, 76799 (1400 N. Valley Mills Dr.)	Regional Office	Lois High
UTAH:		
Salt Lake City, 84147 (125 S. State St.)	......do	Douglas B. Wadsworth
Salt Lake City, 84148 (500 Foothill Blvd.)	Medical Center	William L. Hodson, Jr.
VERMONT:		
White River Junction, 05001	Medical and Regional Office Center ...	Gary DeGasta
VIRGINIA:		
Alexandria, 22314 (1450 Wilkes St.) (Mail: Culpeper National Cemetery, VA).	National Cemetery	Larry Williams
Culpeper, 22701 (305 U.S. Ave.)	......do	Larry Williams
Danville, 24541 (721 Lee St.) (Mail: Salisbury National Cemetery, NC).	......do	Abe C. Stice
Hampton, 23667	Medical Center (medical and domiciliary).	William G. Wright
Hampton, 23669 (Cemetery Rd. at Marshall Ave., VA).	National Cemetery	Homer D. Hardamon
Hampton, 23669 (VA Medical Center) (Mail: Cemetery Rd. at Marshall Ave., VA).	......do	Homer D. Hardamon
Hopewell, 23860 (10th Ave. and Davis St.) (City Point National Cemetery) (Mail: Richmond National Cemetery, VA).	......do	Homer D. Hardamon
Leesburg, 22075 (Balls Bluff National Cemetery) (Mail: Culpeper National Cemetery, VA).	......do	Larry Williams
Mechanicsville, 23111 (Route 156 N.) (Cold Harbor National Cemetery) (Mail: Richmond National Cemetery, VA).	......do	Homer D. Hardamon
Richmond, 23249 (1201 Broad Rock Rd.)	Medical Center	James Dudley
Richmond, 23231 (1701 Williamsburg Rd.)	National Cemetery	Homer D. Hardamon
Richmond, 23231 (8620 Varina Rd.) (Fort Harrison National Cemetery) (Mail: Richmond National Cemetery, VA).	......do	Homer D. Hardamon
Richmond, 23231 (8301 Willis Church Rd.) (Glendale National Cemetery) (Mail: Richmond National Cemetery, VA).	......do	Homer D. Hardamon
Roanoke, 24011 (210 Franklin Rd. SW.)	Regional Office	James Maye
Salem, 24153	Medical Center	John Presley
Sandston, 23150 (400 E. Williamsburg Rd.) (Seven Pines National Cemetery) (Mail: Richmond National Cemetery, VA).	National Cemetery	Homer D. Hardamon
Staunton, 24401 (901 Richmond Ave.) (Mail: Culpeper National Cemetery, VA).	......do	Larry Williams
Triangle, 22172 (R #619, 18424 Joplin Rd.) (Quantico National Cemetery).	......do	Patricia K. Novak
Winchester, 22601 (401A National Ave.) (Mail: Culpeper National Cemetery, VA).	......do	Larry Williams
WASHINGTON:		
American Lake, Tacoma, 98493	Medical Center	Frank Taylor
Seattle, 98174 (915 2d Ave.)	Regional Office	Richard F. Murphy
Seattle, 98108 (4435 Beacon Ave., S.)	Medical Center	Timothy Williams
Spokane, 99205 (N. 4815 Assembly St.)	......do	Joseph M. Manley
Walla Walla, 99362 (77 Wainwright Dr.)	......do	George Marnelli
WEST VIRGINIA:		
Beckley, 25801 (200 Veterans Ave.)	......do	Gerald Husson
Clarksburg, 26301	......do	Michael Newch
Grafton, 26354 (R #2, Box 127) (West Virginia National Cemetery).	National Cemetery	Terry Ellison
Grafton, 26354 (431 Walnut St.) (Mail: West Virginia National Cemetery, WV) (Mail: Grafton National Cemetery, WV).	......do	Terry Ellison
Huntington, 25701 (1540 Spring Valley Dr.)	Medical Center	Phillip S. Elkins
Huntington, 25701 (640 4th Ave.)	Regional Office	Greg Mason

National Facilities—Department of Veterans Affairs—Continued

Address	Type of facility	Director
Martinsburg, 25401	Medical Center (medical and domiciliary).	Richard Dell
WISCONSIN:		
Madison, 53705 (2500 Overlook Ter.) (William S. Middleton Memorial Veterans Hospital).	Medical Center	Nathan L. Geraths
Milwaukee, 53295 (5000 W. National Ave.)	Medical Center (medical and domiciliary).	Russell E. Struble
Milwaukee, 53295 (P.O. Box 6)	Regional Office	Jon A. Baker
Milwaukee, 53295–4000 (5000 W. National Ave.) (Wood National Cemetery).	National Cemetery	Richard A. Anderson
Tomah, 54660	Medical Center	Stanley Q. Johnson
WYOMING:		
Cheyenne, 82001 (2360 E. Pershing Blvd.)	Medical and Regional Office Center ...	Frank Drake
Sheridan, 82801	Medical Center	John Brinkers

Sources of Information

Audiovisuals Persons interested in the availability of VA motion pictures or exhibits for showing outside VA may write the Director, Audio Visuals Service (037), Department of Veterans Affairs, 810 Vermont Avenue NW., Washington, DC 20420. Phone, 202–482–6793 or 6794.

Contracts and Small Business Activities Persons seeking to do business with the Department of Veterans Affairs may contact the Director, Acquisition Policy and Review Service (95), 810 Vermont Avenue NW., Washington, DC 20420. Phone, 202–523–3660. A brochure *Doing Business With the Department of Veterans Affairs,* which describes acquisition opportunities and contact points, is available upon request. The *Handbook for Persons in Business,* prepared with the veteran in mind, which contains information on procurement programs, acquisition regulatory requirements, and general guidance on marketing the Federal Government, and more specifically VA, is also available to veterans upon request. Persons seeking information regarding special contracting and subcontracting programs for small, disadvantaged, 8(a) certified, and women- and veteran-owned businesses may contact the Director, Office of Small and Disadvantaged Business Utilization (00SB). Phone, 202–565–8124.

Employment The Department of Veterans Affairs employs physicians, dentists, podiatrists, optometrists, nurses, nurse anesthetists, physician assistants, expanded-function dental auxiliaries, registered respiratory therapists, certified respiratory technicians, licensed physical therapists, occupational therapists, pharmacists, and licensed practical or vocational nurses under VA's excepted merit system. This system does not require civil service eligibility. Other professional, technical, administrative, and clerical occupations exist in VA that do require civil service eligibility. Persons interested in employment should contact the Human Resources Management Office at their nearest VA facility. All qualified applicants will receive consideration for appointments without regard to race, religion, color, national origin, sex, political affiliation, or any nonmerit factor.

Freedom of Information Act Requests Inquiries should be directed to the Assistant Secretary for Management, Information Management Service (045A4), 810 Vermont Avenue NW., Washington, DC 20420. Phone, 202–535–8272.

Medical Center (Hospital) Design, Construction, and Related Services VA projects requiring services for design, construction, and other related services are advertised in the *Commerce Business Daily.* Architectural/engineering firms interested in designing VA medical center construction projects may write to the Director, A/E Evaluation Staff (087G). Phone, 202–233–3181. Construction contractors should address their inquiries to the Chief, Administrative Services Division (082C). Phone, 202–233–3308. Contact either office at the Department of Veterans Affairs Central Office, 810 Vermont Avenue NW., Washington, DC 20420; or write to the Chief, Supply Service, at any VA medical center or regional office center beginning on page 490.

News Media Representatives of the media outside Washington, DC, may contact VA through the nearest area Office of Public Affairs:

Atlanta (404–347–3236)
Chicago (312–353–4076)
Dallas (214–767–9270)
Denver (303–980–2995)
Los Angeles (310–824–4497)
New York (212–620–6525)

National and Washington, DC, media may contact the Office of Public Affairs in the VA Central Office, 810 Vermont Avenue NW., Washington, DC 20420. Phone, 202–273–5700.

Publications *Annual Report of the Secretary of Veterans Affairs* may be obtained (in single copies), without charge, from the Reports and Information Service (008C2), 810 Vermont Avenue NW., Washington, DC 20420.

The 1995 VA pamphlet *Federal Benefits for Veterans and Dependents* (80–95–1), is for sale by the Superintendent of Documents, Government Printing Office, Washington, DC 20402.

Board of Veterans Appeals Index (I–01–1), an index to appellate decisions, is available on microfiche in annual cumulation from July 1977 through December 1994. The quarterly indexes

may be purchased for $7 and annual cumulative indexes for $22.50. Annual indexes and BVA decisions for 1992 and 1993 are also available on CD–ROM for $30. The VADEX/CITATOR of Appellate Research Materials is a complete printed quarterly looseleaf cumulation of research material which may be purchased for $175 with binder and for $160 without binder. The Vadex Infobase, a computer-searchable version of the VADEX, is also available on diskettes for $100 per copy. These publications may be obtained from Promisel and Korn, Inc., Suite 480, 7201 Wisconsin Avenue, Bethesda, MD 20814. Phone, 301–986–0650.

VA Pamphlet, *A Summary of Department of Veteran Affairs Benefits* (27–82–2), may be obtained, without charge, from any VA regional office.

Interments in VA National Cemeteries, VA NCS–IS–1, provides a list of national cemeteries and information on procedures and eligibility for burial. Copies may be obtained without charge from the National Cemetery System (402E), 810 Vermont Avenue NW., Washington, DC 20420.

Persons may obtain a construction research report listing from the Director, Management and Budget Staff (O82), Office of Facilities, Department of Veterans Affairs, 810 Vermont Avenue NW., Washington, DC 20420. Phone, 202–233–3481.

For further information, contact the Office of Public Affairs, Department of Veterans Affairs, 810 Vermont Avenue NW., Washington, DC 20420. Phone, 202–273–5700.

Independent Establishments and Government Corporations

ADMINISTRATIVE CONFERENCE OF THE UNITED STATES

Suite 500, 2120 L Street NW., Washington, DC 20037–1568
Phone, 202–254–7020

Chairman	THOMASINA V. ROGERS
Executive Director	CONNIE M. HARSHAW, *Acting*
Research Director	JEFFREY S. LUBBERS
General Counsel	GARY J. EDLES
Council:	
Vice Chairman	SALLY KATZEN
Members	SUSAN AU ALLEN, WALTER GELLHORN, WILLIAM B. GOULD IV, C. BOWDEN GRAY, GINGER E. LEW, WILLIAM R. NEALE, JOHN D. PODESTA, JACK QUINN, PAUL A. VANDERMYDE

[For the Administrative Conference of the United States statement of organization, see the *Code of Federal Regulations*, Title 1, Part 301]

The Conference develops recommendations for improving the fairness and effectiveness of procedures by which Federal agencies administer regulatory, benefit, and other Government programs. Conference members are Federal officials, private lawyers, university professors, and other experts in administrative law and government who meet to consider studies of selected problems involving administrative procedures and the regulatory process.

The Administrative Conference of the United States was established as a permanent independent agency by the Administrative Conference Act (5 U.S.C. 591–596) enacted in 1964.

Membership

By statute the Administrative Conference has no fewer than 75 and no more than 101 members, a majority of whom are

Government officials. The Chairman of the Conference is appointed by the President with the advice and consent of the Senate for a 5-year term. The Council, which acts as the executive board, consists of the Chairman and 10 other members appointed by the President for 3-year terms. Federal officials named to the Council may constitute no more than one-half of the total Council membership. Members

ADMINISTRATIVE CONFERENCE OF THE UNITED STATES

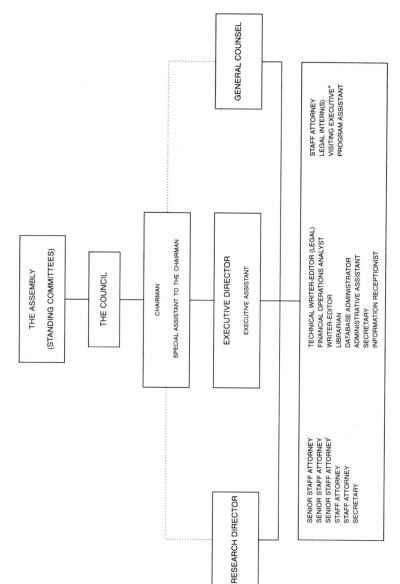

THE ASSEMBLY
(STANDING COMMITTEES)

THE COUNCIL

CHAIRMAN

SPECIAL ASSISTANT TO THE CHAIRMAN

GENERAL COUNSEL

STAFF ATTORNEY
LEGAL INTERN(S)
VISITING EXECUTIVE*
PROGRAM ASSISTANT

EXECUTIVE DIRECTOR

EXECUTIVE ASSISTANT

RESEARCH DIRECTOR

SENIOR STAFF ATTORNEY
SENIOR STAFF ATTORNEY
SENIOR STAFF ATTORNEY
STAFF ATTORNEY
STAFF ATTORNEY
SECRETARY

TECHNICAL WRITER-EDITOR (LEGAL)
FINANCIAL OPERATIONS ANALYST
WRITER-EDITOR
LIBRARIAN
DATABASE ADMINISTRATOR
ADMINISTRATIVE ASSISTANT
SECRETARY
INFORMATION RECEPTIONIST

*Distinguished visiting executive—ceiling exempt.

representing the private sector are appointed by the Chairman, with the approval of the Council, for 2-year terms. The Chairman is the only full-time compensated member.

The entire membership is divided into committees, each assigned a broad area of interest such as adjudication, administration, governmental processes, judicial review, regulation, or rulemaking. The membership meeting in plenary session by statute must meet at least once, and customarily meets twice, each year.

Activities

Subjects for inquiry are developed by the Chairman and approved by the Council. The committees conduct thorough studies of these subjects, propose recommendations, and prepare supporting reports. Recommendations are evaluated by the Council and, if ready for Assembly consideration, are distributed to the membership with the supporting reports and placed on the agenda of the next plenary session. The deliberations of the committees and Assembly are public.

The Chairman is authorized to encourage the departments and agencies to adopt the recommendations of the Conference and is required to transmit to the President and to Congress an annual report and interim reports concerning the activities of the Conference, including reports on the implementation of its recommendations.

Recommendations adopted by the Conference may call for new legislation or for action on the part of affected agencies. A substantial number of recommendations have been implemented and others are in the process of being implemented.

The Chairman may make independent inquiries into procedural matters, including matters proposed by individuals inside or outside the Government. The purpose of such inquiries is to determine whether the problems should be made the subject of Conference study in the interest of developing fair and effective procedures for such cases.

Upon the request of the head of a department or agency, the Chairman is authorized to furnish advice and assistance on matters of administrative procedure. The Conference may collect information and statistics from departments and agencies and publish such reports as it considers useful for evaluating and improving administrative processes. The Conference also serves as a forum for the interchange among departments and agencies of information that may be useful in improving administrative practices and procedures.

Sources of Information

The Conference furnishes upon request copies of its recent recommendations and reports. It also maintains a library where copies of all official Conference documents are available for public inspection. Recommendations of the Conference appear in title 1, part 305, of the 1993 *Code of Federal Regulations*. A listing of recommendations appears (but is not published in full text) in the 1994 *Code of Federal Regulations*.

For further information, contact the Public Information Office, Administrative Conference of the United States, Suite 500, 2120 L Street NW., Washington, DC 20037. Phone, 202-254-7020.

AFRICAN DEVELOPMENT FOUNDATION

1400 Eye Street NW., Washington, DC 20005
Phone, 202-673-3916

Board of Directors:
Chairman   ERNEST G. GREEN

Vice Chair

WILLIE GRACE CAMPBELL

Members of the Board:

CECIL BANKS, MARION DAWSON,
JOHN HICKS, GEORGE MOOSE,
(VACANCY)

Staff:

President

WILLIAM R. FORD

Vice President

CARROLL BOUCHARD

[For the African Development Foundation statement of organization, see the *Code of Federal Regulations,* Title 22, Part 1501]

The African Development Foundation assists and supports indigenous, community-based self-help organizations in their efforts to solve their own development problems.

The African Development Foundation was established by the African Development Foundation Act (22 U.S.C. 290h), as a nonprofit, Government corporation to support the self-help efforts of poor people in African countries. The Foundation became operational in 1984 and is governed by a seven-member Board of Directors, appointed by the President with the advice and consent of the Senate. By law, five Board members are from the private sector and two are from the Government.

The purposes of the Foundation are to:

—strengthen the bonds of friendship and understanding between the people of Africa and the United States;

—support self-help development activities at the local level designed to promote opportunities for community development;

—stimulate and promote effective and expanding participation of Africans in their development process; and

—encourage the establishment and growth of development institutions that are indigenous to particular countries in Africa and that can respond to the requirements of the poor in those countries.

To carry out its purposes, the Foundation makes grants, loans, and loan guarantees to African private groups, associations, or other entities engaged in peaceful activities that enable the people of Africa to develop more fully.

For further information, contact the Public Affairs Officer, African Development Foundation, 10th Floor, 1400 Eye Street NW., Washington, DC 20005. Phone, 202–673–3916.

CENTRAL INTELLIGENCE AGENCY

Washington, DC 20505
Phone, 703–482–1100

Director of Central Intelligence

JOHN M. DEUTCH

Deputy Director of Central Intelligence

GEORGE J. TENET

[For the Central Intelligence Agency statement of organization, see the *Code of Federal Regulations,* Title 32, Part 1900]

The Central Intelligence Agency collects, evaluates, and disseminates vital information on political, military, economic, scientific, and other developments abroad needed to safeguard national security.

The Central Intelligence Agency was established under the National Security Council by the National Security Act of 1947, as amended (50 U.S.C. 401 et seq.). It now functions under that statute, Executive Order 12333 of December 4, 1981, and other laws, regulations, and directives.

The Director of Central Intelligence heads both the Intelligence Community and the Central Intelligence Agency and is the President's principal adviser on intelligence matters. The Director and Deputy Director of Central Intelligence are appointed by the President with the advice and consent of the Senate.

The Central Intelligence Agency, under the direction of the President or the National Security Council:

—advises the National Security Council in matters concerning such intelligence activities of the Government departments and agencies as relate to national security;

—makes recommendations to the National Security Council for the coordination of such intelligence activities of the departments and agencies of the Government as relate to the national security;

—correlates and evaluates intelligence relating to the national security and provides for the appropriate dissemination of such intelligence within the Government;

—collects, produces, and disseminates counterintelligence and foreign intelligence, including information not otherwise obtainable. The collection of counterintelligence or foreign intelligence within the United States shall be coordinated with the Federal Bureau of Investigation as required by procedures agreed upon by the Director of Central Intelligence and the Attorney General;

—collects, produces, and disseminates intelligence on foreign aspects of narcotics production and trafficking;

—conducts counterintelligence activities outside the United States and, without assuming or performing any internal security functions, conducts counterintelligence activities within the United States in coordination with the Bureau as required by procedures agreed upon by the Director of Central Intelligence and the Attorney General;

—coordinates counterintelligence activities and the collection of information not otherwise obtainable when conducted outside the United States by other departments and agencies;

—conducts special activities approved by the President. No agency, except the Central Intelligence Agency (or the Armed Forces of the United States in time of war declared by Congress or during any period covered by a report from the President to the Congress under the War Powers Resolution (50 U.S.C. 1541 et seq.)), may conduct any special activity unless the President determines that another agency is more likely to achieve a particular objective;

—carries out or contracts for research, development, and procurement of technical systems and devices relating to authorized functions;

—protects the security of its installations, activities, information, property, and employees by appropriate means, including such investigations of applicants, employees, contractors, and other persons with similar associations with the Agency, as are necessary;

—conducts such administrative and technical support activities within and outside the United States as are necessary to perform its functions, including procurement and essential cover and proprietary arrangements; and

—performs such other functions and duties relating to intelligence that affect the national security as the National Security Council may from time to time direct.

The Agency has no police, subpoena, or law enforcement powers or internal security functions.

For further information, contact the Central Intelligence Agency, Washington, DC 20505. Phone, 703–482–1100.

COMMODITY FUTURES TRADING COMMISSION

2033 K Street NW., Washington, DC 20581
Phone, 202–254–6387

Chairman	MARY L. SCHAPIRO
Commissioners	JOSEPH B. DIAL, SHELIA C. BAIR, JOHN E. TULL, JR., BARBARA P. HOLUM
General Counsel	ELISSE B. WALTER
Executive Director	SUSAN BAUMANN

[For the Commodity Futures Trading Commission statement of organization, see the *Code of Federal Regulations*, Title 17, Part 140]

The Commodity Futures Trading Commission promotes healthy economic growth, protects the rights of customers, and ensures fairness and integrity in the marketplace through regulation of futures trading. To this end, it also engages in the analysis of economic issues affected by or affecting futures trading.

The Commodity Futures Trading Commission, the Federal regulatory agency for futures trading, was established by the Commodity Futures Trading Commission Act of 1974 (7 U.S.C. 4a). The Commission began operation in April 1975, and its authority to regulate futures trading was renewed by Congress in 1978, 1982, 1986, 1992, and 1995.

The Commission consists of five Commissioners who are appointed by the President, with the advice and consent of the Senate. One Commissioner is designated by the President to serve as Chairman. The Commissioners serve staggered 5-year terms, and by law no more than three Commissioners can belong to the same political party.

The five major operating components that exist within the Commission are: the divisions of enforcement, economic analysis, trading and markets, and the offices of the executive director and the general counsel.

Activities

The Commission regulates trading on the 11 U.S. futures exchanges, which offer active futures and options contracts. It also regulates the activities of numerous commodity exchange members, public brokerage houses (futures commission merchants), Commission-registered futures industry salespeople and associated persons, commodity trading advisers, and commodity pool operators. Some off-exchange transactions involving instruments similar in nature to futures contracts also fall under Commission jurisdiction.

The Commission's regulatory and enforcement efforts are designed to ensure that the futures trading process is fair and that it protects both the rights of customers and the financial integrity of the marketplace. It approves the rules under which an exchange proposes to operate and monitors exchange enforcement of those rules. It reviews the terms of proposed futures contracts, and registers companies and individuals who handle customer funds or give trading advice. The Commission also protects the public by enforcing rules that require

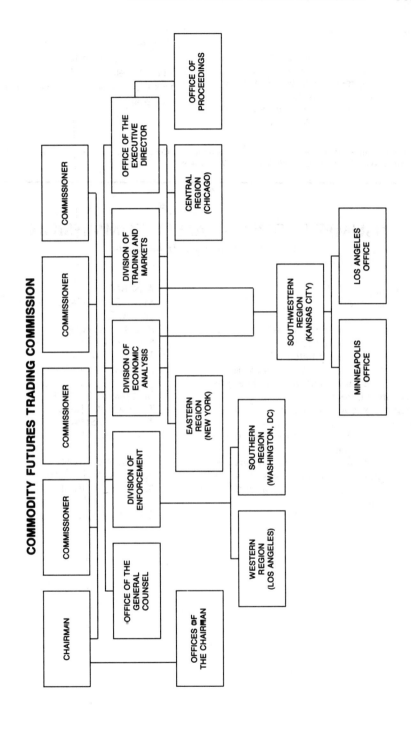

COMMODITY FUTURES TRADING COMMISSION

CHAIRMAN

COMMISSIONER

COMMISSIONER

COMMISSIONER

COMMISSIONER

OFFICE OF THE EXECUTIVE DIRECTOR

OFFICE OF PROCEEDINGS

DIVISION OF TRADING AND MARKETS

DIVISION OF ECONOMIC ANALYSIS

DIVISION OF ENFORCEMENT

OFFICE OF THE GENERAL COUNSEL

OFFICES OF THE CHAIRMAN

CENTRAL REGION (CHICAGO)

EASTERN REGION (NEW YORK)

SOUTHERN REGION (WASHINGTON, DC)

WESTERN REGION (LOS ANGELES)

SOUTHWESTERN REGION (KANSAS CITY)

LOS ANGELES OFFICE

MINNEAPOLIS OFFICE

that customer funds be kept in bank accounts separate from accounts maintained by firms for their own use, and that such customer accounts be marked to present market value at the close of trading each day.

Large regional offices are maintained in Chicago, IL, and New York, NY, where many of the Nation's futures exchanges are located. Smaller regional offices are located in Kansas City, MO, and Los Angeles, CA. A suboffice of the Kansas City regional office is located in Minneapolis, MN.

For further information, contact the Office of Public Affairs, Commodity Futures Trading Commission, 2033 K Street NW., Washington, DC 20581. Phone, 202–254–8630.

CONSUMER PRODUCT SAFETY COMMISSION

East West Towers, 4330 East West Highway, Bethesda, MD 20814
Phone, 301–504–0580

Chairman	ANN BROWN
Commissioners	MARY SHEILA GALL, (3 VACANCIES)
General Counsel	ERIC A. RUBEL
Director, Office of Congressional Relations	ROBERT J. WAGER
Director, Office of the Secretary	SADYE E. DUNN
Freedom of Information Officer	TODD A. STEVENSON
Director, Office of Equal Employment Opportunity and Minority Enterprise	JOHN W. BARRETT, JR.
Executive Director	BERTRAM R. COTTINE
Deputy Executive Director	THOMAS W. MURR, JR.
Inspector General	THOMAS F. STEIN
Director, Office of Human Resources Management	JANET C. BURKE
Director, Office of Information Services	DOUGLAS G. NOBLE
Director, Office of Planning and Evaluation	NICHOLAS V. MARCHICA
Director, Office of Information and Public Affairs	KATHLEEN P. BEGALA
Director, Office of the Budget	EDWARD E. QUIST

Associate Executive Director for Administration	MAUNA V. KAMMER
Associate Executive Director for Field Operations	(VACANCY)
Assistant Executive Director for Compliance	DAVID SCHMELTZER
Assistant Executive Director for Hazard Identification and Reduction	RONALD L. MEDFORD
Associate Executive Director for Engineering Sciences	ANDREW G. STADNIK
Associate Executive Director for Health Sciences	MARY ANN DANELLO
Associate Executive Director for Epidemiology	(VACANCY)
Associate Executive Director for Laboratory Sciences	ANDREW G. ULSAMER
Associate Executive Director for Economic Analysis	WARREN J. PRUNELLA

[For the Consumer Product Safety Commission statement of organization, see the *Code of Federal Regulations,* Title 16, Part 1000]

The Consumer Product Safety Commission protects the public against unreasonable risks of injury from consumer products; assists consumers in evaluating the comparative safety of consumer products; develops uniform safety standards for consumer products and minimizes conflicting State and local regulations; and promotes research and investigation into the causes and prevention of product-related deaths, illnesses, and injuries.

The Consumer Product Safety Commission is an independent Federal regulatory agency established by the Consumer Product Safety Act (15 U.S.C. 2051 *et seq.*). The Commission consists of five Commissioners, appointed by the President with the advice and consent of the Senate, one of whom is appointed Chairman.

In addition to the authority created by the Consumer Product Safety Act, the Commission has responsibility for implementing provisions of the Flammable Fabrics Act (15 U.S.C. 1191),

the Poison Prevention Packaging Act of 1970 (15 U.S.C. 1471), the Federal Hazardous Substances Act (15 U.S.C. 1261), and the act of August 2, 1956 (15 U.S.C. 1211), which prohibits the transportation of refrigerators without door safety devices.

Activities

To help protect the public from unreasonable risks of injury associated with consumer products, the Commission:

CONSUMER PRODUCT SAFETY COMMISSION

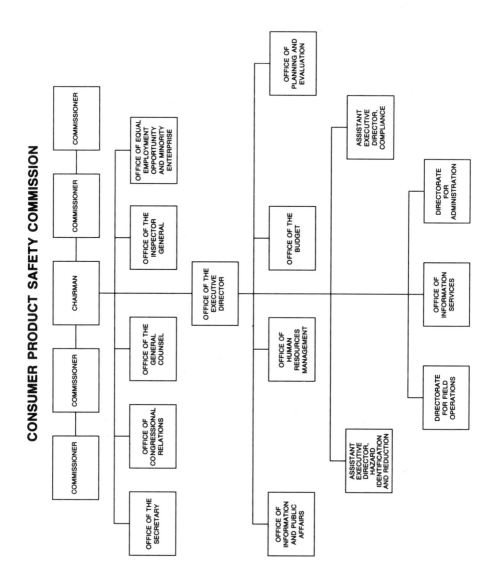

—requires manufacturers to report defects in products that could create substantial hazards;

—requires, where appropriate, corrective action with respect to specific substantially hazardous consumer products already in commerce;

—collects information on consumer product-related injuries and maintains a comprehensive Injury Information Clearinghouse;

—conducts research on consumer product hazards;

—encourages and assists in the development of voluntary standards related to the safety of consumer products;

—establishes, where appropriate, mandatory consumer product standards;

—bans, where appropriate, hazardous consumer products; and

—conducts outreach programs for consumers, industry, and local governments.

Offices

The Commission's headquarters is located at East West Towers, 4330 East West Highway, Bethesda, MD 20814. Regional offices are located in Chicago, IL; New York, NY; and San Francisco, CA. Field offices are maintained in various cities.

Sources of Information

Consumer Information   The Commission operates a toll-free Consumer Product Safety Hotline, 800–638–CPSC; and a teletypewriter for the hearing-impaired, 800–638–8270 (or in Maryland only, 800–492–8140).

General Inquiries   Information on Commission activities may be obtained from the Office of Information and Public Affairs, Consumer Product Safety Commission, Washington, DC 20207. Phone, 301–504–0580.

Reading Room   A public information room is maintained at the Commission.

For further information, contact the Office of Information and Public Affairs, Consumer Product Safety Commission, East West Towers, 4330 East West Highway, Bethesda, MD 20814. Phone, 301–504–0580.

CORPORATION FOR NATIONAL AND COMMUNITY SERVICE

1201 New York Avenue NW., Washington, DC 20525
Phone, 202–606–5000

Board of Directors:

Chairman	JAMES JOSEPH
Members	ANDREA BROWN, THOMAS EHRLICH, CHRIS EVERT, CHRISTOPHER GALLAGHER, TERESA HEINZ, CHRISTINE HERNANDEZ, REATHA CLARK KING, CAROL KINSLEY, LESLIE LENKOWSKY, MARLEE MATLIN, GERALD MCENTEE, ARTHUR NAPARSTEK, WALTER SHORENSTEIN, JOHN ROTHER
Members (*ex officio*)	
(Secretary of Agriculture)	DAN GLICKMAN
(Secretary of Defense)	WILLIAM PERRY
(Secretary of Education)	RICHARD W. RILEY

(Secretary of Health and Human Services)	DONNA E. SHALALA
(Secretary of Housing and Urban Development)	HENRY G. CISNEROS
(Secretary of the Interior)	BRUCE BABBITT
(Secretary of Labor)	ROBERT B. REICH
(Attorney General)	JANET RENO
(Director, Peace Corps)	CHARLES R. BAQUET III, *Acting*
(Administrator, Environmental Protection Agency)	CAROL M. BROWNER
(Chief Executive Officer, Corporation for National and Community Service)	ELI J. SEGAL

Officials

Chief Executive Officer	CATHERINE MILTON
Executive Director/Executive Vice President	SHIRLEY SAGAWA
Deputy Executive Director	TRACY GRAY
Vice President/Director, AmeriCorps*VISTA, National Senior Service Corps and Hope VI	
Vice President/Director, National Civilian Community Corps	DONALD SCOTT
Director, Corporation Field Operations	MALCOLM COLES
Director, Federal Partnerships and Special Programs	SUSAN STROUD
Director, Learn and Serve America	SUSAN STROUD, *Acting*
Director, AmeriCorps*USA Programs	DIANA ALGRA
Director, AmeriCorps Leaders Program	JANET PETERS MAUCERI
Inspector General	LUISE JORDAN
Chief External Affairs Officer	C. RICHARD ALLEN
Director, Congressional and Intergovernmental Affairs	GENE SOFER
Director, Public Affairs	JAY TOSCANO
Director, Public Liaison	MELINDA HUDSON
Chief Financial Officer	GARY KOWALCZYK
Comptroller	DAVID SPEVACEK
Chief Operating Officer	LARRY WILSON
General Counsel	TERRY RUSSELL
Director, Personnel	PHYLLIS BEAULIEU

The Corporation for National and Community Service engages Americans of all backgrounds in community-based service. This service addresses the Nation's educational, public safety, human, and environmental needs to achieve direct and demonstrable results. In doing so, the Corporation fosters civic responsibility, strengthens the ties that bind us together as a people, and provides educational opportunity for those who make a substantial service contribution.

The Corporation for National and Community Service (Corporation) was established by the National and Community Service Act of 1993 (42 U.S.C. 12651 *et seq.*). The Corporation assumed the programs and authorities of the Commission on National and Community Service and effective April 1, 1994, incorporated programs previously administered by ACTION under authority of the Domestic Volunteer Service Act of 1973, as amended (42 U.S.C. 4950). Both ACTION and the Commission for National and Community Service were abolished as Federal agencies.

The Corporation is a Federal corporation and is governed by a 15-

CORPORATION FOR NATIONAL AND COMMUNITY SERVICE

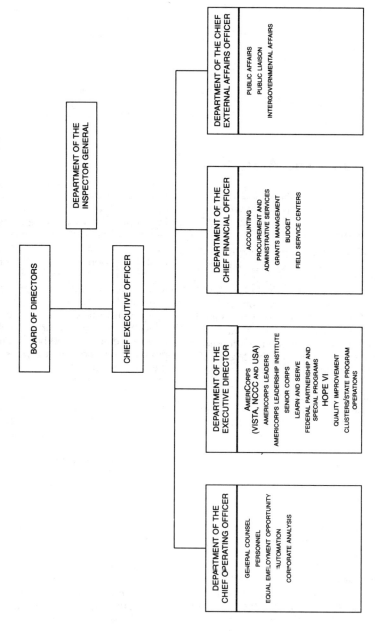

BOARD OF DIRECTORS

DEPARTMENT OF THE INSPECTOR GENERAL

CHIEF EXECUTIVE OFFICER

DEPARTMENT OF THE CHIEF OPERATING OFFICER
- GENERAL COUNSEL
- PERSONNEL
- EQUAL EMPLOYMENT OPPORTUNITY
- AUTOMATION
- CORPORATE ANALYSIS

DEPARTMENT OF THE EXECUTIVE DIRECTOR
- AMERICORPS (VISTA, NCCC AND USA)
- AMERICORPS LEADERS
- AMERICORPS LEADERSHIP INSTITUTE
- SENIOR CORPS
- LEARN AND SERVE
- FEDERAL PARTNERSHIP AND SPECIAL PROGRAMS
- HOPE VI
- QUALITY IMPROVEMENT
- CLUSTERS/STATE PROGRAM OPERATIONS

DEPARTMENT OF THE CHIEF FINANCIAL OFFICER
- ACCOUNTING
- PROCUREMENT AND ADMINISTRATIVE SERVICES
- GRANTS MANAGEMENT
- BUDGET
- FIELD SERVICE CENTERS

DEPARTMENT OF THE CHIEF EXTERNAL AFFAIRS OFFICER
- PUBLIC AFFAIRS
- PUBLIC LIAISON
- INTERGOVERNMENTAL AFFAIRS

member bipartisan Board of Directors, appointed by the President with the advice and consent of the Senate. Each member serves a 5-year term. The membership of the Board is diverse according to race, ethnicity, age, gender, and disability characteristics. The Secretaries of Agriculture, Defense, Education, Health and Human Services, Housing and Urban Development, Interior, and Labor; the Attorney General, the Environmental Protection Agency Administrator, the Peace Corps Director, and the Chief Executive Officer of the Corporation serve as *ex-officio* members of the Board. The Board has overall policy direction over the Corporation's activities and has the power to make all final grant decisions, approve the strategic plan and annual budget, and advise and make recommendations to the President and the Congress regarding changes in the national service laws.

Programs and Activities

The Corporation serves its mission through three major program areas:

AmeriCorps

AmeriCorps is the Nation's national service initiative that engages thousands of Americans of all ages and backgrounds in solving the most pressing community and national problems. AmeriCorps members get things done by providing service to meet educational, public safety, human, and environmental needs. In exchange for 1 or 2 years of service, members will receive service education awards of up to $4,725 per year to help finance their college education or vocational training, or to pay back their student loans. The Corporation has established an Education Award Trust Fund to administer the award monies.

There are three components to AmeriCorps: AmeriCorps*USA is administered through grants, while AmeriCorps*VISTA and AmeriCorps*National Civilian Community Corps are run directly by the Corporation. Currently, some 20,000 members are serving in AmeriCorps.

AmeriCorps*USA   AmeriCorps*USA members accomplish their mission by providing direct service in the four issue areas established by law: education, public safety, human needs, and the environment. Services include: tutoring school-age children; serving as mentor to teen-age parents; developing crime prevention workshops and providing victim assistance; helping the homebound and disabled live independently; coordinating needed services for public housing projects; starting citywide recycling programs; and restoring national parks. Full-time AmeriCorps*USA members must serve at least 1,700 hours during a period of not less than 9 months and not more than 12 months to be eligible for the education award. Part-time members must serve at least 900 hours during a period of not more than 2 years (unless the part-time member is enrolled in an institution of higher education while performing some or all of the service, in which case the member must provide at least 900 hours of service during a period of not more than 3 years).

The Corporation funds AmeriCorps*USA through population-based State allocations; funds distributed to programs selected by the States and submitted to the Corporation through competitive consideration; and programs operated by national nonprofit organizations, professional corps, programs operating in more than one State, and programs operated by Federal agencies. The funds granted to the States, on both formula and competitive bases, are administered by State Commissions on National and Community Service, which subgrant the monies to individual community-based programs. Information regarding annual grants requirements and schedules is published in the *Federal Register*.

AmeriCorps*National Civilian Community Corps (AmeriCorps*NCCC) AmeriCorps*NCCC's mission is to promote civic pride and responsibility through community service. Corps members work in collaboration with community representatives to complete service learning projects in the issue areas of education, public safety, human needs, and the environment—with the primary focus on environmental needs. Corps members, ages 18–24, are recruited nationally and participate in innovative training programs that uniquely combine the best in military training, techniques, Civilian Conservation Corps values, and service learning models. AmeriCorps*NCCC is a residential program, with members living at campuses located at closed or downsized military facilities at Aberdeen, MD; Charleston, SC; Denver, CO; and San Diego, CA. AmeriCorps*NCCC is directly administered by the Corporation.

AmeriCorps*VISTA AmeriCorps*VISTA is a full-time service program which is required by law to address poverty and poverty-related problems. Established in 1965, 4,000 VISTA's are supported directly by the Corporation, but serve with community-based public and private nonprofit organizations through memoranda of agreement between the Corporation and community-based groups. AmeriCorps*VISTA assignments differ from the AmeriCorps*USA and AmeriCorps*NCCC programs in that participants must be assigned to anti-poverty activities and are expected to serve in capacity-building assignments, whereas other AmeriCorps members emphasize direct service. Full-time AmeriCorps*VISTA service is 12 months, with members receiving a living allowance and health and child care; or they may elect to take a $1,200 cash stipend at the close of service rather than an education award.

Learn and Serve America

Learn and Serve America supports service learning by students from kindergarten through graduate school. Service learning is an innovative concept through which students participate in organized service experiences that meet community needs and are supported by a curriculum that allows research, reflection, and discussion of their experiences. The focus of Learn and Serve America is to build a solid foundation for service learning in the curriculum of every school in America. The Corporation awards competitive grants to support Learn and Serve America on an annual basis. Notices of funds availability published in the *Federal Register* provide information concerning application deadlines and program requirements.

School-Based and Community-Based Programs The goal of Learn and Serve America's School-Based and Community-Based Programs is to increase opportunities for school-age youth to learn and develop through service to their communities. The Corporation supports these initiatives through distribution of funds to State education agencies according to a population-based allotment. Grants to State commissions on national service, nonprofit grantmaking entities, Indian tribes, and U.S. territories are competitive.

School-based programs are administered by State education agencies, local education agencies in States not applying for funding, Indian tribes, and U.S. territories. Participants are elementary and secondary school students and out-of-school youth between the ages of 5–17. Schools use Learn and Serve America grants for adult volunteer programs and teacher training in service-learning, along with planning, implementing, and expanding service-learning programs. Community-based programs are administered by State commissions on national and community service and nonprofit organizations.

Higher Education Programs Service Learning at the post-secondary level is supported by grants to institutions of higher learning, consortia of institutions of higher learning, and public and private nonprofit organizations in partnership with institutions of higher education. These grants enable creation or expansion of community service opportunities for students and explore new ways to integrate service into the college curriculum and support model community service programs on campus. The programs are located in 38 States, the District of Columbia, and Puerto Rico.

National Senior Service Corps (Senior Corps)

The three Senior Corps Programs— Retired and Senior Volunteers (RSVP), the Foster Grandparent Program (FGP), and the Senior Companion Program (SCP)—support community service by senior adults. These programs demonstrate the continued resource of seniors, provide valuable community service, and engage the experience, expertise, and commitment of seniors in a continued active involvement in the community. Each of these programs is funded through renewable project grants to public and private nonprofit organizations, who enter into memoranda of agreement with local institutions, including schools, hospitals, senior centers, and other organizations, who directly assign and supervise participants. Most Corporation funding supports continuation projects; new projects are awarded competitively when funds are available.

Retired and Senior Volunteer Program The Retired and Senior Volunteer Program provides part-time, uncompensated service opportunities for persons age 55 or older. Participants, serving in community-based projects across America, serve a wide range of national and community needs, working with persons of all ages.

Foster Grandparent Program The Foster Grandparent Program provides service to children with special needs. Participants must be 60 years of age or older, and must be considered low-income by published Corporation criteria. Participants serve 20-hour weeks, typically 4 hours a day, and provide personal love, attention, and support to children. Children served include those with physical and developmental disabilities, living in conditions of poverty; involved in the

juvenile justice system; teen-age mothers and their children; and Head Start participants. Foster Grandparents receive a stipend of $2.45 per hour and are provided meals, transportation, and physical examinations. They serve in all 50 States, the District of Columbia, Puerto Rico, and the Virgin Islands.

Senior Companion Program The Senior Companion Program engages low-income seniors age 60 and older in service to adults with special needs, with a focus on service to the frail elderly. Eligibility criteria and program benefits for Senior Companions are the same as those provided to Foster Grandparents. Senior Companions provide support, assistance, and companionship to those whom they serve in both in-home and institutional settings. They also provide respite care to caregivers, especially family members of the frail elderly.

Other Corporation Initiatives The Corporation's mission to develop and support an ethic of service in America involves initiatives, special demonstration projects, and other activities, in addition to the three major program areas. These include the new National Service Leadership Institution in San Francisco, CA, the AmeriCorps Leaders Program (and similar leaders programs in AmeriCorps*VISTA and AmeriCorps*NCCC), a disaster response initiative, and short-term summer service intitatives. The Corporation also carries out an extensive training and technical assistance effort to support and assist State Commissions and service programs. Through partnerships with the private sector, other Federal agencies, and the Points of Light Foundation, the Corporation further advocates and advances service in America. The Corporation provides timely information about grants and financial assistance through notices of funds availability in the *Federal Register*.

Sources of Information

General Inquiries To obtain additional information regarding the Corporation's programs and activities, call 1–800–942–2677, or for Senior Corps programs, 1–800–424–8867.

Grants   Notices of funds availability are published in the *Federal Register* for most Corporation programs. Corporation State Program Offices and State Commissions on National and Community Service are located in most States and are the best source of information on programs in specific States or communities.

National Service Recruitment   Persons interested in participating in service activities should call 1–800–942–2677, or contact Corporation State Offices or State Commissions on National and Community Service.

For further information, contact the Corporation for National and Community Service, 1201 New York Avenue NW., Washington, DC 20525. Phone, 202–606–5000.

DEFENSE NUCLEAR FACILITIES SAFETY BOARD
Suite 700, 625 Indiana Avenue NW., Washington, DC 20004
Phone, 202–208–6400

Chairman	JOHN T. CONWAY
Vice Chairman	A.J. EGGENBERGER
Members	JOHN W. CRAWFORD, JR., JOSEPH J. DINUNNO, HERBERT J.C. KOUTS
General Counsel	ROBERT M. ANDERSEN
General Manager	KENNETH M. PUSATERI
Technical Director	GEORGE W. CUNNINGHAM

The Defense Nuclear Facilities Safety Board reviews and evaluates the content and implementation of standards relating to the design, construction, operation, and decommissioning of defense nuclear facilities of the Department of Energy (DOE).

The Defense Nuclear Facilities Safety Board was established as an independent agency on September 29, 1988, by the Atomic Energy Act of 1954, as amended (42 U.S.C. 2286–2286i).

The Board is composed of five members appointed by the President with the advice and consent of the Senate. Members of the Board are appointed from among United States citizens who are respected experts in the field of nuclear safety.

Activities

The Defense Nuclear Facilities Safety Board reviews and evaluates the content and implementation of standards for defense nuclear facilities of DOE; investigates any event or practice at these facilities which may adversely affect public health and safety; and reviews and monitors the design, construction, and operation of facilities. The Board makes recommendations to the Secretary of Energy concerning DOE defense nuclear facilities to ensure adequate protection of public health and safety. In the event that any aspect of operations, practices, or occurrences reviewed by the Board is determined to present an imminent or severe threat to public health and safety, the Board transmits its recommendations directly to the President.

For further information, contact the Defense Nuclear Facilities Safety Board, Suite 700, 625 Indiana Avenue NW., Washington, DC 20004. Phone, 202–208–6400.

DEFENSE NUCLEAR FACILITIES SAFETY BOARD

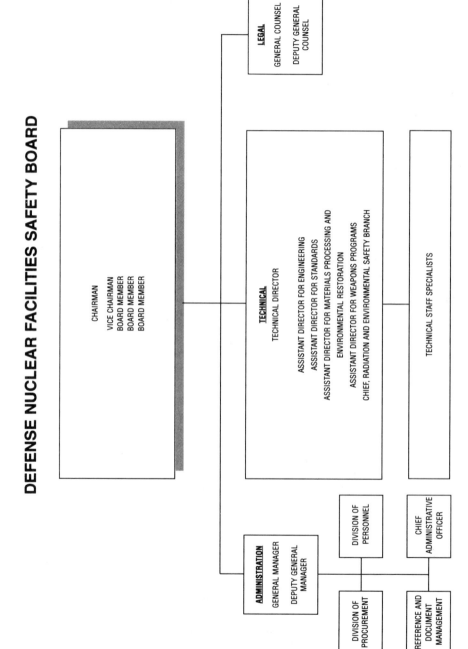

CHAIRMAN
VICE CHAIRMAN
BOARD MEMBER
BOARD MEMBER
BOARD MEMBER

LEGAL
GENERAL COUNSEL
DEPUTY GENERAL COUNSEL

TECHNICAL
TECHNICAL DIRECTOR
ASSISTANT DIRECTOR FOR ENGINEERING
ASSISTANT DIRECTOR FOR STANDARDS
ASSISTANT DIRECTOR FOR MATERIALS PROCESSING AND ENVIRONMENTAL RESTORATION
ASSISTANT DIRECTOR FOR WEAPONS PROGRAMS
CHIEF, RADIATION AND ENVIRONMENTAL SAFETY BRANCH

TECHNICAL STAFF SPECIALISTS

ADMINISTRATION
GENERAL MANAGER
DEPUTY GENERAL MANAGER

DIVISION OF PERSONNEL

DIVISION OF PROCUREMENT

CHIEF ADMINISTRATIVE OFFICER

REFERENCE AND DOCUMENT MANAGEMENT

ENVIRONMENTAL PROTECTION AGENCY

401 M Street SW., Washington, DC 20460
Phone, 202-260-2090

Administrator	CAROL M. BROWNER
Deputy Administrator	FRED J. HANSEN

Staff Offices:

Associate Administrator for Regional Operations and State/Local Relations	SHELLEY H. METZENBAUM
Associate Administrator for Communications, Education and Public Affairs	LORETTA UCELLI
Associate Administrator for Congressional and Legislative Affairs	ROBERT HICKMOTT
Director, Executive Support Office	DIANE N. BAZZLE
Director, Executive Secretariat	SAUNDRA HUDNALL
Chief, Office of Administrative Law Judges	JOHN LOTIS
Director, Office of Civil Rights	DAN RONDEAU
Director, Office of Small and Disadvantaged Business Utilization	LEON H. HAMPTON
Director, Science Advisory Board	DONALD G. BARNES
Director, Pollution Policy	ERIC V. SCHAEFFER
Director, Cooperative Environmental Management	ABBY J. PIRNIE
Assistant Administrator for International Activities	WILLIAM A. NITZE
Principal Deputy Assistant Administrator	ALAN D. HECHT
Deputy Assistant Administrator	ALAN B. SIELEN, *Acting*

Program Offices:

Assistant Administrator for Administration and Resources Management	JONATHAN Z. CANNON
Deputy Assistant Administrators for Administration and Resources Management	KATHLEEN ATERNO
	SALLYANNE HARPER
Director, Office of the Comptroller	KATHRYN SCHMOLL
Director, Office of Human Resources Management	DAVID J. O'CONNOR
Director, Office of Administration	JOHN C. CHAMBERLIN
Director, Office of Grants and Debarment	HARVEY G. PIPPEN
Director, Office of Acquisition Management	BETTY L. BAILEY
Director, Office of Information Resources Management	ALVIN M. DESACHOWITZ
Director, Office of Administration and Resources Management—Research Triangle Park, NC	WILLIAM G. LAXTON
Director, Office of Administration— Cincinnati, OH	WILLIAM M. HENDERSON
Assistant Administrator for Enforcement	STEVEN A. HERMAN
Deputy Assistant Administrators	SCOTT FULTON, MICHAEL M. STAHL
Director, Civil Enforcement	ROBERT VAN HEUVELEN
Director, Criminal Enforcement	EARL E. DEVANEY

Director, Enforcement Capacity and Outreach Office	GERALD A. BRYAN
Director, Office of Federal Activities	RICHARD E. SANDERSON
Director, Office of Federal Facilities Enforcement	BARRY N. BREEN
Director, Office of Compliance	ELAINE G. STANLEY
Director, Office of Regualtory Enforcement	ROBERT VAN HEUVELEN
Director, Office of Site Remediation Enforcement	BRUCE M. DIAMOND
Director, National Enforcement Investigations Center—Denver, CO	FRANK M. COVINGTON
General Counsel	JEAN C. NELSON
Principal Deputy General Counsel	SCOTT FULTON
Assistant Administrator for Policy, Planning and Evaluation	DAVID GARDINER
Deputy Assistant Administrator for Policy, Planning and Evaluation	KARL HAUSKER
Director, Office of Strategic Planning and Environmental Data	FREDERICK W. ALLEN, *Acting*
Director, Office of Policy Analysis	MARYANN FROECHLICH, *Acting*
Director, Office of Regulatory Management and Evaluation	THOMAS E. KELLEY
Inspector General	JOHN C. MARTIN
Deputy Inspector General	(VACANCY)
Assistant Inspector General, Office of Audit	KENNETH A. KONZ
Assistant Inspector General, Office of Investigations	MICHAEL J. FITZSIMMONS
Assistant Inspector General, Office of Management	JOHN C. JONES
Assistant Administrator for Water	BOB PERCIASEPE
Deputy Assistant Administrator for Water	DANA D. MINERVA
Director, Office of Gulf of Mexico Program	DOUGLAS A. LIPKA, *Acting*
Director, Office of Policy and Resources Management	MARK A. LUTTNER
Director, Office of Ground Water and Drinking Water	CYNTHIA C. DOUGHERTY
Director, Office of Wastewater Management	MICHAEL B. COOK
Director, Office of Science and Technology	TUDOR T. DAVIS
Director, American Indian Environmental Office	TERRANCE R. WILLIAMS
Director, Office of Wetlands, Oceans and Watersheds	ROBERT H. WAYLAND III
Assistant Administrator for Solid Waste and Emergency Response	ELLIOTT LAWS
Deputy Assistant Administrator for Solid Waste and Emergency Response	TIMOTHY FIELDS, JR.

Staff Offices:

Director, Office of Organizational Management and Integrity	LAURIE J. MAY
Director, Office of Resources Management and Information	DAVID SUTTON
Director, Office of Policy Analysis and Regulatory Management	MARGARET N. SCHNEIDER
Director, Office of Superfund Revitalization	TIMOTHY FIELDS, JR.

Director, Office of Chemical Emergency Preparedness and Prevention	JAMES L. MAKRIS
Director, Office of Technology Innovation	WALTER W. KOVALICK, JR.
Director, Office of Solid Waste	MICHAEL H. SHAPIRO
Director, Office of Emergency and Remedial Response (Superfund)	STEPHEN D. LUFTIG, *Acting*
Director, Office of Programs Management	THOMAS R. SHECKELLS
Director, Office of Underground Storage Tanks	DAVID W. ZIEGELE
Assistant Administrator for Air and Radiation	MARY D. NICHOLS
Deputy Assistant Administrator for Air and Radiation	RICHARD D. WILSON
Director, Office of Air Quality Planning and Standards	JOHN S. SEITZ
Director, Office of Program Management Operations	JERRY A. KURTWEG
Director, Office of Policy Analysis and Review	ROBERT D. BRENNER
Director, Office of Atmospheric Programs	PAUL STOLPMAN
Deputy Director, Office of Radiation and Indoor Air	STEPHEN D. PAGE, *Acting*
Deputy Director, Office of Mobile Sources—Ann Arbor, MI	CHARLES L. GRAY, JR.
Assistant Administrator for Prevention, Pesticides and Toxic Substances	LYNN R. GOLDMAN
Deputy Assistant Administrator for Pesticides and Toxic Substances	JAMES V. AIDALA
Director, Program Management Operations	MARYLOUISE M. UHLIG
Director, Office of Pesticide Programs	DANIEL BAROLA
Director, Office of Pollution Prevention and Toxics	JOSEPH S. CARRA, *Acting*
Assistant Administrator for Research and Development	ROBERT J. HUGGETT
Deputy Assistant Administrator for Science	JOSEPH K. ALEXANDER
Director, Office of Technology Transfer and Regulatory Support	PETER W. PREUSS
Director, Office of Research Program Management	CARL R. GERBER
Director, Office of Exploratory Research	MELINDA L. McCLANAHAN
Director, Office of Environmental Engineering and Technology Demonstration	ALFRED W. LINDSEY
Director, Office of Environmental Processes and Effects Research	COURTNEY RIORDAN
Director, Office of Modeling, Monitoring Systems, and Quality Assurance	H. MATTHEW BILLS
Director, Office of Health Research	KEN SEXTON
Director, Office of Health and Environmental Assessment	WILLIAM H. FARLAND

[For the Environmental Protection Agency statement of organization, see the *Code of Federal Regulations,* Title 40, Part 1]

The Environmental Protection Agency protects and enhances our environment today and for future generations to the fullest extent possible under the laws enacted by Congress. The Agency's mission is to control and abate pollution in the areas of air,

ENVIRONMENTAL PROTECTION AGENCY

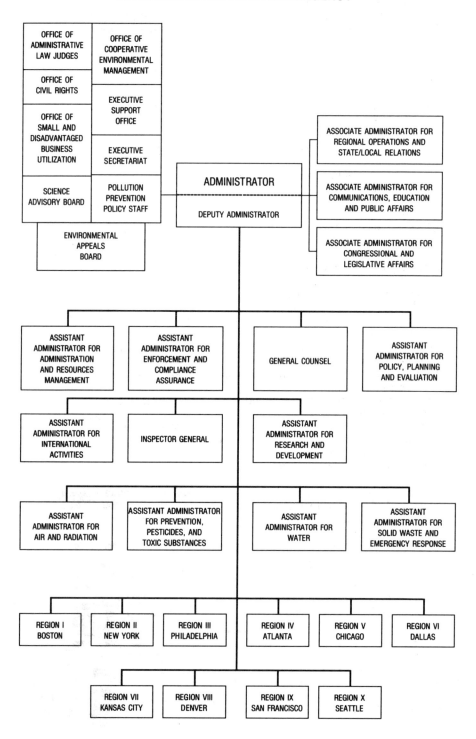

water, solid waste, pesticides, radiation, and toxic substances. Its mandate is to mount an integrated, coordinated attack on environmental pollution in cooperation with State and local governments.

The Environmental Protection Agency was established in the executive branch as an independent agency pursuant to Reorganization Plan No. 3 of 1970 (5 U.S.C. app.), effective December 2, 1970. It was created to permit coordinated and effective governmental action on behalf of the environment. The Agency is designed to serve as the public's advocate for a livable environment.

Activities

Air and Radiation   The air activities of the Agency include:
—development of national programs, technical policies, and regulations for air pollution control;
—enforcement of standards;
—development of national standards for air quality, emission standards for new stationary and mobile sources, and emission standards for hazardous pollutants;
—technical direction, support, and evaluation of regional air activities; and
—provision of training in the field of air pollution control.
Related activities include technical assistance to States and agencies having radiation protection programs, including radon mitigation programs and a national surveillance and inspection program for measuring radiation levels in the environment.

For further information, call 202–260–7400.

Water   The Agency's water quality activities represent a coordinated effort to restore the Nation's waters. The functions of this program include:
—development of national programs, technical policies, and regulations for water pollution control and water supply;
—ground water protection;
—marine and estuarine protection;
—enforcement of standards;
—water quality standards and effluent guidelines development;
—technical direction, support, and evaluation of regional water activities;

—development of programs for technical assistance and technology transfer; and
—provision of training in the field of water quality.

For further information, call 202–260–5700.

Solid Waste and Emergency Response
The Office of Solid Waste and Emergency Response provides policy, guidance, and direction for the Agency's hazardous waste and emergency response programs. The functions of these programs include:
—development of policies, standards, and regulations for hazardous waste treatment, storage, and disposal;
—national management of the Superfund toxic waste cleanup program;
—development of guidelines for the emergency preparedness and "Community Right To Know" programs;
—development of guidelines and standards for underground storage tanks;
—enforcement of applicable laws and regulations;
—analysis of technologies and methods for the recovery of useful energy from solid waste; and
—provision of technical assistance in the development, management, and operation of waste management activities.

For further information, call 202–260–4610.

Prevention, Pesticides and Toxic Substances   The Office of Pesticides and Toxic Substances is responsible for:
—developing national strategies for the control of toxic substances;
—directing the pesticides and toxic substances enforcement activities;
—developing criteria for assessing chemical substances, standards for test protocols for chemicals, rules and procedures for industry reporting and regulations for the control of substances deemed to be hazardous to man or the environment; and
—evaluating and assessing the impact of existing chemicals, new chemicals,

and chemicals with new uses to determine the hazard and, if needed, develop appropriate restrictions.

Additional activities include:
—controlling and regulating pesticides and reducing their use to ensure human safety and protection of environmental quality;
—establishing tolerance levels for pesticides that occur in or on food;
—monitoring pesticide residue levels in food, humans, and nontarget fish and wildlife and their environments; and
—investigating pesticide accidents.

It also coordinates activities under its statutory responsibilities with other agencies for the assessment and control of toxic substances and pesticides.

For further information, call 202–260–2902.

Research and Development The Office of Research and Development is responsible for a national research program in pursuit of technological controls of all forms of pollution. It directly supervises the research activities of the Agency's national laboratories and gives technical policy direction to those laboratories that support the program responsibilities of the regional offices. Close coordination of the various research programs is designed to yield a synthesis of knowledge from the biological, physical, and social sciences that can be interpreted in terms of total human and environmental needs.

General functions include management of selected demonstration programs, planning for Agency environmental quality monitoring programs, coordination of Agency monitoring efforts with those of other Federal agencies, the States, and other public bodies, and dissemination of Agency research, development, and demonstration results.

For further information, call 202–260–7676.

Regional Offices

The Agency's 10 regional offices represent its commitment to the development of strong local programs for pollution abatement. The Regional Administrators are responsible for

accomplishing, within their regions, the national program objectives established by the Agency. They develop, propose, and implement an approved regional program for comprehensive and integrated environmental protection activities.

Regional Offices—Environmental Protection Agency

(Areas included within each region are indicated on the map in Appendix A.)

Region/Address	Administrator
1. Boston, MA (John F. Kennedy Federal Bldg., 02203).	John P. DeVillars
2. New York, NY (26 Federal Plz., 10278).	Jeanne M. Fox
3. Philadelphia, PA (841 Chestnut St., 19107).	Peter H. Kostmayer
4. Atlanta, GA (345 Courtland St. NE., 30365).	John H. Hankinson, Jr.
5. Chicago, IL (230 S. Dearborn St., 60604).	Valdas V. Adamkus
6. Dallas, TX (1445 Ross Ave., 75202).	Jane N. Saginaw
7. Kansas City, KS (726 Minnesota Ave., 66101).	Dennis D. Grams
8. Denver, CO (999 18th St., 80202).	William P. Yellowtail
9. San Francisco, CA (215 Fremont St., 94105).	Felicia Markus
10. Seattle, WA (1200 6th Ave., 98101).	Charles C. Clarke

Sources of Information

Inquiries for information on the following subjects should be directed to the specified office of the Environmental Protection Agency, 401 M Street SW., Washington, DC 20460.

Contracts and Procurement Office of Acquisition Management. Phone, 202–260–5020.

Employment Headquarters Operations and Client Services Division. Phone, 202–260–3144.

Freedom of Information Act Requests Freedom of Information Officer. Phone, 202–260–4048.

Reading Room Information Management and Services Division. Phone, 202–260–5914. Public Reading Room—2430 Mall.

Telephone Directory Available for sale by the Superintendent of Documents, Government Printing Office, Washington, DC 20402.

For further information, contact the Office of Communications, Education and Public Affairs, Environmental Protection Agency, 401 M Street SW., Washington, DC 20460 (phone, 202–260–7963); or write to the Public Information Office of the nearest regional office.

EQUAL EMPLOYMENT OPPORTUNITY COMMISSION

1801 L Street NW., Washington, DC 20507
Phones: 202–663–4900; 202–663–4494 (TDD)

Chairman	GILBERT F. CASELLAS
Executive Director	MARIA BORREO
Executive Officer, Office of the Executive Secretariat	FRANCES HART
Vice Chairman	PAUL M. IGASKI
Special Assistant	JEAN KAMP
Commissioner	PAUL STEVEN MILLER
Executive Assistant	R. PAUL RICHARD
Special Assistants	LISA S. COTTLE, ANDREW V. IMPARTO
Special Assistant/Attorney Advisor	REBECCA L. DICKERSON
Commissioner	R. GAULL SILBERMAN
Special Assistants	SUSAN ADAMS, GARY HOZEMAN, SUSAN MURPHY
Commissioner	JOYCE E. TUCKER
Executive Assistant	CHARLES M. SPEARMAN
Special Assistants	GEORGIA M. RICHARDS, SANDRA S. ZEIGLER
General Counsel	(VACANCY)
Director, Office of Communications and Legislative Affairs	CLAIRE GONZALES
Director, Office of Equal Employment Opportunity	CYNTHIA C. MATTHEWS
Director, Legal Counsel	ELLEN T. VARGYAS
Director, Office of Management	KASSIE BILLINGSLEY, *Acting*
Director, Office of Program Operations	SUSAN REILLY, *Acting*
Director, Office of Federal Operations	RONNIE BLUMENTHAL
Inspector General	ALETHA L. BROWN, *Acting*

The Equal Employment Opportunity Commission eliminates discrimination based on race, color, religion, sex, national origin, disability, or age in hiring, promoting, firing, setting wages, testing, training, apprenticeship, and all other terms and conditions of employment. The Commission conducts investigations of alleged discrimination; makes determinations based on gathered evidence; attempts conciliation when discrimination has taken place; files lawsuits; and conducts voluntary assistance programs for employers, unions, and community organizations. The Commission also has oversight responsibility for all compliance and enforcement activities relating to equal employment opportunity among Federal employees and applicants, including discrimination against individuals with disabilities.

The Equal Employment Opportunity Commission (EEOC) was created by Title VII of the Civil Rights Act of 1964 (42 U.S.C. 2000e–4), and became operational July 2, 1965. Title VII was amended by the Equal Employment Opportunity Act of 1972, the Pregnancy Discrimination Act of 1978, and the Civil Rights Act of 1991.

Executive Order 12067 of June 30, 1978, abolished the Equal Employment Opportunity Coordinating Council and transferred its duties to the Commission with responsibility for providing coherence and direction to the Government's equal employment opportunity efforts.

Reorganization Plan No. 1 of 1978 (5 U.S.C. app.) effective January 1, 1979, transferred Federal equal employment functions from the Civil Service Commission to the EEOC. Authorities for transferred functions include:

—section 717 of Title VII of the Civil Rights Act of 1964 (42 U.S.C. 2000e–16), which prohibits discrimination in employment in the Federal Government on the basis of race, color, religion, sex, or national origin;

—Executive Order 11478 of August 8, 1969, which sets forth the U.S. policy of providing for equal employment opportunity in the Federal Government through affirmative action programs in Federal departments and agencies;

—the Equal Pay Act of 1963 (29 U.S.C. 206) in the Federal sector;

—section 15 of the Age Discrimination in Employment Act of 1967, as amended (29 U.S.C. 621) in the Federal sector; and

—section 501 of the Rehabilitation Act of 1973 (29 U.S.C. 791), which pertains to employment discrimination against individuals with disabilities in the Federal Government.

On July 1, 1979, responsibility for enforcement—in private industry as well as in State and local governments—of the Equal Pay Act of 1963 and the Age Discrimination in Employment Act of 1967 was transferred from the Department of Labor to the Commission. The former act prohibits sex-based pay differences where substantially equal work performed in the same establishment under similar working conditions requires equal skill, effort, and responsibility; and the latter prohibits employment discrimination

against workers or applicants 40 years of age or older. In addition to employers, the age discrimination act covers activities of employment agencies, and both acts cover activities of labor organizations.

The Americans with Disabilities Act of 1990 (ADA) (42 U.S.C. 12101 *et seq.*) was approved on July 26, 1990. Title I of the act has been enforced by EEOC since July 26, 1992, for employers with 25 or more employees; and will become effective on July 26, 1994, for employers with 15 or more employees. Title I governs private employers, State and local governments, employment agencies, labor organizations, and joint labor-management committees. The act prohibits employment discrimination against qualified individuals with disabilities and requires that employers make reasonable accommodations for such qualified individuals if it would not create undue hardship.

The Civil Rights Act of 1991 reversed parts of several U.S. Supreme Court rulings and provided for compensatory and punitive damages for intentional discrimination under Title VII of that act and the ADA.

The Commission operates through 50 field offices, each of which processes charges.

Activities

Enforcement The Commission's field offices receive charges of job discrimination under Title VII, the ADA, the Equal Pay Act of 1963, and the Age Discrimination in Employment Act of 1967. Field offices may initiate investigations to find violations of the acts. Members of the Commission also may initiate charges alleging that a violation of Title VII or the ADA has occurred. Section 501 of the Rehabilitation Act of 1973 covers Federal employees and applicants only.

Charges Under Title VII Title VII prohibits employment discrimination based on race, color, religion, sex, or national origin by private employers, State and local governments, and educational institutions with 15 or more employees, or by the Federal

Government, private and public employment agencies, labor organizations, and joint labor-management committees for apprenticeship and training.

Charges of Title VII violations outside of the Federal sector must be filed with the Commission within 180 days of the alleged violation (or up to 300 days in a State or locality in which a fair employment practices agency is located), and the Commission is responsible for notifying persons so charged within 10 days of the receipt of a new charge. Before investigation, charges must be deferred for 60 days to a State or local fair employment practices agency in States and municipalities where there is a fair employment practices law covering the alleged discrimination. The deferral period is 120 days if the agency has been operating less than 1 year. Under worksharing agreements executed between the Commission and State and local fair employment practices agencies, the Commission routinely will assume jurisdiction over certain charges of discrimination and proceed with its investigation rather than wait for the expiration of the deferral period.

If there is reasonable cause to believe the charge is true, the district, area, or local office attempts to remedy the alleged unlawful practices through informal methods of conciliation, conference, and persuasion. If an acceptable conciliation agreement is not secured, the case is submitted to the Commission for possible litigation. If litigation is approved, the Commission will bring suit in an appropriate Federal district court.

Under Title VII, the Attorney General brings suit when a State or local government, or political subdivision is involved. If the Commission or the Attorney General does not approve litigation or if a finding of no reasonable cause is made, at the conclusion of the administrative procedures (or earlier at the request of the charging party) a Notice of Right-to-Sue is issued that allows the charging party to proceed within 90 days in a Federal district court. In appropriate cases, the Commission may intervene in such civil action if the case is of general public interest. The investigation and conciliation of charges having an industrywide or national impact are coordinated or conducted by Systemic Investigations and Individual Compliance Programs, Office of Program Operations.

Under the provisions of Title VII, section 706(f)(2), as amended by section 4 of the Equal Employment Opportunity Act of 1972 (42 U.S.C. 2000e–5), if it is concluded after a preliminary investigation that prompt judicial action is necessary to carry out the purposes of the act, the Commission or the Attorney General, in a case involving a State or local government, governmental agency or political subdivision, may bring an action for appropriate temporary or preliminary relief pending final disposition of a charge.

Americans with Disabilities Act Charges The Americans with Disabilities Act of 1990 specifically incorporates the powers, remedies, and procedures contained in Title VII of the Civil Rights Act of 1964. Employment discrimination charges based on disability may be filed at any of the Commission's field offices. The Commission will investigate and attempt to conciliate the charges using the same procedures it uses to investigate and conciliate charges filed under Title VII. The litigation procedures under this title apply to charges filed under the act.

Age Discrimination in Employment or Equal Pay Act Charges and Complaints The age discrimination in employment and equal pay acts cover most employees and job applicants in private industry and Federal, State, and local governments.

An age discrimination charge must be filed with the Commission within 180 days of the alleged violation or, in a case where the alleged discriminatory action took place in a State which has its own age discrimination law and authority administering that law, within 300 days of the alleged violation or 30 days after the receipt of a notice of termination of State proceedings, whichever is earlier. A lawsuit must be filed within 2 years of the discriminatory act or 3 years in cases of a willful violation of the law. Under the Civil Rights Act of 1991, a lawsuit must be filed within 90 days of the plaintiff's receipt of notice of final action. The Commission will attempt to eliminate the unlawful practice through informal methods of conciliation, conference, and persuasion. A lawsuit may be brought by the Commission if conciliation fails, or individuals may file suit on their own behalf 90 days after filing a charge with the Commission and the appropriate State agency. Should the Commission take legal action, an individual covered by such action may not file a private suit. If an individual files a complaint of age discrimination, his or her name will be kept confidential, but the individual filing the complaint may not bring a private suit unless he or she elects to file a charge first in accordance with the above requirements.

A lawsuit under the Equal Pay Act of 1963 may be filed by the Commission or by the complainant. There are no prerequisites to individual actions under this law. Wages may be recovered for a period of up to 2 years prior to the filing of a suit, except in the case of willful violation, where 3 years' backpay may be recovered. The name of the individual filing the complaint may be kept confidential at the administrative level.

Complaints Against the Federal Government On April 10, 1992, the Commission published new Federal sector processing regulations codified at 29 CFR 1614, effective October 1, 1992. Federal employees or job applicants who want to file complaints of job discrimination based on race, color, national origin, sex, religion, age, or physical or mental disability must first consult an equal employment opportunity counselor within their agency within 45 calendar days of the alleged discriminatory event or the effective date of the alleged discriminatory personnel action. If the complaint cannot be resolved informally, the person may file a formal complaint within 15 calendar days after the date of receipt of the notice of the right to file a complaint.

An accepted complaint is investigated by the agency and there is a right to a hearing before an EEOC administrative judge before the agency issues its final decision. An individual who wishes to file a complaint under the Equal Pay Act of 1963 must now follow these procedures. An individual may also elect to file suit under the Equal Pay Act of 1963 without prior resort to the agency or to the Commission.

A complaint under the Age Discrimination in Employment Act of 1967 against a Federal agency or department must be filed with the head of the agency, director of equal employment opportunity, head of a field installation, or such other officials as the agency may designate. Federal-sector age discrimination complainants may bypass the administrative complaint process and file a civil action directly in a U.S. district court by first notifying the Commission within 180 calendar days of the alleged discriminatory act and thereafter waiting 30 calendar days before filing suit.

Federal employees may file appeals of final agency decisions or decisions of an arbitrator or the Federal Labor Relations Authority with the Commission's Office of Federal Operations at any time up to 30 calendar days after receipt of the agency notice of final decision. A petition for review of a Merit Systems Protection Board decision may be filed within 30 days of the date that the Board decision becomes final. A request for reopening and reconsideration of any decision of the Commission should be made in writing within 30 days of receipt of such decision. Office of Federal Operations decisions are issued in writing to the complainant, complainant's representative, and the agency. The Office monitors and ensures compliance by Federal agencies with Commission orders and appellate decisions, and provides technical assistance and training to other Federal agencies.

Other Activities The Commission actively promotes voluntary compliance with equal employment opportunity statutes through a variety of educational and technical assistance activities. A distinct activity of the Commission is the Voluntary Assistance Program. This outreach program is designed to provide educational and technical assistance to small and midsize employers and unions—through 1-day seminars on equal employment opportunity laws—about their rights and obligations under all the statutes that the Commission enforces.

Another activity initiated by the Commission is the Expanded Presence Program, which is designed to make the Commission accessible in areas identified as underserved by Commission offices.

In addition to conducting on-site consultations, EEOC co-hosts an annual Federal Dispute Resolution Conference which provides a forum for Federal agencies to meet and exchange ideas on resolving disputes.

Through its Educational Technical Assistance and Training Revolving Fund, the Commission is also able to provide its constituency with advanced and specialized technical assistance offerings. Fees charged for Revolving Fund products are not to exceed the cost of producing the materials or services provided, are to bear a direct relationship to the cost of providing such outreach, and are to be imposed on a uniform basis.

The Commission participates in the development of the employment discrimination law through the issuance of guidelines, publication of significant Commission decisions, and involvement in litigation brought under Title VII, the Equal Pay Act of 1963, the Age Discrimination in Employment Act of 1967, and the Americans with Disabilities Act of 1990.

The Commission has direct liaison with Federal, State, and local governments; employers and union organizations; trade associations; civil rights organizations; and other agencies and organizations concerned with employment of minority group members and women.

The Commission is also a major publisher of data on the employment status of minorities and women. Through six employment surveys (EEO–1 through EEO–6) covering private employers, apprenticeship programs, labor unions, State and local governments, elementary and secondary schools, and colleges and universities, the Commission tabulates and stores data on the ethnic, racial, and sex composition of employees at all job levels within the reported groups.

Research information thus collected is shared with selected Federal agencies, such as the Department of Health and Human Services, the Department of Labor, and others. It is also made available, in appropriate form, for public use.

Field Offices—Equal Employment Opportunity Commission

(DO: District Office; AO: Area Office; LO: Local Office; FO: Field Office)

Office	Address	Director	Telephone
Albuquerque, NM (DO) ...	Suite 900, 505 Marquette NW., 87102	Andres Lopez, *Acting*	505–766–2061
Atlanta, GA (DO)	Suite 1100, 75 Piedmont Ave. NE., 30335	Bernice Kimbrough, *Acting*	404–331–6093
Baltimore, MD (DO)	3d Fl., City Cresent Bldg., 10 S. Howard St., 21201.	Issie L. Jenkins	301–962–3932
Birmingham, AL (DO)	Suite 101, 1900 3d Ave. N., 35203	Warren Bullock	205–731–0082
Boston, MA (AO)	Rm. 100, 10th Fl., 1 Congress St., 02114	Charles L. Looney	617–565–3200
Buffalo, NY (LO)	Suite 350, 6 Fountain Plz., 14203	(Vacancy)	716–846–4441
Charlotte, NC (DO)	5500 Central Ave., 28212	Marsha Drane	704–567–7100
Chicago II (DO)	Suite 0000, 500 W. Madison St., 00001	Cynthia G. Pierre, *Acting* ..	312–353–2713
Cincinnati, OH (AO)	Suite 810, 525 Vine St., 45202	Earl Haley	513–684–2851
Cleveland, OH (DO)	Suite 850, 1660 W. 2d St., 44113–1454	Harold Ferguson	216–522–2001
Dallas, TX (DO)	3d Fl., 207 S. Houston St., 75202–4726	Jacqueline Bradley	214–655–3355
Denver, CO (DO)	2d Fl., 1845 Sherman St., 80203	Francisco J. Flores	303–866–1300
Detroit, MI (DO)	Rm. 1540, 477 Michigan Ave., 48226	Andrew Sheppard, *Acting* .	313–226–7636
El Paso, TX (AO)	Suite 100, Bldg. C, The Commons, 79902	Eliazar Salinas	915–534–6550
Fresno, CA (LO)	Suite 103, 1265 W. Shaw Ave., 93711	David Rodriguez	209–487–5793
Greensboro, NC (LO)	801 Summit Ave., 27405–7813	Daisy Crenshaw	919–333–5174
Greenville, SC (LO)	Suite 530, 15 S. Main St., 29601	Sherald L. Carter	803–241–4400
Honolulu, HI (LO)	Suite 404, 677 Ala Moana Blvd., 96813	Linda K. Kreis	808–541–3120
Houston, TX (DO)	7th Fl., 1919 Smith St., 77002	Harriet L. Ehrlich	713–653–3377
Indianapolis, IN (DO)	Suite 1900, 101 W. Ohio St., 46204–4203	Thomas P. Hadfield	317–226–7212
Jackson, MS (AO)	207 W. Amite St., 39269	Henrene P. Matthews	601–965–4537

Field Offices—Equal Employment Opportunity Commission—Continued
(DO: District Office; AO: Area Office; LO: Local Office; FO: Field Office)

Office	Address	Director	Telephone
Kansas City, MO (AO)	10th Fl., 911 Walnut, 64106	Joseph P. Doherty	816–426–5773
Little Rock, AR (AO)	Suite 621, 320 W. Capitol Ave., 72201	W.P. Brown	501–324–5060
Los Angeles, CA (DO)	4th Fl., 255 E. Temple, 90012	Dorothy Porter	213–894–1000
Louisville, KY (AO)	Suite 268, 600 Martin Luther King, Jr., Pl., 40202	Marcia Hall-Craig, *Acting* ..	502–582–6082
Memphis, TN (DO)	Suite 621, 1407 Union Ave., 38104	Walter Grabon	901–722–2617
Miami, FL (DO)	6th Fl., 1 NE. 1st St., 33132	Federico Costales	305–536–4491
Milwaukee, WI (DO)	Suite 800, 310 W. Wisconsin Ave., 53203	Chester Bailey	414–297–1111
Minneapolis, MN (AO)	Suite 430, 330 S. 2d Ave., 55401–2224	Michael Bloyer	612–335–4040
Nashville, TN (AO)	Suite 202, 50 Vantage Way, 37228	John A. Pahmeyer	615–736–5820
Newark, NJ (AO)	1 Newark Ctr., 21st St., 07102–5233	Corrado Gigante	201–645–6383
New Orleans, LA (DO) ...	Suite 600, 701 Loyola Ave., 70113	Patricia F. Bivins	504–589–2329
New York, NY (DO)	7 World Trade Ctr., 18th St., 10048–0948	Spencer H. Lewis, Jr.	212–748–8500
Norfolk, VA (AO)	1st Fl., SMA Bldg., 252 Monticello Ave., 23510 ...	Kathryne Stokes	804–441–3470
Oakland, CA (LO)	Suite 1170–N, 1301 Clay St., 94612–5217	Joyce Hendy	510–637–3230
Oklahoma City, OK (AO)	531 Couch Dr., 94612	Alma Anderson	405–231–4911
Philadelphia, PA (DO)	10th Fl., 1421 Cherry St., 19102	Johnny J. Butler	215–656–7020
Phoenix, AZ (DO)	Suite 300, 4520 N. Central Ave., 85012	Charles D. Burtner	602–640–5000
Pittsburgh, PA (AO)	Rm. 2038–A, 1000 Liberty Ave., 15222	Eugene V. Nelson	412–644–3444
Raleigh, NC (AO)	1309 Annapolis Dr., 27601	Richard E. Walz	919–856–4064
Richmond, VA (AO)	2d Fl., 3600 W. Broad St., 23230	Gloria Underwood	804–771–2692
San Antonio, TX (DO)	Suite 200, 5410 Fredericksburg Rd., 78229	Pedro Esquivel	512–229–4810
San Diego, CA (LO)	Suite 1550, 401 B St., 92101	Patrick Matarazzo	619–557–7235
San Francisco, CA (DO) .	Suite 500, 901 Market St., 94103	Chester F. Relyea	415–744–6500
San Jose, CA (LO)	96 N. 3d St., 95113	Timothy Riera	408–291–7352
Savannah, GA (LO)	Suite G, 410 Mall Blvd., 31406	Gloria Barnett-Mentor	912–652–4234
Seattle, WA (DO)	Suite 400, Federal Office Bldg., 909 1st Ave., 98104–1061.	Jeanette M. Leino	206–220–6883
St. Louis, MO (DO)	5th Fl., 625 N. Euclid St., 63108	Lynn Bruner	314–425–6585
Tampa, FL (AO)	10th Fl., 501 E. Polk St., 33602	James D. Packwood, Jr. ..	813–228–2310
Washington, DC (FO)	2d Fl., 1400 L St. NW., 20005	Tullio Diaz,*Acting*	202–275–7377

Sources of Information

Employment The Commission selects its employees from various examinations and registers, including mid- and senior-level registers; secretarial, typing, and stenographic registers; and the Equal Opportunity Specialist register. Employment inquiries or applications for positions in the headquarters office should be directed to the Personnel Office, Equal Employment Opportunity Commission, 1801 L Street NW., Washington, DC 20507 (phone, 202–663–4306), or contact the appropriate district office for district office positions.
General Inquiries A nationwide toll-free telephone number links callers with the appropriate field office where

charges may be filed. Phone, 800–669–4000; or 800–669–6820 (TDD).
Information About Survey Forms (EEO–1, 2, 3, 4, 5, and 6). Phone, 202–663–4958.
Media Inquiries Office of Communications and Legislative Affairs, 1801 L Street NW., Washington, DC 20507. Phone, 202–663–4900.
Publications Nationwide toll-free telephone number, 800–669–3362.
Reading Room EEOC Library, 1801 L Street NW., Washington, DC 20507. Phone, 202-663–4630.
Speakers Office of Communications and Legislative Affairs, 1801 L Street NW., Washington, DC 20507. Phone, 202–663–4900.

For further information, contact the Equal Employment Opportunity Commission, 1801 L Street NW., Washington, DC 20507. Phone, 202–663–4900.

EXPORT–IMPORT BANK OF THE UNITED STATES

811 Vermont Avenue NW., Washington, DC 20571
Phone, 1–800–565–EXIM

President and Chairman	KENNETH D. BRODY
First Vice President and Vice Chairman	MARTIN A. KAMARCK
Directors	JULIE D. BELAGA, MARIA LUISA HALEY, RITA M. RODRIGUEZ
Vice Presidents, Project Finance Division	GLEN T. MATSUMOTO DIANNE S. RUDO
General Counsel	CAROL F. LEE
Deputy General Counsel	STEPHEN G. GLAZER
Vice President, Congressional and External Affairs	JACKIE M. CLEGG, *Acting*
Vice President, Public Affairs	CHRISTOPHER DORVAL
Vice President, Management Services and Human Resources	TAMZEN C. REITAN
Director of Equal Opportunity and Diversity Programs	DOLORES BARTNING
Chief Financial Officer	JAMES K. HESS
Deputy, Treasurer-Controller	JOSEPH A. SORBERA
Vice President, Claims and Recoveries	STEPHEN D. PROCTOR
Vice President, Information Management	CANDELARIO TRUJILLO
Senior Vice President, Export Finance Group	RAYMOND J. ALBRIGHT
Chief of Staff	JACKIE M. CLEGG
Vice President, Aircraft Finance Division	MARY C. KILTY, *Acting*
Vice President, Asia and Middle East	TERRENCE J. HULIHAN
Vice President, Europe and Africa	THOMAS E. MORAN
Vice President, Americas	CHARLES A. LEIK
Vice President, Engineering and Environment	JAMES A. MAHONEY
Vice President, Credit Administration	LEILANI L. NEWTON
Vice President, United States Division	JAMES W. CRIST
Vice President, Insurance	WILLIAM W. REDWAY
Senior Vice President, Business Development Group	RICHARD J. FEENEY
Vice President, International Business Development	ARTHUR PILZER
Vice President, Domestic Business Development Group	ROBERT J. KAISER
Vice President, Policy, Planning and Program Development	JAMES C. CRUSE
Director, Quality Review and Secretariat	PATRICIA DELANEY
Vice President, Country Risk Analysis	DANIEL L. BOND

The Export-Import Bank of the United States helps the private sector to create and maintain U.S. jobs by financing exports of the Nation's goods and services. To accomplish this mission, Export-Import Bank offers a variety of loan, guarantee, and insurance programs to support transactions that would not be awarded to U.S. companies without the Bank's assistance.

The Export-Import Bank (Ex-Im Bank), established in 1934, operates as an independent agency of the U.S. Government under the authority of the

Export-Import Bank Act of 1945, as amended (12 U.S.C. 635 et seq.). The Bank has a Board of Directors consisting of a President and Chairman, a First Vice President and Vice Chairman, and three other Directors, all of whom are appointed by the President with the advice and consent of the Senate.

Ex-Im Bank's mission is to help American exporters meet government-supported financing competition from other countries, so that U.S. exports can compete for overseas business on the basis of price, performance, and service. The Bank also fills gaps in the availability of commercial financing for creditworthy export transactions.

Ex-Im Bank is required to find a reasonable assurance of repayment for each transaction it supports. The Bank's legislation requires it to meet the financing terms of competitor export credit agencies, but not to compete with commercial lenders. An export must have a minimum of 50-percent U.S. content in order to be eligible for Ex-Im Bank support. There is no maximum or minimum dollar limit for Ex-Im Bank financing. Legislation restricts the Bank's operation in some countries and its support for military goods and services.

Activities

The Export-Import Bank is authorized to have outstanding, at any one time loans, guarantees, and insurance in aggregate amount not in excess of $75 billion. During fiscal year 1994, the Bank authorized a total of $15 billion in financing, including a wide range of capital goods exports to developing countries.

The Bank supports U.S. exporters through a range of diverse programs, which are offered under four broad categories of export financing:

Working Capital Guarantees   These guarantees are provided to lenders, so that they can provide creditworthy small and medium-sized exporters with

working capital they need to buy, build, or assemble products for export sale.

Export Credit Insurance   This insurance protects the exporter against both the commercial and political risks of a foregn buyer defaulting on payment. The Bank offers a variety of policies: short- and medium-term, single- and multi-buyer, and small business and umbrella policies.

Loan Guarantees   These guarantees encourage sales to creditworthy foreign buyers by providing private sector lenders in medium- and long-term transactions with Ex-Im Bank guarantees against the political and commercial risks of nonpayment. Political-risk-only guarantees are also available.

Direct Loans   These loans provide foreign buyers with competitive, fixed-rate medium- or long-term financing from Ex-Im Bank for their purchases from U.S. exporters. The Bank's direct loans carry the minimum interest rate allowed by the Organization for Economic Cooperation and Development.

Ex-Im Bank has initiated several new programs to broaden the range of customers and types of exporters it supports. The Environmental Exports Program provides enhanced financing terms for environmentally beneficial goods and services. The Bank has also expanded its capabilities in the area of limited recourse project finance, and has adopted a policy of matching foreign tied-aid credits to ensure that U.S. exporters do not lose sales in critical emerging markets. In order to make its programs more readily available, Ex-Im Bank works closely with many State and local governments in its City/State Program.

Regional Offices

The Export-Import Bank operates five regional offices, listed in the table below.

Regional Offices—Export-Import Bank

Region	Address	Telephone
New York	Suite 238, 6 World Trade Ctr., New York, NY 10048	212–466–2950
Miami	P.O. Box 590570, Miami, FL 33159	305–526–7425
Chicago	Suite 2440, 55 W. Monroe St., Chicago, IL 60603	312–353–8081

Regional Offices—Export-Import Bank—Continued

Region	Address	Telephone
Houston	Suite 585, Ashford Crossing II, 1880 S. Dairy Ashford, Houston, TX 77077	713–589–8182
Los Angeles (Long Beach).	Suite 1670, 1 World Trade Ctr., Long Beach, CA 90831	310–498–0141

For further information, contact the Export-Import Bank at 1–800–565–3946, or write to the Business Development Group at 811 Vermont Avenue NW., Washington, DC 20571. Phone, 202–566–8990.

FARM CREDIT ADMINISTRATION

1501 Farm Credit Drive, McLean, VA 22102–5090
Phone, 703–883–4000

Farm Credit Administration Board:

Chairman	MARSHA PYLE MARTIN
Members of the Board	DOYLE L. COOK
	(VACANCY)
Secretary to the Board	FLOYD J. FITHIAN

Staff:

Chief Operating Officer	DOROTHY L. NICHOLS
Director, Office of Congressional and Public Affairs	CHERYL TATES MACIAS
General Counsel	JEAN NOONAN
Associate General Counsels	NANCY E. LYNCH
	KATHLEEN V. BUFFON
Inspector General	ELDON W. STOEHR
Director, Office of Examination and Chief Examiner	DAVID C. BAER
Director, Office of Special Supervision and Corporate Affairs	MICHAEL L. YOUNG
Director, Office of Secondary Market Oversight	SUZANNE J. MCCRORY
Director, Office of Resources Management	LARRY W. EDWARDS

[For the Farm Credit Administration statement of organization, see the *Code of Federal Regulations,* Title 12, Parts 600 and 611]

The Farm Credit Administration is responsible for ensuring the safe and sound operation of the banks, associations, affiliated service organizations, and other entities that collectively comprise what is known as the Farm Credit System, and for protecting the interests of the public and those who borrow from Farm Credit institutions or invest in Farm Credit securities

The Farm Credit Administration was established as an independent financial regulatory agency in the executive branch of the Federal Government by the Farm Credit Act of 1971 (12 U.S.C. 2241 *et seq.*). The Administration carries out its responsibilities by conducting examinations of the various Farm Credit lending institutions, which are Farm Credit Banks, Banks for Cooperatives, the Agricultural Credit Bank, Federal Land Bank Associations, Production Credit Associations, Agricultural Credit Associations, and Federal Land Credit Associations. It also examines the service organizations owned by the Farm Credit

FARM CREDIT ADMINISTRATION

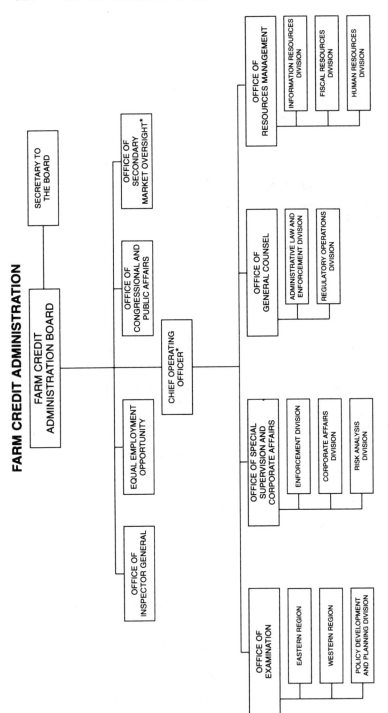

*Reports to the Board for policy and to the CEO for administration.

lending institutions, as well as the National Consumer Cooperative Bank (also known as the National Cooperative Bank (NCB)) and its subsidiaries, including the NCB Development Corporation.

Management of the agency is vested in the Farm Credit Administration Board, whose three full-time members are appointed to 6-year terms by the President, with the advice and consent of the Senate. One member of the Board is designated by the President as Chairman and serves as the Administration's chief executive officer. The Board is responsible for approving rules and regulations, providing for the examination and regulation of and reporting by Farm Credit institutions, and establishing the policies under which the Administration operates. Board meetings are regularly held on the second Thursday of the month and are subject to the Government in the Sunshine Act. Public announcements of these meetings are published in the *Federal Register.*

The lending institutions of the Farm Credit System were established to provide adequate and dependable credit and closely related services to farmers, ranchers, and producers or harvesters of aquatic products; persons engaged in providing on-the-farm services; rural homeowners; and associations of farmers, ranchers, and producers or harvesters of aquatic products, or federations of such associations that operate on a cooperative basis and are engaged in marketing, processing, supply, or business service functions for the benefit of their members. Initially capitalized by the United States Government, the Farm Credit lending institutions are organized as cooperatives and are completely owned by their borrowers. The loan funds provided to borrowers by these institutions are obtained primarily through the sale of securities to investors in the Nation's capital markets.

The Agricultural Credit Act of 1987, as amended (12 U.S.C. 2279aa–1), established the Federal Agricultural Mortgage Corporation (commonly known as "Farmer Mac"). The Corporation, designated as part of the Farm Credit System, is a federally chartered instrumentality of the United States and promotes the development of a secondary market for agricultural real estate and rural housing loans. Farmer Mac also provides guarantees for the timely payment of principal and interest on securities, representing interests in or obligations backed by pools of agricultural real estate loans. The Administration is responsible for the examination and regulation of Farmer Mac to ensure the safety and soundness of its operations.

The Administration administers regulations under which Farm Credit institutions operate. These regulations implement the Farm Credit Act of 1971, as amended, and have the force and effect of law. Similar to other Federal regulators of financial institutions, the Administration's authorities include the power to issue cease-and-desist orders, to levy civil monetary penalties, to remove officers and directors of Farm Credit institutions, and to establish financial and operating reporting requirements. Although it is prohibited from participation in routine management or operations of Farm Credit institutions, the Administration is authorized to become involved in these institutions' management and operations when the Farm Credit Act or its regulations have been violated, when taking an action to correct an unsafe or unsound practice, or when assuming a formal conservatorship over an institution.

The Administration does not operate on funds appropriated by Congress. Its income is derived from assessments collected from the institutions it regulates and examines. In addition to the headquarters office located in McLean, VA, the Administration maintains 6 field offices. They are located in Aurora, CO; Bloomington, MN; Irving, TX; Marietta, GA; Sacramento, CA; and St. Louis, MO.

Authority for the organization and activities of the institutions comprising the cooperative Farm Credit System and that operate under the regulation of the Farm Credit Administration may be found in the Farm Credit Act of 1971, as amended (12 U.S.C. 2001).

Sources of Information

Inquiries for information on the following subjects may be directed to the specified office, Farm Credit Administration, 1501 Farm Credit Drive, McLean, VA 22102–5090.

Contracts and Procurement Inquiries regarding the Administration's procurement and contracting activities should be directed in writing to Contracting and Procurement. Phone, 703–883–4149.

Employment Inquiries regarding employment with the Administration should be directed to the Human Resources Division. Phone, 703–883–4135.

Freedom of Information Requests Requests for agency records must be submitted in writing, clearly identified with "FOIA Request" and addressed to the Office of Congressional and Public Affairs. Phone, 703–883–4056.

Publications Publications and information on the Farm Credit Administration may be obtained by writing the Office of Congressional and Public Affairs. Phone, 703–883–4056.

For further information, contact the Office of Congressional and Public Affairs, Farm Credit Administration, 1501 Farm Credit Drive, McLean, VA 22102–5090. Phone, 703–883–4056.

FEDERAL COMMUNICATIONS COMMISSION

1919 M Street NW., Washington, DC 20554
Phones, 202–418–0200; 202–632–6999 (TDD)

Chairman	REED E. HUNDT
Commissioners	ANDREW C. BARRETT, JAMES H. QUELLO, RACHELLE B. CHONG, SUSAN NESS
Managing Director	ANDREW S. FISHEL
General Counsel	WILLIAM E. KENNARD
Chief Engineer	THOMAS P. STANLEY
Director, Office of Public Affairs	KAREN E. WATSON
Director, Office of Legislative and Intergovernmental Affairs	JUDITH HARRIS
Director, International Bureau	SCOTT BLAKE HARRIS
Inspector General	H. WALKER FEASTER III, *Acting*
Chief, Office of Plans and Policy	ROBERT M. PEPPER
Chairman, Review Board	JOSEPH A. MARINO
Chief, Office of Administrative Law Judges	JOSEPH STIRMER
Chief, Mass Media Bureau	ROY J. STEWART
Chief, Common Carrier Bureau	KATHLEEN M.H. WALLMAN
Chief, Compliance and Information Bureau	BEVERLY G. BAKER
Chief, Wireless Telecommunications Bureau	REGINA KEENEY
Chief, Cable Services Bureau	MEREDITH JONES
Director, Office of Communications Business Opportunities	ANTHONY L. WILLIAMS
Director, Office of Workplace Diversity	HARVEY LEE, *Acting*
Chief, Office of Engineering and Technology	RICHARD M. SMITH

[For the Federal Communications Commission statement of organization, see the *Code of Federal Regulations*, Title 47, Part 0]

FEDERAL COMMUNICATIONS COMMISSION

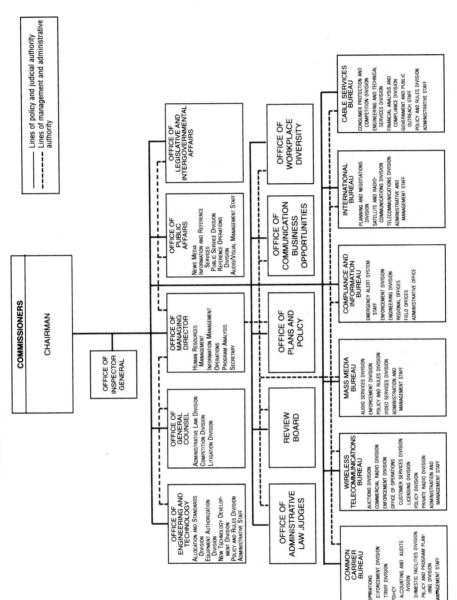

Lines of policy and judicial authority
Lines of management and administrative authority

COMMISSIONERS

CHAIRMAN

OFFICE OF INSPECTOR GENERAL

OFFICE OF LEGISLATIVE AND INTERGOVERNMENTAL AFFAIRS

OFFICE OF PUBLIC AFFAIRS

News Media
Information and Reference Services
Public Service Division
Reference Operations Division
Audio/Visual Management Staff

OFFICE OF MANAGING DIRECTOR

Human Resources Management
Information Management
Operations
Program Analysis
Secretary

OFFICE OF GENERAL COUNSEL

Administrative Law Division
Competition Division
Litigation Division

OFFICE OF ENGINEERING AND TECHNOLOGY

Allocation and Standards Division
Equipment Authorization Division
New Technology Development Division
Policy and Rules Division
Administrative Staff

OFFICE OF WORKPLACE DIVERSITY

OFFICE OF COMMUNICATION BUSINESS OPPORTUNITIES

OFFICE OF PLANS AND POLICY

REVIEW BOARD

OFFICE OF ADMINISTRATIVE LAW JUDGES

CABLE SERVICES BUREAU

Consumer Protection and Competition Division
Engineering and Technical Services Division
Financial Analysis and Compliance Division
Government and Public Outreach Staff
Policy and Rules Division
Administrative Staff

INTERNATIONAL BUREAU

Planning and Negotiations Division
Satellite and Radio-communications Division
Telecommunications Division
Administrative and Management Staff

COMPLIANCE AND INFORMATION BUREAU

Emergency Alert System Staff
Enforcement Division
Engineering Division
Regional Offices
Field Offices
Administrative Office

MASS MEDIA BUREAU

Audio Services Division
Enforcement Division
Policy and Rules Division
Video Services Division
Administration and Management Staff

WIRELESS TELECOMMUNICATIONS BUREAU

Auctions Division
Commercial Radio Division
Enforcement Division
Office of Operations
Customer Services Division
Licensing Division
Policy Division
Private Radio Division
Administration and Management Staff

COMMON CARRIER BUREAU

Operations
Enforcement Division
Tariff Division
Policy
Accounting and Audits Division
Domestic Facilities Division
Policy and Program Planning Division
Management Staff

The Federal Communications Commission regulates interstate and foreign communications by radio, television, wire, satellite, and cable. It is responsible for the orderly development and operation of broadcast services and the provision of rapid, efficient nationwide and worldwide telephone and telegraph services at reasonable rates. Its responsibilities also include the use of communications for promoting safety of life and property and for strengthening the national defense.

The Federal Communications Commission was created by the Communications Act of 1934 (47 U.S.C. 151 *et seq.*) to regulate interstate and foreign communications by wire and radio in the public interest. It was assigned additional regulatory jurisdiction under the provisions of the Communications Satellite Act of 1962 (47 U.S.C. 701–744). The scope of its regulation includes radio and television broadcasting; telephone, telegraph, and cable television operation; two-way radio and radio operators; and satellite communication.

The Commission is composed of five members, who are appointed by the President with the advice and consent of the Senate. One of the members is designated by the President as Chairman.

To assist the Commission in exercising its responsibility in the adjudicatory process, there is a Review Board to review initial decisions and write decisions and the Office of the General Counsel to assist the Commission and individual Commissioners in the disposition of matters arising in cases of adjudication (as defined in the Administrative Procedure Act (5 U.S.C. note prec. 551)) that have been designated for hearings. There also is a corps of administrative law judges, qualified and appointed pursuant to the requirements of the Administrative Procedure Act, who conduct evidentiary adjudicatory hearings and write initial decisions.

Activities

Mass Media   The Mass Media Bureau administers the regulatory program for the following services: amplitude modulation (AM); frequency modulation (FM); television; low-power TV; translators; instructional TV and auxiliary services. The Bureau issues construction permits, operating licenses, and renewals or transfers of such broadcast licenses except for broadcast auxiliary services. The Bureau also oversees compliance by broadcasters with statutes and Commission policies.

For further information, contact the Mass Media Bureau. Phone, 202–632–6460.

Common Carrier Communications   The Common Carrier Bureau administers the regulatory program for interstate common carrier communications by telephone. Common carriers include companies, organizations, or individuals providing communications services to the public for hire, who must serve all who wish to use them at established rates. In providing interstate communications services, common carriers may employ landline wire or electrical or optical cable facilities.

For further information, contact the Common Carrier Bureau. Phone, 202–418–1500.

Wireless Telecommunications   The Wireless Telecommunications Bureau administers all domestic commercial and private wireless telecommunications programs and policies. The commercial wireless services include Cellular, Paging, Personal Communications Services, Specialized Mobile Radio, Air-Ground, and Basic Exchange Telecommunications. The private wireless services include the Land Mobile Radio Services (including Public Safety, Industrial, Land Transportation, and Business), Broadcast Auxiliary, Operational Fixed Microwave and Point-to-Point Microwave, and the Special Radio Services (including Aviation, Marine, Amateur IVDS, and the Personal Radio Service). Additionally, the Bureau serves as the Commission's principal policy and administrative resource with regard to spectrum auctions. The Bureau also implements the compulsory provisions of laws and treaties covering the use of radio for the safety of life and property at sea and in the air. The commercial and amateur radio operator programs are also administered by the Wireless Telecommunications Bureau.

For further information, contact the Wireless Telecommunications Bureau. Phone, 202–418–0600.

International Bureau The International Bureau manages all FCC international telecommunications and satellite programs and policies, and has the principal representational role on behalf of the Commission at international conferences, meetings, and negotiations. The Bureau consists of three divisions: Telecommunications, Satellite and Radiocommunication, and Planning and Negotiations.

The Telecommunications Division develops and administers policy, rules, and procedures for the regulations of telecommunications facilities and services under section 214 of the Communications Act and Cable Landing License Act. In addition, the Division develops and administers regulatory assistance and training programs in conjunction with the administration's Global Information Infrastructure (GII) initiative.

The Satellite and Radiocommunication Division develops and administers policy, rules, standards, and procedures for licensing and regulation of satellite and earth station facilities, both international and domestic, and oversight of Comsat as the U.S. Signatory to INTELSAT and Inmarsat.

The Planning and Negotiations Division represents the Commission in negotiations with Mexico, Canada, and other countries on international agreements that provide for arrangements and procedures for the coordination of radio frequency assignments to prevent and resolve international radio interference involving U.S. licensees and notifies all new changed U.S. radio stations to appropriate administrations and responds to foreign notifications as required and processes high frequency (HF) international broadcast applications and applications to deliver broadcast programs to foreign stations.

For further information, contact the International Bureau. Phone, 202–418–0420.

Cable Services Communications The Cable Services Bureau develops, recommends, and administers policies and programs for the regulation of cable television systems. The Bureau advises and recommends to the Commission, or acts for the Commission under delegated authority, in matters pertaining to the regulation and development of cable television.

With its major divisions—Financial Analysis and Compliance, Consumer Protection and Competition, Policy and Rules, and Engineering and Technical Services, as well as units within the Office of the Bureau Chief—the Cable Services Bureau has the following duties and responsibilities:

—to investigate complaints and answer general inquiries from the public;

—to plan and develop proposed rulemakings and conduct comprehensive studies and analyses (legal, social, and economic) of various petitions for policy or rule changes;

—to process applications for authorizations in the cable television relay service;

—to participate in hearings before Administrative Law Judges, the Review Board, and the Commission;

—to conduct studies and compile data relating to the cable industry for the Commission to develop and maintain an adequate regulatory program;

—to collaborate and coordinate with State and local authorities in matters involving cable television systems; and

—to advise and assist the public, other government agencies, and industry groups on cable television regulation and related matters.

Engineering and Technology The Office of Engineering and Technology administers the Table of Frequency Allocations which specifies the frequency ranges that can be utilized by various radio services. The Office also administers the Experimental Radio Service and the Equipment Authorization Program. The Experimental Radio

Service permits the public to experiment with new uses of radio frequencies. This allows development of radio equipment and exploration of new radio techniques prior to licensing under other regulatory programs. The Equipment Authorization Program includes several specific procedures by which the agency approves radio equipment as a prerequisite to importation, marketing, or use. The procedures range from Commission testing of an equipment sample for compliance with applicable standards, through FCC review of applications and accompanying test reports submitted by the applicants, to a self-authorization procedure whereby a manufacturer certifies that the product complies with the standards.

For further information, contact the Office of Engineering and Technology. Phone, 202–739–0700.

Compliance　Much of the investigative and enforcement work of the Commission is carried out by its field staff. The Field Operations Bureau has 6 regional offices and 35 field offices. It also operates a nationwide fleet of mobile radio direction-finding vehicles for technical enforcement purposes. The field staff, in effect, are the Commission's "eyes and ears" in detecting radio violations and enforcing rules and regulations. Continuous surveillance of the radio spectrum is maintained to detect unlicensed operation and activities or nonconforming transmissions, and to furnish radio bearings on ships and planes in distress. The Field Operations Bureau also administers public service programs aimed at educating Commission licensees, industry, and the general public to improve compliance with FCC rules and regulations.

For further information, contact the Field Operations Bureau. Phone, 202–632–6980.

Regional and Field Offices—Federal Communications Commission

Field Operations Bureau

Regional Office	Address	Regional Director
Atlanta, GA	Suite 310, Koger Center-Gwinnett, 3575 Koger Blvd., Duluth, GA 30136–4958.	Carl E. Pyron
Kansas City, MO	Rm. 320, Brywood Office Twr., 8800 E. 63d St., 64133	Dennis P. Carlton
Kirkland, WA	Rm. 312, 11410 NE. 122d Way, 98034–6927	William C. Johnson
Park Ridge, IL	Rm. 306, Park Ridge Office Ctr., 1550 Northwest Hwy., 60068–1460.	Russell D. Monie
Quincy, MA	NFPA Bldg., 1 Batterymarch Pk., 02169–7495	Joseph P. Casey
San Francisco, CA	Rm. 420, 3777 Depot Rd., Hayward, CA 94545–2756	Serge Marti-Volkoff

Field Office	Address	Engineer in Charge
Allegan, MI	P.O. Box 89, 49010–9437	Melvyn H. Hyman
Anchorage, AK	6721 W. Raspberry Rd., 99502–1896	Marlene Windel
Atlanta, GA	Rm. 320, 3575 Koger Blvd., Duluth, GA, 30136–4958	Fred L. Broce
Baltimore, MD	Rm. 1017, 31 Hopkins Plz., 21201–2802	Robert M. Mroz
Belfast, ME	P.O. Box 470, 04915–0470	Barry A. Bohac
Buffalo, NY	Rm. 1307, 111 W. Huron St., 14202–2398	David A. Viglione
Cerritos, CA	Rm. 660, 1800 Studebaker Rd., 90701–3684	James R. Zoulek
Custer, WA	1330 Loomis Trail Rd., 98240–9303	Jack W. Bazhaw
Dallas, TX	Rm. 1170, 9330 LBJ Fwy., 75243–3429	James D. Wells
Denver, CO	Rm. 860, 165 S. Union Blvd., 80228–2213	Leo E. Cirbo
Douglas, AZ	P.O. Box 6, 85608	Stephen Y. Tsuya
Farmington Hills, MI	24897 Hathaway St., 48335–1552	(Vacancy)
Grand Island, NE	P.O. Box 1588, 68802–1588	James H. Berrie, Jr.
Hato Rey, PR	Rm. 747, Federal Bldg., 00918–1713	William C. Berry
Hayward, CA	Rm. 420, 3777 Depot Rd., 94545–2756	Philip M. Kane
Houston, TX	Rm. 900, 1225 N. Loop West, 77008–1775	Loyd P. Perry
Kansas City, MO	Rm. 320, 8800 E. 63d St., 64133–4895	James A. Dailey
Kingsville, TX	P.O. Box 632, 78363–0632	Oliver K. Long
Kirkland, WA	Rm. 312, 11410 NE. 122d Way, 98034–6927	Gary P. Soulsby
Langhorne, PA	Rm. 404, 2300 E. Lincoln Hwy., 19047–1859	John Rahtes
Laurel, MD	P.O. Box 250, Columbia, MD, 21045–9998	Robert J. Douchis
Livermore, CA	P.O. Box 311, 94551–0311	Thomas N. Stavern
Miami, FL	Rm. 310, 8390 NW. 53d St., 33166–4668	John L. Theimer
New Orleans, LA	Rm. 505, 800 W. Commerce Rd., 70123–3333	James C. Hawkins
New York, NY	201 Varick St., 10014–4870	Alexander J. Zimney
Park Ridge, IL	Rm. 306, 1550 Northwest Hwy., 60068–1460	George M. Moffitt
Portland, OR	Rm. 1782, 1220 SW. 3d Ave., 97204–2898	Charles W. Craig

Field Office	Address	Engineer in Charge
Powder Springs, GA	P.O. Box 85, 30073–0085	Donald E. Taylor
Quincy, MA	1 Batterymarch Pk., 02169–7495	Vincent F. Kajunski
St. Paul, MN	Suite 31, 2025 Sloan Pl., Maplewood, MN 55117–2058	Albert S. Jarratt
San Diego, CA	Rm. 370, 4542 Ruffner St., 92111–2216	William H. Grisby
Tampa, FL	Rm. 1215, 2203 N. Lois Ave., 33607–2356	Ralph M. Barlow
Vero Beach, FL	P.O. Box 1730, 32961–1730	Robert C. McKinney
Virginia Beach, VA	1200 Communications Cir., 23455–3725	J. Jerry Freeman
Waipahu, HI	P.O. Box 1030, 96797–1030	Jack Shedletsky

Sources of Information

Inquiries for information on the special subjects listed in the following paragraphs and those concerning licensing/grant requirements in the various services may be directed to the person or office specified or to the Chief of the Bureau or Office listed below as having responsibility for the service: Federal Communications Commission, 1919 M Street NW., Washington, DC 20554.

Licensing/Grant Responsibility—Federal Communications Commission

Service	Bureau or Office
All broadcasting (except broadcast auxiliary services)	Mass Media Bureau
Cable television relay radio Cable TV rate regulation Cable TV relay services (CARS) Cable signal leakage Cable television questions Registration of cable systems	Cable Services Bureau
Common carrier radio Section 214 of FCC Act	Common Carrier Bureau
Experimental radio	Office of Engineering and Technology
Equipment approval services: Certification Type acceptance Type approval Notification Verification	Office of Engineering and Technology
Amateur radio Auxiliary broadcast services Aviation radio Commercial radio operators Common carrier microwave services Interactive video and data services Land mobile radio Marine radio Private microwave radio	Private Radio Bureau

Advisory Committee Management

Direct inquiries to the Associate Managing Director for Program Analysis. Phone, 202–418–0923.

Consumer Assistance   Inquiries concerning general information on how the Commission works and how the public can participate in the decisionmaking process should be addressed to the Public Service Division, Room 254, 1919 M Street NW., Washington, DC 20554. Phone, 202–418–0200.

Contracts and Procurement   Direct inquiries to the Chief, Acquisitions Branch. Phone, 202–418–0930.

Employment and Recruitment   The Commission's programs require attorneys, electronics engineers, economists, accountants, administrative management and computer specialists, and clerical personnel. Requests for employment information should be directed to the Chief, Personnel Resources Branch. Phone, 202–418–0130. Schools interested in participating in the college recruitment programs of the Commission should direct their inquiries to the Associate Managing Director, Human Resources Management. Phone, 202–418–0100.

Equal Employment Practices by Industry   Direct inquiries to the Chief, Public Service Division. Phone, 202–418–0200.

Internal Equal Employment Practices   Direct Inquiries to the Director, Office of Workplace Diversity. Phone, 202–418–0125.

Ex-Parte Presentations   Information concerning ex-parte presentations should be directed to the Commission's Office of General Counsel. Phone, 202–410–1720.

Fees   Inquiries concerning the Commission's Fee Program should be addressed to the Public Service Division, Room 254, 1919 M Street NW., Washington, DC 20554. Phone, 202–418–0192.

Information Available for Public Inspection   At the Commission's headquarters office in Washington, DC, dockets concerning rulemaking and adjudicatory matters, copies of applications for licenses and grants, and reports required to be filed by licensees and cable system operators are maintained in the public reference rooms—some reports are by law held confidential. General information is also available from the Commission's Internet site @ fcc.gov and through fax-on-demand, 202–418–2830. In addition to the information available at the Commission, each broadcasting station makes available for public reference certain information pertaining to the operation of the station, a current copy of the application filed for license, and nonconfidential reports filed with the Commission. Special requests for inspection of records at the Commission's offices should be directed to the Managing Director. Phone, 202–418–1919. The Library has on file Commission rules and regulations. Phone, 202–418–0450. The Office of Public Affairs distributes publications, public notices, and press releases. Phone, 202–418–0500.

For further information, contact the Public Service Division, Federal Communications Commission, 1919 M Street NW., Washington, DC 20554. Phone, 202–418–0200.

FEDERAL DEPOSIT INSURANCE CORPORATION

550 Seventeenth Street NW., Washington, DC 20429
Phone, 202–393–8400

Board of Directors:

Chairman	RICKI T. HELFER
Vice Chairman	ANDREW C. HOVE, JR.
Directors:	
(Comptroller of the Currency)	EUGENE A. LUDWIG
(Director, Office of Thrift Supervision)	JONATHAN L. FIECHTER, *Acting*
Appointive Director	(VACANCY)

Officials:

Chief Operating Officer and Deputy to the Chairman	DENNIS F. GEER, *Acting*
Chief Financial Officer and Deputy to the Chairman for Financial Policy	WILLIAM A. LONGBRAKE
Deputy to the Chairman for Policy	LESLIE A. WOOLLEY
Deputy to the Vice Chairman	ROGER A. HOOD
Deputy to the Director (Comptroller of the Currency)	THOMAS E. ZEMKE
Deputy to the Director (Office of Thrift Supervision)	WALTER B. MASON
Deputy to the Director (Appointive)	(VACANCY)
Executive Secretary	ROBERT E. FELDMAN, *Acting*
General Counsel	WILLIAM F. KROENER III
Executive Director, Division of Compliance, Resolutions, and Supervision	JOHN W. STONE
Director, Division of Compliance and Consumer Affairs	PAUL L. SACHTLEBEN
Director, Division of Resolutions	ROBERT H. HARTHEIMER, *Acting*
Director, Division of Supervision	STANLEY J. POLING

Director, Division of Depositor and Asset Services	JOHN F. BOVENZI
Director, Division of Finance	STEVEN A. SEELIG
Director, Division of Information Resources Management	CARMEN J. SULLIVAN
Director, Division of Research and Statistics	WILLIAM R. WATSON
Director, Office of Corporate Communications	ALAN J. WHITNEY
Director, Office of Legislative Affairs	ALICE C. GOODMAN
Director, Office of Personnel Management	ALFRED P. SQUERRINI
Director, Office of Equal Employment Opportunity	JOHNNIE B. BOOKER
Director, Office of Training and Educational Services	JANE L. SARTORI
Director, Office of Corporate Services	JAMES A. WATKINS
Inspector General, Office of Inspector General	JAMES A. RENICK, *Acting*

The Federal Deposit Insurance Corporation promotes and preserves public confidence in U.S. financial institutions by insuring bank and thrift deposits up to the legal limit of $100,000; by periodically examining State-chartered banks that are not members of the Federal Reserve System for safety and soundness as well as compliance with consumer protection laws; and by liquidating assets of failed institutions to reimburse the insurance funds for the cost of failures.

The Federal Deposit Insurance Corporation (FDIC) was established under the Banking Act of 1933 in response to numerous bank failures after the Great Depression. FDIC began operations on September 9, 1934, with $150 million from the U.S. Treasury and capital stock subscribed by the 12 Federal Reserve Banks. Congress has increased the limit on deposit insurance five times since 1934, the most current level being $100,000.

The Corporation does not operate on funds appropriated by Congress. Its income is derived from assessments on deposits held by insured banks and from interest on the required investment of its surplus funds in Government securities. It also has authority to borrow from the Treasury up to $30 billion for insurance purposes.

Management of FDIC consists of a Board of Directors that includes the Chairman, Vice Chairman, and Appointive Director. The Comptroller of the Currency, whose office supervises federally chartered or national banks, and the Director of the Office of Thrift Supervision, which supervises federally

chartered savings associations, are also members of the Board. All five Board members are appointed by the President and confirmed by the Senate, with no more than three being from the same political party.

Activities

FDIC insures about $2 trillion of U.S. bank and thrift deposits. The insurance funds are composed of insurance premiums paid by banks and savings associations and the interest on the investment of those premiums in U.S. Government securities, as required by law. FDIC uses the insurance funds, not funds appropriated by Congress, for its operations. Banks pay premiums to the Bank Insurance Fund (BIF) while savings associations pay premiums to the Savings Association Insurance Fund (SAIF). Premiums are determined by an institution's level of capitalization and potential risk to its insurance fund.

FDIC examines about 7,000 commercial and savings banks that are not members of the Federal Reserve System, and are therefore called State-chartered nonmember banks. The

FEDERAL DEPOSIT INSURANCE CORPORATION

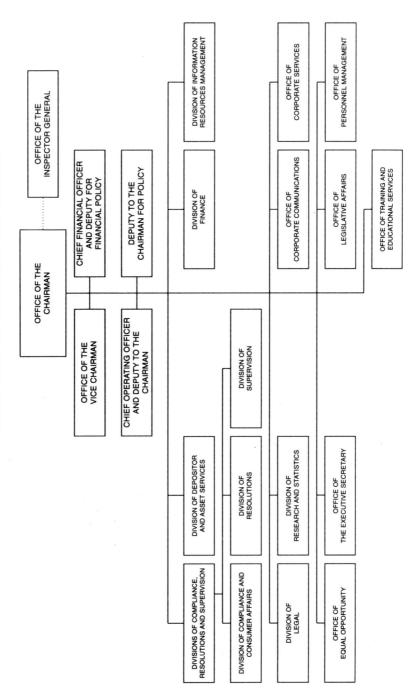

Corporation also has back-up authority to examine other types of financial institutions. The two types of examinations conducted are for safety and soundness, and for compliance with applicable consumer laws such as Truth in Lending, the Home Mortgage Disclosure Act, and the Community Reinvestment Act. Examinations are performed on the institution's premises and off-site through computer data analysis.

A failed bank is generally closed by its chartering authority, and FDIC is named receiver. In that capacity, FDIC attempts to locate a healthy institution to acquire the failed entity. If an acquirer cannot be found, FDIC pays depositors the amount of their insured funds, usually within 1 or 2 business days following the closing. Depositors with funds that exceed the insurance limit often receive an advance dividend, which is a portion of their uninsured funds that is determined by an estimate of the future proceeds from liquidating the failed bank's remaining assets. Depositors with funds in a failed bank that exceed the insurance limit receive a receivership certificate for those funds and partial payments of their uninsured funds as asset liquidation permits.

In addition to its insurance, supervisory, and liquidation responsibilities, FDIC performs other functions relating to State nonmember banks, including:

—approval or disapproval of mergers, consolidations, and acquisitions where the resulting bank is an insured State nonmember;

—approval or disapproval of a proposal by a bank to establish and operate a new branch, close an existing branch, or move its main office from one location to another;

—issuance of enforcement actions, including cease-and-desist orders, for specific violations or practices requiring corrective action, and

—reporting changes in ownership or control of a bank, and reporting any loan secured by 25 percent or more of the bank's stock.

Regional Offices—Federal Deposit Insurance Corporation

Region/Address	Director	Telephone
Supervision		
Atlanta, GA (1 Atlantic Ctr., Suite 1600, 1201 W. Peachtree St. NE., 30309).	Lyle V. Helgerson	404–817–1300
Boston, MA (Westwood Executive Ctr., 200 Lowder Brook Dr., Westwood, MA 02090).	Paul H. Wiechman	617–320–1600
Chicago, IL (Suite 3600, 500 W. Monroe St., 60661)	Simona L. Frank	312–382–7500
Dallas, TX (Suite 1900, 1910 Pacific Ave., 75201)	Kenneth L. Walker	214–220–3342
Kansas City, MO (Suite 1500, 2345 Grand Ave., 64108)	James O. Leese	816–234–8000
Memphis, TN (Suite 1900, 5100 Poplar Ave., 38137)	Cottrell L. Webster	901–685–1603
New York, NY (19th Fl., 452 5th Ave., 10018)	Nicholas J. Ketcha, Jr.	212–704–1200
San Francisco, CA (Suite 2300, 25 Ecker St., 94105)	George J. Masa	415–546–0160
Depositor/Asset Services		
NORTHEAST (111 Founder's Plz., East Hartford, CT 06108)	Gary P. Bowen	203–290–2000
SOUTHEAST (Suite 1300, 1 Atlantic Ctr., 1201 W. Peachtree St. NE., Atlanta GA 30309).	Keith W. Seibold	404–817–2500
MIDWEST (Suite 3200, 500 W. Monroe St., Chicago, IL 60661)	Bart L. Federici	312–382–6000
SOUTHWEST (Suite 1000E, 5080 Spectrum Dr., Dallas, TX 75248)	G. Michael Newton	214–991–0039
WESTERN (4 Park Plz., Jamboree Center, Irvine, CA 92714)	Sandra Waldrop	714–263–7765

Sources of Information

Written requests for general information may be directed to the Office of Corporate Communications, Federal Deposit Insurance Corporation, 550 Seventeenth Street NW., Washington, DC 20429. Information about deposit insurance and other consumer matters is available from the Division of Compliance and Consumer Affairs (DCA) at the same address or any regional office, or DCA's hotline, 1–800–934–3442. For a copy of a bank's quarterly Report of Condition, call 1–800–945–2186. Inquiries about the types of records available to the public, including records available under the Freedom of

Information Act, should be directed to the Office of the Executive Secretary

(phone, 202–898–3811) or any regional office.

For further information, contact the Corporate Communications Office, Federal Deposit Insurance Corporation, 550 Seventeenth Street NW., Washington, DC 20429. Phone, 202–898–6996.

FEDERAL ELECTION COMMISSION

999 E Street NW., Washington, DC 20463
Phones: 202–219–3420; 800–424–9530 (toll-free)

Chairman	DANNY L. MCDONALD
Vice Chairman	LEE ANN ELLIOTT
Commissioners	JOAN D. AIKENS, JOHN WARREN MCGARRY, TREVOR POTTER, SCOTT E. THOMAS
Statutory Officers:	
Staff Director	JOHN C. SURINA
General Counsel	LAWRENCE M. NOBLE
Inspector General	LYNNE A. MCFARLAND

The Federal Election Commission exercises exclusive jurisdiction in the administration and civil enforcement of laws regulating the acquisition and expenditure of campaign funds to ensure compliance by participants in the Federal election campaign process. Its chief mission is to provide public disclosure of campaign finance activities and effect voluntary compliance by providing the public with information on the laws and regulations concerning campaign finance.

The Federal Election Commission is an independent agency established by section 309 of the Federal Election Campaign Act of 1971, as amended (2 U.S.C. 437c). It is composed of six Commissioners appointed by the President with the advice and consent of the Senate. The act also provides for three statutory officers—the Staff Director, the General Counsel, and the Inspector General—who are appointed by the Commission.

Activities

The Commission administers and enforces the Federal Election Campaign Act of 1971, as amended (2 U.S.C. 431 *et seq.*), and the Revenue Act, as amended (26 U.S.C. 1 *et seq.*). These laws provide for the public funding of Presidential elections, public disclosure of the financial activities of political committees involved in Federal

elections, and limitations and prohibitions on contributions and expenditures made to influence Federal elections (Presidency, Senate, and House).

Public Funding of Presidential Elections The Commission oversees the public financing of Presidential elections by certifying Federal payments to primary candidates, general election nominees, and national nominating conventions. It also audits recipients of Federal funds and may require repayments to the U.S. Treasury if a committee makes nonqualified campaign expenditures.

Disclosure The Commission ensures the public disclosure of the campaign finance activities reported by political committees supporting Federal candidates. Committee reports, filed regularly, disclose where campaign money comes from and how it is spent. The Commission places reports on the public record within 48 hours after they are received and computerizes the data contained in the reports.

Contribution Limits and Prohibitions The Commission administers and enforces the law with respect to limits and prohibitions on contributions and expenditures made to influence Federal elections.

Voluntary Compliance The Commission seeks voluntary compliance with the above provisions of the law by providing information through a toll-free telephone line, publications, seminars, regulations (which clarify the law), and advisory opinions (which interpret the law in specific, factual situations).

Enforcement The Commission has exclusive jurisdiction with respect to the civil enforcement of the campaign finance laws. Possible violations of the law are brought to the Commission's attention, either internally (through report review procedures and audits) or externally (through complaints filed by the public or referrals from other government agencies). The Commission seeks to resolve compliance matters through conciliation and may bring suit when conciliation fails. It also defends the law in court.

Sources of Information

Clearinghouse on Election Administration The Clearinghouse compiles and disseminates election administration information related to Federal elections. It also conducts independent contract studies on the administration of elections. For further information, call 202–219–3670, or 800–424–9530 (toll-free).

Congressional Affairs Office This Office serves as primary liaison with Congress and executive branch agencies. The Office is responsible for keeping Members of Congress informed about Commission decisions and, in turn, for informing the Commission on legislative developments. For further information,

call 202–219–4136, or 800–424–9530 (toll-free).

Employment Inquiries regarding employment opportunities should be directed to the Director, Personnel and Labor Management Relations. Phone, 202–219–4290, or 800–424–9530 (toll-free).

General Inquiries The Information Services Division provides information and assistance to Federal candidates, political committees, and the general public. This division answers questions on campaign finance laws, conducts workshops and seminars on the law, and provides publications and forms. Those seeking information or materials should call 202–219–3420, or 800–424–9530 (toll-free).

Media Inquiries The Press Office answers inquiries from print and broadcast media sources around the country, issues press releases on Commission actions and statistical data, responds to informational requests, and distributes other materials. All persons representing media should direct inquiries to the Press Office. For further information, call 202–219–4155, or 800–424–9530 (toll-free).

Public Records The Office of Public Records, located at 999 E Street NW., Washington, DC, provides space for public inspection of all reports and statements relating to campaign finance since 1972. It is open weekdays from 9 a.m. to 5 p.m. and has extended hours during peak election periods. The public is invited to visit the Office or obtain information by calling 202–219–4140, or 800–424–9530 (toll-free).

Reading Room The library contains a collection of basic legal research resources, with emphasis on political campaign financing, corporate and labor political activity, and campaign finance reform. It is open to the public on weekdays between 9 a.m. and 5 p.m. For further information, call 202–219–3312, or 800–424–9530 (toll-free).

For further information, contact Information Services, Federal Election Commission, 999 E Street NW., Washington, DC 20463. Phone, 202–219–3420 or, toll-free, 800–424–9530.

FEDERAL EMERGENCY MANAGEMENT AGENCY

500 C Street SW., Washington, DC 20472
Phone, 202–646–4600

Director	JAMES LEE WITT
General Counsel	JOHN CAREY
Chief Financial Officer	GARY JOHNSON
Inspector General	GEORGE OPFER
Director, Office of Emergency Information and Public Affairs	MAURICE F. GOODMAN
Director, Office of Congressional and Governmental Affairs	MARTHA S. BRADDOCK
Associate Director, Response and Recovery Directorate	RICHARD W. KRIMM
Associate Director, Information Technology Services	JOHN D. HWANG
Associate Director, Mitigation Directorate	RICHARD THOMAS MOORE
Associate Director, Preparedness, Training and Exercises Directorate	KAY GOSS
Associate Director, Operations Support Directorate	BRUCE CAMPBELL
Administrator, Federal Insurance Administration	ELAINE A. MCREYNOLDS
Administrator, United States Fire Administration	CARRYE BROWN

[For the Federal Emergency Management Agency statement of organization, see the *Code of Federal Regulations*, Title 44, Part 2]

The Federal Emergency Management Agency is the central agency within the Federal Government for emergency planning, preparedness, mitigation, response, and recovery. Working closely with State and local governments, FEMA funds emergency programs, offers technical guidance and training, and deploys Federal resources in times of catastrophic disaster. These coordinated activities ensure a broad-based program to protect life and property and provide recovery assistance after a disaster.

The Federal Emergency Management Agency (FEMA) was established by Executive Order 12127 of March 31, 1979, consolidating the Nation's emergency-related programs.

FEMA reports directly to the White House and manages the President's Disaster Relief Fund, the source of most Federal funding assistance after major disasters. FEMA's programs include response to and recovery from major natural disasters and human-caused emergencies, emergency management planning, flood-plain management, hazardous materials planning, dam safety, and multihazard response

planning. Other activities include off-site planning for emergencies at commercial nuclear power plants and the Army's chemical stockpile sites, emergency food and shelter funding for the homeless, plans to ensure the continuity of the Federal Government during national security emergencies, and Federal response to the consequences of major terrorist incidents.

The U.S. Fire Administration (USFA) and its National Fire Academy (NFA) are a part of FEMA, providing national leadership in fire safety and prevention. USFA has responsibility for all fire and emergency medical service programs

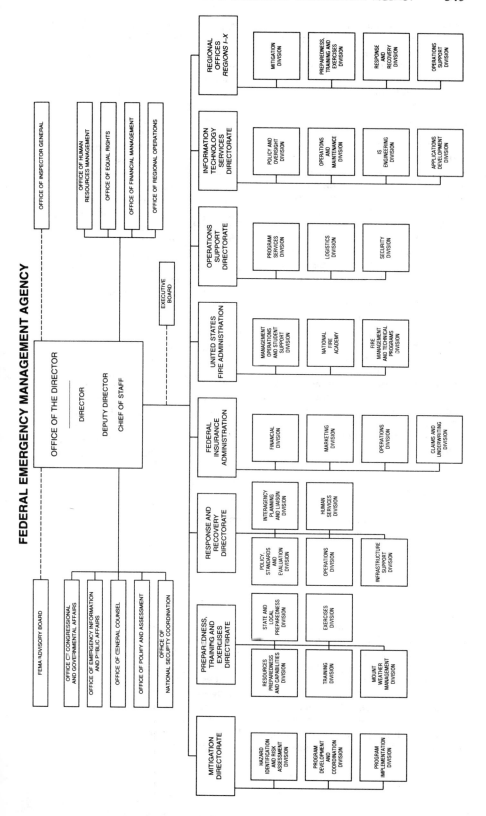

FEDERAL EMERGENCY MANAGEMENT AGENCY

and training activities. The Federal Insurance Administration (FIA) is also a part of FEMA and manages the National Flood Insurance Program and crime insurance programs. The Emergency Management Institute (EMI) at Emmitsburg, Maryland, offers centralized professional courses for the Nation's emergency managers.

FEMA is responsible for coordinating Federal efforts to reduce the loss of life and property through a comprehensive risk-based, all-hazards emergency management program of mitigation, preparedness, response, and recovery. The agency also works to assure the effectiveness and the availability of all-hazard systems and resources in coping with manmade and natural disasters; consolidates the programs aimed at preventing and mitigating the effects of potential disasters with the programs designed to deal with the disasters once they occur; coordinates and plans for the emergency deployment of resources that are used on a routine basis by Federal agencies; and helps to coordinate preparedness programs with State and local governments, private industry, and voluntary organizations. In addition, FEMA provides a Federal focus on fire prevention and public fire safety education.

Activities

The principal activities of FEMA include:
Response and Recovery   This activity provides for the development and maintenance of an integrated operational capability to respond to and recover from the consequences of a disaster, regardless of its cause, in partnership with other Federal agencies, State and local governments, volunteer organizations, and the private sector.
Preparedness, Training, and Exercises This activity provides policy guidance , financial and technical assistance, training, and exercise support required to establish or enhance all-hazard, risk-based emergency management capabilities of Federal, State, and local governments. In addition, this activity maintains a family protection program, utilizing private sector and volunteer

organizations to encourage and assist families and neighborhoods to take actions to increase their emergency preparedness capabilities.
Fire Prevention and Training   This activity prepares Federal, State, and local officials, their staffs, emergency first responders, volunteer groups, and the public to meet the responsibilities of domestic emergencies through planning, mitigation, preparedness, response, and recovery. Educational programs are provided through the National Fire Academy at the National Emergency Training Center and through the field fire training delivery systems.
Operations Support   This activity provides direct support and services which address the common needs of all agency programs, such as administration, acquisition, logistics, information systems, security, and specialized capabilities and integration of the FEMA-wide networks.
Mitigation Programs   This activity provides for the development, coordination, and implementation of policies, plans, and programs to eliminate or reduce the long-term risk to life and property from natural hazards such as floods, earthquakes, hurricanes, and dam failures. A goal of this activity is to encourage and foster mitigation strategies at the State and local levels. This activity provides leadership and direction for management of information resources, ADP, Telecommunications and Systems to accomplish the agency's mission. Provides direct support and services to FEMA's all-hazards emergency management program of mitigation, preparedness, and response and recovery.
Information Technology Services   This activity provides leadership and direction for management of information resources, ADP, telecommunications, and systems to accomplish the agency's mission. It provides direct support and services to FEMA's all-hazards emergency management program of mitigation, preparedness, and response and recovery.
Executive Direction   This activity develops strategies to address public

information issues and provides staff and supporting resources for the general management and administration of the agency in legal affairs; congressional affairs; emergency information and public affairs; policy development; national security; personnel; and financial management.

Regional Offices

Ten regional offices primarily carry out FEMA's programs at the regional, State, and local levels. The regional offices are responsible for accomplishing the national program goals and objectives of the Agency and in supporting development of national policy.

Regional Offices—Federal Emergency Management Agency

Region/Address	Telephone
I. Boston, MA (Rm. 442, J.W. McCormack Post Office and Courthouse Bldg., 02109–4595)	617–223–9540
II. New York, NY (Rm. 1337, 26 Federal Plz., 10278–0002)	212–225–7209
III. Philadelphia, PA (2d Fl., Liberty Sq. Bldg., 105 S. 7th St., 19106–3316)	215–931–5608
IV. Atlanta, GA (Suite 700, 2d Fl., Liberty Sq. Bldg., 1371 Peachtree St., 30309–3108)	404–853–4224
V. Chicago, IL (4th Fl., 175 W. Jackson Blvd., 60604–2698)	312–408–5504

Regional Offices—Federal Emergency Management Agency—Continued

Region/Address	Telephone
VI. Denton, TX (Federal Regional Ctr., 800 N. Loop 288, 76201–3698)	817–898–5104
VII. Kansas, MO (Rm. 200, 911 Walnut St., 64106–2085)	816–283–7061
VIII. Denver, CO (Bldg. 710, Denver Federal Ctr., Box 25267, 80225–0267)	303–235–4812
IX. San Francisco, CA (Bldg. 105, Presidio of San Francisco, 94129–1250)	415–923–7105
X. Bothell, WA (Federal Regional Ctr., 130 228th St. SW., 98021–9796)	206–487–4765

Sources of Information

Inquiries on the following subjects should be directed to the appropriate office of the Federal Emergency Management Agency, 500 C Street SW., Washington, DC 20472.

Acquisition Services Office of Acquisition Management. Phone, 202–646–3744.

Employment Office of Human Resources Management. Phone, 202–646–3964.

Freedom of Information Act Requests Office of General Counsel. Phone, 202–646–3840.

For further information, contact the Office of Emergency Information and Public Affairs, Federal Emergency Management Agency, 500 C Street SW., Washington, DC 20472. Phone, 202–646–4600.

FEDERAL HOUSING FINANCE BOARD

1777 F Street NW., Washington, DC 20006
Phone, 202–408–2500

Board of Directors:
Chairman   (VACANCY)
Members:
    (Secretary of Housing and Urban   HENRY G. CISNEROS
        Development, *ex officio*)

                                                      LAWRENCE U. COSTIGLIO
                                                      (2 VACANCIES)

    Housing and Urban Development   NICOLAS P. RETSINAS
        Secretary's Designee to the Board
    Assistant to the Board Director   MELISSA L. ALLEN

Officials:

Managing Director	RITA I. FAIR
Inspector General	EDWARD KELLEY
General Counsel	BETH L. CLIMO
Director, Office of Examination and Regulatory Oversight	GARY B. TOWNSEND
Director, Office of Policy and Financial Reporting	THOMAS D. SHEEHAN, *Acting*
Director, Office of Housing Finance	SYLVIA C. MARTINEZ
Director, Office of Congressional Affairs	JOHN K. HARDAGE, *Acting*
Director, Office of Public Affairs	(VACANCY)
Director, Office of Administration	PATRICK PIZZELLA
Executive Secretary	ELAINE L. BAKER

[For the Federal Housing Finance Board statement of organization, see the *Code of Federal Regulations,* Title 12, Part 900]

The Federal Housing Finance Board is responsible for the administration and enforcement of the Federal Home Loan Bank Act, as amended.

The Federal Housing Finance Board (Finance Board) was established on August 9, 1989, by the Federal Home Loan Bank Act, as amended by the Financial Institutions Reform, Recovery, and Enforcement Act of 1989 (FIRREA) (12 U.S.C. 1421 *et seq.*), as an independent regulatory agency in the executive branch. The Finance Board succeeded the Federal Home Loan Bank Board for those functions transferred to it by FIRREA.

The Finance Board is governed by a five-member Board of Directors. Four members are appointed by the President with the advice and consent of the Senate for 7-year terms; one of whom is designated as Chairman. The Secretary of the Department of Housing and Urban Development is the fifth member and serves in an *ex officio* capacity.

The Finance Board supervises the Federal Home Loan Banks created in 1932 by the Federal Home Loan Bank Act and issues regulations and orders for carrying out the purposes of the provisions of that act. Savings associations, commercial banks, savings banks, credit unions, insurance companies, and other institutions specified in section 4 of the act that make long-term home-mortgage loans are eligible to become members of the Federal Home Loan Bank. The Finance Board supervises the Federal Home Loan Banks and ensures that they carry out

their housing finance mission, remain adequately capitalized and able to raise funds in the capital markets, and operate in a safe and sound manner. The functions of the Finance Board with respect to the Banks and their members include: prescribing rules and conditions under which the Banks may lend to members and eligible nonmembers; issuing policies governing the Bank System's financial management and investment activities; maintaining Bank System financial and membership data bases and preparing reports on a regular basis; overseeing the implementation of the community investment and affordable housing programs; conducting a biennial review of each member's community support performance; issuing consolidated Federal Home Loan Bank obligations which are joint and several obligations of all Federal Home Loan Banks; annually examining each Federal Home Loan Bank; requiring an independent financial audit of each Bank, the Office of Finance, the Financing Corporation, and the Bank System; appointing six directors to the board of directors of each Bank and conducting the election of the remaining directors by the members; approving dividends paid to each Bank; and approving applications for Bank membership. The Finance Board is not subject to the appropriation process. Its funds are neither appropriated nor

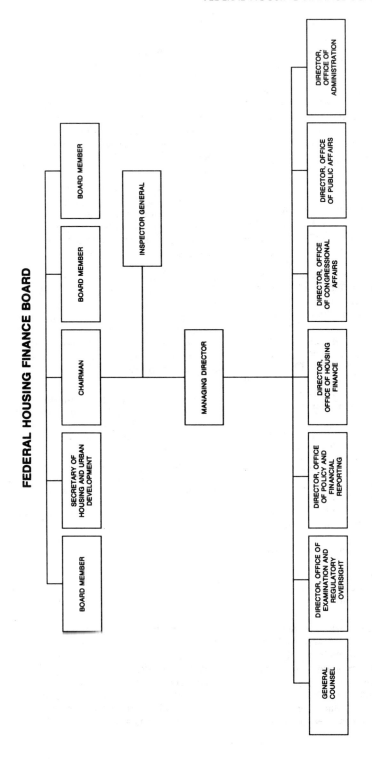

FEDERAL HOUSING FINANCE BOARD

BOARD MEMBER

SECRETARY OF HOUSING AND URBAN DEVELOPMENT

CHAIRMAN

BOARD MEMBER

BOARD MEMBER

INSPECTOR GENERAL

MANAGING DIRECTOR

GENERAL COUNSEL

DIRECTOR, OFFICE OF EXAMINATION AND REGULATORY OVERSIGHT

DIRECTOR, OFFICE OF POLICY AND FINANCIAL REPORTING

DIRECTOR, OFFICE OF HOUSING FINANCE

DIRECTOR, OFFICE OF CONGRESSIONAL AFFAIRS

DIRECTOR, OFFICE OF PUBLIC AFFAIRS

DIRECTOR, OFFICE OF ADMINISTRATION

derived from Government funds, and are not subject to apportionment. The expenses of the Finance Board are paid by assessment against the regional Federal Home Loan Banks.

Regional Banks The System includes 12 regional Federal Home Loan Banks that are mixed-ownership Government corporations. A board of directors, six of whom are appointed by the Finance Board, manages the Banks. The Finance Board conducts the election of the remaining directors.

Capital and Sources of Funds The Bank's principal source of capital is stock, which members are required by law to purchase upon joining the Bank System, and which is redeemed upon a member's withdrawal from the System. The Banks fund their lending activity through the issuance of Bank System consolidated obligations, which are the joint and several liability of the Banks. Member deposits are an additional source of funds. Bank System consolidated debt is issued by the Finance Board through the Office of Finance, the Bank System's fiscal agent. The Bank's consolidated obligations are neither obligations of, nor guaranteed by, the United States.

Operations The Bank's primary activity is extending secured loans to member institutions. Advances are generally collateralized by whole first mortgage loans and mortgage-backed securities, as well as other high-quality assets. In making advances, the Bank System serves as a source of short- and long-term funds for institutions operating in the mortgage markets as originators and holders of mortgage assets. The Bank System does not set standards for the loans its members make; therefore, members have the flexibility to develop responsive credit products and underwriting standards. The Banks also enter into hedging transactions as intermediaries with their members, which assists the members with their asset-liability management.

Under the Affordable Housing Program (AHP), the Banks provide subsidized advances or direct subsidies to Bank members engaged in lending for long-term, owner-occupied and affordable rental housing targeted to households with extremely low or moderate incomes. AHP is a competitive program financed from a specified percentage of each Bank's previous year's net income. For 1995 and beyond, the greater of $100 million or 10 percent of the previous year's net income will be available for the program.

Under the Community Investment Program (CIP), each Bank provides advances priced at the Bank's cost of consolidated obligations of comparable maturities plus reasonable administrative costs, to members engaged in community-oriented mortgage lending. CIP advances are used for loans to finance rental and owner-occupied housing for families whose incomes do not exceed 115 percent of area median income and commercial and economic development activities that benefit low- and moderate-income families or that are located in low- and moderate-income neighborhoods.

To maintain access to long-term advances, Bank members must establish reasonable commitments to residential lending and community support activities. Every 2 years, the Finance Board reviews the community support performance of each member by taking into account factors such as each member's Community Reinvestment Act performance and its lending to first-time homebuyers. The Banks provide technical assistance to their members in meeting the community support standards.

Financing Corporation

The Financing Corporation (FICO) was established by the Competitive Equality Banking Act of 1987 (12 U.S.C. 1441) with the sole purpose of issuing and servicing bonds, the proceeds of which were used to fund thrift resolutions. The principal on the bonds was defeased with capital contributions from the Banks. FICO has a three-member directorate, consisting of the Managing Director of the Office of Finance and two Federal Home Loan Bank presidents.

FICO operates subject to the regulatory authority of the Federal Housing Finance Board.

Sources of Information

Requests for information relating to human resources and procurement should be sent to the Office of Administration, at the address listed below.

For further information, contact the Executive Secretariat, Federal Housing Finance Board, 1777 F Street NW., Washington, DC 20006. Phone, 202–408–2500. Fax, 202–408–2895.

FEDERAL LABOR RELATIONS AUTHORITY

607 Fourteenth Street NW., Washington, DC 20424–0001
Phone, 202–482–6550

Chair	PHYLLIS N. SEGAL
Chief Counsel	SUSAN D. MCCLUSKEY
Special Assistant for External Affairs	HELENANN HIRSCH
Director, Labor-Management Cooperation	CHRISTINA S. MERCHANT
Director of Case Control	ALICIA N. COLUMNA
Member	TONY ARMENDARIZ
Chief Counsel	STEVEN H. SVARTZ
Member	PAMELA TALKIN
Chief Counsel	BARBARA B. FRANKLIN
Chief Administrative Law Judge	SAMUEL A. CHAITOVITZ
Solicitor	DAVID M. SMITH
Executive Director	SOLLY J. THOMAS, JR.
Director of Information Resources and Research Services	HAROLD D. KESSLER
Inspector General	ROBERT G. ANDARY
Office of the General Counsel	
General Counsel	JOSEPH SWERDZEWSKI
Deputy General Counsel	DAVID L. FEDER
Director of Operations and Resources Management	CLYDE B. BLANDFORD, JR.
Deputy Director of Operations, Field Management	NANCY A. SPEIGHT
Executive Assistant	CAROL W. POPE
Assistant General Counsel for Quality and Appeals	MICHAEL D. NOSSAMAN
Federal Service Impasses Panel	
Chair	BETTY BOLDEN
Members	GILBERT CARRILLO, BONNIE P. CASTREY, DOLLY M. GEE, EDWARD F. HARTFIELD, MARY E. JACKSTEIT, STANLEY M. FISHER
Executive Director	LINDA A. LAFFERTY
Foreign Service Labor Relations Board	
Chair	PHYLLIS N. SEGAL
Members	TIA SCHNEIDER DENENBERG (VACANCY)

General Counsel   JOSEPH SWERDZEWSKI

Foreign Service Impasse Disputes Panel

Chair   MARGERY R. GOOTNICK

Members   BETTY BOLDEN, ROBERT S. DEUTSCH, J. DOUGLAS MARCHANT, RALPH H. RUEDY

The Federal Labor Relations Authority oversees the Federal service labor-management relations program. It administers the law that protects the right of employees of the Federal Government to organize, bargain collectively, and participate through labor organizations of their own choosing in decisions affecting them. The Authority also ensures compliance with the statutory rights and obligations of Federal employees and the labor organizations that represent them in their dealings with Federal agencies.

The Federal Labor Relations Authority was created as an independent establishment by Reorganization Plan No. 2 of 1978 (5 U.S.C. app.), effective January 1, 1979, pursuant to Executive Order 12107 of December 28, 1978, to consolidate the central policymaking functions in Federal labor-management relations. Its duties and authority are specified in title VII (Federal Service Labor-Management Relations) of the Civil Service Reform Act of 1978 (5 U.S.C. 7101–7135).

Activities

The Authority provides leadership in establishing policies and guidance relating to the Federal service labor-management relations program. In addition, it determines the appropriateness of bargaining units, supervises or conducts representation elections, and prescribes criteria and resolves issues relating to the granting of consultation rights to labor organizations with respect to internal agency policies and Governmentwide rules and regulations. It also resolves negotiability disputes, unfair labor practice complaints, and exceptions to arbitration awards. The Chair of the Authority serves as the chief executive and administrative officer.

The General Counsel of the Authority investigates alleged unfair labor

practices, files and prosecutes unfair labor practice complaints before the Authority, and exercises such other powers as the Authority may prescribe.

The Federal Service Impasses Panel, an entity within the Authority, is assigned the function of providing assistance in resolving negotiation impasses between agencies and unions. After investigating an impasse, the Panel can either recommend procedures to the parties for the resolution of the impasse or assist the parties in resolving the impasse through whatever methods and procedures, including factfinding and recommendations, it considers appropriate. If the parties do not arrive at a settlement after assistance by the Panel, the Panel may hold hearings and take whatever action is necessary to resolve the impasse.

The Foreign Service Labor Relations Board and the Foreign Service Impasse Disputes Panel administer provisions of chapter 2 of the Foreign Service Act of 1980 (22 U.S.C. 3921), concerning labor-management relations. This chapter establishes a statutory labor-management relations program for Foreign Service employees of the United States Government. Administrative and staff support is provided by the Federal Labor Relations Authority and the Federal Service Impasses Panel.

FEDERAL LABOR RELATIONS AUTHORITY

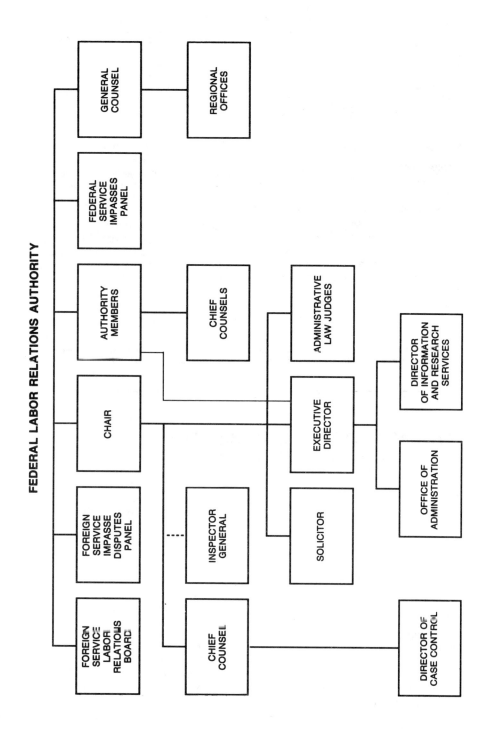

Regional Offices—Federal Labor Relations Authority

City/Address	Director	Telephone
Atlanta, GA (Suite 122, 1371 Peachtree St. NE., 30309–3102)	Brenda M. Robinson	404–347–2324
Boston, MA (Suite 1500, 99 Summer St., 02110)	Edward S. Davidson	617–424–5730
Chicago, IL (Suite 1150, Xerox Ctr., 55 W. Monroe, 60603)	William E. Washington	312–353–6306
Dallas, TX (Suite 926, 525 Griffin St., 75202)	James Petrucci	214–767–4996
Denver, CO (Suite 100, 1244 Speer Blvd., 80204)	Marjorie K. Thompson	303–844–5224
San Francisco, CA (Suite 220, 901 Market St., 94103)	Ronald T. Smith	415–744–4000
Washington, DC (Suite 400, 1255 22d St. NW., 20037)	Michael W. Doheny	202–653–8500

Sources of Information

Employment Employment inquiries and applications may be sent to the Director of Personnel. Phone, 202–482–6660.

Publications The Authority will assist in arranging reproduction of documents and ordering transcripts of hearings. Requests for publications should be submitted to the Director, Information Resources and Research Services. Phone, 202–482–6550.

Reading Room Anyone desiring to inspect formal case documents or read agency publications may use facilities of the Authority's offices.

Speakers To give agencies, labor organizations, and other interested persons a better understanding of the Federal service labor-management relations program and the Authority's role and duties, its personnel participate as speakers or panel members before various groups. Requests for speakers or panelists should be submitted to the Office of the Chair (phone, 202–482–6500); or to the Deputy General Counsel (phone, 202–482–6680).

For further information, contact the Director of Information Resources and Research Services, Federal Labor Relations Authority, 607 Fourteenth Street NW., Washington, DC 20424–0001. Phone, 202–482–6550.

FEDERAL MARITIME COMMISSION

800 North Capitol Street NW., Washington, DC 20573–0001
Phone, 202–523–5707

Chairman	WILLIAM D. HATHAWAY
Commissioners	HAROLD J. CREEL, JR., MING C. HSU, JOE SCROGGINS, JR., DELMOND J.H. WON
General Counsel	ROBERT D. BOURGOIN
Secretary	JOSEPH C. POLKING
Director, Office of Informal Inquiries, Complaints, and Informal Dockets	JOSEPH T. FARRELL
Chief Administrative Law Judge	NORMAN D. KLINE
Director, Office of Equal Employment Opportunity	MARY A. JACKSON
Inspector General	TONY P. KOMINOTH
Managing Director	EDWARD PATRICK WALSH
Deputy Managing Director	BRUCE A. DOMBROWSKI
Director, Bureau of Economics and Agreements Analysis	AUSTIN SCHMITT
Director, Bureau of Tariffs, Certification and Licensing	BRYANT L. VANBRAKLE
Director, Bureau of Investigations	NORMAN W. LITTLEJOHN

Director, Bureau of Hearing Counsel   WILLIAM JARREL SMITH, JR.
Director, Bureau of Administration   SANDRA L. KUSUMOTO

The Federal Maritime Commission regulates the waterborne foreign and domestic offshore commerce of the United States, assures that United States international trade is open to all nations on fair and equitable terms, and protects against unauthorized, concerted activity in the waterborne commerce of the United States. This is accomplished through maintaining surveillance over steamship conferences and common carriers by water; assuring that only the rates on file with the Commission are charged; reviewing agreements between persons subject to the Shipping Act of 1984 and the Shipping Act, 1916; guaranteeing equal treatment to shippers, carriers, and other persons subject to the shipping statutes; and ensuring that adequate levels of financial responsibility are maintained for indemnification of passengers.

The Federal Maritime Commission was established by Reorganization Plan No. 7 of 1961 (5 U.S.C. app.), effective August 12, 1961. It is an independent agency that regulates shipping under the following statutes: the Shipping Act of 1984 (46 U.S.C. app. 1701–1720); the Shipping Act, 1916 (46 U.S.C. app. 801 *et seq.*); the Merchant Marine Act, 1920 (46 U.S.C. app. 861 *et seq.*); the Foreign Shipping Practices Act of 1988 (46 U.S.C. app. 1710a); the Intercoastal Shipping Act, 1933 (46 U.S.C. app. 843 *et seq.*); the Merchant Marine Act, 1936 (46 U.S.C. app. 1101 *et seq.*); and certain provisions of the act of November 6, 1966 (46 U.S.C. app. 817(d) and 817(e)).

Activities

Agreements   The Commission reviews for legal sufficiency agreements filed under section 15 of the Shipping Act, 1916 (46 U.S.C. app. 814), and section 5 of the Shipping Act of 1984 (46 U.S.C. app. 1704), including conference, interconference, and cooperative working agreements among common carriers, terminal operators, and other persons subject to the shipping statutes. The Commission also monitors activities under all effective (1984 act) or approved (1916 act) agreements for compliance with the provisions of law and its rules, orders, and regulations.

Tariffs   The Commission accepts or rejects tariff filings, including filings dealing with service contracts, of common carriers engaged in the foreign and domestic offshore commerce of the United States, or conferences of such carriers. The Commission regulates the rate of return of carriers in the domestic offshore trades. Special permission applications may be submitted for relief from statutory and/or Commission tariff requirements. The Commission monitors the activities of controlled carriers under section 9 of the Shipping Act of 1984 (46 U.S.C. app. 1708, 1709, 1714).

Licenses   The Commission issues licenses to persons, partnerships, corporations, or associations desiring to engage in ocean freight forwarding activities.

Passenger Indemnity   The Commission administers the passenger indemnity provisions of the act of November 6, 1966, which require shipowners and operators to obtain certificates of financial responsibility to pay judgments for personal injury or death or to refund fares in the event of nonperformance of voyages.

Informal Complaints   The Commission reviews alleged or suspected violations of the shipping statutes and rules and regulations of the Commission and may take administrative action to institute formal proceedings, to refer matters to other governmental agencies, or to bring about voluntary agreement between the parties.

Formal Adjudicatory Procedure   The Commission conducts formal investigations and hearings on its own motion and adjudicates formal complaints in accordance with the

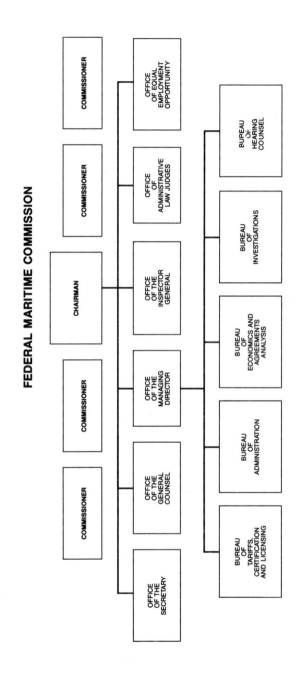

FEDERAL MARITIME COMMISSION

Administrative Procedure Act (5 U.S.C. note prec. 551).

Rulemaking The Commission promulgates rules and regulations to interpret, enforce, and ensure compliance with shipping and related statutes by common carriers and other persons subject to the statutes.

Investigation, Audit, and Financial and Economic Analyses The Commission prescribes and administers programs to ensure compliance with the provisions of the shipping statutes. These programs include the submission of information; field investigations and audits of activities and practices of common carriers, conferences, terminal operators, freight forwarders, and other persons subject to the shipping statutes; and rate analyses, studies, and economic reviews of current and prospective trade conditions, including the extent and nature of competition in various trade areas.

International Affairs The Commission conducts investigations of foreign governmental and foreign carrier practices that adversely affect the U.S. shipping trade and, in conjunction with the Department of State, conducts activities to effect the elimination of discriminatory practices on the part of foreign governments against United States-flag shipping and to achieve comity between the United States and its trading partners.

District Offices—Federal Maritime Commission

District	Address	Officer in Charge
Houston	Suite 110, Box 14, 14960 Heathrow Forest Pky., Houston, TX 77032–3842 ...	Donald H. Butler
Los Angeles	Suite 270, 11 Golden Shore, Long Beach, CA 90802	Michael A. Murphy
Miami	Suite 302, 18441 NW. 2d Ave., Miami, FL 33169	Richard L. Larson
New Orleans	Suite 2260, 365 Canal St., New Orleans, LA 70130	(Vacancy)
New York	Suite 614, 6 World Trade Ctr., New York, NY 10048–0949	Martin J. Keenaghan
Puerto Rico	Rm. 762, U.S. District Courthouse, 150 Carlos Chardon Ave., Hato Rey, PR 00918–2254.	Lorraine Jiménez
San Francisco	Suite 1250, 455 Market St., San Francisco, CA 94105–2441	Carlos D. Niemeyer

Sources of Information

Employment Employment inquiries may be directed to the Office of Personnel, Federal Maritime Commission, 800 North Capitol Street NW., Washington, DC 20573–0001. Phone, 202–523–5773.

Informal Complaints Phone, 202–523–5807.

Publications The *Thirty-third Annual Report (1994)* is a recent publication of the Federal Maritime Commission.

For further information, contact the Office of the Secretary, Federal Maritime Commission, 800 North Capitol Street NW., Washington, DC 20573–0001. Phone, 202–523–5725. Fax, 202–523–0014.

FEDERAL MEDIATION AND CONCILIATION SERVICE

2100 K Street NW., Washington, DC 20427
Phone, 202–606–8100

Director	JOHN CALHOUN WELLS
Deputy Director	FLOYD WOOD

The Federal Mediation and Conciliation Service represents the public interest by promoting the development of sound and stable labor-management relationships;

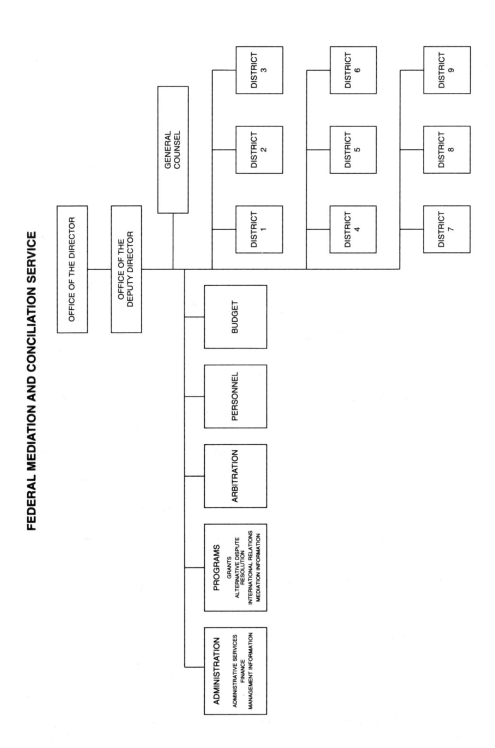

FEDERAL MEDIATION AND CONCILIATION SERVICE

preventing or minimizing work stoppages by assisting labor and management to settle their disputes through mediation; advocating collective bargaining, mediation, and voluntary arbitration as the preferred processes for settling issues between employers and representatives of employees; developing the art, science, and practice of dispute resolution; and fostering constructive joint relationships of labor and management leaders to increase their mutual understanding and solution of common problems.

The Federal Mediation and Conciliation Service was created by the Labor Management Relations Act, 1947 (29 U.S.C. 172). The Director is appointed by the President with the advice and consent of the Senate.

Activities

The Federal Mediation and Conciliation Service helps prevent disruptions in the flow of interstate commerce caused by labor-management disputes by providing mediators to assist disputing parties in the resolution of their differences. Mediators have no law enforcement authority and rely wholly on persuasive techniques.

The Service offers its facilities in labor-management disputes to any industry affecting interstate commerce, either upon its own motion or at the request of one or more of the parties to the dispute, whenever in its judgment such dispute threatens to cause a substantial interruption of commerce. The Labor Management Relations Act requires that parties to a labor contract must file a dispute notice if agreement is not reached 30 days in advance of a contract termination or reopening date. The notice must be filed with the Service and the appropriate State or local mediation agency. The Service is required to avoid the mediation of disputes that would have only a minor effect on interstate commerce if State or other conciliation services are available to the parties.

For further information, contact one of the district offices listed below.

Mediation   The mediator's efforts are directed toward the establishment of sound and stable labor-management relations on a continuing basis. In this work the mediator has a more basic function: encouraging and promoting better day-to-day relations between labor and management, thereby helping to reduce the incidence of work stoppages. Issues arising in negotiations may then be faced as problems to be settled through mutual effort rather than issues in dispute.

For further information, contact the Office of Public Affairs. Phone, 202–606–8100.

Arbitration   The Service, on the joint request of employers and unions, will also assist in the selection of arbitrators from a roster of private citizens who are qualified as neutrals to adjudicate matters in dispute.

For further information, contact the Office of Arbitration Services. Phone, 202–606–5111.

District Offices—Federal Mediation and Conciliation Service

District/Address	Director	Telephone
1. New York, NY (2d Fl., 1633 Broadway, 10019)	Kenneth C. Kowalski	212–399–5038
2. Philadelphia, PA (Rm. 3456, 600 Arch St., 19106)	John F. McDermott	215–607 7000
3. Atlanta, GA (Suite 318, 1720 Peachtree St. NW., 30309)	C. Richard Barnes	404–347–2473
4. Independence, OH (Suite 100, 6161 Oak Tree Blvd., 44131)	W. Kenneth Evans	216–522–4800
5. Hinsdale, IL (Suite 203, 908 N. Elm St., 60521)	Daniel O'Leary	708–887–4750
6. Minneapolis, MN (Suite 3950, 1300 Godward St., 55413)	Maureen Labenski	612–370–3300
7. St. Louis (Creve Coeur), MO (Suite 325, 12140 Woodcrest Executive Dr., 63141).	William B. Weier, *Acting*	314–576–1012
8. Glendale, CA (Suite 610, Glendale Financial Sq., 225 W. Broadway, 91204).	Joseph E. Medine, *Acting*	213–965–3814
9. Seattle, WA (Rm. 310, 2001 6th Ave., 98121)	Norman A. Lee	206–553–5800

For further information, contact the Office of Public Affairs, Federal Mediation and Conciliation Service, 2100 K Street NW., Washington, DC 20427. Phone, 202–606–8100. Fax, 202–606–4251.

FEDERAL MINE SAFETY AND HEALTH REVIEW COMMISSION

1730 K Street NW., Washington, DC 20006
Phone, 202–653–5625

Chairman	MARYLU JORDAN
Commissioners	JOYCE A. DOYLE, MARK L. MARKS,
	(VACANCY)
Chief Administrative Law Judge	PAUL MERLIN
General Counsel	L. JOSEPH FERRARA
Executive Director	RICHARD L. BAKER
Administrative Officer	REGINA M. CLARKE

The Federal Mine Safety and Health
Review Commission is an independent,
quasi-judicial agency established by the
Federal Mine Safety and Health Act of
1977 (30 U.S.C. 801 *et seq.*). That act,
enforced by the Secretary of Labor
through the Mine Safety and Health
Administration, governs compliance with
occupational safety and health standards
in the Nation's surface and underground
coal, metal, and nonmetal mines.

The Commission consists of five
members who are appointed by the
President with the advice and consent of
the Senate and who serve staggered, 6-
year terms. The Chairman is selected
from among the Commissioners.

The Commission and its Office of
Administrative Law Judges are charged
with deciding cases brought pursuant to
the act by the Mine Safety and Health
Administration, mine operators, and
miners or their representatives. These
cases generally involve review of the
Administration's enforcement actions
including citations, mine closure orders,
and proposals for civil penalties issued
for violations of the act or the mandatory
safety and health standards promulgated
by the Secretary. The Commission also
has jurisdiction over discrimination
complaints filed by miners or their
representatives in connection with their
safety and health rights under the act,
and over complaints for compensation
filed on behalf of miners idled as a result

of mine closure orders issued by the
Administration.

Activities

Cases brought before the Commission
are assigned to the Office of
Administrative Law Judges, and hearings
are conducted pursuant to the
requirements of the Administrative
Procedure Act (5 U.S.C. 554, 556) and
the Commission's procedural rules (29
CFR Part 2700).

A judge's decision becomes a final but
nonprecedential order of the
Commission 40 days after issuance
unless the Commission has directed the
case for review in response to a petition
or on its own motion. If a review is
conducted, a decision of the
Commission becomes final 30 days after
issuance unless a party adversely
affected seeks review in the U.S. Circuit
Court of Appeals for the District of
Columbia or the Circuit within which
the mine subject to the litigation is
located.

As far as practicable, hearings are held
at locations convenient to the affected
mines. The Office of Administrative Law
Judges has two offices: the Falls Church
Office, 2 Skyline, 5203 Leesburg Pike,
Falls Church, VA 22041; and the Denver
Office, Colonnade Center, Room 280,
1244 Speer Boulevard, Denver, CO
80204.

**For further information, contact the Executive Director, Federal Mine Safety and Health Review
Commission, Sixth Floor, 1730 K Street NW., Washington DC 20006. Phone, 202–653–5625.**

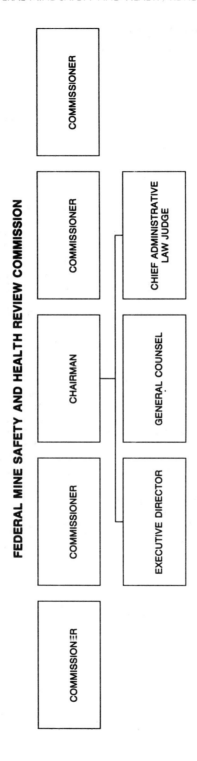

FEDERAL MINE SAFETY AND HEALTH REVIEW COMMISSION

COMMISSIONER

COMMISSIONER

CHAIRMAN

COMMISSIONER

COMMISSIONER

CHIEF ADMINISTRATIVE LAW JUDGE

GENERAL COUNSEL

EXECUTIVE DIRECTOR

FEDERAL RESERVE SYSTEM

Board of Governors of the Federal Reserve System
Twentieth Street and Constitution Avenue NW., Washington, DC 20551
Phone, 202-452-3000

Board of Governors

Chairman	ALAN GREENSPAN
Vice Chairman	ALAN S. BLINDER
Members	EDWARD W. KELLEY, JR., LAWRENCE B. LINDSEY, SUSAN M. PHILLIPS, JANET L. YELLEN, (VACANCY)

Official Staff:

Assistants to the Board	JOSEPH R. COYNE, DONALD J. WINN, THEODORE E. ALLISON
General Counsel	J. VIRGIL MATTINGLY, JR.
Secretary	WILLIAM W. WILES
Associate Secretaries	JENNIFER J. JOHNSON BARBARA R. LOWREY
Director, Division of Consumer and Community Affairs	GRIFFITH L. GARWOOD
Director, Division of Banking Supervision and Regulation	RICHARD SPILLENKOTHEN
Associate Director (Bank Holding Companies)	DON E. KLINE
Associate Director (Regulation)	FREDERICK M. STRUBLE
Director, Division of Monetary Affairs	DONALD L. KOHN
Deputy Director	DAVID E. LINDSEY
Director, Division of Research and Statistics	MICHAEL J. PRELL
Deputy Director	EDWARD C. ETTIN
Staff Director, Division of International Finance	EDWIN M. TRUMAN
Senior Associate Directors	LARRY J. PROMISEL CHARLES J. SIEGMAN
Staff Director, Office of Staff Director for Management	S. DAVID FROST
Director, Division of Information Resources Management	STEPHEN R. MALPHRUS
Director, Division of Human Resources Management	DAVID L. SHANNON
Associate Director	JOHN R. WEIS
Controller	GEORGE E. LIVINGSTON
Inspector General, Office of the Inspector General	BRENT L. BOWEN
Director, Division of Support Services	ROBERT E. FRAZIER
Director, Division of Federal Reserve Bank Operations and Payment Systems	CLYDE H. FARNSWORTH, JR.
Deputy Director, Finance and Control	DAVID L. ROBINSON

Officers of the Federal Reserve Banks

Chairmen and Federal Reserve Agents:

Atlanta	LEO BENATAR
Boston	JEROME H. GROSSMAN
Chicago	ROBERT M. HEALEY
Cleveland	A. WILLIAM REYNOLDS

Dallas	CECE SMITH
Kansas City	HERMAN CAIN
Minneapolis	GERALD A. RAUENHORST
New York	MAURICE R. GREENBERG
Philadelphia	JAMES M. MEAD
Richmond	HENRY J. FAISON
St. Louis	ROBERT H. QUENON
San Francisco	JUDITH M. RUNSTAD

Presidents:

Atlanta	ROBERT P. FORRESTAL
Boston	CATHY E. MINEHAN
Chicago	MICHAEL E. MOSKOW
Cleveland	JERRY L. JORDAN
Dallas	ROBERT D. MCTEER, JR.
Kansas City	THOMAS M. HOENIG
Minneapolis	GARY H. STERN
New York	WILLIAM J. MCDONOUGH
Philadelphia	EDWARD G. BOEHNE
Richmond	J. ALFRED BROADDUS, JR.
St. Louis	THOMAS C. MELZER
San Francisco	ROBERT T. PARRY

Federal Open Market Committee

Chairman	ALAN GREENSPAN
Vice Chairman	WILLIAM J. MCDONOUGH
Members	THOMAS M. HOENIG, EDWARD W. KELLEY, JR., LAWRENCE B. LINDSEY, THOMAS C. MELZER, CATHY E. MINEHAN, SUSAN M. PHILLIPS, MICHAEL H. MOSCOW, (VACANCY)

Official Staff:

Secretary and Economist	DONALD L. KOHN
Deputy Secretary	NORMAND R.V. BERNARD
Assistant Secretaries	JOSEPH R. COYNE
	GARY P. GILLUM
General Counsel	J. VIRGIL MATTINGLY, JR.
Deputy General Counsel	THOMAS C. BAXTER, JR.
Economists	MICHAEL J. PRELL
	EDWIN M. TRUMAN
Manager, System Open Market Account	PETER R. FISHER
President, Federal Advisory Council	ANTHONY P. TERRACCIANCO
Chairman, Consumer Advisory Council	JAMES L. WEST
President, Thrift Institutions Advisory Council	CHARLES JOHN KOCH

The Federal Reserve System, the central bank of the United States, is charged with administering and making policy for the Nation's credit and monetary affairs. Through its supervisory and regulatory banking functions, the Federal Reserve helps to maintain the banking industry in sound condition, capable of responding to the Nation's domestic and international financial needs and objectives.

The Federal Reserve System was established by the Federal Reserve Act (12 U.S.C. 221), approved December 23, 1913. The System serves as the Nation's central bank. The powers of central banks vary widely, but their major

responsibility is in the execution of
monetary policy. Central banks typically
perform a number of other functions,
such as the transfer of funds, handling
Government deposits and debt issues,
supervising and regulating banks, and
acting as lender of last resort.

It is the responsibility of the Federal
Reserve System to contribute to the
strength and vitality of the U.S.
economy. By influencing the lending
and investing activities of depository
institutions and the cost and availability
of money and credit, the Federal Reserve
System can help promote the full use of
human and capital resources, the growth
of productivity, relatively stable prices,
and equilibrium in the Nation's
international balance of payments.
Through its supervisory and regulatory
banking functions, the Federal Reserve
System helps maintain a commercial
banking system that is responsive to the
Nation's financial needs and objectives.

The System consists of seven parts: the
Board of Governors in Washington, DC;
the 12 Federal Reserve Banks and their
25 branches and other facilities situated
throughout the country; the Federal
Open Market Committee; the Federal
Advisory Council; the Consumer
Advisory Council; the Thrift Institutions
Advisory Council; and the Nation's
financial institutions, including
commercial banks, savings and loan
associations, mutual savings banks, and
credit unions.

Board of Governors

Broad supervisory powers are vested in
the Board of Governors, which has its
offices in Washington, DC. The Board is
composed of seven members appointed
by the President with the advice and
consent of the Senate. The Chairman of
the Board of Governors is, by Executive
Order 11269 of February 14, 1966, a
member of the National Advisory
Council on International Monetary and
Financial Policies.

The Board determines general
monetary, credit, and operating policies
for the System as a whole and formulates
the rules and regulations necessary to
carry out the purposes of the Federal

Reserve Act. The Board's principal duties
consist of monitoring credit conditions;
supervising the Federal Reserve Banks,
member banks, and bank holding
companies; and regulating the
implementation of certain consumer
credit protection laws.

Power To Influence Credit Conditions
Pursuant to the Depository Institutions
Deregulation and Monetary Control Act
of 1980, referred to as the Monetary
Control Act of 1980 (12 U.S.C. 226
note), the Board is given the power,
within statutory limitations, to fix the
requirements concerning reserves to be
maintained by depository institutions on
transaction accounts or nonpersonal time
deposits. Another important instrument
of credit control is found in open market
operations. The members of the Board of
Governors also are members of the
Federal Open Market Committee, whose
work and organization are described on
page 570. The Board of Governors
reviews and determines the discount rate
charged by the Federal Reserve Banks.
For the purpose of preventing excessive
use of credit for the purchase or carrying
of securities, the Board is authorized to
regulate the amount of credit that may
be initially extended and subsequently
maintained on any security (with certain
exceptions).

Supervision of Federal Reserve Banks
The Board is authorized to make
examinations of the Federal Reserve
Banks, to require statements and reports
from such Banks, to supervise the issue
and retirement of Federal Reserve notes,
to require the establishment or
discontinuance of branches of Reserve
Banks, and to exercise supervision over
all relationships and transactions of those
Banks with foreign branches. The Board
of Governors reviews and follows the
examination and supervisory activities of
the Federal Reserve Banks aimed at
further coordination of policies and
practices.

Supervision of Bank Holding Companies
The Bank Holding Company Act of 1956
gave the Federal Reserve primary
responsibility for supervising and
regulating the activities of bank holding
companies. This act was designed to

achieve two basic objectives: to control the expansion of bank holding companies by avoiding the creation of monopoly or restraining trade in banking; and to limit the expansion of bank holding companies to those nonbanking activities that are closely related to banking, thus maintaining a separation between banking and commerce. A company that seeks to become a bank holding company must obtain the prior approval of the Federal Reserve. Any company that qualifies as a bank holding company must register with the Federal Reserve System and file reports with the System. To preserve the traditional separation of banking and commerce, the Congress amended the Bank Holding Act in December 1970.

Supervision of Member Banks The Board has jurisdiction over the admission of State banks and trust companies to membership in the Federal Reserve System, the termination of membership of such banks, the establishment of branches by such banks, and the approval of bank mergers and consolidations where the resulting institution will be a State member bank. It receives copies of condition reports submitted by them to the Federal Reserve Banks. It has power to examine all member banks and the affiliates of member banks and to require condition reports from them. It has authority to require periodic and other public disclosure of information with respect to an equity security of a State member bank that is held by 500 or more persons. It establishes minimum standards with respect to installation, maintenance, and operation of security devices and procedures by State member banks. Also, it has authority to issue cease-and-desist orders in connection with violations of law or unsafe or unsound banking practices by State member banks and to remove directors or officers of such banks in certain circumstances, and it may, in its discretion, suspend member banks from the use of the credit facilities of the Federal Reserve System for making undue use of bank credit for speculative purposes or for any other purpose

inconsistent with the maintenance of sound credit conditions.

The Board may grant authority to member banks to establish branches in foreign countries or dependencies or insular possessions of the United States, to invest in the stocks of banks or corporations engaged in international or foreign banking, or to invest in foreign banks. It also charters, regulates, and supervises certain corporations that engage in foreign or international banking and financial activities.

The Board is authorized to issue general regulations permitting interlocking relationships in certain circumstances between member banks and organizations dealing in securities or between member banks and other banks.

Other Activities Under the Change in Bank Control Act of 1978 (12 U.S.C. 1817(j)), the Board is required to review other bank stock acquisitions.

Under the Truth in Lending Act (15 U.S.C. 1601), the Board is required to prescribe regulations to ensure a meaningful disclosure by lenders of credit terms so that consumers will be able to compare more readily the various credit terms available and will be informed about rules governing credit cards, including their potential liability for unauthorized use.

Under the International Banking Act of 1978 (12 U.S.C. 3101), the Board has authority to impose reserve requirements and interest rate ceilings on branches and agencies of foreign banks in the United States, to grant loans to them, to provide them access to Federal Reserve services, and to limit their interstate banking activities.

The Board also is the rulemaking authority for the Equal Credit Opportunity Act, the Home Mortgage Disclosure Act, the Fair Credit Billing Act, the Expedited Funds Availability Act, and certain provisions of the Federal Trade Commission Act as they apply to banks.

Expenses To meet its expenses and pay the salaries of its members and its employees, the Board makes semiannual assessments upon the Reserve Banks in proportion to their capital stock and surplus.

Federal Open Market Committee

The Federal Open Market Committee is comprised of the Board of Governors and five of the presidents of the Reserve Banks. The Chairman of the Board of Governors is traditionally the Chairman of the Committee. The president of the Federal Reserve Bank of New York serves as a permanent member of the Committee. Four of the twelve Reserve Bank presidents rotate annually as members of the Committee.

Open market operations of the Reserve Banks are conducted under regulations adopted by the Committee and pursuant to specific policy directives issued by the Committee, which meets in Washington at frequent intervals. Purchases and sales of securities in the open market are undertaken to supply bank reserves to support the credit and money needed for long-term economic growth, to offset cyclical economic swings, and to accommodate seasonal demands of businesses and consumers for money and credit. These operations are carried out principally in U.S. Government obligations, but they also include purchases and sales of Federal agency obligations and bankers' acceptances. All operations are conducted in New York, where the primary markets for these securities are located; the Federal Reserve Bank of New York executes transactions for the Federal Reserve System Open Market Account in carrying out these operations.

Under the Committee's direction, the Federal Reserve Bank of New York also undertakes transactions in foreign currencies for the Federal Reserve System Open Market Account. The purposes of these operations include helping to safeguard the value of the dollar in international exchange markets and facilitating growth in international liquidity in accordance with the needs of an expanding world economy.

Federal Reserve Banks

The 12 Federal Reserve Banks are located in Atlanta, Boston, Chicago, Cleveland, Dallas, Kansas City, Minneapolis, New York, Philadelphia, Richmond, San Francisco, and St. Louis.

Branch banks are located in Baltimore, Birmingham, Buffalo, Charlotte, Cincinnati, Denver, Detroit, El Paso, Helena, Houston, Jacksonville, Little Rock, Los Angeles, Louisville, Memphis, Miami, Nashville, New Orleans, Oklahoma City, Omaha, Pittsburgh, Portland, Salt Lake City, San Antonio, and Seattle.

Directors and Officers of Reserve Banks The Board of Directors of each Reserve Bank is composed of nine members, equally divided into three designated classes: class A, class B, and class C. Directors of class A are representative of the stockholding member banks. Directors of class B must be actively engaged in their districts in commerce, agriculture, or some other industrial pursuit, and may not be officers, directors, or employees of any bank. Class C directors may not be officers, directors, employees, or stockholders of any bank. The six class A and class B directors are elected by the stockholding member banks, while the three class C directors are appointed by the Board of Governors. The terms of office of the directors are so arranged that the term of one director of each class expires each year.

One of the class C directors appointed by the Board of Governors is designated as Chairman of the Board of Directors of the Reserve Bank and as Federal Reserve agent, and in the latter capacity he is required to maintain a local office of the Board of Governors on the premises of the Reserve Bank. Another class C director is appointed by the Board of Governors as deputy chairman. Each Reserve Bank has as its chief executive officer a president appointed for a term of 5 years by its Board of Directors with the approval of the Board of Governors.

Reserves on Deposit In accordance with provisions of the Monetary Control Act of 1980 (12 U.S.C. 226 note), the Reserve Banks receive and hold on deposit the reserve or clearing account deposits of depository institutions. These banks are permitted to count their vault cash as part of their required reserve.

Extensions of Credit The Monetary Control Act of 1980 (12 U.S.C. 226

note) directs the Federal Reserve to open its discount window to any depository institution that is subject to Federal Reserve reserve requirements on transaction accounts or nonpersonal time deposits.

Discount window credit provides for Federal Reserve lending to eligible depository institutions under two basic programs. One is the adjustment credit program; the other supplies more extended credit for certain limited purposes.

Short-term adjustment credit is the primary type of Federal Reserve credit. It is available to help borrowers meet temporary requirements for funds. Borrowers are not permitted to use adjustment credit to take advantage of any spread between the discount rate and market rates.

Extended credit is provided through three programs designed to assist depository institutions in meeting longer term needs for funds. One provides seasonal credit—for periods running up to 9 months—to smaller depository institutions that lack access to market funds. A second program assists institutions that experience special difficulties arising from exceptional circumstances or practices involving only that institution. Finally, in cases where more general liquidity strains are affecting a broad range of depository institutions—such as those whose portfolios consist primarily of longer term assets—credit may be provided to address the problems of particular institutions being affected by the general situation.

Currency Issue The Reserve Banks issue Federal Reserve notes, which constitute the bulk of money in circulation. These notes are obligations of the United States and are a prior lien upon the assets of the issuing Federal Reserve Bank. They are issued against a pledge by the Reserve Bank with the Federal Reserve agent of collateral security including gold certificates, paper discounted or purchased by the Bank, and direct obligations of the United States.

Other Powers The Reserve Banks are empowered to act as clearinghouses and as collecting agents for depository institutions in the collection of checks and other instruments. They are also authorized to act as depositories and fiscal agents of the United States and to exercise other banking functions specified in the Federal Reserve Act. They perform a number of important functions in connection with the issue and redemption of United States Government securities.

Federal Advisory Council

The Federal Advisory Council acts in an advisory capacity, conferring with the Board of Governors on general business conditions.

The Council is composed of 12 members, one from each Federal Reserve district, being selected annually by the Board of Directors of the Reserve Bank of the district. The Council is required to meet in Washington, DC, at least four times each year, and more often if called by the Board of Governors.

Consumer Advisory Council

The Consumer Advisory Council confers with the Board of Governors several times each year on the Board's responsibilities in the field of consumer credit protection. The Council was established by Congress in 1976 at the suggestion of the Board and replaced the Advisory Committee on Truth in Lending that was established by the 1968 Truth in Lending Act.

The Council is composed of 30 members from all parts of the country. It advises the Board on its responsibilities under such laws as Truth in Lending, Equal Credit Opportunity, and Home Mortgage Disclosure.

Thrift Institutions Advisory Council

The Thrift Institutions Advisory Council is an advisory group established by the Board in 1980 made up of representatives from nonbank depository thrift institutions, which includes savings and loans, mutual savings bankers, and credit unions. The Council meets at least four times each year with the Board of

Governors to discuss developments relating to thrift institutions, the housing industry and mortgage finance, and certain regulatory issues.

Sources of Information

Employment Written inquiries regarding employment should be addressed to the Director, Division of Personnel, Board of Governors of the Federal Reserve System, Washington, DC 20551.

Procurement Firms seeking business with the Board should address their inquiries to the Director, Division of Support Services, Board of Governors of the Federal Reserve System, Washington, DC 20551.

Publications Among the publications issued by the Board are *The Federal Reserve System—Purposes and*

Functions, and a series of pamphlets including *Guide to Business Credit and the Equal Credit Opportunity Act; Consumer Handbook; Making Deposits: When Will Your Money Be Available;* and *When Your Home Is On the Line: What You Should Know About Home Equity Lines of Credit.* Copies of these pamphlets are available free of charge. Information regarding publications may be obtained in Room MP–510 (Martin Building) of the Board's headquarters. Phone, 202–452–3244.

Reading Room A reading room where persons may inspect records that are available to the public is located in Room B–1122 at the Board's headquarters, Twentieth Street and Constitution Avenue NW., Washington, DC. Information regarding the availability of records may be obtained by calling 202–452–3684.

For further information, contact the Office of Public Affairs, Board of Governors, Federal Reserve System, Washington, DC 20551. Phone, 202–452–3204 or 202–452–3215.

FEDERAL RETIREMENT THRIFT INVESTMENT BOARD

1250 H Street NW., Washington, DC 20005
Phone, 202–942–1600

Chairman	JAMES H. ATKINS
Members	SHIRLEY CHILTON-ODELL, SCOTT B. LUKINS, STEPHEN L. NORRIS, (VACANCY)

Officials:

Executive Director	ROGER W. MEHLE
General Counsel	JOHN J. O'MEARA
Deputy General Counsel	JAMES B. PETRICK
Associate General Counsel (Programs)	DAVID L. HUTNER, *Acting*
Director of Accounting	DAVID L. BLACK
Director of Administration	STRAT D. VALAKIS
Director of Automated Systems	JOHN W. WITTERS
Director of Benefits and Program Analysis	ALISONE M. CLARKE
Director of Communications	VEDA R. CHARROW
Director of External Affairs	THOMAS J. TRABUCCO
Director of Investments	PETER B. MACKEY

The Federal Retirement Thrift Investment Board administers the Thrift Savings Plan, which provides Federal employees the opportunity to save for additional retirement security.

The Federal Retirement Thrift Investment Board was established as an independent agency by the Federal Employees' Retirement System Act of 1986 (5 U.S.C. 8472). The act vests responsibility for the agency in six named fiduciaries: the five Board members and the Executive Director. The five members of the Board, one of whom is designated as Chairman, are appointed by the President with the advice and consent of the Senate and serve on the Board on a part-time basis. The members appoint the Executive Director, who is responsible for the management of the agency and the Plan.

Activities

The Thrift Savings Plan is a tax-deferred, defined contribution plan that was established as one of the three parts of the Federal Employees' Retirement System. For employees covered under the System, savings accumulated through the Plan make an important addition to the retirement benefits provided by Social Security and the System's Basic Annuity. Civil Service Retirement System employees may also take advantage of the Plan to supplement their annuities.

The Board operates the Thrift Savings Plan and manages the investments of the Thrift Savings Fund solely for the benefit of participants and their beneficiaries. As part of these responsibilities, the Board maintains an account for each Plan participant, makes loans, purchases annuity contracts, and provides for the payment of benefits.

For further information, contact the Director of External Affairs, Federal Retirement Thrift Investment Board, 1250 H Street NW., Washington, DC 20005. Phone, 202–942–1640.

FEDERAL TRADE COMMISSION

Pennsylvania Avenue at Sixth Street NW., Washington, DC 20580
Phone, 202–326–2222 (Public Reference Branch)

Chairman	ROBERT PITOFSKY
Executive Assistant	JAMES C. HAMILL
Commissioners	MARY L. AZCUENAGA, ROSCOE B. STAREK III, JANET T. STEIGER, CHRISTINE A. VARNEY
Executive Director	ROBERT S. WALTON III
Deputy Executive Director for Management	ROSEMARIE STRAIGHT
Deputy Executive Director for Planning and Information	ALAN PROCTOR
Director, Bureau of Competition	WILLIAM J. BAER
Deputy Director	MARY LOU STEPTOE
Deputy Director	MARK D. WHITENER, *Acting*
Director, Bureau of Consumer Protection	JOAN Z. BERNSTEIN
Deputy Director	LYDIA B. PARNES
Director, Bureau of Economics	JONATHAN B. BAKER
General Counsel	STEVEN CALKINS
Deputy General Counsel	JAY C. SHAFFER
Director, Office of Legislative Affairs	DORIAN HALL, *Acting*
Director, Office of Public Affairs	MURFY ALEXANDER

Secretary of the Commission	DONALD S. CLARK
Chief Administrative Law Judge	LEWIS F. PARKER
Inspector General	FREDERICK J. ZIRKEL

[For the Federal Trade Commission statement of organization, see the *Code of Federal Regulations*, Title 16, Part 0]

The objective of the Federal Trade Commission is to maintain competitive enterprise as the keystone of the American economic system, and to prevent the free enterprise system from being fettered by monopoly or restraints on trade or corrupted by unfair or deceptive trade practices. The Commission is charged with keeping competition both free and fair.

The purpose of the Federal Trade Commission is expressed in the Federal Trade Commission Act (15 U.S.C. 41–58) and the Clayton Act (15 U.S.C. 12), both passed in 1914 and both successively amended in the years that have followed. The Federal Trade Commission Act prohibits the use in or affecting commerce of "unfair methods of competition" and "unfair or deceptive acts or practices." The Clayton Act outlaws specific practices recognized as instruments of monopoly. As an administrative agency, acting quasi-judicially and quasi-legislatively, the Commission was established to deal with trade practices on a continuing and corrective basis. It has no authority to punish; its function is to prevent, through cease-and-desist orders and other means, those practices condemned by the law of Federal trade regulation. However, court-ordered civil penalties up to $10,000 may be obtained for each violation of a Commission order or trade regulation rule.

The Federal Trade Commission was organized as an independent administrative agency in 1914 pursuant to the Federal Trade Commission Act. Related duties subsequently were delegated to the Commission by various statutes, including: the Wheeler-Lea Act, the Trans-Alaska Pipeline Authorization Act, the Clayton Act, the Export Trade Act, the Wool Products Labeling Act, the Fur Products Labeling Act, the Textile Fiber Products Identification Act, the Fair Packaging and Labeling Act, the Lanham Trade-Mark Act of 1946, the Consumer Credit Protection Act, the Robinson-Patman Act, the Hobby Protection Act, the Magnuson-Moss Warranty-Federal

Trade Commission Improvement Act, the Federal Trade Commission Improvements Act of 1980, the Smokeless Tobacco Health Education Act of 1986, the Telephone Disclosure and Dispute Resolution Act, the Federal Trade Commission Improvements Act of 1994, the International Antitrust Enforcement Assistance Act of 1994, the Telemarketing and Consumer Fraud and Abuse Prevention Act, and the Federal Trade Commission Act Amendments of 1994.

The Commission is composed of five members. Each member is appointed by the President, with the advice and consent of the Senate, for a term of 7 years. Not more than three of the Commissioners may be members of the same political party. One Commissioner is designated by the President as Chairman of the Commission and is responsible for its administrative management.

Activities

The Commission's principal functions are to:

—promote competition in or affecting commerce through the prevention of general trade restraints such as price-fixing agreements, boycotts, illegal combinations of competitors, and other unfair methods of competition;

—safeguard the public by preventing the dissemination of false or deceptive advertisements of consumer products and services generally, and food, drug, cosmetics, and therapeutic devices, particularly, as well as other unfair or deceptive practices;

—prevent pricing discrimination; exclusive-dealing and tying

FEDERAL TRADE COMMISSION

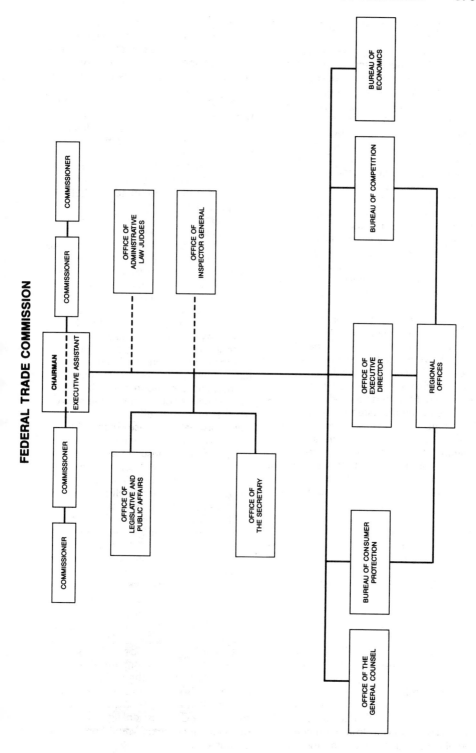

arrangements; corporate mergers, acquisitions, or joint ventures, when such practices or arrangements may substantially lessen competition or tend to create a monopoly; interlocking directorates or officers' positions that may restrain competition; the payment or receipt of illegal brokerage; and discrimination among competing customers in the furnishing of or the payment for services or facilities used to promote the resale of a product;

—enjoin various fraudulent telemarketing schemes;

—bring about truthful labeling of textile, wool, and fur products;

—regulate packaging and labeling of certain consumer commodities within the purview of the Fair Packaging and Labeling Act so as to prevent consumer deception and to facilitate value comparisons;

—supervise the registration and operation of associations of American exporters engaged in export trade;

—achieve accurate credit cost disclosure by consumer creditors (retailers, finance companies, non-Federal credit unions, and other creditors not specifically regulated by another Government agency) as called for in the Truth in Lending Act to ensure a meaningful basis for informed credit decisions, and to regulate the issuance of and liability for the use of credit cards so as to prohibit their fraudulent use in or affecting commerce;

—protect consumers against circulation of inaccurate or obsolete credit reports and ensure that consumer reporting agencies exercise their responsibilities in a manner that is fair and equitable and in conformity with the Fair Credit Reporting Act, the Fair Credit Billing Act, the Equal Credit Opportunity Act, and the Fair Debt Collection Practices Act; and

—gather and make available to the Congress, the President, and the public, factual data concerning economic and business conditions.

Enforcement The Commission's law enforcement work falls into two general categories: actions to foster voluntary compliance with the law, and formal administrative litigation leading to mandatory orders against offenders.

For the most part, compliance with the law is obtained through voluntary and cooperative action by way of staff level advice, which is not binding on the Commission; advisory opinions by the Commission; and through issuance of guides and policy statements delineating legal requirements as to particular business practices.

The formal litigation is similar to that in Federal courts. Cases are instituted either by issuance of an administrative complaint or by filing a Federal district court complaint charging the person, partnership, or corporation with violating one or more of the statutes administered by the Commission. Cases may be settled by consent orders. If the charges in an administrative matter are not contested, or if the charges are found to be true after an administrative hearing in a contested case, a cease-and-desist order may be issued requiring discontinuance of the unlawful practices and may include other related requirements. Federal district court charges are resolved through either settlements or court-ordered injunctive or other equitable relief.

Legal Case Work Cases before the Commission may originate through complaint by a consumer or a competitor; the Congress; or from Federal, State, or municipal agencies. Also, the Commission itself may initiate an investigation into possible violation of the laws it administers. No formality is required in submitting a complaint. A letter giving the facts in detail, accompanied by all supporting evidence in possession of the complaining party, is sufficient. It is the general policy of the Commission not to disclose the identity of any complainant, except as permitted by law or Commission rules.

Upon receipt of a complaint, various criteria are applied in determining whether the particular matter should be investigated. Within the limits of available resources, investigations are initiated that are considered to best support the Commission's goals of maintaining competition and protecting consumers.

The Commission's investigations commonly include requests for voluntary production of relevant information and materials. The Commission also has the authority to issue compulsory process in the form of subpeonas, civil investigative demands, or orders to file reports. The Commission may bring suit in a United States district court to enforce its compulsory process. Also, the Commission often cooperates with other law enforcement agencies, both domestic and, to the extent permitted by U.S. law, foreign and international.

On completion of an investigation, staff will recommend Commission action. The staff may recommend that the matter be closed. If that recommendation is approved, a closing letter is usually sent to the individual or company that was the subject of the investigation. The staff may instead recommend that the Commission approve the settlement of a case, usually by acceptance of an agreement containing a consent order to cease and desist. Such consent orders frequently provide that the respondent does not admit any violation of the law, but agrees to be bound by an order requiring the discontinuance of the challenged practices, and, in some cases, other corrective action.

If the Commission determines that some action other than closing the investigation is appropriate, but no consent agreement can be negotiated, the Commission may issue a formal complaint alleging that the respondent has violated one or more of the laws administered by the Commission. The respondent is then served with a copy of the complaint, often accompanied by a proposed cease-and-desist order to be used if the allegations of law violations are proved. The Commission's counsel supporting the complaint and respondents may negotiate a consent agreement after the issuance of the formal complaint. Otherwise, the case is heard by an administrative law judge, who conducts a trial that is open to the public, and issues an initial decision.

The initial decision becomes the decision of the Commission at the end of 30 days unless the respondent or the counsel supporting the complaint appeals the decision to the Commission, or the Commission by order stays the effective date or places the case on its own docket for review. In the Commission's decision on such an appeal or review, the initial decision may be sustained, modified, or reversed. If the complaint is sustained or modified, a cease-and-desist order is issued. If an initial decision dismissing a complaint is sustained, no cease-and-desist order is issued.

Under the Federal Trade Commission Act, an order to cease and desist or to take other corrective action—such as affirmative disclosure, divestiture, or restitution—becomes final 60 days after date of service upon the respondent, unless within that period the respondent petitions an appropriate United States court of appeals to review the order, and also petitions the Commission to stay the order pending review. If the Commission does not stay the order, the respondent may seek a stay from the reviewing appeals court. The appeals court has the power to affirm, modify, or set the order aside. If the appeals court upholds the Commission's order, the respondent may seek certiorari to the Supreme Court and ask that the appeals court or the Supreme Court continue to stay the order. Provisions requiring divestiture are automatically stayed until any judicial review is complete. Violations of a cease-and-desist order, after it becomes effective, subject the offender to suit by the Government in a United States district court for the recovery of a civil penalty of not more than $10,000 for each violation and, where the violation continues, each day of its continuance is a separate violation.

In addition to, or in lieu of, the administrative proceeding initiated by a formal complaint, the Commission may, in some cases, request that a United States district court issue a preliminary or permanent injunction to halt the use of allegedly unfair or deceptive practices, to prevent an anticompetitive merger from taking place, or to prevent violations of any other statutory obligations enforced by the Commission.

The Commission also has specific authority to ask the United States district court to enjoin the dissemination of advertisements of food, drugs, cosmetics, and devices intended for use in the diagnosis, prevention, or treatment of disease, whenever it has reason to believe that such a proceeding would be in the public interest. Preliminary injunctions remain in effect until a cease-and-desist order is issued and becomes final, or until the complaint is dismissed by the Commission or the order is set aside by the court on review.

Further, the dissemination of a false advertisement of a food, drug, device, or cosmetic, where the use of the commodity advertised may be injurious to health or where there is intent to defraud or mislead, constitutes a misdemeanor. Conviction subjects the offender to a fine of not more than $5,000, or imprisonment of not more than 6 months, or both. Succeeding convictions may result in a fine of not more than $10,000, or imprisonment for not more than 1 year, or both. The statute provides that the Commission shall certify this type of case to the Attorney General for institution of appropriate court proceedings.

Compliance Activities   Through systematic and continuous review, the Commission obtains and maintains compliance with its cease-and-desist orders. All respondents against whom such orders have been issued are required to file reports with the Commission to substantiate their compliance. In the event compliance is not obtained, or if the order is subsequently violated, civil penalty proceedings may be instituted.

Trade Regulation Rules   The Commission is authorized to issue trade regulation rules specifically defining acts or practices that are unfair or deceptive. A rule may also specify steps to prevent such practices from occurring. Such rules may be limited to certain industries or be applicable to all businesses within the Commission's jurisdiction. Rules are promulgated under specific procedures providing for participation of interested parties, including oral hearings and comments. The Commission's decision to issue a rule may be appealed to a United States court of appeals. In most cases, once a rule has become final, the Commission can seek the institution of a civil proceeding in a United States district court for knowing violations of the rule and seek civil penalties of up to $10,000 per violation and consumer redress.

Cooperative Procedures   In carrying out the statutory directive to "prevent" the use in or affecting commerce of unfair practices, the Commission makes extensive use of voluntary and cooperative procedures. Through these procedures business and industry may obtain authoritative guidance and a substantial measure of certainty as to what they may do under the laws administered by the Commission.

Whenever it is practicable, the Commission will furnish a formal advisory opinion as to whether a proposed course of conduct, if pursued, would be likely to result in further action by the Commission. An advisory opinion is binding upon the Commission with respect to the person or group to whom the opinion is issued with regard to the acts, practices, or conduct described in the request, where all relevant facts were completely and accurately presented to the Commission, until the advice has been rescinded or revoked and notice has been given to the requester. No enforcement action will be initiated by the Commission concerning any conduct undertaken by the requester in good faith reliance upon the advice of the Commission where such conduct is discontinued promptly upon notification of rescission or revocation of the Commission's approval.

Industry guides are administrative interpretations in laymen's language of laws administered by the Commission for the guidance of the public in conducting its affairs in conformity with legal requirements. They provide the basis for voluntary and simultaneous abandonment of unlawful practices by members of a particular industry or industry in general. Failure to comply with the guides may result in corrective action by the Commission under applicable statutory provisions.

Consumer Protection Consumer protection is one of the two main missions of the Commission. The Commission works to increase the usefulness of advertising by ensuring it is truthful and not misleading; reduce instances of fraudulent, deceptive, or uniform marketing practices; and prevent creditors from using unlawful, practices when granting credit, maintaining credit information, collecting debts, and operating credit systems. Consumer Protection initiates investigations in many areas of concern to consumers, including health claims in food advertising; environmental advertising and labeling; general advertising issues; health care fraud; telemarketing, business opportunity, and franchise and investment fraud; mortgage lending and discrimination; enforcement of Commission orders; and enforcement of credit statutes and trade rules.

The Commission has issued and enforces many trade rules important to consumers. The Used Car Rule requires that dealers display a buyers guide containing warranty information on the window of each vehicle offered for sale to consumers. The Mail Order Rule requires companies to ship merchandise that consumers order by mail or telephone within a certain time, and sets out requirements for notifying consumers about delays and offering them the option of agreeing to the delays or cancelling their orders. The Funeral Rule requires that price and other specific information regarding funeral arrangements be made available to consumers to help them make informed choices and pay only for services they select. The Franchise Rule requires the seller to provide each prospective franchisee with a basic disclosure document containing detailed information about the nature of its business and terms of the proposed franchise relationship. The R–Value Rule requires manufacturers to disclose the R–value (a measure of resistance to heat flow) of their home-insulation products. Under the Cooling-Off Rule, consumers can cancel purchases of $25 or more made door-to-door, or at places other than the seller's usual place of business, within 3 business days of purchase.

Under the Consumer Protection mission, the Commission also enforces a number of specific laws that help consumers. One such law is the Consumer Credit Protection Act, which establishes, among other things, rules for the use of credit cards, the disclosure of the terms on which open- and closed-end credit is granted, and the disclosure of the reasons a business uses in determining not to grant credit.

The Truth in Lending Act is one part of the Consumer Credit Protection Act. Its purpose is to ensure that every customer who has need for consumer credit is given meaningful information with respect to the cost of that credit. In most cases the credit cost must be expressed in the dollar amount of finance charges, and as an annual percentage rate computed on the unpaid balance of the amount financed. The Truth in Lending Act was amended in October 1970 to regulate the issuance, holder's liability, and the fraudulent use of credit cards.

The Fair Credit Reporting Act, another part of the Consumer Credit Protection Act, represents the first Federal regulation of the vast consumer reporting industry, covering all credit bureaus, investigative reporting companies, detective and collection agencies, lenders' exchanges, and computerized information reporting companies. The purpose of this act is to ensure that consumer reporting activities are conducted in a manner that is fair and equitable, upholding the consumer's right to privacy as against the informational demands of others.

Maintaining Competition (Antitrust) The second major mission of the Commission is to encourage competitive forces in the American economy. Under the Federal Trade Commission Act, the Commission seeks to prevent unfair practices that may keep one company from competing with others. Under the Federal Trade Commission Act and the Clayton Act, the Commission attempts to prevent mergers of companies if the result may be to lessen competition. Under some circumstances, companies planning to merge must first give notice to the Commission and the Department of Justice's Antitrust Division and provide certain information concerning the operations of the companies involved.

The Commission also enforces the provisions of the Robinson-Patman Act, a part of the Clayton Act prohibiting companies from discriminating among other companies that are its customers in terms of price or other services provided. **Economic Factfinding** The Commission makes economic studies of conditions and problems affecting competition in the economy. Reports of this nature may be used to inform legislative proposals, part of a rulemaking record, in response to requests of the Congress and statutory directions, or for the information and guidance of the Commission and the executive branch of the Government as well as the public. The reports have provided the basis for significant legislation and, by spotlighting poor economic or regulatory performance,

they have also led to voluntary changes in the conduct of business, with resulting benefits to the public.
Competition and Consumer Advocacy To promote competition, consumer protection, and the efficient allocation of resources, the Commission has an active program designed to advocate the consumer interest in a competitive marketplace by encouraging courts, legislatures, and government administrative bodies to consider efficiency and consumer welfare as important elements in their deliberations.

The Commission uses these opportunities to support procompetitive means of regulating the Nation's economy, including the elimination of anticompetitive regulations that reduce the welfare of consumers and the implementation of regulatory programs that protect the public and preserve as much as possible the discipline of competitive markets. The competition and consumer advocacy program relies on persuasion rather than coercion.

Regional Offices—Federal Trade Commission

Region	Address	Director
ATLANTA—Alabama, Florida, Georgia, Mississippi, North Carolina, South Carolina, Tennessee, Virginia	Rm. 1000, 1718 Peachtree St. NW., Atlanta, GA 30367	Paul K. Davis, *Acting*
BOSTON—Connecticut, Maine, Massachusetts, New Hampshire, Rhode Island, Vermont	Suite 1184, 10 Causeway St., Boston, MA 02222–1073	Phoebe D. Morse
CHICAGO—Illinois, Indiana, Iowa, Kentucky, Minnesota, Missouri, Wisconsin	Suite 1437, 55 E. Monroe St., Chicago, IL 60603	C. Steven Baker
CLEVELAND—Delaware, District of Columbia, Maryland, Michigan, Ohio, Pennsylvania, West Virginia	Suite 520–A, 668 Euclid Ave., Cleveland, OH 44114	Phillip L. Broyles
DALLAS—Arkansas, Louisiana, New Mexico, Oklahoma, Texas	Suite 500, 100 N. Central Expressway, Dallas, TX 75201	Thomas B. Carter
DENVER—Colorado, Kansas, Montana, Nebraska, North Dakota, South Dakota, Utah, Wyoming	Suite 1523, 1961 Stout St., Denver, CO 80294–0101	Claude C. Wild III
LOS ANGELES—Arizona, southern California	Suite 13209, 11000 Wilshire Blvd., Los Angeles, CA 90024	Sue L. Frauens, *Acting*
NEW YORK—New Jersey, New York	Suite 1300, 150 William St., New York, NY 10038	Michael J. Bloom
SAN FRANCISCO—Northern California, Hawaii, Nevada	Suite 570, 901 Market St., San Francisco, CA 94103	Jeffrey A. Klurfeld
SEATTLE—Alaska, Idaho, Oregon, Washington	2806 Federal Bldg., 915 2d Ave., Seattle, WA 98174	Charles A. Harwood

Sources of Information

Contracts and Procurement   Persons seeking to do business with the Federal Trade Commission should contact the Division of Procurement and General Services, Federal Trade Commission, Washington, DC 20580. Phone, 202–326–2275.

Employment   Civil service registers are used in filling positions for economists, accountants, investigators, and other professional, administrative, and clerical personnel. The Federal Trade Commission employs a sizable number of attorneys under the excepted appointment procedure. All employment inquiries should be directed to the Director of Personnel, Federal Trade Commission, Washington, DC 20580. Phone, 202–326–2022.

General Inquiries Persons desiring information on consumer protection, restraint of trade questions, or to register a complaint, should contact the Federal Trade Commission or the nearest regional office.

Publications A copy of the *Federal Trade Commission—"Best Sellers,"* which lists publications of interest to the general public, is available free upon request from the Public Reference Section, Federal Trade Commission, Washington, DC 20580. Phone, 202–326–2222. TTY, 202–326–2502.

Over 140 of the Commission's consumer publications are also available online. The FTC Consumerline gopher service is located on the Internet at CONSUMER.FTC.GOV 2416. For World Wide Web access, the Uniform Resource Locator is GOPHER:// CONSUMER.FTC.GOV:2416.

For further information, contact the Director, Office of Public Affairs, Federal Trade Commission, Pennsylvania Avenue at Sixth Street NW., Washington, DC 20580. Phone, 202–326–2180.

GENERAL SERVICES ADMINISTRATION

General Services Building, Eighteenth and F Streets NW., Washington, DC 20405
Phone, 202–708–5082

Administrator of General Services	ROGER W. JOHNSON
Deputy Administrator	THURMAN M. DAVIS, *Acting*
Chief of Staff	BARBARA O. SILBY
Special Counsel, Office of Ethics	ALLIE B. LATIMER
Associate Administrator for Equal Employment Opportunity	YVONNE T. JONES
Associate Administrator for Enterprise Development	MIRINDA JACKSON, *Acting*
Deputy Director for Small and Disadvantaged Business Utilization	MIRINDA JACKSON
Deputy Director for Training and Compliance	ROSALINDA CASTILLO
Associate Administrator for Congressional and Intergovernmental Affairs	WILLIAM R. RATCHFORD
Associate Administrator for Public Affairs	HENRY CONNORS, *Acting*
Associate Administrator for Management Services and Human Resources	MARLENE M. JOHNSON
Deputy Associate Administrator	JACK J. LANDERS
Director of Workplace Initiatives	FAITH WOHL
Director of Personnel	GAIL P. LOVELACE
Director of Management Controls and Evaluation	JOHN H. DAVENJAY
Director of Management Services	GREGORY L. KNOTT
Director of Quality Management and Training	JON R. HALSALL
Controller	JON A. JORDAN
Director of the Executive Secretariat	ERIC DODDS
Director of Labor Management Partnership and Information Technology	DONALD P. HEFFERNAN
Associate Administrator for FTS2000	ROBERT J. WOODS

Deputy Associate Administrator	WILLIAM P. CUNNANE
Inspector General	WILLIAM R. BARTON
Deputy Inspector General	JOEL S. GALLAY
Assistant Inspector General for Auditing	WILLIAM E. WHYTE, JR.
Assistant Inspector General for Investigations	JAMES E. HENDERSON
Assistant Inspector General for Quality Management	LAWRENCE J. DEMPSEY
Assistant Inspector General for Administration	JAMES E. LE GETTE
Counsel to the Inspector General	KATHLEEN S. TIGHE,
Director, Internal Evaluation Program	ANDREW A. RUSSONIELLO
Chairman, GSA Board of Contract Appeals	STEPHEN M. DANIELS
Vice Chairman	ROBERT W. PARKER
Board Counsel	WILBUR T. MILLER
Clerk of the Board	BEATRICE JONES
Chief Financial Officer	DENNIS J. FISCHER
Director of Budget	WILLIAM B. EARLY, JR.
Director of Finance	ROBERT E. SUDA
Director of Financial Management	CAROLE A. HUTCHINSON
Director of Financial Management Systems	WILLIAM J. TOPOLEWSKI
Associate Administrator for Acquisition Policy	IDA USTAD
Executive Officer	A. TONI HAZLEWOOD
Director of GSA Acquisition Policy	PAUL M. LYNCH
Director of Federal Acquisition Policy	C. ALLEN OLSON
Director, Federal Acquisition Institute	JOHN BLUMENSTEIN, *Acting*
General Counsel	EMILY CLARK HEWITT
Special Counsel to the General Counsel	MICKI CHEN
Associate General Counsel for General Law	LAURENCE HARRINGTON
Associate General Counsel for Personal Property	VINCENT CRIVELLA
Associate Administrator for Real Property	SHARON A. ROACH

INFORMATION TECHNOLOGY SERVICE

General Services Building, Eighteenth and F Streets NW., Washington, DC 20405
Phone, 202–501–1000

Commissioner, Information Technology Service	JOE M. THOMPSON
Deputy Commissioner	G. MARTIN WAGNER
Senior Advisor	IRA JEKOWSKY
Business Industry Outreach Director	JOEL ODOM
Deputy Commissioner for Information Technology Policy and Leadership	FRANCIS A. MCDONOUGH
Assistant Commissioner	FRED L. SIMS
Deputy Commissioner for Emerging Technology Implementation	RONALD L. PIASECKI
Deputy Commissioner (Controller) for Resources Management	LINDA F. VANDENBURG
Assistant Commissioner	SHEREEN G. REMEZ
Deputy Commissioner for Information Technology Acquisition	JAMES ARRINGTON, *Acting*
Deputy Chief Information Officer for GSA-Wide Information Technology	DONALD L. VENNEBERG
Deputy Commissioner for Information Security	THOMAS R. BURKE, *Acting*
Deputy Commissioner for Information Technology Integration	LAWRENCE S. COHAN

Deputy Assistant Commissioner   CHARLES A. SELF
Deputy Commissioner for Local   DON HARDESTY
   Telecommunications
Deputy Assistant Commissioner   JAMES EDWARDS

FEDERAL SUPPLY SERVICE

*1941 Jefferson Davis Highway, Arlington, VA; Mailing address: Washington, DC 20406
Phone, 703–305–6667*

Commissioner, Federal Supply Service	FRANK P. PUGLIESE, JR.
Deputy Commissioner	DONNA D. BENNETT
Chief of Staff	PATRICIA M. MEAD
Controller	JOHN B. CONRAD, *Acting*
Director of Transportation Audits	JEFFREY THURSTON
Assistant Commissioner for Distribution Management	BRIAN FREEMAN
Assistant Commissioner for Business Management and Marketing	REBECCA R. RHODES, *Acting*
Assistant Commissioner for Quality and Contract Administration	F. DONALD GENOVA, *Acting*
Assistant Commissioner for Acquisition	WILLIAM N. GORMLEY
Assistant Commissioner for FSS Information Systems	RAYMOND J. HANLEIN

PUBLIC BUILDINGS SERVICE

*General Services Building, Eighteenth and F Streets NW., Washington, DC 20405
Phone, 202–501–1100*

Commissioner, Public Buildings Service	KENNETH R. KIMBROUGH
Deputy Commissioner	DAVID L. BIBB
Chief of Staff	ANN W. EVERETT
Controller	THOMAS M. SHERMAN
Acquisition Executive	SHARON R. JENKINS
Assistant Commissioner for Business Development	JAMES A. WILLIAMS
PBS Chief Information Officer	STEVEN R. MEAD
Assistant Commissioner for Commercial Broker	HILARY W. PEOPLES, *Acting*
Assistant Commissioner for the Federal Protective Service	GARRETT J. DAY
Assistant Commissioner for Fee Developer	JAMES B. STEWART, *Acting*
Assistant Commissioner for Property Disposal	BRIAN K. POLLY
Assistant Commissioner for Governmentwide Real Property Policy	ROBERT J. DILUCHIO
Assistant Commissioner for Portfolio Management	JUNE V. HUBER
Assistant Commissioner for Property Management	JAMES F. STEELE

[For the General Services Administration statement of organization, see the *Code of Federal Regulations,* Title 41, Part 105–53]

*The General Services Administration establishes policy for and provides economical
and efficient management of Government property and records, including
construction and operation of buildings; procurement and distribution of supplies;*

GENERAL SERVICES ADMINISTRATION

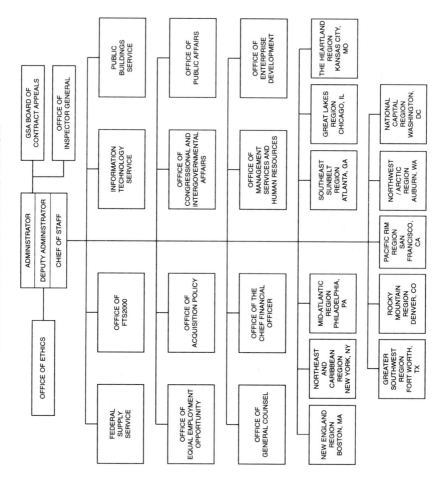

utilization and disposal of property; transportation, traffic, and communications management; and management of the Governmentwide automatic data processing resources program. Its functions are carried out at three levels of organization: the central office, regional offices, and field activities.

The General Services Administration (GSA) was established by section 101 of the Federal Property and Administrative Services Act of 1949 (40 U.S.C. 751).

Acquisition Policy   The Office of Acquisition Policy plans, directs, and coordinates a comprehensive, agencywide acquisition policy program, including the establishment of major agency acquisition goals and objectives.

The Office of Acquisition Policy has a major role in developing, maintaining, issuing, and administering guiding principles via the Federal Acquisition Regulation (FAR), which is applicable to all Federal agencies. It chairs the Civilian Agency Acquisition Council and provides administrative support through the FAR Secretariat. The Office develops GSA implementing and supplementing principles required by FAR, which is published as the General Services Administration Acquisition Regulation.

The Office manages the agency's internal system for the suspension and debarment of nonresponsive contractors and a Governmentwide system for exchanging information on debarred, suspended, and ineligible parties. The Office also is responsible for overseeing the agency's acquisition information system and serves as agency coordinator for the Federal Procurement Data System.

The Office's Federal Acquisition Institute fosters and promotes Governmentwide career management and training programs to develop a professional workforce and coordinates Governmentwide studies to improve the procurement process.

For further information, call 202–501–1043.

Enterprise Development   The mission of the Office of Enterprise Development is to promote and facilitate programs and activities that support an environment that provides "Access to Opportunity" to small, minority, and women business owners to participate in GSA contracting nationwide. To accomplish this, the Office plans, implements, and evaluates comprehensive agencywide procurement preference programs, including: the Small Business Program, the Women in Business Program, the Minority Business Enterprise Program, the Subcontracting Program, and the Mandatory Source Program, among others.

The Office coordinates and develops policies that regulate the operation and implementation of the Small Business Programs under sections 8 and 15 of the Small Business Act. The Office, through the Business Service Center Program, provides assistance, information, and counseling to small businesses interested in pursuing Federal Government contracts, and conducts outreach, seminars, liaison, and source listing for small and disadvantaged businesses.

The Business Service Centers assist agency procurement officials in the establishment of subcontracting plans and act as liaisons between GSA and the Small Business Administration. The Business Service Centers conduct on-site reviews of vendor subcontracting plans to ensure compliance with the terms of the approved plan.

For further information, call 202–501–1021.

Business Service Center Directory

Region	Address	Telephone
NATIONAL CAPITAL REGION—Washington, DC	7th and D Sts. SW., 20407	202–708–5804
NEW ENGLAND REGION—Boston, MA	10 Causeway St., 02222	617–565–8100
NORTHEAST AND CARIBBEAN REGION—New York, NY	26 Federal Plz., 10278	212–264–1234
MID–ATLANTIC REGION—Philadelphia, PA	Rm. 808, 100 Penn Sq. E., 19107–3396	215–656–5523
SOUTHEAST SUNBELT REGION—Atlanta, GA	Rm. 2900, 401 W. Peachtree St. NW., 30303	404–331–5103

Business Service Center Directory—Continued

Region	Address	Telephone
GREAT LAKES REGION—Chicago, IL	230 S. Dearborn St., 60604	312–353–5383
THE HEARTLAND REGION—Kansas City, MO	1500 E. Bannister Rd., 64131	816–926–7203
GREATER SOUTHWEST REGION—Fort Worth, TX	819 Taylor St., 76102	817–334–3284
ROCKY MOUNTAIN REGION—Denver, CO	Denver Federal Ctr., 80225–0006	303–326–7408
PACIFIC RIM REGION—San Francisco, CA	525 Market St., 94105	415–744–5060
NORTHWEST/ARCTIC REGION—Auburn, WA	GSA Ctr., 98001	206–931–7957

Contract Appeals   The General Services Administration Board of Contract Appeals is responsible for resolving disputes arising out of contracts with the General Services Administration, the Department of the Treasury, the Department of Education, the Department of Commerce, and other independent Government agencies. The Board is also empowered to hear and decide protests arising out of automatic data processing procurements Governmentwide. Although the Board is located within the agency, it functions as an independent tribunal.

For further information, contact the Board of Contract Appeals (G), General Services Administration, Washington, DC 20405. Phone, 202–501–0720.

Ethics   The Office of Ethics is responsible for developing and directing the agency's programs governing employee standards of ethical conduct.

For further information, call 202–501–0765.

Equal Employment Opportunity   The Office of Equal Employment Opportunity is responsible for the agency's equal employment opportunity program.

For further information, call 202–501–0767.

FTS2000   The Office of Federal Telecommunications System 2000 (FTS2000) provides common-user, long-distance telecommunications services. The FTS2000 program offers the Federal Government low-cost, state-of-the-art, integrated voice, data, and video telecommunications. Program services are provided through two multi-billion dollar, 10-year contracts that were awarded to the American Telephone & Telegraph Company (AT&T) and Sprint in December 1988.

This Office provides leadership, policy, program direction, and program oversight for ensuring a timely, high-quality, innovative, and cost-effective Governmentwide program for intercity telecommunications services.

For further information, call 703–760–7790.

Information Technology Service
The Information Technology Service is responsible for the coordination and direction of a comprehensive, Governmentwide program for the management, procurement, and utilization of automated data processing and local telecommunications equipment and services; planning and directing programs for improving Federal records and information management practices; and providing information to the public through the Federal Information Center.
Governmentwide Information Resources Management Assistance   The General Services Administration provides Governmentwide programs to assist Federal agencies in managing their information resources. The Office of Information Technology Integration (ITI) provides technical and contracting assistance through three complementary programs: the Federal Systems Integration and Management System (FEDSIM); the Federal Computer Acquisition Center (FEDCAC); and the Federal Information System Support Program (FISSP). This assistance is provided on a reimbursable, nonmandatory basis to agencies utilizing the system.
FEDSIM provides technical and contractual services to Federal agencies in acquisition, integration, management, and the use of information systems and information technology.

FEDCAC competitively conducts large dollar value information processing resources acquisitions for Federal agencies. These acquisitions include systems hardware; systems software; and associated services such as maintenance, training, and systems analysis support.

FISSP allows ITI to consolidate relatively small, quick-reaction, technical services project requirements for other agencies in order to reduce costs.

For further information, contact the Office of Information Technology Integration, Suite 1100, 5203 Leesburg Pike, Falls Church, VA 22041. Phone, 703–756–4100.

Information Technology Policy and Leadership The Service plans, develops, and directs a Governmentwide program to help agencies improve their acquisition, management, and use of information technology. The Service develops and issues Governmentwide policies and regulations on information technology acquisition, management, and use. It promotes the development of a technologically competent Federal workforce through management assistance programs, such as the Trail Boss Program, that help Federal agencies prepare for, conduct, and implement major information technology acquisitions.

For further information, contact the Office of Information Technology Policy and Leadership. Phone, 201–501–0202.

Information Technology Acquisition The Service plays a major role in the Governmentwide procurement of Federal Information Processing (FIP) and telecommunications hardware, software, and services. In providing its acquisition services, the agency seeks out and obtains the best buys; obtains the best leasing and/or purchase price arrangements; negotiates long-term procurement actions to achieve cost reductions; and continually strives to improve Federal procurement practices.

For further information, contact the Office of Information Technology Acquisition. Phone, 202–501–1072.

Telecommunications Services The Service develops policies and procedures and defines standards for GSA's Local Service Program. Under this program, the agency provides telecommunications services and products to Federal agencies at locations where it is economically beneficial. The Service also plays a major role in Governmentwide activities.

The Service is presently moving forward with an Aggregated Systems Procurement Program that replaces local telecommunications systems and upgrades service at selected locations nationwide. It has implemented the replacement of the large tariffed system in the Nation's Capital with the Washington Interagency Telecommunications System and has placed purchase-of-telecommunications-services contracts nationwide except for the New England area and Alaska to satisfy the Government's requirements for customer-provided telecommunications equipment and services. These requirements can be satisfied in New England using the Aggregated Systems Procurement Program contract and in Alaska using other telecommunications contracts. The Service also administers a nationwide telecommunications support services contract.

The Service manages and administers the National Security Emergency Preparedness Telecommunications Program activities. It ensures that the agency supports Governmentwide national security and domestic emergency plans, including those promulgated by the National Communications System.

For further information, contact the Office of Local Telecommunications Services. Phone, 202–606–9000.

Information Security The Office of Information Security provides worldwide support to all Government activities conducting sensitive and classifies national security, diplomatic, and Department of Defense missions. The Office provides a comprehensive range of services for information systems and participates in the development of Governmentwide information security policies in support of Federal, civil, and Department of Defense activities. This

Office provides the technical expertise, personnel, logistics, training, and facilities necessary to manage and support critical Government communications.

For further information, contact the Office of Information Security. Phone, 202–708–7000.

Office of Emerging Technology The Office of Emerging Technology plans, manages, and directs activities that promote the identification, development, and use of current and emerging technologies in the Federal Government. The Office develops strategies for integrating Federal, State, and local government applications to form a synergetic approach to use information technology to improve the delivery of government services; compiles trend information of emerging technologies to support efforts to improve government services; identifies information technology tools, applications, and effective implementation strategies to improve government performance; plans, develops, and implements multiagency and intergovernmental information technology pilots and prototypes to validate concept of operation and assess the viability for Governmentwide implementation; and establishes benchmarks on best practices of governmental applications of information technology. The Office oversees the implementation of new and proven information technology applications that will improve the delivery of government services provided by Federal, State, local, and tribal governments. The Office also serves as the Governmentwide program offices for Electronic Commerce, Electronic Mail, Information Technology Accommodations and the Security Infrastructure Program Management Office.

For further information, contact the Office of Emerging Technology. Phone, 202–501–0308.

Federal Information Center Program
The Federal Information Center Program, a clearinghouse for information about the Federal Government, can eliminate the maze of referrals that people have experienced in contacting the Federal Government. Persons with questions

about a Government program or agency, and who are unsure of which office can help, may call the Center. A specialist will either answer the question or locate an expert who can.

Residents of more than 80 metropolitan areas have direct access to the Center via toll-free (800) telephone service, and callers in four States—Iowa, Kansas, Missouri, and Nebraska—have statewide toll-free service. Users of telecommunications devices for the deaf (TDD/TTY) may call a nationwide toll-free number: 800–326–2996.

For further information, call the Federal Information Center number for your area.

Federal Information Centers—General Services Administration

(Review the areas listed below. If your area is listed, call 800–688–9889. If your area is not listed, call 301–722–9000. TDD/TTY users should call 800–326–2996.)

State	City
ALABAMA	Birmingham, Mobile
ALASKA	Anchorage
ARIZONA	Phoenix
ARKANSAS	Little Rock
CALIFORNIA	Los Angeles, Sacramento, San Diego, San Francisco, Santa Ana
COLORADO	Colorado Springs, Denver, Pueblo
CONNECTICUT	Hartford, New Haven
DELAWARE	Wilmington
FLORIDA	Fort Lauderdale, Jacksonville, Miami, Orlando, St. Petersburg, Tampa, West Palm Beach
GEORGIA	Atlanta
HAWAII	Honolulu
IDAHO	Boise
ILLINOIS	Chicago
INDIANA	Gary, Indianapolis
IOWA	From all points
KANSAS	From all points
KENTUCKY	Louisville
LOUISIANA	New Orleans
MAINE	Portland
MARYLAND	Baltimore
MASSACHUSETTS	Boston
MICHIGAN	Detroit, Grand Rapids
MINNESOTA	Minneapolis
MISSISSIPPI	Jackson
MISSOURI	St. Louis
MONTANA	Billings
NEBRASKA	Omaha
NEVADA	Las Vegas
NEW HAMPSHIRE	Portsmouth
NEW JERSEY	Newark, Trenton
NEW MEXICO	Albuquerque
NEW YORK	Albany, Buffalo, New York, Rochester, Syracuse
NORTH CAROLINA	Charlotte
NORTH DAKOTA	Fargo
OHIO	Akron, Cincinnati, Cleveland, Columbus, Dayton, Toledo
OKLAHOMA	Oklahoma City, Tulsa
OREGON	Portland
PENNSYLVANIA	Philadelphia, Pittsburgh
RHODE ISLAND	Providence

Federal Information Centers—General Services Administration—Continued

(Review the areas listed below. If your area is listed, call 800–688–9889. If your area is not listed, call 301–722–9000. TDD/TTY users should call 800–326–2996.)

State	City
SOUTH CAROLINA	Greenville
SOUTH DAKOTA	Sioux Falls
TENNESSEE	Chattanooga, Memphis, Nashville
TEXAS	Austin, Dallas, Fort Worth, Houston, San Antonio
UTAH	Salt Lake City
VERMONT	Burlington
VIRGINIA	Norfolk, Richmond, Roanoke
WASHINGTON	Seattle, Tacoma
WEST VIRGINIA	Huntington
WISCONSIN	Milwaukee
WYOMING	Cheyenne

Federal Information Relay Service (FIRS)

The Federal Information Relay Service serves as an intermediary between hearing individuals and individuals who are deaf, hard of hearing, and speech-impaired for nationwide communications with and within the Federal Government. The Service enables Federal employees to conduct official duties and allows the general public to conduct business with the Federal Government and its agencies. FIRS also encourages direct communications between individuals using telecommunications devices for the deaf (TDD/TTY's) by maintaining an on-line bulletin board and by publishing an annual directory of Federal TDD/TTY telephone numbers.

To utilize the Federal Information Relay Service, call 800–877–8339 (toll-free). To obtain a FIRS brochure call 800–877–0996 (toll-free). These numbers serve both voice and TDD/TTY calls.

To access the Federal Information Relay Service bulletin board of TDD/TTY numbers, call 800–877–8845 (toll-free).

For a free copy of the directory, write to: U.S. Government TDD Directory, Dept. 588B, Customer Information Center, Pueblo, CO 81009.

For further information, contact the Office of Emerging Technology. Phone, 202–501–1937 (voice) or 202–501–2860 (TDD).

Specialized Data Centers

The Service operates several programs that collect and maintain information on equipment of interest to the public and the private sector.

The Federal Procurement Data Center provides information regarding goods and services bought by the Federal Government. The Center is a unique source of consolidated information about Federal purchases, and the data is readily available through reports prepared by the Center.

The Federal Equipment Data Center operates the Automatic Data Processing Equipment Data System Program, which collects and maintains information regarding general-purpose processing equipment being used by the Federal Government. Information is collected and disseminated on federally operated domestic assistance programs, such as grants, and is available in an annual catalog and through a nationally accessible computer system.

For further information, contact the Automated External Information Division. Phone, 703–235–2870.

Domestic Assistance Catalog

The Federal Domestic Assistance Catalog Program collects and disseminates information on all federally operated domestic assistance programs such as grants, loans, and insurance. This information is published annually in the Catalog of Federal Domestic Assistance, and is available through the Federal Assistance Programs Retrieval System, a nationally accessible computer system.

For further information, contact the Federal Domestic Assistance Catalog staff. Phone, 202–708–5126.

Federal Supply Service

The Federal Supply Service (FSS) provides leadership, through policy, guidance, and service delivery, which assures that the Federal Government's requirements for personal property and administrative services are effectively met at the least overall cost to the taxpayer. Towards this goal, FSS operates a worldwide supply system to contract for and distribute personal property and services to Federal agencies. FSS provides Governmentwide programs for transportation, mail and travel management, transportation audits, Federal fleet management, and management of aircraft owned or operated by civilian agencies in support of their missions; and administers a Governmentwide property management program for the utilization of excess personal property and the donation and sale of surplus personal property.

The Service provides over $8 billion annually in common-use goods and services. The Supply and Procurement business line of FSS uses the aggregate purchasing power of the Government to establish sources of supply for commonly used business, operational, administrative, and financial supplies and services. Over 98 percent of the support provided by the business line is for commercial items and services, and 90 percent is delivered directly to customers. Almost 80 percent of the supply and procurement business volume is from orders directly placed by customers, under contracts established by FSS. FSS also operates a distribution system that makes 5 million deliveries a year of common office supplies, direct to customer desktops, within 48 hours of their orders. Another 7 million customer deliveries are made within 2 weeks from over 15,000 high-demand items, including overnight support for national emergencies and disaster relief. In compliance with applicable laws, regulations, and Executive orders, FSS helps the Government conserve energy, recycle used materials, and purchase products that are environmentally sound.

Each year FSS establishes numerous multimillion-dollar contracts for environmentally oriented products—ranging from recycled items such as retread tires, office supplies, and insulation, to shipping boxes with recycled content, to energy and water saving devices, and to reformulated industrial products.

To eliminate unnecessary expenditures and maximize the utilization of federally owned personal property, FSS directs and coordinates, on a worldwide basis, a Government property management program. Under this program, excess personal property valued at approximately $12.3 billion annually is available for transfer to other agencies and, when no longer needed by the Federal Government, is allocated to the States for donation to eligible recipients or disposed of through competitive public sales.

The Federal Supply Service administers Governmentwide programs for transportation and travel management, transportation audits, and fleet management to meet the requirements of Federal agencies.

To provide agencies with economical fleet management services, FSS manages an Interagency Fleet Management System (IMFS) comprised of approximately 145,000 vehicles, ranging from compact sedans to buses and ambulances. As part of the services provided, GSA acquires the vehicles, ensures that fuel and maintenance/repair services are available, and disposes of the vehicles when due for replacement. In conjunction with the Department of Energy, FSS introduced alternative fuel vehicles (AFV'S) into the Federal fleet, and currently has over 10,000 in use.

The FSS Fleet Management Program is also responsible for developing regulations and procedures governing the management and oversight of all Federal Government motor vehicles, except those exempted under the Federal Property and Administrative Services Act of 1949, as amended.

As the Government's civilian freight manager, FSS provides rating and routing services to customer agencies at 20–50 percent off commercial rates, as well as small package overnight delivery service at a savings of 70 percent below commercial rates.

In addition, FSS coordinates Governmentwide policy development for the management of Government aircraft through the Interagency Committee for Aviation Policy. Through its Federal Aviation Management Information System, FSS stores aircraft and facility inventory, cost and utilization data, and contract, rental, and charter data pertinent to all civilian agency aircraft.

For further information, contact the Federal Supply Service, Washington, DC 20406. Phone, 703–305–6646.

Public Buildings Service

The Public Buildings Service (PBS) is responsible for the design, construction, management, operation, alteration, extension, and remodeling, owned and leased, in which accommodations for Government activities are provided, and where authorized, for the acquisition, use, custody, and accountability of GSA/ PBS real property and related personal property. It has responsibility for 260 million square feet of space, excluding external parking areas, in about 7,300 federally owned or leased buildings, in addition to approximately $6.4 billion in construction projects currently underway. The President issued Executive Order 12512, dated April 12, 1985, which gave PBS the responsibility to provide leadership in the development and maintenance of needed property management information systems for the Government.

For further information, call 202–501–1100.

Office of the Commercial Broker

The Commercial Broker acquires real property through leases and purchases and directs the development of procedures and specifications related to real property acquisitions, including leasing, building purchases, site acquisition, and easements; marketing vacant space; outleasing vacant space; appraisals and initial assignments of space; lease acquisition delegations; space planning; requirements development; buildout of space; cost estimates; installation of telecommunications/local area networks; furniture procurement, and disposal.

For further information, contact the Office of Real Property Development. Phone, 202–501–1025.

Office of Property Management

The Office of Property Management develops and administers programs to: manage and operate Government-owned and leased property; processes related to maintaining space assignments after initial occupancy; manage and administer leases and outleases; ensure service delivery to tenants; distribute rent bills; administer day-to-day operation of occupancy agreements with client agencies; safeguard Federal employees

from hazardous exposure to GSA operations or services and environmental matters related to building operations and alterations; fire protection for all facilities and personnel; alter buildings, systems, and space after initial tenant occupancy; design and construction of alterations, excluding major modernizations; assist regions on procurement issues related to contracting; procure construction, building services, professional services, and architect-engineer services; provide oversight of delegations of authority to agencies for operation and management of Government-owned and/or -operated buildings; guide delegated agencies in lease management, administrative contracting officer, and contracting officer's representative activities.

For further information, contact the Office of Property Management. Phone, 202–501–0971.

Office of the Fee Developer

The Office of the Fee Developer plans, directs, and coordinates the nationwide operation of the Fee Developer business line within PBS. This Office represents the Fee Developer in agency dealings of national scope with other executive branch agencies, the legislative and judicial branches, and other Government and private-sector interests. It plans, guides, and accommodates temporary and extraordinary real property planning and development efforts requiring enhanced national emphasis and direction, when required by the PBS Commissioner. The Office defines, articulates, advocates, promotes, and interprets PBS vision and principles for excellence in public architecture, engineering, and construction. The Office of Fee Developer maintains arrangements for eliciting advisory input from nationally renowned design professionals on major product design commissions and design solutions; fosters design quality through sponsorship of award, peer review, and other similar programs; and directs, coordinates, and performs all personnel management and administrative support functions for the Office of the Fee Developer.

For further information, contact the Office of the
Fee Developer. Phone, 202–501–0887.

Office of the Federal Protective Service

The Office of the Federal Protective Service develops and administers guidelines and standards for uniformed force operations, investigates criminal offenses not involving GSA employees, and conducts limited pre-appointments. The Office conducts preliminary investigations of accidents, incidents, and criminal complaints occurring on GSA-controlled property. The Federal Protective Service coordinates with appropriate Federal Emergency Management Agency representatives for security and law enforcement requirements. It gathers protective intelligence information pertaining to demonstrations, bomb threats, and other criminal activities. The Office provides centralized communication, alarm monitoring, and coordination for State and Federal officials regarding Federal facilities. The Office of the Federal Protective Service develops a nationwide physical security protection program and coordinates a nationwide Occupant Emergency Program.

For further information, contact the Office of the
Federal Protective Service. Phone, 202–501–0907.

Office of Property Disposal

The Office of Property Disposal develops and administers programs related to the utilization of excess and surplus real property; disposal of surplus real property by sale, exchange, lease, assignment, transfer, permit; protection and maintenance of excess and surplus property pending disposition disposal of Defense Industrial Reserve Plants; and disposal services to agencies which have their own disposal authorities on a reimbursable basis, e.g., seized, forfeited, or foreclosed. The Office directs the development of a national plan to market properties and buildings. It also establishes national benchmarking standards and a customer liaison program.

For further information, contact the Office of
Property Disposal. Phone, 202–501–0210.

Office of Portfolio Management

The Office of Portfolio Management plans, directs, coordinates, and evaluates the programs, functions, and activities of the portfolio management business line at the national level. The Office conducts strategic and business planning; makes capital investment decisions and obtains capital resources; manages the national portfolio of real estate and art assets; obtains the support of other service providers; evaluates portfolio and service provider performance; and provides guidance and assistance to regional portfolio managers and other business lines.

For further information, contact the Office of
Portfolio Management. Phone, 202–501–0018.

Office of Business Development

The Office of Business Development directs the policy and management of the National Account Executive and Regional Account Manager programs; facilitates the development of strategic partnerships with client agencies; performs research and analysis of PBS' long-term strategic and business direction, directs the national real property strategic marketing plans and programs; develops and implements national customer outreach and public relations programs to form partnerships with key customers and raise agencies' awareness of current and future alternatives with the real estate portfolio.

For further information, contact the Office of
Business Development. Phone, 202–501–0018.

Office of Governmentwide Real Property Policy

The Office of Governmentwide Real Property Policy provides executive direction and comprehensive management over the area of Governmentwide real property policy and related activities and is responsible for the development, coordination, administration, and issuance of Governmentwide real property for customers within GSA and other Federal agencies. The Office evaluates the implementation and effectiveness of real property policies and the need for continuous improvement; directs, coordinates, develops, and administers GSA's legislative plan; represents GSA and customer agencies with the Office of Management and Budget and Congress on real property matters; ensures that the PBS position on legislation is consistent with the Governmentwide policy; and

ensures the testimony on real property issues is consistent with Governmentwide real property policy.

For further information, contact the Office of Governmentwide Real Property Policy. Phone, 202–501–0856.

Regional Offices Regional offices are located in 11 U.S. cities. Within its area of jurisdiction, each regional office is responsible for executing assigned programs.

Regional Offices—General Services Administration

Headquarters	Address	Administrator
New England Region	Boston, MA (10 Causeway St., 02222)	Robert J. Dunfey, Jr.
Northeast and Caribbean Region.	New York, NY (26 Federal Plz., 10278)	Karen R. Adler
Mid-Atlantic Region	Philadelphia, PA (100 Penn Sq. E., 19107–3396)	Paul Chistolini
Southeast Sunbelt Region .	Atlanta, GA (Suite 2800, 401 W. Peachtree St. NW., 30365)	Carol A. Dortch
Great Lakes Region	Chicago, IL (230 S. Dearborn St., 60604)	William C. Burke
The Heartland Region	Kansas City, MO (1500 E. Bannister Rd., 64131)	Glen W. Overton
Greater Southwest Region .	Fort Worth, TX (819 Taylor St., 76102)	John Pouland
Rocky Mountain Region	Denver, CO (Denver Federal Ctr., 80225–0006)	Polly B. Baca
Pacific Rim Region	San Francisco, CA (525 Market St., 94105)	Kenn N. Kojima
Northwest/Arctic Region	Auburn, WA (GSA Ctr., 98002)	L. Jay Pearson
National Capital Region	Washington, DC (7th and D Sts. SW., 20407)	Thurman M. Davis

Sources of Information

Consumer Information Center

Organized under the Office of Public Affairs is the Consumer Information Center, a program that assists Federal agencies in the release of relevant and useful consumer information and generates increased public awareness of this information. The Center publishes quarterly the *Consumer Information Catalog,* which is free to the public and lists more than 200 free or low-cost Federal consumer interest publications. Topics include health, food, nutrition, money management, employment, Federal benefits, the environment, and education. The *Catalog* is widely distributed through congressional offices, Federal facilities, educators, State and local governmental consumer offices, and private nonprofit organizations. For a free copy of the *Catalog,* write to Consumer Information Catalog, Pueblo, CO 81009. Phone, 719–948–4000. Bulk copies are free to nonprofit organizations.

For help in accessing CIC information electronically, send e-mail to cic.info@pueblo.gsa.gov. Put the words

"SEND INFO" in the body of the message.

Contracts Individuals seeking to do business with the General Services Administration may obtain detailed information from the Business Service Centers listed on page 585. Inquiries concerning programs to assist small business should be directed to one of the Business Service Centers.

Employment Inquiries and applications should be directed to the Personnel Operations Division (CPS), Office of Personnel, General Services Administration, Washington, DC 20405. Schools interested in the recruitment program should contact the Personnel Operations Division (CPS), Office of Personnel, Washington, DC 20405 (phone, 202–501–0370), and/or the appropriate regional office listed above.

Fraud and Waste Contact the Inspector General's Office at (800–424–5210 (toll free) or 202–501–1780 (in the Washington, DC, metropolitan area)).

Freedom of Information and Privacy Act Requests Inquiries concerning policies pertaining to Freedom of Information Act and Privacy Act matters should be addressed to the General Services

Administration (CAIR), Attn: GSA FOIA or Privacy Act Officer, Room 7102, Washington, DC 20405. Phone, 202–501–2691. TDD callers may use the Federal Information Relay Service (phone, 202–708–9300; fax, 202–501–2727). FOIA or Privacy Act requests concerning GSA regions should be directed to the FOIA or Privacy Act officers for the particular region. (*See* the listing on page 593.)

Public and News Media Inquiries   The Office of Public Affairs is responsible for the coordination of responses to inquiries from both the general public and news media, as well as for maintaining an information network with agency employees with regard to items of interest to the Federal worker. The Office, through its Office of Media Relations, issues news releases. Its Office of Communications is responsible for printing the *GSA Update,* a weekly bulletin of noteworthy items designed to keep agency employees apprised of pertinent issues, and *GSA Today,* a quarterly employee magazine.

Publications   Many publications are available at moderate prices through the bookstores of the Government Printing Office or from customer supply centers. Others may be obtained free or at production cost from a Business Service Center or a Federal Information Center. (*See* pages 585 and 588, respectively.)

The telephone numbers and addresses of the Federal Information Centers and of the Government Printing Office bookstores are listed in local telephone directories. If a publication is not distributed by any of the centers or stores, inquiries should be directed to the originating agency's service or office. The addresses for inquiries are:

Public Buildings Service (P), General Services Administration, Washington, DC 20405

Federal Supply Service (F), General Services Administration, Washington, DC 20406

Office of Finance (BC), General Services Administration, Washington, DC 20405

Information Technology Service (K), General Services Administration, Washington, DC 20405

Those who would like a brief index of publications or who are not certain of the service or office of origin should write to the Director of Publications, Office of Communications (XS), General Services Administration, Washington, DC 20405. Phone, 202–501–1235.

Small Business Activities   Inquiries concerning programs to assist small businesses should be directed to one of the Business Service Centers listed on page 585.

Speakers   Inquiries and requests for speakers should be directed to the Office of Public Affairs (X), General Services Administration, Washington, DC 20405 (phone, 202–501–0705); or contact the nearest regional office.

For further information concerning the General Services Administration, contact the Office of Public Affairs (X), General Services Administration, Washington, DC 20405. Phone, 202–501–0705.

INTER–AMERICAN FOUNDATION

901 North Stuart Street, Arlington, VA 22203
Phone, 703–841–3800

Board of Directors:

Chair	MARÍA OTERO
Vice Chair	NEIL H. OFFEN
Directors	HARRIET C. BABBITT, MARK SCHNEIDER, ANN BROWNELL SLOANE, NORTON STEVENS, ALEXANDER F. WATSON, PATRICIA HILL WILLIAMS, FRANK D. YTURRIA

Staff:

President	GEORGE A. EVANS
Vice President for Programs	LINDA BORST
Vice President for Learning and Dissemination	ANNE TERNES
Vice President for Financial Management and Systems	WINSOME WELLS, *Acting*
General Counsel	ADOLFO A. FRANCO

The Inter-American Foundation is an independent Federal agency that supports social and economic development in Latin America and the Caribbean. It makes grants primarily to private, indigenous organizations that carry out self-help projects benefiting poor people.

The Inter-American Foundation was created by Congress in 1969 (22 U.S.C. 290f) to support the self-help efforts of poor people in Latin America and the Caribbean. The Foundation was established because of congressional concern that traditional programs of development assistance were not reaching poor people. Instead of working through governments, the Foundation responds directly to the initiatives of the poor by supporting local and private organizations. Approximately 75 percent of the Foundation's funds are derived from congressional appropriations and the remainder from the Social Progress Trust Fund of the Inter-American Development Bank.

The Foundation is governed by a nine-member Board of Directors appointed by the President with the advice and consent of the Senate. By law, six members of the Board are from private organizations and three are from the Government.

The Foundation has made 3,811 grants, totaling nearly $410 million through fiscal year 1994 in 36 countries of Latin America and the Caribbean. Most grants are made to private, grassroots organizations, including community associations and small urban enterprises or to larger organizations that work with local groups and provide them with credit, technical assistance, training, and marketing services. A small number of grants each year are made to centers in Latin America and the Caribbean for research on the problems of poor people and grassroots development.

For further information, contact the Office of the President, Inter-American Foundation, 901 North Stuart Street, Arlington, VA 22203. Phone, 703–841–3810.

INTERSTATE COMMERCE COMMISSION

Twelfth Street and Constitution Avenue NW., Washington, DC 20423
Phone, 202–927–7119

Chairman	LINDA J. MORGAN
Vice Chairman	GUS A. OWEN
Commissioners	J.J. SIMMONS III, GAIL C. MCDONALD, (VACANCY)
Chief of Staff and Chief Executive Officer	AMY NORTHCUTT
Deputy Chief Executive Officer	J.B. ROBINSON
Counsel to the Chief Executive Officer/ Privacy/Freedom of Information Act Officer	JOHN M. ATKISSON
Chief, Section of Facility and Systems Services	DON HIRST
Chief, Section of Financial Services	AUBREY HERNDON
Chief, Section of Personnel Services	J.B. ROBINSON
Director, Office of Compliance and Enforcement	BERNARD GAILLARD
Associate Director	THOMAS T. VINING
Deputy Director, Section of Operations, Insurance, and Tariffs	DIXIE HORTON
Deputy Director, Section of Investigations and Enforcement	CHARLES E. WAGNER
Director, Office of Economic and Environmental Analysis	MILAN P. YAGER
Associate Director	LELAND GARDNER
Deputy Director, Section of Costing and Financial Information	WARD L. GINN
Deputy Director, Section of Research and Analysis	THOMAS A. SCHMITZ
Deputy Director, Section of Environmental Analysis	ELAINE K. KAISER
Director, Office of Human Relations	ALEXANDER W. DOBBINS
Director, Office of Proceedings	DAVID M. KONSCHNIK
Assistant to the Director, Section of Administration	JULIA M. FARR
Deputy Director, Section of Legal Counsel I	JOSEPH H. DETTMAR
Deputy Director, Section of Legal Counsel II	BERYL GORDON
Director, Office of Congressional and Press Services	RICHARD S. FITZSIMMONS
Director, Office of Public Assistance	DAN G. KING
General Counsel	HENRI F. RUSH
Deputy General Counsel	ELLEN D. HANSON
Inspector General	JAMES J. MCKAY
Secretary	VERNON A. WILLIAMS
Assistant Secretary	ANNE K. QUINLAN
Chief, Section of Records	EDWARD C. FERNANDEZ

Chief, Section of Licensing   (VACANCY)
Chief, Section of Publications   ELLEN R. KEYS

[For the Interstate Commerce Commission statement of organization, see the *Code of Federal Regulations,* Title 49, Part 1011]

The Interstate Commerce Commission regulates interstate surface transportation, including trains, trucks, buses, water carriers, household goods transporters, freight forwarders, transportation brokers, and pipelines that are not regulated by the Federal Energy Regulatory Commission. The regulatory laws vary depending on the type of transportation; however, they generally involve certification of carriers seeking to provide transportation for the public and regulation of their rates, adequacy of service, and carrier consolidations. The Commission assures that the public receives shipping rates and services that are fair and reasonable.

The Interstate Commerce Commission was created as an independent regulatory agency by act of February 4, 1887 (49 U.S.C. 10301 *et seq.*), now known as the Interstate Commerce Act.

The Commission's responsibilities include regulation of carriers engaged in transportation in interstate commerce and in foreign commerce to the extent that it takes place within the United States. Surface transportation under the Commission's jurisdiction includes railroads, trucking companies, bus lines, household goods transporters, freight forwarders, water carriers, transportation brokers, and pipelines that are not regulated by the Federal Energy Regulatory Commission.

The Commission's authority has been strengthened and its jurisdiction broadened by subsequent legislation, such as the Hepburn Act, the Panama Canal Act, the Motor Carrier Act of 1935, and the Transportation Acts of 1920, 1940, and 1958.

However, in more recent legislation, beginning with the Railroad Revitalization and Regulatory Reform Act of 1976 (45 U.S.C. 801), the Commission's statutory mandate has been altered to provide for less regulation over carrier rates and practices. This fundamental shift in national transportation policy has proceeded in the Motor Carrier Act of 1980, the Staggers Rail Act of 1980, the Household Goods Transportation Act of 1980, the Bus Regulatory Reform Act of 1982, the Surface Freight Forwarder Deregulation Act of 1986, the Negotiated Rates Act of 1993, and the Trucking Industry Regulatory Reform Act of 1994. These measures provided for a sharply reduced Federal role in regulating the trucking, railroad, and bus industries.

The Chairman is designated by the President from among the five Commissioners. The Commissioners elect their own Vice Chairman annually and may delegate certain duties and functions to individual Commissioners or to boards consisting of not less than three eligible employees.

Field offices are maintained in various cities to monitor the utilization of railroad freight cars in order to avoid severe shortages, investigate violations of the Interstate Commerce Act and related laws, and provide assistance to the public in its use of regulated carriers that provide transportation by railroad, highway, and waterway.

Activities

In broad terms and within prescribed legal limits, Commission regulations encompass transportation economics and service.

In the transportation economics area, the Commission settles controversies over rates and charges among regulated carriers, shippers, receivers of freight, passengers, and others. It rules upon applications for mergers, consolidations, and acquisitions of control. It prescribes accounting rules and awards reparations and administers laws relating to railroad bankruptcy. It acts to prevent unlawful discrimination, destructive competition,

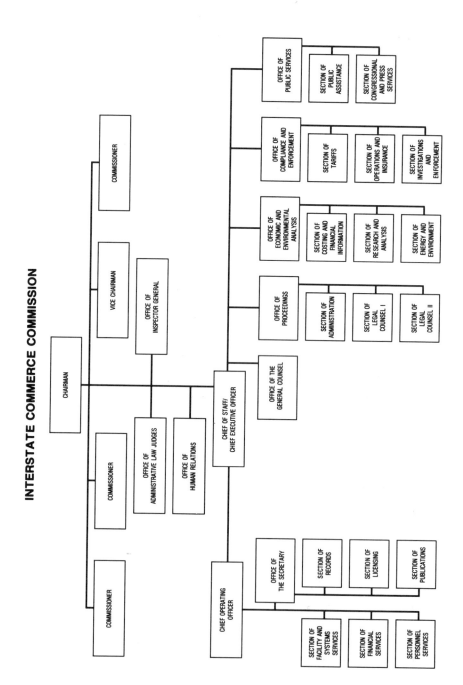

INTERSTATE COMMERCE COMMISSION

and rebating. It also has jurisdiction over the use, control, supply, movement, distribution, exchange, interchange, and return of railroad equipment. Under certain limited conditions, the Commission is authorized to direct the handling and movement of traffic over a railroad and its distribution over other lines of railroads.

In the transportation service area, the Commission grants the right to operate railroads, trucking companies, bus lines, household goods transporters, freight forwarders, water carriers, and transportation brokers. It also approves applications to construct and abandon railroad lines.

Although public hearings on matters before the Commission may be held at any point throughout the country, final decisions are made at the Washington, DC, headquarters in all formal proceedings. These cases include rulings upon rate changes, applications to engage in for-hire transport, carrier mergers, adversary proceedings on complaint actions, and punitive measures taken in enforcement matters.

Regional Offices—Interstate Commerce Commission

Headquarters/Address	Director
CENTRAL—Rm. 1304, 219 S. Dearborn St., Chicago, IL 60604	William Redmond, Jr.
EASTERN—Rm. 16400, 3535 Market St., Philadelphia, PA 19104	Richard M. Biter
WESTERN—Suite 500, 211 Main St., San Francisco, CA 94105	John H. Kirkemo

Sources of Information

Consumer Affairs The Commission maintains a staff at each of its regional offices to handle complaints from the public regarding the transportation services provided by carriers.

Among the many consumer-oriented services are a series of advisory bulletins alerting the public and prospective transportation users to the existence of certain transportation problems. There is also a regulation requiring household goods carriers to furnish an information bulletin to each prospective customer. These public advisories may be obtained

from the Office of Compliance and Enforcement, Interstate Commerce Commission, Washington, DC 20423. Phone, 202–927–5500.

Contracts and Procurement Inquiries regarding the Commission's procurement and contracting activities should be addressed to the Chief Operating Officer, Interstate Commerce Commission, Washington, DC 20423. Phone, 202–927–5370.

Employment Applications for employment may be sent to the Chief, Section of Personnel Services, Interstate Commerce Commission, Washington, DC 20423. Phone, 202–927–7288.

Publications A complete list of publications, including explanatory material on the operation and activities of the Interstate Commerce Commission and on special consumer-related fields, such as household goods movements and small shipments, is available. It may be obtained from the Office of Public Services, Room 3130, Interstate Commerce Commission, Washington, DC 20423. Phone, 202–927–5350.

Reading Rooms The library and several rooms at ICC Headquarters are available for records inspection and copying. Requests for access to public records should be made at the Office of the Secretary, Room 2215, ICC Building; or write to the Secretary, Interstate Commerce Commission, Washington, DC 20423. Phone, 202–927–7428.

Small Business Activities The Commission maintains an Office of Public Services to help the small business owner or transportation firm in such matters as how to file protests on rates, how to file for new operating authority or extensions, or how to obtain adequate service where there is none. Inquiries should be addressed to the Office of Public Services, Room 3119, Interstate Commerce Commission, Washington, DC 20423. Phone, 202–927–7597.

Speakers Requests for speakers to discuss subjects relating to the Commission's organization, operations, procedures, and regulations should be directed to the Office of Public Services, Room 3130, Interstate Commerce

Commission, Washington, DC 20423. Phone, 202–927–5350.

For further information, contact the Office of Public Services, Interstate Commerce Commission, Room 3130, Twelfth Street and Constitution Avenue NW., Washington, DC 20423. Phone, 202–927–5350.

MERIT SYSTEMS PROTECTION BOARD
1120 Vermont Avenue NW., Washington, DC 20419
Phone, 202–653–7124

Chairman	BENJAMIN L. ERDREICH
Chief Counsel to the Chairman	STEVEN L. KATZ
Counsel to the Chairman	WILLIAM B. WILEY
Legal Specialist to the Chairman	DENISE L. MILLER
Executive Assistant to the Chairman	ANITA L. BOLES
Vice Chairman	(VACANCY)
Legal Counsel	(VACANCY)
Special Advisor	(VACANCY)
Member	ANTONIO C. AMADOR
Chief Counsel	MARK KELLEHER
Executive Assistant	PEDRO VARGAS
Counsel	ALAN FORST
Office of the Chairman:	
Chief Administrative Law Judge, Office of Regional Operations	PAUL G. STREB
Director, Office of Appeals Counsel	STEPHEN E. ALPERN
Director, Planning and Resources Management Services	DARRELL L. NETHERTON
Director, Financial and Administrative Management	ROBERT W. LAWSHE
Director, Information Resources Management	BARBARA B. WADE
Director, Human Resources Management	MARSHA SCIALDO BOYD
Director, Office of Policy and Evaluation	EVANGELINE W. SWIFT
Clerk of the Board	ROBERT E. TAYLOR
General Counsel	LLEWELLYN M. FISCHER
Deputy General Counsel and Legislative Counsel	MARY L. JENNINGS
Deputy Legislative Counsel	SUSAN L. WILLIAMS
Director, Office of Equal Employment Opportunity	JANICE E. FRITTS

[For the Merit Systems Protection Board statement of organization, see the *Code of Federal Regulations*, Title 5, Part 1200]

The Merit Systems Protection Board protects the integrity of Federal merit systems and the rights of Federal employees working in the systems. In overseeing the personnel practices of the Federal Government, the Board conducts special studies of the merit systems, hears and decides charges of wrongdoing and employee appeals of adverse agency actions, and orders corrective and disciplinary actions when appropriate.

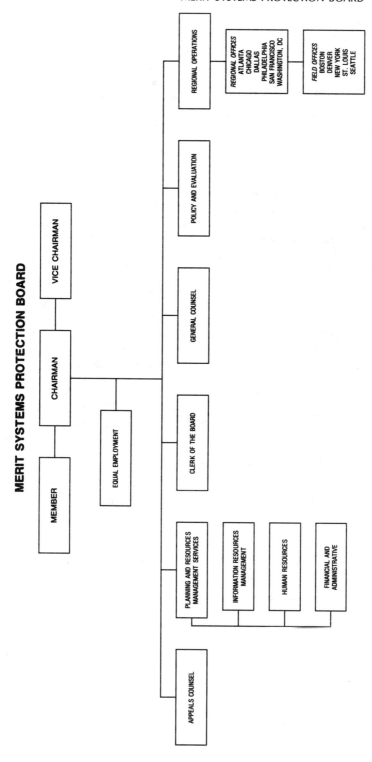

MERIT SYSTEMS PROTECTION BOARD

- MEMBER
- CHAIRMAN
- VICE CHAIRMAN
- EQUAL EMPLOYMENT
- APPEALS COUNSEL
- PLANNING AND RESOURCES MANAGEMENT SERVICES
  - INFORMATION RESOURCES MANAGEMENT
  - HUMAN RESOURCES
  - FINANCIAL AND ADMINISTRATIVE
- CLERK OF THE BOARD
- GENERAL COUNSEL
- POLICY AND EVALUATION
- REGIONAL OPERATIONS
  - *REGIONAL OFFICES* ATLANTA CHICAGO DALLAS PHILADELPHIA SAN FRANCISCO WASHINGTON, DC
  - *FIELD OFFICES* BOSTON DENVER NEW YORK ST. LOUIS SEATTLE

The Merit Systems Protection Board is a successor agency to the United States Civil Service Commission, established by act of January 16, 1883 (22 Stat. 403). Reorganization Plan No. 2 of 1978 (5 U.S.C. app.), effective January 1, 1979, pursuant to Executive Order 12107 of December 28, 1978, redesignated part of the Commission as the Merit Systems Protection Board. The Board's duties and authority are specified in 5 U.S.C. 1201–1206.

Activities

The Board has responsibility for hearing and adjudicating appeals by Federal employees of adverse personnel actions, such as removals, suspensions, and demotions. It also resolves cases involving reemployment rights, the denial of periodic step increases in pay, actions against administrative law judges, and charges of prohibited personnel practices, including charges in connection with whistleblowing. The Board has the authority to enforce its decisions and to order corrective and disciplinary actions. An employee or applicant for employment involved in an appealable action that also involves an allegation of discrimination may ask the Equal Employment Opportunity Commission to review a Board decision. Final decisions and orders of the Board can be appealed to the U.S. Court of Appeals for the Federal Circuit.

The Board reviews regulations issued by the Office of Personnel Management and has the authority to require agencies to cease compliance with any regulation that could constitute a prohibited personnel practice. It also conducts special studies of the civil service and other executive branch merit systems and reports to the President and the Congress on whether the Federal work force is being adequately protected against political abuses and prohibited personnel practices.

Regional Offices—Merit Systems Protection Board

Region	Address	Director	Telephone
Atlanta, GA	401 W. Peachtree St. NW., 30308	Thomas J. Lanphear	404–730–2751
Chicago, IL	31st Fl., 230 S. Dearborn St., 60604	Martin W. Baumgaertner	312–353–2923
Dallas, TX	Rm. 6F20, 1100 Commerce St., 75242	Paula A. Latshaw	214–767–0555
Falls Church, VA (Washington Regional Office).	Suite 1109, 5203 Leesburg Pike, 22041	P.J. Winzer	703–756–6250
Philadelphia, PA	Rm. 501, 2d and Chestnut Sts., 19106	Lonnie L. Crawford, Jr.	215–597–9960
San Francisco, CA	Rm. 2800, 525 Market St., 94105	Denis Marachi	415–774–3081

Field Offices—Merit Systems Protection Board

Region	Address	Chief Administrative Judge	Telephone
Boston, MA	Suite 1810, 99 Summer St., 02110	William Carroll	617–424–5700
Denver, CO	Suite 100, 12567 W. Cedar Dr., Lakewood, CO 80228.	Joseph H. Hartman	303–969–5101
New York, NY	Rm. 3137, 26 Federal Plz., 10278	Sean P. Walsh	212–264–9372
Seattle, WA	Rm. 1840, 915 2d Ave., 98174	Carl Berkenwald	206–220–7975
St. Louis, MO	Suite 410, 911 Washington Ave., 63101	Jack Salyer, *Acting*	314–425–4295

For further information, contact the Merit Systems Protection Board, 1120 Vermont Avenue NW., Washington, DC 20419. Phone, 202–653–7124.

NATIONAL AERONAUTICS AND SPACE ADMINISTRATION

300 E Street SW., Washington, DC 20546
Phone, 202–358–1000

Administrator	DANIEL S. GOLDIN
Deputy Administrator	J.R. DAILEY, *Acting*
Associate Deputy Administrator	J.R. DAILEY
Associate Deputy Administrator (Technical)	MICHAEL I. MOTT
Chief Scientist	FRANCE A. CORDOVA
Chief Engineer	DAVID H. MOBLEY
Chief Information Officer	JOHN C. LYNN
NASA Chief Financial Officer	ARNOLD H. HOLTZ
Comptroller	MALCOLM L. PETERSON
Deputy Chief Financial Officer	KENNETH J. WINTER
Director, Systems and Cost Analysis Division	DAVID J. PINE
Director, Financial Management Division	(VACANCY)
Director, Resource Analysis Division	PATRICIA A. NASH
Chief, Budget Operations Office	BOBBY C. BALES
Associate Administrator for Policy and Plans	ALAN M. LADWIG
Director for Special Projects and Staff Director, NASA Advisory Council	ANNE L. ACCOLA
Associate Administrator for Legislative Affairs	JEFFREY LAWRENCE
Deputy Associate Administrator	LYNN W. HENNINGER
Deputy Associate Administrator (Programs)	MARY D. KERWIN
Deputy Associate Administrator (Policy)	PHYLLIS A. LOVE
Director, Congressional Liaison Division	MARY D. KERWIN, *Acting*
Director, Legislation Division	MICHAEL A. MAGUIRE
Director, Congressional Inquiries Division	HELEN ROTHMAN
Director, Outreach Division	PHYLLIS A. LOVE, *Acting*
Associate Administrator for Life and Microgravity Sciences and Applications	HARRY C. HOLLOWAY
Deputy Associate Administrator (Operations and Space Flight)	ARNAULD E. NICOGOSSIAN
Deputy Associate Administrator (Programs)	(VACANCY)
Director, Policy and Program Management	ARNAULD E. NICOGOSSIAN, *Acting*
Director, Life and Biomedical Sciences and Applications Division	JOAN VERNIKOS
Director, Microgravity Sciences and Applications Division	ROBERT C. RHOME
Director, Flight Systems Division	EDWARD A. REEVES
Director, Aerospace Medicine and Occupational Health Division	EARL W. FERGUSION, *Acting*
Associate Administrator for Mission to Planet Earth	CHARLES F. KENNEL
Deputy Associate Administrator (Programs)	WILLIAM F. TOWNSEND
Deputy Associate Administrator (Management)	MICHAEL B. MANN
Assistant Associate Administrator (External Coordination)	LISA R. SHAFFER, *Acting*
Assistant Associate Administrator (Program Integration)	DOUGLAS R. NORTON

Director, Flight Systems Division	MICHAEL R. LUTHER
Director, Operations, Data and Information Systems Division	DIXON M. BUTLER
Director, Science Division	ROBERT C. HARRISS
Associate Administrator for Space Science	WESLEY T. HUNTRESS
Deputy Associate Administrator	A.V. DIAZ
Assistant Associate Administrator	MARY E. KICZA
Cassini Program Director	EARLE K. HUCKINS
Director, Solar System Exploration Division	JURGEN RAHE
Director, Astrophysics Division	DANIEL W. WEEDMAN
Director, Space Physics Division	GEORGE L. WITHBROE
Associate Administrator for Continual Improvement	LAWRENCE J. ROSS, *Acting*
Director, Internal Total Quality Management Division	JOSEPH MCELWEE
Director, Benchmarking and External Programs Division	JOHN W. GAFF
General Counsel	EDWARD A. FRANKLE
Deputy General Counsel	GEORGE E. REESE
Associate General Counsel (General Law)	ROBERT M. STEPHENS
Associate General Counsel (Contracts)	DAVID P. FORBES
Associate General Counsel (Intellectual Property)	JOHN G. MANNIX
Associate General Counsel (Commercial)	JUNE W. EDWARDS
Associate Administrator for Procurement	DEIDRE A. LEE
Deputy Associate Administrator	THOMAS S. LUEDTKE
Director, Program Operations Division	A. FOSTER FOURNIER
Director, Acquisition Liaison Division	W. LEE EVEY
Director, Analysis Division	ROGER P. WILSON, *Acting*
Director, Contract Management Division	ANNE C. GUENTHER
Director, Headquarters Acquisition Division	LAURA D. LAYTON
Associate Administrator for Small and Disadvantaged Business Utilization	RALPH C. THOMAS III
Associate Administrator for Space Access and Technology	JOHN E. MANSFIELD
Deputy Associate Administrator	GREGORY M. RECK
Director, Flight Integration Office	JACK LEVINE
Director, Launch Vehicles Office	CHARLES R. GUNN
Director, Technology Transfer and Commercial Development Division	ROBERT L. NORWOOD
Director, Spacecraft Systems Division	SAMUEL L. VENNERI
Director, Space Processing Division	EDWARD A. GABRIS
Director, Space Transportation Division	GARY PAYTON
Director, Management Operations Division	MARTIN STEIN
Senior Executive for Advanced Concept Division	IVAN BEKEY
Associate Administrator for Public Affairs	LAURIE BOEDER
Deputy Associate Administrator	GEOFFREY H. VINCENT
Deputy Associate Administrator (New Initiatives)	BRUCE HENDERSON
Director, Program Management Division	WALTER A. MAULL, *Acting*
Director, Media Services Division	JAMES W. MCCULLA

Director, Public Services Division — PAULA CLEGGETT-HALEIM, *Acting*

Director, Television Development Division — THOMAS J. BENTSEN, *Acting*

Associate Administrator for Space Flight — J. WAYNE LITTLES

Deputy Associate Administrator — RICHARD J. WISNIEWSKI

Deputy Associate Administrator (Space Station Program) — WILBUR C. TRAFTON

Deputy Associate Administrator (Space Shuttle) — BRYON D. O'CONNOR

Associate Administrator for Management Systems and Facilities — BENITA A. COOPER

Deputy Associate Administrator — MICHAEL D. CHRISTENSEN

Director, Environmental Management Division — ROBERT E. HAMMOND

Director, Information Resources Management Division — RUSSELL S. RICE

Director, Facilities Engineering Division — WILLIAM W. BRUBAKER

Director, Security, Logistics and Industrial Relations Division — JEFFREY E. SUTTON

Director, Headquarters Operations Division — (VACANCY)

Director, Resources and Management Controls Office — TIMOTHY M. SULLIVAN

Director, Aircraft Management Office — JAMES T. BODDIE, JR.

Associate Administrator for Safety and Mission Assurance — FREDERICK D. GREGORY

Deputy Associate Administrator — MICHAEL A. GREENFIELD

Director, Aerospace Safety Advisory Panel — FRANK L. MANNING

Director, Engineering and Quality Management Division — DANIEL R. MULVILLE

Director, Resources Management Office — DALE E. MOORE

Director, Space Flight Safety and Mission Assurance Division — RICHARD U. PERRY

Director, Payloads and Aeronautics Division — J. CHARLES SAWYER, JR., *Acting*

Director, Safety and Risk Management Division — JAMES D. LLOYD

Director, Software Independent Verification Facility — CHARLES W. MERTZ

Associate Administrator for Aeronautics — ROBERT E. WHITEHEAD, *Acting*

Deputy Associate Administrator — ROBERT E. WHITEHEAD

Deputy Associate Administrator (Management) — RICHARD A. REEVES

Chief Engineer — (VACANCY)

Director, Institutions Division — (VACANCY)

Director, Resources and Management Office — GLENN C. FULLER

Director, Strategy and Policy Office — JAY M. HENN

Director, High Performance Computing and Communications Office — LEE B. HOLCOMB

Director, High Speed Research Division — LOUIS J. WILLIAMS

Director, Subsonic Transportation Division — RAY V. HOOD, *Acting*

Director, High Performance Aircraft and Flight Projects Division — RICHARD S. CHRISTIANSEN, *Acting*

Director, Critical Technologies Division — RICHARD S. CHRISTIANSEN, *Acting*

Associate Administrator for Space Communications — CHARLES T. FORCE

Deputy Associate Administrator	(VACANCY)
Director, Program Integration Division	DAVID W. HARRIS
Director, Administration and Resources Management Division	RONALD R. DAPICE
Director, Communications and Data Systems Division	CHARLES T. FORCE, *Acting*
Director, Ground Networks Division	ROBERT M. HORNSTEIN
Director, Space Network Division	WILSON LUNDY
Associate Administrator for Human Resources and Education	SPENCE M. ARMSTRONG
Director, Education Division	FRANKLIN C. OWENS
Director, Management Systems Division	STANLEY S. KASK, JR.
Director, National Service Center	TYRONE C. TAYLOR
Director, Personnel Division	VICKI A. NOVAK
Director, Training and Development Division	CARSON K. EOYANG
Associate Administrator for Equal Opportunity Programs	YVONNE B. FREEMAN
Deputy Associate Administrator	(VACANCY)
Director, Diversity Policy and Strategic Planning Division	JAMES A. WESTBROOKS
Director, Discrimination Complaints Division	OCEOLA S. HALL
Director, Minority University Research and Education Division	BETTIE L. WHITE
Inspector General	(VACANCY)
Deputy Inspector General	LEWIS D. RINKER
Assistant Inspector General for Auditing	(VACANCY)
Assistant Inspector General for Investigations	(VACANCY)
Assistant Inspector General for Management	(VACANCY)
Associate Administrator for External Relations	JOHN D. SHUMACHER, *Acting*
Deputy Associate Administrator	JOHN D. SHUMACHER
Director, Defense Affairs Division	CONRAD O. FORSYTHE
Director, Management Support Office	SHIRLEY A. PEREZ
Director, International Relations Division	BETH A. MASTERS
Director, Space Flight Division	LYNN F.H. CLINE
Director, Special Studies Division	SYLVIA K. KRAEMER
Director, Mission to Planet Earth Division	LISA R. SHAFFER

NASA Centers

Director, Ames Research Center	KEN K. MUNECHIKA
Director, George C. Marshall Space Flight Center	G. PORTER BRIDWELL
Director, Goddard Space Flight Center	JOHN M. KLINEBERG
Manager, NASA Management Office, Jet Propulsion Laboratory	KURT LINDSTROM
Director, John F. Kennedy Space Center	JAY F. HONEYCUTT
Director, Langley Research Center	PAUL F. HOLLOWAY
Director, Lewis Research Center	DONALD J. CAMPBELL
Director, Lyndon B. Johnson Space Center	CAROLYN HUNTOON

Director, John C. Stennis Space Center

Director, Dryden Flight Research Center

ROY S. ESTESS

KENNETH J. SZALAI

[For the National Aeronautics and Space Administration statement of organization, see the *Code of Federal Regulations,* Title 14, Part 1201]

The National Aeronautics and Space Administration conducts research for the solution of problems of flight within and outside the Earth's atmosphere and develops, constructs, tests, and operates aeronautical and space vehicles. It conducts activities required for the exploration of space with manned and unmanned vehicles and arranges for the most effective utilization of the scientific and engineering resources of the United States with other nations engaged in aeronautical and space activities for peaceful purposes.

The National Aeronautics and Space Administration was established by the National Aeronautics and Space Act of 1958, as amended (42 U.S.C. 2451 *et seq.*).

NASA Headquarters

Planning, coordinating, and controlling Administration programs are vested in Headquarters. Directors of NASA centers are responsible for the execution of agency programs, largely through contracts with research, development, and manufacturing enterprises. A broad range of research and development activities are conducted in NASA Centers by Government-employed scientists, engineers, and technicians to evaluate new concepts and phenomena and to maintain the competence required to manage contracts with private enterprises.

Planning, directing, and managing research and development programs are the responsibility of seven program offices, all of which report to and receive overall guidance and direction from the Administrator. The overall planning and direction of institutional operations at NASA Centers and management of agencywide institutional resources are the responsibility of the appropriate Institutional Associate Administrator under the overall guidance and direction of the Administrator.

Aeronautics The Office of Aeronautics is responsible for conducting programs that pioneer the identification, development, verification, transfer, application, and commercialization of high-payoff aeronautics technologies.

The Office seeks to promote economic growth and security and to enhance U.S. competitiveness through safe, superior, and environmentally compatible U.S. civil and military aircraft, and through a safe, efficient national aviation system. In addition, the Office is responsible for managing the Ames, Dryden Flight, Langley, and Lewis Research Centers.

For further information, call 202–358–2693.

Space Access and Technology The Office of Space Access and Technology pioneers innovative space technologies and proactively transfers those technologies to aerospace and nonaerospace applications. This Office is responsible for planning and assessing technology development requirements and providing management and executive leadership for activities across the Agency which satisfy these requirements; and for developing partnerships with industry, academia, and other Government agencies.

For further information, call 202–358–4566.

Life and Microgravity Sciences and Applications The Office of Life and Microgravity Sciences and Applications is responsible for NASA's programs concerned with life and microgravity sciences and their possible commercial applications, life support research and technologies, space human factors, occupational health issues, and aerospace medicine. The Office provides planning, development, integration, and operations support for science payloads on the space shuttle, free flyers, space station, and other advanced carriers. The

NATIONAL AERONAUTICS AND SPACE ADMINISTRATION

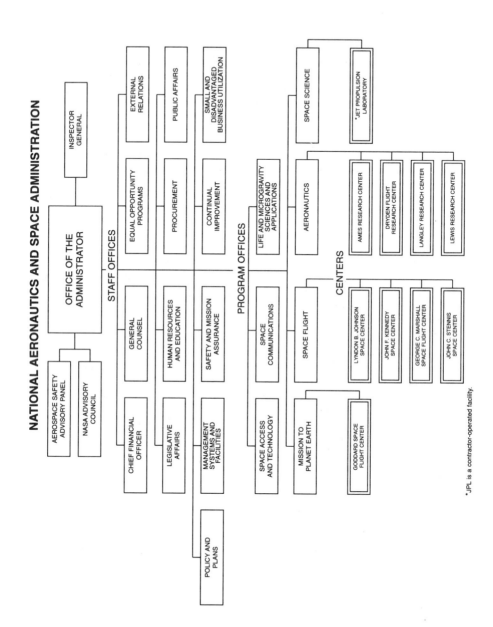

*JPL is a contractor-operated facility.

Office also establishes all requirements and standards for design, development, and operation of human space flight systems and facilities.

For further information, call 202–358–2530.

Mission to Planet Earth The Office of Mission to Planet Earth conducts NASA's programs that study global climate change and integrated functioning of the Earth as a system. This includes developing and managing remote sensing satellites and instruments, aircraft and ground measurements and research, as well as data and information systems needed to support the objectives of the U.S. Global Change Research Program. The Office also has institutional management responsibility for the Goddard Space Flight Center and maintains contact with the National Academy of Sciences and other science advisory and coordinating boards and committees.

For further information, call 202–358–1770.

Space Science The Office of Space Science is responsible for conducting programs and research designed to understand the origin, evolution, and structure of the universe and the solar system. The Office also manages NASA's activities at the Jet Propulsion Laboratory and maintains contacts with the Space Studies Board of the National Academy of Sciences and with other science advisory boards and committees.

For further information, call 202–358–1409.

Space Flight The Office of Space Flight (OSF) is NASA's principal organization for space flight operations and utilization involving human space flight. It consists of the following programmatic missions: flight to and from space for people and cargo, operating habitable space facilities, and managing the utilization of these facilities in support of NASA's space missions, such as space missions from and to Earth. OSF operates the space shuttle and the *Spacelab* and is currently developing the U.S. segment of the international space station. The Office is also responsible for institutional management of the Kennedy Space

Center, Marshall Space Flight Center, Johnson Space Flight Center, and the Stennis Space Center.

In further executing its responsibilities, the Office plans, directs, and executes the development, acquisition, testing, and operation of all elements of the Space Shuttle Program; plans, directs, and manages execution of prelaunch, launch, flight landing, post-flight operations, and payload assignments; maintains and upgrades the design of ground and flight systems throughout the operational period; procures recurring system hardware; manages *Spacelab* development, procurement, and operations; develops and implements necessary policy with other government and commercial users of the space shuttle; and coordinates all associated research. OSF is working with the Russian Space Agency to plan and execute a series of joint missions that will involve flying cosmonauts aboard the space shuttle and astronauts aboard the *Mir* space station. In 1995, a U.S. astronaut was launched aboard a Russian rocket to *Mir* for a 90-day stay aboard the space station, followed by a shuttle docking mission to *Mir* to exchange crew members. This mission will be the first of up to seven joint missions, precursors to assembly and utilization of the international space station.

NASA is leading an international effort to build and deploy a permanently manned space station into Earth's orbit. Elements of the space station will be provided by Canada, Japan, Italy, Russia, and nine European nations represented by the European Space Agency. The space station will be a permanent outpost in space where humans will live and work productively for extended periods of time. It will provide an advanced research laboratory to explore space and employ its resources, as well as the opportunity to learn to build, operate, and maintain systems in space. U.S. elements of the space station will be launched aboard the space shuttle and assembled in orbit. The first flight is scheduled for 1997.

For further information, call 202–358–2015.

Space Communications   The Office of Space Communications is responsible for meeting requirements critical to NASA's aeronautics and space flight missions. They include spacecraft operations and control centers, ground and space communications, data acquisition and processing, flight dynamics and trajectory analyses, spacecraft tracking, and applied research and development of new technology. The Space Network with its constellation of Tracking and Data Relay Satellites, Deep Space Network, Spaceflight Tracking and Data Network, and various other facilities currently provide for the requirements for NASA's space missions. A global communications system links tracking sites, control centers, and data processing facilities that provide real-time data processing for mission control, orbit and attitude determination, and routine processing of telemetry data for space missions.

For further information, call 202–358–4758.

NASA Centers

Ames Research Center   The Center, located at Moffett Field, CA, provides leadership for NASA in aeronautics and astronautics research and technology development. The Center fulfills this mission through the development and operation of unique national facilities and the conduct and management of leading edge research and technology programs. These activities are vital to the achievement of the Nation's aeronautics and space goals, and to its security and economic prosperity.

Dryden Flight Research Center   The Center, which is located in Edwards, CA, conducts safe, timely aerospace flight research and aircraft operations in support of agency and national needs. It assures preeminent flight research capability through effective management and maintenance of unique national expertise and facilities, and provides operational landing support for the national space transportation system.

Goddard Space Flight Center   The Center, which is located in Greenbelt, MD, conducts Earth-orbiting spacecraft and experiment development and flight operations. It develops and operates tracking and data acquisition systems and conducts supporting mission operations. It also develops and operates Spacelab payloads; space physics research programs; Earth science and applications programs; life science programs; information systems technology; sounding rockets and sounding rocket payloads; launch vehicles; balloons and balloon experiments; planetary science experiments; and sensors for environmental monitoring and ocean dynamics.

Jet Propulsion Laboratory   The Laboratory, which is operated under contract by the California Institute of Technology in Pasadena, CA, develops spacecraft and space sensors and conducts mission operations and ground-based research in support of solar system exploration, Earth science and applications, Earth and ocean dynamics, space physics and astronomy, and life science and information systems technology. The Laboratory also is responsible for the operation of the Deep Space Network in support of NASA projects.

Lyndon B. Johnson Space Center   The Center, which is located in Houston, TX, is the host center for the Space Station Program Office, and manages development and operation of the space shuttle, a manned space transportation system developed for the United States by NASA. The shuttle is designed to reduce the cost of using space for commercial, scientific, and defense needs. This Center is responsible for the development, production, delivery, and flight operation of the orbiter vehicle, that portion of the space shuttle that is designed to take crew and experiments into space, place satellites in orbit, retrieve ailing satellites, etc. The shuttle crew (up to seven people) includes pilots, mission specialists, and payload specialists. Crew personnel (other than payload specialists) are recruited, selected, and trained by the Center. It is also responsible for design, development, and testing of spaceflight payloads and associated systems for manned flight; for planning and conducting manned spaceflight missions; and for directing medical, engineering, and scientific experiments that are helping man understand and improve the environment.

John F. Kennedy Space Center   The Center in Florida designs, constructs, operates, and maintains space vehicle facilities and ground support equipment for launch and recovery operations. The Center is also responsible for prelaunch operations, launch operations, and payload processing for the space shuttle and expendable launch vehicle programs, and landing operations for the space shuttle orbiter; also recovery and refurbishment of the reusable solid rocket booster.

Langley Research Center   The Center, located in Hampton, VA, performs research in long-haul aircraft technology; general aviation commuter aircraft technology; military aircraft and missile (systems) technology; National Aero-Space Plane; fundamental aerodynamics; computational fluid dynamics; propulsion/airframe integration; unsteady aerodynamics and aeroelasticity; hypersonic propulsion; aerospace acoustics; aerospace vehicle structures and materials; computational structural mechanics; space structures and dynamics; controls/structures interaction; aeroservoelasticity; interdisciplinary research; aerothermodynamics; aircraft flight management and operating procedures; advanced displays; computer science; electromagnetics; automation and robotics; reliable, fault-tolerant systems and software; aircraft flight control systems; advanced space vehicle configurations; advanced space station development; technology experiments in space; remote sensor and data acquisition and communication technology; space electronics and control systems; planetary entry technology; nondestructive evaluation and measurements technology; atmospheric sciences; Earth radiation budget; atmospheric dynamics; space power conversion and transmission;

space environmental effects; and systems analysis of advanced aerospace vehicles.

Lewis Research Center   The Center, located in Cleveland, OH, is a center of excellence in aeronautics, space systems, and microgravity science and technology. The Center also conducts research in critical disciplines of materials, structures, internal fluid mechanics instrumentation, and controls and electronics. All of these efforts are supported by unique research and development facilities.

George C. Marshall Space Flight Center   The Center, which is located in Huntsville, AL, manages, develops, and tests the external tank, solid rocket booster, and main engines, which are major portions of the space shuttle project; oversees the development of the *Spacelab*; and conducts research in structural systems, materials science engineering, electronics, guidance, navigation, and control.

John C. Stennis Space Center   The Center, which is located in Bay St. Louis, MS, plans and manages research and development activities in the field of space and terrestrial applications; space flight; and research in oceanography, meteorology, and environmental sciences.

Sources of Information

Contracts and Small Business Activities   Inquiries regarding contracting for small business opportunities with the Administration should be directed to the Associate Administrator for Small and Disadvantaged Business Utilization, NASA Headquarters, 300 E Street SW., Washington, DC 20546. Phone, 202–358–2088.

Employment   Direct all inquiries to the Personnel Director of the nearest NASA Center or, for the Washington, DC, metropolitan area, to the Chief, Headquarters Personnel Branch, NASA Headquarters, Washington, DC 20546. Phone, 202–358–1562.

Publications, Speakers, Films, and Exhibit Services   Several publications concerning these services can be obtained by contacting the Public Affairs Officer of the nearest NASA Center.

Publications include *NASA Directory of Services for the Public, NASA Film List,* and *NASA Educational Publications List.* The Headquarters telephone directory and certain publications and picture sets are available for sale from the Superintendent of Documents, Government Printing Office, Washington, DC 20402. Telephone directories for NASA Centers are available only from the Centers. Publications and documents not available for sale from the

Superintendent of Documents or the National Technical Information Service (Springfield, VA 22151) may be obtained from the NASA Center's Information Center in accordance with the Administration regulation concerning freedom of information (14 CFR, part 1206).

Reading Room   NASA Headquarters Information Center, Room 1H23, 300 E Street SW., Washington, DC 20546. Phone, 202–358–1000.

For further information, contact the Headquarters Information Center, National Aeronautics and Space Administration, Washington, DC 20546. Phone, 202–358–1000.

NATIONAL ARCHIVES AND RECORDS ADMINISTRATION

Seventh Street and Pennsylvania Avenue NW., Washington, DC 20408
Phone, 202–501–5400

Archivist of the United States	JOHN W. CARLIN
Deputy Archivist of the United States	RALPH C. BLEDSOE, *Acting*
Executive Director, National Historical Publications and Records Commission	GERALD W. GEORGE
Assistant Archivist for Federal Records Centers	DAVID F. PETERSON
Assistant Archivist for Public Programs	LINDA N. BROWN
Director of the Federal Register	RICHARD L. CLAYPOOLE
Assistant Archivist for Special and Regional Archives	RAYMOND A. MOSLEY
Assistant Archivist for Presidential Libraries	RICHARD A. JACOBS, *Acting*
Assistant Archivist for Records Administration	JAMES W. MOORE
Assistant Archivist for the National Archives	MICHAEL J. KURTZ
Assistant Archivist for Policy and Information Resources Management Services	RALPH C. BLEDSOE
Assistant Archivist for Administrative Services	ADRIENNE C. THOMAS
Inspector General	ROBERT C. TAYLOR, *Acting*

[For the National Archives and Records Administration statement of organization, see the *Federal Register* of June 25, 1985, 50 FR 26278]

The National Archives and Records Administration establishes policies and procedures for managing U.S. Government records. The National Archives assists Federal agencies in documenting their activities, administering records management programs, scheduling records, and retiring noncurrent records to Federal Records Centers. The agency accessions, arranges, describes, preserves, and makes available to the public the historically valuable records of the three branches of Government; manages the Presidential Libraries system; assists the National Historical Publications and Records Commission in its grant program for State and local records and edited publications of the papers of prominent Americans; and publishes the laws, regulations, and Presidential and other public documents.

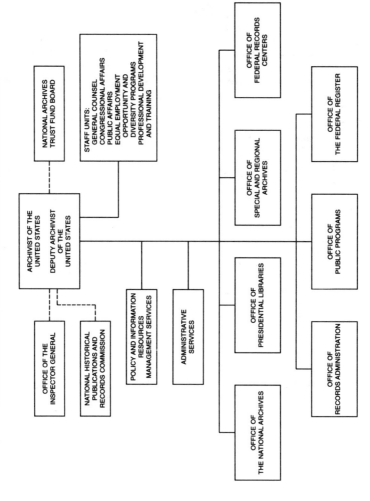

NATIONAL ARCHIVES AND RECORDS ADMINISTRATION

The National Archives and Records Administration was established by act of October 19, 1984 (44 U.S.C. 2101 et seq.), effective April 1, 1985, as an independent agency in the executive branch of the Government. It is the successor agency to the National Archives Establishment, which was created by act of June 19, 1934 (48 Stat. 1122), and subsequently incorporated into the General Services Administration as the National Archives and Records Service by section 104 of the Federal Property and Administrative Services Act of 1949 (63 Stat. 381), approved June 30, 1949.

Activities

Archival Program   The National Archives maintains the historically valuable records of the U.S. Government dating from the Revolutionary War era to the recent past; arranges and preserves records and prepares finding aids to facilitate their use; makes records available for use in research rooms in all of its facilities; answers written and oral requests for information contained in its holdings; and, for a fee, provides copies of records. In addition, many important records are available on microfilm. Most of the historically valuable records in the agency's custody are maintained in the Washington, DC, area. Records that are primarily of regional or local interest are, however, maintained in 13 regional archives, the locations of which are listed below.

Regional Archives—National Archives and Records Administration

City/Address	Director	Telephone
Anchorage, AK (654 W. 3d Ave., 99501)	Thomas C. Wiltsey	907–271–2441
New York, NY (201 Varick St., 10014)	Robert Morris	212–337–1300
Chicago, IL (7358 S. Pulaski Rd., 60629)	Peter W. Bunce	312–581–7816
Denver, CO (Denver Federal Ctr., 80225)	Joel Barker	303–236–0817
East Point, GA (1557 St. Joseph Ave., 30344)	Gayle P. Peters	404–763–7477
Fort Worth, TX (501 W. Felix St., 76115)	Kent Carter	817–334–5525
Kansas City, MO (2312 E. Bannister Rd., 64131)	R. Reed Whitaker	816–926–6272
Laguna Niguel, CA (24000 Avila Rd., 92677)	Diane Nixon	714–643–4241
Philadelphia, PA (9th and Market Sts., 19107)	Robert J. Plowman	215–597–3000
Pittsfield, MA (100 Dan Fox Dr., 01201)	Jean Nudd	413–445–6885
San Bruno, CA (1000 Commodore Dr., 94066)	Waverly Lowell	415–876–9018
Seattle, WA (6125 Sand Point Way NE., 98115)	Phillip E. Lothyan	206–526–6507
Waltham, MA (380 Trapelo Rd., 02154)	James K. Owens	617–647–8100

For further information concerning records in the National Archives, contact the Reference Services Branch. Phone, 202–501–5400.

Presidential Libraries   Through the Presidential libraries, which are located at sites selected by the Presidents and built with private funds, the agency preserves and makes available the records and personal papers of a particular President's administration. In addition to providing reference services on Presidential documents, each library prepares documentary and descriptive publications and operates a museum to exhibit documents, historic objects, and other memorabilia of interest to the public.

The records of each President since Herbert Hoover are administered by the agency. Once considered personal papers, all Presidential records created on or after January 20, 1981, are declared by law to be owned and controlled by the United States and are required to be transferred to the National Archives at the end of the administration, pursuant to the Presidential Records Act of 1978 (44 U.S.C. 2201 et seq.).

Presidential Libraries—National Archives and Records Administration

Library	Address	Director	Telephone
Herbert Hoover Library	West Branch, IA 52358	Timothy G. Walch, Acting .	319–643–5301

Presidential Libraries—National Archives and Records Administration—Continued

Library	Address	Director	Telephone
Franklin D. Roosevelt Library	Hyde Park, NY 12538	Verne W. Newton	914–229–8114
Harry S. Truman Library	Independence, MO 64050	Larry J. Hackman	816–833–1400
Dwight D. Eisenhower Library	Abilene, KS 67410	Daniel D. Holt	913–263–4751
John F. Kennedy Library	Boston, MA 02125	Bradley Gerratt	617–929–4545
Lyndon B. Johnson Library	Austin, TX 78705	Harry J. Middleton	512–482–5137
Gerald R. Ford Library	Ann Arbor, MI 48109	Frank H. Mackaman	313–741–2218
Gerald R. Ford Museum	Grand Rapids, MI 49504	James R. Kratsas	616–451–9263
Nixon Presidential Materials Staff ...	Washington, DC 20408	William H. Cunliffe, *Acting*	301–713–6950
Jimmy Carter Library	Atlanta, GA 30307	Donald B. Schewe	404–331–3942
Ronald Reagan Library	Simi Valley, CA 93065	Richard N. Smith	805–522–8444
Bush Presidential Materials Project	College Station, TX 77840	David Alsobrook, *Acting* ..	409–260–9554

For further information, contact the Office of Presidential Libraries. Phone, 202–501–5700.

Federal Records Centers   Federal agencies retire certain noncurrent records to low-cost storage in Federal records centers in accordance with established disposition schedules. The centers provide reference services, including loan or return of records to the agency of origin; prepare authenticated reproductions of documents; and furnish information from records. The Federal records centers dispose of records of transitory value and transfer to the Office of the National Archives those that have enduring value. The centers also offer technical assistance workshops and advice on file maintenance, storage, records disposition practices, and vital records. Reimbursable microfilming services are available from most centers.

Federal Records Centers—National Archives and Records Administration

City/Address	Director	Telephone
Bayonne, NJ (Bldg. 22, Military Ocean Terminal, 07002)	Karen L. Lucas, *Acting*	201–823–7161
Chicago, IL (7358 S. Pulaski Rd., 60629)	David E. Kuehl	312–353–0164
Dayton, OH (3150 Springboro Rd., 45439)	Denis Pauskauskas	513–225–2878
Denver, CO (Bldg. 48, Denver Federal Ctr., 80225)	Robert Svenningsen	303–236–0801
East Point, GA (1557 St. Joseph Ave., 30344)	William R. Craig, *Acting* ..	404–763–7438
Fort Worth, TX (Bldg. 1, Fort Worth Federal Ctr., 76115)	James W. Mouat	817–334–5515
Kansas City, MO (2312 E. Bannister Rd., 64131)	John J. Allshouse	816–926–7271
Laguna Niguel, CA (24000 Avila Rd., 92677)	Sharon L. Roadway	714–643–4220
Philadelphia, PA (14700 Townsend Rd., 19151)	David S. Weber	215–951–5588
Pittsfield, MA (100 Dan Fox Dr., 01201)	Gregory L. Schildmeyer ..	413–445–6885
San Bruno, CA (1000 Commodore Dr., 94066)	David D. Drake	415–876–9015
Seattle, WA (6125 Sand Point Way NE., 98115)	Steven M. Edwards	206–526–6503
St. Louis, MO (National Personnel Records Ctr., 9700 Page Ave., 63132)	David L. Petree	314–538–4201
Suitland, MD (Washington National Records Ctr., 4205 Suitland Rd., 20409) ...	Ferris Stovel	301–457–7000
Waltham, MA (380 Trapelo Rd., 02154)	Diane Leblanc	617–457–7000

For further information, contact the Office of Federal Records Centers. Phone, 301–713–7200.

Records Administration   The agency develops standards and guidelines for the management and disposition of recorded information to ensure proper documentation of the organization, policies, and activities of the Government. It appraises Federal records and approves records disposition schedules. It also monitors archival records not in the agency's custody, inspects agency records and records management practices, develops records management training programs, and provides guidance and assistance with respect to proper records management.

For further information, contact the Office of Records Administration. Phone, 301–713–7100.

Laws, Regulations, and Presidential Documents   The agency prepares and publishes a wide variety of public documents. Upon issuance, acts of Congress are published immediately in slip law (pamphlet) form and then cumulated and published for each session of Congress in the *United States Statutes at Large*.

Each Federal workday, the *Federal Register* publishes current Presidential proclamations and Executive orders, Federal agency regulations having general applicability and legal effect, proposed agency rules, and documents that are required by statute to be published. All Federal regulations in force are published annually in codified form in the *Code of Federal Regulations.*

Presidential speeches, news conferences, messages, and other materials made public by the White House are published each week in the *Weekly Compilation of Presidential Documents* and annually in the *Public Papers of the Presidents.*

The *Codification of Presidential Proclamations and Executive Orders* furnishes, in one comprehensive source, proclamations and Executive orders having general applicability and continuing legal effect, with effective amendments incorporated into their texts. The most current volume covers the period from April 13, 1945, to January 20, 1989.

The *United States Government Manual,* published annually, serves as the official handbook of the Federal Government, providing extensive information on agencies of the legislative, judicial, and executive branches.

For further information, contact the Office of the Federal Register. Phone, 202–523–4534; TDD, 202–523–5229; Fax, 202–523–6866.

Public Programs   The agency has an extensive exhibits program. The Declaration of Independence, Constitution, and Bill of Rights are on permanent display in the National Archives Building. The 1297 Magna Carta, on indefinite loan, is also on display. The agency exhibits numerous other documents on a variety of historical themes in its other facilities.

For further information, contact the Office of Public Programs. Phone, 202–501–5200.

Other Activities

National Archives Trust Fund Board
The National Archives Trust Fund Board receives monies from the sale of reproductions of historic documents, audiovisual materials, and publications about the records, as well as gifts. The Board invests these funds and uses income to support archival functions such as the preparation of publications that make information about historic records more widely available. Members of the Board are the Archivist of the United States, the Secretary of the Treasury, and the Chairman of the National Endowment for the Humanities.

For further information, contact the Secretary, National Archives Trust Fund Board. Phone, 301–713–6405.

National Historical Publications and Records Commission   The agency supports the initiatives of this statutory commission in making plans, estimates, and recommendations for historical works and in cooperating with and encouraging various non-Federal agencies and institutions in gathering and publishing papers and other documents important for the study of American history. The Commission awards grants to promote a variety of historically oriented projects, such as archival programs, documentary publications projects, and archival and editorial education.

The Commission provides grant money for printed and microfilm publications of the papers of important American diplomats, politicians, reformers, scientists, and labor figures, as well as corporate and organizational records. A subsidy program provides grants to nonprofit presses to help support publication costs of sponsored editions.

The Commission makes grants to State and local governments, historical societies, archives, libraries, and associations for the preservation, arrangement, and description of historical records.

Educational programs sponsored by the Commission include an institute to train scholars in documentary editing, and fellowships in the fields of documentary editing and archival administration.

For further information, contact the National Historical Publications and Records Commission. Phone, 202–501–5600.

Sources of Information

Calendar of Events The National Archives Calendar of Events is published monthly. To be added to the mailing list, call 202–501–5525. For a recorded announcement of events at the National Archives Building and the National Archives at College Park, call 202–501–5000. For the hearing impaired, call 202–501–5450 for the announcement of events at the Archives Building and 301–713–7343 for events at the College Park building.

Speakers and Presentations Community and school outreach programs are presented upon request. Interested groups in the Washington, DC, area should call 202–501–5205. Groups outside the Washington, DC, area should contact the regional archive or Presidential library in their areas (*See* listings on pages 614 and 615, respectively).

Education specialists present workshops at regional and national conferences of humanities professionals and as in-service training for teachers. For further information, contact the Education Branch by calling 202–501–6729.

Publications Agency publications, including facsimiles of certain documents, finding aids to the records, microfilm copies of many important records, and *Prologue,* a scholarly journal published quarterly, are available from the Publications Distribution Staff (NECD), National Archives, Room G–9, Washington, DC 20408. Phone, 1–800–234–8861 (toll free) or 202–501–5235. Fax, 202–501–7170. Records management publications are available from the Office of Records Administration by calling 301–713–7100.

Teaching Materials Education specialists have developed low-cost documentary teaching materials for classroom use. Each kit deals with an historical event or theme and includes document facsimiles and teaching aids. For further information, contact the

Education Branch by calling 202–501–6729.

Tours Individuals or groups may request general or specialty tours behind the scenes at the National Archives Building. The tours are given by reservation only, and individuals are requested to make reservations at least 3 weeks in advance. The tours are given at 10:15 a.m. or 1:15 p.m., Monday through Friday. Call 202–501–5205 between 9 a.m. and 4 p.m., Monday through Friday, to make reservations. Tours of the National Archives at College Park, MD, may be arranged by calling the number above between 9 a.m. and 4 p.m., Monday through Friday.

Audiovisual Sales and Rentals The National Audiovisual Center, which distributes federally produced motion pictures, filmstrips, slide sets, and video and audio tapes, was transferred from the National Archives and Records Administration to the National Technical Information Service, Department of Commerce. For information about available products and services, call 1–800–553–NTIS (toll free).

Museum Shops Publications, document facsimiles, and souvenirs are available for sale in the National Archives Building, at each Presidential library, and at some regional archives.

Educational Opportunities Several courses are offered on archival and records management principles and on using the resources of the institution.

"Going to the Source: An Introduction to Research in Archives," is a 4-day, annual course on doing research in primary sources. The course provides experience with documents, microfilm, finding aids, and research methodology to researchers from such varied positions as public policy analysts, museum curators, and historical novelists. For further information, contact the Education Branch by calling 202–501–6729.

"Introduction to Genealogy" is a half-day course offered several times a year to introduce genealogists to the records in the National Archives that can further their research in family history. There are also several half-day workshops each month that focus on specific aspects of genealogical research. For further information, contact the Education Branch by calling 202–501–6172.

The secondary school program annually offers an 8-day workshop, "Primarily Teaching," to introduce educators to the holdings of the National Archives and provide strategies for teaching with primary sources. For further information, contact the Education Branch by calling 202–501–6729.

The "Modern Archives Institute" is a 2-week course for archivists that introduces students to the principles and techniques of archival work. It is offered twice a year, in February and June, for a fee. Students are advised to register 3 months in advance. Inquiries should be sent to the Professional Development and Training Staff, National Archives and Records Administration, 8601 Adelphi Road, Room 3110, College Park, MD 20740–6001. Phone 301–713–7390.

A 2-day files improvement workshop and a 3-day records disposition workshop are designed for any Federal Government employee with responsibility for the records creation, filing, and disposition process. For further information, contact the Agency Services Division. Phone, 301–713–7100. Similar training is offered by the Federal records centers for agency field employees. For further information, contact any Federal records center listed on page 615.

A half-day program is offered by the Office of the Federal Register to provide public instruction on how to research Federal regulations that directly affect them. The program, "The Federal Register: What It Is And How To Use It," is conducted in Washington, DC, and in major regional cities. For further information, call 202–523–4534.

The National Historical Publications and Records Commission Institute for the Editing of Historical Documents is held for 2 weeks each summer at the University of Wisconsin, Madison. Admission is competitive and applicants should hold a masters degree in American history or American studies or have equivalent training. Tuition is $350. The Commission also offers three fellowships annually in advanced documentary editing and two fellowships in mid-level archival administration. The editorial fellows work with document publication projects supported or endorsed by the Commission. The archival fellows work at a historical records repository in such areas as appraisal, collection development, personnel administration, budget preparation, and external affairs. The fellows receive stipends and fringe benefits for a 9- to 10-month period. The fellowships are jointly funded by the Commission and the Andrew W. Mellon Foundation. For further information, contact the National Historical Publications and Records Commission, National Archives and Records Administration, Washington, DC 20408. Phone, 202–501–5600.

Volunteer Service Opportunities   A wide variety of opportunities are available for volunteers. At the National Archives Building and the National Archives at College Park, MD, volunteers conduct tours, provide information in the Exhibition Hall, work with staff archivists in processing historic documents, and serve as genealogical aides in the genealogical orientation room. For further information, call 202–501–5205. Similar opportunities exist in the Presidential libraries and at some of the regional archives.

Congressional and Public Affairs Congressional Affairs maintains contact with, and responds to, inquiries from congressional offices. For congressional inquiries, call 202–501–5506. Fax, 202–273–3139.

Public Affairs maintains contact with and responds to media inquiries and issues press releases and other literature. For media inquiries call 202–501–5525. Public Affairs also maintains contact with organizations representing the archival profession, scholarly organizations, and other groups served by the National Archives.

Reference Services   Records are available for research purposes in reading rooms at the National Archives Building, Seventh Street and

Pennsylvania Avenue NW., Washington, DC; at the National Archives at College Park, 8601 Adelphi Road, College Park, MD; at the Washington National Records Center in Suitland, MD; and at each Presidential library, Federal records center, and regional archives. Written requests for information may be sent to any of these units; however, if uncertainty exists as to which unit in Washington, DC, and Maryland to address, send reference requests to the National Archives, User Services Division, Room 3360, 8601 Adelphi Rd, College Park, MD 20470–6001.

The Nixon Presidential Materials Staff also has a reading room at the National Archives at College Park, located in room 1320 (phone, 301–713–6950). Some Nixon materials are available for public inspection, but researchers are advised to contact the staff in advance to ascertain the availability of materials before visiting the facility. Requests for additional information should be directed to the Reference Services Branch, National Archives and Records Administration, Washington, DC 20408. Phone, 202–501–5400.

Inquiries concerning the holdings and services of the National Archives can be made electronically. The e-mail address is inquire@arch2.nara.gov. In addition, information about the National Archives and its holdings is available on the Internet via the NARA gopher, CLIO. To access CLIO via the Internet, point your gopher client at gopher.nara.gov, port 70 (the default). To access the National Archives gopher CLIO via the World Wide Web point your gopher client at www.nara.gov. A third service, fax-on-demand, is an interactive fax retrieval system that allows users to select and receive by fax a wide variety of agency-related information. To use the fax-on-demand service, call 301–713–6905 from the fax machine handset and follow the voice instructions. One of the options that can be selected is a list of

the available documents. There is no charge for using fax-on-demand, other than for telephone service.

Freedom of Information Act/Privacy Act Requests Requests should be directed as follows:

Administrative records of the National Archives and Records Administration: Administrative Service, National Archives at College Park, 8601 Adelphi Road, College Park, MD 20740–6001. Phone, 301–713–6750. Fax, 301–713–7389.

Historical records in the custody of the Office of the National Archives: Office of the National Archives, National Archives at College Park, 8601 Adelphi Road, College Park, MD 20740–6001. Phone, 301–713–7000.

Historical records in the custody of a Presidential library: the library that has custody of the records (*See* pages 614 and 615 for addresses.).

Records in the custody of the Federal records centers: the Federal agency that transferred the records to the Federal records center.

Contracts Individuals seeking to do business with the agency may obtain detailed information from the Acquisitions Staff, National Archives at College Park, 8601 Adelphi Road, College Park, MD 20740–6001. Phone, 301–713–6755.

Employment For job opportunities nationwide, contact the nearest agency facility or the Personnel Operations Branch, Room 2002, 9700 Page Boulevard, St. Louis, MO 63132. Phone, 800–634–4898 (toll free); TDD, 314–538–4799.

Records Administration Information Center Upon request, the Records Administration Information Center provides individualized assistance in answering records management questions. For further information, call 301–713–6677.

For further information, write or visit the National Archives and Records Administration, Seventh Street and Pennsylvania Avenue NW., Washington, DC 20408. Phone, 202–501–5400.

NATIONAL CAPITAL PLANNING COMMISSION

Suite 301, 801 Pennsylvania Avenue NW., Washington, DC 20576
Phone, 202–724–0174

Chairman	HARVEY B. GANTT
Members	ARRINGTON DIXON, PATRICIA ELWOOD, ROBERT A. GAINES, MARGARET G. VANDERHYE
Ex Officio:	
(Secretary of the Interior)	BRUCE BABBITT
(Secretary of Defense)	WILLIAM J. PERRY
(Administrator of General Services)	ROGER W. JOHNSON
(Chairman, Senate Committee on Governmental Affairs)	WILLIAM V. ROTH, JR.
(Chairman, Committee on Government Reform and Oversight)	WILLIAM F. CLINGER
(Mayor of the District of Columbia)	MARION S. BARRY, JR.
(Chairman, Council of the District of Columbia)	DAVID A. CLARKE
Staff:	
Executive Director	REGINALD W. GRIFFITH
Executive Assistant	PRISCILLA A. BROWN
Assistant Executive Director for Operations	ROBERT E. GRESHAM
Director for Intergovernmental and Public Affairs	DAVID JULYAN
Executive Officer	ALLISON HOPKINS, *Acting*
General Counsel	SANDRA H. SHAPIRO
Secretariat	RAE N. ALLEN
Director, Long-Range Planning Division	EDWARD C. HROMANIK
Director, Technical Planning Services Division	GEORGE H.F. OBERLANDER
Director, Planning Review and Implementation Division	RONALD E. WILSON
Director, Planning Information and Technology Division	(VACANCY)

[For the National Capital Planning Commission statement of organization, see the *Code of Federal Regulations*, Title 1, Part 456.2]

The National Capital Planning Commission is the central agency for conducting planning and development activities for the Federal Government in the National Capital region. The region includes the District of Columbia and all land areas within the boundaries of Montgomery and Prince Georges Counties in Maryland and Fairfax, Loudoun, Prince William, and Arlington Counties in Virginia.

The National Capital Planning Commission was established as a park planning agency by act of June 6, 1924, as amended (40 U.S.C. 71 *et seq.*). Two years later its role was expanded to include comprehensive planning. In 1952, under the National Capital Planning Act, the Commission was designated the central planning agency for the Federal and District of Columbia governments.

NATIONAL CAPITAL PLANNING COMMISSION

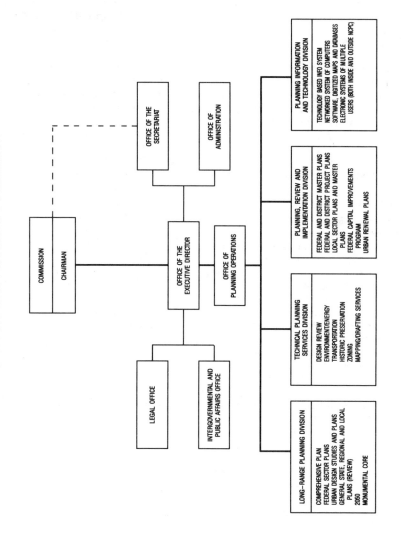

In 1973, the National Capital Planning Act was amended by the District of Columbia Home Rule Act, which made the Mayor of the District of Columbia the chief planner for the District; however, the Commission continues to serve as the central planning agency for the Federal Government in the National Capital region.

The Commission is composed of five appointed and seven *ex officio* members. Three citizen members, including the Chairman, are appointed by the President and two by the mayor of the District of Columbia. Presidential appointees include one resident each from Maryland and Virginia and one from anywhere in the United States; however, the two mayoral appointees must be District of Columbia residents.

Activities

The Commission has three primary functions: comprehensive planning to ensure the orderly development of the Federal Establishment and protection of Federal interests in the National Capital region, plan and program review, and preparation of the Federal Capital Improvements Program.

Comprehensive Planning   The Comprehensive Plan is a statement of policies dealing with the growth and development of the National Capital and consists of both Federal and District elements. It is an important planning tool that provides a framework for policy decisions regarding physical development proposed by Federal, State, local, and regional agencies.

Plan and Program Review   The Commission's plan and program review function consists of reviewing plans and programs proposed by Federal, State, regional, and local agencies or jurisdictions in the National Capital region. This function provides the Commission with an opportunity to coordinate plan and program proposals.

Following this review the Commission, with regard to certain types of projects, provides the sponsoring agency with comments and recommendations. Approval by the Commission must be obtained prior to construction of Federal

public buildings in the District of Columbia and District of Columbia buildings in the central area of the District.

Each Federal or District project comes to the Commission for review at several stages. The first submission by an agency may be a master plan for an entire installation or facility. Plans for construction of individual projects implementing a master plan are submitted to the Commission at both the preliminary and the final stages.

Federal Capital Improvements Programming   Another comprehensive planning activity is the preparation, adoption, and updating of the Five-Year Federal Capital Improvements Program, a "budget" schedule for Federal physical improvements throughout the National Capital region. It is prepared by the Commission in order to systematically review proposed Federal agency projects with regard to timing, location, and financing, and to coordinate agency development plans throughout the region.

A Federal Capital budget represents the first year of the 5-year program and consists of capital outlay requests for the region contained in the President's fiscal year Federal budget transmitted to Congress. The program for the second through fifth years incorporates Commission recommendations to Federal agencies and the Office of Management and Budget for subsequent budget submissions to Congress.

Additional Activities   Other Commission responsibilities include review of all proposed zoning regulations, map changes, and amendments to the District of Columbia zoning ordinance in order to ensure consistency of zoning regulations with Federal interests and with the Comprehensive Plan.

The Commission also:
—adopts urban renewal area boundaries;
—prepares, adopts, and modifies urban renewal plans;
—approves the Permanent System of Highways Plan;
—recommends proposed street and alley closings;

—approves transfers of jurisdiction between Federal and District agencies; —approves the sale of surplus property and park land; and —acquires land for parks and parkways in the National Capital region.

The Commission serves the entire National Capital region by coordinating Federal planning and development with the planning activities of State, local, and regional agencies and jurisdictions.

For further information, contact the Public Affairs Officer, National Capital Planning Commission, Suite 301, 801 Pennsylvania Avenue NW., Washington, DC 20576. Phone, 202–724–0174. Fax, 202–724–0195.

NATIONAL CREDIT UNION ADMINISTRATION

1775 Duke Street, Alexandria, VA 22314–3428
Phone, 703–518–6300

Chairman	NORMAN E. D'AMOURS
Vice Chairman	SHIRLEE BOWNÉ
Member of the Board	ROBERT H. SWAN
Executive Director	KARL HOYLE
Secretary to the Board	BECKY BAKER
Executive Assistant to the Vice Chairman	JOHN BUTLER
Executive Assistant to the Board Member	RUSSELL CLARK
General Counsel	ROBERT FENNER
Director, Public and Congressional Affairs	ROBERT E. LOFTUS
Director, Office of Examination and Insurance	DAVID M. MARQUIS
Inspector General	H. FRANK THOMAS
Controller	JANE WALTERS
Director, Office of Community Development and Low-Income Credit Unions	PETER MAJKA
Director, Office of Investment Services	JAMES FEENEY
Director, Office of Technology Information Systemss	DOUG VERNER
Director, Office of Administration	JAMES L. BAYLEN
Director, Office of Human Resources	DOROTHY FOSTER
Director, Office of Training and Development	ROBERT POMPA
Director, Office of Corporate Credit Unions	H. ALLEN CARVER

[For the National Credit Union Administration statement of organization, see the *Code of Federal Regulations*, Title 12, Part 720]

The National Credit Union Administration Board is responsible for chartering, insuring, supervising, and examining Federal credit unions and administering the National Credit Union Share Insurance Fund. The Board also manages the Central Liquidity Facility, a mixed-ownership Government corporation whose purpose is to supply emergency loans to member credit unions.

The National Credit Union Administration was established by act of March 10, 1970 (12 U.S.C. 1752), and reorganized by act of November 10, 1978 (12 U.S.C. 226), as an independent agency in the executive branch of the Federal Government. It regulates and insures all Federal credit unions and insures State-chartered credit unions that apply and qualify for share insurance.

Activities

Chartering The Administration's Board grants Federal credit union charters to groups sharing a common bond of occupation or association, or groups within a well-defined neighborhood, community, or rural district. A preliminary investigation is made to determine if certain minimum standards are met before granting a Federal charter.

For further information, contact the appropriate regional office listed in the table below.

Supervision Supervisory activities are carried out through annual examiner contacts and through periodic policy and regulatory releases from the Administration. The Administration also maintains a warning system designed to identify emerging problems as well as to monitor operations between examinations.

Examinations The Administration conducts annual examinations of Federal credit unions to determine their solvency and compliance with laws and regulations and to assist credit union management and operations.

For further information, contact the Director, Office of Examination and Insurance. Phone, 703-518-6360.

Share Insurance The act of October 19, 1970 (12 U.S.C. 1781 et seq.), provides for a program of share insurance. The insurance is mandatory for Federal credit unions and for State-chartered credit unions in many States and is optional for other State-chartered credit unions that meet Administration standards. Credit union members' accounts are insured up to $100,000. The National Credit Union Share Insurance Fund requires each insured credit union to place and maintain a 1-percent deposit of its insured savings with the Fund.

For further information, contact the Director, Office of Examination and Insurance. Phone, 703-518-6360.

Regional Offices—National Credit Union Administration

Region	Address	Director	Telephone	Fax
1. ALBANY—Connecticut, Maine, Massachusetts, New Hampshire, New York, Rhode Island, Vermont	9 Washington Sq., Washington Ave. Ext., Albany, NY 12205	Layne L. Bumgardner	518-464-4180	518-464-4195
2. CAPITAL—Delaware, District of Columbia, Maryland, New Jersey, Pennsylvania, Virginia, West Virginia	No. 206, 1775 Duke St., Alexandria, VA 22314	Robert Schafer	202-682-1900	703-838-0401
3. ATLANTA—Alabama, Arkansas, Florida, Georgia, Kentucky, Louisiana, Mississippi, North Carolina, Puerto Rico, South Carolina, Tennessee, Virgin Islands	Suite 1600, 7000 Central Pky., Atlanta, GA 30328	H. Allen Carver	404-396-4042	
4. CHICAGO—Illinois, Indiana, Michigan, Missouri, Ohio, Wisconsin	Suite 155, 4225 Napperville Road, Lisle, IL 60532	Nicholas Veghts	708-245-1000	708-245-1015
5. AUSTIN—Arizona, Colorado, Iowa, Kansas, Minnesota, Nebraska, New Mexico, North Dakota, Oklahoma, South Dakota, Texas, Utah, Wyoming	Suite 5200, 4807 Spicewood Springs Rd., Austin, TX 78759-8490	John S. Ruffin	512-482-4500	512-482-4511
6. PACIFIC—Alaska, American Samoa, California, Guam, Hawaii, Idaho, Montana, Nevada, Oregon, Washington	No. 1350, 2300 Clayton Rd., Concord, CA 94520	Daniel L. Murphy	510-825-6125	510-486-3729

Sources of Information

Consumer Complaints The Administration investigates the complaints of members who are unable to resolve problems with their Federal credit union when these problems relate to a possible violation of the Federal Credit Union Act or consumer protection regulations. Complaints should be sent directly to the appropriate regional office.

Employment Inquiries and applications for employment should be directed to the Office of Human Resources, National Credit Union Administration, 1775 Duke Street, Alexandria, VA 22314-3428.

Federally Insured Credit Unions   A list of federally insured credit union names, addresses, asset level, and number of members is available for review at NCUA's Alexandria and regional offices. Copies of the listing are available at a nominal fee from NCUA, Publications, 1775 Duke Street, Alexandria, VA 22314–3428. Phone, 703–518–6340.

Publications   NCUA publications are available in hard copy, or using a computer and modem, via the NCUA Bulletin Board. To view and download NCUA publications from the Bulletin

Board, log onto the system at 703–518–6480. For assistance, contact the systems operator at 703–518–6335. A list of publications and hard copies are available through the NCUA, Office of Administration, 1775 Duke Street, Alexandria, VA 22314–3428. Phone, 703–518–6340.

Starting a Federal Credit Union
Groups interested in forming a Federal credit union may obtain free information by writing to the appropriate regional office.

For further information concerning the National Credit Union Administration, contact the Office of Public and Congressional Affairs, National Credit Union Administration, 1775 Duke Street, Alexandria, VA 22314–3428. Phone, 703–518–6330.

NATIONAL FOUNDATION ON THE ARTS AND THE HUMANITIES

NATIONAL ENDOWMENT FOR THE ARTS
1100 Pennsylvania Avenue NW., Washington, DC 20506
Phone, 202–682–5400

Chairman	JANE ALEXANDER
Chief of Staff	ALEXANDER CRARY
Congressional Liaison	DICK WOODRUFF
General Counsel	KAREN CHRISTENSEN
Inspector General	LEON LILLY
Director, Millennium Projects	BRIAN O'DOHERTY
Director, Policy, Planning and Research	OLIVE MOSIER
Director, Civil Rights Division	ANGELIA RICHARDSON
Director, Research Division	TOM BRADSHAW
Librarian	JEANNE MCCONNELL
Director, Public Affairs	CHERIE SIMON
Director, Public Information	OLIVIA BAISDEN
Director, Special Projects	ROSEMARY CRIBBEN
Senior Deputy Chairman	ANA STEELE
Associate Deputy Chairman for Program Coordination	A.B. SPELLMAN
Budget Officer	AARON FINEMAN
Director, Council and Panel Operations	YVONNE SABINE
Deputy Chairman for Programs	SUSAN CLAMPITT
Director, Dance	CYNTHIA MAYEDA, *Acting*
Director, Design	SAMINA QURAESHI
Director, Folk and Traditional Arts	DANIEL SHEEHY
Director, Literature	GIGI BRADFORD
Director, Media Arts	BRIAN O'DOHERTY
Director, Museums	JENNIFER DOWLEY
Director, Music	OMUS HIRSHBEIN

Director, Opera-Musical Theater   OMUS HIRSHBEIN
Director, Presenting   OMUS HIRSHBEIN
Director, Theater   KERYL MCCORD
Director, Visual Arts   JENNIFER DOWLEY
Deputy Chairman for Public Partnership   SCOTT SANDERS
Director, Arts in Education   DOUGLAS HERBERT
Director, Challenge/Advancement   LEE DENNISON
Director, Expansion Arts   PATRICE POWELL
Director, Federal Liaison   MARIANNE KLINK
Director, International   MERIANNE LITEMAN
Director, Local Arts Agencies   DIANE MATARAZA
Director, Special Constituencies   PAULA TERRY
Director, State and Regional   EDWARD DICKEY
Deputy Chairman for Management   LARRY BADEN
Director, Administrative Services   MURRAY WELSH
Director, Contracts and Procurement   BILL HUMMEL
Director, Finance   MARVIN MARKS
Grants Officer   DONNA DIRICCO, *Acting*
Director, Human Resources   MAXINE JEFFERSON
   Director, Arts Administration Fellows   ANYA NYKYFORIAK
   Director, Personnel   LEON WILLIAMS
Director, Information Management   RUTH REED
Coordinators, Management Systems   MARTHA JONES
                                                            KATHY PLOWITZ-WORDEN

NATIONAL ENDOWMENT FOR THE HUMANITIES
1100 Pennsylvania Avenue NW., Washington, DC 20506
Phone, 202–606–8400

Chairman   SHELDON HACKNEY
Deputy Chairman   JUAN MESTAS
   General Counsel   MICHAEL SHAPIRO
   Director of Congressional Liaison   ANN S. YOUNG
   Director, Office of Planning and Budget   STEPHEN F. CHERRINGTON
   Director, Office of Communications Policy   GARY KRULL
   Director, Federal/State Partnership   CAROLE WATSON
   Director, Division of Education Programs   JAMES HERBERT
   Director, Division of Public Programs   MARSHA SEMMEL
   Director, Division of Research Programs   GUINEVERE L. GRIEST
   Director, Division of Preservation and   GEORGE FARR
      Access
   Accounting Officer   D. RAY GLEASON
   Administrative Services Officer   BARRY MAYNES
   IRM Systems Officer   WILLIAM J. KINSELLA
   Equal Employment Opportunity Officer   MARGARET V. HORNE
   Grants Officer   DAVID WALLACE
   Director of Personnel   TIMOTHY G. CONNELLY
Inspector General   SHELDON BERNSTEIN

INSTITUTE OF MUSEUM SERVICES
Room 510, 1100 Pennsylvania Avenue NW., Washington, DC 20506
Phone, 202–606–8536

Director   DIANE B. FRANKEL
Director, Policy, Planning, and Budget   LINDA BELL

Public Information Officer and Congressional Liaison	MAMIE BITTNER
Executive Assistant, National Museum Services Board and Administrative Assistant	S. WILLIAM LANEY
Program Director	REBECCA DANVERS
Assistant Program Director	MARY ESTELLE KENNELLY

[For the National Foundation on the Arts and the Humanities statement of organization, see the *Code of Federal Regulations*, Title 45, Part 1100]

The National Foundation on the Arts and the Humanities encourages and supports national progress in the humanities and the arts.

The National Foundation on the Arts and the Humanities was created as an independent agency by the National Foundation on the Arts and the Humanities Act of 1965 (20 U.S.C. 951). The Foundation consists of a National Endowment for the Arts, a National Endowment for the Humanities, a Federal Council on the Arts and the Humanities, and an Institute of Museum Services. Each Endowment has its own Council, composed of the Endowment Chairman and 26 other members appointed by the President, which advises the Chairman with respect to policies and procedures and reviews applications for financial support while making recommendations thereon.

The Federal Council on the Arts and Humanities consists of 20 members, including the two Endowment Chairmen and the Director of the Institute of Museum Services, and is designed to coordinate the activities of the two Endowments and related programs of other Federal agencies. Four members are excluded from the Federal Council when it is considering matters under the Arts and Artifacts Indemnity Act (20 U.S.C. 971).

National Endowment for the Arts

The National Endowment for the Arts supports the visual, literary, and performing arts to benefit all Americans by fostering artistic excellence and developing the Nation's finest creative talent; by preserving and transmitting our diverse cultural heritage; by making the arts more accessible to all Americans; by promoting the vitality of arts institutions; and by making the arts intrinsic to education.

The Arts Endowment serves as a catalyst to increase opportunities for artists and resources for arts organizations. It promotes involvement in the arts by citizens, public and private organizations, and States and local communities. The agency awards grants to nonprofit arts organizations in support of outstanding performances, exhibitions, projects, and programs; provides fellowships to exceptionally talented American artists to stimulate the creation of new works of art, to expand the Nation's artistic resources, and to promote preservation of the country's cultural heritage; and funds projects whose goal is to educate, formally or informally, both children and adults in the arts. Also, it disburses program funds to State arts agencies and local and regional organizations in order to promote broad dissemination of the arts across America. Its grantmaking is conducted through the following programs: Challenge and Advancement, Dance, Design Arts, Expansion Arts, Folk Arts, International, Literature, Media Arts, Museums, Opera-Musical Theater, Presenting and Commissioning, Theater, Visual Arts, Arts in Education, Local Arts Agencies, and State and Regional.

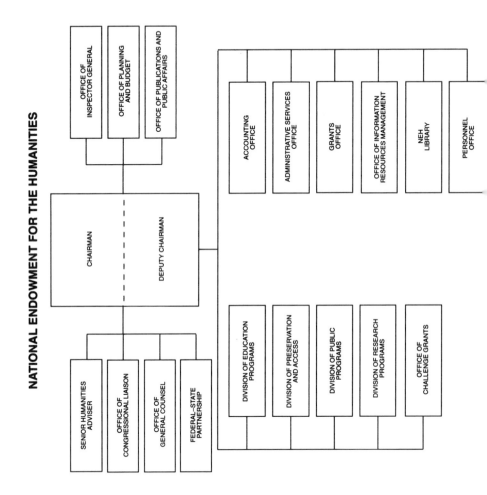

NATIONAL ENDOWMENT FOR THE HUMANITIES

Sources of Information

Grants Persons interested in applying for a grant in the arts should contact the appropriate program at the National Endowment for the Arts by calling 202–682–5464 for further information.

Publications A report of the National Endowment for the Arts is issued annually and may be obtained from the Superintendent of Documents, Government Printing Office, Washington, DC 20402.

A Program Announcement containing information for prospective applicants may be obtained by writing to the National Endowment for the Arts, requesting the publication entitled *Guide to Programs,* Washington, DC 20506.

Employment Information The Office of Personnel Management registers from which employees are most often appointed are Secretary, Mid-Level Administrative Examination, and Senior-Level Examination.

For further information, contact the Public Information Office, National Endowment for the Arts, 1100 Pennsylvania Avenue NW., Washington, DC 20506. Phone, 202–682–5400.

National Endowment for the Humanities

The National Endowment for the Humanities is an independent, grant-making agency established by Congress in 1965 to support research, education, and public programs in the humanities.

According to the agency's authorizing legislation, the term "humanities" includes, but is not limited to, the study of the following: language, both modern and classical; linguistics; literature; history; jurisprudence; philosophy; archeology; comparative religion; ethics; the history, criticism, and theory of the arts; and those aspects of the social sciences that employ historical or philosophical approaches.

The Endowment makes grants to individuals, groups, or institutions— schools, colleges, universities, museums, public television stations, libraries, public agencies, and nonprofit private groups—to increase understanding and appreciation of the humanities. Its grant-making is conducted through four operating divisions—Education Programs, Public Programs, Preservation and Access, and Research Programs, through the Office of Federal/State Partnership and the Office of Challenge Grants.

Education Grants Grants in the Division of Education Programs support efforts in elementary and secondary schools as well as in institutions of higher education to improve instruction in humanities disciplines and to

disseminate results of exemplary education programs. This Division also supports college and school teacher seminars that provide for collegial interaction.

For further information, call 202–606–8373.

Research Projects of longer duration, often involving collaboration between scholars, fall within the domain of the Division of Research Programs, which awards grants for the preparation of publication of important texts in the humanities, the organization of collections and the preparation of reference materials, the conduct of collaborative or coordinated research, the support of centers where scholars may conduct their research, and the support of international organizations for the exchange of scholars. This Division also supports individual scholars, teachers, and other interpreters of the humanities for full-time, independent study or research.

For further information, call 202–606–8200.

Public Grants The Division of Public Programs strives to fulfill the Endowment's mandate "to increase public understanding of the humanities" by supporting those institutions and organizations that develop and present humanities programming for general audiences.

For further information, call 202–606–8267.

Federal/State Partnership Grants Humanities committees in each of the 50 States, the Virgin Islands, Puerto Rico, the District of Columbia, the Northern Mariana Islands, American Samoa, or Guam, receive annual grants from the Division of State Programs, which they then re-grant to support humanities programs at the local level.

For further information, call 202–606–8254.

Challenge Grants Nonprofit institutions interested in developing new sources of long-term support for educational, scholarly preservation and public programs in the humanities may be assisted in these efforts by a Challenge Grant.

For further information, call 202–606–8309.

Preservation and Access The Division of Preservation and Access expands Endowment support in attacking the problem of deteriorating humanities resources. Cooperative projects set in a national framework with an emphasis on the preservation of America's past and the work of American scholars, using both Federal and private funds, are particularly encouraged.

For further information, call 202–606–8570.

Sources of Information

Employment The Office of Personnel Management registers from which employees are most often appointed are: Clerk-Typist, Mid-Level Administrative Register, and Senior-Level Register.

Grants Those interested in applying for a grant in the humanities should request information, guidelines, and application forms from the Endowment's Public Information Office, Room 402, 1100 Pennsylvania Avenue NW., Washington, DC 20506. Phone, 202–606–8400.

Publications An annual report for the National Endowment for the Humanities is issued annually and may be obtained from the Endowment's Public Information Office, Room 402, 1100 Pennsylvania Avenue NW., Washington, DC 20506. Phone, 202–606–8400.

Overview of Endowment Programs, which contains information for prospective applicants, may be obtained by writing to the Public Information Office, at the address given above.

Humanities, a bimonthly review of issues in the humanities published by the Endowment, is available by subscription ($15 domestic, $18.75 foreign) through the Superintendent of Documents, P.O. Box 371954, Pittsburgh, PA 15250– 7954.

For further information, contact the Public Information Office, National Endowment for the Humanities, Room 402, 1100 Pennsylvania Avenue NW., Washington, DC 20506. Phone, 202–606–8400.

Institute of Museum Services

The Institute of Museum Services is an independent, grant-making agency established by Congress in 1976 to assist museums in maintaining, increasing, and improving their services to the public.

The Institute of Museum Services (IMS) was created by the Museum Services Act (20 U.S.C. 961 note). In December 1981, pursuant to title II of the act of Dec. 23, 1981 (20 U.S.C. 961, 962), the Institute was established as an

independent agency within the National Foundation on the Arts and the Humanities. The Institute's Director is appointed by the President with the advice and consent of the Senate, and is authorized to make grants to museums subject to policy directives and priorities set by the National Museum Services Board. The Board is comprised of 15 Presidentially appointed nonvoting members and 5 *ex officio* nonvoting members.

The Institute awards grants on a competitive basis to support the efforts of museums to conserve the Nation's historic, scientific, and cultural heritage; to maintain and expand their educational role; and to ease the financial burden borne by museums as a result of their increasing use by the public. The Institute awards grants to all types of museums, including but not limited to art, history, general, children's, natural history, science and technology, historic houses, zoos and aquariums, botanical gardens and arboretums, nature centers, and planetariums.

The Institute currently makes grants in seven categories: General Operating Support, Conservation Project Support, Museum Assessment Program, Professional Services Program, Conservation Assessment Program, Technical Assistance, and Museum Leadership Initiatives. General Operating Support grants are 2-year competitive awards that maintain or improve the operations of museums. Conservation Project Support grants are annual competitive awards, for projects lasting up to 2 years, that provide funds for various conservation efforts. Museum Assessment Program grants are one-time awards made to museums to provide for an independent, professional assessment of their programs and operations. Conservation Assessment Program grants are one-time awards made to museums to assess the condition of their environment and collections, to identify conservation needs and priorities. Professional Services Program grants provide funding to national, regional, State, or local private, nonprofit professional museum organizations and associations for proposals designed to strengthen museum services. Technical Assistance grants provide funds to small, emerging minority and rural museums for training and other implementation activities. Museum Leadership Initiatives support projects that establish mentoring relationships between at least two parties, one of whom is a museum staff member.

Sources of Information

Grants, Contracts, and Cooperative Agreements   Those interested in applying for Institute of Museum Services funding should contact the Program Office, Institute of Museum Services, Room 609, 1100 Pennsylvania Avenue NW., Washington, DC 20506. Phone, 202–606–8539.

For further information, contact the Program Director, Institute of Museum Services, Room 609, 1100 Pennsylvania Avenue NW., Washington, DC 20506. Phone, 202–606–8539.

NATIONAL LABOR RELATIONS BOARD

1099 Fourteenth Street NW., Washington, DC 20570
Phone, 202–273–1000 (Central Locator); 202–273–4300 (TDD)

Chairman	WILLIAM B. GOULD IV
Members	MARGARET A. BROWNING, CHARLES I. COHEN, JOHN C. TRUESDALE, JAMES M. STEPHENS
Executive Secretary	JOSEPH E. MOORE, *Acting*
Solicitor	JEFFREY D. WEDEKIND, *Acting*
Inspector General	JOHN E. HIGGINS, JR., *Acting*
Director, Division of Information	DAVID B. PARKER

Chief Administrative Law Judge .... DAVID S. DAVIDSON
General Counsel .... FRED L. FEINSTEIN
  Deputy General Counsel .... MARY JOYCE CARLSON
  Associate General Counsel, Division of ... ROBERT E. ALLEN
    Advice
  Associate General Counsel, Division of ... LINDA R. SHER, *Acting*
    Enforcement Litigation
  Associate General Counsel, Division of ... WILLIAM G. STACK
    Operations Management
  Director, Division of Administration .... GLORIA J. JOSEPH
  Director, Equal Employment Opportunity .. BARBARA T. GAINEY

[For the National Labor Relations Board statement of organization, see the *Federal Register* of June 14, 1979, 44 FR 34215]

The National Labor Relations Board administers the Nation's principal labor law, the National Labor Relations Act. The Board is vested with the power to prevent and remedy unfair labor practices committed by private sector employers and unions and to safeguard employees' rights to organize and determine, through secret ballot elections, whether to have unions as their bargaining representative.

The National Labor Relations Board (NLRB) is an independent agency created by the National Labor Relations Act of 1935 (Wagner Act) (29 U.S.C. 167), as amended by acts of 1947 (Taft-Hartley Act), 1959 (Landrum-Griffin Act), and 1974 (Health Care Amendments).

The act affirms the right of employees to self-organization and collective bargaining through representatives of their own choosing, to engage in other protected, concerted activities, or to refrain from such activities. The act prohibits certain unfair labor practices by employers and labor organizations or their agents. It authorizes the Board to designate appropriate units for collective bargaining and to conduct secret ballot elections to determine whether employees desire representation by a labor organization.

As of July 1, 1971, the Postal Reorganization Act (39 U.S.C. note prec. 101) conferred jurisdiction upon the Board over unfair labor practice charges and representation elections affecting U.S. Postal Service employees. As of August 25, 1974, jurisdiction over all privately operated health care institutions was conferred on the Board by an amendment to the act (29 U.S.C. 152 *et seq.*).

Activities

Under the act, NLRB has two principal functions: preventing and remedying unfair labor practices by employers and labor organizations or their agents; and conducting secret ballot elections among employees in appropriate collective-bargaining units to determine whether or not they desire to be represented by a labor organization in bargaining with employers about their wages, hours, and working conditions. The agency also conducts secret ballot elections among employees who have been covered by a union-security agreement to determine whether or not they wish to revoke their union's authority to make such agreements. In jurisdictional disputes between two or more unions, the Board determines which competing group of workers is entitled to perform the work involved.

Two major, separate components comprise NLRB. The Board itself has five members appointed by the President and primarily acts as a quasi-judicial body in deciding cases on the basis of formal records in administrative proceedings. The General Counsel, also appointed by the President, is independent from the Board.

Under the general supervision of the General Counsel, 33 regional directors and their staffs process representation, unfair labor practice, and jurisdictional dispute cases. (Some regions have subregional or resident offices.) They issue complaints in unfair labor practice cases; seek settlement of unfair labor practice charges; obtain compliance with Board orders and court judgments; and petition district courts for injunctions to prevent or remedy unfair labor practices. The regional directors direct hearings in representation cases; conduct elections pursuant to the agreement of the parties or the decision-making authority delegated to them by the Board or pursuant to Board directions; and issue certifications of representatives when unions win or certify the results when unions lose employee elections. They process petitions for bargaining unit clarification, for amendment of certification, and for rescission of a labor organization's authority to make a union-shop agreement. They also conduct national emergency employee referendums.

NLRB can act only when it is formally requested to do so. Individuals, employers, or unions may initiate cases by filing charges of unfair labor practices or petitions for employee representation elections with the Board field offices serving the area where the case arises.

In the event that a regional director declines to proceed on a representation petition, the party filing the petition may appeal to the Board. When a regional director declines to proceed on an unfair labor practice charge, the charging party may appeal to the General Counsel.

For details concerning filing such appeals with those Washington, DC, offices, parties may contact the field office most convenient to them. Field office addresses and telephone numbers are listed below.

Administrative law judges conduct hearings in unfair labor practice cases, make findings of fact and conclusions of law, and recommend remedies for violations found. Their decisions can be appealed to the Board for a final agency determination. The Board's decisions are subject to review in the U.S. Courts of Appeals.

Field Offices—National Labor Relations Board

(RD: Regional Director; OC: Officer-in-Charge; RO: Resident Officer)

Office/Address	Director/Officer	Telephone
Albany, NY (Clinton Ave. at N. Pearl St., 12207)	Thomas J. Sheridan (RO)	518–472–2215
Albuquerque, NM (505 Marquette Ave. NW., 87102)	Robert A. Reisinger (RO)	505–766–3800
Anchorage, AK (222 W. 7th Ave., 99513)	Minoru Hayashi (RO)	907–271–5015
Atlanta, GA (101 Marietta St. NW., 30323)	Martin M. Arlook (RD)	404–331–2896
Baltimore, MD (103 S. Gay St., 8th Fl., 21202)	Louis J. D'Amico (RD)	410–962–2822
Birmingham, AL (1900 3d Ave N., 3d Fl., 35203)	C. Douglas Marshall (RO)	205–731–1492
Boston, MA (10 Causeway St., 02222)	Rosemary Pye (RD)	617–565–6700
Brooklyn, NY (1 Metro Tech Ctr., Jay St. & Myrtle Ave., 11201)	Alvin P. Blyer (RD)	718–330–7713
Buffalo, NY (111 W. Huron St., 14202)	(Vacancy) (RD)	551–846–4931
Chicago, IL (200 W. Adams St., 60606)	Elizabeth Kinney (RD)	312–353–7570
Cincinnati, OH (550 Main St., 45202)	Richard Ahearn (RD)	513–684–3686
Cleveland, OH (1240 E. 9th St., 44199)	Frederick Calatrello (RD)	216–522–3715
Denver, CO (600 17th St., 80202)	Arthur R. DePalma (RD)	303–844–3551
Des Moines, IA (210 Walnut St., 50309)	Morris E. Petersen (RO)	515–284–4391
Detroit, MI (477 Michigan Ave., 48226)	William C. Schaub (RD)	313–226–3200
El Paso, TX (700 E. San Antonio Ave., 79901)	Laureano A. Medrano (RO)	915–534–6434
Fort Worth, TX (819 Taylor St., 76102)	Michael Dunn (RD)	817–334–2921
Grand Rapids, MI (82 Ionia NW., 49503)	David L. Basso (RO)	616–456–2679
Hartford, CT (1 Commercial Plz., 06103)	Peter B. Hoffman (RD)	203–240–3522
Hato Rey, PR (150 Carlos E. Chardon Ave., 00918)	Mary Zelma Asseo (RD)	809–766–5347
Honolulu, HI (300 Ala Moana Blvd., 96850)	Thomas W. Cestare (OC)	808–541–2814
Houston, TX (440 Louisiana St., 77002)	Ruth F. Small (RO)	713–238–9632
Indianapolis, IN (575 N. Pennsylvania St., 46204)	Saundria Bordone (RD)	317–226–7430
Jacksonville, FL (400 W. Bay St., 32202)	James L. McDonald (RD)	904–232–3768
Las Vegas, NV (600 Las Vegas Blvd. S., 89101)	Kenneth A. Rose (RO)	702–388–6416
Little Rock, AR (TCBY Twr., 425 W. Capitol St., 72201–3489)	Thomas H. Smith, Jr. (RO)	501–324–6311
Los Angeles, CA (Region 31) (11000 Wilshire Blvd., 90024)	James J. McDermott (RD)	310–575–7352
Los Angeles, CA (Region 21) (888 Figueroa St., 90017)	Victoria E. Aguayo (RD)	213–894–5200
Memphis, TN (1407 Union Ave., 38104)	Gerard P. Fleischut (RD)	901–722–2725
Miami, FL (51 SW. 1st Ave., 33130)	Hector O. Nava (RO)	305–536–5391
Milwaukee, WI (310 W. Wisconsin Ave., 53203)	Phillip Bloedorn, Acting (RD)	414–297–3861
Minneapolis, MN (110 S. 4th St., 55401)	Ronald M. Sharp (RD)	612–348–1757
Nashville, TN (801 Broadway, 37203)	Alton W. Barksdale (RO)	615–736–5922
Newark, NJ (970 Broad St., 07102)	William A. Pascarell (RD)	201–645–2100
New Orleans, LA (1515 Poydras St., 70112)	Hugh Frank Malone (RD)	504–589–6361

Field Offices—National Labor Relations Board—Continued
(RD: Regional Director; OC: Officer-in-Charge; RO: Resident Officer)

Office/Address	Director/Officer	Telephone
New York, NY (26 Federal Plz., 10278)	Daniel Silverman (RD)	212–264–0300
Oakland, CA (1301 Clay St., 94612)	James S. Scott (RD)	510–637–3300
Overland Park, KS (8600 Farley St., 66212)	F. Rozier Sharp (RD)	913–236–3000
Peoria, IL (300 Hamilton Blvd., 61602)	Glenn A. Zipp (RD)	309–671–7080
Philadelphia, PA (615 Chestnut St., 19106)	Peter W. Hirsch (RD)	215–597–7601
Phoenix, AZ (234 N. Central Ave., 85004)	Roy H. Garner (RD)	602–379–3361
Pittsburgh, PA (1000 Liberty Ave., 15222)	Gerald Kobell (RD)	412–644–2977
Portland, OR (222 SW. Columbia St., 97201)	Delano D. Eyer (OC)	503–326–3085
San Antonio, TX (615 E. Houston St., 78205)	Ruben R. Armendariz (RO)	210–229–6140
San Diego, CA (555 W. Beech St., 92101)	Claude R. Marston (RO)	619–557–6184
San Francisco, CA (901 Market St., 94103)	Robert H. Miller (RO)	415–744–6810
Seattle, WA (915 2d Ave., 98174)	John D. Nelson (RD)	206–220–6300
St. Louis, MO (611 N. 10th St., 63101)	Ralph R. Tremain (RD)	314–425–4167
Tampa, FL (201 E. Kennedy Blvd., 33602)	Rochelle Kenton (RD)	813–228–2641
Tulsa, OK (111 W. 5th St., 74103)	Francis Molenda (RO)	918–581–7951
Washington, DC (2120 L St. NW., 20037)	Steven L. Shuster (RO)	202–254–7612
Winston-Salem, NC (251 N. Main St., 27101)	Willie L. Clark, Jr. (RD)	910–631–5201

Sources of Information

Contracts Prospective suppliers of goods and services may inquire about agency procurement and contracting practices by writing to the Chief, Procurement and Facilities Branch, National Labor Relations Board, Washington, DC 20570. Phone, 202–273–4040.

Employment The Board appoints administrative law judges from a register established by the Office of Personnel Management. The agency hires attorneys, stenographers, and typists for all its offices; field examiners for its field offices; and administrative personnel for its Washington office. Inquiries regarding college and law school recruiting programs should be directed to the nearest regional office. Employment inquiries and applications may be sent to any regional office or the Washington personnel office.

Publications Anyone desiring to inspect formal case documents or read agency publications may use facilities of the Washington or field offices. The agency will assist in arranging reproduction of documents and order transcripts of hearings. The Board's offices offer free informational leaflets in limited quantities: *The National Labor Relations Board and YOU (Unfair Labor Practices), The National Labor Relations Board and YOU (Representation Cases), Your Government Conducts an Election for You on the Job,* and *The National Labor Relations Board—What It Is, What It Does.* The Superintendent of Documents, Government Printing Office, Washington, DC 20402, sells *A Guide to Basic Law and Procedures Under the NLRA,* the *Annual Report,* the *Classified Index of National Labor Relations Board Decisions and Related Court Decisions,* volumes of Board decisions, and a number of subscription services, including the *NLRB Casehandling Manual* (in three parts), the *Weekly Summary of NLRB Cases,* the *NLRB Election Report,* and *An Outline of Law and Procedure in Representation Cases.*

Speakers To give the public and persons appearing before the agency a better understanding of the National Labor Relations Act and the Board's policies, procedures, and services, Washington and regional office personnel participate as speakers or panel members before bar associations, labor, educational, civic, or management organizations, and other groups. Requests for speakers or panelists may be made to Washington officials or to the appropriate regional director.

For further information, contact the Information Division, National Labor Relations Board, 1099 Fourteenth Street NW., Washington, DC 20570. Phone, 202–273–1991.

NATIONAL MEDIATION BOARD

Suite 250 East, 1301 K Street NW., Washington, DC 20572
Phone, 202-523-5920

Chairwoman	MAGDALENA G. JACOBSEN
Members	ERNEST W. DUBESTER
	KENNETH B. HIPP
Chief of Staff	STEPHEN E. CRABLE
Chief Operating Officer	GERILYN E. JOHNSON
General Counsel	RONALD M. ETTERS
Hearing Officer/Assistant to General Counsel	JOYCE M. KLEIN
Senior Hearing Officers/Legal Counsels	MARY L. JOHNSON
	ROLAND WATKINS
Director of Arbitration	ROY J. CARVATTA
Director, Information Resources Management	DONALD L. WEST
Public Information Officer	THORNTON L. TOWNSEND

National Railroad Adjustment Board

Room 1364, 219 South Dearborn Street, Chicago, IL 60604
Phone, 312-886-7302

The National Mediation Board, in carrying out the provisions of the Railway Labor Act, assists in maintaining a free flow of commerce in the railroad and airline industries by resolving disputes that could disrupt travel or imperil the economy. The Board also handles railroad and airline employee representation disputes, and provides administrative and financial support in adjusting minor grievances in the railroad industry under section 153 of the Railway Labor Act.

The National Mediation Board was created on June 21, 1934, by an act amending the Railway Labor Act, as amended (45 U.S.C. 151–158, 160–162, 1181–1188).

The Board's major responsibilities include the mediation of disputes over wages, hours, and working conditions that arise between rail and air carriers and organizations representing their employees; and the investigation of representation disputes and certification of employee organizations as representatives of crafts or classes of carrier employees.

Disputes arising out of grievances or interpretation or application of agreements concerning rates of pay, rules, or working conditions in the railroad industry are referable to the National Railroad Adjustment Board. This Board is divided into four divisions

and consists of an equal number of representatives of the carriers and of national organizations of employees. In deadlocked cases the National Mediation Board is authorized to appoint a referee to sit with the members of the division for the purpose of making an award.

In the airline industry no national airline adjustment board has been established for settlement of grievances. Over the years the employee organizations and air carriers with established bargaining relationships have agreed to grievance procedures with final jurisdiction resting with a system board of adjustment. The Board is frequently called upon to name a neutral referee to serve on a system board when the parties are deadlocked and cannot agree on such an appointment themselves.

Activities

Mediation Disputes   The National Mediation Board is charged with mediating disputes between carriers and labor organizations relating to initial contract negotiations or subsequent changes in rates of pay, rules, and working conditions. When the parties fail to reach accord in direct bargaining either party may request the Board's services or the Board may on its own motion invoke its services. Thereafter, negotiations continue until the Board determines that its efforts to mediate have been unsuccessful, at which time it seeks to induce the parties to submit the dispute to arbitration. If either party refuses to arbitrate, the Board issues a notice stating that the parties have failed to resolve their dispute through mediation. This notice commences a 30-day cooling-off period after which self-help is normally available to either or both parties.

Employee Representation   If a dispute arises among a carrier's employees as to who is to be the representative of such employees, it is the Board's duty to investigate such dispute and to determine by secret-ballot election or other appropriate means whether or not and to whom a representation certification should be issued. In the course of making this determination, the Board must determine the craft or class in which the employees seeking representation properly belong.

Additional Duties   Additional duties of the Board include the interpretation of agreements made under its mediatory auspices; the appointment of neutral referees when requested by the National Railroad Adjustment Board; the appointment of neutrals to sit on system boards and special boards of adjustment; and finally, the duty of notifying the President when the parties have failed to reach agreement through the Board's mediation efforts and that the labor dispute, in the judgment of the Board, threatens substantially to interrupt interstate commerce to a degree such as to deprive any section of the country of essential transportation service. In these cases, the President may, at his discretion, appoint an Emergency Board to investigate and report to him on the dispute. Self-help is barred for 60 days after appointment of the Emergency Board.

Section 9A of the Railway Labor Act (45 U.S.C. 159a) provides emergency dispute procedures covering publicly funded and operated commuter railroads and their employees. That section attempts to resolve contract disputes between the parties through a series of emergency board procedures with a maximum 8-month status quo period. Section 9A is invoked only after all other procedures under the act have been exhausted.

Sources of Information

Publications   Available for public distribution are the following documents: *Determinations of the National Mediation Board* (21 volumes); *Interpretations Pursuant to Section 5, Second of the Act* (2 volumes); Annual Reports of the National Mediation Board including the Report of the National Railroad Adjustment Board; *The Railway Labor Act at Fifty;* and *The National Mediation Board at Fifty—Its Impact on Railroad and Airline Labor Disputes.*

Reading Room   At the Board's headquarters in Washington, DC, copies of collective-bargaining agreements between labor and management of various rail and air carriers are available for public inspection, by appointment, during office hours (1 to 4 p.m., Monday through Friday).

For further information, contact the Chief of Staff, National Mediation Board, Suite 250 East, 1301 K Street NW., Washington, DC 20572. Phone, 202–523–5920. Fax, 202–523–1494.

NATIONAL RAILROAD PASSENGER CORPORATION (AMTRAK)

60 Massachusetts Avenue NE., Washington, DC 20002
Phone, 202–906–3000

Board of Directors:

Chairman	THOMAS M. DOWNS
Members	GOV. THOMAS R. CARPER, DANIEL W. COLLINS, SYLVIA A. DE LEON, ROBERT KILEY, CELESTE P. MCLAIN, ROY M. NEEL, DON J. PEASE
Secretary of Transportation (*ex officio*)	FEDERICO PEÑA

Officers:

President and Chairman	THOMAS M. DOWNS
Executive Vice President and Chief Operating Officer	DENNIS F. SULLIVAN
Chief Financial Officer	ELIZABETH C. REVEAL
Vice President, Corporate Management and Corporate Secretary	ANNE W. HOEY
Vice President, Government and Public Affairs	THOMAS J. GILLESPIE, JR.
Vice President, Human Resources	DENNIS R. WRIGHT
Vice President, Contract Services	RONALD J. HARTMAN
Vice President, Passenger Marketing and Sales	ROBERT K. WEHRMAN
Vice President, Reengineering	NORRIS W. OVERTON
Chief Executive Officer—West Coast Strategic Business Unit	GILBERT O. MALLERY
Chief Executive Officer—Northeast Corridor Strategic Business Unit	GEORGE D. WARRINGTON
Chief Executive Officer—Intercity Rail Service Strategic Business Unit	ARTHUR F. MCMAHON
General Counsel	STEPHEN C. ROGERS

[For the National Railroad Passenger Corporation statement of organization, see the *Code of Federal Regulations*, Title 49, Part 700]

The National Railroad Passenger Corporation was established to develop the potential of modern rail service in meeting the Nation's intercity passenger transportation needs.

The National Railroad Passenger Corporation (Amtrak) was created by the Rail Passenger Service Act of 1970, as amended (45 U.S.C. 541), and was incorporated under the laws of the District of Columbia to provide a balanced national transportation system by developing, operating, and improving U.S. intercity rail passenger service.

Amtrak is governed by a nine-member board of directors: The Secretary of Transportation serves as an *ex officio* member and Amtrak's president serves as Chairman; three members (representing labor, State Governors, and the business community) are appointed by the President with the advice and consent of the Senate; two members represent commuter authorities; and two members are selected by the preferred stockholder. The Corporation is managed by its president along with the executive vice president, chief financial officer, six vice presidents, and three chief executive officers of the strategic business units (SBU's).

The three SBU's, the Northeast Corridor, the Intercity, and the West, were created during Amtrak's restructuring in the fall of 1994 in order to increase profitability. Each SBU has a chief executive officer who has control over business decisions in his area. The SBU's have been successful in the Northeast Corridor, which has expanded operations south—through Richmond to Newport News.

Amtrak operates an average of 212 trains per day, serving over 540 station locations, over a system of approximately 24,500 route miles. Of this route system, Amtrak now owns a right-of-way of 2,611 track miles in the Northeast Corridor (Washington-New York-Boston; New Haven-Springfield; Philadelphia-Harrisburg), and several small track segments in the East, purchased pursuant to the Regional Rail Reorganization Act of 1973 (45 U.S.C. 701 et seq.) and the Railroad Revitalization and Regulatory Reform Act of 1976 (45 U.S.C. 801 et seq.).

Amtrak owns or leases its stations and owns its own repair and maintenance facilities. The Corporation employs a total work force of approximately 25,000 and provides all reservation, station, and on-board service staffs, as well as train and engine operating crews. Outside the Northeast Corridor, Amtrak has historically contracted with 21 privately owned railroads for the right to operate over their track and has compensated each railroad for its total package of services. Under contract, these railroads are responsible for the condition of the roadbed and for coordinating the flow of traffic.

In fiscal year 1994, Amtrak transported over 22 million people approximately 6 billion passenger miles. In addition,

under contracts with several transit agencies, Amtrak carried over 33 million commuters.

Although Amtrak's basic route system was originally designated by the Secretary of Transportation in 1971, modifications have been made to the Amtrak system and to individual routes that have resulted in more efficient and cost-effective operations. Currently, in the face of ongoing budget constraints, new service will only be added if a State agrees to share any losses associated with the new service or if the new service does not substantially add to Amtrak's need for Federal assistance.

Amtrak began operation in 1971 with an antiquated fleet of equipment inherited from private railroads; some cars were nearly 30 years old. Since then, the fleet has been modernized and new state-of-the-art single- and bi-level passenger cars and locomotives have been added.

Systemwide ridership is steadily rising, and Amtrak is finding it increasingly difficult to meet the demands of increased travel patterns with its limited passenger fleet. To ease these equipment constraints, the Corporation is working to identify innovative funding sources in order to acquire additional passenger cars and locomotives.

There is no rail passenger system in the world that makes a profit; Amtrak is no exception. However, Amtrak has made significant progress in reducing its dependence on Federal support, while at the same time improving the quality of service. Every year Amtrak moves further toward increasing the ratio of its earned revenue to total costs. As a result, Amtrak's appropriation for the current fiscal year is 45 percent below that for fiscal year 1978 (in constant dollars). One of Amtrak's highest priorities is to make the Corporation even more self-sufficient in the future.

For further information, contact the Public Affairs Department, Amtrak, 60 Massachusetts Avenue NE., Washington, DC 20002. Phone, 202–906–3860.

NATIONAL SCIENCE FOUNDATION
4201 Wilson Boulevard, Arlington, VA 22230
Phone, 703–306–1234

National Science Board

Chairman	FRANK H.T. RHODES
Vice Chairman	MARY ANNE FOX
Members	PERRY L. ADKISSON, BERNARD F. BURKE, F. ALBERT COTTON, THOMAS B. DAY, JAMES J. DUDERSTADT, SANFORD D. GREENBERG, PHILLIP A. GRIFFITHS, CHARLES E. HESS, JOHN E. HOPCROFT, SHIRLEY MALCOM, EVE L. MENGER, CLAUDIA I. MITCHELL-KERNAN, DIANA NATALICIO, JAIME OAXACA, JAMES L. POWELL, IAN M. ROSS, HOWARD E. SIMMONS, ROBERT M. SOLOW, WARREN M. WASHINGTON, JOHN A. WHITE, JR., RICHARD N. ZARE, (VACANCY)
(Ex officio)	NEAL F. LANE
Executive Officer	MARTA C. CEHELSKY
Inspector General	LINDA G. SUNDRO
Deputy Inspector General and Senior Legal Advisor	PHILIP L. SUNSHINE
Assistant Inspector General for Audit	CLIFFORD L. BENNETT
Assistant Inspector General for Oversight	JAMES J. ZWOLENIK

Officials:

Director	NEAL F. LANE
Deputy Director	ANNE C. PETERSEN
Senior Science Adviser	KARL A. ERB
Assistant to the Director for Science Policy and Planning	JUDITH SUNLEY
Assistant to the Director for Human Resource Development	WILLIAM A. LESTER
Staff Associate	THOMAS N. COOLEY
General Counsel	LAWRENCE RUDOLPH
Director, Office of Legislative and Public Affairs	JOEL M. WIDDER, *Acting*
Director, Division of Public Affairs	JOEL M. WIDDER, *Acting*
Director, Division of Legislative Affairs	JOEL M. WIDDER
Director, Office of Policy Support	SUSAN B. COZZENS
Director, Office of Science and Technology Infrastructure	NATHANIEL G. PITTS
Director, Office of Polar Programs	CORNELIUS W. SULLIVAN
Deputy Director, Office of Polar Programs	CAROL A. ROBERTS
Assistant Director for Mathematical and Physical Sciences	WILLIAM C. HARRIS
Executive Officer	THOMAS A. WEBER

Director, Division of Physics	ROBERT A. EISENSTEIN
Director, Division of Chemistry	JANET G. OSTERYOUNG
Director, Division of Materials Research	JOHN H. HOPPS, JR.
Director, Division of Astronomical Sciences	HUGH M. VAN HORN
Director, Division of Mathematical Sciences	DONALD J. LEWIS
Assistant Director for Geosciences	ROBERT W. CORELL
Deputy Assistant Director	THOMAS J. BAERWALD
Director, Division of Atmospheric Sciences	RICHARD S. GREENFIELD
Director, Division of Earth Sciences	JAMES F. HAYS
Director, Division of Ocean Sciences	DONALD F. HEINRICHS, *Acting*
Assistant Director for Biological Sciences	MARY E. CLUTTER
Executive Officer	JAMES L. EDWARDS
Director, Division of Biological Instrumentation and Resources	JAMES H. BROWN
Director, Division of Molecular and Cellular Biosciences	JULIUS H. JACKSON
Director, Division of Integrative Biology and Neuroscience	BRUCE L. UMMINGER
Director, Division of Environmental Biology	JOANN P. ROSKOSKI, *Acting*
Assistant Director for Engineering	JOSEPH BORDOGNA
Deputy Assistant Director for Engineering	ELBERT L. MARSH
Director, Division of Engineering Education and Centers	MARSHALL M. LIH
Director, Division of Electrical and Communications Systems	LAWRENCE S. GOLDBERG
Director, Division of Chemical and Transport Systems	KENNETH R. HALL
Director, Division of Civil and Mechanical Systems	OSCAR W. DILLON, *Acting*
Director, Division of Design, Manufacture, and Industrial Innovation	BRUCE M. KRAMER
Director, Division of Bioengineering and Environmental Systems	JANIE M. FOUKE
Director, Office of Small Business Research and Development	DONALD SENICH
Director, Office of Small and Disadvantaged Business Utilization	JOSEPH BORDOGNA
Assistant Director for Computer and Information Science and Engineering	PAUL R. YOUNG
Deputy Assistant Director	MERRELL L. PATRICK, *Acting*
Head, Office of Cross-Disciplinary Activities	JOHN CHERNIAVSKY
Director, Division of Advanced Scientific Computing	ROBERT R. BORCHERS
Director, Division of Computer and Computation Research	RICHARD B. KIEBURTZ
Director, Division of Information, Robotics, and Intelligent Systems	YI-TZUU CHIEN
Director, Division of Microelectronic Information Processing Systems	BERNARD CHERN
Director, Division of Networking and Communications Research and Infrastructure	GEORGE O. STRAWN
Assistant Director for Social, Behavioral, and Economic Sciences	CORA B. MARRETT
Executive Officer	MARGARET L. WINDUS, *Acting*

Director, Division of Social, Behavioral, and Economic Research	ALLAN KORNBERG
Director, Division of Science Resources Studies	KENNETH BROWN
Director, Division of International Programs	MARCEL BARDON
Assistant Director for Education and Human Resources	LUTHER S. WILLIAMS
Deputy Assistant Director	JANE T. STUTSMAN
Office Administrator, Office of Systemic Reform	PEIRCE A. HAMMOND, *Acting*
Director, Division of Elementary, Secondary, and Informal Science Education	MARGARET B. COZZENS
Director, Division of Graduate Education and Research Development	TERENCE L. PORTER
Director, Division of Human Resource Development	ROOSEVELT CALBERT
Director, Division of Research, Evaluation, and Dissemination	DARYL E. CHUBIN
Director, Division of Undergraduate Education	ROBERT WATSON
Chief Financial Officer, Office of Budget, Finance, and Award Management	JOSEPH L. KULL
Deputy Chief Financial Officer	ALBERT A. MUHLBAUER
Director, Division of Financial Management	ALBERT A. MUHLBAUER
Director, Division of Grants and Agreements	WILLIAM B. COLE
Director, Division of Contracts, Policy, and Oversight	ROBERT B. HARDY
Director, Budget Division	EDWARD L. BLANSITT
Director, Office of Information and Resource Management	CONSTANCE K. McLINDON
Deputy Director	GERARD R. GLASER
Director, Division of Human Resource Management	JOHN F. WILKINSON
Director, Division of Information Systems	FRED WENDLING
Director, Division of Administrative Services	ROBERT E. SCHMITZ

[For the National Science Foundation statement of organization, see the *Federal Register* of February 8, 1993, 58 FR 7587–7595; May 27, 1993, 58 FR 30819; and May 2, 1994, 59 FR 22690]

The National Science Foundation promotes the progress of science and engineering through the support of research and education programs. Its major emphasis is on high-quality, merit-selected research—the search for improved understanding of the fundamental laws of nature upon which our future well-being as a nation depends. Its educational programs are aimed at ensuring increased understanding of science and engineering at all educational levels, maintaining an adequate supply of scientists, engineers, and science educators to meet our country's needs.

The National Science Foundation was established as an independent agency by the National Science Foundation Act of 1950 (42 U.S.C. 1861–1875).

The purposes of the Foundation are: to increase the Nation's base of scientific and engineering knowledge and strengthen its ability to conduct research in all areas of science and engineering; to develop and help implement science and engineering education programs that can better prepare the Nation for meeting the challenges of the future; and to promote international cooperation through science and engineering. In its role as a leading Federal supporter of

NATIONAL SCIENCE FOUNDATION

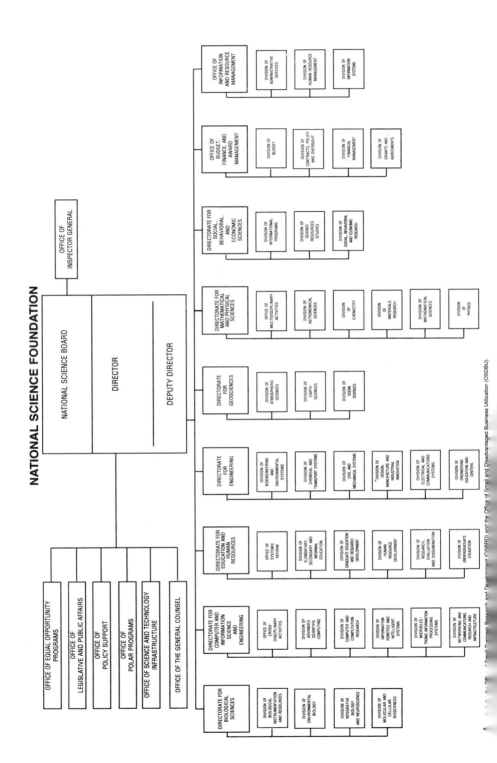

science and engineering, the agency also has an important role in national policy planning.

The Foundation consists of a National Science Board and a Director. The National Science Board is composed of 24 part-time members and the Director *ex officio.* Members are appointed by the President with the advice and consent of the Senate, for 6-year terms. They are selected because of their records of distinguished service and eminence in science, engineering, education, research management, or public affairs to be broadly representative of the views of national science and engineering leadership.

Both the Director and the Deputy Director are appointed by the President with the advice and consent of the Senate, to a 6-year term and an unspecified term, respectively.

The National Science Foundation Act assigns policymaking functions for the Foundation to the National Science Board, within the framework of applicable policies set forth by the President and the Congress, and assigns the administration of the Foundation to the Director. By statute the Director of the Foundation is a member of the Board and Chairman of the Executive Committee of the Board.

The Board also has a broad, national policy responsibility to monitor and make recommendations to promote the health of U.S. science and engineering research and education.

The Foundation's Office of Inspector General is responsible for conducting and supervising audits, inspections, and investigations relating to the programs and operations of the Foundation, including allegations of misconduct in science.

Activities

The National Science Foundation initiates and supports fundamental, long-term, merit-selected research in all the scientific and engineering disciplines. This support is made through grants, contracts, and other agreements awarded to universities, colleges, academic consortia, and nonprofit and small business institutions. Most of this research is directed toward the resolution of scientific and engineering questions concerning fundamental life processes, natural laws and phenomena, fundamental processes influencing the human environment, and the forces affecting people as members of society as well as the behavior of society as a whole.

The Foundation encourages cooperative efforts by universities, industries, and government. It also promotes the application of research and development for better products and services that improve the quality of life and stimulate economic growth.

The Foundation promotes the development of research talent through support of undergraduate and graduate students, as well as postdoctoral researchers. It administers special programs to identify and encourage participation by groups underrepresented in science and technology and to strengthen research capability at smaller institutions, small businesses, undergraduate colleges, and universities.

The Foundation supports major national and international science and engineering activities, including the U.S. Antarctic Program, the Ocean Drilling Program, global geoscience studies, and others. Cooperative scientific and engineering research activities support exchange programs for American and foreign scientists and engineers, execution of jointly designed research projects, participation in the activities of international science and engineering organizations, and travel to international conferences.

Support is provided through contracts and cooperative agreements with national centers where large facilities are made available for use by qualified scientists and engineers. Among the types of centers supported by the Foundation are astronomy and atmospheric sciences, biological and engineering research, science and technology, supercomputers, and long-term ecological research sites.

The Foundation provides competitively awarded grants for repair, renovation, or, in exceptional cases, replacement of facilities used for research and research training at academic and nonprofit institutions.

The Foundation's science and engineering education activities include grants for research and development activities directed to model instructional materials for students and teachers and the application of advanced technologies to education. Grants also are available for teacher preparation and enhancement and informal science education activities. Funding is also provided for college science instrumentation, course and curriculum improvement, faculty and student activities, and minority resource centers. In addition, studies of the status of math, science, and engineering education are supported.

The National Science Foundation presents annually the Alan T. Waterman Award to an outstanding young scientist or engineer for support of research and study. Periodically the National Science Board presents the honorary Vannevar Bush Award to a person who, through public service activities in science and technology, has made an outstanding contribution toward the welfare of mankind and the Nation. The two awards are designed to encourage individuals to seek to achieve the Nation's objectives in scientific and engineering research and education.

The Foundation also provides support for the President's Committee on the National Medal of Science.

Sources of Information

Board and Committee Minutes Summary minutes of the open meetings of the Board may be obtained from the National Science Board Office. Phone, 703–306–2000. Summary minutes of the Foundation's advisory groups may be obtained from the contacts listed in the notice of meetings published in the *Federal Register.* General information about the Foundation's advisory groups may be obtained from the Division of Human Resource Management, Room 315, Arlington, VA 22230. Phone, 703–306–1181.

Contracts The Foundation publicizes contracting and subcontracting opportunities in the *Commerce Business Daily* and other appropriate publications. Organizations seeking to undertake contract work for the Foundation should contact either the Division of Contracts, Policy, and Oversight (phone, 703–306–1242) or the Division of Administrative Services (phone, 703–306–1122), National Science Foundation, Arlington, VA 22230.

Employment Inquiries may be directed to the Division of Human Resource Management, National Science Foundation, Room 315, Arlington, VA 22230. Phone, 703–306–1182, or, for the hearing impaired (TDD), 703–306–0189. NSF vacancy hotline numbers are 703–306–0080 or 1–800–628–1487.

Fellowships Consult *NSF Guide to Programs* and appropriate announcements and brochures for postdoctoral fellowship opportunities that may be available through some Foundation divisions. Beginning graduate and minority graduate students wishing to apply for fellowships should contact the Directorate for Education and Human Resources. Phone, 703–306–1694.

Freedom of Information Act Requests Requests for agency records should be submitted in accordance with the Foundation FOIA regulation at 45 CFR, part 612. Such requests should be clearly identified with "FOIA REQUEST" and be addressed to the Office of Legislative and Public Affairs, National Science Foundation, Room 1245, Arlington, VA 22230. Phone, 703–306–1070.

Grants Individuals or organizations who plan to submit grant proposals should refer to the *NSF Guide to Programs, Grant Proposal Guide* (NSF 94–2), and appropriate program brochures and announcements that may be obtained as indicated in the Reference to Publications on page 645.

Office of Inspector General General inquiries may be directed to the Office of Inspector General, National Science Foundation, Room 1135, Arlington, VA 22230. Phone, 703–306–2100.

Privacy Act Requests   Requests for personal records should be submitted in accordance with the Foundation Privacy Act regulation at 45 CFR, part 613. Such requests should be clearly identified with "PRIVACY ACT REQUEST" and be addressed to the Privacy Act Officer, National Science Foundation, Room 485, Arlington, VA 22230. Phone, 703–306–1243.

Publications   The National Science Board assesses the status and health of science and its various disciplines, including such matters as human and material resources, in reports submitted to the President for submission to the Congress. The most recent report is *Science and Engineering Indicators, 1993.*

The National Science Foundation issues brochures that announce and describe new programs, critical dates, and application procedures for competitions. Single copies of these brochures, including *Publications of the National Science Foundation,* can be ordered in a variety of ways: phone, 703–306–1130; fax, 703–644–4278; via Internet: PUBS@NSF.GOV, or by writing to: National Science Foundation, Forms and Publications, Room P15, 4201 Wilson Boulevard, Arlington, VA 22230. These brochures are available electronically on the World Wide Web: NSF Home Page; Internet; Gopher; or the Science and Technology Information System (STIS). For more information about accessing NSF publications electronically, request the flyer *Getting NSF Information and Publication,* NSF 95–64.

Other Foundation publications include: the *Grant Policy Manual* (NSF 88–47), which contains comprehensive statements of Foundation grant administration policy, procedures, and guidance; *Guide to Programs,* which summarizes information about support programs; the quarterly *Antarctic Journal of the United States* and its annual review issue; and the *NSF Annual Report.* These publications are available from the Superintendent of Documents, Government Printing Office, Washington, DC 20402.

Reading Room   A collection of Foundation policy documents and staff instructions, as well as current indexes, are available to the public for inspection and copying during regular business hours, 8:30 a.m. to 5:00 p.m., Monday through Friday, in the National Science Foundation Library, Room 225, Arlington, VA 22230. Phone, 703–306–0658.

Small Business Activities   The Office of Small Business Research and Development provides information on opportunities for Foundation support to small businesses with strong research capabilities in science and technology. Phone, 703–306–1391. The Office of Small and Disadvantaged Business Utilization oversees agency compliance with the provisions of the Small Business Act and the Small Business Investment Act of 1958, as amended (15 U.S.C. 631, 661, 683). Phone, 703–306–1391.

For further information, contact the National Science Foundation Information Center, 4201 Wilson Boulevard, Second Floor, Arlington, VA 22230. Phone, 703–306–1234; TDD, 703–306–0189; or send e-mail message to INFO@NSF.GOV.

NATIONAL TRANSPORTATION SAFETY BOARD

490 L'Enfant Plaza SW., Washington, DC 20594
Phone, 202–382–6600

Chairman   JAMES E. HALL
Vice Chairman   ROBERT T. FRANCIS II

Members	JOHN A. HAMMERSCHMIDT, (2 VACANCIES)
Managing Director	KENNETH V. JORDAN
Deputy Managing Director	RONALD S. BATTOCCHI
Director, Office of Government Affairs	PETER GOELZ
Director, Office of Public Affairs	JULIE BEAL
Deputy Director	ALAN M. POLLOCK
General Counsel	DANIEL D. CAMPBELL
Deputy General Counsel	DAVID BASS
Director, Office of Aviation Safety	WILLIAM G. LAYNOR, *Acting*
Deputy Director	RONALD SCHLEEDE, *Acting*
Director, Office of Research and Engineering	BERNARD S. LOEB
Deputy Director	VERNON ELLINGSTAD
Director, Office of Safety Recommendations	BARRY M. SWEEDLER
Deputy Director	RICHARD VAN WOERKOM
Director, Office of Surface Transportation Safety	JAMES A. ARENA
Deputy Director	RALPH E. JOHNSON
Director, Office of Administration	B. MICHAEL LEVINS
Deputy Director	(VACANCY)
Chief Administrative Law Judge	WILLIAM E. FOWLER, JR.

[For the National Transportation Safety Board statement of organization, see the *Code of Federal Regulations*, Title 49, Part 800]

The National Transportation Safety Board seeks to assure that all types of transportation in the United States are conducted safely. The Board investigates accidents, conducts studies, and makes recommendations to Government agencies, the transportation industry, and others on safety measures and practices.

The National Transportation Safety Board was established in 1967 and made totally independent on April 1, 1975, by the Independent Safety Board Act of 1974 (49 U.S.C. app. 1901).

The Safety Board consists of five members appointed by the President with the advice and consent of the Senate for 5-year terms. The President designates two of these members as Chairman and Vice Chairman of the Board for 2-year terms. The designation of the Chairman is made with the advice and consent of the Senate.

Activities

Accident Investigation The Board is responsible for investigating, determining probable cause, making safety recommendations, and reporting the facts and circumstances of:

—U.S. civil aviation and certain public-use aircraft accidents;

—railroad accidents in which there is a fatality or substantial property damage, or that involve a passenger train;

—pipeline accidents in which there is a fatality, substantial property damage, or significant injury to the environment;

—highway accidents, including railroad grade-crossing accidents that the Board selects in cooperation with the States;

—major marine casualties, and marine accidents involving a public vessel and a nonpublic vessel, in accordance with regulations prescribed jointly by the Board and the U.S. Coast Guard; and

—other transportation accidents that are catastrophic, involve problems of a recurring character, or otherwise should be investigated in the judgment of the Board.

Safety Problem Identification In addition, the Board makes recommendations on matters pertaining to transportation safety and is a catalyst for transportation accident prevention by conducting safety studies and special

NATIONAL TRANSPORTATION SAFETY BOARD

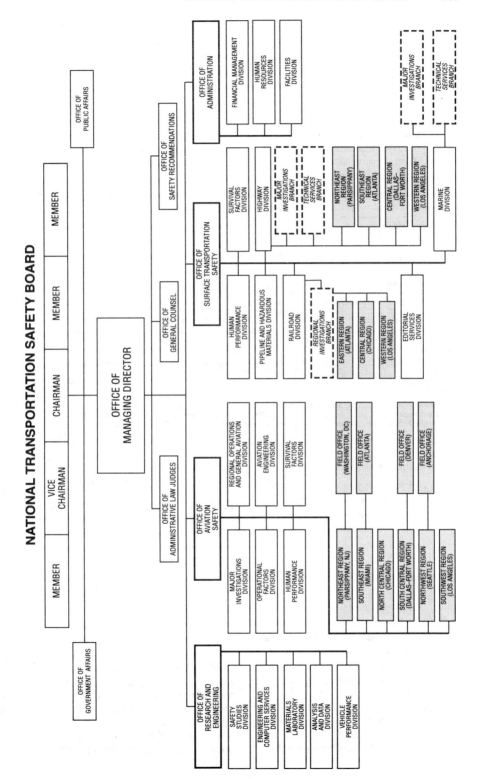

investigations, assessing techniques of accident investigation and publishing recommended procedures for these investigations, establishing regulatory requirements for reporting accidents, evaluating the transportation safety consciousness and efficacy of other Government agencies in the prevention of accidents, evaluating the adequacy of safeguards and procedures concerning the transportation of hazardous materials and the performance of other

Government agencies charged with ensuring the safe transportation of such materials, and reporting annually to the Congress on its activities.

Certificate, Civil Penalty, or License Appeal   The Board also reviews on appeal the suspension, amendment, modification, revocation, or denial of certain certificates, licenses, or assessments of civil penalties issued by the Secretary or an Administrator of the Department of Transportation.

Regional/Field Offices—National Transportation Safety Board
(R: Regional Director; FC: Field Chief)

Region/Field Office	Address	Officer
AVIATION:		
North Central Region	31 W. 775 North Ave., West Chicago, IL 60185	Carl Dinwiddie (R)
South Central Region	Suite 300, 1200 Copeland Rd., Arlington, TX 76011	Tommy McFall (R)
South Central Field	Suite 500, 4760 Oakland St., Denver, CO 80239	Norm Wiemeyer (FC)
Southwest Region	Suite 555, 1515 W. 190th St., Gardena, CA 90248	Gary Mucho (R)
Southeast Region	Suite B–103, 8405 NW. 53d St., Miami, FL 33166	Jorge Prellezo (R)
Southeast Field	Suite 321, 1720 Peachtree St. NW., Atlanta, GA 30309	Preston Hicks (FC)
Northeast Region	Suite 203, 2001 Rte. 46, Parsippany, NJ 07054	Dennis Jones (R)
Northeast Field	490 L'Enfant Plz. SW., Washington, DC 20594	Jodi Reeves (FC)
Northwest Region	Rm. 201, 19518 Pacific Hwy. S., Seattle, WA 98188	Keith McGuire (R)
Northwest Field	Box 11, Rm. 142, 222 W. 7th Ave., Anchorage, AK 99513	Jim LaBelle (FC)
RAILROAD:		
Central Region	31 W. 775 North Ave., West Chicago, IL 60185	Russ Seipler (R)
Western Region	Suite 555, 1515 W. 190th St., Gardena, CA 90248	Dave Watson (R)
Eastern Region	Suite 321, 1720 Peachtree St. NW., Atlanta, GA 30309	Mark Garcia (R)
HIGHWAY:		
Central Region	Suite 300, 1200 Copeland Rd., Arlington, TX 76011	Kennith Rogers (R)
Western Region	Suite 555, 1515 W. 190th St., Gardena, CA 90248	Ronald Robinson (R)
Southeast Region	Suite 321, 1720 Peachtree St. NW., Atlanta, GA 30309	Jay Golden (R)
Northeast Region	Suite 203, 2001 Rte. 46, Parsippany, NJ 07054	Frank Ghiorsi (R)

Sources of Information

Contracts and Procurement   Inquiries regarding the Board's procurement and contracting activities should be addressed to the Contracting Officer, Budget and Financial Policy, National Transportation Safety Board, Washington, DC 20594. Phone, 202–382–6707.

Employment   Send applications for employment to the Human Resources Division, National Transportation Safety Board, Washington, DC 20594. Phone, 202–382–6718.

Publications   Publications are provided free of charge to the following categories of subscribers: Federal, State, or local transportation agencies; international transportation organizations or foreign governments; educational institutions or public libraries; nonprofit public safety

organizations; and the news media. Persons in these categories who are interested in receiving copies of Board publications should contact the Public Inquiries Branch, National Transportation Safety Board, Washington, DC 20594. Phone, 202–382–6735.

All other persons interested in receiving publications must purchase them from the National Technical Information Service, 5285 Port Royal Road, Springfield, VA 22161. Orders may be placed by telephone to the Subscription Unit, 703–487–4630, or to the sales desk on 703–487–4768.

Reading Room   The Public Reference Room of the Board is available for record inspection or photocopying. It is located in Room 5111 at the Board's Washington, DC, headquarters and is open 9:00 a.m. to 4:00 p.m. every business day. Requests for access to public records should be made in person at Room 5111, or by writing the Public Inquiries Branch, National Transportation Safety Board, Washington, DC 20594. Phone, 202–382–6735.

For further information, contact the Office of Public Affairs, National Transportation Safety Board, 490 L'Enfant Plaza SW., Washington, DC 20594. Phone, 202–382–0660. Fax, 202–287–2617.

NUCLEAR REGULATORY COMMISSION
Washington, DC 20555
Phone, 301–415–7000

Chairman	IVAN SELIN
Executive Assistant	DENNIS K. RATHBUN
Legal Assistant	KATHRYN WINSBERG
Commissioner	KENNETH C. ROGERS
Legal Assistant	MYRON KARMAN
Commissioner	E. GAIL DE PLANQUE
Legal Assistant	E. NEIL JENSEN
Chairman, Advisory Committee on Reactor Safeguards	THOMAS S. KRESS
Chairman, Advisory Committee on Nuclear Waste	MARTIN J. STEINDLER
Chief Administrative Judge, Atomic Safety and Licensing Board Panel	B. PAUL COTTER, JR.
Chairman, Advisory Committee on Medical Uses of Isotopes	BARRY SIEGEL, M.D. [1]
Director, Office of Commission Appellate Adjudication	JOHN F. CORDES, JR., *Acting*
Inspector General	DAVID C. WILLIAMS
General Counsel	KAREN D. CYR
Secretary of the Commission	JOHN C. HOYLE
Director, Office of International Programs	CARLTON R. STOIBER
Director, Office of Congressional Affairs	DENNIS K. RATHBUN
Director, Office of Public Affairs	WILLIAM M. BEECHER
Executive Director for Operations	JAMES M. TAYLOR
Deputy Executive Director for Nuclear Reactor Regulation, Regional Operations and Research	JAMES L. MILHOAN
Deputy Executive Director for Nuclear Materials Safety, Safeguards and Operations Support	HUGH L. THOMPSON, JR.
Assistant for Operations	JAMES L. BLAHA
Regional Administrator, Region I (King of Prussia, PA)	THOMAS T. MARTIN
Regional Administrator, Region II (Atlanta, GA)	STEWART D. EBNETER
Regional Administrator, Region III (Lisle, IL)	JOHN B. MARTIN
Regional Administrator, Region IV (Arlington, TX)	LEONARD J. CALLAN

[1] Contact Larry W. Camper, NMSS/NRC.

Director, Walnut Creek, CA, Field Office (Region IV)	KENNETH E. PERKINS, JR.
Director, Office of Investigations	GUY P. CAPUTO
Director, Office of Enforcement	JAMES LIEBERMAN
Deputy Chief Financial Officer/Controller, Office of the Controller	RONALD M. SCROGGINS
Director, Office of Administration	PATRICIA G. NORRY
Director, Office of Information Resources Management	GERALD F. CRANFORD
Director, Office of Small Business and Civil Rights	VANDY MILLER
Director, Office for Analysis and Evaluation of Operational Data	EDWARD L. JORDAN
Director, Office of Personnel	PAUL E. BIRD
Director, Office of State Programs	RICHARD L. BANGART
Director, Office of Nuclear Material Safety and Safeguards	CARL J. PAPERIELLO
Deputy Director, Office of Nuclear Material Safety and Safeguards	MALCOLM R. KNAPP
Director, Division of Fuel Cycle Safety and Safeguards	ROBERT F. BURNETT
Director, Division of Industrial and Medical Nuclear Safety	DONALD A. COOL
Director, Division of Waste Management	JOHN T. GREEVES
Director, Office of Nuclear Reactor Regulation	WILLIAM T. RUSSELL
Deputy Director, Office of Nuclear Reactor Regulation	FRANK J. MIRAGLIA, JR.
Associate Director for Projects	ROY P. ZIMMERMAN
Director, Division of Reactor Projects—I/II	STEVEN A. VARGA
Director, Division of Reactor Projects—III/IV	JACK W. ROE
Director, Division of Project Support	BRIAN K. GRIMES
Associate Director for Advanced Reactors and License Renewal	DENNIS M. CRUTCHFIELD
Associate Director for Inspection and Technical Assessment	ASHOK C. THADANI
Director, Division of Engineering	BRIAN SHERON
Director, Division of Systems Safety and Analysis	GARY M. HOLLAHAN
Director, Division of Technical Support	RICHARD L. SPESSARD
Director, Division of Reactor Controls and Human Factors	BRUCE A. BOGER
Director, Inspection and Support Programs	FRANCIS P. GILLESPIE
Director, Office of Nuclear Regulatory Research	DAVID L. MORRISON
Deputy Director	THEMIS P. SPEIS
Director, Division of Engineering Technology	LAWRENCE C. SHAO
Director, Division of Systems Technology	M. WAYNE HODGES
Director, Division of Regulatory Applications	BILL M. MORRIS

[For the Nuclear Regulatory Commission statement of organization, see the *Code of Federal Regulations,* Title 10, Part I]

The Nuclear Regulatory Commission licenses and regulates civilian use of nuclear energy to protect public health and safety and the environment. This is achieved by licensing persons and companies to build and operate nuclear reactors and other

NUCLEAR REGULATORY COMMISSION

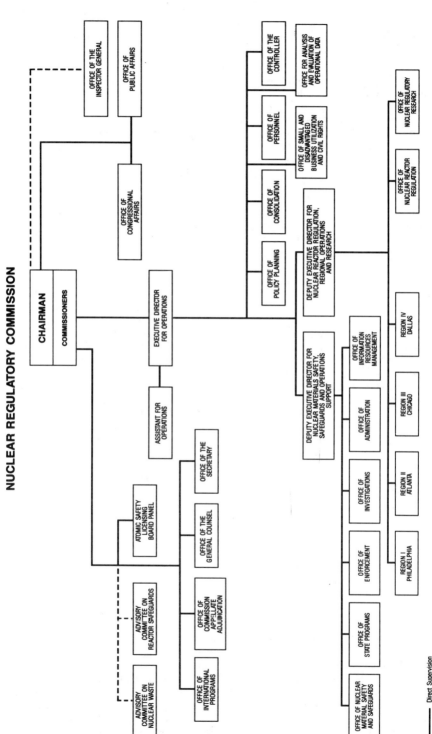

OFFICE OF THE INSPECTOR GENERAL

OFFICE OF PUBLIC AFFAIRS

OFFICE OF CONGRESSIONAL AFFAIRS

CHAIRMAN

COMMISSIONERS

EXECUTIVE DIRECTOR FOR OPERATIONS

ASSISTANT FOR OPERATIONS

ATOMIC SAFETY LICENSING BOARD PANEL

OFFICE OF THE SECRETARY

OFFICE OF THE GENERAL COUNSEL

OFFICE OF COMMISSION APPELLATE ADJUDICATION

ADVISORY COMMITTEE ON REACTOR SAFEGUARDS

ADVISORY COMMITTEE ON NUCLEAR WASTE

OFFICE OF INTERNATIONAL PROGRAMS

OFFICE OF THE CONTROLLER

OFFICE FOR ANALYSIS AND EVALUATION OF OPERATIONAL DATA

OFFICE OF PERSONNEL

OFFICE OF SMALL AND DISADVANTAGED BUSINESS UTILIZATION AND CIVIL RIGHTS

OFFICE OF CONSOLIDATION

OFFICE OF POLICY PLANNING

DEPUTY EXECUTIVE DIRECTOR FOR NUCLEAR REACTOR REGULATION, REGIONAL OPERATIONS AND RESEARCH

OFFICE OF NUCLEAR REGULATORY RESEARCH

OFFICE OF NUCLEAR REACTOR REGULATION

DEPUTY EXECUTIVE DIRECTOR FOR NUCLEAR MATERIALS SAFETY, SAFEGUARDS AND OPERATIONS SUPPORT

OFFICE OF INFORMATION RESOURCES MANAGEMENT

OFFICE OF ADMINISTRATION

OFFICE OF INVESTIGATIONS

OFFICE OF ENFORCEMENT

OFFICE OF STATE PROGRAMS

OFFICE OF NUCLEAR MATERIAL SAFETY AND SAFEGUARDS

REGION IV DALLAS

REGION III CHICAGO

REGION II ATLANTA

REGION I PHILADELPHIA

——— Direct Supervision
- - - Coordination

facilities and to own and use nuclear materials. The Commission makes rules and sets standards for these types of licenses. It also carefully inspects the activities of the persons and companies licensed to ensure that they do not violate the safety rules of the Commission.

The Nuclear Regulatory Commission (NRC) was established as an independent regulatory agency under the provisions of the Energy Reorganization Act of 1974 (42 U.S.C. 5801) and Executive Order 11834 of January 15, 1975, effective January 19, 1975. Transferred to the Commission were all licensing and related regulatory functions formerly assigned to the Atomic Energy Commission, which was established by the Atomic Energy Act of 1946 (60 Stat. 755), as amended by the Atomic Energy Act of 1954, as amended (42 U.S.C. 2011 *et seq.*).

The Commission's major program components are the Office of Nuclear Reactor Regulation, the Office of Nuclear Material Safety and Safeguards, and the Office of Nuclear Regulatory Research, which were created by the Energy Reorganization Act of 1974. Headquarters offices are located in suburban Maryland, and there are four regional offices.

The Commission ensures that the civilian uses of nuclear materials and facilities are conducted in a manner consistent with the public health and safety, environmental quality, national security, and the antitrust laws. The major share of the Commission's effort is focused on regulating the use of nuclear energy to generate electric power.

Activities

The Nuclear Regulatory Commission fulfills its responsibilities through a system of licensing and regulatory activities that include:

—licensing the construction and operation of nuclear reactors and other nuclear facilities, such as nuclear fuel cycle facilities and nonpower test and research reactors, and overseeing their decommissioning;

—licensing the possession, use, processing, handling, and export of nuclear material;

—licensing the siting, design, construction, operation, and closure of low-level radioactive waste disposal sites under NRC jurisdiction and the construction, operation, and closure of the geologic repository for high-level radioactive waste;

—licensing the operators of nuclear power and nonpower test and research reactors;

—inspecting licensed facilities and activities;

—conducting the principal U.S. Government research program on light-water reactor safety;

—conducting research to provide independent expertise and information for making timely regulatory judgments and for anticipating problems of potential safety significance;

—developing and implementing rules and regulations that govern licensed nuclear activities;

—investigating nuclear incidents and allegations concerning any matter regulated by the NRC;

—enforcing NRC regulations and the conditions of NRC licenses;

—conducting public hearings on matters of nuclear and radiological safety, environmental concern, common defense and security, and antitrust matters;

—maintaining the NRC Incident Response Program, including the NRC Operations Center;

—collecting, analyzing, and disseminating information about the operational safety of commercial nuclear power reactors and certain nonreactor activities; and

—developing effective working relationships with the States regarding reactor operations and the regulation of nuclear material, including assurance that adequate regulatory programs are maintained by those States that exercise, by agreement with the Commission, regulatory control over certain nuclear materials in the State.

Sources of Information

Contracts and Procurement Detailed information on how to do business with the Commission may be obtained by calling the Director, Division of Contracts, at 301–415–7305. Information on programs to assist small business is available from the Director, Office of Small Business and Civil Rights, Mail Stop T2F18, Nuclear Regulatory Commission, Washington, DC 20555–0001. Phone, 301–415–7380.

Employment The Commission's employment activities are exempt from civil service requirements and are conducted under an independent merit system. However, employees receive Federal employee benefits (retirement, group life insurance, and health benefits) on the same basis as other Federal employees. Applicants with veterans preference are accorded the preference granted to them by the Veterans' Preference Act of 1944 (58 Stat. 387).

Recruitment is continual, and applications from individuals qualified for Commission needs are accepted whenever they are received. In addition to receiving applications from candidates at all grade levels throughout the year, the agency recruits annually from colleges as appropriate to fill needs for interns and entry-level professionals.

Employment inquiries, applications, and requests from schools for participation in the recruitment program may be directed to the Director, Office of Personnel, Mail Stop T3A2, Nuclear Regulatory Commission, Washington, DC 20555–0001. Phone, 301–415–7516.

Freedom of Information Act Requests Requests for copies of records should be directed to the Chief, FOIA/LPDR Branch, Mail Stop T6D8, Nuclear Regulatory Commission, Washington, DC 20555–0001. Phone, 301–415–7169.

Publications The NRC *Annual Report,* NUREG–1145, provides a summary of major agency activities for the year. *Nuclear Regulatory Commission Issuances,* NUREG–0750 (monthly— four indexes and 2 hard-bound editions), a compilation of adjudications and other issuances for the Commission, including Atomic Safety and Licensing Boards, is available for sale from the Government Printing Office, either by subscription or on a single-issue basis. Other subscription items available from the Government Printing Office include: *Licensed Operating Reactors-Status Summary Report* (annual), NUREG–0020; *Licensee, Contractor and Vendor Inspection Status Report* (quarterly), NUREG–0040; *Report to Congress on Abnormal Occurrences* (quarterly), NUREG–0090; *Regulatory and Technical Reports* (quarterly), NUREG–0304; *Title List of Documents Made Publicly Available* (monthly), NUREG–0540; *U.S. Nuclear Regulatory Commission Rules and Regulations; U.S. NRC Telephone Directory,* NUREG/BR–0046; and the *Weekly Information Report.* Pricing and ordering information may be obtained by writing to the Superintendent of Documents, Government Printing Office, P.O. Box 37082, Washington, DC 20013–7082. Phone, 202–512–1800.

The Commission produces a variety of scientific, technical, and administrative information publications dealing with licensing and regulating civilian nuclear power. Information on agency publications can be obtained from *Title List of Documents Made Publicly Available,* NUREG–0540. This document, published monthly, includes docketed material associated with civilian nuclear power plants and other uses of radioactive materials, and nondocketed material received and generated by the Commission pertinent to its role as a regulatory agency. Single copies of monthly issues of NUREG–0540 are available for purchase from the Government Printing Office and from the National Technical Information Service, Springfield, VA 22161. Phone, 703–487–4099. Subscription service for the *Standard Review Plan,* NUREG–0800, is handled exclusively by the National Technical Information Service.

Active *Regulatory Guides* may be purchased from the Government Printing Office or, as they are issued, on standing orders from the National Technical Information Service. These *Regulatory Guides* are published in 10 subject areas: Power Reactors, Research and Test Reactors, Fuels and Materials Facilities, Environmental and Siting, Materials and Plant Protection, Products, Transportation, Occupational Health, Antitrust and Financial Review, and General.

Single copies of some draft publications, such as *Draft Environmental Statements* and *Draft Regulatory Guides*, are available without charge, based on supply, from the Nuclear Regulatory Commission, Distribution and Mail Services Section, Washington, DC 20555–0001. Interested persons may be placed on a Commission mailing list for *Draft Regulatory Guides* by writing to the Distribution and Mail Services Section, NRC, Washington, DC 20555–0001.

Nuclear Regulatory Commission Regulatory Agenda (NUREG–0936), published in the *Federal Register* each April and October, is updated semiannually.

Documents in the NUREG series may be purchased from the Superintendent of Documents, Government Printing Office, P.O. Box 37082, Washington, DC 20013–7082. Copies are also available from the National Technical Information Service, 5285 Port Royal Road, Springfield, VA 22161. Persons may obtain information regarding the status of any regulation or petition for rulemaking before the Commission by calling 301–415–7158.

Reading Rooms The Headquarters Public Document Room maintains an extensive collection of documents related to NRC licensing proceedings and other significant decisions and actions, and documents from the regulatory activities of the former Atomic Energy Commission. Books, journals, trade publications, or documents on industry standards are not stocked in the Reading Room. Persons interested in detailed, technical information about nuclear facilities and other licensees find this specialized research center to be a major resource. Located at 2120 L Street NW., Washington, DC, the Public Document Room is open Monday through Friday from 7:45 a.m. to 4:15 p.m., except on Federal holidays.

Documents from the collection may be reproduced, with some exceptions, on paper, microfiche, or diskette for a nominal fee. The Public Document Room also offers an order subscription service for selected serially published documents and reports. Certain items of immediate interest, such as press releases and meeting notices, are posted in the Reading Room and on an electronic bulletin board via FedWorld, a Governmentwide computer bulletin board system. Contact FedWorld at 703–487–4608 for access to the Public Document Room bulletin board.

Reference librarians are available to assist users with information requests. The computerized online Bibliographic Retrieval System includes extensive indices to the collection and an online ordering module for the placement of orders for the reproduction and delivery of specific documents. Off-site access to the Bibliographic Retrieval System (at 1200, 2400, and 9600 baud) is available for searches 24 hours a day, including weekends and holidays. Access to the system may be arranged by calling the number listed below.

For additional information regarding the Public Document Room contact the Nuclear Regulatory Commission, Public Document Room, Washington, DC 20555. Phone, 202–634–3273 or toll free, 800–397–4209; via Internet, pdr@nrc.gov; or fax, 202–634–3343.

In addition, the Commission maintains approximately 87 local public document rooms around the country. The document rooms are located in libraries in cities and towns near commercially operated nuclear power reactors and certain nonpower reactor facilities. They contain detailed information specific to the nearby facilities, which are either licensed or under regulatory review. Power reactor and high-level radioactive waste local public document rooms also contain a microfiche file of all publicly available NRC documents issued since January 1981. A list of local public document rooms is available from the Director, Division of Freedom of Information and Publications Services, Nuclear Regulatory Commission, Washington, DC 20555–0001. To obtain specific information about the availability of documents at the local public document rooms, NRC's Local Public Document Room Program staff may be contacted directly by calling toll-free, 800–638–8081.

For further information, contact the Office of Public Affairs, Nuclear Regulatory Commission, Washington, DC 20555–0001. Phone, 301–504–2240.

OCCUPATIONAL SAFETY AND HEALTH REVIEW COMMISSION

1120 Twentieth Street NW., Washington, DC 20036–3419
Phone, 202–606–5100

Chairman	STUART E. WEISBERG
Commissioners	VELMA MONTOYA
	(VACANCY)
Executive Director	WILLIAM J. GAINER
Chief Administrative Law Judge	IRVING SOMMER
General Counsel	EARL R. OHMAN, JR.
Executive Secretary	RAY H. DARLING, JR.
Public Affairs Specialist	LINDA A. WHITSETT

The Occupational Safety and Health Review Commission works to ensure the timely and fair resolution of cases involving the alleged exposure of American workers to unsafe or unhealthy working conditions.

The Occupational Safety and Health Review Commission is an independent, quasi-judicial agency established by the Occupational Safety and Health Act of 1970 (29 U.S.C. 651–678).

The Commission is charged with ruling on cases forwarded to it by the Department of Labor when disagreements arise over the results of safety and health inspections performed by the Department's Occupational Safety and Health Administration. Employers have the right to dispute any alleged job safety or health violation found during the inspection by the Administration, the penalties it proposed, and the time given by the agency to correct any hazardous situation. Employees and representatives of employees may initiate a case by challenging the propriety of the time the Administration has allowed for correction of any violative condition.

The Occupational Safety and Health Act covers virtually every employer in the country. Enforced by the Secretary of Labor, the act is an effort to reduce the incidence of personal injuries, illness, and deaths among working men and women in the United States that result from their employment. It requires employers to furnish to each of their employees a working environment free from recognized hazards that are causing or likely to cause death or serious physical harm to the employees and to comply with occupational safety and health standards promulgated under the act.

Activities

The Commission was created to adjudicate enforcement actions initiated under the act when they are contested by employers, employees, or representatives of employees. A case arises when a citation is issued against an employer as the result of an Occupational Safety and Health Administration inspection and it is contested within 15 working days.

The Commission is more of a court system than a simple tribunal, for within

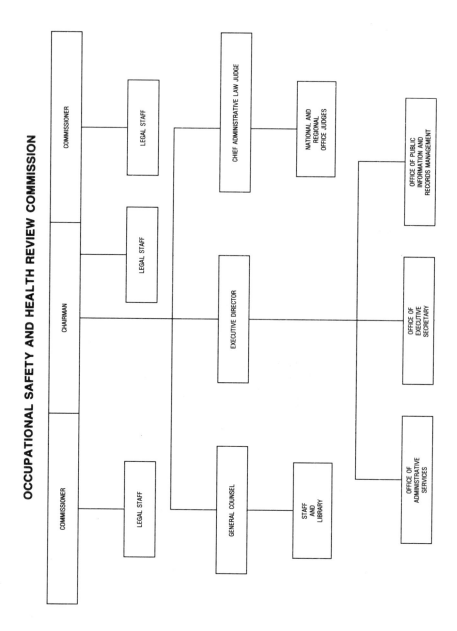

OCCUPATIONAL SAFETY AND HEALTH REVIEW COMMISSION

the Commission there are two levels of adjudication. All cases that require a hearing are assigned to an administrative law judge, who decides the case. Ordinarily the hearing is held in the community where the alleged violation occurred or as close as possible. At the hearing, the Secretary of Labor will generally have the burden of proving the case. After the hearing, the judge must issue a decision, based on findings of fact and conclusions of law.

A substantial number of the decisions of the judges become final orders of the Commission. However, each decision is subject to discretionary review by the three members of the Commission upon the direction of any one of the three, if done within 30 days of the filing of the decision. When that occurs, the Commission issues its own decision.

Once a case is decided, any person adversely affected or aggrieved thereby may obtain a review of the decision in the United States Courts of Appeals.

The principal office of the Commission is in Washington, DC. There are also four regional offices where Commission judges are stationed.

Review Commission Judges—Occupational Safety Review Commission

City/Address	Telephone
Atlanta, GA (1365 Peachtree St. NE., 30309)	404–347–4197
Boston, MA (John W. McCormack Post Office and Courthouse, 02110)	617–223–9746
Dallas, TX (1100 Commerce St., 75242)	214–767–5271
Denver, CO (1050 17th St., 80265)	303–844–2281

Sources of Information

Publications Copies of the Commission's *Rules of Procedure, Guide to the Rules of Procedure,* decisions, *Annual Report to the President,* and pamphlets explaining the functions of the Commission are available from the Commission's Public Affairs Specialist at the Commission's Washington office.

For further information, contact the Public Affairs Specialist, Occupational Safety and Health Review Commission, 1120 Twentieth Street NW., Washington, DC 20036–3419. Phone, 202–606–5398. Fax, 202–606–5050.

OFFICE OF GOVERNMENT ETHICS

Suite 500, 1201 New York Avenue NW., Washington, DC 20005–3917
Phone, 202–523–5757

Director	STEPHEN D. POTTS
Deputy Director	DONALD E. CAMPBELL
General Counsel	F. GARY DAVIS
Deputy General Counsel	JANE S. LEY
Associate Director for Administration	ROBERT E. LAMMON
Associate Director for Education	BARBARA A. MULLEN-ROTH
Associate Director for Program Assistance and Review	JACK COVALESKI

[For the Office of Government Ethics statement of organization, see the *Code of Federal Regulations,* Title 5, Part 2600]

The Office of Government Ethics provides overall direction of executive branch policies in preventing conflicts of interest on the part of officers and employees of all executive agencies. The Office is the principal agency for administering the Ethics in Government Act for the executive branch.

The Office of Government Ethics is a separate executive agency established under the Ethics in Government Act of 1978, as amended (5 U.S.C. app. 401).

The Director of the Office is appointed by the President with the advice and consent of the Senate for a 5-year term, and is required to submit to Congress a biennial report concerning the implementation of the Director's functions and responsibilities.

Activities

The chief responsibilities of the Office are:

—developing, in consultation with the Attorney General and the Office of Personnel Management, rules and regulations to be promulgated by the President or the Director of the Office of Government Ethics pertaining to standards of ethical conduct of executive agencies, public and confidential financial disclosure of executive branch officials, executive agency ethics training programs, and the identification and resolution of conflicts of interest;

—monitoring and investigating compliance with the executive branch financial disclosure requirements of the Ethics in Government Act of 1978, as amended;

—providing ethics program assistance and information to executive branch agencies through a desk officer system;

—conducting periodic reviews of the ethics programs of executive agencies;

—ordering corrective action on the part of agencies and employees that the Director of the Office deems necessary, including orders to establish or modify an agency's ethics program;

—providing guidance on and promoting understanding of ethical standards in executive agencies through an extensive program of Government ethics advice, education, and training;

—evaluating the effectiveness of the Ethics Act, the conflict of interest laws, and other related statutes; and

—recommending appropriate new legislation or amendments.

Sources of Information

The Office of Government Ethics provides advisory letters and memoranda and formal advisory opinions in an annually updated publication, *The Informal Advisory Letters and Memoranda and Formal Opinions of the United States Office of Government Ethics,* available from the Government Printing Office. In addition, the Office publishes a periodic newsletter on Government ethics, offers a free ethics electronic bulletin board service (phone via modem, 202–523–1186), and has available ethics publications, instructional videotapes, and a CD–ROM. The Office also, upon request, provides copies of executive branch public financial disclosure reports (SF 278's) in accordance with the Ethics Act and the Office's regulations.

For further information, contact the Office of Government Ethics, Suite 500, 1201 New York Avenue NW., Washington, DC 20005–3917. Phone, 202–523–5757; hearing-impaired, 202–532–1200. Fax, 202–523–6325..

OFFICE OF PERSONNEL MANAGEMENT

1900 E Street NW., Washington, DC 20415–0001
Phone, 202–606–1800

Director	JAMES B. KING
Deputy Director	LORRAINE A. GREEN
General Counsel	LORRAINE LEWIS
Director, Office of Congressional Relations	IRA N. FOREMAN
Director, Office of Communications	JANICE R. LACHANCE

Director, Office of International Affairs	CARMEN LOMELLIN
Inspector General	PATRICK E. MCFARLAND
Chief Financial Officer	J. GILBERT SEAUX
Chairman, Federal Prevailing Rate Advisory Committee	ANTHONY F. INGRASSIA
Director, Office of Merit Systems and Oversight and Effectiveness	CAROL J. OKIN
Associate Director for Investigations Service	PATRICIA W. LATTIMORE, *Acting*
Associate Director for Retirement and Insurance Service	CURTIS J. SMITH
Associate Director for Employment Service	LEONARD R. KLEIN
Associate Director, Human Resources Systems Service	ALLEN HEUERMAN, *Acting*
Associate Director, Workforce Training Service	JUDITH M. JAFFE
Director, Office of Executive Resources	CURTIS J. SMITH
Director, Office of Contracting and Administrative Services	LYNN L. FURMAN
Director, Office of Information Technology	GLENN SUTTON, *Acting*
Director, Office of Human Resources and Equal Employment Opportunity	WILLIAM R. IRVIN

[For the Office of Personnel Management statement of organization, see the *Federal Register* of Jan. 5, 1979, 44 FR 1501]

The Office of Personnel Management administers a merit system for Federal employment that includes recruiting, examining, training, and promoting people on the basis of their knowledge and skills, regardless of their race, religion, sex, political influence, or other nonmerit factors. The Office's role is to ensure that the Federal Government provides an array of personnel services to applicants and employees. Through a range of programs designed to develop and encourage the effectiveness of the Government employee, the Office supports Government program managers in their personnel management responsibilities and provides benefits to employees and to retired employees and their survivors.

The Office of Personnel Management was created as an independent establishment by Reorganization Plan No. 2 of 1978 (5 U.S.C. app.), effective January 1, 1979, pursuant to Executive Order 12107 of December 28, 1978. Transferred to OPM were many of the functions of the former United States Civil Service Commission. The Office's duties and authority are specified in the Civil Service Reform Act of 1978 (5 U.S.C. 1101).

The five regional offices carry out programs in the field. In addition the Office has service centers in key locations, Federal job information and testing centers, and other field duty stations.

Office of the Inspector General   The Office of the Inspector General conducts comprehensive and independent audits, investigations, and evaluations relating to

the programs and operations of the agency. The Office is responsible for administrative actions against health care providers who commit sanctionable offenses with respect to the Federal Employees' Health Benefits Program or other Federal programs. The Office keeps the Director and Congress fully informed about problems and deficiencies in the administration of agency programs and operations, and the necessity for corrective action.

For further information, contact the Office of the Inspector General. Phone, 202–606–1200.

Activities

Examining and Staffing   The Office of Personnel Management is responsible for managing, nationwide in partnership with departments and agencies, the examining of applicants for competitive

OFFICE OF PERSONNEL MANAGEMENT

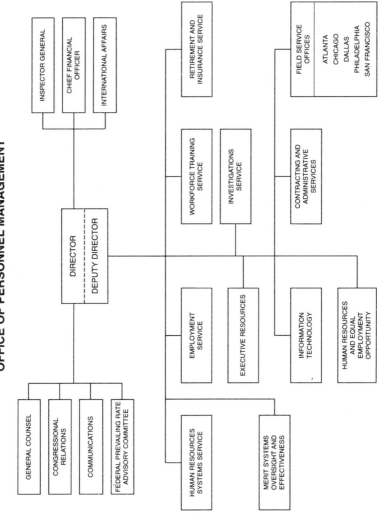

positions in the Federal civil service at General Schedule grades 1 through 15 and for Federal wage system positions. In addition to administering examinations, the Office is also responsible for:
—establishing basic qualification standards for all occupations;
—establishing conditions for delegating examining authority to agencies;
—providing policy direction and guidance for promotion, reassignment, transfer, and reinstatement of employees already recruited into the competitive civil service; and
—authorizing agencies to fill positions outside the competitive service when examining is impracticable or when the positions are policy-determining or confidential in nature.

The Office also administers the Qualification Review Board examining process for career Senior Executive Service appointments and conducts a competitive examination of applicants for administrative law judge positions.

Personnel Investigations   Personnel investigations are used in support of the selection and appointment processes. They serve several purposes:
—to determine the suitability of applicants under consideration for appointment;
—to check on applicants or employees under consideration for appointment to positions having either national security and/or public trust requirements; and
—to enforce civil service regulations.

Recruiting and Affirmative Employment The Office provides leadership, direction, and policy for Governmentwide recruiting programs. These programs include general external and internal recruiting, academic relations, and comparable programs designed to reach the Nation's population, including programs for students, people with disabilities, veterans, women, and minorities. Policy, guidance, and technical assistance are provided to agencies in implementing the following programs: generic recruiting initiatives, student employment, disabled veterans

affirmative action, and Federal equal opportunity recruitment. The Office is also responsible for assuring that recruiting and affirmative employment practices are integral parts of all Federal personnel management activities.

Employee Development and Training The Office plans, promotes, sets standards, and evaluates Governmentwide programs and policies for the development and training of Federal employees. It offers a wide variety of training and development management services such as career development programs and contractual access to the private sector for courses and instructional technology application. It also provides training and development information and coordination services. Through a nationwide network of interagency training centers, a European center, management development centers, and the Federal Executive Institute, it offers a broad range of Government-related courses.

Personnel Systems   The Office sets policy for, administers, and provides leadership and guidance to agencies on systems to support the manager's personnel management responsibilities. It also provides administrative support to special advisory bodies, including the Federal Prevailing Rate Advisory Committee, the Federal Salary Council, and the National Partnership Council. These include:
—white and blue collar pay systems, including Senior Executive Service and special occupational pay systems; geographical adjustments and locality payments; special rates to address recruitment and retention problems; allowances and differentials, including recruitment and relocation bonuses, retention allowances, and hazardous duty/environmental pay; and premium pay;
—annual and sick leave, court leave, military leave, leave transfer and leave bank programs, family and medical leave, excused absence, holidays, and scheduling of work—including flexible and compressed work schedules;
—performance management, covering appraisal systems, performance pay and

awards, administration of the Presidential Rank Awards Program for Senior Executives, and incentive awards for suggestions, inventions, and special acts;
—research and demonstration projects and other innovative practices to explore potential improvements in personnel systems and better and simpler ways to manage Federal personnel;
—classification policy and standards for agencies to determine the series and grades for Federal jobs;
—labor-management relations, including labor-management partnerships and consulting with unions on Governmentwide issues;
—systems and techniques for resolving disputes with employees;
—quality of worklife initiatives, such as employee health and fitness, work and family, AIDS in the workplace, and employee assistance programs;
—information systems to support and improve Federal personnel management decisionmaking; and
—Governmentwide instructions for personnel processing and recordkeeping, and for release of personnel data under the Freedom of Information Act and the Privacy Act.

Oversight The Office assesses agencies' effectiveness in personnel management at the Governmentwide, agency, and installation levels to gather information for policy development and program refinement, ensure compliance with personnel laws and regulations, enhance agency capability for self-evaluation, and assist agencies in operating personnel programs which effectively support accomplishment of their primary missions.

Employee Benefits The Office also manages numerous activities that directly affect the well-being of the Federal employee and indirectly enhance employee effectiveness. These include health benefits, life insurance, and retirement benefits.

Other Personnel Programs The Office administers the Senior Executive Service and is responsible for oversight and providing assistance on a variety of Governmentwide executive personnel management matters. It coordinates the temporary assignment of employees between Federal agencies and State, local, and Indian tribal governments; institutions of higher education; and other eligible organizations for up to 2 years, for work of mutual benefit to the participating organizations. It administers the Presidential Management Intern Program, which provides 2-year, excepted appointments with Federal agencies to recipients of graduate degrees in appropriate disciplines. In addition, the Office of Personnel Management administers the Federal Merit System Standards, which apply to certain grant-aided State and local programs.

Field Service—Office of Personnel Management

Region	Address	Director
ATLANTA—Alabama, Florida, Georgia, Mississippi, North Carolina, South Carolina, Tennessee, Virginia	75 Spring St. SW., Atlanta, GA 30303–3109	Ronald E. Brooks
CHICAGO—Illinois, Indiana, Iowa, Kansas, Kentucky, Michigan, Minnesota, Missouri, Nebraska, North Dakota, Ohio, South Dakota, West Virginia, Wisconsin,	230 S. Dearborn St., Chicago, IL 60604–0001	Steven R. Cohen
DALLAS—Arizona, Arkansas, Colorado, Louisiana, Montana, New Mexico, Oklahoma, Texas, Utah, Wyoming	1100 Commerce St., Dallas, TX 75242–0001	Felix R. Garza, *Acting*
PHILADELPHIA—Connecticut, Delaware, Maine, Maryland, Massachusetts, New Hampshire, New Jersey, New York, Pennsylvania, Puerto Rico, Rhode Island, Vermont, Virgin Islands	600 Arch St., Philadelphia, PA 19106–1596	Rose N. Gwin, *Acting*
SAN FRANCISCO—Alaska, California, Hawaii, Idaho, Nevada, Oregon, Washington, Pacific Ocean area	7th Fl., 120 Howard St., San Francisco, CA 94105–0001	Joseph S. Patti

Sources of Information

Contracts Contact the Chief, Contracting Division, Office of Personnel Management, Washington, DC 20415–0001 (phone, 202–606–2240); or the appropriate field service center office.

Employment A network of service centers and Federal Job Test Centers, located in major metropolitan areas, provides Federal employment information. To obtain the appropriate telephone number, check the blue pages under U.S. Government, Office of Personnel Management. For information about employment opportunities within the Office of Personnel Management, contact the Director for Human Resources (phone, 202–606–2400); or the appropriate field service center.

Publications The Office issues publications addressed to a variety of audiences ranging from applicants for employment to the heads of Federal agencies.

The Chief, Publications Services Division, can provide information about Federal personnel management publications. For further information, call 202–606–1822.

Reading Room The Office of Personnel Management Library maintains collections of historical and current information on personnel management and the Federal civil service, including legislative information. The Library also serves as a reading room for those interested in Office publications available to the public. The Superintendent of Documents, Government Printing Office, Washington, DC 20402, sells subscriptions to *Personnel Literature.*

For further information, contact the Office of Communications, Office of Personnel Management, 1900 E Street NW., Washington, DC 20415–0001. Phone, 202–606–1800.

OFFICE OF SPECIAL COUNSEL

Suite 300, 1730 M Street NW., Washington, DC 20036–4505
Phones: Locator, 202–653–7188; Toll-free, 1–800–872–9855

Special Counsel	KATHLEEN DAY KOCH
Executive Assistant	ROBERT J. MURPHY
Deputy Special Counsel	JAMES A. KAHL
Associate Special Counsel for Prosecution	WILLIAM E. REUKAUF
Associate Special Counsel for Investigation	ROBERT D. L'HEUREUX
Associate Special Counsel for Planning and Advice	ERIN MCDONNELL
Director for Management	WILLIAM L. DEAN
Director, Legislative and Public Affairs	MICHAEL G. LAWRENCE

The Office of Special Counsel investigates allegations of certain activities prohibited by civil service laws, rules, or regulations and litigates before the Merit Systems Protection Board.

Activities

The Office of Special Counsel (OSC) was established on January 1, 1979, by Reorganization Plan No. 2 of 1978 (5 U.S.C. app.). The Civil Service Reform Act of 1978 (5 U.S.C. 1101 note), which became effective on January 11, 1979, enlarged its functions and powers. Pursuant to provisions of the Whistleblower Protection Act of 1989 (5 U.S.C. 1211 *et seq.*), OSC functions as an independent investigative and prosecutorial agency within the executive branch which litigates before the Merit Systems Protection Board.

OFFICE OF SPECIAL COUNSEL

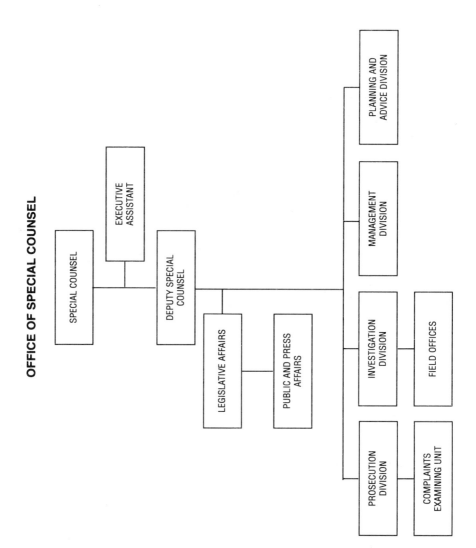

The primary role of OSC is to protect employees, former employees, and applicants for employment from prohibited personnel practices, especially reprisal for whistleblowing. OSC's basic areas of statutory responsibility are:

—receiving and investigating allegations of prohibited personnel practices and other activities prohibited by civil service law, rule, or regulation and, if warranted, initiating corrective or disciplinary action;

—providing a secure channel through which information evidencing a violation of any law, rule or regulation, gross mismanagement, gross waste of funds, abuse of authority, or substantial and specific danger to public health or safety may be disclosed without fear of retaliation and without disclosure of identity, except with the employee's consent; and

—enforcing the provisions of the Hatch Act.

Sources of Information

Field offices are located in Dallas, TX (Room 7C30, 1100 Commerce Street, 75242; phone, 214–767–8871) and Oakland, CA (Suite 365S, 1301 Clay Street, 94612–5217; phone, 510–637–3460).

For further information, contact the Office of Special Counsel, Suite 300, 1730 M Street NW., Washington, DC 20036–4505. Phone, 202–653–7188; or toll-free, 1–800–872–9855.

PANAMA CANAL COMMISSION

Suite 1050, 1825 Eye Street NW., Washington, DC 20006–5402
Phone, 202–634–6441

Official in Washington:
Secretary   MICHAEL RHODE, JR.

Officials in the Republic of Panama:
Administrator   GILBERTO GUARDIA
Deputy Administrator   RAYMOND P. LAVERTY

[For the Panama Canal Commission statement of organization, see the *Code of Federal Regulations*, Title 35, Part 9]

The Panama Canal Commission operates, maintains, and improves the Panama Canal to provide efficient, safe, and economical transit service for the benefit of world commerce.

The Panama Canal Commission was established as an independent agency in the executive branch of the Government by the Panama Canal Act of 1979 (22 U.S.C. 3601)

The Commission is supervised by a nine-member Board of which not fewer than five members are nationals of the United States, with the remaining members being nationals of the Republic of Panama. All members of the Board are appointed by the President. The members who are United States nationals are appointed with the advice and consent of the Senate.

Activities

The Commission was established by Congress on October 1, 1979, to carry out the responsibilities of the United States with respect to the Panama Canal under the Panama Canal Treaty of 1977. In fulfilling these obligations, the Commission manages, operates, and maintains the Canal, its complementary works, installations, and equipment, and

PANAMA CANAL COMMISSION

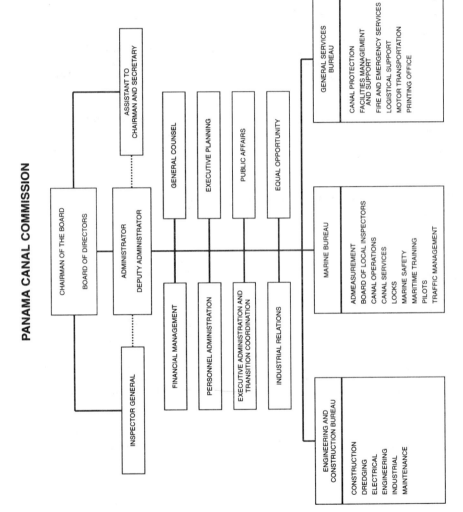

CHAIRMAN OF THE BOARD
BOARD OF DIRECTORS

ASSISTANT TO
CHAIRMAN AND SECRETARY

ADMINISTRATOR
DEPUTY ADMINISTRATOR

INSPECTOR GENERAL

GENERAL COUNSEL

EXECUTIVE PLANNING

PUBLIC AFFAIRS

EQUAL OPPORTUNITY

FINANCIAL MANAGEMENT

PERSONNEL ADMINISTRATION

EXECUTIVE ADMINISTRATION AND
TRANSITION COORDINATION

INDUSTRIAL RELATIONS

GENERAL SERVICES
BUREAU

CANAL PROTECTION
FACILITIES MANAGEMENT
AND SUPPORT
FIRE AND EMERGENCY SERVICES
LOGISTICAL SUPPORT
MOTOR TRANSPORTATION
PRINTING OFFICE

MARINE BUREAU

ADMEASUREMENT
BOARD OF LOCAL INSPECTORS
CANAL OPERATIONS
CANAL SERVICES
LOCKS
MARINE SAFETY
MARITIME TRAINING
PILOTS
TRAFFIC MANAGEMENT

ENGINEERING AND
CONSTRUCTION BUREAU

CONSTRUCTION
DREDGING
ELECTRICAL
ENGINEERING
INDUSTRIAL
MAINTENANCE

provides for the orderly transit of vessels through the Canal. This U.S. agency will perform these functions until the treaty terminates on December 31, 1999, at which time the Republic of Panama will assume full responsibility for the Canal.

Sources of Information

Marine Operations Director, Marine Bureau, Panama. Phone, 011–507–52–4500.

Economic and Marketing Information Director, Office of Executive Planning, Panama. Phone, 011–507–52–7961.
Procurement Office of Logistical Support, 4400 Dauphine Street, New Orleans, LA 70146–6800. Phone, 504–948–5299.
Panama Canal Commission Unit 2300, APO AA 34011–2300. Telex, 3034 PCCAMRM PG.

For further information, contact the Office of the Secretary, Panama Canal Commission, Suite 1050, 1825 Eye Street NW., Washington, DC 20006–5402. Phone, 202–634–6441.

PEACE CORPS
1990 K Street NW., Washington, DC 20526
Phone (Locator), 202–606–3886

Director	CHARLES R. BAQUET III, *Acting*
Deputy Director	CHARLES R. BAQUET III
General Counsel	BRIAN J. SEXTON
Inspector General	CHARLES C. MADDOX, *Acting*
Special Assistant to the Director	THOMAS EDWARDS
Director of Congressional Relations	JOAN TIMONEY
Director of Communications	CELIA FISCHER
Director of Private Sector Relations	AMY RULE
Associate Director for International Operations	JOHN P. HOGAN
Regional Director/Africa Operations	SANDRA ROBINSON
Regional Director/Inter-American Operations	VICTOR JOHNSON
Regional Director/Asia and Pacific Operations	MARGARET GOODMAN
Regional Director/Europe, Central Asia and Mediterranean Operations	FRED O'REGAN

Director of Training and Program Support	HOWARD ANDERSON
Chief Financial Officer	ELLEN YAFFE
Deputy Chief Financial Officer	LANA HURDLE
Director of Financial Services	YVONNE VAUGHAN
Associate Director for Management	STANLEY D. SUYAT
Director of Human Resource Management	SHARON BARBEE FLETCHER
Director of Information Resources Management	RON CONNER
Director of Contracts	PAUL ALLMAN
Director of Administrative Services	JOSE LARACUENTE
Associate Director for Volunteer Support	JUDY HARRINGTON
Director of Medical Services	DAVID GOOTNICK, M.D.
Director of Special Services	BARBARA PICKETT
Director of Domestic Programs	CHRISTOPHER HEDRICK
Associate Director for Volunteer Recruitment and Selection	PATRICIA GARAMENDI
Director of Placement	LIZ LOSTOMBO

[For the Peace Corps statement of organization, see the *Code of Federal Regulations,* Title 22, Part 302]

The Peace Corps' purpose is to promote world peace and friendship, to help other countries in meeting their needs for trained men and women, and to promote understanding between the American people and other peoples served by the Peace Corps. The Peace Corps Act emphasizes the Peace Corps' commitment toward programming to meet the basic needs of those living in the countries where volunteers work.

The Peace Corps was established by the Peace Corps Act of 1961, as amended (22 U.S.C. 2501), and was made an independent agency by title VI of the International Security and Development Cooperation Act of 1981 (22 U.S.C. 2501–1).

The Peace Corps consists of a Washington, DC, headquarters; 13 area offices; and overseas operations in more than 90 countries. Its presence in foreign countries fluctuates as programs are added or withdrawn.

Activities

To fulfill the Peace Corps mandate, men and women are trained for a 9- to 14-week period in the appropriate local language, the technical skills necessary for their particular job, and the cross-cultural skills needed to adjust to a society with traditions and attitudes different from their own. Volunteers serve for a period of 2 years, living among the people with whom they work. Volunteers are expected to become a part of the community through their voluntary service.

PEACE CORPS

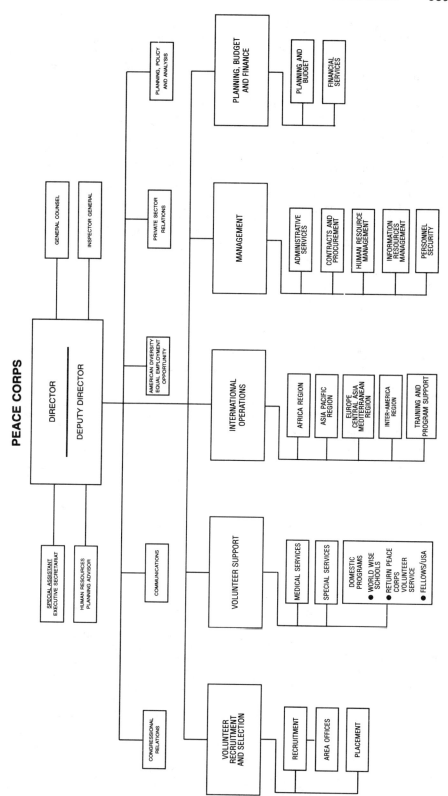

Thousands of volunteers serve throughout Central and South America, the Caribbean, Africa, Asia, the Pacific, Central and Eastern Europe, Russia, Ukraine, the Baltics, and Central Asia. They work in six program areas, including: education, agriculture, health, small business development, urban development, and the environment. Community-level projects are designed to incorporate the skills of volunteers with the resources of host-country agencies and other international assistance organizations to help solve specific development problems, often in conjunction with private volunteer organizations.

In the United States, the Peace Corps is working to promote an understanding of people in other countries. Through its World Wise Schools Program, volunteers are matched with elementary and junior high schools in the United States to encourage an exchange of letters, pictures, music, and artifacts. Participating students increase their knowledge of geography, languages, and different cultures, as well as to gain an appreciation for volunteerism.

The Peace Corps offers other domestic programs involving former volunteers, universities, local public school systems, and private businesses and foundations in a partnership to help solve some of our most pressing domestic problems across the United States.

To help support Peace Corps' domestic program and community needs overseas, the Peace Corps Office of Private Sector Relations works with schools, civic groups, businesses, and neighborhood and youth organizations in the United States to facilitate their support of Peace Corps initiatives here and abroad.

Area Offices—Peace Corps

Office	Address	Telephone
ATLANTA (Alabama, Georgia, Mississippi, South Carolina, Florida, Tennessee).	Rm. 2324, 101 Marietta St. NW., Atlanta, GA 30323).	404–331–2932
BOSTON (Maine, Massachusetts, New Hampshire, Rhode Island, Vermont).	Rm. 450, 10 Causeway St., Boston, MA 02222	617–565–5555
CHICAGO (Illinois, Indiana)	Suite 450, 55 W. Monroe St., Chicago, IL 60603	312–353–4990
DALLAS (Arkansas, Louisiana, New Mexico, Oklahoma, Texas).	Rm. 230, 400 N. Ervay St., P.O. Box 638, Dallas, TX 75221.	214–767–5435
DENVER (Colorado, Montana, North Dakota, South Dakota, Utah, Wyoming).	Rm. 550, 140 E. 19th Ave., Denver, CO 80203	303–866–1057
DETROIT (Michigan, Ohio, Kentucky)	Rm. M–74, P.V. McNamara Bldg., 477 Michigan Ave., Detroit, MI 48226.	313–226–7928
KANSAS CITY (Iowa, Kansas, Missouri, Nebraska) .	Suite 565, 500 State Ave., Kansas City, KS 66101 .	913–551–5700
LOS ANGELES (Arizona, southern California)	Suite 8104, 11000 Wilshire Blvd., Los Angeles, CA 90024.	310–235–7444
MINNEAPOLIS (Minnesota, Wisconsin)	Suite 420, 330 2d Ave. S., Minneapolis, MN 55401	612–348–1480
NEW YORK (Connecticut, New York, New Jersey, Pennsylvania, Puerto Rico).	Rm. 611, 6 World Trade Ctr., New York, NY 10048	212–466–2477
ROSSLYN, VA (District of Columbia, Maryland, Delaware, North Carolina, Virginia, West Virginia).	Suite 400, 1400 Wilson Blvd., Arlington, VA 22209 .	703–235–9191
SAN FRANCISCO (Hawaii, Nevada, northern California).	Rm. 533, 211 Main St., San Francisco, CA 94105 ..	415–744–2677
SEATTLE (Alaska, Idaho, Oregon, Washington)	Rm. 1776, 2001 6th Ave., Seattle, WA 98121	206–553–5490

Sources of Information

Becoming a Peace Corps Volunteer Persons interested in becoming a Peace Corps volunteer should write to the area office serving their community or call 1–800–424–8580, extension 2293.

Employment Persons interested in employment with the Peace Corps should address inquiries to: Peace Corps, Office of Human Resource Management, Washington, DC 20526. Phone, 202–606–3950. For recorded employment opportunities, call 202–606–3214.

General Inquiries Information or assistance may be obtained by contacting the Peace Corps' Washington, DC, headquarters or any of its area offices. Frequently, information is available from local post offices.

For further information, contact the Press Office, Peace Corps, 1990 K Street NW., Washington, DC 20526. Phone, 202–606–3010; or toll-free, 1–800–424–8580. Fax, 202–606–3108.

PENNSYLVANIA AVENUE DEVELOPMENT CORPORATION

Suite 1220 North, 1331 Pennsylvania Avenue NW., Washington, DC 20004–1703
Phone, 202–724–9091

Board of Directors:

Chairman	RICHARD A. HAUSER
Vice Chairman	EDWARD E. ALLISON
Directors	CATHERINE M. BOUCREE, ELEANOR LYONS WILLIAMS, PETER TERPELUK, JR., JAYNE B. IKARD, WALTER J. GANZI, JR., JEANNETTE NAYLOR COPE

Officials:

Executive Director	LESTER M. HUNKELE III
Assistant Director, Legal	ROBERT E. MCCALLY
Assistant Director, Development	JERRY M. SMEDLEY
Director, Finance and Administration	ALEXANDER K. MILIN
Director, Public Improvements	RICHARD SITEK
Director, Design and Planning	JAN F. FRANKINA
Director, Corporate Affairs and Congressional Relations	ANNE P. HARTZELL
Administrative Officer/Secretary, Board of Directors	DIANE G. SMITH

The Pennsylvania Avenue Development Corporation is a Federal agency responsible for revitalizing Pennsylvania Avenue between the White House and the Capitol. A comprehensive plan, prepared by the agency and approved by Congress in 1975, guides development in a 21-block section of Pennsylvania Avenue and the adjacent blocks north of the avenue.

The Pennsylvania Avenue Development Corporation was established as a wholly owned Federal corporation by the Pennsylvania Avenue Development Corporation Act of 1972, as amended (40 U.S.C. 871).

The Corporation is governed by a 15-member Board of Directors. Eight members are appointed by the President from the private sector for 6-year terms; seven serve by virtue of their positions in the Federal or District of Columbia Governments. There are also eight nonvoting members representing Federal and District organizations with expertise in planning, cultural, and architectural matters.

Activities

The Corporation's activities to revitalize Pennsylvania Avenue take two forms. First, using funds appropriated by Congress, the Corporation undertakes projects which improve the public areas and ambience of Pennsylvania Avenue. These projects include repaving and landscaping the avenue and adjacent areas, facilitating traffic patterns, and preserving the designated historic landmarks. Also, it has completed seven parks and open spaces along the avenue and sponsors people-oriented activities within the area.

PENNSYLVANIA AVENUE DEVELOPMENT CORPORATION

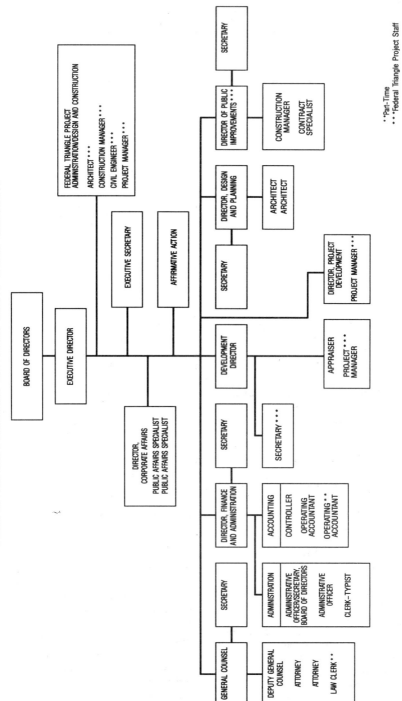

* *Part-Time
* * *Federal Triangle Project Staff

The second part of the Corporation's activity involves a partnership with the private sector to develop projects compatible with the Pennsylvania Avenue Plan. It uses funds borrowed from the United States Treasury to assemble land for housing, office buildings, retail uses, hotels, and community arts space. The Corporation makes public offerings of development opportunities on sites, and either sells the property or enters into long-term leases with developers selected to carry out individual projects. The proceeds from the leases or sales are used to retire the agency's debt to the Treasury.

In carrying out the plan, the Corporation works closely with a number of Federal agencies, including the Commission of Fine Arts, the National Capital Planning Commission, the Advisory Council on Historic Preservation, and the National Park Service. It also works closely in the implementation of the plan with relevant agencies of the District of Columbia government.

The Federal Triangle Development Act, approved August 21, 1987, gave the Corporation the authority to plan and implement, in consultation with the General Services Administration, the development of a 3.1-million-square-foot complex for Federal offices and trade-related activities.

Sources of Information

Publications The *Pennsylvania Avenue Plan* (1974), as approved by Congress in May 1975, and published *Amendments to the Pennsylvania Avenue Plan* (November 1990) describe the program for comprehensive revitalization of the designated area. Copies of these documents, as well as the Corporation's annual report and other supplementary materials, are available upon request.

For further information, contact the Director of Corporate Affairs, Pennsylvania Avenue Development Corporation, Suite 1220 North, 1331 Pennsylvania Avenue NW., Washington, DC 20004–1703. Phone, 202–724–9062.

PENSION BENEFIT GUARANTY CORPORATION

1200 K Street NW., Washington, DC 20005
Phone, 202–326–4000

Board of Directors:	
Chairman (Secretary of Labor)	ROBERT B. REICH
Members:	
(Secretary of the Treasury)	ROBERT E. RUBIN
(Secretary of Commerce)	RONALD H. BROWN
Officials:	
Executive Director	MARTIN SLATE
Deputy Executive Director and Chief Negotiator	NELL HENNESSY
Deputy Executive Director and Chief Operating Officer	WILLIAM B. POSNER
Deputy Executive Director and Chief Financial Officer	N. ANTHONY CALHOUN
Deputy Executive Director and Chief Management Officer	JOHN SEAL
Assistant Executive Director for Legislative and Congressional Affairs	JUDY SCHUB
Director, Budget Department	HENRY R. THOMPSON

Director, Case Operations and Compliance Department	ANNA L. GILREATH, *Acting*
Director, Communications and Public Affairs Department	JUDITH WELLES
Director, Contracts and Controls Review Department	DALE WILLIAMS
Director, Corporate Finance and Negotiations Department	ANDREA E. SCHNEIDER
Director, Corporate Policy and Research Department	STUART A. SIRKIN
Director, Facilities and Services Department	JANET A. SMITH
Director, Financial Operations Department	EDWARD L. KNAPP
General Counsel	JAMES J. KEIGHTLEY
Director, Human Resources Department	R. FRANK TOBIN
Director, Information Resources Management Department	CRIS BIRCH, *Acting*
Inspector General	WAYNE ROBERT POLL
Director, Insurance Operations Department	BENNIE L. HAGANS
Director, Organization Review and Analysis Department	SHERLINE M. BRICKUS
Director, Participant and Employer Appeals Department	HARRIET D. VERBURG
Director, Procurement Department	ROBERT W. HERTING

The Pension Benefit Guaranty Corporation guarantees payment of nonforfeitable pension benefits in covered private–sector defined benefit pension plans.

The Pension Benefit Guaranty Corporation is a self-financing, wholly owned Government corporation subject to the Government Corporation Control Act (31 U.S.C. 9101–9109). The Corporation, established by Title IV of the Employee Retirement Income Security Act of 1974 (29 U.S.C. 1301–1461), is governed by a Board of Directors consisting of the Secretaries of Labor, Commerce, and the Treasury. The Secretary of Labor is Chairman of the Board. A seven-member Advisory Committee, composed of two labor, two business, and three public members appointed by the President, advises the agency on various matters.

Activities

Coverage   PBGC insures most private-sector defined benefit pension plans that provide a pension benefit based on factors such as age, years of service, and salary.

The Corporation administers two insurance programs separately covering single-employer and multiemployer plans. More than 41 million workers participate in approximately 58,000 covered plans.

Single-Employer Insurance   Under the single-employer program, the Corporation guarantees payment of certain pension benefits if an insured plan terminates without sufficient assets to pay those benefits. However, the law limits the total monthly benefit that the agency may guarantee for one individual to $2,573.86 per month, at age 65, for a plan terminating during 1995, and sets other restrictions on PBGC's guarantee. The Corporation may also pay some benefits above the guaranteed amount depending on amounts recovered from the employer responsible for the plan.

A plan administrator may terminate a single-employer plan in a "standard" or "distress" termination if certain procedural and legal requirements are met. In either termination, the plan administrator must inform participants in writing at least 60 days prior to the date the administrator proposes to terminate the plan. Only a plan which has sufficient assets to pay all benefit liabilities may terminate in a standard

PENSION BENEFIT GUARANTY CORPORATION

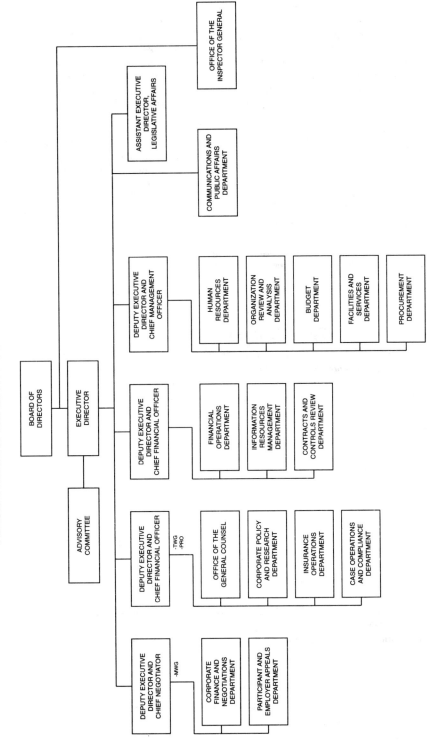

termination. The Corporation also may institute termination proceedings in certain specified circumstances. **Multiemployer Insurance**   Under title IV, as originally enacted, the Corporation guaranteed nonforfeitable benefits for multiemployer plans in a similar fashion as for single-employer plans. However, the multiemployer program was revised in 1980 by the Multiemployer Pension Plan Amendments Act (29 U.S.C. 1001 note) which changed the insurable event from plan termination to plan insolvency. The Corporation now provides financial assistance to plans that are unable to pay nonforfeitable benefits. The plans are obligated to repay such assistance. The act also made employers withdrawing from a plan liable to the plan for a portion of its unfunded vested benefits. **Premium Collections**   All defined benefit pension plans insured by PBGC are required to pay premiums to the Corporation according to rates set by Congress. The annual premium per plan participant for multiemployer pension plans is $2.60 for plan years beginning after September 26, 1988. The basic premium for all single-employer plans is $19 per participant per year. Underfunded single-employer plans must also pay an additional premium equal to $9 per $1,000 of unfunded vested benefits, subject to a cap that will be phased out by the end of 1997.

For further information, contact the Pension Benefit Guaranty Corporation, 1200 K Street NW., Washington, DC 20005–4026. Phone, 202–326–4000.

POSTAL RATE COMMISSION

1333 H Street NW., Washington, DC 20268–0001
Phone, 202–789–6800; Fax, 202–789–6861

Chairman	EDWARD J. GLEIMAN
Special Counsel	JAMES PIERCE MYERS
Vice Chairman	W.H. LEBLANC III
Special Assistant	JOHN B. KEELEY
Commissioner	GEORGE W. HALEY
Special Assistant	IRVIN H. BROMALL
Commissioner	H. EDWARD QUICK, JR.
Special Assistant	(VACANCY)
Commissioner	WAYNE A. SCHLEY
Special Assistant	TREVOR E. NORRIS
Special Assistant to the Commission	ROBERT W. MITCHELL
Chief Administrative Officer and Secretary	MARGARET P. CRENSHAW
Legal Advisor	STEPHEN L. SHARFMAN
Director, Office of Rates, Analysis and Planning	ROBERT COHEN
Assistant Director, Office of Rates, Analysis and Planning	WILLIAM FERGUSON
Director, Office of the Consumer Advocate	W. GAIL WILLETTE

Assistant Director, Office of the Consumer Advocate	E. RAND COSTICH
Personnel Officer	CYRIL J. PITTACK

[For the Postal Rate Commission statement of organization, see the *Code of Federal Regulations,* Title 39, Part 3002]

The major responsibility of the Postal Rate Commission is to submit recommended decisions to the United States Postal Service Governors on postage rates, fees, and mail classifications.

The Postal Rate Commission is an independent agency created by the Postal Reorganization Act, as amended (39 U.S.C. 3601–3604). It is composed of five Commissioners, appointed by the President with the advice and consent of the Senate, one of whom is designated as Chairman.

The Commission promulgates rules and regulations, establishes procedures, and takes other actions necessary to carry out its obligations. Acting upon requests from the U.S. Postal Service, or on its own initiative, the Commission recommends and issues advisory opinions to the Board of Governors of the U.S. Postal Service changes in rates or fees in each class of mail or type of service. It studies and submits recommended decisions on establishing or changing the mail classification schedule and holds on-the-record hearings that are lawfully required to attain sound and fair recommendations. The Commission also initiates studies on postal matters, such as cost theory and operations; receives, studies, and conducts hearings; and issues recommended decisions and reports to the Postal Service on complaints received from interested persons relating to postage rates, postal classifications, and problems of national scope regarding postal services. Additionally, the Commission has appellate jurisdiction to review Postal Service determinations to close or consolidate small post offices.

Sources of Information

Employment The Commission's programs require attorneys, economists, statisticians, accountants, industrial engineers, marketing specialists, and administrative and clerical personnel. Requests for employment information should be directed to the Personnel Officer.

Electronic Information Service The Commission maintains a Bulletin Board Service (OCA BBS) that provides information on electronic documents or data provided by or to the Commission on current proceedings. Phone, 202–789–6891.

Reading Room Facilities for inspection and copying of records that are available to the public are located in Suite 300, 1333 H Street NW., Washington, DC. The room is open from 8 a.m. to 4:30 p.m., Monday through Friday, except legal holidays.

Rules of Practice and Procedure The Postal Rate Commission's Rules of Practice and Procedure governing the conduct of proceedings before the Commission may be found in part 3001 of title 39 of the *Code of Federal Regulations.*

For further information, contact the Secretary, Postal Rate Commission, 1333 H Street NW., Washington, DC 20268–0001. Phone, 202–789–6840.

RAILROAD RETIREMENT BOARD

844 North Rush Street, Chicago, IL 60611–2092
Phone, 312–751–4776
Office of Legislative Affairs: Suite 500, 1310 G Street NW., Washington, DC 20005–3004
Phone, 202–272–7742

Chairman	GLEN L. BOWER
Labor Member	V.M. SPEAKMAN, JR.
Management Member	JEROME F. KEVER
Inspector General	MARTIN J. DICKMAN
General Counsel	CATHERINE C. COOK
Deputy General Counsel	STEVEN A. BARTHOLOW
Director, Hearings and Appeals	DALE G. ZIMMERMAN
Director, Legislative Affairs	MARIAN P. GIBSON
Director, Programs	KENNETH P. BOEHNE, *Acting*
Director, Retirement and Survivor Programs	ROBERT J. DUDA
Director, Retirement Benefits	KENNETH J. ZOLL
Director, Survivor Benefits	CHARLENE T. KUKLA
Director, Disability and Medicare Operations	JOHN R. FELDHEIM
Director, Unemployment and Sickness Insurance	(VACANCY)
Director, Taxation	JOHN L. THORESDALE
Director, Field Service	RONALD J. DAMMON
Director, Administration	KENNETH P. BOEHNE
Chief Actuary	FRANK J. BUZZI
Chief Financial Officer	PETER A. LARSON
Chief Information Officer	(VACANCY)
Director, Research and Employment Accounts	BOBBY V. FERGUSON
Director, Personnel	JOHN F. MALICH
Director, Quality Assurance	(VACANCY)
Director, Supply and Service	HENRY M. VALIULIS
Director, Public Affairs	WILLIAM G. POULOS
Equal Opportunity Manager	LEO FRANKLIN
Secretary to the Board	BEATRICE E. EZERSKI

[For the Railroad Retirement Board statement of organization, see the *Code of Federal Regulations*, Title 20, Part 200]

The Railroad Retirement Board administers comprehensive retirement-survivor and unemployment-sickness benefit programs for the Nation's railroad workers and their families.

The Railroad Retirement Board was established by the Railroad Retirement Act of 1934, as amended (42 U.S.C. 201—228z–1, 231 *et seq.*).

The Board derives statutory authority from the Railroad Retirement Act of 1974 (45 U.S.C. 231–231v) and the Railroad Unemployment Insurance Act (45 U.S.C. 351–368). It administers these acts and participates in the administration of the Social Security Act and the Health Insurance for the Aged Act insofar as they affect railroad retirement beneficiaries.

RAILROAD RETIREMENT BOARD

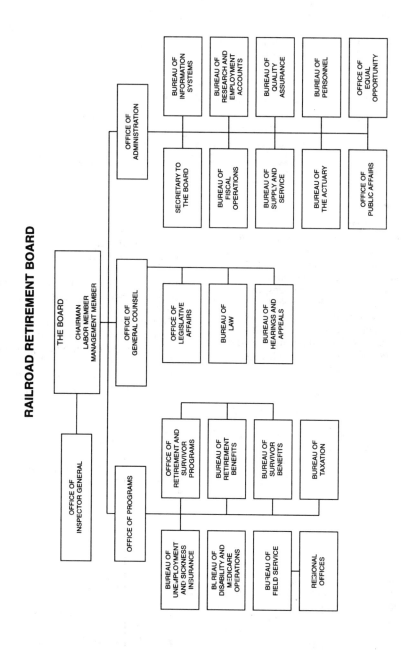

The Board is composed of three members appointed by the President with the advice and consent of the Senate—one upon recommendations of representatives of employees; one upon recommendations of carriers; and one, the Chairman, as a public member.

Field Organization   The Board maintains direct contact with railroad retirement beneficiaries through its field offices located across the country. Field personnel explain benefit rights and responsibilities on an individual basis, assist employees applying for benefits, and answer questions related to the benefit programs.

Regional Offices—Railroad Retirement Board

City	Address	Director	Telephone
Atlanta, GA	Suite 2304, 101 Marietta St., 30323–3011	Patricia Lawson	404–331–2691
Cleveland, OH	Rm. 989, 1240 E. 9th St., 44199–2093	Kevin B. McCrone	216–522–4043
Kansas City, MO	Rm. 257, 601 E. 12th St., 64106–2882	Daniel H. Hauser	816–426–3278
Oakland, CA	Suite 390N, 1301 Clay St., 94612–5227	Donald R. Wedl	510–637–2982
Philadelphia, PA	Suite 670, 1421 Cherry St., 19102–1413	Richard D. Baird	215–656–6946

Activities

The Railroad Retirement Act provides for the payment of annuities to individuals who have completed at least 10 years of creditable service and have ceased compensated service upon their attainment of specified ages, or at any age if permanently disabled for all employment. In some circumstances occupational disability annuities or supplemental annuities are provided for longer term or career employees.

A spouse's annuity is provided, under certain conditions, for the wife or husband of an employee annuitant. Divorced spouses may also qualify.

Survivor annuities are awarded to the qualified spouses, children, and parents of deceased career employees. Various lump-sum benefits are also provided under certain conditions.

Benefits are provided under the Railroad Unemployment Insurance Act to individuals who are unemployed in a benefit year, but who are ready and willing to work, and to individuals who are unable to work because of sickness or injury, based upon qualifying railroad earnings in a preceding 1-year period.

The Board maintains, through its field offices, a placement service for unemployed railroad personnel.

Sources of Information

Benefit Inquiries   Inquiries concerning claims for railroad retirement and survivor benefits should be directed to the Office of Retirement and Survivor Programs, Congressional Inquiry Section (phone, 312–751–4973). Inquiries concerning unemployment and sickness claims should be directed to the Bureau of Unemployment and Sickness Insurance, Adjudication, Systems and Procedures Section (phone, 312–751–4810).

To locate the nearest field office, individuals should check with their rail employer, local union official, local post office, or one of the regional offices listed above. Most offices are open to the public from 9 a.m. to 3:30 p.m., Monday through Friday. The Board also relies on railroad labor groups and employers for assistance in keeping railroad personnel informed about its benefit programs.

Employment   Inquiries and applications for employment should be directed to the Director of Personnel, Railroad Retirement Board, 844 North Rush Street, Chicago, IL 60611–2092. Phone, 312–751–4570.

Legislative Assistance   Information regarding legislative matters may be obtained through the Office of Legislative Affairs (phone, 202–272–7742).

Publications   General information pamphlets on benefit programs may be obtained from the Board's field offices or Chicago headquarters. Requests for annual reports or statistical data should be directed to the Director of Public Affairs at the Chicago headquarters.

Electronic Information Services
Railroad Retirement Board information is available through America Online and CompuServe. With America Online, select "Clubs & Interests," then "AARP Online," "Software Library," and then "Government Resources." With CompuServe, enter "GO TRAINNET".

Select the Library Section, and then "RR Retirement Board."
Telecommunications Devices for the Deaf (TDD) The Board provides TDD services from 9 a.m. to 3:30 p.m. (CST/CDT) daily. Phone 312–751–4701 for beneficiary inquiries and 312–751–4334 for employment inquiries.

For further information, contact the Office of Public Affairs, Railroad Retirement Board, 844 North Rush Street, Chicago, IL 60611–2092. Phone, 312–751–4776.

RESOLUTION TRUST CORPORATION
801 Seventeenth Street NW., Washington, DC 20434
Phone, 202–416–6900

Chief Executive Officer	JOHN E. RYAN, *Acting*
Deputy Chief Executive Officer	JOHN E. RYAN
General Counsel	(VACANCY)
Vice President (Division of Asset Management and Sales)	THOMAS HORTON
Chief Financial Officer	DONNA H. CUNNINGHAME

The Resolution Trust Corporation was established to manage and resolve failed savings associations that were insured by the Federal Savings and Loan Insurance Corporation before the enactment of the Financial Institutions Reform, Recovery, and Enforcement Act of 1989, and for which a conservator or receiver is appointed between January 1, 1989, and July 1, 1995. The Corporation will terminate all functions no later than December 31, 1995.

The Resolution Trust Corporation (Corporation) was established on August 9, 1989, by the Financial Institutions Reform, Recovery, and Enforcement Act of 1989 (12 U.S.C. 1441a).

The Corporation is an agency of the United States for purposes of subchapter II, chapters 5 and 7, of title 5 of the United States Code, when it is acting as a corporation. When the Corporation is acting as a conservator or receiver of an insured depository institution, it is deemed to be a Federal agency to the same extent as the Federal Deposit Insurance Corporation when acting in the same capacity.

The Corporation is a mixed-ownership Government corporation for purposes of 31 U.S.C. 9105, 9107, and 9108, notwithstanding the fact that no Federal funds are permitted to be invested in the Corporation.

Under the direction of the Chief Executive Officer, the duties of the Corporation include:

—managing and resolving all cases involving depository institutions, the accounts of which were insured by the former Federal Savings and Loan Insurance Corporation prior to August 9, 1989, and which have been or will be in conservatorship or receivership as of January 1, 1989, through July 1, 1995;

—conducting the operations of the Corporation in such a way as to maximize the return of value from the sale or other disposition of depository institutions or their assets, while minimizing the impact on real estate and financial markets and minimizing losses to the Government;

—making efficient use of funds
provided by the Resolution Funding
Corporation or the Treasury; and

—maximizing the availability and
affordability of residential real property
for low- and moderate-income
individuals.

For further information, contact the Corporate Communications Office, Resolution Trust Corporation, 801 Seventeenth Street NW., Washington, DC 20434. Phone, 202–416–7557.

SECURITIES AND EXCHANGE COMMISSION
450 Fifth Street NW., Washington, DC 20549
Phone, 202–942–4150

Chairman	ARTHUR LEVITT
Commissioners	RICHARD Y. ROBERTS, STEVEN M.H. WALLMAN, (2 VACANCIES)
Secretary	JONATHAN G. KATZ
Executive Director	JAMES M. MCCONNELL
Chief of Staff	MICHAEL SCHLEIN
General Counsel	SIMON M. LORNE
Director, Division of Corporation Finance	LINDA C. QUINN
Director, Division of Enforcement	WILLIAM R. MCLUCAS
Director, Division of Investment Management	BARRY P. BARBASH
Director, Division of Market Regulation	BRANDON BECKER
Chief Accountant	(VACANCY)
Chief Administrative Law Judge	BRENDA P. MURRAY
Chief Economist	SUSAN E. WOODWARD
Director, Office of International Affairs	MICHAEL D. MANN
Director, Office of Public Affairs, Policy Evaluation and Research	JENNIFER KIMBALL
Director, Office of Legislative Affairs	KATHRYN FULTON
Inspector General	WALTER STACHNIK
Director, Office of Equal Employment Opportunity	JESSICA KOLE, *Acting*
Director, Office of Consumer Affairs	NANCY M. SMITH
Associate Executive Director, Office of Administrative and Personnel Management	FERNANDO L. ALEGRIA, JR.
Associate Executive Director, Office of the Comptroller	LAWRENCE H. HAYNES
Associate Executive Director, Office of Filings and Information Services	WILSON A. BUTLER
Associate Executive Director, Office of Information Technology	(VACANCY)

[For the Securities and Exchange Commission statement of organization, see the *Code of Federal Regulations,* Title 17, Part 200]

The Securities and Exchange Commission administers Federal securities laws that seek to provide protection for investors; to ensure that securities markets are fair and honest; and, when necessary, to provide the means to enforce securities laws through sanctions.

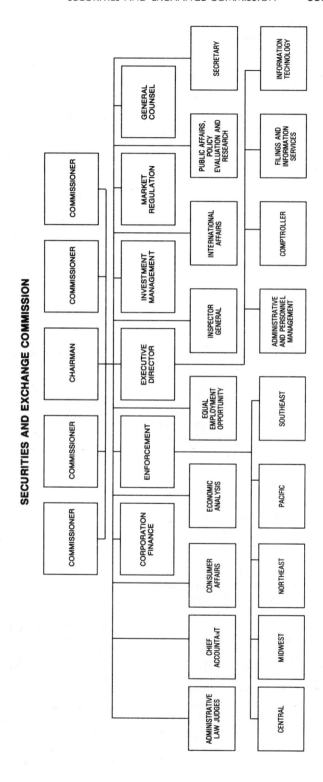

SECURITIES AND EXCHANGE COMMISSION

The Securities and Exchange Commission was created under authority of the Securities Exchange Act of 1934 (15 U.S.C. 78a–78jj) and was organized on July 2, 1934. The Commission serves as adviser to United States district courts in connection with reorganization proceedings for debtor corporations in which there is a substantial public interest. The Commission also has certain responsibilities under section 15 of the Bretton Woods Agreements Act of 1945 (22 U.S.C. 286k--1) and section 851(e) of the Internal Revenue Code of 1954 (26 U.S.C. 851(e)).

The Commission is vested with quasi-judicial functions. Persons aggrieved by its decisions in the exercise of those functions have a right of review by the United States Courts of Appeals.

Activities

Full and Fair Disclosure The Securities Act of 1933 (15 U.S.C. 77a) requires issuers of securities and their controlling persons making public offerings of securities in interstate commerce or through the mails, directly or by others on their behalf, to file with the Commission registration statements containing financial and other pertinent data about the issuer and the securities being offered. It is unlawful to sell such securities unless a registration statement is in effect. There are limited exemptions, such as government securities, nonpublic offerings, and intrastate offerings, as well as certain offerings not exceeding $1.5 million. The effectiveness of a registration statement may be refused or suspended after a public hearing if the statement contains material misstatements or omissions, thus barring sale of the securities until it is appropriately amended.

Registration of securities does not imply approval of the issue by the Commission or that the Commission has found the registration disclosures to be accurate. It does not insure investors against loss in their purchase, but serves rather to provide information upon which investors may make an informed and realistic evaluation of the worth of the securities.

Persons responsible for filing false information with the Commission subject themselves to the risk of fine or imprisonment or both. Similarly, persons connected with the public offering may be liable for damages to purchasers of the securities if the disclosures in the registration statement and prospectus are materially defective. Also, the above act contains antifraud provisions that apply generally to the sale of securities, whether or not registered (15 U.S.C. 77a *et seq.*).

Regulation of Securities Markets The Securities Exchange Act of 1934 assigns to the Commission broad regulatory responsibilities over the securities markets, the self-regulatory organizations within the securities industry, and persons conducting a business in securities. Persons who execute transactions in securities generally are required to register with the Commission as broker-dealers. Securities exchanges and certain clearing agencies are required to register with the Commission, and associations of brokers or dealers are permitted to register with the Commission. The act also provides for the establishment of the Municipal Securities Rulemaking Board to formulate rules for the municipal securities industry.

The Commission oversees the self-regulatory activities of the national securities exchanges and associations, registered clearing agencies, and the Municipal Securities Rulemaking Board. In addition, the Commission regulates industry professionals, such as securities brokers and dealers, certain municipal securities professionals, government securities brokers and dealers, and transfer agents.

The act authorizes national securities exchanges, national securities associations, clearing agencies, and the Municipal Securities Rulemaking Board to adopt rules that are designed, among other things, to promote just and equitable principles of trade and to protect investors. The Commission is required to approve or disapprove most proposed rules of these self-regulatory organizations and has the power to abrogate or amend existing rules of the national securities exchanges, national securities associations, and the Municipal Securities Rulemaking Board. In addition, the Commission has broad rulemaking authority over the activities of brokers, dealers, municipal securities dealers, securities information processors, and transfer agents. The Commission may regulate such securities trading practices as short sales and stabilizing transactions. It may regulate the trading of options on national securities exchanges and the activities of members of exchanges who trade on the trading floors. The Commission may adopt rules governing broker-dealer sales practices in dealing with investors. The Commission also is authorized to adopt rules concerning the financial responsibility of brokers and dealers and reports made by them.

The act also requires the filing of registration statements and annual and other reports with national securities exchanges and the Commission by companies whose securities are listed upon the exchanges, and by companies that have assets of $5 million or more and 500 or more shareholders of record. In addition, companies that distributed securities pursuant to a registration statement declared effective by the Commission under the Securities Act of 1933 must also file annual and other reports with the Commission. Such applications and reports must contain financial and other data prescribed by the Commission as necessary or appropriate for the protection of investors and to ensure fair dealing. In addition, the solicitation of proxies, authorizations, or consents from holders of such registered securities must be made in accordance with rules and regulations prescribed by the Commission. These rules provide for disclosures to securities holders of information relevant to the subject matter of the solicitation.

Disclosure of the holdings and transactions by officers, directors, and large (10-percent) holders of equity securities of companies also is required, and any and all persons who acquire more than 5 percent of certain equity securities are required to file detailed information with the Commission and any exchange upon which such securities may be traded. Moreover, any person making a tender offer for certain classes of equity securities is required to file reports with the Commission if, as a result of the tender offer, such person would own more than 5 percent of the outstanding shares of the particular class of equity security involved. The Commission also is authorized to promulgate rules governing the repurchase by a corporate issuer of its own securities.

Regulation of Mutual Funds and Other Investment Companies The Investment Company Act of 1940 (15 U.S.C. 80a–1—80a–64) requires investment companies to register with the Commission and regulates their activities to protect investors. The regulation covers sales load, management contracts, composition of boards of directors, and capital structure.

The act prohibits investment companies from engaging in various transactions, including transactions with affiliated persons, unless the Commission first determines that such transactions are fair. In addition, the act provides a somewhat parallel but less stringent regulation of business development companies.

Under the act, the Commission may institute court action to enjoin the consummation of mergers and other plans of reorganization of investment companies if such plans are unfair to securities holders. It also may impose sanctions by administrative proceedings against investment company management for violations of the act and other Federal securities laws and file court actions to enjoin acts and practices of management officials involving breaches of fiduciary duty and personal misconduct and to disqualify such officials from office.

Regulation of Companies Controlling Utilities The Public Utility Holding Company Act of 1935 (15 U.S.C. 79a—79z–6) provides for regulation by the Commission of the purchase and sale of securities and assets by companies in electric and gas utility holding company systems, their intrasystem transactions and service, and management arrangements. It limits holding companies to a single coordinated utility system and requires simplification of complex corporate and capital structures and elimination of unfair distribution of voting power among holders of system securities.

The issuance and sale of securities by holding companies and their subsidiaries, unless exempt (subject to conditions and terms that the Commission is empowered to impose) as an issue expressly authorized by the State commission in the State in which the issuer is incorporated, must be found by the Commission to meet certain statutory standards.

The purchase and sale of utility properties and other assets may not be made in contravention of rules, regulations, or orders of the Commission regarding the consideration to be received, maintenance of competitive conditions, fees and commissions, accounts, disclosure of interest, and similar matters. In passing upon proposals for reorganization, merger, or consolidation, the Commission must be satisfied that the objectives of the act generally are complied with and that the terms of the proposal are fair and equitable to all classes of securities holders affected.

Regulation of Investment Advisers   The Investment Advisers Act of 1940 (15 U.S.C. 80b–1—80b–21) provides that persons who, for compensation, engage in the business of advising others with respect to securities must register with the Commission. The act prohibits certain fee arrangements, makes fraudulent or deceptive practices on the part of investment advisers unlawful, and requires, among other things, disclosure of any adverse personal interests the advisers may have in transactions that they effect for clients. The act authorizes the Commission, by rule, to define fraudulent and deceptive practices and prescribe means to prevent those practices.

Rehabilitation of Failing Corporations   Chapter 11, section 1109(a), of the Bankruptcy Code (11 U.S.C. 1109) provides for Commission participation as a statutory party in corporate reorganization proceedings administered in Federal courts. The principal functions of the Commission are to protect the interests of public investors involved in such cases through efforts to ensure their adequate representation, and to participate in legal and policy issues that are of concern to public investors generally.

Representation of Debt Securities Holders   The interests of purchasers of publicly offered debt securities issued pursuant to trust indentures are safeguarded under the provisions of the Trust Indenture Act of 1939 (15 U.S.C. 77aaa–77bbbb). This act, among other things, requires the exclusion from such indentures of certain types of exculpatory clauses and the inclusion of certain protective provisions. The independence of the indenture trustee, who is a representative of the debt holder, is assured by proscribing certain relationships that might conflict with the proper exercise of his duties.

Enforcement Activities   The Commission's enforcement activities are designed to secure compliance with the Federal securities laws administered by the Commission and the rules and regulations adopted thereunder. These activities include measures to:

—compel obedience to the disclosure requirements of the registration and other provisions of the acts;

—prevent fraud and deception in the purchase and sale of securities;

—obtain court orders enjoining acts and practices that operate as a fraud upon investors or otherwise violate the laws;

—suspend or revoke the registrations of brokers, dealers, investment companies, and investment advisers who willfully engage in such acts and practices;

—suspend or bar from association persons associated with brokers, dealers, investment companies, and investment advisers who have violated any provision of the Federal securities laws; and

—prosecute persons who have engaged in fraudulent activities or other willful violations of those laws.

In addition, attorneys, accountants, and other professionals who violate the securities laws face possible loss of their privilege to practice before the Commission.

To this end, private investigations are conducted into complaints or other indications of securities violations. Evidence thus established of law violations is used in appropriate administrative proceedings to revoke registration or in actions instituted in Federal courts to restrain or enjoin such activities. Where the evidence tends to establish criminal fraud or other willful violation of the securities laws, the facts are referred to the Attorney General for criminal prosecution of the offenders. The Commission may assist in such prosecutions.

Regional/District Offices—Securities and Exchange Commission

(R: Regional Director; D: District Administrator)

Region/District	Address	Officer	Telephone
1. NORTHEAST (NEW YORK, NY)	Suite 1300, 7 World Trade Ctr., 10048	Richard H. Walker (R)	202–748–8000
Boston, MA	Suite 600, 73 Tremont St., 02108–3912	Juan Marcel Marcelino (D)	617–424–5900
Philadelphia, PA	Suite 1005 E., Curtis Ctr., 601 Walnut St., 19106–3322	Donald M. Hoerl (D)	215–597–3100
2. SOUTHEAST (MIAMI, FL)	Suite 200, 1401 Brickell Ave., 33131	Charles V. Senatore (R)	305–536–4700
Atlanta, GA	Suite 1000, 3475 Lenox Rd. NE., 30326–1232	Richard P. Wessel (D)	404–842–7600
3. MIDWEST (CHICAGO, IL)	Suite 1400, Northwestern Atrium Ctr., 500 W. Madison St., 60661–2511	Mary Keefe (R)	312–353–7390
4. CENTRAL (DENVER, CO)	Suite 4800, 1801 California St., 80202–2648	Robert H. Davenport (R)	303–391–6800
Fort Worth, TX	Suite 1900, 801 Cherry St., 76102	T. Christopher Browne (D)	817–334–3821
Salt Lake City, UT	500 Key Bank Twr., 50 S. Main St., 84144–0402	Kenneth D. Israel (D)	801–524–5796
5. PACIFIC (LOS ANGELES, CA)	Suite 1100, 5670 Wilshire Blvd., 90036–3648	Elaine M. Cacheris (R)	213–965–3998
San Francisco, CA	11th Fl., 44 Montgomery St., 94104	David B. Bayless (D)	415–705–2500

Sources of Information

Inquiries regarding the following matters should be directed to the appropriate office, Securities and Exchange Commission, 450 Fifth Street NW., Washington, DC 20549.

Consumer Activities Publications detailing the Commission's activities, which include material of assistance to the potential investor, are available from the Publications Unit. In addition, the Office of Consumer Affairs answers questions from investors, assists investors with specific problems regarding their relations with broker dealers and companies, and advises the Commission and other offices and divisions regarding problems frequently encountered by investors and possible regulatory solutions to such problems. Phone, 202–942–7040. Toll-free consumer information line, 1–800–SEC–0330. Fax, 202–942–9634.

Contracts Contact the Office of Administrative and Personnel Management. Phone, 202–942–4000.

Employment With the exception of the attorney category, positions are in the competitive civil service and are filled generally by selection from lists of eligibles established as a result of appropriate civil service examinations. The Commission operates a college and law school recruitment program, including on-campus visitations for interview purposes. Inquiries should be directed to the Office of Administrative and Personnel Management. Phone, 202–942–4000. Fax, 202–942–9630.

Investor Information and Protection Complaints and inquiries may be directed to headquarters or to any regional or district office. Registration statements and other public documents filed with the Commission are available for public inspection in the public reference room at the home office. Much of the information also is available at the

Northeast and Midwest regional offices. Copies of the public material may be purchased from the Commission's contract copying service at prescribed rates.

Publications *Official Summary*—A monthly summary of securities transactions and holding of officers, directors, and principal stockholders ($26 per issue) is available through the Superintendent of Documents, Government Printing Office,

Washington, DC 20402. Phone, 202–512–1800.

Reading Rooms The Commission maintains a public reference room and also a library (phone, 202–942–7090; fax, 202–942–9629), where additional information may be obtained.

Small Business Activities Information on security laws that pertain to small businesses in relation to securities offerings may be obtained from the Commission. Phone, 202–942–2950.

For further information, contact the Office of Public Affairs, Securities and Exchange Commission, 450 Fifth Street NW., Washington, DC 20549. Phone, 202–942–0020. Fax, 202–942–9654.

SELECTIVE SERVICE SYSTEM

National Headquarters, Arlington, VA 22209–2425
Phone, 703–235–2555

Director	GIL CORONADO
Deputy Director	(VACANCY)
Executive Director	G. HUNTINGTON BANISTER
Inspector Counsel	ALFRED RASCON
Financial Manager	JOSEPH S. TROPEA
Counselor and General Counsel	HENRY N. WILLIAMS
Director for Planning, Analysis and Evaluation	RICHARD S. FLAHAVAN
Director for Information Management	NORMAN W. MILLER
Director for Operations	COL. STEVEN L. MELANCON
Director for Resource Management	B. FAYE REDDING
Director for Public and Congressional Affairs	LEWIS C. BRODSKY

[For the Selective Service System statement of organization, see the *Code of Federal Regulations*, Title 32, Part 1605]

The purpose of the Selective Service System is to be prepared to supply to the Armed Forces human resources adequate to ensure the security of the United States, with concomitant regard for the maintenance of an effective national economy.

The Selective Service System was established by the Military Selective Service Act (50 U.S.C. app. 451–471a). The act authorizes the registration of male citizens of the United States and all other male persons who are in the United States and who are between the ages of 18½ to 26 years. The act exempts members of the active Armed Forces and foreign diplomatic and consular personnel from registration and liability for training and service. Likewise

exempted are nonimmigrant aliens. Proclamation 4771 of July 2, 1980, requires male persons born after January 1, 1960, and who have attained age 18 to register. Registration is conducted at post offices within the United States and at United States Embassies and consulates outside the United States.

The act imposes liability for training and service in the Armed Forces upon registrants who are between the ages of 18 ½ years to 26 years, except those

SELECTIVE SERVICE SYSTEM

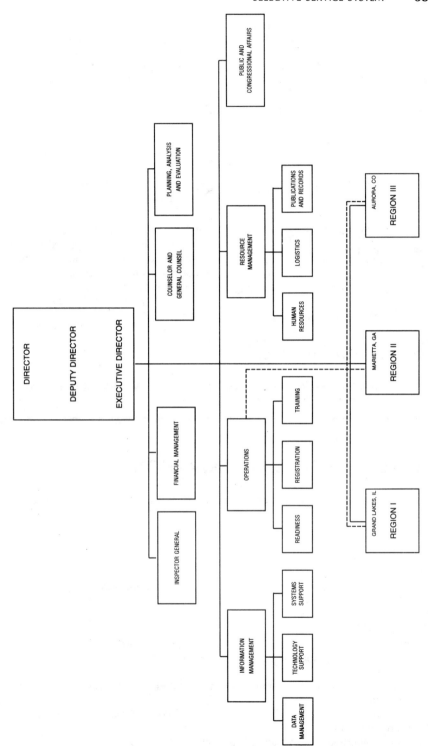

who are exempted or deferred. Persons who have been deferred remain liable for training and service until age 35. Aliens are not liable for training and service until they have remained in the United States for more than 1 year. Conscientious objectors who are found to be opposed to any service in the Armed Forces are required to perform civilian work in lieu of induction into the Armed Forces.

The authority to induct registrants, including doctors and allied medical specialists, expired July 1, 1973.

Regional Offices—Selective Service System

Region/Address	Director	Telephone
I. Great Lakes, IL (Rm. M–29, Bldg. 1, 2701 Sheridan Rd., 60088–5027).	Lt. Col. Ronald V. Meilstrup, USAFR.	708–688–4540
II. Marietta, GA (Rm. A–210, 805 Walker St., 30060–2731)	Lt. Col. Keith A. Scragg, USAFR	404–590–6602
III. Aurora, CO (Bldg. T–318, Fitzsimons Army Medical Ctr., 80045–5001).	Lt. Col. Wayne McDonald, USAFR.	303–361–8155

Sources of Information

Employment Inquiries and applications should be directed to the Director, Selective Service System, Attn: RMH, Arlington, VA 22209–2425. Phone, 703–235–2258.
Procurement Inquiries should be directed to the Director, Selective Service System, Attn: RML, Arlington, VA 22209–2425. Phone, 703–235–2207.

Publications Selective Service Regulations appear in chapter XVI of title 32 of the *Code of Federal Regulations*.
Requirements of Law Persons desiring information concerning the requirements of the Military Selective Service Act should contact the National Headquarters of the Selective Service System.

For further information, contact the Office of Public and Congressional Affairs, Selective Service System, Arlington, VA 22209–2425. Phone, 703–235–2053.

SMALL BUSINESS ADMINISTRATION

409 Third Street SW., Washington, DC 20416
Phones: Personnel locator, 202–205–6600; Answer desk, 800–U–ASK–SBA (toll-free); Fraud-waste, 202–205–7151

Administrator	PHILIP LADER
Deputy Administrator	CASSANDRA M. PULLEY
Chief of Staff	MISSY KINCAID
Counselor to the Administrator	JEANNE SADDLER
Associate Administrator for Field Operations	(VACANCY)
Director, Executive Secretariat	SUSAN M. CLIFFORD
Chief Counsel for Advocacy	JERE W. GLOVER
General Counsel	JOHN T. SPOTILA
Assistant Administrator for Congressional and Legislative Affairs	MARY K. SWEDIN
Associate Administrator for Communications and Public Liaison	WILLIAM F. COMBS
Assistant Administrator for Public Communications	JANIS F. KEARNEY
Assistant Administrator for Marketing/Outreach	IRMA R. MUNOZ

Chief Financial Officer and Associate Deputy Administrator for Management and Administration	JOHN D. WHITMORE
Deputy Associate Deputy Administrator for Management and Administration	DOUGLAS CRISCITELLO
Assistant Administrator for Human Resources	CAROLYN J. SMITH
Assistant Administrator for Administration	CALVIN JENKINS
Assistant Administrator for Information Resources Management	LAWRENCE E. BARRETT
Associate Deputy Administrator for Economic Development	MARY JEAN RYAN
Deputy Associate Deputy Administrator for Economic Development	PATRICIA FORBES
Associate Administrator for Surety Guarantees	DOROTHY D. KLEESCHULTE
Associate Administrator for Financial Assistance	JOHN R. COX
Associate Administrator for Investment	ROBERT D. STILLMAN
Associate Administrator for Business Initiatives	MONIKA HARRISON
Assistant Administrator for International Trade	JEANNE SCLATER
Assistant Administrator for Veterans Affairs	LEON J. BECHET
Associate Administrator for Small Business Development Centers	JOHNNIE ALBERTSON
Assistant Administrator for Women's Business Ownership	(VACANCY)
Assistant Administrator for Native American Affairs	QUANAH STAMPS
Associate Deputy Administrator for Government Contracting and Minority Enterprise Development	ROBERT L. NEAL, JR.
Deputy to the Associate Deputy Administrator for GC/MED	ROBERT J. MOFFITT
Associate Administrator for Government Contracting	THOMAS DUMARESQ
Associate Administrator for Minority Small Business and Capital Ownership Development	HERBERT MITCHELL
Assistant Administrator for Technology	RICHARD J. SHANE, *Acting*
Assistant Administrator for Size Standards	GARY M. JACKSON
Inspector General	JAMES S. HOOBLER
Associate Administrator for Disaster Assistance	BERNARD KULIK
Assistant Administrator for Hearings and Appeals	MONA MITNICK, *Acting*
Assistant Administrator for Equal Employment Opportunity and Civil Rights Compliance	ERLINE M. PATRICK

[For the Small Business Administration statement of organization, see the *Code of Federal Regulations*, Title 13, Part 101]

The fundamental purposes of the Small Business Administration are to aid, counsel, assist, and protect the interests of small business; ensure that small business concerns receive a fair portion of Government purchases, contracts, and subcontracts, as well as of the sales of Government property; make loans to small business concerns, State and local development companies, and the victims of floods or other catastrophes, or of certain types of economic injury; and license, regulate, and make loans to small business investment companies.

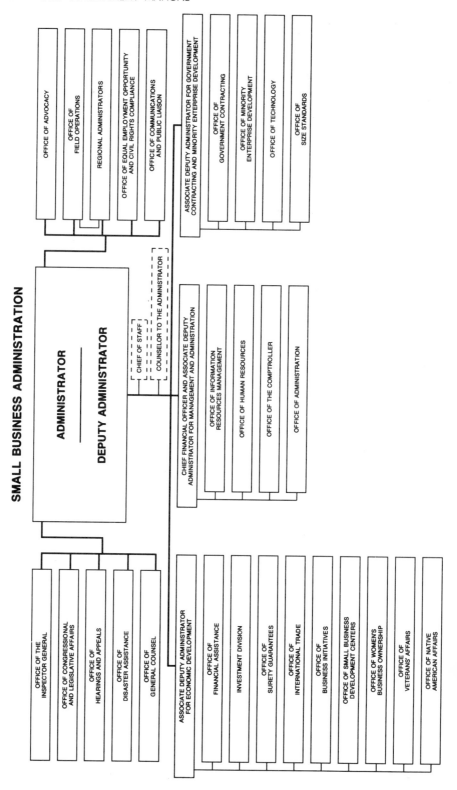

SMALL BUSINESS ADMINISTRATION

ADMINISTRATOR

DEPUTY ADMINISTRATOR

CHIEF OF STAFF

COUNSELOR TO THE ADMINISTRATOR

OFFICE OF ADVOCACY

OFFICE OF FIELD OPERATIONS

REGIONAL ADMINISTRATORS

OFFICE OF EQUAL EMPLOYMENT OPPORTUNITY AND CIVIL RIGHTS COMPLIANCE

OFFICE OF COMMUNICATIONS AND PUBLIC LIAISON

ASSOCIATE DEPUTY ADMINISTRATOR FOR GOVERNMENT CONTRACTING AND MINORITY ENTERPRISE DEVELOPMENT

OFFICE OF GOVERNMENT CONTRACTING

OFFICE OF MINORITY ENTERPRISE DEVELOPMENT

OFFICE OF TECHNOLOGY

OFFICE OF SIZE STANDARDS

CHIEF FINANCIAL OFFICER AND ASSOCIATE DEPUTY ADMINISTRATOR FOR MANAGEMENT AND ADMINISTRATION

OFFICE OF INFORMATION RESOURCES MANAGEMENT

OFFICE OF HUMAN RESOURCES

OFFICE OF THE COMPTROLLER

OFFICE OF ADMINISTRATION

OFFICE OF THE INSPECTOR GENERAL

OFFICE OF CONGRESSIONAL AND LEGISLATIVE AFFAIRS

OFFICE OF HEARINGS AND APPEALS

OFFICE OF DISASTER ASSISTANCE

OFFICE OF GENERAL COUNSEL

ASSOCIATE DEPUTY ADMINISTRATOR FOR ECONOMIC DEVELOPMENT

OFFICE OF FINANCIAL ASSISTANCE

INVESTMENT DIVISION

OFFICE OF SURETY GUARANTEES

OFFICE OF INTERNATIONAL TRADE

OFFICE OF BUSINESS INITIATIVES

OFFICE OF SMALL BUSINESS DEVELOPMENT CENTERS

OFFICE OF WOMEN'S BUSINESS OWNERSHIP

OFFICE OF VETERANS' AFFAIRS

OFFICE OF NATIVE AMERICAN AFFAIRS

The Small Business Administration (SBA) was created by the Small Business Act of 1953 and derives its present existence and authority from the Small Business Act (15 U.S.C. 631 et seq.). It also derives its authority from the Small Business Investment Act of 1958 (15 U.S.C. 661). The Secretary of Commerce has delegated to the Administration certain responsibilities and functions under section 202 of the Public Works and Economic Development Act of 1965 (42 U.S.C. 3142) and is further authorized to delegate to the Administrator certain responsibilities and functions under chapter 3 of the Trade Act of 1974 (19 U.S.C. 2101).

Activities

Financial Assistance The Administration provides guaranteed, direct, or immediate participation loans to small business concerns to help them finance plant construction, conversion, or expansion and acquire equipment, facilities, machinery, supplies, or materials. It also provides them with working capital. Since enactment of the act of June 4, 1976 (90 Stat. 663), farming enterprises are included within the term "small business concerns."

The Administration is authorized to make direct loans to individuals with disabilities and nonprofit organizations employing these individuals in the production of goods or services. Direct loans are also available to Vietnam and disabled veterans and to eligible section 8(a) contractors. The Administration may provide loans to finance residential or commercial construction or rehabilitation for sale; loans to small business concerns located in urban or rural areas, with high proportions of unemployed or low-income individuals, or owned by low-income individuals; extensions and revolving lines of credit for export purposes to enable small business concerns to develop foreign markets and obtain pre-export financing; and guarantee loans to qualified employee trusts with respect to small business concerns. The Administration may finance small firms that manufacture, sell, install, service, or

develop specific energy measures including engineering, architectural, consulting, or other professional services connected with eligible energy measures.

The Administration may also provide assistance to small business concerns needing small-scale financing and technical assistance through loans and grants to private, nonprofit organizations who, in turn, make microloans and provide technical assistance to eligible concerns.

Under the provisions of sections 501–506 of the Small Business Investment Act (15 U.S.C. 695, 696), loans are made to State and local development companies, who, likewise, assist small business concerns by providing long-term loans for the acquisition of land and buildings, construction, conversion or expansion of facilities, and the purchase of machinery and equipment.

For further information, contact the Office of Financial Assistance. Phone, 202–205–6490.

Disaster Assistance The Administration also lends money to help the victims of floods, riots, or other catastrophes repair or replace most disaster-damaged property. Direct loans with subsidized interest rates are made to assist small businesses and small agricultural cooperatives without credit elsewhere that have sustained substantial economic injury resulting from natural disasters.

For further information, contact the Office of Disaster Assistance. Phone, 202–205–6734.

Investment The Administration licenses, regulates, and provides financial assistance to small business investment companies, and section 301(d) licensees (formerly minority enterprise small business investment companies). The sole function of these investment companies is to provide venture capital in the form of equity financing, long-term loan funds, and management services to small business concerns.

For further information, contact the Investment Division. Phone, 202–205–6510.

Surety Bonds Through its Surety Bond Guarantee Program, the Administration helps to make the contract bonding process accessible to small and emerging contractors who find bonding unavailable. It will guarantee to reimburse a qualified surety up to 90 percent of losses incurred under bid, payment, or performance bonds issued to small contractors on contracts valued up to $1.25 million. The contracts may be for construction, supplies, manufacturing, or services provided by either a prime contractor or subcontractor for governmental or nongovernmental work.

For further information, contact the Office of Surety Guarantee. Phone, 202–205–6540.

Government Contracting The Administration works closely with purchasing agencies of the Federal Government and with the Nation's leading contractors in developing policies and procedures that will increase the number of contracts going to small business.

The Administration provides a wide range of services to small firms to help them obtain and fulfill Government contracts and subcontracts. It sets aside suitable Government purchases for competitive award to small business concerns and provides an appeal procedure for a low-bidding small firm whose ability to perform a contract is questioned by the contracting officer. The Administration develops subcontract opportunities for small businesses by maintaining close contact with prime contractors and referring qualified small firms to them. It cooperates with Federal agencies in setting procurement goals for small businesses, small disadvantaged businesses, and small women-owned businesses for prime contracts and subcontracts.

The Administration maintains a computerized small business source referral system that provides qualified sources for Federal Government and large business procurements. It cooperates with Government agencies in ensuring that small firms have an opportunity to procure a fair share of Government property, such as timber, royalty oil, strategic materials, and mineral leases, that is sold to the private

sector. The Administration also works with Federal agencies to ensure that small firms have a fair opportunity to acquire surplus Government property.

For further information, contact the Office of Government Contracting. Phone, 202–205–6460.

Business Initiatives The Administration develops and cosponsors courses and conferences, prepares informational leaflets and booklets, and encourages research into the operations of small business concerns. It counsels and conducts management workshops and courses for established as well as prospective businesspersons, and enlists the volunteer aid of retired and active executives in assisting small businesses with management and technical services. It also contracts with college and university schools of business for counseling services by qualified students. The Administration utilizes the private sector to obtain maximum leverage from all programs in achieving goals and in meeting the needs of the small business community.

For further information, contact the Office of Business Initiatives. Phone, 202–205–6665.

Minority Enterprise Development Sections 7(j) and 8(a) of the Small Business Act provide the authority for the Minority Enterprise Development Program. The Development Program is a multi-faceted program designed to promote business ownership by socially and economically disadvantaged persons. Its components include the 8(a) program, the 7(j) management and technical assistance program, and the minority outreach program.

Participation in the 8(a) program is available to small businesses that are at least 51 percent unconditionally owned, controlled, and managed by one or more individuals determined by SBA to be socially and economically disadvantaged. In order to gain approval for participation in the 8(a) program, the firms must sell goods and/or services that the Federal Government purchases, and demonstrate the potential for successful business development.

Program participants receive a wide variety of services from SBA including management and technical assistance, loans, and Federal contracts. Under 8(a) program authority, SBA contracts with Federal Government entities to provide goods and services and, in turn, subcontracts the performance of these contracts to 8(a) program participants. Information regarding the program and 8(a) program applications are provided by SBA's district offices. The Administration's Division of Certification and Eligibility addresses issues related to 8(a) program eligibility. The Division of Program Development handles matters related to 8(a) contract awards and the business development of 8(a) participant firms.

Under section 7(j) program authority, SBA provides management and technical assistance to section 8(a) program participants, other socially and economically disadvantaged persons, and those businesses operating in low-income or high-unemployment areas. The Administration enters into cooperative agreements and contracts with qualified organizations and individuals, including businesses, State and local governments, educational institutions, Indian tribes, and nonprofit organizations to provide this assistance. At the local level, services are provided on a one-to-one basis in the areas of bookkeeping and accounting services, production, engineering and technical advice, feasibility studies, marketing analysis and advertising expertise, legal services, and specialized management training. At the regional and national levels, SBA funds innovative programs to provide for services in such areas as transition management for 8(a) firms, competitive marketing strategies, financing, comprehensive business plans, and financial management services. The Administration's Division of Management and Technical Assistance administers the 7(j) program.

The minority outreach program provides a broad range of assistance to firms owned by socially and economically disadvantaged individuals by providing information and networking opportunities through a variety of programs. The Administration has combined its efforts with those of private industry, banks, local communities, and other Federal agencies to provide this assistance. The Administration's outreach efforts include publishing a newsletter, entering into cooperative agreements with major corporations to establish an information network with SBA regarding contracting opportunities for firms owned by disadvantaged individuals. The network would provide an electronic bulletin board to disseminate information about potential Federal and private sector contracting opportunities, and would sponsor numerous events designed to foster business development for economically disadvantaged firms. The Division of Minority Small Business Outreach, working in conjunction with other program divisions, is responsible for the Administration's outreach efforts.

For further information, contact the Office of Minority Enterprise Development. Phone, 202–205–6410.

Advocacy The Office of Advocacy evaluates the impact on small businesses of legislative proposals and other public policy issues by preparing policy papers and by conducting research having an impact on small business. The Office conducts economic and statistical research into matters affecting the competitive strength of small business. The Office also researches the effect of Federal laws, programs, and regulations on small business and makes recommendations to Federal agencies for appropriate adjustments to meet the needs of small business.

The Chief Counsel for Advocacy is the Government's principal advocate of small business. The Office promotes the position of small business with Federal agencies and State and local governments; maintains liaison with trade and professional organizations; and serves as the major source of information about the Government for small business.

The Chief Counsel for Advocacy has specific responsibilities for monitoring the performance of Federal agencies under the Regulatory Flexibility Act (5 U.S.C. 601) and the patent and trademark laws amendments (35 U.S.C. 301).

For further information, contact the Office of Advocacy. Phone, 202–205–6533.

Women's Business Ownership The Women's Business Ownership Program, with a constituency of more than 5 million women business owners generating over $278.1 billion in gross receipts, was formed to implement a national policy to support women entrepreneurs. It operates under the authority and mandate of Executive Order 12138 of May 18, 1979, and the Small Business Act (15 U.S.C. 631). Its functions are carried out by the Office of Women's Business Ownership and their network of district and regional representatives.

The Office develops and coordinates a national program to increase the strength, profitability, and visibility of women-owned businesses, while making maximum use of existing government and private-sector resources.

The Office develops and recommends national pilot programs in the private sector to provide training and counseling in the initiation, management, and financing of women-owned businesses. It encourages access to capital formation through trade organizations and management consultants who provide financial education and counseling tailored to the needs of women business owners. The Office seeks out and adapts existing small business skills development programs to the needs of potential and actual women business owners and encourages delivery through existing private-sector organizations, SCORE, SBDC, ACE, and SBA regional and district offices throughout the country.

The Office also has created a national mentoring program, the Women's Network for Entrepreneurial Training, which links seasoned entrepreneurs to women business owners ready for expansion.

To accomplish this mainstreaming approach, the Office cooperates with existing Administration programs to develop, implement, and evaluate all activities to ensure equal access for women business owners.

In conjunction with the Office of International Trade, the Office of Women's Business Ownership supports the expansion of women-owned businesses into the global marketplace by offering training conferences and resources to prepare such businesses for exporting services and products overseas.

The Women's Business Ownership Act of 1988 and the Women's Business Development Act of 1991 authorized SBA to establish demonstration projects to provide long-term training and counseling for women, and a guaranteed loan program for loans not exceeding $50,000. It also established a National Women's Business Council, whose mission is to submit annual recommendations to the President and Congress on ways to improve opportunities for women-owned businesses, and to develop a long-range strategy for supporting such businesses.

In addition, the Office is responsible for negotiating with Federal agencies to set annual Governmentwide goals to increase Federal prime contracts with women-owned businesses. It is responsible for increasing and monitoring the number of women in the Administration-operated Procurement Automated Source System from which Government agencies and major corporations extract profiles of potential bidders.

For further information, contact the Office of Women's Business Ownership. Phone, 202–205–6673.

Veterans Affairs The main objective of the Veterans Affairs program is to advocate for assistance to veterans in business or those who wish to start businesses. The Office of Veterans Affairs monitors and reviews the Administration's financial, procurement, and management assistance programs for "special consideration" for veterans. These efforts include the development and implementation of procurement and other specialized training, consultant services, and conferences tailored to the special needs of veterans. The Office also maintains liaison with Federal agencies, State and local governments, and private organizations to ensure maximum use of existing programs to assist veterans, and it advocates new and more effective programs to benefit veteran small business.

For further information, contact the Office of Veterans Affairs. Phone, 202–205–6773.

Innovation, Research and Technology The Office of Innovation, Research and Technology has authority and responsibility for coordinating and monitoring the Governmentwide activities of the Small Business Innovation Research Program (SBIR). In accordance with the Small Business Research and Development Enhancement Act of 1992, as amended (15 U.S.C. 631 note), the Office develops and issues policy directives for the general conduct of the programs within the Federal Government and maintains a source file and information program to provide each interested and qualified small business concern with information on opportunities to compete for SBIR program awards. The Office also coordinates with each participating Federal agency in developing a master release schedule of all program solicitations; publishes the *Presolicitation Announcement* quarterly, which contains pertinent facts on upcoming solicitations; and surveys and monitors program operations within the Federal Government and reports on the progress of the program each year to Congress.

The program has four main objectives: to expand and improve the small business innovation research program; to emphasize the program's goal of increasing private sector commercialization of technology developed through Federal research and development; to increase small business participation in Federal research and development; and to improve the Federal Government's dissemination of information concerning the small business innovation research program, particularly with regard to program participation by women-owned small business concerns and by socially and economically disadvantaged small business concerns.

For further information, contact the Office of Technology. Phone, 202–205–6450.

International Trade The Office of International Trade develops and recommends agency policy regarding the International Trade Program. To this end, the Office develops plans, operating procedures, and standards to effectively strengthen and improve the agency's International Trade Program for small business; develops new methods and techniques for assisting small businesses entering international markets; and plans, develops, and implements programs to encourage small business participation in international trade. To assure that adequate consideration is given to small business interests in the Federal Government's export expansion program, the Office coordinates the Administration's International Trade Program with the Departments of Commerce and Agriculture, the Export-Import Bank of the United States, the Agency for International Development, and with other Federal and State agencies and private organizations concerned with international trade.

The Office also develops programs in cooperation with operating units of the Department of Commerce and other Federal and State agencies to assure that small businesses will be afforded maximum opportunities and benefits from participation in trade shows, fairs, and missions, and other domestic and overseas export development activities.

For further information, contact the Office of International Trade. Phone, 202–205–6720.

Small Business Development Centers Small Business Development Centers provide counseling and training to existing and prospective small business owners. These services are available at approximately 750 geographically dispersed locations, including Puerto Rico and the Virgin Islands. The Office of Small Business Development Centers develops national policies and goals in accordance with the Small Business Development Center Act of 1980 (15 U.S.C. 631 note). It establishes standards for the selection and performance of Centers; monitors compliance with applicable Office of Management and Budget circulars and laws; and implements new approaches to improve operations of existing centers.

The Office is responsible for coordinating program efforts with other internal activities of the Administration, as well as with the activities of other Federal agencies, and maintains liaison with other Federal, State, and local agencies and private organizations whose activities relate to Small Business Development Centers. It also assesses how the program is affected by substantive developments and policies in other areas of the agency, in other government agencies, and in the private sector.

For further information, contact the Office of Small Business Development Centers. Phone, 202–205–6766.

Field Offices—Small Business Administration

(RO: Regional Office; DO: District Office; BO: Branch Office; POD: Post of Duty)

Office	Address	Officer in Charge	Telephone
I. BOSTON, MA (RO)	9th Fl., 155 Federal St., 02110	Patrick McGowan	617–451–2030
Augusta, ME (DO)	Rm. 512, 40 Western Ave., 04330	Leroy G. Perry	207–622–8378
Boston, MA (DO)	Rm. 265, 10 Causeway St., 02222–1093.	(Vacancy)	617–565–5590
Concord, NH (DO)	Suite 202, 143 N. Main St., 03302–1257.	William K. Phillips	603–225–1400
Hartford, CT (DO)	2d Fl., 330 Main St., 06106	JoAnn Vanvechten	203–240–4700
Montpelier, VT (DO)	Rm. 205, 87 State St., 05602	Kenneth Silvia	802–828–4422
Providence, RI (DO)	5th Fl., 380 Westminister Mall, 02903	Joseph Loddo	401–528–4561
Springfield, MA (BO)	Rm. 212, 1550 Main St., 01103	Harold Webb	413–785–0268
II. NEW YORK, NY (RO)	Rm. 31–08, 26 Federal Plz., 10278	Thomas M. Bettridge	212–264–1450
Buffalo, NY (DO)	Rm. 1311, 111 W. Huron St., 14202	Franklin J. Sciortino	716–846–4301
Elmira, NY (BO)	4th Fl., 333 E. Water St., 14901	James J. Cristofaro	607–734–8130
Hato Rey, PR (DO)	Rm. 691, Federal Bldg., Carlos Chardon Ave., 00918.	Carlos E. Chardon	809–766–5572
Melville, NY (BO)	Rm. 102E, 35 Pinelawn Rd., 11747	Bert Haggerty	516–454–0750
New York, NY (DO)	Rm. 3100, 26 Federal Plz., 10278	Aubrey A. Rogers	212–264–2454
Newark, NJ (DO)	4th Fl., 60 Park Pl., 07102	Francisco Marrero	201–645–2434
Rochester, NY (BO)	Rm. 410, 100 State St., 14614	Peter Flihan	716–263–6700
Albany, NY (POD)	Rm. 815, Clinton and Pearl Sts., 12207.	(Vacancy)	518–472–6300
Camden, NJ (POD)	2600 Mt. Ephraim Ave., 08104	(Vacancy)	609–757–5183
St. Croix, VI (POD)	Suite 7, 4200 United Shopping Plz., 00820–4487.	Carl Christensen	809–778–5380
St. Thomas, VI (POD)	Rm. 210, Federal Office Bldg., Veterans Dr., 00802.	(Vacancy)	809–774–8530
Syracuse, NY (DO)	Rm. 1071, 100 S. Clinton St., 13260	B.J. Paprocki	315–423–5383
III. PHILADELPHIA, PA (RO)	Suite 201, Allendale Sq., 475 Allendale Rd., King of Prussia, 19406.	Susan M. McCann	215–962–3710
Baltimore, MD (DO)	3d Fl., 10 N. Calvert St., 21202	Charles J. Gaston	410–962–4392
Clarksburg, WV (DO)	5th Fl., 168 W. Main St., 26301	Gregory Walter	304–623–5631
King of Prussia, PA (DO)	Suite 201, Allendale Sq., 475 Allendale Rd., 19406.	Clifton Toulson, Jr.	215–962–3710
Pittsburgh, PA (DO)	5th Fl., 960 Penn Ave., 15222	Joseph M. Kopp	412–644–2780
Richmond, VA (DO)	Rm. 3015, 400 N. 8th St., 23240	Dratin Hill, Jr.	804–771–2400
Washington, DC (DO)	1110 Vermont Ave. NW., 20036	Wilfredo Gonzalez	202–606–4000
Charleston, WV (BO)	Rm. 309, 550 Eagan St., 25301	Bill Durham	304–347–5220
Harrisburg, PA (BO)	Rm. 309, 100 Chestnut St., 17101	(Vacancy)	717–782–3840
Wilkes-Barre, PA (BO)	Rm. 2327, 20 N. Pennsylvania Ave., 18702.	(Vacancy)	717–826–6497
Wilmington, DE (BO)	Suite 412, 920 N. King St., 19801	(Vacancy)	302–573–6295
IV. ATLANTA, GA (RO)	5th Fl., 1375 Peachtree St. NE., 30367–8102.	Billy M. Paul	404–347–4999
Atlanta, GA (DO)	6th Fl., 1720 Peachtree Rd. NW., 30309.	(Vacancy)	404–347–4749
Birmingham, AL (DO)	Suite 200, 2121 8th Ave. N., 35203–2398.	James C. Barksdale	205–731–1344
Charlotte, NC (DO)	Suite A2015, 200 N. College St., 28202–2137.	Gary Cook	704–344–6563
Columbia, SC (DO)	Rm. 358, 1835 Assembly St., 29201	Elliott Cooper	803–765–5376
Coral Gables, FL (DO)	Suite 501, 1320 S. Dixie Hwy., 33146–2911.	Charles Anderson	305–536–5521
Jackson, MS (DO)	Suite 400, 101 W. Capitol St., 39201	Janita Stewart	601–965–4378
Jacksonville, FL (DO)	Suite 100–B, 7825 Baymeadows Way, 32256–7504.	Thomas Short	904–443–1900

Field Offices—Small Business Administration—Continued
(RO: Regional Office; DO: District Office; BO: Branch Office; POD: Post of Duty)

Office	Address	Officer in Charge	Telephone
Louisville, KY (DO)	Rm. 188, 600 Dr. M.L. King, Jr., Pl., 40202.	William Federhofer	502–582–5971
Nashville, TN (DO)	Suite 201, 50 Vantage Way, 37228–1500.	(Vacancy)	615–736–5881
Gulfport, MS (BO)	Suite 1001, 1 Hancock Plz., 39501–7758.	(Vacancy)	601–863–4449
Statesboro, GA (POD) ...	Rm. 225, 52 N. Main St., 30458	(Vacancy)	912–489–8719
Tampa, FL (POD)	Suite 104, 501 E. Polk St., 33602–3945.	(Vacancy)	813–228–2594
West Palm Beach, FL (POD).	Suite 402, 5601 Corporate Way, 33407–2044.	(Vacancy)	407–689–3922
V. CHICAGO, IL (RO)	Rm. 1975, 300 S. Riverside Plz., 60606–6611.	Peter Barca	312–353–0357
Chicago, IL (DO)	Rm. 1250, 500 W. Madison St., 60661–2511.	John L. Smith	312–353–4528
Cincinnati, OH (BO)	Suite 870, 525 Vine St., 45202	(Vacancy)	513–684–2814
Cleveland, OH (DO)	Suite 630, 1111 Superior Ave., 44199 .	Gilbert Goldberg	216–522–4180
Columbus, OH (DO)	Suite 1400, 2 Nationwide Plz., 43215–2592.	Frank D. Ray	614–469–6860
Detroit, MI (DO)	Rm. 515, 477 Michigan Ave., 48226 ...	Dwight Reynolds	313–226–6075
Indianapolis, IN (DO)	Suite 100, 429 N. Pennsylvania, 46204–1873.	Janice Wolfe	317–226–7272
Madison, WI (DO)	Rm. 213, 212 E. Washington Ave., 53703.	Curtis A. Charter	608–264–5261
Minneapolis, MN (DO) ...	Suite 610, 100 N. 6th St., 55403–1563	Edward A. Daum	612–370–2324
Marquette, MI (BO)	300 S. Front St., 49885	Paul Jacobson	906–225–1108
Milwaukee, WI (BO)	Suite 400, 310 W. Wisconsin Ave., 53203.	Michael Kiser	414–297–3941
Springfield, IL (BO)	Suite 302, 511 W. Capitol St., 62704 ..	D.I. Brookhart	217–492–4416
VI. DALLAS, TX (RO)	Bldg. C, 8625 King George Dr., 75235–3391.	James W. Breedlove	214–767–7611
Albuquerque, NM (DO) ..	Suite 320, 625 Silver Ave. SW., 87102	Tommy W. Dowell	505–766–1870
Dallas, TX (DO)	Suite 114, 4300 Amon Carter Blvd., 76155.	James S. Reed	817–885–6500
El Paso, TX (DO)	Suite 320, 10737 Gateway W., 79935 .	Carlos Mendoza	915–540–5676
Harlingen, TX (DO)	Rm. 500, 222 E. Van Buren St., 78550	Miguel Cavazos	512–427–8533
Houston, TX (DO)	Suite 550, 9301 Southwest Fwy., 77074–1591.	Milton Wilson	713–773–6500
Little Rock, AR (DO)	Suite 100, 2120 Riverfront Dr., 72202 .	Joseph Foglia	501–324–5278
Lubbock, TX (DO)	Suite 200, 1611 10th St., 79401	(Vacancy)	806–743–7462
New Orleans, LA (DO) ...	Suite 2000, 1661 Canal St., 70112	Abby Carter	504–589–6685
Oklahoma City, OK (DO)	Suite 670, 200 NW. 5th St., 73102	Ray Harshman	405–231–4301
San Antonio, TX (DO)	Suite 200, 7400 Blanco Rd., 78216	Rodney Martin	210–229–4535
Corpus Christi, TX (BO) .	Suite 1200, 606 N. Carancahus, 78476	(Vacancy)	512–888–3331
Fort Worth, TX (BO)	Rm. 8A–27, 819 Taylor St., 76102	(Vacancy)	817–334–3777
Austin, TX (POD)	Rm. 520, 300 E. 8th St., 78701	Jay Ferguson	512–482–5288
Marshall, TX (POD)	Rm. 103, 505 E. Travis, 75670	(Vacancy)	903–935–5257
Shreveport, LA (POD)	Rm. 8A–08, 500 Fannin St., 71101	Bobby Boling	318–676–3196
VII. KANSAS CITY, MO (RO) ..	13th Fl., 911 Walnut St., 64106	Bruce W. Kent	816–426–3316
Cedar Rapids, IA (DO) ..	Suite 100, 373 Collins Rd. NE., 52402–3147.	James Thomson	319–393–8630
Des Moines, IA (DO)	Rm. 749, 210 Walnut St., 50309	Conrad E. Lawlor	515–284–4422
Kansas City, MO (DO) ...	Suite 501, 323 W. 8th St., 64105	Dorothy Kleeschulte	816–374–6708
Omaha, NE (DO)	11145 Mill Valley Rd., 68154	Glenn Davis	402–221–4691
St. Louis, MO (DO)	Rm. 242, 815 Olive St., 63101	Robert L. Andrews	314–539–6600
Wichita, KS (DO)	Suite 510, 100 E. English St., 67202 ...	Elizabeth Aver	316–269–6273
Springfield, MO (BO)	Suite 110, 620 S. Glenstone St., 65802–3200.	Dean Cotton	417–864–7670
VIII. DENVER, CO (RO)	7th Fl., North Twr., 633 17th St., 80202–3607.	Thomas J. Redder	303–294–7022
Casper, WY (DO)	Rm. 4001, 100 East B St., 82602–2839.	James Gallogly	307–261–5761
Denver, CO (DO)	Suite 426, 721 19th St., 80202–2599 ..	Antonio Valdez	303–844–3984
Fargo, ND (DO)	Rm. 218, 657 2d Ave. N., 58108–3086	James L. Stai	701–239–5131
Helena, MT (DO)	Rm. 528, 301 S. Park, 59626	Jo Alice Mospan	406–449–5381
Salt Lake City, UT (DO) .	Rm. 2237, 125 S. State St., 84138–1195.	Stan Nakano	801–524–5804
Sioux Falls, SD (DO)	Suite 101, 101 S. Main Ave., 57102–0527.	(Vacancy)	605–330–4231
IX. SAN FRANCISCO, CA (RO).	20th Fl., 71 Stevenson St., 94105–2939.	Viola Canales	415–744–6402
Fresno, CA (DO)	Suite 107, 2719 N. Air Fresno Dr., 93727–1547.	Peter Bergin	209–487–5189

Field Offices—Small Business Administration—Continued
(RO: Regional Office; DO: District Office; BO: Branch Office; POD: Post of Duty)

Office	Address	Officer in Charge	Telephone
Glendale, CA (DO)	Suite 1200, 330 N. Brand Blvd., 91203–2304.	Alberto Alvarado	213–894–2956
Honolulu, HI (DO)	Rm. 2213, 300 Ala Moana Blvd., 96850–4981.	Andrew Poe Poe	808–541–2990
Las Vegas, NV (DO)	Rm. 301, 301 E. Stewart St., 89125–2527.	Patrick Allison	702–388–6611
Phoenix, AZ (DO)	Suite 800, 2828 N. Central Ave., 85004–1025.	James P. Guyer	602–640–2316
San Diego, CA (DO)	Suite 4–S–29, 880 Front St., 92188–0270.	George P. Chandler, Jr.	619–557–7252
San Francisco, CA (DO)	4th Fl., 211 Main St., 94105–1988	Mark Quinn	415–744–6820
Santa Ana, CA (DO)	Suite 160, 901 W. Civic Center Dr.	John S. Waddell	714–836–2494
Agana, GU (BO)	Rm. 508, 238 Archbishop F.C. Flores St., 96910.	(Vacancy)	671–472–7277
Sacramento, CA (DO)	Rm. 215, 660 J St., 95814–2413	Roberta L. Conner	916–551–1426
Reno, NV (POD)	Rm. 238, 50 S. Virginia St., 89505–3216.	Art Ereckson	702–784–5268
Tucson, AZ (POD)	Rm. 7–H, 300 W. Congress St., 85701–1319.	Ivan P. Hankins	602–670–4759
Ventura, CA (POD)	Suite 10, 6477 Telephone Rd., 93003–4459.	Teddy Lutz	805–642–1866
X. SEATTLE, WA (RO)	Park Place Blvd., S–1805, 1200 6th Ave., 98101–1128.	Gretchen Sorensen	206–553–5676
Anchorage, AK (DO)	Rm. 67, 222 W. 8th Ave., 99513–7559	Frank Cox	907–271–4022
Boise, ID (DO)	Suite 290, 1020 Main St., 83702–5745	Thomas Bergdoll	208–334–1696
Portland, OR (DO)	Suite 500, 222 SW. Columbia, 97201–6605.	John L. Gilman	503–326–2682
Seattle, WA (DO)	Rm. 1792, 915 2d Ave., 98174–1088 ..	Robert P. Meredith	206–220–6520
Spokane, WA (DO)	10th Fl. E., W. 601 1st Ave., 99204–0317.	Robert Wiebe	509–353–2800

Disaster Area Offices

Office	Address	Telephone
Atlanta, GA	Suite 300, 1 Baltimore Pl., 30308	404–347–3771
Fort Worth, TX	Suite 102, 4400 Amon Carter Blvd., 76155	817–885–7600
Niagara Falls, NY	3d Fl., 360 Rainbow Blvd. S., 14303	716–282–4612
Sacramento, CA	Suite 208, 1825 Bell St., 95825	916–978–4571

Regional Administrators

Region/Address	Administrator	Telephone
I. BOSTON, MA (9th Fl., 155 Federal St., 02110)	Patrick K. McGowan	617–451–2030
II. NEW YORK, NY (Rm. 31–08, 26 Federal Plz., 10278)	Thomas M. Bettridge	212–264–1450
III. PHILADELPHIA, PA (Suite 201, 475 Allendale Rd., Allendale Sq., King of Prussia, PA 19406.	Susan M. McCann	610–962–3710
IV. ATLANTA, GA (5th Fl., 1375 Peachtree St. NE., 30367–8120) ..	Billy M. Paul	404–347–4999
V. CHICAGO, IL (Rm. 1975, 300 S. Riverside Plz., 60606–6611) ..	Peter Barca	312–353–0357
VI. DALLAS, TX (Bldg. C, 8625 King George Dr., 75235–3391)	James W. Breedlove	214–767–7611
VII. KANSAS CITY, MO (13th Fl., 911 Walnut St., 64106)	Bruce W. Kent	816–234–6380
VIII. DENVER, CO (7th Fl., 633 17th St., 80202–2939)	Thomas J. Redder	303–294–7022
IX. SAN FRANCISCO, CA (20th Fl., 71 Stevenson St., 94105–2939).	Viola Canales	415–744–6402
X. SEATTLE, WA (Park Pl. Bldg., S–1805, 1200 6th Ave., 98101–1128).	Gretchen Sorensen	206–553–2872

For further information, contact the Office of Public Communications, Small Business Administration, 409 Third Street SW., Washington, DC 20416. Phone, 202–205–6533.

SOCIAL SECURITY ADMINISTRATION

6401 Security Boulevard, Baltimore, MD 21235
Phone, 410–965–1234

Commissioner of Social Security	SHIRLEY A. CHATER
Principal Deputy Commissioner	LAWRENCE H. THOMPSON
Deputy Commissioner for Finance, Assessment, and Management	JOHN R. DYER
Deputy Commissioner for Operations	JANICE L. WARDEN
Deputy Commissioner for Systems	RENATO A. DIPENTIMA
Deputy Commissioner for Human Resources	RUTH A. PIERCE
Inspector General	JUNE GIBBS-BROWN, *Acting*
General Counsel	ARTHUR FRIED
Deputy Commissioner for Programs, Policy, Evaluation and Communications	CAROLYN W. COLVIN
Deputy Commissioner for Legislation and Congressional Affairs	JUDY L. CHESSER
Chief Financial Officer	JOHN R. DYER

[For the Social Security Administration statement of organization, see the *Code of Federal Regulations*, Title 20, Part 422]

The Social Security Administration administers the Federal retirement, survivors, disability, and health insurance programs for the aged, disadvantaged, and physically and mentally challenged. It is responsible for studying the problems of poverty, insecurity, and health care needs of those individuals and how they can be resolved through social insurance and related programs, and for making recommendations towards the most effective methods of improving social and economic security through social insurance.

The Administration also assigns Social Security numbers and birth registration documents to U.S. citizens and maintains a record, for tax purposes, of reported earnings for each individual assigned a social security number.

The Social Security Administration was established by Reorganization Plan No. 2 of 1946 (5 U.S.C. app.), effective July 16, 1946. It was made an independent agency in the executive branch by the Social Security Independence and Program Improvement Act of 1994 (42 U.S.C. 901), effective March 31, 1995.

The Administration is headed by a Commissioner, appointed by the President with the advice and consent of the Senate.

In administering the programs necessary to carry out its regulatory responsibilities, the Commissioner is assisted by a Deputy Commissioner, who performs duties assigned or delegated by the Commissioner; a Chief Financial Officer; and an Inspector General.

To assist the Commission in exercising its responsibilities, there is a Social Security Advisory Board to advise the Commissioner on policies related to old-age, survivors, and disability insurance programs under title II of the Social Security Act and the supplemental security program under title XVI of that act. The Board is composed of seven members, one of whom is designated by the President as Chairman.

Activities

Medicare   The Social Security Administration administers a national program of contributory social insurance whereby employees, employers, and the self-employed pay contributions that are pooled in special trust funds. When earnings stop or are reduced because the worker retires, dies, or becomes disabled, monthly cash benefits are paid to partially replace part of the earnings the family has lost.

Part of the contributions go into a separate hospital insurance trust fund, so that when workers and their dependents become 65 years old they will have help with their hospital bills. They may also elect to receive help with doctor bills and other medical expenses by paying a percentage of supplementary medical insurance premiums, while the Federal Government pays the remainder. Together, these two programs are often referred to as "Medicare." Under certain conditions, Medicare protection also is provided to people who are receiving social security or railroad retirement monthly benefits based on a disability. The responsibility for the administration of the Medicare Program has been transferred to the Health Care Financing Administration. By agreement with the Department of Labor, the Administration is also involved in certain aspects of the administration of the black lung benefits provisions of the Federal Coal Mine Health and Safety Act of 1969, as amended (30 U.S.C. 901).

Old-Age Survivors and Disability This insurance program provides monthly benefits to retired and disabled workers, their spouses and children, and to survivors of insured workers.

Supplemental Security Income The agency administers this program for the aged, blind, and disabled. This basic Federal payment program is financed out of general revenue, rather than a special trust fund. Some States, choosing to provide payments to supplement the benefits, have agreements with the Administration under which it administers the supplemental payments for the States.

Appellate Decisions The Social Security Administration also provides administrative direction to a national organization of administrative law judges, who conduct independent hearings and decide appealed determinations involving the benefit provisions of Administration programs. The Administration, through its Appeals Council, reviews such appealed determinations and renders the Secretary's final decision.

Regional Offices

Social Security Administration operations are decentralized to provide appropriate services at the local level. The United States is divided into 10 regions, each headed by a Regional Commissioner. The Regional Commissioner is the principal agency representative at the regional level, responsible for effective Administration contact with HHS, other Federal agencies, State disability determination services, and State welfare agencies. Regional Commissioners implement national operational and management plans for providing services directly to the public and coordinate regional operations so that they are effective and consistent with national and regional requirements, as well as systems and policy directives.

Each region contains, under the overall direction of the Regional Commissioner, a network of district offices, branch offices, and teleservice centers, which serve as the contact between the Administration and the public. These installations have responsibility for:

—informing people of the purposes and provisions of programs and their rights and responsibilities thereunder;

—assisting with claims filed for retirement, survivors, health, or disability insurance benefits, black lung benefits, or supplemental security income;

—developing and adjudicating claims;

—assisting certain beneficiaries in claiming reimbursement for medical expenses;

—conducting development of cases involving earnings records, coverage, and fraud-related questions;

—making rehabilitation service referrals; and

—assisting claimants in filing appeals on Administration determinations of benefit entitlement or amount.

Sources of Information

Inquiries on the following subjects may be directed to the appropriate office, Social Security Administration, 6401 Security Boulevard, Baltimore, MD 21235.

Contracts and Small Business Activities Contact the Office of Acquisitions and Grants. Phone, 410–965–9457.

Employment A variety of civil service registers and examinations are used in hiring new employees. Specific employment information may be obtained from the Office of Personnel. Phone, 410–965–4506.

Publications The Social Security Administration collects a substantial volume of economic, demographic, and other data in furtherance of its program mission. Basic data on employment and earnings, beneficiaries and benefit payments, utilization of health services, and other items of program interest are published regularly in the *Social Security Bulletin,* its *Annual Statistical Supplement,* and in special releases and reports that appear periodically on selected topics of interest to the general

public. Additional information may be obtained from the Publications Staff, Office of Research and Statistics, Room 209, 4301 Connecticut Avenue NW., Washington, DC 20008. Phone, 202–282–7138.

The Office of Public Affairs has published numerous pamphlets concerning Administration programs. Single copies may be obtained at any of over 1,300 local offices.

Reading Rooms Requests for information, for copies of records, or to inspect or copy records may be made at any local office or the Headquarters Contact Unit, Room G–44, Altmeyer Building. Phone, 800–2345–SSA (toll-free answering service).

Speaker and Films It is the Administration's policy to make speakers, films, and exhibits available to public or private organizations, community groups, schools, etc., throughout the Nation. Requests for this service should be directed to the nearest Social Security Office or the Office of Public Affairs.

For further information concerning the Social Security Administration, contact the Office of Public Inquiries, Social Security Administration, 6401 Security Boulevard, Baltimore, MD 21235. Phone, 410–965–7700.

TENNESSEE VALLEY AUTHORITY

400 West Summit Hill Drive, Knoxville, TN 37902
Phone, 615–632–2101

One Massachusetts Avenue NW., Washington, DC 20444–0001
Phone, 202–898–2999

Chairman	CRAVEN CROWELL
Directors	JOHNNY H. HAYES
	WILLIAM H. KENNOY
Senior Vice President, Communications	ALAN CARMICHAEL
Chief Operating Officer	J.W. DICKEY
Chief Nuclear Officer	OLIVER D. KINGSLEY, JR.
Chief Financial Officer	DAVID N. SMITH
Chief Administrative Officer	NORMAN A. ZIGROSSI

The Tennessee Valley Authority conducts a unified program of resource development for the advancement of economic growth in the Tennessee Valley region. The

Authority's program of activities includes flood control, navigation development, electric power production, fertilizer development, recreation improvement, and forestry and wildlife development. While its power program is financially self-supporting, other programs are financed primarily by appropriations from Congress.

The Tennessee Valley Authority is a wholly owned Government corporation created by act of May 18, 1933 (16 U.S.C. 831–831dd). All functions of the Authority are vested in its three-member Board of Directors, the members of which are appointed by the President with the advice and consent of the Senate. The President designates one member as Chairman.

While its electric power program is required to be financially self-supporting, other programs are financed primarily by appropriations.

A system of dams built by the Authority on the Tennessee River and its larger tributaries provides flood regulation on the Tennessee and contributes to regulation of the lower Ohio and Mississippi Rivers. The system maintains a continuous 9-foot-draft channel for navigation for the length of the 650-mile Tennessee River main stream, from Paducah, KY, to Knoxville, TN. The dams harness the power of the rivers to produce electricity. They also provide other benefits, including a major asset for outdoor recreation.

The Authority operates the river control system and provides assistance to State and local governments in reducing local flood problems. It also works with cooperating agencies to encourage full and effective use of the navigable waterway by industry and commerce.

The Authority is the wholesale power supplier for many local municipal and cooperative electric systems serving customers in parts of seven States. It supplies power to several Federal installations and industries whose power requirements are large or unusual. Power to meet these demands is supplied from dams, coal-fired powerplants, nuclear powerplants, combustion turbine installations, and a pumped-storage hydroelectric project operated by the Authority, U.S. Corps of Engineers dams in the Cumberland Valley; and Aluminum Company of America dams,

whose operation is coordinated with the Authority's system.

In economic and community development programs, the Authority provides technical assistance in areas including industrial development, regional waste management, tourism promotion, community preparedness, and vanpool organization. It works with local communities and groups to develop maximum use of available area resources. Working with regional learning centers, businesses, and industries, the agency has identified skills that are needed in the high-technology job market and has set up training centers.

At Muscle Shoals, AL, the Authority operates a national laboratory for development of new and improved fertilizers and processes. Research results are made available to industry. Fertilizers produced in the demonstration facilities are distributed for use in research and educational programs, principally farm test demonstrations and demonstrations conducted through cooperative and wholesale fertilizer distributors. It also conducts a major bioenergy research program.

In cooperation with other agencies, the Authority conducts research and development programs in forestry, fish and game, watershed protection, health services related to its operations, and economic development of Tennessee Valley communities.

In the western parts of Kentucky and Tennessee, the Authority operates Land Between the Lakes—a demonstration project in outdoor recreation, environmental education, and natural resource management.

Sources of Information

Citizen Participation   Regional Communications, ET PB 25H, 400 West Summit Hill Drive, Knoxville, TN 37902–1499. Phone, 615–632–8000.

Contracts   Division of Purchasing, CST 17N 08B, P.O. Box 11127, 605 Chestnut Street, Chattanooga, TN 37401–2127. Phone, 615–751–2624. This office will direct inquiries to the appropriate procurement officer.

Electric Power Supply and Rates   Power Group, LP 2S 180G, 1101 Market Street, Chattanooga, TN 37402–2801. Phone, 615–751–8678 or 3531.

Employment   Human Resources Services, ET 5D 93U, 400 West Summit Hill Drive, Knoxville, TN 37902–1499 (and personnel offices at other major locations and construction projects). Phone, 615–632–3341.

Environmental and Energy Education/ Information   TVA Energy Education/ Information Programs, Forestry Building, Ridgeway Road, Norris, TN 37828. Phone, 615–632–1599.

Environmental Quality   Resource Development, SPB 2S 201P, 309 Walnut Street, Knoxville, TN 37902–1499. Phone, 615–632–6578.

Fertilizer and Agriculture   National Fertilizer and Environmental Research Center, Muscle Shoals, AL 35660–1010. Phone, 205–386–2593.

Local Economic Development and Regional Planning   Valley Resource Center, OCH 2E 62E, 601 Summit Hill Drive, Knoxville, TN 37902–1499 (phone, 615–632–4400); Minority Economic Development, OCH E 3B 7B,

601 Summit Hill Drive, Knoxville, TN 37902–1499 (phone, 615–632–4405).

Maps   Maps and Surveys Department, HB 2N 200A, 311 Broad Street, Chattanooga, TN 37402–2801. Phone, 615–751–2133.

Medical Program   Medical Services, EB 6W 4A, 20 East Eleventh Street, Chattanooga, TN 37402–2801. Phone, 615–751–2091.

Publications   Regional Communications, ET PB 25H, 400 West Summit Hill Drive, Knoxville, TN 37902–1499. Phone, 615–632–8000.

Recreation, Shoreline Development, Regulation of Floating Structures, and Land and Land Rights   Land Resources, Forestry Building, Ridgeway Road, Norris, TN 37828. Phone, 615–632–1802.

Technical Library Services   Technical Library, WT 2D 15B, 400 West Summit Hill Drive, Knoxville, TN 37902–1499 (phone, 615–632–3033); Chattanooga Office Complex, SP 1N 30A, 1101 Market Street, Chattanooga, TN 37402–2801 (phone, 615–751–4913); National Fertilizer and Environmental Research Center, Room A100, NFD 1A 100E, Muscle Shoals, AL 35660–1010 (phone, 205–386–2871); Land Between the Lakes, 100 Van Morgan Drive, Golden Pond, KY 42211–9001 (phone, 502–924–5602).

For further information, contact Regional Communications, Tennessee Valley Authority, 400 West Summit Hill Drive, Knoxville, TN 37902–1499 (phone, 615–632–8000); or the Washington Office, 412 First Street SE., Washington, DC 20444–2003 (phone, 202–479–4412).

THRIFT DEPOSITOR PROTECTION OVERSIGHT BOARD

808 Seventeenth Street NW., Washington, DC 20232
Phone, 202–416–2650

Chairman	ROBERT E. RUBIN
Board of Directors:	
(Secretary of the Treasury)	ROBERT E. RUBIN
(Chairman of the Board of Governors of the Federal Reserve System)	ALAN GREENSPAN
(Director, Office of Thrift Supervision)	JONATHAN L. FIECHTER, *Acting*

(Chief Executive Officer, Resolution Trust Corporation)	JOHN E. RYAN, *Acting*
(Chairman, Federal Deposit Insurance Corporation)	RICKI T. HELFER
Independent Member	ROBERT C. LARSON
	(VACANCY)
Executive Director	DIETRA L. FORD
General Counsel	RICHARD H. FARINA
Deputy Executive Directors:	
Government Affairs and Public Liaison	KENNETH COLBURN
Finance	THOMAS ELZEY
Oversight and Evaluation	NEAL PETERSON

The principal duties of the Oversight Board are to review and evaluate the overall strategies, policies, and goals of the Resolution Trust Corporation and to approve, prior to implementation, the Corporation's financial plans, budgets, and periodic financing requests. The Oversight Board also reviews the Resolution Trust Corporation's overall performance, including its management activities, internal controls, and performance relative to budget plans. In addition, the Board monitors the implementation by the Corporation of the 10-point Management Reform Program instituted by the Secretary of the Treasury in his role as Oversight Board Chairman. It also regularly reports to Congress on the Resolution Trust Corporation's programs, progress, and funding needs.

The Thrift Depositor Protection Oversight Board, formerly the Oversight Board (of the Resolution Trust Corporation), was established as an instrumentality of the United States on August 9, 1989, by the Financial Institutions Reform, Recovery, and Enforcement Act of 1989 (12 U.S.C. 1441a).

The Board is governed by a seven-member directorate consisting of the Secretary of the Treasury, who is its Chairperson; the Chairman of the Board of Governors of the Federal Reserve System; the Chief Executive Officer of the Resolution Trust Corporation; the Chairman of the Federal Deposit Insurance Corporation; the Director of the Office of Thrift Supervision; and two independent members appointed by the President, with the advice and consent of the Senate.

The day-to-day operations of the Board are conducted through its Executive Director and other officers and staff. The Board is required to transmit periodic reports to the Congress and the President, including: reports under the Inspector General Act; annual audits of Resolution Trust Corporation's financial statements; annual reports on Oversight Board and Corporation operations; semiannual reports (which are followed by appearances before the Senate and House Banking Committees); quarterly submissions of the Corporation's operating plans; quarterly reports on severely troubled institutions supervised by the Office of Thrift Supervision; and quarterly budget reports.

Activities

The Thrift Depositor Protection Oversight Board:

—reviews and evaluates overall strategies, policies, and goals of the RTC for case resolutions, management and disposition of assets, and use of private contractors;

—approves, prior to implementation, RTC financial plans, budgets, and periodic financing requests;

—reviews RTC's regulations and procedures, not including its internal administrative practices or procedures or its determinations or actions with respect to case-specific matters;

—reviews RTC's overall performance including its management activities, internal controls, and performance relative to approved budget plans;

THRIFT DEPOSITOR PROTECTION OVERSIGHT BOARD

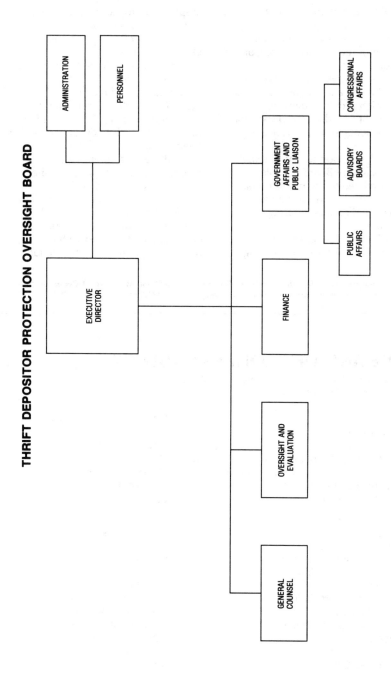

—establishes and maintains a national advisory board to advise the Oversight Board on policies and programs for the disposition of real property assets of RTC institutions;

—directs the operations of six regional advisory boards and a national advisory board, which provide advice to RTC and the Oversight Board on the disposition of real estate acquired from insolvent savings and loans;

—provides support for the Affordable Housing Advisory Board on policies and programs related to the provision of affordable housing, including the operation of affordable housing programs;

—provides advice regarding the merger of RTC's Affordable Housing

Disposition Program into the Federal Deposit Insurance Corporation at the termination of RTC operations in December 1995;

—maintains an Audit Committee to monitor RTC internal controls, monitors audit findings and recommendations of the RTC Inspector General and the General Accounting Office and RTC's responses to such findings, monitors the financial operations of RTC, and regularly reports findings and recommendations to RTC and the Oversight Board; and

—directs activities of the Resolution Funding Corporation (REFCORP), a mixed-ownership Government corporation established with the sole purpose of providing financing for RTC.

For further information, contact the Director of Government and Public Affairs, Thrift Depositor Protection Oversight Board, 808 Seventeenth Street NW., Washington, DC 20232. Phone, 202–416–2622.

TRADE AND DEVELOPMENT AGENCY
Room 309, State Annex 16, Washington, DC 20523–1602
Phone, 703–875–4357

Director	J. JOSEPH GRANDMAISON
Deputy Director	NANCY D. FRAME
General Counsel	KENNETH FRIES
Assistant Director for Management Operations	DEIRDRE E. CURLEY
Special Assistant for Policy/Public Affairs	STEVEN MAVIGILIO
Congressional Liaison Officer	ERIKA M. GASPAR
Export Promotion Director	EDWARD CABOT
Regional Directors:	
Africa and Middle East	JOHN RICHTER
Central, Eastern, and Southern Europe	GEOFFREY JACKSON
New Independent States, South Asia, Mongolia, and India	DANIEL D. STEIN
East Asia and Pacific Islands	FREDERICK EBERHART
Latin America and Caribbean	ALBERT W. ANGULO
Special Projects	BARBARA R. BRADFORD
Economist/Evaluation Officer	DAVID DENNY
Financial Manager	NOREEN ST. LOUIS
Contracting Officer	DELLA GLENN
Administrative Officer	(VACANCY)

The Trade and Development Agency's mission is to promote economic development in, and simultaneously export U.S. goods and services to, developing and middle-income nations in the following regions of the world: Africa/Middle East,

TRADE AND DEVELOPMENT AGENCY

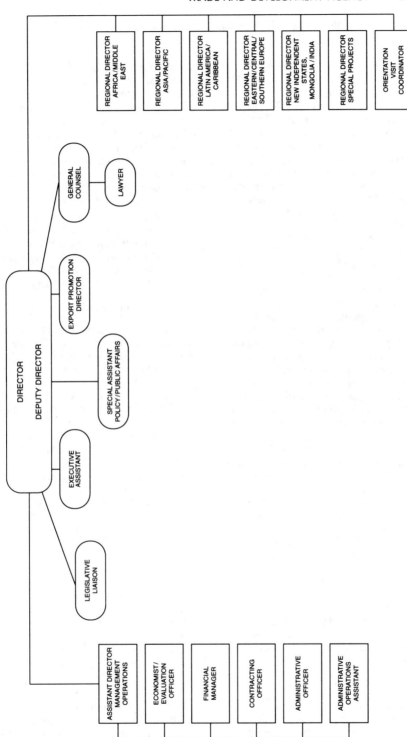

*Asia/Pacific, Central Europe, Latin America and the Caribbean, and the New
Independent States (NIS).*

The Trade and Development Agency
(TDA) was established on July 1, 1980,
as a component organization of the
International Development Cooperation
Agency. Section 2204 of the Omnibus
Trade and Competitiveness Act of 1988
(22 U.S.C. 2421) made the organization
a separate component agency. The
organization was renamed and made an
independent agency within the executive
branch of the Federal Government on
October 28, 1992, by the Foreign
Assistance Act of 1961 as amended by
the Jobs Through Exports Act of 1992
(22 U.S.C. 2421).

The Trade and Development Agency
assists in the creation of jobs for
Americans by helping U.S. companies
pursue exports and other overseas
business opportunities. TDA funds
feasibility studies, orientation visits,
training grants, conferences, symposia,
and various forms of technical assistance
that supports specific projects. This
enables American businesses to become
involved in the planning of infrastructure
and industrial projects in middle-income
and developing nations. Working closely
with a foreign nation sponsor, TDA
makes its funds available on the
condition that the foreign entity contracts
with a U.S. firm to perform the actual
work on the project. This affords
American firms market entry, exposure,
and information, thus helping them to
establish a position in markets that are
otherwise difficult to penetrate.

TDA's focus is the planning and
design engineering phase of major
infrastructure and industrial projects.
TDA is involved in several sectors:
agriculture, aviation, energy,
environment, health care, manufacturing,
mining and minerals development,
telecommunications, transportation, and
water resources.

Activities

TDA funds feasibility studies, which
evaluate the technical, economic, and
financial aspects of a development
project. These studies advise the host

nation about the availability of U.S.
goods and services and is required by
financial institutions in assessing the
creditworthiness of the undertaking.
Costs for a study are shared between
TDA and the U.S. firm developing the
project. TDA funding activities are based
upon an official request for assistance
made by the sponsoring government or
private sector organization of a
developing or middle-income nation.

TDA makes decisions on funding
requests for feasibility studies based on
the recommendations contained in the
definitional mission or desk study report,
the advice of the U.S. Embassy, our
internal analysis, and budget capabilities.

Sources of Information

Requests for proposals (RFP's) to conduct
feasibility studies funded by TDA are
listed in the *Commerce Business Daily
(CBD)*. Information on definitional
mission opportunities can be obtained
by calling TDA's "DM Hotline" at 703–
875–7447. Small and minority U.S. firms
that wish to be included in TDA's
consultant database and considered for
future solicitations should contact TDA's
Contracts Office at 703–875–4357.

In an effort to provide timely
information on Agency-supported
projects, TDA publishes the *TDA
BiWeekly* and a calendar of events. They
are available together on a paid
subscription basis (703–875–4246). A
quarterly publication, *TDA Update,*
contains current items of interest on a
variety of program activities. Region- or
sector-specific fact sheets and case
studies also are available. An annual
report summarizes the Agency's
activities.

Regional program inquiries should be
directed to the assigned Country
Manager at 703–875–4357; fax, 703–
875–4009.

TDA's library maintains final reports
on all TDA activities. These are available
for public review Monday through Friday
from 8:30 a.m. to 5:30 p.m. Copies of

completed feasibility studies must be purchased through the Department of Commerce's National Technical Information Service (NTIS).

For further information, contact the Trade and Development Agency, Room 309, State Annex 16, Washington, DC 20523–1602. Phone, 703–875–4357.

UNITED STATES ARMS CONTROL AND DISARMAMENT AGENCY

320 Twenty-first Street NW., Washington, DC 20451
Phone, 202–647–8677

Director	JOHN D. HOLUM
Deputy Director	RALPH EARLE II
Special Advisor	LISA FARRELL
Special Assistant	CAROLEEN NORD
Executive Assistant	VICTOR ALESSI
Executive Secretary	BARBARA STARR
Senior Military Advisor	COL. CHARLES CICCOLELLA, USA
Chairman, Scientific and Policy Advisory Committee	(VACANCY)
Principal Deputy Director, On-Site Inspection Agency	JOERG H. MENZEL
Assistant Director, Nonproliferation and Regional Arms Control Bureau	LAWRENCE SCHEINMAN
Assistant Director, Multilateral Affairs Bureau	LORI MURRAY
Assistant Director, Strategic and Eurasian Affairs Bureau	MICHAEL NACHT
Assistant Director, Intelligence, Verification and Information Support Bureau	AMY SAND
General Counsel	MARY ELIZABETH HOINKES, *Acting*
Director of Congressional Affairs	IVO SPALATIN
Director of Public Affairs	MARY DILLION
Administrative Director	CATHLEEN LAWRENCE
U.S. Commissioner, Standing Consultative Commission	STANLEY RIVELES
U.S. Representative to the Conference on Disarmament	STEPHEN LEDOGAR
U.S. Representative to the Special Verification Commission and the Joint Compliance and Inspection Commission	STEVEN STEINER
Special Representative, Chief Science Advisor	JAMES SWEENEY

[For the United States Arms Control and Disarmament Agency statement of organization, see the *Code of Federal Regulations,* Title 22, Part 601]

The United States Arms Control and Disarmament Agency formulates and implements arms control nonproliferation and disarmament policies that promote the national security of the United States and its relations with other countries. To effectively carry out its responsibilities, the Agency prepares and participates in discussions and negotiations with foreign countries on such issues as strategic arms

UNITED STATES ARMS CONTROL AND DISARMAMENT AGENCY

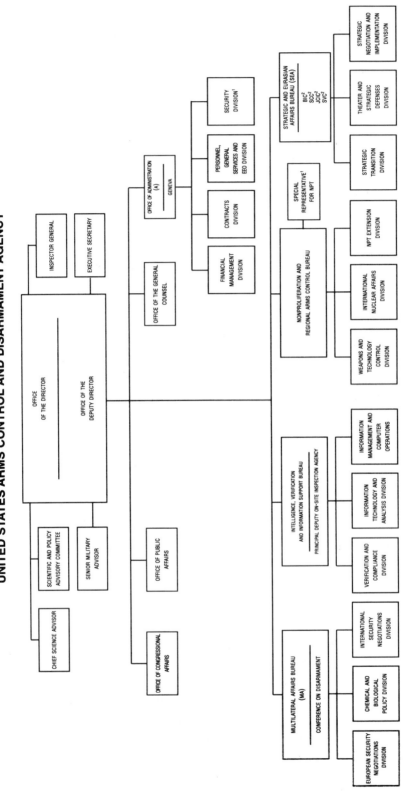

[1] Special reporting access to the Deputy Director.
[2] Direct access to the Director.

limitations, conventional force reductions in Europe, prevention of the spread of nuclear weapons to countries that do not now possess them, prohibition on chemical weapons, and the international arms trade.

The United States Arms Control and Disarmament Agency was established by act of September 26, 1961 (22 U.S.C. 2561), in response to congressional feeling that the Nation's national security efforts could be most effectively executed by lawfully centralizing arms control and disarmament responsibilities.

Activities

The Agency conducts studies and provides advice relating to arms control, nonproliferation and disarmament policy formulation; prepares for and manages United States participation in international negotiations in the arms control nonproliferation and disarmament field; disseminates and coordinates public information about arms control nonproliferation and disarmament; and prepares for, operates, or directs, as needed, U.S. participation in international control systems that may result from United States arms control or disarmament activities.

In addition to directing the activities described above, the Director functions as the principal adviser to the President, the National Security Advisor, and the Secretary of State in arms control nonproliferation and disarmament matters. Under the direction of the Secretary of State, the Director also has primary responsibility within the Government for such matters.

In support of its activities, the Agency conducts research and studies or, through contracts and agreements, arranges for involvement by private or public institutions or persons. It also coordinates such efforts by or for other Government agencies, and analyzes selected defense programs for their arms control pursuits.

The Arms Control and Disarmament Act also provides for the establishment of a Scientific and Policy Advisory Committee—not to exceed 15 members, appointed by the President—to advise the President, the Secretary of State, and the Director of the Agency on matters affecting arms control, disarmament, and world peace.

Sources of Information

Contracts Individuals seeking to do business with the Agency or to obtain information on research contracts may contact the Contracting Office (phone, 703–235–3288) at the address shown below.

Publications Copies of publications such as *World Military Expenditures* (annual series), *Documents on Disarmament* (annual series), *Arms Control and Disarmament Agreements,* the Agency's newsletter *ACDA Update,* and the Agency's Annual Report may be ordered from the Superintendent of Documents, Government Printing Office, Washington, DC 20402, (phone, 202–783–3238); or from the Office of Public Affairs (phone, 202–647–8677) at the address shown below.

Speakers Officers of the Agency will address audiences in all parts of the country, workload permitting. Phone, 202–647–4800.

For further information, contact the United States Arms Control and Disarmament Agency, 320 Twenty-first Street NW., Washington, DC 20451. Phone, 202–647–8677.

UNITED STATES COMMISSION ON CIVIL RIGHTS

624 Ninth Street NW., Washington, DC 20425
Phone, 202–376–8177

Chairperson	MARY FRANCES BERRY
Vice Chairman	CRUZ REYNOSO
Commissioners	CARL A. ANDERSON, ARTHUR A. FLETCHER, ROBERT P. GEORGE, CONSTANCE HORNER, RUSSELL REDENBAUGH, CHARLES PEI WANG
Staff Director	MARY K. MATHEWS
General Counsel	(VACANCY)
Solicitor	MIGUEL A. SAPP
Assistant Staff Director for Civil Rights Evaluation	FREDERICK ISLER, *Acting*
Chief, Civil Rights Evaluation	(VACANCY)
Assistant Staff Director for Management	(VACANCY)
Chief, Public Affairs Unit	CHARLES RIVERA
Assistant Staff Director for Congressional Affairs	JAMES S. CUNNINGHAM
Chief, Regional Programs Coordination	CAROL-LEE HURLEY
Director, Eastern Regional Division	EDWARD DARDEN, *Acting*
Director, Central Regional Division	MELVIN L. JENKINS
Director, Midwestern Regional Division	CONSTANCE D. DAVIS
Director, Rocky Mountain Regional Division	KI-TAEK CHUN, *Acting*
Director, Southern Regional Division	BOBBY DOCTOR
Director, Western Regional Division	PHILIP MONTEZ

[For the Commission on Civil Rights statement of organization, see the *Code of Federal Regulations*, Title 45, Part 701]

The Commission on Civil Rights collects and studies information on discrimination or denials of equal protection of the laws because of race, color, religion, sex, age, handicap, national origin, or in the administration of justice in such areas as voting rights, enforcement of Federal civil rights laws, and equal opportunity in education, employment, and housing.

The Commission on Civil Rights was first created by the Civil Rights Act of 1957, as amended, and reestablished by the United States Commission on Civil Rights Act of 1983, as amended (42 U.S.C. 1975).

Activities

The Commission makes findings of fact but has no enforcement authority. Findings and recommendations are submitted to the President and Congress, and many of the Commission's recommendations have been enacted, either by statute, Executive order, or regulation. The Commission evaluates Federal laws and the effectiveness of Government equal opportunity programs. It also serves as a national clearinghouse for civil rights information.

Regional Programs The Commission maintains six regional divisions.

UNITED STATES COMMISSION ON CIVIL RIGHTS

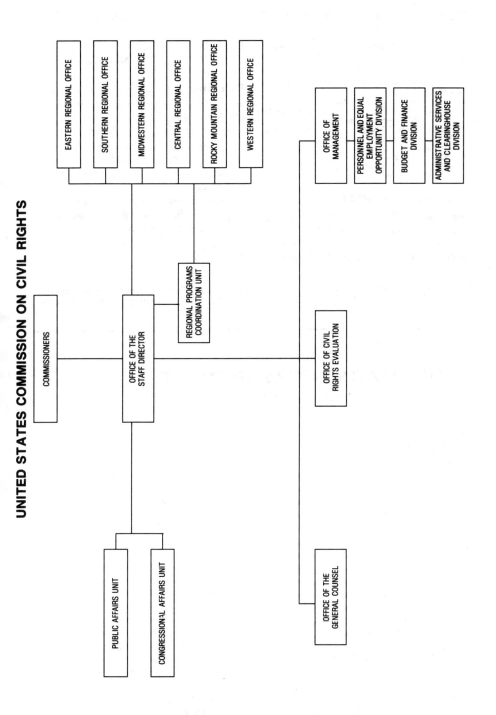

Regional Divisions—Commission on Civil Rights

Region/Address	Telephone
CENTRAL—Rm. 3103, 911 Walnut St., Kansas City, MO 64106	816–426–5253
EASTERN—Rm. 500, 624 9th St. NW., Washington, DC 20425	202–376–7533
MIDWESTERN—Suite 410, 55 W. Monroe St., Chicago, IL 60603	312–353–8311
ROCKY MOUNTAIN—Suite 710, 1700 Broadway, Denver, CO 80290	303–866–1040
SOUTHERN—Rm. 2821, 101 Marietta St., Atlanta, GA 30303	404–730–2476
WESTERN—Rm. 810, 3660 Wilshire Blvd., Los Angeles, CA 90010	213–894–3437

Sources of Information

Complaints Complaints alleging denials of civil rights may be reported to Complaints Referral, 624 Ninth Street NW., Washington, DC 20425. Phone, 202–376–8513; 800–552–6843 (toll-free).

Employment Personnel Office, Room 510, 624 Ninth Street NW., Washington, DC 20425. Phone, 202–376–8364.

Publications Commission publications are made available upon request from the Administrative Services and Clearinghouse Division, Room 550, 624 Ninth Street NW., Washington, DC 20425. Phone, 202–376–8105. A catalog of publications may be obtained from this office.

Reading Room The National Civil Rights Clearinghouse Library is located in Room 602, 624 Ninth Street NW., Washington, DC 20425. Phone, 202–376–8110.

For further information, contact the Public Affairs Unit, United States Commission on Civil Rights, Room 730, 624 Ninth Street NW., Washington, DC 20425. Phone, 202–376–8312; hearing-impaired (TTY), 202–376–8116 .

UNITED STATES INFORMATION AGENCY

301 Fourth Street SW., Washington, DC 20547
Phone, 202–619–4700

Director	JOSEPH D. DUFFEY
Chief of Staff	IRIS J. BURNETT
Deputy Director	PENN KEMBLE
Counselor	DONNA M. OGLESBY
Executive Secretary	MARY ELLEN CONNELL
Chairman, U.S. Advisory Commission on Public Diplomacy	LEWIS MANILOW
Vice Chairman, U.S. Advisory Commission on Public Diplomacy	WILLIAM HYBL
Director, Office of Civil Rights	HATTIE P. BALDWIN
Inspector General	MARIAN C. BENNETT
General Counsel	LES JIN
Director, Office of Congressional and Intergovernmental Affairs	DOUGLAS WILSON
Director, Office of Public Liaison	KIMBERLY MARTEAU
Director, Office of Research	ANN T. PINCUS
Deputy Director	STEPHEN M. SHAFFER
Associate Director for Broadcasting	JOSEPH B. BRUNS, *Acting*
Deputy Associate Director	JOSEPH B. BRUNS
Chief of Staff	JANIE FRITZMAN
Senior Adviser	JOYCE KRAVITZ
Director, Office of Administration	DENNIS D. SOKOL
Director, Office of Personnel	JANIE FRITZMAN, *Acting*
Director, Office of Budget	JAMES ATHERTON

Director, Office of Policy	STEVE MUNSON
Director, Office of International Training	CHERYL MARLIN
Director, Office of Planning	JAMES HUZEN
Director, Office of Program Review	FRANK CUMMINS
Director, Office of External Affairs	JOSEPH D. O'CONNELL, JR.
Director, Office of Engineering and Technical Operations	ROBERT KAMOSA
Director, Voice of America	GEOFFREY COWAN
Director, Office of Television and Film Service	CHARLES W. FOX III
Director, Office of Cuba Broadcasting	RICHARD LOBO
Director, Radio Marti	ROLANDO BONACHEA
Director, TV Marti	ANTONIO DIEGUEZ
Associate Director for Information	ROBERT BARRY FULTON
Deputy Associate Director	MYRON L. HOFFMANN
Director, Geographic Liaison	PAMELA H. SMITH
Director, Thematic Programs	C. ANTHONY JACKSON
Director, Information Resources	JUDITH S. SIEGEL
Director, Support Services	LEWIS LUCHS
Executive Officer	KYRA V. EBERLE
Associate Director for Educational and Cultural Affairs	JOHN P. LOIELLO
Deputy Associate Director	DELL PENDERGRAST
Executive Director, Cultural Property Staff	MARIE PAPAGEORGE KOUROUPAS
Staff Director, J. William Fulbright Foreign Scholarship Board	RALPH H. VOGEL
Director, Office of Citizen Exchanges	ROBERT SCHIFFER
Director, Office of International Visitors	LULA RODRIGUEZ
Director, Office of Academic Programs	BARRY BALLOW, *Acting*
Director, Office of Arts America	ROBIN BERRINGTON
Director, Office of Policy and Evaluation	DAVID MICHAEL WILSON
Executive Officer	J. DAVID WHITTEN
Associate Director for Management	HENRY HOWARD
Deputy Associate Director	JOANN CLIFTON
Director, Office of Administration	EILEEN KEANE BINNS
Director, Office of Technology	DANIEL S. CAMPBELL
Director, Office of Personnel	JAN BRAMBILLA, *Acting*
Comptroller, Office of the Comptroller	STANLEY M. SILVERMAN
Director, Office of Security	LARRY CARNAHAN, *Acting*
Director, Office of Contracts	(VACANCY)
Executive Officer	DANIEL D. DUNNING
Director, Office of African Affairs	ROBERT LAGAMMA
Deputy Director	CORNELIUS WALSH
Director, Office of American Republics Affairs	DONALD R. HAMILTON
Deputy Director	JOHN DWYFR
Director, Office of East Asian and Pacific Affairs	GEORGE F. BEASLEY
Deputy Director	LOUISE CRANE
Director, Office of West European and Canadian Affairs	JOHN P. HARROD
Deputy Director	C. MILLER CROUCH
Director, Office of East European and NIS Affairs	ANNE M. SIGMUND
Deputy Director	MORRIS E. JACOBS

Director, Office of North African, Near Eastern   KENT D. OBEE
and South Asian Affairs
Deputy Director   WILLIAM D. CAVNESS, JR.

[For the United States Information Agency statement of organization, see the *Code of Federal Regulations,*
Title 22, Part 504]

The mission of the United States Information Agency is to understand, inform, and influence foreign communities in promotion of the national interest; and to broaden the dialog between Americans, their institutions, and counterparts abroad. In support of that mission, the Agency conducts academic and cultural exchanges, international broadcasting, and a wide variety of informational programs. The Agency is known as the U.S. Information Service overseas.

The legislative mandates of the United States Information Agency (USIA) derive from the United States Information and Educational Exchange Act of 1948 (22 U.S.C. 1431), and the Mutual Educational and Cultural Exchange Act of 1961 (22 U.S.C. 2451). The U.S. Information and Educational Exchange Act's purpose is to increase mutual understanding between the people of the United States and the people of other countries. It prohibits, with certain exceptions approved by Congress, dissemination within the United States of materials produced by the Agency for distribution overseas. It also requires the Agency to make its overseas program materials available for public inspection at its Washington, DC, headquarters. The Mutual Educational and Cultural Exchange Act authorizes educational and cultural exchanges between the United States and other countries as well as United States participation in international fairs and expositions abroad.

The five executive level offices of the Agency are the Office of Public Liaison, Office of the General Counsel, Office of Congressional and Intergovernmental Affairs, Office of the Inspector General, and the Office of Research.

Activities

The activities of the U.S. Information Agency are based on two key premises, as follows: First, that foreign public opinion is important and that USIA should work to understand it—with the hope that our understanding will be a factor in policy formation; to seek to

inform others about American life and values, policies, and interests as a nation; and, if possible, to eliminate misperception and move others to action in ways that serve the national interest; and second, that mutual understanding borne of people-to-people communication matters, and that USIA should serve as a facilitator to bring Americans and their academic and other nongovernmental sector institutions into substantive contact with influential counterparts abroad through exchanges and other programs.

On this basis, USIA works to:
—explain and advocate U.S. policies in terms that are credible and meaningful in foreign cultures;
—provide information about the United States, its people, values, and institutions;
—build lasting relationships and understanding between Americans and U.S. institutions and their counterparts overseas through the exchange of people and ideas; and
—advise on foreign attitudes and their implications for U.S. policies.

To accomplish its purposes, the Agency conducts a variety of activities overseas, including educational and academic exchanges, international radio and television broadcasting, English teaching, the distribution of transcripts and official texts of significant U.S. Government policy statements, maintaining information resource centers overseas with online reference capabilities, assisting the mass media in bringing information about U.S. foreign policy to audiences around the world,

UNITED STATES INFORMATION AGENCY

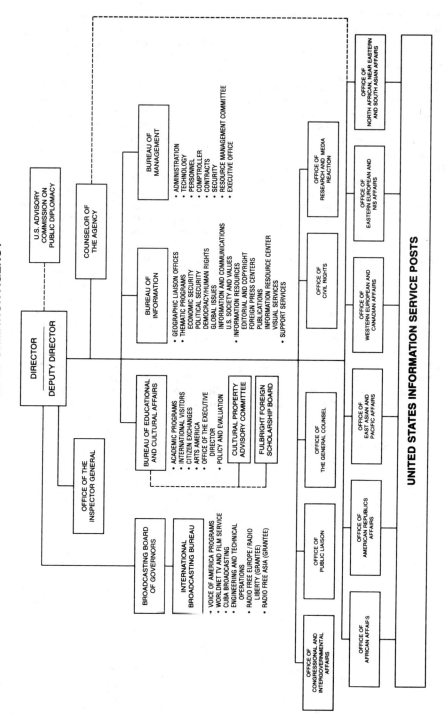

DIRECTOR
DEPUTY DIRECTOR

U.S. ADVISORY COMMISSION ON PUBLIC DIPLOMACY

COUNSELOR OF THE AGENCY

OFFICE OF THE INSPECTOR GENERAL

BROADCASTING BOARD OF GOVERNORS

INTERNATIONAL BROADCASTING BUREAU
• VOICE OF AMERICA PROGRAMS
• WORLDNET TV AND FILM SERVICE
• CUBA BROADCASTING
• ENGINEERING AND TECHNICAL OPERATIONS
• RADIO FREE EUROPE/RADIO LIBERTY (GRANTEE)
• RADIO FREE ASIA (GRANTEE)

BUREAU OF EDUCATIONAL AND CULTURAL AFFAIRS
• ACADEMIC PROGRAMS
• INTERNATIONAL VISITORS
• CITIZEN EXCHANGES
• ARTS AMERICA
• OFFICE OF THE EXECUTIVE DIRECTOR
• POLICY AND EVALUATION

CULTURAL PROPERTY ADVISORY COMMITTEE

FULBRIGHT FOREIGN SCHOLARSHIP BOARD

BUREAU OF INFORMATION
• GEOGRAPHIC LIAISON OFFICES
• THEMATIC PROGRAMS
  ECONOMIC SECURITY
  POLITICAL SECURITY
  DEMOCRACY/HUMAN RIGHTS
  GLOBAL ISSUES
  INFORMATION AND COMMUNICATIONS
  U.S. SOCIETY AND VALUES
• INFORMATION RESOURCES
  EDITORIAL AND COPYRIGHT
  FOREIGN PRESS CENTERS
  PUBLICATIONS
  INFORMATION RESOURCE CENTER
  VISUAL SERVICES
• SUPPORT SERVICES

BUREAU OF MANAGEMENT
• ADMINISTRATION
• TECHNOLOGY
• PERSONNEL
• COMPTROLLER
• CONTRACTS
• SECURITY
• RESOURCE MANAGEMENT COMMITTEE
• EXECUTIVE OFFICE

OFFICE OF CONGRESSIONAL AND INTERGOVERNMENTAL AFFAIRS

OFFICE OF PUBLIC LIAISON

OFFICE OF THE GENERAL COUNSEL

OFFICE OF CIVIL RIGHTS

OFFICE OF RESEARCH AND MEDIA REACTION

OFFICE OF AFRICAN AFFAIRS

OFFICE OF AMERICAN REPUBLICS AFFAIRS

OFFICE OF EAST ASIAN AND PACIFIC AFFAIRS

OFFICE OF WESTERN EUROPEAN AND CANADIAN AFFAIRS

OFFICE OF EASTERN EUROPEAN AND NIS AFFAIRS

OFFICE OF NORTH AFRICAN, NEAR EASTERN AND SOUTH ASIAN AFFAIRS

UNITED STATES INFORMATION SERVICE POSTS

and facilitating linkages between American and foreign nongovernmental institutions.

Functional Elements

The four major functional elements of the Agency are the International Bureau of Broadcasting (comprised of the Voice of America, the WORLDNET Television Service, Radio and TV Marti, Radio Free Europe (RFE), and Radio Liberty (RL)), the Bureau of Educational and Cultural Affairs, the Bureau of Information, and the Bureau of Management.

International Broadcasting Bureau Established by the United States International Broadcasting Act of 1994, the International Broadcasting Bureau consists of the Voice of America, the Office of Cuba Broadcasting, and the Television and Film Service. Beginning October 1, 1995, the Bureau will include Radio Free Europe and Radio Liberty.

The *Voice of America (VOA)* is the International Broadcasting Bureau's functional element for worldwide radio broadcasting. VOA operates in accordance with the act of January 27, 1948, as amended (22 U.S.C. 1463) which requires that it serve as a consistently reliable, authoritative, accurate, objective, and comprehensive news source. It must present a balanced and comprehensive projection of significant American thought and institutions. VOA produces and broadcasts radio programs in English and 46 foreign languages for overseas audiences, and to over 2000 affiliate stations worldwide. Its programming includes world and regional news, reports from correspondents on the scene, analyses of worldwide events, feature programs, music, and editorials.

The *Office of Cuba Broadcasting* is located within the Voice of America. It oversees all programming broadcast for Cuba on VOA's Radio Marti and TV Marti programs. In keeping with the principles of the VOA charter, both services offer their audiences accurate and objective news reports and features on American culture and opinion. Radio Marti broadcasts on medium and shortwave frequencies. TV Marti is available on VHF (very high frequency) and international satellite.

The *Television and Film Service* is responsible for organizing and directing the International Broadcasting Bureau's worldwide television and film activities. The areas of responsibility encompass: producing programs and interactive press conferences for the WORLDNET satellite delivery system; newsfiles in English, Spanish, French, Arabic, Ukrainian, and Russian; producing and acquiring films and videotapes for direct projection or placement overseas; providing facilitative assistance to visiting foreign television and film producers; operating television news bureaus at foreign press centers; providing assistance to foreign broadcasters in the production and telecast of cooperative television programs; serving as the Bureau's primary point of contact with American motion picture and television industries; and coordinating with other U.S. and foreign government agencies on the dissemination of information overseas through motion pictures and television.

Bureau of Information The Bureau of Information is comprised of four offices responsible for most of USIA's information production and support services, including: pamphlets and other special publications; the U.S. Speakers and Professionals-in-Residence Programs; teleconference programs, including the use of new digital video technology; the *Wireless File,* a daily text and backround service; Foreign Press Centers in Washington, New York, and Los Angeles. The Information Bureau is structured to respond rapidly and comprehensively to field requirements by exploiting the latest technologies and greatest range of expertise to acquire, produce, and distribute information to USIS field posts in support of the vital interests of the United States. The Information Bureau focuses on representing enduring American values, particularly individual freedom and equality under the law, and on promoting democratization, market economics, human rights, the rule of law and the peaceful resolution of disputes.

Our products and services are produced and offered to the field based on country resource allocations, country plan themes, and post requirements.

The *Office of Geographic Liaison* includes six area teams: American Republics, East Asia, Near East and South Asia, Africa, Eastern Europe/NIS, and Western Europe, which serve as the primary contact points with the field. The Office contains regional elements of the *Wireless File*. Regional publications officers in Washington advise and assist the posts in the development of book and related print media activities. Regional library officers in the field advise posts on the operations of reference and documentation centers and libraries. A Washington-based regional librarian is assigned to each geographic unit. As part of the total support unit, the Geographic Liaison Office works in close cooperation with all other Information Bureau core teams and the Agency in general. The six geographic teams are designed to be responsive to the Agency's overseas posts and to identify and provide appropriate products and services.

The *Office of Thematic Programs* is composed of six teams that coincide with the themes represented in the Policy Office and the country plan process. The six teams are Economic Security, Political Security, Democracy/ Human Rights, Information and Communications, U.S. Society and Values, and Global Issues. The Thematic teams tailor products and services to the needs of country, regional, and global audiences.

The *Office of Information Resources* includes five core teams: Foreign Press Centers, Information Resource Center (i.e., USIA library), Publications team (including book programs), the Visual Support Services team, and the Editorial and Copyright Services team. The teams facilitate for the field the free flow of targeted information relevant to influential audiences abroad, through the acquisition, production and promotion of print materials (e.g., books and pamphlets), materials in electronic form (e.g., CD–ROM and data banks), or through support of overseas journalists

and resident correspondents through the Foreign Press Centers.

The *Office of Support Services* provides a wide array of support to all other core teams of the Information Bureau, to field posts, and to other Agency elements. The services from the four support teams include administrative support, telecommunications and computer support, printing, training, and program evaluation and development.

Bureau of Educational and Cultural Affairs   The Bureau of Educational and Cultural Affairs administers programs authorized by the Mutual Educational and Cultural Exchange Act of 1961 (the Fulbright-Hays Act), including academic exchanges, short-term professional exchanges, youth exchanges, cooperative projects with private organizations, and English-teaching programs. It also provides staff support for the Presidentially appointed J. William Fulbright Foreign Scholarship Board and for the Cultural Property Advisory Committee. The Bureau consists of four major offices:

The *Office of Academic Programs* develops and coordinates a wide variety of academic educational exchange and English language-teaching programs. It oversees the administration of more than 7,000 grants each year to U.S. citizens to study, teach, and conduct research abroad, and for foreign nationals to conduct similar activities in the United States. The best known of the exchanges supported by this office is the Fulbright Program which operates in more than 120 countries. The Office of Academic Programs maintains a worldwide information network about educational opportunities in the United States, and supports programs which enhance the experiences of foreign students enrolled in U.S. colleges and universities. The Office also encourages and supports U.S.-based studies at foreign universities and other institutions of higher learning. Worldwide support for English language training is provided through overseas-based language consultants, development of English language teaching materials, and a variety of teacher training seminars and fellowships.

The *Office of International Visitors* arranges informative visits to the United States for more than 5,000 influential foreign leaders each year in such fields as government, economics, labor, journalism, the arts, and education. Selected individuals, who are nominated by United States Information Service posts, travel throughout the country meeting counterparts in their fields of interest. They also meet with Americans in their homes or other informal settings. The Office also manages the Agency's two reception centers; serves as the Agency's liaison with the large network of public and private organizations involved in the international visitor program; and arranges programs in the United States for United Nations fellows and foreign government trainees.

The *Office of Citizen Exchanges* provides funding to American nonprofit institutions for international exchange and training programs which support agency goals and objectives. Nonprofit institutions may submit proposals only in response to requests for proposals (RFP's) published by the Office, and these proposals are judged among others in the competition. Programs usually involve professional, nonacademic exchanges—often with study tours, workshops, and internships as key components, and taking place in multiple phases overseas and in the United States. Emphasis is usually on nontechnical themes such as democracy-building, journalism, the role of government, or conflict resolution. The Office also administers all high school exchange programs sponsored by USIA, including major special initiatives in East Europe and the former Soviet Union, and the Congress-Bundestag program with Germany.

The *Office of Arts America* administers fine and performing arts programs, sending performing arts groups and fine arts exhibitions on overseas tours. Arts America identifies and recruits specialists in the fields of literature, film, and the visual and performing arts to speak at or work with host country institutions in their fields of expertise. The Office also awards grants to American nonprofit institutions involved in the international exchange of performing and visual artists and encourages linkages between U.S. and foreign cultural institutions. Arts America also represents the Agency in the Fund for U.S. Artists at International Festivals and Exhibitions.

The *Office of Policy and Evaluation* provides policy analysis, coordination, and evaluation of the activities and programs of the Bureau of Educational and Cultural Affairs. The Office also analyzes U.S. Government- funded international exchanges and training programs with the objective of promoting better coordination among government agencies. The Office is responsible for advising the Associate Director on conceptual approaches to the Bureau's activities and on the development and implementation of its policies. It coordinates activities with the Bureau to ensure consistency of approach; evaluates the success, strengths, and weaknesses of programs; and provides staff support to the Cultural Property Advisory Committee, which advises the Director on U.S. efforts to curb illicit trade in artifacts.

Overseas Posts

Principally an overseas agency, USIA's work is carried out by its foreign service officers and staff assigned to American missions abroad. Overseas posts engage in political advocacy of American foreign policy objectives and conduct cultural and educational exchanges and informational activities in support of those objectives. The Agency maintains 212 posts in 147 countries.

Sources of Information

Administrative Regulations Inquiries regarding administrative staff manuals and instructions to staff affecting members of the public that were issued, adopted, or promulgated on or after July 5, 1967, should be directed to the Directives, Forms and Records Management Staff, United States Information Agency, Washington, DC 20547. Phone, 202–619–5680.

Contracts Contact the Office of Contracts, United States Information Agency, Washington, DC 20547. Phone, 202–205–5498.

Employment For information concerning employment opportunities, contact the Domestic Personnel Division, Office of Personnel, United States Information Agency, Washington, DC 20547. Phone, 202–619–4659. For Voice of America (VOA) and the Television and Film Service (WORLDNET TV) employment information, contact the Office of Personnel, International Broadcasting Bureau, United States Information Agency, Washington, DC 20547. Phone, 202–619–3117. For Office of Cuba Broadcasting, contact the Office of Personnel, Office of Cuba Broadcasting, United States Information Agency, Washington, DC 20547. Phone, 202–401–7114.

International Audiovisual Programs For information concerning a certification program under international agreement to facilitate the export and import of qualified visual and auditory materials of an educational, scientific, and cultural character, contact the Chief Attestation Officer of the United States, United States Information Agency, Washington, DC 20547. Phone, 202–475–0221.

For further information, contact the Office of Public Liaison, United States Information Agency, Washington, DC 20547. Phone, 202–619–4355.

UNITED STATES INTERNATIONAL DEVELOPMENT COOPERATION AGENCY

320 Twenty-first Street NW., Washington, DC 20523–0001
Phone, 202–647–1850

Director, U.S. International Development Cooperation Agency	J. BRIAN ATWOOD, *Acting*
Deputy Director	(VACANCY)

AGENCY FOR INTERNATIONAL DEVELOPMENT

320 Twenty-first Street NW., Washington, DC 20523–0001
Phone, 202–647–1850

Administrator	J. BRIAN ATWOOD
Deputy Administrator	CAROL LANCASTER
Counselor	KELLY C. KAMMERER
Chief of Staff	RICHARD L. MCCALL, JR.
Executive Secretary	AARON S. WILLIAMS
Assistant to the Administrator, Bureau for Program and Policy Coordination	COLIN BRADFORD
Assistant Administrator for Management	LARRY E. BYRNE
Assistant Administrator for Africa	JOHN F. HICKS
Assistant Administrator for Asia and the Near East	MARGARET CARPENTER
Assistant Administrator for Europe and the New Independent States	THOMAS A. DINE
Assistant Administrator for Latin America and the Caribbean	MARK SCHNEIDER
Assistant Administrator for Humanitarian Response	DOUGLAS M. STAFFORD

Assistant Administrator for Global Programs, Field Support and Research	SALLY SHELTON
Assistant Administrator for Legislative and Public Affairs	JILL BUCKLEY
Director, Office of Small and Disadvantaged Business Utilization	IVAN R. ASHLEY
Director, Office of Equal Opportunity Programs	JESSALYN L. PENDARVIS
General Counsel	WANDRA G. MITCHELL
Inspector General	JEFFREY RUSH, JR.

OVERSEAS PRIVATE INVESTMENT CORPORATION

1100 New York Avenue NW., Washington, DC 20527
Phone, 202–336–8400; Fax, 202–408–9859

President and Chief Executive Officer	RUTH R. HARKIN
Executive Vice President	CHRISTOPHER FINN
Vice President, Investment Development	MERRYL R. BURPOE, *Acting*
Vice President and General Counsel	CHARLES D. TOY
Vice President and Treasurer	MILDRED O. CALLEAR
Vice President, Finance	ROBERT O. DRAGGON
Vice President, Insurance	DANIEL W. RIORDAN
Vice President, Management Services	RICHARD K. CHILDRESS
Chairman of the Board	J. BRIAN ATWOOD

[For the Agency for International Development statement of organization, see the *Federal Register* of Aug. 26, 1987, 52 FR 32174]

The United States International Development Cooperation Agency (IDCA) was established by Reorganization Plan No. 2 of 1979 (5 U.S.C. app., effective October 1, 1979) to be a focal point within the U.S. Government for economic matters affecting U.S. relations with developing countries. The Agency's functions are policy planning, policymaking, and policy coordination on international economic issues affecting developing countries. The Director of the Agency serves as the principal international development adviser to the President and the Secretary of State, receiving foreign policy guidance from the Secretary of State. The U.S. Agency for International Development and the Overseas Private Investment Corporation are component agencies of the U.S. International Development Cooperation Agency.

Agency for International Development

The U.S. Agency for International Development (USAID) administers U.S. foreign economic and humanitarian assistance programs worldwide in the developing world, Central and Eastern Europe, and the New Independent States of the former Soviet Union. The Agency functions under an Administrator, who concurrently serves as the Acting Director of IDCA.

Programs

USAID meets its post-Cold War era challenges by utilizing its strategy for achieving sustainable development in developing countries. The Agency supports programs in four areas: population and health, broad-based economic growth, environment, and democracy. USAID also provides humanitarian assistance and aid to countries in crisis and transition.

UNITED STATES INTERNATIONAL DEVELOPMENT COOPERATION AGENCY

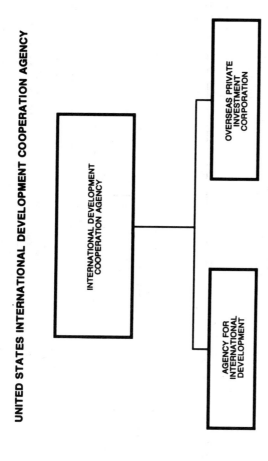

AGENCY FOR INTERNATIONAL DEVELOPMENT

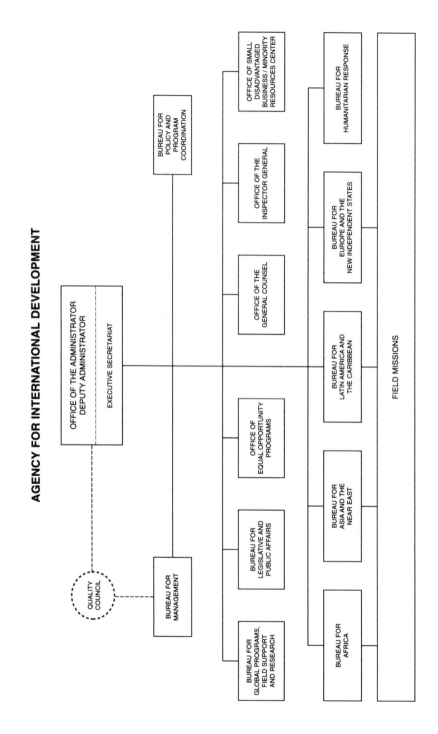

Population and Health USAID contributes to a cooperative global effort to stabilize world population growth and support women's reproductive rights. The types of population and health programs supported vary with the particular needs of individual countries and the kinds of approaches that local communities initiate and support. Most USAID resources will be directed to the following areas: support for voluntary family planning systems, reproductive health care, needs of adolescents and young adults, infant and child health, and education for girls and women.

Economic Growth USAID will promote broad-based economic growth by addressing the factors that enhance the capacity for growth and by working to remove the obstacles that stand in the way of individual opportunity. In this context, programs will concentrate on strengthening market economies, expanding economic opportunities for the less advantaged in developing countries, and building human skills and capacities to facilitate broad-based participation.

Environment USAID environmental programs will support two strategic goals: reducing long-term threats to the global environment, particularly loss of biodiversity and climate change; and promoting sustainable economic growth locally, nationally, and regionally by addressing environmental, economic, and developmental practices that impede development and are unsustainable. Globally, USAID programs will focus on the reducing sources and enhancing sinks of greenhouse gas emissions and on promoting innovative approaches to the conservation and sustainable use of the planet's biological diversity. The approach to national environmental problems will differ on a country-by-country basis, depending on a particular country's environmental priorities. Country strategies may include improving agricultural, industrial, and natural resource management practices that play a central role in environmental degradation; strengthening public policies and institutions to protect the environment; holding dialogues with country governments on environmental issues and with international agencies on the environmental impact of lending practices and the design and implementation of innovative mechanisms to support environmental work; and environmental research and education.

Democracy The Agency's strategic objective in the democracy area is the transition to and consolidation of democratic regimes throughout the world. Programs will focus on some of the following types of problems: human rights abuses; misperceptions about democracy and free-market capitalism; lack of experience with democratic institutions; the absence or weakness of intermediary organizations; nonexistent, ineffectual, or undemocratic political parties; disenfranchisement of women, indigenous peoples, and minorities; failure to implement national charter documents; powerless or poorly defined democratic institutions; tainted elections; and the inability to resolve conflicts peacefully.

Humanitarian Assistance and Post-Crisis Transitions USAID will provide humanitarian assistance that saves lives, reduces suffering, helps victims return to self-sufficiency, and reinforces democracy. Programs will focus on disaster prevention, preparedness, and mitigation; timely delivery of disaster relief and short-term rehabilitation supplies and services; preservation of basic institutions of civil governance during disaster crisis; support for democratic institutions during periods of national transition; and building and reinforcement of local capacity to anticipate and handle disasters and their aftermath.

Overseas Organizations

USAID country organizations are located in countries where a bilateral program is being implemented. The in-country organizations are subject to the direction and guidance of the chief U.S. diplomatic representative in the country, usually the Ambassador. The organizations report to the Agency's Assistant Administrators for the four geographic bureaus—the Bureaus for Africa, Asia and Near East, Europe and the New Independent States, and Latin America and the Caribbean.

There are three types of country organizations: AID missions, offices of the USAID representative, and USAID sections of the embassy. USAID missions are located in countries in which the U.S. economic assistance program is major, continuing, and usually involves multiple types of aid in several sectors. Each mission is headed by a mission director, who has been delegated program planning, implementation, and representation authorities. Offices of the USAID representative are located in countries in which the economic assistance program is moderate, declining, or has limited objectives. The offices are usually headed by a USAID Representative, who also has delegated authority for program implementation and representation. USAID sections of the embassy are located in countries where the assistance program is very small or is being phased out. Program planning and implementation authorities are delegated to the chief U.S. diplomatic representative who is assisted by the USAID affairs officer.

The overseas program activities that involve more than one country are administered by regional offices. These offices may also perform country organizational responsibilities for assigned countries. Generally, the offices are headed by a regional development officer.

Development Assistance Coordination and Representative Offices provide liaison with various international organizations and represent U.S. interests in development assistance matters. Such offices may be only partially staffed by Agency personnel and may be headed by employees of other U.S. Government agencies.

Country Organizations—U.S. Agency for International Development

(Missions, Offices, or Sections of Embassy)

Country	Officer in Charge [1]
Albania/Tirana	Dianne M. Blane (OR)
Angola/Luanda	Bill Masten (CO)
Armenia/Yerevan	Fred E. Winch (OR)

Country Organizations—U.S. Agency for International Development—Continued

(Missions, Offices, or Sections of Embassy)

Country	Officer in Charge [1]
Bangladesh/Dhaka	Richard Brown (MD)
Belize/Belize City	Robert Dakan (OR)
Benin/Cotonou	Thomas F. Cornell (OR)
Bolivia/La Paz	Lewis Lucke, *Acting* (MD)
Botswana/Gaborone	Howard R. Handler (MD)
Brazil/Brasilia	Edward Kadunc (OR)
Burkina Faso/Ouagadougou	Thomas C. Luche (OR)
Bulgaria/Sofia	John A. Tennant (OR)
Burundi/Bujumbura	Myron Golden (MD)
Cambodia/Phnom Penh	Joseph Goodwin (OR)
Cape Verde/Praia	Barbara Kennedy (OR)
Chad/N'Djamena	Richard Frankel, *Acting* (OR)
Chile/Santiago	Thomas Nicastro (OR)
Colombia/Bogotá	Lars Klassen (OR)
Costa Rica/San Jose	Stephen Wingert (MD)
Croatia/Zagreb	Charles R. Aaneson (OR)
Czech Republic/Prague	James F. Bednar (OR)
Dominican Republic/Santo Domingo.	Marilyn Zak (MD)
Ecuador/Quito	John Sanbrailo (MD)
Egypt/Cairo	John Westley (MD)
El Salvador/San Salvador	Carl Leonard, *Acting* (MD)
Estonia/Tallinn	Adrian deGraffenreid (OR)
Ethiopia/Addis Ababa	Margaret Bonner (MD)
FYR Macedonia/Skopje	Linda Gregory (OR)
Gambia/Banjul	Rose Marie Depp (OR)
Ghana/Accra	Barbara Sandovaln (MD)
Guatemala/Guatemala City	William Rhodes (MD)
Guinea/Conakry	Thomas E. Park (MD)
Guinea-Bissau/Bissau	Michael F. Lukomski (OR)
Guyana, Georgetown	Mosina Jordan (MD)
Haiti/Port-au-Prince	Larry Crandall (MD)
Honduras/Tegucigalpa	Marshall Brown (MD)
Hungary/Budapest	David L. Cowles (OR)
India/New Delhi	Walter Bollinger (MD)
Indonesia/Jakarta	Charles F. Weden (MD)
Israel/Jerusalem (West Bank)	Christopher Crowley (MD)
Israel/Tel Aviv (Gaza)	Christopher Crowley (MD)
Jamaica/Kingston	Carol Tyson (MD)
Jordan/Amman	William T. Oliver, Jr. (MD)
Kazakhstan/Almaty	Craig G. Buck (MD)
Kenya/Nairobi	George E. Jones (MD)
Latvia/Riga	Baudouin De Marcken (OR)
Lesotho/Maseru	F. Gary E. Lewis, *Acting* (MD)
Liberia/Monrovia	Lowell Lynch (OR)
Lithuania/Vilnius	John Cloutier (OR)
Madagascar/Antananarivo	Donald R. MacKenzie (MD)
Malawi/Lilongwe	Cynthia Rozell (MD)
Mali/Bamako	Joel Schlesinger (MD)
Mexico/Mexico City	Arthur Danart (OR)
Mongolia/Ulaanbaatar	Charles Howell (OR)
Morocco/Rabat	Michael Farbman (MD)
Mozambique/Maputo	Roger Carlson (MD)
Namibia/Windhoek	Edward Spriggs (OR)
Nepal/Kathmandu	Frederick Machmer (MD)
Nicaragua/Managua	George Carner (MD)
Niger/Niamey	James Anderson (MD)
Nigeria/Lagos	Stephen Spielman (AAO)
Oman/Muscat	Mark S. Matthews (OR)
Pakistan-Afghanistan/Islamabad.	John Blackton (MD)
Panama/Panama City	David Mutchler (MD)
Paraguay/Asuncion	Richard Nelson (OR)
Peru/Lima	George Wachtenheim (MD)
Philippines/Manila	Kenneth Schofield (MD)
Philippines/Manila (ASEAN)	Dennis Zvinakis (OR)
Poland/Warsaw	Donald Pressley (OR)
Romania/Bucharest	Richard J. Hough (OR)
Russia/Moscow	James A. Norris (MD)

Country Organizations—U.S. Agency for International Development—Continued
(Missions, Offices, or Sections of Embassy)

Country	Officer in Charge[1]
Rwanda/Kigali	Myron Golden (MD)
Senegal/Dakar	Anne Williams (MD)
Slovakia/Bratislava	Patricia Lerner (OR)
Slovenia/Ljublana	Michael Zak (OR)
Somalia/Mogadishu	Richard Ullrich (MD)
South Africa/Pretoria	Leslie A. Dean (MD)
Sri Lanka/Colombo	David Cohen (MD)
Swaziland/Mbabane	Jack Royer, *Acting* (MD)
Tanzania/Dar es Salaam	Mark Wentling (MD)
Thailand/Bangkok	Linda Lion (MD)

Country Organizations—U.S. Agency for International Development—Continued
(Missions, Offices, or Sections of Embassy)

Country	Officer in Charge[1]
Tunisia/Tunis	David Painter, *Acting* (MD)
Uganda/Kampala	Donald Clark (MD)
Ukraine/Kiev	Gary F. Huger (MD)
Yemen/Sanaa	William D. McKinney (OR)
Zambia/Lusaka	Joseph Stepanek (MD)
Zimbabwe/Harare	Peter Benedict (MD)

[1] MD: Mission Director; D: Director; OR: Office of the AID Representative; DO: Development Officer; RD: Regional Director; AAO: AID Affairs Officer for Section of Embassy; CO: Coordinator in Washington

International Organizations—Agency for International Development
(Selected Regional Organizations)
(A: Advisor; C: Counselor; ED: Executive Director; MD: Mission Director; AID R: AID Representative; RD: Regional Director)

Country	Officer in Charge
Regional Offices	
Regional Economic Development Services Offices	
Office for East and Southern Africa—Nairobi, Kenya	Fred C. Fisher (RD)
Office for West and Central Africa—Cote d'Ivoire, Abidjan	Williard Pearson (RD)
Caribbean Regional Development Office/Bridgetown—Bridgetown, Barbados	Paul Bisek, *Acting* (RD)
Development Assistance Coordination and Representation Offices	
U.S. Mission to the United Nations Agencies for Food and Agriculture—Rome, Italy	Hugh Smith (ED)
Office of the U.S. Representative to the Development Assistance Committee of the Organization for Economic Cooperation and Development—Paris, France.	Dennis Brennan (AID R)
Office of the AID Development Adviser to the U.S. Executive Director to the Asian Development Bank—Manila, Philippines.	Terry Barker (A)
U.S. Mission to the European Office of the United Nations and Other International Organizations—Geneva, Switzerland.	(Vacancy) (AID R)
AID Office for Development Cooperation—Tokyo, Japan	Paul White (C)

Overseas Private Investment Corporation

[For the Overseas Private Investment Corporation statement of organization, see the *Code of Federal Regulations*, Title 22, Chapter VII]

The Overseas Private Investment Corporation (OPIC) is a self-sustaining, Federal agency whose purpose is to promote economic growth in developing countries by encouraging U.S. private investment in those nations. The Corporation assists American investors in three principal ways: financing investment projects through direct loans and/or guaranties; insuring investment projects against a broad range of political risks; and providing a variety of investor services. All of these programs are designed to reduce the perceived stumbling blocks and risks associated with overseas investment.

Organized as a corporation and structured to be responsive to private business, OPIC's mandate is to mobilize and facilitate the participation of U.S.

private capital and skills in the economic and social development of developing countries and emerging economies. Currently, OPIC programs are available for new business enterprises or expansion in some 140 countries worldwide. OPIC encourages American overseas private investment in sound business projects, thereby improving U.S. global competitiveness, creating American jobs and increasing U.S. exports. OPIC does not support projects that will result in the loss of domestic jobs or have a negative impact on the host country's environment or workers' rights.

The Corporation is governed by a 15-member Board of Directors—8 appointed from the private sector and 7 from the Federal Government.

Activities

By reducing or eliminating certain perceived political risks for investors and providing financing and assistance not otherwise available, the Corporation helps to reduce the unusual risks and problems that can make investment opportunities in the developing areas less attractive than in advanced countries. At the same time, it reduces the need for government-to-government lending programs by involving the U.S. private sector in establishing capital-generation and strengthening private-sector economies in developing countries.

The Corporation insures U.S. investors against the political risks of expropriation, inconvertibility of local currency holdings, and damage from war, revolution, insurrection, or civil strife. It also offers a special insurance policy to U.S. contractors and exporters against arbitrary drawings of letters of credit posted as bid, performance, or advance payment guaranties. Other special programs are offered for minerals exploration, oil and gas exploration, and development and leasing operations.

The Corporation offers U.S. lenders protection against both commercial and political risks by guaranteeing payment of principal and interest on loans (up to $200 million) made to eligible private enterprises.

Its Direct Investment loans, offered to small- and medium-sized businesses, generally cover terms of from 7 to 12 years, and usually range from $2 million to $6 million with varying interest rates, depending on assessment of the commercial risks of the project financed.

Programs are available only for a new facility, expansion or modernization of an existing plant, or technological or service products designed to generate investment which will produce significant new benefits for host countries.

Sources of Information

U.S. International Development Cooperation Agency

General Inquiries   Inquiries may be directed to the Office of External Affairs, U.S. International Development Cooperation Agency, Washington, DC 20523–0001. Phone, 202–647–1850.

Agency for International Development

Congressional Affairs   Congressional inquiries may be directed to the Bureau for Legislative and Public Affairs, Agency for International Development, Washington, DC 20523–0001. Phone, 202–647–8440.

Contracting and Small Business Inquiries   For information regarding contracting opportunities, contact the Office of Small and Disadvantaged Business Utilization, Agency for International Development, Washington, DC 20523–0001. Phone, 703–875–1551.

Employment   For information regarding employment opportunities, contact the Workforce Planning, Recruitment and Personnel Systems Division, Office of Human Resources, Agency for International Development, Washington, DC 20523–0001. Phone, 202–663–2400.

General Inquiries   General inquiries may be directed to the Bureau for Legislative and Public Affairs, Agency for International Development, Washington, DC 20523–0001. Phone, 202–647–1850.

News Media   Inquiries from the media only should be directed to the Press Relations Division, Bureau for Legislative and Public Affairs, Agency for International Development, Washington, DC 20523–0001. Phone, 202–647–4274.

Overseas Private Investment Corporation

General Inquiries   Inquiries should be directed to the Information Office, Overseas Private Investment Corporation,

1100 New York Avenue NW.,
Washington, DC 20527. Phone, 202–
336–8799.

Publications   OPIC programs are further
detailed in the *Annual Report* and the
Program Summary. These publications
are available free of charge.

UNITED STATES INTERNATIONAL TRADE COMMISSION

500 E Street SW., Washington, DC 20436
Phone, 202–205–2000

Chairman	PETER S. WATSON
Vice Chairman	JANET A. NUZUM
Commissioners	DAVID B. ROHR, DON E. NEWQUIST, CAROL T. CRAWFORD, LYNN M. BRAGG
Director of Operations	ROBERT ROGOWSKY
Director of Investigations	LYNN FEATHERSTONE
General Counsel	LYN SCHLITT
Executive Liaison	WILLIAM T. HART
Congressional Liaison	JEFFREY M. MENATH
Chief Administrative Law Judge	JANET D. SAXON
Secretary	DONNA R. KOEHNKE
Inspector General	JANE ALTENHOFEN
Director, Office of Public Affairs	MARGARET M. O'LAUGHLIN
Director, Office of Economics	PETER MORICI
Director, Office of Industries	M. VERN SIMPSON, JR.
Division Chief, Agriculture and Forest Products	CATHY L. JABARA
Division Chief, Minerals, Metals, Machinery, and Miscellaneous Manufactures	LARRY L. BROOKHART
Division Chief, Energy, Chemicals, and Textiles	JOHN J. GERSIC
Division Chief, Services, Electronics, and Transportation	NORMAN MCLENNAN
Director, Office of Tariff Affairs and Trade Agreements	EUGENE A. ROSENGARDEN
Director, Office of Unfair Import Investigations	LYNN LEVINE
Director, Trade Remedy Assistance Office	ELIZABETH SELTZER
Director, Office of Administration	STEPHEN MCLAUGHLIN, *Acting*

*The United States International Trade Commission furnishes studies, reports, and
recommendations involving international trade and tariffs to the President, the
Congress, and other Government agencies. In this capacity, the Commission
conducts a variety of investigations, public hearings, and research projects pertaining
to the international trade policies of the United States.*

The United States International Trade
Commission is an independent agency
created by act of September 8, 1916 (39
Stat. 795), and originally named the
United States Tariff Commission. The
name was changed to the United States
International Trade Commission by
section 171 of the Trade Act of 1974 (19
U.S.C. 2231). The Commission's present
powers and duties are provided for

UNITED STATES INTERNATIONAL TRADE COMMISSION

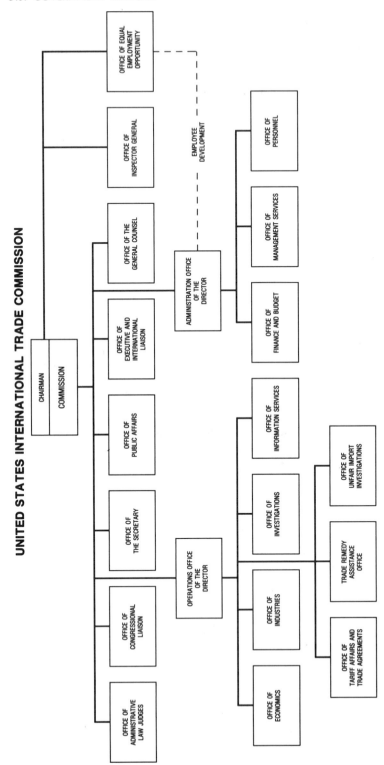

largely by the Tariff Act of 1930 (19 U.S.C. 1654); the Agricultural Adjustment Act (7 U.S.C. 601); the Trade Expansion Act of 1962 (19 U.S.C. 1801); the Trade Act of 1974 (19 U.S.C. 2101); the Trade Agreements Act of 1979 (19 U.S.C. 2501); and the Omnibus Trade and Competitiveness Act of 1988 (19 U.S.C. 2901).

Six Commissioners are appointed by the President with the advice and consent of the Senate for 9-year terms, unless appointed to fill an unexpired term. The Chairman and Vice Chairman are designated by the President for 2-year terms, and succeeding Chairmen may not be of the same political party. The Chairman generally is responsible for the administration of the Commission. Not more than three Commissioners may be members of the same political party (19 U.S.C. 1330).

Activities

The Commission performs a number of functions pursuant to the statutes referred to above. Under the Tariff Act of 1930, the Commission is given broad powers of investigation relating to the customs laws of the United States and foreign countries; the volume of importation in comparison with domestic production and consumption; the conditions, causes, and effects relating to competition of foreign industries with those of the United States; and all other factors affecting competition between articles of the United States and imported articles. The Commission is required to make available to the President and to the Committee on Ways and Means of the House of Representatives and to the Committee on Finance of the Senate, whenever requested, all information at its command and is directed to make such investigations and reports as may be requested by the President or by either of said committees or by either branch of the Congress. The Omnibus Trade and Competitiveness Act of 1988 amended several of the statutes administered by the Commission and, in addition, required the Commission to conduct

several industry competitiveness investigations.

In order to carry out these responsibilities, the Commission is required to engage in extensive research, conduct specialized studies, and maintain a high degree of expertise in all matters relating to the commercial and international trade policies of the United States.

Trade Negotiations   The Commission advises the President as to the probable economic effect on the domestic industry and consumers of modification of duties and other barriers to trade that may be considered for inclusion in any proposed trade agreement with foreign countries (19 U.S.C. 2151).

Generalized System of Preferences   The Commission advises the President with respect to every article that may be considered for preferential removal of the duty on imports from designated developing countries as to the probable economic effect the preferential removal of duty will have on the domestic industry and on consumers (19 U.S.C. 2151, 2163).

Industry Adjustment to Import Competition (Global Safeguard Actions)   The Commission conducts investigations upon petition on behalf of an industry, a firm, a group of workers, or other entity representative of an industry to determine whether an article is being imported in such increased quantities as to be a substantial cause of serious injury or threat thereof to the domestic industry producing an article like or directly competitive with the imported article (19 U.S.C. 2251–2254). If the Commission's finding is affirmative, it recommends to the President the action that would address such injury and be most effective in facilitating positive adjustment by the industry to import competition. The President has discretion to take action that could be in the form of an increase in duties, imposition of a quota, negotiation of orderly marketing agreements, or provision of adjustment assistance to groups of workers, firms, or communities. If the President does not provide relief or does not provide relief in the form recommended by the

Commission, Congress may, by means of a joint resolution disapproving the action of the President, direct the President to provide the relief recommended by the Commission (19 U.S.C. 2251–2254).

The Commission reports with respect to developments within an industry that has been granted import relief and advises the President of the probable economic effect of the reduction or elimination of the tariff increase that has been granted. The President may continue, modify, or terminate the import relief previously granted.

Imports from NAFTA Countries (Bilateral Safeguard Actions) The Commission conducts investigations to determine whether, as a result of the reduction or elimination of a duty provided for under the North American Free Trade Agreement (NAFTA), a Canadian article or a Mexican article, as the case may be, is being imported into the United States in such increased quantities and under such conditions so that imports of the article constitute a substantial cause of serious injury or (except in the case of a Canadian article) a threat of serious injury to the domestic industry producing an article that is like or directly competitive with the imported article (19 U.S.C. 3351–3356). If the Commission's determination is in the affirmative, the Commission recommends to the President the relief which is necessary to prevent or remedy serious injury. Such relief generally would take the form of the suspension of any further reduction in the rate of duty for such article from the subject country provided for in NAFTA, or an increase in the rate of duty on such article from such country to the lesser of the general column 1 rate of duty on such article or the column 1 rate of duty in effect immediately prior to the entry into force of NAFTA. Commission investigations under these provisions are similar procedurally to those conducted under the global safeguard action provisions.

Market Disruption From Communist Countries The Commission conducts investigations to determine whether increased imports of an article produced in a Communist country are causing market disruption in the United States (19 U.S.C. 2436). If the Commission's determination is in the affirmative, the President may take the same action as in the case of serious injury to an industry, except that the action would apply only to imports of the article from the Communist country. Commission investigations conducted under this provision are similar procedurally to those conducted under the global safeguard action provisions.

East-West Trade Monitoring System The Commission monitors imports into the United States from nonmarket-economy countries and makes a report at least once each calendar quarter on the effect of such imports on the production of like or directly competitive articles in the United States and on employment within the industry (19 U.S.C. 2240).

Imported Articles Subsidized or Sold at Less Than Fair Value The Commission conducts preliminary investigations under the Tariff Act of 1930 to determine whether there is reasonable indication of material injury to, threat of material injury to, or material retardation of the establishment of an industry in the United States by reason of imports of foreign merchandise allegedly being subsidized or sold at less than fair value (19 U.S.C. 1671, 1673, 1675). If the Commission's determination is affirmative, and the Secretary of Commerce further determines that the foreign merchandise is being subsidized or is being, or is likely to be, sold at less than its fair value, or there is reason to believe or suspect such unfair practices are occurring, then the Commission conducts final investigations to determine whether a U.S. industry is materially injured or threatened with material injury, or its establishment is materially retarded by reason of such imports.

If the Secretary of Commerce determines to suspend an investigation upon acceptance of an agreement to eliminate the injurious effect of subsidized imports or imports sold at less than fair value, the Commission may conduct an investigation to determine whether the injurious effect of imports of the merchandise that was the subject of the suspended investigation is eliminated completely by the agreement. The Commission also conducts investigations to determine whether in light of changed circumstances such a suspension agreement continues to eliminate completely the injurious effect of imports of the merchandise.

The Commission conducts investigations to determine whether changed circumstances exist that indicate that an industry in the United States would not be threatened with material injury, or the establishment of such an industry would not be materially retarded, if the countervailing duty order or antidumping order resulting from affirmative final determinations by the Commission and Secretary of Commerce were modified or revoked.

With regard to imports of articles from countries not party to the Agreement on Interpretation and Application of Articles VI, XVI, and XXIII of the General Agreement on Tariffs and Trade, the Commission determines, with respect to any such duty-free article that the Secretary of Commerce has determined is being subsidized, whether an industry in the United States is materially injured or threatened with material injury, or its establishment is materially retarded by reason of such imports (19 U.S.C. 1303).

Import Interference With Agricultural Programs   The Commission conducts investigations at the direction of the President to determine whether any articles are being or are practically certain to be imported into the United States under such conditions and in such quantities as to render or tend to render ineffective, or to materially interfere with, programs of the Department of Agriculture for agricultural commodities or products thereof, or to reduce substantially the amount of any product processed in the United States from such commodities or products, and makes findings and recommendations (7 U.S.C. 624). The President may restrict the imports in question by imposition of either import fees or quotas. Such fees or quotas may be applied only against

countries that are not members of the World Trade Organization.

Unfair Practices in Import Trade   The Commission applies U.S. statutory and common law of unfair competition to the importation of products into the United States and their sale (19 U.S.C. 1337). The statute declares unlawful unfair methods of competition and unfair acts in the importation or sale of products in the United States, the threat or effect of which is to destroy or substantially injure a domestic industry, prevent the establishment of such an industry, or restrain or monopolize trade and commerce in the United States. The statute also declares as unlawful per se infringement of a valid and enforceable U.S. patent, copyright, registered trademark, or maskwork; no resulting injury need be found. If the Commission determines that there is a violation of the statute, it is to direct that the articles involved be excluded from entry into the United States, or it may issue cease-and-desist orders directing the person engaged in such violation to cease and desist from engaging in such unfair methods or acts.

Provision is made for the Commission to make certain public interest determinations that could result in the withholding of an exclusion or cease-and-desist order. The President may, within 60 days after the issuance of a Commission order, disapprove the order for policy reasons. Commission determinations of violation are subject to court review.

Uniform Statistical Data   The Commission, in cooperation with the Secretary of the Treasury and the Secretary of Commerce, establishes for statistical purposes an enumeration of articles imported into the United States and exported from the United States, and seeks to establish comparability of such statistics with statistical programs for domestic production (19 U.S.C. 1484).

In conjunction with such activities, the three agencies are to develop concepts for an international commodity code for reporting transactions in international trade and to report thereon to the Congress (19 U.S.C. 1484).

Harmonized Tariff Schedule of the United States, Annotated   The Commission issues a publication containing the U.S. tariff schedules and related matters and considers questions concerning the arrangement of such schedules and the classification of articles (19 U.S.C. note prec. 1202, 1484).

International Trade Studies   The Commission conducts studies, investigations, and research projects on a broad range of topics relating to international trade, pursuant to requests of the President, the House Ways and Means Committee, the Senate Finance Committee, either branch of the Congress, or on its own motion (19 U.S.C. 1332). Public reports of these studies, investigations, and research projects are issued in most cases.

The Commission also keeps informed of the operation and effect of provisions relating to duties or other import restrictions of the United States contained in various trade agreements (19 U.S.C. 2482). Occasionally the Commission is required by statute to perform specific trade-related studies.

Industry and Trade Summaries   The Commission prepares and publishes, from time to time, a series of summaries of trade and tariff information (19 U.S.C. 1332). These summaries contain descriptions (in terms of the Tariff Schedules of the United States) of the thousands of products imported into the United States, methods of production, and the extent and relative importance of U.S. consumption, production, and

trade, together with certain basic factors affecting the competitive position and economic health of domestic industries.

Sources of Information

Inquiries should be directed to the specific organizational unit or to the Secretary, United States International Trade Commission, 500 E Street SW., Washington, DC 20436. Phone, 202–205–2000.

Contracts   The Chief, Contracting and Procurement Division, has responsibility for contract matters. Phone, 202–205–2730.

Employment   Information on employment can be obtained from the Director, Office of Personnel. The agency employs international economists, attorneys, accountants, commodity and industry specialists and analysts, and clerical and other support personnel. Phone, 202–205–2651.

Publications   The Commission publishes results of investigations concerning various commodities and subjects; it also publishes a series of reports on chemicals. Other publications include *Industry and Trade Summaries,* an annual report to the Congress on the operation of the trade agreements program; and an annual report to Congress of Commission activities. Specific information regarding these publications can be obtained from the Office of the Secretary.

Reading Rooms   Reading rooms are open to the public in the Office of the Secretary and in the Commission Library.

For further information, contact the Secretary, United States International Trade Commission, 500 E Street SW., Washington, DC 20436. Phone, 202–205–2000.

UNITED STATES POSTAL SERVICE

475 L'Enfant Plaza SW., Washington, DC 20260–0010
Phone, 202–268–2000

Board of Governors:
Chairman of the Board   SAM WINTERS
Vice Chairman of the Board   TIRSO DEL JUNCO, M.D.

Secretary of the Board	DAVID F. HARRIS
Governors	SUSAN E. ALVARADO, LEGREE S. DANIELS, EINAR V. DYHRKOPP, BERT H. MACKIE, NORMA PACE
Postmaster General	MARVIN RUNYON
Deputy Postmaster General	MICHAEL S. COUGHLIN

Management:

Chief Operating Officer and Executive Vice President	WILLIAM J. HENDERSON
Chief Financial Officer and Senior Vice President	MICHAEL J. RILEY
Chief Marketing Officer and Senior Vice President	LOREN E. SMITH
Senior Vice President and General Counsel	MARY S. ELCANO
Vice President, Consumer Advocate	(VACANCY)
Senior Vice President, Corporate Relations	LARRY M. SPEAKES
Vice President, Diversity Development	ROBERT F. HARRIS
Vice President, Engineering	WILLIAM J. DOWLING
Vice President, Facilities	RUDOLPH K. UMSCHEID
Vice President, Information Systems	RICHARD D. WEIRICH
Vice President, Labor Relations	JOSEPH J. MAHON, JR.
Vice President, Legislative Affairs	GERALD J. MCKIERNAN
Vice President, Marketing Systems	(VACANCY)
Vice President, Product Management	(VACANCY)
Vice President, Purchasing	DARRAH PORTER
Vice President, Quality	NORMAN E. LORENTZ
Vice President, Technology Applications	ROBERT A.F. REISNER
Judicial Officer	JAMES A. COHEN
Chief Postal Inspector	KENNETH J. HUNTER
Deputy Chief Inspector, Criminal Investigations	JEFFREY J. DUPILKA
Deputy Chief Inspector, Operations Support	RECIE SPRINGFIELD, JR.
Deputy Chief Inspector, Audit	KENNETH C. WEAVER

Area Operations:

Vice President, Allegheny Area	JON STEELE
Vice President, Great Lakes Area	WILLIAM J. GOOD
Vice President, Mid-Atlantic Area	HENRY A. PANKEY
Vice President, Mid-West Area	WILLIAM J. BROWN
Vice President, New York Metro Area	JOHN F. KELLY
Vice President, Northeast Area	NANCY L. GEORGE
Vice President, Pacific Area	GENE R. HOWARD
Vice President, Southeast Area	DAVID C. BAKKE
Vice President, Southwest Area	CHARLES K. KERNAN
Vice President, Western Area	CRAIG G. WADE
Vice President, Controller	M. RICHARD PORRAS
Vice President, Human Resources	GAIL G. SONNENBERG
Vice President, Operations Redesign	DIANE M. REGAN
Vice President, Operations Support	ALLEN R. KANE

Vice President, Sales   JOHN R. WARGO
Vice President, Workforce, Planning and   JAMES C. WALTON
    Service Management

[For the United States Postal Service statement of organization, see the *Code of Federal Regulations,* Title 39, Parts 221–226]

The United States Postal Service provides mail processing and delivery services to individuals and businesses within the United States. The Service is committed to serving customers through the development of efficient mail-handling systems and operates its own planning and engineering programs. It is also the responsibility of the Postal Service to protect the mails from loss or theft and to apprehend those who violate postal laws.

The Postal Service was created as an independent establishment of the executive branch by the Postal Reorganization Act (39 U.S.C. 101 *et seq.*), approved August 12, 1970. The United States Postal Service commenced operations on July 1, 1971.

The Postal Service has approximately 745,000 employees and handles about 177 billion pieces of mail annually. The chief executive officer of the Postal Service, the Postmaster General, is appointed by the nine Governors of the Postal Service, who are appointed by the President with the advice and consent of the Senate for overlapping 9-year terms. The Governors and the Postmaster General appoint the Deputy Postmaster General, and these 11 people constitute the Board of Governors.

In addition to the national headquarters, there are area and district offices supervising approximately 40,000 post offices, branches, stations, and community post offices throughout the United States.

Activities

In order to expand and improve service to the public, the Postal Service is engaged in customer cooperation activities, including the development of programs for both the general public and major customers. The Consumer Advocate, a postal ombudsman, represents the interest of the individual mail customer in matters involving the Postal Service by bringing complaints and suggestions to the attention of top postal management and solving the problems of individual customers. To provide postal services responsive to public needs, the Postal Service operates its own planning, research, engineering, real estate, and procurement programs specially adapted to postal requirements, and maintains close ties with international postal organizations.

The Postal Service is the only Federal agency whose employment policies are governed by a process of collective bargaining under the National Labor Relations Act. Labor contract negotiations, affecting all bargaining unit personnel, as well as personnel matters involving employees not covered by collective bargaining agreements, are administered by Labor Relations or Human Resources.

The United States Postal Inspection Service is the Federal law enforcement agency which has jurisdiction in criminal matters affecting the integrity and security of the mail, and operates as the Inspector General for the Postal Service. Postal Inspectors enforce more than 100 Federal statutes involving mail fraud, mail bombs, child pornography, illegal drugs, mail theft, and other postal crimes, as well as being responsible for the protection of all postal employees. Inspectors also audit postal contracts and financial accounts.

UNITED STATES POSTAL SERVICE

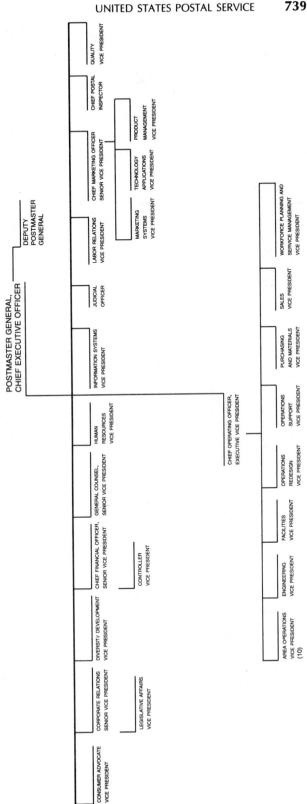

Postal Inspection Service—United States Postal Service

Division Office	Address	Telephone
Atlanta, GA	P.O. Box 16489, 30321–0489	404–765–7369
Boston, MA	P.O. Box 2217, 02205–2217	617–654–5825
Buffalo, NY	1200 Main Place Twr., 14202–3796	716–853–5300
Charlotte, NC	2901 I–85 South GMF, 28228–3000	704–329–9120
Chicago, IL	433 W. Van Buren St., MPO, 60669–2201	312–765–4500
Cincinnati, OH	P.O. Box 14487, 45250–0487	513–684–5700
Cleveland, OH	P.O. Box 5726, 44101–0726	216–443–4000
Denver, CO	P.O. Box 329, 80201–0329	303–295–5320
Detroit, MI	P.O. Box 330119, 48232–6119	313–226–8184
Fort Worth, TX	P.O. Box 162929, 76161–2929	817–625–3400
Houston, TX	P.O. Box 1276, 77251–1276	713–238–4400
Kansas City, MO	Suite 850, 3101 Broadway, 64111–2416	816–932–0400
Los Angeles, CA	P.O. Box 2000, Pasadena, CA 91102–2000	818–405–1200
Memphis, TN	P.O. Box 3180, 38173–0180	901–576–2077
Miami, FL	6th Fl., 3400 Lakeside Dr., Miramar, FL 33027–3242	305–436–7200
Newark, NJ	P.O. Box 509, 07101–0509	201–596–5400
New Orleans, LA	P.O. Box 51690, 70151–1690	504–589–1200
New York, NY	P.O. Box 555, James Farley Bldg., 10116–0555	212–330–3844
Philadelphia, PA	P.O. Box 7500, 19101–9000	215–895–8450
Phoenix, AZ	P.O. Box 20666, 85036–0666	602–223–3660
Pittsburgh, PA	1001 California Ave., 15290–9000	412–359–7900
Richmond, VA	P.O. Box 25009, 23260–5009	804–775–6267
St. Louis, MO	1106 Walnut St., 63199–2201	314–539–9300
St. Paul, MN	P.O. Box 64558, 55164–2201	612–293–3200
San Diego, CA	P.O. Box 2110, 92112–2110	619–233–0610
San Francisco, CA	P.O. Box 882000, 94188–2000	415–550–5700
San Juan, PR	P.O. Box 363667, 00936–3667	809–749–7600
Seattle, WA	P.O. Box 400, 98111–4000	206–442–6300
Tampa, FL	P.O. Box 22526, 33622–2526	813–281–5200
Washington, DC	P.O. Box 96096, 20066–6096	202–636–2300

Sources of Information

Inquiries on the following information should be directed to the specified office, U.S. Postal Service, 475 L'Enfant Plaza SW., Washington, DC 20260.
Consumer Information Contact the Consumer Advocate. Phone, 202–268–2284. Information on past and present schemes used to defraud the public is available through Congressional and Public Affairs, Postal Inspection Service. Phone, 202–268–4293.
Contracts and Small Business Activities Contact Purchasing. Phone, 202–268–4633.
Employment General information about jobs such as clerk, letter carrier, etc., including information about programs for veterans, may be obtained by contacting the nearest post office.

Individuals interested in working at the Postal Headquarters in Washington, DC, may obtain information by calling 202–268–3218

Information about Inspection Service employment may be obtained from the Chief Postal Inspector. Phone, 202–268–4267.
Films Contact Corporate Relations for films available for loan to the public. Phone, 202–268–2189.
Philatelic Information Contact Stamp Services. Phone, 202–268–2312.
Philatelic Sales Contact Philatelic Fulfillment, Kansas City, MO 64144–9998. Phone, 816–455–0970.
Publications Pamphlets on mailability, postage rates and fees, and many other topics may be obtained free of charge from the nearest post office.

Most postal regulations are contained in Postal Service manuals covering domestic mail, international mail, postal operations, administrative support, employee and labor relations, financial management, and procurement. These manuals and other publications including the *National Five-Digit ZIP Code and Post Office Directory*

(Publication 65) may be purchased from the Superintendent of Documents, Government Printing Office, Washington, DC 20402–0001. (The *National Five-Digit ZIP Code and Post*

Office Directory is also available through local post offices.)

Reading Rooms Located on 11th Floor North, Library. Phone, 202–268–2900.

For further information, contact the U.S. Postal Service, 475 L'Enfant Plaza SW., Washington, DC 20260. Phone, 202–268–2000.

Boards, Commissions, and Committees

Note: This is a listing of Federal boards, centers, commissions, councils, panels, study groups, task forces, etc., not listed elsewhere in the *Manual*, which were established by congressional or Presidential action, whose functions are not strictly limited to the internal operations of a parent department or agency, and which are authorized to publish documents in the *Federal Register*. While the editors have attempted to compile a complete and accurate listing, suggestions for improving coverage of this guide are welcome. Please address your comments to the Office of the Federal Register, National Archives and Records Administration, Washington, DC 20408. Phone, 202–523–5230.

Federal advisory committees, as defined by the Federal Advisory Committee Act, as amended (5 U.S.C. app.), have not been included here. A complete listing of these committees can be found in the *Twenty-third Annual Report of the President on Federal Advisory Committees for Fiscal Year 1994*. For further information on Federal advisory committees and this report, contact the Committee Management Secretariat, General Services Administration, General Services Building (CAM), Room 7114, Washington, DC 20405. Phone, 202–273–3556.

Administrative Committee of the Federal Register
National Archives, Washington, DC 20408. Phone, 202–523–4534.

Advisory Commission on Intergovernmental Relations
800 K Street NW., Suite 450 South, Washington, DC 20575. Phone, 202–653–5540.

Advisory Council on Historic Preservation
1100 Pennsylvania Avenue NW., Room 809, Washington, DC 20004. Phone, 202–606–8503.

American Battle Monuments Commission
20 Massachusetts Avenue NW., Pulaski Building, Suite 5119, Washington, DC 20314–0001. Phone, 202–761–0533.

Appalachian Regional Commission
1666 Connecticut Avenue NW., Washington, DC 20235. Phone, 202–884–7799.

Architectural and Transportation Barriers Compliance Board [1]
1331 F Street NW., Suite 1000, Washington, DC 20004–1111. Phone, 202–272–5434.

Arctic Research Commission
4350 North Fairfax Drive, Suite 630, Arlington, VA 22203. Phone, 703–525–0111.

---

[1] Also known as the Access Board.

Arthritis and Musculoskeletal Interagency Coordinating Committee
National Institutes of Health, Building 31, Room 4C32, Bethesda, MD 20892. Phone, 301–496–0801.

Barry M. Goldwater Scholarship and Excellence in Education Foundation
6225 Brandon Avenue, Suite 315, Springfield, VA 22150–2519. Phone, 703–756–6012.

Board for International Broadcasting
1201 Connecticut Avenue NW., Suite 400, Washington, DC 20036. Phone, 202–254–8040.

Citizens' Stamp Advisory Committee
United States Postal Service, 475 L'Enfant Plaza SW., Room 4474–E, Washington, DC 20260–2437. Phone, 202–268–2312.

Commission of Fine Arts
441 F Street NW., Pension Building, Suite 312, Washington, DC 20001. Phone, 202–504–2200.

Committee on Foreign Investment in the United States
15th Street and Pennsylvania Avenue NW., Main Treasury Building, Room 5100, Washington, DC 20220. Phone, 202–622–1860.

Committee for the Implementation of Textile Agreements
14th Street and Constitution Avenue NW., Department of Commerce, Room 3001A, Washington, DC 20230. Phone, 202–482–3737.

Committee for Purchase From People Who Are Blind or Severely Disabled
1735 Jefferson Davis Highway, Crystal Square 3, Suite 403, Arlington, VA 22202–3461. Phone, 703–603–7740.

Coordinating Council on Juvenile Justice and Delinquency Prevention
633 Indiana Avenue NW., Department of Justice, Office of Juvenile Justice and Delinquency Prevention, Washington, DC 20531. Phone, 202–307–0668.

Delaware River Basin Commission
Office of the United States Commissioner: 1010 Massachusetts Avenue NW., Suite 100, Washington, DC 20001. Phone, 202–343–5761.
Office of the Executive Director: P.O. Box 7360, West Trenton, NJ 08628. Phone, 609–883–9500; (FTS) 483–2077.

Endangered Species Committee
1849 C Street NW., Department of the Interior, Room 4429, Washington, DC 20240. Phone, 202–208–4077.

Export Administration Review Board
14th Street and Constitution Avenue NW., Herbert C. Hoover Building, Room 2639, Washington, DC 20230. Phone, 202–482–5863.

Federal Financial Institutions Examination Council
2100 Pennsylvania Avenue NW., Suite 200, Washington, DC 20037. Phone, 202–634–6526.

Federal Financing Bank
15th Street and Pennsylvania Avenue NW., Main Treasury Building, Room 3054, Washington, DC 20220. Phone, 202–622–2470.

Federal Interagency Committee on Education
400 Maryland Avenue SW., Department of Education, Federal Office Building 6, Room 3061, Washington, DC 20202–3600. Phone, 202–401–3679.

Federal Laboratory Consortium for Technology Transfer
1850 M Street NW., Suite 800, Washington DC 20036. Phone, 202–331–4220 Fax, 202–331–4290..

Federal Library and Information Center Committee
Library of Congress, Washington, DC 20540–5100. Phone, 202–707–4800.

Franklin Delano Roosevelt Memorial Commission
FH 825–A, Hart Senate Office Building, Washington, DC 20510. Phone, 202–228–2491.

Harry S Truman Scholarship Foundation

712 Jackson Place NW., Washington, DC 20006. Phone, 202–395–4831.

Illinois and Michigan Canal National Heritage Corridor Commission

15701 South Independence Boulevard, Lockport, IL 60441. Phone, 815–740–2047.

Indian Arts and Crafts Board

Department of the Interior, 1849 C Street NW., Room 4004–MIB, Washington, DC 20240. Phone, 202–208–3773.

Information Security Oversight Office

750 17th Street NW., Suite 530, Washington, DC 20006. Phone, 202–634–6150.

Interagency Committee on Employment of People with Disabilities

1801 L Street NW., Equal Employment Opportunity Commission, Federal Sector Programs, Room 5238, Washington, DC 20507. Phone, 202–663–4560; or 202–663–4593 (TDD).

Interagency Savings Bonds Committee

999 F Street NW., Washington, DC 20226. Phone, 202–219–3472.

J. William Fulbright Foreign Scholarship Board

301 Fourth Street SW., United States Information Agency, Room 247, Washington, DC 20547. Phone, 202–619–4290.

James Madison Memorial Fellowship Foundation

2000 K Street NW., Suite 303, Washington, DC 20006. Phone, 202–653–8700.

Japan-United States Friendship Commission

1120 Vermont Avenue NW., Suite 925, Washington, DC 20005. Phone, 202–275–7712.

Joint Board for the Enrollment of Actuaries

Department of the Treasury, Washington, DC 20220. Phone, 202–376–1421.

Marine Mammal Commission

1825 Connecticut Avenue NW., Room 512, Washington, DC 20009. Phone, 202–606–5504.

Migratory Bird Conservation Commission

1849 C Street NW., 622 ARLSQ, Washington, DC 20240. Phone, 703–358–1716.

Mississippi River Commission

1400 Walnut Street, P.O. Box 80, United States Army Corps of Engineers, Lower Mississippi Valley Division, Vicksburg, MS 39180. Phone, 601–634–5758.

National Archives Trust Fund Board

8601 Adelphi Road, Room 4100, College Park, MD 20740–6001. Phone, 301–713–6405.

National Commission on Libraries and Information Science

1110 Vermont Avenue NW., Suite 820, Washington, DC 20005. Phone, 202–606–9200.

National Communications System

701 South Courthouse Road, Arlington, VA 22204–2198. Phone, 703–602–2817.

National Council on Disability

1331 F Street NW., Suite 1050, Washington, DC 20004. Phone, 202–272–2004; or (TDD) 202–272–2074.

National Historical Publications and Records Commission

Seventh Street and Pennsylvania Avenue NW., National Archives Building, Room 607, Washington, DC 20408. Phone, 202–501–5600.

National Occupational Information Coordinating Committee

2100 M Street NW., Suite 156, Washington, DC 20037. Phone, 202–653–5665.

National Park Foundation

1101 17th Street NW., Suite 1102, Washington, DC 20036–4704. Phone, 202–785–4500.

Northwest Power Planning Council
851 Southwest Sixth Avenue, Suite 1100, Portland, OR 97204–1348. Phone, 503–222–5161.

Office of Navajo and Hopi Indian Relocation
P.O. Box KK, Flagstaff, AZ 86002. Phone, 520–779–2721.

Office of Women's Business Ownership
409 Third Street SW., Sixth Floor, Washington, DC 20416. Phone, 202–205–6673.

Permanent Committee for the Oliver Wendell Holmes Devise
Library of Congress, Manuscript Division, Washington, DC 20540. Phone, 202–707–5383.

Physician Payment Review Commission
2120 L Street NW., Suite 200, Washington, DC 20037. Phone, 202–653–7220.

President's Committee on Employment of People With Disabilities
1331 F Street NW., Suite 300, Washington, DC 20004–1107. Phone, 202–376–6200; or (TDD) 202–376–6205.

President's Council on Integrity and Efficiency
Office of Management and Budget, New Executive Office Building, Room 6025, Washington, DC 20503. Phone, 202–395–6911.

President's Foreign Intelligence Advisory Board
Old Executive Office Building, Room 340, Washington, DC 20500. Phone, 202–456–2352.

Prospective Payment Assessment Commission
300 Seventh Street SW., Suite 301B, Washington, DC 20024. Phone, 202–401–8986.

Regulatory Information Service Center
750 17th Street NW., Suite 500, Washington, DC 20006. Phone, 202–395–6220.

Susquehanna River Basin Commission
Office of the United States Commissioner: 1010 Massachusetts Avenue NW., Suite 100, Washington, DC 20001. Phone, 202–343–4091.
Office of the Executive Director: 1721 North Front Street, Harrisburg, PA 17102–2391. Phone, 717–238–0422 (non-FTS).

Textile Trade Policy Group
600 17th Street NW., Winder Building, Room 300, Washington, DC 20506. Phone, 202–395–3026.

Trade Policy Committee
Office of Policy Coordination, 600 17th Street NW., Winder Building, Room 414, Washington, DC 20506. Phone, 202–395–7210.

United States Holocaust Memorial Museum
100 Raoul Wallenberg Place SW., Washington, DC 20024. Phone, 202–488–0400.

United States Nuclear Waste Technical Review Board
1100 Wilson Boulevard, Suite 910, Arlington, VA 22209. Phone, 703–235–4473.

Veterans Day National Committee
Department of Veterans Affairs (80D), 810 Vermont Avenue NW., Washington, DC 20420. Phone, 202–273–5735.

White House Commission on Presidential Scholars
400 Maryland Avenue SW., Federal Office Building 6, Room 2189, Washington, DC 20202. Phone, 202–401–1395.

QUASI-OFFICIAL AGENCIES

Note: This section contains organizations that are not Executive agencies under the definition in 5 U.S.C. 105 but that are required by statute to publish certain information on their programs and activities in the *Federal Register*.

LEGAL SERVICES CORPORATION

750 First Street NE., Washington, DC 20002–4250
Phone, 202–336–8800

President	ALEXANDER D. FORGER
Vice President	MARTHA BERGMARK
Secretary	PATRICIA BATIE
Comptroller/Treasurer	DAVID RICHARDSON
Director, Office of Program Evaluation, Analysis and Review	JOHN TULL
Director, Office of Program Services	MERCERIA LUDGOOD
Inspector General	EDOUARD QUATREVAUX
General Counsel	VICTOR FORTUNO
Director, Communications	JAMES LAMB
Director, Government Relations	GAIL LASTER

[For the Legal Services Corporation statement of organization, see the *Code of Federal Regulations*, Title 45, Part 1601]

The Legal Services Corporation provides quality legal assistance for noncriminal proceedings to those who would otherwise be unable to afford such assistance.

The Legal Services Corporation is a private, nonprofit organization established by the Legal Services Corporation Act of 1974, as amended (42 U.S.C. 2996), to provide financial support for legal assistance in noncriminal proceedings to persons financially unable to afford legal services.

The Corporation is governed by an 11-member Board of Directors, appointed by the President with the advice and consent of the Senate. Each member serves for a term of 3 years, except that five of the members first appointed—as designated by the President at the time of appointment—serve 2-year terms. The President of the Corporation, appointed by the Board of Directors, is the chief executive officer and serves as an *ex officio* Board member.

The Corporation provides financial assistance to qualified programs furnishing legal assistance to eligible clients and makes grants to and contracts with individuals, firms, corporations, and

747

organizations for the purpose of providing legal assistance to these clients.

The Corporation establishes maximum income levels for clients based on family size, urban and rural differences, and cost-of-living variations. Using these maximum income levels and other financial factors, the Corporation's recipient programs establish criteria to determine the eligibility of clients and priorities of service based on an appraisal of the legal needs of the eligible client community.

For further information, contact the Office of Communications, Legal Services Corporation, 750 First Street NE., Washington, DC 20002–4250. Phone, 202–336–8800.

SMITHSONIAN INSTITUTION
1000 Jefferson Drive SW., Washington, DC 20560
Phone, 202–357–1300

Board of Regents:

The Chief Justice of the United States (*Chancellor*)	WILLIAM H. REHNQUIST
The Vice President of the United States	ALBERT GORE, JR.
Members of the Senate	DANIEL PATRICK MOYNIHAN, THAD COCHRAN, ALAN K. SIMPSON
Members of the House of Representatives	SAM JOHNSON, NORMAN Y. MINETA, BOB LIVINGSTON
Citizen Members	JEANNINE SMITH CLARK, BARBER B. CONABLE, HANNA HOLBORN GRAY, MANUEL L. IBÁÑEZ, SAMUEL C. JOHNSON, HOMER A. NEAL, FRANK A. SHRONTZ, WESLEY SAMUEL WILLIAMS, JR., (VACANCY)

Officials:

The Secretary	I. MICHAEL HEYMAN
The Inspector General	THOMAS D. BLAIR
Director, Office of Planning, Management and Budget	CAROLE WHARTON
Counselor to the Secretary for Electronic Communications and Special Projects	MARC PACHTER
Counselor to the Secretary for Latino Affairs	MIGUEL BRETOS
Executive Assistant to the Secretary	JAMES M. HOBBINS
Executive Secretary to the Secretary	BARBARA SEDERBORG
Under Secretary	CONSTANCE NEWMAN
General Counsel	JAMES DOUGLAS, *Acting*
Director, Office of Government Relations	JOHN BERRY
Director, Office of Communications	DAVID J. UMANSKY
Senior Information Officer	LEE DENNY
Director, Visitor Information and Associates Reception Center	MARY GRACE POTTER
Assistant Secretary for Finance and Administration	NANCY SUTTENFIELD
Executive Assistant for Administration	CAROLYN JONES

Director, Office of Sponsored Projects	ARDELLE FOSS
Director, Office of Equal Employment and Minority Affairs	ERA MARSHALL
Director, Office of Human Resources	SUSAN ROEHMER
Director, Office of Information Technology	VINCENT J. MARCALUS
Director, Office of Printing and Photographic Services	JAMES H. WALLACE, JR.
Director, Office of Contracting and Property Management	JOHN W. COLBERT
Director, Travel Services Office	JUDITH PETROSKI
Director of Facilities Services	RICHARD RICE, *Acting*
Director, Office of Design and Construction	WILLIAM L. THOMAS, *Acting*
Director, Office of Plant Services	PATRICK J. MILLER
Director, Office of Protection Services	MICHAEL J. SOFIELD, *Acting*
Director, Mail Order Division	(VACANCY)
Assistant Directors, Museum Shops	ROLAND BANSCHER
	JOSEPH CARPER
Director, Office of Architectural History and Historic Preservation	CYNTHIA R. FIELD
Director, Office of Environmental Management and Safety	F. WILLIAM BILLINGSLEY
Treasurer	SUDEEP ANAND
Comptroller	LESLIE CASSON
Risk Manager, Office of Risk and Asset Management	JACQUELINE YOUNG
Senior Business Officer, Office of Business Management	NANCY JOHNSON
Director, Office of Product Development and Licensing	HANNAH MULLIN, *Acting*
Assistant Provost for Arts and Humanities	TOM L. FREUDENHEIM
Director, Anacostia Museum	STEVEN NEWSOME
Director, Archives of American Art	RICHARD WATTENMAKER
Director, Cooper-Hewitt, National Design Museum	DIANNE PILGRIM
Director, Freer Gallery of Art and Arthur M. Sackler Gallery	MILO C. BEACH
Director, Hirshhorn Museum and Sculpture Garden	JAMES T. DEMETRION
Director, National Museum of African Art	SYLVIA WILLIAMS
Associate Director for Collections and Research (NMAFA)	ROY SIEBER
Director, National Air and Space Museum	MARTIN O. HARWIT
Director, National Museum of American Art	ELIZABETH BROUN
Curator In Charge, Renwick Gallery	MICHAEL W. MONROE
Director, National Museum of American History	SPENCER CREW
Director, National Museum of the American Indian	W. RICHARD WEST, JR.
Director, National Portrait Gallery	ALAN M. FERN
Director, Office of Exhibits Central	JOHN COPPOLA
Director, Center for Museum Studies	REX ELLIS
Director, Smithsonian Institution Traveling Exhibition Service	ANNA R. COHN
Director, Institutional Studies Office	ZAHAVA DOERING
Provost	ROBERT S. HOFFMANN

Assistant Provost for the Sciences	ROSS B. SIMONS
Editor, Joseph Henry Papers Project	MARC ROTHENBERG
Director, American Studies Program	WILCOMB E. WASHBURN
Director, National Zoological Park	MICHAEL H. ROBINSON
Director, National Museum of Natural History	DONALD ORTNER, *Acting*
Director, Smithsonian Man and the Biosphere Program	FRANCISCO DALLMEIER
Director, Office of Fellowships and Grants	ROBERTA RUBINOFF
Director, Smithsonian Environmental Research Center	DAVID L. CORRELL
Director, Smithsonian Astrophysical Observatory	IRWIN I. SHAPIRO
Director, Smithsonian Tropical Research Institute	IRA RUBINOFF
Director, Conservation Analytical Laboratory	LAMBERTUS VAN ZELST
Deputy Director, Conservation Analytical Laboratory	ALAN W. POSTLETHWAITE
Director, Smithsonian Institution Libraries	BARBARA SMITH
Director, Museum Support Center	VINCENT WILCOX
Coordinator, International Environmental Science Program	JOAN ZAVALA
Director, Environmental Awareness Program	JUDITH GRADWOHL
Director, Smithsonian Institution Archives	ETHEL W. HEDLIN
Coordinator, The National Collections Program (Smithsonian Institution Archives)	WILLIAM TOMPKINS
Assistant Provost for Educational and Cultural Programs	JAMES EARLY
Director, Office of Elementary and Secondary Education	ANN BAY
Director, Center for Folklife Programs and Cultural Studies	RICHARD KURIN
Director, National Science Resources Center	DOUGLAS LAPP
Director, Wider Audience Development Program	MARSHALL WONG
Director, Office of Special Events and Conference Services	KATHERINE KIRLIN, *Acting*
Director, Office of International Relations	FRANCINE BERKOWITZ
Coordinator, International Center	FRANCINE BERKOWITZ
Director, Office of Telecommunications	PAUL B. JOHNSON
Director, Smithsonian Institution Press	DANIEL GOODWIN, *Acting*
Deputy Director, Smithsonian Institution Press	VINCENT L. MACDONNELL
Editor, Smithsonian Magazine	DONALD B. MOSER
Publisher, Smithsonian Magazine	RON WALKER
Director, The Smithsonian Associates	MARA MAYOR
Associate Director for Marketing and Membership, The Smithsonian Associates	HOLLY SHAHEEN
Associate Director for Educational and Cultural Programs, The Smithsonian Associates	CAROL BOGASH
Deputy Director, The Smithsonian Associates	BARBARA TUCELING

Assistant Secretary for Institutional Advancement	ALICE GREEN BURNETTE
Director, National Campaign for the National Museum of the American Indian	JOHN L. COLONGHI
Director, Office of Development	MARIE MATTSON
The John F. Kennedy Center for the Performing Arts [1]	
Chairman	JAMES D. WOLFENSOHN
President	LAWRENCE J. WILKER
National Gallery of Art [1]	
President	ROBERT H. SMITH
Director	EARL A. POWELL III
Woodrow Wilson International Center for Scholars [1]	
Director	CHARLES BLITZER
Deputy Director	SAMUEL WELLS
Deputy Director for Planning and Management	DEAN W. ANDERSON
Chairman, Board of Trustees	JOSEPH H. FLOM

The Smithsonian Institution is an independent trust instrumentality of the United States that fosters the increase and diffusion of knowledge. History, technology, science, and the arts are represented in exhibits through the conduct of research, publication of studies, and participation in cooperative international programs of scholarly exchange.

The Smithsonian Institution was created by act of August 10, 1846 (20 U.S.C. 41 et seq.), to carry out the terms of the will of James Smithson of England, who in 1829 had bequeathed his entire estate to the United States "to found at Washington, under the name of the Smithsonian Institution, an establishment for the increase and diffusion of knowledge." On July 1, 1836, Congress accepted the legacy and pledged the faith of the United States to the charitable trust.

After accepting the trust property for the United States, Congress vested responsibility for administering the trust in the Smithsonian Board of Regents, composed of the Chief Justice, the Vice President, three Members of the Senate, three Members of the House of Representatives, and nine citizen members appointed by joint resolution of Congress.

To carry out Smithson's mandate, the Institution:
—performs fundamental research;
—publishes the results of studies, explorations, and investigations;
—preserves for study and reference more than 140 million items of scientific, cultural, and historical interest;
—maintains exhibits representative of the arts, American history, technology, aeronautics and space exploration, and natural history; and
—engages in programs of education and national and international cooperative research and training, supported by its trust endowments and gifts, grants and contracts, and funds appropriated to it by Congress.

Activities

Anacostia Museum The Museum is located in the historic Fort Stanton neighborhood of southeast Washington.

---

[1] Administered under a separate Board of Trustees.

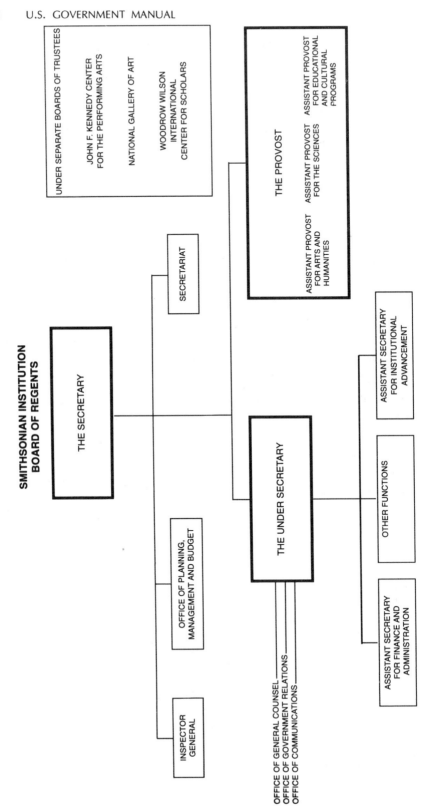

SMITHSONIAN INSTITUTION
BOARD OF REGENTS

THE SECRETARY

UNDER SEPARATE BOARDS OF TRUSTEES

JOHN F. KENNEDY CENTER FOR THE PERFORMING ARTS

NATIONAL GALLERY OF ART

WOODROW WILSON INTERNATIONAL CENTER FOR SCHOLARS

THE PROVOST

ASSISTANT PROVOST FOR ARTS AND HUMANITIES

ASSISTANT PROVOST FOR THE SCIENCES

ASSISTANT PROVOST FOR EDUCATIONAL AND CULTURAL PROGRAMS

SECRETARIAT

INSPECTOR GENERAL

OFFICE OF PLANNING, MANAGEMENT AND BUDGET

THE UNDER SECRETARY

OFFICE OF GENERAL COUNSEL
OFFICE OF GOVERNMENT RELATIONS
OFFICE OF COMMUNICATIONS

ASSISTANT SECRETARY FOR FINANCE AND ADMINISTRATION

OTHER FUNCTIONS

ASSISTANT SECRETARY FOR INSTITUTIONAL ADVANCEMENT

The Museum serves as a national resource for exhibitions, scholarly and applied research, historical documentation, and interpretive and educational programs relating to African-American history and culture. The African-American church, the Harlem Renaissance, African-American inventors, and works by renowned artists such as Sam Gilliam have been the subjects of exhibitions by the Museum.

The Research Department, open for use by scholars, supports exhibition design and educational programs. It conducts independent studies of African-American history, minority and ethnic studies, and the history of Anacostia and Washington, DC.

The Education Department designs, prepares, and schedules programs that enhance current exhibitions and develops independent programs and activities to serve the needs and interests of the immediate neighborhood, as well as the broader community. These activities include guided tours, demonstrations, lectures, storytelling, teacher seminars, family workshops, conservation seminars, and performing arts programs.

For further information, contact the Anacostia Museum, 1901 Fort Place SE., Washington, DC 20020. Phone, 202–287–3369.

Archives of American Art   The Archives contains the Nation's largest collection of documentary materials reflecting the history of visual arts in the United States. The Archives gathers, preserves, and microfilms the papers of artists, craftsmen, collectors, dealers, critics, museums, and art societies. These papers consist of manuscripts, letters, notebooks, sketchbooks, business records, clippings, exhibition catalogs, tape-recorded interviews, and photographs of artists and their work. The extensive microfilm holdings include bodies of materials not belonging to the Archives but recorded by it with permission of the owner.

The Archives' chief processing and reference center is in the Smithsonian's Museum of American Art and Portrait Gallery Building. The Archives has administrative offices in both Washington and New York. Regional branch offices, each with a complete set of microfilm duplicating the archives' collections, are located in Boston, Detroit, New York, and San Marino, California.

For further information, contact the Archives of American Art, Smithsonian Institution, Washington, DC 20560. Phone, 202–357–2781.

Arthur M. Sackler Gallery   The museum of Asian art opened to the public September 1987 on the National Mall. Changing exhibitions drawn from major collections in the United States and abroad, as well as from the permanent holdings of the Sackler Gallery, are displayed in the distinctive new museum. The Gallery's growing permanent collection is founded on a group of art objects from China, South and Southeast Asia, and the ancient Near East that was given by the late Arthur M. Sackler, a medical researcher, publisher, and art collector. Dr. Sackler's gift included Chinese jades, bronzes, ancient Near Eastern ceramics, gold and silver, and sculpture from South and Southeast Asia. The collection has expanded to include Persian manuscripts; Japanese paintings; ceramics, prints, and textiles; and paintings and metalware from China, Japan, and South and Southeast Asia.

Programs at the Gallery include loan exhibitions and major international shows offering both surveys of distinctive Asian traditions and comparative exhibitions showing the art of different centuries, geographic areas, and types of patronage. Many exhibitions are accompanied by public programs and scholarly symposia.

For further information, contact the Arthur M. Sackler Gallery, 1050 Independence Avenue SW., Washington, DC 20560. Phone, 202–357–4880.

Conservation Analytical Laboratory   The Laboratory provides a focus within the Smithsonian Institution for conservation of the millions of artifacts in the collections. It provides chemical analyses to curators for cataloging purposes, and to conservators for establishing the nature of a particular example of deterioration and for determining whether commercial materials proposed for use in prolonged contact with artifacts are truly safe. It treats many hundreds of artifacts each year and, upon request, supports other conservators in the Institution with advice and specialized materials. It collaborates with archeologists, curators, and university and government laboratories in archeometric studies.

For further information, contact the Director, Conservation Analytical Laboratory, Museum Support Center, 4210 Silver Hill Road, Suitland, MD 20560. Phone, 301–238–3700.

Cooper-Hewitt, National Design Museum The Museum is located in New York City. Its collection consists of more than 165,000 items. It maintains a reference library of about 50,000 volumes relating to design, ornament, and architecture, and a picture library of several million photographs and clippings, as well as a series of archives devoted to color material and industrial design. The Museum is not only a major assemblage of decorative art materials but also a research laboratory serving professionals and students of design. The regularly changing exhibitions always relate to some aspect of design. The museum is open daily except Mondays and major holidays.

For further information, contact the Cooper-Hewitt, National Design Museum, 2 East Ninety-First Street, New York, NY 10128. Phone, 212–860–6868.

Freer Gallery of Art The building, the original collection, and an endowment were the gift of Charles Lang Freer. The Gallery houses one of the world's most renowned collections of Asian art as well as an important group of ancient Egyptian glass, early Christian manuscripts, and the works of James McNeill Whistler together with other 19th and early 20th century American artists.

More than 26,000 objects in the Asian collection represent the arts of East Asia, the Near East, and South and Southeast Asia, including paintings, manuscripts, scrolls, screens, ceramics, metalwork, glass, jade, lacquer, and sculpture. Members of the staff conduct research on objects in the collection and publish

results in scholarly journals and books. They arrange special exhibitions and present lectures in their fields of specialization.

For further information, contact the Freer Gallery of Art, Twelfth Street and Jefferson Drive SW., Washington, DC 20560. Phone, 202–357–4880.

Hirshhorn Museum and Sculpture Garden The Museum houses major collections of art consisting primarily of American and European painting and sculpture of the past 100 years. The nucleus of the collection is the gift of more than 7,000 works of art presented in 1966 to the people of the United States by Joseph H. Hirshhorn (1899–1981).

Supplementing the permanent collection are loan exhibitions focusing on contemporary painting and sculpture as well as on art movements of the modern era. There is an active program of public service and education, including docent tours through the Museum to introduce visitors to the collections, lectures on contemporary art and artists, films of historic and artistic interest, and others. The Museum houses a collection research facility, a specialized 10,000-volume art library, and a photographic archive—available for consultation by prior appointment.

For further information, contact the Hirshhorn Museum and Sculpture Garden, Eighth Street and Independence Avenue SW., Washington, DC 20560. Phone, 202–357–3091.

National Museum of African Art This is the only art museum in the United States dedicated exclusively to portraying the rich, creative heritage of Africa.

Established in 1964 and incorporated as a bureau of the Smithsonian in 1979, the Museum opened its new location on the National Mall in September 1987. Its research components, collection, exhibitions, and public programs establish the Museum as a primary source for the examination and discovery of the arts and culture of sub-Saharan Africa. In recent years, works of outstanding aesthetic quality have been added to a collection numbering about 7,000 works in wood, metal, fired clay, ivory, and fiber. Examples of sub-Saharan traditional art include a wooden figure of a Zairian Yombe carver; a Lower Niger Bronze Industry vessel, with chameleons; and a memorial grave figure of a colonial officer from the Cameroon grassfields.

The Eliot Elisofon Photographic Archives includes some 100,000 slides, photos, and film segments on Africa. There is also a specialized library of 18,000 volumes and periodicals.

For further information, contact the Museum of African Art, 950 Independence Avenue SW., Washington, DC 20560. Phone, 202–357–4600.

National Air and Space Museum

Created to memorialize the development of aviation and space flight, the Museum collects, displays, and preserves aeronautical and space flight artifacts of historical significance as well as documentary and artistic materials related to air and space. The exhibitions and study collections record human conquest of the air from its tentative beginnings to recent achievements by high altitude aircraft, guided missiles, rockets, satellites, and manned space flight. The principal areas in which work is concentrated include flight craft of all types, manned and unmanned; space flight vehicles; and propulsion systems.

The Langley Theater, with a giant screen presentation, and the 70-foot domed Einstein Planetarium are featured.

For further information, contact the National Air and Space Museum, Seventh Street and Independence Avenue SW., Washington, DC 20560. Phone, 202–357–1745.

National Museum of American Art

This museum is devoted to American painting, sculpture, folk art, photography, and graphic art from the 18th century to the present. A portion of the Museum's permanent collection of over 35,000 works is exhibited in its extensive galleries, and the remainder is available for study by scholars. Various aspects of American art are examined through numerous temporary exhibitions, accompanied by carefully documented publications. The Department of Educational Programs conducts tours for schoolchildren, university students, and the general public. It also has a program for junior interns. A research program for

visiting scholars, both predoctoral and postdoctoral, is maintained, and training for university interns in all aspects of museum operations, including conservation, is carried on under staff supervision.

The Renwick Gallery presents special exhibitions of contemporary American crafts, with accompanying publications, as well as a selection of objects, dating from 1900 to the present, from its permanent collection. It also maintains an active film and lecture program.

Guided tours of the galleries and special educational programs for schools and organizations are provided.

For further information, contact the National Museum of American Art, Eighth and G Streets NW., Washington, DC 20560. Phone, 202–357–1959.

National Museum of American History

The Museum's exhibits offer a unique view of the American experience. Important elements of the collections present the European background, but emphasis is placed upon the growth of the United States, upon the men and women who have shaped our heritage, upon science and the arts, and upon the remaking of our world through technology.

Exhibits draw upon strong collections in the sciences and engineering, agriculture, manufacturing, transportation, medicine, printing, photography, ceramics, coins and stamps, and glass. Outstanding holdings include Whitney's cotton gin, Morse's telegraph, the John Bull locomotive, and a great variety of scientific instruments. Political, social, military, and cultural history are also well represented. Major installations treat everyday life in America just after the Revolutionary War, science in American life, and the diverse origins of the American people. The Museum offers changing exhibits on a wide range of subjects including news reporting, information technology, American music, and American cars and trains. Demonstrations, films, and performances highlight many aspects of the museum.

Scholars may be aided in the use of the Museum's research collections and specialized library facilities by appointment.

For further information, contact the National Museum of American History, Twelfth Street and Constitution Avenue NW., Washington, DC 20560. Phone, 202–357–2510.

National Museum of the American Indian The Museum was established by act of November 28, 1989 (20 U.S.C. 80q *et seq.*), and will eventually be located in a museum to be built on the National Mall in Washington, DC, near the turn of the century. In the meantime, some of the Museum's collections are on view in the George Gustav Heye Center located in the Alexander Hamilton U.S. Custom House in lower Manhattan in New York City. The Museum, whose collections were transferred from the former Museum of the American Indian, Heye Foundation, in New York City, is dedicated to the collection, preservation, study, and exhibition of the living cultures, history, and arts of the native peoples of the Americas.

Highlights include Northwest Coast carvings; Eskimo masks; pottery and weaving from the Southwest; painted hides and garments from the Plains; goldwork from Colombia, Mexico, and Peru; and Amazonian featherwork.

For information on hours and admission fees, call 212–668–6624 (in New York City) or 202–357–2700 (in Washington, DC).

For further information, contact the National Museum of the American Indian, Suite 7103, 470 L'Enfant Plaza SW., Washington, DC 20560. Phone, 202–287–2523.

National Museum of Natural History This museum serves as a national and international center for the natural sciences. Among the exhibits are halls devoted to the Ice Age; the rise of Western civilization; mammals; birds; dinosaurs and other extinct animals and plants; sea life; South American, Asian, African, and Pacific cultures; gems and minerals; and American Indians. Notable attractions include a 3,000-gallon tank containing a living coral reef; a live-insect zoo; a discovery room, where persons of all ages may touch and handle natural history specimen.

The Museum maintains the largest natural history reference collections in the Nation available to qualified researchers. Systematic and biological studies at the museum are providing new information that is of use in conservation, monitoring pollution, food production, improvement of medical knowledge, and other problems.

A Global Volcanism Network gathers information about volcanic activity and other geophysical events and informs scientists around the world via a monthly bulletin and other publications. The Museum also administers the Smithsonian Marine Station at Link Port, Florida, which conducts marine biological research along the Florida coast.

The Museum staff participates in joint educational programs with universities by teaching courses, training graduate students, and conducting science seminars.

For further information, contact the National Museum of Natural History, Tenth Street and Constitution Avenue NW., Washington, DC 20560. Phone, 202–357–2664.

National Portrait Gallery The Gallery was established by act of April 27, 1962 (20 U.S.C. 75a), as a museum of the Smithsonian Institution "for the exhibition and study of portraiture depicting men and women who have made significant contributions to the history, development, and culture of the people of the United States." It is housed in one of the oldest Government structures in Washington—the former U.S. Patent Office Building, constructed between 1836 and 1867—on the very site that Pierre L'Enfant, in his original plan for the city, had designated for a pantheon to honor the Nation's immortals.

The first floor of the Gallery is devoted to major loan exhibitions, changing exhibitions from the Gallery's collection of paintings, sculpture, prints, photographs, and drawings as well as several galleries with special portrait collections. On the second floor are featured the permanent collection of portraits of eminent Americans and the Hall of Presidents containing portraits and associative items of our Chief Executives. The two-story Victorian Renaissance Great Hall on the third floor is used for special events and exhibitions.

Publications include richly illustrated catalogs for major shows, an illustrated checklist of portraits in the collection, and educational materials designed to be used as teaching guides.

A 45,000-volume library is shared with the National Museum of American Art. The education department offers outreach programs for elementary and secondary schools, senior citizen groups, hospitals, and nursing homes; walk-in or group tours; and programs for handicapped audiences.

For general information and descriptive brochures on the Gallery's activities, contact the Public Affairs Office, National Portrait Gallery, Eighth and F Streets NW., Washington, DC 20560. Phone, 202–357–1915.

National Postal Museum   The Smithsonian's newest museum houses the Nation's postal history and philatelic collection, the largest of its kind in the world, with more than 16 million objects. The 75,000 square-foot museum is devoted to the history of America's mail service. Five major galleries include exhibits on mail service in colonial times and the Civil War, the Pony Express, the evolution of modern mail service, automation, mail transportation, the art of letters, and displays of the Museum's priceless stamp collection.

Highlights include three mail planes, a replica of a railway mail car, a mudwagon, an airmail beacon, displays of letters and greeting cards, foreign and domestic mail boxes, and more than 5,000 U.S. and foreign issue stamps and covers.

For further information, contact the National Postal Museum, 2 Massachusetts Avenue NE., Washington, DC 20560. Phone, 202–633–9361.

National Zoological Park   The Park covers an area of approximately 165 acres of parkland along Rock Creek, 2 miles north of the center of Washington. In addition, it operates a 3,000-acre conservation and research center near Front Royal, VA. Its collection is outstanding and is composed of

approximately 4,500 living mammals, birds, amphibians, and reptiles of 480 species. Research objectives include investigations in animal behavior, ecology, nutrition, reproductive physiology, pathology, and clinical medicine. Conservation-oriented studies cover maintenance of wild populations and long-term captive breeding and care of endangered species.

For further information, contact the National Zoological Park, 3001 Connecticut Avenue NW., Washington, DC 20008. Phone, 202–673–4721.

American Studies Program   This office conducts a graduate program in the material aspects of American civilization for graduate students enrolled in cooperating universities. Interested students should apply to the American studies departments of the George Washington University or the University of Maryland or the Office of American Studies, Smithsonian Institution, Washington, DC 20560.

For further information, contact the Office of American Studies, National Postal Museum, 2 Massachusetts Avenue NE., Washington, DC 20560. Phone, 202–633–9386.

Office of Fellowships and Grants   This office develops and administers the numerous Smithsonian programs designed to assist scholars and students from the United States and throughout the world in utilizing the Institution's unique resources. These academic programs, which include long- and short-term appointments, are an important complement to those offered by universities and support participants' research in art, history, and science.

Predoctoral, postdoctoral, and graduate student fellowship programs provide scholars and students the opportunity to conduct research on independently conceived projects at Smithsonian facilities in conjunction with the Institution's research staff.

The Office of Fellowships and Grants offers internships aimed at increasing minority participation in ongoing Smithsonian research activities and fields of interest. In addition, it administers all internships funded by stipends. In addition to these programs, the Office administers other research opportunity programs for many of the Smithsonian bureaus.

For further information, contact the Office of Fellowships and Grants, Suite 7300, 955 L'Enfant Plaza SW., Washington, DC 20560. Phone, 202–287–3271.

Center for Folklife Programs and Cultural Studies   The Center is responsible for research, documentation, and presentation of American folklife traditions. It produces Folkways Recordings, prepares publications based on the papers, films, tapes, and other materials amassed during previous Festivals of American Folklife and directs the planning, development, and presentation of future folklife programs.

For further information, contact the Center for Folklife Programs and Cultural Studies, Suite 2600, 955 L'Enfant Plaza, Washington, DC 20560. Phone, 202–287–3424.

International Center   The International Center supports Smithsonian activities abroad and coordinates the Smithsonian's international interests, particularly those that do not fall within the scope of a single Smithsonian bureau or museum. The International Center provides a meeting place and an organizational channel to bring together the world's scholars, museum professionals, decisionmakers, and the general public, to attend and participate in conferences, public forums, lectures, performances, exhibitions, films, and workshops. Through the International Center, the Smithsonian seeks to encourage a broadening of public understanding of the histories, cultures, and natural environments of regions throughout the world.

For further information, contact the Office of International Relations, Room 3123, 1100 Jefferson Drive SW., Washington, DC 20560. Phone, 202–357–4281.

Center for Museum Studies   The Center provides professional guidance and technical assistance to museums on collections and their management, exhibition techniques, educational activities, and operational methods. It conducts training programs for museum professionals and administers a central

intern referral and placement service. The Center also supports programs in museum careers. It cooperates with American and foreign museums and governmental agencies on museum matters and houses the Museum Reference Center, the Nation's only museological library.

For further information, contact the Center for Museum Studies, 900 Jefferson Drive SW., Room 2235, Washington, DC 20560. Phone, 202–357–3101.

Smithsonian Institution Archives   The Archives, which is open by appointment to the scholarly community and the general public, is the official depository for the Institution's records. These records are essential to an understanding of the growth of the Institution. They are equally significant for their documentation of the development of science and art in America, particularly during the 19th century, a process in which the Smithsonian played a major part. In addition to its official records, the Archives holds a substantial number of private papers that further document the Smithsonian's role through the lives of eminent scientists, such as Joseph Henry, Spencer F. Baird, Samuel P. Langley, Charles D. Walcott, and Charles Greeley Abbot. Holdings are described in the *Guide to Smithsonian Archives,* Smithsonian Institution Press, 1978.

For further information, contact the Smithsonian Institution Archives, 900 Jefferson Drive SW., Washington, DC 20560. Phone, 202–357–1420.

Smithsonian Astrophysical Observatory   The Observatory is located in Cambridge, MA, on the grounds of the Harvard College Observatory. Since 1973, the observatories have coordinated research activities under a single director in a cooperative venture known as the Harvard-Smithsonian Center for Astrophysics.

The Center's research activities are organized in seven divisions, as follows: atomic and molecular physics, radio and geoastronomy, high-energy astrophysics, optical and infrared astronomy, planetary sciences, solar and stellar physics, and theoretical astrophysics.

Data-gathering facilities include a major observatory in Arizona, optical and radio astronomy facilities in Massachusetts, and a radio astronomy and submillimeter-wave facility in Hawaii. The Smithsonian Astrophysical Observatory's observational capabilities are complemented by library, computation, and laboratory facilities in Cambridge.

Research results are published in the *Center Preprint Series* and other technical and nontechnical bulletins, and distributed to scientific and educational institutions around the world. As a further service to international science, the Smithsonian Astrophysical Observatory serves as the headquarters for the International Astronomical Union's Central Telegram Bureau and the Minor Planet Center. The Central Telegram Bureau provides rapid international dissemination of news about the discovery of comets, novae, and other astronomical phenomena. The Minor Planet Center is the principal source for all positional observations of asteroids as well as for establishing their orbits and ephemerides.

The Public Affairs Office coordinates an extensive public education program. A variety of "open nights" are held in Cambridge and at other facilities.

Information about these activities and other general materials for students and teachers may be obtained from the Information Officer, Smithsonian Astrophysical Observatory, 60 Garden Street, Cambridge, MA 02138. Phone, 617–495–7461.

Smithsonian Environmental Research Center

The Center measures physical, chemical, and biological interactions in the environment and determines how these interactions control biological responses. This research is carried out in a 2,600-acre facility in Edgewater, MD, where the ecology of land/water interactions is studied for an estuary and its adjacent watersheds.

For further information, contact the Smithsonian Environmental Research Center, P.O. Box 28, Edgewater, MD 21037. Phone, 301–261–4190.

Smithsonian Institution Libraries

The libraries of the Smithsonian Institution include approximately 1.4 million volumes with strengths in natural history,

museology, history of science, and humanities. The systems' administrative services and Central Reference and Loan are located in the National Museum of Natural History with branch libraries located in each of the major Smithsonian museums and research units including the Cooper-Hewitt, National Design Museum, New York City; the Smithsonian Astrophysical Observatory, Cambridge, MA; and the Smithsonian Tropical Research Institute, Republic of Panama. Inquiries on special subjects or special collections should be addressed to the appropriate branch library or to Central Reference and Loan.

For further information, contact the Smithsonian Institution Libraries, Tenth Street and Constitution Avenue NW., Washington, DC 20560. Phone, 202–357–2240.

Smithsonian Institution Traveling Exhibition Service

The purpose of the Service is to provide to educational, scientific, and cultural institutions exhibitions and other services that will enrich their programs and enable them to offer a greater variety of cultural experiences to their audiences. The Service circulates the best possible exhibits at the lowest possible rental fees.

More than 75 exhibitions of paintings, sculptures, prints, drawings, decorative arts, history, children's art, natural history, photography, science, and technology are circulated every year. Lists of available exhibitions and information for future bookings can be obtained directly from the Smithsonian Institution Traveling Exhibition Service, Washington, DC 20560.

For further information, contact the Smithsonian Institution Traveling Exhibition Service, Room 3146, 1100 Jefferson Drive SW., Washington, DC 20560. Phone, 202–357–3168.

Smithsonian Tropical Research Institute

The Institute, a research organization devoted to the study and support of tropical biology, education, and conservation, focuses broadly on the evolution of patterns of behavior and ecological adaptations. The tropics offer a rich natural laboratory for these purposes. Panama further offers its unique zoogeographic characteristics—

landbridge to terrestrial life forms of two continents and water barriers to marine life of two oceans.

The Institute provides a base of operations and an intellectual center for exploring the frontiers of biology across the varied land and seascapes of the tropical world. It operates the Barro Colorado Nature Monument, a 12,000-acre tropical forest research preserve including Barro Colorado Island and adjacent peninsulas in Gatun Lake, Republic of Panama. The Institute also maintains a research and conference center in Ancon, including one of the world's finest tropical biology libraries. In addition, there are two marine biology laboratories, one on the Atlantic side of the isthmus at Galeta Island and the other at Fort Amador on the Pacific side. The Institute's scientific staff conducts research in these areas as well as in other parts of Central and South America, the Pacific, Asia, and Africa, where comparative studies are clarifying the distinctive biological role of the tropics.

For a brochure describing the Institute's activities and illustrating some of the facilities and habitats available, contact the Director, Smithsonian Tropical Research Institute, Unit 0948 APO AA 34002–0948. Phone, 507–62–3049 (international operator assistance required).

The John F. Kennedy Center for the Performing Arts The Center, the sole official memorial in Washington to President Kennedy, is an independent bureau of the Smithsonian Institution, administered by a 49-member Board of Trustees.

In a public/private partnership, the Federal Government provides appropriated fund support for the maintenance and operation of the physical facilities of the Presidential monument, while the Board of Trustees is responsible for raising private funds for all of the artistic initiatives. Additional funds for programming and education are derived through box office sales and other earned income, and other government grants. The Center's Board is responsible for administration of the building and for performing arts programming and education.

Since its opening in 1971, the Center has presented a year-round program of the finest in music, dance, and drama from the United States and abroad. Facilities include the Opera House, the Eisenhower Theater, the American Film Institute Theater, the Terrace Theater, the Theater Lab, and the Concert Hall, home of the Center's affiliate, the National Symphony Orchestra.

The Center's Education Department includes the nationwide American College Theater Festival, Youth and Family Programs, the National Symphony Orchestra Education Program, and the Kennedy Center Alliance for Arts Education, designed to increase participation by students throughout the country in Center activities and to establish the Center as a focal point for strengthening the arts in education at all levels.

The Kennedy Center box offices are open daily, and general information and tickets may be obtained by calling 202–467–4600 or 202–416–8524 (TDD). Full-time students, senior citizens over the age of 65, enlisted personnel of grade E–4 and below, fixed low-income groups, and the disabled may purchase tickets for most performances at a 50-percent discount through the Specially Priced Ticket Program. This program is designed to make the Center accessible to all, regardless of economic circumstance.

Visitor services are provided by the Friends of the Kennedy Center. Tours are available free of charge between 10 a.m. and 1 p.m. daily.

National Gallery of Art The National Gallery of Art is governed by a Board of Trustees composed of five Trustees and the Secretary of State, the Secretary of the Treasury, the Chief Justice of the United States, and the Secretary of the Smithsonian Institution. It houses one of the finest collections in the world, illustrating Western man's achievements in painting, sculpture, and the graphic arts. The collections, beginning with the 13th century, are rich in European old master paintings and French, Spanish, Italian, American, and British 18th- and 19th-century paintings; sculpture from the late Middle Ages to the present; Renaissance medals and bronzes; Chinese porcelains; and about 75,000 works of graphic art from the 12th to the 20th centuries. The collections are acquired by private donation rather than by government funds, which serve solely to operate and maintain the building and its collections.

The National Gallery's West Building, designed by John Russell Pope in neoclassical style, was a gift to the Nation from Andrew W. Mellon, who also bequeathed his collection to the gallery in 1937. On March 17, 1941, President Franklin D. Roosevelt accepted the completed building and works of art on behalf of the people of the United States of America.

The National Gallery's East Building, designed by I.M. Pei, was accepted by President Jimmy Carter in June of 1978 as a gift of Paul Mellon and the late Ailsa Mellon Bruce, son and daughter of the gallery's founder, and the Andrew W. Mellon Foundation. The East Building provides space for temporary exhibitions, the gallery's growing collections, the Center for the Advanced Study in the Visual Arts, including greatly expanded library and photographic archives, and administrative and curatorial offices.

A professor-in-residence position is filled annually by a distinguished scholar in the field of art history; graduate and postgraduate research is conducted under a fellowship program; programs for schoolchildren and the general public are conducted daily; and an Extension Service distributes loans of audiovisual materials, including films, slide lectures, and slide sets throughout the world. Publications, slides, and reproductions may be obtained through the Publications Service.

For general information on the National Gallery of Art and its activities, call 202–737–4215.

Woodrow Wilson International Center for Scholars The Center, located in Washington, DC, is the Nation's official memorial to its 28th President. The Center's mandate is to integrate the world of learning with the world of public affairs. Through meetings and conferences, the Center brings scholars together with Members of Congress, Government officials, business leaders, and other policymakers. Through publication of books and the *Wilson Quarterly* and a nationally broadcast radio program, the results of the Center's research and meetings are made publicly available.

The Center awards approximately 40 residential fellowships annually to individuals with project proposals representing the entire range of superior scholarship, with a strong emphasis on the humanities and social sciences.

Applications from any country are welcome. Persons with outstanding capabilities and experience from a wide variety of backgrounds (including government, the corporate world, academia, and other professions) are eligible for appointment. For academic participants, eligibility is limited to the postdoctoral level.

The Center prefers its fellows to be in residence for the academic year— September to May or June—although a few fellowships are available for shorter periods of not less than 4 months.

The Center holds one round of competitive selection per year. The deadline for the receipt of applications is October 1, and decisions on appointments are announced in March of the following year.

For further information, contact the Fellowship Office, Woodrow Wilson Center, Washington, DC 20560. Phone, 202–357–2841; Fax, 202–357–4439.

Sources of Information

Contracts and Small Business Activities Information may be obtained from the Director, Office of Contracting and Property Management, Smithsonian Institution, Washington, DC 20560, regarding procurement of supplies; contracts for construction, services, exhibits, research, etc.; and property management and utilization services for all Smithsonian Institution organizations except as follows: John F. Kennedy Center for the Performing Arts, Washington, DC 20566; Supply Officer, National Gallery of Art, Sixth Street and

Constitution Avenue NW., Washington, DC 20565. Phone, 202–287–3343.

Education and Research Refer to statements on the Office of Fellowships and Grants, the American Studies Program, the Center for Folklife Programs and Cultural Studies, the Woodrow Wilson International Center for Scholars, and other offices. For information, write to the Directors of these offices at the Smithsonian Institution, Washington, DC 20560. For information regarding Kennedy Center Education Programs, both in Washington, DC, and in nationwide touring productions and training, contact the John F. Kennedy Center for the Performing Arts, Washington, DC 20566 (phone, 202–416–8000).

The Center for Advanced Study in the Visual Arts was founded in 1979, as part of the National Gallery of Art, to promote study of the history, theory, and criticism of art, architecture, and urbanism through the formation of a community of scholars. The activities of the Center for Advanced Study, which include the fellowship program, meetings, research, and publications, are privately funded. For further information, contact the Center for Advanced Study in the Visual Arts, National Gallery of Art, Washington, DC 20565. Phone, 202–842–6480; or fax, 202–842–6733.

Employment Employment information for the Washington, DC, metropolitan area may be obtained from the Office of Human Resources, Smithsonian Institution, Suite 2100, 955 L'Enfant Plaza SW., Washington, DC 20560. Phone, 202–287–3100. Employment information for the following locations may be obtained by contacting the organizations directly as follows: the Cooper-Hewitt, National Design Museum, 2 East 91st Street, New York, NY 10028 (phone, 212–860–6868); Smithsonian Astrophysical Observatory, Personnel Department, 160 Concord Avenue, Cambridge, MA 02138 (phone, 617–495–7371); Personnel Office, National Gallery of Art, Fourth Street and Constitution Avenue NW., Washington, DC 20565 (phone, 202–842–6298); or for the hearing impaired

(TDD), 202–789–3021); and the John F. Kennedy Center for the Performing Arts, Human Resources Department, Washington, DC 20566 (phone, 202–416–8610).

Films The National Gallery of Art circulates films, slide programs, videos, teaching packets, and videodiscs to schools and civic organizations throughout the country. Contact the Department of Education Resources, National Gallery of Art, Washington, DC 20565. Phone, 202–842–6273. Please write to request a free catalog of programs.

Memberships For information about membership in The Smithsonian Associates Resident Program, write to The Smithsonian Associates, Room 3077, 1100 Jefferson Drive SW., Washington, DC 20560. Phone, 202–357–3030. The Resident program offers a wide variety of performing arts events, courses, lectures, seminars, symposia, films, and guided tours with noted specialists. Additional activities include a lecture series for retirees; classes, workshops, films, and summer camp sessions for young people; and family and adult/child activities. Membership benefits include a minimum 25-percent discount for most paid events and admission priority; free lectures, docent-led tours, films, and museum shop parties; a subscription to *Smithsonian* magazine; monthly copies of the *Associate,* the award-winning guide to Resident Associate activities; free parking on a space-available basis for members participating in The Smithsonian Associate activities on weeknights and weekends, with valid membership card and event ticket, beginning one-half hour before the announced starting time of the event, in the west lot of the National Museum of Natural History; dining privileges at the Associates' Court; and free admission to the Cooper-Hewitt, National Design Museum in New York City. Additionally, all members receive discounts on museum shop purchases; *Smithsonian Catalog* items; Smithsonian Institution Press publications and records; and subscription discounts on the *Wilson Quarterly* and *Air and Space* magazine.

Members over the age of 60 receive additional discounts on most paid events. The Smithsonian Associates also offer volunteer opportunities and special services for individuals with disabilities.

For information about The Smithsonian Associates National Program, contact The Smithsonian Associates, Room 3045, 1100 Jefferson Drive SW., Washington, DC 20560. Phone, 202–357–4800. National membership benefits include a subscription to *Smithsonian* magazine; information services from the Associates' Reception Center; eligibility to travel on international and U.S. study tours and seminars guided by expert study leaders; the opportunity to visit Washington, DC, on a Smithsonian "Anytime" Weekend; discounted tickets for Smithsonian educational events nationwide; and dining privileges in the Associates' Court. The Contributing Membership offers additional opportunities to support the Smithsonian Institution. Contributing members, at various levels, receive an array of benefits—from receiving quarterly issues of *Smithsonian Institution Research Reports* to being invited to the annual James Smithson weekend and other special events. For information about the Contributing Membership, write to the address at the beginning of this paragraph. Phone, 202–357–1699.

The Young Benefactors offers individuals between the ages of 25 and 45 the opportunity to increase their understanding of the Institution and to participate in unique fundraising events which assist the Institution in achieving its goals. For additional information about the Young Benefactors, write to The Smithsonian Associates, Room 3045, 1100 Jefferson Drive SW., Washington, DC 20560. Phone, 202–357–1351.

The Circle of the National Gallery of Art is a membership program which provides support for special projects for which Federal funds are not available. Since its inception in 1986, the Circle has provided support for scholarly exhibitions, acquisitions of works of art, publications, films, and symposia at the Gallery's Center for Advanced Study in the Visual Arts. For more information

about membership in the Circle of the National Gallery of Art, please write to The Circle, National Gallery of Art, Washington, DC 20565; or call 202–737–4215.

Information about activities of the Friends of the National Zoo and their magazine, *The Zoogoer,* is available by writing to them at the National Zoological Park, Washington, DC 20008. Phone, 202–673–4960.

Information about the national and local activities of Friends of the Kennedy Center (including the bimonthly *Kennedy Center News* for members) is available at the information desks within the Center or by writing to Friends of the Kennedy Center, Washington, DC 20566.

Photographs Color and black and white photographs and slides (including illustrated slide lectures) are available to Government agencies, research and educational institutions, publishers, and the general public from the Smithsonian. Subjects include photographs of the Smithsonian's scientific, technological, historical, and art collections as well as pictures dating back more than 130 years taken from its photographic archives. Information, order forms, and price lists may be obtained from Photographic Services, Smithsonian Institution, Washington, DC 20560. Phone, 202–357–1933.

Publications The Smithsonian Institution Press and the Office of Public Affairs publish *Smithsonian Year,* the Institution's annual report, along with a supplement that lists current titles. The Press also publishes books and studies related to the sciences, technology, history, air and space, and the arts at a wide range of prices. A book catalog and a list of studies are available from Publications Sales, Smithsonian Institution Press, 1111 North Capitol Street, Washington, DC 20002. Phone, 202–287–3738.

An events highlight advertisement, which appears on the next-to-last Friday of the month, is published in the *Washington Post* by the Office of Public Affairs.

A brief guide to the Smithsonian Institution, published in English and several foreign languages; a visitor's guide for individuals with disabilities; the *Smithsonian Institution Research Reports* (containing news of current research projects in the arts, sciences, and history that are being conducted by Smithsonian staff); and *Smithsonian Runner* (a newsletter about Native American-related activities at the Smithsonian) are available from the Office of Public Affairs, 900 Jefferson Drive SW., Washington, DC 20560. Phone, 202–357–2627.

For the monthly Calendar of Events of the National Museum of American Art and the Renwick Gallery, which also gives information on museum publications, write the Office of Public Affairs, National Museum of American Art, Smithsonian Institution, Washington, DC 20560. Phone, 202–357–2247.

For the newsletter *Art to Zoo* for teachers from fourth through eighth grades, write to the Office of Elementary and Secondary Education, Room 1163, Arts and Industries Building, Washington, DC 20560. Phone, 202–357–2425.

The Gallery Shops, National Gallery of Art (phone, 202–842–6466), makes available quality reproductions and publications about the Gallery's collections. The Information Office provides a monthly Calendar of Events and several brochures including *Brief Guide to the National Gallery of Art* and *An Invitation to the National Gallery of Art* (the latter in several foreign languages).

Radio and Telephone   *Radio Smithsonian* produces award-winning radio series and specials about the arts, sciences, and human culture for national broadcast on public radio.

Dial-A-Museum, 202–357–2020; a taped telephone message with daily announcements on new exhibits and special events.

Smithsonian Skywatchers Report, 202–357–2000; a taped telephone message with weekly announcements on stars, planets, and worldwide occurrences of short-lived natural phenomena.

Spanish listing of Smithsonian events, call 202–633–9126.

Concerts from the National Gallery is broadcast 4 weeks after the performance on Radio Station WGTS, 91.9 FM, Sundays at 7:00 p.m., November through July.

Speakers   The Bureau maintains a roster of staff and volunteers available to speak about the Center and its activities.

Education Office, National Gallery of Art, Fourth Street and Constitution Avenue NW., Washington, DC 20565. (They provide gallery talks and lectures.) Phone, 202–842–6246.

Museum aides give slide and musical presentations in area schools and senior citizen facilities. National Portrait Gallery, Eighth and F Streets NW., Washington, DC 20560. Phone, 202–357–2920.

Special Functions   Inquiries regarding the use of Kennedy Center facilities for special functions may be directed to the Office of Special Events, John F. Kennedy Center for the Performing Arts, Washington, DC 20566. Phone, 202–416–8000.

Theater Operations   Inquiries regarding the use of the Kennedy Center's theaters may be addressed to the Booking Coordinator, John F. Kennedy Center for the Performing Arts, Washington, DC 20566. Phone, 202–416–8000.

Tours   For tour information, contact the appropriate office listed below:

Education, Anacostia Museum, 1901 Fort Place SE., Washington, DC 20020. Phone, 202–287–3369.

Division of Museum Programs, National Museum of American Art, Smithsonian Institution, Washington, DC 20560. Phone, 202–357–3111.

Curator of Education, National Portrait Gallery, Eighth and F Streets NW., Washington, DC 20560. Phone, 202–357–2920.

Friends of the National Zoo, National Zoological Park, 3000 Connecticut Avenue NW., Washington, DC 20008. Phone, 202–673–4960.

Education Office, National Gallery of Art, Washington, DC 20565. Phone, 202–842–6247.

Office of Education, National Museum of Natural History, Tenth Street and Constitution Avenue NW., Washington, DC 20560. Phone, 202–357–3045.

Office of Public Programs (tour scheduling), National Museum of

American History, Fourteenth Street and Constitution Avenue NW., Washington, DC 20560. Phone, 202–357–1481; or for the hearing-impaired (TTY), 202–357–1563.

Office of Education, Hirshhorn Museum and Sculpture Garden, Eighth Street and Independence Avenue SW., Washington, DC 20560. Phone, 202–357–3235.

Department of Education, Smithsonian Environmental Research Center, RR4, Box 28, Edgewater, MD 21037. Phone, 202–261–4190, ext. 42.

Membership Department, Cooper-Hewitt, National Design Museum, 2 East Ninety-first Street, New York, NY 10028. Phone, 212–860–6868.

Office of Volunteer Services (tour scheduling), National Air and Space Museum, Seventh Street and Independence Avenue SW., Washington, DC 20560. Phone, 202–357–1400.

Department of Education, National Museum of African Art, 950 Independence Avenue SW., Washington, DC 20560. Phone, 202–357–4600.

Tour Information, Friends of the Kennedy Center, Washington, DC 20566. Phone, 202–416–8000.

Visitor Information   The Smithsonian Information Center, located in the original Smithsonian building, provides a general orientation and assistance for members and the public relative to the national collections, museum events, and programs. Write to the Smithsonian Information Center, 1000 Jefferson Drive SW., Washington, DC 20560. Phone, 202–357–2700; or for the hearing impaired (TTY), 202–357–1729.

The Visitor Services Office of the National Gallery of Art provides individual assistance to those with special needs, responds to written and telephone requests, supplies crowd control for ticketed exhibitions and programs, and provides information to those planning to visit the Washington, DC, area. For more information, write to the National Gallery of Art, Office of Visitor Services, Washington, DC 20565. Phone, 202–842–6681; or for the hearing impaired (TDD), 202–842–6176.

Volunteer Service Opportunities   The Smithsonian Institution welcomes volunteers and offers a variety of service opportunities. Persons may serve as tour guides or information volunteers, or may participate in an independent program in which their educational and professional backgrounds are matched with curatorial or research requests from within the Smithsonian. For information, write to the Visitor Information and Associates' Reception Center, 1000 Jefferson Drive SW., Washington, DC 20560. Phone, 202–357–2700; or for the hearing-impaired (TTY), 202–357–1729.

Volunteers at the National Gallery of Art may select from providing such services as giving tours of the permanent Gallery collection for children and adults in English or foreign languages; serving as art information specialists at the art information desks throughout the West and East buildings; and assisting the library staff on assorted projects. For further details, write the Education Division, National Gallery of Art, Washington, DC 20565. Phone, 202–842–6246; or for the hearing impaired (TDD), 202–842–6176. For library volunteering inquiries, phone 202–842–6510.

For information about volunteer opportunities at the Kennedy Center, write to Friends of the Kennedy Center, Washington, DC 20566. Phone, 202–416–8000.

For further information, members of the press may contact the Office of Public Affairs, Smithsonian Institution, 900 Jefferson Drive SW., Washington, DC 20560. Phone, 202–357–2627. All other inquiries should be directed to the Smithsonian Visitor Information Center, 1000 Jefferson Drive SW., Washington, DC 20560. Phone, 202–357–2700; or for the hearing impaired (TTY), 202–357–1729.

STATE JUSTICE INSTITUTE

Suite 600, 1650 King Street, Alexandria, VA 22314
Phone, 703–684–6100

Board of Directors:

Chairman	JOHN F. DAFFRON, JR.
Vice Chairman	DAVID A. BROCK
Secretary	JANICE L. GRADWOHL
Executive Committee Member	TERRENCE B. ADAMSON
Members	JOSEPH F. BACA, ROBERT N.
	BALDWIN, VIVI L. DILWEG,
	CARLOS R. GARZA, KEITH
	MCNAMARA, FLORENCE R.
	MURRAY, SANDRA A. O'CONNOR

Officers:

Executive Director	DAVID I. TEVELIN
Deputy Director	RICHARD VAN DUIZEND

The State Justice Institute was established to further the development and adoption of improved judicial administration in the State courts of the United States.

The State Justice Institute was created by the State Justice Institute Act of 1984 (42 U.S.C. 10701) as a private, nonprofit corporation to further the development and improvement of judicial administration in the State courts.

The Institute is supervised by a Board of Directors consisting of 11 members appointed by the President with the advice and consent of the Senate. The Board is statutorily composed of six judges, a State court administrator, and four members of the public, of whom no more than two can be of the same political party.

The goals of the Institute are to:
—direct a national program of assistance to ensure that all U.S. citizens have ready access to a fair and effective judicial system;
—foster coordination and cooperation with the Federal Judiciary;
—serve as a clearinghouse and information center for the dissemination of information regarding State judicial systems; and
—encourage education for judges and support personnel of State court systems.

To accomplish these broad objectives, the Institute is authorized to provide funds, through grants, cooperative agreements, and contracts, to State courts and organizations that can assist in the achievement of improving judicial administration of the State courts.

Sources of Information

Inquiries concerning the following programs and activities should be directed to the specified office of the State Justice Institute, Suite 600, 1650 King Street, Alexandria, VA 22314. Phone, 703–684–6100.

Grants—Chief/Program Division.
Publications, Consumer Information—Publications Coordinator/Office of the Executive Director.
Speakers, Privacy Act/Freedom of Information Act Requests—Executive Secretary/Office of the Executive Director.
Employment/Personnel—Personnel Specialist/Finance and Management Division.

To access the electronic bulletin board, dial 703–739–2303 or 2304. Instructions may be obtained from the Publications Coordinator by calling 703–684–6100.

For further information, contact the Publications Coordinator, State Justice Institute, Suite 600, 1650 King Street, Alexandria, VA 22314. Phone, 703–684–6100.

UNITED STATES INSTITUTE OF PEACE

1550 M Street NW., Washington, DC 20005–1708
Phone, 202–457–1700; Fax, 202–429–6063

Board of Directors:
Public Members:

Chairman	CHESTER A. CROCKER
Vice Chairman	MAX M. KAMPELMAN
Members	DENNIS L. BARK, THEODORE M. HESBURGH, WILLIAM R. KINTNER, CHRISTOPHER PHILLIPS, ELSPETH DAVIES ROSTOW, MARY LOUISE SMITH, W. SCOTT THOMPSON, ALLEN WEINSTEIN

Ex officio:

Director, U.S. Arms Control and Disarmament Agency	JOHN D. HOLUM
Assistant Secretary of State for Intelligence and Research	TOBY TRISTER GATI
President, National Defense University	LT. GEN. ERVIN J. ROKKE, USAF
Principal Deputy Under Secretary of Defense for Policy	WALTER B. SLOCOMBE

Officials:

President	RICHARD H. SOLOMON
Executive Vice President	HARRIET HENTGES
Vice President	CHARLES E. NELSON
Director, Education and Training	(VACANCY)
Director, Research and Studies	(VACANCY)
Director, Special Programs	KENNETH M. JENSEN
Director, Grants Program	DAVID R. SMOCK
Director, Jennings Randolph Fellowship Program for International Peace	JOSEPH L. KLAITS
Director, Jeannette Rankin Library Program	MARGARITA STUDEMEISTER
Director, Administration	BERNICE J. CARNEY
Director, Public Affairs and Information	WILSON GRABILL, *Acting*
Director, Rule of Law Initiative	NEIL J. KRITZ, *Acting*
Senior Scholar for Religion, Ethics, and Human Rights	DAVID LITTLE
Senior Scholar for Preventive Diplomacy and Early Warning	MICHAEL LUND

The United States Institute of Peace was established to promote research, policy analysis, education, and training on international peace and conflict resolution.

The United States Institute of Peace is an independent, Federal institution created and funded by Congress to develop and disseminate knowledge about international peace and conflict

resolution. The Institute addresses this mandate in three principal ways:
—by expanding basic and applied knowledge about the origins, nature, and processes of peace and war, encompassing the widest spectrum of approaches and insights;
—by disseminating this knowledge to officials, policymakers, diplomats, and others engaged in efforts to promote international peace; and
—by supporting education and training programs and providing information for secondary and university-level teachers and students and the general public.

The Institute's primary activities are grantmaking, fellowships, in-house research projects, public education and outreach activities, publications, and library services.

The Grants Program provides financial support for research, information services, education, and training. Eligible grantees include nonprofit organizations; official public institutions, including public schools, colleges, universities, libraries, and State and local agencies; and individuals.

The Jennings Randolph Program for International Peace provides fellowships to scholars, doctoral candidates, practitioners, and other professionals to undertake research and other appropriate forms of work on issues of international peace and the management of international conflicts. The Research and Studies Program conducts conferences, seminars, and study groups on issues of short- and long-term significance.

The Jeannette Rankin Library Program has four main components: a specialized research library; a network with and support for other libraries, both private and public; an oral history resource; and bibliographic as well as other data bases.

The Public Affairs Office fulfills requests for speakers, media services, and general inquiries, and conducts outreach programs in Washington, DC, and elsewhere. Institute-directed activities under the Education and Training Program include educational video programs, teacher training projects, and a National Peace Essay Contest for high school students. Institute publications include the *Biennial Report to Congress and the President;* a newsletter, *Peace Watch;* periodic papers on selected topics, *Peaceworks;* and monographs, books, and special reports generated from Institute-sponsored projects.

For further information, contact the Office of Public Affairs and Information, United States Institute of Peace, Suite 700, 1550 M Street NW., Washington, DC 20005-1708. Phone, 202-457-1700.

SELECTED MULTILATERAL ORGANIZATIONS

MULTILATERAL INTERNATIONAL ORGANIZATIONS IN WHICH THE UNITED STATES PARTICIPATES

Explanatory note: Descriptions of most of the organizations listed below may be found in the publication entitled *United States Contributions to International Organizations.*

The United States participates in the organizations named below in accordance with the provisions of treaties, other international agreements, congressional legislation, or executive arrangements. In some cases, no financial contribution is involved.

Various commissions, councils, or committees subsidiary to the organizations listed here are not named separately on this list. These include the international bodies for narcotics control, which are subsidiary to the United Nations.

I. United Nations, Specialized Agencies, and International Atomic Energy Agency

United Nations
Food and Agricultural Organization
International Maritime Organization
International Atomic Energy Agency
International Civil Aviation Organization
International Fund for Agricultural
 Development (IFAD)
International Labor Organization
International Telecommunication Union
United Nations Industrial Development
 Organization (UNIDO)
Universal Postal Union
World Health Organization
World Intellectual Property Organization
World Meteorological Organization

II. Peacekeeping

United Nations Forces in Cyprus
United Nations Disengagement Observer
 Force (UNDOF) and UNIFIL
Multinational Force and Observers
United Nations Iran-Iraq Military
 Observer Group (UNIIMOG)
United Nations Observer Group in
 Central America (UNOGCA)

III. Inter-American Organizations

Organization of American States
Inter-American Indian Institute
Inter-American Institute for Cooperation
 on Agriculture
Inter-American Tropical Tuna
 Commission
Pan American Health Organization
 (PAHO)
Pan American Institute of Geography
 and History
Pan American Railway Congress
 Association
Postal Union of the Americas and Spain
 and Portugal

IV. Regional Organizations

NATO
North Atlantic Assembly
Colombo Plan for Cooperative Economic
 and Social Development in Asia and
 the Pacific
Organization for Economic Cooperation
 and Development (OECD)
South Pacific Commission

V. Other International Organizations

Bureau of International Expositions
Commission for the Conservation of
  Antarctic Marine Living Resources
Customs Cooperation Council (CCC)
Fund for the Protection of the World
  Cultural and Natural Heritage
General Agreement on Tariffs and Trade
  (GATT)
Hague Conference on Private
  International Law
International Agency for Research on
  Cancer
International Bureau of the Permanent
  Court of Arbitration
International Bureau for the Publication
  of Customs Tariffs
International Bureau of Weights and
  Measures
International Center for the Study of the
  Preservation and the Restoration of
  Cultural Property (ICCROM)
International Coffee Organization (ICO)
International Commission for the
  Conservation of Atlantic Tunas
International Cotton Advisory Committee
International Council for the Exploration
  of the Seas (ICES)
International Council of Scientific
  Unions and Its Associated Unions (20)
International Criminal Police
  Organization (INTERPOL)
International Hydrographic Organization
International Institute for Cotton
International Institute for the Unification
  of Private Law
International Jute Organization
International Lead and Zinc Study Group
International Natural Rubber
  Organization
International North Pacific Fisheries
  Commission
International Office of Epizootics
International Office of Vine and Wine
International Organization for Legal
  Metrology
International Rubber Study Group
International Seed Testing Association
International Sugar Organization
International Tropical Timber
  Organization
International Union for the Protection of
  New Varieties of Plants (UPOV)
International Whaling Commission
International Wheat Council

Interparliamentary Union
North Atlantic Ice Patrol
North Atlantic Salmon Conservation
  Organization
Permanent International Association of
  Navigation Congresses
United Nations Compensation
  Commission
World Tourism Organization (WTO)

VI. Special Voluntary Programs

Colombo Plan Drug Advisory Program
Consultative Group on International
  Agricultural Research
Convention on International Trade in
  Endangered Species of Wild Fauna
  and Flora (CITES)
International Organization for Migration
  (IOM)
International Atomic Agency Technical
  Assistance and Cooperation Fund
OAS Special Cultural Fund
OAS Special Development Assistance
  Fund
OAS Special Multilateral Fund
  (Education and Science)
OAS Special Projects Fund (Mar del
  Plata)
PAHO Special Health Promotion Funds
United Nations Capital Development
  Fund (UNCDF)
United Nations Center for Human
  Settlements (Habitat) (UNCHS)
United Nations Children's Fund
  (UNICEF)
United Nations Development Fund for
  Women (UNIFEM)
United Nations Development Program
  (UNDP)
United Nations Educational and Training
  Program for South Africa
United Nations Environment Program
  (UNEP)
United Nations/Food and Agricultural
  Organization World Food Program
  (WFP)
United Nations Fund for Drug Abuse
  Control (UNFDAC)
United Nations High Commissioner for
  Refugees Program (UNHCR)
United Nations Relief and Works Agency
  (UNRWA)
United Nations Trust Fund for South
  Africa
United Nations Volunteers (UNV)
WHO Special Programs

WMO Voluntary Cooperation Program

African Development Bank

Headquarters: Abidjan, Côte d'Ivoire

President: Babacar Ndiaye

The African Development Bank (AFDB) was established in 1963 and, by charter amendment, opened its membership to non-African countries in 1982. AFDB's mandate is to contribute to the economic development and social progress of its regional members. AFDB members[1] total 76—including 51 African countries and 25 non-regional countries. Ownership of the Bank, by charter, is two-thirds African and one-third non-regional.

The African Development Fund (AFDF), the concessional lending affiliate, was established in 1973 to complement AFDB operations by providing concessional financing for high-priority development projects in the poorest African countries. AFDF membership consists of 26 member countries and AFDB, which represents its African members and is allocated half of the votes.

The United States became a member of AFDF in 1976 by virtue of the African Development Fund Act (22 U.S.C. 290g note) and, in February 1983, became a member of AFDB by virtue of the African Development Bank Act (22 U.S.C. 290i note).

Asian Development Bank

Headquarters: 6 ADB Avenue, 1501 Mandaluyong, Metro Manila, Philippines. Phone, 632–711–3851

President: Mitsuo Sato

The Agreement establishing the Asian Development Bank came into effect on August 22, 1966, when it was ratified by 15 governments. The Bank commenced operations on December 19, 1966. The United States became a member by virtue of the Asian Development Bank Act of March 16, 1966 (22 U.S.C. 285). The Bank now has 55 member

---

[1] AFDB membership totals include the former Socialist Federal Republic of Yugoslavia.

countries—39 from Asia and 16 from outside the region.

The purpose of the Bank is to foster economic growth and contribute to the acceleration of economic development of the developing member countries in Asia, collectively and individually. The Bank, including its concessional loan window, lends about $5 billion annually and provides over $100 million per year in technical assistance.

Correspondence to the Asian Development Bank should be mailed to P.O. Box 789, 1099 Manila, Philippines.

Inter-American Defense Board

2600 Sixteenth Street NW., Washington, DC 20441. Phone, 202–939–6600

Chairman: Maj. Gen. John C. Ellerson, USA

The Inter-American Defense Board is a permanently constituted, international organization, autonomous within the inter-American system, composed of army, navy, and air officers appointed by the governments of American Republics. Its constitutional sources are: Resolution XXXIX of the Meeting of Foreign Ministers at Rio de Janeiro in January 1942; Resolution XXXIV of the Ninth International Conference of American States held in Bogotá, Colombia, in April 1948; and Resolution III of the Fourth Meeting of Consultation of Ministers of Foreign Affairs, held in Washington, DC, March–April 1951.

The Board studies and recommends to the governments of the American Republics measures necessary for close military collaboration in preparation for the collective self-defense of the American continents.

Inter-American Development Bank

Headquarters: 1300 New York Avenue NW., Washington, DC 20577. Phone, 202–623–1000

President: Enrique V. Iglesias

The Inter-American Development Bank (IDB) is an international financial institution established in 1959 to help accelerate economic and social development in Latin America and the

Caribbean. It is based in Washington, DC.

The Bank has 28 member countries in the Western Hemisphere and 18 outside of the region.

In its 34 years of operation, IDB has helped to provide, secure, and organize financing for projects that represent a total investment of more than $178 billion. The Bank has also fostered a more equitable distribution of the benefits of development, and has been a pioneer in financing social projects.

The Bank's highest authority is its Board of Governors, on which each member country is represented. Its 12-member Board of Executive Directors is responsible for the conduct of the Bank's operations.

The Bank's field offices represent its dealings with local authorities and borrowers and supervise the implementation of Bank-supported projects.

International Bank for Reconstruction and Development

Headquarters: 1818 H Street NW., Washington, DC 20433. Phone, 202–477–1234

President: James D. Wolfensohn

The International Bank for Reconstruction and Development (IBRD), also known as the World Bank, officially came into existence on December 27, 1945.

IBRD's purpose is to promote economic, social, and environmental progress in developing nations by raising productivity so that their people may live better and fuller lives. It does this by lending funds at market-determined interest rates, providing advice, and serving as a catalyst to stimulate outside investments. IBRD's resources come primarily from funds raised in the world capital markets, its retained earnings, and repayments on its loans.

During the Bank's 1994 fiscal year, it made new loan commitments totaling $14,244 million in support of sound development projects, primarily in middle-income developing countries.

International Development Association
The International Development

Association (IDA) came into existence on September 24, 1960, as an affiliate of IBRD. IDA's resources consist of subscriptions and supplementary resources in the form of general replenishments, mostly from its more industrialized and developed members; special contributions by its richer members; repayments on earlier credits; and transfers from its net earnings.

IDA promotes economic development, increases productivity, and raises the standard of living in the least developed areas of the world. It does this by financing their developmental requirements on concessionary terms, which are more flexible and bear less heavily on the balance of payments than those of conventional loans, thereby furthering the objectives of IBRD and supplementing its activities.

During the World Bank's 1994 fiscal year, IDA made new commitments totaling $6,592 million, primarily in the poorest countries in sub-Saharan Africa and Asia.

International Finance Corporation

Headquarters: 1818 H Street NW., Washington, DC 20433. Phone, 202–477–1234

President: James D. Wolfensohn
Executive Vice President: Jannik Lindbaek

The International Finance Corporation (IFC), an affiliate of the World Bank, was established in July 1956 to promote productive private enterprise in developing countries.

IFC pursues its objective principally through direct debt and equity investments in projects that establish new businesses or expand, modify, or diversify existing businesses. It also encourages cofinancing by other investors and lenders. For every dollar of financing approved by IFC for its own account, other investors and lenders provide about $5.43.

Additionally, advisory services and technical assistance are provided by IFC to developing member countries in areas such as capital market development, privatization, corporate restructuring, and foreign direct investment.

During the World Bank's 1994 fiscal year, IFC made new debt and equity commitments for its own account of $2.5 billion supporting 231 new projects. The entire size of these projects totalled approximately $15.8 billion.

International Monetary Fund

700 Nineteenth Street NW., Washington, DC 20431. Phone, 202–623–7000

Managing Director and Chairman of the Executive Board: Michel Camdessus

The Final Act of the United Nations Monetary and Financial Conference, signed at Bretton Woods, NH, on July 22, 1944, set forth the original Articles of Agreement of the International Monetary Fund. The Agreement became effective on December 27, 1945, when the President, authorized by the Bretton Woods Agreements Act (22 U.S.C. 286) accepted membership for the United States in the Fund, the Agreement having thus been accepted by countries having approximately 80 percent of the quotas. The inaugural meeting of the Board of Governors was held in March 1946, and the first meeting of the Executive Directors was held May 6, 1946.

On May 31, 1968, the Board of Governors approved an amendment to the Articles of Agreement for the establishment of a facility based on Special Drawing Rights (SDR's) in the Fund and for modification of certain rules and practices of the Fund. The amendment became effective on July 28, 1969, and the Special Drawing Account became operative on August 6, 1969. The United States acceptance of the amendment and participation in the Special Drawing Account were authorized by the Special Drawing Rights Act (22 U.S.C. 286 *et seq.*).

On April 30, 1976, the Board of Governors approved a second amendment to the Articles of Agreement, which entered into force on April 1, 1978. United States acceptance of this amendment was authorized by the Bretton Woods Agreements Act Amendments (22 U.S.C. 286e–5). This amendment gave members the right to adopt exchange arrangements of their choice while placing certain obligations on them regarding their exchange rate policies, over which IMF was to exercise firm surveillance. The official price of gold was abolished and the SDR account was promoted as the principal reserve asset of the international monetary system.

On June 28, 1990, the Board of Governors approved a third amendment to the Articles of Agreement, under which a member's voting rights and certain related rights may be suspended by a 70-percent majority of the executive board if the member, having been declared ineligible to use the general resources of the Fund, persists in its failure to fulfill any of its obligations under the Articles.

On November 11, 1992, the third amendment to IMF's Articles of Agreement took effect, increasing quotas by approximately 50 percent under the Ninth General Review to SDR's 145 billion (equivalent to approximately $202 billion). As of March 31, 1995, IMF had 179 member countries.

The purposes of the Fund are to promote international monetary cooperation through a permanent institution that provides the machinery for consultation and collaboration on international monetary problems; to facilitate the expansion and balanced growth of international trade; to promote exchange stability; to assist in the establishment of a multilateral system of payments for current transactions between members; and to give confidence to members by making the Fund's resources temporarily available to them under adequate safeguards.

In accordance with these purposes, the Fund seeks to shorten the duration and lessen the degree of imbalance in the international balances of payments of members.

The Fund provides financial assistance to aid its members in handling balance-of-payment difficulties through a variety of facilities that are designed to address specific problems. These lending mechanisms include stand-by and extended arrangements, as well as separate facilities to provide compensatory and contingency financing to countries suffering temporary declines in their export earnings, to support structural adjustment programs in the poorest countries, and to promote systemic transformation in the formerly centrally planned economies during the transition to a market economy.

For further information, contact the Chief, Public Affairs Division, External Relations Department, International Monetary Fund, 700 Nineteenth Street NW., Washington, DC 20431. Phone, 202–623–7300.

International Organization for Migration

Headquarters: 17 Route des Morillons, Grand-Saconnex, Geneva; mailing address—P.O. Box 71, CH1211, Geneva 19, Switzerland

Director General: James N. Purcell, Jr.

Washington Office: Suite 1110, 1750 K Street NW., Washington, DC 20006. Phone, 202–862–1826
Chief of Mission: Hans-Petter Boe

New York Office: Suite 1610, 122 E. 42d Street, New York, NY 10168. Phone, 212–681–7000
Chief of Mission: Richard E. Scott

The International Organization for Migration (IOM), formerly the Intergovernmental Committee for Migration (ICM), was created in 1951 at a conference in Brussels sponsored by the Governments of the United States and Belgium.

IOM is a technical, nonpolitical organization that plans and operates refugee resettlement, national migration, and emergency relief programs at the request of its member states and in cooperation with other international organizations.

IOM has four major objectives: the processing and movement of refugees to countries offering them permanent resettlement opportunities; the promotion of orderly migration to meet the specific needs of both emigration and immigration countries; the transfer of technology through migration in order to promote the economic, educational, and social advancement of countries in the process of development, particularly in Latin America and Africa; and the provision of a forum to states and other partners to discuss experiences, exchange views, and devise measures to promote cooperation and coordination of efforts on migration issues.

IOM has a membership of 54 governments; 41 other governments have observer status. Operational offices are located in 60 countries, including some nonmember countries.

Multilateral Investment Guarantee Agency

Headquarters: 1818 H Street NW., Washington, DC 20433. Phone, 202–477–1234

President: James D. Wolfensohn
Executive Vice President: Akira Iida

The Multilateral Investment Guarantee Agency (MIGA), an affiliate of the World Bank, was formally constituted in April 1988.

MIGA's basic purpose is to facilitate the flow of private investment for productive purposes to developing member countries by offering long-term political risk insurance to investors, such as coverage against risks of expropriation, currency transfer, and war and civil disturbance; and by providing advisory and consultative services.

During the World Bank's 1994 fiscal year, MIGA issued 38 guarantees with a maximum contingent liability of $372.6 million to facilitate aggregate direct investment of approximately $1.3 billion.

Organization of American States

General Secretariat: 1889 F Street NW., Washington, DC 20006. Phone, 202–458–3000. Fax, 202–458–3967

Secretary General: César Gaviria
Assistant Secretary General: Christopher Thomas
Executive Secretary for Economic and Social Affairs: Lorne McDonnough, *Acting*
Executive Secretary for Education, Science, and Culture: Leonel Zuñiga, *Acting*
Assistant Secretary for Management: Phillip McLean
Assistant Secretary for Legal Affairs: William M. Berenson, *Acting*

The Organization of American States (OAS) is a regional, intergovernmental

MULTILATERAL ORGANIZATIONS

organization whose primary purposes are to strengthen the peace and security of the continent; to promote and consolidate representative democracy, with due respect for the principle of nonintervention; to prevent possible causes of difficulties and to conciliate disputes that may arise among the member states; to provide for common action by those states in the event of aggression; to seek the solution of political, juridical, and economic problems that may arise among them; to promote, by cooperative action, their economic, social, and cultural development; and to achieve an effective limitation of conventional weapons that will make it possible to devote the largest amount of resources to the economic and social development of the member states. With roots dating from 1890, the first OAS Charter was signed in 1948. Two subsequent protocols of amendment, Buenos Aires 1967 and Cartagena de Indias 1985, gave it its present form. Two additional protocols of amendment, Washington 1992 and Managua 1993, are currently in the ratification process. The Protocol of Washington will incorporate provisions for the protection of democratically constituted governments and will include the eradication of extreme poverty, which constitutes an obstacle to the full democratic development of the peoples of the hemisphere, among the essential purposes of the Organization. The Protocol of Managua will establish the Inter-American Council for Integral Development in replacement of the current Inter-American Councils for Economic and Social Affairs and Education, Science and Culture.

The OAS member states are Argentina, Antigua and Barbuda, Commonwealth of the Bahamas, Barbados, Belize, Bolivia, Brazil, Canada, Chile, Colombia, Costa Rica, Cuba, Commonwealth of Dominica, Dominican Republic, Ecuador, El Salvador, Grenada, Guatemala, Guyana, Haiti, Honduras, Jamaica, Mexico, Nicaragua, Panama, Paraguay, Peru, St. Kitts and Nevis, St. Lucia, St. Vincent and the Grenadines, Suriname, Trinidad and Tobago, the United States of America, Uruguay, and

Venezuela. The present Government of Cuba is excluded from participation by a decision of the Eighth Meeting of Consultation of Ministers of Foreign Affairs in 1962. Thirty-three non-American countries and the European Union are Permanent Observers.

The principal organs of the OAS are:
—the General Assembly, which is normally composed of the foreign ministers of the member states and meets at least once a year to decide the general action and policy of the Organization;
—the Meeting of Consultation of Ministers of Foreign Affairs, which meets on call to consider urgent matters of common interest or threats to the peace and security of the hemisphere;
—the Permanent Council, which meets twice a month at OAS headquarters;
—the Inter-American Economic and Social Council and the Inter-American Council For Education, Science, and Culture, which meet once a year;
—the Inter-American Juridical Committee;
—the Inter-American Commission on Human Rights; and
—the General Secretariat, which is the central and permanent organ, headquartered in Washington, DC.

OAS has six specialized organizations that handle technical matters of common interest to the American States. OAS also holds specialized conferences on specific technical matters.

For further information, contact the Director, Department of Public Information, Organization of American States, Seventeenth Street and Constitution Avenue NW., Washington, DC 20006. Phone, 202–458–3760. Fax, 202–458–6421.

United Nations

United Nations, New York, NY 10017. Phone, 212 963 1234

Secretary-General: Boutros Boutros-Ghali

United Nations Office at Geneva: Palais des Nations, 1211 Geneva 10, Switzerland

Director-General: Antoine Blanca

United Nations Office at Vienna: Vienna International Centre, P.O. Box 500, A–1400, Vienna, Austria

Director-General: Giorgio Giacomelli

Washington, DC, Office: U.N. Information Centre, Suite 400, 1775 K Street NW., Washington, DC 20006. Phone, 202–331– 8670; Fax, 202–331–9191

Director: Michael Stopford

The United Nations is an international organization that was set up in accordance with the Charter [1] drafted by governments represented at the Conference on International Organization meeting at San Francisco. The Charter was signed on June 26, 1945, and came into force on October 24, 1945, when the required number of ratifications and accessions had been made by the signatories. Amendments increasing membership of the Security Council and the Economic and Social Council came into effect on August 31, 1965.

The United Nations now consists of 185 member states of which 51 are founding members.

Purpose The purposes of the United Nations set out in the Charter are: to maintain international peace and security; to develop friendly relations among nations; to achieve international cooperation in solving international problems of an economic, social, cultural, or humanitarian character and in promoting respect for human rights; and to be a center for harmonizing the actions of nations in the attainment of these common ends.

Organization
The principal organs of the United Nations are:

General Assembly All states that are members of the United Nations are members of the General Assembly. Its functions are to consider and discuss any matter within the scope of the Charter of the United Nations and to make

[1] Charter of the United Nations, together with the Statute of the International Court of Justice (Department of State Publication No. 2353, International Organization and Conference Series III, 21), June 26, 1945. Available for sale from the Superintendent of Documents, Government Printing Office, Washington, DC 20402. Phone, 202–783– 3238.

recommendations to the members of the United Nations and other organs. It approves the budget of the organization, the expenses of which are borne by the members as apportioned by the General Assembly.

The General Assembly may call the attention of the Security Council to situations likely to endanger international peace and security, may initiate studies, and may receive and consider reports from other organs of the United Nations. Under the "Uniting for Peace" resolution adopted by the General Assembly in November 1950, if the Security Council fails to act on an apparent threat to or breach of the peace or act of aggression because of lack of unanimity of its five permanent members, the Assembly itself may take up the matter within 24 hours—in emergency special session—and recommend collective measures, including, in case of a breach of the peace or act of aggression, use of armed force when necessary to maintain or restore international peace and security.

The General Assembly has held to date 50 regular sessions, 18 special sessions, and 11 emergency special sessions. It normally meets in regular annual session in September.

Security Council The Security Council consists of 15 members of which 5—the People's Republic of China, France, the Union of Soviet Socialist Republics, the United Kingdom, and the United States of America—are permanent members and are elected each year. The 10 nonpermanent members are elected for 2-year terms by the General Assembly. The primary responsibility of the Security Council is to act on behalf of the members of the United Nations in maintenance of international peace and security. Measures that may be employed by the Security Council are outlined in the Charter.

The Security Council, together with the General Assembly, also elects the judges of the International Court of Justice and makes a recommendation to the General Assembly on the appointment of the Secretary General of the organization.

The Security Council first met in London on January 17, 1946, and is so organized as to be able to function continuously.

Economic and Social Council This organ is responsible, under the authority of the General Assembly, for the economic and social programs of the United Nations. Its functions include making or initiating studies, reports, and recommendations on international economic, social, cultural, educational, health, and related matters; promoting respect for and observance of human rights and fundamental freedoms for all; calling international conferences and preparing draft conventions for submission to the General Assembly on matters within its competence; negotiating agreements with the specialized agencies and defining their relationship with the United Nations; coordinating the activities of the specialized agencies; and consulting with nongovernmental organizations concerned with matters within its competence. The Council consists of 54 members of the United Nations elected by the General Assembly for 3-year terms; 18 are elected each year.

The Council usually holds two regular sessions a year. It has also held a number of special sessions.

Trusteeship Council The Trusteeship Council was initially established to consist of any member states that administer trust territories, permanent members of the Security Council that do not administer trust territories, and enough other nonadministering countries elected by the General Assembly for 3-year terms to ensure that membership would be equally divided between administering and nonadministering members. At present, the participating members of the Council are the United Kingdom, China, France, the Union of Soviet Socialist Republics, and the United States.

Of the original 11 trust territories, all except the Trust Territory of the Pacific Islands, which is administered by the United States, have attained the goals of the trusteeship system, either as independent states or as parts of such states.

The Council functions under authority of the General Assembly. It considers reports from the member administering the Trust Territory, examines petitions from inhabitants of the Trust Territory, and provides for periodic inspection visits to the Trust Territory. The Council has held 61 regular sessions and a number of special sessions.

International Court of Justice The International Court of Justice is the principal judicial organ of the United Nations. It has its seat at The Hague, the Netherlands. All members of the United Nations are *ipso facto* parties to the Statute of the Court. Nonmembers of the United Nations may become parties to the Statute of the Court on conditions prescribed by the General Assembly on the recommendation of the Security Council.

The jurisdiction of the Court comprises all cases that the parties refer to it and all matters specially provided for in the Charter of the United Nations or in treaties and conventions in force.

The Court consists of 15 judges known as "members" of the Court. They are elected for 9-year terms by the General Assembly and the Security Council, voting independently, and may be reelected.

Secretariat The Secretariat consists of a Secretary-General and "such staff as the Organization may require." The Secretary-General, who is appointed by the General Assembly on the recommendation of the Security Council, is the chief administrative officer of the United Nations. He acts in that capacity for the General Assembly, the Security Council, the Economic and Social Council, and the Trusteeship Council. Under the Charter, the Secretary-General "may bring to the attention of the Security Council any matter that in his opinion may threaten the maintenance of international peace and security."

SELECTED BILATERAL ORGANIZATIONS

International Boundary Commission, United States and Canada

United States Section: 1250 23d Street NW., Suite 405, Washington, DC 20037. Phone, 202–736–9100.

Canadian Section: 615 Booth Street, Room 130, Ottawa, ON K1A 0E9. Phone, 613–995–4960.

International Boundary and Water Commission, United States and Mexico

United States Section: 4171 North Mesa Street, Suite C–310, El Paso, TX 79902–1441. Phone, 915–534–6700.

Mexican Section: Avenida Universidad, No. 2168, Ciudad Juárez, Chihuahua, Mexico 32320; or P.O. Box 10525, El Paso, TX 79995. Phone, 011–52–161–37311.

International Joint Commission—United States and Canada

United States Section: 1250 23d Street NW., Suite 100, Washington, DC 20440. Phone, 202–736–9000.

Canadian Section: 100 Metcalfe Street, Ottawa, ON K1P 5M1. Phone, 613–995–2984.

Regional Office: 100 Ouellette Avenue, Windsor, ON N9A 6T3; or P.O. Box 32869, Detroit MI 48232. Phone, 519–256–7821 or 313–226–2170.

Joint Mexican-United States Defense Commission

United States Section: 1111 Jefferson Davis Highway, Suite 509, Arlington, VA 22202. Phone, 703–604–0482 or 703–604–0483.

Mexican Section: 1911 Pennsylvania Avenue NW., Mexican Embassy, Sixth Floor, Washington, DC 20006. Phone, 202–728–1748.

Permanent Joint Board on Defense— United States and Canada

United States Section: 1111 Jefferson Davis Highway, Suite 511, Arlington, VA 22202. Phone, 703–604–0488.

Canadian Section: National Defense Headquarters, 101 Colonel By Drive, Ottawa, ON K1A 0K2.

Appendices

APPENDIX A: Standard Federal Regions and Federal Executive Boards

Standard Federal Regions

Standard Federal administrative regions were established to achieve more uniformity in the location and geographic jurisdiction of Federal field offices. Standard regions are a basis for promoting more systematic coordination among agencies and Federal, State, and local governments and for securing management improvements and economies through greater interagency and intergovernmental cooperation. Boundaries were drawn and regional office locations designated for 10 regions, and agencies are required to adopt the uniform system when changes are made or new offices established. A map showing the standard boundaries is printed on the following page.

The regional structures of agencies not conforming to the uniform regional system can be found in the tables accompanying their descriptions, when provided by the agency.

For further information, contact the General Management Division, Office of Management and Budget, New Executive Office Building, Washington, DC 20503. Phone, 202–395–5090.

Federal Executive Boards

Federal Executive Boards (FEB's) were established by Presidential directive (a memorandum for heads of Federal departments and agencies dated November 13, 1961) to improve internal Federal management practices and to provide a central focus for Federal participation in civic affairs in major metropolitan centers of Federal activity. They carry out their functions under the supervision and control of the Office of Personnel Management (OPM).

Federal Executive Boards are composed of heads of Federal field offices in the metropolitan area. A Chairman is elected annually from among the membership to provide overall leadership to the Board's operations. Committees and task forces carry out interagency projects consistent with the Board's missions.

Federal Executive Boards serve as a means for disseminating information within the Federal Government and for promoting discussion of Federal policies and activities of importance to all Federal executives in the field.

Currently, Federal Executive Boards are located in 28 metropolitan areas that are important centers of Federal activity. These areas are: Albuquerque-Santa Fe, Atlanta, Baltimore, Boston, Buffalo, Chicago, Cincinnati, Cleveland, Dallas-Fort Worth, Denver, Detroit, Honolulu-Pacific, Houston, Kansas City, Los Angeles, Miami, New Orleans, New York, Newark, Oklahoma City, Philadelphia, Pittsburgh, Portland, St. Louis, San Antonio, San Francisco, Seattle, and the Twin Cities (Minneapolis-St. Paul).

Federal Executive Associations, Councils, or Committees have been locally organized in over 100 other metropolitan areas to perform functions similar to the Federal Executive Boards but on a lesser scale of organization and activity.

For further information, contact the Assistant for Regional Operations, Office of Personnel Management, Room 5H22L, 1900 E Street NW., Washington, DC 20415–0001. Phone, 202–606–1001.

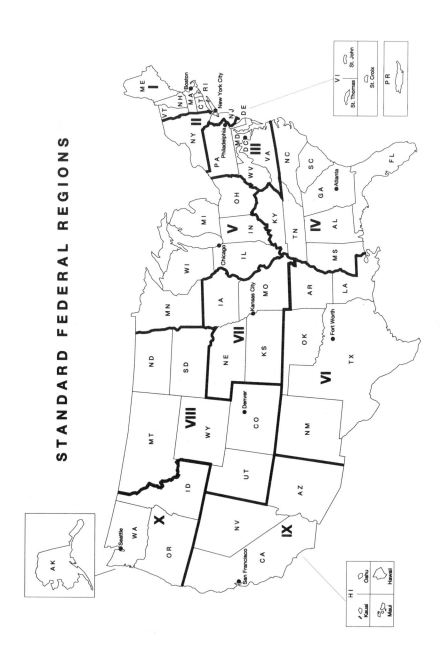

APPENDIX B: Commonly Used Abbreviations and Acronyms

ABMC	American Battle Monuments Commission
ACDA	United States Arms Control and Disarmament Agency
ACF	Administration for Children and Families
ACUS	Administrative Conference of the United States
ACYF	Administration on Children, Youth, and Families
ADA	Americans with Disabilities Act of 1990
ADB	Asian Development Bank
ADD	Administration on Developmental Disabilities
AEDS	Atomic Energy Detection System
AFAA	Air Force Audit Agency
AFBCMR	Air Force Review Board for Correction of Military Records
AFCARA	Air Force Civilian Appellate Review Agency
AFDB	African Development Bank
AFDC	Aid to Families with Dependent Children
AFDF	African Development Fund
AFIS	American Forces Information Service
AFPC	Armed Forces Policy Council
AFPEO	Air Force Program Executive Office
AFPPS	American Forces Press and Publications Service
AFRRI	Armed Forces Radiobiology Research Institute
AFRTS	Armed Forces Radio and Television Service

AFSC	Armed Forces Staff College
AGRICOLA	Agricultural OnLine Access
AIDS	Acquired Immune Deficiency Syndrome
AmeriCorps NCCC	AmeriCorps* National Civilian Community Corps
AMS	Agricultural Marketing Service
Amtrak	National Railroad Passenger Corporation
ANA	Administration for Native Americans
AOA	Administration on Aging
APHIS	Animal and Plant Health Inspection Service
ARC	Appalachian Regional Commission
ARPA	Advanced Research Projects Agency
ARS	Agricultural Research Service
ATSDR	Agency for Toxic Substances and Disease Registry
BEA	Bureau of Economic Analysis
BHRD	Bureau of Health Resources Development
BIA	Bureau of Indian Affairs
BIB	Board for International Broadcasting
BJA	Bureau of Justice Assistance
BJS	Bureau of Justice Statistics
BLM	Bureau of Land Management
BLMRCP	Bureau of Labor-Management Relations and Cooperative Programs
BLS	Bureau of Labor Statistics
BPA	Bonneville Power Administration
BSC's	Business Service Centers

783

BTS — Bureau of Transportation Statistics

BVA — Board of Veterans' Appeals

C⁴ — Command, Control, Communication, and Computer Systems

CALS/CE — Computer-Aided Acquisition and Logistic Support/Concurrent Engineering Program

CBO — Congressional Budget Office

CCC — Commodity Credit Corporation; Customs Cooperation Council

CCEA — Cabinet Council on Economic Affairs

CCR — Commission on Civil Rights

CDBG — Community Development Block Grants

CDC — Centers for Disease Control

CEA — Council of Economic Advisers

CEOS — Child Exploitation and Obscenity Section (Justice)

CEQ — Council on Environmental Quality

CFA — Commission of Fine Arts

CFR — *Code of Federal Regulations*

CFSA — Consolidated Farm Service Agency

CFTC — Commodity Futures Trading Commission

CG — Commanding General

CHAMPVA — Civilian Health and Medical Program of the Veterans Administration

CIDS — Computer Information Delivery Service

CIO — Central Imagery Office

C³I — Command, Control, Communications, and Intelligence

C⁴I — Communication, Command, Control, Computer, and Intelligence

CIA — Central Intelligence Agency

CIC — Consumer Information Center

CMHS — Center for Mental Health Services

CNO — Chief of Naval Operations

Conrail — Consolidated Rail Corporation

COPS — Office of Community Oriented Policing Service (Justice)

CPSC — Consumer Product Safety Commission

CRS — Congressional Research Service; Community Relations Service

CSA — Community Services Administration

CSAP — Center for Substance Abuse Prevention

CSAT — Center for Substance Abuse Treatment

CSREES — Cooperative State Research, Education, and Extension Service

CUFT — Center for the Utilization of Federal Technology

DA — Department of the Army

DAU — Defense Acquisition University

DCAA — Defense Contract Audit Agency

DCASR's — Defense Contract Administration Services Regions

DCMC — Defense Contract Management Command

DCS — Defense Communications System

DEA — Drug Enforcement Administration

DIA — Defense Intelligence Agency

DINFOS — Defense Information School

DIPEC — Defense Industrial Plant Equipment Center

DIS — Defense Investigative Service

DISA — Defense Information Services Activity; Defense Information Systems Agency

DISAM — Defense Institute of Security Assistance Management

DLA — Defense Logistics Agency

DLSA — Defense Legal Services Agency

DMA	Defense Mapping Agency	FCA	Farm Credit Administration
DMFO	Defense Medical Facilities Office	FCC	Federal Communications Commission
DMS	Defense Mapping School	FCIA	Foreign Credit Insurance Association
DMSA	Defense Medical Support Activity	FCIC	Federal Crop Insurance Corporation
DMSSC	Defense Medical Systems Support Center	FDA	Food and Drug Administration
DNA	Defense Nuclear Agency	FDIC	Federal Deposit
DOC	Department of Commerce		Insurance Corporation
DOD	Department of Defense	FEB's	Federal Executive Boards
DODDS	Department of Defense Dependents Schools	FEC	Federal Election Commission
DOE	Department of Energy	FEDRIP	Federal Research in Progress Database
DOL	Department of Labor	FEMA	Federal Emergency
DOT	Department of Transportation		Management Agency
DSAA	Defense Security Assistance Agency	FERC	Federal Energy Regulatory Commission
DSMC	Defense Systems Management Command	FFB	Federal Financing Bank
		FGIS	Federal Grain Inspection Service
DTSA	Defense Technology Security Administration	FHA	Federal Housing Administration
EDA	Economic Development Administration	FHWA	Federal Highway Administration
EEOC	Equal Employment Opportunity Commission	FIA	Federal Insurance Administration
EIA	Energy Information Administration	FIC	Federal Information Centers
EO	Executive order •	FIRS	Federal Information Relay Service
EOUSA	Executive Office for United States Attorneys	FICO	Financing Corporation
EPA	Environmental Protection Agency	FLETC	Federal Law Enforcement Training Center
EPIC	El Paso Intelligence Center	FLRA	Federal Labor Relations Authority
ERA	Economic Regulatory Administration	FMC	Federal Maritime Commission
ERS	Economic Research Service	FMCS	Federal Mediation and Conciliation Service
ES	Extension Service	FmHA	Farmers Home Administration
ESA	Employment Standards Administration	FMS	Financial Management Service
ETA	Employment and Training Administration	FNMA	Federal National Mortgage Association
Eximbank	Export-Import Bank of the United States	FOIA	Freedom of Information Act
FAA	Federal Aviation Administration	FOMC	Federal Open Market Committee
Farmer Mac	Federal Agricultural Mortgage Corporation	FPRS	Federal Property Resources Service
FAS	Foreign Agricultural Service	FR	*Federal Register*
FBI	Federal Bureau of Investigation	FRA	Federal Railroad Administration

FRS	Federal Reserve System	ICES	International Council for the Exploration of the Seas
FSIS	Food Safety and Inspection Service		
FSLIC	Federal Savings and Loan Insurance Corporation	ICO	International Coffee Organization
FSS	Federal Supply Service	IDA	International Development Association; Institute for Defense Analyses
FSTS	Federal Secure Telephone Service		
FTC	Federal Trade Commission	IDCA	United States International Development Cooperation Agency
FTS	Federal Telecommunications System		
FWS	Fish and Wildlife Service	IEVS	Income Eligibility Verification Systems
GAO	General Accounting Office	IFAD	International Fund for Agricultural Development
GATT	General Agreement on Tariffs and Trade		
GIPSA	Grain Inspection, Packers and Stockyards Administration	IFC	International Finance Corporation
		IGDOD	Inspector General, Department of Defense
GNMA	Government National Mortgage Association	IHA's	Indian Housing Authorities
GPO	Government Printing Office	IHS	Indian Health Service
GSA	General Services Administration	ILAB	Bureau of International Labor Affairs
HCFA	Health Care Financing Administration	ILO	International Labor Organization
HDS	Office of Human Development Services	IMF	International Monetary Fund
HHS	Department of Health and Human Services	IMS	Institute of Museum Services
HIV	Human Immunodeficiency Virus	INF	Intermediate-range nuclear forces
HRA	Health Resources Administration	INS	Immigration and Naturalization Service
HUD	Department of Housing and Urban Development	INTERPOL	International Criminal Police Organization
HUMINT	Defense Human Intelligence Service	IOM	International Organization for Migration
IAEA	International Atomic Energy Agency	IRMC	Information Resources Management College
IAF	Inter-American Foundation	IRMS	Information Resources Management Service
IBRD	International Bank for Reconstruction and Development	IRS	Internal Revenue Service
		ITA	International Trade Administration
ICAF	Industrial College of the Armed Forces	ITAR	International Traffic in Arms Regulations
ICAO	International Civil Aviation Organization	ITU	International Telecommunication Union
IDB	Inter-American Development Bank		
ICC	Interstate Commerce Commission	IVHS	Intelligent Vehicle-Highway System
		JAG	Judge Advocate General

JCWS   Joint and Combined Warfighting School

JCEWS   Joint Command, Control, and Electronic Warfare School

JCS   Joint Chiefs of Staff

JCSOS   Joint and Combined Staff Officer School

JCWS   Joint and Combined Warfighting School

JICST   Japan International Center of Science and Technology

JMIC   Joint Military Intelligence College

JTC³A   Joint Tactical Command, Control, and Communications Agency

MA   Maritime Administration

MASINT   Central Measurement and Signals Intelligence Office

MBDA   Minority Business Development Agency

MBFR   Mutual and balanced force reduction

MED   Office of Medical Services (State)

MHSS   Military Health Services System

MIGA   Multilateral Investment Guarantee Agency

MMS   Minerals Management Service

MSHA   Mine Safety and Health Administration

MSPB   Merit Systems Protection Board

MSSD   Model Secondary School for the Deaf

MTB   Materials Transportation Bureau

NARA   National Archives and Records Administration

NASA   National Aeronautics and Space Administration

NASS   National Agricultural Statistics Service

NATO   North Atlantic Treaty Organization

NBS   National Biological Service; National Bureau of Standards

NCB   National Cooperative Bank

NCC   National Coordinating Committee

NCI   National Cancer Institute

NCIC   National Cartographic Information Center

NCJRS   National Criminal Justice Reference Service

NCPC   National Capital Planning Commission

NCS   National Cemetery System

NCUA   National Credit Union Administration

NDU   National Defense University

NEH   National Endowment for the Humanities

NEL   National Engineering Laboratory

NHI   National Highway Institute

NHPRC   National Historical Publications and Records Commission

NHTSA   National Highway Traffic Safety Administration

NIC   National Institute of Corrections

NIE   National Institute of Education

NIH   National Institutes of Health

NIJ   National Institute of Justice

NIS   Naval Investigative Service

NIST   National Institute of Standards and Technology

NLM   National Library of Medicine

NLRB   National Labor Relations Board

NMCS   National Military Command System

NML   National Measurement Laboratory

NNMC   National Naval Medical Center

NOAA   National Oceanic and Atmospheric Administration

NOS   National Ocean Survey

NPS   National Park Service

NRC   Nuclear Regulatory Commission

NRCS   Natural Resources Conservation Service

NRWA   National Rural Water Association

NSA   National Security Agency

NSC   National Security Council

NSF   National Science Foundation

NSTL   National Space Technology Laboratories

NTIA   National Telecommunications and Information Administration

NTID   National Technical Institute for the Deaf

NTIS   National Technical Information Service (Commerce)

NTSB   National Transportation Safety Board

NWC   National War College

OA   Office of Administration

OAS   Organization of American States

OASTP   Office of the Assistant Secretary for Technology Policy

OCC   Office of the Comptroller of the Currency (Treasury)

OCDETF   Organized Crime Drug Enforcement Task Forces

OCHAMPUS   Office of Civilian Health and Medical Program of the Uniformed Services

OCS   Office of Community Services; Officer Candidate School; Outer Continental Shelf

OCSE   Office of Child Support Enforcement

OECD   Organization for Economic Cooperation and Development

OECI   Office of Economic Conversion (Commerce)

OES   Office of Employment Security

OFA   Office of Family Assistance

OFCC   Office of Federal Contract Compliance

OFM   Office of Financial Management

OFR   Office of the Federal Register

OGE   Office of Government Ethics

OGPS   Office of Grants and Program Systems

OJJDP   Office of Juvenile Justice and Delinquency Prevention

OJP   Office of Justice Programs

OMB   Office of Management and Budget

OMIS   Office of Management and Information Systems

OPFI   Office of Program and Fiscal Integrity

OPIC   Overseas Private Investment Corporation

OPM   Office of Personnel Management

OPO's   Organ procurement organizations

ORM   Office of Regional Management

ORR   Office of Refugee Relief; Office of Refugee Resettlement

OSC   Office of Special Counsel

OSCE   Office of Child Support Enforcement

OSDBU   Office of Small and Disadvantaged Business Utilization

OSF   Office of Space Flight

OSHA   Occupational Safety and Health Administration

OSHRC   Occupational Safety and Health Review Commission

OSM   Office of Surface Mining Reclamation and Enforcement

OSSD   Office of Space Systems Development

OSTP   Office of Science and Technology Policy

OT   Office of Transportation

OTA   Office of Technology Assessment; Office of Technical Assistance

OTAA   Office of Trade Adjustment Assistance

OTS   Office of Thrift Supervision

OVC   Office for Victims of Crime

OVI   Office of Voluntarism Initiatives

OWBO   Office of Women's Business Ownership

PADC   Pennsylvania Avenue Development Corporation

PAHO   Pan American Health Organization
PBGC   Pension Benefit Guaranty Corporation
PBS   Public Buildings Service
PCC   Panama Canal Commission
PHA's   Public Housing Agencies
PHS   Public Health Service
PLBB   Patent Licensing Bulletin Board
PRC   Postal Rate Commission
PTO   Patent and Trademark Office
PWBA   Pension and Welfare Benefits Administration
RBCDS   Rural Business and Cooperative Development Service
RDA   Rural Development Administration
REA   Rural Electrification Administration
REFCORP   Resolution Funding Corporation
RETRF   Rural Electrification and Telephone Revolving Fund
RFE   Radio Free Europe
RHCDS   Rural Housing and Community Development Service
RICO   Racketeer Influenced and Corrupt Organizations
RIT   Rochester Institute of Technology
RL   Radio Liberty
ROTC   Reserve Officer Training Corps
RRB   Railroad Retirement Board
RSA   Rehabilitation Services Administration
RSPA   Research and Special Programs Administration (Transportation)
RTB   Rural Telephone Bank
RTC   Resolution Trust Corporation
RUS   Rural Utilities Service
SAIF   Savings Association Insurance Fund
SAMHSA   Substance Abuse and Mental Health Services Administration
SAO   Smithsonian Astrophysical Observatory

SAVE   Systematic Alien Verification for Entitlement
SBA   Small Business Administration
SEC   Securities and Exchange Commission
SERC   Smithsonian Environmental Research Center
SGLI   Servicemen's Group Life Insurance
SIDS   Sudden Infant Death Syndrome
SITES   Smithsonian Institution Traveling Exhibition Service
SLS   Saint Lawrence Seaway Development Corporation
SPC   South Pacific Commission
SRDC   State Rural Development Councils
SSA   Social Security Administration
SSI   Supplemental Security Income Program
SSS   Selective Service System
START   Strategic arms reduction talks
Stat.   United States Statutes at Large
TDA   Trade and Development Agency
TFCS   Treasury Financial Communication System
TSI   Transportation Safety Institute
TVA   Tennessee Valley Authority
UDAG   Urban Development Action Grants
UIS   Unemployment Insurance Service
U.N.   United Nations [1]
UNESCO   United Nations Educational, Scientific and Cultural Organization
UNICEF   United Nations Children's Fund (formerly United Nations International Children's Emergency Fund)

---

[1] Acronyms for other U.N. agencies can be found under Selected Multilateral Organizations, beginning on page 769.

UNICOR	Federal Prison Industries, Inc.	USTTA	United States Travel and Tourism Administration
UPU	Universal Postal Union	VA	Department of Veterans Affairs
USA	United States Army		
USAF	United States Air Force	VETS	Veterans' Employment and Training Service
USAID	United States Agency for International Development	VGLI	Veterans Group Life Insurance
U.S.C.	United States Code	VISTA	Volunteers in Service to America
USCG	United States Coast Guard	VOA	Voice of America
USDA	United States Department of Agriculture	WAPA	Western Area Power Administration
		WHO	World Health Organization
USES	United States Employment Service	WHS	Washington Headquarters Services
USGS	United States Geological Survey	WIC	Special supplemental food program for Women, Infants, and Children
USIA	United States Information Agency		
USITC	United States International Trade Commission	WIN	Work Incentive program
		WMO	World Meteorological Organization
USMC	United States Marine Corps	WTO	World Tourism Organization
USN	United States Navy	WWMCCS	Worldwide Military Command and Control System
USNCB	United States National Central Bureau		
USRA	United States Railway Association	YCC	Youth Conservation Corps

APPENDIX C: Federal Executive Agencies Terminated, Transferred, or Changed in Name Subsequent to March 4, 1933

NOTE: Italicized terms indicate obsolete agencies, organizations, and entities. In most instances, explanatory remarks are written at those terms elsewhere in this appendix. Dates prior to March 4, 1933, are included to provide additional information about the agencies.

This appendix is indexed in a format considered to be useful to the reader. Entries are carried at the most significant term in their titles, or when there is more than one significant term, the entry is carried at the first significant term. Thus, **Bureau of the Budget** is found at **Budget, Bureau of the**, and **Bureau of Agricultural Engineering** is found at **Agricultural Engineering, Bureau of**. Reader comments on the format are encouraged and should be sent to the address shown on page IV of the *Manual*.

Accounts, Bureau of Functions transferred to *Bureau of Government Financial Operations* by Treasury Order 229 of Jan. 14, 1974.

Acquisition, Office of Under Secretary of Defense for Renamed Office of Under Secretary of Defense for Acquisition and Technology by act of Nov. 30, 1993 (107 Stat. 1728).

ACTION Established by Reorg. Plan No. 1 of 1971 (5 U.S.C. app.), effective July 1, 1971. Reorganized by act of Oct. 1, 1973 (87 Stat. 405). Functions relating to SCORE and ACT programs transferred to Small Business Administration by EO 11871 of July 18, 1975 (40 FR 30915). Functions exercised by the Director of ACTION prior to Mar. 31, 1995, transferred to the Corporation for National and Community Service (107 Stat. 888 and Proclamation 6662 of Apr. 4, 1994 (57 FR 16507)).

Acts of Congress *See* State Department

Advisory Board, Commission, Committee. *See other part of title*

Aeronautical Board Organized in 1916 by agreement of *War* and Navy Secretaries. Placed under supervision of President by military order of July 5, 1939. Dissolved by Defense Secretary's letter of July 27, 1948, and functions transferred to *Munitions Board* and *Research and Development Board*. Military order of July 5, 1939, revoked by military order of Oct. 18, 1948.

Aeronautics, Bureau of Established in Navy Department by act of July 12, 1921 (42 Stat. 140). Abolished by act of Aug. 18, 1959 (73 Stat. 395) and functions transferred to *Bureau of Naval Weapons*.

Aeronautics, National Advisory Committee for Established by act of Mar. 3, 1915 (38 Stat. 930). Terminated by act of July 29, 1958 (72 Stat. 432),

and functions transferred to National Aeronautics and Space Administration, established by same act.

Aeronautics Administration, Civil *See* Aeronautics Authority, Civil

Aeronautics Authority, Civil Established under act of June 23, 1938 (52 Stat. 973). Renamed *Civil Aeronautics Board* and Administrator transferred to Commerce Department by Reorg. Plan Nos. III and IV of 1940, effective June 30, 1940. Office of Administrator designated *Civil Aeronautics Administration* by Department Order 52 of Aug. 29, 1940. *Administration* transferred to *Federal Aviation Agency* by act of Aug. 23, 1958 (72 Stat. 810). Functions of *Board* under act of Aug. 23, 1958 (72 Stat. 775), transferred to National Transportation Safety Board by act of Oct. 15, 1966 (80 Stat. 931). Functions of *Board* terminated or transferred— effective in part Dec. 31, 1981; in part Jan. 1, 1983; and in part Jan. 1, 1985—by act of Aug. 23, 1958 (92 Stat. 1744). Most remaining functions transferred to Transportation Secretary, remainder to U.S. Postal Service. Termination of *Board* finalized by act of Oct. 4, 1984 (98 Stat. 1703).

Aeronautics Board, Civil *See* Aeronautics Authority, Civil

Aeronautics Branch Established in Commerce Department to carry out provisions of act of May 20, 1926 (44 Stat. 568). Renamed *Bureau of Air Commerce* by Secretary's administrative order of July 1, 1934. Personnel and property transferred to *Civil Aeronautics Authority* by EO 7959 of Aug. 22, 1938.

Aeronautics and Space Council, National Established by act of July 29, 1958 (72 Stat. 427). Abolished by Reorg. Plan No. 1 of 1973, effective June 30, 1973.

Agricultural Stabilization and Conservation Service Established on June 5, 1961, by Secretary of

791

Agriculture under authority of revised statutes (5 U.S.C. 301) and Reorg. Plan No. 2 of 1953 (5 U.S.C. app.). Abolished by Secretary's Memorandum 1010–1 dated October 20, 1994. Functions assumed by Consolidated Farm Service Agency.

Aging, Administration on   Established by *Health, Education, and Welfare Secretary* on Oct. 1, 1965, to carry out provisions of act of July 14, 1965 (79 Stat. 218). Reassigned to *Social and Rehabilitation Service* by Department reorganization of Aug. 15, 1967. Transferred to Office of Assistant Secretary for Human Development by Secretary's order of June 15, 1973. Transferred to the Office of the Secretary of Health and Human Services by Secretary's reorganization notice dated Apr. 15, 1991.

Aging, Federal Council on   Established by Presidential memorandum of Apr. 2, 1956. Reconstituted at Federal level by Presidential letter of Mar. 7, 1959, to *Health, Education, and Welfare Secretary*. Abolished by EO 11022 of May 15, 1962, which established *President's Council on Aging*.

Aging, Office of   Established by *Health, Education, and Welfare Secretary* June 2, 1955, as *Special Staff on Aging*. Terminated Sept. 30, 1965, and functions assumed by Administration on Aging.

Aging, President's Council on   Established by EO 11022 of May 14, 1962. Terminated by EO 11022, which was revoked by EO 12379 of Aug. 17, 1982.

Agricultural Adjustment Administration   Established by act of May 12, 1933 (48 Stat. 31). Consolidated into *Agricultural Conservation and Adjustment Administration* as *Agricultural Adjustment Agency*, Agriculture Department, by EO 9069 of Feb. 23, 1942. Grouped with other agencies to form *Food Production Administration* by EO 9280 of Dec. 5, 1942. Transferred to *War Food Administration* by EO 9322 of Mar. 26, 1943. Administration terminated by EO 9577 of June 29, 1945, and functions transferred to Agriculture Secretary. Transfer made permanent by Reorg. Plan No. 3 of 1946, effective July 16, 1946. Functions of *Agricultural Adjustment Agency* consolidated with *Production and Marketing Administration* by Secretary's Memorandum 1118 of Aug. 18, 1945.

Agricultural Adjustment Agency   *See Agricultural Adjustment Administration*

Agricultural Advisory Commission, National   Established by EO 10472 of July 20, 1953. Terminated Feb. 4, 1965, on resignation of members.

Agricultural Chemistry and Engineering, Bureau of   *See Agricultural Engineering, Bureau of*

Agricultural Conservation and Adjustment Administration   Established by EO 9069 of Feb. 23, 1942, consolidating *Agricultural Adjustment Agency, Sugar Agency, Federal Crop Insurance Corporation,* and *Soil Conservation Service.* Consolidated into *Food Production Administration* by EO 9280 of Dec. 5, 1942.

Agricultural Conservation Program Service   Established by Agriculture Secretary Jan. 21, 1953, from part of *Production and Marketing*

Administration. Merged with *Commodity Stabilization Service* by Secretary's Memorandum 1446, supp. 2, of Apr. 19, 1961.

Agricultural Developmental Service, International   Established by Agriculture Secretary's memorandum of July 12, 1963. Functions and delegations of authority transferred to Foreign Agricultural Service by Secretary's memorandum of Mar. 28, 1969. Functions transferred by Secretary to *Foreign Economic Development Service* Nov. 8, 1969.

Agricultural Economics, Bureau of   Established by act of May 11, 1931 (42 Stat. 532). Functions transferred to other units of Agriculture Department, including *Consumer and Marketing Service* and Agricultural Research Service, under Secretary's Memorandum 1320, supp. 4, of Nov. 2, 1953.

Agricultural Engineering, Bureau of   Established by act of Feb. 23, 1931 (46 Stat. 1266). Merged with *Bureau of Chemistry and Soils* by Secretarial order of Oct. 16, 1938, to form *Bureau of Agricultural Chemistry and Engineering.*

Agricultural and Industrial Chemistry, Bureau of   *Bureau of Chemistry* and *Bureau of Soils,* created in 1901, combined into *Bureau of Chemistry and Soils* by act of Jan. 18, 1927 (44 Stat. 976). Soils units transferred to other agencies of Agriculture Department and remaining units of *Bureau of Chemistry and Soils* and *Bureau of Agricultural Engineering* consolidated with *Bureau of Agricultural Chemistry and Engineering* by Secretary's order of Oct. 16, 1938. In February 1943 agricultural engineering research made part of *Bureau of Plant Industry, Soils, and Agricultural Engineering,* and organization for continuing agricultural chemistry research relating to crop utilization named *Bureau of Agricultural and Industrial Chemistry,* in accordance with *Research Administration* Memorandum 5 issued pursuant to EO 9069 of Feb. 23, 1942, and in conformity with Secretary's Memorandums 960 and 986. Functions transferred to *Agricultural Research Service* under Secretary's Memorandum 1320, supp. 4, of Nov. 2, 1953.

Agricultural Library, National   Established by Agriculture Secretary's Memorandum 1496 of Mar. 23, 1962. Consolidated into *Science and Education Administration* by Secretary's order of Jan. 24, 1978. Reestablished as National Agricultural Library by Secretary's order of June 16, 1981. Became part of Agricultural Research Service in 1994 under Department of Agriculture reorganization.

Agricultural Marketing Administration   Established by EO 9069 of Feb. 23, 1942, consolidating *Surplus Marketing Administration, Agricultural Marketing Service,* and *Commodity Exchange Administration. Division of Consumers' Counsel* transferred to *Administration* by Secretary's memorandum of Feb. 28, 1942. Consolidated into *Food Distribution Administration* in Agriculture Department by EO 9280 of Dec. 5, 1942.

Agricultural Marketing Service   Established by Agriculture Secretary pursuant to act of June 30, 1939 (53 Stat. 939). Merged into *Agricultural Marketing Administration* by EO 9069 of Feb. 23, 1942. Renamed *Consumer and Marketing Service* by

Secretary's Memorandum 1567, supp. 1, of Feb. 8, 1965. Reestablished as Agricultural Marketing Service by Agriculture Secretary on Apr. 2, 1972, under authority of Reorg. Plan No. 2 of 1953 (67 Stat. 633).

Agricultural Relations, Office of Foreign See **Agricultural Service, Foreign**

Agricultural Research Administration Established by EO 9069 of Feb. 23, 1942. Superseded by Agricultural Research Service.

Agricultural Research Service Established by Agriculture Secretary's Memorandum 1320, supp. 4, of Nov. 2, 1953. Consolidated into *Science and Education Administration* by Secretary's order of Jan. 24, 1978. Reestablished as Agricultural Research Service by Secretarial order of June 16, 1981.

Agricultural Service, Foreign Established by act of June 5, 1930 (46 Stat. 497). Economic research and agricultural attaché activities administered by *Foreign Agricultural Service Division, Bureau of Agricultural Economics,* until June 29, 1939. Transferred by Reorg. Plan No. II of 1939, effective July 1, 1939, from Agriculture Department to State Department. Economic research functions of *Division* transferred to *Office of Foreign Agricultural Relations* June 30, 1939. Functions of *Office* transferred to Foreign Agricultural Service Mar. 10, 1953. Agricultural attachés placed in Agriculture Department by act of Aug. 28, 1954 (68 Stat. 908).

Agricultural Stabilization and Conservation Service Established June 5, 1961, by the Secretary of Agriculture under authority of revised statutes (5 U.S.C. 301) and Reorg. Plan No. 2 of 1953 (5 U.S.C. app.). Abolished and functions assumed by the *Farm Service Agency* by Secretary's Memorandum 1010–1 dated Oct. 20, 1994 (59 FR 60297, 60299).

Agricultural Statistics Division Transferred to *Bureau of Agricultural Economics* by EO 9069 of Feb. 23, 1942.

Agriculture, Division of See **Farm Products, Division of**

Air Commerce, Bureau of See **Aeronautics Branch**

Air Coordinating Committee Established Mar. 27, 1945, by interdepartmental memorandum; formally established by EO 9781 of Sept. 19, 1946. Terminated by EO 10883 of Aug. 11, 1960, and functions transferred for liquidation to *Federal Aviation Agency.*

Air Force Management Engineering Agency Established in 1975 in Air Force as separate operating unit. Made subordinate unit of Air Force Military Personnel Center (formerly Air Force Manpower and Personnel Center) in 1978. Reestablished as separate operating unit of Air Force, effective Mar. 1, 1985, by Secretarial order.

Air Force Manpower and Personnel Center Certain functions transferred on activation of Air Force Management Engineering Agency, which was made separate operating unit from Air Force Manpower and Personnel Center (later Air Force Military Personnel Center) in April 1985 by general order of Chief of Staff.

Air Force Medical Service Center Renamed Air Force Office of Medical Support by Program Action Directive 85–1 of Mar. 6, 1985, approved by Air Force Vice Chief of Staff.

Air Mail, Bureau of Established in Interstate Commerce Commission to carry out provisions of act of June 12, 1934 (48 Stat. 933). Personnel and property transferred to *Civil Aeronautics Authority* by EO 7959 of Aug. 22, 1938.

Air Patrol, Civil Established in *Civilian Defense Office* by Administrative Order 9 of Dec. 8, 1941. Transferred to *War Department* as auxiliary of Army Air Forces by EO 9339 of Apr. 29, 1943. Transferred to Air Force Department by Defense Secretary's order of May 21, 1948. Established as civilian auxiliary of U.S. Air Force by act of May 26, 1948 (62 Stat. 274).

Air Safety Board Established by act of June 23, 1938 (52 Stat. 973). Functions transferred to *Civil Aeronautics Board* by Reorg. Plan No. IV of 1940, effective June 30, 1940.

Airways Modernization Board Established by act of Aug. 14, 1957 (71 Stat. 349). Transferred to *Federal Aviation Agency* by EO 10786 of Nov. 1, 1958.

Alaska, Board of Road Commissioners for Established in *War Department* by act of Jan. 27, 1905 (33 Stat. 616). Functions transferred to Interior Department by act of June 30, 1932 (47 Stat. 446), and delegated to *Alaska Road Commission.* Functions transferred to Commerce Department by act of June 29, 1956 (70 Stat. 377), and terminated by act of June 25, 1959 (73 Stat. 145).

Alaska, Federal Field Committee for Development Planning in Established by EO 11182 of Oct. 2, 1964. Abolished by EO 11608 of July 19, 1971.

Alaska, Federal Reconstruction and Development Planning Commission for Established by EO 11150 of Apr. 2, 1964. Abolished by EO 11182 of Oct. 2, 1964, which established *President's Review Committee for Development Planning in Alaska* and *Federal Field Committee for Development Planning in Alaska.*

Alaska, President's Review Committee for Development Planning in Established by EO 11182 of Oct. 2, 1964. Superseded by *Federal Advisory Council on Regional Economic Development* established by EO 11386 of Dec. 28, 1967. EO 11386 revoked by EO 12553 of Feb. 25, 1986.

Alaska Communication System Operational responsibility vested in Army Secretary by act of May 26, 1900 (31 Stat. 206). Transferred to Air Force Secretary by Defense Secretary's reorganization order of May 24, 1962.

Alaska Engineering Commission See **Alaska Railroad**

Alaska Game Commission Established by act of Jan. 13, 1925 (43 Stat. 740). Expired Dec. 31, 1959, pursuant to act of July 7, 1958 (72 Stat. 339).

Alaska International Rail and Highway Commission Established by act of Aug. 1, 1956 (70 Stat. 888). Terminated June 30, 1961, under terms of act.

Alaska Power Administration Established by Interior Secretary in 1967. Transferred to Energy Department by act of Aug. 4, 1977 (91 Stat. 578).

Alaska Railroad Built pursuant to act of Mar. 12, 1914 (38 Stat. 305), which created *Alaska Engineering Commission*. Placed under Interior Secretary by EO 2129 of Jan. 26, 1915, and renamed Alaska Railroad by EO 3861 of June 8, 1923. Authority to regulate tariffs granted to Interstate Commerce Commission by EO 11107 of Apr. 25, 1963. Authority to operate Railroad transferred to Transportation Secretary by act of Oct. 15, 1966 (80 Stat. 941), effective Apr. 1, 1967. Railroad purchased by State of Alaska, effective Jan. 5, 1985.

Alaska Road Commission *See* **Alaska, Board of Road Commissioners for**

Alcohol, Bureau of Industrial Established by act of May 27, 1930 (46 Stat. 427). Consolidated into *Bureau of Internal Revenue* by EO 6166 of June 10, 1933. Consolidation deferred until May 11, 1934, by EO 6639 of Mar. 10, 1934. Order also transferred to Internal Revenue Commissioner certain functions imposed on Attorney General by act of May 27, 1930, with relation to enforcement of criminal laws concerning intoxicating liquors remaining in effect after repeal of 18th amendment; personnel of, and appropriations for, *Bureau of Industrial Alcohol;* and necessary personnel and appropriations of *Bureau of Prohibition,* Justice Department.

Alcohol, Commissioner of Industrial Office created in Treasury Department by act of May 27, 1930 (46 Stat. 427). Abolished by EO 6639 of Mar. 10, 1934.

Alcohol, Drug Abuse, and Mental Health Administration Established by *Health, Education, and Welfare Secretary* by act of May 21, 1972 (88 Stat. 134). Functions transferred to Health and Human Services Department by act of Oct. 17, 1979 (93 Stat. 695). Established as an agency of the Public Health Service by act of Oct. 27, 1986 (100 Stat. 3207–106). Renamed Substance Abuse and Mental Health Services Administration by act of July 10, 1992 (106 Stat. 325).

Alcohol Abuse and Alcoholism, National Institute on Established within the National Institute of Mental Health, *Health, Education, and Welfare Department* by act of Dec. 31, 1970 (84 Stat. 1848). Removed from within the National Institute of Mental Health and made an entity within the Alcohol, Drug Abuse, and Mental Health Administration by act of May 14, 1974 (88 Stat. 1356). Functions transferred to Health and Human Services Department by act of Oct. 17, 1979 (93 Stat. 695). (*See also* act of Oct. 27, 1986; 100 Stat. 3207–106.) Abolished by act of July 10, 1992 (106 Stat. 331). Reestablished by act of July 10, 1992 (106 Stat. 359).

Alcohol Administration, Federal *See* **Alcohol Control Administration, Federal**

Alcohol Control Administration, Federal Established by EO 6474 of Dec. 4, 1933. Abolished Sept. 24, 1935, on induction into office of Administrator, *Federal Alcohol Administration,* as provided in act of Aug. 29, 1935 (49 Stat. 977). Abolished by Reorg. Plan No. III of 1940, effective June 30, 1940, and functions consolidated with activities of Internal Revenue Service.

Alexander Hamilton Bicentennial Commission Established by act of Aug. 20, 1954 (68 Stat. 746). Terminated Apr. 30, 1958.

Alien Property, Office of Transferred to Civil Division, Justice Department, by Attorney General Order 249–61 of Sept. 1, 1961. Abolished by EO 11281 of May 13, 1966, and foreign funds control functions transferred to Office of Foreign Assets Control, Treasury Department. Remaining functions continued by Civil Division, Justice Department. Remaining functions abolished by act of Aug. 23, 1988 (102 Stat. 1370).

Alien Property Custodian Appointed by President Oct. 22, 1917, under authority of act of Oct. 6, 1917 (40 Stat. 415). Office transferred to *Alien Property Division,* Justice Department, by EO 6694 of May 1, 1934. Powers vested in Attorney General by EO 8136 of May 15, 1939. Authority vested in Attorney General by EO's 6694 and 8136 transferred by EO 9142 of Apr. 21, 1942, to *Office of Alien Property Custodian, Office for Emergency Management,* as provided for by EO 9095 of Mar. 11, 1942.

Alien Property Custodian, Office of Established in *Office for Emergency Management* by EO 9095 of Mar. 11, 1942. Terminated by EO 9788 of Oct. 14, 1946, and functions transferred to Justice Department. Transfer made permanent by Reorg. Plan No. 1 of 1947, effective July 1, 1947.

Alien Property Division *See* **Alien Property Custodian**

American Republics, Office for Coordination of Commercial and Cultural Relations between the Established by *Council of National Defense* order approved by President Aug. 16, 1940. Succeeded by *Office of the Coordinator of Inter-American Affairs, Office for Emergency Management,* established by EO 8840 of July 30, 1941. Renamed *Office of Inter-American Affairs* by EO 9532 of Mar. 23, 1945. Information functions transferred to State Department by EO 9608 of Aug. 31, 1945. Terminated by EO 9710 of Apr. 10, 1946, and functions transferred to State Department, functioning as *Institute of Inter-American Affairs.* Transferred to *Foreign Operations Administration* by Reorg. Plan No. 7, effective Aug. 1, 1953.

American Revolution Bicentennial Administration *See* **American Revolution Bicentennial Commission**

American Revolution Bicentennial Commission Established by act of July 4, 1966 (80 Stat. 259). *American Revolution Bicentennial Administration* established by act of Dec. 11, 1973 (87 Stat. 697), to replace *Commission. Administration* terminated June 30, 1977, pursuant to terms of act. Certain continuing functions transferred to Interior Secretary by EO 12001 of June 29, 1977.

American Studies, Office of   Renamed American Studies Program by Smithsonian Institution administrative order in 1990.

Anacostia Neighborhood Museum   Renamed Anacostia Museum by Smithsonian Institution announcement of Apr. 3, 1987.

Animal Industry, Bureau of   Established in Agriculture Department by act of May 29, 1884 (23 Stat. 31). Functions transferred to Agricultural Research Service by Secretary's Memorandum 1320, supp. 4, of Nov. 2, 1953.

Apprenticeship, Federal Committee on   Previously known as *Federal Committee on Apprentice Training,* established by EO 6750–C of June 27, 1934. Functioned as part of *Division of Labor Standards,* Labor Department, established as of Aug. 16, 1937 (50 Stat. 664). Transferred to *Office of Administrator, Federal Security Agency,* by EO 9139 of Apr. 18, 1942. Transferred to *Bureau of Training, War Manpower Commission,* by EO 9247 of Sept. 17, 1942. Returned to Labor Department by EO 9617 of Sept. 19, 1945.

Architect, Office of the Supervising   *See* Construction Branch

Archive of Folksong   Renamed Archive of Folk Culture by administrative order of Deputy Librarian of Congress, effective Sept. 21, 1981.

Archives Council, National   Established by act of June 19, 1934 (48 Stat. 1122). Transferred to General Services Administration by act of June 30, 1949 (63 Stat. 378). Terminated on establishment of Federal Records Council by act of Sept. 5, 1950 (64 Stat. 583).

Archives Establishment, National   *Office of Archivist of the U.S.* and *National Archives* created by act of June 19, 1934 (48 Stat. 1122). Transferred to General Services Administration by act of June 30, 1949 (63 Stat. 381), and incorporated as *National Archives and Records Service* by order of General Services Administrator, together with functions of *Division of the Federal Register, National Archives Council, National Historical Publications Commission,* National Archives Trust Fund Board, *Trustees of the Franklin D. Roosevelt Library,* and Administrative Committee of the Federal Register. Transferred from General Services Administration to National Archives and Records Administration by act of Oct. 19, 1984 (98 Stat. 2283), along with certain functions of Administrator of General Services transferred to Archivist of the United States, effective Apr. 1, 1985.

Archives and Records Service, National   *See* Archives Establishment, National

Archives Trust Fund Board, National   *See* Archives Establishment, National

Area Redevelopment Administration   Established May 8, 1961, by Commerce Secretary pursuant to act of May 1, 1961 (75 Stat. 47) and Reorg. Plan No. 5 of 1950, effective May 24, 1950. Terminated

Aug. 31, 1965, by act of June 30, 1965 (79 Stat. 195). Functions transferred to Economic Development Administration in Commerce Department by Department Order 4–A, effective Sept. 1, 1965.

Arlington Memorial Amphitheater Commission   Established by act of Mar. 4, 1921 (41 Stat. 1440). Abolished by act of Sept. 2, 1960 (74 Stat. 739), and functions transferred to Defense Secretary.

Arlington Memorial Bridge Commission   Established by act of Mar. 4, 1913 (37 Stat. 885; D.C. Code (1951 ed.) 8–158). Abolished by EO 6166 of June 10, 1933, and functions transferred to *Office of National Parks, Buildings, and Reservations.*

Armed Forces Medical Library   Founded in 1836 as *Library of the Surgeon General's Office,* U.S. Army. Later known as *Army Medical Library,* then *Armed Forces Medical Library* in 1952. Personnel and property transferred to National Library of Medicine established in Public Health Service by act of Aug. 3, 1956 (70 Stat. 960).

Armed Forces Museum Advisory Board, National   Established by act of Aug. 30, 1961 (75 Stat. 414). Functions discontinued due to lack of funding.

Armed Services Renegotiation Board   Established by Defense Secretary's directive of July 19, 1948. Abolished by Defense Secretary's letter of Jan. 18, 1952, and functions transferred to *Renegotiation Board.*

Army, Communications Command, U.S.   Renamed U.S. Army Information Systems Command by Department General Order No. 26 of July 25, 1984.

Army Materiel Development and Readiness Command, U.S.   Renamed U.S. Army Materiel Command by Department General Order No. 28 of Aug. 15, 1984.

Army and Navy, Joint Board   Placed under direction of President by military order of July 5, 1939. Abolished Sept. 1, 1947, by joint letter of Aug. 20, 1947, to President from Secretaries of *War* and *Navy.*

Army and Navy Staff College   Established Apr. 23, 1943, and operated under Joint Chiefs of Staff. Redesignated the National War College, effective July 1, 1946.

Army Specialist Corps   Established in *War Department* by EO 9078 of Feb. 26, 1942. Abolished by *War Secretary* Oct. 31, 1942, and functions merged into central *Officer Procurement Service.*

Arthritis, Diabetes, and Digestive and Kidney Diseases, National Institute of   *See* **Arthritis, Metabolism, and Digestive Diseases, National Institute of**

Arthritis, Metabolism, and Digestive Diseases, National Institute of   Renamed *National Institute of Arthritis, Diabetes, and Digestive and Kidney Diseases* by Secretary's order of June 15, 1981, pursuant to act of Dec. 19, 1980 (94 Stat. 3184).

Renamed National Institute of Diabetes and Digestive and Kidney Diseases and National Institute of Arthritis and Musculoskeletal and Skin Diseases by act of Nov. 20, 1985 (99 Stat. 820).

Arts, Advisory Committee on the Established under authority of act of Sept. 20, 1961 (75 Stat. 527). Terminated July 1973 by act of Oct. 6, 1972. Formally abolished by Reorg. Plan No. 2 of 1977, effective Apr. 1, 1978.

Arts, National Council on the Established in Executive Office of the President by act of Sept. 3, 1964 (78 Stat. 905). Transferred to National Foundation on the Arts and the Humanities by act of Sept. 29, 1965 (79 Stat. 845).

Assay Commission, Annual Established initially by act of Apr. 2, 1792 (1 Stat. 250) and by act of Feb. 12, 1873 (Revised Statute sec. 3647; 17 Stat. 432). Terminated and functions transferred to Treasury Secretary by act of Mar. 14, 1980 (94 Stat. 98).

Assistance, Bureau of Public Renamed *Bureau of Family Services* by order of *Health, Education, and Welfare Secretary,* effective Jan. 1, 1962. Functions redelegated to *Social and Rehabilitation Service* by Secretary's reorganization of Aug. 15, 1967.

Assistance Coordinating Committee, Adjustment Established by act of Jan. 3, 1975 (88 Stat. 2040). Inactive since 1981.

Assistance Payments Administration Established by *Health, Education, and Welfare Secretary's* reorganization of Aug. 15, 1967. Transferred by *Secretary's* reorganization of Mar. 8, 1977 (42 FR 13262), from *Social and Rehabilitation Service* to Social Security Administration.

Athletics, Interagency Committee on International Established by EO 11117 of Aug. 13, 1963. Terminated by EO 11515 of Mar. 13, 1970.

Atlantic-Pacific Interoceanic Canal Study Commission Established by act of Sept. 22, 1964 (78 Stat. 990). Terminated Dec. 1, 1970, pursuant to terms of act.

Atomic Energy Commission Established by act of Aug. 1, 1946 (60 Stat. 755). Abolished by act of Oct. 11, 1974 (88 Stat. 1237) and functions transferred to *Energy Research and Development Administration* and Nuclear Regulatory Commission.

Aviation, Interdepartmental Committee on Civil International Established by Presidential letter of June 20, 1935. Terminated on organization of *Civil Aeronautics Authority.*

Aviation Agency, Federal Established by act of Aug. 23, 1958 (72 Stat. 731). Transferred to Transportation Secretary by act of Oct. 15, 1966 (80 Stat. 931). *Agency* reestablished as Federal Aviation Administration by act of Jan 12, 1983 (96 Stat. 2416).

Aviation Commission, Federal Established by act of June 12, 1934 (48 Stat. 938). Terminated Feb. 1, 1935, under provisions of act.

Beltsville Research Center Established to operate with other agencies of Agriculture Department under

Agricultural Research Administration. Consolidated into *Agricultural Research Administration,* Agriculture Department, by EO 9069 of Feb. 23, 1942.

Biological Survey, Bureau of Established by Secretary's order July 1, 1885, as part of *Division of Entomology,* Agriculture Department. Made separate bureau by act of Apr. 23, 1904 (33 Stat. 276). Transferred to Interior Department by Reorg. Plan No. II of 1939, effective July 1, 1939. Consolidated with *Bureau of Fisheries* into *Fish and Wildlife Service* by Reorg. Plan No. III of 1940, effective June 30, 1940.

Biological Survey, National Established in the Interior Department by Secretarial Order 3173 of Sept. 29, 1993. Renamed National Biological Service by Secretarial order in 1995.

Blind, Inc., American Printing House for the Established in 1858 as privately owned institution in Louisville, KY. Functions of Treasury Secretary, except that relating to perpetual trust funds, transferred to *Federal Security Agency* by Reorg. Plan No. II of 1939, effective July 1, 1939. Functions performed by *Health, Education, and Welfare Department* transferred to Education Department.

Blind-made Products, Committee on Purchases of Established by act of June 25, 1938 (52 Stat. 1196). Renamed *Committee for Purchase of Products and Services of the Blind and Other Severely Handicapped* by act of June 23, 1971 (85 Stat. 77). Renamed *Committee for Purchase from the Blind and Other Severely Handicapped* by act of July 25, 1974 (88 Stat. 392). Renamed Committee for Purchase From People Who Are Blind or Severely Disabled by act of Oct. 29, 1992 (106 Stat. 4486).

Blind and Other Severely Handicapped, Committee for Purchase of Products and Services of the See **Blind-made Products, Committee on Purchases of**

Blockade and Supply Division Established by State departmental order of Aug. 27, 1943, in *Office of Foreign Economic Coordination.* Office abolished by departmental order of Nov. 6, 1943, pursuant to EO 9380 of Sept. 25, 1943, which established *Foreign Economic Administration.*

Board. See other part of title

Bond and Spirits Division Established as *Taxes and Penalties Unit,* as announced by Assistant to Attorney General in departmental circular of May 25, 1934, pursuant to EO 6639 of May 10, 1934. Abolished by administrative order of October 1942, and functions transferred to Tax, Claims, and Criminal Divisions, Justice Department.

Bonneville Power Administration Established by Interior Secretary pursuant to act of Aug. 20, 1937 (50 Stat. 731). Transferred to Energy Department by act of Aug. 4, 1977 (91 Stat. 578).

Boston National Historic Sites Commission Established by joint resolution of June 16, 1955 (69 Stat. 137). Terminated June 16, 1960, by act of Feb. 19, 1957 (71 Stat. 4).

Brazil-U.S. Defense Commission, Joint Established in May 1942 by agreement between the U.S. and Brazil. Terminated in September 1977 at direction of Brazilian Government.

Broadcast Bureau Merged with *Cable Television Bureau* to form Mass Media Bureau by Federal Communications Commission order, effective Nov. 30, 1982.

Broadcast Intelligence Service, Foreign *See* Broadcast Monitoring Service, Foreign

Broadcast Monitoring Service, Foreign Established in Federal Communications Commission by Presidential directive of Feb. 26, 1941. Renamed *Foreign Broadcast Intelligence Service* by FCC order of July 28, 1942. Transferred to *War Department* by Secretarial order of Dec. 30, 1945. Act of May 3, 1945 (59 Stat. 110), provided for liquidation 60 days after Japanese armistice. Transferred to *Central Intelligence Group* Aug. 5, 1946, and renamed *Foreign Broadcast Information Service.*

Budget, Bureau of the Established by act of June 10, 1921 (42 Stat. 20), in Treasury Department under immediate direction of President. Transferred to Executive Office of the President by Reorg. Plan No. I of 1939, effective July 1, 1939. Reorganized by Reorg. Plan No. 2 of 1970, effective July 1, 1970, and renamed Office of Management and Budget.

Buildings Administration, Public Established as part of *Federal Works Agency* by Reorg. Plan No. I of 1939, effective July 1, 1939. Abolished by act of June 30, 1949 (63 Stat. 380), and functions transferred to General Services Administration.

Buildings Branch, Public Organized in *Procurement Division*, established in Treasury Department by EO 6166 of June 10, 1933. Consolidated with *Branch of Buildings Management*, National Park Service, to form *Public Buildings Administration, Federal Works Agency*, under Reorg. Plan No. I of 1939, effective July 1, 1939.

Buildings Commission, Public Established by act of July 1, 1916 (39 Stat. 328). Abolished by EO 6166 of June 10, 1933, and functions transferred to *Office of National Parks, Buildings, and Reservations*, Interior Department. Functions transferred to *Public Buildings Administration, Federal Works Agency*, under Reorg. Plan No. I of 1939, effective July 1, 1939.

Buildings Management, Branch of Functions of National Park Service (except those relating to monuments and memorials) consolidated with *Public Buildings Branch, Procurement Division*, Treasury Department, to form *Public Buildings Administration, Federal Works Agency*, in accordance with Reorg. Plan No. I of 1939, effective July 1, 1939.

Buildings and Public Parks of the National Capital, Office of Public Established by act of Feb. 26, 1925 (43 Stat. 983), by consolidation of *Office of Public Buildings and Grounds* under Chief of Engineers, U.S. Army, and *Office of Superintendent of State, War, and Navy Department Buildings.* Abolished by EO 6166 of June 10, 1933, and

functions transferred to *Office of National Parks, Buildings, and Reservations*, Interior Department.

Bureau. *See other part of title*

Business, Cabinet Committee on Small Established by Presidential letter of May 31, 1956. Dissolved January 1961.

Business Administration, Domestic and International *See* Business and Defense Services Administration

Business Cooperation, Division of Established in *National Recovery Administration* by EO 7075 of June 15, 1935. Transferred to Commerce Department by EO 7252 of Dec. 21, 1935. By same order, functions of *Division* ordered terminated by Apr. 1, 1936. *Committee of Industrial Analysis* created by EO 7323 of Mar. 21, 1936, to complete work of *Division.*

Business and Defense Services Administration Established by Commerce Secretary Oct. 1, 1953, and operated under Department Organization Order 40–1. Abolished by Department Organization Order 40–1A of Sept. 15, 1970, and functions transferred to *Bureau of Domestic Commerce.* Functions transferred to *Domestic and International Business Administration*, effective Nov. 17, 1972. *Administration* terminated by Secretary's order of Dec. 4, 1977, and functions assumed by *Industry and Trade Administration.*

Business Economics, Office of Established by Commerce Secretary Jan. 17, 1946. Renamed *Office of Economic Analysis* Dec. 1, 1953. Transferred to *Social and Economic Statistics Administration* along with Bureau of the Census and renamed Bureau of Economic Analysis on Jan. 1, 1972.

Business Operations, Bureau of International Established by Commerce Secretary Aug. 8, 1961, by Departmental Orders 173 and 174. Abolished by Departmental Order 182 of Feb. 1, 1963, which established *Bureau of International Commerce.* Functions transferred to *Domestic and International Business Administration*, effective Nov. 17, 1972.

Cable Television Bureau Merged with *Broadcast Bureau* by Federal Communications Commission order to form Mass Media Bureau, effective Nov. 30, 1982.

California Debris Commission Established by act of Mar. 1, 1893 (27 Stat. 507). Abolished by act of Nov. 17, 1986 (100 Stat. 4229), and functions transferred to Interior Secretary.

Canal Zone Government Established by act of Aug. 24, 1912 (37 Stat. 561). Abolished by act of Sept. 27, 1979 (93 Stat. 454).

Capital Housing Authority, National Established by act of June 12, 1934 (48 Stat. 930). Made agency of District of Columbia government by act of Dec. 24, 1973 (87 Stat. 779), effective July 1, 1974.

Capital Park Commission, National Established by act of June 6, 1924 (43 Stat. 463). *National Capital Park and Planning Commission* named successor by act of Apr. 30, 1926 (44 Stat. 374). Functions transferred to National Capital Planning Commission by act of July 19, 1952 (66 Stat. 781).

Capital Park and Planning Commission, National See Capital Park Commission, National

Capital Regional Planning Council, National Established by act of July 19, 1952 (66 Stat. 785). Terminated by Reorg. Plan No. 5 of 1966, effective Sept. 8, 1966.

Capital Transportation Agency, National Established by act of July 14, 1960 (74 Stat 537). Authorized to establish rapid rail transit system by act of Sept. 8, 1965 (79 Stat. 663). Functions transferred to Washington Metropolitan Area Transit Authority by EO 11373 of Sept. 20, 1967.

Career Executive Board Established by EO 10758 of Mar. 4, 1958. Terminated July 1, 1959, and EO 10758 revoked by EO 10859 of Feb. 5, 1960.

Caribbean Organization Act of June 30, 1961 (75 Stat. 194), provided for acceptance by President of Agreement for the Establishment of the Caribbean Organization, signed at Washington, June 21, 1960. Article III of Agreement provided for termination of Caribbean Commission, authorized by Agreement signed Oct. 30, 1946, on first meeting of Caribbean Council, governing body of Organization. Terminated, effective Dec. 31, 1965, by resolution adopted by Council.

Cemeteries and Memorials in Europe, National Supervision transferred from War Department to American Battle Monuments Commission by EO 6614 of Feb. 26, 1934, which transfer was deferred to May 21, 1934, by EO 6690 of Apr. 25, 1934.

Cemeteries and Parks, National War Department functions regarding National Cemeteries and Parks located in continental U.S. transferred to Office of National Parks, Buildings, and Reservations, Interior Department, by EO 6166 of June 10, 1933.

Censorship, Office of Established by EO 8985 of Dec. 19, 1941. Terminated by EO 9631 of Sept. 28, 1945.

Censorship Policy Board Established by EO 8985 of Dec. 19, 1941. Terminated by EO 9631 of Sept. 28, 1945.

Census, Bureau of the See Census Office

Census Office Established temporarily within the Interior Department in accordance with act of Mar. 3, 1899. Established as a permanent office by act of Mar. 6, 1902. Transferred from Interior Department to Department of Commerce and Labor by act of Feb. 14, 1903. Remained in Commerce Department under provisions of Reorganization Plan No. 5 of May 24, 1950, effective May 24, 1950.

Center. See other part of title

Central. See other part of title

Chemistry and Soils, Bureau of See Agricultural and Industrial Chemistry, Bureau of

Chesapeake Bay Center for Environmental Studies Established in 1965 in Annapolis, MD, as part of

Smithsonian Institution by Secretarial order. Merged with Radiation Biology Laboratory by Secretarial Order July 1, 1983, to form Smithsonian Environmental Research Center.

Child Development, Office of See Children's Bureau

Child Support Enforcement, Office of Established in Health, Education, and Welfare Department by act of Jan. 4, 1975 (88 Stat. 2351). Replaced by Family Support Administration.

Children's Bureau Established by act of Apr. 9, 1912 (37 Stat. 79). Placed in Labor Department by act of Mar. 4, 1913 (37 Stat. 737). Transferred, with exception of child labor functions, to Social Security Administration, Federal Security Agency, by Reorg. Plan No. 2 of 1946, effective July 16, 1946. Continued under Administration when Agency functions assumed by Health, Education, and Welfare Department. Reassigned to Welfare Administration by Department reorganization of Jan. 28, 1963. Reassigned to Social and Rehabilitation Service by Department reorganization of Aug. 15, 1967. Reassigned to Office of Child Development by Department reorganization order of Sept. 17, 1969.

China, U.S. Court for Established by act of June 30, 1906 (34 Stat. 814). Transferred to Justice Department by EO 6166 of June 10, 1933, effective Mar. 2, 1934. Act of June 30, 1906, repealed effective Sept. 1, 1948 (62 Stat. 992).

Christopher Columbus Quincentenary Jubilee Commission Established by act of Aug. 7, 1984 (98 Stat. 1257). Terminated pursuant to terms of act.

Civil defense. See Defense

Civil Rights, Commission on Established by act of Sept. 9, 1957 (71 Stat. 634). Terminated in 1983 and reestablished by act of Nov. 30, 1983 (97 Stat. 1301). Renamed United States Commission on Civil Rights by act of Nov. 2, 1994 (108 Stat. 4683).

Civil Service Commission, U.S. Established by act of Jan. 16, 1883 (22 Stat. 403). Redesignated as Merit Systems Protection Board and functions transferred to Board and Office of Personnel Management by Reorg. Plan No. 2 of 1978, effective Jan. 1, 1979.

Civil War Centennial Commission Established by act of Sept. 7, 1957 (71 Stat. 626). Terminated May 1, 1966, pursuant to terms of act.

Civilian Conservation Corps Established by act of June 28, 1937 (50 Stat. 319). Made part of Federal Security Agency by Reorg. Plan No. I of 1939, effective July 1, 1939. Liquidation provided for by act of July 2, 1942 (56 Stat. 569), not later than June 30, 1943.

Civilian Production Administration Established by EO 9638 of Oct. 4, 1945. Consolidated with other agencies to form Office of Temporary Controls, Office for Emergency Management, by EO 9809 of Dec. 12, 1946.

Civilian Service Awards Board, Distinguished Established by EO 10717 of June 27, 1957.

Terminated by EO 12014 of Oct. 19, 1977, and functions transferred to *U.S. Civil Service Commission.*

Claims, U.S. Court of Established Feb. 25, 1855 (10 Stat. 612). Abolished by act of Apr. 2, 1982 (96 Stat. 26) and trial jurisdiction transferred to *U.S. Claims Court* and appellate functions merged with those of *U.S. Court of Customs and Patent Appeals* to form U.S. Court of Appeals for the Federal Circuit. *U.S. Claims Court* renamed U.S. Court of Federal Claims by act of Oct. 29, 1992 (106 Stat. 4516).

Claims Commission of the United States, International Established in State Department by act of Mar. 10, 1950 (64 Stat. 12). Abolished by Reorg. Plan No. 1 of 1954, effective July 1, 1954, and functions transferred to Foreign Claims Settlement Commission of the United States.

Claims Settlement Commission of the United States, Foreign Established by Reorg. Plan No. 1 of 1954, effective July 1, 1954. Transferred to Justice Department by act of Mar. 14, 1980 (94 Stat. 96).

Clark Sesquicentennial Commission, George Rogers Established by Public Resolution 51 (45 Stat. 723). Expenditures ordered administered by Interior Department by EO 6166 of June 10, 1933.

Classification Review Committee, Interagency Established by EO 11652 of Mar. 8, 1972. Abolished by EO 12065 of June 28, 1978.

Clemency Board, Presidential Established in Executive Office of the President by EO 11803 of Sept. 16, 1974. Final recommendations submitted to President Sept. 15, 1975, and *Board* terminated by EO 11878 of Sept. 10, 1975.

Coal Commission, National Bituminous Established under authority of act of Aug. 30, 1935 (49 Stat. 992). Abolished by Reorg. Plan No. II of 1939, effective July 1, 1939, and functions transferred to *Bituminous Coal Division,* Interior Department.

Coal Consumers' Counsel, Office of the Bituminous Established by act of Apr. 11, 1941 (55 Stat. 134), renewing provisions of act of Apr. 23, 1937 (50 Stat. 72) for 2 years to continue functions of *Consumers' Counsel Division,* Interior Department. Functions continued by acts of Apr. 24, 1943 (57 Stat. 68), and May 21, 1943 (57 Stat. 82). Terminated Aug. 24, 1943.

Coal Division, Bituminous Established July 1, 1939, by Interior Secretary's Order 1394 of June 16, 1939, as amended by Order 1399, of July 5, 1939, pursuant to act of Apr. 3, 1939 (53 Stat. 562) and Reorg. Plan No. II of 1939, effective July 1, 1939. Administered functions vested in *National Bituminous Coal Commission* by act of Apr. 23, 1937 (50 Stat. 72). Act extended to Aug. 24, 1943, on which date it expired.

Coal Labor Board, Bituminous Established by act of July 12, 1921 (42 Stat. 140). Abolished as result of U.S. Supreme Court decision, May 18, 1936, in case of *Carter* v. *Carter Coal Company et al.*

Coal Leasing Planning and Coordination, Office of Established Mar. 22, 1978, by Interior Departmental

Manual Release 2075. Abolished Aug. 4, 1981, by Departmental Manual Release 2342.

Coal Mine Safety Board of Review, Federal Established by act of July 16, 1952 (66 Stat. 697). Inactive after Mar. 30, 1970, pursuant to act of Dec. 30, 1969 (83 Stat. 803).

Coal Mines Administration Established by Interior Secretary July 1, 1943. Abolished by Secretary's Order 1977 of Aug. 16, 1944, as amended by Order 1982 of Aug. 31, 1944, and functions assumed by *Solid Fuels Administration for War. Administration* reestablished in Interior Department by EO 9728 of May 21, 1946. Terminated June 30, 1947, by act of Mar. 27, 1942 (56 Stat. 176).

Coal Research, Office of Established in Interior Department by act of July 7, 1960 (74 Stat. 336). Functions transferred to *Energy Research and Development Administration* by act of Oct. 11, 1974 (88 Stat. 1237).

Coast and Geodetic Survey *See* Coast Survey

Coast Guard, U.S. Transferred from Treasury Department to Navy Department by EO 8929 of Nov. 1, 1941. Returned to Treasury Department by EO 9666 of Dec. 28, 1945. Transferred to Transportation Department by act of Oct. 15, 1966 (80 Stat. 931).

Coast Survey Established by act of Feb. 10, 1807 (2 Stat. 413). Redesignated as *Coast and Geodetic Survey* by act of June 20, 1878 (20 Stat. 206). Transferred to *Environmental Science Services Administration* by Reorg. Plan No. 2 of 1965, effective July 13, 1965.

Codification Board Established by act of June 19, 1937 (50 Stat. 304). Abolished by Reorg. Plan No. II of 1939, effective July 1, 1939, and functions transferred to *Division of the Federal Register.*

Coinage, Joint Commission on the Established by act of July 23, 1965 (79 Stat. 258). Expired Jan. 4, 1975, pursuant to act of Oct. 6, 1972 (88 Stat. 776).

Collection of Fine Arts, National Established within Smithsonian Institution by act of Mar. 24, 1937 (50 Stat. 51). Renamed National Museum of American Art in Smithsonian Institution by act of Oct. 13, 1980 (94 Stat. 1884).

Columbia Institution for the Instruction of the Deaf and Dumb, and the Blind Established by act of Feb. 16, 1857 (11 Stat. 161). Renamed *Columbia Institution for the Instruction of the Deaf and Dumb* by act of Feb. 23, 1865 (13 Stat. 436). Renamed *Columbia Institution for the Deaf* by act of Mar. 4, 1911 (36 Stat. 1422). Renamed *Gallaudet College* by act of June 18, 1954 (68 Stat. 265). Functions of *Health, Education, and Welfare Department* transferred to Education Department by act of Oct. 17, 1979 (93 Stat. 695). Renamed Gallaudet University by act of Aug. 4, 1986 (100 Stat. 781).

Commander in Chief, U.S. Fleet, and Chief of Naval Operations Duties of two positions prescribed by EO 8984 of Dec. 18, 1941. Combined under one officer by EO 9096 of Mar. 12, 1942.

Commerce, Bureau of Domestic   *See* **Business and Defense Services Administration**

Commerce, Bureau of Foreign   Established by Commerce Secretary Oct. 12, 1953, by Reorg. Plan No. 5 of 1950, effective May 24, 1950. Abolished by department order of Aug. 7, 1961, and functions vested in *Bureau of International Programs* and *Bureau of International Business Operations.*

Commerce, Bureau of Foreign and Domestic   Established by act of Aug. 23, 1912 (37 Stat. 407). Functions reassigned to other offices of Commerce Department due to internal reorganizations.

Commerce, Bureau of International   *See* **Business Operations, Bureau of International**

Commerce Commission, Interstate   Certain functions as cited in act of Oct. 15, 1966 (80 Stat. 931) transferred to Commerce Secretary. Functions relating to railroad and pipeline safety transferred to Federal Railroad Administrator and motor carrier safety to Federal Highway Administrator by act.

Commerce Department, Solicitor for   Transferred from Justice Department to Commerce Department by EO 6166 of June 10, 1933.

Commerce Service, Foreign   Established in *Bureau of Foreign and Domestic Commerce,* Commerce Department, by act of Mar. 3, 1927 (44 Stat. 1394). Transferred to State Department as part of Foreign Service by Reorg. Plan No. II of 1939, effective July 1, 1939.

Commercial Company, U.S.   Established Mar. 27, 1942, as subsidiary of *Reconstruction Finance Corporation.* Transferred to *Office of Economic Warfare* by EO 9361 of July 15, 1943. *Office* consolidated into *Foreign Economic Administration* by EO 9380 of Sept. 25, 1943. Functions returned to *Corporation* by EO 9630 of Sept. 27, 1945, until June 30, 1948.

Commercial Policy, Executive Committee on   Established by Presidential letter of Nov. 11, 1933, to Secretary of State. Abolished by EO 9461 of Aug. 7, 1944.

Commercial Services, Office of Foreign   Established by Commerce Secretary Feb. 1, 1963, and operated under Department Organization Order 40–4. Abolished Sept. 15, 1970, by Department Organization Order 40–2A and functions transferred to Bureau of International Commerce.

Commercial Standards Division   Transferred with *Division of Simplified Trade Practice* from *National Bureau of Standards* to Commerce Secretary by Reorg. Plan No. 3 of 1946, effective July 16, 1946, to permit reassignment to *Office of Domestic Commerce.* Functions transferred to *National Bureau of Standards* by Commerce Department Order 90, June 7, 1963, pursuant to Reorg. Plan No. 5 of 1950, effective May 24, 1950.

Commission.   *See other part of title*

Committee.   *See also other part of title*

Committee Management Secretariat   Established in Office of Management and Budget Jan. 5, 1973, by

act of Oct. 6, 1972 (86 Stat. 772). Functions transferred to General Services Administrator by Reorg. Plan No. 1 of 1977, effective Apr. 1, 1978. Reassigned to *National Archives and Records Service* by GSA order of Feb. 22, 1979. Transferred in Archives to Office of the Federal Register by GSA order of Oct. 14, 1980. Transferred to Office of the Archivist of the United States by GSA order of Sept. 24, 1982. Reassigned to Office of Program Initiatives, GSA, by GSA order of May 18, 1984. Transferred to Office of Management Services, GSA, by GSA order of Apr. 7, 1986.

Commodities Corporation, Federal Surplus   *See* **Relief Corporation, Federal Surplus**

Commodity Credit Corporation   Organized by EO 6340 of Oct. 16, 1933, and managed in close affiliation with *Reconstruction Finance Corporation.* Transferred to Agriculture Department by Reorg. Plan No. I of 1939, effective July 1, 1939.

Commodity Exchange Administration   *See* **Grain Futures Administration**

Commodity Exchange Authority   *See* **Grain Futures Administration**

Commodity Exchange Commission   Established by act of Sept. 21, 1922 (42 Stat. 998). Functions transferred to Commodity Futures Trading Commission by act of Oct. 23, 1974 (88 Stat. 1414).

Commodity Stabilization Service   Established Nov. 2, 1953, by Secretary's Memorandum 1320, supp. 4. Renamed Agricultural Stabilization and Conservation Service by Secretary's Memorandum 1458 of June 14, 1961, effective June 5, 1961.

Communication Agency, International   *See* **Information Agency, U.S.**

Communications Program, Joint Tactical   Combined with *Joint Interoperability of the Tactical Command and Control Systems Programs* to form Joint Tactical Command, Control, and Communications Agency in July 1984, pursuant to Defense Department Directive 5154.28.

Community Development Corporation   Established in Housing and Urban Development Department by act of Dec. 31, 1970 (84 Stat. 1791). Renamed *New Community Development Corporation* by act of Aug. 22, 1974 (88 Stat. 725). Abolished Nov. 30, 1983, by act of Nov. 30, 1983 (97 Stat. 1238), and functions transferred to Assistant Secretary for Community Planning and Development, Housing and Urban Development Department.

Community Development Corporation, New   *See* **Community Development Corporation**

Community Facilities, Bureau of   Established in 1945 by *Federal Works Administrator.* Transferred by act of June 30, 1949 (63 Stat. 380), to General Services Administration, functioning as *Community Facilities Service.* Certain functions transferred to various agencies, including Interior Department, Housing and Home Finance Agency, and *Federal Security Agency* by Reorg. Plans Nos. 15, 16, and 17 of 1950, effective May 24, 1950.

Community Facilities Administration Established in *Housing and Home Finance Agency* by Administrator's Organizational Order 1 of Dec. 23, 1954. Terminated by act of Sept. 9, 1965 (79 Stat. 667), and functions transferred to Housing and Urban Development Department.

Community Organization, Committee on Established in *Office of Defense Health and Welfare Services* Sept. 10, 1941. Functions transferred to *Federal Security Agency* by EO 9338 of Apr. 29, 1943.

Community Relations Service Established in Commerce Department by act of July 2, 1964 (78 Stat. 241). Transferred to Justice Department by Reorg. Plan No. 1 of 1966, effective Apr. 22, 1966.

Community Service, Commission on National and Established by act of Nov. 16, 1990 (104 Stat. 3168). Abolished by act of Sept. 21, 1993, and functions vested in the Board of Directors or the Executive Director prior to Oct. 1, 1993, transferred to the Corporation for National and Community Service (107 Stat. 873, 888).

Community Services, Office of Established in Health and Human Services Department by act of Aug. 13, 1981 (95 Stat. 516). Replaced by Family Support Administration.

Community Services Administration Established by act of Jan. 4, 1975 (88 Stat. 2291) as successor to *Office of Economic Opportunity*. Abolished as independent agency through repeal of act of Aug. 20, 1964 (except titles VIII and X of such act) by act of Aug. 13, 1981 (95 Stat. 519).

Community Services Administration Functions concerning Legal Services Program transferred to Legal Services Corporation by act of July 25, 1974 (88 Stat. 389). Renamed *Public Services Administration* by *Health, Education, and Welfare* departmental notice of Nov. 3, 1976. Transferred to *Office of Human Development* by Secretary's reorganization of Mar. 8, 1977 (42 FR 13262).

Community War Services Established in *Office of the Administrator* under EO 9338 of Apr. 29, 1943, and *Federal Security Agency* order. Terminated Dec. 31, 1946, by act of July 26, 1946 (60 Stat. 695).

Conciliation Service, U.S. Established by act of Mar. 4, 1913 (37 Stat. 738). Functions transferred to Federal Mediation and Conciliation Service, established by act of June 23, 1947 (61 Stat. 153).

Conservation and Renewable Energy Office Renamed Energy Efficiency and Renewable Energy Office by Assistant Secretary's memorandum of Mar. 3, 1993.

Constitution, Commission on the Bicentennial of the United States Established by act of Sept. 29, 1983, as amended (97 Stat. 722). Terminated by act of Dec. 3, 1991 (105 Stat. 1232).

Constitution, transfer of functions *See* **Statutes at Large and other matters**

Construction, Collective Bargaining Committee in Established by EO 11849 of Apr. 1, 1975. Inactive since Jan. 7, 1976. Formally abolished by EO 12110 of Dec. 28, 1978.

Construction, Equipment and Repairs, Bureau of Established in Navy Department by act of Aug. 31, 1842 (5 Stat. 579). Abolished by act of July 5, 1862 (12 Stat. 510), and functions distributed among *Bureau of Equipment and Recruiting, Bureau of Construction and Repair,* and *Bureau of Steam Engineering*.

Construction Branch Established in Treasury Department in 1853 and designated *Bureau of Construction* under control of *Office of Supervising Architect* by Sept. 30, 1855. *Office* incorporated into *Public Buildings Branch, Procurement Division,* by EO 6166 of June 10, 1933. Transferred to *Federal Works Agency* by Reorg. Plan No. I of 1939, effective July 1, 1939, when *Public Buildings Branch* of *Procurement Division, Bureau of Buildings Management,* National Park Service, Interior Department—so far as latter concerned with operation of public buildings for other departments or agencies—and *U.S. Housing Corporation* consolidated with *Public Buildings Administration, Federal Works Agency.*

Construction Industry Stabilization Committee Established by EO 11588 of Mar. 29, 1971. Abolished by EO 11788 of June 18, 1974.

Construction and Repair, Bureau of Established by act of July 5, 1862 (12 Stat. 510), replacing *Bureau of Construction, Equipment and Repairs.* Abolished by act of June 20, 1940 (54 Stat. 492), and functions transferred to *Bureau of Ships.*

Consumer Advisory Council Established by EO 11136 of Jan. 3, 1964. *Office of Consumer Affairs* established in Executive Office of the President by EO 11583 of Feb. 24, 1971, and Council reestablished in *Office.*

Consumer Affairs, Office of Established by EO 11583 of Feb. 24, 1971. Transferred to *Health, Education, and Welfare Department* by EO 11702 of Jan. 25, 1973.

Consumer Affairs Staff, National Business Council for Established in Commerce Department by departmental organization order of Dec. 16, 1971. Terminated by departmental order of Dec. 6, 1973, due to lack of funding.

Consumer agencies Consumer agencies of *National Emergency Council* and *National Recovery Administration* reorganized and functions transferred, together with those of *Consumers' Advisory Board, NRA,* and *Cabinet Committee on Price Policy,* to *Consumers' Division, NRA,* by EO 7120 of July 30, 1935. Division transferred to Labor Department by EO 7252 of Dec. 21, 1935. Transferred to *Division of Consumers' Counsel, Agricultural Adjustment Administration,* Agriculture Department, by Labor Secretary's letter of Aug. 30, 1938, to Agriculture Secretary. Continued as *Consumer Standards Project* until June 30, 1941. Research on consumer standards continued by *Consumer Standards Section, Consumers' Counsel Division,* transferred to *Agricultural Marketing*

Administration by administrative order of Feb. 28, 1942. Other project activities discontinued.

Consumer Cooperative Bank, National   Established by act of Aug. 20, 1978 (92 Stat. 499). Removed from mixed-ownership, Government corporation status by acts of Sept. 13, 1982 (96 Stat. 1062) and Jan. 12, 1983 (96 Stat. 2478).

Consumer Interests, President's Committee on   Established by EO 11136 of Jan. 3, 1964. Abolished by EO 11583 of Feb. 24, 1971.

Consumer and Marketing Service   Established by Agriculture Secretary Feb. 2, 1965. Renamed Agricultural Marketing Service Apr. 2, 1972, by Secretary's order and certain functions transferred to Animal and Plant Health Inspection Service.

Consumers' Counsel   Established in *National Bituminous Coal Commission* by act of Aug. 30, 1935 (49 Stat. 993). Office abolished by Reorg. Plan No. II of 1939, effective July 1, 1939, and functions transferred to Office of Solicitor, Interior Department, to function as *Consumers' Counsel Division* under direction of Interior Secretary. Functions transferred to *Office of the Bituminous Coal Consumers' Counsel* June 1941 by act of Apr. 11, 1941 (55 Stat. 134).

Consumers' Counsel Division   *See* **Consumers' Counsel**

Consumers' Counsel, Division of   Established by act of May 12, 1933 (48 Stat. 31). Transferred by order of Agriculture Secretary from *Agricultural Adjustment Administration* to supervision of *Director of Marketing*, effective Feb. 1, 1940. Transferred to *Agricultural Marketing Administration* by administrative order of Feb. 28, 1942.

Consumers' Problems, Adviser on   *See* **Consumer agencies**

Contract Committee Government   *See* **Contract Compliance, Committee on Government**

Contract Compliance, Committee on Government   Established by EO 10308 of Dec. 3, 1951. Abolished by EO 10479 of Aug. 13, 1953, which established successor *Government Contract Committee.* Abolished by EO 10925 of Mar. 6, 1961, and records and property transferred to *President's Committee on Equal Employment Opportunity.*

Contract Settlement, Office of   Established by act of July 1, 1944 (58 Stat. 651). Transferred to *Office of War Mobilization and Reconversion* by act of Oct. 3, 1944 (58 Stat. 785). Terminated by EO 9809 of Dec. 12, 1946, and Reorg. Plan No. 1 of 1947, effective July 1, 1947, and functions transferred to Treasury Department. Functions transferred to General Services Administration by act of June 30, 1949 (63 Stat. 380).

Contract Settlement Advisory Board   Established by act of July 1, 1944 (58 Stat. 651). Transferred to Treasury Department by EO 9809 of Dec. 12, 1946, and by Reorg. Plan No. 1 of 1947, effective July 1, 1947. Transferred to General Services Administration by act of June 30, 1949 (63 Stat. 380) and established as *Contract Review Board.* Renamed

Board of Contract Appeals in 1961 by Administrator's order. Board established as independent entity within General Services Administration Feb. 27, 1979, pursuant to act of Nov. 1, 1978 (92 Stat. 2383).

Contract Settlement Appeal Board, Office of   Established by act of July 1, 1944 (58 Stat. 651). Transferred to Treasury Department by EO 9809 of Dec. 12, 1946, and by Reorg. Plan No. 1 of 1947, effective July 1, 1947. Functions transferred to General Services Administration by act of June 30, 1949 (63 Stat. 380). Abolished by act of July 14, 1952 (66 Stat. 627).

Contract Termination Board, Joint   Established Nov. 12, 1943, by *Director of War Mobilization.* Functions assumed by *Office of Contract Settlement.*

Contracts Division, Public   Established in Labor Department to administer act of June 30, 1936 (49 Stat. 2036). Consolidated with Wage and Hour Division by Secretarial order of Aug. 21, 1942. Absorbed by Wage and Hour Division by Secretarial order of May 1971.

Cooperation Administration, International   Established by State Department Delegation of Authority 85 of June 30, 1955, pursuant to EO 10610 of May 9, 1955. Abolished by act of Sept. 4, 1961 (75 Stat. 446), and functions redelegated to Agency for International Development pursuant to Presidential letter of Sept. 30, 1961, and EO 10973 of Nov. 3, 1961.

Cooperative State Research Service   Established in the Department of Agriculture. Incorporated into Cooperative State, Research, Education, and Extension Service under Department of Agriculture reorganization in 1995.

Coordinating Service, Federal   *Office of Chief Coordinator* created by Executive order promulgated in *Bureau of the Budget* Circular 15, July 27, 1921, and duties enlarged by other *Bureau* circulars. Abolished by EO 6166 of June 10, 1933. Contract form, Federal traffic, and surplus property functions transferred to *Procurement Division* by order of Treasury Secretary, approved by President Oct. 9, 1933, issued pursuant to EO's 6166 of June 10, 1933, and 6224 of July 27, 1933.

Copyright Royalty Tribunal   Established as an independent entity within the legislative branch by act of Oct. 19, 1976 (90 Stat. 2594). Abolished by act of Dec. 17, 1993 (107 Stat. 2304), and functions transferred to copyright arbitration royalty panels.

Copyrighted Works, National Commission on New Technological Uses of   Established by act of Dec. 31, 1974 (88 Stat. 1873). Terminated Sept. 29, 1978, pursuant to terms of act.

Corporate Payments Abroad, Task Force on Questionable   Established by Presidential memorandum of Mar. 31, 1976. Terminated Dec. 31, 1976, pursuant to terms of memorandum.

Corporation, Federal Facilities   Established in Treasury Department by EO 10539 of June 22, 1954. Placed under supervision of Director appointed by General Services Administrator by EO

10720 of July 11, 1957. Dissolved by act of Aug. 30, 1961 (75 Stat. 418), and functions transferred to Administrator of General Services.

Corregidor-Bataan Memorial Commission Established by act of Aug. 5, 1953 (67 Stat. 366). Terminated May 6, 1967, by act of Dec. 23, 1963 (77 Stat. 477).

Cost Accounting Standards Board Established by act of Aug. 15, 1970 (84 Stat. 796). Terminated Sept. 30, 1980, due to lack of funding.

Cost of Living Council Established by EO 11615 of Aug. 15, 1971. Abolished by EO 11788 of June 18, 1974.

Cotton Stabilization Corporation Organized June 1930 under laws of Delaware by *Federal Farm Board* pursuant to act of June 15, 1929 (46 Stat. 11). Certificate of dissolution filed with Corporation Commission of Delaware Dec. 27, 1934.

Council. *See other part of title*

Courts Under act of Aug. 7, 1939 (53 Stat. 1223), and revised June 25, 1948 (62 Stat. 913), to provide for administration of U.S. courts, administrative jurisdiction over all continental and territorial courts transferred to Administrative Office of the U.S. Courts, including U.S. courts of appeals and district courts, District Court for the Territory of Alaska, U.S. District Court for the District of the Canal Zone, District Court of Guam, District Court of the Virgin Islands, Court of Claims, Court of Customs and Patent Appeals, and Customs Courts.

Credit Unions, Bureau of Federal *See* **Credit Union System, Federal**

Credit Union System, Federal Established by act of June 26, 1934 (48 Stat. 1216), to be administered by *Farm Credit Administration.* Transferred to Federal Deposit Insurance Corporation by EO 9148 of Apr. 27, 1942, and Reorg. Plan No. 1 of 1947, effective July 1, 1947. Functions transferred to *Bureau of Federal Credit Unions, Federal Security Agency,* established by act of June 29, 1948 (62 Stat. 1091). Functions transferred to *Health, Education, and Welfare Department* by Reorg. Plan No. 1 of 1953, effective Apr. 11, 1953. Functions transferred to National Credit Union Administration by act of Mar. 10, 1970 (84 Stat. 49).

Crime, National Council on Organized Established by EO 11534 of June 4, 1970. Terminated by EO 12110 of Dec. 28, 1978.

Critical Materials Council, Nation Established within Executive Office of the President by act of July 31, 1984 (98 Stat. 1250). *Office* abolished in Sept. 1993 due to lack of funding and functions transferred to the Office of Science and Technology Policy.

Crop Production Loan Office Authorized by Presidential letters of July 26, 1918, and July 26, 1919, to Agriculture Secretary. Further authorized by act of Mar. 3, 1921 (41 Stat. 1347). Transferred to Farm Credit Administration by EO 6084 of Mar. 27, 1933.

Cultural Center, National Established in Smithsonian Institution by act of Sept. 2, 1958 (72 Stat. 1698). Renamed John F. Kennedy Center for the Performing Arts by act of Jan. 23, 1964 (78 Stat. 4).

Customs, Bureau of Functions relating to award of numbers to undocumented vessels, vested in *Collectors of Customs,* transferred to Commandant of Coast Guard by EO 9083 of Feb. 27, 1942. Transfer made permanent by Reorg. Plan No. 3 of 1946, effective July 16, 1946. Redesignated U.S. Customs Service by Treasury Department Order 165–23 of Apr. 4, 1973.

Customs Court, U.S. Formerly established as Board of General Appraisers by act of June 10, 1890 (26 Stat. 136). Renamed *U.S. Customs Court* by act of May 26, 1926 (44 Stat. 669). Renamed U.S. Court of International Trade by act of Oct. 10, 1980 (94 Stat. 1727).

Customs and Patent Appeals, U.S. Court of Established by act of Mar. 2, 1929 (45 Stat. 1475). Abolished by act of Apr. 2, 1982 (96 Stat. 28) and functions merged with appellate functions of *U.S. Court of Claims* to form U.S. Court of Appeals for the Federal Circuit.

Dairy Industry, Bureau of *Bureau of Dairying* established in Agriculture Department by act of May 29, 1924 (43 Stat. 243). *Bureau of Dairy Industry* designation first appeared in act of May 11, 1926 (44 Stat. 499). Functions transferred to Agricultural Research Service by Secretary's Memorandum 1320, supp. 4, of Nov. 2, 1953.

Defense Advanced Research Projects Agency Established as a separate agency of the Department of Defense by DOD Directive 5105.41 dated July 25, 1978. Renamed Advanced Research Projects Agency by Defense Secretary's order dated July 13, 1993.

Defense, Advisory Commission to the Council of National *See* **Defense, Council of National**

Defense, Council of National Established by act of Aug. 29, 1916 (39 Stat. 649). *Advisory Commission*—composed of Advisers on Industrial Production, Industrial Materials, Employment, Farm Products, Price Stabilization, Transportation, and Consumer Protection—established by *Council* pursuant to act and approved by President May 29, 1940. Commission decentralized by merging divisions with newly created national defense units. Agencies evolved from *Commission,* except *Office of Agricultural War Relations* and *Office of Price Administration,* made units of *Office for Emergency Management. Council* inactive.

Defense, Office of Civilian Established in *Office for Emergency Management* by EO 8757 of May 20, 1941. Terminated by EO 9562 of June 4, 1945.

Defense Administration, Federal Civil Established in *Office for Emergency Management* by EO 10186 of Dec. 1, 1950; subsequently established as independent agency by act of Jan. 12, 1951 (64 Stat. 1245). Functions transferred to *Office of Defense and Civilian Mobilization* by Reorg. Plan No. 1 of 1958, effective July 1, 1958.

Defense Advisory Council, Civil Established by act of Jan. 12, 1951 (64 Stat. 1245). Transferred to *Office of Defense and Civilian Mobilization* by Reorg. Plan No. 1 of 1958, effective July 1, 1958.

Defense Aid Reports, Division of Established in *Office for Emergency Management* by EO 8751 of May 2, 1941. Abolished by EO 8926 of Oct. 28, 1941, which created *Office of Lend-Lease Administration.*

Defense Air Transportation Administration Established Nov. 12, 1951, by Commerce Department Order 137. Abolished by Amendment 3 of Sept. 13, 1962, to Department Order 128 (revised) and functions transferred to *Office of the Under Secretary of Commerce for Transportation.*

Defense Atomic Support Agency Renamed Defense Nuclear Agency by General Order No. 1 of July 1, 1971.

Defense Audiovisual Agency Established by Defense Department Directive 5040.1 of June 12, 1979. Abolished by Secretary's memorandum of Apr. 19, 1985, and functions assigned to the military departments.

Defense Audit Service Established by Defense Department directive of Oct. 14, 1976. Abolished by Deputy Secretary's memorandum of Nov. 2, 1982, and functions transferred to Office of the Inspector General.

Defense Civil Preparedness Agency Functions transferred from Defense Department to Federal Emergency Management Agency by EO 12148 of July 20, 1979.

Defense and Civilian Mobilization Board Established by EO 10773 of July 1, 1938. Redesignated *Civil and Defense Mobilization Board* by act of Aug. 26, 1958 (72 Stat. 861). Abolished by *Office of Emergency Preparedness* Circular 1200.1 of Oct. 31, 1962.

Defense Communications Agency Established by direction of the Secretary of Defense on May 12, 1960. Renamed Defense Information Systems Agency by DOD Directive 5105.19 dated June 25, 1991.

Defense Communications Board Established by EO 8546 of Sept. 24, 1940. Renamed *Board of War Communications* by EO 9183 of June 15, 1942. Abolished by EO 9831 of Feb. 24, 1947, and property transferred to Federal Communications Commission.

Defense Coordinating Board, Civil Established by EO 10611 of May 11, 1955. EO 10611 revoked by EO 10773 of July 1, 1958.

Defense Electric Power Administration Established by Interior Secretary's Order 2605 of Dec. 4, 1950. Abolished June 30, 1953, by Secretary's Order 2721 of May 7, 1953. Reestablished by Departmental Manual Release No. 253 of Aug. 6, 1959. Terminated by Departmental Manual Release No. 1050 of Jan. 10, 1977.

Defense Fisheries Administration Established by Interior Secretary's Order 2605 of Dec. 4, 1950. Abolished June 30, 1953, by Secretary's Order 2722 of May 13, 1953.

Defense Health and Welfare Services, Office of Established by EO 8890 of Sept. 3, 1941. Terminated by EO 9338 of Apr. 29, 1943, and functions transferred to *Federal Security Agency.*

Defense Homes Corporation Incorporated pursuant to President's letter to Treasury Secretary of Oct. 18, 1940. Transferred to *Federal Public Housing Authority* by EO 9070 of Feb. 24, 1942.

Defense Housing Coordination, Division of Established in *Office for Emergency Management* by EO 8632 of Jan. 11, 1941. Functions transferred to *National Housing Agency* by EO 9070 of Feb. 24, 1942.

Defense Housing Coordinator Office established July 21, 1940, by *Advisory Commission to Council of National Defense.* Functions transferred to *Division of Defense Housing Coordination, Office for Emergency Management,* by EO 8632 of Jan. 11, 1941.

Defense Housing Division, Mutual Ownership Established by Administrator of *Federal Works Agency* under provisions of act of June 28, 1941 (55 Stat. 361). Functions transferred to *Federal Public Housing Authority, National Housing Agency,* by EO 9070 of Feb. 24, 1942.

Defense Manpower Administration Established by Labor Secretary by General Order 48, pursuant to EO 10161 of Sept. 9, 1950, and Reorg. Plan No. 6 of 1950, effective May 24, 1950. General Order 48 revoked by General Order 63 of Aug. 25, 1953, which established *Office of Manpower Administration* in .Department.

Defense Materials Procurement Agency Established by EO 10281 of Aug. 28, 1951. Abolished by EO 10480 of Aug. 14, 1953, and functions transferred to General Services Administration.

Defense Materials Service *See* **Emergency Procurement Service**

Defense Mediation Board, National Established by EO 8716 of Mar. 19, 1941. Terminated on creation of *National War Labor Board, Office for Emergency Management* by EO 9017 of Jan. 12, 1942. Transferred to Labor Department by EO 9617 of Sept. 19, 1945. *Board* terminated by EO 9672 of Dec. 31, 1945, which established *National Wage Stabilization Board* in Labor Department. Terminated by EO 9809 of Dec. 12, 1946, and functions transferred to Labor Secretary and Treasury Department, effective Feb. 24, 1947.

Defense Minerals Administration Established by Interior Secretary's Order 2605 of Dec. 4, 1950. Functions assigned to *Defense Materials Procurement Agency.* Functions of exploration for critical and strategic minerals redelegated to Interior Secretary and administered by *Defense Minerals Exploration Administration* by Secretary's Order 2726 of June 30, 1953. Termination of program announced by Secretary June 6, 1958. Certain activities continued in *Office of Minerals Exploration,* Interior Department.

Defense Minerals Exploration Administration See **Defense Minerals Administration**

Defense Mobilization, Office of Established in Executive Office of the President by EO 10193 of Dec. 16, 1950. Superseded by *Office of Defense Mobilization* established by Reorg. Plan No. 3 of 1953, effective June 12, 1953, which assumed functions of former *Office, National Security Resources Board,* and critical materials stockpiling functions of Army, Navy, Air Force, and Interior Secretaries and of *Army and Navy Munitions Board.* Consolidated with *Federal Civil Defense Administration* into *Office of Defense and Civilian Mobilization* by Reorg. Plan No. 1 of 1958, effective July 1, 1958, and offices of Director and Deputy Director terminated.

Defense Mobilization Board Established by EO 10200 of Jan. 3, 1951, and restated in EO 10480 of Aug. 14, 1953. Terminated by EO 10773 of July 1, 1958.

Defense Plant Corporation Established by act of June 25, 1940 (54 Stat. 572). Transferred from *Federal Loan Agency* to Commerce Department by EO 9071 of Feb. 24, 1942. Returned to *Federal Loan Agency* pursuant to act of Feb. 24, 1945 (59 Stat. 5). Dissolved by act of June 30, 1945 (59 Stat. 310), and functions transferred to *Reconstruction Finance Corporation.*

Defense Plants Administration, Small Established by act of July 31, 1951 (65 Stat. 131). Terminated July 31, 1953, by act of June 30, 1953 (67 Stat. 131). Functions relating to liquidation transferred to Small Business Administration by EO 10504 of Dec. 1, 1953.

Defense Production Administration Established by EO 10200 of Jan. 3, 1951. Terminated by EO 10433 of Feb. 4, 1953, and functions transferred to *Office of Defense Mobilization.*

Defense Property Disposal Service Renamed Defense Reutilization and Marketing Service by Defense Logistics Agency General Order 10–85, effective July 1, 1985.

Defense Public Works Division Established in *Public Works Administration.* Transferred to *Office of Federal Works Administrator* by administrative order of July 16, 1941. Abolished by administrative order of Mar. 6, 1942, and functions transferred to *Office of Chief Engineer, Federal Works Agency.*

Defense Purchases, Office for the Coordination of National Established by order of *Council of National Defense,* approved June 27, 1940. Order revoked Jan. 7, 1941, and records transferred to Executive Office of the President.

Defense Research Committee, National Established June 27, 1940, by order of *Council of National Defense.* Abolished by order of *Council* June 28, 1941, and reestablished in *Office of Scientific Research and Development* by EO 8807 of June 28, 1941. *Office* terminated by EO 9913 of Dec. 26,

1947, and property and records transferred to *National Military Establishment.*

Defense Resources Committee Established by Administrative Order 1496 of June 15, 1940. Replaced by *War Resources Council* by Administrative Order 1636 of Jan. 14, 1942. Inactive.

Defense Solid Fuels Administration Established by Interior Secretary's Order 2605 of Dec. 4, 1950. Abolished June 29, 1954, by Secretary's Order 2764.

Defense Stockpile Manager, National Established by act of Nov. 14, 1986 (100 Stat. 4067). Functions transferred from General Services Administrator to Defense Secretary by EO 12626 of Feb. 25, 1988.

Defense Supplies Corporation Established under act of June 25, 1940 (54 Stat. 572). Transferred from *Federal Loan Agency* to Commerce Department by EO 9071 of Feb. 24, 1942. Returned to *Federal Loan Agency* by act of Feb. 24, 1945 (59 Stat. 5). Dissolved by act of June 30, 1945 (59 Stat. 310), and functions transferred to *Reconstruction Finance Corporation.*

Defense Supply Agency Renamed Defense Logistics Agency by DOD Directive 5105.22 of Jan. 22, 1977.

Defense Supply Management Agency Established in Defense Department by act of July 1, 1952 (66 Stat. 318). Abolished by Reorg. Plan No. 6 of 1953, effective June 30, 1953, and functions transferred to Defense Secretary.

Defense Transport Administration Established Oct. 4, 1950, by order of Commissioner of Interstate Commerce Commission in charge of *Bureau of Service,* pursuant to EO 10161 of Sept. 9, 1950. Terminated by DTA Commissioner's order, effective July 1, 1955, and functions transferred to Bureau of Safety and Service, Interstate Commerce Commission.

Defense Transportation, Office of Established in *Office for Emergency Management* by EO 8989 of Dec. 18, 1941. Terminated by EO 10065 of July 6, 1949.

Director. *See other part of title*

Disarmament Administration, U.S. Established in State Department. Functions transferred to U.S. Arms Control and Disarmament Agency by act of Sept. 26, 1961 (75 Stat. 638).

Disarmament Problems, President's Special Committee on Established by President Aug. 5, 1955. Dissolved in February 1958.

Disaster Assistance Administration, Federal Functions transferred from Housing and Urban Development Department to Federal Emergency Management Agency by EO 12148 of July 20, 1979.

Disaster Loan Corporation Grouped with other agencies to form *Federal Loan Agency* by Reorg. Plan No. I of 1939, effective July 1, 1939. Transferred to Commerce Department by EO 9071 of Feb. 24, 1942. Returned to *Federal Loan Agency* by act of Feb. 24, 1945 (59 Stat. 5). Dissolved by act of June 30, 1945 (59 Stat. 310), and functions transferred to *Reconstruction Finance Corporation.*

Disease Control, Center for   Established within the Public Health Service by *Health, Education, and Welfare Secretary* on July 1, 1973. Renamed *Centers for Disease Control* by Health and Human Services Secretary's notice of Oct. 1, 1980 (45 FR 67772). Renamed Centers for Disease Control and Prevention by act of Oct. 27, 1992 (106 Stat. 3504).

Displaced Persons Commission   Established by act of June 25, 1948 (62 Stat. 1009). Terminated Aug. 31, 1952, pursuant to terms of act.

District of Columbia   Established by acts of July 16, 1790 (1 Stat. 130), and Mar. 3, 1791. *Corporations of Washington and Georgetown* and *levy court of Washington County* abolished in favor of territorial form of government in 1871. Permanent commission government established July 1, 1878. District Government created as municipal corporation by act of June 11, 1878 (20 Stat. 102). Treated as branch of U.S. Government by various statutory enactments of Congress. District Government altered by Reorg. Plan No. 3 of 1967, effective Nov. 3, 1967. Charter for local government in District of Columbia provided by act of Dec. 24, 1973 (87 Stat. 774).

District of Columbia, Highway Commission of the   Established by act of Mar. 2, 1893 (27 Stat 532). *National Capital Park and Planning Commission* named successor by act of Apr. 30, 1926 (44 Stat. 374). Functions transferred to National Capital Planning Commission by act of July 19, 1952 (66 Stat. 781).

District of Columbia, Reform-School of the   Established by act of May 3, 1876 (19 Stat. 49). Renamed *National Training School for Boys* by act of May 27, 1908 (35 Stat. 380). Transferred to Justice Department by Reorg. Plan No. II of 1939, effective July 1, 1939, to be administered by Director of Bureau of Prisons.

District of Columbia Auditorium Commission   Established by act of July 1, 1955 (69 Stat. 243). Final report submitted to Congress Jan. 31, 1957, pursuant to act of Apr. 27, 1956 (70 Stat. 115).

District of Columbia Redevelopment Land Agency   Established by act of Aug. 2, 1946 (60 Stat. 790). Agency established as instrumentality of District Government by act of Dec. 24, 1973 (87 Stat. 774), effective July 1, 1974.

District of Columbia-Virginia Boundary Commission   Established by act of Mar. 21, 1934 (48 Stat. 453). Terminated Dec. 1, 1935, to which date it had been extended by Public Resolution 9 (49 Stat. 67).

Division.   *See other part of title*

Domestic Council   Established in Executive Office of the President by Reorg. Plan No. 2 of 1970, effective July 1, 1970. Abolished by Reorg. Plan No. 1 of 1977, effective Mar. 26, 1978, and functions transferred to President and staff designated as *Domestic Policy Staff.* Pursuant to EO 12045 of Mar. 27, 1978, *Staff* assisted President in performance of transferred functions. Renamed Office of Policy Development in 1981. Abolished in Feb. 1992 by

President's reorganizational statement, effective May 1992.

Domestic Policy Staff   *See* **Domestic Council**

Dominican Customs Receivership   Transferred from *Division of Territories and Island Possessions,* Interior Department, to State Department by Reorg. Plan No. IV of 1940, effective June 30, 1940.

Drug Abuse, National Institute on   Established within the National Institute of Mental Health, *Health, Education, and Welfare Department* by act of Mar. 21, 1972 (86 Stat. 85). Removed from within the National Institute of Mental Health and made an entity within the Alcohol, Drug Abuse, and Mental Health Administration by act of May 14, 1974 (88 Stat. 136). Functions transferred to Health and Human Services Department by act of Oct. 17, 1979 (93 Stat. 695). (*See also* act of Oct. 27, 1986; 100 Stat. 3207–106.) Abolished by act of July 10, 1992 (106 Stat. 331). Reestablished by act of July 10, 1992 (106 Stat. 361).

Drug Abuse, President's Advisory Commission on Narcotic and   Established by EO 11076 of Jan. 15, 1963. Terminated November 1963 under terms of order.

Drug Abuse Control, Bureau of   Established in Food and Drug Administration, Health and Human Services Department, to carry out functions of act of July 15, 1965 (79 Stat. 226). Functions transferred to *Bureau of Narcotics and Dangerous Drugs,* Justice Department, by Reorg. Plan No. 1 of 1968, effective Apr. 8, 1968. Abolished by Reorg. Plan No. 2 of 1973, effective July 1, 1973, and functions transferred to Drug Enforcement Administration.

Drug Abuse Law Enforcement, Office of   Established by EO 11641 of Jan. 28, 1972. Terminated by EO 11727 of July 6, 1973, and functions transferred to Drug Enforcement Administration.

Drug Abuse Policy, Office of   Established in Executive Office of the President by act of Mar. 19, 1976 (90 Stat. 242). Abolished by Reorg. Plan No. 1 of 1977, effective Mar. 26, 1978, and functions transferred to President.

Drug Abuse Prevention, Special Action Office for   Established by EO 11599 of June 17, 1971, and act of Mar. 21, 1972 (86 Stat. 65). Terminated June 30, 1975, pursuant to terms of act.

Drug Abuse Prevention, Treatment, and Rehabilitation, Cabinet Committee on   Established Apr. 27, 1976, by Presidential announcement. Terminated by Presidential memorandum of Mar. 14, 1977.

Drug Law Enforcement, Cabinet Committee for   Established Apr. 27, 1976, pursuant to Presidential message to Congress of Apr. 27, 1976. Abolished by Presidential memorandum of Mar. 14, 1977.

Drugs, Bureau of Narcotics and Dangerous   *See* **Drug Abuse Control, Bureau of**

Drugs and Biologics, National Center for   Renamed *Center for Drugs and Biologics* by Food and Drug

Administration notice of Mar. 9, 1984 (49 FR 10166). Reestablished as Center for Drug Evaluation and Research and Center for Biologics Evaluation and Research by Secretary's notice of Oct. 6, 1987 (52 FR 38275).

Drunk Driving, Presidential Commission on Established by EO 12358 of Apr. 14, 1982. Terminated Dec. 31, 1983, by EO 12415 of Apr. 5, 1983.

Dryden Research Center, Hugh L. Formerly separate field installation of National Aeronautics and Space Administration. Made component of Ames Research Center by NASA Management Instruction 1107.5A of Sept. 3, 1981.

Economic Administration, Foreign Established in *Office for Emergency Management* by EO 9380 of Sept. 25, 1943. Functions of *Office of Lend-Lease Administration, Office of Foreign Relief and Rehabilitation Operations, Office of Economic Warfare* (together with *U.S. Commercial Company, Rubber Development Corporation, Petroleum Reserves Corporation,* and *Export-Import Bank of Washington* and functions transferred thereto by EO 9361 of July 15, 1943), and foreign economic operations of *Office of Foreign Economic Coordination* transferred to *Administration.* Foreign procurement activities of *War Food Administration* and Commodity Credit Corporation transferred by EO 9385 of Oct. 6, 1943. Terminated by EO 9630 of Sept. 27, 1945, and functions redistributed to State, Commerce, and Agriculture Departments and *Reconstruction Finance Corporation.*

Economic Analysis, Office of *See* **Business Economics, Office of**

Economic Cooperation Administration Established by act of Apr. 3, 1948 (62 Stat. 138). Abolished by act of Oct. 10, 1951 (65 Stat. 373), and functions transferred to *Mutual Security Agency* pursuant to EO 10300 of Nov. 1, 1951.

Economic Coordination, Office of Foreign *See* **Board of Economic Operations**

Economic Defense Board Established by EO 8839 of July 30, 1941. Renamed *Board of Economic Warfare* by EO 8982 of Dec. 17, 1941. *Board* terminated by EO 9361 of July 15, 1943, and *Office of Economic Warfare* established in *Office for Emergency Management. Office of Economic Warfare* consolidated with *Foreign Economic Administration* by EO 9380 of Sept. 25, 1943.

Economic Development, Office of Regional Established by Commerce Secretary Jan. 6, 1966, pursuant to act of Aug. 26, 1965 (79 Stat. 552). Abolished by Department Order 5A, Dec. 22, 1966, and functions vested in Economic Development Administration.

Economic Development Service, Foreign Established by order of Agriculture Secretary Nov. 8, 1969. Abolished by order of Secretary Feb. 6, 1972, and functions transferred to Economic Research Service.

Economic Growth and Stability, Advisory Board on Established by Presidential letter to Congress of June

1, 1953. Superseded by *National Advisory Board on Economic Policy* by Presidential direction Mar. 12, 1961. *Cabinet Committee on Economic Growth* established by President Aug. 21, 1962, to succeed *Board.*

Economic Management Support Center Established by Agriculture Secretary's Memorandum 1836 of Jan. 9, 1974. Consolidated with other Department units into *Economics, Statistics, and Cooperatives Service* by Secretary's Memorandum 1927, effective Dec. 23, 1977.

Economic Operations, Board of Established by State departmental order of Oct. 7, 1941. Abolished by departmental order of June 24, 1943, and functions transferred to *Office of Foreign Economic Coordination* established by same order. *Office* abolished by departmental order of Nov. 6, 1943, pursuant to EO 9380 of Sept. 25, 1943.

Economic Opportunity, Office of Established in Executive Office of the President by act of Aug. 20, 1964 (78 Stat. 508). All OEO programs except three transferred by administrative action to *Health, Education, and Welfare,* Labor, and Housing and Urban Development Departments July 6, 1973. Community Action, Economic Development, and Legal Services Programs transferred to *Community Services Administration* by act of Jan. 4, 1975 (88 Stat. 2310).

Economic Policy, Council on Established by Presidential memorandum of Feb. 2, 1973. Functions absorbed by *Economic Policy Board* Sept. 30, 1974.

Economic Policy, Council on Foreign Established Dec. 22, 1954, by Presidential letter of Dec. 11, 1954. Abolished by President Mar. 12, 1961, and functions transferred to Secretary of State.

Economic Policy, Council on International Established in Executive Office of the President by Presidential memorandum of January 1971. Reestablished by act of Aug. 29, 1972 (86 Stat. 646). Terminated Sept. 30, 1977, on expiration of statutory authority.

Economic Policy, National Advisory Board on *See* **Economic Growth and Stability, Advisory Board on**

Economic Policy Board, President's Established by EO 11808 of Sept. 30, 1974. Terminated by EO 11975 of Mar. 7, 1977.

Economic Research Service Established by Agriculture Secretary's Memorandum 1446, supp. 1, of Apr. 3, 1961. Consolidated with other Agriculture Department units into *Economics, Statistics, and Cooperatives Service* by Secretary's Memorandum 1927, effective Dec. 23, 1977. Redesignated as Economic Research Service by Secretarial order of Oct. 1, 1981.

Economic Security, Advisory Council on Established by EO 6757 of June 29, 1934. Terminated on approval of act of Aug. 14, 1935 (49 Stat. 620) Aug. 14, 1935.

Economic Security, Committee on Established by EO 6757 of June 29, 1934. Terminated as formal agency in April 1936, as provided in act, but continued informally for some time thereafter.

Economic Stabilization, Office of Established in *Office for Emergency Management* by EO 9250 of Oct. 3, 1942. Terminated by EO 9620 of Sept. 20, 1945, and functions transferred to *Office of War Mobilization and Reconversion*. Reestablished in *Office for Emergency Management* by EO 9699 of Feb. 21, 1946. Transferred by EO 9762 of July 25, 1946, to *Office of War Mobilization and Reconversion*. Consolidated with other agencies to form *Office of Temporary Controls* by EO 9809 of Dec. 12, 1946.

Economic Stabilization Agency Established by EO 10161 of Sept. 9, 1950, and EO 10276 of July 31, 1951. Terminated, except for liquidation purposes, by EO 10434 of Feb. 6, 1953. Liquidation completed Oct. 31, 1953, pursuant to EO 10480 of Aug. 14, 1953.

Economic Stabilization Board Established by EO 9250 of Oct. 3, 1942. Transferred to *Office of War Mobilization and Reconversion* by EO 9620 of Sept. 20, 1945. Returned to *Office of Economic Stabilization* on reestablishment by EO 9699 of Feb. 21, 1946. *Board* returned to *Office of War Mobilization and Reconversion* by EO 9762 of July 25, 1946. Functions terminated by EO 9809 of Dec. 12, 1946.

Economic Warfare, Board of *See* **Economic Defense Board**

Economic Warfare, Office of *See* **Economic Defense Board**

Economics, Bureau of Industrial Established by Commerce Secretary Jan. 2, 1980, in conjunction with Reorg. Plan No. 3 of 1979, effective Oct. 1, 1980, and operated under Department Organization Order 35–5B. Abolished at bureau level by Secretarial order, effective Jan. 22, 1984 (49 FR 4538). Industry-related functions realigned and transferred from Under Secretary for Economic Affairs to Under Secretary for International Trade. Under Secretary for Economic Affairs retained units to support domestic macroeconomic policy functions.

Economics, Statistics, and Cooperatives Service Renamed *Economics and Statistics Service* by Agriculture Secretary's Memorandum 2025 of Sept. 17, 1980. Redesignated as Economic Research Service and *Statistical Reporting Service* by Secretarial order of Oct. 1, 1981.

Economy Board, Joint Placed under direction of President by military order of July 5, 1939. Abolished Sept. 1, 1947, by joint letter of Aug. 20, 1947, from Secretaries of *War* and *Navy* to President.

Education, Federal Board for Vocational Established by act of Feb. 23, 1917 (39 Stat. 929). Functions transferred to Interior Department by EO 6166 of June 10, 1933. Functions assigned to *Commissioner of Education* Oct. 10, 1933. *Office of Education* transferred from Interior Department to *Federal Security Agency* by Reorg. Plan No. I of

1939, effective July 1, 1939. *Board* abolished by Reorg. Plan No. 2 of 1946, effective July 16, 1946.

Education, National Institute of Established by act of June 23, 1972 (86 Stat. 327). Transferred to Office of Educational Research and Improvement, Education Department, by act of Oct. 17, 1979 (93 Stat. 678), effective May 4, 1980.

Education, Office of Established as independent agency by act of Mar. 2, 1867 (14 Stat. 434). Transferred to Interior Department by act of July 20, 1868 (15 Stat. 106). Transferred to *Federal Security Agency* by Reorg. Plan No. I of 1939, effective July 1, 1939. Functions of *Federal Security Administrator* administered by *Office of Education* relating to student loans and defense-related education transferred to *War Manpower Commission* by EO 9247 of Sept. 17, 1942.

Education, Office of Bilingual Abolished by act of Oct. 17, 1979 (93 Stat. 675), and functions transferred to Office of Bilingual Education and Minority Languages Affairs, Education Department.

Education Beyond the High School, President's Committee on Established by act of July 26, 1956 (70 Stat. 676). Terminated Dec. 31, 1957. Certain activities continued by *Bureau of Higher Education, Office of Education.*

Education Division Established in *Health, Education, and Welfare Department* by act of June 23, 1972 (86 Stat. 327). Functions transferred to Education Department by act of Oct. 17, 1979 (93 Stat. 677).

Education Statistics, National Center for Established in the Office of the Assistant Secretary, Health and Human Services Department, by act of Aug. 21, 1974 (88 Stat. 556). Transferred to the Office of Educational Research and Improvement, Education Department, by act of Oct. 17, 1979 (93 Stat. 678), effective May 4, 1980. Renamed *Center for Education Statistics* by act of Oct. 17, 1986 (100 Stat. 1579). Renamed National Center for Education Statistics by act of Apr. 28, 1988 (102 Stat. 331).

Educational and Cultural Affairs, Bureau of Established by Secretary of State in 1960. Terminated by Reorg. Plan No. 2 of 1977, effective July 1, 1978, and functions transferred to *International Communication Agency*, effective Apr. 1, 1978.

Educational and Cultural Affairs, Interagency Council on International Established Jan. 20, 1964, by Foreign Affairs Manual Circular, under authority of act of Sept. 21, 1961 (75 Stat. 527). Terminated Oct. 1973 following creation of Subcommittee on International Exchanges by National Security Council directive.

Educational Exchange, U.S. Advisory Commission on Established by act of Jan. 27, 1948 (62 Stat. 10). Abolished by act of Sept. 21, 1961 (75 Stat. 538), and superseded by U.S. Advisory Commission on International Educational and Cultural Affairs.

Efficiency, Bureau of Organized under act of Feb. 28, 1916 (39 Stat. 15). Abolished by act of Mar. 3,

1933 (47 Stat. 1519), and records transferred to *Bureau of the Budget.*

Elderly, Committee on Mental Health and Illness of the Established by act of July 29, 1975 (89 Stat. 347). Terminated Sept. 30, 1977.

Electoral votes for President and Vice President, transfer of functions See **State Department**

Electric Home and Farm Authority Incorporated Aug. 1, 1935, under laws of District of Columbia. Designated as U.S. agency by EO 7139 of Aug. 12, 1935. Continued by act of June 10, 1941 (55 Stat. 248). Grouped with other agencies in *Federal Loan Agency* by Reorg. Plan. No. I of 1939, effective July 1, 1939. Functions transferred to Commerce Department by EO 9071 of Feb. 24, 1942. Terminated by EO 9256 of Oct. 13, 1942.

Electric Home and Farm Authority, Inc. Organized Jan. 17, 1934, under laws of State of Delaware by EO 6514 of Dec. 19, 1933. Dissolved Aug. 1, 1935, and succeeded by *Electric Home and Farm Authority.*

Emergency Administration of Public Works, Federal Established by act of June 16, 1933 (48 Stat. 200). Operation continued by subsequent legislation, including act of June 21, 1938 (52 Stat. 816). Consolidated with *Federal Works Agency* as *Public Works Administration* by Reorg. Plan No. I of 1939, effective July 1, 1939. Functions transferred to *Office of Federal Works Administrator* by EO 9357 of June 30, 1943.

Emergency Conservation Work Established by EO 6101 of Apr. 5, 1933. Succeeded by *Civilian Conservation Corps.*

Emergency Council, National Established by EO 6433–A of Nov. 17, 1933. Consolidated with *Executive Council* by EO 6889–A of Oct. 29, 1934. Abolished by Reorg. Plan No. II of 1939, effective July 1, 1939, and functions (except those relating to *Radio Division* and *Film Service*) transferred to Executive Office of the President.

Emergency Council, Office of Economic Adviser to National Established by EO 6240 of Aug. 3, 1933, in connection with *Executive Council,* which later consolidated with *National Emergency Council.* Records and property used in preparation of statistical and economic summaries transferred to *Central Statistical Board* by EO 7003 of Apr. 8, 1935.

Emergency Management, Liaison Officer for Resignation of Liaison Officer for Emergency Management accepted by Presidential letter of Nov. 3, 1943, and no successor appointed. Liaison facilities terminated pursuant to optional provisions of administrative order of Jan. 7, 1941.

Emergency Management, Office for Established in Executive Office of the President by administrative order of May 25, 1940, in accordance with EO 8248 of Sept. 8, 1939. Inactive.

Emergency Mobilization Preparedness Board Established Dec. 17, 1981, by the President.

Abolished by Presidential directive of Sept. 16, 1985.

Emergency Planning, Office of Established as successor to *Office of Civil and Defense Mobilization* by act of Sept. 22, 1961 (75 Stat. 630). Renamed *Office of Emergency Preparedness* by act of Oct. 21, 1968 (82 Stat. 1194). Terminated by Reorg. Plan No. 2 of 1973, effective July 1, 1973, and functions transferred to the Treasury and Housing and Urban Development Departments and General Services Administration.

Emergency Preparedness, Office of See **Emergency Planning, Office of**

Emergency Procurement Service Established Sept. 1, 1950, by Administrator of General Services. Renamed *Defense Materials Service* Sept. 7, 1956. Functions transferred to *Property Management and Disposal Service* July 29, 1966. Service abolished July 1, 1973, and functions transferred to Federal Supply Service, Public Buildings Service, and Federal Property Resources Service.

Emergency Relief Administration, Federal Established by act of May 12, 1933 (48 Stat. 55). Expired June 30, 1938, having been liquidated by *Works Progress Administrator* pursuant to act of May 28, 1937 (50 Stat. 352).

Employee-Management Relations Program, President's Committee on the Implementation of the Federal Established by EO 10988 of Jan. 17, 1962. Terminated upon submission of report to President June 21, 1963.

Employees' Compensation, Bureau of Transferred from *Federal Security Agency* to Labor Department by Reorg. Plan No. 19 of 1950, effective May 24, 1950. Functions absorbed by Employment Standards Administration Mar. 13, 1972.

Employees' Compensation Appeals Board Transferred from *Federal Security Agency* to Labor Department by Reorg. Plan No. 19 of 1950, effective May 24, 1950.

Employees' Compensation Commission, U.S. Established by act of Sept. 7, 1916 (39 Stat. 742). Abolished by Reorg. Plan No. 2 of 1946, effective July 16, 1946, and functions transferred to *Federal Security Administrator.*

Employment Board, Fair Established by *U.S. Civil Service Commission* pursuant to EO 9980 of July 26, 1948. Abolished by EO 10590 of Jan. 18, 1955.

Employment of the Physically Handicapped, President's Committee on Established by EO 10640 of Oct. 10, 1955, continuing *Committee* established by act of July 11, 1949 (63 Stat. 409). Superseded by President's Committee on Employment of the Handicapped established by EO 10994 of Feb. 14, 1962.

Employment Policy, President's Committee on Government Established by EO 10590 of Jan. 18, 1955. Abolished by EO 10925 of Mar. 6, 1961, and functions transferred to *President's Committee on Equal Employment Opportunity.*

Employment Practice, Committee on Fair
Established in *Office of Production Management* by
EO 8802 of June 25, 1941. Transferred to *War
Manpower Commission* by Presidential letter
effective July 30, 1942. Committee terminated on
establishment of *Committee on Fair Employment
Practice, Office for Emergency Management*, by EO
9346 of May 27, 1943. Terminated June 30, 1946,
by act of July 17, 1945 (59 Stat. 743).

Employment Security, Bureau of   Transferred from
Federal Security Agency to Labor Department by
Reorg. Plan No. 2 of 1949, effective Aug. 20, 1949.
Abolished by Labor Secretary's order of Mar. 14,
1969, and functions transferred to *Manpower
Administration.*

Employment Service, U.S.   Established in Labor
Department in 1918 by departmental order.
Abolished by act of June 6, 1933 (48 Stat. 113), and
created as bureau with same name. Functions
consolidated with unemployment compensation
functions of *Social Security Board, Bureau of
Employment Security*, and transferred to *Federal
Security Agency* by Reorg. Plan No. I of 1939,
effective July 1, 1939. *Service* transferred to *Bureau
of Placement, War Manpower Commission*, by EO
9247 of Sept. 17, 1942. Returned to Labor
Department by EO 9617 of Sept. 19, 1945.
Transferred to *Federal Security Agency* by act of
June 16, 1948 (62 Stat. 443), to function as part of
Bureau of Employment Security, Social Security
Administration. *Bureau*, including *U.S. Employment
Service*, transferred to Labor Department by Reorg.
Plan No. 2 of 1949, effective Aug. 20, 1949.
Abolished by reorganization of *Manpower
Administration*, effective Mar. 17, 1969, and
functions assigned to *U.S. Training and Employment
Service.*

Employment Stabilization Board, Federal
Established by act of Feb. 10, 1931 (46 Stat. 1085).
Abolished by EO 6166 of June 10, 1933. Abolition
deferred by EO 6623 of Mar. 1, 1934, until
functions of *Board* transferred to *Federal
Employment Stabilization Office*, established in
Commerce Department by same order. *Office*
abolished by Reorg. Plan No. I of 1939, effective
July 1, 1939, and functions transferred from
Commerce Department to *National Resources
Planning Board*, Executive Office of the President.

Employment Stabilization Office, Federal.   *See*
Employment Stabilization Board, Federal

Employment and Training, Office of Comprehensive
Established in Labor Department. Terminated due to
expiration of authority for appropriations after fiscal
year 1982. Replaced by *Office of Employment and
Training Programs.*

Employment and Training Programs, Office of
Renamed Office of Job Training Programs by
Employment and Training Administration
reorganization in Labor Department, effective June
1984.

Endangered Species Scientific Authority
Established by EO 11911 of Apr. 13, 1976.
Terminated by act of Dec. 28, 1979 (93 Stat. 1228),
and functions transferred to Interior Secretary.

Energy Administration, Federal   Established by act
of May 7, 1974 (88 Stat. 96). Assigned additional
responsibilities by acts of June 22, 1974 (88 Stat.
246), Dec. 22, 1975 (89 Stat. 871), and Aug. 14,
1976 (90 Stat. 1125). Terminated by act of Aug. 4,
1977 (91 Stat. 577), and functions transferred to
Energy Department.

Energy Conservation, Office of   Established by
Interior Secretarial Order 2953 May 7, 1973.
Functions transferred to *Federal Energy
Administration* by act of May 7, 1974 (88 Stat. 100).

Energy Data and Analysis, Office of   Established by
Interior Secretarial Order 2953 of May 7, 1973.
Functions transferred to *Federal Energy
Administration* by act of May 7, 1974 (88 Stat. 100).

Energy Policy Office   Established in Executive
Office of the President by EO 11726 of June 29,
1973. Abolished by EO 11775 of Mar. 26, 1974.

Energy Programs, Office of   Established by
Commerce Department Organization Order 25–7A,
effective Sept. 24, 1975. Terminated by act of Aug.
4, 1977 (91 Stat. 581), and functions transferred to
Energy Department.

Energy Research and Development Administration
Established by act of Oct. 11, 1974 (88 Stat. 1234).
Assigned responsibilities by acts of Sept. 3, 1974 (88
Stat. 1069, 1079), Oct. 26, 1974 (88 Stat. 1431),
and Dec. 31, 1974 (88 Stat. 1887). Terminated by
act of Aug. 4, 1977 (91 Stat. 577), and functions
transferred to Energy Department.

Energy Resources Council   Established in Executive
Office of the President by act of Oct. 11, 1974 (88
Stat. 1233). Establishing authority repealed by act of
Aug. 4, 1977 (91 Stat. 608), and *Council* terminated.

**Energy Supplies and Resources Policy, Presidential
Advisory Committee on**   Established July 30, 1954,
by President. Abolished Mar. 12, 1961, by President
and functions transferred to Interior Secretary.

Enforcement Commission, National   Established by
General Order 18 of *Economic Stabilization
Administrator*, effective July 30, 1952. Functions
transferred to Director, *Office of Defense
Mobilization*, and Attorney General by EO 10494 of
Oct. 14, 1953.

Engineering, Bureau of   *See* **Steam Engineering,
Bureau of**

Entomology, Bureau of   *See* **Entomology and Plant
Quarantine, Bureau of**

Entomology and Plant Quarantine, Bureau of
Bureau of Entomology and *Bureau of Plant
Quarantine* created by acts of Apr. 23, 1904 (33
Stat. 276), and July 7, 1932 (47 Stat. 640),
respectively. Consolidated with disease control and
eradication functions of *Bureau of Plant Industry* into
Bureau of Entomology and Plant Quarantine by act
of Mar. 23, 1934 (48 Stat. 467). Functions
transferred to Agricultural Research Service by
Secretary's Memorandum 1320, supp. 4, of Nov. 2,
1953.

Environment, Cabinet Committee on the *See* **Environmental Quality Council**

Environmental Financing Authority Established by act of Oct. 18, 1972 (86 Stat. 899). Expired June 30, 1975, pursuant to terms of act.

Environmental Quality Council Established by EO 11472 of May 29, 1969. Renamed *Cabinet Committee on the Environment* by EO 11514 of Mar. 5, 1970. EO 11514 terminated by EO 11541 of July 1, 1970.

Environmental Science Services Administration Established in Commerce Department by Reorg. Plan No. 2 of 1965, effective July 13, 1965, by consolidating *Weather Bureau* and *Coast and Geodetic Survey*. Abolished by Reorg. Plan No. 4 of 1970, effective Oct. 3, 1970, and functions transferred to National Oceanic and Atmospheric Administration.

Equal Employment Opportunity, President's Committee on Established by EO 10925 of Mar. 6, 1961. Abolished by EO 11246 of Sept. 24, 1965, and functions transferred to Labor Department and *U.S. Civil Service Commission.*

Equal Opportunity, President's Council on Established by EO 11197 of Feb. 5, 1965. Abolished by EO 11247 of Sept. 24, 1965, and functions transferred to Justice Department.

Equipment, Bureau of Established as *Bureau of Equipment and Recruiting* by act of July 5, 1862 (12 Stat. 510), replacing *Bureau of Construction, Equipment and Repairs.* Designated as *Bureau of Equipment* in annual appropriation acts commencing with fiscal year 1892 (26 Stat. 192) after cognizance over enlisted personnel matters transferred, effective July 1, 1889, to *Bureau of Navigation.* Functions distributed among bureaus and offices in Navy Department by act of June 24, 1910 (61 Stat. 613). Abolished by act of June 30, 1914 (38 Stat. 408).

Ethics, Office of Government Established in the Office of Personnel Management by act of Oct. 26, 1978 (92 Stat. 1862). Changed to independent executive agency status by act of Nov. 3, 1988 (102 Stat. 3031).

European Migration, Intergovernmental Committee for Renamed Intergovernmental Committee for Migration by Resolution 624, passed by Intergovernmental Committee for European Migration Council, effective Nov. 11, 1980.

Evacuation, Joint Committee on *See* **Health and Welfare Aspects of Evacuation of Civilians, Joint Committee on**

Exchange Service, International Established in 1849 in Smithsonian Institution. Renamed Office of Publications Exchange by Secretary's internal directive of Jan. 11, 1985.

Executive Branch of the Government, Commission on Organization of the Established by act of July 7, 1947 (61 Stat. 246). Terminated June 12, 1949, pursuant to terms of act. Second *Commission on Organization of the Executive Branch of the Government* established by act of July 10, 1953 (67

Stat. 142). Terminated June 30, 1955, pursuant to terms of act.

Executive Council Established by EO 6202–A of July 11, 1933. Consolidated with *National Emergency Council* by EO 6889–A of Oct. 29, 1934.

Executive Exchange, President's Commission on *See* **Personnel Interchange, President's Commission on**

Executive orders *See* **State Department**

Executive Organization, President's Advisory Council on Established by President Apr. 5, 1969. Terminated May 7, 1971.

Executives, Active Corps of Established in ACTION by act of Oct. 1, 1973 (87 Stat. 404). Transferred to Small Business Administration by EO 11871 of July 18, 1975.

Exhibits, Supervisor of Established by Interior Department. Abolished in 1941 due to lack of funding.

Export Control, Administrator of Functions delegated to Administrator by Proc. 2413 of July 2, 1940, transferred to *Office of Export Control, Economic Defense Board,* by EO 8900 of Sept. 15, 1941. Renamed *Board of Economic Warfare* by EO 8982 of Dec. 17, 1941. *Board* terminated by EO 9361 of July 15, 1943.

Export Control, Office of *See* **Export Control, Administrator of**

Export-Import Bank of Washington Organization of District of Columbia banking corporation directed by EO 6581 of Feb. 2, 1934. Certificate of incorporation filed Feb. 12, 1934. Grouped with other agencies to form *Federal Loan Agency* by Reorg. Plan No. I of 1939, effective July 1, 1939. Transferred to Commerce Department by EO 9071 of Feb. 24, 1942. Functions transferred to *Office of Economic Warfare* by EO 9361 of July 15, 1943. Established as permanent independent agency by act of July 31, 1945 (59 Stat. 526). Renamed Export-Import Bank of the U.S. by act of Mar. 13, 1968 (82 Stat. 47).

Export-Import Bank of Washington, DC, Second Authorized by EO 6638 of Mar. 9, 1934. Abolished by EO 7365 of May 7, 1936, and records transferred to *Export-Import Bank of Washington,* effective June 30, 1936.

Export Marketing Service Established by Agriculture Secretary Mar. 28, 1969. Merged with Foreign Agricultural Service by Secretary's memorandum of Dec. 7, 1973, effective Feb. 3, 1974.

Exports and Requirements, Division of Established in *Office of Foreign Economic Coordination* by State Departmental order of Feb. 1, 1943. Abolished by departmental order of Nov. 6, 1943, pursuant to EO 9380 of Sept. 25, 1943.

Extension Service Established by act of May 14, 1914 (38 Stat. 372). Consolidated into *Science and Education Administration* by Secretary's order of Jan. 24, 1978. Reestablished as *Extension Service* by

Secretarial order of June 16, 1981. Became part of Cooperative State, Research, Education, and Extension Service under Department of Agriculture's reorganization in 1995.

Facts and Figures, Office of Established in *Office for Emergency Management* by EO 8922 of Oct. 24, 1941. Consolidated with *Office of War Information* in *Office for Emergency Management* by EO 9182 of June 13, 1942.

Family Security Committee Established in *Office of Defense Health and Welfare Services* Feb. 12, 1941, by administrative order. Terminated Dec. 17, 1942.

Family Services, Bureau of *See* **Assistance, Bureau of Public**

Family Support Administration Established on Apr. 4, 1986, in Health and Human Services Department under authority of section 6 of Reorganization Plan No. 1 of 1953, effective Apr. 11, 1953 (*see also* 51 FR 11641). Merged into Administration for Children and Families by Secretary's reorganization notice dated Apr. 15, 1991.

Farm Board, Federal Established by act of June 15, 1929 (46 Stat. 11). Renamed Farm Credit Administration and certain functions abolished by EO 6084 of Mar. 27, 1933. Administration placed under Agriculture Department by Reorg. Plan No. I of 1939, effective July 1, 1939. Made independent agency in the executive branch of the Government, to be housed in the Agriculture Department, by act of Aug. 6, 1953 (67 Stat. 390). Removed from Agriculture Department by act of Dec. 10, 1971 (85 Stat. 617).

Farm Credit Administration *See* **Farm Board, Federal**

Farm Loan Board, Federal Established in Treasury Department to administer act of July 17, 1916 (39 Stat. 360). Offices of appointed members of *Board,* except member designated as *Farm Loan Commissioner,* abolished by EO 6084 of Mar. 27, 1933, and *Board* functions transferred to *Farm Loan Commissioner,* subject to jurisdiction and control of Farm Credit Administration. Title changed to *Land Bank Commissioner* by act of June 16, 1933. Abolished by act of Aug. 6, 1953 (67 Stat. 393).

Farm Loan Bureau, Federal Established in Treasury Department under supervision of *Federal Farm Loan Board* and charged with execution of act of July 17, 1916 (39 Stat. 360). Transferred to *Farm Credit Administration* by EO 6084 of Mar. 27, 1933.

Farm Loan Commissioner *See* **Farm Loan Board, Federal**

Farm Mortgage Corporation, Federal Established by act of Jan. 31, 1934 (48 Stat. 344). Transferred to Agriculture Department by Reorg. Plan No. I of 1939, effective July 1, 1939, to operate under supervision of Farm Credit Administration. Abolished by act of Oct. 4, 1961 (75 Stat. 773).

Farm Products, Division of (Also known as *Division of Agriculture*) Established by *Advisory Commission to Council of National Defense* pursuant to act of Aug. 29, 1916 (39 Stat. 649).

Office of Agricultural Defense Relations (later known as *Office for Agricultural War Relations*) established in Agriculture Department by Presidential letter of May 5, 1941, which transferred to Agriculture Secretary functions previously assigned to *Division of Agriculture.* Functions concerned with food production transferred to *Food Production Administration* and functions concerned with food distribution transferred to *Food Distribution Administration* by EO 9280 of Dec. 5, 1942.

Farm Security Administration *See* **Resettlement Administration**

Farm Service Agency Established by Secretary's Memorandum 1010–1 dated Oct. 20, 1994, under authority of the act of Oct. 13, 1994 (7 U.S.C. 6901), and assumed certain functions of the *Agricultural Stabilization and Conservation Service,* the *Farmers' Home Administration,* and the *Federal Crop Insurance Corporartion.* Renamed Consolidated Farm Service Agency by Acting Administrator on Dec. 19, 1994.

Farmer Cooperative Service Established by Agriculture Secretary's Memorandum 1320, supp. 4, of Dec. 4, 1953. Consolidated with other Agriculture Department units into *Economics, Statistics, and Cooperatives Service* by Secretary's Memorandum 1927, effective Dec. 23, 1977.

Farmers' Home Administration. *See* **Resettlement Administration**

Federal. *See also other part of title*

Federal Advisory Council Established in *Federal Security Agency* by act of June 6, 1933 (48 Stat. 116). Transferred to Labor Department by Reorg. Plan No. 2 of 1949, effective Aug. 20, 1949.

Federal Crop Insurance Corporation Established by act of Feb. 16, 1938. Consolidated with the *Agricultural Stabilization and Conservation Service* and *Federal Crop Insurance Corporation* in 1995 to form the *Farm Service Agency* pursuant to act of Oct. 13, 1994 (108 Stat. 3178).

Federal Grain Inspection Service Established in the Agriculture Department by act of Oct. 21, 1976 (90 Stat. 2868). Abolished by Secretary's Memorandum 1010–1 dated Oct. 20, 1994, and program authority and functions transferred to the Grain Inspection, Packers and Stockyards Administration.

Federal Register, Administrative Committee of the *See* **Archives Establishment, National**

Federal Register, Division of the Established by act of July 26, 1935 (49 Stat. 500). Transferred to General Services Administration as part of *National Archives and Records Service* by act of June 30, 1949 (63 Stat. 381). Renamed Office of the Federal Register by order of General Services Administrator, Feb. 6, 1959. Transferred to National Archives and Records Administration by act of Oct. 19, 1984 (98 Stat. 2283).

Federal Register, Office of the *See* **Federal Register, Division of the**

Federal Reserve Board   Renamed Board of Governors of the Federal Reserve System, and Governor and Vice Governor designated as Chairman and Vice Chairman, respectively, of Board by act of Aug. 23, 1935 (49 Stat. 704).

Field Services, Office of   Established by Commerce Secretary Feb. 1, 1963, by Department Organization Order 40–3. Terminated by Department Organization Order 40–1A of Sept. 15, 1970, and functions transferred to *Bureau of Domestic Commerce.*

Filipino Rehabilitation Commission   Established by act of June 29, 1944 (58 Stat. 626). Inactive pursuant to terms of act.

Film Service, U.S.   Established by *National Emergency Council* in September 1938. Transferred to *Office of Education, Federal Security Agency,* by Reorg. Plan No. II of 1939, effective July 1, 1939. Terminated June 30, 1940.

Films, Coordinator of Government   Director of *Office of Government Reports* designated *Coordinator of Government Films* by Presidential letter of Dec. 18, 1941. Functions transferred to *Office of War Information* by EO 9182 of June 13, 1942.

Financial Operations, Bureau of Government   Renamed Financial Management Service by Treasury Secretary's Order 145–21, effective Oct. 10, 1984.

Fire Administration, U.S.   *See* **Fire Prevention and Control Administration, National**

Fire Council, Federal   Established by EO 7397 of June 20, 1936. Transferred July 1, 1939, to *Federal Works Agency* by EO 8194 of July 6, 1939, with functions under direction of *Federal Works Administrator.* Transferred with *Federal Works Agency* to General Services Administration by act of June 30, 1949 (63 Stat. 380). Transferred to Commerce Department by EO 11654 of Mar. 13, 1972.

Fire Prevention and Control, National Academy for   Established in Commerce Department by act of Oct. 29, 1974 (88 Stat. 1537). Transferred to Federal Emergency Management Agency by Reorg. Plan No. 3 of 1978, effective Apr. 1, 1979.

Fire Prevention and Control Administration, National   Renamed U.S. Fire Administration by act of Oct. 5, 1978 (92 Stat. 932). Transferred to Federal Emergency Management Agency by Reorg. Plan No. 3 of 1978, effective Apr. 1, 1979.

Fish Commission, U.S.   *Commissioner of Fish and Fisheries* established as head of *U.S. Fish Commission* by joint resolution of Feb. 9, 1871 (16 Stat. 594). *Commission* established as *Bureau of Fisheries* in *Department of Commerce and Labor* by act of Feb. 14, 1903 (32 Stat. 827). Labor Department created by act of Mar. 4, 1913 (37 Stat. 736), and *Bureau* remained in Commerce Department. Transferred to Interior Department by Reorg. Plan No. II of 1939, effective July 1, 1939. Consolidated with *Bureau of Biological Survey* into *Fish and Wildlife Service* by Reorg. Plan No. III of 1940, effective June 30, 1940.

Fish and Wildlife Service   Established by Reorg. Plan No. III of 1940, effective June 30, 1940, consolidating *Bureau of Fisheries* and *Bureau of Biological Survey.* Succeeded by U.S. Fish and Wildlife Service.

Fisheries, Bureau of   *See* **Fish Commission, U.S.**

Fisheries, Bureau of Commercial   Organized in 1959 under U.S. Fish and Wildlife Service, Interior Department. Abolished by Reorg. Plan No. 4 of 1970, effective Oct. 3, 1970, and functions transferred to National Oceanic and Atmospheric Administration.

Fishery Coordination, Office of   Established in Interior Department by EO 9204 of July 21, 1942. Terminated by EO 9649 of Oct. 29, 1945.

Flood Indemnity Administration, Federal   Established in *Housing and Home Finance Agency* by Administrator's Organizational Order 1, effective Sept. 28, 1956, redesignated as Administrator's Organizational Order 2 on Dec. 7, 1956, pursuant to act of Aug. 7, 1956 (70 Stat. 1078). Abolished by Administrator's Organizational Order 3, effective July 1, 1957, due to lack of funding.

Food, Cost of Living Council Committee on   Established by EO 11695 of Jan. 11, 1973. Abolished by EO 11788 of June 18, 1974.

Food, Drug, and Insecticide Administration   Established by act of Jan. 18, 1927 (44 Stat. 1002). Renamed Food and Drug Administration by act of May 27, 1930 (46 Stat. 422). Transferred from Agriculture Department to *Federal Security Agency* by Reorg. Plan No. IV of 1940, effective June 30, 1940. Transferred to *Health, Education, and Welfare Department* by Reorg. Plan No. 1 of 1953, effective Apr. 11, 1953.

Food Distribution Administration   Established in Agriculture Department by EO 9280 of Dec. 5, 1942, consolidating *Agricultural Marketing Administration, Sugar Agency,* distribution functions of *Office for Agricultural War Relations,* regulatory work of *Bureau of Animal Industry,* and food units of *War Production Board.* Consolidated with other agencies by EO 9322 of Mar. 26, 1943, to form *Administration of Food Production and Distribution.*

Food and Drug Administration *See* **Food, Drug, and Insecticide Administration**

Food Industry Advisory Committee   Established by EO 11627 of Oct. 15, 1971. Abolished by EO 11781 of May 1, 1974.

Food and Nutrition Service   Established Aug. 8, 1969, by Secretary of Agriculture under authority of 5 U.S.C. 301 and Reorg. Plan No. 2 of 1953 (5 U.S.C. app.). Abolished by Secretary's Memorandum 1010–1 dated Oct. 20, 1994. Functions assumed by Food and Consumer Service.

Food Production Administration   Established in Agriculture Department by EO 9280 of Dec. 5, 1942, which consolidated *Agricultural Adjustment Agency,* Farm Credit Administration, *Farm Security Administration,* Federal Crop Insurance Corporation, Soil Conservation Service, and food production activities of *War Production Board, Office of Agricultural War Relations,* and *Division of Farm Management and Costs, Bureau of Agricultural Economics.* Consolidated with other agencies by EO 9322 of Mar. 26, 1943, to form *Administration of Food Production and Distribution.*

Food Production and Distribution, Administration of Established by consolidation of *Food Production Administration, Food Distribution Administration,* Commodity Credit Corporation, and Extension Service, Agriculture Department, by EO 9322 of Mar. 26, 1943, under direction of Administrator, directly responsible to President. Renamed *War Food Administration* by EO 9334 of Apr. 19, 1943. Terminated by EO 9577 of June 29, 1945, and functions transferred to Agriculture Secretary. Transfer made permanent by Reorg. Plan No. 3 of 1946, effective July 16, 1946.

Food Safety and Quality Service Renamed Food Safety and Inspection Service by Agriculture Secretary's memorandum of June 19, 1981.

Foods, Bureau of Renamed Center for Food Safety and Applied Nutrition by Food and Drug Administration notice of Mar. 9, 1984 (49 FR 10166).

Foreign. *See also other part of title*

Foreign Aid, Advisory Committee on Voluntary Established by President May 14, 1946. Transferred from State Department to Director, *Mutual Security Agency,* and later to Director, *Foreign Operations Administration,* by Presidential letter of June 1, 1953.

Foreign Operations Administration Established by Reorg. Plan No. 7 of 1953, effective Aug. 1, 1953, and functions transferred from *Office of Director of Mutual Security, Mutual Security Agency, Technical Cooperation Administration, Institute of Inter-American Affairs.* Abolished by EO 10610 of May 9, 1955, and functions and offices transferred to State and Defense Departments.

Foreign Scholarships, Board of Renamed J. William Fulbright Foreign Scholarship Board by act of Feb. 16, 1990 (104 Stat. 49).

Forest Reservation Commission, National Established by act of Mar. 1, 1911 (36 Stat. 962). Terminated by act of Oct. 22, 1976 (90 Stat. 2961), and functions transferred to Agriculture Secretary.

Forests, Director of Established by Administrative Order 1283 of May 18, 1938. Made part of *Office of Land Utilization,* Interior Department, by Administrative Order 1466 of Apr. 15, 1940.

Freedmen's Hospital Established by act of Mar. 3, 1871 (16 Stat. 506; T. 32 of D.C. Code). Transferred from Interior Department to *Federal Security Agency* by Reorg. Plan No. IV of 1940, effective June 30, 1940.

Fuel Yards Established by act of July 1, 1918 (40 Stat. 672). Transferred from *Bureau of Mines,* Commerce Department, to *Procurement Division,* Treasury Department, by EO 6166 of June 10, 1933, effective Mar. 2, 1934.

Fuels Coordinator for War, Office of Solid *See* **Fuels Administration for War, Solid**

Fuels Corporation, U.S. Synthetic Established by act of June 30, 1980 (94 Stat. 636). Terminated Apr. 18, 1986, by act of Dec. 19, 1985 (99 Stat. 1249), and functions transferred to Treasury Secretary.

Fund-Raising Within the Federal Service, President's Committee on Established by EO 10728 of Sept. 6, 1957. Abolished by EO 10927 of Mar. 18, 1961, and functions transferred to *U.S. Civil Service Commission.*

Gallaudet College *See* **Columbia Institution for the Instruction of the Deaf and Dumb, and the Blind**

General Programs, Office of Renamed Office of Public Programs by the Chairman, National Endowment for the Humanities, in January 1991.

Geographic Board, U.S. Established by EO 27–A of Sept. 4, 1890. Abolished by EO 6680 of Apr. 17, 1935, and duties transferred to *U.S. Board on Geographical Names,* Interior Department, effective June 17, 1934. *Board* abolished by act of July 25, 1947 (61 Stat. 457), and duties assumed by *Board on Geographic Names.*

Geographical Names, U.S. Board on *See* **Geographic Board, U.S.**

Geography, Office of Function of standardizing foreign place names placed in Interior Department conjointly with *Board on Geographic Names* by act of July 25, 1947 (61 Stat. 456). Functions transferred to Defense Department by memorandum of understanding by Interior and Defense Departments and *Bureau of the Budget* Mar. 9, 1968.

Geological Survey Established in the Interior Department by act of Mar. 3, 1879 (20 Stat. 394). Renamed United States Geological Survey by acts of Nov. 13, 1991 (105 Stat. 1000) and May 18, 1992 (106 Stat. 172).

Germany, Mixed Claims Commission, U.S. and Established by agreement of Aug. 10, 1922, between U.S. and Germany. Duties extended by agreement of Dec. 31, 1928. Time limit for filing claims expired June 30, 1928. All claims disposed of by Oct. 30, 1939. Terminated June 30, 1941.

Goethals Memorial Commission Established by act of Aug. 4, 1935 (49 Stat. 743). Placed under jurisdiction of *War Department* by EO 8191 of July 5, 1939.

Government. *See other part of title*

Grain Futures Administration Established in Agriculture Department under provisions of act of Sept. 21, 1922 (42 Stat. 998). Superseded by *Commodity Exchange Administration* by order of Secretary, effective July 1, 1936. Consolidated with other agencies into *Commodity Exchange Branch, Agricultural Marketing Administration,* by EO 9069 of Feb. 23, 1942. Functions transferred to Agriculture Secretary by EO 9577 of June 29, 1945. Transfer made permanent by Reorg. Plan No. 3 of 1946, effective July 16, 1946. Functions transferred to *Commodity Exchange Authority* by Secretary's

Memorandum 1185 of Jan. 21, 1947. Functions transferred to Commodity Futures Trading Commission by act of Oct. 23, 1974 (88 Stat. 1414).

Grain Stabilization Corporation   Organized as Delaware corporation to operate in connection with *Federal Farm Board* pursuant to act of June 15, 1929 (46 Stat. 11). Terminated by filing of certificate of dissolution with Corporation Commission of State of Delaware Dec. 14, 1935.

Grants and Program Systems, Office of   Abolished and functions transferred to Cooperative State Research Service, Agriculture Department, by Secretarial Memorandum 1020–26 of July 1, 1986.

Grazing Service   Consolidated with *General Land Office* into Bureau of Land Management, Interior Department, by Reorg. Plan No. 3 of 1946, effective July 16, 1946.

Great Lakes Basin Commission   Established by EO 11345 of Apr. 20, 1967. Terminated by EO 12319 of Sept. 9, 1981.

Great Lakes Pilotage Administration   Established in Commerce Department to administer act of June 30, 1960 (74 Stat. 259). Administration of act transferred to Transportation Secretary by act of Oct. 15, 1966 (80 Stat. 931).

Handicapped, National Center on Education Media and Materials for the   Established by agreement between *Health, Education, and Welfare Secretary* and Ohio State University, pursuant to acts of Aug. 20, 1969 (83 Stat. 102) and Apr. 13, 1970 (84 Stat. 187). Authorization deleted by act of Nov. 29, 1975 (89 Stat. 795), and Secretary authorized to enter into agreements with non-Federal organizations to establish and operate centers for handicapped.

Handicapped, National Council on the   Established in *Health, Education, and Welfare Department* by act of Nov. 6, 1978 (92 Stat. 2977). Transferred to Education Department by act of Oct. 17, 1979 (93 Stat. 677). Reorganized as independent agency by act of Feb. 22, 1984 (98 Stat. 26).

Handicapped Employees, Interagency Committee on   Alternately renamed Interagency Committee on Employment of People with Disabilities by EO 12704 of Feb. 26, 1990.

Handicapped Individuals, White House Conference on   Established by act of Dec. 7, 1974 (88 Stat. 1617). Terminated Dec. 30, 1977, pursuant to terms of act.

Handicapped Research, National Institute of   Renamed National Institute on Disability and Rehabilitation Research by act of Oct. 21, 1986 (100 Stat. 1820).

Health, Cost of Living Council Committee on   Established by EO 11695 of Jan. 11, 1973. Abolished by EO 11788 of June 18, 1974.

Health, Education, and Welfare, Department of   Established by Reorganization Plan No. 1 of 1953 (5 U.S.C. app.), effective Apr. 11, 1953. Renamed Health and Human Services Department by act of Oct. 17, 1979 (93 Stat. 695).

Health, Welfare, and Related Defense Activities, Office of the Coordinator of   *Federal Security Administrator* designated as Coordinator of health, welfare, and related fields of activity affecting national defense, including aspects of education under *Federal Security Agency,* by *Council of National Defense,* with approval of President, Nov. 28, 1940. Office of Coordinator superseded by *Office of Defense Health and Welfare Services,* established in *Office for Emergency Services* by EO 8890 of Sept. 3, 1941.

Health Care Technology, National Council on   Established by act of July 1, 1944, as amended (92 Stat. 3447). Renamed *Council on Health Care Technology* by act of Oct. 30, 1984 (98 Stat. 2820). Name lowercased by act of Oct. 7, 1985 (99 Stat. 493). Terminated by act of Dec. 19, 1989 (103 Stat. 2205).

Health Facilities, Financing, Compliance, and Conversion, Bureau of   Renamed Bureau of Health Facilities by Health and Human Services Department Secretarial order of Mar. 12, 1980 (45 FR 17207).

Health Industry Advisory Committee   Established by EO 11695 of Jan. 11, 1973. Abolished by EO 11781 of May 1, 1974.

Health Manpower, Bureau of   Renamed Bureau of Health Professions by Health and Human Services Department Secretarial order of Mar. 12, 1980 (45 FR 17207).

Health and Medical Committee   Established by *Council of National Defense* order of Sept. 19, 1940. Transferred to *Federal Security Agency* by *Council* order approved by President Nov. 28, 1940. Reestablished in *Office of Defense Health and Welfare Services, Office for Emergency Management,* by EO 8890 of Sept. 3, 1941. *Committee* transferred to *Federal Security Agency* by EO 9338 of Apr. 29, 1943.

Health Resources Administration   Established in Public Health Service. Abolished by Health and Human Services Department Secretarial reorganization of Aug. 20, 1982 (47 FR 38409), and functions transferred to Health Resources and Services Administration.

Health Service, Public   Originated by act of July 16, 1798 (1 Stat. 605). Transferred from Treasury Department to *Federal Security Agency* by Reorg. Plan No. I of 1939, effective July 1, 1939.

Health Services Administration   Established in Public Health Service. Abolished by Health and Human Services Department Secretarial reorganization of Aug. 20, 1982 (47 FR 38409), and functions transferred to Health Resources and Services Administration.

Health Services Industry, Committee on the   Established by EO 11627 of Oct. 15, 1971. Abolished by EO 11695 of Jan. 11, 1973.

Health Services and Mental Health Administration   Established in Public Health Service Apr. 1, 1968. Abolished by *Health, Education, and Welfare Department* reorganization order and functions transferred to *Centers for Disease Control, Health*

Resources Administration, and *Health Services Administration,* effective July 1, 1973.

Health Services Research, National Center for Established by act of July 23, 1974 (88 Stat. 363). Transferred from *Health Resources Administration* to Office of the Assistant Secretary for Health by *Health, Education, and Welfare Department* reorganization, effective Dec. 2, 1977. Renamed *National Center for Health Services Research and Health Care Technology Assessment* by Secretary's order, pursuant to act of Oct. 30, 1984 (98 Stat. 2817). Terminated by act of Dec. 19, 1989 (103 Stat. 2205).

Health Statistics, National Center for Established by act of July 23, 1974 (88 Stat. 363). Transferred from *Health Resources Administration* to Office of the Assistant Secretary for Health by *Health, Education, and Welfare Department* reorganization, effective Dec. 2, 1977. Transferred to *Centers for Disease Control* by Secretary's notice of Apr. 2, 1987 (52 FR 13318).

Health and Welfare Activities, Interdepartmental Committee to Coordinate Appointed by President Aug. 15, 1935, and reestablished by EO 7481 of Oct. 27, 1936. Terminated in 1939.

Health and Welfare Aspects of Evacuation of Civilians, Joint Committee on Established August 1941 as joint committee of *Office of Defense Health and Welfare Services* and *Office of Civilian Defense.* Reorganized in June 1942 and renamed *Joint Committee on Evacuation. Office of Defense Health and Welfare Services* abolished by EO 9388 of Apr. 29, 1943, and functions transferred to *Federal Security Agency. Committee* terminated.

Heart and Lung Institute, National Renamed National Heart, Lung, and Blood Institute by act of Apr. 22, 1976 (90 Stat. 402).

Heritage Conservation and Recreation Service Established by Interior Secretary Jan. 25, 1978. Abolished by Secretarial Order 3060 of Feb. 19, 1981, and functions transferred to National Park Service.

Highway Safety Agency, National Established in Commerce Department by act of Sept. 9, 1966 (80 Stat. 731). Functions transferred to Transportation Department by act of Oct. 15, 1966 (80 Stat. 931). Functions transferred to *National Highway Safety Bureau* by EO 11357 of June 6, 1967. *Bureau* renamed National Highway Traffic Safety Administration by act of Dec. 31, 1970 (84 Stat. 1739).

Highway Safety Bureau, National *See* **Highway Safety Agency, National**

Home Economics, Bureau of Human Nutrition and *See* **Home Economics, Office of**

Home Economics, Office of Renamed *Bureau of Home Economics* by Secretary's Memorandum 436, effective July 1, 1923, pursuant to act of Feb. 26, 1923 (42 Stat. 1289). Redesignated *Bureau of Human Nutrition and Home Economics* February 1943 in accordance with *Research Administration* Memorandum 5 issued pursuant to EO 9069 of Feb.

23, 1942, and in conformity with Secretary's Memorandums 960 and 986. Functions transferred to Agricultural Research Service by Secretary's Memorandum 1320, supp. 4, of Nov. 2, 1953.

Home Loan Bank Administration, Federal *See* **Home Loan Bank Board, Federal**

Home Loan Bank Board *See* **Home Loan Bank Board, Federal**

Home Loan Bank Board, Federal Established by acts of July 22, 1932 (47 Stat. 725), June 13, 1933 (48 Stat. 128), and June 27, 1934 (48 Stat. 1246). Grouped with other agencies to form *Federal Loan Agency* by Reorg. Plan No. I of 1939, effective July 1, 1939. Functions transferred to *Federal Home Loan Bank Administration, National Housing Agency,* by EO 9070 of Feb. 24, 1942. Abolished by Reorg. Plan No. 3, effective July 27, 1947, and functions transferred to *Home Loan Bank Board, Housing and Home Finance Agency.* Renamed *Federal Home Loan Bank Board* and made independent agency by act of Aug. 11, 1955 (69 Stat. 640). Abolished by act of Aug. 9, 1989 (103 Stat. 354, 415), and functions transferred to Office of Thrift Supervision, Resolution Trust Corporation, Federal Deposit Insurance Corporation, and Federal Housing Finance Board.

Home Loan Bank System, Federal Grouped with other agencies to form *Federal Loan Agency* by Reorg. Plan No. I of 1939, effective July 1, 1939. Functions transferred to *Federal Home Loan Bank Administration, National Housing Agency,* by EO 9070 of Feb. 24, 1942. Transferred to *Housing and Home Finance Agency* by Reorg. Plan No. 3 of 1947, effective July 27, 1947.

Home Mortgage Credit Extension Committee, National Voluntary Established by act of Aug. 2, 1954 (68 Stat 638). Terminated Oct. 1, 1965, pursuant to terms of act.

Home Owners' Loan Corporation Established by act of June 13, 1933 (48 Stat. 128), under supervision of *Federal Home Loan Bank Board.* Grouped with other agencies to form *Federal Loan Agency* by Reorg. Plan No. I of 1939, effective July 1, 1939. Transferred to *Federal Home Loan Bank Administration, National Housing Agency,* by EO 9070 of Feb. 24, 1942. Board of Directors abolished by Reorg. Plan No. 3 of 1947, effective July 27, 1947, and functions transferred, for liquidation of assets, to *Home Loan Bank Board, Housing and Home Finance Agency.* Terminated by order of *Home Loan Bank Board Secretary,* effective Feb. 3, 1954, pursuant to act of June 30, 1953 (67 Stat. 121).

Homesteads, Division of Subsistence Established by act of June 16, 1933 (48 Stat. 205). Interior Secretary authorized to administer section 208 of act by EO 6209 of July 21, 1933. *Federal Subsistence Homesteads Corporation* created by Secretary's order of Dec. 2, 1933, and organization incorporated under laws of Delaware. Transferred to *Resettlement Administration* by EO 7041 of May 15, 1935.

Homesteads Corporation, Federal Subsistence *See* **Homesteads, Division of Subsistence**

Hospitalization, Board of Federal   Organized Nov. 1, 1921. Designated as advisory agency to *Bureau of the Budget* May 7, 1943. Terminated June 30, 1948, by Director's letter of May 28, 1948.

Housing, President's Committee on Equal Opportunity in   Established by EO 11063 of Nov. 20, 1962. Inactive as of June 30, 1968.

Housing Administration, Federal   Established by act of June 27, 1934 (48 Stat. 1246). Grouped with other agencies to form *Federal Loan Agency* by Reorg. Plan No. I of 1939, effective July 1, 1939. Functions transferred to *Federal Housing Administration, National Housing Agency*, by EO 9070 of Feb. 24, 1942. Transferred to *Housing and Home Finance Agency* by Reorg. Plan No. 3, effective July 27, 1947. Functions transferred to Housing and Urban Development Department by act of Sept. 9, 1965 (79 Stat. 667).

Housing Administration, Public   Established as constituent agency of *Housing and Home Finance Agency* by Reorg. Plan No. 3 of 1947, effective July 27, 1947. Functions transferred to Housing and Urban Development Department by act of Sept. 9, 1965 (79 Stat. 667).

Housing Agency, National   Established by EO 9070 of Feb. 24, 1942, to consolidate housing functions relating to *Federal Home Loan Bank Board, Federal Home Loan Bank System, Federal Savings and Loan Insurance Corporation, Home Owners' Loan Corporation, U.S. Housing Corporation, Federal Housing Administration, U.S. Housing Authority, Defense Homes Corporation, Division of Defense Housing Coordination, Central Housing Committee, Farm Security Administration* with respect to nonfarm housing, *Public Buildings Administration, Division of Defense Housing, Mutual Ownership Defense Housing Division, Office of Administrator of Federal Works Agency*, and *War* and *Navy* Departments with respect to housing located off military installations. Agency dissolved on creation of *Housing and Home Finance Agency* by Reorg. Plan No. 3 of 1947, effective July 27, 1947.

Housing Authority, Federal Public   Established by EO 9070 of Feb. 24, 1942. Public housing functions of *Federal Works Agency, War* and *Navy* Departments (except housing located on military installations), and *Farm Security Administration* (nonfarm housing) transferred to *Authority*, and *Defense Homes Corporation* administered by *Authority's* Commissioner. Functions transferred to *Public Housing Administration, Housing and Home Finance Agency*, by Reorg. Plan No. 3 of 1947, effective July 27, 1947.

Housing Authority, U.S.   Established in Interior Department by act of Sept. 1, 1937 (50 Stat. 888). Transferred to *Federal Works Agency* by Reorg. Plan No. I of 1939, effective July 1, 1939. Transferred to *Federal Public Housing Authority, National Housing Agency*, by EO 9070 of Feb. 24, 1942. Office of Administrator abolished by Reorg. Plan No. 3 of 1947, effective July 27, 1947, and functions transferred to *Public Housing Administration, Housing and Home Finance Agency*.

Housing Corporation, U.S.   Incorporated July 10, 1918, under laws of New York. Transferred from Labor Department to Treasury Department by EO 7641 of June 22, 1937. Transferred from Treasury Department to *Public Buildings Administration, Federal Works Agency*, by EO 8186 of June 29, 1939. Functions transferred for liquidation to *Federal Home Loan Bank Administration, National Housing Agency*, by EO 9070 of Feb. 24, 1942. Terminated Sept. 8, 1952, by Secretary, *Home Loan Bank Board*.

Housing Council, National   Established in *Housing and Home Finance Agency* by Reorg. Plan No. 3 of 1947, effective July 27, 1947. Terminated by Reorg. Plan No. 4 of 1965, effective July 27, 1965, and functions transferred to President.

Housing Division   Established in *Public Works Administration* by act of June 16, 1933 (48 Stat. 195). Functions transferred to *U.S. Housing Authority* by EO 7732 of Oct. 27, 1937.

Housing Expediter, Office of the   Established in *Office of War Mobilization and Reconversion* by Presidential letter of Dec. 12, 1945, to *Housing Expediter*. Functions of *Housing Expediter* defined by EO 9686 of Jan. 26, 1946. *Housing Expediter* confirmed in position of *National Housing Administrator* Feb. 6, 1946. *Office of the Housing Expediter* established by act of May 22, 1946 (60 Stat. 208). Functions of *Office* and *National Housing Administrator* segregated by EO 9820 of Jan. 11, 1947. Housing functions of *Civilian Production Administration* transferred to *Office* by EO 9836 of Mar. 22, 1947, effective Apr. 1, 1947. Rent control functions of *Office of Temporary Controls* transferred to *Office* by EO 9841 of Apr. 23, 1947. *Office* terminated by EO 10276 of July 31, 1951, and functions transferred to *Economic Stabilization Agency*.

Housing and Home Finance Agency   Established by Reorg. Plan No. 3 of 1947, effective July 27, 1947. Terminated by act of Sept. 9, 1965 (79 Stat. 667), and functions transferred to Housing and Urban Development Department.

Howard University   Established by act of Mar. 2, 1867 (14 Stat. 438). Functions of Interior Department transferred to *Federal Security Agency* by Reorg. Plan No. IV of 1940, effective June 30, 1940. Functions of *Health, Education, and Welfare Department* transferred to Education Department by act of Oct. 17, 1979 (93 Stat. 678).

Human Development, Office of   Established in *Health, Education, and Welfare Department*. Renamed Office of Human Development Services and component units transferred to or reorganized under new administrations in Office by Secretary's reorganization order of July 26, 1977. Merged into the Administration for Children and Families by Health and Human Services Department Secretary's reorganization notice dated Apr. 15, 1991.

Human Development Services, Office of   *See* **Human Development, Office of**

Hydrographic Office   Jurisdiction transferred from *Bureau of Navigation* to Chief of Naval Operations by EO 9126 of Apr. 8, 1942, and by Reorg. Plan

No. 3 of 1946, effective July 16, 1946. Renamed U.S. Naval Oceanographic Office by act of July 10, 1962 (76 Stat. 154).

Immigration, Bureau of   Established as branch of Treasury Department by act of Mar. 3, 1891 (26 Stat. 1085). Transferred to *Department of Commerce and Labor* by act of Feb. 14, 1903 (34 Stat. 596). Made *Bureau of Immigration and Naturalization* by act of June 29, 1906 (37 Stat. 736). Made separate division after Labor Department created by act of Mar. 4, 1913 (37 Stat. 736). Consolidated into Immigration and Naturalization Service, Labor Department, by EO 6166 of June 10, 1933. Transferred to Justice Department by Reorg. Plan No. V of 1940, effective June 14, 1940.

Immigration, Commissioners of   Offices of commissioners of immigration of the several ports created by act of Aug. 18, 1894 (28 Stat. 391). Abolished by Reorg. Plan No. III of 1940, effective June 30, 1940, and functions transferred to *Bureau of Immigration and Naturalization,* Labor Department.

Immigration and Naturalization, Bureau of   *See* **Immigration, Bureau of**

Immigration and Naturalization, District Commissioner of   Created by act of Aug. 18, 1894 (28 Stat. 391). Abolished by Reorg. Plan No. III of 1940, effective June 30, 1940. Functions administered by Immigration and Naturalization Commissioner, Justice Department, through district immigration and naturalization directors.

Immigration and Naturalization Service   *See* **Immigration, Bureau of**

Import Programs, Office of   Established by Commerce Secretary Feb. 14, 1971. Functions transferred to *Domestic and International Business Administration,* effective Nov. 17, 1972.

Indian Claims Commission   Established by act of Aug. 13, 1946 (60 Stat. 1049). Terminated by act of Oct. 8, 1976 (90 Stat. 1990), and pending cases transferred to *U.S. Court of Claims* Sept. 30, 1978.

Indian Commissioners, Board of   Established by section 2039, Revised Statutes. Abolished by EO 6145 of May 25, 1933.

Indian Medical Facilities   Functions transferred from Interior Department to *Health, Education, and Welfare Department,* to be administered by Surgeon General of Public Health Service, by act of Aug. 5, 1954 (68 Stat. 674).

Indian Opportunity, National Council on   Established by EO 11399 of Mar. 6, 1968. Terminated Nov. 26, 1974, by act of Nov. 26, 1969 (83 Stat. 220).

Indian Policy Review Commission, American   Established by act of Jan. 2, 1975 (88 Stat. 1910). Terminated June 30, 1977, pursuant to terms of act.

Industrial Analysis, Committee of   Established by EO 7323 of Mar. 21, 1936. Terminated Feb. 17, 1937.

Industrial Cooperation, Coordinator for   Established by EO 7193 of Sept. 26, 1935. Continued by EO 7324 of Mar. 30, 1936. Terminated June 30, 1937.

Industrial Emergency Committee   Established by EO 6770 of June 30, 1934. Consolidated with *National Emergency Council* by EO 6889–A of Oct. 29, 1934.

Industrial Pollution Control Council Staff, National   Established by Commerce Department Organization Order 35–3 of June 17, 1970. *Staff* abolished by departmental organization order of Sept. 10, 1973. Council inactive.

Industrial Recovery Board, National   Established by EO 6859 of Sept. 27, 1934. Terminated by EO 7075 of June 15, 1935.

Industrial Recovery Board, Special   Established by EO 6173 of June 16, 1933. Functions absorbed by *National Emergency Council* under terms of EO 6513 of Dec. 18, 1933.

Industrial Relations, Office of   Activated in Navy Department Sept. 14, 1945. Superseded June 22, 1966, by creation of *Office of Civilian Manpower Management.*

Industry and Trade Administration   *See* **Business and Defense Services Administration**

Information, Committee for Reciprocity   Established by EO 6750 of June 27, 1934; reestablished by EO 10004 of Oct. 5, 1948, which revoked EO 6750. Superseded by EO 10082 of Oct. 5, 1949; abolished by EO 11075 of Jan. 15, 1963, which revoked EO 10082.

Information, Coordinator of   Established by Presidential order of July 11, 1941. Functions exclusive of foreign information activities transferred by military order of June 13, 1942, to jurisdiction of Joint Chiefs of Staff, *War Department,* as *Office of Strategic Services.* Foreign information functions transferred to *Office of War Information* by EO 9182 of June 13, 1942.

Information, Division of   Established pursuant to Presidential letter of Feb. 28, 1941, to *Liaison Officer, Office of Emergency Management.* Abolished by EO 9182 of June 13, 1942. Functions relating to public information on war effort transferred and consolidated with *Office of War Information,* and publication services relating to specific agencies of OEM transferred to those agencies.

Information, Office of Coordinator of   Transferred, exclusive of foreign information activities, to *Office of War Information* by EO 9182 of June 13, 1942. Designated *Office of Strategic Services* and transferred to jurisdiction of Joint Chiefs of Staff by military order of June 13, 1942. Terminated by EO 9621 of Sept. 20, 1945, and functions distributed to State and *War* Departments.

Information Administration, International   Transferred from State Department to U.S. Information Agency by Reorg. Plan No. 8 of 1953, effective Aug. 1, 1953.

Information Agency, U.S.   Established by Reorg. Plan No. 8 of 1953, effective Aug. 1, 1953. Abolished by Reorg. Plan No. 2 of 1977, effective Apr. 1, 1978; replaced by and functions transferred to *International Communication Agency*. Redesignated U.S. Information Agency by act of Aug. 24, 1982 (96 Stat. 291).

Information and Public Affairs, Office of   Merged with *Office of Intergovernmental Affairs* to form Office of Public and Intergovernmental Affairs by Labor Secretary's Order 1–85 of June 5, 1985.

Information Resources Management, Office of   *See* **Telecommunications Service, Automated Data**

Information Resources Management Service   Established in the General Services Administration. Renamed Information Technology Service in 1995.

Information Security Committee, Interagency   Established by EO 12065 of June 28, 1978. Abolished by EO 12356 of Apr. 2, 1982.

Information Security Oversight Office   Established in General Services Administration by EO 12065 of June 28, 1978. EO 12065 revoked by EO 12356 of Apr. 2, 1982, which provided for continuation of Office.

Information Service, Government   *See* **Information Service, U.S.**

Information Service, Interim International   Established in State Department by EO 9608 of Aug. 31, 1945. Abolished Dec. 31, 1945, pursuant to terms of order.

Information Service, U.S.   Established in March 1934 as division of *National Emergency Council*. Transferred to *Office of Government Reports* by Reorg. Plan No. II of 1939, effective July 1, 1939. Consolidated, along with other functions of *Office*, into *Division of Public Inquiries, Bureau of Special Services, Office of War Information*, by EO 9182 of June 13, 1942. *Bureau of Special Services* renamed *Government Information Service* and transferred to *Bureau of the Budget* by EO 9608 of Aug. 31, 1945. Service transferred to *Office of Government Reports* by EO 9809 of Dec. 12, 1946.

Insane, Government Hospital for the   Established by act of Mar. 3, 1855 (10 Stat. 682). Renamed Saint Elizabeths Hospital by act of July 1, 1916 (39 Stat. 309). Transferred from Interior Department to *Federal Security Agency* by Reorg. Plan No. IV of 1940, effective June 30, 1940. Transferred to *Health, Education, and Welfare Department* by Reorg. Plan No. 1 of 1953, effective Apr. 11, 1953. Functions redelegated to National Institute of Mental Health by Secretary's reorganization order of Aug. 9, 1967. Property and administration transferred to District of Columbia Government by act of Nov. 8, 1984 (98 Stat. 3369).

Installations, Director of   Established in Defense Department by act of July 14, 1952 (66 Stat. 625). Abolished by Reorg. Plan No. 6 of 1953, effective June 30, 1953, and functions transferred to Defense Secretary.

Insular Affairs, Bureau of   Transferred from *War Department* to *Division of Territories and Island Possessions*, Interior Department, by Reorg. Plan No. II of 1939, effective July 1, 1939.

Insurance Administrator, Federal   Established by act of Aug. 1, 1968 (82 Stat. 567). Functions transferred to Federal Emergency Management Agency by Reorg. Plan No. 3 of 1978, effective Apr. 1, 1979.

Integrity and Efficiency, President's Council on   Established by EO 12301 of Mar. 26, 1981 (46 FR 19211). Abolished and reestablished by EO 12625 of Jan 27, 1988 (53 FR 2812). Abolished and reestablished by EO 12805 of May 11, 1992 (57 FR 20627).

Intelligence Activities, President's Board of Consultants on Foreign   Established by EO 10656 of Feb. 6, 1956. EO 10656 revoked by EO 10938 of May 4, 1961, and *Board* terminated. Functions transferred to President's Foreign Intelligence Advisory Board.

Intelligence Advisory Board, President's Foreign   Established by EO 11460 of Mar. 20, 1969. Abolished by EO 11984 of May 4, 1977. Reestablished by EO 12331 of Oct. 20, 1981.

Intelligence Authority, National   Established by Presidential directive of Jan. 22, 1946. Terminated on creation of Central Intelligence Agency under National Security Council by act of July 26, 1947 (61 Stat. 497).

Intelligence Group, Central   Terminated on creation of Central Intelligence Agency by act of July 26, 1947 (61 Stat. 497).

Inter-American Affairs, Institute of   *See* **American Republics, Office for Coordination of Commercial and Cultural Relations between the**

Inter-American Affairs, Office of   *See* **American Republics, Office for Coordination of Commercial and Cultural Relations between the**

Inter-American Affairs, Office of the Coordinator of   *See* **American Republics, Office for Coordination of Commercial and Cultural Relations between the**

Interagency.   *See other part of title*

Interdepartmental.   *See also other part of title*

Interdepartmental Advisory Council   Established January 1941 to advise *Coordinator of Health, Welfare, and Related Defense Activities*. Terminated on creation of *Office of Defense Health and Welfare Service* Sept. 3, 1941.

Interest and Dividends, Committee on   Established by EO 11695 of Jan. 11, 1973. Abolished by EO 11781 of May 1, 1974.

Intergovernmental Affairs, Office of   Merged with *Office of Information and Public Affairs* to form Office of Public and Intergovernmental Affairs by Labor Secretary's Order 1–85 of June 5, 1985.

Intergovernmental Relations, Commission on   Established by act of July 10, 1953 (67 Stat. 145).

Final report submitted to Congress by June 30, 1955, pursuant to act of Feb. 7, 1955 (69 Stat. 7).

Intergovernmental Relations, Office of   Established by EO 11455 of Feb. 14, 1969. Functions transferred to *Domestic Council* by EO 11690 of Dec. 14, 1972.

Interim Compliance Panel   Established by Dec. 30, 1969 (83 Stat. 774). Terminated June 30, 1976, pursuant to terms of act.

Internal Revenue Service   Functions relating to alcohol, tobacco, firearms, and explosives transferred to Bureau of Alcohol, Tobacco and Firearms by Treasury departmental order July 1, 1972.

Internal Security Division   Established July 9, 1945, by transfer of functions from Criminal Division. Abolished Mar. 22, 1973, and functions transferred to Criminal Division, Justice Department.

International.   *See also other part of title*

International Activities, Office of   Renamed *Office of Service and Protocol* by Smithsonian Institution Secretary's internal directive of Jan. 11, 1985.

International Development, Agency for   Transferred from State Department to U.S. International Development Cooperation Agency by Reorg. Plan No. 2 of 1979, effective Oct. 1, 1979. Continued as agency within IDCA by IDCA Delegation of Authority No. 1 of Oct. 1, 1979.

Investigation, Bureau of   Established by act of May 22, 1908 (35 Stat. 235). Functions consolidated with investigative functions of *Bureau of Prohibition, Division of Investigation,* Justice Department, by EO 6166 of June 10, 1933, effective Mar. 2, 1934.

Investigation, Division of   Designated as Federal Bureau of Investigation in Justice Department by act of Mar. 22, 1935 (49 Stat. 77).

Investigation and Research, Board of   Established by act of Sept. 18, 1940 (54 Stat. 952). Extended to Sept. 18, 1944, by Proc. 2559 of June 26, 1942.

Investigations, Division of   Established by administrative order of Apr. 27, 1933. Abolished Jan. 17, 1942, by administrative order and functions transferred to *Branch of Field Examination, General Land Office,* Interior Department.

Investments, Office of Foreign Direct   Established in Commerce Department Jan. 2, 1968, by Departmental Organization Order 25–3 to carry out provisions of EO 11387 of Jan. 1, 1968. Controls on foreign investments terminated Jan. 29, 1974.

Jamestown-Williamsburg-Yorktown National Celebration Commission   Established by act of Aug. 13, 1953 (67 Stat. 576). Terminated upon submission of final report to Congress Mar. 1, 1958.

Joint.   *See also other part of title*

Joint Resolutions of Congress   *See* **State Department**

Judicial Procedure, Commission on International Rules of   Established by act of Sept. 2, 1958 (72 Stat. 1743). Terminated Dec. 31, 1966, by act of Aug. 30, 1964 (78 Stat. 700).

Justice Assistance, Research, and Statistics, Office of   Established in Justice Department by act of Dec. 27, 1979 (93 Stat. 1201). Abolished by act of Oct. 12, 1984 (98 Stat. 2091).

Kennedy, Commission To Report Upon the Assassination of President John F.   Established by EO 11130 of Nov. 29, 1963. Report submitted Sept. 24, 1964, and *Commission* discharged by Presidential letter of same date.

Labor, President's Committee on Migratory   Appointed by Presidential letter of Aug. 26, 1954. Formally established by EO 10894 of Nov. 15, 1960. Terminated Jan. 6, 1964, by Labor Secretary in letter to members, with approval of President.

Labor and Commerce, Department of   Established by act of Feb. 14, 1903 (32 Stat. 825). Reorganized into separate Departments of Labor and Commerce by act of Mar. 4, 1913 (37 Stat. 736).

Labor Department, Solicitor for   Transferred from Justice Department to Labor Department by EO 6166 of June 10, 1933.

Labor-Management Advisory Committee   Established by EO 11695 of Jan. 11, 1973. Abolished by EO 11788 of June 18, 1974.

Labor-Management Policy, President's Advisory Committee on   Established by EO 10918 of Feb. 16, 1961. Abolished by EO 11710 of Apr. 4, 1973.

Labor-Management Relations Services, Office of   Established by Labor Secretary's Order 3–84 of May 3, 1984. Renamed *Bureau of Labor-Management Relations and Cooperative Programs* by Secretarial Order 7–84 of Sept. 20, 1984 (49 FR 38374).

Labor-Management Services Administration   *Office of Pension and Welfare Benefit Programs* transferred from *Administration* and constituted as separate unit by Labor Secretary's Order 1–84 of Jan. 20, 1984 (49 FR 4269). Remaining labor-management relations functions reassigned by Labor Secretary's Order 3–84 of May 3, 1984.

Labor Organization, International   Established in 1919 by Treaty of Versailles with U.S. joining in 1934. U.S. membership terminated Nov. 1, 1977, at President's direction.

Labor Relations Council, Federal   Established by EO 11491 of Oct. 29, 1969. Abolished by Reorg. Plan No. 2 of 1978, effective Jan. 1, 1979, and functions transferred to Federal Labor Relations Authority.

Labor Standards, Apprenticeship Section, Division of   Transferred to *Federal Security Agency* by EO 9139 of Apr. 18, 1942, functioning as *Apprentice Training Service.* Transferred to *War Manpower Commission* by EO 9247 of Sept. 17, 1942, functioning in *Bureau of Training.* Returned to Labor Department by EO 9617 of Sept. 19, 1945.

Labor Standards, Bureau of   Established by Labor departmental order in 1934. Functions absorbed by Occupational Safety and Health Administration in May 1971.

Land Bank Commissioner   *See* **Farm Loan Board, Federal**

Land Law Review Commission, Public   Established by act of Sept. 19, 1964 (78 Stat. 982). Terminated Dec. 31, 1970, pursuant to terms of act.

Land Office, General   Consolidated with *Grazing Service* into Bureau of Land Management, Interior Department, by Reorg. Plan No. 3 of 1946, effective July 16, 1946.

Land Office, Office of Recorder of the General   Created in Interior Department by act of July 4, 1836 (5 Stat. 111). Abolished by Reorg. Plan No. III of 1940, effective June 30, 1940, and functions transferred to *General Land Office.*

Land Policy Section   Established in 1934 as part of *Program Planning Division, Agricultural Adjustment Administration.* Personnel taken over by *Resettlement Administration* in 1935.

Land Problems, Committee on National   Established by EO 6693 of Apr. 28, 1934. Abolished by EO 6777 of June 30, 1934.

Land Program, Director of   Basis of program found in act of June 16, 1933 (48 Stat. 200). *Special Board of Public Works* established by EO 6174 of June 16, 1933. Land Program established by *Board* by resolution passed Dec. 28, 1933, and amended July 18, 1934. *Federal Emergency Relief Administration* designated to administer program Feb. 28, 1934. Land Program transferred to *Resettlement Administration* by EO 7028 of Apr. 30, 1935. Functions of *Administration* transferred to Agriculture Secretary by EO 7530 of Dec. 31, 1936. Land conservation and land-utilization programs administered by *Administration* transferred to *Bureau of Agricultural Economics* by Secretary's Memorandum 733. Administration of land programs placed under Soil Conservation Service by Secretary's Memorandum 785 of Oct. 6, 1938.

Land Use Coordination, Office of   Established by Agriculture Secretary's Memorandum 725 of July 12, 1937. Abolished Jan. 1, 1944, by General Departmental Circular 21 and functions administered by *Land Use Coordinator.*

Land Use and Water Planning, Office of   Established in Interior Department by Secretarial Order No. 2953 of May 7, 1973. Abolished by Secretarial Order No. 2988 of Mar. 11, 1976.

Law Enforcement Assistance Administration   Established by act of June 19, 1968 (82 Stat. 197). Operations closed out by Justice Department due to lack of appropriations and remaining functions transferred to *Office of Justice Assistance, Research, and Statistics.*

Law Enforcement Training Center, Consolidated Federal   Renamed Federal Law Enforcement Training Center by Amendment No. 1 of Aug. 14,

1975, to Treasury Department Order 217 (Revision 1).

Legislative Affairs, Office of   Renamed Office of Intergovernmental and Legislative Affairs Feb. 24, 1984, by Attorney General's Order 1054–84 (49 FR 10177).

Lend-Lease Administration, Office of   Established by EO 8926 of Oct. 28, 1941, to replace *Division of Defense Aid Reports.* Consolidated with *Foreign Economic Administration* by EO 9380 of Sept. 25, 1943.

Lewis and Clark Trail Commission   Established by act of Oct. 6, 1964 (78 Stat. 1005). Terminated October 1969 by terms of act.

Lighthouses, Bureau of   Established in Commerce Department by act of Aug. 7, 1789 (1 Stat. 53). Consolidated with U.S. Coast Guard by Reorg. Plan No. II of 1939, effective July 1, 1939.

Lincoln Sesquicentennial Commission   Established by joint resolution of Sept. 2, 1957 (71 Stat. 587). Terminated Mar. 1, 1960, pursuant to terms of joint resolution.

Liquidation, Director of   Established in *Office for Emergency Management* by EO 9674 of Jan. 4, 1946. Terminated by EO 9744 of June 27, 1946.

Liquidation Advisory Committee   Established by EO 9674 of Jan. 4, 1946. Terminated by EO 9744 of June 27, 1946.

Loan Agency, Federal   Established by Reorg. Plan No. I of 1939, effective July 1, 1939, by consolidating *Reconstruction Finance Corporation*— including subordinate units of *RFC Mortgage Company, Disaster Loan Corporation, Federal National Mortgage Association, Defense Plant Corporation, Defense Homes Corporation, Defense Supplies Corporation, Rubber Reserve Company, Metals Reserve Company,* and *War Insurance Corporation* (later known as *War Damage Corporation*)—with *Federal Home Loan Bank Board, Home Owners' Loan Corporation, Federal Savings and Loan Insurance Corporation, Federal Housing Administration, Electric Home and Farm Authority,* and *Export-Import Bank of Washington. Federal Home Loan Bank Board, Federal Savings and Loan Insurance Corporation, Home Owners' Loan Corporation, Federal Housing Administration,* and *Defense Homes Corporation* transferred to *National Housing Agency* by EO 9070 of Feb. 24, 1942. *Reconstruction Finance Corporation* and its units (except *Defense Homes Corporation*), *Electric Home and Farm Authority,* and *Export-Import Bank of Washington* transferred to Commerce Department by EO 9071 of Feb. 24, 1942. *RFC* and units returned to *Federal Loan Agency* by act of Feb. 24, 1945 (59 Stat. 5). *Agency* abolished by act of June 30, 1947 (61 Stat. 202), and all property and records transferred to *Reconstruction Finance Corporation.*

Loan Fund, Development   Established in *International Cooperation Administration* by act of Aug. 14, 1957 (71 Stat. 355). Created as independent corporate agency by act of June 30, 1958 (72 Stat. 261). Abolished by act of Sept. 4,

1961 (75 Stat. 445), and functions redelegated to Agency for International Development.

Loan Policy Board Established by act of July 18, 1958 (72 Stat. 385). Abolished by Reorg. Plan No. 4 of 1965, effective July 27, 1965, and functions transferred to Small Business Administration.

Longshoremen's Labor Board, National Established in Labor Department by EO 6748 of June 26, 1934. Terminated by Proc. 2120 of Mar. 11, 1935.

Low-Emission Vehicle Certification Board Established by act of Dec. 31, 1970 (84 Stat. 1701). Terminated by act of Mar. 14, 1980 (94 Stat. 98).

Lowell Historic Canal District Commission Established by act of Jan. 4, 1975 (88 Stat. 2330). Expired January 1977 pursuant to terms of act.

Loyalty Review Board Established Nov. 10, 1947, by *U.S. Civil Service Commission,* pursuant to EO 9835 of Mar. 21, 1947. Abolished by EO 10450 of Apr. 27, 1953.

Management Improvement, Advisory Committee on Established by EO 10072 of July 29, 1949. Abolished by EO 10917 of Feb. 10, 1961, and functions transferred to *Bureau of the Budget.*

Management Improvement, President's Advisory Council on Established by EO 11509 of Feb. 11, 1970. Inactive as of June 30, 1973.

Manpower, President's Committee on Established by EO 11152 of Apr. 15, 1964. Terminated by EO 11515 of Mar. 13, 1970.

Manpower Administration Renamed Employment and Training Administration by Labor Secretary's Order 14–75 of Nov. 12, 1975.

Manpower Management, Office of Civilian Renamed Office of Civilian Personnel by Navy Secretary's Notice 5430 of Oct. 1, 1976.

Marine Affairs, Office of Established by Interior Secretary Apr. 30, 1970, to replace *Office of Marine Resources,* created by Secretary Oct. 22, 1968. Abolished by Secretary Dec. 4, 1970.

Marine Corps Memorial Commission, U.S. Established by act of Aug. 24, 1947 (61 Stat. 724). Terminated by act of Mar. 14, 1980 (94 Stat. 98).

Marine Inspection and Navigation, Bureau of *See* Navigation and Steamboat Inspection, Bureau of

Marine Resources and Engineering Development, National Council on Established in Executive Office of the President by act of June 17, 1966 (80 Stat. 203). Terminated Apr. 30, 1971, due to lack of funding.

Maritime Administration Established in Commerce Department by Reorg. Plan No. 21 of 1950, effective May 24, 1950. Transferred to Transportation Department by act of Aug. 6, 1981 (95 Stat. 151).

Maritime Advisory Committee Established by EO 11156 of June 17, 1964. Terminated by EO 11427 of Sept. 4, 1968.

Maritime Board, Federal *See* Maritime Commission, U.S.

Maritime Commission, U.S. Established by act of June 29, 1936 (49 Stat. 1985), as successor agency to *U.S. Shipping Board* and *U.S. Shipping Board Merchant Fleet Corporation.* Training functions transferred to Commandant of Coast Guard by EO 9083 of Feb. 27, 1942. Functions further transferred to *War Shipping Administration* by EO 9198 of July 11, 1942. Abolished by Reorg. Plan No. 21 of 1950, effective May 24, 1950, which established *Federal Maritime Board* and *Maritime Administration* as successor agencies. *Board* abolished, regulatory functions transferred to Federal Maritime Commission, and functions relating to subsidization of merchant marine transferred to Commerce Secretary by Reorg. Plan No. 7 of 1961, effective Aug. 12, 1961.

Maritime Labor Board Authorized by act of June 23, 1938 (52 Stat. 968). Mediatory duties abolished by act of June 23, 1941 (55 Stat. 259); title expired June 22, 1942.

Marketing Administration, Surplus Established by Reorg. Plan No. III of 1940, effective June 30, 1940, consolidating functions vested in *Federal Surplus Commodities Corporation* and *Division of Marketing and Marketing Agreements, Agricultural Adjustment Administration.* Consolidated with other agencies into *Agricultural Marketing Administration* by EO 9069 of Feb. 23, 1942.

Marketing and Marketing Agreements, Division of Established in Agriculture Department by act of June 3, 1937 (50 Stat. 246). Consolidated with *Federal Surplus Commodities Corporation* into *Surplus Marketing Administration* by Reorg. Plan No. III of 1940, effective June 30, 1940.

Mediation, U.S. Board of Established by act of May 20, 1926 (44 Stat. 577). Abolished by act of June 21, 1934 (48 Stat. 1193), and superseded by National Mediation Board, July 21, 1934.

Medical Information Systems Program Office, Tri-Service Renamed Defense Medical Systems Support Center by memorandum of Assistant Defense Secretary (Health Affairs) May 3, 1985.

Medical Services Administration Established by *Health, Education, and Welfare Secretary's* reorganization of Aug. 15, 1967. Transferred from *Social and Rehabilitation Service* to Health Care Financing Administration by Secretary's reorganization of Mar. 8, 1977 (42 FR 13262).

Medicine and Surgery, Department of Established in the *Veterans Administration* by act of Sept. 2, 1958 (72 Stat. 1243). Renamed *Veterans Health Services and Research Administration* in the Veterans Affairs Department by act of Oct. 25, 1988 (102 Stat. 2640). Renamed Veterans Health Administration by act of May 7, 1991 (105 Stat. 187).

Memorial Commission, National Established by Public Resolution 107 of Mar. 4, 1929 (45 Stat. 1699). Terminated by EO 6166 of June 10, 1933, and functions transferred to *Office of National Parks, Buildings, and Reservations,* Interior Department.

Mental Health, National Institute of Established by act of July 3, 1946 (60 Stat. 425). Made entity within the Alcohol, Drug Abuse, and Mental Health Administration by act of May 14, 1974 (88 Stat. 135). Functions transferred to Health and Human Services Department by act of Oct. 17, 1979 (93 Stat. 695). (*See also* act of Oct. 27, 1986; 100 Stat. 3207–106.) Abolished by act of July 10, 1992 (106 Stat. 331). Reestablished by act of July 10, 1992 (106 Stat. 364).

Metals Reserve Company Established June 28, 1940, by act of Jan. 22, 1932 (47 Stat. 5). Transferred from *Federal Loan Agency* to Commerce Department by EO 9071 of Feb. 24, 1942. Returned to *Federal Loan Agency* by act of Feb. 24, 1945 (59 Stat. 5). Dissolved by act of June 30, 1945 (59 Stat. 310), and functions transferred to *Reconstruction Finance Corporation*.

Metric Board, U.S. Established by act of Dec. 23, 1975 (89 Stat. 1007). Terminated Oct. 1, 1982, due to lack of funding.

Mexican-American Affairs, Interagency Committee on Established by Presidential memorandum of June 9, 1967. Renamed *Cabinet Committee on Opportunities for Spanish-Speaking People* by act of Dec. 30, 1969 (83 Stat. 838). Terminated Dec. 30, 1974, pursuant to terms of act.

Mexican Claims Commission, American Established by act of Dec. 18, 1942 (56 Stat. 1058). Terminated Apr. 4, 1947, by act of Apr. 3, 1945 (59 Stat. 59).

Mexican Claims Commission, Special Established by act of Apr. 10, 1935 (49 Stat. 149). Terminated by EO 7909 of June 15, 1938.

Mexico Commission for Border Development and Friendship, U.S.- Established through exchange of notes of Nov. 30 and Dec. 3, 1966, between U.S. and Mexico. Terminated Nov. 5, 1969.

Micronesian Claims Commission Established by act of July 1, 1971 (85 Stat. 92). Terminated Aug. 3, 1976, pursuant to terms of act.

Migration, Intergovernmental Committee for European Renamed Intergovernmental Committee for Migration by Resolution 624, passed by *Intergovernmental Committee for European Migration Council,* effective Nov. 11, 1980.

Migration, International Committee for Created in 1951. Renamed International Organization for Migration pursuant to article 29, paragraph 2, of the ICM constitution, effective Nov. 14, 1989.

Migratory Bird Conservation Commission Chairmanship transferred from Agriculture Secretary to Interior Secretary by Reorg. Plan No. II of 1939, effective July 1, 1939.

Military Air Transport Service Renamed Military Airlift Command in U.S. Air Force by HQ MATS/MAC Special Order G–164 of Jan. 1, 1966.

Military Appeals, United States Court of Established under Article I of the Constitution of the United States pursuant to act of May 5, 1950, as amended. Renamed United States Court of Appeals for the Armed Forces by act of Oct. 5, 1994 (108 Stat. 2831).

Military Establishment, National Established as executive department of the Government by act of July 26, 1947 (61 Stat. 495). Designated Department of Defense by act of Aug. 10, 1949 (63 Stat. 579).

Military Purchases, Interdepartmental Committee for Coordination of Foreign and Domestic Informal liaison committee created on Presidential notification of Dec. 6, 1939, to Treasury and *War* Secretaries and Acting Navy Secretary. Committee dissolved in accordance with Presidential letter to Treasury Secretary Apr. 14, 1941, following approval of act of Mar. 11, 1941 (55 Stat. 31).

Military Renegotiation Policy and Review Board Established by directive of Defense Secretary July 19, 1948. Abolished by Defense Secretary's letter of Jan. 18, 1952, which transferred functions to *Renegotiation Board.*

Military Sea Transportation Service Renamed Military Sealift Command in U.S. Navy by COMSC notice of Aug. 1, 1970.

Militia Bureau Established in 1908 as *Division of Militia Affairs, Office of War Secretary.* Superseded in 1933 by National Guard Bureau.

Mine Health and Safety Academy, National Transferred from Interior Department to Labor Department by act of July 25, 1979 (93 Stat. 111).

Minerals Exploration, Office of Established by act of Aug. 21, 1958 (72 Stat. 700). Functions transferred to *Geological Survey* by Interior Secretary's Order 2886 of Feb. 26, 1965.

Minerals Mobilization, Office of Established by Interior Secretary pursuant to act of Sept. 8, 1950 (64 Stat. 798) and EO 10574 of Nov. 5, 1954, and by order of *Office of Defense Mobilization.* Succeeded by *Office of Minerals and Solid Fuels* Nov. 2, 1962. *Office of Minerals Policy Development* combined with *Office of Research and Development* in Interior Department May 21, 1976, under authority of Reorg. Plan No. 3 of 1950, to form *Office of Minerals Policy and Research Analysis.* Abolished Sept. 30, 1981, by Secretarial Order 3070 and functions transferred to Bureau of Mines.

Minerals Policy and Research Analysis, Office of *See* **Minerals Mobilization, Office of**

Minerals and Solid Fuels, Office of Established by Interior Secretary Oct. 26, 1962. Abolished and functions assigned to Deputy Assistant Secretary—Minerals and Energy Policy, Office of the Assistant Secretary—Mineral Resources, effective Oct. 22, 1971.

Mines, Bureau of Established in Interior Department by act of May 16, 1910 (36 Stat. 369). Transferred to Commerce Department by EO 4239 of June 4, 1925. Transferred to Interior Department by EO 6611 of Feb. 22, 1934. Renamed United States Bureau of Mines by act of May 18, 1992 (106 Stat. 172).

Mining Enforcement and Safety Administration
Established by Interior Secretary's Order 2953 of May 7, 1973. Terminated by departmental directive Mar. 9, 1978, and functions transferred to Mine Safety and Health Administration, Labor Department, established by act of Nov. 9, 1977 (91 Stat. 1319).

Minority Business Enterprise, Office of   Renamed Minority Business Development Agency by Commerce Secretarial Order DOO–254A of Nov. 1, 1979.

Mint, Bureau of the   Renamed U.S. Mint by Treasury Secretarial order of Jan. 9, 1984 (49 FR 5020).

Missile Sites Labor Commission   Established by EO 10946 of May 26, 1961. Abolished by EO 11374 of Oct. 11, 1967, and functions transferred to Federal Mediation and Conciliation Service.

Missouri Basin Survey Commission   Established by EO 10318 of Jan. 3, 1952. Final report of *Commission* submitted to President Jan. 12, 1953, pursuant to EO 10329 of Feb. 25, 1952.

Missouri River Basin Commission   Established by EO 11658 of Mar. 22, 1972. Terminated by EO 12319 of Sept. 9, 1981.

Mobilization, Office of Civil and Defense   *See* **Mobilization, Office of Defense and Civilian**

Mobilization, Office of Defense and Civilian
Established by Reorg. Plan No. 1 of 1958, effective July 1, 1958. Redesignated as *Office of Civil and Defense Mobilization* by act of Aug. 26, 1958 (72 Stat. 861), consolidating functions of *Office of Defense Mobilization* and *Federal Civil Defense Administration*. Civil defense functions transferred to Defense Secretary by EO 10952 of July 20, 1961, and remaining organization redesignated *Office of Emergency Planning* by act of Sept. 22, 1961 (75 Stat. 630).

Mobilization Policy, National Advisory Board on   Established by EO 10224 of Mar. 15, 1951. EO 10224 revoked by EO 10773 of July 1, 1958.

Monetary and Financial Problems, National Advisory Council on International   Established by act of July 31, 1945 (59 Stat. 512). Abolished by Reorg. Plan No. 4 of 1965, effective July 27, 1965, and functions transferred to President. Functions assumed by National Advisory Council on International Monetary and Financial Policies, established by EO 11269 of Feb. 14, 1966.

Monument Commission, National   Established by act of Aug. 31, 1954 (68 Stat. 1029). Final report submitted in 1957, and audit of business completed September 1964.

Monuments in War Areas, American Commission for the Protection and Salvage of Artistic and Historic   Established by President June 23, 1943; announced by Secretary of State Aug. 20, 1943. Activities assumed by State Department Aug. 16, 1946.

Mortgage Association, Federal National   Chartered Feb. 10, 1938, by act of June 27, 1934 (48 Stat.

1246). Grouped with other agencies to form *Federal Loan Agency* by Reorg. Plan No. I of 1939, effective July 1, 1939. Transferred to Commerce Department by EO 9071 of Feb. 24, 1942. Returned to *Federal Loan Agency* by act of Feb. 24, 1945 (59 Stat. 5). Transferred to *Housing and Home Finance Agency* by Reorg. Plan No. 22 of 1950, effective July 10, 1950. Rechartered by act of Aug. 2, 1954 (68 Stat. 590) and made constituent agency of *Housing and Home Finance Agency*. Transferred with functions of *Housing and Home Finance Agency* to Housing and Urban Development Department by act of Sept. 9, 1965 (79 Stat. 667). Made Government-sponsored, private corporation by act of Aug. 1, 1968 (82 Stat. 536).

Motor Carrier Claims Commission   Established by act of July 2, 1948 (62 Stat. 1222). Terminated Dec. 31, 1952, by acts of July 11, 1951 (65 Stat. 116), and Mar. 14, 1952 (66 Stat. 25).

Mount Rushmore National Memorial Commission
Established by act of Feb. 25, 1929 (45 Stat. 1300). Expenditures ordered administered by Interior Department by EO 6166 of June 10, 1933. Transferred to National Park Service, Interior Department, by Reorg. Plan No. II of 1939, effective July 1, 1939.

Munitions Board   Established in Defense Department by act of July 26, 1947 (61 Stat. 499). Abolished by Reorg. Plan No. 6 of 1953, effective June 30, 1953, and functions vested in Defense Secretary.

Munitions Board, Joint Army and Navy   Organized in 1922. Placed under direction of President by military order of July 5, 1939. Reconstituted Aug. 18, 1945, by order approved by President. Terminated on establishment of *Munitions Board* by act of July 26, 1947 (61 Stat. 505).

Museum of History and Technology, National
Renamed National Museum of American History in Smithsonian Institution by act of Oct. 13, 1980 (94 Stat. 1884).

Museum Services, Institute of   Established by act of June 23, 1972 (86 Stat. 327). Transferred to Office of Educational Research and Improvement, Education Department, by act of Oct. 17, 1979 (93 Stat. 678), effective May 4, 1980. Transferred to National Foundation on the Arts and the Humanities by act of Dec. 23, 1981 (95 Stat. 1414).

Narcotics, Bureau of   Established in Treasury Department by act of June 14, 1930 (46 Stat. 585). Abolished by Reorg. Plan No. 1 of 1968, effective Apr. 8, 1968, and functions transferred to *Bureau of Narcotics and Dangerous Drugs*, Justice Department.

Narcotics Control, Cabinet Committee on International   Established by Presidential memorandum of Aug. 17, 1971. Terminated by Presidential memorandum of Mar. 14, 1977.

National.   *See other part of title*

Naval Material, Office of   Established by act of Mar. 5, 1948 (62 Stat. 68). Abolished by Defense Department reorg. order of Mar. 9, 1966, and functions transferred to Navy Secretary (31 FR 7188).

Naval Material Command   See **Naval Material Support Establishment**

Naval Material Support Establishment   Established by Navy Department General Order 5 of July 1, 1963 (28 FR 7037). Replaced by *Naval Material Command* pursuant to General Order 5 of Apr. 29, 1966 (31 FR 7188). Functions realigned to form Office of Naval Acquisition Support, and termination of *Command* effective May 6, 1985.

Naval Observatory   Jurisdiction transferred from *Bureau of Navigation* to Chief of Naval Operations by EO 9126 of Apr. 8, 1942, and by Reorg. Plan No. 3 of 1946, effective July 16, 1946.

Naval Oceanography Command   Renamed Naval Meteorology and Oceanography Command in 1995.

Naval Petroleum and Oil Shale Reserves, Office of   Established by Navy Secretary, as required by law (70A Stat. 457). Jurisdiction transferred to Energy Department by act of Aug. 4, 1977 (91 Stat. 581).

Naval Weapons, Bureau of   Established by act of Aug. 18, 1959 (73 Stat. 395), to replace *Bureau of Ordnance and Aeronautics.* Abolished by Defense Department reorg. order of Mar. 9, 1966, and functions transferred to Navy Secretary (31 FR 7188), effective May 1, 1966.

Navigation, Bureau of   Created by act of July 5, 1884 (23 Stat. 118), as special service under Treasury Department. Transferred to *Department of Commerce and Labor* by act of Feb. 4, 1903 (32 Stat. 825). Consolidated with *Bureau of Navigation and Steamboat Inspection* by act of June 30, 1932 (47 Stat. 415).

Navigation, Bureau of   Renamed Bureau of Naval Personnel by act of May 13, 1942 (56 Stat. 276).

Navigation and Steamboat Inspection, Bureau of   Renamed *Bureau of Marine Inspection and Navigation* by act of May 27, 1936 (49 Stat. 1380). Functions transferred to *Bureau of Customs,* Treasury Department, and U.S. Coast Guard by EO 9083 of Feb. 28, 1942. Transfer made permanent and *Bureau* abolished by Reorg. Plan. No. 3 of 1946, effective July 16, 1946.

Navy Commissioners, Board of   Established by act of Feb. 7, 1815 (3 Stat. 202). Abolished by act of Aug. 31, 1842 (5 Stat. 579).

Navy Department   Defense housing functions transferred to *Federal Public Housing Authority, National Housing Agency,* by EO 9070 of Feb. 24, 1942.

Neighborhoods, National Commission on   Established by act of Apr. 30, 1977 (91 Stat. 56). Terminated May 4, 1979, pursuant to terms of act.

Neighborhoods, Voluntary Associations and Consumer Protection, Office of   Abolished and certain functions transferred to Office of the Assistant Secretary for Housing—Federal Housing Commissioner and Office of the Assistant Secretary for Community Planning and Development. Primary enabling legislation, act of Oct. 31, 1978 (92 Stat. 2119), repealed by act of Aug. 13, 1981 (95 Stat.

398). Abolishment of *Office* and transfer of functions carried out by Housing and Urban Development Secretarial order.

New England River Basins Commission   Established by EO 11371 of Sept. 6, 1967. Terminated by EO 12319 of Sept. 9, 1981.

Nicaro Project   Responsibility for management of Nicaro nickel producing facilities in Oriente Province, Cuba, transferred from *Office of Special Assistant to the Administrator (Nicaro Project)* to *Defense Materials Service* by General Services Administrator, effective July 7, 1959. Facilities expropriated by Cuban Government and nationalized Oct. 26, 1960.

Northern Mariana Islands Commission on Federal Laws   Created by joint resolution of Mar. 24, 1976 (90 Stat. 263). Terminated upon submission of final report in August 1985.

Nursing Research, National Center for   Renamed National Institute of Nursing Research by act of June 10, 1993 (107 Stat. 178).

Nutrition Division   Functions transferred from *Health, Education, and Welfare Department* to Agriculture Department by EO 9310 of Mar. 3, 1943.

Ocean Mining Administration   Established by Interior Secretarial Order 2971 of Feb. 24, 1975. Abolished by Department Manual Release 2273 of June 13, 1980.

Oceanography, Interagency Committee on   Established by *Federal Council for Science and Technology* pursuant to EO 10807 of Mar. 13, 1959. Absorbed by *National Council on Marine Resources and Engineering Development* pursuant to Vice Presidential letter of July 21, 1967.

Office.   See also other part of title

Office Space, President's Advisory Commission on Presidential   Established by act of Aug. 3, 1956 (70 Stat. 979). Terminated June 30, 1957, by act of Jan. 25, 1957 (71 Stat. 4).

Official Register   Function of preparing *Official Register* vested in Director of the Census by act of Mar. 3, 1925 (43 Stat. 1105). Function transferred to *U.S. Civil Service Commission* by EO 6166 of June 10, 1933. Yearly compilation and publication required by act of Aug. 28, 1935 (49 Stat. 956). Act repealed by act of July 12, 1960 (74 Stat. 427), and last *Register* published in 1959.

Ohio River Basin Commission   Established by EO 11578 of Jan. 13, 1971. Terminated by EO 12319 of Sept. 9, 1981.

Oil and Gas, Office of   Established by Interior Secretary May 6, 1946, in response to Presidential letter of May 3, 1946. Transferred to *Federal Energy Administration* by act of May 7, 1974 (88 Stat. 100).

Oil Import Administration   Established in Interior Department by Proc. 3279 of Mar. 10, 1959. Merged into *Office of Oil and Gas* Oct. 22, 1971.

Oil Import Appeals Board Established by Commerce Secretary Mar. 13, 1959, and made part of Office of Hearings and Appeals Dec. 23, 1971.

Operations Advisory Group Established by EO 11905 of Feb. 18, 1976. Abolished by Presidential Directive No. 2 of Jan. 20, 1977.

Operations Coordinating Board Established by EO 10483 of Sept. 2, 1953, which was superseded by EO 10700 of Feb. 25, 1957. EO 10700 revoked by EO 10920 of Feb. 18, 1961, and *Board* terminated.

Ordnance, Bureau of *See* **Ordnance and Hydrography, Bureau of**

Ordnance and Hydrography, Bureau of Established in Navy Department by act of Aug. 31, 1842 (5 Stat. 579). Replaced under act of July 5, 1862 (12 Stat. 510), by *Bureau of Ordnance* and *Bureau of Navigation.* Abolished by act of Aug. 18, 1959 (73 Stat. 395), and functions transferred to *Bureau of Naval Weapons.*

Organization, President's Advisory Committee on Government Established by EO 10432 of Jan. 24, 1953. Abolished by EO 10917 of Feb. 10, 1961, and functions transferred to *Bureau of the Budget* for termination.

Organizations Staff, International Functions merged with Foreign Agricultural Service by Agriculture Secretary's memorandum of Dec. 7, 1973, effective Feb. 3, 1974.

Overseas Private Investment Corporation Transferred as separate agency to U.S. International Development Cooperation Agency by Reorg. Plan No. 2 of 1979, effective Oct. 1, 1979.

Oversight Board (for the Resolution Trust Corporation) Established by act of Aug. 9, 1989 (103 Stat. 363). Renamed Thrift Depositor Protection Oversight Board by act of Dec. 12, 1991 (105 Stat. 1767).

Pacific Northwest River Basins Commission Established by EO 11331 of Mar. 6, 1967. Terminated by EO 12319 of Sept. 9, 1981.

Packers and Stockyards Administration Established by Agriculture Secretary's Memorandum 1613, supp. 1, of May 8, 1967. Certain functions consolidated into Agricultural Marketing Service by Secretary's Memorandum 1927 of Jan. 15, 1978. Remaining functions incorporated into the Grain Inspection, Packers and Stockyards Administration by Secretary's Memorandum 1010–1 dated Oct. 20, 1994.

Panama Canal Operation of piers at Atlantic and Pacific terminals transferred to Panama Railroad by EO 7021 of Apr. 19, 1935. Panama Canal reestablished as *Canal Zone Government* by act of Sept. 26, 1950 (64 Stat. 1038).

Panama Canal Company Established by act of June 29, 1948 (62 Stat. 1076). Abolished and superseded by Panama Canal Commission (93 Stat. 454).

Panama Railroad Company Incorporated Apr. 7, 1849, by New York State Legislature. Operated under private control until 1881, when original *French Canal Company* acquired most of its stock.

Company and its successor, *New Panama Canal Company,* operated railroad as common carrier and also as adjunct in attempts to construct canal. In 1904 their shares of stock in *Panama Railroad Company* passed to ownership of U.S. as part of assets of *New Panama Canal Company* purchased under act of June 28, 1902 (34 Stat. 481). Remaining shares purchased from private owners in 1905. *Panama Railroad Company* reincorporated by act of June 29, 1948 (62 Stat. 1075) pursuant to requirements of act of Dec. 6, 1945 (59 Stat. 597). Reestablished as *Panama Canal Company* by act of Sept. 26, 1950 (64 Stat. 1038). Army Secretary directed to discontinue commercial operations of *Company* by Presidential letter of Mar. 29, 1961.

Paperwork, Commission on Federal Established by act of Dec. 27, 1974 (88 Stat. 1789). Terminated January 1978 pursuant to terms of act.

Park Service, National Functions in District of Columbia relating to space assignment, site selection for public buildings, and determination of priority in construction transferred to *Public Buildings Administration, Federal Works Agency,* under Reorg. Plan No. I of 1939, effective July 1, 1939.

Park Trust Fund Board, National Established by act of July 10, 1935 (49 Stat. 477). Terminated by act of Dec. 18, 1967 (81 Stat. 656), and functions transferred to National Park Foundation.

Parks, Buildings, and Reservations, Office of National Established in Interior Department by EO 6166 of June 10, 1933. Renamed National Park Service by act of Mar. 2, 1934 (48 Stat. 362).

Parole, Board of Established by act of June 25, 1948 (62 Stat. 854). Abolished by act of Mar. 15, 1976 (90 Stat. 219), and functions transferred to U.S. Parole Commission.

Patent Office Provisions of first patent act administered by State Department, with authority for granting patents vested in board comprising Secretaries of State and *War* and Attorney General. Board abolished, authority transferred to Secretary of State, and registration system established by act of Feb. 21, 1793 (1 Stat. 318). *Office* made bureau in State Department in October 1802, headed by *Superintendent of Patents. Office* reorganized in 1836 by act of June 4, 1836 (5 Stat. 117) under *Commissioner of Patents. Office* transferred to Interior Department in 1849. *Office* transferred to Commerce Department by EO 4175 of Mar. 17, 1925.

Patents Board, Government Established by EO 10096 of Jan. 23, 1950. Abolished by EO 10930 of Mar. 24, 1961, and functions transferred to Commerce Secretary.

Pay Board Established by EO 11627 of Oct. 15, 1971. Abolished by EO 11695 of Jan. 11, 1973.

Peace Corps Established in State Department by EO 10924 of Mar. 1, 1961, and continued by act of Sept. 22, 1961 (75 Stat. 612), and EO 11041 of Aug. 6, 1962. Functions transferred to ACTION by Reorg. Plan No. 1 of 1971, effective July 1, 1971. Made independent agency in executive branch by act of Dec. 29, 1981 (95 Stat. 1540).

Pennsylvania Avenue, Temporary Commission on Established by EO 11210 of Mar. 25, 1956. Inactive as of Nov. 15, 1969, due to lack of funding.

Pension and Welfare Benefit Programs, Office of *See* Labor-Management Services Administration

Pensions, Commissioner of Provided for by act of Mar. 2, 1833 (4 Stat. 668). Continued by act of Mar. 3, 1835 (4 Stat. 779), and other acts as *Office of the Commissioner of Pensions.* Transferred to Interior Department as bureau by act of Mar. 3, 1849 (9 Stat. 395). Consolidated with other bureaus and agencies into *Veterans Administration* by EO 5398 of July 21, 1930.

Pensions, Office of the Commissioner of *See* Pensions, Commissioner of

Perry's Victory Memorial Commission Created by act of Mar. 3, 1919 (40 Stat. 1322). Administration of Memorial transferred to National Park Service by act of June 2, 1936 (49 Stat. 1393). *Commission* terminated by terms of act and membership reconstituted as advisory board to Interior Secretary.

Personal Property, Office of *See* Supply Service, Federal

Personnel, National Roster of Scientific and Specialized Established by *National Resources Planning Board* pursuant to Presidential letter of June 18, 1940, to Treasury Secretary. After Aug. 15, 1940, administered jointly by *Board* and *U.S. Civil Service Commission.* Transferred to *War Manpower Commission* by EO 9139 of Apr. 18, 1942. Transferred to Labor Department by EO 9617 of Sept. 19, 1945. Transferred with *Bureau of Employment Security* to *Federal Security Agency* by act of June 16, 1948 (62 Stat. 443). Transferred to Labor Department by Reorg. Plan No. 2 of 1949, effective Aug. 20, 1949, and became inactive. Roster functions transferred to National Science Foundation by act of May 10, 1950 (64 Stat. 154). Reactivated in 1950 as *National Scientific Register* by *Office of Education, Federal Security Agency,* through *National Security Resources Board* grant of funds, and continued by National Science Foundation funds until December 1952, when *Register* integrated into Foundation's National Register of Scientific and Technical Personnel project in Division of Scientific Personnel and Education.

Personnel Administration, Council of Established by EO 7916 of June 24, 1938, effective Feb. 1, 1939. Made unit in *U.S. Civil Service Commission* by EO 8467 of July 1, 1940. Renamed *Federal Personnel Council* by EO 9830 of Feb. 24, 1947. Abolished by act of July 31, 1953 (67 Stat. 300), and personnel and records transferred to *Office of Executive Director, U.S. Civil Service Commission.*

Personnel Council, Federal *See* Personnel Administration, Council of

Personnel Interchange, President's Commission on Established by EO 11451 of Jan. 19, 1969. Continued by EO 12136 of May 15, 1979, and renamed *President's Commission on Executive Exchange.* Continued by EO 12493 of Dec. 5, 1984. Abolished by EO 12760 of May 2, 1991.

Personnel Management, Liaison Office for Established by EO 8248 of Sept. 8, 1939. Abolished by EO 10452 of May 1, 1953, and functions transferred to *U.S. Civil Service Commission.*

Petroleum Administration for Defense Established under act of Sept. 8, 1950 (64 Stat. 798) by Interior Secretary's Order 2591 of Oct. 3, 1950, pursuant to EO 10161 of Sept. 9, 1950. Continued by Secretary's Order 2614 of Jan. 25, 1951, pursuant to EO 10200 of Jan. 3, 1951, and PAD Delegation 1 of Jan. 24, 1951. Abolished by Secretary's Order 2755 of Apr. 23, 1954.

Petroleum Administration for War *See* Petroleum Coordinator for War, Office of

Petroleum Administrative Board Established Sept. 11, 1933, by Interior Secretary. Terminated Mar. 31, 1936, by EO 7076 of June 15, 1935. Interior Secretary authorized to execute functions vested in President by act of Feb. 22, 1935 (49 Stat. 30) by EO 7756 of Dec. 1, 1937. Secretary also authorized to establish *Petroleum Conservation Division* to assist in administering act. Records of *Petroleum Administrative Board* and *Petroleum Labor Policy Board* housed with *Petroleum Conservation Division, Office of Oil and Gas,* acting as custodian for Interior Secretary.

Petroleum Coordinator for War, Office of Interior Secretary designated *Petroleum Coordinator for National Defense* by Presidential letter of May 28, 1941, and approved *Petroleum Coordinator for War* by Presidential letter of Apr. 20, 1942. *Office* abolished by EO 9276 of Dec. 2, 1942, and functions transferred to *Petroleum Administration for War,* established by same EO. *Administration* terminated by EO 9718 of May 3, 1946.

Petroleum Labor Policy Board Established by Interior Secretary, as *Administrator of Code of Fair Competition for Petroleum Industry,* on recommendation of Planning and Coordination Committee Oct. 10, 1933. Reorganized by Secretary Dec. 19, 1933, and reorganization confirmed by order of Mar. 8, 1935. Terminated Mar. 31, 1936, when *Petroleum Administrative Board* abolished by EO 7076 of June 15, 1935.

Petroleum Reserves Corporation Established June 30, 1943, by *Reconstruction Finance Corporation.* Transferred to *Office of Economic Warfare* by EO 9360 of July 15, 1943. *Office* consolidated into *Foreign Economic Administration* by EO 9380 of Sept. 25, 1943. Functions transferred to *Reconstruction Finance Corporation* by EO 9630 of Sept. 27, 1945. RFC's charter amended Nov. 9, 1945, to change name to *War Assets Corporation. Corporation* designated by *Surplus Property Administrator* as disposal agency for all types of property for which *Reconstruction Finance Corporation* formerly disposal agency. Domestic surplus property functions of *Corporation* transferred to *War Assets Administration* by EO 9689 of Jan. 31, 1946. *Reconstruction Finance Corporation Board of Directors* ordered by President to dissolve *War Assets Corporation* as soon after Mar. 25, 1946, as practicable.

Philippine Alien Property Administration
Established in *Office for Emergency Management* by
EO 9789 of Oct. 14, 1946. Abolished by EO 10254
of June 15, 1951, and functions transferred to Justice
Department.

Philippine War Damage Commission   Established
by act of Apr. 30, 1946 (60 Stat. 128). Terminated
Mar. 31, 1951, by act of Sept. 6, 1950 (64 Stat.
712).

Physical Fitness, Committee on   Established in
Office of Federal Security Administrator by EO 9338
of Apr. 29, 1943. Terminated June 30, 1945.

Physical Fitness, President's Council on   *See* **Youth
Fitness, President's Council on**

Planning Board, National   Established by
Administrator of Public Works July 30, 1933.
Terminated by EO 6777 of June 30, 1934.

Plant Industry, Bureau of   Established by act of
Mar. 2, 1902 (31 Stat. 922). Soil fertility and soil
microbiology work of *Bureau of Chemistry and Soils*
transferred to *Bureau* by act of May 17, 1935. Soil
chemistry and physics and soil survey work of
Bureau of Chemistry and Soils transferred to *Bureau*
by Secretary's Memorandum 784 of Oct. 6, 1938. In
February 1943 engineering research of *Bureau of
Agricultural Chemistry and Engineering* transferred to
*Bureau of Plant Industry, Soils, and Agricultural
Engineering* by Research Administration
Memorandum 5 issued pursuant to EO 9069 of Feb.
23, 1942, and in conformity with Secretary's
Memorandums 960 and 986. Functions transferred
to Agricultural Research Service by Secretary's
Memorandum 1320, supp. 4, of Nov. 2, 1953.

**Plant Industry, Soils, and Agricultural Engineering,
Bureau of**   *See* **Plant Industry, Bureau of**

Plant Quarantine, Bureau of   *See* **Entomology and
Plant Quarantine, Bureau of**

Policy Development, Office of   *See* **Domestic
Council**

Post Office Department   *See* **Postal Service**

Postal Savings System   Established by act of June
25, 1910 (36 Stat. 814). System closed by act of
Mar. 28, 1966 (80 Stat. 92).

Postal Service   Created July 26, 1775, by
Continental Congress. Temporarily established by
Congress by act of Sept. 22, 1789 (1 Stat. 70), and
continued by subsequent acts. *Post Office
Department* made executive department under act of
June 8, 1872 (17 Stat. 283). Offices of First, Second,
Third, and Fourth Assistant Postmasters General
abolished and Deputy Postmaster General and four
Assistant Postmasters General established by Reorg.
Plan No. 3 of 1949, effective Aug. 20, 1949.
Reorganized as U.S. Postal Service in executive
branch by act of Aug. 12, 1970 (84 Stat. 719),
effective July 1, 1971.

Power Administration, Southeastern   Established by
Interior Secretary in 1943 to carry out functions
under act of Dec. 22, 1944 (58 Stat. 890).

Transferred to Energy Department by act of Aug. 4,
1977 (91 Stat. 578).

Power Administration, Southwestern   Established
by Interior Secretary in 1943 to carry out functions
under act of Dec. 22, 1944 (58 Stat. 890).
Transferred to Energy Department by act of Aug. 4,
1977 (91 Stat. 578).

Power Commission, Federal   Established by act of
June 10, 1920 (41 Stat. 1063). Terminated by act of
Aug. 4, 1977 (91 Stat. 578), and functions
transferred to Energy Department.

Preparedness, Office of   Renamed *Federal
Preparedness Agency* by General Services
Administrator's order of June 26, 1975.

Preparedness Agency, Federal   Functions
transferred from General Services Administration to
Federal Emergency Management Agency by EO
12148 of July 20, 1979.

Presidential.   *See other part of title*

President's.   *See other part of title*

Press Intelligence, Division of   Established in
August 1933. Made division of *National Emergency
Council* July 10, 1935. Continued in *Office of
Government Reports* by Reorg. Plan No. II of 1939,
effective July 1, 1939. Transferred to *Office of War
Information* by EO 9182 of June 13, 1942,
functioning in *Bureau of Special Services. Office*
abolished by EO 9608 of Aug. 31, 1945, and *Bureau*
transferred to *Bureau of the Budget.* Upon
reestablishment of *Office of Government Reports,* by
EO 9809 of Dec. 12, 1946, *Division of Press
Intelligence* made unit of *Office.*

Price Administration, Office of   Established by EO
8734 of Apr. 11, 1941, combining *Price Division*
and *Consumer Division* of *National Defense
Advisory Commission.* Renamed *Office of Price
Administration* by EO 8875 of Aug. 28, 1941, which
transferred *Civilian Allocation Division* to *Office of
Production Management.* Consolidated with other
agencies into *Office of Temporary Controls* by EO
9809 of Dec. 12, 1946, except *Financial Reporting
Division,* transferred to Federal Trade Commission.

Price Commission   Established by EO 11627 of
Oct. 15, 1971. Abolished by EO 11695 of Jan. 11,
1973.

Price Decontrol Board   Established by act of July
25, 1946 (60 Stat. 669). Effective period of act of
Jan. 30, 1942 (56 Stat. 23), extended to June 30,
1947, by joint resolution of June 25, 1946 (60 Stat.
664).

**Price Stability for Economic Growth, Cabinet
Committee on**   Established by Presidential letter of
Jan. 28, 1959. Abolished by Presidential direction
Mar. 12, 1961.

Price Stabilization, Office of   Established by
General Order 2 of *Economic Stabilization
Administrator* Jan. 24, 1951. *Director of Price
Stabilization* provided for in EO 10161 of Sept. 9,
1950. Terminated Apr. 30, 1953, by EO 10434 of
Feb. 6, 1953, and provisions of acts of June 30,

1952 (66 Stat. 296) and June 30, 1953 (67 Stat. 131).

Prices and Costs, Committee on Government Activities Affecting Established by EO 10802 of Jan. 23, 1959. Abolished by EO 10928 of Mar. 23, 1961.

Priorities Board Established by order of *Council of National Defense,* approved Oct. 18, 1940, and by EO 8572 of Oct. 21, 1940. EO 8572 revoked by EO 8629 of Jan. 7, 1941.

Prison Industries, Inc., Federal Established by EO 6917 of Dec. 11, 1934. Transferred to Justice Department by Reorg. Plan No. II of 1939, effective July 1, 1939.

Prison Industries Reorganization Administration Functioned from Sept. 26, 1935, to Sept. 30, 1940, under authority of act of Apr. 8, 1935 (49 Stat. 115), and of EO's 7194 of Sept. 26, 1935, 7202 of Sept. 28, 1935, and 7649 of June 29, 1937. Terminated due to lack of funding.

Private Sector Programs, Office of Functions transferred to the Office of Citizen Exchanges within the Bureau of Educational and Cultural Affairs, USIA, by act of Feb. 16, 1990 (104 Stat. 56).

Processing tax *Agricultural Adjustment Administration's* function of collecting taxes declared unconstitutional by U.S. Supreme Court Jan. 6, 1936. Functions under acts of June 28, 1934 (48 Stat. 1275), Apr. 21, 1934 (48 Stat. 598), and Aug. 24, 1935 (49 Stat. 750) discontinued by repeal of these laws by act of Feb. 10, 1936 (49 Stat. 1106).

Processing Tax Board of Review Established in Treasury Department by act of June 22, (49 Stat. 1652). Abolished by act of Oct. 21, 1942 (56 Stat. 967).

Proclamations *See* **State Department**

Procurement, Commission on Government Established by act of Nov. 26, 1969 (83 Stat. 269). Terminated Apr. 30, 1973, due to expiration of statutory authority.

Procurement and Assignment Service Established by President Oct. 30, 1941. Transferred from *Office of Defense Health and Welfare Services* to *War Manpower Commission* by EO 9139 of Apr. 18, 1942. Transferred to *Federal Security Agency* by EO 9617 of Sept 19, 1945, which terminated *Commission.*

Procurement Division Established in Treasury Department by EO 6166 of June 10, 1933. Renamed *Bureau of Federal Supply* by Treasury Department Order 73 of Nov. 19, 1946, effective Jan. 1, 1947. Transferred to General Services Administration as Federal Supply Service by act of June 30, 1949 (63 Stat. 380).

Procurement Policy, Office of Federal Established within Office of Management and Budget by act of Aug. 30, 1974 (88 Stat. 97). Abolished due to lack of funding and functions transferred to Office of Management and Budget by act of Oct 28, 1993 (107 Stat. 1236).

Product Standards Policy, Office of Formerly separate operating unit under Assistant Secretary for Productivity, Technology and Innovation, Commerce Department. Transferred to *National Bureau of Standards* by departmental reorganization order, effective Apr. 27, 1982.

Production Areas, Committee for Congested Established in Executive Office of the President by EO 9327 of Apr. 7, 1943. Terminated Dec. 31, 1944, by act of June 28, 1944 (58 Stat. 535).

Production Authority, National Established in Commerce Department Sept. 11, 1950, by EO's 10161 of Sept. 9, 1950, 10193 of Dec. 16, 1950, and 10200 of Jan. 3, 1951. Abolished by Commerce Secretary's order of Oct. 1, 1953, and functions merged into *Business and Defense Services Administration.*

Production Management, Office of Established in *Office for Emergency Management* by EO 8629 of Jan. 7, 1941. Abolished by EO 9040 of Jan. 24, 1942, and personnel and property transferred to *War Production Board.*

Production and Marketing Administration Established by Agriculture Secretary's Memorandum 1118 of Aug. 18, 1945. Functions transferred under Department reorganization by Secretary's Memorandum 1320, supp. 4, of Nov. 2, 1953.

Productivity Council, National Established by EO 12089 of Oct. 23, 1978. EO 12089 revoked by EO 12379 of Aug. 17, 1982.

Programs, Bureau of International Established by Commerce Secretary Aug. 8, 1961, by Departmental Orders 173 and 174. Abolished by Departmental Order 182 of Feb. 1, 1963, which established *Bureau of International Commerce.* Functions transferred to *Domestic and International Business Administration,* effective Nov. 17, 1972.

Prohibition, Bureau of Established by act of May 27, 1930 (46 Stat. 427). Investigative functions consolidated with functions of *Bureau of Investigation* into *Division of Investigation,* Justice Department, by EO 6166 of June 10, 1933, which set as effective date Mar. 2, 1934, or such later date as fixed by President. All other functions performed by *Bureau of Prohibition* ordered transferred to such division in Justice Department as deemed desirable by Attorney General.

Property, Office of Surplus Established in *Procurement Division,* Treasury Department, by EO 9425 of Feb. 19, 1944, and act of Oct. 3, 1944 (58 Stat. 765), under general direction of *Surplus Property Board* established by same legislation. Transferred to Commerce Department by EO 9541 of Apr. 19, 1945. Terminated by EO 9643 of Oct. 19, 1945, and activities and personnel transferred to *Reconstruction Finance Corporation.*

Property Administration, Surplus *See* **War Property Administration, Surplus**

Property Board, Surplus *See* **War Property Administration, Surplus**

Property Council, Federal Established by EO 11724 of June 25, 1973, and reconstituted by EO 11954 of Jan. 7, 1977. Terminated by EO 12030 of Dec. 15, 1977.

Property Management and Disposal Service *See* **Emergency Procurement Service**

Property Office, Surplus Established in *Division of Territories and Island Possessions,* Interior Department, under Regulation 1 of *Surplus Property Board,* Apr. 2, 1945. Transferred to *War Assets Administration* by EO 9828 of Feb. 21, 1947.

Property Review Board Established by EO 12348 of Feb. 25, 1982. EO 12348 revoked by EO 12512 of Apr. 29, 1985.

Provisions and Clothing, Bureau of Established by acts of Aug. 31, 1842 (5 Stat. 579), and July 5, 1862 (12 Stat. 510). Designated *Bureau of Supplies and Accounts* by act of July 19, 1892 (27 Stat. 243). Abolished by Defense Department reorg. order of Mar. 9, 1966, and functions transferred to Navy Secretary (31 FR 7188).

Public. *See other part of title*

Publications Commission, National Historical Established by act of Oct. 22, 1968 (82 Stat. 1293). Renamed National Historical Publications and Records Commission by act of Dec. 22, 1974 (88 Stat. 1734).

Puerto Rican Hurricane Relief Commission Established by act of Dec. 21, 1928 (45 Stat. 1067). No loans made after June 30, 1934, and *Commission* abolished June 3, 1935, by Public Resolution 22 (49 Stat. 320). Functions transferred to *Division of Territories and Island Possessions,* Interior Department. After June 30, 1946, collection work performed in *Puerto Rico Reconstruction Administration.* Following termination of *Administration,* remaining collection functions transferred to Agriculture Secretary by act of July 11, 1956 (70 Stat. 525).

Puerto Rico, U.S.-Puerto Rico Commission on the Status of Established by act of Feb. 20, 1964 (78 Stat. 17). Terminated by terms of act.

Puerto Rico Reconstruction Administration Established in Interior Department by EO 7057 of May 28, 1935. Terminated Feb. 15, 1955, by act of Aug. 15, 1953 (67 Stat. 584).

Radiation Biology Laboratory *See* **Radiation and Organisms, Division of**

Radiation Council, Federal Established by EO 10831 of Aug. 14, 1959, and act of Sept. 23, 1959 (73 Stat. 688). Abolished by Reorg. Plan No. 3 of 1970, effective Dec. 2, 1970, and functions transferred to Environmental Protection Agency.

Radiation and Organisms, Division of Established by Secretarial order of May 1, 1929, as part of Smithsonian Astrophysical Observatory. Renamed *Radiation Biology Laboratory* by Secretarial order of Feb. 16, 1965. Merged with *Chesapeake Center for*

Environmental Studies by Secretarial order of July 1, 1983, to form Smithsonian Environmental Research Center.

Radio Commission, Federal Established by act of Feb. 23, 1927 (44 Stat. 1162). Abolished by act of June 19, 1934 (48 Stat. 1102), and functions transferred to Federal Communications Commission.

Radio Division Established by *National Emergency Council* July 1, 1938. Transferred to *Office of Education, Federal Security Agency,* by Reorg. Plan No. II of 1939, effective July 1, 1939. Terminated June 30, 1940, by terms of act of June 30, 1939 (53 Stat. 927).

Radio Propagation Laboratory, Central Transferred from *National Bureau of Standards* to *Environmental Science Services Administration* by Commerce Department Order 2–A, effective July 13, 1965.

Radiological Health, National Center for Devices and Renamed Center for Devices and Radiological Health by Food and Drug Administration notice of Mar. 9, 1984 (49 FR 10166).

Rail Public Counsel, Office of Established by act of Feb. 5, 1976 (90 Stat. 51). Terminated Dec. 1, 1979, due to lack of funding.

Railroad Administration, U.S. *See* **Railroads, Director General of**

Railroad and Airline Wage Board Established by Economic Stabilization Administrator's General Order 7 of Sept. 27, 1951, pursuant to act of Sept. 8, 1950 (64 Stat. 816). Terminated Apr. 30, 1953, by EO 10434 of Feb. 6, 1953, and acts of June 30, 1952 (66 Stat. 296), and June 30, 1953 (67 Stat. 131).

Railroads, Director General of Established under authority of act of Aug. 29, 1916 (39 Stat. 645). Organization of *U.S. Railroad Administration* announced Feb. 9, 1918. Office abolished by Reorg. Plan No. II of 1939, effective July 1, 1939, and functions transferred to Treasury Secretary.

Railway Association, U.S. Established by act of Jan. 2, 1974 (87 Stat. 985). Terminated Apr. 1, 1987, by act of Oct. 21, 1986 (100 Stat. 1906).

Railway Labor Panel, National Established by EO 9172 of May 22, 1942. EO 9172 revoked by EO 9883 of Aug. 11, 1947.

Real Estate Board, Federal Established by EO 8034 of Jan. 14, 1939. Abolished by EO 10287 of Sept. 6, 1951.

Reclamation, Bureau of *See* **Reclamation Service**

Reclamation Service Established July 1902 in *Geological Survey* by Interior Secretary, pursuant to act of June 17, 1902 (32 Stat. 388). Separated from Survey in 1907 and renamed *Bureau of Reclamation* June 1923. Power marketing functions transferred to Energy Department by act of Aug. 4, 1977 (91 Stat. 578). *Bureau* renamed *Water and Power Resources Service* by Secretarial Order 3042 of Nov. 6, 1979. Renamed Bureau of Reclamation by Secretarial Order 3064 of May 18, 1981.

Reconciliation Service Established by Director of Selective Service pursuant to EO 11804 of Sept. 16, 1974. Program terminated Apr. 2, 1980.

Reconstruction Finance Corporation Established Feb. 2, 1932, by act of Jan. 22, 1932 (47 Stat. 5). Grouped with other agencies to form *Federal Loan Agency* by Reorg. Plan No. I of 1939, effective July 1, 1939. Transferred to Commerce Department by EO 9071 of Feb. 24, 1942. Returned to *Federal Loan Agency* by act of Feb. 24, 1945 (59 Stat. 5). *Agency* abolished by act of June 30, 1947 (61 Stat. 202), and functions assumed by *Corporation*. Functions relating to financing houses or site improvements, authorized by act of Aug. 10, 1948 (61 Stat. 1275), transferred to *Housing and Home Finance Agency* by Reorg. Plan No. 23 of 1950, effective July 10, 1950. *Corporation* Board of Directors, established by act of Jan. 22, 1932 (47 Stat. 5), abolished by Reorg. Plan No. 1 of 1951, effective May 1, 1951, and functions transferred to Administrator and *Loan Policy Board* established by same plan, effective Apr. 30, 1951. Act of July 30, 1953 (67 Stat. 230), provided for *RFC* succession until June 30, 1954, and for termination of its lending powers Sept. 28, 1953. Certain functions assigned to appropriate agencies for liquidation by Reorg. Plan No. 2 of 1954, effective July 1, 1954. *Corporation* abolished by Reorg. Plan No. 1 of 1957, effective June 30, 1957, and functions transferred to *Housing and Home Finance Agency,* General Services Administration, Small Business Administration, and Treasury Department.

Records and Information Management, Office of Functions transferred from *National Archives and Records Service* to *Automated Data and Telecommunications Service* by General Services Administrator's decision, effective Jan. 10, 1982, regionally and Apr. 1, 1982, in Washington, DC.

Recovery Administration, Advisory Council, National Established by EO 7075 of June 15, 1935. Transferred to Commerce Department by EO 7252 of Dec. 21, 1935, and functions ordered terminated not later than Apr. 1, 1936, by same order. *Committee of Industrial Analysis* created by EO 7323 of Mar. 21, 1936, to complete work of *Council.*

Recovery Administration, National Established by President pursuant to act of June 16, 1933 (48 Stat. 194). Provisions of title I of act repealed by Public Resolution 26 of June 14, 1935 (49 Stat. 375), and extension of *Administration* in skeletonized form authorized until Apr. 1, 1936. *Office of Administrator, National Recovery Administration,* created by EO 7075 of June 15, 1935. *Administration* terminated by EO 7252 of Dec. 21, 1935, which transferred *Division of Review, Division of Business Corporation,* and *Advisory Council* to Commerce Department for termination of functions by Apr. 1, 1936. *Consumers' Division* transferred to Labor Department by same order.

Recovery Review Board, National Established by EO 6632 of Mar. 7, 1934. Abolished by EO 6771 of June 30, 1934.

Recreation, Bureau of Outdoor Established in Interior Department by act of May 28, 1963 (77 Stat.

49). Terminated by Secretary's order of Jan. 25, 1978, and functions assumed by *Heritage Conservation and Recreation Service.*

Recreation and Natural Beauty, Citizens' Advisory Committee on Established by EO 11278 of May 4, 1966. Terminated by EO 11472 of May 29, 1969.

Recreation and Natural Beauty, President's Council on Established by EO 11278 of May 4, 1966. Terminated by EO 11472 of May 29, 1969.

Recreation Resources Review Commission, Outdoor Established by act of June 28, 1958 (72 Stat. 238). Final report submitted to President January 1962 and terminated Sept. 1, 1962.

Regional Action Planning Commissions Authorized by act of Aug. 26, 1965 (79 Stat. 552). Federal role abolished through repeal by act of Aug. 13, 1981 (95 Stat. 766). At time of repeal, eight commissions—Coastal Plains, Four Corners, New England, Old West Ozarks, Pacific Northwest, Southwest Border, Southwest Border Region, and Upper Great Lakes—affected.

Regional Councils, Federal Established by EO 12314 of July 22, 1981. Abolished by EO 12407 of Feb. 22, 1983.

Regional Operations, Executive Director of Established in Food and Drug Administration by *Health, Education, and Welfare Secretary's* order of May 20, 1971. Merged into Office of Regulatory Affairs by Health and Human Services Secretary's order of Nov. 5, 1984.

Regulatory Council, U.S. Disbanded by Vice Presidential memorandum of Mar. 25, 1981. Certain functions continued in Regulatory Information Service Center.

Regulatory Relief, Presidential Task Force on Establishment announced in President's remarks Jan. 22, 1981. Disbanded and functions transferred to Office of Management and Budget in August 1983.

Rehabilitation Services Administration Functions transferred from *Health, Education, and Welfare Department* to Office of Special Education and Rehabilitative Services, Education Department, by act of Oct. 17, 1979 (93 Stat. 678), effective May 4, 1980.

Relief Corporation, Federal Surplus Organized under powers granted to President by act of June 16, 1933 (48 Stat. 195). Charter granted by State of Delaware Oct. 4, 1933, and amended Nov. 18, 1935, changing name to *Federal Surplus Commodities Corporation* and naming Agriculture Secretary, Administrator of Agricultural Adjustment Administration, and Governor of Farm Credit Administration as Board of Directors. Continued as agency under Agriculture Secretary by acts of June 28, 1937 (50 Stat. 323) and Feb. 16, 1938 (52 Stat. 38). Consolidated with *Division of Marketing and Marketing Agreements* into *Surplus Marketing Administration* by Reorg. Plan No. III of 1940, effective June 30, 1940. Merged into *Agricultural Marketing Administration* by EO 9069 of Feb. 23, 1942.

Relief and Rehabilitation Operations, Office of Foreign Established in State Department as announced by White House Nov. 21, 1942. Consolidated with *Foreign Economic Administration* by EO 9380 of Sept. 25, 1943.

Renegotiation Board Established by act of Mar. 23, 1951 (65 Stat. 7). Terminated Mar. 31, 1979, by act of Oct. 10, 1978 (92 Stat. 1043).

Rent Advisory Board Established by EO 11632 of Nov. 22, 1971. Abolished by EO 11695 of Jan. 11, 1973.

Rent Stabilization, Office of Established by General Order 9 of *Economic Stabilization Administrator* July 31, 1951, pursuant to act of June 30, 1947 (61 Stat. 193), and EO's 10161 of Sept. 9, 1950, and 10276 of July 31, 1951. Abolished by EO 10475 of July 31, 1953, and functions transferred to *Office of Defense Mobilization. Office of Research and Development* combined with *Office of Minerals Policy Development* in Interior Department May 21, 1976, under authority of Reorg. Plan No. 3 of 1950, effective May 24, 1950, to form *Office of Minerals Policy and Research Analysis.* Abolished Sept. 30, 1981, by Secretarial Order 3070 and functions transferred to *Bureau of Mines.*

Reports, Office of Government Established July 1, 1939, to perform functions of *National Emergency Council* abolished by Reorg. Plan No. II of 1939, effective July 1, 1939. Established as administrative unit of Executive Office of the President by EO 8248 of Sept. 8, 1939. Consolidated with *Office of War Information, Office for Emergency Management,* by EO 9182 of June 13, 1942. Reestablished in Executive Office of the President by EO 9809 of Dec. 12, 1946, which transferred to it functions of *Media Programming Division* and *Motion Picture Division, Office of War Mobilization and Reconversion,* and functions transferred from *Bureau of Special Services, Office of War Information,* to *Bureau of the Budget* by EO 9608 of Aug. 31, 1945. Subsequent to enactment of act of July 30, 1947 (61 Stat. 588), functions of *Office* restricted to advertising and motion picture liaison and operation of library. Terminated June 30, 1948.

Research, Office of University Transferred from *Office of Program Management and Administration,* Research and Special Programs Administration, to Office of Economics, Office of the Assistant Secretary for Policy and International Affairs, under authority of Transportation Department appropriation request for FY 1985, effective Oct. 1, 1984.

Research and Development Board Established in Defense Department by act of July 26, 1947 (61 Stat. 499). Abolished by Reorg. Plan No. 6 of 1953, effective June 30, 1953, and functions vested in Defense Secretary.

Research and Development Board, Joint Established June 6, 1946, by charter of Secretaries of War and Navy. Terminated on creation of *Research and Development Board* by act of July 26, 1947 (61 Stat. 506).

Research and Intelligence Service, Interim Established in State Department by EO 9621 of Sept. 20, 1945. Abolished Dec. 31, 1945, pursuant to terms of order.

Research Resources, Division of Established in National Institutes of Health, Health and Human Services Department. Renamed National Center for Research Resources by Secretarial notice of Feb. 23, 1990 (55 FR 6455) and act of June 10, 1993 (107 Stat. 178).

Research Service, Cooperative State Established by Agriculture Secretary's Memorandum 1462, supp. 1, of Aug. 31, 1961. Consolidated into *Science and Education Administration* by Secretary's order of Jan. 24, 1978. Reestablished as Cooperative State Research Service by Secretarial order of June 16, 1981.

Research and Service Division, Cooperative Functions transferred to Agriculture Secretary in *Farmer Cooperative Service* by act of Aug. 6, 1953 (67 Stat. 390).

Resettlement Administration Established by EO 7027 of Apr. 30, 1935. Functions transferred to Agriculture Department by EO 7530 of Dec. 31, 1936. Renamed *Farm Security Administration* by Secretary's Memorandum 732 of Sept. 1, 1937. Abolished by act of Aug. 14, 1946 (60 Stat. 1062) and functions incorporated into the *Farmers' Home Administration,* effective Jan. 1, 1947. *Farmers' Home Administration* abolished, effective Dec. 27, 1994, under authority of Secretary's Memorandum 1010–1 dated Oct. 20, 1994 (59 FR 66441). Functions assumed by the Consolidated Farm Service Agency and the Rural Housing and Community Development Service.

Resolution Trust Corporation Established by act of Aug. 9, 1989 (103 Stat. 369). Board of Directors of the Corporation abolished by act of Dec. 12, 1991 (105 Stat. 1769).

Resources Board and Advisory Committee, National Established by EO 6777 of June 30, 1934. Abolished by EO 7065 of June 7, 1935, and functions transferred to *National Resources Committee.*

Resources Committee, National Established by EO 7065 of June 7, 1935. Abolished by Reorg. Plan No. I of 1939, effective July 1, 1939, and functions transferred to *National Resources Planning Board* in Executive Office of the President. *Board* terminated by act of June 26, 1943 (57 Stat. 169).

Resources Planning Board, National *See Resources Committee, National*

Retired Executives, Service Corps of Established in ACTION by act of Oct. 1, 1973 (87 Stat. 404). Transferred to Small Business Administration by EO 11871 of July 18, 1975.

Retraining and Reemployment Administration Established by EO 9427 of Feb. 24, 1944, and act of Oct. 3, 1944 (58 Stat. 788). Transferred from *Office of War Mobilization and Reconversion* to Labor Department by EO 9617 of Sept. 19, 1945. Terminated pursuant to terms of act.

Revenue Sharing, Office of Established by Treasury Secretary to administer programs authorized by acts of Oct. 20, 1972 (86 Stat. 919), and July 22, 1976 (90 Stat. 999). Transferred from Office of the Secretary to Assistant Secretary (Domestic Finance) by Treasury Department Order 242, rev. 1, of May 17, 1976.

Review, Division of Established in *National Recovery Administration* by EO 7075 of June 15, 1935. Transferred to Commerce Department by EO 7252 of Dec. 21, 1935, and functions terminated Apr. 1, 1936. *Committee of Industrial Analysis* created by EO 7323 of Mar. 21, 1936, to complete work of *Division.*

RFC Mortgage Company Organized under laws of Maryland Mar. 14, 1935, pursuant to act of Jan. 22, 1932 (47 Stat. 5). Grouped with other agencies to form *Federal Loan Agency* by Reorg. Plan No. I of 1939, effective July 1, 1939. Transferred to Commerce Department by EO 9071 of Feb. 24, 1942. Returned to *Federal Loan Agency* by act of Feb. 24, 1945 (59 Stat. 5). Assets and liabilities transferred to *Reconstruction Finance Corporation* by act of June 30, 1947 (61 Stat. 207).

River Basins, Neches, Trinity, Brazos, Colorado, Guadalupe, San Antonio, Nueces, and San Jacinto, and Intervening Areas, U.S. Study Commission on Established by act of Aug. 28, 1958 (72 Stat. 1058). Terminated June 30, 1962.

River Basins, Savannah, Altamaha, Saint Marys, Apalachicola-Chattahoochee, and Perdido-Escambia, and Intervening Areas, U.S. Study Commission on Established by act of Aug. 28, 1958 (72 Stat. 1090). Terminated Dec. 23, 1962.

Road Inquiry, Office of Established by Agriculture Secretary under authority of act of Aug. 8, 1894 (28 Stat. 264). Federal aid for highways to be administered by Agriculture Secretary through *Office of Public Roads and Rural Engineering* authorized by act of July 11, 1916 (39 Stat. 355), known as *Bureau of Public Roads* after July 1918. Transferred to *Federal Works Agency* by Reorg. Plan No. I of 1939, effective July 1, 1939, and renamed *Public Roads Administration.* Transferred to General Services Administration as *Bureau of Public Roads* by act of June 30, 1949 (63 Stat. 380). Transferred to Commerce Department by Reorg. Plan No. 7 of 1949, effective Aug. 20, 1949. Transferred to Transportation Secretary by act of Oct. 15, 1966 (80 Stat. 931), and functions assigned to Federal Highway Administration.

Roads, Bureau of Public *See* **Road Inquiry, Office of**

Roads Administration, Public *See* **Road Inquiry, Office of**

Roads and Rural Engineering, Office of Public *See* **Road Inquiry, Office of**

Rock Creek and Potomac Parkway Commission Established by act of Mar. 14, 1913 (37 Stat. 885). Abolished by EO 6166 of June 10, 1933, and functions transferred to *Office of National Parks, Buildings, and Reservations,* Interior Department.

Roosevelt Centennial Commission, Theodore Established by joint resolution of July 28, 1955 (69 Stat. 383). Terminated Oct. 27, 1959, pursuant to terms of act.

Roosevelt Library, Franklin D. Functions assigned to National Park Service by Reorg. Plan No. 3 of 1946, effective July 16, 1946, transferred to General Services Administration by Reorg. Plan No. 1 of 1963, effective July 27, 1963.

Roosevelt Library, Trustees of the Franklin D. Established by joint resolution of July 18, 1939 (53 Stat. 1063). Transferred to General Services Administration by act of June 30, 1949 (63 Stat. 381). Abolished by act of Mar. 5, 1958 (72 Stat. 34), and Library operated by *National Archives and Records Service,* General Services Administration.

Rubber Development Corporation Establishment announced Feb. 20, 1943, by Commerce Secretary. Organized under laws of Delaware as subsidiary of *Reconstruction Finance Corporation.* Assumed all activities of *Rubber Reserve Company* relating to development of foreign rubber sources and procurement of rubber therefrom. Functions transferred to *Office of Economic Warfare* by EO 9361 of July 15, 1943. *Office* consolidated into *Foreign Economic Administration* by EO 9380 of Sept. 25, 1943. *Office* returned to *Reconstruction Finance Corporation* by EO 9630 of Sept. 27, 1945. Certificate of incorporation expired June 30, 1947.

Rubber Producing Facilities Disposal Commission Established by act of Aug. 7, 1953 (67 Stat. 408). Functions transferred to *Federal Facilities Corporation* by EO 10678 of Sept. 20, 1956.

Rubber Reserve Company Established June 28, 1940, under act of Jan. 22, 1932 (47 Stat. 5). Transferred from *Federal Loan Agency* to Commerce Department by EO 9071 of Feb. 24, 1942. Returned to *Federal Loan Agency* by act of Feb. 24, 1945 (59 Stat. 5). Dissolved by act of June 30, 1945 (59 Stat. 310), and functions transferred to *Reconstruction Finance Corporation.*

Rural Areas Development, Office of Established by Agriculture Secretary's memorandum in 1961 (revised Sept. 21, 1962). Renamed *Rural Community Development Service* by Secretary's Memorandum 1570 of Feb. 24, 1965.

Rural Community Development Service Established by Agriculture Secretary's Memorandum 1570 of Feb. 25, 1965, to supersede *Office of Rural Areas Development.* Abolished Feb. 2, 1970, by Secretary's Memorandum 1670 of Jan. 30, 1970, and functions transferred to other agencies in department.

Rural Development Administration Established within Agriculture Department by Secretary's Memorandum 1020–34 dated Dec. 31, 1991. Abolished Dec. 27, 1994 (59 FR 66441) under authority of Secretary's Memorandum 1010–1 dated Oct. 20, 1994. Functions assumed by the Rural Business and Cooperative Development Service.

Rural Development Committee *See* **Rural Development Program, Committee for**

Rural Development Policy, Office of   Established initially as *Office of Rural Development Policy Management and Coordination,* Farmers Home Administration, by Agriculture Secretary's Memorandum 1020–3 of Oct. 26, 1981. Abolished in 1986 due to lack of funding.

Rural Development Program, Committee for   Established by EO 10847 of Oct. 12, 1959. Abolished by EO 11122 of Oct. 16, 1963, which established *Rural Development Committee. Committee* superseded by EO 11307 of Sept. 30, 1966, and functions assumed by Agriculture Secretary.

Rural Development Service   Established by Agriculture Secretarial order in 1973. Functions transferred to *Office of Rural Development Coordination and Planning,* Farmers Home Administration, by Secretarial order in 1978.

Rural Electrification Administration   Established by EO 7037 of May 11, 1935. Functions transferred by EO 7458 of Sept. 26, 1936, to *Rural Electrification Administration* established by act of May 20, 1936 (49 Stat. 1363). Transferred by Reorg. Plan No. II of 1939, effective July 1, 1939. Abolished by Secretary's Memorandum 1010–1 dated Oct. 20, 1994, and functions assumed by Rural Utilities Service.

Rural Rehabilitation Division   Established April 1934 by act of May 12, 1933 (48 Stat. 55). Functions transferred to *Resettlement Administration* by *Federal Emergency Relief Administrator's* order of June 19, 1935.

Saint Elizabeths Hospital   *See* **Insane, Government Hospital for the**

Saint Lawrence Seaway Development Corporation   Established by act of May 13, 1954 (68 Stat. 92). Commerce Secretary given direction of general policies of *Corporation* by EO 10771 of June 20, 1958. Transferred to Transportation Department by act of Oct. 15, 1966 (80 Stat. 931).

Salary Stabilization, Office of   *See* **Salary Stabilization Board**

Salary Stabilization Board   Established May 10, 1951, by *Economic Stabilization Administrator's* General Order 8. Stabilization program administered by *Office of Salary Stabilization.* Terminated Apr. 30, 1953, by EO 10434 of Feb. 6, 1953, and acts of June 30, 1952 (66 Stat. 296), and June 30, 1953 (67 Stat. 131).

Sales Manager, Office of the General   Established by Agriculture Secretary Feb. 29, 1976. Consolidated with Foreign Agricultural Service by Secretary's Memorandum 2001 of Nov. 29, 1979.

Savings Bonds, Interdepartmental Committee for the Voluntary Payroll Savings Plan for the Purchase of U.S.   Established by EO 11532 of June 2, 1970. Superseded by EO 11981 of Mar. 29, 1977, which established Interagency Committee for the Purchase of U.S. Savings Bonds.

Savings and Loan Advisory Council, Federal   Established by act of Oct. 6, 1972 (86 Stat. 770).

Continued by act of Dec. 26, 1974 (88 Stat. 1739). Terminated by act of Aug. 9, 1989 (103 Stat. 422).

Savings and Loan Insurance Corporation, Federal   Established by act of June 27, 1934 (48 Stat. 1246). Grouped with other agencies to form *Federal Loan Agency* by Reorg. Plan No. I of 1939, effective July 1, 1939. Transferred to *Federal Home Loan Bank Administration, National Housing Agency,* by EO 9070 of Feb. 24, 1942. Board of Trustees abolished by Reorg. Plan No. 3 of 1947, effective July 27, 1947, and functions transferred to *Home Loan Bank Board.* Abolished by act of Aug. 9, 1989 (103 Stat. 354).

Savings Bonds Division, United States   Established by Departmental Order 62 of Dec. 26, 1945, as successor to the War and Finance Division, War Savings Staff, and Defense Savings Staff. Functions transferred to Bureau of Public Debt by Departmental Order 101–05 of May 11, 1994, and *Division* renamed Savings Bond Marketing Office.

Science, Engineering, and Technology, Federal Coordinating Council for   Established by act of May 11, 1976 (90 Stat. 471). Abolished by Reorg. Plan No. 1 of 1977, effective Feb. 26, 1978, and functions transferred to President. Functions redelegated to Director of the Office of Science and Technology Policy and Federal Coordinating Council for Science, Engineering, and Technology, established by EO 12039 of Feb. 24, 1978.

Science, Engineering, and Technology Panel, Intergovernmental   Established by act of May 11, 1976 (90 Stat. 465). Abolished by Reorg. Plan No. 1 of 1977, effective Feb. 26, 1978, and functions transferred to President. Functions redelegated to Director of Office of Science and Technology Policy by EO 12039 of Feb. 24, 1978, which established Intergovernmental Science, Engineering, and Technology Advisory Panel.

Science Advisory Committee, President's   Established by President Apr. 20, 1951, and reconstituted Nov. 22, 1957. Terminated with *Office of Science and Technology,* effective July 1, 1973.

Science Exhibit-Century 21 Exposition, U.S.   Established Jan. 20, 1960, by Commerce Department Order 167. Abolished by revocation of order on June 5, 1963.

Science and Technology, Federal Council for   *See* **Scientific Research and Development, Interdepartmental Committee on**

Science and Technology, Office of   Established by Reorg. Plan No. 2 of 1962, effective June 8, 1962. *Office* abolished by Reorg. Plan No. 1 of 1973, effective June 30, 1973, and functions transferred to National Science Foundation.

Science and Technology, President's Committee on   Established by act of May 11, 1976 (90 Stat. 468). Abolished by Reorg. Plan No. 1 of 1977, effective Feb. 26, 1978, and functions transferred to President.

Scientific Research and Development, Interdepartmental Committee on   Established by EO 9912 of Dec. 24, 1947. EO 9912 revoked by EO

10807 of Mar. 13, 1959, which established *Federal Council for Science and Technology.* Abolished by act of May 11, 1976 (90 Stat. 472).

Scientific Research and Development, Office of Established in *Office for Emergency Management* by EO 8807 of June 28, 1941. Terminated by EO 9913 of Dec. 26, 1947, and property transferred to *National Military Establishment* for liquidation.

Scientists and Engineers, National Committee for the Development of Established by President Apr. 3, 1956. Renamed *President's Committee on Scientists and Engineers* May 7, 1957. Final report submitted Dec. 17, 1958, and expired Dec. 31, 1958.

Scientists and Engineers, President's Committee on *See* **Scientists and Engineers, National Committee for the Development of**

Screw Thread Commission, National Established by act of July 18, 1918 (40 Stat. 912). Terminated by EO 6166 of June 10, 1933, and records transferred to Commerce Department, effective Mar. 2, 1934. Informal Interdepartmental Screw Thread Committee established on Sept. 14, 1939, consisting of *War,* Navy, and Commerce Department representatives.

Security, Commission on Government Established by act of Aug. 9, 1955 (69 Stat. 595). Terminated Sept. 22, 1957, pursuant to terms of act.

Security, Office of the Director for Mutual *See* **Security Agency, Mutual**

Security Agency, Federal Established by Reorg. Plan No. I of 1939, effective July 1, 1939, grouping under one administration *Office of Education, Public Health Service, Social Security Board, U.S. Employment Service, Civilian Conservation Corps,* and *National Youth Administration.* Abolished by Reorg. Plan No. 1 of 1953, effective Apr. 11, 1953, and functions and units transferred to *Health, Education, and Welfare Department.*

Security Agency, Mutual Established and continued by acts of Oct. 10, 1951 (65 Stat. 373) and June 20, 1952 (66 Stat. 141). *Agency* and *Office of Director for Mutual Security* abolished by Reorg. Plan No. 7 of 1953, effective Aug. 1, 1953, and functions transferred to *Foreign Operations Administration,* established by same plan.

Security and Individual Rights, President's Commission on Internal Established by EO 10207 of Jan. 23, 1951. Terminated by EO 10305 of Nov. 14, 1951.

Security Resources Board, National Established by act of July 26, 1947 (61 Stat. 499). Transferred to Executive Office of the President by Reorg. Plan No. 4 of 1949, effective Aug. 20, 1949. Functions of *Board* transferred to Chairman and *Board* made advisory to him by Reorg. Plan No. 25 of 1950, effective July 10, 1950. Functions delegated by Executive order transferred to *Office of Defense Mobilization* by EO 10438 of Mar. 13, 1953. *Board* abolished by Reorg. Plan No. 3 of 1953, effective June 12, 1953, and remaining functions transferred to *Office of Defense Mobilization.*

Security Training Commission, National Established by act of June 19, 1951 (65 Stat. 75). Expired June 30, 1957, pursuant to Presidential letter of Mar. 25, 1957.

Seed Loan Office Authorized by Presidential letters of July 26, 1918, and July 26, 1919, to Agriculture Secretary. Further authorized by act of Mar. 3, 1921 (41 Stat. 1347). Office transferred to Farm Credit Administration by EO 6084 of Mar. 27, 1933.

Selective Service Appeal Board, National Established by EO 9988 of Aug. 20, 1948. Inactive as of Apr. 11, 1975.

Selective Service Records, Office of *See* **Selective Service System**

Selective Service System Established by act of Sept. 16, 1940 (54 Stat. 885). Placed under jurisdiction of *War Manpower Commission* by EO 9279 of Dec. 5, 1942, and designated *Bureau of Selective Service.* Designated Selective Service System, separate agency, by EO 9410 of Dec. 23, 1943. Transferred for liquidation to *Office of Selective Service Records* established by act of Mar. 31, 1947 (61 Stat. 31). Transferred to Selective Service System by act of June 24, 1948 (62 Stat. 604).

Self-Help Development and Technical Development, Office of Established in *National Consumer Cooperative Bank* by act of Aug. 20, 1978 (92 Stat. 499). Abolished by act of Aug. 13, 1981 (95 Stat. 437), and assets transferred to Consumer Cooperative Development Corporation, Commerce Department, Dec. 30, 1982.

Services, Bureau of Special *See* **Office of War Information**

Services, Division of Central Administrative Established by *Liaison Officer for Emergency Management* pursuant to Presidential letter of Feb. 28, 1941. Terminated by EO 9471 of Aug. 25, 1944, and functions discontinued or transferred to constituent agencies of *Office for Emergency Management* and other agencies.

Shipbuilding Stabilization Committee Originally organized by *National Defense Advisory Commission* in 1940. Established August 1942 by *War Production Board.* Transferred to Labor Department from *Civilian Production Administration,* successor agency to *Board,* by EO 9656 of Nov. 15, 1945. Terminated June 30, 1947.

Shipping Board, U.S. Established by act of Sept. 7, 1916 (39 Stat. 729). Abolished by EO 6166 of June 10, 1933, and functions, including those with respect to *U.S. Shipping Board Merchant Fleet Corporation,* transferred to *U.S. Shipping Board Bureau,* Commerce Department, effective Mar. 2, 1934. Separation of employees deferred until Sept. 30, 1933, by EO 6245 of Aug. 9, 1933. Functions assumed by *U.S. Maritime Commission* Oct. 26, 1936, pursuant to act of June 29, 1936 (49 Stat. 1985).

Shipping Board Bureau, U.S. *See* **Shipping Board, U.S.**

Shipping Board Emergency Fleet Corporation, U.S. Established Apr. 16, 1917, under authority of act of Sept. 7, 1916 (39 Stat. 729). Renamed *U.S. Shipping Board Merchant Fleet Corporation* by act of Feb. 11, 1927 (44 Stat. 1083). Terminated Oct. 26, 1936, under provisions of act of June 29, 1936 (49 Stat. 1985), and functions transferred to *U.S. Maritime Commission.*

Shipping Board Merchant Fleet Corporation, U.S. *See* **Shipping Board Emergency Fleet Corporation, U.S.**

Ships, Bureau of Established by act of June 20, 1940 (54 Stat. 493), to replace *Bureau of Engineering* and *Bureau of Construction and Repair.* Abolished by Defense Department reorg. order of Mar. 9, 1966, and functions transferred to Navy Secretary (31 FR 7188).

Simpson Historical Research Center, Albert F. Renamed Headquarters USAF Historical Research Center by Defense Secretary's special order of Dec. 16, 1983.

Smithsonian Symposia and Seminars, Office of Renamed Office of Interdisciplinary Studies by Smithsonian Institution announcement of Mar. 16, 1987.

Social Development Institute, Inter-American Established by act of Dec. 30, 1969 (83 Stat. 821). Renamed Inter-American Foundation by act of Feb. 7, 1972 (86 Stat. 34).

Social Protection, Committee on Established in *Office of Defense Health and Welfare Services* by administrative order June 14, 1941. Functions transferred to *Federal Security Agency* by EO 9338 of Apr. 29, 1943.

Social and Rehabilitation Service Established by *Health, Education, and Welfare Secretary's* reorganization of Aug. 15, 1967. Abolished by Secretary's reorganization of Mar. 8, 1977 (42 FR 13262), and constituent units—*Medical Services Administration, Assistance Payments Administration, Office of Child Support Enforcement,* and *Public Services Administration*—transferred.

Social Security Administration *See* **Social Security Board**

Social Security Board Established by act of Aug. 14, 1935 (49 Stat. 620). Incorporated into *Federal Security Agency* by Reorg. Plan No. I of 1939, effective July 1, 1939. *Social Security Board* abolished and Social Security Administration established by Reorg. Plan No. 2 of 1946 (5 U.S.C. app.), effective July 16, 1946, and functions of the *Board* transferred to *Federal Security Administrator.* Social Security Administration transferred from *Federal Security Agency* by Reorganization Plan No. 1 of 1953 (5 U.S.C. app.), effective Apr. 11, 1953, to the *Department of Health, Education, and Welfare.* Social Security Administration became an independent agency in the executive branch by act of Aug. 15, 1994 (108 Stat. 1464), effective Mar. 31, 1995.

Soil Conservation Service *See* **Soil Erosion Service**

Soil Erosion Service Established in Interior Department following allotment made Aug. 25, 1933. Transferred to Agriculture Department by Interior Secretary's administrative order of Mar. 25, 1935. Made *Soil Conservation Service* by order of Agriculture Secretary, Apr. 27, 1935, pursuant to provisions of act of Apr. 27, 1935 (49 Stat. 163). Certain functions of *Soil Conservation Service* under jurisdiction of Interior Department transferred from Agriculture Department to Interior Department by Reorg. Plan No. IV of 1940, effective June 30, 1940. *Soil Conservation Service* abolished by act of Oct. 13, 1994 (108 Stat. 3225) and functions assumed by the Natural Resources Conservation Service.

Soils, Bureau of *See* **Agricultural and Industrial Chemistry, Bureau of** and **Plant Industry, Bureau of**

Solicitor General, Office of Assistant Established in Justice Department by act of June 16, 1933 (48 Stat. 307). Terminated by Reorg. Plan No. 2 of 1950, effective May 24, 1950.

Space Science, Office of *See* **Space and Terrestrial Applications, Office of**

Space Science Board Renamed Space Studies Board by authority of the National Research Council, National Academy of Sciences, effective May 8, 1989.

Space Station, Office of Established in the National Aeronautics and Space Administration. Abolished in 1990 and remaining functions transferred to the Office of Space Flight.

Space Technology Laboratories, National Renamed John C. Stennis Space Center by EO 12641 of May 20, 1988.

Space and Terrestrial Applications, Office of Combined with *Office of Space Science* to form Office of Space Science and Applications by National Aeronautics and Space Administrator's announcement of Sept. 29, 1981.

Space Tracking and Data Systems, Office of Renamed Office of Space Operations by National Aeronautics and Space Administrator's announcement of Jan. 9, 1987.

Space Transportation Operations, Office of Combined with *Office of Space Transportation Systems* to form Office of Space Transportation Systems, National Aeronautics and Space Administration, effective July 1982.

Space Transportation Systems, Office of *See* **Space Transportation Operations, Office of**

Spanish-Speaking People, Cabinet Committee on Opportunities for *See* **Mexican-American Affairs, Interagency Committee on**

Special. *See other part of title*

Specifications Board, Federal Established by *Bureau of the Budget* Circular 42 of Oct. 10, 1921. Transferred from *Federal Coordinating Service* to *Procurement Division* by Treasury Secretary's order of Oct. 9, 1933. *Board* superseded by *Federal Specifications Executive Committee,* set up by

Director of Procurement under Circular Letter 106 of July 16, 1935.

Sport Fisheries and Wildlife, Bureau of Established in Interior Department by act of Aug. 8, 1956 (70 Stat. 1119). *Bureau* replaced by U.S. Fish and Wildlife Service pursuant to act of Apr. 22, 1974 (88 Stat. 92).

Standards, National Bureau of *See* **Weights and Measures, Office of Standard**

State Department Duty of Secretary of State of procuring copies of all statutes of the States, as provided for in act of Sept. 28, 1789 (R.S. 206), abolished by Reorg. Plan No. 20 of 1950, effective May 24, 1950. Functions of numbering, editing, and distributing proclamations and Executive orders transferred from State Department to *Division of the Federal Register, National Archives,* by EO 7298 of Feb. 18, 1936. Duty of Secretary of State of publishing Executive proclamations and treaties in newspapers in District of Columbia, provided for in act of July 31, 1876 (19 Stat. 105), abolished by Reorg. Plan No. 20 of 1950, effective May 24, 1950. Functions concerning publication of U.S. Statutes at Large, acts and joint resolutions in pamphlet form known as slip laws, and amendments to the Constitution; electoral votes for President and Vice President; and Territorial papers transferred from State Department to General Services Administrator by Reorg. Plan No. 20 of 1950. (*See also* **Archives Establishment, National**)

State and Local Cooperation, Division of Established by *Advisory Commission to Council of National Defense* Aug. 5, 1940. Transferred to *Office of Civilian Defense.*

State and Local Government Cooperation, Committee on Established by EO 11627 of Oct 15, 1971. Abolished by EO 11695 of Jan. 11, 1973.

State Technical Services, Office of Established by Commerce Secretary Nov. 19, 1965, pursuant to act of Sept. 14, 1965 (79 Stat. 697). Abolished by Secretary, effective June 30, 1970.

Statistical Board, Central Organized Aug. 9, 1933, by EO 6225 of July 27, 1933. Transferred to *Bureau of the Budget* by Reorg. Plan No. I of 1939, effective July 1, 1939. Expired July 25, 1940, and functions taken over by *Division of Statistical Standards, Bureau of the Budget.*

Statistical Committee, Central Established by act of July 25, 1935 (49 Stat. 498). Abolished by Reorg. Plan No. I of 1939, effective July 1, 1939, and functions transferred to *Bureau of the Budget.*

Statistical Policy Coordination Committee Established by EO 12013 of Oct. 7, 1977. Abolished by EO 12318 of Aug. 21, 1981.

Statistical Reporting Service Established by Agriculture Secretary's Memorandum 1446, supp. 1, part 3, of 1961. Consolidated with other departmental units into *Economics, Statistics, and Cooperatives Service* by Secretary's Memorandum 1927, effective Dec. 23, 1977. Redesignated as *Statistical Reporting Service* by Secretary's order of

Oct. 1, 1981. Renamed National Agricultural Statistics Service.

Statistics Administration, Social and Economic Established Jan. 1, 1972, by Commerce Secretary. Terminated by Commerce Department Organization Order 10–2, effective Aug. 4, 1975 (40 FR 42765). Bureau of Economic Analysis and Bureau of the Census restored as primary operating units of Commerce Department by Organization Orders 35–1A and 2A, effective Aug. 4, 1975.

Statutes at Large *See* **State Department**

Statutes of the States *See* **State Department**

Steam Engineering, Bureau of Established in Navy Department by act of July 5, 1862 (12 Stat. 510). Redesignated as *Bureau of Engineering* by act of June 4, 1920 (41 Stat. 828). Abolished by act of June 20, 1940 (54 Stat. 492), and functions transferred to *Bureau of Ships.*

Steamboat Inspection Service President authorized to appoint *Service* by act of June 28, 1838 (5 Stat. 252). Treasury Secretary authorized to establish boards of local inspectors at enumerated ports throughout the U.S. by act of Feb. 28, 1871 (16 Stat. 440). Authority to appoint boards of local inspectors delegated to *Secretary of Commerce and Labor* by act of Mar. 4, 1905 (33 Stat. 1026). Consolidated with *Bureau of Navigation and Steamboat Inspection* by act of June 30, 1932 (47 Stat. 415).

Stock Catalog Board, Federal Standard Originated by act of Mar. 2, 1929 (45 Stat. 1461). Transferred from *Federal Coordinating Service* to *Procurement Division* by Treasury Secretary's order of Oct. 9, 1933.

Strategic Defense Initiative Organization Established in 1986 as a separate agency of the Department of Defense. Renamed Ballistic Missile Defense Organization by Deputy Secretary's memorandum in May 1993.

Strategic Services, Office of *See* **Information, Office of Coordinator of**

Subversive Activities Control Board Established by act of Sept. 23, 1950 (64 Stat. 987). Terminated June 30, 1973, due to lack of funding.

Sugar Division Created by act of May 12, 1933 (48 Stat. 31), authorized by act of Sept. 1, 1937 (50 Stat. 903). Taken from *Agricultural Adjustment Administration* and made independent division of Agriculture Department by Secretary's Memorandum 783, effective Oct. 16, 1938. Placed under *Agricultural Conservation and Adjustment Administration* by EO 9069 of Feb. 23, 1942, functioning as *Sugar Agency.* Functions transferred to *Food Distribution Administration* by EO 9280 of Dec. 5, 1942.

Sugar Rationing Administration Established by Agriculture Secretary's Memorandum 1190 of Mar. 31, 1947, under authority of act of Mar. 31, 1947 (61 Stat. 35). Terminated Mar. 31, 1948, on expiration of authority.

Supplies and Accounts, Bureau of *See* **Provisions and Clothing, Bureau of**

Supplies and Shortages, National Commission on Established by act of Sept. 30, 1974 (88 Stat. 1168). Terminated Mar. 31, 1977, pursuant to terms of act.

Supply, Bureau of Federal *See* **Procurement Division**

Supply, Office of Renamed Office of Procurement and Property by Smithsonian Institution announcement of Nov. 4, 1986.

Supply Committee, General Established by act of June 17, 1910 (36 Stat. 531). Abolished by EO 6166 of June 10, 1933, effective Mar. 2, 1934, and functions transferred to *Procurement Division, Treasury Department.*

Supply Priorities and Allocations Board Established in *Office for Emergency Management* by EO 8875 of Aug. 28, 1941. Abolished by EO 9024 of Jan. 16, 1942, and functions transferred to *War Production Board.*

Supply Service, Federal Renamed *Office of Personal Property* by General Services Administration order, effective Sept. 28, 1982; later renamed *Office of Federal Supply and Services* by GSA order of Jan. 22, 1983; then redesignated Federal Supply Service.

Surveys and Maps, Federal Board of *See* **Surveys and Maps of the Federal Government, Board of**

Surveys and Maps of the Federal Government, Board of Established by EO 3206 of Dec. 30, 1919. Renamed *Federal Board of Surveys and Maps* by EO 7262 of Jan. 4, 1936. Abolished by EO 9094 of Mar. 10, 1942, and functions transferred to Director, *Bureau of the Budget.*

Space System Development, Office of Established in the National Aeronautics and Space Administration. Renamed Office of Space Access and Technology in 1995.

Tariff Commission, U.S. Established by act of Sept. 8, 1916 (39 Stat. 795). Renamed U.S. International Trade Commission by act of Jan. 3, 1975 (88 Stat. 2009).

Tax Appeals, Board of Established as an independent agency within the executive branch by act of June 2, 1924 (43 Stat. 336). Continued by acts of Feb. 26, 1926 (44 Stat. 105) and Feb. 10, 1939 (53 Stat. 158). Renamed *Tax Court of the United States* by act of Aug. 16, 1954 (68A Stat. 879). Renamed United States Tax Court by act of Dec. 30, 1969 (83 Stat. 730).

Technical Cooperation Administration Transferred from State Department to *Mutual Security Agency* by EO 10458 of June 1, 1953. Transferred to *Foreign Operations Administration* by Reorg. Plan No. 7 of 1953, effective Aug. 1, 1953.

Technical Services, Office of Designated unit of Office of the Commerce Secretary by Department Order 179, July 23, 1962. Functions transferred to *National Bureau of Standards* by Order 90 of Jan. 30, 1964.

Technology, Automation, and Economic Progress, National Commission on Established by act of Aug. 19, 1964 (78 Stat. 463). Terminated January 1966 pursuant to terms of act.

Telecommunications Advisor to the President Established in Executive Office of the President by EO 10297 of Oct. 9, 1951. EO 10297 revoked by EO 10460 of June 16, 1953, and functions transferred to Director of *Office of Defense Mobilization.*

Telecommunications Management, Director of Established in *Office of Emergency Planning* by EO 10995 of Feb. 16, 1962. Assignment of radio frequencies delegated to Government agencies and foreign diplomatic establishments by EO 11084 of Feb. 16, 1963. Abolished by Reorg. Plan No. 1 of 1970, effective Apr. 20, 1970.

Telecommunications Policy, Office of Established in Executive Office of the President by Reorg. Plan No. 1 of 1970, effective Apr. 20, 1970. Abolished by Reorg. Plan No. 1 of 1977, effective Mar. 26, 1978, and certain functions transferred to President with all other functions transferred to Commerce Department.

Telecommunications Service, Automated Data Renamed *Office of Information Resources Management* by General Services Administration order of Aug. 17, 1982. Later renamed Information Resources Management Service.

Temporary Controls, Office of Established in *Office for Emergency Management* by EO 9809 of Dec. 12, 1946, consolidating *Office of War Mobilization and Reconversion, Office of Economic Stabilization, Office of Price Administration,* and *Civilian Production Administration.* Functions with respect to Veterans' Emergency Housing Program transferred to *Housing Expediter* by EO 9836 of Mar. 22, 1947. Functions with respect to distribution and price of sugar products transferred to Agriculture Secretary by act of Mar. 31, 1947 (61 Stat. 36). Office terminated by EO 9841 of Apr. 23, 1947, and remaining functions redistributed.

Temporary Emergency Court of Appeals Established by act of Dec. 22, 1971 (85 Stat. 749). Abolished by act of Oct. 29, 1992, effective Apr. 30, 1993 (106 Stat. 4507). Court's jurisdiction and pending cases transferred to the United States Court of Appeals for the Federal Circuit.

Territorial Affairs, Office of Established by Interior Secretarial Order 2951 of Feb. 6, 1973. Abolished by Departmental Manual Release 2270 of June 6, 1980, and functions transferred to Office of Assistant Secretary for Territorial and International Affairs.

Territorial papers *See* **State Department**

Territories, Office of Established by Interior Secretary July 28, 1950. Functions reassigned to *Deputy Assistant Secretary for Territorial Affairs* in *Office of the Assistant Secretary—Public Land Management,* Interior Department, by Secretarial Order 2942, effective July 1, 1971.

Terrorism, Cabinet Committee To Combat Established by Presidential memorandum of Sept.

25, 1972. Terminated by National Security Council memorandum of Sept. 16, 1977.

Textile Industry, Board of Inquiry for the Cotton
Established by EO 6840 of Sept. 5, 1934. Abolished by EO 6858 of Sept. 26, 1934.

Textile National Industrial Relations Board
Established by administrative order of June 28, 1934. Abolished by EO 6858 of Sept. 26, 1934, which created *Textile Labor Relations Board* in connection with Labor Department. *Board* terminated July 1, 1937, and functions absorbed by *U.S. Conciliation Service,* Labor Department.

Textile National Industrial Relations Board, Cotton
Established by original Code of Fair Competition for the Cotton Textile Industry, as amended July 10, 1934. Abolished by EO 6858 of Sept. 26, 1934.

Textile Work Assignment Board, Cotton
Amendments to Code of Fair Competition for Cotton Textile Industry approved by EO 6876 of Oct. 16, 1934, and *Cotton Textile Work Assignment Board* appointed by *Textile Labor Relations Board. Board* expired June 15, 1935.

Textile Work Assignment Board, Silk   Appointed by *Textile Labor Relations Board* following President's approval of amendments to Code of Fair Competition for Silk Textile Industry by EO 6875 of Oct. 16, 1934. Terminated June 15, 1935.

Textile Work Assignment Board, Wool   Established by EO 6877 of Oct. 16, 1934. Terminated June 15, 1935.

Textiles, Office of   Established by Commerce Secretary Feb. 14, 1971. Functions transferred to *Domestic and International Business Administration,* effective Nov. 17, 1972.

Trade, Special Adviser to the President on Foreign
Established by EO 6651 of Mar. 23, 1934. Terminated on expiration of *National Recovery Administration.*

Trade Administration, International   *See* **Business and Defense Services Administration**

Trade Agreements, Interdepartmental Committee on
Established by Secretary of State in 1934 and reestablished by EO 9832 of Feb. 25, 1947. Abolished by EO 11075 of Jan. 15, 1963.

Trade and Developent Program   Established by act of Sept. 4, 1961, as amended (88 Stat. 1804). Designated separate entity within the U.S. International Development Cooperation Agency by act of Sept. 4, 1961, as amended (102 Stat. 1329). Renamed Trade and Development Agency by act of Oct. 28, 1992 (106 Stat. 3657).

Trade Expansion Act Advisory Committee
Established by EO 11075 of Jan. 15, 1963. Abolished by EO 11846 of Mar. 27, 1975, and records transferred to Trade Policy Committee established by same EO.

Trade Negotiations, Office of the Special Representative for   Renamed Office of the U.S. Trade Representative by EO 12188 of Jan. 4, 1980.

Trade Policy Committee   Established by EO 10741 of Nov. 25, 1957. Abolished by EO 11075 of Jan. 15, 1963.

Traffic Safety, President's Committee for
Established by Presidential letter of Apr. 14, 1954. Continued by EO 10858 of Jan. 13, 1960. Abolished by EO 11382 of Nov. 28, 1967.

Traffic Safety Agency, National   Established in Commerce Department by act of Sept. 9, 1966 (80 Stat. 718). Activity transferred to Transportation Department by act of Oct. 15, 1966 (80 Stat. 931). Responsibility placed in *National Highway Safety Bureau* by EO 11357 of June 6, 1967.

Training and Employment Service, U.S.   Established in *Manpower Administration,* Labor Department, Mar. 17, 1969. Abolished by Secretary's letter of Dec. 6, 1971, and functions assigned to *Office of Employment Development Programs* and *U.S. Employment Service.*

Training School for Boys, National   *See* **District of Columbia, Reform-School of the**

Transportation, Federal Coordinator of   Established by act of June 16, 1933 (48 Stat. 211). Expired June 16, 1936, under provisions of Public Resolution 27 (49 Stat. 376).

Transportation, Office of   Established in Agriculture Department by Secretary's Memorandum 1966 dated Dec. 12, 1978. Abolished by Secretary's Memorandum 1030–25 dated Dec. 28, 1990.

Transportation and Communications Service
Established by General Services Administrator Oct. 19, 1961. Abolished by Administrator's order, effective July 15, 1972. Motor equipment, transportation, and public utilities responsibilities assigned to Federal Supply Service; telecommunications function assigned to *Automated Data Telecommunications Service.*

Transportation and Public Utilities Service
Abolished by General Services Administration order of Aug. 17, 1982. Functions transferred to various GSA organizations.

Transportation Safety Board, National   Established in Transportation Department by act of Oct. 15, 1966 (80 Stat. 935). Abolished by act of Jan. 3, 1975 (88 Stat. 2156), which established independent National Transportation Safety Board.

Travel Service, U.S.   Replaced by U.S. Travel and Tourism Administration, Commerce Department, pursuant to act of Oct. 16, 1981 (95 Stat. 1014).

Treasury, Office of the Assistant Secretary of the— Electronics and Information Technology
Established by Secretary's Order 114–1 of Mar. 14, 1983. Abolished by Secretary's Order 114–3 of May 17, 1985, and functions transferred to Office of the Assistant Secretary for Management. Certain provisions effective Aug. 31, 1985 (50 FR 23573).

Treasury, Solicitor of the   Position established when certain functions of *Solicitor of the Treasury* transferred to Justice Department by EO 6166 of June 10, 1933. *Solicitor of the Treasury* transferred from Justice Department to Treasury Department by same order. *Office of Solicitor of the Treasury* abolished by act of May 10, 1934 (48 Stat. 758), and functions transferred to General Counsel, Treasury Department.

Treasury Secretary, Assistant Office abolished by Reorg. Plan No. III of 1940, effective June 30, 1940, and functions transferred to Fiscal Assistant Secretary, Treasury Department.

Treaties *See* **State Department**

Typhus Commission, U.S. of America Established in *War Department* by EO 9285 of Dec. 24, 1942. Abolished June 30, 1946, by EO 9680 of Jan. 17, 1946.

U.S. *See other part of title*

Uniformed Services University of the Health Sciences, School of Medicine of the Renamed F. Edward Hébert School of Medicine by act of Sept. 24, 1983 (97 Stat. 704).

United Nations Educational, Scientific and Cultural Organization U.S. membership in UNESCO authorized by act of July 30, 1946 (60 Stat. 712). Announcement of U.S. intention to withdraw made Dec. 28, 1983, in accordance with UNESCO constitution. Official U.S. withdrawal effective Dec. 31, 1984, by Secretary of State's letter of Dec. 19, 1984. U.S. maintains status as observer mission in UNESCO.

United States Court of Military Appeals Established under Article I of the Constitution of the United States pursuant to act of May 5, 1950, as amended (10 U.S.C. 867). Renamed United States Court of Appeals for the Armed Forces by act of Oct. 5, 1995 (108 Stat. 2831).

Upper Mississippi River Basin Commission Established by EO 11659 of Mar. 22, 1972. Terminated by EO 12319 of Sept. 9, 1981.

Urban Affairs, Council for Established in Executive Office of the President by EO 11452 of Jan. 23, 1969. Terminated by EO 11541 of July 1, 1970.

Urban Mass Transportation Administration Functions regarding urban mass transportation established in the Department of Housing and Urban Development by act of July 9, 1964 (78 Stat. 302). Most functions transferred to Transportation Department by Reorg. Plan No. 2 of 1968, effective June 30, 1968 (82 Stat. 1369), and joint responsibility assigned to Transportation and Housing and Urban Development Departments for functions relating to research, technical studies, and training. Transportation and Housing and Urban Development Under Secretaries agreed in November 1969 that Transportation Department should be focal point for urban mass transportation grant administration; at which time functions transferred to the Department of Transportation. Renamed Federal Transit Administration by act of Dec. 18, 1991 (105 Stat. 2088).

Urban Renewal Administration Established in *Housing and Home Finance Agency* by Administrator's Organizational Order 1 of Dec. 23,

1954. Functions transferred to Housing and Urban Development Department by act of Sept. 9, 1965 (78 Stat. 667), and *Administration* terminated.

Utilization and Disposal Service Established July 1, 1961, by Administrator of General Services and assigned functions of Federal Supply Service and Public Buildings Service. Functions transferred to *Property Management and Disposal Service* July 29, 1966.

Veterans Administration Legal work in defense of suits against the U.S. arising under act of June 7, 1924 (43 Stat. 607), transferred to Justice Department by EO 6166 of June 10, 1933. Transfer deferred to Sept. 10, 1933, by EO 6222 of July 27, 1933. Established as an independent agency under the President by Executive Order 5398 of July 21, 1930, in accordance with the act of July 3, 1930 (46 Stat. 1016) and the act of Sept. 2, 1958 (72 Stat. 1114). Made an executive department in the executive branch and redesignated Veterans Affairs Department by act of Oct. 25, 1988 (102 Stat. 2635).

Veterans Education Appeals Board *See* **Veterans Tuition Appeals Board**

Veterans Employment Service Renamed Veterans' Employment and Training Service by Labor Secretary's Order 4–83 of Mar. 24, 1983 (48 FR 14092).

Veterans Health Administration *See* **Medicine and Surgery, Department of**

Veterans Health Services and Research Administration *See* **Medicine and Surgery, Department of**

Veterans Placement Service Board Established by act of June 22, 1944 (58 Stat. 293). Abolished by Reorg. Plan No. 2 of 1949, effective Aug. 20, 1949, and functions transferred to Labor Secretary.

Veterans Tuition Appeals Board Established by act of Aug. 24, 1949 (63 Stat. 654). Functions assumed by *Veterans Education Appeals Board* established by act of July 13, 1950 (64 Stat. 336). *Board* terminated by act of Aug. 28, 1957 (71 Stat. 474).

Veterinary Medicine, Bureau of Established in Food and Drug Administration, *Health, Education, and Welfare Department*. Renamed Center for Veterinary Medicine by FDA notice of Mar. 9, 1984 (49 FR 10166).

Virgin Islands Public works programs under act of Dec. 20, 1944 (58 Stat. 827), transferred from General Services Administrator to Interior Secretary by Reorg. Plan No. 15 of 1950, effective May 24, 1950.

Virgin Islands Company Established in 1934. Reincorporated as Government corporation by act of June 30, 1949 (63 Stat. 350). Program terminated June 30, 1965, and *Corporation* dissolved July 1, 1966.

Virgin Islands Corporation *See* **Virgin Islands Company**

Visitor Facilities Advisory Commission, National
Established by act of Mar. 12, 1968 (82 Stat. 45).
Expired Jan. 5, 1975, pursuant to act of Oct. 6, 1972
(86 Stat. 776).

Vocational Rehabilitation, Office of Established to
administer provisions of act of July 6, 1943 (57 Stat.
374). Other duties delegated by acts of Aug. 3, 1954
(68 Stat. 652), Nov. 8, 1965 (79 Stat. 1282), July 12,
1960 (74 Stat. 364), and July 10, 1954 (68 Stat.
454). Redesignated *Vocational Rehabilitation
Administration* Jan. 28, 1963. Made component of
newly created *Social and Rehabilitation Service* as
Rehabilitation Services Administration by *Health,
Education, and Welfare Department* reorganization
of Aug. 15, 1967.

Vocational Rehabilitation Administration *See*
Vocational Rehabilitation, Office of

Voluntary Citizen Participation, State Office of
Renamed State Office of Voluntarism in ACTION by
notice of Apr. 18, 1986 (51 FR 13265), effective
May 18, 1986.

Volunteer Service, International, Secretariat for
Established in 1962 by International Conference on
Middle Level Manpower called by President.
Terminated Mar. 31, 1976, due to insufficient
funding.

Volunteers in Service to America Established by
act of Nov. 8, 1966 (80 Stat. 1472). *Service*
administered by *Office of Economic Opportunity*
and functions transferred to ACTION by Reorg. Plan
No. 1 of 1971, effective July 1, 1971.

Wage Adjustment Board Established May 29,
1942, by Labor Secretary at Presidential direction of
May 14, 1942, to accomplish purpose of act of Mar.
3, 1931 (46 Stat. 1494), as amended by acts of Aug.
30, 1935 (49 Stat. 1011), and Jan. 30, 1942 (56 Stat.
23). Disbanded on termination of *National Wage
Stabilization Board.*

Wage and Price Stability, Council on Established
in Executive Office of the President by act of Aug.
24, 1974 (88 Stat. 750). Abolished by EO 12288 of
Jan. 29, 1981. Funding ceased beyond June 5, 1981,
by act of June 5, 1981 (95 Stat. 74), and
authorization for appropriations repealed by act of
Aug. 13, 1981 (95 Stat. 432).

Wage and Price Stability Program *See* **Wage and
Price Stability, Council on**

Wage Stabilization Board Established by EO
10161 of Sept. 9, 1950. Reconstituted by EO 10377
of July 25, 1952. Terminated Apr. 30, 1953, by EO
10434 of Feb. 6, 1953, and acts of June 30, 1952
(66 Stat. 296), and June 30, 1953 (67 Stat. 131).

Wage Stabilization Board, National *See* **Defense
Mediation Board, National**

Wallops Flight Center, Wallops Island, VA
Formerly separate field installation of National
Aeronautics and Space Administration. Made
component of Goddard Space Flight Center by
NASA Management Instruction 1107.10A of Sept. 3,
1981.

War, Solid Fuels Administration for Established in
Interior Department by EO 9332 of Apr. 19, 1943.
Absorbed *Office of Solid Fuels Coordinator for War*
(originally established as *Office of Solid Fuels
Coordinator for National Defense*) pursuant to
Presidential letter of Nov. 5, 1941; later changed by
Presidential letter of May 25, 1942. Terminated by
EO 9847 of May 6, 1947.

War Assets Administration Established in *Office for
Emergency Management* by EO 9689 of Jan. 31,
1946. Functions transferred to *Surplus Property
Administration* by Reorg. Plan No. 1 of 1947,
effective July 1, 1947, and agency renamed *War
Assets Administration.* Abolished by act of June 30,
1949 (63 Stat. 738), and functions transferred for
liquidation to General Services Administration.

War Assets Corporation *See* **Petroleum Reserves
Corporation**

War Claims Commission Established by act of July
3, 1948 (62 Stat. 1240). Abolished by Reorg. Plan
No. 1 of 1954, effective July 1, 1954, and functions
transferred to Foreign Claims Settlement Commission
of the U.S.

War Commodities Division Established in *Office of
Foreign Economic Coordination* by State
Departmental Order of Aug. 27, 1943. *Office*
abolished by departmental order of Nov. 6, 1943,
pursuant to EO 9380 of Sept. 25, 1943, which
established *Foreign Economic Administration* in
Office for Emergency Management.

War Communications, Board of *See* **Defense
Communications Board**

War Contracts Price Adjustment Board Established
by act of Feb. 25, 1944 (58 Stat. 85). Abolished by
act of Mar. 23, 1951 (65 Stat. 7), and functions
transferred to *Renegotiation Board,* established by
same act, and General Services Administrator.

War Damage Corporation *See* **War Insurance
Corporation**

War Department Established by act of Aug. 7,
1789 (1 Stat. 49), succeeding similar department
established prior to adoption of the Constitution.
Three military departments—Army; Navy, including
naval aviation and U.S. Marine Corps; and Air
Force—reorganized under *National Military
Establishment* by act of July 26, 1947 (61 Stat. 495).

War Finance Corporation Established by act of
Apr. 5, 1918 (40 Stat. 506). Functions and
obligations transferred by Reorg. Plan No. II of 1939,
effective July 1, 1939, to Treasury Secretary for
liquidation not later than Dec. 31, 1939.

War Food Administration *See* **Food Production
and Distribution, Administration of**

War Information, Office of Established in *Office of
Emergency Management* by EO 9182 of June 13,
1942, consolidating *Office of Facts and Figures;
Office of Government Reports; Division of
Information, Office for Emergency Management;* and
*Foreign Information Service—Outpost, Publications,
and Pictorial Branches, Coordinator of Information.*
Abolished by EO 9608 of Aug. 31, 1945. *Bureau of*

Special Services and functions with respect to review of publications of Federal agencies transferred to *Bureau of the Budget.* Foreign information activities transferred to State Department.

War Insurance Corporation Established Dec. 13, 1941, by act of June 10, 1941 (55 Stat. 249). Charter filed Mar. 31, 1942. Renamed *War Damage Corporation* by act of Mar. 27, 1942 (56 Stat. 175). Transferred from *Federal Loan Agency* to Commerce Department by EO 9071 of Feb. 24, 1942. Returned to *Federal Loan Agency* by act of Feb. 24, 1945 (59 Stat. 5). *Agency* abolished by act of June 30, 1947 (61 Stat. 202), and functions assumed by *Reconstruction Finance Corporation.* Powers of *War Damage Corporation,* except for purposes of liquidation, terminated as of Jan. 22, 1947.

War Labor Board, National *See* **Defense Mediation Board, National**

War Manpower Commission Established in *Office for Emergency Management* by EO 9139 of Apr. 18, 1942. Terminated by EO 9617 of Sept. 19, 1945, and functions, except *Procurement and Assignment Service,* transferred to Labor Department.

War Mobilization, Office of Established by EO 9347 of May 27, 1943. Transferred to *Office of War Mobilization and Reconversion* by EO 9488 of Oct. 3, 1944.

War Mobilization and Reconversion, Office of Established by act of Oct. 3, 1944 (58 Stat. 785). Consolidated with other agencies by EO 9809 of Dec. 12, 1946, to form *Office of Temporary Controls. Media Programming Division* and *Motion Picture Division* transferred to *Office of Government Reports,* reestablished by same order. Certain other functions transferred to President and Commerce Secretary.

War Mobilization and Reconversion Advisory Board, Office of Established by act of Oct. 3, 1944 (58 Stat. 788). Transferred to *Office of Temporary Controls* by EO 9809 of Dec. 12, 1946.

War Plants Corporation, Smaller Established by act of June 11, 1942 (56 Stat. 351). Functions transferred by EO 9665 of Dec. 27, 1945, to *Reconstruction Finance Corporation* and Commerce Department. Abolished by act of June 30, 1947 (61 Stat. 202), and functions transferred for liquidation to General Services Administration by Reorg. Plan No. 1 of 1957, effective July 1, 1957.

War and Post War Adjustment Policies, Advisory Unit on Established in *Office of War Mobilization* by Presidential direction Nov. 6, 1943. Report submitted Feb. 15, 1944, and Unit Director and Assistant Director submitted letter to Director of *War Mobilization* ending their work May 12, 1944.

War Production Board Established in *Office for Emergency Management* by EO 9024 of Jan. 16, 1942. *Board* terminated and successor agency, *Civilian Production Administration,* established by EO 9638 of Oct. 4, 1945.

War Property Administration, Surplus Established in *Office of War Mobilization* by EO 9425 of Feb. 19, 1944. Terminated on establishment of *Surplus*

Property Board by act of Oct. 3, 1944 (58 Stat. 768). *Surplus Property Administration* established in *Office of War Mobilization and Reconversion* by act of Sept. 18, 1945 (59 Stat. 533), and *Board* abolished. Domestic functions of *Administration* merged into *War Assets Corporation, Reconstruction Finance Corporation,* by EO 9689 of Jan. 31, 1946. Foreign functions transferred to State Department by same order. Transfers made permanent by Reorg. Plan No. 1 of 1947, effective July 1, 1947.

War Refugee Board Established in Executive Office of the President by EO 9417 of Jan. 22, 1944. Terminated by EO 9614 of Sept. 14, 1945.

War Relations, Agricultural, Office for *See* **Farm Products, Division of**

War Relief Agencies, President's Committee on Established by Presidential letter of Mar. 13, 1941. *President's War Relief Control Board* established by EO 9205 of July 25, 1942, to succeed *Committee. Board* terminated by EO 9723 of May 14, 1946, and functions transferred to State Department.

War Relief Control Board, President's *See* **President's Committee on War Relief Agencies**

War Relocation Authority Established in *Office for Emergency Management* by EO 9102 of Mar. 18, 1942. Transferred to Interior Department by EO 9423 of Feb. 16, 1944. Terminated by EO 9742 of June 25, 1946.

War Resources Board Established in August 1939 as advisory committee to work with *Joint Army and Navy Munitions Board.* Terminated by President Nov. 24, 1939.

War Resources Council *See* **Defense Resources Committee**

War Shipping Administration Established in *Office for Emergency Management* by EO 9054 Feb. 7, 1942. Terminated by act of July 8, 1946 (60 Stat. 501), and functions transferred to *U.S. Maritime Commission,* effective Sept. 1, 1946.

Water, Office of Saline Established to perform functions vested in Interior Secretary by act of July 29, 1971 (85 Stat. 159). Merged with *Office of Water Resources Research* to form *Office of Water Research and Technology* by Secretary's Order 2966 of July 26, 1974.

Water Commission, National Established by act of Sept. 26, 1968 (82 Stat. 868). Terminated Sept. 25, 1973, pursuant to terms of act.

Water Policy, Office of Established by Interior Department Manual Release 2374 of Dec. 29, 1981, under authority of Assistant Secretary. Abolished by Secretarial Order No. 3096 of Oct. 19, 1983, and functions transferred to *Geological Survey* and *Office of Policy Analysis.*

Water Pollution Control Administration, Federal Established under *Health, Education, and Welfare* Secretary by act of Oct. 2, 1965 (79 Stat. 903). Transferred to Interior Department by Reorg. Plan No. 2 of 1966, effective May 10, 1966. Renamed *Federal Water Quality Administration* by act of Apr.

3, 1970. Abolished by Reorg. Plan No. 3 of 1970, effective Dec. 2, 1970, and functions transferred to Environmental Protection Agency.

Water and Power Resources Service Renamed Bureau of Reclamation May 18, 1981, by Interior Secretarial Order 3064.

Water Quality Administration, Federal See **Water Pollution Control Administration, Federal**

Water Research and Technology, Office of Established by Interior Secretarial Order 2966 of July 26, 1974. Abolished by Secretarial order of Aug. 25, 1982, and functions transferred to Bureau of Reclamation, Geological Survey, and *Office of Water Policy.*

Water Resources Council Established by act of July 22, 1965 (89 Stat 575). Inactive as of Oct. 1, 1982.

Water Resources Research, Office of Established to perform functions vested in Interior Secretary by act of July 17, 1964 (78 Stat. 329). Merged with *Office of Saline Water* to form *Office of Water Research and Technology* by Secretary's Order 2966 of July 26, 1974.

Watergate Special Prosecution Force Established by Attorney General order, effective May 25, 1973. Terminated by Attorney General order, effective June 20, 1977.

Waterways Corporation, Inland Incorporated under act of June 3, 1924 (43 Stat. 360). Transferred from *War Department* to Commerce Department by Reorg. Plan No. II of 1939, effective July 1, 1939. *Corporation* sold to *Federal Waterways Corporation* under contract of July 24, 1953. Renamed *Federal Barge Lines, Inc.* Liquidated by act of July 19, 1963 (77 Stat. 81).

Weather Bureau Established in Agriculture Department by act of Oct. 1, 1890 (26 Stat. 653). Transferred to Commerce Department by Reorg. Plan No. IV of 1940, effective June 30, 1940. Functions transferred to *Environmental Science Services Administration* by Reorg. Plan No. 2 of 1965, effective July 13, 1965.

Weather Control, Advisory Committee on Established by act of Aug. 13, 1953 (67 Stat. 559). Act of Aug. 28, 1957 (71 Stat. 426), provided for termination by Dec. 31, 1957.

Weights and Measures, Office of Standard Renamed *National Bureau of Standards* by act of Mar. 3, 1901 (31 Stat. 1449). Bureau transferred from Treasury Department to *Department of Commerce and Labor* by act of Feb. 14, 1903 (32 Stat. 825). Bureau established within the Department of Commerce by act of Mar. 4, 1913 (37 Stat. 736). Renamed National Institute of Standards and Technology by act of Aug. 23, 1988 (102 Stat. 1827).

Welfare Administration Established by *Health, Education, and Welfare Secretary's* reorganization of Jan. 28, 1963. Components consisted of *Bureau of Family Services, Children's Bureau, Office of Juvenile Delinquency and Youth Development,* and *Cuban Refugee Staff.* These functions reassigned to

Social and Rehabilitation Service by Department reorganization of Aug. 15, 1967.

Wilson Memorial Commission, Woodrow Established by act of Oct. 4, 1961 (75 Stat. 783). Terminated on submittal of final report to President and Congress Sept. 29, 1966.

Women, Interdepartmental Committee on the Status of Established by EO 11126 of Nov. 1, 1963. Terminated by EO 12050 of Apr. 4, 1978.

Women, President's Commission on the Status of Established by EO 10980 of Dec. 14, 1961. Submitted final report to President Oct. 11, 1963.

Women's Army Auxiliary Corps Established by act of May 14, 1942 (56 Stat. 278). Repealed in part and superseded by act of July 1, 1943 (57 Stat. 371), which established *Women's Army Corps. Corps* abolished by Defense Secretary Apr. 24, 1978, pursuant to provisions of 10 U.S.C. 125A.

Women's Business Enterprise Division Renamed *Office of Women's Business Enterprise* by Small Business Administrator's reorganization, effective Aug. 19, 1981. Renamed Office of Women's Business Ownership Aug. 19, 1982.

Women's Reserve Established in U.S. Coast Guard by act of Nov. 23, 1942 (56 Stat. 1020).

Women's Year, 1975, National Commission on the Observance of International Established by EO 11832 of Jan. 9, 1975. Continued by act of Dec. 23, 1975 (89 Stat. 1003). Terminated Mar. 31, 1978, pursuant to terms of act.

Wood Utilization, National Committee on Established by Presidential direction in 1925. Abolished by EO 6179–B of June 16, 1933.

Work Projects Administration See **Works Progress Administration**

Work-Training Programs, Bureau of Abolished by reorganization of *Manpower Administration* and functions assigned to *U.S. Training and Employment Service,* effective Mar. 17, 1969.

Working Life, Productivity and Quality of, National Center for Established by act of Nov. 28, 1975 (89 Stat. 935). Authorized appropriations expired Sept. 30, 1978, and functions assumed by *National Productivity Council.*

Works, Advisory Committee on Federal Public Established by President Oct. 5, 1955. Abolished by President Mar. 12, 1961, and functions assigned to *Bureau of the Budget.*

Works Administration, Federal Civil Established by EO 6420–B of Nov. 9, 1933. Function of employment expired March 1934. Function of settling claims continued under *Works Progress Administration.*

Works Administration, Public See **Emergency Administration of Public Works, Federal**

Works Agency, Federal Established by Reorg. Plan No. I of 1939, effective July 1, 1939. Functions relating to defense housing transferred to *Federal*

Public Housing Authority, National Housing Agency, by EO 9070 of Feb. 24, 1942. Abolished by act of June 30, 1949 (63 Stat. 380), and functions transferred to General Services Administration.

Works Emergency Housing Corporation, Public Established by EO 6470 of Nov. 29, 1933. Incorporated under laws of State of Delaware. Abolished and liquidated as of Aug. 14, 1935, by filing of certificate of surrender of corporate rights.

Works Emergency Leasing Corporation, Public Incorporated Jan. 3, 1934, under laws of Delaware by direction of Administrator of Public Works. Terminated with filed certificate of dissolution with secretary of state of Delaware Jan. 2, 1935.

Works Progress Administration Established by EO 7034 of May 6, 1935, and continued by subsequent yearly emergency relief appropriation acts. Renamed *Work Projects Administration* by Reorg. Plan No. I of 1939, effective July 1, 1939, which provided for consolidation of *Works Progress Administration* into *Federal Works Agency.* Transferred by President to *Federal Works Administrator* Dec. 4, 1942.

Works, Special Board of Public *See* **Land Program, Director of**

Yards and Docks, Bureau of Established by acts of Aug. 31, 1842 (5 Stat. 579), and July 5, 1862 (12 Stat. 510). Abolished by Defense Department reorg.

order of Mar. 9, 1966, and functions transferred to Navy Secretary (31 FR 7188).

Youth Administration, National Established in *Works Progress Administration* by EO 7086 of June 26, 1935. Transferred to *Federal Security Agency* by Reorg. Plan No. I of 1939, effective July 1, 1939. Transferred to *Bureau of Training, War Manpower Commission,* by EO 9247 of Sept. 17, 1942. Terminated by act of July 12, 1943 (57 Stat. 539).

Youth Crime, President's Committee on Juvenile Delinquency and Established by EO 10940 of May 11, 1961. Terminated by EO 11529 of Apr. 24, 1970.

Youth Fitness, President's Council on Established by EO 10673 of July 16, 1956. Renamed *President's Council on Physical Fitness* by EO 11074 of Jan. 8, 1963. Renamed President's Council on Physical Fitness and Sports by EO 11398 of Mar. 4, 1968.

Youth Opportunity, President's Council on Established by EO 11330 of Mar. 5, 1967. Inactive as of June 30, 1971; EO 11330 revoked by EO 12379 of Aug. 17, 1982.

Youth Programs, Office of Established in Interior Department by Secretarial Order No. 2985 of Jan. 7, 1965. Functions moved to Office of Historically Black College and University Programs and Job Corps, Office of the Secretary, by Departmental Manual Release 2788 of Mar. 22, 1988.

APPENDIX D: Agencies Appearing in the Code of Federal Regulations

(This section contains an alphabetical listing of agencies appearing in the *Code of Federal Regulations* (CFR). The listing was revised as of March 15, 1995.)

Agency	CFR Title, Subtitle or Chapter
ACTION	45, XII
Administrative Committee of the Federal Register	1, I
Administrative Conference of the United States	1, III
Advanced Research Projects Agency	32, I
Advisory Commission on Intergovernmental Relations	5, VII
Advisory Committee on Federal Pay	5, IV
Advisory Council on Historic Preservation	36, VIII
African Development Foundation	22, XV
Federal Acquisition Regulation	48, 57
Agency for International Development	22, II
Federal Acquisition Regulation	48, 7
Agricultural Marketing Service	7, I, IX, X, XI
Agricultural Research Service	7, V
Agriculture Department	
Agricultural Marketing Service	7, I, IX, X, XI
Agricultural Research Service	7, V
Animal and Plant Health Inspection Service	7, III; 9, I
Commodity Credit Corporation	7, XIV
Consolidated Farm Service Agency	7, VII, XVIII
Cooperative State Research, Education, and Extension Service	7, XXXIV
Economic Analysis Staff	7, XXXIX
Economic Research Service	7, XXXVII
Economics Management Staff	7, XL
Energy, Office of	7, XXIX
Environmental Quality, Office of	7, XXXI
Federal Acquisition Regulation	48, 4
Federal Crop Insurance Corporation	7, IV
Finance and Management, Office of	7, XXX
Food and Consumer Service	7, II
Food Safety and Inspection Service	9, III
Foreign Agricultural Service	7, XV
Foreign Economic Development Service	7, XXI
Forest Service	36, II
General Sales Manager, Office of	7, XXV
Grain Inspection, Packers and Stockyards Administration	7, VIII; 9, II
Grants and Program Systems, Office of	7, XXXII
Information Resources Management, Office of	7, XXVII
Inspector General, Office of	7, XXVI
International Cooperation and Development, Office of	7, XXII
National Agricultural Library	7, XLI
National Agricultural Statistics Service	7, XXXVI
Operations, Office of	7, XXVIII
Rural Business and Cooperative Development Service	7, XVIII
Rural Development Administration	7, XLII
Rural Housing and Community Development Service	7, XVIII
Rural Telephone Bank	7, XVI
Rural Utilities Service	7, XVII, XVIII
Secretary of Agriculture, Office of	7, Subtitle A
Soil Conservation Service	7, VI
Transportation, Office of	7, XXXIII
World Agricultural Outlook Board	7, XXXVIII

Agency	CFR Title, Subtitle or Chapter
National Security Council	32, XXI; 47, 2
Presidential Documents	3
Science and Technology Policy, Office of	32, XXIV; 47, II
Trade Representative, Office of the United States	15, XX
Export Administration, Bureau of	15, VII
Export-Import Bank of the United States	12, IV
Family Assistance, Office of	45, II
Farm Credit Administration	12, VI
Farm Credit System Insurance Corporation	12, XIV
Farmers Home Administration	7, XVIII
Federal Acquisition Regulation	48, 1
Federal Aviation Administration	14, I
Federal Claims Collection Standards	4, II
Federal Communications Commission	47, I
Federal Contract Compliance Programs, Office of	41, 60
Federal Crop Insurance Corporation	7, IV
Federal Deposit Insurance Corporation	5, XXII; 12, III
Federal Election Commission	11, I
Federal Emergency Management Agency	44, I
Federal Acquisition Regulation	48, 44
Federal Employees Group Life Insurance Federal Acquisition Regulation	48, 21
Federal Employees Health Benefits Acquisition Regulation	48, 16
Federal Energy Regulatory Commission	18, I
Federal Financial Institutions Examination Council	12, XI
Federal Financing Bank	12, VIII
Federal Highway Administration	23, I, II; 49, III
Federal Home Loan Mortgage Corporation	1, IV
Federal Housing Enterprise Oversight Office	12, XVII
Federal Housing Finance Board	12, IX
Federal Information Resources Management Regulations	41, Subtitle E, Ch. 201
Federal Inspector for the Alaska Natural Gas Transportation System, Office of	10, XV
Federal Labor Relations Authority, and General Counsel of the Federal Labor Relations Authority	5, XIV; 22, XIV
Federal Law Enforcement Training Center	31, VII
Federal Maritime Commission	46, IV
Federal Mediation and Conciliation Service	29, XII
Federal Mine Safety and Health Review Commission	29, XXVII
Federal Pay, Advisory Committee on	5, IV
Federal Prison Industries, Inc.	28, III
Federal Procurement Policy Office	48, 99
Federal Property Management Regulations	41, 101
Federal Property Management Regulations System	41, Subtitle C
Federal Railroad Administration	49, II
Federal Register, Administrative Committee of	1, I
Federal Register, Office of	1, II
Federal Reserve System	12, II
Federal Retirement Thrift Investment Board	5, VI, LXXVI
Federal Service Impasses Panel	5, XIV
Federal Trade Commission	5, XLVII; 16, I
Federal Transit Administration	49, VI
Federal Travel Regulation System	41, Subtitle F
Finance and Management, Office of	7, XXX
Fine Arts, Commission on	45, XXI
Fiscal Service	31, II
Fish and Wildlife Service, United States	50, I, IV
Fishery Conservation and Management	50, VI
Fishing and Whaling, International Regulatory Agencies	50, III
Food and Drug Administration	21, I
Food and Consumer Service	7, II
Food Safety and Inspection Service	9, III
Foreign Agricultural Service	7, XV
Foreign Assets Control, Office of	31, V
Foreign Claims Settlement Commission of the United States	45, V
Foreign Economic Development Service	7, XXI
Foreign Service Grievance Board	22, IX

Agency	CFR Title, Subtitle or Chapter
Foreign Service Impasse Disputes Panel	22, XIV
Foreign Service Labor Relations Board	22, XIV
Foreign-Trade Zones Board	15, IV
Forest Service	36, II
General Accounting Office	4, I, II
General Sales Manager, Office of	7, XXV
General Services Administration	
Contract Appeals, Board of	48, 61
Federal Acquisition Regulation	48, 5
Federal Information Resources Management Regulations	41, Subtitle E, Ch. 201
Federal Property Management Regulations System	41, 101, 105
Federal Travel Regulation System	41, Subtitle F
Payment From a Non-Federal Source for Travel Expenses	41, 304
Payment of Expenses Connected With the Death of Certain Employees	41, 303
Relocation Allowances	41, 302
Travel Allowances	41, 301
Geological Survey	30, IV
Government Ethics, Office of	5, XVI
Government National Mortgage Association	24, III
Grain Inspection, Packers and Stockyards Administration	7, VIII; 9, II
Grants and Program Systems, Office of	7, XXXII
Great Lakes Pilotage	46, III
Harry S. Truman Scholarship Foundation	45, XVIII
Health and Human Services, Department of	45, Subtitle A
Child Support Enforcement, Office of	45, III
Children and Families, Administration for	45, II, III, IV, X
Community Services, Office of	45, X
Family Assistance, Office of	45, II
Federal Acquisition Regulation	48, 3
Food and Drug Administration	21, I
Health Care Financing Administration	42, IV
Human Development Services, Office of	45, XIII
Inspector General (Health Care), Office of	42, V
Public Health Service	42, I
Refugee Resettlement, Office of	45, IV
Social Security Administration	20, III
Health Care Financing Administration	42, IV
Housing and Urban Development, Department of	24, Subtitle B
Community Planning and Development, Office of Assistant Secretary for	24, V, VI
Equal Opportunity, Office of Assistant Secretary for	24, I
Federal Acquisition Regulation	48, 24
Federal Housing Enterprise Oversight, Office of	12, XVII
Government National Mortgage Association	24, III
Housing—Federal Housing Commissioner, Office of Assistant Secretary for	24, II, VIII, X, XX
Inspector General, Office of	24, XII
Mortgage Insurance and Loan Programs Under the Emergency Homeowners' Relief Act	24, XV
Public and Indian Housing, Office of Assistant Secretary for	24, IX
Secretary, Office of	24, Subtitle A, VII
Solar Energy and Energy Conservation Bank	24, XI
Housing—Federal Housing Commissioner, Office of Assistant Secretary for	24, II, VIII, X, XX
Human Development Services, Office of	45, XIII
Immigration and Naturalization Service	8, I
Independent Counsel, Office of	28, VII
Indian Affairs, Bureau of	25, I
Indian Affairs, Office of Assistant Secretary	25, VI
Indian Arts and Crafts Board	25, II
Information Agency, United States	22, V
Federal Acquisition Regulation	48, 19
Information Resources Management, Office of	7, XXVII
Information Security Oversight Office	32, XX
Inspector General	

NAME INDEX

NOTE: Separate listings of Senators and Representatives can be found beginning on pages 32 and 34, respectively. Any other references to said persons can be found in this index.

AGENCY/SUBJECT INDEX

NOTE: This index does not include material appearing in Appendices B–D.

RECENT CHANGES

Personnel actions brought to the attention of *Manual* editors July 5–Aug. 31, 1994

Page	Position	Action

Library of Congress

53   Registrar of Copyrights and Associate Librarian of Congress   Marybeth Peters appointed July 29 (effective Aug. 7).

Supreme Court of the United States

69   Associate Justice   Stephen G. Breyer confirmed July 29, vice Harry A. Blackmun.

U.S. Courts of Appeals

72   U.S. Circuit Judge for the Second Circuit   Guido Calabresi confirmed July 18.

72   U.S. Circuit Judge for the Second Circuit   Jose A. Cabranes confirmed August 9, vice Richard J. Cardamone.

Office of Management and Budget

96   Deputy Director for Management   John A. Koskinen confirmed July 15, vice Philip Lader.

Energy Department

273   Chief Financial Officer   Joseph F. Vivona confirmed July 21 (new position).

273   Assistant Secretary, Fossil Energy   Patricia Fry Godley confirmed July 21, vice James G. Randolph.

Health and Human Services Department

293   Administrator, Substance Abuse and Mental Health Services Administration   Nelba Chavez confirmed July 14, vice Frederick K. Goodwin.

Justice Department

365   Associate Attorney General   John R. Schmidt confirmed July 21, vice Webster L. Hubbell.

Treasury Department

483   Deputy Secretary   Roger C. Altman resigned Aug. 17.

490   Director of the Mint   Philip N. Diehl confirmed June 24, vice David J. Ryder.

Federal Labor Relations Authority

585   Member, designation as Chairman   Phyllis N. Segal confirmed July 15, vice Jean McKee.

Thrift Depositor Protection Oversight Board

733   Chief Executive Officer, Resolution Trust Corporation   Roger C. Altman resigned Aug. 17.

United States Arms Control and Disarmament Agency

738   Assistant Director   Michael Nacht confirmed July 14, vice Linton F. Brooks.

738   Assistant Director   Amy Sands confirmed July 14, vice Manfred Eimer.

738   Assistant Director   Lawrence Scheinman confirmed July 14, vice Bradley Gordon.